W9-CIQ-514

What's New in This Book?

While revising this book to cover the change from Excel 5 in Windows 3.x to Excel 7 in Windows 95, the author has seized every opportunity to improve and enhance the book:

☐ All chapters and all program code examples are completely revised throughout for the Windows 95 operating system.

☐ Enhancements based on reader feedback from the first edition are included throughout the book. As well as expanding various discussions, many tips and notes were added in response to reader comments or queries.

☐ Chapter 13, "Arrays," was completely rewritten to give readers a more solid understanding of what an array is and when and how to use arrays in your VBA programs.

☐ Chapter 14, "Debugging and Testing Macros," includes a much more thorough explanation of using the VBA Debugger than previous book to help you find and correct problems in your programs.

☐ Chapter 15, "Dialog Boxes and Custom Controls," has expanded coverage of using dialog sheets to create custom dialog boxes, and improved code examples for using dialog box controls.

☐ Chapter 16, "Menus and Toolbars," was rewritten to give you a more complete and understandable coverage of the important VBA objects and commands that enable you to create customized menus and toolbars in your Excel VBA programs.

☐ Chapter 19, "Working with Other Applications: OLE and OLE Automation," was revised to reflect using OLE operations in the Windows 95 environment. New code examples show how to use Excel VBA to control objects in Access 95 (the latest addition to the VBA family of host applications).

☐ Chapter 20, "Working with Other Applications: DDE, DLLs, and Sending Keystrokes," has been revised to use the new Windows 95 32-bit DLL calls.

☐ The sample application in Appendix B has been revised to show how easily you can convert an Excel VBA application into an Excel add-in program.

Teach Yourself Excel Programming with Visual Basic for Applications

in 21 Days

Teach Yourself
Excel Programming with Visual Basic for Applications
in 21 Days

Matthew Harris

SAMS PUBLISHING

201 West 103rd Street
Indianapolis, Indiana 46290

To Laura Maria Earle, whose loving support has made a world of difference.

Copyright © 1996 by Sams Publishing

FIRST EDITION

All rights reserved. No part of this book shall be reproduced, stored in a retrieval system, or transmitted by any means, electronic, mechanical, photocopying, recording, or otherwise, without written permission from the publisher. No patent liability is assumed with respect to the use of the information contained herein. Although every precaution has been taken in the preparation of this book, the publisher and author assume no responsibility for errors or omissions. Neither is any liability assumed for damages resulting from the use of the information contained herein. For information, address Sams Publishing, 201 W. 103rd St., Indianapolis, IN 46290.

International Standard Book Number: 0-672-30782-0

Library of Congress Catalog Card Number: 95-72329

99 98 97 96   4 3 2 1

Interpretation of the printing code: the rightmost double-digit number is the year of the book's printing; the rightmost single-digit, the number of the book's printing. For example, a printing code of 96-1 shows that the first printing of the book occurred in 1996.

Composed in AGaramond and MCPdigital by Macmillan Computer Publishing

Printed in the United States of America

Trademarks

All terms mentioned in this book that are known to be trademarks or service marks have been appropriately capitalized. Sams Publishing cannot attest to the accuracy of this information. Use of a term in this book should not be regarded as affecting the validity of any trademark or service mark.

Publisher and President	*Richard K. Swadley*
Acquisitions Manager	*Greg Wiegand*
Development Manager	*Dean Miller*
Managing Editor	*Cindy Morrow*
Marketing Manager	*Gregg Bushyeager*

Acquisitions Editor/ Development Editor
Sunthar Visuvalingam

Production Editor
Anne Owen

Technical Reviewer
Robert Bogue

Editorial Coordinator
Bill Whitmer

Technical Edit Coordinator
Lynette Quinn

Formatter
Frank Sinclair

Editorial Assistants
Sharon Cox
Andi Richter
Rhonda Tinch-Mize

Cover Designer
Tim Amhrein

Book Designer
Gary Adair
Michele Laseau

Production Team Supervisor
Brad Chinn

Production
Mary Ann Abramson
Mona Brown
Michael Brumitt
Jason Hand
Louisa Klucznik
Steph Mineart
Bobbi Satterfield
Andrew Stone
Mark Walchle

Indexer
Jeanne Clark
Cheryl Dietsch

Overview

Week 1 at a Glance   **1**

Day   1   Getting Started   3

       2   Writing and Editing Simple Macros   23

       3   Understanding Data Types, Variables, and Constants   61

       4   Operators and Expressions   101

       5   Visual Basic for Applications and Excel Functions   137

       6   Function Procedures and User-Defined Functions   177

       7   Working with Objects   211

Week 1 in Review   **245**

Week 2 at a Glance   **253**

Day   8   Making Decisions in Visual Basic for Applications   255

       9   Repeating Actions in Visual Basic: Loops   295

       10   Data Types and Variables: Advanced Topics   339

       11   Modular Programming Techniques   385

       12   Managing Files with Visual Basic for Applications   429

       13   Arrays   469

       14   Debugging and Testing Macros   521

Week 2 in Review   **549**

Week 3 at a Glance   **567**

Day   15   Dialog Boxes and Custom Controls   569

       16   Menus and Toolbars   619

       17   Error Handling   667

       18   Working with Excel   703

       19   Working with Other Applications: OLE and OLE Automation   735

       20   Working with Other Applications: DDE, DLLs, and Sending Keystrokes   767

       21   Using Automatic Procedures, Event Procedures, and Add-Ins   799

Week 3 in Review   **829**

Appendixes

       A   Answers   839

       B   Sample Application   903

          Index   935

Contents

Week 1 at a Glance   1

Day   1   Getting Started   3

Macros and Programming Languages 4

    What Is a Macro? 4

    A Brief History of Visual Basic for Applications 5

Why Learn Visual Basic for Applications in Excel? 7

Recording a New Excel Macro 9

    Setting Up the Macro's Starting Conditions 10

    Starting the Macro Recorder 11

    Naming the New Macro and Selecting Options 12

    Recording Your Actions 15

    Stopping the Macro Recorder 16

Macro Source Code 17

Running a Macro 18

Summary 19

    Q&A 20

Workshop 21

    Quiz 21

    Exercises 22

Day   2   Writing and Editing Simple Macros   23

Understanding Excel's Visual Basic for Applications Environment 24

    Understanding Modules 24

    Examining the Visual Basic for Applications Toolbar and Menu

    Commands 25

Editing Macros 32

    Finding Recorded Macros 32

    Parts of a Recorded Macro 34

    Editing Macro Text 37

    Moving or Copying a Macro from One Module to Another 39

    Moving or Copying an Entire Module Sheet 40

    Protecting Your Macro Source Code.. 41

Writing New Macros 41

    Inserting a New Module Sheet 41

    Selecting an Existing Module Sheet 42

    Writing the Macro Text 43

Running a Macro While Editing 46

Displaying Messages to a Macro's User 46

Understanding Error Messages While Writing, Editing, or Running a

    Macro 48

    Syntax Errors 48

    Runtime Errors 51

Recording New Actions in an Existing Macro 52

Printing Your Macros 55

Summary 56

    Q&A 56

Workshop 57

    Quiz 57

    Exercises 58

Day 3   Understanding Data Types, Variables, and Constants   61

Examining Visual Basic Data Types.. 62

    Dates 65

    Numbers.. 66

    Text Strings 68

    Logical Values 68

    Variant Data 69

Understanding Variables... 69

    What Is a Variable? 69

    Choosing Variable Names 71

    Creating Variables.. 73

    Scope: Determining Which Variables Are Available 76

    Persistence: Determining How Long Variables Retain Their Value...... 81

    Requiring Explicit Variable Declaration 81

    Specifying the Data Type of a Variable 84

Understanding Constants 87

    Creating Named Constants 88

    Constant Scope 89

    Writing Literal Constants 90

    Specifying the Data Type of a Constant 92

    Understanding Predefined Constants 93

    Using the Object Browser to Find Available Predefined Constants 94

Getting Data from Your Procedure's User 95

Summary 98

    Q&A 98

Workshop... 99

    Quiz 99

    Exercises 100

Day 4   Operators and Expressions   101

Understanding Operators and Expressions 102

Data Type Compatibility.. 104

Visual Basic's Automatic Data Conversions 105

    Numeric Type Conversions 107

    String and Number Conversions.. 108

    Boolean Conversions 108

    Date Conversions 108

The Assignment Operator (=) 109

Arithmetic Operators 112

Addition (+) 112
Subtraction (-) 113
Multiplication (*) 114
Division (/) 115
Integer Division (\) 115
Modulo Division (*Mod*) 116
Exponentiation (^) 116
Comparison Operators 116
String Comparisons 118
The *Like* Operator 121
The *Is* Operator 123
Logical Operators 124
Understanding Truth Tables 125
And 125
Or 126
Not 126
Xor 127
Eqv 127
Imp 128
String Concatenation Operators 128
Using String Concatenation 128
String Concatenation Operators 130
Understanding Operator Precedence and Complex Expression
Evaluation 131
Summary 134
Q&A 134
Workshop 135
Quiz 135
Exercises 136

Day   5   Visual Basic for Applications and Excel Functions   137

Understanding Functions 138
Using Functions in Assignments and Expressions 139
Understanding Function Arguments and Function Results 142
Ignoring a Function's Result 143
Using a Function's Named Arguments 145
Using Visual Basic for Applications' Functions 147
Mathematical Functions 147
Data Conversion Functions 148
Date and Time Functions 151
User Interaction Functions 153
String Functions 156
Disk, Directory Information, and Other Functions 157
Using Excel's Functions 157
Using the Object Browser to Insert Function Calls 159
Viewing and Inserting Visual Basic's Functions 160
Viewing and Inserting Excel's Functions 162

Using Functions to Manipulate Strings 163
   Removing Extraneous Space Characters 164
   Getting the Length of a String 165
   Comparing and Searching Strings 166
   Breaking a String into Smaller Parts 169
   Using String Characters You Cannot Type at the Keyboard 170
Summary 172
   Q&A 173
Workshop 174
   Quiz 174
   Exercises 175

Day 6   Function Procedures and User-Defined Functions   177

Understanding Function Procedures and User-Defined Functions 178
Creating Function Procedures 179
   Writing a Function Procedure 180
   Creating User-Defined Functions for Excel 183
   Declaring a Data Type for a Function's Result 184
   Declaring Data Types for a Function's Arguments 186
   Creating Optional Arguments 187
   Understanding and Controlling How VBA Passes Arguments 190
Using Function Procedures in Visual Basic for Applications 193
   Using the Object Browser to Find and Insert Your Function
     Procedures 194
   Using the Object Browser to Display a Function's Code 195
   Entering a Function Procedure Description with the Object
     Browser 196
Using User-Defined Functions in Excel 198
   Changing a User-Defined Function's Category 199
Designing Function Procedures and User-Defined Functions 200
   Designing Functions for Excel 202
Understanding Recursion 203
   Analyzing a Recursive Function's Operation 204
   Avoiding Accidental Recursion and Other Recursion Problems 206
Summary 207
   Q&A 208
Workshop 209
   Quiz 209
   Exercises 209

Day 7   Working with Objects   211

Understanding Objects 212
   Object Properties 213
   Object Methods 214
Using Objects 215
   Using Object Properties 217
   Using Object Methods 220

Declaring Object Variables 224
Using Objects in Expressions and Assignments 224
Referring to Objects by Using *With...End With* 228
Working with Object Collections and Object Containers 230
Adding to Collections 233
Referring to Specific Objects in a Collection or Container 234
Using the Object Browser with Objects, Methods, and Properties 235
Summary 238
Q&A 239
Workshop 241
Quiz 241
Exercises 241

Week 1 in Review   **245**

Week 2 at a Glance   **253**

Day   8   Making Decisions in Visual Basic for Applications   255

Understanding Visual Basic for Applications' Decision-Making
Commands 256
Making Simple Choices 258
Choosing a Single Branch Using *If...Then* 258
Choosing between Branches Using *If...Then...Else* 261
Making Complex Choices 264
Nested *If...Then* Statements 264
Using *If...Then...ElseIf* 267
Using the *Select...Case* Statement 268
Unconditional Branching 273
Ending Procedures, Functions, and Entire Programs Early 277
Using the *Exit* Statement 278
Using the *End* Statement 280
Using *MsgBox* to Let Users Make Choices 283
Summary 288
Q&A 289
Workshop 290
Quiz 290
Exercises 291

Day   9   Repeating Actions in Visual Basic: Loops   295

Understanding Looping Commands 296
Fixed Repetition: the *For* Loops 299
Using the *For...Next* Loop 299
Using the *For Each...Next* Loop 308
Flexible Repetition: The *Do* Loops 311
Understanding How Visual Basic for Applications Tests the Loop
Determinant 312
Using Loops That Test Conditions Before Execution 315
Using Loops That Test Conditions after Execution 321

Ending Loops Early 326
Nesting Loops 329
Nesting *For* Loops 329
Nesting *Do* Loops 332
Summary 335
Q&A 335
Workshop 336
Quiz 337
Exercises 337

Day 10 Data Types and Variables: Advanced Topics   **339**

Getting Information about Variables and Expressions 340
Using Visual Basic for Application's Data Information Functions 342
Determining the Specific Data Type of a Variable or Expression 346
Understanding the Special *Empty* and *Null* Values 353
Defensive Programming: Preventing Errors before They Happen 355
Checking Arguments and Other Internal Values 356
Validating User Input 357
Validating Other Input 362
Preserving Variables between Function and Procedure Calls 362
Creating Your Own Data Types 369
Defining a User-Defined Data Type 370
Declaring Variables That Have a User-Defined Type 372
Using Variables with User-Defined Types 372
Summary 381
Q&A 381
Workshop 382
Quiz 382
Exercises 383

Day 11 Modular Programming Techniques   **385**

Using Modules More Effectively 386
Creating Procedure and Function Libraries 388
Making Library Procedures and Functions Available 389
Advanced Scope Rules for Cross-Module Programming 397
Understanding Private and Public Scope 397
Overriding Visual Basic for Application's Scope Rules 399
Understanding and Avoiding Circular References 404
Understanding and Using Module Qualifiers 406
Understanding Structured Programming Techniques 407
Understanding Procedures That Call Other Procedures 408
Top-Down Design and Step-Wise Refinement 410
Using Modules to Organize Your Programming Projects 413
Using Procedure Arguments to Communicate Data
between Procedures 414
Understanding When and Why You Should Use Argument Lists
with Your Procedures 414

Specifying a Procedure's Argument List 415
Using Procedures That Have Arguments 416
Summary 424
Q&A 424
Workshop 426
Quiz 426
Exercises 427

Day   12   Managing Files with Visual Basic for Applications   429

Understanding File Management 430
What Is File Management? 430
Reviewing Visual Basic for Applications' File Management
Capabilities 431
Working with File Attributes 432
Understanding File Attributes 433
Getting a File's Attributes 435
Changing a File's Attributes 438
Getting or Finding Filenames 441
Using the *GetOpenFilename* Method 441
Using the *GetSaveAsFilename* Method 445
Using the *Dir* Function to Find Files 448
Working with Disk Drives and Directories 452
Getting the Current Directory Path and Drive Letter 452
Changing the Current Directory 453
Changing the Current Disk Drive 454
Creating Disk Directories 455
Removing Disk Directories 456
Copying and Deleting Files 457
Copying a File 457
Deleting a File 459
Renaming or Moving Files 460
Getting Information about Files 462
Getting a File's Time and Date Stamp 462
Getting the Length of a File 463
Summary 465
Q&A 465
Workshop 466
Quiz 466
Exercises 466

Day   13   Arrays   469

Understanding Arrays 470
Understanding Single-Dimensional Arrays 470
Understanding Multi-Dimensional Arrays 472
Static and Dynamic Arrays 474
The *Option Base* Statement 475
Declaring Arrays 476
Using Arrays 478

Using *ReDim* with Dynamic Arrays 486
The *LBound* and *UBound* Functions 492
Using *Erase* to Clear or Remove Arrays 494
Using Arrays as Arguments to Procedures and Functions 496
Sorting Arrays 498
Searching Arrays 506
    Using Linear Searches 506
    Using Binary Searches 510
Summary 515
    Q&A 515
Workshop 517
    Quiz 517
    Exercises 518

Day 14 Debugging and Testing Macros 521

Basic Types of Program Bugs 522
Using the Break Mode 523
    Entering Break Mode from an Error Dialog Box 524
    Setting and Using Breakpoints 526
    Using the *Stop* Statement 527
    Entering Break Mode Using the Step Into Command 528
    Entering Break Mode by Interrupting Code Execution 528
    Ending Break Mode 529
Using the Step Into Command 529
Using the Step Over Command 534
Understanding and Using Watched Variables 535
    Adding a Watch Expression 536
    Editing a Watch Expression 539
    Deleting a Watch Expression 539
    Using the Instant Watch 539
Tracing Procedure Calls 540
Using the Immediate Pane 541
    Using the *Debug.Print* Statement 542
Summary 546
    Q&A 546
Workshop 546
    Quiz 547
    Exercises 547

Week 2 in Review 549

Week 3 at a Glance 567

Day 15 Dialog Boxes and Custom Controls 569

Understanding Custom Dialog Box Controls 570
Creating Custom Dialog Boxes 574
    Inserting a New Dialog Sheet 575
    Using the Forms Toolbar 576
    Adding Controls to the Custom Dialog Box 578

Editing Custom Dialog Box Controls 580
Controlling the Tab Order 582
Setting Control Properties Interactively 584
Displaying a Custom Dialog Box with VBA 587
Using VBA with Custom Dialog Box Controls 588
Attaching VBA Procedures to Dialog Box Controls 588
Using the Edit Box Control 591
Using Option Button Controls and Group Boxes 595
Using Check Box Controls 600
Using Scrollbar and Spinner Controls with Dynamically Updated
   Labels in a Floating Dialog Box 604
Using List Box Controls 612
Summary 615
Q&A 615
Workshop 616
Quiz 616
Exercises 617

Day   16   Menus and Toolbars   619

Understanding Menu Structures 620
The Parts of a Menu 620
VBA Menu Objects and Properties 621
Excel's Built-In Menus 624
Custom Menu Bars 624
Using the Interactive Menu Editor 625
Managing Custom and Built-In Menu Bars 626
Adding a New Menu Bar 627
Displaying a Menu Bar 627
Deleting a Menu Bar 628
Resetting a Built-In Menu Bar 629
A Blank Menu Bar Example 629
Managing Menus with VBA 631
Adding Menus 631
Deleting Menus 633
A Menu Bar with Non-Working Menus 633
Managing Menu Items 635
Adding Menu Items 636
Specifying a Menu Item's Event Procedure 637
Displaying Hints for Menu Item Commands in the Status Bar 638
Deleting Menu Items 638
Enabling or Disabling Menu Items 639
Checking Menu Items 639
Renaming Menu Items 640
Adding Submenus 640
Putting It Together: A Functioning Menu Example 641
Understanding Toolbars 645
Toolbar Objects, Properties and Methods 646
Accessing Excel's Built-In Toolbars 648

Creating and Managing Toolbars 648
    Creating a Custom Toolbar 649
    Hiding, Displaying, and Positioning Toolbars 650
    Deleting a Toolbar 653
    Restoring a Built-In Toolbar 654
    Adding Toolbar Buttons 655
    Deleting Toolbar Buttons 656
    Manipulating Toolbar Buttons 656
Putting It Together: A Working Toolbar 657
Summary 663
    Q&A 663
Workshop 664
    Quiz 664
    Exercises 664

Day   17   Error Handling   667

Strategies for Error Handling 668
The *On Error GoTo* Statement 670
The *Resume* Statement 671
Finding the Runtime Error's Type, Message, and Location 674
    Determining the Runtime Error Type: Using the *Err* Function 674
    Getting the Runtime Error Message Text:
      Using the *Error* Function 677
    Determining the Runtime Error Location: Using the *Erl* Function 678
Forcing Runtime Errors and Creating User-Defined Error Codes:
    The *Error* Statement 679
Putting It Together: Examples of Error Handling 681
    Handling Fatal Errors 681
    Resolving Runtime Errors without Halting 685
    Retrying the Error-Causing Statement 687
    Resuming Execution at a Specified Point 689
    Forcing a Runtime Error 691
Summary 697
    Q&A 698
Workshop 699
    Quiz 699
    Exercises 699

Day   18   Working with Excel   703

Working with Workbook Objects 704
    Returning a Workbook Object 704
    Opening a Workbook 705
    Creating a New Workbook 707
    Activating a Workbook 708
    Saving a Workbook 709
    Closing a Workbook 711
Working with Worksheet Objects 712
    Returning a Worksheet Object 712

Activating a Worksheet 714
Creating a New Worksheet 715
Renaming a Worksheet 715
Copying and Moving a Worksheet 716
Deleting a Worksheet 717
Methods That Return Range Objects 718
Using the *Range* Method 718
Using the *Cells* Method 720
Using the *Offset* Method 722
Other Methods and Properties That Return Ranges 723
Working with Cells and Ranges 724
Selecting a Cell or Range 724
Working with Values and Formulas 724
Defining a Range Name 726
Cutting, Copying, and Clearing Data 727
Summary 730
Q&A 730
Workshop 732
Quiz 732
Exercises 732

Day   19   Working with Other Applications: OLE and OLE Automation   735

What Is OLE? 736
A Brief History of OLE 736
How Does Visual Basic for Applications Fit In? 739
Adding Linked and Embedded Objects 739
Using the *Add* Method for the *OLEObjects* Collection 739
Looking Up an Object's Class Type 741
Inserting a New Embedded Object 744
Inserting an Existing File as an Embedded Object 746
Inserting an Existing File as a Linked Object 747
Working with Linked and Embedded Objects 748
Using OLE Object Properties 749
Using OLE Object Methods 752
Using OLE Automation 756
Accessing OLE Automation Objects 756
Accessing Objects Directly 757
Creating a New OLE Automation Object 758
Accessing an Existing OLE Automation Object 761
Summary 762
Q&A 763
Workshop 764
Quiz 764
Exercises 765

Day 20 **Working with Other Applications: DDE, DLLs, and Sending Keystrokes** **767**

Starting Another Application 768
Activating a Running Application 770
Using Dynamic Data Exchange 773
    DDE: The Basics 773
    Initiating and Terminating a Link between VBA
      and a DDE Server 774
    Controlling the Server Application 778
    Exchanging Data with the DDE Server Application 780
Sending Keystrokes to an Application 784
Accessing DLLs from Visual Basic for Applications 788
    Declaring DLL Procedures 789
    Some DLL Examples 790
Summary 793
    Q&A 794
Workshop 796
    Quiz 796
    Exercises 796

Day 21 **Using Automatic Procedures, Event Procedures, and Add-Ins** **799**

What Are Automatic Procedures and Event Procedures? 800
Working with Automatic Procedures 801
    Auto_Open Procedures 801
    Auto_Close Procedures 803
Working with Event Procedures 804
    The *OnSheetActivate* Property 805
    The *OnSheetDeactivate* Property 807
    The *OnWindow* Property 809
    The *OnKey* Method 810
    The *OnDoubleClick* Property 813
    The *OnTime* Method 814
    The *OnEntry* Property 816
    The *OnCalculate* Property 819
Working with Add-In Applications 820
    Creating an Add-In Application 821
    Controlling Add-Ins with Visual Basic 821
Summary 823
    Q&A 824
Workshop 826
    Quiz 826
    Exercises 826

Week 3 in Review **829**

Appendixes

A	**Answers**	**839**

Day 1 840
  Quiz 840
  Exercises 841
Day 2 842
  Quiz 842
  Exercises 844
Day 3 846
  Quiz 846
  Exercises 847
Day 4 850
  Quiz 850
  Exercises 851
Day 5 851
  Quiz 851
  Exercises 852
Day 6 854
  Quiz 854
  Exercises 855
Day 7 857
  Quiz 857
  Exercises 858
Day 8 860
  Quiz 860
  Exercises 861
Day 9 864
  Quiz 864
  Exercises 864
Day 10 869
  Quiz 869
  Exercises 870
Day 11 874
  Quiz 874
  Exercises 875
Day 12 878
  Quiz 878
  Exercises 879
Day 13 880
  Quiz 880
  Exercises 880
Day 14 883
  Quiz 883
  Exercises 883

Day 15 884
    Quiz 884
    Exercises 884
Day 16 887
    Quiz 887
    Exercises 888
Day 17 889
    Quiz 889
    Exercise 890
Day 18 891
    Quiz 891
    Exercises 892
Day 19 894
    Quiz 894
    Exercises 896
Day 20 896
    Quiz 896
    Exercises 897
Day 21 898
    Quiz 898
    Exercises 899

B   **Sample Application**   **903**

Creating the Sample Application 904
Entering the Code Listings 905
    The Constants Module 905
    The AnimalMain Module 906
    The AnimalRetrieval Module 911
    The LearnNewAnimals Module 916
    The ListAnimals Module 920
    The Functions Module 922
    The Automatic Module 923
Creating the Guess The Animal Game's Dialog Boxes 925
    The DialogMain Dialog Box 925
    The DialogRules Dialog Box 927
    The DialogList Dialog Box 928
    The DialogNewAnimal Dialog Box 928
Using the Game 929
Converting Guess The Animal to an Add-In Program 930
How Guess The Animal Works 931

Index   **935**

Acknowledgments

I would like to thank all of the individuals at Sams who worked on this book for their hard work and dedication to quality books.

About the Author

Matthew Harris

Matthew Harris, a consultant living in Oakland, California, has been involved with the microcomputer industry since 1980. He has provided programming, technical support, training, and consulting services to the 1990 International AIDS Conference, the University of California at San Francisco, and many private companies, both large and small. A certified hardware technician, Mr. Harris began programming applications for IBM PCs and compatibles in 1983 and has written both commercially distributed applications and in-house applications for many clients. He also has taught classes on using MS-DOS and on programming in BASIC and Pascal. Mr. Harris is the author of *The Disk Compression Book* and is the co-author of *Using FileMaker Pro 2.0 for Windows* (both published by Que Books). Mr. Harris is a contributing author to *Using Word for Windows 6, Using Excel 5, Excel Professional Techniques, Using Paradox 4.5 for DOS, Using Paradox for Windows 5.0, The Paradox Developer's Guide, Using MS-DOS 6, Unveiling Windows 95,* and *Using Access 7 for Windows,* all published by Que Books. Mr. Harris can be reached via CompuServe at 74017,766 or through the Internet at 74017.766@compuserve.com.

How To Use This Book

If you want to automate routine tasks, automate OLE and other types of data exchanges between applications, or write complete programs that handle all aspects of performing complex tasks, you've made a wise decision in choosing this book. As you can guess from its title, this book is structured so that you can teach yourself the Visual Basic for Applications programming language for Excel in 21 days. By working through the daily lessons' examples, quizzes, and exercises, you'll learn how to write macro programs and develop add-in programs for Excel 7.

This book concentrates exclusively on Visual Basic for Applications programming in Excel 7. The first and most important reason this book concentrates on Excel 7 is because this book is designed for people who have never programmed before, as well as for those people who are new to Visual Basic for Applications (VBA) programming. Excel 7's programming environment is the easiest and most congenial environment for both beginning programmers and for beginning VBA programmers. Excel's Macro Recorder (a feature not found in Access) enables you to record VBA program code, giving you a quick leg up to writing and developing your own programs. Excel's Dialog Sheets (for creating dialog boxes) are easy to use, and relieve you from many of the difficulties of creating dialog boxes that you encounter in other dialects of Visual Basic for Applications. In Excel, you can write and then directly execute VBA programs; other versions of VBA (such as Access) don't permit you to directly execute your VBA code. Excel 7 is a clean, simple environment in which to learn a new programming language. A secondary reason that this book concentrates on Excel 7 programming is the simple fact that Excel is probably the single most widespread VBA product on the market.

Use this book as the gateway to the world of Visual Basic for Applications programming. If you've never written a computer program before, this book will show you how. If you've used other programming languages but haven't programmed in VBA before, this book gets you started in Visual Basic for Applications as quickly and easily as possible. After you've mastered the skills and techniques presented in this book, you'll have the knowledge and confidence to tackle Visual Basic for Applications programming in more challenging environments—such as Access 7.

To get started in this book, you need to know how to use Excel 7 and also know how to use Windows 95. You don't need any previous programming experience to learn how to write programs in VBA because at the same time this book teaches you VBA, it also teaches you fundamental programming concepts and good programming techniques. Each daily lesson builds on material in previous lessons—as do many of the examples. You start by recording and refining simple macros, such as formatting data in Excel worksheet cells, and progress to creating custom dialog boxes, menus, and toolbars as well as add-in applications. Notes, Tips, Cautions, and DOs and DON'Ts provide excellent coverage of topics from experienced programmers.

Syntax

Syntax blocks show you how to use a specific Visual Basic for Applications language element. The following is an example of what a syntax block looks like.

The following is a sample syntax line:

```
Sub ProcName ( [ByVal ¦ ByRef] [argname] )
```

The syntax line means that you should type everything exactly as it appears, with these exceptions:

☐ You must supply a name that you define, or supply a specific data item for each placeholder. Placeholders are indicated by italics. In the sample line, both *ProcName* and *argname* are placeholders.

☐ Items enclosed in square brackets are optional. In the sample line, ByVal ¦ ByRef is an optional element and so is *argname*.

☐ The vertical bar (¦) symbol indicates alternate items. When two or more alternate items appear, you can use any one of them. In the sample line above, you could include either ByVal or ByRef, but not both.

Listings

Listings present Visual Basic for Applications procedures or functions that demonstrate the programming commands or topics under discussion. Listings have two elements associated with them:

The Type icon denotes the new program for you to enter.

The Analysis icon denotes the explanation of how the listing's program code works, including why code was written one way rather than another way.

Q&A and Workshops

Each day's lesson ends with special features that reinforce what you've learned that day and which develop your Visual Basic for Applications programming skills by putting them to practical use. The Q&A section provides answers to common questions and problems.

The Workshop presents quizzes to test your mastery of new concepts, and exercises that help you apply your new programming skills by writing code—the best way to learn VBA (answers for both quiz questions and exercises are in Appendix A, "Answers").

Special BUG BUSTER exercises invite you to locate a *bug*, or a program defect, in the listed program—you often learn more from solving a problem than any amount of reading or lecturing.

Conventions

This book uses several typographical conventions to help you differentiate Visual Basic code from regular English text, and to distinguish different parts of the program code from one another; special type styles are also used to identify important concepts and new terms.

- ☐ Words and symbols that are part of the Visual Basic for Applications programming language are printed in a monospace font.

- ☐ Placeholders—terms used to represent what you actually type within the program code—are printed in an *italic monospace* font.

- ☐ Variable names or procedure names that you create are printed in **monospace bold** whenever they appear in a regular text paragraph—program code listings are printed entirely in monospace font.

- ☐ New terms or important concepts are printed in an *italic* font. Literal values in the text, such as the name of a worksheet, or the name of a named range of data in an Excel worksheet are also typeset in an *italic* font.

- ☐ For menu commands—such as **F**ile | **O**pen—in Excel or another Windows program, each command is separated from the next submenu command by a vertical bar, and the menu command's hotkey is emphasized in bold. Hotkeys for dialog box command buttons and other controls are also emphasized in bold.

As you get ready for your first week of learning how to program in Visual Basic for Applications, you need only two things: Excel 7 and this book. If you don't have Excel 7 (or Excel 5, in a pinch), you can still use this book, but its value to you will be limited. You cannot learn a programming language well by just reading a book. To learn Visual Basic for Applications, you must actually record and edit macros, and enter and run your own procedures written from scratch. The examples and exercises in this book offer you the hands-on experience you need to master Visual Basic for Applications programming in Excel. You'll also gain many skills that you'll be able to apply to VBA programming in Access 7 or Microsoft Project.

This book is arranged so that each day ends with several quiz questions and some exercises. At the end of each lesson, you should be able to answer all the quiz questions and complete all the exercises. Appendix A, "Answers," includes answers to all the quiz questions and solutions to most of the exercises. In the exercise solutions for most of the early lessons, you'll find additional programming explanations and tips related to the specific exercise solution.

Make every attempt to complete every exercise; this book uses several of the program solutions for exercises in early chapters as the basis for additional exercises, examples, or explanations in later chapters. For example, Day 2 makes use of a macro that you create while performing Exercise 1 from Day 1.

What's Ahead?

The first week covers basic material that you need to know to get started recording, editing, and writing Visual Basic for Applications (VBA) macros and procedures. The lessons in the first week also explain how to create user-defined functions for your Excel worksheets and Access databases.

In Day 1, "Getting Started," and Day 2, "Writing and Editing Simple Macros," you learn how to record and edit a VBA macro, how to recognize the basic elements of a VBA procedure, and how to get started writing your own VBA macros without recording. These two chapters also introduce you to some of the features of VBA's Object Browser, an important tool for VBA programming. Day 2 also shows you how to make your macros display simple messages on-screen.

In Day 3, "Understanding Data Types, Variables, and Constants," you learn about variables, and how to use them to store data temporarily in your VBA macros and procedures. You also learn about the different types of data that VBA can store and manipulate, and how to use constants to simplify the way you include unchanging values in your VBA statements. Day 3 also describes how to get input from your VBA macro's user. In Day 4, "Operators and Expressions," you learn how to incorporate variables and constants into expressions that calculate new values.

Day 5, "Visual Basic for Applications and Excel Functions," explains all about the various functions VBA provides for you to convert values from one data type to another, to get information about VBA or Excel, and to perform various other tasks. You also learn how to access the built-in worksheet functions of Excel. You learn what a function is, and how to use function results in your expressions. In Day 6, "Function Procedures and User-Defined Functions," you learn how to create your own custom functions for use in your VBA macros and procedures, and how to create and use custom functions for your Excel worksheets.

The first week's lessons end with Day 7, "Working with Objects." Day 7 teaches you what program objects are, and how to recognize and understand various object references that you'll see in the macros you record. This lesson teaches you about object properties and methods, and explains how to retrieve or change the values of an object's property or how to use an object's methods.

This is a lot of material to cover in just one week, but if you take the information one chapter a day, you should have no problems.

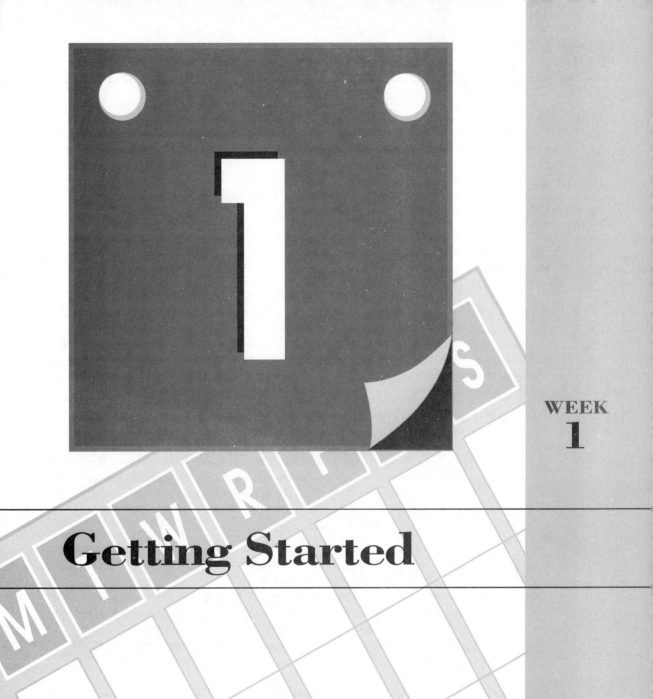

Getting Started

Welcome to *Teach Yourself Excel Programming with Visual Basic for Applications in 21 Days.* In this lesson for the first day, you learn:

- [ ] What macros are and how they are used.
- [ ] How Visual Basic for Applications relates to and enhances macros.
- [ ] Why you need to add Visual Basic for Applications program commands to recorded macros, and why to use Visual Basic for Applications to program macros without recording.
- [ ] How to record and run a macro.

Macros and Programming Languages

Before you start writing your own macros, you should have a good understanding of what a macro is and how a Visual Basic for Applications (VBA) programmed macro differs from a recorded macro.

What Is a Macro?

Eventually—regardless of the operating system or software applications you use—you'll notice that you execute the same sequences of commands over and over in order to accomplish routine tasks. Rather than enter a command sequence every time you want to perform a task, you can create a *macro* to make an application execute the sequence of commands on its own. Macros enable you to enter a single command that accomplishes the same task that would otherwise require you to enter several commands manually.

> **Note:** Recorded command sequences were originally called *macro-commands*; modern usage has shortened the term to the simpler *macro*. (The term *macro* is found as a prefix for several words in the English language; it is derived from the Greek word meaning *enlarged* or *elongated.*) In the context of computers and application software, *macro* is always understood to mean a macro-command.

Macros provide benefits other than convenience. Because computers are much better suited to performing repetitive tasks than human beings are, recording repeated sequences of commands in a macro increases the accuracy of the work you perform, as well as the speed. Once you record the correct series of commands, you can count on the computer to repeat the sequence flawlessly each time it executes the macro. Another benefit from using macros is that a human operator is not usually needed while a macro executes. If the macro is particularly long, or performs operations that require substantial computer processing time (such as database queries and

sorts), you are free to leave the computer and do something else, or to switch to a different application and continue working on some other task.

A macro recorder records *all* of the user's actions—including mistakes and false starts. When an application program plays back a macro, it performs each recorded command in the exact sequence you originally performed them. Early macro recorders had a serious drawback: if you recorded a lengthy series of actions that contained a minor mistake, the only way to remove the mistake was to record the macro all over again. Also, if you needed to make a minor change in a long macro, you had to rerecord the entire macro. Often, rerecording a long macro simply led to additional mistakes in the new recording. For these reasons, software developers added the capability to edit macros to their macro recorders, so you could more easily correct minor mistakes or make other changes in a macro without rerecording it entirely.

> **Note:** Not every application contains a macro recorder. Microsoft Access 7, for example, uses a *macro builder* instead of a macro recorder like the one found in Excel 7. In Access's macro builder, you select the actions that you want the macro to carry out from a predefined list of commands instead of having the application record actions as you perform them.

A Brief History of Visual Basic for Applications

Visual Basic for Applications (VBA), although still a new product, comes from a background with a history almost as long as that of the entire computer industry. Visual Basic for Applications is a modern dialect of the BASIC programming language that was first developed in the early 1960s. (BASIC is an acronym for *B*eginner's *A*ll-Purpose *S*ymbolic *I*nstruction *C*ode.)

Although, by today's standards, the original BASIC programming language was severely limited, it was easy to learn and understand, and rapidly became very widespread. Versions of BASIC were (and still are) produced for use on all types of computers. Microsoft's GWBASIC (GW stands for *G*raphics *W*orkshop) was one of the first programming languages available for the computers that evolved into the modern-day personal computer. GWBASIC was supplied with MS-DOS versions prior to Version 5.0. Early PC computers manufactured by IBM even contained a version of BASIC built into the computer's ROM (Read-Only Memory) chips.

Over the years, the original design and specifications for BASIC have been improved. As the technology for programming languages advanced and changed, various software publishers added to the capabilities of the original BASIC. Modern dialects of BASIC usually have many

or all of the features found in other programming languages of more recent origin, such as Pascal or C.

In the late 1980s, Microsoft published a tremendously enhanced version of the BASIC language, called QuickBASIC. QuickBASIC incorporated almost all the features found in state-of-the-art software development systems. Microsoft now includes a version of QuickBASIC with DOS Versions 6.0 and higher (but not in Windows 95).

After several versions of QuickBASIC, in 1992 Microsoft introduced Visual Basic for Windows. As with QuickBASIC, Visual Basic for Windows added state-of-the-art features, and was closely integrated with the Windows environment. Visual Basic provides commands for creating and controlling the necessary elements of a Windows program: dialog boxes, menu bars, drop-down lists, command buttons, checkboxes, toolbars, and so on. In particular, Visual Basic incorporated the necessary commands to use Object Linking and Embedding (OLE) and Dynamic Data Exchange (DDE) to communicate or share data with other Windows applications. Visual Basic is essentially a new programming language for Windows, with its roots in BASIC.

At the same time BASIC was evolving and improving, so were the macro recorders used in applications programs. Over the years, application macros gradually became more complex and sophisticated in response to users' desires to make macros more flexible in function and easier to maintain. Many macro languages began to include capabilities similar to those usually found only in complete programming languages.

Many applications' macro languages differ greatly from product to product, however. This means you might need to learn several different macro languages; as a result, you might experience a loss in productivity while you learn the new macro language. To eliminate the need to learn a new macro language for each product, Microsoft began to incorporate elements of the BASIC programming language in the macro languages of its products. The macro language for Microsoft's Word for Windows is still known as WordBasic, for example, while the macro language for Microsoft Access 2.0 was known as Access Basic. (Microsoft Access 7 now uses Visual Basic for Applications as its programming language, although it still includes a special macro language system, as well.)

To unify the macro languages in its Windows applications, and to integrate those applications' macro languages with Windows' DDE and OLE, Microsoft has created a special version of the Visual Basic language, called Visual Basic for Applications (abbreviated VBA). Excel 5 was the first released product to include Visual Basic for Applications (VBA). With the release of Microsoft Office 95, VBA is now implemented in Microsoft Access 7 as well as Excel 7 and Microsoft Project.

Visual Basic for Applications is essentially the same as Visual Basic for Windows, with some slight differences. VBA macro programs are stored in a file format used by the application you wrote the Visual Basic for Applications macro in, rather than individual text files. For example, VBA macro programs created in Excel 7 are stored in an Excel workbook file; VBA programs in Access 7 are stored in an Access database file.

To run a Visual Basic for Applications macro program, you must start it by using the application you wrote the macro in. For example, you cannot start an Excel VBA macro from any program other than Excel—although another application could use OLE Automation to cause Excel to execute a particular macro (or send a DDE message). Although the core features of VBA remain the same in each application, each different application adds special commands and objects (depending on the specific application) to Visual Basic for Applications. For example, VBA in Excel 7 contains many commands that pertain only to worksheets and the tasks that you can perform with a worksheet. Similarly, VBA in Access 7 contains commands that pertain only to database manipulation.

By having only one macro programming language in all of its products, Microsoft ensures that a great deal of what you learn about Visual Basic for Applications in one application applies to using VBA in another application. In fact, Visual Basic 4 (the most recent version of Visual Basic) also supports VBA, so that you can easily convert any programs you write in VBA to a complete Visual Basic program.

Why Learn Visual Basic for Applications in Excel?

Because you can use an Excel macro recorder to record your actions in a macro and then later play them back, it may at first seem unnecessary to learn VBA. Recorded macros alone, however, cannot always fill your needs. A recorded macro can only play back each action you perform, in the same sequence you originally performed the actions, without deviation. You can use Visual Basic for Applications to enhance your recorded macros, greatly increasing their flexibility and power.

Recorded macros are inflexible, so they cannot respond to changed or changing conditions. You can make a macro programmed in VBA, however, that will evaluate various predetermined conditions and choose a different series of actions based on those conditions. If you execute an Excel macro, for example, that attempts to select a worksheet named "Sales Chart" when there is no such worksheet in the current workbook, your recorded macro will fail to execute correctly, and Excel will display an error message dialog box. By adding VBA programming to this recorded macro, you could make it first test for the existence of the specified worksheet before selecting it, or even insert and rename a new worksheet if the desired worksheet did not exist.

Note: If you have experience with Microsoft Access, using Access' Macro Builder may seem a bit like programming, but it isn't. The Access Macro Builder only allows you to select actions from a predefined list. The macros you create with the Access Macro Builder have many of the same limitations that recorded macros have—they lack the flexibility of VBA's decision-making commands and the capability to repeat actions efficiently.

When it comes to repetitive actions within the macro itself, recorded macros are rather limited. If you want a recorded macro to repeat an action several times, you must manually repeat that action the desired number of times when you record the macro. The macro then always repeats the action the same number of times, every time you execute the macro, until you edit the macro or rerecord it. In contrast, a macro programmed in VBA can use predetermined conditions—or input from the macro's user—to repeat an action a flexible number of times, or to choose whether the action should be performed at all.

As an example, you might want to record a macro to change the width of several adjacent columns in an Excel worksheet. If you want the macro to change the width of the first three columns in the worksheet, you must manually repeat the resizing operation for each of the three columns as you record the macro. The recorded macro will only (and always) change the width of the first three columns of a worksheet—you cannot use the same macro to change the width of two columns or four columns. Also, if you changed the width of the first three columns, your recorded macro will only operate on the first three columns—you cannot use the same macro to change the width of the second through fourth columns rather than the first through third. By adding Visual Basic for Applications programming to this recorded macro, you can create a macro that asks you how many, and which, columns to resize, and even enables you to specify the new column width.

These two examples represent a couple of the simplest tasks that you can perform with VBA in your macros. There are many circumstances under which you will want to add decision-making and efficient repetition to recorded macros. The only way to get these features is to manually add VBA program statements to your recorded macro.

In addition to enhancing specific recorded macros, you can also use VBA to connect, organize, and control several recorded macros that you use to perform a complex overall task made up of several smaller tasks. For example, you might regularly import data from a database program into an Excel worksheet, format the data for display, generate a chart from the data, and then print the chart and formatted report.

To pull all these individual tasks together to create a single task performed by a single macro, you might first record a separate macro for each of the individual tasks—a macro to import the data, another macro to format the data for display, another macro to create the chart, and yet another macro to print the data. Next, you would organize the recorded macros so that they are executed in the proper sequence by a single macro that you write with VBA.

You can also use Visual Basic for Applications to control the execution of other applications and to automate the sharing of data between applications by using OLE and DDE, as explained later in this book.

Recording a New Excel Macro

Before you can enhance a macro with Visual Basic for Applications, you must first record a macro to enhance. This section shows you what you need to know to use Excel's macro recorder, in general, and also takes you through the steps of recording a specific macro.

Typically, recording a macro involves four major steps:

1. *Set up the starting conditions for the macro.* Setting up the starting conditions for a macro means establishing the same conditions in your work environment that you expect to exist at the time you later play back the recorded macro. Setting up the starting conditions for an Excel macro might involve any or all of the following actions (or others not listed): opening a workbook, selecting a specific worksheet, selecting a specific range of cells, selecting a specific chart sheet, and so on.

2. *Start the macro recorder.* You provide a name for the new macro and select the location to store the recorded macro at the same time you start the macro recorder.

3. *Perform the actions that you want recorded for later use.* You can record into a macro any action that you can perform by using the keyboard or mouse—including executing previously recorded macros. The specific actions that you perform depend on the task that you want to record.

4. *Stop the macro recorder.* When you stop the macro recorder, your actions are no longer recorded and stored in the macro. Once you stop the macro recorder, the new recorded macro is immediately available for use.

Setting Up the Macro's Starting Conditions

Before recording any macro, you must set up the conditions under which you will run the macro. (*Running* or *executing* a macro means playing back the recorded instructions in the macro.) Remember that the VBA Macro Recorder records *all* the actions you perform. A recorded Excel macro, for example, could include activities such as opening a workbook, selecting a worksheet, and selecting a range of cells on the worksheet. If you didn't want to include these activities in the recorded macro, you would have to perform them *before* starting the macro recorder.

For example, if you want to record a general-purpose macro that will change the character font and type size of the text in whatever worksheet cell or range of cells is currently selected, the starting condition for that macro is an open workbook with a selected range of cells on the active worksheet. To establish the starting conditions for this macro, therefore, you should open a workbook and select cells before starting the macro recorder.

If you start the macro recorder and then open a workbook, select a worksheet, and select cells, those actions become part of the recorded macro. The recorded macro then always opens the same workbook and applies the character formatting to the same worksheet and range of cells—your recorded macro ends up being specific to that particular workbook, worksheet, and range of cells, instead of being a general-purpose tool to apply the character formatting to any selected range of cells.

As a specific example, assume that you frequently apply a 12-point bold Arial font as the character formatting style for worksheet cells you want to draw attention to, without changing any other part of the cells' formatting. In this case, you can't use a named style (accessed through the Format | Style menu command) to apply the desired character formatting because you'd affect *all* of the cells' attributes (such as date or currency formatting), not just the character format—instead, you must set the font attributes manually each time. To reduce the amount of time required to format the text, you decide to record a macro that selects the 12-point bold Arial font and applies that character formatting to whatever cell or range of cells happens to be currently selected. Because you want this macro to work on any selected cell or range of cells, the starting conditions for this macro are that there is an open workbook with a selected range of cells on the active worksheet.

To set up the starting conditions for this specific example, open any workbook and select any cell on any worksheet. Figure 1.1 shows a sample workbook opened, with cell B4 selected. By selecting a cell on a worksheet, you have created the necessary starting conditions to record this general-purpose macro for applying character formatting to any selected cell or range of cells.

Figure 1.1.
Set up the starting conditions for the text formatting macro before you start the Macro Recorder.

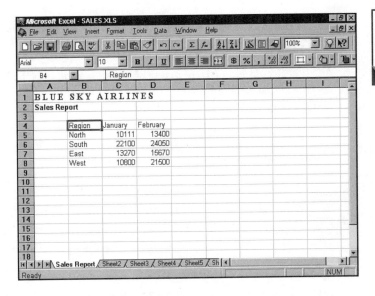

Starting the Macro Recorder

To start recording a new macro, choose the **T**ools | **R**ecord Macro | **R**ecord New Macro command. Excel displays the Record New Macro dialog box shown in Figure 1.2. (The next section explains the options in this dialog box.)

You can also start the Macro Recorder whenever the Visual Basic Toolbar is displayed by clicking the Record Macro button. Excel displays the Visual Basic Toolbar whenever a module sheet is active; you can also display or hide toolbars with the **V**iew | **T**oolbars command.

Tip: If no files are open and the **T**ools menu is not shown on Excel's main menu bar, the **R**ecord Macro command appears on the **F**ile menu.

Figure 1.2.
In the Record New Macro dialog box, enter the name for the new macro and add any comments about what the macro does.

Naming the New Macro and Selecting Options

The first Record New Macro dialog box option to fill in is the **M**acro Name. By default, VBA selects a macro name consisting of the word **Macro** followed by a number corresponding to the number of macros you've recorded in this work session. You should enter a name for the macro that conveys some meaning about what the macro does. For example, if you are recording a macro to generate a chart from sales data in a worksheet, you might enter the name **MakeSalesChart** in the **M**acro Name text box.

> **Note:** You can enter a macro name up to 46 characters in length in the **M**acro Name text box. Macro names must begin with a letter, although they can contain numbers. Macro names cannot include spaces or punctuation characters.

In the specific example of creating a general-purpose macro to apply the 12-point bold Arial font, you should enter the name **FormatArialBold12** in the **M**acro Name text box. This name lets you know fairly clearly what the macro does.

The second option to fill in is the **D**escription text box. The information in this text box is not directly used by the macro; it is just a place to keep some notes and comments about what the macro does. When you record a macro, VBA fills in a default description stating the date that the macro was recorded and by which user. (VBA uses the name entered in the User **N**ame text box on the General tab of the Options dialog box; if this text box is empty, VBA uses the user name you entered when you logged on to Windows 95. You can display the Options dialog box by choosing the **T**ools | **O**ptions command.)

For the **FormatArialBold12** example, leave the original information in place but add this additional text in the **D**escription text box:

```
Applies 12-point bold Arial font to active cell or range.
```

DO	DON'T

DO use a meaningful name for your recorded macro, one that reflects the action the macro carries out. A name such as **MakeSalesChart** or **FormatArialBold12** communicates much more than default names such as **Macro1**.

DO be sure to enter any special prerequisites for the macro in the **D**escription text box, such as whether or not a particular workbook should be opened before using the macro.

The Record New Macro dialog box has additional options not shown in its initial display. To see the additional options, click the **O**ptions button. Figure 1.3 shows Excel's Record New Macro dialog box after clicking the **O**ptions button.

Figure 1.3.

Use the Record New Macro options to control where Excel stores the recorded macro, to assign a menu choice and shortcut key to the macro, and to select the language used to record the macro.

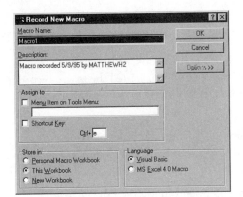

If you're certain you'll use the macro you are about to record with great frequency, you may want to attach the macro to a menu choice on the **T**ools menu, assign a shortcut key to run the macro, or both. Usually, you should not assign a macro to a menu choice or shortcut key unless you really do expect to use the macro with great frequency—if you assign all your macros to shortcut keys or a menu choice on the **T**ools menu, you'll quickly run out of unassigned keys or end up with menus that are too long to be useful.

To assign the macro to a choice on the **T**ools menu, select the Men**u** Item on Tools Menu check box and enter the name for the menu choice in the accompanying text box.

To assign the macro to a shortcut key, select the Shortcut **K**ey check box and enter the keystroke you want to use to run this macro. (All shortcut keys are really the combination of the keystroke you enter plus the Ctrl key—if you enter **a** as the shortcut key for a macro, the actual shortcut keystroke is Ctrl+a.)

Next, choose where you want the recorded macro stored. As you can see in Figure 1.3, you can choose to store the macro in the **P**ersonal Macro Workbook, This **W**orkbook (the workbook that was active when you started the Macro Recorder), or in a **N**ew Workbook (a completely new workbook file).

Store the new macro in the Personal macro workbook to help ensure that it is available at all times, no matter which files you have open. When you select the **P**ersonal Macro Workbook option, Excel stores the macro in a special workbook file named PERSONAL.XLS in the startup folder. (Excel automatically opens workbook files stored in its startup folder—\EXCEL\XLSTART—each time you start Excel.) If you select this option and the PERSONAL.XLS workbook file does not already exist, Excel creates it for you.

Note: You may not notice that the PERSONAL.XLS workbook is open because, by default, Excel hides the PERSONAL workbook file after creating it. (Refer to Excel's online help for information on hiding and unhiding workbook files.)

Storing the recorded macro in a new workbook causes Excel to create a new workbook and store the macro in that workbook. Although Excel stores the macro in a new workbook, the workbook that was active when you started the macro recorder remains the active workbook; any actions you record are performed in that workbook and not in the new workbook created to store the macro.

Regardless of which workbook you choose to store the new recorded macro in, the macro is attached to the workbook as a VBA *module sheet*. Modules are described in more detail in the next lesson.

Because you intend to use the **FormatArialBold12** macro in all your worksheets, the macro should be available all the time. Therefore, you should choose the **P**ersonal Macro Workbook option to store the **FormatArialBold12** macro in the PERSONAL.XLS workbook.

DO	**DON'T**

DO store general-purpose macros in the Personal macro file.

DO store macros that relate specifically to a single workbook, project, or similar file in the file to which the macro relates.

In the Language option group, make sure that the **V**isual Basic option button is selected. Any other macro language options provided in this control group are to provide backward compatibility with previous versions of Excel's macro language. You cannot add Visual Basic for Applications program enhancements to a macro unless the macro is recorded in the Visual Basic for Applications language.

Figure 1.4 shows the Record New Macro dialog box filled in for the **FormatArialBold12** example macro.

Figure 1.4.

The completed Record New Macro dialog box for the sample ***FormatArialBold12*** *macro.*

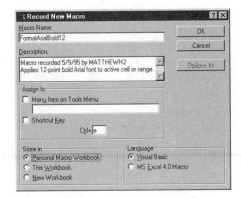

Recording Your Actions

When you are satisfied with the options you've selected in the Record New Macro dialog box, choose the OK button; Excel now displays the Stop Recorder toolbar and begins recording your actions. The Macro Recorder stores each action you perform in the new macro until you stop the Macro Recorder.

Figure 1.5 shows the Stop Recorder toolbar displayed during a macro recording session (the macro being recorded in Figure 1.5 is the **FormatArialBold12** example macro). Notice that the word *Recording* appears in the status bar at the bottom-left side of the Excel window to help remind you that Excel is recording all your actions.

Figure 1.5.

*Excel displays the Stop Recorder toolbar and the word **Recording** in the status bar while you record a macro.*

For the specific example of the **FormatArialBold12** macro, perform these actions:

1. Choose the Format | Cells command to display the Format Cells dialog box.

2. If the Font options are not already displayed, click the Font tab to display the Font options. (Figure 1.6 shows the Format Cells dialog box with the Font options displayed.)

3. Select **Arial** in the **F**ont list.

4. Select **Bold** in the F**o**nt Style list.

5. Select **12** in the **S**ize list.

6. Choose OK to close the Format Cells dialog box and apply the changes to the selected cell in the worksheet.

Figure 1.6.
Excel's Format Cells dialog box, showing the Font options filled in for the
FormatArialBold12
macro.

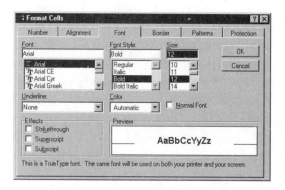

Stopping the Macro Recorder

As mentioned in the preceding section, as soon as you choose the OK button in the Record New Macro dialog box, Excel begins recording the macro and displays the Stop Recorder toolbar. The Stop Recorder toolbar contains only one button—the Stop Macro button.

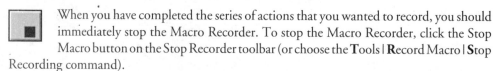

When you have completed the series of actions that you wanted to record, you should immediately stop the Macro Recorder. To stop the Macro Recorder, click the Stop Macro button on the Stop Recorder toolbar (or choose the **T**ools | **R**ecord Macro | **S**top Recording command).

For the **FormatArialBold12** example macro, you should stop the Macro Recorder immediately after you choose OK to close the Format Cells dialog box.

| **DO** | **DON'T** |

DO remember to stop the Macro Recorder as soon as you complete the series of actions you want to record; the recorder continues to record all your actions until you stop it.

DON'T forget that Excel stores the completed macro in the location you chose in the Record New Macro dialog box.

Macro Source Code

When you record a macro, the Macro Recorder stores a series of text instructions that describe, in the Visual Basic for Applications programming language, the various actions you perform while the recorder is on. This text description of your commands is called the *source code* for the macro. Later, when you run the macro, VBA reads the recorded instructions in the source code and executes each instruction in sequence, thereby duplicating the actions that you performed when you recorded the macro.

The following lines list the source code produced when you record the **FormatArialBold12** macro in Excel. Notice that the name and the description of the macro that you entered in the Record New Macro dialog box is included at the beginning of the recorded macro source code.

```
'
' FormatArialBold12 Macro
' Macro recorded 5/9/95 by MATTHEWH2
' Applies 12-point bold Arial font to active cell or range.
'
'
Sub FormatArialBold12()
    With Selection.Font
        .Name = "Arial"
        .FontStyle = "Bold"
        .Size = 12
        .Strikethrough = False
        .Superscript = False
        .Subscript = False
        .OutlineFont = False
        .Shadow = False
        .Underline = xlNone
        .ColorIndex = xlAutomatic
    End With
End Sub
```

Don't be dismayed if this source code listing doesn't make a lot of sense to you right now. You can record and execute macros without ever looking at the macro's source code, or even knowing what it does. The next lesson explains the various parts of a macro and also explains how to locate the source code for a particular macro and display it for editing or inspection.

Note: If you performed any actions other than those specified in the preceding numbered steps, your recorded macro will contain additional statements corresponding to your additional actions.

Running a Macro

After you have recorded a macro, you can run the macro. Running the macro causes Excel to carry out all the instructions recorded in the macro.

To run a macro, choose the **Tools | M**acro command to display the Macro dialog box, shown in Figure 1.7. In the Macro dialog box, select the macro you want to run in the **M**acro Name/ Reference list, and then choose the **R**un button to execute that macro. (Other buttons in the Macro dialog box are described in following lessons.)

Figure 1.7.
Use the Macro dialog box to
select a macro to run. Only
the macros available in open
workbooks are listed.

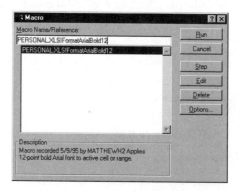

For example, to run the **FormatArialBold12** macro you just recorded, first select a new cell on the worksheet (preferably one that contains some text, so you can see the changes made to the text in the cell by the **FormatArialBold12** macro). Next, choose the **Tools | M**acro command to display the Macro dialog box, and then select the **FormatArialBold12** macro in the **M**acro Name/Reference list. Finally, choose the **R**un button to execute the **FormatArialBold12** macro. The text in whatever cell was selected when you ran the **FormatArialBold12** macro has its formatting changed to 12-point bold Arial font.

The Macro dialog box lists the macros stored in workbooks that are currently open, including workbooks that are opened but hidden. The name of the workbook that contains the macro is listed in front of the macro name in the **Macro Name/Reference** list if the macro is not in the current workbook. If the macro you want is not listed, you must open the workbook that the macro is stored in to make the macro available before you open the Macro dialog box.

The **FormatArialBold12** macro should be listed if you stored it in the Personal macro workbook; if the PERSONAL.XLS workbook is not the active workbook, then you may need to select **PERSONAL.XLS!FormatArialBold12** in the **Macro** Name/Reference list in order to run the `FormatArialBold12` macro.

If you used the options in the Record New Macro dialog box to create a menu item on the **Tools** menu, or to assign a shortcut key to the macro, you can also run that specific macro by choosing the appropriate command from the **Tools** menu or by pressing the assigned shortcut key combination. As with the macros listed in the Macro dialog box, only macros stored in a currently open workbook (it does not have to be the active workbook) are added to the **Tools** menu or have their hotkeys activated.

This means, for example, that if you create a macro named **MakeSalesChart** in a workbook named SALES and assign the **MakeSalesChart** macro to a choice on the **Tools** menu named *Sales Chart*, the Sales Chart choice appears on the **Tools** menu only if the SALES workbook is open.

> **Note:** Excel macros are available only if the workbook in which the macro is stored is currently open. The workbook does not have to be the active workbook in order for its macros to be available, nor does the workbook have to be visible.

As you may already know, you can also run macros by assigning them to custom toolbar buttons and by creating custom menu choices for the macros. You can also assign a macro to a button or graphic object placed directly into an Excel 7 worksheet. Day 16, "Menus and Toolbars," describes how to assign a macro to a toolbar button, menu command, or graphic object on a worksheet or form from a programmer's point of view. Refer to Excel's online help for more information about using interactive features to assign macros to menus and toolbar buttons.

Summary

Today you learned about the history of the Visual Basic for Applications programming language, and you learned how macro languages gradually became complex enough to be considered programming languages. Microsoft has greatly increased the power and convenience of the macro languages in its products by incorporating the Visual Basic programming language in the macro language for several of its new products. Adding Visual Basic decision-making and looping structures to recorded macros increases their power. By using Visual Basic for Applications, you can create macro programs to suit a wide variety of needs.

In this lesson, you learned how to record an Excel macro and how to run a macro that you have previously recorded. These are the most basic skills you need to get started with VBA. Many of the macros that you use your VBA programming skills on will begin with a macro that you recorded. The next lesson teaches you how to edit a recorded macro.

Q&A

Q What is a VBA host application?

A A VBA *host application* is any application that contains Visual Basic for Applications. Microsoft's Excel, Access, and Project are now all VBA host applications.

Q Do all VBA host applications have a macro recorder?

A No. Microsoft's Access 7, for example, does not have a macro recorder.

Q Is recording a macro the only way to create an Excel macro?

A No. You can also create a macro by writing it directly on a module sheet. The material covered in the next lesson describes how to create a macro without recording.

Q When recording an Excel macro, do I have to leave the Macro Recorder toolbar on the screen?

A No. If you want, click the top-right corner of the Macro Recorder toolbar to close it, or use the **View** | **Toolbars** command to hide the Macro Recorder toolbar. When you are ready to stop recording the macro, use the **Tools** | **Record Macro** | **S**top Recording command.

Q Can I give a macro a different name after I have recorded it?

A Yes, although you can only rename a macro by editing the macro source code directly, as described in the next lesson. Renaming a macro, however, may cause some minor problems. If your macro is assigned to menu commands, a shortcut key, or to buttons or graphic objects on a worksheet, these custom controls will still try to run the macro using its old name. If you rename a macro, you will have to reassign each custom control and menu to the new macro name. For this reason, it is much better to spend a little time carefully choosing a macro's name, rather than count on renaming the macro later.

Q Is it possible to assign an Excel macro to a menu command on the Tools menu or to a shortcut key after I record it?

A Yes. Use the Macro dialog box to assign a macro to a choice on the **Tools** menu or to assign a shortcut key. Choose the **Tools** | **M**acro command to open the Macro dialog

box, select the macro you want to assign to a **Tools** menu choice or shortcut key command in the **M**acro Name/Reference list, and then choose the **O**ptions button. Select the desired menu choice or shortcut key in the Assign-to group, and then choose OK.

Q **If I do assign an Excel macro to a choice on the Tools menu or to a shortcut key when I record the macro, can I later change or remove the menu command and shortcut key after I record the macro?**

A Yes. You can also use the **O**ptions button in the Macro dialog box to change the **T**ools menu choice or shortcut key assigned to a macro. Follow the procedure described in the preceding question to open the Macro dialog box and access the menu and shortcut key assignment options. To change the menu choice name or the shortcut key, edit the appropriate options. To remove the menu choice or shortcut key assignment, clear the check box for the option you want to remove.

Q **Can I assign a macro to a menu other than the Tools menu?**

A Yes, you can assign a macro to a menu choice on any menu in your application. You can even create completely new custom menus for your application. To assign macros to menus other than the **T**ools menu, you must use the Visual Basic menu editor. Using the menu editor is described in the lesson for Day 16.

Workshop

The Workshop section presents Quiz questions to help you cement your new knowledge, and Exercises to give you experience using what you have learned. Try to understand the questions and exercises before moving on to the next lesson. Answers are in Appendix A.

Quiz

1. What were the reasons recorded macros evolved toward programming languages?
2. How does Visual Basic for Applications differ from Visual Basic?
3. List three benefits obtained by adding Visual Basic program elements to a recorded macro.
4. Can you assign an Excel macro to a menu when you first record it? If so, to which menu?
5. Which macros would you expect to find listed in Excel's Macro dialog box?

Exercises

1. Record a new Excel macro as follows:

   Start the Macro Recorder, setting the options in the Record New Macro dialog box so that the macro is stored in the personal macro file.

   Give the macro the name **NewFile**.

   Record the following actions:

   Choose the **File** | **New** command to create a new workbook, and then use the **File** | Save **As** command to save the workbook (use the name NEWFILE).

   Immediately after saving the file, choose the **File** | **Close** command to close the file.

   Stop the Macro Recorder.

2. Use the Windows 95 Explorer (or just use a window on the desktop) to delete the file (NEWFILE) you just created when you recorded the macro in Exercise 1. Now run the **NewFile** macro you just recorded. What happens? (Hint: Use the Explorer or the **File** | **O**pen command to check the contents of the folder where you saved the new file in Exercise 1.)

3. Now run the **NewFile** macro again. What happens? (Hint: Choose Cancel or End in each dialog box that appears.)

Writing and Editing Simple Macros

Now that you know how to record and run a macro, and you understand the benefits of adding VBA programming to your macros, you are ready to learn how to edit existing macros and how to create new macros without recording. In today's lesson you learn:

☐ How to use the Visual Basic Toolbar and menu commands to edit or write macros, and how to record new commands into an existing macro.

☐ What types of error messages you can expect to see when editing or running a macro, and how to solve the problems that produce those error messages.

☐ How to enable a macro to display simple messages for the user to read.

Understanding Excel's Visual Basic for Applications Environment

In Day 1, you learned how to record and run an Excel macro. Before you edit or write macros, you need to learn more about where macros are stored. You also need to have a general understanding of the VBA menu commands and toolbar buttons, and how they fit into Excel.

Note: This book concentrates exclusively on VBA programming in Excel because Excel is probably the most common, and definitely the most friendly VBA programming environment.

Understanding Modules

You know from Day 1 that Visual Basic for Applications macros are stored as part of the workbook files in which Excel normally keeps its data. Excel 7 stores macros in special workbook sheets called *modules*. A VBA module contains the macro *source code*—the text representation of the instructions in the macro. Each of your Excel 7 workbook files can contain none, one, or several modules; in turn, each module can contain the source code for none, one, or several VBA macros.

When you record a macro, you can specify only the workbook that Excel stores the recorded macro in (the personal macro workbook, current workbook, or a new workbook, as explained in Day 1). Excel chooses the module sheet in which it stores the recorded macro, creating that module sheet, if necessary.

Understanding how Excel 7 gives names to the module sheets it creates will help you locate your recorded macros when you want to view or edit them. When Excel 7 creates the module sheet in which it stores the recorded macro, it gives the module sheet the name *ModuleN*, where *N* is the number of macro sheets created for this workbook during the current work session. (A module's name, like a worksheet's name, is the text displayed in the sheet's tab at the bottom of the workbook window.)

For example, the first time you store a recorded macro in the personal macro workbook (which is named PERSONAL.XLS), Excel creates a module sheet named *Module1* to store the recorded macro. If you continue to record macros in the same work session and store them in the personal macro workbook, Excel continues to store the recorded macros in the same *Module1* module sheet—until you choose a different workbook to store a recorded macro in. If, later in the same work session, you again choose to store recorded macros in the personal macro workbook, Excel adds another module sheet, named *Module2*, to the PERSONAL.XLS workbook.

If a workbook already contains a module sheet with the same name Excel has chosen for a new module sheet, Excel raises the number in the sheet name until the name for the new module sheet no longer conflicts with the names of existing module sheets. For instance, if you start a new Excel work session, and then choose to store a recorded macro in the personal macro workbook, Excel initially chooses the name *Module1* for the new module sheet—because the new sheet is the first module sheet created for the PERSONAL.XLS workbook in the current work session. If, however, the PERSONAL.XLS workbook already contains module sheets named *Module1* and *Module2*, Excel raises the number in the sheet name so there is no conflict with existing names; the new module sheet gets the name *Module3*.

> **Note:** Excel uses the same rules for choosing the name of a module sheet that you insert manually with the **Insert | Macro | Module** command as when Excel creates a module sheet to store a recorded macro. Inserting module sheets is described later in this lesson.

Examining the Visual Basic for Applications Toolbar and Menu Commands

Apart from being just a place to keep the source code for the macros you record, module sheets also provide the "workshop" in which you edit, write, and debug your macros. This section introduces the Visual Basic for Applications commands and programming resources available to you.

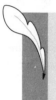

Except for the commands used to record and run a macro, all other commands that relate to using VBA appear only when the active window displays a module sheet. Whenever you display a module in the active window, Excel enters VBA programming mode. In VBA programming mode, Excel changes some of the available menu commands—adding commands that pertain only to VBA and module sheets, and removing commands that pertain only to worksheet or chart sheets and their data. At the same time, Excel also displays the Visual Basic toolbar.

The following sections give you an overview of the Visual Basic menus and toolbar.

> **Note:** Other VBA applications, such as Access 7, also display the Visual Basic toolbar and alter their menus when the active window is a VBA module window. Not every VBA host application has exactly the same menu commands available, but all are highly similar—that's the whole point of using VBA in the first place.

Introducing Visual Basic Menu Commands

Figure 2.1 shows the Excel 7 module sheet produced as a result of recording the `FormatArialBold12` macro in lesson 1. Compare this figure with Figure 2.2, which shows a blank worksheet in the same workbook. Notice that the main menu bar (across the top of the screen) in Figure 2.1 is different from the main menu bar in Figure 2.2—Excel has removed the F**o**rmat and **D**ata menu choices, and added the **R**un choice to the main menu.

Microsoft Excel - Personal.xls
File Edit View Insert Run Tools Window Help
'
' FormatArialBold12 Macro
' Macro recorded 5/9/95 by MATTHEWH2
' Applies 12-point bold Arial font to active cell or range.
'
'
Sub FormatArialBold12()
With Selection.Font
.Name = "Arial"
.FontStyle = "Bold"
.Size = 12
.Strikethrough = False
.Superscript = False
.Subscript = False
.OutlineFont = False
.Shadow = False
.Underline = xlNone
.ColorIndex = xlAutomatic
Module1
Ready
NUM

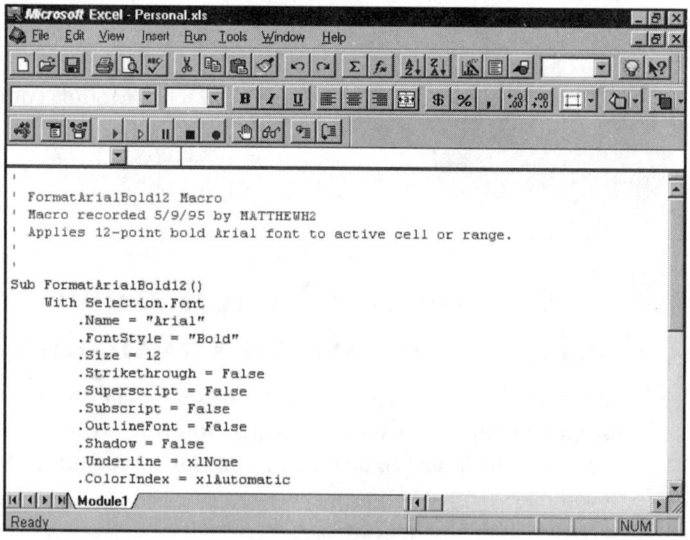

Figure 2.1.
Displaying a VBA module sheet changes Excel's main menu bar and causes Excel to display the Visual Basic toolbar.

Figure 2.2.

A blank Excel 7 worksheet. Notice the difference in the main menu bar between this figure and Figure 2.1.

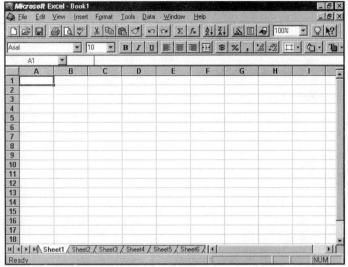

The **F**ormat and **D**ata choices do not appear on Excel's main menu when displaying a module sheet because the commands on these menus are not meaningful in a VBA module. For instance, it makes no sense to sort the source code in a module sheet, or to apply fancy text formatting to the macro instructions; Excel therefore prohibits such actions by removing the menu choices that give you access to formatting and data manipulation commands. Similarly, the commands accessible through the **R**un menu choice are only meaningful and useful when the active window displays a VBA module; Excel does not, therefore, display the **R**un choice on the main menu unless a module sheet is displayed.

Other main menu choices—such as the **E**dit, **V**iew, and **T**ools menus—remain on the main menu, but the commands available from those menus change when the active window displays a module sheet. Only commands meaningful in the context of a VBA module remain on the menus. The next few sections summarize each of the menu choices that Excel changes or adds when it enters VBA programming mode.

Don't be dismayed if the purpose or meaning of the commands described in the next few sections doesn't make much sense to you right now. Almost all of the VBA menu commands described in the following paragraphs are used to carry out activities that you have not yet learned about. Each lesson fully describes the menu commands relevant to the topics in that lesson. Right now, you just need to get acquainted with which menus change and what the new available choices are. If you're adventurous, go ahead and try some of these commands—just be sure you practice on a workbook that doesn't contain irreplaceable data.

The Edit Menu

In VBA programming mode, Excel doesn't display the Format menu. The Sheet command, however, is the one command from the Format menu that is relevant to a module sheet—unlike adding fancy typefaces to your source code, it does make sense to be able to rename, hide, or unhide a module sheet.

Excel therefore puts the Sheet command on the Edit menu instead of the Format menu while Excel is in VBA programming mode. To rename, hide, or unhide a module sheet, use the Edit | Sheet command instead of the Format | Sheet command.

The View Menu

Excel adds three commands to the View menu while in VBA programming mode. These commands are useful when you test or debug your macro programs. (*Debugging* is the name given to the process of finding and correcting errors in a program; Day 14 describes how to debug your VBA macros.)

The following list summarizes the three commands that Excel adds to the View menu:

- [ ] **Procedure Definition.** The Procedure Definition command takes you to the module sheet containing the definition of a particular procedure. As you learn later in this lesson, the term *procedure* specifies a particular type of macro.

- [ ] **Object Browser.** The Object Browser command activates the Visual Basic Object Browser. The Object Browser allows you to determine which macros are currently available. The section "Finding Recorded Macros" later in this lesson describes the Object Browser in more detail. Later lessons describe other features of the Object Browser.

- [ ] **Debug Window.** The Debug Window command opens the Debug window, which is part of the program debugging tools that VBA provides you. Day 14 describes how to use the Debug window to help you find and correct errors in your macros.

The Run Menu

The Run menu appears on the Excel main menu only when Excel is in VBA programming mode; that is, whenever the current window displays a module sheet. Most of the commands on the Run menu relate to program debugging. The Run menu contains these commands:

- [ ] **Start.** The Start command causes VBA to start running the macro you are currently editing—that is, VBA runs whatever macro currently contains the text insertion point.

- [ ] **End.** The End command stops a running macro (or stops the macro recorder, if it is running).

- [ ] **Reset.** The Reset command also stops a running macro but resets all of the macro's variables. (You learn about variables in the next lesson.)

□ **S**tep Into. This debugging command enables you to view the execution of each instruction in a macro.

□ Step **O**ver. This debugging command enables you to execute all of the instructions in a macro without pausing at each individual instruction in the macro.

□ Toggle **B**reakpoint. Marks a place in the macro where you want the execution of instructions to halt; this command is used only for debugging your VBA code.

□ **C**lear All Breakpoints. Removes all of the breakpoints in a module; used only when debugging.

The last four commands in the above list—**S**tep Into, Step **O**ver, Toggle **B**reakpoint, and **C**lear All Breakpoints—are used only when debugging a macro. These commands allow you to closely control the execution of a macro, enabling you to stop and start the macro at specified points, and to trace the execution of a macro step by step. Each of the debugging commands is described in detail in Day 14.

The Tools Menu

Excel adds six commands to the **T**ools menu when in VBA programming mode. The following list summarizes those commands:

□ **A**dd Watch. Use this command in conjunction with the last four commands on the **R**un menu to help you in the debugging process. This command enables you to inspect data that your macro produces, while the macro is still running.

□ **E**dit Watch. This command enables you to alter the specific data item that you select for inspection with the **A**dd Watch command.

□ Instant **W**atch. Like Add Watch, this command enables you to inspect data that your macro produces while the macro is still running.

□ References. The References command allows you to specify which Excel workbooks are referenced by the module you are currently working on. As you learn in later lessons, macros in one module can run macros stored in another module.

□ Ma**k**e Add-In. The Ma**k**e Add-In command, as its name implies, enables you to create an add-in program from macros you have written or recorded, or a combination of both. Day 21 describes how to use this command.

□ Menu E**d**itor. The Menu E**d**itor command activates the Menu Editor, which allows you to customize Excel's menus. Use the Menu Editor to create menu choices that execute macros you have written or recorded. Day 16 describes how to use the Menu Editor.

□ Attach **T**oolbars. The Attach **T**oolbars command allows you to attach custom toolbars to a particular workbook so that the toolbar is available whenever that workbook is open. Day 16 also describes how to create custom toolbars.

Introducing the Visual Basic Toolbar

Choosing a command button with a mouse is easier for many users than choosing a menu command. Excel therefore provides the most important and frequently used VBA commands as buttons on the Visual Basic toolbar. If you're working extensively with VBA, you may find that using the command buttons on the Visual Basic toolbar speeds up your work.

Usually, Excel automatically displays the Visual Basic toolbar whenever the active window displays a module sheet—that is, whenever Excel is in VBA programming mode. You can, however, use the **View | Toolbars** command to override this behavior. If you or another user hides the Visual Basic Toolbar by using the **View | Toolbars** command, Excel may not display the Visual Basic toolbar when you display a module sheet.

If Excel doesn't display the Visual Basic toolbar when you display a module sheet, use the **View | Toolbars** command to display it. To display the Visual Basic toolbar, follow these steps:

1. Choose the **View | Toolbars** command. Excel displays the Toolbars dialog box.
2. Select the check box to the left of the Visual Basic toolbar name in the **Toolbars** list.
3. Choose OK. Excel closes the Toolbars dialog box and displays the Visual Basic toolbar in its last visible position.

> **Tip:** You can also display the Toolbars dialog box by right-clicking (clicking the right mouse button) on any visible toolbar and then choosing Toolbars from the resulting pop-up menu.

Figure 2.3 shows the Visual Basic toolbar in its default configuration for Excel 7. Figure 2.3 shows the Visual Basic toolbar in a floating window (also called an *undocked* toolbar); refer to Figure 2.1 for a view of the Visual Basic toolbar in a fixed position (also called a *docked* toolbar). Refer to your Excel documentation or on-line help for information on displaying, moving, docking, and undocking toolbars.

Figure 2.3.

The Visual Basic toolbar contains buttons for the most important and most commonly used VBA commands.

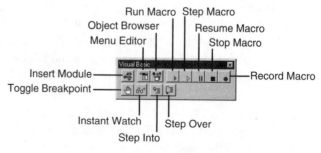

The Visual Basic toolbar has 12 buttons. Each button's action is summarized below:

☐ *Insert Module.* This button inserts a module sheet in front of the currently active sheet. Choosing this button is the same as using the **I**nsert | **M**acro | **M**odule command to insert a module sheet.

☐ *Menu Editor.* This button starts the Menu Editor. Choosing this button is the same as using the **T**ools | Menu E**d**itor command. You use the menu editor to customize your application's menus.

☐ *Object Browser.* This button starts the Object Browser. Choosing this button is the same as using the **V**iew | **O**bject Browser command. You use the Object Browser to see a list of the macros currently available, among other tasks.

☐ *Run Macro.* Use this button to run a macro. If the active window displays a module, choosing this button is the same as using the **R**un | **S**tart command. If the active window is not a module, choosing this button has the same effect as using the **T**ools | **M**acro command to display the Macro dialog box you learned about in lesson 1.

☐ *Step Macro.* Use this button when you debug your macros. Choosing this button starts VBA's break mode and displays the Debug window. Day 14 describes debugging macros.

☐ *Resume Macro.* This button resumes the execution of a paused macro; you usually use this button only while debugging macros.

☐ *Stop Macro.* Use this button to stop a running macro; if the macro recorder is running, this button stops the macro recorder.

☐ *Record Macro.* Use this button to start the macro recorder. Choosing this button is the same as using the **T**ools | **M**acro | **R**ecord Macro command to start the macro recorder.

☐ *Toggle Breakpoint, Instant Watch, Step Into, Step Over.* You use these last few buttons on the Visual Basic toolbar only when you are testing and debugging your macros. Usually, you use these buttons in conjunction with the Debug window described in Day 14. The Toggle Breakpoint button corresponds to the **R**un | Toggle **B**reakpoint command; Instant Watch corresponds to the **T**ools | Instant **W**atch command; and the Step Into and Step Over buttons correspond to the commands of the same name on the **R**un menu.

As with the menu commands, don't let yourself be disturbed if the purpose or meaning for any of the buttons on the Visual Basic toolbar isn't completely clear to you right now. Each lesson fully describes the commands and toolbar buttons that relate to the topics covered in that lesson. This section is only intended to acquaint you with the controls available from the Visual Basic toolbar.

Editing Macros

Before you can edit a macro, you must display the module sheet that contains the macro you want to edit, and then locate the macro in the module. For example, in order to edit the **FormatArialBold12** macro you recorded in Day 1, you first must display the module sheet in the PERSONAL.XLS workbook (where the recorded macro was stored) that contains the **FormatArialBold12** macro source code.

This section first describes how to display a VBA macro and then acquaints you with the various parts of a recorded macro before explaining how to edit the macro itself.

Finding Recorded Macros

Before you can display and edit a particular macro, you first must display the module sheet containing that macro. As you learned at the beginning of this lesson, Excel creates new module sheets, as necessary, to store the macros that you record. Because of the way Excel inserts and names new module sheets in a workbook, you may end up with several different modules in a single workbook, all of which have very similar names. As a result, you may sometimes find it difficult to determine which module sheet contains a particular macro.

As an example, when you recorded the **FormatArialBold12** macro in lesson 1, you stored it in the PERSONAL.XLS workbook. If this was the first macro you ever recorded and stored in PERSONAL.XLS, Excel stored the **FormatArialBold12** macro in a module sheet named *Module1*. If you then recorded the **NewFile** macro from Exercise 1.1 in the same Excel working session, Excel also stored it in the *Module1* module sheet. If you exited Excel between the time you recorded **FormatArialBold12** and the time you recorded **NewFile**, Excel stored the **NewFile** macro in a different module sheet (most likely *Module2*).

As you can see, if you wanted to edit the **NewFile** macro, you might not be able to tell immediately which module sheet in PERSONAL.XLS contains the source code for **NewFile** without actually looking at all of the module sheets in the workbook.

Instead of hunting through all of the text in all of the module sheets looking for a particular macro that you want to edit, you can use the Object Browser to locate the macro you want to display or edit.

To use the Object Browser to locate and display a macro, follow these steps:

1. Display any module sheet in the active window. You have to perform this step because the commands to access the Object Browser only appear when Excel is in VBA programming mode.

2. Choose the **V**iew | **O**bject Browser command. Excel displays the Object Browser dialog box shown in Figure 2.4.

Figure 2.4.
Use the Object Browser dialog box to help locate macros and the modules they are stored in.

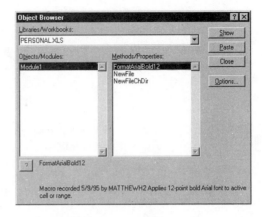

3. Select the workbook containing the macro you want to display or edit in the **L**ibraries/ Workbooks drop-down list. The Object Browser now displays a list of all of the module sheets in the selected workbook in the **O**bjects/Modules list box.

4. Select a module sheet in the **O**bjects/Modules list box. The Object Browser now displays a list of all of the macros in the selected module in the **M**ethods/Properties list box.

5. Select the macro you want to display or edit in the **M**ethods/Properties list box.

6. To view the source code for the selected macro, choose the **S**how command button.

As soon as you choose the **S**how button, VBA displays the module sheet that contains the macro you selected in the **M**ethods/Properties list, and places the insertion point near the beginning of the macro's source code. If necessary, VBA unhides the module sheet or workbook so you can view the module sheet and macro. If the macro you are looking for does not appear in the **M**ethods/Properties list box, try a different module or workbook.

For example, to view the source code for the **FormatArialBold12** macro you recorded on Day 1, follow the steps above, making the following choices in the specified steps:

☐ In step 3, select the PERSONAL.XLS workbook in the **L**ibraries/Workbooks drop-down list.

☐ In step 4, if PERSONAL.XLS has more than one module sheet listed in the **O**bjects/ Modules list box, select each module in the **O**bjects/Modules list in turn, until you see the **FormatArialBold12** macro name appear in the **M**ethods/Properties list.

☐ In step 5, select **FormatArialBold12** in the **M**ethods/Properties list.

After you select the **FormatArialBold12** macro name and choose the **S**how button in the Object Browser dialog box, your screen should appear similar to the one shown in Figure 2.1. (The exact appearance of your screen may differ, but you should see the macro source code for **FormatArialBold12**.)

> ✓ **Tip:** The Libraries/Workbooks drop-down list shows all opened workbooks—including hidden workbooks. If the workbook containing the macro you want to edit does not appear on the Libraries/Workbooks drop-down list, you have not opened that workbook file.

 You can also start the Object Browser by clicking the Object Browser command button on the Visual Basic toolbar.

Once you display the macro you want to edit, you can use the scroll bars to position the macro in the window. You can also use the **Edit | Find** command to search for a macro name in a module sheet. Using the **Edit | Find** command to search for text in a module sheet works the same as searching for text in an Excel worksheet. (Refer to Excel's online help for information on the **Edit | Find** command.)

DO	DON'T

DO remember that Excel hides the Personal macro workbook (PERSONAL.XLS) by default. To display or edit a macro in the Personal macro workbook, either use the Object Browser to show the macro, or choose the **Window | Unhide** command (**File | Unhide**, if no unhidden workbooks are open) to manually unhide the Personal macro workbook.

DO use the **Window | Hide** command to hide the Personal macro workbook when you finish editing or viewing macros in that workbook. Hiding the Personal macro workbook not only keeps your workspace uncluttered, but also helps prevent accidental changes to your macros.

Parts of a Recorded Macro

If you examine several recorded macros, you'll notice they all have several features in common. Listing 2.1 shows the source code for the **FormatArialBold12** macro you recorded in Day 1, and Listing 2.2 shows how the source code for the **NewFile** macro recorded as a result of performing Exercise 1.1 might appear (line 8 will not appear in the **NewFile** macro if you did not change the drive and directory when you recorded the macro).

2

Note: The macro source code in actual module sheets does not include a number in front of each line; line numbers appear in all of the listings in this book to make it easier to identify and discuss particular lines in the various macro example listings. Also, in some of the recorded macro listings (such as Listing 2.2), you may see the symbol ➡. This symbol indicates that the code line in the listing is really one single line in your VBA module but that the code line had to be divided in order to fit in this book.

Listing 2.1. The FormatArialBold12 macro.

```
 1:    '
 2:    ' FormatArialBold12 Macro
 3:    ' Macro recorded 5/9/95 by MATTHEWH2
 4:    ' Applies 12-point bold Arial font to active cell or range.
 5:    '
 6:    '
 7:    Sub FormatArialBold12()
 8:        With Selection.Font
 9:            .Name = "Arial"
10:            .FontStyle = "Bold"
11:            .Size = 12
12:            .Strikethrough = False
13:            .Superscript = False
14:            .Subscript = False
15:            .OutlineFont = False
16:            .Shadow = False
17:            .Underline = xlNone
18:            .ColorIndex = xlAutomatic
19:        End With
20:    End Sub
```

Listing 2.2. The NewFile macro.

```
 1:    '
 2:    ' NewFile Macro
 3:    ' Macro recorded 5/12/95 by MATTHEWH2
 4:    ' Creates a new workbook, then saves it with the name NEWFILE
 5:    '
 6:    Sub NewFile()
 7:        Workbooks.Add
 8:        ChDir "C:\VBA21"
 9:        ActiveWorkbook.SaveAs Filename:="C:\VBA21\NEWFILE.xls",
➡FileFormat _
10:            :=xlNormal, Password:="", WriteResPassword:="", _
11:            ReadOnlyRecommended:=False, CreateBackup:=False
12:        ActiveWorkbook.Close
13:    End Sub
```

The first six lines in Listing 2.1 are comments, as are the first six lines in Listing 2.2. A *comment* is a line in a VBA macro that does not actually contain instructions that are part of the macro. You use comments to provide documentation within the macro's source code about that macro. Notice that each comment line begins with an apostrophe (') character. VBA treats any text that follows an apostrophe as a comment, beginning from the apostrophe to the end of the line.

A recorded macro always begins with comment lines that state the name of the macro and contain the text that you entered in the **D**escription text box of the Record New Macro dialog box at the time you recorded the macro. The specific number and content of comment lines in a recorded macro depend on the length of the description you entered.

In Listing 2.1, line 7 is the actual beginning of the recorded macro; in Listing 2.2, line 6 is the beginning of the recorded macro. Every VBA macro begins with the keyword Sub, followed by the macro name. (A *keyword* is a word that is part of the VBA programming language, rather than a word—such as a macro name—that the user creates.) The macro name, in turn, is always followed by a pair of empty parentheses; the purpose and use of these parentheses is explained fully in Days 6 and 11. For now, you need only know that the parentheses always appear after the macro name in a recorded macro.

The line that contains the Sub keyword and the macro's name is referred to as the macro *declaration* line, because this is the line that makes the macro's existence known to VBA. Line 7 is the macro declaration line in Listing 2.1; line 6 is the macro declaration line in Listing 2.2.

Immediately following the macro's declaration is the *body* of the macro. In Listing 2.1, lines 8 through 19 make up the body of the **FormatArialBold12** macro; in Listing 2.2, lines 7 through 12 make up the body of the **NewFile** macro. Each line in the macro's body consists of one or more VBA statements. A VBA *statement* is a series of keywords and other symbols that, together, make up a single complete instruction to VBA—sort of like a single sentence in the English language. Just as a paragraph is made up of several sentences, so is a VBA macro made up of several statements. The VBA statements in a recorded macro contain the instructions that perform actions equivalent to the actions you performed while you recorded the macro.

For instance, line 9 in Listing 2.1 selects the Arial font, line 10 selects the Bold font style, and so on. In Listing 2.2, line 7 creates a new workbook, and lines 8 through 11 (also in Listing 2.2) are the equivalent of setting various workbook properties.

After the body of the macro comes the line containing the End Sub keywords, which tell VBA that it has reached the end of the macro. The macro in Listing 2.1 ends in line 20, and the macro in Listing 2.2 ends in line 14.

When you run a macro, VBA begins with the first line in the body of the macro (the first line after the macro declaration), and executes the instructions in that line sequentially, from left to right. VBA then moves on to the next line, and executes the instructions in that line, and so on until it reaches the end of the macro, signified by the End Sub statement.

Take another look at lines 9 and 10 in Listing 2.2. Notice the underscore (_) character at the end of each of these lines. Notice also that there is a space preceding the underscore, separating it from the other text on the line. This special combination of a space character followed by an underscore at the end of a line is called the *line continuation* symbol and signals to VBA that the next line of the macro is to be joined to the current line to form a single statement.

In Listing 2.2, lines 9 and 10 together are actually a single statement—in this case, the command that saves the workbook and sets several options for the saved workbook. In order to make the macro more readable, the macro recorder divided this single *logical* line into several *physical* lines by using the line continuation symbol. Without the line continuation symbol dividing the single logical line into several shorter physical lines, the line for this statement would extend beyond the edge of even a maximized module sheet window, requiring you to scroll the window to see the entire statement. Later, when you write your own macros, you can use the line continuation character yourself, to help make your macros more readable.

As you have probably already noticed, many of the lines in both recorded macros are indented from the left edge of the sheet. Each level of indentation helps separate one part of the macro from another. Notice that the entire body of each macro is indented between the Sub...End Sub keywords. This helps your eye pick out the body of the macro. At other points (lines 9 through 18 in Listing 2.1) the statements are indented even further. This second, greater level of indentation helps you identify all of the statements enclosed by the With...End With keywords. (Days 7 and 11 describe the With...End With statement.) At yet another point (lines 11 and 12 in Listing 2.2), the text is again indented, this time to help pick out the statement divided over two lines with the line continuation symbol.

The macro recorder automatically indents the code it produces in order to make the recorded macro more understandable to a human reader. As you write your own macros, you also should indent your code to help identify various sections of your macro. There is no requirement that you indent lines; the macros in Listings 2.1 and 2.2 would run just as well if all of the lines began flush with the left edge of the sheet. Line indenting is just a formatting convention adopted by good programmers to make their programs easier to understand and maintain.

If you use a color monitor when you view a recorded macro on-screen, you will notice that different parts of the macro's text are displayed with different colors. Comments are displayed with green text, whereas the Sub, End Sub, and other VBA keywords are displayed with blue text. The remaining text in the macro does not contain VBA keywords, and is displayed in black text to indicate that it contains data and program statements created by the user. VBA color-codes the text on-screen so you can more easily tell what part of a macro or statement you are looking at.

Editing Macro Text

Editing macro source code in a module is much like editing text in any dialog text box or in a worksheet cell. Editing text in a VBA module sheet is exactly like editing text in the Windows

Notepad or in WordPad. Use any of the keyboard, mouse, or **E**dit menu commands to add, delete, select, cut, copy, or paste text in a module that you would use in the Windows Notepad or WordPad.

> **Tip:** You can use the **E**dit | **F**ind command to locate specific words or phrases within a module, or use the **E**dit | **R**eplace command to replace specific words or phrases.

Any changes you make in a module are saved whenever you save the workbook file containing the module.

As an example of editing a macro, assume you want to add a comment to the macro shown in Listing 2.2, explaining what the command in line 8 does. To add the comment for line 8, follow these steps:

1. Move the insertion point to the end of line 7.
2. Press Enter to insert a blank line in the macro in front of line 8.
3. Type an apostrophe (')—all comments begin with an apostrophe.
4. Now type the comment, in this case, type the sentence:

   `Next line changes current directory to C:\VBA21.`

Listing 2.3 shows the modified **NewFile** macro; the added comment is now line 8.

Listing 2.3. Adding a comment to the NewFile macro.

```
 1:   '
 2:   ' NewFile Macro
 3:   ' Macro recorded 5/12/95 by MATTHEWH2
 4:   ' Creates a new workbook, then saves it with the name NEWFILE
 5:   '
 6:   Sub NewFile()
 7:       Workbooks.Add
 8:       'Next line changes current directory to C:\VBA21
 9:       ChDir "C:\VBA21"
10:       ActiveWorkbook.SaveAs Filename:="C:\VBA21\NEWFILE.xls",
➥FileFormat _
11:           :=xlNormal, Password:="", WriteResPassword:="", _
12:           ReadOnlyRecommended:=False, CreateBackup:=False
13:       ActiveWorkbook.Close
14:   End Sub
```

DO	DON'T

DO add comments to the body of a macro while it is still fresh in your mind what actions you recorded, especially if you record long macros. Adding comments to recorded macros will make it easier to change the macro later, if you need to.

DO add comments that explain the purpose or reason for any changes you make to a recorded macro. Again, these comments make it easier to determine which parts of a macro you edited and what those changes accomplish.

As you add this comment to the **NewFile** macro, notice that when you insert the new line and begin typing, the text you type is black. When you move the insertion point to any other line—whether by pressing Enter, using the arrow keys, or clicking the mouse—the new comment line turns green. This is because VBA examines each new line you type (or existing lines that you alter) whenever the insertion point leaves the line.

VBA examines each new or altered line in the macro to determine whether the line is syntactically correct. (*Syntax* is the name given to the rules for arranging words and symbols in a programming—or human—language.) If the new or changed line does have the correct syntax, VBA then color-codes the parts of the line using the color-coding scheme described earlier. If there is a syntax error in the line, VBA color codes the line red and may display one of several possible syntax error messages. Syntax error messages are described in more detail later in this lesson.

Moving or Copying a Macro from One Module to Another

Before you edit a macro, you might want to make a backup copy of the macro's source code—especially if you plan to make extensive changes in the macro, or if the macro is long or performs complex actions. If you make a copy of the macro source code text, you can easily go back to the original recorded version of the macro if your changes don't work out as you anticipated.

The best way to copy a single macro is to use the Windows Clipboard, following these steps:

1. Display the macro you want to copy.
2. Select all of the macro's source code text. Make sure you include all of the macro, including the Sub and End Sub lines and all of the lines between.
3. Use the **Edit | C**opy command to copy the macro text to the Windows Clipboard.
4. Now display the module sheet you want to copy the macro to.
5. Use the **Edit | P**aste command to paste the macro text into the module.

You can use the technique just described to copy a macro into the same module, a different module in the same workbook, or a module in a different workbook. You can also use this technique to paste macro text into other Windows applications, such as Windows Notepad.

DO	**DON'T**

DO make a backup copy of a macro if you are not certain how your changes will work out, or if your macro was difficult to record.

DON'T make a backup copy of a macro in the same module sheet that contains the original macro. If a module contains two or more macros with the same name, VBA cannot determine which macro to run and displays an error message stating that there is an *ambiguous name* in the module.

Moving or Copying an Entire Module Sheet

If you want to copy or move an entire module sheet—that is, to copy or move all of the macros in a module—then use the **Edit | M**ove or Copy Sheet command. Copying a module sheet is just like copying an Excel worksheet. Follow these steps:

1. Select the module sheet you want to copy or move. To copy or move more than one module sheet, select the sheets by holding down the Ctrl key and clicking the module sheets' name tabs.

2. Choose the **Edit | M**ove or Copy command to open the Move or Copy dialog box (shown in Figure 2.5).

Figure 2.5.

Use the Move or Copy dialog box to move or copy a module (and all the macros it contains) to the same or a different workbook.

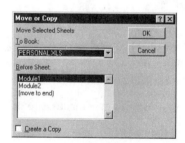

3. Choose which workbook is to receive the module sheet in the **T**o Book drop-down list. The **T**o Book drop-down list shows all of the currently open, unhidden workbooks.

4. Choose the sheet in front of which to insert the selected module sheet(s) in the **B**efore Sheet list box.

5. Select the Create Copy check box if you want to copy the selected modules; leave Create Copy unselected if you want to move the selected modules.

6. Choose OK. Excel copies or moves the selected module sheet(s).

Protecting Your Macro Source Code

If you don't want people who use your macros to be able to change the macro's source code, or if you just want to prevent accidental changes to the macro source code, you can hide or protect the entire workbook or individual module sheets within a workbook. Use the **Tools | Protection** command to protect a workbook, or to protect some or all of your module sheets, individually. (Hiding and protecting module sheets is the same as hiding or protecting any Excel worksheet; refer to your Excel documentation or online help for information on hiding and protecting workbooks and other sheets.)

> **Note:** Protecting a workbook or module sheet does not prevent a user from unhiding that workbook or module sheet. If you want to create macros you can distribute without anyone being able to read or change the source code, you should construct an add-in program. Day 21, "Using Automatic Procedures, Event Procedures, and Add-Ins," describes how to create an add-in program.

Writing New Macros

To write a macro of your own without using the macro recorder, you can type the macro in an existing module sheet, or create a new module sheet to contain the macro.

Inserting a New Module Sheet

If the workbook you want to store a macro in does not already contain a module sheet, you must insert a module sheet before you can write a macro in that workbook. You might also insert a new module sheet if the existing module sheets are getting full (a module can contain a maximum of about 4,000 lines), or if you just want to create the new macro in its own module.

If you need (or decide) to write your macro in a new module sheet, follow these two steps to add a module sheet:

1. Open the workbook file you want to store the macro in.

2. Choose the **Insert | Macro | Module** command (or click the Insert Module button on the Visual Basic toolbar). Excel adds a new module sheet to the workbook, inserting it

in front of whatever sheet was active at the time you inserted the new module, and making the new module the active sheet.

Whenever Excel displays a module sheet, it enters VBA programming mode. Because Excel makes any new sheet the active sheet, Excel enters VBA programming mode immediately after you insert the module.

DO	DON'T

DO rename a new module sheet immediately after inserting it, giving it a descriptive name so you can more easily identify the macros in that module. (Excel names module sheets you insert by following the same naming rules explained earlier in this chapter for automatically inserted modules; therefore your new module sheet receives a name like *Module1*, which doesn't tell you a lot about the macros in that module.)

DO remember that you rename an Excel 7 module sheet the same way you rename any Excel sheet: double-click the sheet's name tab, or choose the **Edit | Sheet | Rename** command to display the Rename Sheet dialog box; enter the new module name in the **Name** text box, and choose OK. (Remember, Excel moves the **Sheet** command from the **Format** menu to the **Edit** menu when in VBA programming mode.)

Selecting an Existing Module Sheet

To write a new macro in an existing module sheet, you must first select the module sheet in which you want to write the macro. Selecting the module sheet makes it the active sheet, and causes Excel to enter VBA programming mode.

Select module sheets the same way you select any other sheet in Excel. To select an existing module sheet to write a new macro in, open the workbook that contains the module you want to select, and simply click the module sheet's name tab. Excel makes it the active sheet.

Tip: If you are certain you have opened the correct workbook, but you don't see the module you want to select, the module sheet may be hidden. You must unhide the module sheet to select it. Unhide a module sheet the same way you unhide any other Excel sheet: use the **Edit | Sheet | Unhide** command in VBA programming mode (or the **Format | Sheet | Unhide** command when a worksheet is the active sheet).

Writing the Macro Text

To write the source code text for the macro—whether you add the macro to a new or existing module sheet—position the insertion point at the place in the module where you want to type the new macro.

You can type the new macro source code anywhere in a module sheet, as long as you make sure that you insert the new macro *after* the End Sub statement that ends the preceding macro, and *before* the Sub statement which begins the next macro in the module. Many users find it easiest to simply add new macros to the end of the module.

When you write a macro, you must specify the macro's name and include the Sub keyword at the beginning of the macro and the End Sub keywords at the end of the macro. If you omit any of these three elements, the syntax of your macro will not be correct, and VBA will display an error message when you attempt to run the macro.

The classic first program in any programming language is a program that displays the message *Hello, World!* on the screen. Listing 2.4 shows just such a VBA macro program.

To enter this macro program yourself, follow these steps:

1. Open any Excel workbook, or create a new workbook.
2. Choose the **Insert | Macro | Module** command to insert a new module sheet in the workbook. Excel inserts the new module and makes it the active sheet.
3. Choose the **Edit | Sheet | Rename** command to display the Rename Sheet dialog box.
4. Enter the name **FirstProgram** in the **N**ame text box.
5. Choose OK. Excel renames the new module sheet.
6. Make sure the insertion point is at the beginning of a blank line, and type the text shown in Listing 2.4, pressing Enter at the end of each line to start a new line.

   Type the source code from Listing 2.4 into the module sheet exactly as it appears in the listing, but without the line numbers. (Remember, the line numbers are not part of the macro listings, the numbers are included in this book only to make it easier to identify and discuss specific parts of a macro.)

Listing 2.4. The HelloMacro procedure.

```
1: Sub HelloMacro()
2:     MsgBox "Hello, World!"
3: End Sub
```

The first line in Listing 2.4 is the macro declaration. Remember, the *macro declaration* (also called a *procedure declaration*) is the statement that tells VBA about the existence of the macro, and indicates the beginning of the macro's source code.

Every macro declaration must begin with the Sub keyword, followed by a space and then the name of the macro. In Listing 2.4, the macro's name is **HelloMacro**. The final part of the macro declaration is the pair of empty parentheses. These parentheses are required; you learn about their purpose in Days 6 and 11. (If you don't include the parentheses, VBA adds them to the macro declaration when the insertion point leaves the declaration line.)

For a macro declaration to be syntactically correct, the Sub keyword must be the first word on the line, and the macro declaration must be the only VBA statement in the line, although you can add a comment after the declaration.

Note: You can add comments to the end of a line that contains a VBA statement by typing a space, an apostrophe (`'`), and then the comment itself. Comments formatted this way are called *trailing comments*. The following macro fragment shows a trailing comment:

```
ChDir "E:\" 'changes the current directory to E:\
```

The second line in Listing 2.4 forms the body of the macro and is the only statement in the macro that does any work. The body of a macro may consist of none, one, or many statements. The MsgBox statement displays a message in a dialog box on-screen; a later section of this chapter describes the MsgBox statement.

The third and final line of the **HelloMacro** macro, End Sub, completes the macro. This line signals VBA that this is the end of the macro; VBA stops executing the macro when it reaches this line. Like the macro declaration, the End Sub statement must be the first two words in the line, and must be on a line by itself, although you can add a trailing comment after it.

Note: Sub procedures are saved whenever the workbook file that contains the macro is saved.

Understanding the Terms *Macro* and *Procedure*

So far, this book has used the term *macro* to refer to both macros you record and macros you write. There is another term, however, that helps distinguish between recorded macros and macros you write yourself. Strictly speaking, the term macro applies only to instructions that you record with the macro recorder (or assemble in

something like Access' Macro Builder). Macros you write from scratch are more accurately referred to as *sub procedures*, or just *procedures*. The rest of this book uses the term *macro* to refer to code that you record with the macro recorder, and uses the term *procedure* to refer to VBA code you write yourself.

After you enter the source code for the **HelloMacro** sub procedure, run it by using the technique you learned in Day 1:

1. Choose the **T**ools | **M**acro command to display the Macro dialog box.
2. Select the **HelloMacro** procedure in the **M**acro Name/Reference list.
3. Choose the **R**un command button.

When VBA executes the **HelloMacro** sub procedure from Listing 2.4, it displays the dialog box shown in Figure 2.6. Choose the OK button to clear the dialog box and end the macro.

Figure 2.6.

The **HelloMacro** *procedure shown in Listing 2.4 displays its message in this dialog box.*

DO	**DON'T**

DO remember to include the End Sub statement to end your sub procedures. Omitting the End Sub statement can lead to a variety of problems.

DO avoid problems caused by accidentally omitting the End Sub statement by writing the macro declaration line and the line with the End Sub keywords at the same time, and then insert the body of the macro between these two lines.

Notice that, even in this short procedure, the body of the procedure is indented to set it off from the procedure declaration and ending. You should always indent your code to make it more readable. Compare Listing 2.4 with the following listing; you can see that even short procedures are more readable when properly indented.

```
1:  Sub HelloMacro()
2:  MsgBox "Hello, World!"
3:  End Sub
```

The Auto Indent Feature

The VBA text editor contains a feature called *auto indenting*, which helps you format your source code with various indentation levels. If auto indenting is turned on, whenever you press Enter to begin a new line, the insertion point in the new line automatically moves to match the indentation level of the line above it. (Press Backspace to return to a previous level of indentation.)

To turn auto indenting on or off, select or clear the **A**uto Indent check box on the Module General tab of the Options dialog box. (Choose the **T**ools | **O**ptions command to open the Options dialog box.) Auto indent is on by default when you install Excel.

Running a Macro While Editing

Whether you are writing or editing a macro, you'll need to run the macro to test the result of your efforts. You already know how to use the Macro dialog box to run a macro or procedure; you can also run a macro or procedure directly from the module sheet, as you are editing.

To run a macro while editing, follow these steps:

1. Make sure the insertion point is positioned somewhere in the procedure you want to run, either in the body of the procedure, in the declaration line of the procedure, or in the `End Sub` statement of the procedure.

2. Choose the **R**un | **S**tart command. VBA executes the entire procedure, from beginning to end.

For example, to run the `HelloMacro` procedure, position the insertion point anywhere in the procedure's source code, and then choose the **R**un | **S**tart command.

You can also run a procedure while editing by positioning the insertion point anywhere in the procedure's source code and then clicking the Run Macro button on the Visual Basic toolbar.

 If the insertion point is not inside a macro's or procedure's source code when you use the **R**un | **S**tart command or the Run Macro button, Excel can't tell which macro or procedure you want to run, and displays the Macro dialog box instead.

Displaying Messages to a Macro's User

Listing 2.4 includes the VBA `MsgBox` statement, which you can use to make your macros and procedures display a message on-screen. Messages or other information that a macro or

procedure displays on-screen, sends to a printer, or writes to a disk file is called *output*. The MsgBox statement is the simplest form of on-screen output you can include in your VBA procedures.

The MsgBox statement is like a procedure that is built in to VBA. The line in the **HelloMacro** procedure that contains the MsgBox statement causes VBA to run, or *call*, that built-in procedure. The MsgBox statement from Listing 2.4 is shown again, below:

```
MsgBox "Hello, World!"
```

The quoted text on the line after the procedure name MsgBox is the text of the message to be displayed by MsgBox. VBA passes this additional information on to the MsgBox procedure for its use. Additional information passed on for use by a procedure that your source code calls is referred to as an *argument* for that procedure. The text "Hello, World!" is the argument for the MsgBox procedure. (Days 6 and 11 describe how to write your own procedures that use arguments.) The double quotation marks (") in the "Hello World!" argument indicate that the text enclosed in quotation marks is data in the macro, rather than instructions that VBA is supposed to carry out.

Refer again to Figure 2.6, and notice that the title bar of the dialog box displayed by the MsgBox statement contains the words *Microsoft Excel*. By default, a dialog box displayed by MsgBox has a title indicating the application that is running the VBA macro or procedure—Microsoft Excel, in this case.

You can change the title of the dialog box that MsgBox displays. Listing 2.5 shows the **HelloMacro** procedure from Listing 2.4 with the MsgBox statement altered so that the dialog box shown in Figure 2.7 appears. Compare Figure 2.7 with Figure 2.6, and notice that the title of the MsgBox dialog box is now *Greeting Box*.

 Listing 2.5. Displaying a customized title bar with MsgBox.

```
1:  Sub HelloMacro()
2:      MsgBox "Hello, World!", , "Greeting Box"
3:  End Sub
```

Figure 2.7.

The MsgBox statement in Listing 2.5 displays this dialog box. Notice that the title of this dialog box is different from the one shown in Figure 2.6.

The MsgBox statement (line 2 of Listing 2.5) in the procedure now looks somewhat different from its previous form, although it still performs the same purpose in the macro—to display a message to the macro's user. In Listing 2.5, the MsgBox statement now contains three arguments after it; each argument is separated from the others with a comma.

The first argument of the MsgBox statement is the same as it was in Listing 2.4, and is the text to be displayed by MsgBox. Because this variation of the MsgBox statement has more than one argument, the first argument is followed by a comma; *argument lists* in VBA procedures are separated by commas, just as items in a list in the English language are separated by commas.

The second argument of the MsgBox statement is optional; this example omits the optional second argument. Because the optional argument is left out, a single space character is shown in the argument list as a place holder. This blank space indicates to VBA that the optional argument in the list is missing. A comma follows the place-holding space character to separate it from the next argument in the list. (If you do not type the space character between the two commas, VBA adds it for you—but you do have to type both commas yourself.)

The optional second argument in the MsgBox statement specifies how many and what type of command buttons appear in the dialog box displayed by MsgBox. When you omit the optional second argument (as in this example), the dialog box that MsgBox displays contains only one command button—the OK button. (You'll learn more about the optional command button argument for MsgBox in Days 5 and 8.)

The third and final argument in the MsgBox statement specifies the title for the dialog box (refer to Figure 2.7). Like the first argument, the text for the dialog box title bar is enclosed in double quotation marks ("). VBA always recognizes quoted text as data, rather than text that contains program instructions. If you omit the quotation marks for either the MsgBox message text or the text for the dialog box's title bar, VBA displays an error message. Because the third argument is also the last argument, no comma after the third argument is needed.

Understanding Error Messages While Writing, Editing, or Running a Macro

As you write or edit your macros and procedures, you may make various mistakes as you create or alter the statements in your macros and procedures. VBA can detect many of these errors as you write the macro and detects other errors as you run the macro.

Syntax Errors

Syntax is the name given to the specific order of words and symbols that makes up a valid VBA statement. Some of the most common errors you encounter while writing or editing VBA procedures are *syntax errors*—error messages that inform you of incorrect syntax in a VBA statement, such as missing commas, missing quotation marks, missing arguments, and so on.

Whenever you write a new line of code, or change an existing line of code, VBA *parses* the line when the insertion point leaves the new or changed line. (*Parsing* is the name given to the process of breaking a VBA statement into its component parts and determining which parts of the line are keywords, variables, or data; the process is similar to parsing a sentence in English to determine its component parts—nouns, verbs, adjectives, and so on.)

When VBA successfully parses a line of code in a macro without finding any errors, it color-codes the various parts of the line. VBA keywords are shown in blue, comments are shown in green, and data or other statements are shown in black text. If, however, VBA detects a syntax error in the line during the parsing process, VBA color-codes the entire line in red and displays a dialog box containing an error message.

Examine the following macro fragment, which shows an incorrectly written `MsgBox` statement:

```
MsgBox "Hello, World!", , Greeting Box
```

In this example, the quotation marks required around the text specifying the title of the dialog box were accidentally omitted. As a result, VBA cannot determine that the two words in the last argument are data; instead, VBA assumes that the word `Greeting` is a variable name. (A *variable* is a way of naming a memory location used to store data. Variables are described in the next chapter.)

Because VBA assumes the third argument is a variable named `Greeting`, it expects a comma or the end of the argument list for the `MsgBox` procedure. Instead, VBA finds a space character, followed by what appears to be another variable name. VBA colors the entire line red to indicate that it contains an error, highlights the word or symbol at the place in the line where VBA determines the error exists, and then displays the error dialog box shown in Figure 2.8. You can see the highlighted word `Box` in the macro text where VBA detected the error.

Figure 2.8.

VBA displays error messages about syntax errors as you type or change each line.

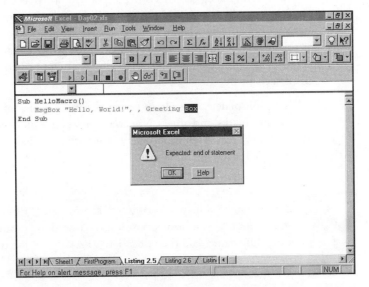

If you receive a syntax error message like this, choose the **H**elp button to access VBA's online help system and get more information about the specific syntax error encountered. To clear the error dialog box, choose the OK button.

After you clear the error dialog box from the screen, try to fix the syntax error. You can move the insertion point from the line after clearing the syntax error dialog box, but the line remains colored red to indicate that it contains an error. VBA won't parse the line containing the syntax error again until you run the procedure or until you again edit that line. VBA only parses lines in a procedure when you move the insertion point away from the line immediately after making changes, or when you run the procedure.

Tip: You can turn the syntax checking feature on and off. Although it is highly recommended that you leave the syntax checking turned on (it can save you a great deal of time and frustration later) you can disable syntax checking by selecting the **T**ools | **O**ptions command to display the Options dialog box. To disable syntax checking, select the Module General tab (if necessary) to display the Module General options, and clear the **D**isplay Syntax Errors check box. Choose OK when you have finished setting the Module General options.

When VBA is executing a procedure and encounters a line containing a syntax error, VBA stops executing the procedure, displays the module containing the procedure that has the syntax error, selects the specific line in the module where it detected the error, and then displays another syntax error dialog box.

The syntax error dialog box that VBA displays for a syntax error it encounters while executing a procedure usually contains much less detail about the specific error than the syntax error dialog box that VBA displays when it first detects the syntax error after you write or change the line. For this reason—and to avoid problems caused when a macro's or procedure's execution is unexpectedly terminated—you should always attempt to correct syntax errors the first time VBA detects them.

VBA is capable of detecting a large variety of syntax errors, informing you of missing commas, missing quote marks, and others. Not every syntax error message is so explicit, however. In some cases, VBA can't always tell you what's wrong with the syntax of a particular statement, only that there is a syntax error.

Tip: If you need help resolving syntax errors with a specific VBA keyword or built-in procedure (like MsgBox), position the insertion point over the keyword or procedure name, and then press F1. VBA displays the online help for that keyword or procedure (if there is any).

Runtime Errors

It is possible for you to create a syntactically correct VBA statement that still doesn't execute properly. Errors that only show up when you actually run the procedure or macro are called *runtime* errors. There are many different types of runtime errors. Runtime errors are usually caused by missing procedure arguments, arguments of the wrong data type, missing keywords, attempts to access non-existent disk drives or directory folders, or errors in logic.

Study the following VBA statement, which again contains an improperly formed MsgBox statement:

```
MsgBox "Hello, World!", "Greeting Box"
```

In this example, VBA finds nothing wrong with the syntax of the MsgBox statement: The data text is properly enclosed in quotation marks, and the argument list is correctly separated with commas. (Because all arguments except the first argument for MsgBox are optional, VBA accepts two arguments for MsgBox as correct syntax.) When VBA attempts to execute the statement in this line, however, it displays the error dialog box shown in Figure 2.9.

Figure 2.9.
VBA detects some errors only while the procedure is running and consequently displays a runtime error dialog box.

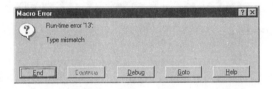

This dialog box informs you that an error occurred while VBA was running the procedure, and displays a message describing the error. In this case, the specific error is a *type mismatch*. If you look again at the MsgBox statement above, you'll notice that the place-holding comma for the optional command button argument of MsgBox is missing (compare this to line 2 of Listing 2.5).

When VBA executes this statement, it parses the quoted text "Greeting Box" as the second argument of MsgBox, instead of as the third argument, because of the missing place-holding comma. Because the command button argument must be a number, not text, VBA complains that the type of the data passed to the MsgBox procedure does not match the type of data expected for that argument. (Data types are explained in more detail in the next chapter.)

The error dialog box for runtime errors contains several command buttons. The following list summarizes each of these buttons:

- ☐ **End**—Choose this command button to end the procedure.
- ☐ **Continue**—Choose this command button to continue the procedure. Some runtime errors allow you to continue running the procedure; for most runtime errors, however, this command button is disabled.

☐ **D**ebug—Choose this command button to use the VBA Debugger to help track down and solve the causes of whatever problem caused the runtime error. Using the Debugger is described in Day 14.

☐ **G**oto—Choose this command button to go to the line in the procedure source code that produced the runtime error. VBA displays the module sheet that contains the procedure that produced the error, positions the text in the module so that the offending line is displayed, and selects that line.

☐ **H**elp—This command accesses the VBA online help system and displays the help topic describing the precise runtime error that has occurred. Use this button to get more information if it is not clear to you what the runtime error message means.

If you don't understand why the use of a particular VBA keyword or procedure causes a runtime error, you can get help with that specific keyword or procedure by positioning the insertion point over that word and pressing F1. VBA displays the online help topic for that keyword or procedure, if any.

Recording New Actions in an Existing Macro

One of the easiest ways to add new instructions to an existing macro is to simply record the additional instructions directly into the existing macro.

Although the macro recorder does not necessarily produce the most attractive or efficient code, recording actions directly into an existing macro helps reduce syntax and runtime errors produced by writing the code manually. You can record new actions directly in a macro to help reduce the amount of editing and testing time required to make your macro work correctly. You can also replace or modify a large part of a previously recorded macro. To do this, you first edit the macro to remove the instructions that you want replace, and then record the new instructions directly into the macro.

Yet another reason to record new actions directly into a macro procedure is to ensure that a recorded macro ends up in a particular module sheet. When you simply record a new macro, Excel chooses which module to add the new macro to (as described at the beginning of this lesson). To ensure that a recorded macro ends up stored in a particular module sheet, you can write the macro declaration yourself, and then record the macro actions directly into the macro body.

To record new actions directly into an existing macro or procedure, follow these steps:

1. Display the module sheet that contains the macro or procedure you want to add to.
2. Place the insertion point at the location in the macro or procedure where you want the new recorded instructions to begin.

3. Choose the **Tools | R**ecord Macro | **M**ark Position for Recording command. This command marks the position in the macro where the Macro Recorder inserts the new recorded instructions.

4. Set up any starting conditions required for the new instructions that you will record (setting up starting conditions was described in Day 1).

5. Choose the **Tools | R**ecord Macro | **R**ecord at Mark command. This command starts the Macro Recorder and inserts the new recorded actions at the previously marked position in the module sheet.

6. Now perform any and all of the actions that you want to record into the macro.

7. When you finish performing all of the actions you want to record, choose the **Tools | R**ecord Macro | **S**top Recording command, or click the Stop Macro button.

To view the new recorded VBA instructions, display the module sheet and macro that you placed the recording mark in.

DO	**DON'T**

DO remember that the recorder records *all* your actions, including mistakes and false starts, so plan your actions ahead of time.

The **NewBook** recorded macro shown in Listing 2.6 contains the single VBA instruction (line 8) that causes Excel to create a new workbook—this macro has the same effect as choosing the **File | N**ew command. To record this macro yourself, start the Macro Recorder as you learned to do in Day 1, name the macro **NewBook**, choose the **File | N**ew command, choose OK to create a new workbook, and then immediately stop the Macro Recorder.

Listing 2.6. The NewBook macro creates a new workbook file.

```
1:  '
2:  ' NewBook Macro
3:  ' Macro recorded 5/12/95 by Matthew Harris
4:  ' Creates a new workbook
5:  '
6:  '
7:  Sub NewBook()
8:      Workbooks.Add
9:  End Sub
```

The **NewBook** macro doesn't really provide any advantage over just choosing the **File | N**ew command to create a new workbook; by adding more recorded instructions to it, however, you can increase its utility.

Assume that you decide to add instructions to the **NewBook** macro so that it not only creates a new workbook, but also inserts a module sheet into the new workbook (Excel doesn't add module sheets to new workbooks automatically). At this point, you don't know enough about VBA to know which statements to add to the **NewBook** macro so that it will carry out the desired additional actions. You can, however, record the instructions that add a module sheet to a workbook directly into the existing **NewBook** macro.

To record the new actions directly into the **NewBook** macro, follow these steps:

1. Use the Object Browser to display the source code for the **NewBook** macro, as you learned to do earlier in this lesson.

2. Move the insertion point to the location where you want to insert the new recorded instructions.

   For the **NewBook** macro, you want to add the new instructions after the existing statements in the macro, but before the end of the macro, so you place the insertion point at the beginning of the End Sub statement at the end of the macro (line 9 in Listing 2.6). The Macro Recorder will insert all new recorded instructions in front of the End Sub line.

3. Choose the **T**ools | **R**ecord Macro | **M**ark Position for Recording command. The Macro Recorder marks the current position for recording, although no visible mark appears on the module sheet.

4. Choose the **T**ools | **R**ecord Macro | **R**ecord at Mark command. The Macro Recorder begins recording your actions, inserting the code into the **NewBook** macro at the marked location.

5. Choose the **I**nsert | **M**acro | **M**odule command. (This is the new action inserted into the existing macro.)

6. Stop the Macro Recorder.

After stopping the Macro Recorder, the **NewBook** macro appears as shown in Listing 2.7. Notice that the Macro Recorder added one VBA statement to the macro (line 9 in Listing 2.7). This new line corresponds to the one action you performed—inserting a module sheet—and is the code inserted by the Macro Recorder at the mark.

Listing 2.7. The NewBook macro with recorded code inserted directly.

```
1:   '
2:   ' NewBook Macro
3:   ' Macro recorded 5/12/95 by Matthew Harris
4:   ' Creates a new workbook
5:   '
6:   '
7:   Sub NewBook()
8:       Workbooks.Add
```

```
 9:      Modules.Add
10:  End Sub
```

The recording mark remains in effect until you close the workbook containing the mark, or until you mark another location. As the Macro Recorder adds the new recorded instructions to the macro, it moves the recording mark forward so that the recording mark remains at the end of the new recorded instructions. You can therefore record several actions, stop the Macro Recorder, and then start the Macro Recorder again to record more instructions at the recording mark in the same macro. The Macro Recorder inserts the additional recorded instructions into the macro after the previous group of recorded instructions.

To insert new recorded actions into a different macro or module, simply follow the process described above again: place the insertion point in the macro where you want to insert the new recorded actions, place the recording mark with the **Tools | Record Macro | Mark** Position for Recording command, and then start the macro recorder to record at the mark.

Printing Your Macros

At some point in time, you'll probably want to print some of your macros. You might want to print a macro for archival or documentation purposes, to show to a colleague, or to study. (Studying the macros produced by the Excel Macro Recorder is a good way to help yourself learn VBA.)

When you print a macro, you must print the entire module sheet that contains the macro. If you want, you can print more than one module sheet at once, although all of the module sheets must be in the same workbook.

To print a module sheet, follow these steps:

1. Select the module sheet or sheets you want to print. (You can select several module sheets at once by holding down the Ctrl key and clicking on the sheets' name tabs to select them.)

2. Choose the **File | Print** command. Excel displays the Print dialog box.

3. To print only the selected module sheets, select the Selecte**d** Sheet(s) option in the Print What area of the Print dialog box. Leave this option unselected if you want to print the entire workbook (including worksheets as well as module sheets).

4. Fill in the other options in the Print dialog box as you would for any other printing job.

5. Choose OK. Excel prints the selected module sheets, or the entire workbook, depending on whether you chose the Selecte**d** Sheet(s) option in Step 3.

When you print a module sheet, you cannot print selected text, nor can you preview the printed module sheet. You can only print an entire module sheet, and the printed output from the module sheet is always formatted the same way (except for page margins, headers and footers, which you can control through the Page Setup dialog box).

Summary

In today's lesson, you learned how Excel module sheets are used by the Excel macro recorder. You were then introduced to the VBA menu and toolbar commands before you learned how to locate, display, and edit a macro. You also learned how to make copies of individual macros or entire module sheets.

Next, you learned how to get started writing your own macros without recording. You then learned how to make your macros display messages for the macro's user, followed by a discussion and explanation of the syntax and runtime errors you are likely to encounter as you write, edit, and run your macros. You learned how—and the reasons why—to insert new recorded instructions directly into an existing macro, and, finally, you learned how to make a printed copy of your module sheets.

Q&A

Q I don't like the colors that VBA uses to color-code the different parts of a macro. Can I change the colors used?

A Yes, you can change the colors that VBA uses to identify different parts of a macro. Choose the **T**ools | **O**ptions command to display the Options dialog box, and then select the Module Format tab, if necessary, to bring the module formatting options to the front. Select the item whose color you want to change in the **C**ode Colors list, and then select the color for the text in the **F**oreground and **B**ackground drop-down list boxes. Usually, you should select only the foreground color and leave the background color set to **Automatic**. When you are satisfied with your changes, choose OK.

Q I don't like the display font for the macros in my module sheets. Is there any way to change the display font and point size?

A Yes, you can change the display font and size used in the module sheets. Like the color options, the font and point size options are found on the Module Format tab of the Options dialog box, which is opened by the **T**ools **O**ptions command. Select the display font in the **F**ont drop-down list, and choose the point size in the **S**ize drop-down list. A sample of the text appears in the lower-right area of the Module Format tab.

Q Do I have to indent code the same way the recorder does?

A No, you don't have to indent code the same way the recorder does; in fact, you don't have to indent your macro code at all.

There is nothing in VBA that requires you to indent your code; indenting code is merely a formatting convention used to make the code more readable for human beings. If you prefer a different indenting style, go ahead and use that style. It is highly recommended, however, that you do indent your code in some fashion, in order to make it easier to understand.

Q When should I insert a new module to write a macro?

A Insert a new module for a macro whenever you want to start a new category of macros, or if a module is getting full—a module sheet can contain up to 4,000 lines of code, approximately.

Q I don't want to print the entire module sheet; how can I print only one macro?

A To print a single macro instead of an entire module sheet, use the **Edit | Copy** command to copy the macro text to the Windows Clipboard. You can then either paste the macro text into a module sheet so that it is the only macro in the module, or paste the macro text into an application such as Windows Notepad, Windows WordPad, or a word processor.

Q How can I select the font and formatting used when I print a module?

A Although you can use the Page Setup dialog box to alter the margins, headers, footers, and page orientation, you cannot change the font or formatting used to print a module. Modules always print in the same font used on-screen, and with only the formatting that you put in the module by indenting your code, leaving blank lines, and so on. If, for some reason, you must change the font or print formatting of a macro or module sheet, use the **Edit | Copy** command to copy the text from the module sheet to the Windows Clipboard, and then paste the text into a word processor (such as Windows Write, Word for Windows, WordPerfect for Windows, etc.) and use the word processor's features to change fonts and formatting in the module.

Workshop

The Workshop section presents Quiz questions to help you cement your new knowledge, and Exercises to give you experience using what you have learned. Answers are in Appendix A.

Quiz

1. What is a VBA module?
2. What is the purpose of adding comments to a recorded macro? Should you use comments in macros that you write yourself?

3. What is a VBA keyword?

4. What are the required parts of a macro?

5. What is a macro declaration?

6. What is the body of a macro, and where is it found?

7. What important tool does VBA provide to help you locate specific macros?

8. Why is recorded VBA source code indented? Why should you indent your source code?

9. What is the purpose of the MsgBox procedure?

10. What is an argument? What is an argument list?

11. What is the line continuation symbol, and what is it used for?

12. What is a syntax error?

13. What is a runtime error?

14. Give three reasons why you might want to record new macro instructions directly into a macro.

Exercises

1. Insert a new module sheet in the PERSONAL.XLS workbook (you may need to unhide this workbook first). Rename the module sheet so it has the name *VBHelp*. Now type in the following program listing (omitting the line numbers):

```
1:  ' ProgHelp macro
2:  ' This macro opens the VBA Help
3:  ' reference at the table of contents
4:  '
5:  Sub ProgHelp()
6:      Application.Help "VBA_XL.HLP"
7:  End Sub
```

When you have finished entering the macro, run it. You should see the Visual Basic Reference online help file opened at its table of contents. (Remember to hide the PERSONAL.XLS workbook when you are done with this exercise.)

2. Write a macro to display the message I am a Visual Basic message in a dialog box with a single button and the title VBA Message.

3. **BUG BUSTER:** Find the error in the following macro (enter the macro in a module and run it to help find the error):

```
1:  Sub Broken()
2:      MsgBox Yet Another Message
3:  End Sub
```

4. Write a macro that uses `MsgBox` to display the message `recorded instructions complete`. Next, mark a recording location in the macro immediately before the `MsgBox` statement, and then record the actions necessary to open the SAMPLES.XLS sample file provided with Excel 7. After you stop the macro recorder, close the SAMPLES.XLS workbook, and then run the resulting macro. What happens?

Understanding Data Types, Variables, and Constants

In this lesson, you learn about the types of data that VBA can manipulate, and how to add temporary data storage to your VBA procedures. In this lesson, you learn:

☐ What a data type is and what data types are inherent to VBA.

☐ What a variable is and how to create and use variables in your procedures.

☐ What a constant is and how to create and use constants in your procedures.

☐ How to get input from your macro's user and store that input in a variable—an important first step in adding interactive decision-making to your programs.

Examining Visual Basic Data Types

Before you learn about variables, you should understand how VBA stores different kinds of information. VBA stores data in a way that distinguishes between numbers, dates, and text. *Data type* is the term that refers to the specific kinds of data that VBA can store and manipulate—such as text and numbers.

Table 3.1 summarizes VBA's data types, shows how much memory each type consumes, briefly describes the data type, and gives the range of values that data type can store. For data types that store numbers, the range of possible values indicates the largest and smallest number that VBA can store using that data type. For non-numeric data types, the value range indicates the upper and lower limits of values that VBA can store using those types.

Note: A *byte* is the typical unit used to measure computer memory and disk storage. A byte consists of eight *bits* (binary digits); a single alphabetic character typically requires a single byte of storage.

Table 3.1. Visual Basic data types.

Type Name	Size in Bytes	Description and Value Range
Array	As required by the type and number of array elements	Each array element's range is the same as the base type. The number of elements in an array has no fixed limit.
Boolean	2 (16 bits)	Stores logical values; may contain only the values True or False.

Type Name	Size in Bytes	Description and Value Range
Currency	8 (64 bits)	−922,337,203,685,477.5808 to 922,337,203,685,477.5807.
Date	8 (64 bits)	Stores a combination of date and time information. Dates may range from January 1, 0100 to December 31, 9999. Times may range from 00:00:00 to 23:59:59.
Double	8 (64 bits)	Negative numbers: from $-1.79769313486232 \times 10^{308}$ to $-4.94065645841247 \times 10^{-324}$. Positive numbers: from $4.94065645841247 \times 10^{-324}$ to $1.79769313486232 \times 10^{308}$.
Integer	2 (16 bits)	Whole numbers from −32,768 to 32,767.
Long	4 (32 bits)	Whole numbers from −2,147,483,648 to 2,147,483,647.
Object	4 (32 bits)	Used to access any object recognized by VBA. Stores the memory address of the object.
Single	4 (32 bits)	Negative numbers: from -3.402823×10^{38} to $-1.401298 \times 10^{-45}$. Positive numbers: from 1.401298×10^{-45} to 3.402823×10^{38}.
String	1 byte per character	Used to store text. May contain 0 characters up to approximately 2 billion characters. In Windows 3.1, string length is a maximum of 65,535 (64K) characters.

continues

Table 3.1. continued

Type Name	Size in Bytes	Description and Value Range
Variant	16 bytes, plus 1 byte per character	The Variant type can store any other data type. The range for Variants depends on the data actually stored: If text, the range is that of a string type; if numeric, the range is that of a Double type.

Later in this section, each data type listed in Table 3.1 (except Object and Array types) is described in more detail. The Object and Array types are described in their own separate lessons. Arrays are the topic of Day 13, while Objects are the topic of Day 7.

Scientific Notation

In Table 3.1, you may see a way of representing numbers—called *scientific notation*—that is unfamiliar to you. In scientific notation, which is used for very large and very small numbers, values are represented without leading or trailing zeros, and there is only one digit to the left of the decimal. The number is multiplied by 10 raised to some power (the *exponent*) to show where the decimal point actually lies. Scientific notation is compact and readable, compared to a number in standard notation with 300 zeroes after it.

Keep in mind that a negative exponent results in a smaller number; a positive exponent results in a larger number. You cannot use superscript characters in source code, so VBA uses a variation of scientific notation devised especially for computers. In VBA's scientific notation, use the letter *E* followed by the exponent, instead of writing ×*10*. The following table gives examples of numbers in VBA scientific notation and standard notation.

-1.23E2	-123
-1.23E-2	-0.0123
2.5E10	25,000,000,000
7E9	7,000,000,000
2.5E-10	0.00000000025
1.7E1	17
1.7E0	1.7

You can convert most of the data types listed in Table 3.1 to another data type. The next lesson shows how VBA automatically converts data and briefly describes how to manually convert data types. This lesson focuses on the different data types themselves: their qualities, their limits, and their uses.

Dates

VBA uses the Date data type to store dates and times. Date type data uses up 8 bytes of memory for every date/time combination stored.

Note: As you work with VBA Date type information, be aware that VBA's Date types aren't the same as the date types used in Excel, although they have many similarities.

When VBA displays dates (by using MsgBox, for example), the date displays in the short date format your computer system uses. Similarly, VBA displays the time information stored with a date using the 12- or 24-hour time format for your computer. (In Windows 95, you can change the date and time formats by choosing the Regional Settings icon in the Windows 95 Control Panel.)

Usually, you need not be concerned with how VBA stores Date type information—you simply display, store, or otherwise manipulate a date; VBA automatically handles all details of converting the serial date number into year, month, day, and time information for you.

VBA's Date data type is a *serial date*. (Serial dates store a date as a number of days from a given starting date, instead of keeping track of months and years separately.) The base date for VBA's Date type is December 30, 1899. VBA uses negative numbers to represent dates before 12/30/1899, and positive numbers to represent dates after that. The number *0* represents the date 12/30/1899, itself. In this scheme, January 1, 1900 is represented by the number *2* (1/1/1900 is 2 days after 12/30/1899); the number *-2*, however, is the date 12/28/1899 (two days before 12/30/1899).

Note: VBA always uses the same base date for its Date type serial dates, regardless of Excel's date scheme (or the date scheme of any other VBA host application). Excel also uses serial dates, but the base date for Excel's serial dates is January 1, 1900. (You can also set Excel for compatibility with the Macintosh date system, which uses serial dates from January 1, 1904.) Regardless of the base date for Excel's dates, Date types in VBA always use 12/30/1899 as the base date.

In the serial date number stored in a Date data type, the whole part of the number (digits to the left of the decimal) is the total number of days from the base date. Optionally, a VBA serial date can have digits to the right of the decimal; these digits indicate the time of day as a fraction of a day. One hour is 1/24 of a day—approximately 0.0416. Similarly, one minute is 1/1440 of a day, and a second is 1/86400 of a day.

You can subtract dates from each other, or add or subtract numbers to a date to change its value. For instance, if you want to determine the number of days between two dates, simply subtract the earlier date from the later date. VBA knows, because the values are Date type values, that the intent of the computation is to obtain the difference, in days, between the two dates. Similarly, if you want to find out the date 60 days from a given date, just add 60 to the date—VBA computes a date 60 days later.

VBA provides several built-in procedures (described in Day 5) to extract separately the year, month, day, hours, minutes, and seconds stored by a Date type.

Numbers

VBA has five different numeric data types: Integer, Long, Single, Double, and Currency. A numeric data type stores numbers using various formats, depending on the specific numeric type. Numeric data types provide a compact and efficient way to store numbers. The numeric data type that occupies the most memory (and has the greatest range of possible values) takes up no more than 8 bytes of memory to store numbers that may have as many as 300 digits. The following paragraphs describe each of the numeric types in more detail.

Integers and Long Integers

An *integer* is a whole number, without any fractional part. The numbers *1*, *3768*, and *12* are all integers; the numbers *1.5*, *3.14*, and *17.2* are not integers. (The number *1.0* is not an integer, even though the fractional part is zero—integers never contain a decimal point, even if the decimal fraction is zero.)

VBA provides two different integer data types: Integer and Long integer. The *Integer* data type requires two bytes of memory to store a number; the range of numbers you can store as an Integer data type is from –32,768 up to 32,767. Because the range for an Integer data type is fairly limited, VBA provides another, larger integer type: the *Long integer*. A Long integer (referred to simply as a *Long*) uses 4 bytes of memory to store a number, and has a value range from –2,147,483,648 to 2,147,483,647.

Integer and Long integer data types have a couple of advantages over other numeric data types: integers require less memory to store a number than VBA's other numeric data types, and mathematical and comparison operations on Integer or Long data type numbers are faster than those for floating-point numeric types. Integer and Long data types have many uses; most

frequently, you use them for cumulative counting operations, because of their compact size and faster speed in arithmetic operations. Use an Integer or Long type for numbers that do not have a fractional part.

VBA automatically converts Integer and Long data types into text when you display them using procedures such as MsgBox. The next lesson contains more information about VBA's automatic data type conversions.

Floating-Point Numbers

Floating-point numbers can have any number of digits before or after the decimal point (within the range limits of the specific data type). Floating-point numbers get their name from the fact that the decimal point "floats" from one position to another, depending on whether the value stored is large or small. The numbers *11.0123, -1107.1, 0.0125,* and *435.67876* are all floating-point numbers. Floating-point numbers are also sometimes called *real* numbers. Use floating-point data types any time you need to store a number that has a fractional part.

VBA has two different floating-point data types: Single and Double. The Single data type requires 4 bytes of memory, and can store negative numbers from -3.402823×10^{38} to $-1.401298 \times 10^{-45}$, and positive numbers from 1.401298×10^{-45} to 3.402823×10^{38}. Numbers stored using the Single data type are called *single-precision* numbers. The Double data type requires 8 bytes of memory, and can store negative numbers from $-1.79769313486232 \times 10^{308}$ to $-4.94065645841247 \times 10^{-324}$, and positive numbers from $4.94065645841247 \times 10^{-324}$ to $1.79769313486232 \times 10^{308}$. Numbers stored using the Double data type are called *double-precision* numbers.

Although single- and double-precision numbers have greater ranges than other numeric data types, they have a couple of minor disadvantages. Operations performed on floating-point numbers are somewhat slower than similar operations on other numeric data types. Also, numbers stored as floating-point data types can be subject to small rounding errors. Like the integer data types, VBA automatically converts Single and Double values into text when you display them with procedures like MsgBox. If a floating-point number is very large or very small, VBA displays the number in scientific notation.

The Currency Data Type

VBA's Currency data type is a *fixed-point* number, that is, the decimal point always occurs in the same place—there are always four places to the right of the decimal point. Use the Currency data type to store numbers when accuracy is extremely important, as is true with money calculations.

The Currency data type requires 8 bytes of memory, and can store numbers from $-922,337,203,685,477.5808$ to $922,337,203,685,477.5807$. Mathematical operations on Currency data type numbers have little or no rounding errors, and are therefore somewhat more accurate than floating-point numbers. Rounding errors with Currency type numbers typically occur only when you multiply or divide Currency type numbers by values with a different numeric type. Like all the other numeric data types, VBA automatically converts Currency values into text when you display them.

Text Strings

Any text data stored in a VBA program is called a *string*. Strings get their names because text data is commonly regarded as a string of characters. A string may contain any kind of text characters: letters of the alphabet, digits, punctuation, or various symbols. Strings in VBA code are always enclosed in double quotation marks ("). "Fred and Wilma", "3.14", "Robert Silverberg", and "16,000.00" are all strings. There are two categories of string: variable-length strings, which grow or shrink in size as the string they store changes size, and fixed-length strings that always remain the same size. All strings in VBA are variable-length strings, unless you specify a fixed length, as described later in this chapter.

String data types play an important role in most VBA programs. Most user input (in dialog boxes, worksheet cells, and so on) is string data. Also, because you can only display text on-screen, all other data types must be converted to string data before you can display them. Many of VBA's built-in procedures—like MsgBox—use string data in all or some of their arguments.

VBA provides several operators to concatenate (connect together) and compare strings; VBA also has several built-in procedures to help you extract substrings from larger strings, search for characters or words in a string, change the case of letters in a string, and so on. The next lesson describes VBA's string operators, and Day 5 describes VBA's string manipulation procedures.

Logical Values

Typically, a VBA program makes decisions by testing whether various conditions are true or false. To simplify testing various conditions, and to provide a means of storing the results of such tests, VBA provides a logical data type. Logical values of True and False are referred to as *Boolean* values. (The name comes from a mathematician named Boole who developed a system of logical mathematics.) The VBA logical data type is also called the *Boolean* data type.

VBA's Boolean data type requires 2 bytes of memory, and may have one of two values: True or False. If you display a Boolean data type on-screen, VBA automatically converts it to a string containing either the word *True* or *False*. Boolean values are produced as the result of a comparison operation. (A comparison operation is when you compare one thing to another, such as comparing two numbers to see which is greater, or comparing two strings to see which is alphabetically lower.) Tomorrow's lesson describes VBA's various comparison operations.

Variant Data

The Variant data type is a special data type that can store any of the data types listed in Table 3.1, including Object and Array types. VBA uses the Variant data type for all variables, unless you explicitly declare the data type for the variable, as described later in this chapter.

Variant data types take on the characteristics of the particular data type they are currently storing. If a Variant data type contains string data, for example, the Variant takes on the characteristics of a string. If a Variant data type contains numeric data, the Variant takes on the characteristics of a numeric data type—usually a Double, although Variants may also have the characteristics of Integer, Long, Single, or Currency types.

A Variant data type uses the most compact representation possible for the data it contains. If VBA stores a whole number in a Variant, the number is handled as an Integer or as a Long, depending on its size. For instance, VBA treats the number 15 in a Variant type as an Integer; it would treat the number 1,000,000 in a Variant type as a Long.

VBA stores most floating-point numbers in a Variant as the Double data type. VBA includes the Variant data type so that you don't always have to be concerned with specifying the data types of variables you use in your code. Any variable for which you do not specifically declare the data type becomes a Variant data type.

Although Variant data types are convenient, and relieve you of some work when writing your procedures, they do require more memory than any other data type, except for large strings and arrays. (Arrays are described fully in Day 13.) Also, mathematical and comparison operations on Variant data types are slower than similar operations performed on any other data type. In general, you should avoid using Variant variables—relying on Variant variable data types can lead you into sloppy programming habits and make it difficult to find and eliminate bugs in your programs.

Understanding Variables

Variables are important because they provide a computer program with a way to temporarily store and manipulate data. This section gives you an understanding of what a variable is, and how to create variables.

What Is a Variable?

A *variable* is a name given by you, the programmer, to an area of the computer's memory used to store data of any type. Think of a variable as a pigeon-hole in which you can put any single item of data and save it for later use. The variable's name is the identifying label for that pigeon-hole. The contents of the pigeon-hole (the value of the variable) can change, but the name of the variable remains the same. VBA variables may store any of the data types listed in Table 3.1.

In some senses, a variable is like a named worksheet cell. In Excel, you can give a name to a cell in a worksheet, and then refer to that worksheet cell by its name so you don't have to use—or even remember—the cell's actual row and column address each time you want to refer to the data or formula in that worksheet cell.

In the same way, a VBA variable is a name that refers to a specific memory location in your computer so that you don't have to worry about the actual memory address of the stored data—you use the variable name to refer to whatever data is stored in that memory location. VBA handles all of the details of finding specific memory locations in your computer for you. You never have to worry about the specific address of a variable's data—just use the variable name to refer to the stored data.

You use variables in VBA statements the same way you use variables in algebraic equations. The variable represents a numeric quantity, text, date, or other information that is not known exactly at the time you write the statement, but will be present and available when VBA executes the statement.

Whenever a variable name appears in a VBA statement, VBA inserts into the statement the actual value currently stored in the memory location referred to by the variable. In the following example, if the variable **AnyNum** contains the number *2*, then the entire statement evaluates to the number *4*:

```
AnyNum + 2
```

When VBA executes the above statement, it substitutes the number *2* (stored in the variable named **AnyNum**) into the statement, adds it to the number *2* that is written directly into the statement, and comes up with the result: *4*. If the variable **AnyNum** contains the number *4* instead, then the same statement (AnyNum + 2) evaluates to *6*.

As another, more complex example of how you use variables, examine the following formula, which computes what percentage one number is of another number (you may recall this formula, or one like it, from your high-school mathematics courses):

```
Percent = (Part ÷ Whole) × 100
```

In this sample statement, the variables named **Part** and **Whole** represent two different numbers. The formula in this statement computes what percentage **Part** is of the **Whole**—the variable named **Percent** stores the result of the computation. When VBA executes this statement, it retrieves whatever numbers are stored in the memory locations referred to by **Part** and **Whole**, and inserts them into the statement before performing any computations.

If the variable **Part** contains the number 5 and **Whole** contains the number 20, then VBA substitutes values when it executes the statement to create the following interim statement (VBA stores such interim statements internally, and discards them when it has finished executing the statement—you will never see the interim statements that VBA constructs):

```
Percent = (5 ÷ 20) × 100
```

Next, VBA performs the computation and stores the result in the memory location referred to by the **Percent** variable: 5 divided by 20 is 0.25, and 0.25 multiplied by 100 is 25; therefore, the value that VBA ends up storing in the **Percent** variable is the number *25*. Any number previously stored in the **Percent** variable is replaced by this new value.

Note: VBA doesn't really use the division (÷) and multiplication (×) symbols shown in the sample formula in this section, because you can't type these symbols at the keyboard. Instead, VBA uses the slash (/) and the asterisk (*) to indicate division and multiplication. Day 4 describes all of the arithmetic operation symbols that VBA uses, and their meanings. This chapter uses the standard division (÷) and multiplication (×) symbols so you can focus on the discussions of variables and their use, without worrying about what unfamiliar symbols might mean.

3

Choosing Variable Names

With only a few restrictions, you can choose any name you want for a variable. This section first explains VBA's rules and limitations for variable names, and then gives you some guidelines for naming your variables.

Understanding Identifiers

An *identifier* is a name you give to the elements in your procedures and modules that you create—such as variables. The term *identifier* comes from the fact that the names you create identify specific memory locations (in the case of a variable name), groups of instructions (in the case of a macro or procedure name), or other program elements.

The same rules and guidelines explained in this section for choosing a variable name also apply to choosing other identifier names. Later lessons refer you to these rules for creating identifiers.

A variable name must follow these rules:

☐ The variable name must begin with a letter of the alphabet.

☐ After the first letter, the variable name may consist of any combination of digit, letter, or underscore (_) characters.

☐ Variable names may not contain spaces, a period (.), or any of the symbols VBA uses to indicate mathematical or comparison operations (=, +, −, and so on).

☐ Variable names may not exceed 255 characters in length.

☐ A variable's name cannot duplicate certain VBA keywords. If you choose variable names that duplicate these keywords—called *restricted keywords*—VBA displays one of several possible syntax error messages.

☐ A variable's name must be unique within its *scope*. That is, the variable name must be unique within the procedure or module in which you declare the variable. If you inadvertently give two variables the same name in the same procedure, or you give a variable a name that is the same as a macro or procedure name in the same module, VBA displays an error message when you run the macro.

Some examples of valid variable names are:

```
MyVar
PayDate
New_Item
Percent
Whole
Part
Line12
```

The following examples are *not* valid variable names:

```
New Item       'Not valid because it contains a space character
5thDimension   'Does not begin with a letter
Dim            'duplicates a VBA restricted keyword
Week/Day       'Contains an invalid character: VBA interprets the slash character
               ' as a division operation
```

Names for variables are not *case-sensitive*, that is, the capitalization of the variable name does not matter. The variable names `MyVar` and `myvar` are the same, as far as VBA is concerned. In fact, VBA regularizes the capitalization of variable names in your code, based on the capitalization you used the last time you typed the variable name. For example, if you type the variable name `MyVar`, and then later type the variable name as `myvar`, VBA changes the previous `MyVar` to `myvar`.

When you choose names for variables, try to make the name as descriptive as possible; choose names like `PcntProfit` rather than `X` or `Y`. A good name for a variable that stores a value representing a temperature in degrees Celsius, for example, is `CelsiusTemp` or, possibly, `DegreesC`. In the percentage formula example in the preceding section, the variable names `Part` and `Whole` were chosen to reflect the purpose and use of the numbers they store.

DO	DON'T

DO remember that, although capitalization of variable names (or other identifiers) does not matter to VBA, adding capitalization can make your code much easier for a human being to read and understand.

> **DO** remember to take advantage of the underscore (_); you can use the underscore as a substitute for a space character to make your variable names (and other identifiers) more readable. The second and third identifiers following are much more readable than the first, due to adding capital letters and underscores:
>
> ```
> verylongidentifiername
> VeryLongIdentifierName
> Very_Long_Identifier_Name
> ```

Creating Variables

The simplest way to create a variable is to just use the variable in a VBA statement. VBA creates a variable, and reserves memory for the variable's storage location, the first time the variable appears in a VBA statement—usually a statement that stores a data value in the variable.

Storing a data value in a variable is called *assigning the variable* or *making an assignment.* You make an assignment to a variable by using the assignment operator, represented by the equals sign (=). The following line is an example of assigning a value to a variable:

```
MyVar = 15
```

This statement stores the numeric value 15 in the memory location specified by the variable name **MyVar**. If this is the first statement in a procedure to use this variable, then VBA creates the variable, reserves a memory location to store the variable's data, and then stores the number 15 in the new memory location specified by the variable name.

If the **MyVar** variable already exists, then VBA simply stores the number 15 in the memory location referred to by **MyVar**. The new value replaces whatever was previously stored in **MyVar**; the previous contents of **MyVar** are lost.

Creating a variable by just using it in a statement is called an *implicit variable declaration.* By using the variable in a statement, you are implicitly telling (declaring to) VBA that you want to create that variable. All variables that VBA creates with an implicit variable declaration have the Variant data type. Implicit variable declaration is also known less formally as *on-the-fly* variable declaration.

Implicit variable declaration is convenient but has potential problems. One such problem occurs when you have a variable named **MyValue**, for example, and later misspell its name as **MValue**. Depending on exactly where the misspelled variable name occurs in your code, VBA might produce a runtime error or simply create a new variable. If VBA does create a new variable, you may end up with subtle problems in your code that are very difficult to find.

Implicit variable declaration also causes problems if you write an assignment statement mistakenly believing that you are implicitly declaring a new variable when you are really using a previously created variable. In this case, you inadvertently destroy the previously stored value—this kind of problem usually does not result in a runtime error, but instead tends to result in other problems whose cause is difficult to locate.

For these reasons, and others, VBA provides a way for you to make *explicit* variable declarations. Declaring variables explicitly provides these advantages:

☐ Explicit declaration speeds up the execution of your code. VBA creates all of the variables declared explicitly in a module or procedure before it executes the procedure's code. The speed of your code's execution increases by the amount of time otherwise required to analyze and create an implicitly declared variable.

☐ Explicit declaration helps avoid errors due to misspelling a variable name, as described in the preceding paragraphs.

☐ Explicit variable declarations make your code easier to read and understand. By seeing all the variable declarations at the beginning of a module or procedure, a human reader can more easily determine which variables are used in that module or procedure.

☐ Explicitly declaring a variable helps regularize the variable name's capitalization. If you declare a variable explicitly, VBA always changes the capitalization of the variable name in a VBA statement to match the capitalization of the variable name in the variable declaration instead of using the capitalization from the last time you typed the variable name. For example, if you explicitly declare a variable capitalized as `MyValue`, and then later type the variable name as `myvalue`, VBA changes `myvalue` to match the capitalization in the explicit declaration: `MyValue`.

Note: Although Variant data types can store Date type data, a Variant may not correctly store a date obtained from Excel. For example, VBA won't recognize a date from an Excel worksheet cell as a date unless the Excel date is formatted with one of Excel's date formats. A Date type, however, will correctly store the Excel date from the worksheet cell regardless of its formatting. Conversely, when you insert a date value from VBA into an Excel worksheet cell, the date information is not correctly interpreted if it comes from a Variant data type instead of a Date type. For these reasons, you should always explicitly declare variables you use for dates as a Date data type. (Specifying the data type of a variable is explained later in this chapter.)

To explicitly declare a variable, use VBA's `Dim` statement with the following syntax:

Syntax

```
Dim name
```

name is any valid variable identifier. For example:

```
Dim PcntProfit
```

The statement above tells VBA to create a variable named **PcntProfit**. (The `Dim` keyword, by the way, is an abbreviation of the word *dimension*.) All variables that you create with this form of the `Dim` keyword are Variant type variables. (You'll learn how to create variables with specific data types later in this lesson.)

> **Note:** Whenever VBA creates a new variable, it *initializes* the variable: strings are set to contain no characters, numbers are set to 0, Boolean variables are initialized to `False`, and dates are initialized to December 30, 1899.

If you wish, you can declare several variables on the same line, separating each variable name with a comma, as shown in the following syntax example:

Syntax

```
Dim name1, name2, nameN
```

name1, *name2*, and *nameN* are any valid VBA variable names. You may list as many variable names as you desire. The following `Dim` statement declares three different variables (**PcntProfit**, **Gross_Income**, and **Total_Costs**):

```
Dim PcntProfit, Gross_Income, Total_Costs
```

You can only declare a variable once in a particular procedure or module. As long as the `Dim` statement comes before any statements that actually use the variable, you can place the `Dim` statement anywhere in a procedure. The best programming practice, however, gathers all explicit variable declarations into a single area at the beginning of a procedure.

Listing 3.1 shows the **HelloMacro** procedure from yesterday's lesson, modified to explicitly declare a variable named **HelloMsg**, which it uses to store the text the `MsgBox` statement will display. (The **HelloMacro** procedure in Listing 3.1 displays the dialog box shown in Figure 3.1.)

Listing 3.1. The `HelloMacro` procedure, with an explicit variable declaration.

```
1:  Sub HelloMacro()
2:      Dim HelloMsg    'stores text for the MsgBox message
3:      HelloMsg = "Hello, World!"
4:      MsgBox HelloMsg, , "Greeting Box"
5:  End Sub
```

Analysis The Dim statement appears in line 2 of Listing 3.1. When VBA executes this statement, it creates the variable **HelloMsg**, and reserves memory storage space for it. (The **HelloMsg** variable is a Variant type; unless you specify the variable's type as described later in this lesson, VBA always creates Variant type variables.) Line 2 includes a trailing comment that indicates the purpose of the variable.

Line 3 of Listing 3.1 makes an assignment to the **HelloMsg** variable; this line stores the string "Hello, World!" in the memory location referred to by the **HelloMsg** variable. Next, line 4 uses the **HelloMsg** variable as one of the arguments for the MsgBox procedure. When VBA executes line 4, it retrieves the string stored in **HelloMsg**, and then passes that string on to MsgBox as its first argument. MsgBox displays the same message dialog box as before—although MsgBox now gets its first argument from a variable, that variable contains the same string information that was previously written directly into the MsgBox statement.

Figure 3.1.

*The **HelloMacro** procedure displays this dialog box.*

DO	DON'T

DO add comments explaining how a procedure uses a particular variable—even if the variable has a properly descriptive name. Comments increase the readability of your procedures (and make it easier to change them if you later need to).

DON'T assume that, just because VBA initializes a newly created variable, that the new variable contains any particular value.

DO always manually initialize a variable by making an assignment to it, before using that variable in other operations.

Scope: Determining Which Variables Are Available

The term *scope* refers to the area of a VBA procedure or module in which a given variable, procedure, or other identifier is accessible. This section discusses the two basic scope levels: procedure-level and module-level. Variables, procedures, and identifiers that are available only inside a procedure have procedure-level scope, and those that are available to all procedures in a module have module-level scope.

Procedure-Level Scope

A variable declared inside a procedure is available only inside that procedure. The **HelloMsg** variable shown in line 2 of Listing 3.1, for example, is only available in the **HelloMacro** procedure; no other procedure can access that variable. In fact, the **HelloMsg** variable really exists only while VBA is actually executing the **HelloMacro** procedure. The **HelloMsg** variable is therefore said to have *procedure-level* scope.

Although it may not seem so at first, VBA restricts the availability of variables through its scope rules to help simplify things for you, the programmer. Because a variable with procedure-level scope is not available to any procedure except the procedure in which you declare the variable, you don't have to worry quite so much about duplicate variable names.

The rules for choosing variable names tell you that a variable's name must be unique within its scope. For variables with procedure-level scope, this means that you cannot declare two variables with the same name in the same procedure. (Obviously, neither VBA nor a human being can tell which variable you intend to use if they both have the same name.)

Because procedure-level scope restricts a variable's availability to the procedure in which you declare the variable, however, you can safely use the same variable name in *different* procedures. Look at Listing 3.2, which shows two complete procedures. (**HelloMacro** in this listing displays the same dialog box shown previously in Figure 3.1.)

 Listing 3.2. Procedure-level scope.

```
1:  Sub HelloMacro()
2:      Dim HelloMsg     'stores text for the MsgBox message
3:      HelloMsg = "Hello, World!"
4:      MsgBox HelloMsg, , "Greeting Box"
5:  End Sub
6:
7:  Sub HelloDave()
8:      Dim HelloMsg     'stores text for the MsgBox message
9:      HelloMsg = "Hello, Dave!"
10:     MsgBox HelloMsg, , "Greeting Box"
11: End Sub
```

 Lines 1 through 5 contain the same **HelloMacro** procedure from Listing 3.1, which works exactly the same. A second procedure, **HelloDave** has been added to the module, and begins on line 7 of Listing 3.2. The **HelloDave** procedure works exactly the same as the **HelloMacro** procedure; it just displays a different text message in its dialog box.

Notice in lines 2 and 8 that both procedures use the Dim statement to declare variables named **HelloMsg**. This is reasonable, because the variable name **HelloMsg** is a good, descriptive name for the variable's contents and purpose in both procedures.

Because the **HelloMsg** variables are declared inside separate procedures and have procedure-level scope, there is no ambiguity about which variable VBA should use. In the **HelloMacro** procedure, VBA uses the **HelloMsg** variable declared locally in that procedure (line 2 of the listing). In the **HelloDave** procedure, VBA uses the **HelloMsg** variable declared locally in that procedure (line 8).

Module-Level Scope

Sometimes, you'll want to have several procedures access the same variable. Often, it's more efficient to compute a value once, store it in a variable, and then use that variable in several procedures than it is to compute the same value over and over again.

For example, you might write several procedures, all of which need to use a value for the gross sales income for your company. One procedure might use the figure for gross sales to compute the percent of profit earned, another procedure might use the gross sales figure to compute gross profits, yet another procedure would use the gross sales figure to compute net profits, and so on.

If you declare a **Sales** variable to store the computed figure for gross sales inside a procedure, then the **Sales** variable has procedure-level scope, and no other procedure can access the value stored in **Sales**. This means that your procedures for computing percent profit, gross profit, and net profit each must compute the value for gross sales themselves. Obviously, computing the gross sales figure repeatedly is wasted time and effort.

Instead, it would be more efficient to create a procedure that computes only the figure for gross sales, and then stores that figure in a variable named **Sales**, which is available to all of the other procedures. This way, you compute the value for **Sales** only once; when the percent profit procedure needs this value, it uses the value stored in the **Sales** variable; the separate procedures for computing gross profit and net profit also would use the previously computed figure stored in the **Sales** variable.

VBA enables you to declare variables that several procedures can access at once. When a variable is available to all of the procedures in a module, the variable is said to have *module-level* scope. VBA limits the scope of a module-level variable to the module in which you declare the variable. (VBA does provide ways you can force a variable to have even greater scope; Day 11 describes those techniques.)

To make a variable available to all of the procedures in a particular module, place the Dim statement for that variable at the beginning of the module, before any procedure declarations. Listing 3.3 shows an entire module that contains two simple procedures and a single module-level variable declaration (both procedures have the same output as shown in Figure 3.1).

> **Note:** The area at the beginning of a module, before any macro or procedure declarations, is referred to as the *definition*, or *declaration* area of the module because this is where you place module-level variable declarations and other directives to VBA that affect the entire module.

Listing 3.3. Module-level variable scope.

```
1:  Dim HelloMsg    'used by all procedures in this module
2:
3:  Sub HelloMacro()
4:      HelloMsg = "Hello, World!"
5:      MsgBox HelloMsg, , "Greeting Box"
6:  End Sub
7:
8:  Sub HelloDave()
9:      HelloMsg = "Hello, Dave!"
10:     MsgBox HelloMsg, , "Another Message Box"
11: End Sub
```

In this listing, lines 3 through 6 contain the **HelloMacro** procedure, and lines 8 through 11 contain the **HelloDave** procedure. Notice that neither of these procedures contain any Dim statements. Instead, line 1 uses a Dim statement to declare a module-level variable named **HelloMsg**.

Because line 1 declares the **HelloMsg** variable at a module-level, it is available to all of the procedures in the same module. In lines 4 and 5, in the **HelloMacro** procedure, VBA uses the module-level **HelloMsg** variable. Similarly, in lines 9 and 10 of the **HelloDave** procedure, VBA uses the same module-level **HelloMsg** variable.

Using Variables with the Same Name at Different Scope Levels

A variable name must be unique within its scope. Just as you cannot declare two variables with the same name in the same procedure, you cannot declare two module-level variables with the same name in the same module—and for the same reasons.

You can, however, safely have variables with the same name at *different* scope levels. When variables have the same name but different scope, VBA uses the variable with the most *local* scope. You've already partially seen how this works in Listing 3.2, which shows two different procedures, each of which declares its own variable, but uses the same name for the variable. You saw that, because the variables have procedure-level scope, each procedure can use only its own *local* variable. Listing 3.4 shows an entire module containing three procedures, all of which use variables with the same names.

Listing 3.4. Combined module-level and procedure-level scope.

```
 1: Dim HelloMsg     'used by all procedures in this module
 2:                  'that do not have their own HelloMsg variable
 3: Sub HelloMacro()
 4:     HelloMsg = "Hello, World!"
 5:     MsgBox HelloMsg, , "Greeting Box"
 6: End Sub
 7:
 8: Sub HelloDave()
 9:     HelloMsg = "Hello, Dave!"
10:     MsgBox HelloMsg, , "Another Message Box"
11: End Sub
12:
13: Sub AnotherMessage()
14:     Dim HelloMsg     'local declaration: this procedure uses this variable
15:     HelloMsg = "Yet Another Message"
16:     MsgBox HelloMsg, , "Yet Another Message Box"
17: End Sub
```

Listing 3.4 shows three different procedures. You've already seen the first two procedures in Listing 3.3. The third procedure, **AnotherMessage** begins in line 13 and ends in line 17. The **AnotherMessage** procedure works the same as the preceding procedures, displaying a message in a dialog box by using a MsgBox statement.

Notice that line 1 of the listing declares a module-level variable, **HelloMsg**. Line 14, in the **AnotherMessage** procedure, also declares a variable named **HelloMsg**. When VBA executes the **HelloMacro** procedure, it uses the **HelloMsg** variable declared in line 1. **HelloMacro** has no variables declared locally, there is no possible ambiguity, and therefore VBA uses the module-level variable. Similarly, when VBA executes the **HelloDave** procedure, it also uses the **HelloMsg** variable declared in line 1.

The **AnotherMessage** procedure, however, contains its own **HelloMsg** variable declaration (line 14). When VBA executes lines 15 and 16, therefore, it resolves any ambiguity about which **HelloMsg** variable to use by using the most local variable: the **HelloMsg** variable declared at procedure-level in line 14 of the **AnotherMessage** procedure.

The module-level **HelloMsg** variable declared in line 1 is not accessible to the **AnotherMessage** procedure.

Note: Procedure-level variables are frequently referred to as *local* variables, because their declarations are local to the currently executing procedure.

Persistence: Determining How Long Variables Retain Their Value

Persistence is the term used to refer to the length of time that any given variable retains the value assigned to it. Values assigned to variables persist only as long as the variable is active within its scope.

When you declare a variable inside a procedure, that variable exists only while VBA is executing the procedure containing that particular variable. When VBA executes a procedure, it reserves memory space for all the variables declared locally in that procedure, whether the variables are declared explicitly or implicitly. When VBA stops executing that particular procedure, VBA returns the memory used by the procedure's local variables to the general pool of available computer memory, and the procedure's local variables cease to exist.

For instance, when VBA begins executing the **HelloMacro** procedure in Listing 3.1, it reserves memory space for the **HelloMsg** variable. When VBA finishes executing **HelloMacro**, it returns the memory reserved for the **HelloMsg** variable to the general pool of available memory, essentially destroying whatever value was stored in **HelloMsg**.

Procedure-level variables are created each time a procedure begins to execute, and destroyed whenever the procedure stops executing. Stated in more technical terms, a local variable is undefined (or *out of context*) until the procedure that declares it begins to execute. When the procedure that declares the variable stops executing, the variable is once again undefined.

Variables that you declare at the module level persist for as long as VBA is executing a procedure or macro in that module. When VBA executes a macro procedure, it actually looks through the entire module that contains the procedure it is executing, and creates any module-level variables. As long as VBA is executing a procedure in that module, the values stored in the module-level variables are retained.

Requiring Explicit Variable Declaration

Although implicit variable declaration (declaring variables by just using them) is convenient, it does have some inherent problems. As long as you can declare variables implicitly, you run the risk of inadvertently creating a new variable when you really intended to use an existing variable, or of using an existing variable when you really intended to create a new one. Both of these mistakes lead to bugs in your code that are very difficult to track down. (A *bug* is any defect in your code that prevents it from executing correctly, or results in erroneous computations.)

Earlier, you learned how to use the Dim statement to declare variables and help reduce the problems associated with implicit declaration. Using Dim to declare variables alone won't always help you detect or prevent the subtle errors related to implicit variable declaration, as long as VBA allows you to declare variables implicitly.

To help you detect errors associated with implicit variable declaration at all times, VBA provides the `Option Explicit` command. When you use `Option Explicit`, VBA requires you to declare all variables with a `Dim` statement before you use them. The `Option Explicit` command essentially prohibits implicit variable declaration anywhere in a module that contains the `Option Explicit` command.

To require explicit declaration for all variables in a module, add the `Option Explicit` command in the definition area of the module—that is, at the beginning of the module, before any macro or variable declarations. Listing 3.5 shows the same module from Listing 3.3, but with the `Option Explicit` command added.

Listing 3.5. The `Option Explicit` module command.

```
1:  Option Explicit    'requires that all variables in this module be declared
    ↪explicitly
2:  Dim HelloMsg    'used by all procedures in this module
3:
4:  Sub HelloMacro()
5:      HelloMsg = "Hello, World!"
6:      MsgBox HelloMsg, , "Greeting Box"
7:  End Sub
8:
9:  Sub HelloDave()
10:      HelloMsg = "Hello, Dave!"
11:      MsgBox HelloMsg, , "Another Message Box"
12: End Sub
```

Analysis
Except for line 1, the procedures in this module work exactly the same as described for Listing 3.2.

Line 1 of the module in Listing 3.5 contains the `Option Explicit` command. Because of this command, all of the variables in this module must be declared with the `Dim` statement. If you add an implicit variable declaration to this module, VBA displays a runtime error message stating that the variable is undeclared.

Note: Commands such as `Option Explicit`, which don't actually cause VBA to perform an action, but instead tell VBA how it should operate are called *compiler directives*. The VBA compiler is the part of VBA that reads your source code and *compiles* it into the machine instructions that your computer needs to carry out the specified task. A compiler directive simply instructs VBA about specific rules that you want VBA to follow when it compiles your source code.

The `Option Explicit` command affects only the module in which it appears. If the workbook that contains this module also contains other modules, the other modules are unaffected by the `Option Explicit` command in line 1. You must include the `Option Explicit` command in each module for which you want to require variable declarations.

DO	DON'T

DO use the `Option Explicit` command in your modules. Requiring yourself to declare variables explicitly helps reduce your opportunities to make a mistake, and consequently helps you write bug-free code.

Tip: Because including `Option Explicit` in all of your modules is so helpful, VBA provides a way to automatically include `Option Explicit` in every new module sheet you create. To make VBA add the `Option Explicit` command to each new module, select the **R**equire Variable Declaration option in the Module General tab of the Options dialog box. To set the **R**equire Variable Declaration option, follow these steps:

1. Choose the Tools | **O**ptions command. Excel displays the Options dialog box.
2. Click the Module General tab to display the module sheet options, if necessary.
3. Select the **R**equire Variable Declaration check box.
4. Choose OK. Excel closes the Options dialog box.

Now, each time you—or the Macro Recorder—insert a new module into a workbook, VBA automatically adds the `Option Explicit` command at the beginning of the module.

Selecting the **R**equire Variable Declaration option in the Options dialog box only affects new modules; if you want to require variables to be explicitly declared in a module you created previously, you must add `Option Explicit` by editing that module yourself.

Specifying the Data Type of a Variable

All variables in VBA, whether implicitly or explicitly declared, are of the Variant data type, unless you specify the variable's data type in the statement that declares the variable. So far, you've seen examples of variables declared both implicitly and explicitly. In all of these examples, the variables were *untyped*, that is, their data types were not specified. All of these variables were therefore of the Variant type, because untyped variables in VBA are always Variant data types.

Declaring *typed* variables (variables whose data type you specify) offers several advantages:

☐ Typed variables make your program code faster. Because you tell VBA the type of the variable when you declare it, your program is speeded up by the amount of time VBA would otherwise spend analyzing a Variant type variable to determine its specific type.

☐ Typed variables make your program code more efficient. Variant variables can take up much more memory than variables of specific types. A typed variable uses up only as much memory as required by that specific type. Using typed variables can greatly reduce the amount of memory that your VBA program requires; in some cases, using typed variables may make the difference between whether your procedure has enough memory to work or not.

☐ Typed variables make your program code easier to read and understand.

☐ Programs that use typed variables help you prevent bugs. Typed variables help reveal certain kinds of programmer error—such as incompatible mixes of data types—because VBA displays runtime errors that would not occur if the variables were untyped.

There are other reasons why you may want to declare typed variables. For example, although Variant data types can store dates, a Variant variable may not correctly store a date from Excel. VBA variables explicitly declared with the Date type do not have this problem.

You declare a variable's type in the same statement you use to declare the variable. You can declare a typed variable either when you declare the variable implicitly, or when you declare the variable explicitly, with Dim. When you declare String type variables, you can also specify a particular length for the string.

Using *Dim* to Declare Typed Variables

To declare a variable and its type with the Dim statement, add the keyword **As** after the variable name, and then type the name of the data type that you want the variable to have. The general syntax to use the Dim statement to declare a typed variable is:

Syntax

```
Dim varname As type
```

varname represents any valid VBA variable name, and *type* represents any one of VBA's data type names. (Table 3.1 lists the names of all of VBA's data types.)

The following lines show examples of the correct syntax for typed variable declarations:

```
Dim PcntProfit As Single
Dim Gross_Sales As Currency
Dim PayDay As Date
Dim Message As String
Dim Counter As Integer
```

If you want, you can also declare several typed variables with a single Dim statement, as shown in the following line; separate each variable and type declaration from the next with a comma (,):

```
Dim PcntProfit As Single, Gross_Sales As Currency, Message As String
```

DO	DON'T

DO declare the data type for each variable individually when you declare several typed variables in a single Dim statement. If you omit the data type, VBA creates a variable with a Variant data type. In the following line, for example, **NetValue** has the Variant data type:

```
Dim NetValue, PcntProfit As Single
```

Using Type Definition Characters to Declare Typed Variables

You can also specify the type of a variable when you declare the variable implicitly, by adding a special symbol—called a *type definition character*—to the end of the variable's name. Table 3.2 lists VBA's type definition characters and the types they indicate.

Table 3.2. Type definition characters.

Definition Character	Type
!	Single
@	Currency
#	Double
$	String
%	Integer
&	Long Integer

Notice that there are only six type definition characters; there are no type definition characters for Boolean, Date, Object, or Array data types. Type definition characters may only appear at the end of a variable name.

Listing 3.6 shows yet another variation of the **HelloMacro** procedure from Day 2.

Listing 3.6. Explicit and Implicit type declaration.

```
1:  Sub HelloMacro()
2:      Dim HelloMsg As String
3:      HelloMsg = "Hello, World!"
4:      Title$ = "Greeting Box"
5:      MsgBox HelloMsg, , Title$
6:  End Sub
```

This version of **HelloMacro** works much the same as previous versions. Line 1 contains the procedure declaration. In line 2, a Dim statement explicitly declares the **HelloMsg** variable. Because the Dim statement includes the As keyword and the type name String, the **HelloMsg** variable has the String data type. Line 3 assigns text for the message to the **HelloMsg** string variable.

Line 4 implicitly declares the **Title$** variable at the same time it assigns text for the message dialog box title to the variable. Because the **Title$** variable name ends with the type definition character for a string, this variable also has the String data type. Finally, line 5 uses the MsgBox statement to display the message dialog box; in this statement, both the text for the message and the dialog box's title bar come from variables: **HelloMsg** and **Title$**, respectively.

If either line 3 or line 4 tried to assign numeric or date type data to the **HelloMsg** or the **Title$** variables, VBA would display a type mismatch runtime error, and halt the execution of the macro.

Once you add a type definition character to a variable, you must include the type definition character each time you use the variable name. If the type definition character were left out of the **Title$** variable name in line 5 (where **Title$** is used for the first time after its implicit typed declaration), VBA would have displayed a runtime error, and stopped executing the macro.

Tip: You can also use type definition characters in Dim statements to specify the data type of a variable. The following two Dim statements have the same effect—to declare a variable named **Count** with the Integer data type:

```
Dim Count As Integer
```

```
Dim Count%
```

(If you put both of these lines in the same procedure, VBA produces a runtime error complaining that there is a duplicate variable declaration.)

Note: Once you declare a typed variable, whether you declare the variable explicitly or implicitly and no matter how you specify the type, the variable retains that same data type for as long as it exists. You cannot redeclare a variable or respecify its data type.

Using *Dim* to Declare Fixed-Length String Variables

Whether you declare String data type variables by using Dim or the $ type definition character, the string variables you create are all, by default, variable-length strings.

Variable-length string variables change size, depending on the size of the string stored by the variable. For some purposes, you'll want to use a fixed-length string. Fixed-length strings always have the same size. Fixed-length strings are useful if you want to ensure that the text stored in the string variable always contains the same number of characters.

You can use fixed-length strings to help line up information into columns for display, for example, or to ensure that string data stored in a particular variable never exceeds a certain length. There is only one way to declare a fixed-length string variable; you must use the Dim statement. The following line demonstrates the general syntax to create a fixed-length string:

Syntax

```
Dim varname As String * N
```

varname is any valid variable name, and *N* is any number from 1 up to the maximum string length of approximately 2 billion characters. (Formerly 65,000 (64K) characters in Windows 3.1).

The following statement is an example of a fixed-length string declaration:

```
Dim LastName As String * 30
```

An asterisk (*) followed by a number after the String keyword tells VBA to create the string variable as a fixed-length string having the specified length (in this case, 30 characters).

Understanding Constants

A *constant* is a value in a macro program that does not change. The procedure examples presented so far use string constants like "Hello World!" and "Greeting Box". Constants like this are referred to as *literal constants* because you write the literal value directly into your code.

Other examples of literal constants include the numbers 36, 3.14, 212, and the dates #12/31/93# or #October 28, 1994#. If you examine most recorded macros, you'll find other examples of literal constants (frequently, literal string constants). You can only change constants by editing the macro.

You use constants, like the string constants in the `HelloMacro` procedure, to provide data in a procedure that does not change—the opposite of a variable, which you use to provide data that does change. You can use constants as arguments for procedures or in mathematical and comparison operations.

Constants do not have to be literal constants; VBA allows you to create *named constants*. A named constant, like a variable, has a name that you give to it; that name represents a specific, unchanging value. Also like a variable, VBA substitutes the specific value referred to by the constant's name into a statement at the point in the statement where VBA encounters the named constant. Unlike a variable, however, the value of a named constant never changes; like a literal constant, the only way to change the value associated with a named constant is to edit the procedure.

Use named constants to improve the readability and understandability of your procedures. For example, a procedure that performs geometric calculations is much easier to read and understand if you use a named constant, `Pi`, instead of the literal constant `3.14`.

You also use named constants to make it easier to update and maintain your procedures and programs. For instance, if you have a VBA program that computes a tax liability for your company, it's possible that the tax rate might change sometime in the future. If you put the tax rate in your program as a literal constant, you may have difficulty updating your program to use the new tax rate—you'll have to search through the entire program and change every occurrence of the tax rate value. If, instead, you use a named constant for the tax rate, then you only have to change the value for the tax rate in one location—the statement that declares the named constant—to update your program to use the new tax rate.

In general, you should use named constants instead of literal constants for values that you use repeatedly in a procedure or module, or for values that are difficult to remember or whose meaning is not immediately clear.

Creating Named Constants

To choose the name for a constant, observe the same rules and guidelines that you follow to choose a variable name. (Refer to the section "Creating Variables" earlier in this lesson for an explanation of the rules for choosing identifier names.)

Like a variable, you must declare a named constant before you can use it. Unlike a variable, however, you must always declare named constants explicitly by using the `Const` keyword. The next line shows the general syntax to declare a named constant:

SAMS
PUBLISHING

Sams Learning Center

3

Syntax

```
Const name = value
```

name represents any valid identifier, and *value* represents any data value: numeric, string, or date. The next few lines show several named constant declarations:

```
Const BoilingPoint = 212
Const SalesTax = 8.25
Const Greeting = "Hello"
```

Each constant declaration begins with the Const keyword, is followed by the constant's name, an equals sign (=), and the value assigned to the constant.

If you wish, you can declare several constants with the same Const statement by separating each constant declaration and value assignment with a comma (,). The following line has the same effect as the three separate lines shown previously:

```
Const BoilingPoint = 212, SalesTax = 8.25, Greeting = "Hello"
```

You can specify a literal value for a named constant, include previously defined constants, or use any of VBA's mathematical or comparison operations as part of the constant declaration—with the following restrictions: you cannot concatenate strings, use variables, or use the Is operator in a constant declaration. (String concatenation, mathematical and logical operators, and the Is operator are described in the next lesson.)

The following constant declarations, for example, show both the use of a previously defined constant, and the use of a mathematical operator in the constant declaration:

```
Const BoilingPoint = 212
Const DangerZone = BoilingPoint + 50
```

Constant Scope

Like variables, you can declare named constants inside your procedures, or in the definition and declaration area at the beginning of a module. A constant declared inside a procedure has procedure-level scope and a constant declared in the definition and declaration area at the beginning of a module has module-level scope. Named constants follow the same scope rules as do variables, in all respects.

Because one of the major purposes for using a named constant is to avoid repeating or duplicating literal constant values throughout your procedures, you'll usually want to have your named constants available to all procedures in a module. Therefore, you should usually place constant declarations at the module-level, so they have the greatest scope.

Whenever VBA encounters a named constant in a statement, it inserts the value associated with the constant into the statement. Examine Listing 3.7, following, which shows an entire module. This macro procedure calculates the area of a circle and stores the value in a variable.

Type

Listing 3.7. Using constants: Computing the area of a circle.

```
1:  Const Pi = 3.14
2:  Dim CircleArea As Single
3:
4:  Sub Calc_CircleArea()
5:      Dim Radius As Single
6:      Radius = 5
7:      CircleArea = Pi * (Radius * Radius)
8:      MsgBox CircleArea, ,"Area of a Circle"
9:  End Sub
```

Analysis

Line 1 in Listing 3.7 declares a module-level constant, `Pi`, which represents an approximation of the number π. Line 7 of the listing contains a statement that computes the area of a circle; when VBA executes this statement, it inserts the value *3.14* at the location occupied by the constant name, `Pi`. When VBA executes the `Calc_CircleArea` procedure, the `MsgBox` statement in line 8 displays the number *78.5*. Notice that the `CircleArea` variable is declared at the module level, so that the value computed in the `Calc_CircleArea` procedure is available to other macros in the same module.

Writing Literal Constants

Even if you never use a literal constant in your macros and procedures—an unlikely event—you must still write literal constants when you declare named constants. There are a few rules you must observe when you write literal constants; the following paragraphs describe the rules for writing String constants, numeric constants, Date constants, and Boolean constants.

String Constants

To write literal string constants in your macro programs, follow these rules:

☐ String constants must be enclosed in double quotation marks (`"`). The following example is not legal, because it doesn't have quotation marks:

```
This is not a valid string constant.
```

☐ A blank string constant (called a *null string*, or an *empty string*) is indicated by two quotation marks together, with nothing between them: `""`.

☐ A string constant must be all on the same line. You cannot use the line-continuation symbol to continue a literal string constant to another line. Neither of the following examples are valid, because they split the string constant over more than one line:

```
"This is not a
valid string constant"
"Neither is this a _
valid string constant"
```

If you included any of the examples from the above list in a procedure, VBA would display a runtime error, and stop executing the procedure. The following example is a valid string constant:

```
"This string constant is valid."
```

Numeric Constants

These rules apply to literal numeric constants; a numeric constant may contain any of VBA's numeric types.

☐ Numeric constants must consist only of the number characters 0 through 9.

☐ A numeric constant may optionally begin with a minus sign (–) and may contain a decimal point.

☐ You may use scientific notation for numeric constants.

No other symbols or characters are allowed in a numeric constant. The following examples are valid numeric constants:

```
12
-14.3
6.6E2
```

☐ Do not use dollar signs or whole-number separators in numeric constants. The following are not valid numeric constants:

```
$656        'not valid: contains a dollar sign
6,560       'not valid: contains a whole-number separator
```

Date Constants

VBA recognizes date constants in any one of several different formats; you must enclose all date constants, however, in pound signs (#). The following lines show some of the date constant formats that VBA can recognize:

```
#2-5-58 21:17#
#February 5, 1958 9:17pm#
#Mar-31-94#
#15 April 1994#
```

No matter which of the above formats you write the literal data constant in, VBA reformats the date constant (when you move the insertion point away from the line after writing the constant) to conform to one of the following two formats, depending on whether or not the date constant also contains time information:

```
#2/5/58 9:17:00 PM#
#2/5/58#
```

If you omit the pound signs (#) when you write a literal date constant, VBA cannot correctly interpret the date constant as a date. Instead, VBA tries to evaluate the date information as variable names, numeric constants, and mathematical operators. For example, VBA attempts to interpret the following date—which is missing the pound signs—as a mathematical expression involving division:

`3/15/94`

Don't enclose literal date constants in quotation marks, either, or VBA will interpret the date as a string constant, instead of a date constant. For example, VBA interprets the following line as a string constant, not a date:

`"3/15/94"`

Boolean Constants

There are only two valid Boolean constants: `True` and `False`. Your VBA program statements must always use the keywords `True` and `False` to express the desired Boolean value as a constant. When you write the keywords in your macros, remember to spell the word out in full, and don't use quotation marks.

Specifying the Data Type of a Constant

When you declare a named constant, or write a literal constant, VBA considers the value represented by the constant to have the data type most consistent with the expression assigned to the constant. For example, VBA treats a constant containing a string as a string data type when determining whether the constant is appropriately combined with other data values.

Occasionally, you may want to specify the data type of a constant. Declaring a specific data type for a constant can improve the accuracy of a calculation—by declaring a constant with a Double data type, for example, VBA computes the result of mathematical operations involving that constant by using the greater range of the Double data type. You may also want to specify that a constant be an Integer, Long, Currency, or other type to ensure that the results of mathematical operations that use that constant have a particular type. (As explained in the next lesson, VBA determines the data type for the result of a computation based on the data type of the values in the computation.)

You may use Boolean, Integer, Long, Single, Double, Currency, Date, or String data types for constants (but not Object or Array types). Declaring a type for a constant is similar to declaring the type for a variable, except that the declaration begins with the keyword `Const`. The general syntax for declaring a constant is:

Syntax

```
Const name As type = value
```

In the above syntax sample, *name* is any valid constant name, *type* is the name of any one of VBA's data types, and *value* is the value you want to assign to the constant. The following line illustrates a valid constant declaration with a specific type:

```
Const Pi As Double = 3.14
```

This example declares the constant **Pi** as a Double data type. You can also use type definition characters to specify the data type of a constant, as shown in the following example (which has the same effect as the line above):

```
Const Pi# = 3.14
```

Understanding Predefined Constants

VBA provides several *predefined constants*. A predefined constant is a named constant that has already been defined for you. In addition to the constants that VBA predefines, Excel also predefines several constants for use with Excel workbooks, charts, and so on.

Note: Other VBA host applications also include predefined constants that pertain to that particular host application. Access 7, for example, provides predefined constants that relate to various database activities and properties.

Constants predefined by VBA all begin with the letters *vb* to indicate that they are defined by Visual Basic for Applications. As an example, the constants vbOKOnly, vbOKCancel, and vbAbortRetryIgnore are all defined by VBA. Predefined constants make it easier to use some of VBA's built-in procedures, like the MsgBox statement you've already seen, and the InputBox statement you'll learn about later in this lesson.

Although none of the MsgBox examples have used it so far, you may recall from earlier discussions that MsgBox has an optional argument which specifies the number of buttons in the dialog box; typically, you use VBA's predefined constants for the buttons argument in MsgBox. (Day 6 describes how to use the buttons argument for MsgBox.) Excel 7 constants all begin with the letters *xl*, so that you know they are defined by Excel. Some of the Excel constants include xlChart, xlCountrySetting, and xlWorksheet.

Note: Use constants defined by VBA, Excel, or another VBA host application the same way you use constants that you declare yourself. Specific predefined constants are described throughout this book in the chapters that cover the topics that those predefined constants relate to.

Using the Object Browser to Find Available Predefined Constants

To see a complete list of predefined constants available, whether defined by VBA or Excel, use the Object Browser, following these steps:

1. Display any module sheet in the active window.

2. Choose the **View | O**bject Browser command. VBA displays the Object Browser dialog box. Figure 3.2 shows the Object Browser dialog box with the list of VBA constants displayed.

 You can also open the Object Browser dialog box by clicking the Object Browser button on the Visual Basic toolbar.

Once you've opened the Object Browser dialog box, follow these additional steps to view the VBA predefined constants:

1. Select **VBA** in the **L**ibraries/Workbooks drop-down list of the Object Browser dialog box.

2. Select **Constants** in the **O**bjects/Modules list.

3. To get more information about a particular predefined constant, select the constant in the **M**ethods/Properties list.

   Once you select a constant in the **M**ethods/Properties list, the selected constant name appears at the bottom of the Object Browser dialog box, along with a brief description of the constant's purpose (see Figure 3.2).

Figure 3.2.

Use the Object Browser to view lists of constants defined by VBA, Excel, or another VBA host application.

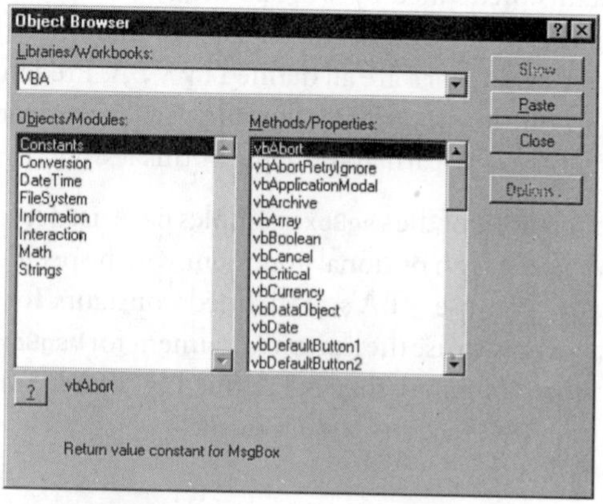

> **Note:** The VBA predefined constants are the same in all VBA host applications. Predefined constants for a specific application, such as Excel, are only available when you're working with VBA in that application. For example, you won't find the Excel xlWorksheet constant listed in the Object Browser in Access 7—the xlWorksheet constant is only available when you're using VBA in Excel.

If there is online help available for the item selected in the **M**ethods/Properties list, the button with a question mark on it (at the bottom of the Object Browser dialog box, underneath the **Ob**jects/Modules list) is enabled, as shown in Figure 3.2. Click this button to access the help topic for the selected item. Not all objects in the Object Browser have additional help available.

To view a list of constants predefined by Excel, follow the same procedure just described, but choose **Excel** in the Libraries/Workbooks drop-down list, instead of **VBA**.

Getting Data from Your Procedure's User

In Day 2, you learned how to make your procedures display messages by using VBA's MsgBox statement; several examples in this chapter have also used MsgBox. Earlier in this lesson, you learned how to create variables and constants. Now you're ready to learn how to use these elements together to get information from your procedure's user.

Obtaining data, storing it in a variable, and displaying the results of actions performed on or as a result of the user's entered data are the essential elements required to write interactive procedures. (An *interactive* procedure is one that exchanges information with its user; that is, the procedure interacts with its user by displaying messages and receiving input.) Interactive procedures are often more useful than macros created exclusively by recording. By getting information from the user, an interactive procedure can perform the same operations using different data.

Data entered by a user is called *input*. To get input from your procedure's user, use the InputBox function. (A *function* is a special type of VBA procedure that returns a value.) The InputBox function displays a dialog box which contains text that prompts the user to input some value, and a text box to enter the value in. The dialog box that InputBox displays also contains OK and Cancel command buttons.

When you use InputBox, you supply the string used to prompt the user for input. Optionally, you may also supply a string argument that InputBox uses as the title of the dialog box it displays.

The syntax for the InputBox function is:

```
stringvar = InputBox (Prompt [, Title])
```

stringvar represents any variable that can store a string (either a String type variable, or a Variant type). The *Prompt* argument represents any string value (literal, constant, or variable). InputBox displays this string as the prompt in the dialog box; you must always supply the *Prompt* argument—it is a *required argument*.

The *Title* argument is an optional second argument for InputBox. (All optional elements in the syntax lines are enclosed in square brackets.) *Title* also represents any string value, literal, constant, or variable. InputBox displays the text in this string in the title bar of the dialog box. If you omit the *Title* argument, VBA displays the word Input in the title bar of the InputBox dialog.

Listing 3.8 shows an entire module containing a single procedure, a module-level constant declaration, and a module-level variable declaration. This procedure, like the one in Listing 3.7, computes the area of a circle. Unlike the procedure in Listing 3.7—which always computes the area of a circle with a radius of 5 units—this procedure gets the radius of the circle from the procedure's user.

Type

Listing 3.8. Getting input with the InputBox statement.

```
1:  Const Pi As Single = 3.14      'an approximation of the value pi.
2:  Dim CircleArea As Single        'stores the computed area of a circle
3:
4:  Sub Calc_CircleArea()
5:      Const BoxTitle = "Area of a Circle"
6:      Dim Radius As Single, Temp As String
7:      Temp = InputBox("Enter circle radius", BoxTitle)
8:      Radius = CSng(Temp)
9:      CircleArea = Pi * (Radius * Radius)
10:     MsgBox CircleArea, , BoxTitle
11: End Sub
```

Analysis

Line 1 of Listing 3.8 declares the module-level constant **Pi**. Line 2 declares the module-level variable **CircleArea**. These items are declared at the module level so that they are available throughout the module—other procedures in the same module may need access to the value for π, and another procedure may need to use the value for the circle's area once it has been calculated.

Line 4 contains the actual procedure declaration; as before, this procedure is named **Calc_CircleArea**. Line 5 declares a procedure-level constant, **BoxTitle**; this constant is only available locally, within the **Calc_CircleArea** procedure. **BoxTitle** was declared locally in this procedure because it is unlikely this constant will be used in any other procedure; its purpose—

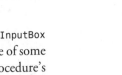

to supply fixed text for the title bars of all dialog boxes displayed by `Calc_CircleArea`—is rather specific to `Calc_CircleArea`. Line 6 declares all of the variables used locally in this procedure (`Radius` and `Temp`) and also specifies the data types for those variables.

Pay close attention to line 7 of Listing 3.8. This statement calls the InputBox function. InputBox displays its first argument as text in the dialog box, prompting the user to enter a value of some kind. In this statement, InputBox displays the text Enter circle radius to let the procedure's users know what value they are expected to enter. InputBox displays the second argument as the title of the dialog box. Here, the string value represented by the constant `BoxTitle` is used for the InputBox dialog box title.

DO   **DON'T**

DO try to make the prompt text for the InputBox function as clear and descriptive as possible regarding the type of value you expect your procedure's user to type in.

When the InputBox statement in line 7 executes, it displays the dialog box shown in Figure 3.3. The user types a number into the text box and chooses either the OK or Cancel command buttons to close the dialog box, as with any other Windows dialog box.

Figure 3.3.
This is the input dialog box displayed by the InputBox *function in line 7 of Listing 3.8.*

Whenever you call a function, you must somehow use the value returned by the function. (The value returned by a function is called the *function result*.) Frequently, you use a function result by assigning it to a variable, as shown in line 7 with the InputBox function, which has its result assigned to the `Temp` variable.

The function result of InputBox is always a string (this is why the `Temp` variable was declared as a String). Refer again to Figure 3.3. If the user chooses the OK command button, then InputBox returns whatever the user typed into the text box as the function result. If the user chooses the Cancel command button (or presses Esc or uses the Close button in the dialog box), then InputBox returns an empty string as the function result.

Because the `Temp` variable was explicitly declared as a String type, the string value must be converted to a numeric value before you can use it in mathematical computations. Line 8 of Listing 3.8 does exactly that, using VBA's built-in CSng function to convert the user's input to a Single type number. CSng is one of several data conversion functions described in more detail in Day 5.

Finally, line 9 computes the area of the circle, and assigns the result to `CircleArea`. Line 10 uses `MsgBox` to display the computed area. Notice that the `MsgBox` statement in line 10 uses the same `BoxTitle` constant to specify the title for the `MsgBox` dialog box as was used in line 7 for `InputBox`.

This is an ideal use for a constant—using a constant for the title bar ensures that all of the title bars in this particular procedure are the same, and avoids having to type the entire title more than once. Incidentally, the amount of computer memory that VBA would have needed to store the literal constants for duplicate title bar strings is also saved.

Summary

Today you learned about the different types of data that VBA can manipulate and store. You learned that a variable is a named memory storage location used to temporarily store information that a procedure is working with. You also learned how to name and declare variables, and how to specify a variable's data type. This chapter explained the scope rules that determine a variable's availability, and how long VBA retains the values stored in a variable. You learned about literal constants and the rules governing writing literal constants of different types. You also learned what a named constant is, how to declare named constants, and how to specify a constant's type. Finally, you learned how to use VBA's `InputBox` function to obtain input from a macro's user.

Q&A

Q Do I have to declare the data types of variables or named constants?

A No, you don't have to specify a data type when you declare a variable or a constant. If you don't specify a data type when you declare a variable, then VBA creates a Variant type variable. If you don't specify a data type when you declare a constant, then VBA chooses the most compatible data type for the value represented by the constant. It is often a good idea to declare the type of both variables and constants, however. If for no other reason, declaring the data type of a variable helps you think through exactly what you expect to use the variable for.

Q How do I know which data type to use when I declare a variable?

A Choose the data type for a variable based on the kinds of information you want to store in that variable. If the variable will store text information, use the String data type; if the variable will hold numbers representing dollar or other money values, use the Currency type, and so on. If you know that numeric values stored in a particular variable will not exceed certain ranges, choose the smallest numeric data type that has a range equivalent to, or only slightly greater than, the range of values you expect to store in the variable in order to conserve computer memory.

This last suggestion also helps you detect possible errors in your program. If you declare a variable as an Integer data type because you do not expect it to store values outside the Integer range, and then later get number overflow errors when your procedure runs, the error messages may indicate a bug in the procedure. (*Overflow* occurs when a number is too large to be stored in the data type used for it.)

Q When and where should I declare variables?

A You should develop the habit of declaring all of your variables all of the time; use the `Option Explicit` command to require variable declaration, as described earlier in this chapter. (All of the examples in this book, from this point on, use only explicitly declared variables.) Declaring all variables explicitly is good programming technique. By declaring your variables ahead of time, you not only get the benefits described earlier in the chapter, but you force yourself into doing a little planning ahead, as well—which can save you a great deal of time and frustration later on.

Declare variables at the beginning of the procedure or module that you want to use that variable in. Unless you specifically want a variable to be available throughout a module, you should declare all of your variables locally within a procedure instead of at module-level.

Q If the function result from `InputBox` is always a String data type, does that mean I can't get other data types from my macro's user?

A Yes, and no. It is true that the function result of `InputBox` is always a string. However, VBA provides a variety of ways to translate data from one data type to another, such as the `CSng` function used in Listing 3.8. Usually, you can convert the strings returned by `InputBox` into any other data type except Object and Array—depending on the specific contents of the returned string. By converting the returned strings, you can use `InputBox` to obtain dates, currency values, and integer or floating-point numeric values.

Workshop

The Workshop section presents Quiz questions to help you cement your new knowledge, and Exercises to give you experience using what you have learned. Answers are in Appendix A.

Quiz

1. How many numeric data types are there in VBA?
2. What is the difference between the Integer and Single data types? Integer and Long?
3. What is a type definition character?
4. What does it mean to declare a variable implicitly? What about explicitly?
5. What rules does VBA impose on identifier names? What other guidelines should you follow when choosing an identifier name?

6. What are the advantages of explicitly declaring a variable?

7. What are the advantages of specifying the type of a variable, whether it is declared explicitly or implicitly?

8. Why should you use named constants in your macro programs?

9. What is the purpose of the `InputBox` function?

10. Which of the `InputBox` arguments described in this lesson is required?

11. What data type is always returned by the `InputBox` function?

Exercises

1. Based on the stated use for a data item, decide whether the item is a variable or a constant, and then choose names and write typed declarations for each of the following (where possible, write the typed declaration both with and without using type definition characters):

   ```
   (a) a computed count of columns in a worksheet
   (b) the computed total sales, in dollars, of the East
       Coast division of a company
   (c) the projected number of respondents from a
       marketing survey
   (d) the computed surface area of a cylinder
   (e) the multiplier to convert inches to centimeters
   (f) the computed profit, expressed as a percentage,
       for the first quarter of the year
   (g) the self-employment tax rate
   ```

2. From scratch, write a procedure named **EchoThis** that uses `InputBox` to get a sentence (or a word) from the user, and then display the user's input with `MsgBox`.

3. In the Personal macro workbook, record a macro named **OpenSheet3** that performs the following actions: open any existing workbook file, and then select a worksheet named *Sheet3* (use a different sheet name, if necessary). Stop the recorder. Now edit the macro (you may need to unhide the PERSONAL.XLS workbook, first) so that it uses `InputBox` to ask the user for a filename, and then opens the workbook file whose name the user typed in. (HINTS: First examine the recorded macro statements to determine which statement opens the file. Insert your `InputBox` statement ahead of the file-opening statement. Assign the result from `InputBox` to a variable, and then substitute that variable for the literal constant filename that was recorded in the macro.)

   Run the edited macro to test it. Be sure you enter a valid filename when you test your macro.

4. Modify the **NewFile** macro you recorded in Exercise 1 of Day 1 so that it uses `InputBox` to get the filename for the new file that the macro creates and saves from the user.

Operators and Expressions

By now, you know how to record and edit macros, how to write simple macros of your own, and how to create and use constants and variables. Now you are ready to learn how to combine variables and constants together to create new values. In this lesson, you learn:

☐ What an expression is and how to construct expressions.

☐ What the various arithmetic, comparison, string, and logical operators are, how they work, and how to use them in expressions.

☐ About data type compatibility in expressions and how VBA can sometimes automatically convert data into compatible types.

☐ How VBA determines the data type of an expression and how to override VBA's type determination.

☐ How VBA determines the order of operations performed in complex expressions and how to alter the evaluation order.

As you read this particular lesson, don't try to memorize all the facts in this chapter. If you can answer all the quiz questions and perform the exercises at the end of today's lesson, you'll have mastered the most important aspects of the information presented here. As you continue with later lessons in this book, and with your VBA programming in general, refer back to this chapter to brush up on specific details.

Understanding Operators and Expressions

An *expression* is a value or group of values that expresses a single quantity. Every expression *evaluates to* (results in) a single quantity or value. The expression 2+2, for example, evaluates to 4. Expressions are made up of any one or more of the following building blocks:

Constants (literal or named)
Variables (of any data type)
Operators
Arrays
Array elements
Functions

All expressions result in a single value that has one of the data types you learned about in Day 3. Expressions also may evaluate to one of the special values, Empty or Null. VBA provides the keywords Empty and Null to indicate special conditions in a variable or expression. The Empty value represents an uninitialized Variant type variable, or the result of an expression that contains an uninitialized Variant type variable. The Null value represents an expression that contains invalid data. Day 10 describes the Empty and Null keywords and the values they represent in more detail.

Some examples of expressions include the following:

Expression	Description
5	Contains one value and evaluates to the number 5.
"5"	Contains one value and evaluates to the character 5.
"To" & "day"	Contains two string values and one operator; evaluates to the single string *Today*.
c * (p/100)	Results in a number obtained by multiplying the contents of variable **c** by the value obtained after dividing the contents of variable **p** by the constant 100.
CStr(1200)	Uses a VBA function and evaluates to the function result—in this case, a single string value of 1200 (CStr converts numbers to equivalent strings).
MyValue <= 7	Evaluates to a logical value; in this case indicating whether the contents of variable **MyValue** are less than or equal to the constant number value 7.

In the preceding examples, notice that the number 5 is not the same as the alphanumeric character "5"; the first is a numeric data type (specifically, an Integer) while the second is a String data type (even though it contains only one character).

You use *operators* to combine, compare, or otherwise manipulate specific values within an expression. Operators get their name because they are the symbols that indicate specific mathematical or other operations to be carried out on various values in an expression. When you use an operator in an expression, the data items—whether variables or constants—that the operator acts on are called the *operands*; most operators require two operands. In the expression 2 + 1, for example, the numbers 2 and 1 are the operands of the addition operator (+). An expression may contain none, one, or several operators.

You use expressions to perform calculations and compare values, and to supply values as arguments for VBA's various functions and procedures. All expressions evaluate to a single value with a specific data type. In VBA, an expression is sort of like a sentence in English. All of your VBA statements contain one or more expressions—every example you've seen in this book so far contains at least one expression.

All Visual Basic expressions evaluate to a value that has one of Visual Basic's data types. The following list summarizes the different types of VBA expressions:

- [ ] A *date expression* is any expression that evaluates to a Date type value. Date expressions may include date constants, variables that contain dates or numbers, numeric constants, dates returned by functions, and arithmetic operators.

☐ A *numeric expression* is any expression that evaluates to a number of any type—Integer, Long, Single, Double, or Currency. Numeric expressions may include variables that contain numbers, numeric constants, functions that return numbers, and arithmetic operators. Numeric expressions may also include string expressions that VBA can convert to a number. (If all the characters in a string are digits, then VBA can convert the string to a numeric value; for example, VBA can convert the string "36" to the number 36.)

☐ A *string expression* is any expression that evaluates to a String type value. String expressions may include variables that contain strings, string constants, functions that return strings, or string concatenation operators. String expressions may also include numeric expressions that VBA can convert to a string.

☐ A *logical expression* is any expression that evaluates to a Boolean type value: True or False. Logical expressions can consist of variables that contain Boolean values, Boolean constants, functions that return Boolean values, comparison operators, or logical operators.

☐ An *object expression* is any expression that evaluates to a reference to a specific object. Objects and object expressions are described in Day 7.

Data Type Compatibility

Not all data types are compatible with each other; you cannot combine incompatible data types in the same expression. For example, it makes no sense to arithmetically add the string "fruit fly" to the number 12—the expression is not meaningful, and VBA cannot evaluate it.

Many data types are compatible with each other, however. For example, you can combine different numeric data types in the same expression—VBA automatically handles the necessary data type conversions among the different numeric types. VBA can also sometimes automatically convert other data types so that all the types in an expression are compatible, although it cannot always do so. String and Date types, for example, are compatible with numeric types only under specific conditions, described later in this chapter.

Keeping track of, and knowing, the data type of an expression is fairly important because expressions that contain incompatible data types cause VBA to produce a *type mismatch* runtime error when your procedure executes. When VBA encounters an expression containing different data types, it first tries to resolve any data type difference by converting values in the expression into compatible data types. If VBA cannot successfully resolve the type differences by converting data types, then VBA displays the type mismatch runtime error, and your procedure stops executing.

If you assign the result of an expression to a variable, and the variable type is incompatible with the type of the expression result, VBA also displays a type mismatch error. Similarly, using the result of an expression as an argument for a function or procedure also results in a type mismatch error if the argument data type and the expression result have incompatible data types.

The following expression, for example, is not valid because it attempts to combine a string with a number:

```
"128" + 256
```

If your procedure contains an expression like this, VBA generates a type mismatch runtime error, and your procedure stops executing.

Either of the following modifications to the previous expression are valid, although the two expressions produce very different results:

```
"128" + "256"    'Evaluates to the string "128256"
128 + 256        'Evaluates to the number 384
```

VBA provides a variety of functions for converting information of one data type to another, such as strings to numbers, numbers into strings, and so on (in the preceding lesson, you saw the CSng function used to convert a string to a Single numeric type). VBA's data conversion functions are described in more detail in Day 5.

Visual Basic's Automatic Data Conversions

VBA uses various different rules to automatically convert data into compatible types. VBA chooses the data conversion rules applied to a particular expression based on the specific data types and operators used in an expression.

VBA can perform automatic data type conversions most readily when an expression contains Variant type variables because the data type of a Variant is not fixed. When an expression contains literal constants, typed variables, or typed constants, VBA applies stricter data type conversion rules because the data type of these items is fixed. (Remember, a *typed variable* or a *typed constant* is one for which you have explicitly declared the data type with either the As keyword or a type definition character, as described in the preceding lesson.)

Whenever an expression contains elements whose data types are fixed, VBA tries to convert the other data types in the expression to be compatible with the fixed data type; the data type of the expression result will also have the data type of the fixed data types in the expression.

The following expressions help illustrate how the data types and operator affect the data type conversions that VBA makes, and how VBA determines the expression result type:

Expression	Description and Result Type
Num + Str	Produces type mismatch when Num is a declared numeric type and Str is a declared String type.
	Performs string concatenation when Num is a Variant and Str is a declared String type; result is a String type.
	Performs arithmetic addition when Num is a declared numeric type and Str is a Variant, or when both Num and Str are Variant type; result is a numeric type.
Num + "3"	Produces type mismatch when Num is a declared numeric type.
	Performs string concatenation when Num is a Variant type; result is a String type.
	(Notice that this expression never results in arithmetic addition.)
3 + Str	Produces type mismatch when Str is a declared String type.
	Performs arithmetic addition when Str is a Variant type; result is a numeric type.
	(Notice that this expression never results in string concatenation.)
Num & Str	Always performs string concatenation, regardless of the variable types; result is a String type.
	This expression never produces a type mismatch error.

Pay special attention to the last item in the preceding list. This expression uses the string concatenation operator (&), which joins two strings together. Because you can use this operator *only* with strings, VBA converts the data types in the expression to strings, regardless of their original data type, and whether or not any variables in the expression have specific types. (String concatenation is described in more detail later in this chapter.) As each operator is described in the later sections of this chapter, any special data conversion rules that VBA applies for that specific operator are also described.

You may notice that most of the expressions in the above list produce a type mismatch error only when both of the operands in the expression have specific and different types. You may also notice that the expressions do not produce type mismatch errors when one of the operands is a Variant type variable. As mentioned before, VBA can most readily perform automatic data type conversions on Variant data types. Do not, however, use Variant data types merely to avoid type mismatch errors.

> ### Taking Advantage of Type Mismatch Errors
>
> Type mismatch errors aren't necessarily a tragedy; in fact, type mismatch errors can be of great use to you. In Day 3, you were told that one of the reasons for declaring the specific data type of a variable is to help locate certain kinds of programmer errors. Mixing data types in a single expression may not always be what you intended, especially since mixing data types in a single expression may not always produce a desirable result.
>
> Suppose, in the expression 3 + Str, you intended to concatenate the character 3 with a string stored in the variable Str, but accidentally omitted the quotation marks around the digit character 3. Instead of a string constant, you have mistakenly included a numeric constant in the expression. This expression never performs string concatenation, which is what you actually desired. If the Str variable is specifically declared as having the String type, however, VBA generates a type mismatch error when it evaluates this expression, revealing your mistake so that you can correct it.

Numeric Type Conversions

VBA usually converts all numeric data types to the greatest precision type in the expression, and then gives the expression's result that type. For example, if an expression contains numeric values with Integer and Single types, the expression result is Single—the greatest precision type in the expression.

Note: *Precision* refers to the number of significant digits that a numeric data type can store.

If you assign the result of a numeric expression to a variable that has a lower precision than the expression's actual result type, VBA rounds the expression result until its precision matches the expected type. For example, if you assign a numeric expression that results in a Double type number to an Integer type variable, VBA rounds the double-precision number until it is an Integer. The following statement illustrates this:

```
Num% = 1 + 1.51    'Stores the integer 3 in Num%
```

In the preceding line, the actual expression result is a Double type number: 2.51. VBA rounds this number to 3 so that it is compatible with the Integer data type of the variable that stores the expression result. (% is the type definition character for an Integer, remember.)

String and Number Conversions

If VBA converts a number to a string, VBA creates a string containing all of the digits of the number, and the decimal (if the number has one). The number 412.72, for example, converts to the string "412.72". If the number is very large or very small, VBA may create a string representation of the number in scientific notation—the number 0.0000000003937, for example, converts to the string "3.937E-11".

VBA can convert a string to a number only if the string contains the character representation of a number in either decimal format or scientific notation. The strings "98.6", "12", "-16.7", "1.2E10" all represent numbers, and VBA can convert them to numbers. The strings "1,024", "$74.50", and "Fred and Ethel" cannot be converted to numbers because they contain non-numeric characters.

Boolean Conversions

When VBA converts Boolean type values to numbers, the value True converts to -1, and the value False converts to 0. When VBA converts a number to a Boolean type, zero converts to False and any other value converts to True. When VBA converts Boolean type values to strings, VBA uses the string "True" for True and "False" for False. VBA cannot convert string expressions to a Boolean type; VBA can only convert numeric expressions into Boolean values. When you use Boolean type values in arithmetic expressions, VBA always converts them to numbers, even if all other parts of the expression are also Boolean variables or constants.

Date Conversions

When VBA converts a Date data type to a number, the resulting numeric value is a Double type number that contains the number of days from December 30, 1899—a negative number represents a date earlier than 12/30/1899. The number's decimal portion (if any) expresses the time of day as a fraction of a day; 0 is midnight, and 0.5 is noon. VBA's conversion of numeric data types into Date data types is simply the inverse of the Date to number conversion just described.

Note: If an expression results in a value outside the range of the data type for that expression, VBA displays a numeric overflow or underflow error message at runtime, and your procedure stops executing. (*Overflow* occurs when a number is too large for its data type; *underflow* occurs when a number is too small.)

If the expression contains a literal constant, you can occasionally solve this problem by using a type definition character with the literal constant to force the expression

to evaluate to a numeric type with a greater range. For example, in an expression like the following (where the variable `Num` is declared as an Integer data type) VBA treats the expression result as an Integer data type because all the operands in the expression have the Integer type:

```
Num * 2      'this expression result is of Integer type
```

If `Num` contains a value large enough that multiplying it by two produces a number greater than 32,767, VBA displays an overflow runtime error message and stops executing your procedure. The next expression, however, uses a type definition character to alter the data type of the constant operand in the expression:

```
Num * 2&      'this expression result is of the Long type
```

Because VBA always assigns a data type to the expression result that is the same as the data type in the expression with the greatest range, this second expression has a result that is of the Long data type.

The Assignment Operator (=)

The preceding lesson briefly acquainted you with the assignment operator (=). You use the assignment operator to assign an expression result to a variable, or to assign the value stored in one variable to another variable. The assignment operator stores whatever value is represented by an expression or variable on the right side of the assignment operator (=) in the memory location referred to by the variable on the left side of the operator.

Note: The assignment operator (=) does *not* fulfill the same function you may be accustomed to from working with algebraic equations. In algebra, the equal sign (=) indicates quantities that are equal to each other, and you solve an equation to find the numbers that will make the equality statement true—the action represented by the equal sign (=) in an algebraic equation is actually a test for equality (described later in this lesson), not an assignment operation. The assignment operation always indicates that a value is to be stored in a specified memory location, indicated by the variable at the left side of the assignment operator.

The assignment operation has two different syntax forms, both of which are equally acceptable and accomplish the same purpose. The first form of the assignment operation uses the keyword `Let`, and has the following general syntax:

```
Let varname = expression
```

varname represents any VBA variable, and *expression* represents any VBA expression. This syntax is the original form of the assignment operation, used in the earliest versions of the BASIC programming language. The following VBA statement is an example of a `Let` assignment statement:

```
Let X = Y        'assigns value represented by Y to the variable X
```

The second form for assignment operations is much more common in VBA programming, and is the form used throughout this book. The general syntax of this more common form of the assignment statement is:

```
varname = expression
```

varname represents any variable, and *expression* represents any expression. The following statements are examples of this simpler, more common assignment statement (the first line assigns the contents of **Y** to **X**; the second line assigns to **MyVar** the result of adding 12 to the contents of **YourVar**):

```
X = Y
MyVar = 12 + YourVar
```

In both forms of the assignment statement, the variable on the left side of the assignment operator (=) receives and stores the value that results from evaluating the expression on the right side of the assignment operator. When VBA executes an assignment statement, it first evaluates the expression on the right side of the assignment operator (=), and then stores the expression result in the variable whose name appears at the left side of the assignment operator.

Always keep in mind that VBA evaluates the expression on the right side of the assignment operator *before* storing any data in the variable on the left side of the assignment operator (=). This is an important concept. In many procedures, you will find assignment statements similar to these:

```
Count = Count + 1
GrossTotal = GrossTotal + SubTotal
```

You might use assignment statements like these if you keep a running count of something, or if you compute a grand total by adding together several subtotal figures. It may not be immediately obvious to you what value ends up stored in the variable in a statement like this, or whether or not VBA can even execute these statements.

Statements like these work because VBA computes the expression result on the right side of the assignment operator (=) first, and then assigns the value to the variable on the left of the assignment operator. For example, assume that the variable **Count** contains the value 9 at the time VBA executes the following statement:

```
Count = Count + 1
```

First, VBA evaluates the expression on the right side of the assignment operator. To evaluate the expression, VBA retrieves the current value—9—stored in the **Count** variable, and then adds 1

to it, resulting in the number 10. Next, VBA assigns this new value to the **Count** variable, completing the assignment operation. When VBA has finished executing this assignment statement, **Count** contains the numeric value 10 (the previous contents of **Count**, if any, are replaced by this new value).

Rather than reading an assignment statement as *x equals y*, many programmers learn to read assignment statements as *x gets y* or *let x be equal to y*. These last two ways of reading assignment statements reflect the action of the assignment operation more clearly—if you develop the mental habit of reading assignment statements this way, you may find it easier to understand the program statements that you encounter in recorded macros, examples in this book, or other VBA source code that you may want to read and understand.

You will see and use the shorter form of the assignment operation much more commonly than the longer form, mostly because the short form involves less typing. The long form of the assignment operation, with the keyword Let, is often recommended for beginning programmers because it helps distinguish the assignment operation from the equality comparison operation—both of which use the same symbol to indicate the desired operation.

Although the two operations use the same symbol, do not confuse the assignment operator with the equal sign (=) used to test for equality. The following two statements are *not* the same. The first statement assigns the value 5 to the variable **MyVal**; the second statement is a logical expression that evaluates as either True or False, depending on whether **MyVal** already contains the number 5:

```
MyVal = 5        'assigns the number 5 to MyVal
(MyVal = 5)      'compares contents of MyVal to the number 5
```

Note that the second line preceding is not actually a complete VBA statement (although it is a complete expression) because the result of the logical expression is not used in any way—a line like this in one of your procedures would produce a syntax error. To make a syntactically valid VBA statement, the statement must use the expression result in some fashion: assign it to a variable, use it as a function or procedure argument, and so on.

When you assign an expression result to a variable with a specific data type, the expression result must have a data type compatible with the variable receiving the assignment. Often, VBA can convert the data type of an expression result to a type compatible with the variable receiving the assignment, if the expression result and variable do not already have compatible types. Variant type variables, by their nature, can receive assignments of any data type; the Variant takes on the data type of the expression result assigned to it.

Some additional points to remember about assignments are:

☐ You can assign any numeric variable or expression to any other numeric type variable, or to a Variant type variable. If you assign a numeric expression to a typed variable with a lower precision or range (such as assigning a Double to a Long type), then VBA rounds the value to match the precision of the variable receiving the assignment.

☐ If you assign a Variant variable containing a number to a String type variable, VBA automatically converts the number to a string. (Typed numeric variables or numeric constants assigned to a String type variable produce a type mismatch error.)

Arithmetic Operators

VBA can perform all the standard arithmetic operations: addition, subtraction, multiplication, and division; VBA also has a mathematical operator to raise numbers to a specified power, and provides additional special math operators for integer and modulo division. Table 4.1 summarizes VBA's arithmetic operators. (In the table, N is any valid VBA numeric expression.)

Table 4.1. Arithmetic operators.

Operator	Syntax	Name/Description
+	N1 + N2	Adds N1 to N2.
-	N1 - N2	Subtracts N2 from N1; also indicates unary minus.
*	N1 * N2	Multiplies N1 by N2.
/	N1 / N2	Divides N1 by N2.
\	N1 \ N2	Integer Division. Divides N1 by N2, discarding any fractional part so that the result is an integer.
Mod	N1 Mod N2	Modulo Division. Divides N1 by N2, returning only the remainder of the division operation.
^	N1 ^ N2	Exponentiation. Raises N1 to the N2 power.

The following sections describe each of these operators in detail.

Addition (+)

The addition operator (+) performs simple addition. Both operands must be numeric expressions or strings that VBA can convert to a number. You can also use the addition operator to perform arithmetic with Date data types. The following sample expressions illustrate the correct syntax for the addition operator:

```
MyVal + 1          'adds 1 to the contents of MyVal
MyVal + YourVal    'adds the contents of MyVal and YourVal
```

The data type of an addition expression's result usually is the same as the most precise data type in the expression. If an expression contains both Integer and Long data types, for example, then the result of that expression is a Long data type. There are some exceptions to this rule, however, particularly if the expression includes Variant type variables. The following list summarizes these exceptions:

- ☐ The data type result of adding a Single and a Long is a Double.

- ☐ If you add a Date data type to any other data type, the expression always results in a Date type.

- ☐ If you assign the result of an addition expression to a Variant variable that currently has an Integer type, and if the expression result is greater than (overflows) the range of values for the Integer type, then VBA converts the result to a Long. After assignment, the Variant variable also has the Long data type.

- ☐ If you assign the result of an addition expression to a Variant variable that currently has a Long, Single, or Date type, and if the expression result overflows the range of the numeric type, then VBA converts the result to a Double. After assignment, the Variant variable also has the Double data type.

- ☐ If either operand in the addition expression is Null or evaluates to Null, then the addition expression also results in Null. (Null is a special value that you can assign only to Variant type variables to indicate that they do not contain valid data. Null is described in more detail in Day 10.)

> **Note:** The order of precision for VBA's numeric data types, from least precise to most precise is: Integer, Long, Single, Double, Currency.

Some additional examples of valid addition expressions are:

```
Now + 1              'expression result is Date type
PcntProfit + 0.5     '
#1/1/94# + 60        'adds 60 days to the literal date 1/1/94
```

In the first example in the preceding code, Now is a VBA function that returns a Date value corresponding to the current date and time (according to your computer's clock).

Subtraction (-)

The subtraction operator (-) fulfills two different purposes. You use the subtraction operator either to subtract one number from another, or to indicate the unary minus.

A *unary minus* is the minus sign you place in front of a number to indicate that it is a negative number. In VBA, you can also place the minus sign in front of a variable or other expression to indicate that the value of the variable or expression should be negated. Placing the unary minus in front of a variable or expression is the same as multiplying that number by -1. The following expressions illustrate the unary minus:

```
-1               'a negative literal constant
-MyVal           'negates whatever number is stored in MyVal
-(MyVal +10)     'negates the result of adding 10 to MyVal
```

4

The last two expressions above show how you can use the unary minus to negate a numeric variable's value or the result of an expression. If **MyVal** contains the number 5, then the result of the second expression above is -5 and the result of the third expression is -15.

The next few sample expressions illustrate the subtraction operator used to perform subtraction:

```
Now - 60            'expression result is a Date type
40 - MyVal          'the difference between 40 and MyVal
AnyVal - SomeVal    'the difference between AnyVal and SomeVal
```

Both operands in a subtraction expression must be numeric variables or expressions, or a string expression that VBA can convert to a number. You can also use the subtraction operator to perform arithmetic with dates. The data type of a subtraction expression's result usually is the same as the most precise data type in the expression.

VBA follows the same rules for determining the data type of a subtraction expression's result as it does for expressions that use the addition operator, with the following additional rules:

☐ If one of the operands in the subtraction expression is a Date type, then the data type of the expression result is Date.

☐ If both operands in the subtraction expression are Date types, then the data type of the expression result is Double.

Note: Although you can concatenate (join) two strings together with the (+) operator, you cannot use the (-) operator to divide or split apart a string. Instead, you must use VBA's Mid, Left, or Right functions to split strings apart. These functions are described in the next lesson.

Multiplication (*)

The multiplication operator (*) multiplies two numbers together; the result of a multiplication expression is the product of the two operands. Both operands in a multiplication expression must be numeric expressions or strings that VBA can convert to a number. The following sample expressions illustrate the correct syntax for the multiplication operator:

```
4 * 10              'multiplies 4 by 10; result is 40
NumVal * 2          'result is product of NumVal and 2
NumVal * OtherVal   'result is product of NumVal and OtherVal
```

The data type of a multiplication expression's result usually is the same as the most precise data type in the expression. VBA follows the same rules for determining the data type of a multiplication expression's result as it does for expressions that use the addition operator. In multiplication expressions, all Variant variables that contain Date type values are converted to numeric values.

Division (/)

This division operator (/) is sometimes referred to as the *floating-point* or *real number* division operator to help distinguish it from the integer division operator described in the next section. The floating-point division operator performs standard arithmetic division on its operands. In division expressions, the first operand is divided by the second operand; the expression result is the quotient. Both operands in a floating-point division expression must be numeric expressions or strings that VBA can convert to a number. The following expressions illustrate the use of the division operator:

```
9 / 3          'Divides 9 by 3
NumVal / 17    'Divides the value in the NumVal variable by 17
Minutes / 60   'Divides the value in the Minutes variable by 60
```

If either operand in a floating-point division expression has the value Null, then the expression result is also Null. The data type result of a floating-point division operation is usually Double, with the following exception: If both of the operands in the division expression have the Integer or Single type, then the floating-point division expression result is Single, unless the expression result overflows (or underflows) the value range for a Single. If the result overflows the range for a Single, then VBA converts the result to a Double data type.

Integer Division (\)

Integer division is essentially the same as floating-point division, except that expressions that use the integer division operator (\) always result in a whole number, with no fractional part. Both operands in an integer division expression must be numeric expressions or strings that VBA can convert to a number. The following sample expressions illustrate the correct syntax for the integer division operator:

```
4 \ 2.5        'Divides 4 by 2.5; returns the value 1
6 \ NumVal     'Divides 6 by contents of NumVal
MyVal \ NumVal 'Divides MyVal by NumVal
```

In integer division, VBA rounds each operand (if necessary) to an Integer or Long number before performing the division operation. For example, in the integer division expression 19.5 \ 2, VBA rounds the value 19.5 to 20, before carrying out the division operation; the result of this expression is 10.

VBA discards any fractional remainder resulting from an integer division expression result. For example, the floating-point division expression 18 / 5 evaluates to 3.6, but the integer division expression 18 \ 5 evaluates to 3. Notice that VBA does not round the integer division quotient; it simply truncates the result so that it is a whole number.

The data type result of an integer division expression is either an Integer or a Long; VBA uses the smallest data type that will accommodate the expression result. If either operand in an integer division expression is Null, then the expression result is also Null.

Modulo Division (*Mod*)

Modulo division is the complement of integer division. In modulo division, the expression returns only the remainder of the division operation as an integer. Both operands in a modulo division expression must be numeric expressions or strings that VBA can convert to a number. The following sample expressions illustrate the modulo division operator:

```
4 Mod 2            'returns the value 0
5.4 Mod 3          'returns the value 2
6 Mod NumVal       'if NumVal contains 5, returns 1
MyVal Mod NumVal   'Divide MyVal by NumVal, return remainder
```

In modulo division, VBA rounds each operand (if necessary) to an Integer or Long number before performing the division operation, just like integer division. For example, in the second sample expression preceding, VBA rounds the number 5.4 to 5 before performing the division operation; 3 goes into 5 once, with 2 as a remainder—the expression therefore returns 2 as the expression result.

The data type result of a modulo division expression is either an Integer or a Long; VBA uses the smallest data type that accommodates the expression result. If either operand in a modulo division expression is Null, then the expression result is also Null.

Exponentiation (^)

The exponentiation operator (^) raises a number to a specified power. Exponentiation says how many times a number should be multiplied by itself—2^3 is the same as 2×2×2. To write 2^3 as a VBA statement, use the following expression:

```
2 ^ 3
```

Both operands in an exponentiation expression must be numeric expressions or strings that VBA can convert to a number. The operand to the left of the exponentiation operator may be a negative number only if the operand on the right side of the exponentiation operator is an integer. If either operand is Null, then the expression result is also Null; otherwise, the data type result of an exponentiation expression is a Double data type.

Comparison Operators

Comparison operators are also sometimes referred to as *relational* operators. Most often, you use comparison operations to establish the criterion for making a decision, or to formulate a description of the conditions under which a group of commands are to be repeated (looping). (Day 8 describes VBA's decision-making statements; Day 9 describes VBA's looping statements.)

The result of any comparison operation is a Boolean type value: True or False. You use comparison operators to compare literal, constant, or variable values of any similar type.

Table 4.2 lists all the comparison operators available in VBA, and describes their function (in the table, E represents any valid VBA expression).

Table 4.2. Comparison operators.

Operator	Syntax	Name/Description
=	E1 = E2	Equal to. True if E1 is equal to E2, false otherwise.
<	E1 < E2	Less than. True if E1 is less than E2, false otherwise.
<=	E1 <= E2	Less than or equal to. True if E1 is less than or equal to E2, false otherwise.
>	E1 > E2	Greater than. True if E1 is greater than E2, false otherwise.
>=	E1 >= E2	Greater than or equal to. True if E1 is greater than or equal to E2, false otherwise.
<>	E1 <> E2	Not equal to. True if E1 is not equal to E2, false otherwise.
Is	E1 Is E2	Is. Both operands must be Object type values. True if E1 refers to the same object as E2, false otherwise.
Like	E1 Like E2	Like. Both operands must be String type values. True if E1 matches the pattern contained in E2.

If both operands in a comparison expression have the same data type, then VBA performs a straightforward comparison for that data type. If both operands are strings, for example, VBA makes a string comparison; if both operands are Dates, then VBA makes a date comparison, and so on.

The following sample expressions illustrate the use of and syntax for various comparison operators:

```
MyVal = 2            'evaluates to True if MyVal contains 2
4 <> 5               'evaluates to True: 4 does not equal 5
NumVal < 17          'True if NumVal is less than 17
"Sam" < "Joe"    'False; "Joe" is alphabetically less than "Sam"
"Fred" < "Freddy"     'True; "Fred" is shorter than "Freddy"
Now > #5/30/1995#   'True if Now is greater than May 30, 1995
```

The first three sample expressions provide examples of numeric comparison, the next two examples are string comparisons, and the final sample expression is a date comparison.

Note: Remember that VBA date values can include time information. When you compare date values, VBA actually compares the date *and* time information. For this reason, even if the month, day, and year of two dates are the same, they may not be equal to each other if the time portion of the date value is different. For example, the date #1/1/94# is less than the date #1/1/94 9:00:00 AM#. In the first date, no time value is supplied and VBA assumes that the time is 00:00:00. Even though the year, month, and day is the same in the second date, it has a later time, and is therefore greater than the first date.

To compare only the year, month, and day part of a Date type value, you can use VBA's CInt or CLng functions to convert the serial date value to an Integer or Long number. Converting a serial date to a whole number isolates the year, month, and day information; you can then directly compare these numbers to compare the dates that they represent. (VBA's serial date numbers were described in Day 3; data type conversion functions are described in Day 5.)

In numeric comparison expressions, the specific type of a numeric value in the expression is not important. However, if you compare values with different data types—such as comparing an Integer to a String, or a Variant to some other type—you may receive type mismatch errors, or results other than those you expect.

If both operands in a comparison expression have definite types (either because they are constants or typed variables), and those types are not compatible, VBA displays a type mismatch error. The following expressions, for example, produce type mismatch errors because they attempt to compare incompatible data types:

```
1 > "zero"
NumVal% <= StrVal$
```

If one or both of the operands in a comparison expression is a Variant type variable, VBA will try to convert the Variant data to a compatible type, if necessary. If a data conversion is necessary, and VBA can't convert the Variant to a compatible type, it displays a runtime error message.

Because you cannot always easily tell whether or not VBA will perform a numeric comparison or a string comparison when you mix numeric and string values in a comparison expression, you should always use one of VBA's type conversion functions (like CStr) to explicitly convert values to numbers or strings, so that both operands in a comparison expression have the same data type. (Conversion functions are described in the next lesson.)

String Comparisons

Comparing strings is a little more complicated than comparing numbers. In VBA, a string is equal to another string only when both strings contain exactly the same characters in exactly the same order, and both strings are exactly the same length.

Examine the following expressions:

```
"abc" = "abc"      'True: both strings are the same
"abc" = "abc "     'False: the strings are not the same
```

In the first expression, the strings are equal to each other—both strings contain the same characters in the same order and are the same length. In the second expression, the strings are not equal to each other—the string on the right side of the operator has an additional space character at the end of the string. VBA does *not* ignore leading or trailing space characters when it compares strings.

When VBA compares strings with relational operators, it compares each string from left to right, character by character. In essence, VBA sorts the two strings alphabetically. VBA considers whichever string comes first in alphabetical order to be the "lesser" string. If two strings are different lengths, but otherwise identical, the shorter of the two strings is the "lesser" string. The next few sample expressions help illustrate how string comparisons work:

```
"abc" < "abc "     'True: the string on the left is shorter
"abcd" > "abc"     'True: the string on the left is longer
"aaa" < "aab"      'True: 1st string is less than the 2nd string
"aab" < "abb"      'True
"abb" < "abc"      'True
```

DO   DON'T

DO pay attention when you compare fixed- and variable-length strings. Remember that a fixed-length string always contains the same number of characters, and that a variable-length string increases or decreases in size, depending on the size of the string stored in it. Examine the following VBA code fragment:

```
Dim FixLen As String * 10, VarLen As String
FixLen = "test"
VarLen = "test"
MsgBox (FixLen = VarLen)      'displays False
```

Because **FixLen** is *always* 10 characters in length, it is longer than **VarLen**, which is only 4 characters long. VBA considers **FixLen** to be greater than **VarLen**. To avoid this type of problem with both fixed- and variable-length strings, use the Trim function to remove leading and trailing blanks from a string, as shown following (the Trim function is described more fully in the next chapter):

```
Dim FixLen As String * 10, VarLen As String
FixLen = "test"
VarLen = "test"
MsgBox (Trim(FixLen) = VarLen)      'displays True
```

Binary and Text String Comparison

So far, the string comparison expressions shown include only strings consisting of lowercase characters. VBA offers two different ways to deal with comparing characters of different cases. The first technique that VBA uses to compare strings is called a *binary* compare, and is the default comparison technique.

To understand how binary comparison works, you need to remember that all information in your computer must be stored as a number. To store text, your computer uses a scheme in which each character that your computer can display has a unique number. The letters *a* through *z* all have unique consecutive numbers, as do the letters *A* through *Z*. Typically, the uppercase letters *A* through *Z* have lower numbers than the lowercase letters *a* through *z*. The number corresponding to a particular letter or other character is called the *character code* for that character.

When VBA performs a binary comparison of string information, it uses the actual binary number equivalent for each character as it compares each pair of characters. Because the uppercase letters have lower binary numbers, uppercase letters alphabetize before lowercase letters. In other words, when VBA performs a binary string comparison, the string `"AAA"` is less than the string `"aaa"`.

The second type of comparison that VBA offers is called *text* comparison. In a text comparison, VBA does not use the binary number equivalent for each character; instead, VBA considers uppercase letters to be equivalent to lowercase letters. In a text comparison, the string `"AAA"` is equal to the string `"aaa"`. The next two sample expressions help illustrate the difference between binary and text string comparisons:

```
"Fred" = "fred"    'False in a binary comparison,
                   'True in a text comparison
"Fred" < "fred"    'True in a binary comparison,
                   'False in a text comparison
```

Choosing the String Comparison Technique

Syntax

To control whether VBA uses binary or text comparison, use the `Option Compare` command:

```
Option Compare [Text ¦ Binary]
```

To specify binary string comparisons, use the `Binary` keyword; to specify text comparisons, use the `Text` keyword. The `Option Compare` command must appear on a line by itself, at the module level:

```
Option Compare Text
```

You can only use the `Option Compare` commands at the module level, and they affect only the comparisons made by procedures in that particular module. Typically, you place the `Option Compare` command in the definition and declaration area of your module, before any variable or procedure declarations. If neither `Option Compare` command is present, VBA uses binary comparisons.

The *Like* Operator

The Like operator gives you the ability to perform a special type of string comparison operation. You can only use the Like operator with strings.

The Like operator tests a string to determine whether or not it matches a specified pattern. You can use the Like operator to perform searches through text data to find all the words or phrases that match a particular pattern—a search of this type is often referred to as a *fuzzy search*.

Syntax

The general syntax for the Like operator is:

```
StrExpr1 Like StrExpr2
```

StrExpr1 represents any valid VBA string expression. *StrExpr2* represents a string expression specially constructed to specify a pattern that the Like operator compares to *StrExpr1*.

The Like expression evaluates True if the first operand (*StrExpr1*) matches the pattern in the second operand (*StrExpr2*); otherwise, the expression evaluates to False. Both operands in the expression must be string expressions, or VBA displays a type mismatch error.

You specify the pattern to compare a string to by using various special characters. The following expression is True when **AnyStr** contains strings such as "Fred", "Ferdinand", "Food", "Fraud", and so on:

```
AnyStr Like "F*d"
```

The next expression evaluates True when **AnyStr** contains strings such as "cut", "cot", "cat", and so on:

```
AnyStr Like "c?t"
```

VBA expects the operand to the right of the Like operator to contain a string expression that specifies a pattern. Table 4.3 summarizes the techniques and symbols for constructing matching patterns for the Like operator:

Table 4.3. Pattern-matching characters for the Like operator.

Pattern Character(s)	Matches up with
#	Any single digit, 0 through 9
*	Any number of characters in any combination, or no characters
?	Any single character
[list]	list is a list of specific characters. Matches any single character in list.
[!list]	list is a list of specific characters. Matches any single character *not* in list.

Operators and Expressions

Use the last two pattern character specifications in Table 4.3 to list individual characters that you want to match, or not match. The following expressions show how to use the square brackets with a character list.

This expression is `True` if **AnyStr** contains "big" or "bid", and `False` if it contains "bit" or "bin":

```
AnyStr Like "bi[dg]"
```

The next expression is `True` if **AnyStr** contains "big", "bid", or "bin", `False` if it contains "bit":

```
AnyStr Like "bi[!t]"
```

The following expression is `True` if **AnyStr** contains "bin" or "bit", `False` if **AnyStr** contains "bid" or "big":

```
AnyStr Like "bi[!dg]"
```

You can also use the square brackets to specify a range of characters to match or not match:

```
AnyStr Like "bi[a-f]"
AnyStr Like "bi[!a-f]"
```

The first example above is `True` whenever **AnyStr** contains one of the strings "bia", "bib", "bic", "bid", "bie", or "bif", and `False` otherwise. The second example expression is the inverse of the first, and is `False` whenever **AnyStr** contains one of the strings "bia", "bib", "bic", "bid", "bie", or "bif". The second expression is `True` for any string that contains the first two letters bi and does *not* end with the letters a through f.

When you specify a range of characters, you must specify the range from lowest to highest character. For example, the range pattern [a-f] is valid, but [f-a] is not. VBA ignores pairs of square brackets with nothing inside ([]).

Because the left bracket ([), question mark (?), number sign (#), and asterisk (*) characters have special meanings in the pattern string, you must enclose them inside square brackets if you want to make them part of the pattern to match. For example, if you wanted to find out if a string ended with a question mark, you would use the following expression (which is `True` if **AnyStr** contains any number or combination of characters ending with a question mark):

```
AnyStr Like "*[?]"
```

The right bracket (]) and exclamation mark (!) characters also have special meanings in the pattern string; to match these characters, make sure that they are *outside* the square brackets of a character list. For example, to determine whether a string ends with an exclamation mark, you would use the following expression (which is `True` if **AnyStr** contains any number or combination of characters ending with an exclamation mark):

```
AnyStr Like "*!"
```

To match a hyphen character in the pattern string, place the hyphen at the beginning or end of a character list, inside the square brackets. Placing the hyphen in any other location specifies a range of characters. The next expression shows how to match a hyphen character (this expression is True if **AnyStr** contains "big-headed", "pig-headed", "plug-ugly", "tag-along", and so on):

```
AnyStr Like "*g[-]*"     'True
```

The results of string comparisons that use the Like operator are also affected by the Option Compare setting. If the comparison option is set for binary string comparisons, the Like operator distinguishes between upper- and lowercase letters. If the comparison option is set for text comparison, the Like operator is not case-sensitive.

Whether or not VBA is currently using binary or text comparison also affects what characters the Like operator includes in various ranges that you might specify. If, for example, you have specified the range [e-i], and the comparison option is set for binary comparison, then only the characters *e, f, g, h,* and *i* match the specified range. If the comparison option is set for text comparison, however, the range includes several more characters—*E, e, È, è, É, é, Ê, ê, Ë, ë, F, f, G, g, H, h, I,* and *i* are all included in the range [e-i] when the Option Compare Text option is on. Notice that the characters Ì, ì, Í, í, Î, î, Ï, and ï are not included in the range; the specified range ended with the letter *i*, and accented characters are higher in the alphabetic sort order than unaccented characters.

> **Note:** If you only want to find out whether a string is part of another string, use the VBA Instr function instead of the Like comparison operator. For example, if you simply want to determine whether the string *big* is part of the string *bigger,* use the Instr function. Day 5 describes VBA functions.

The *Is* Operator

VBA has one final comparison operator: the Is operator. You can only use the Is operator to compare Object type expressions. Expressions that include the Is operator always result in a Boolean value.

The Is operator expression evaluates to True when both object expressions refer to the same object; it evaluates to False otherwise. VBA provides the Is operator because none of the other comparison operators are meaningful when used with Object type expressions. Object expressions are really memory addresses that refer to a specific object in Excel (or another VBA host application). Day 7 explains objects more fully.

Logical Operators

Most often, you use VBA's logical operators to combine the results of individual comparison expressions in order to build up complex criteria for making a decision within your procedure, or for establishing the conditions under which a group of statements will repeat.

You can use any valid expression that has a Boolean result as the operands for a logical operator, or a number that VBA can convert to a Boolean value. VBA considers 0 to be equivalent to the Boolean value False, and any other numeric value equivalent to the Boolean value True.

Usually, the result of a logical operation is a Boolean type value, although some logical operations may result in the special value Null if one or more of the operands are Null. Because VBA treats the special value Empty as 0, VBA treats operands in logical expressions that contain Empty as if they contain the Boolean value False.

Table 4.4 lists the logical operators available in VBA, along with their syntax and a brief description of how the operator works. (In the table, E represents any valid expression with a Boolean result, such as a comparison operation.)

Table 4.4. Logical operators.

Operator	Syntax	Name/Description
And	E1 And E2	Conjunction. True if both E1 and E2 are true; returns false otherwise.
Or	E1 Or E2	Disjunction. True if either or both E1 or E2 is true; returns false otherwise.
Not	Not E1	Negation. True if E1 is false, false if E1 is true.
Xor	E1 Xor E2	Exclusion. True if E1 is true or E2 is true, but not both; returns false otherwise.
Eqv	E1 Eqv E2	Equivalence. True if E1 is the same value as E2; returns false otherwise.
Imp	E1 Imp E2	Implication. False whenever E1 is true and E2 is false; returns true otherwise.

Note: The VBA logical operators And, Not, and Or are similar to the AND, NOT, and OR functions built into Excel. Excel does not, however, have equivalent functions for the VBA Eqv, Imp, or Xor operators.

Understanding Truth Tables

The following sections describe each of VBA's logical operators in more detail. First, however, it is important that you know how to read a Boolean truth table. A *truth table* is a table that shows all the possible combinations of values for a particular type of logical expression, and their results.

Most truth tables have three columns: the first column is for the value of the first operand, the second column is for the value of the second operand, and the last column always contains the value of the expression result. Each row in the table is for a particular combination of values. Examine the following line from the And operator's truth table:

```
False True False
```

In this line, the first operand is False, the second operand is True, and the result of the And operation when the operands have the given values is False. This line in the truth table says that the result of the expression False And True is False.

And

The And operator performs a logical conjunction. The result of the And operation is True only when both of its operands are true; otherwise it is False.

The And operator has the following general syntax:

Syntax

Operand1 And *Operand2*

Operand1 and *Operand2* are any valid VBA logical expressions. (A *logical expression* is any VBA expression that results in a Boolean type value: True or False.) The following truth table shows the results of the And operation:

Operand1	Operand2	Expression Result
True	True	True
True	False	False
False	True	False
False	False	False

Use the And operator to find out whether or not two different conditions are true at the same time. For example, you would use the And operator in an expression like the following:

```
(Gross_Sales < 50000) And (Net_Profit < 10000)
```

The preceding expression evaluates True if both the value contained in **Gross_Sales** is less than 50,000 *and* the value contained in **Net_Profit** is less than 10,000.

Notice that the two operands in this expression are comparison expressions; notice also the parentheses around the expressions that make up the And operator's operands. Parentheses tell VBA to evaluate the expression inside the parentheses *before* evaluating other parts of the expression. Also, the parentheses help make the expression more readable for a human being, by grouping together the related parts of the expression. Parentheses used to group parts of an expression into a sub-expression are a common feature in expressions of all types: numeric, string, date, and comparison, as well as logical expressions.

Or

The Or operator performs a logical disjunction, more frequently referred to as an *inclusive or*. The result of the Or operation is True whenever either or both operands is True; otherwise the result is False.

The Or operator has the following general syntax:

`Operand1 Or Operand2`

Operand1 and *Operand2* are any valid VBA logical expressions. The following truth table shows the results of the Or operation:

Operand1	Operand2	Expression Result
True	True	True
True	False	True
False	True	True
False	False	False

Use the Or operator to find out whether one or the other of two different conditions is true. For example, you would use the Or operator in an expression like the following:

`(Gross_Sales < 50000) Or (Net_Profit < 10000)`

The preceding statement evaluates True if either the value contained in **Gross_Sales** is less than 50,000 *or* the value contained in **Net_Profit** is less than 10,000.

Not

The Not operator performs logical negation; it inverts whatever value it is used with. The Not operator uses only one operand, and results in True whenever the operand is False, or False whenever the operand is True.

The Not operator has the following general syntax:

`Not Operand1`

Operand1 is any valid VBA logical expression. The following truth table shows the results of the Not operation:

Operand1	Expression Result
True	False
False	True

Xor

The Xor operator performs a logical exclusion, more frequently referred to as an *exclusive or*. The result of the Xor operation is True when either—but not both—operand is true; otherwise, the result is False.

Syntax

The Xor operator has the following general syntax:

`Operand1 Xor Operand2`

Operand1 and *Operand2* are any valid VBA logical expressions. The following truth table shows the results of the Xor operation:

Operand1	Operand2	Expression Result
True	True	False
True	False	True
False	True	True
False	False	False

Eqv

The Eqv operator performs a logical equivalence operation; using the Eqv operator is similar to a test for equality. The result of the Eqv operation is True whenever both operands are the same; otherwise, the result is False.

Syntax

The Eqv operator has the following general syntax:

`Operand1 Eqv Operand2`

Operand1 and *Operand2* are any valid VBA logical expressions. The following truth table shows the results of the Eqv operation:

Operand1	Operand2	Expression Result
True	True	True
True	False	False
False	True	False
False	False	True

If either operand expression in an Eqv operation expression is Null, then the expression result is also Null.

Imp

The Imp operator performs a logical implication. The Imp operator tests the relationship between two logical values when the truth of one value implies the truth of another value; as a result, the Imp operation produces the value True only when the second operand does not contradict the first operand. The Imp operator has the following syntax:

Syntax

```
Operand1 Imp Operand2
```

Operand1 and *Operand2* are any valid VBA logical expressions. The following truth table shows the results of the Imp operation:

Operand1	Operand2	Expression Result
True	True	True
True	False	False
False	True	True
False	False	True

If P and Q are variables containing logical values, then the results of the two expressions following are equivalent:

```
P Imp Q
Not (P And (Not Q))
```

These expressions are equivalent because logical implication says that, if one condition exists, then a second condition must also exist. The result of a logical implication can be true even when the first condition is false, as long as the second condition is true. However, the result of logical implication cannot be true if the first condition is true and the second condition is false. The effects of logical implication are not nearly as intuitive or easy to understand as the other logical operators; fortunately, use of the logical implication operator is rarely necessary.

String Concatenation Operators

VBA lets you join strings together to form larger strings. Joining one string to another is called *concatenating* the strings. String concatenation is extremely useful and generally quite straight-forward, although there are a few issues you need to be aware of.

Using String Concatenation

One of the most frequent uses for string concatenation is to assemble strings from various sources within your procedure to create customized messages for display. Listing 4.1 shows a procedure that asks the user for a workbook filename, opens that workbook, and then selects a particular sheet for the user (in this case, a sheet named *Sales Report*).

Listing 4.1. String concatenation.

```
 1:  '
 2:  'String Concatenation Demonstration
 3:  '
 4:  Sub Open2DataEntry()
 5:    Const Title$ = "Data Entry Setup"
 6:    Const ShtName = "Sales Report"
 7:    Dim FName As String
 8:    FName = InputBox("Enter the name of workbook to open:", _
 9:                     Title$)
10:    Workbooks.Open Filename:=FName
11:    ActiveWorkbook.Sheets(ShtName).Select
12:    MsgBox "Workbook " & FName & " opened, " & ShtName & _
13:           " selected.", , _
14:           Title$ & " Complete"
15: End Sub
```

Analysis Line 4 contains the procedure declaration. Line 5 declares a string constant used to supply the title bar for the various dialog boxes this procedure displays. Line 6 declares a string constant used to specify the name of the worksheet to select. Line 7 declares a variable to store the workbook name that the user enters. Lines 8 and 9 contain a single statement which uses the InputBox function to obtain a filename from the procedure's user. Line 10 opens the workbook file, using the workbook filename obtained from the user in line 8. Line 11 selects the *Sales Report* worksheet.

(The instruction to open a workbook file in line 10 was copied from a recorded macro; the literal string in the original recorded macro was replaced with the **FName** variable so that different file names could be supplied to this command, depending on the user's input. The instruction in line 11 to select the *Sales Report* worksheet was constructed in the same way.)

In lines 12 through 14, notice how the MsgBox statement uses concatenated strings to assemble a message for the user and to assemble a new title bar for the MsgBox dialog box. (The MsgBox statement in lines 12 through 14 is one VBA statement—notice the line continuation symbol at the end of lines 12 and 13.)

The string expression in lines 12 and 13 for the MsgBox procedure's first argument combines literal strings with the string in the **FName** variable and with the string indicated by the **ShtName** constant to form a single text string that VBA passes on to MsgBox. The string concatenation expression in line 14 constructs the MsgBox procedure's second argument, specifying the dialog box's title. The string expression in line 14 combines the string indicated by the constant **Title$** with a literal string constant.

If you run this procedure, and enter the name **SALES.XLS** when the procedure prompts you to enter a filename, then the MsgBox statement in lines 12 through 14 displays the dialog box shown in Figure 4.1. (This example assumes that you actually have a workbook named SALES.XLS in the current folder; otherwise, VBA displays a runtime error. If you experiment with this listing, make sure you enter a valid workbook name.)

Figure 4.1.

The MsgBox *statement in
lines 12 through 14 of
Listing 4.1 displays this
dialog box if you enter the
filename SALES.XLS.*

String Concatenation Operators

VBA provides two different operators for string concatenation; the following paragraphs describe each of these concatenation operators and their preferred usage.

The Preferred Concatenation Operator: (&)

You can only use the ampersand (&) operator to concatenate strings; this operator has no other purpose or function in VBA. All of the examples in this book use the ampersand operator for string concatenation—this is the preferred string concatenation operator because it leaves no doubt as to what operation you intend. The general syntax for the ampersand operator is:

`Operand1 & Operand2`

`Operand1` and `Operand2` represent any valid string or numeric expression. If one or both of the operands is a numeric expression, VBA converts the number to a string before performing the concatenation operation. The data type result of string concatenation is always a String data type. If an operand in a string concatenation expression is `Null` or `Empty`, then VBA treats that operand as a zero-length string (that is, a string that does not contain any characters). Listing 4.1, in the preceding section, contains several examples of the & operator.

> **Note:** If you don't separate the & operator from the variable name in front of it with at least one space, VBA assumes that you want to use the ampersand (&) as a Long type definition character, instead of as a string concatenation operator. This situation has varying results: In some cases, VBA converts the variable or expression result to a Long data type number, in other cases VBA displays a runtime or syntax error of some kind. If you have declared all of your variables with specific types (as is good programming practice), VBA will display an error message.

The Addition Operator Used for String Concatenation: (+)

You can also use the plus (+) operator to concatenate strings. The + operator has syntax and operand requirements the same as those for the & operator, with one major exception. The + operator for string concatenation is a historic inheritance from the original versions of the

BASIC programming language. These early versions of BASIC did not make a great distinction between string concatenation and addition. In VBA, however, the primary purpose of the plus (+) operator is for arithmetic addition. Whenever VBA encounters an expression that uses the + operator, it first tries to perform arithmetic addition. VBA only performs string concatenation with the + operator if one of the operands is a string expression and cannot be converted to a number, or if both operands are strings.

DO	DON'T

DO use the & operator for string concatenation to avoid ambiguity about the operation you intend, and to ensure that VBA performs string concatenation.

DON'T use the + operator for string concatenation, because expressions that use the + operator may be ambiguous to both VBA and a human reader.

Understanding Operator Precedence and Complex Expression Evaluation

A *complex expression* is simply any expression built up from two or more other expressions. Just as you build complete sentences in English by assembling words and phrases together, you create complex expressions in VBA by assembling various simpler expressions. Many of the expressions that you write will be complex expressions—especially when you write the expressions that determine decision-making or looping control in your procedures, or if you need to write expressions that represent various mathematical formulas.

To learn how VBA evaluates complex expressions, study the following expression, which is the VBA implementation of the formula for computing the volume of a sphere (**Radius** is a variable containing the radius of the sphere; **Pi** is a named constant):

```
(4 / 3) * Pi * Radius ^ 3
```

Notice that this expression contains four operators acting on five different values. Since each operator requires two operands, you may wonder how VBA evaluates this expression, which has an odd number of operands in it. The answer is fairly simple—VBA groups values in the expression operator by operator, performs the indicated operation, and substitutes the resulting value into the expression. You may recall this process (called *reducing the terms of an expression*) from your high-school or college mathematics courses.

VBA uses standard *operator precedence* rules to determine which operations in the expression to evaluate first. VBA always evaluates expressions enclosed in parentheses first. In the above expression for computing the volume of a sphere, VBA evaluates the expression 4 / 3 first because it is enclosed in parentheses. After performing the division operation, VBA substitutes the resulting value—1.333333—into the expression. The interim expression that VBA computes internally, shown following, now has three operators and four different values:

```
1.333333 * Pi * Radius ^ 3
```

Next, VBA performs the exponentiation operation: `Radius ^ 3`. VBA performs the exponentiation operation now, because the exponentiation operator has the highest priority of the remaining operators in the expression, according to VBA's rules of operator precedence. As VBA performs the exponentiation operation, it retrieves whatever value is stored in **Radius**, and raises it to the third power. VBA then substitutes that value into the expression. If **Radius** contains the number 2, then the resulting value of the expression `Radius ^ 3` is 8 (2 raised to the third power). The interim expression that VBA computes internally, shown following, now has two operators and three different values:

```
1.333333 * Pi * 8
```

Finally, VBA performs the two multiplication operations in the expression. The multiplication operators, as you might guess, have the same priority level in VBA's operator precedence rules. There are no remaining parentheses in the expression, either. In this situation, VBA determines which operation to perform first by performing the operations in order, from left to right.

The leftmost multiplication operation is the expression `1.333333 * Pi`. VBA therefore performs this multiplication operation first. If the constant **Pi** contains the value 3.14, then the result of this multiplication operation is 4.186665. The interim expression that VBA computes internally, shown following, now has one operator and two different values:

```
4.186665 * 8
```

There is only one operation left to perform. VBA performs the final multiplication operation—`4.186665 * 8`—obtaining the number 33.493324.

VBA has now evaluated the expression to a single value, and returns that value as the expression's result.

The preceding analysis of how VBA evaluates a complex expression illustrates VBA's rules for determining the *evaluation order* of an expression, which are summarized as follows:

☐ Parts of an expression enclosed in parentheses are always evaluated first. If the expression enclosed in parentheses is another complex expression, VBA applies these same rules to the expression within the parentheses.

☐ Specific operations are performed depending on the operator's precedence. The precedence of VBA's various operators is shown in Table 4.5.

☐ When operators have equal precedence, they are evaluated in order from left to right.

| DO | DON'T |

DO use parentheses to override VBA's normal order of evaluation, whenever necessary—VBA always evaluates expressions enclosed in parentheses first.

DO group values in an expression with parentheses any time you are uncertain how VBA will evaluate the expression, or any time the evaluation order of an expression is not immediately obvious.

DO remember that grouping expressions with parentheses is an important way to make your procedures more readable and easier to understand.

VBA evaluates expressions in this general order:

- ☐ Arithmetic operators, first.
- ☐ String concatenation operators, second.
- ☐ Comparison operators, third.
- ☐ Logical operators, last.

Table 4.5 lists the exact operator precedence that VBA uses. Read the operator precedence from the top of the table to the bottom. Operators are listed from highest precedence to lowest precedence. Operators listed on the same line have equal precedence.

Table 4.5. Operator precedence from highest to lowest.

Operator	Comments
^	Exponentiation, highest priority
–	Unary minus
*, /	Multiplication and division have equal precedence; they are evaluated as they are encountered from left to right.
\	
Mod	
+, –	Addition and subtraction have equal precedence; they are evaluated as they are encountered from left to right.
&	All string concatenation is performed after any arithmetic operations in the expression, and before any comparison or logical operations.

continues

133

Table 4.5. continued

Operator	Comments
<, <=, >, >=, =, <>, Is, Like	All comparison operators have equal precedence, and they are evaluated as they are encountered from left to right. Use parentheses to group comparison operators in expressions.
Not	
And	
Or	
Xor	
Eqv	
Imp	

Summary

In this lesson, you learned what expressions and operators are, and you learned how to use operators. You learned about each of VBA's arithmetic, string, comparison, and logical operators in detail.

Today's lesson explained why knowing the data type of an expression result is important, and explained the rules that VBA uses to determine the data type of an expression result for each operator and operand type involved. You learned how data type compatibilities can affect the results of an expression, and you also learned that VBA can often automatically convert values into compatible data types.

Finally, you learned how VBA evaluates complex expressions, and you learned the rules that VBA uses to determine which operations in a complex expression to perform first.

Q&A

Q Do I need to memorize all the data type and data conversion rules that VBA uses when it evaluates expressions?

A No, you don't need to memorize this information. It is important, however, that you have a basic understanding of what these rules are, and how VBA applies them, even if you don't memorize all the fine details. This knowledge helps you write programs that are bug-free. By knowing how VBA evaluates expressions and determines expression results, you can control the numeric precision of expression results and therefore increase the accuracy of your program's computations. This knowledge also helps you identify the source of various different program errors that you might experience.

Q I'm not sure that I understand how to use the logical or comparison operators.

A You don't usually use logical and comparison operators in expressions in the same way that you use arithmetic or string concatenation operators. With arithmetic or string operators, you typically assign the expression result to a variable or use it as a procedure or function argument. More typically, however, you use the results of expressions with logical and comparison operators to determine the existence or absence of a certain condition—such as whether or not a particular count has exceeded a preset value, or whether or not the user entered a particular response to a prompt. Logical and comparison expressions are essential components of the decision-making and looping commands described in Days 8 and 9.

Q How do I know which string concatenation operator to use?

A Always use the ampersand (&) operator for string concatenation. VBA provides the plus (+) operator for string concatenation in order to make it easier to translate programs from other dialects of the BASIC programming language into VBA, if necessary.

Workshop

The Workshop section presents Quiz questions to help you cement your new knowledge, and Exercises to give you experience using what you have learned. Answers are in Appendix A.

Quiz

1. What is an expression? An expression result?
2. How many different values may an expression contain? How are the values in an expression connected together?
3. Can a single value, such as a literal constant or a variable, be considered an expression?
4. What can you use the result of an expression for? Must you use the result of an expression?
5. What are the two uses of the equals sign (=) as an operator?
6. What is the difference between the / operator and the \ operator?
7. If **NumVal** and **StrVal** are both Variant type variables, and **NumVal** contains 17, and **StrVal** contains "23", what is the result of each the following expressions?

```
(a) NumVal < 5
(b) NumVal + StrVal
(c) NumVal & StrVal
(d) NumVal - (5 + (6 * 2))
(e) StrVal & "Skidoo"
```

Exercises

1. Add parentheses to each of the following expressions so that they produce the indicated result:

Expression	Result
(a) 3 * 5 - 7	-6
(b) 4.7 + 26 / 10	3.07
(c) 312 / 47 + 16 - 2	5.114754
(d) 17 - 5 - 44 / 2 ^ 2	100

2. Write, from scratch, a procedure named **ThreeWords**. This procedure should use three different InputBox statements to get three words from the user; assemble the three words into a single string (with spaces between each word), and then display the assembled string on-screen with a MsgBox statement. In your procedure, declare a named string constant for the string "Input: ". Use this string constant and the string concatenation operator to alter the title of each of the three dialog boxes displayed by the InputBox statement so that the title of the first dialog box is "Input: First Word", the second dialog box is "Input: Second Word", and the third dialog box is "Input: Third Word".

Visual Basic for Applications and Excel Functions

You've already used one of VBA's built-in functions: InputBox. Now that you know all about expressions, you're ready to learn how to incorporate functions into your expressions. Today you learn:

☐ What a function is and how to use functions in expressions.

☐ How to use the Object Browser to determine what functions are available.

☐ How to save typing time and programming effort by using the Object Browser to insert VBA functions and their argument lists into your code.

☐ How to utilize the most important VBA functions to convert data from one type to another or to manipulate strings.

Understanding Functions

A *function* is a built-in formula that operates on expressions and generates values. A function always *returns* a value, which VBA inserts into your program at the point where the function name occurs. VBA functions fall into several groups, according to the type of operation or calculation they perform. You use functions to provide values in an expression, and to perform tasks such as:

☐ Converting text strings to other data types.

☐ Getting information about text strings.

☐ Converting other data types to text strings.

☐ Formatting numbers or other data types for display.

☐ Manipulating or generating date values.

☐ Performing trigonometric, logarithmic, statistical, financial, and other calculations.

☐ Getting information about files, disk drives, or the environment in which VBA is currently running.

This chapter summarizes each of the different categories of functions, and describes in detail the most important VBA functions and their uses. Later lessons describe other functions summarized in this chapter, as they become relevant to the topics of those lessons. Also, as you will learn in the next lesson, you can create your own functions for use in your VBA procedures.

In the examples and text so far, you have encountered examples of both VBA procedures and VBA functions. Don't let yourself get confused between the terms *function* and *procedure*. Generally, a procedure carries out a specific task (or group of tasks), just as a particular menu command in Excel carries out a specific task. A function, on the other hand, usually operates on one or more values, and provides a specific value in return, like a formula in an Excel worksheet cell.

Using Functions in Assignments and Expressions

To use a function, simply type the function name in a VBA statement—along with any arguments the function requires—at the point in the statement where you want to use the function result. (Putting a function name in a VBA statement to invoke a function is referred to as *calling* the function.) The following statements show typical uses of functions:

```
Tomorrow = Now + 1
AnyStr = CStr(AnyValue)
```

In the first statement, the Now function obtains the date and time from your computer system's clock, and returns that information as a Date type value. When VBA executes this statement, it inserts the date value returned by the Now function into the expression at the point occupied by the Now keyword. VBA then evaluates the expression, adding one to the date returned by Now, and assigning that result to the variable **Tomorrow**. If today is August 8, 1995, then, after the execution of this statement, the date value stored in **Tomorrow** is August 9, 1995.

The second statement uses the CStr function, which converts its argument into a string and then returns that string. When VBA executes this statement, it passes the value stored in the **AnyValue** variable to the CStr function. CStr converts the value into a string, and returns that string as the function result. For instance, if **AnyValue** contains the number 12, then CStr returns the string "12". VBA then inserts the string returned by CStr into the expression at the point occupied by the CStr keyword. In this case, the function result is the only value in the expression, so VBA simply assigns the string value returned by CStr to the variable **AnyStr**.

The next statement is another example of the way you typically use functions:

```
MsgBox TypeName(AnyVar)
```

This statement uses the VBA TypeName function, which returns a string containing the name of the data type of its argument. When VBA executes this statement, it first calls the TypeName function, passing whatever value is stored in the **AnyVar** variable to the TypeName function. TypeName determines what data type was passed to it, and returns a string stating the name of the data type. VBA then inserts the string returned by TypeName into the statement at the point occupied by the TypeName function name. Because the TypeName function name is placed in the statement as the argument to the MsgBox procedure, VBA passes the result of the TypeName function as an argument to MsgBox. If the variable **AnyVar** is a Variant type variable, then TypeName returns the string "Variant", and the MsgBox procedure displays the word Variant on-screen.

These three examples illustrate some important facts about functions:

☐ You can use a function result as part of an expression.

☐ You can assign a function result to a variable.

☐ You can use a function result to supply a value in another procedure's or function's argument list.

☐ Functions have their argument lists enclosed in parentheses.

Essentially, you can use a function to supply a value anywhere in any VBA statement where you can legitimately use a constant or variable value. Listing 5.1 shows a complete procedure to further demonstrate how you use functions in expressions.

Listing 5.1. Using functions.

```
 1:  Sub FuncDemo()
 2:      Dim vDate
 3:      Dim tDate As Date
 4:      vDate = CStr(Now)
 5:      tDate = Time
 6:      MsgBox "Today's date: " & vDate
 7:      MsgBox "The current time: " & tDate
 8:      MsgBox "The variable vDate is type: " & TypeName(vDate)
 9:      MsgBox "The variable tDate is type: " & TypeName(tDate)
10:  End Sub
```

 Line 1 contains the procedure declaration for the **FuncDemo** procedure. Lines 2 and 3 declare variables for **FuncDemo** to use. Line 2 declares the variable **vDate**; this variable is a Variant type because the variable declaration does not specify a data type. Line 3 declares the variable **tDate**; this variable is a Date type.

Line 4 is the first statement in **FuncDemo** that performs any work. When VBA executes line 4, it first calls the Now function, which returns the current date and time from your computer system's clock as a Date type value. VBA then inserts the result from the Now function into the statement. Because the Now function appears in the statement as the argument to the CStr function, VBA passes the Now function's result to the CStr function—CStr returns the string equivalent of whatever argument is passed to it. In this case, the argument is a Date type value (the Now function result), so CStr returns a string containing the current date and time. If today is August 8, 1995, and the time is 8:12 AM, then the CStr function in line 4 returns the string 8/8/95 8:12:00 AM. To complete the execution of the statement in line 4, VBA assigns the result of the CStr function to the **vDate** variable.

When VBA executes the statement in line 5, it first calls the Time function, which returns the time of day from your computer system's clock as a Date type value. If the current time is 8:12 AM, then the Time function in line 5 returns the value 8:12:00 AM as a Date data type. VBA then assigns the Date value returned by the Time function to the **tDate** variable.

Line 6 uses the MsgBox procedure to display a literal string concatenated with the value stored in the **vDate** variable. Notice the use of the ampersand (&) string concatenation operator. When VBA executes this statement, it first concatenates the literal string with the string contained in

the **vDate** variable (remember, line 4 stored the current date and time in the **vDate** variable by using the CStr function to convert the date returned by the Now function into a string). Next, VBA passes the single string resulting from the string concatenation expression as the argument to the MsgBox procedure. If today is September 20, 1995, and the time is 10:11 PM and 29 seconds, then the MsgBox statement in line 6 displays the dialog box shown in Figure 5.1

Figure 5.1.

The MsgBox *statement in Line 6 of Listing 5.1 displays this dialog box, showing the current date and time (according to your computer's clock).*

Line 7 also uses MsgBox. When VBA executes this statement, it first evaluates the expression that supplies the argument to MsgBox. This time, the string expression consists of a literal string concatenated with a Date type value. Because the expression contains the string concatenation operator (&), VBA correctly assumes that the intent of this expression is to produce a String type value; VBA therefore automatically converts the value in **tDate** into a string, and then performs the specified concatenation operation. Next, VBA passes the string resulting from the concatenation expression as the argument to MsgBox. If the current time is 6:33 PM exactly, then the MsgBox procedure in line 7 displays a dialog box similar to the one in Fig. 5.1, but containing the message The current time: 6:33:00 PM on-screen.

Lines 8 and 9 also use MsgBox. This time, each line displays a message stating the data type of a variable. When VBA executes line 8, it first calls the TypeName function. The argument for the TypeName function is the **vDate** variable. TypeName analyzes the contents of the **vDate** variable, and returns a string that contains the name of the data type of the information stored by **vDate**. The **vDate** variable contains string data, so the TypeName function returns a string containing the word String. VBA next inserts the string returned by TypeName into the expression that forms the argument for the MsgBox procedure. Now, VBA finishes evaluating the expression by concatenating the literal string with the string returned by TypeName. The MsgBox procedure in line 8 then displays the dialog box shown in Figure 5.2.

Figure 5.2.

The MsgBox *statement in Line 8 of Listing 5.1 displays this dialog box, revealing the data type of the data stored in the **vDate** variable.*

VBA executes line 9 similarly. Because **tDate** is a Date type variable, the `TypeName` function returns the string `Date`. The `MsgBox` statement in line 9 therefore displays the message `The variable tDate is type: Date`.

DO	**DON'T**

DO remember that the `TypeName` function reports on the type of data *stored* by a variable, not the type of the variable itself. Line 8 of Listing 5.1 correctly reports that the data stored in the variable is a string, which is correct; `TypeName` can't help you determine whether or not the variable type is a string (in this case it's a Variant type containing a string).

DON'T forget to include the parentheses around a function's argument list (see "Ignoring a Function's Result" later in this chapter).

Understanding Function Arguments and Function Results

As you've seen in the examples so far, and in Listing 5.1, some functions require one or more arguments, others do not. Functions that do not require arguments usually just retrieve a value that is not otherwise available. The `Time` function (which returns the current time from your computer's clock), for example, does not require any arguments. To use a function that does not use any arguments, just type the function name into your program, as in the following statement:

```
TimeNow = Time
```

Other functions require that you supply one or more values for them to act on. The `Sqr` function, for example, returns the square root of a number—in order for `Sqr` to calculate a square root, you must supply a number for `Sqr` to act on, as shown in the next statement:

```
Root = Sqr(AnyNum)
```

You supply values to a function through the function's argument list. Enclose the argument list in parentheses, and—if there is more than one argument—separate each argument in the list with a comma, as you learned to do in Day 2 with the `MsgBox` procedure.

The data type of a value returned by a function depends on the specific function. Most functions return Variant type data values, although other functions return specific data types such as String, Double, and Integer. VBA, frequently, can automatically convert a function's result to a data type compatible with other values in the expression that contains the function—just like

VBA converts data types in variable assignments and expression evaluation. All the data type compatibility rules you learned in Day 4 that apply to Variant and typed variables and constants also apply to the values returned by functions.

Ignoring a Function's Result

Normally, you must use the value returned by a function in some way—either by including the function result in an expression, an argument list, or by assigning it to a variable. In some cases, however, you may want to ignore the result returned by a function.

Day 2 mentioned that VBA's MsgBox procedure has an optional second argument that allows you to specify how many command buttons appear in the message dialog box. You can use the command button argument in the MsgBox procedure to display a message that asks the user a question, and enables the user to respond to your question by choosing a command button in the message dialog box.

If you use this optional command button argument for MsgBox, then you must be able to obtain a value from MsgBox that indicates which button the user chose. In fact, the MsgBox procedure is really a function—most of the time you use the MsgBox function, however, you ignore its result.

All the examples and procedure listings in this book so far have omitted the command buttons argument from the MsgBox statements; when you omit the buttons argument, MsgBox displays a dialog box that contains only one button. Because the dialog box, as used so far, contained only one button, it didn't matter what the result of the MsgBox function was, and so all of the MsgBox statements so far have ignored the MsgBox function's result, using MsgBox statements similar to the following (which simply consists of the MsgBox function name, followed by its argument list):

```
MsgBox AnyText, , AnyTitle
```

VBA provides several predefined constants for specifying the buttons in the MsgBox dialog box (Day 8 describes these constants in more detail). One of these constants, vbYesNo, indicates to MsgBox that it should include a **Y**es button and a **N**o button in the dialog box that it displays. The following statement produces the dialog box shown in Figure 5.3:

```
MsgBox "Do you see two buttons?", vbYesNo, "Button Demonstration"
```

Figure 5.3.

A MsgBox dialog box, showing the result of including the buttons argument.

There's only one problem with this statement: the result of the user's choice is *not* returned in any way—this statement still ignores the MsgBox function result.

To retrieve the MsgBox function result, you must change this statement in two ways: you must add parentheses around the argument list, and alter the statement so that it uses the function result in some way. Typically, you'll assign the MsgBox function result to a variable, so you can later test the function result in another statement to determine which button your procedure's user actually chose. The next line shows the MsgBox statement altered so that it returns a value (notice the line continuation symbol—this is a single VBA statement):

```
Response = MsgBox ("Do you see two buttons?", vbYesNo, _
                   "Button Demonstration")
```

When VBA executes this statement, it displays the same dialog box shown in Figure 5.3. When the user chooses either the **Y**es button or the **N**o button, VBA closes the dialog box, and stores a number representing the chosen button in the **Response** variable.

Notice that the first MsgBox statement, which ignores the MsgBox function result, does not have any parentheses around the argument list, and that the second MsgBox statement, which uses the MsgBox function result, *does* have parentheses around the argument list.

These two MsgBox statements illustrate an important fact about functions: By omitting the parentheses around the function's argument list, you tell VBA that you want to ignore the function's result. When you omit the parentheses around the argument list, VBA treats the function call as if it were a call to a procedure, and does not return the function result.

If you look again at the function examples earlier in this chapter, and at the functions used in Listing 5.1, you'll notice that all of the statements that call a VBA function include parentheses around the function's argument list, even when the argument list contains only one argument. Functions that do not have arguments do not require parentheses when you call them.

You can't ignore the result of every VBA function—nor would you necessarily want to. Ignoring the result of a function is only useful with functions (such as MsgBox) that carry out some task as part of producing their return value. You ignore the function result when you want the function to carry out its task, but you don't care about the result of that task. The MsgBox function, as an example, carries out the task of displaying a message on-screen in a dialog box as part of the task involved in returning a choice from the user. MsgBox is also useful if all you want to do is just display a message; in this case, you use the function to display a message, but ignore its result. (Day 8 explains how to use MsgBox to enable your program's user to make choices affecting the execution of your program.)

If you try to ignore the result of a function that has no arguments (like the Now function) or any other function whose result cannot be ignored, VBA displays one of several possible runtime errors, depending on the specific function, although you'll usually receive a type mismatch or

syntax error. Typically, VBA prevents you from ignoring the result of any function whose name is a VBA keyword (such as CStr and other conversion functions), and those functions whose only purpose is to provide some returned value, such as the mathematical functions.

Using a Function's Named Arguments

You learned in Day 2 that you must list a procedure's arguments in a specific order. Similarly, you must also list a function's arguments in a specific order. Functions that use more than one argument depend on the position of a value in the argument list to determine which argument that value represents. For instance, you've learned that for MsgBox, the first argument is the message to display, the second argument is the number and type of buttons for the dialog box, and the third argument is the title of the dialog box.

Even though the second MsgBox argument specifying the command buttons for the dialog box is optional, and has been omitted in almost all of the examples and exercises so far, you still must include place-holding commas for the second argument in the argument list. As you saw in Day 2, omitting the place-holding commas for the second argument causes a type mismatch error.

As you may have discovered by now, it's often easy to inadvertently omit place-holding commas or to transpose argument values in functions that have optional arguments or have several arguments. When you omit or transpose arguments in a function's argument list, you may get type mismatch errors or, worse, no error at all. Sometimes, transposing values (such as row and column coordinates) in a function's argument list does not produce any type of runtime error—your program simply produces the wrong answer and you can't figure out why.

To help prevent programmer errors, and to make it easier to use functions that have optional arguments, VBA provides an alternative to listing the values in an argument list in a specific order. You can also pass argument values to a function by using the function's *named arguments*. The following lines show two MsgBox statements that have exactly the same effect; the first statement uses the standard method of listing arguments, and the second statement uses the named argument method of listing arguments (both statements ignore the MsgBox function result):

```
MsgBox AnyMsg, , AnyTitle
MsgBox prompt:=AnyMsg, Title:=AnyTitle
```

The second statement uses named arguments for the message (or prompt) that MsgBox displays, and for the title argument that specifies the title for the message dialog box by assigning a value to each named argument. The argument name for the MsgBox title, for example, is Title; the expression Title:=AnyTitle assigns the contents of the variable **AnyTitle** as the argument value that VBA passes to MsgBox to be used as the dialog box's title.

Similarly, the argument name for the MsgBox prompt text is prompt, and the expression prompt:=AnyMsg assigns the contents of the variable **AnyTitle** as the argument value that VBA passes to MsgBox to be used as the text displayed by the message dialog box.

5

145

Note: The symbol that assigns a value to a named argument (:=) is not exactly the same as the regular assignment operator (=). If you omit the colon (:) when you assign a value to a named argument, VBA does not necessarily detect a syntax error, but is unable to interpret the statement correctly. When VBA executes the statement, it displays one of several possible runtime errors—frequently a type mismatch error.

When you use named arguments, you don't have to include place-holding commas for optional arguments. Notice, in the second statement on the preceding page, that there is no place-holder comma between the arguments for the prompt and title, as there is in the first statement. In fact, named arguments do not have to appear in any particular order. In the second statement, you could list the `Title` argument before the `prompt` argument, as shown below:

```
MsgBox Title:=AnyTitle, prompt:=AnyMsg
```

`MsgBox` still uses the value assigned to the `Title` argument as the dialog box title. When you use named arguments, VBA uses the name of the argument to determine what value that argument represents.

The `InputBox` function also has named arguments, as do all of the VBA functions. The following statement shows an `InputBox` statement that uses named arguments:

```
User_Input = InputBox(prompt:=AnyText, Title:=AnyTitle)
```

Notice that this statement includes parentheses around the argument list. You must always include parentheses around the argument list when you use a function's result, whether or not you use named arguments when you call the function.

DO   DON'T

DO remember that VBA uses the name of the argument to determine what value that argument represents.

DO include parentheses around a function's argument list whenever you use the function's result.

Note: You cannot mix named arguments with a standard argument list in the same function call. You must either use named arguments or a standard argument list for each individual function call, although you do not have to use the same method of listing arguments in every function call.

To determine the names of a function's arguments, search VBA's online help for the particular function name, or use the Object Browser to paste the function's name and complete named argument list into your program code as described in the section "Using The Object Browser to Insert Function Calls," later in this chapter.

Using Visual Basic for Applications' Functions

VBA's various built-in functions fall into several different categories, based on the general purpose of the functions in that category (such as mathematical, data conversion, date and time, interaction, string, and disk information). The next few sections discuss each function category, and include a table listing the functions and summarizing their actions.

Unfortunately, discussing every VBA function in detail is beyond the capacity of this book. Fortunately, though, most of the VBA functions—such as the mathematical functions—are fairly self-explanatory, and don't require much explanation. Other functions, such as some of the data type conversion functions, are discussed in more detail. VBA's string manipulation functions are of sufficient importance that a separate section of this lesson has been devoted to explaining their use.

Tip: To get more information about a specific function, type the function name, highlight it, and then press F1. VBA displays the online reference with that particular function as the current topic.

5

Mathematical Functions

VBA provides a standard selection of mathematical functions. Use these functions in expressions or to provide arguments for other functions in any of the ways already described. Table 5.1 summarizes the mathematical functions available in VBA. In the table, N stands for any valid numeric expression; all function arguments are required unless otherwise noted.

Table 5.1. VBA's mathematical functions.

Function(Arguments)	Returns/Action
Abs(N)	Returns the absolute value of N.
Atn(N)	Returns the Arctangent of N, as an angle in radians.

continues

Table 5.1. continued

Function(Arguments)	Returns/Action
Cos(N)	The Cosine of the angle N, where N is an angle measured in radians.
Exp(N)	Returns the constant *e* raised to the power N. (*e* is the base of natural logarithms, and is approximately equal to 2.718282.)
Fix(N)	Returns the integer part of N by rounding; if N is negative, Fix returns the nearest negative integer greater than or equal to N.
Int(N)	Returns the integer part of N by rounding; if N is negative, Int returns the nearest negative integer less than or equal to N.
Log(N)	Returns the natural logarithm of N.
Rnd(N)	Returns a random number; argument is optional. Rnd is used to provide a random factor in programs that simulate some real-world event, such as stock market simulations. Use the Rnd function only after initializing VBA's random number generator with the Randomize statement.
Sgn(N)	Returns the sign of a number: -1 if N is negative, 1 if N is positive, 0 if N is 0.
Sin(N)	Returns the Sine of an angle; N is an angle measured in radians.
Sqr(N)	Returns the square root of N. VBA displays a runtime error if N is negative. (By mathematical definition, negative numbers cannot have a square root.)
Tan(N)	Returns the Tangent of an angle; N is an angle measured in radians.

Data Conversion Functions

Visual Basic provides several functions to convert one data type into another. Use these data conversion functions to resolve type mismatch errors and to maintain explicit control over the data types in your expressions.

For example, if you receive a type mismatch error for a particular assignment statement, you may be able to convert the expression on the right side of the assignment operator to a type that is compatible with the variable on the left side of the assignment operator by using one of the conversion functions. In the following statement, for example, the variable **AnyStr$** is a String type variable, so assigning the number 12 to it directly results in a type mismatch error. Instead,

the statement uses the CStr function to convert the number 12 to the string "12" in order to avoid the type mismatch error:

```
AnyStr$ = CStr(12)
```

As another example, you may want to keep the result of an expression within the range of a Single numeric type (most numeric expressions result in a Double); in this case you would use the CSng function to convert the expression result to a single-precision number, as shown in this statement:

```
AnySingle = CSng(412/14)
```

Table 5.2 summarizes VBA's conversion functions. In the table, N stands for any numeric expression, S stands for any string expression, and E stands for an expression of any type. Each function's arguments are required unless otherwise noted.

Table 5.2. Data conversion functions.

Function(Arguments)	Returns/Action
Asc(S)	Returns the character code number corresponding to the first letter of the string S. The letter A, for example, has the character code 65.
Chr(N)	Returns a string containing the character that corresponds to the character code N, which must be a number between 0 and 255, inclusive. The character code 65, for example, returns the letter A.
Format(E, S)	Returns a string containing the value represented by E, formatted according to instructions contained in S. You can use Format to convert numbers like 1000 to strings like $1,000.00.
Hex(N)	Returns a string containing the hexadecimal representation of N.
Oct(N)	Returns a string containing the octal representation of N.
RGB(N, N, N)	Returns a Long integer representing an RGB color value. N in each argument must be an integer between 0 and 255, inclusive. From left to right, the arguments are the values for red, green, and blue.
Str(N)	Returns the string equivalent of the numeric expression N.
Val(S)	Returns a numeric value corresponding to the number represented by the string S. S must contain only digits and a single decimal point, otherwise VBA cannot convert the number.

Table 5.2. continued

Function(Arguments)	Returns/Action
CBool(N)	Returns the Boolean equivalent of the numeric expression N.
CCur(E)	Returns a numeric value of type Currency; E may be any valid numeric expression, or a string expression that can be converted to a number.
CDate(E)	Returns a Date type value. E may be any valid expression (either a string or number) that represents a date within the range 1/1/100 through 12/31/9999, inclusive.
CDbl(E)	Returns a numeric value of type Double; E may be any valid numeric expression, or a string expression that can be converted to a number.
CInt(E)	Returns a numeric value of type Integer; E may be any valid numeric expression, or a string expression that can be converted to a number.
CLng(E)	Returns a numeric value of type Long; E may be any valid numeric expression, or a string expression that can be converted to a number.
CSng(E)	Returns a numeric value of type Single; E may be any valid numeric expression, or a string expression that can be converted to a number.
CStr(E)	Returns a String type value; E may be any valid numeric or string expression.
CVar(E)	Returns a Variant type value; E may be any valid numeric or string expression.

The most frequent conversion functions you'll use are the functions (grouped together at the end of Table 5.2) that begin with the letter C—for *convert*—followed by an abbreviation of a type name: CStr, CSng, CDbl, and so on. Consider the following statement, which produces a type mismatch error at runtime:

```
AnyStr$ = 1.25
```

A type mismatch error occurs in this statement because number and string types are not compatible with each other (remember, the $ is the String type-definition character). To make this assignment, you must explicitly convert the number to a string with the CStr function, as shown below:

```
AnyStr$ = CStr(1.25)
```

When VBA executes the above statement, it first executes the `CStr` function and inserts the function result into the expression on the right side of the assignment operator. Now both values in the assignment expression are of the String data type, and VBA is able to complete the assignment operation.

> **Note:** Using typed variables and type conversion functions requires you, the programmer, to be aware of when VBA converts data types in your code from one type to another. As you learned in Day 4, relying exclusively on VBA's automatic type conversion rules may not produce the results you want or expect because some operators—such as the plus sign (+)—behave differently depending on the data type of the values in the expression. Using typed variables and type conversion functions helps you avoid or locate subtle errors resulting from data type conversions you did not anticipate.

Date and Time Functions

Use VBA's date and time functions to obtain the current date or time, to break a date value into its component parts, or to convert strings and numbers to Date type values.

Table 5.3 summarizes VBA's date and time functions and their effects. In the table, N is any valid numeric expression, and D is any valid date expression (including Date type values, numbers, or strings that VBA can convert to a date). All function arguments are required, unless otherwise noted.

Table 5.3. Date and time functions.

Function(Arguments)	Returns/Action
Date	Returns the current date from your computer system's clock. (You may also use this function as a procedure to set your computer system's clock. Refer to VBA's online help for details.)
Time	Returns the current time from your computer system's clock as a Date value. (You may also use this function as a procedure to set your computer system's clock. Refer to VBA's online help for details.)
Now	Returns the current date and time from your computer system's clock.

continues

Table 5.3. continued

Function(Arguments)	Returns/Action
Year(D)	Returns an integer containing the year part of the date expression. The year is returned as a number between 100 and 9999.
Month(D)	Returns an integer containing the month part of the date expression. The month is returned as a number between 1 and 12, inclusive.
Day(D)	Returns an integer containing the day part of the date expression. The day is returned as a number between 1 and 31, inclusive.
Weekday(D)	Returns an integer containing the day of the week for the date in the date expression. The weekday is returned as a number between 1 and 7, inclusive; 1 is Sunday, 2 is Monday, and so on.
Hour(D)	Returns an integer containing the hour part of the time contained in the date expression. The hour is returned as a number between 0 and 23, inclusive. If the date expression does not contain a value for the time, then Hour returns 0.
Minute(D)	Returns an integer containing the minutes part of the time contained in the date expression. The minutes are returned as a number between 0 and 59, inclusive. If the date expression does not contain a value for the time, Minute returns 0.
Second(D)	Returns an integer containing the seconds part of the time contained in the date expression. The seconds are returned as a number between 0 and 59, inclusive. If the date expression does not contain a value for the time, Second returns 0.
DateSerial(N, N, N)	Returns a serial date value for a specified date. From left to right, the arguments represent the year, month, and day. The year argument must be a whole number between 100 and 9999, month must be between 1 and 12, and day must be between 1 and 31 (all ranges are inclusive).
TimeSerial(N, N, N)	Returns a serial time value for a specified time. From left to right, the arguments represent the hours, minutes, and seconds. The hour argument must be a whole number between 0 and 23, minutes and seconds must both be numbers between 0 and 59 (all ranges are inclusive).

Function(Arguments)	Returns/Action
DateValue(E)	Returns a date value equivalent to the date specified by E, which must be any string, number, or constant representing a date.
TimeValue(E)	Returns a date value containing the time specified by E, which must be any string, number, or constant representing a time.
Timer	Returns a number representing the number of seconds since midnight, according to your computer system's clock.

User Interaction Functions

You're already acquainted with VBA's interactive functions for input and output: InputBox and MsgBox. These are the only user interaction functions in VBA.

InputBox

Both MsgBox and InputBox have several optional arguments that have not yet been described. The complete general syntax for the InputBox function is shown below:

Syntax

```
InputBox(Prompt [, Title, Default, XPos, YPos, HelpFile, Context])
```

Prompt is any string expression. The Prompt argument is the only required argument for InputBox—all of the other arguments are optional. The square brackets in the argument list of the syntax example indicate that the remaining arguments are optional.

You're already familiar with the Prompt and Title arguments; the first is a string used to tell the user what information you expect them to enter; the second is a string used as the title for the input dialog box.

The Default argument is also any string expression; use the Default argument to provide a default value for the user's input. The following statement, for example, asks the user to enter a filename, and suggests the name NEWFILE. The dialog box produced by this statement, showing the default value, is shown in Figure 5.4.

```
User_Input = InputBox("Enter a file name: ", _
                      "Make a File", "NEWFILE")
```

Figure 5.4.

Use the optional arguments for InputBox to specify a default value for the user's input.

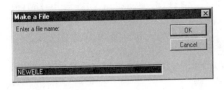

As you may have noticed, the `InputBox` dialog box displays in the center of the screen. You may want the dialog box to display in another position on-screen, especially if you have opened other dialog boxes on-screen that you'd like to have remain visible. Staggering input dialog boxes as they're opened helps your procedure's user keep track of where they are in a particular sequence of dialog boxes.

The *XPos* and *YPos* arguments may be any numeric expression. These arguments allow you to specify where in the active window the input dialog box appears. *XPos* and *YPos* provide the coordinates for the top-left corner of the dialog box. *XPos* is the horizontal distance from the left edge of the window; *YPos* is the vertical distance from the top of the window. Both distances are measured in *twips*; one twip equals 1/20 of a point (a point is a measurement of printing type size). Because a point is 1/72 of an inch, a twip is therefore approximately equal to 0.0007 inches.

> **Caution:** Be careful if you specify the position of the `InputBox` dialog box. It is possible for you to specify positions for the *XPos* and *YPos* arguments so large that the dialog box does not appear on-screen at all because its position is beyond the right hand or bottom edge of the window. Although the dialog box is not visible, it *is* active—none of the controls you can see on-screen will work until you respond to the "invisible" dialog box.

The last two optional arguments for the `InputBox` function are the *HelpFile* and *Context* arguments. *HelpFile* is a string expression that contains the name of a Windows help file— usually this is a help file that you have written using the Windows Help File compiler. *Context* is a numeric expression specifying the topic in the help file that pertains to the dialog box you are displaying—for example, 0 is usually the table of contents for a help file.

If you specify either *HelpFile* or *Context*, you must specify both. Whenever you specify a help file for an input dialog box, VBA automatically adds a **H**elp command button to the dialog box. (VBA does not include the Windows Help Compiler—if you want to create your own custom help files, you must obtain the Windows Help Compiler separately from Microsoft.)

To use named arguments for `InputBox`, just use the argument names given in the syntax example above: `Prompt`, `Title`, `Default`, `XPos`, `YPos`, `HelpFile`, and `Context`. The following statement produces the same dialog box shown in Figure 5.4, but uses named arguments:

```
User_Input = InputBox(prompt:="Enter a file name: ", _
        Title:="Make a File", Default:="NEWFILE")
```

MsgBox

The complete argument list for `MsgBox` is similar to that for `InputBox`, and is shown here:

SAMS
PUBLISHING

Sams
Learning
Center

Syntax

```
MsgBox (Prompt [, Buttons, Title, HelpFile, Context])
```

The only required argument for MsgBox is the *Prompt* argument, which can be any string expression; all other arguments are optional. The *Title*, *HelpFile*, and *Context* arguments in MsgBox have the same purpose and requirements as their counterparts in the InputBox function. Notice that MsgBox does not have arguments for the dialog box position; the MsgBox dialog box always displays near the center of the window. Notice also that MsgBox has a *Buttons* argument, instead of a *Default* argument.

In MsgBox, the *Buttons* argument is a numeric expression that specifies how many and what kind of buttons appear in the MsgBox dialog box. The *Buttons* argument also specifies the default button in the dialog box, and whether or not the dialog box contains the standard Windows Critical, Information, Exclamation, or Question icons for cautionary and user-query messages. The following statement, for example, displays the dialog box shown in Figure 5.5.

```
User_Input = MsgBox("Choose a button", vbYesNo, "Button Test")
```

This statement uses the vbYesNo constant, which is one of the predefined constants that VBA provides expressly for use with MsgBox. Using these VBA constants, and using the value returned by the MsgBox function, is described in Day 8.

Figure 5.5.

The MsgBox function provides options to specify how many and what kinds of command buttons appear in the dialog box.

Button Test

Choose a button

[Yes]   [No]

5

DO   **DON'T**

DO use the named arguments for InputBox and MsgBox to make using their various arguments simpler, and to make your VBA statements easier for a human being to read and understand.

DO use the line continuation symbol to put each named argument on a separate line whenever your statements begin to get excessively long:

```
User_Input = MsgBox(Prompt:="Choose a button", _
                    Buttons:=vbYesNo, _
                    Title:="Button Test")
```

This statement is easy for a human being to read and understand; many of the examples later in this book use formatting like this to make them more understandable.

String Functions

You use VBA's string functions to find strings inside other strings, to compare strings to each other, and to copy selected portions of strings. Because string data is so important as user input, filenames, names of worksheets, names of modules, and named ranges of data, you will use VBA's string functions frequently. This section just summarizes the available string functions; a later section gives more detail on how to use the most important and useful string functions.

In Table 5.4, N is any valid numeric expression, and S is any valid string expression. Unless otherwise noted, all function arguments are required.

Table 5.4. String functions.

Function(Arguments)	Returns/Action
InStr(N1, S1, S2, N2)	Returns the position of S1 in S2. N1 is the starting position for the search; N2 specifies whether to perform a case-sensitive search. N1 and N2 are optional. If N2 is omitted, the search uses the current setting of Option Compare.
LCase(S)	Returns a String type containing a copy of S with all upper-case characters converted to lowercase characters.
Left(S, N)	Returns a string; copies N characters from S, beginning with the leftmost character of S.
Len(S)	Returns the number of characters in S.
LTrim(S)	Returns a copy of the string S, after removing any space characters from the left side of the string (leading spaces).
Mid(S, N1, N2)	Returns a string; copies N2 characters from S, beginning with the character position in S specified by N1. N2 is optional; if you omit N2 then Mid returns all of the characters in string S, from position N1 to the end of the string.
Right(N, S)	Returns a string; copies N characters from S, beginning with the rightmost character of S. For example, Right("outright",5) returns the string "right".
RTrim(S)	Returns a copy of the string S, after removing any space characters from the right side of the string (trailing spaces).
Space(N)	Returns a string of spaces N characters long.
StrComp(S1, S2, N)	Compares S1 to S2 and returns a number indicating the comparison result: -1 if S1 < S2, 0 if S1 = S2, 1 if S1 > S2. N is optional; it indicates whether to make a case-sensitive comparison. If N is

Function(Arguments)	Returns/Action
	omitted, strings are compared using the current Option Compare setting.
String(N, S)	Returns a string N characters long of the character specified by the first character in S. For example, String(5, "x") returns the string xxxxx.
Trim(S)	Returns a copy of the string S, after removing both leading and trailing space characters from the string.
UCase(S)	Returns S with all lowercase characters converted to uppercase characters.

Disk, Directory Information, and Other Functions

Occasionally, your programs may need to obtain information about a disk drive, locate a particular file, or make a list of files. VBA provides several different disk and directory information functions to help you accomplish these tasks. Day 12 gives information on managing files and disk directories from your VBA programs.

VBA provides several other functions not mentioned in this chapter. These additional functions allow you to communicate with other applications, get information about runtime errors, get information about arrays, and to manipulate various Excel application objects. Later lessons discuss these other functions, as they become relevant.

5

Using Excel's Functions

In addition to the functions built into Visual Basic for Applications, Excel also makes some of its functions available to VBA. Excel has a wide variety of functions that perform mathematical, logical, financial, and statistical operations on data in worksheets. Excel makes many, but not all, of these functions available to VBA.

Note: Other VBA host applications, like Access 7, also make some or all of their functions available to VBA in the same way that Excel does. Almost all of the information in this section about using Excel's functions in VBA applies to other VBA applications, as well. Other applications will, of course, have different functions than those found in Excel.

Visual Basic for Applications and Excel Functions

The functions that Excel makes available to VBA are not part of VBA, they are part of Excel. Other software applications that include VBA for Applications (like Microsoft Project) may also make their functions—if they have any—available to VBA. The functions available to VBA in one host application may not be available in another host application. If you intend to write VBA programs that any host application can run, don't use functions from the host application because they may not be available in every application. For instance, if you want to write a procedure that you can use in either Excel, Access, or Microsoft Project, don't use Excel functions in your VBA statements.

To use a function that belongs to Excel (or any host application), you access the function in VBA through the `Application` program object. The `Application` object in VBA represents the host application and all its resources. (Objects are explained in more detail in Day 7; using Excel objects is explained in Day 18.)

The following statement uses the Excel `Max` function, which returns the largest number in its argument list:

```
MsgBox Application.Max(4, 1, 3, 2)    'Displays 4
```

In this statement, notice that the keyword `Application` is followed by a period (.) and then the name of the function, `Max`, without any spaces. The period—called a *dot separator*—indicates that the statement refers to the `Max` function, which is part of the `Application` object. When you use Excel's functions in your VBA macro programs, you must include the `Application` keyword and the dot separator (.) in front of every Excel function name.

Note: You cannot ignore the result of an Excel function. You must always include the parentheses in a call to an Excel function, and you must always use the function result in some way, either as a value in an expression, an argument for another function or procedure, or in an assignment statement.

You may have already noticed that Excel has many functions that have the same names as some of the functions listed in Tables 5.1 through 5.4. This situation may be true in other host applications as well: the host application has functions whose names duplicate the names of functions inherent to VBA.

Because you must always specify the `Application` keyword when you use an Excel function, there is never any ambiguity for either VBA or for a human reader as to which function your statement refers to. Even when a VBA and an Excel function have the same name, you can easily tell which function is in use:

```
Rslt = Log(AnyNum)
Rslt = Application.Log(AnyNum)
```

The first statement calls the VBA `Log` function; the second statement calls Excel's `Log` function. To use the VBA version of a function, just use the function name by itself; to use Excel's version of a function, include the `Application` keyword.

> **Caution:** Excel (or other application) functions that have the same name as VBA functions do not necessarily carry out the same tasks or produce the same results. For example, the Excel `LOG` function is different from the VBA `Log` function, and they return different answers—the Excel `LN` function is the one that matches the effects of VBA's `Log` function. Carefully review the action and result of Excel's and VBA's functions before you use one in place of the other; otherwise, your procedures may produce erroneous results.

Not every Excel function is available to VBA. Some Excel functions that duplicate VBA functions are simply not available because there is no point in making them available. As an example, the Excel functions `Date`, `Year`, `Month`, `Day`, `Hour`, `Minute`, and `Second` all duplicate VBA's `Date`, `Year`, `Month`, `Day`, `Hour`, `Minute`, and `Second` functions in both behavior and purpose. None of these Excel functions is available to VBA. Occasionally, some host application functions are not available to VBA, whether or not they duplicate VBA functions.

If you are uncertain whether a particular Excel function is available to VBA, use the Object Browser (as described in the next section of this chapter) to see if the **Methods/Properties** list includes the function you want when **Application** is selected in the **Objects/Modules** list and **Excel** is selected in the **Libraries/Workbooks** text box. If the function you want is not listed, then it is not available to VBA.

To find out what functions Excel (or any other application) has available, and to find out what the uses and purposes of those functions are, use the online help system and search for the word *functions*.

Using the Object Browser to Insert Function Calls

The number of functions available to you through both VBA and Excel is substantial—combined, there are literally several hundreds of functions available.

Obviously, it is difficult (if not impossible) to memorize the purpose, use, and arguments for this many different functions. Most people end up memorizing the names and arguments of only those functions that they use frequently, and then rely on a general knowledge of available functions to help them locate a specific function for a specific purpose, as needed.

VBA provides the Object Browser to help you locate available functions and determine what their argument lists and named arguments are. The Object Browser is an important tool that also allows you to access any online help available for specific functions, and to paste a "template" for the function call into your procedure's source code, including all of the function's named arguments.

Viewing and Inserting Visual Basic's Functions

To insert a function call into your VBA source code, you start the Object Browser the same way you have already learned: choose the **V**iew | **O**bject Browser command—which appears on the **V**iew menu only when the current sheet is a module—or click the Object Browser button on the Visual Basic toolbar, if the toolbar is displayed.

Whichever technique you use to start the Object Browser, VBA displays the Object Browser dialog box shown in Figure 5.6.

Figure 5.6.

Use the Object Browser to determine which functions are available and to insert a function call with all its named arguments into your program source code.

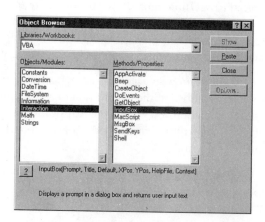

Note: The Object Browser dialog box lists *all* of the procedures, constants, and commands available—not just functions. As a result, you will see many more items listed in the Object Browser than just the functions described in this chapter. Many of the items you see listed are described in later lessons.

You've already learned how to use the Object Browser to view the predefined constants that VBA provides; viewing the available functions is very similar. To view the available VBA functions, follow these steps:

1. Select **VBA** in the **L**ibraries/Workbooks drop-down list box at the top of the Object Browser dialog box.

   The **O**bjects/Modules list now shows the various categories of functions, procedures, and constants defined by VBA.

2. Select the function category in which you are interested (Constants, Conversion, DateTime, FileSystem, Information, Interaction, Math, or Strings) in the **O**bjects/Modules list. Figure 5.6 shows the **Interaction** category selected.

3. Select the specific function you want to use—or want to get more information about—in the **M**ethods/Properties list. Figure 5.6 shows the InputBox function selected.

At the bottom of the Object Browser dialog box in Figure 5.6, notice that the InputBox function name and complete argument list appear, along with a simple explanation of the function's action and return value. Each name that appears in the argument list is the name to use for the function's named arguments. The Object Browser always uses this area of the dialog box to show you the correct argument syntax and named arguments for whatever function you select in the **M**ethods/Properties list, along with a brief explanation of the function's purpose. (Not every function displays explanatory text—Excel's functions, for example, do not display any explanatory text, although the Object Browser does display the Excel function syntax and named arguments.)

Refer again to Figure 5.6, and notice the command button with a question mark on it at the bottom left of the Object Browser dialog box. Whenever this button is enabled, there is online help available for the item selected in the **M**ethods/Properties list. Choose this button to view whatever help is available for the selected item. The online help for VBA functions describes any limitations on the range or data type of the function arguments, explains which arguments are optional, and explains how to interpret the function's return values.

To paste the function name and the function's complete argument list into your program source code, follow these steps:

1. Position the insertion point in your module at the place where you want to use the function's result.

2. Open the Object Browser dialog box and select the function that you want to paste into your source code in the **M**ethods/Properties list, as described above.

3. Choose the **P**aste button. VBA closes the Object Browser dialog box and pastes the selected function name into your source code at the insertion point, including all of the function's named arguments, both required and optional.

With the InputBox function selected as shown in Figure 5.6, choosing the **P**aste button inserts the following text into your module at the insertion point:

```
InputBox(Prompt:=, Title:=, Default:=, XPos:=, YPos:=, HelpFile:=, Context:=)
```

To use the pasted function, simply delete from the argument list any optional arguments that you don't intend to use, and then either replace the remaining argument names with the argument values, or use the named arguments by adding the assigned values to the argument list. The two statements below show a pasted InputBox function modified both ways—use whichever method most suits your needs (the second example has had a VBA line continuation symbol added):

```
InputBox("Enter a file name:", "Get File", "NEWFILE")
InputBox(Prompt:="Enter a file name:", Title:="Get File", _
         Default:="NEWFILE")
```

DO	**DON'T**

DO remember that the Object Browser inserts only the function name, argument list, and parentheses into your VBA source code.

DO remember to add any assignment expressions, variables, or other elements to make the pasted function and argument list into a syntactically valid statement.

Viewing and Inserting Excel's Functions

To use the Object Browser to view the functions that Excel makes available to VBA, or to paste an Excel function into your source code, follow these steps:

1. Open the Object Browser dialog box.

2. Select **Excel** in the **L**ibraries/Workbooks drop-down list box at the top of the Object Browser dialog box.

    The **O**bjects/Modules list now shows the various categories of functions, procedures, constants, and other program objects defined by Excel.

3. Select the **Application** category in the **O**bjects/Modules list. (See Figure 5.7.)

4. Select the specific Excel function you want to use—or want to get more information about—in the **M**ethods/Properties list. Figure 5.7 shows the Excel SUM function selected.

Because you can only access Excel's functions in VBA through the Application object (which is the repository of all of Excel's resources) you must select **Application** in the **O**bjects/Modules list to display the Excel functions (as shown in Figure 5.7). The Object Browser then lists all of the functions, commands, and other resources that Excel makes available through the Application object.

Figure 5.7.

You can also use the Object Browser to view and insert functions from Excel.

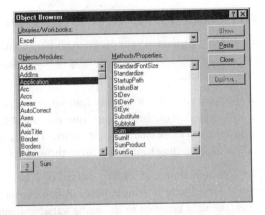

DO   **DON'T**

DO remember that you can only access Excel's functions when you include the `Application` keyword and the period (.) in front of the function name.

DO add the `Application` keyword and the period (.) whenever you use the Object Browser to paste an Excel function into your source code. The Object Browser pastes only the function name and arguments into your source code.

Using Functions to Manipulate Strings

Manipulating string data is an important part of many programs, especially programs that interact with a human user. Interactive programs need to manipulate string data for two reasons: to formulate messages you want to display to the user, and because the user's input (via `InputBox`) comes into your program as string data.

The more effectively you can manipulate string data, the more likely you are to be able to display attractive, coherent messages for your program's user. Also, the greater your skill in string manipulation, the more likely you will be able to successfully analyze the strings that your program's user enters.

VBA provides many different functions as tools to help you manipulate string data. VBA's string functions were summarized in Table 5.4, earlier in this chapter. This and the next section describe how to use the most important string functions and some of the data conversion functions to perform both simple and complex operations on string data in your programs.

Removing Extraneous Space Characters

Occasionally, string data in your program ends up containing extraneous space characters either at the end of the string or at the beginning of the string. These leading and trailing spaces occur for different reasons.

One of the most common sources of leading or trailing space characters occurs when you use the InputBox function to obtain input from the user. InputBox returns *all* of the text a user types, including any extra space characters. If the user types extra spaces before or after the actual input value, then the InputBox function returns those extra spaces as part of its return string.

Another common source of leading or trailing spaces in string data occurs when you use the contents of a fixed-length string variable. A fixed-length string always has the same length, and VBA pads the data assigned to the string variable (usually with trailing spaces) to fill out the declared string length, if necessary. As a result, whenever you use a fixed-length string there is a good chance it will contain trailing spaces.

Extraneous leading or trailing spaces in a string may cause a variety of difficulties—some only cosmetic, others more serious. When you assemble strings for display, the extra space characters may cause large gaps in your text, resulting in an unattractive and hard-to-read display. In other cases, extraneous leading and trailing spaces can affect string comparisons, the reported length of the string, and several other factors. These effects may cause the string value to be unusable in some other expression, or they may just cause your procedure to produce erroneous results. Either way, you can have a potentially serious problem.

VBA provides a trio of functions specifically for the purpose of removing—that is, trimming—unwanted leading and trailing spaces from a string. The first function, RTrim, removes space characters from the right side of the string (trailing spaces). The second function, LTrim, removes space characters from the left side of the string (leading spaces). The third function, Trim, removes both leading and trailing spaces from the string.

These string-trimming functions do not actually change the string—you pass the string you want trimmed as a function argument, and the function returns a *copy* of the string with the extra spaces removed. The procedure in Listing 5.2 demonstrates the use of the string-trimming functions.

Listing 5.2. Demonstration of RTrim, LTrim, and Trim functions.

```
1:  Sub TrimDemo()
2:      Dim ExSpace As String
3:      ExSpace = "    mad dog    "
4:      MsgBox "{" & ExSpace & "}"
5:      MsgBox "{" & RTrim(ExSpace) & "}"
6:      MsgBox "{" & LTrim(ExSpace) & "}"
7:      MsgBox "{" & Trim(ExSpace) & "}"
8:  End Sub
```

 Line 1 contains the procedure declaration for **TrimDemo**. Line 2 declares a string variable, and line 3 assigns a string with both leading and trailing spaces (four each) to the **ExSpace** variable. Line 4 uses MsgBox to display the unaltered **ExSpace** string. The string expression for the MsgBox argument concatenates a pair of curly braces around the **ExSpace** string to help show whether or not there are leading or trailing spaces in the string. When VBA executes this MsgBox statement, it displays the dialog box shown in Figure 5.8.

Figure 5.8.
The procedure in Listing 5.2 starts out by displaying this dialog box to show that the string stored in ExSpace *has leading and trailing space characters in it.*

Lines 5 through 7 of Listing 5.2 each use one of the three string-trimming functions to remove leading and trailing spaces from the **ExSpace** string; each line uses MsgBox to display the result of the string-trimming function. Keep in mind that the contents of the string variable **ExSpace** don't change—the string-trimming functions return a copy of the string in **ExSpace** with the extraneous characters removed.

DO	DON'T

DO remember that when you compare strings with VBA's comparison operators, VBA considers the longer string to be greater than the other string, provided the two strings are otherwise identical.

DO use the Trim function to remove leading and trailing spaces from strings before you compare them. By using the Trim function, you ensure that the string comparison is not affected by leading or trailing spaces that aren't usually significant to a human being, but are significant to your computer.

Getting the Length of a String

Frequently, you will need to know the length of a string (that is, how many characters are in the string), especially when you are formatting messages for the user, or when formatting string data that your procedure inserts into an Excel worksheet or other document. VBA provides the Len function to allow you to obtain the length of a string. The following statement shows the general syntax for the Len function:

```
Len(String)
```

String represents any valid VBA string expression. The following statement shows the `Len` function used in an assignment statement:

```
StrLen = Len("Frederick")    'returns 9
```

Again, fixed-length strings are a special case. Because a fixed-length string is always the same length, the `Len` function always returns the declared length of the string. For example, if you declare **FirstName** as a string variable 20 characters in length, the `Len` function always returns **20** as the length of the string in **FirstName**, even if the name stored in the variable is *Bob*, which is only three characters long—the rest of the 20-character length is all space characters.

Usually, when you use the `Len` function, your intent is to find out how many characters are in the string, *excluding* any leading or trailing spaces. Continuing with the **FirstName** example, if you wanted to know the actual length of the name stored in the variable, use a statement similar to the following:

```
NameLen = Len(Trim(FirstName))
```

In this statement, the `Trim` function removes any leading or trailing spaces from the string in the variable, and the `Len` function reports the length of the trimmed string. If **FirstName** contains *Bob*, then **NameLen** would end up with the value **3**.

Comparing and Searching Strings

Day 4 explained how to compare strings using comparison operators, and explained the effects of the `Option Compare Binary` and `Option Compare Text` settings.

VBA also provides a couple of functions to help you compare strings. The first function, `StrComp`, simply compares two different strings. In some circumstances, you may want to use `StrComp` instead of the comparison operators (=, <, or >) to compare strings, because `StrComp` allows you to specify whether to perform a binary or text comparison, overriding the module-level `Option Compare` setting for just that particular comparison.

For example, you may have decided that you want most of your string comparisons to ignore the case (upper or lower) of the characters when comparing strings; consequently, you added the `Option Compare Text` statement to your module. You may then wish to perform a specific string comparison that *is* case-sensitive; you then use VBA's `StrComp` function, and specify a case-sensitive comparison.

Using the *StrComp* Function

The general syntax for the `StrComp` function is:

SAMS PUBLISHING

StrComp(*String1, String2* [, *Compare*])

String1 and *String2* represent any two string expressions you want to compare. The optional *Compare* argument may be either the number 0 or the number 1. A 0 specifies binary comparison, and 1 specifies text comparison. If you omit the *Compare* argument, StrComp uses the current Option Compare setting. StrComp has the following return values:

☐ -1 if *String1* is less than *String2*

☐ 0 if *String1* and *String2* are equal to each other

☐ 1 if *String1* is greater than *String2*

The procedure in Listing 5.3 demonstrates the StrComp function.

Type

Listing 5.3. Demonstration of StrComp function.

```
1:  Sub Demo_StrComp()
2:      Const Dflt = "Suggested"
3:      Dim UserStr As String
4:      UserStr = InputBox(Prompt:="Enter some text:", _
5:                         Title:="String Comparison", _
6:                         Default:=Dflt)
7:      MsgBox StrComp(UserStr, Dflt, 1)
8:  End Sub
```

Analysis

Line 1 contains the procedure declaration for **Demo_StrComp**. Line 2 declares a constant, **Dflt**, for use as the default prompt in a later InputBox statement. Line 3 declares a string variable, **UserStr**, to hold the result of the InputBox function. Lines 4 through 6 are a single statement that calls the InputBox function to obtain a string from the user. The InputBox function call uses named arguments for InputBox, and specifies the prompt, dialog box title, and suggested default value for the InputBox dialog box. The statement assigns the result of the InputBox function to the **UserStr** variable.

Line 7 contains the StrComp function call; the statement uses MsgBox to simply display the StrComp function's returned value directly on-screen. The StrComp function call in line 7 uses all of the possible arguments for StrComp. This statement passes the **UserStr** variable and the **Dflt** constant to StrComp for comparison. Line 7 also specifies that StrComp should perform a text comparison (1 indicates a text comparison). This procedure reveals whether the user accepted the suggested default value for the InputBox function, or if the user entered a string lesser or greater than the string in the suggested default.

DO	**DON'T**
DO consider creating module-level constant declarations for the StrComp function's return values and for the text comparison argument—this is an ideal use for named constants.	

5

Visual Basic for Applications and Excel Functions

Using the *InStr* Function

VBA's other string comparison function, InStr, helps you determine whether one string contains another string. This function is useful in a number of circumstances. For example, use InStr if you want to determine whether a string the user entered contains a particular word. As another example, use InStr if you want to determine whether or not a string contains characters that would prevent it from being converted to a number.

The general syntax for the InStr function is:

```
InStr([Start, ] String1, String2 [, Compare])
```

String1 and *String2* are any valid string expressions. InStr searches *String1* to see if it contains *String2*. The optional *Start* argument is any numeric expression; this argument, if supplied, tells InStr at what character position in *String1* the search should begin. The optional *Compare* argument specifies whether or not InStr should use binary or text comparison while searching for *String2* in *String1*. Like the StrComp function, a 0 specifies binary comparison, and a 1 specifies text comparison. If you include either the *Start* or the *Compare* arguments, you must include both.

InStr returns a number indicating the character position in *String1* where *String2* was found; if InStr does not find *String2* within *String1*, then InStr returns 0.

Listing 5.4 demonstrates the use of InStr.

Type

Listing 5.4. Demonstration of InStr function.

```
1:  Sub Demo_InStr()

2:      Const Dflt = "Suggested"
3:      Dim UserStr As String
4:      UserStr = InputBox(Prompt:="Enter some text:", _
5:                         Title:="String Comparison", _
6:                         Default:=Dflt)
7:      MsgBox InStr(1, UserStr, Dflt, 1)
8:  End Sub
```

Analysis

Line 1 contains the procedure declaration for **Demo_InStr**. Lines 2 and 3 declare a string constant and string variable for use with the InputBox function. Lines 4 through 6 contain a single statement that calls the InputBox function to obtain a string from the user, and stores that string in the **UserStr** variable.

Line 7 contains the InStr function call; the function's returned value is simply displayed on-screen (line 8). The InStr function call in line 7 uses all of the possible arguments for InStr. In this statement, InStr searches to see if the string in **UserStr** contains the string indicated by the

Dflt constant, and uses a text comparison. Because this call to InStr includes the optional comparison argument, the statement also includes the starting position for the search. InStr begins searching for the **Dflt** string in the first character position of the **UserStr**.

If **UserStr** contains the string Suggested text, then InStr returns 1. If **UserStr** contains the string This text was Suggested, then InStr returns 15. If **UserStr** contains the string This is some text, then InStr returns 0. Finally, InStr function result is passed as the argument to MsgBox (still in line 7), which displays the result of the call to InStr.

Breaking a String into Smaller Parts

In many procedures, you will need to break a string into its component parts. For example, you may need to analyze a string that the user enters to determine if it contains more than one word and then, if it does, separate out the individual words that the user entered. You'll see samples of this type of string manipulation in later lessons and sample code listings.

The *Left* Function

VBA provides three functions to help you extract *substrings* from larger strings. (A substring is any string that is—or can be—part of a larger string.) The first of VBA's substring functions is the Left function, which returns a copy of a specified portion of a string. The general syntax for the Left function is:

Syntax

```
Left(string, length)
```

string represents any valid string expression, and *length* is any numeric expression. The Left function returns a copy of *string*, beginning with the first character in *string*, and continuing for the number of characters specified by *length*. If *length* is a number greater than the actual length of *string*, then Left returns the entire *string*.

In the following statement, Left copies the first 17 characters of the string **OldStr**, and returns those characters as a string; this statement assigns the function result of Left to the variable **NewStr**. If **OldStr** contains the string The quick red fox jumps over the lazy brown dog, then **NewStr** contains The quick red fox after VBA executes this statement.

```
NewStr = Left(OldStr, 17)
```

The *Right* Function

The next VBA substring function is the Right function. The general syntax for the Right function is:

```
Right(string, length)
```

In the above syntax sample, *string* represents any valid string expression, and *length* is any numeric expression. The Right function returns a copy of *string*, beginning with the *last* character in the string, and continuing *from right to left* for the number of characters specified by *length*. If *length* is a number greater than the actual length of *string*, then Right returns the entire *string*. The Right function always copies characters from the end of the string, working back towards the beginning of the string—without reversing the order of the characters.

In the following statement, the Right function returns the last four characters of the string stored in **OldStr**. If the **OldStr** variable contains the string hairball, this statement stores the string ball in **NewStr**.

```
NewStr = Right(OldStr, 4)
```

The *Mid* Function

You may want to extract a substring from somewhere in the middle of a string, rather than from the left or right end of the string. Such a situation might occur if you are extracting individual words from a line of text. To extract a substring from the middle of another string, VBA provides the Mid function. The Mid function has the following general syntax:

```
Mid(string, start [, length])
```

In this syntax sample, *string* represents any string expression, while *start* and *length* represent any numeric expression. The Mid function returns a copy of *string*, beginning at the character position in *string* specified by *start*. The optional *length* argument specifies how many characters Mid copies from *string*. If you omit *length* (or *length* is greater than the remaining length of *string*), Mid copies all of the remaining characters in *string*, from the position indicated by *start* to the end of *string*. If *start* contains a number greater than the actual length of *string*, then Mid returns an empty string.

The following statement shows an example of the Mid function:

```
NewStr = Mid(OldStr, 3, 4)
```

In the above statement, if **OldStr** contains the string unknowingly, then this statement stores the string know in **NewStr**.

Using String Characters You Cannot Type at the Keyboard

Sometimes you need to include a character in a string for which there is no key on the keyboard—such as a Greek letter, the symbol for Yen, or the copyright symbol.

You may also need to include a character in a string that already has some special meaning to VBA—like the double quotation mark symbol ("). You can't include characters like the double quotation mark (") directly in a string because VBA always assumes that this character starts or ends a string. The following statement, for example, will not execute without producing a runtime or syntax error:

```
MsgBox "This "cannot" work"
```

Although this statement might be intended to display the string This "cannot" work on-screen, VBA can't execute it. Because the double quotation mark (") tells VBA that a literal string is either beginning or ending, VBA parses the MsgBox argument above into three pieces: a string (This), a variable name (**cannot**), and another string (work).

To include characters that you cannot type at the keyboard, or that have special meanings to VBA, in a string, you use the VBA Chr function. The Chr function has the following general syntax:

Syntax

```
Chr(charcode)
```

In this syntax sample, *charcode* represents any numeric expression that is a valid code for the character set used by your computer. *charcode* must be a number between 0 and 255. As you may remember from the discussion about binary and text string comparison, your computer stores letters internally as numbers, and uses a scheme where every character has its own unique number. The Chr function takes the code for a particular character as its argument, and then returns a string containing just the character specified by the numeric code passed to Chr.

To see a list of the character codes that VBA recognizes, and their corresponding characters, open the VBA online help system and search for the topic *character sets*. Looking up the character code for the double quote mark (") reveals that it has code 34. By using the Chr function to supply the double quote mark, the following statement displays the message: This "will" work:

```
MsgBox "This " & Chr(34) & "will" & Chr(34) & " work"
```

Once you have used the Chr function to get the desired character as a string, you can use the string concatenation operator (&) to assemble that character into a string. The following statement, for example, adds the copyright symbol to the beginning of the literal string, and displays the result on-screen (see Figure 5.9):

```
MsgBox Chr(169) & "1995, Blue Sky Enterprises"
```

Figure 5.9.

Use the Chr function and concatenated strings to add characters to strings that you can't type at the keyboard.

You can also control how messages that you display are formatted, by adding special characters to the string. One of the characters you can produce with the Chr function is the carriage-return character (character code 13). This is the character that your computer generates whenever you press the Enter key on your keyboard, and—when used in text—indicates the start of a new line. As shown in Figure 5.10, the following statement uses Chr to add a carriage-return character to a concatenated string so that the resulting dialog box contains two lines of text (this is a single statement, notice the line continuation symbol at the end of the first line):

```
MsgBox "This is the first line" & Chr(13) & _
       "This is the second line"
```

Figure 5.10.

You can also use the Chr function to add characters in strings that affect how text is formatted when displayed or printed.

DO   **DON'T**

DO declare module-level constants for the character code numbers you use frequently. Using module-level constants helps make your programs more readable and easier to maintain. A module that makes frequent use of the copyright symbol and the carriage return code, for example, might contain the following module-level declarations:

```
Const CRightSym As Integer = 169    'copyright symbol
Const CR As Integer = 13    'carriage-return
```

The two examples already given would then appear as follows (and would have the same results shown in Figures 5.9 and 5.10, respectively):

```
MsgBox Chr(CRightSym) & "1994, Blue Sky Enterprises"
MsgBox "This is the first line" & Chr(CR) & _
       "This is the second line"
```

Summary

In this lesson you learned what a function is and how to use functions in expressions. You also learned how to ignore the result of a function, and more importantly, how to use a function's named arguments to simplify using optional arguments. Next, you reviewed the various categories of functions available.

You also learned how to access the functions that Excel makes available, and how to use the Object Browser to determine exactly which functions are available, and to insert the function name and its named arguments into your source code. Finally, today's lesson showed you how important effective string manipulation can be, and showed you the essentials of using VBA's string manipulation functions.

Q&A

Q In the Tables of VBA functions, I noticed that there are two different functions that convert numbers to strings: Str and CStr. Which one should I use?

A Usually, you should use the CStr function. The CStr function uses the international settings in your computer system (accessed through the Regional Settings icon in Windows 95 Control Panel) to determine which symbol your computer uses to indicate the decimal place in a number. If you change the nationality settings for your computer system—and therefore change the decimal separator character—the CStr function will still correctly convert numbers to strings. The Str function, on the other hand, assumes that the number decimal separator character is a period (.) and always uses that character. Str is provided mostly for backward compatibility with older dialects of BASIC.

Q I also noticed, in the Tables of VBA functions, that there is more than one function to convert strings to numbers: Val, CInt, CLng, CSng, CDbl, and CCur. Which one should I use?

A The situation with Val and the other functions that convert strings to numbers is similar to that with Str and CStr. The Val function assumes that the decimal number separator is a period (.), whereas the other functions use whatever number separator is specified by the international settings for your computer system. In general, you should use the CInt, CLng, CSng, CDbl, and CCur functions instead of Val. Both Str and Val are included in VBA to maintain compatibility with early versions of the BASIC programming language; the CStr, CInt, CLng, CSng, CDbl, and CCur functions are newer and more effective additions to the language.

Q I'm not sure I understand how named arguments differ from a standard argument list.

A A standard argument list simply contains the values to be passed to the function, separated by commas, and arranged in a specific order. VBA determines which value to use for each argument based on its position in the argument list. With named arguments, you use the specific name of an argument to identify the value for that argument. When you use named arguments, you do not have to list them in any particular order.

Q I'm not sure I understand how to use the `HelpFile` and `Context` arguments in the `InputBox` and `MsgBox` functions.

A Unless you purchase the Windows Help Compiler from Microsoft, it is unlikely that these arguments will be of any use to you. The `HelpFile` argument specifies the name of a file that you have previously prepared by using the Windows Help Compiler. The `Context` argument specifies the help topic that you want displayed when the user chooses the **Help** button. When the user chooses the **Help** button, VBA activates the Windows Help program—the same program used by every Windows application to display their online help files—and displays the help topic specified by the context number. To get some idea of how this works, enter the following procedure (without the line numbers) and run it:

```
1:  Sub Demo_HelpButton()
2:    Dim msgText As String
3:    msgText = "Help button gets VB Help Contents"
4:    MsgBox Prompt:=msgText, _
5:           Title:="Help Button Demonstration", _
6:           HelpFile:="VBA_XL.HLP", _
7:           Context:=0
8:  End Sub
```

If you choose the **Help** button in the dialog box displayed by the above procedure, you will see the table of contents for VBA's online help. VBA's online help is stored in the file VBA_XL.HLP and the context 0 is the table of contents.

Q Do I have to use all of the named arguments that the Object Browser pastes in?

A No. Just delete the optional named arguments you don't want to use. If you delete a required argument, VBA displays an error message when you run your procedure.

Workshop

Answers are in Appendix A.

Quiz

1. List three tasks that you would typically use a function to help you perform.
2. Where in a VBA statement can you use the value returned by a function?
3. How do you tell VBA that you want to ignore a function's result? Can you ignore the result of every VBA function?
4. What is the difference between the functions provided by VBA and the functions provided by the host application, such as Excel?
5. What is the VBA keyword that you must use in order to access a host application function, such as an Excel function?

6. Is it possible to ignore the result of an application function, such as an Excel function?

7. What use is the Object Browser to you?

8. Why is manipulating string data important?

Exercises

1. Add the data conversion functions to the following statements so that no type mismatch errors occur, and the expression has the stated value (HINT: write a procedure that uses a MsgBox statement to display the result of each expression):

```
(a) Sum$ = 12 + 15      'Sum$ should contain "27"
(b) Num% = "47" + "52"  'Num% should contain 99
(c) Num@ = 12.98 * "16"     'Num@ should contain 207.68
(d) Root! = Sqr(User_Input$)'If User_Input$ contains "4",
                            'then Root! should contain 2.
```

2. Write a procedure that obtains 3 numbers from the user, and then displays the smallest of the numbers entered. Use the Excel MIN function to determine the smallest number. In your procedure, use the named arguments for InputBox and MsgBox.

3. Write a procedure that obtains a word or phrase from the user and then displays: the first three characters of the user's input, the last four characters of the user's input, and the four characters after the first two characters of the input string.

4. Write a procedure that obtains a string from the user, and then displays the result of searching the entire string for the letter "L." (In this exercise, just display the numeric result of the InStr function.)

5

6

Function Procedures and User-Defined Functions

On Day 5, you learned what a function is and how to use the built-in functions of both VBA and Excel. In this lesson, you learn how to create your own customized functions, and how to make those functions available not only for your own VBA programs, but for use within Excel, as well. Today, you'll learn:

☐ How to create function procedures with named arguments, optional arguments, and specific data type results, and how to ensure that your function procedures are usable by Excel or any Visual Basic host application.

☐ How to use your custom function procedures in your VBA procedures or from Excel (or any host application).

☐ Tips and requirements for designing functions in general, and specifically functions for Excel.

☐ What a recursive function is and what benefits and problems are associated with recursive functions.

Understanding Function Procedures and User-Defined Functions

Before you start writing your own customized functions, you need to become acquainted with the terminology and concepts used to discuss the functions that you write in VBA. Although there is really only one way to create custom functions in VBA, you can—by observing certain guidelines and restrictions—create a specific variety of customized functions suitable for use by Excel, or any other VBA host application.

A *function procedure* is a special kind of VBA procedure that returns a result. Your function procedures—just like the built-in VBA functions—may have optional arguments, or use named arguments. You can use your function procedures to supply values in expressions and assignments, or as arguments to other functions and procedures. You write the program statements that determine the arguments the function uses, the actions the function performs, and the value that the function returns.

You can even use function procedures you create in your Excel worksheets, much the same way you use Excel's built-in worksheet functions. For Excel to use your function procedures, the code in the function procedure must adhere to certain guidelines and restrictions, however.

From Excel's point of view, the VBA function procedures that it uses are *user-defined functions*. This term distinguishes the function procedures you write from the built-in Excel functions. Although all user-defined functions are also function procedures, not all function procedures meet the requirements for a user-defined function.

Function procedure is the most general term for functions you create; the term *user-defined function* describes a specific type of function procedure—one that Excel can use. You cannot use function procedures that do not meet the requirements for a user-defined function in an Excel worksheet formula—you can only use those functions in statements in your own procedures.

Usually, you create function procedures to perform computations, get information, or to format data—just like the built-in VBA functions. For example, you may have a VBA program in Excel that analyzes energy consumption data. In this program, you may have several places that convert natural gas consumption measured in therms to measurements in BTUs. Instead of typing the formula for converting therms to BTUs in your program every place that you use that formula—which increases the chance that you'll make a typing mistake that results in an erroneous computation somewhere—you can write a function procedure that accepts a value in therms as an argument, and then returns a value in BTU as the function result.

Similarly, formulas to convert feet to centimeters, pounds to kilograms, Fahrenheit to Celsius, or that compute profit margins, commissions, discounts, and so on are all possible uses for function procedures.

You can also replace long, complicated worksheet formulas with a single user-defined function. It is usually easier to use and remember a single user-defined function name than a complex formula. As an example, you might have a worksheet with a range named *Sales* and a range named *Costs*, each of which contains the sales figures and costs for a particular quarter of the year. You might then enter a formula in the worksheet, similar to the following, that computes the percent profit using the named ranges in the worksheet:

```
=((SUM(Sales) -SUM(Costs))/SUM(Costs))*100
```

A formula of this length is fairly tedious to enter—and this formula is actually quite simple compared to some of the formulas that many Excel users use. The more often you use this formula, the more likely you are to make a typing mistake when you enter it. Also, it is not necessarily obvious what this formula does when you first see it. You can eliminate these problems by creating a VBA user-defined function for Excel. For example, you might create a function named `Calc_PcntProfit` that receives the range names as arguments, and then returns the result of the formula's computation as the function result. A user-defined function like this is easier to use and remember than the longer Excel formula.

Creating Function Procedures

You cannot use the macro recorder to record a function procedure, although you can edit a recorded macro and turn it into a function procedure. Most of the time, though, you create your function procedures by writing the function procedure directly into a VBA module.

Writing a Function Procedure

Function procedures are very similar to the VBA procedures you already know how to write. The main difference between a function procedure and other procedures—apart from the fact that functions return a value and procedures do not—is that you enclose a function procedure with the keywords Function and End Function instead of the Sub and End Sub keywords you are already familiar with.

Syntax

The general syntax for a function procedure is:

```
Function name([arglist])
    'VBA Statements
    [name = expression]
End Function
```

Every function procedure begins with the restricted keyword Function, followed by the name of the function procedure. *name* represents the name you choose for the function procedure. Function names must follow the same rules as any other identifier name in VBA: they must begin with a letter, may not contain spaces or any of the arithmetic, logical, or relational operator symbols, and may not duplicate any of VBA's restricted keywords.

After the function's name comes the function's argument list, enclosed in parentheses. In the syntax sample, *arglist* represents the argument list for your function procedure. *arglist* is optional—you don't have to write functions that use arguments, although you probably will want to. If you do include the argument list, separate each argument name with a comma (,).

The optional syntax element *name = expression* represents the *function assignment*, which tells VBA what value the function should return. Although this part of a function is, technically, optional, you should always include a function assignment statement in your function procedures. Finally, the function declaration ends with the keywords End Function.

> **Note:** Even if a function has no arguments—like VBA's Now, Date, or Time functions—you must include parentheses for the argument list in the function declaration. For instance, you might write a function procedure that returns the name of the file containing the current workbook, so you can insert the filename into a worksheet cell. A function like this doesn't need arguments—it doesn't require any outside information to do its job. Such a function would have a declaration like this:
>
> ```
> Function ThisBookName()
> ```

Usually, a function's purpose is to perform some computation or other manipulation of specific data, and to return the result of that manipulation. As you already know, you pass information to VBA's built-in functions by specifying values in the function's argument list. When you declare a function procedure, you list a name for each argument you intend to pass to your function, separating each argument name in the list with a comma. Argument names must follow the naming conventions that apply to any VBA identifier.

The names that you provide in the argument list are like variables: they refer to whatever value you provide at the time your function is called in a VBA statement or by Excel. Whenever the argument name appears in a statement inside the function, VBA behaves as if the argument name is a variable containing the value provided in the argument list in the statement that called your function.

> **Note:** Argument names have the same scope as variables declared locally within the function procedure—that is, argument variables are not accessible outside the function procedure in whose argument list they are declared.

Look again at the previous syntax sample, and the line containing the statement: *name = expression*. This line represents the *function assignment*. *name* is the function's name, and *expression* is any expression that produces the value you want the function to return. The function assignment tells VBA what value the function will return. Notice that the function assignment uses the function procedure's name as if it were a variable and assigns a value to it. Function procedures may have none, one, or several different function assignment statements.

The first function example you'll study helps manipulate strings. As you may remember from the preceding lesson, the Len function reports the length of a string—including any leading or trailing spaces. If you want to find the length of a string *excluding* leading and trailing spaces, you could use *nested* function calls (one function call inside another) like this:

```
StrLen = Len(Trim(AnyStr))
```

In the above statement, the Trim function first trims any leading and trailing spaces from the string stored in the variable **AnyStr**; the result from the Trim function provides the argument for the Len function so that the string length returned by Len excludes leading and trailing spaces.

This type of operation is a good candidate for a function procedure. Using a single call to your custom function procedure is simpler and easier than repeatedly writing the nested function call shown above. Listing 6.1 shows just such a simple function procedure, **SLen**, which returns the length of a string, excluding leading or trailing spaces.

Listing 6.1. A simple function procedure: SLen.

```
1:   Function SLen(tStr)
2:       SLen = Len(Trim(tStr))
3:   End Function
```

Line 1 contains the function declaration for **SLen**. The line begins with the required `Function` keyword, followed by the function name. After the function name is the opening parenthesis, which tells VBA that this is the start of the function's argument list. Next is the argument name **tStr**. The argument name tells VBA that one argument must be passed to the function procedure when it is called. Finally, line 1 ends with the closing parenthesis, which ends the function's argument list.

Line 2 of the **SLen** function is the line that does all of the function's work, and also contains the function assignment for **SLen**. When VBA evaluates the expression `Len(Trim(tStr))`, it takes the string received through the **tStr** argument and passes it to the VBA `Trim` function to remove any leading or trailing spaces. The result of the `Trim` function is, in turn, used as the argument for the `Len` function. VBA then assigns the result of the `Len` function to the function name, **Slen**— **SLen** therefore returns the length of the argument string, excluding any leading or trailing spaces.

When VBA evaluates the expression `Len(Trim(tStr))`, and assigns the expression's result to the **SLen** function name in line 2, VBA is performing the *function assignment*. The function assignment tells VBA what value the function should return.

Finally, line 3 ends the function procedure with the keywords `End Function`. After VBA executes this line, execution returns to whatever procedure statement called the **SLen** function, and VBA inserts the **SLen** function result in that statement.

DO	DON'T

DO make sure that you include a function assignment statement in your function procedures. There is no point in writing a function procedure that does not return a result.

DO remember that VBA doesn't generate any error messages if you forget to include a function assignment statement in your function procedure—you must make sure you include the function assignment yourself.

To use the **SLen** function, you would use a statement similar to the following, which displays the result of **SLen** for the string "　　　mad dog　　　":

```
MsgBox SLen("    mad dog    ")
```

In this statement, the argument string has four leading and trailing spaces each, and the length of the string (as reported by VBA's Len function) is 15. The **SLen** function reports the length of the string without its leading and trailing spaces; the above statement displays the number 7.

Creating User-Defined Functions for Excel

Function procedures that follow certain restrictions on their activities are called user-defined functions (abbreviated UDF), and are the only function procedures that Excel can use in a worksheet cell's formula.

All restrictions on user-defined functions stem from one basic restriction: a UDF cannot alter Excel's environment in any way. This means that a user-defined function cannot select, insert, delete, or format any data in any worksheet, chart sheet, or other sheet. A UDF also cannot add, delete, or rename sheets or workbooks, nor change screen views, and so on. For example, you cannot use a function procedure as a user-defined function in Excel if it selects cells or changes the current worksheet in any way.

In addition, a UDF may not set object properties or use object methods—in most cases, setting object properties or using object methods results in changes to Excel's environment (objects, methods, and properties are described in the next lesson). A user-defined function may, however, retrieve object property values, and execute any object methods that do not change Excel's environment.

Usually, a user-defined function should only make calculations or perform manipulations based on data received through its argument list or retrieved from Excel. You could use the **SLen** function shown in Listing 6.1 as a user-defined function—it meets all of the requirements.

Note: Neither VBA nor Excel displays an error message if you use a function procedure that does not actually meet the restrictions for user-defined functions as a UDF. Instead, your function is just unable to return a result. For example, if you try to insert a value in an Excel worksheet cell by using a function procedure that violates the rules for user-defined functions, the cell displays the Excel #VALUE! error message, which indicates only that the function or formula for that cell is unable to return a valid result.

Declaring a Data Type for a Function's Result

Unless you specify otherwise, the result that your function procedure returns has the Variant data type. As you learned in Day 3, values stored or handled as Variant data types take up more memory than any other data type, and also require more time to handle.

You can specify the data type of a function result for the same reasons you specify the data type of variables and constants: to speed up the execution of your code, to use memory more efficiently, to make your code easier to understand, and to help catch programmer errors by forcing an awareness of when VBA converts data from one type to another. Consider declaring a specific data type result for all of the function procedures that you write.

To specify the data type of a function's return value, simply add the keyword As and the desired data type name to the end of the function declaration line.

Syntax

Including the function type declaration, the general syntax for a function declaration is:

```
Function name([arglist]) [As type]
```

All the other parts of the function declaration syntax are the same as shown previously. *type* represents the name of any VBA data type. *name* and *arglist* are the same as described previously.

VBA prohibits you from assigning an incompatible data type to the function's result in any function procedure that has a declared data type for its result. If, for example, you mistakenly write a function assignment statement so that you assign, say, an Integer to the result of a function with a declared String type result, then VBA displays a type mismatch error.

If you assign a data type that is not the same as the declared return type for the function procedure but is otherwise compatible, then VBA converts the value to the type specified for the function when it returns the function result. For example, if you assign a Double data type to a function whose result you declared as a Long, then VBA does not produce any errors; it just converts the Double to a Long type when it returns the function result.

Declaring the data type of a function result has one other effect: if the function procedure ends without executing a function assignment statement, then VBA returns a zero-length string for String type functions, and 0 for function procedures that return a numeric data type. (An untyped function procedure that ends without executing a function assignment statement returns a Variant type result containing the special value Empty.)

Listing 6.2 shows the **SLen** function modified so that it always returns a value of the Long data type.

Listing 6.2. Specifying the data type of the Slen function result.

```
1:   Function SLen(tStr) As Long
2:   'returns length of tStr, excluding leading/trailing spaces
3:       SLen = Len(Trim(tStr))
4:   End Function
```

Line 1 contains the function declaration for **SLen**. This function has the same name and argument list as the function in Listing 6.1, but this time, the data type of the function's result is also declared. After the closing parenthesis that ends the function's argument list, the As keyword appears, followed by the Long type name. This tells VBA that the **SLen** function should always return a result with the Long data type.

The Long data type was chosen as the data type for the **SLen** function result for two reasons. First, because the length of a string is always a whole number—you can never have a fractional part of a character. Second, because an Integer type does not have enough range to hold the maximum possible string length—the largest positive number an Integer data type can represent is 32,767, but strings may be up to approximately 2 billion characters in length. The Long data type, therefore, is the smallest data type that still accommodates the entire possible range of values that the function might return.

Line 2 is a comment line stating the purpose and action of the function procedure.

Line 3 works exactly the same as line 2 in listing 6.1. Because this version of **SLen** has a data type specified for its return value, VBA would display a type mismatch error if you assigned, say, a string value to **SLen** in line 3, instead of a numeric value.

Without the typed function result, if you did assign a String type value instead of a numeric value to the function result, VBA would accept the string in the function assignment to **SLen**, and **SLen** would return that string value as its result. If you then used the **SLen** result in an arithmetic expression, the arithmetic expression might result in an erroneous computation, or a runtime error of some kind. Tracing errors caused by function return values of an unexpected data type can be difficult because the error may propagate through several function or procedure calls before producing a noticeable error. Declaring the data type of a function's result helps you prevent and detect the source of such errors.

DO	DON'T

DO choose a data type for the result of your function procedures that requires the least amount of memory, but still accommodates the full range of possible values that the function might return. For general-purpose numeric or mathematical functions, a Double type for the function result is fairly typical.

DO consider how you intend to use the function when you choose the data type for the function's result—the intended use of a function procedure may affect your choice for the function's data type. For example, if you intend to use your function procedure solely to perform some type of financial computation, you should declare a Currency type for the function result.

DO include a line or two of comments for each function or other procedure that you write in order to document your VBA code, and to help you if you later need to modify the code. (Although the purpose and operation of a function you write today may seem obvious, it may not seem so obvious three months from now.)

Declaring Data Types for a Function's Arguments

Unless you specify otherwise, VBA passes all of a function procedure's arguments into the function procedure as Variant data types. Like a function procedure's result, you can also declare specific data types for each argument in the function procedure's argument list.

You use arguments with specific data types for the same (by now) familiar reasons that you use for typing variables or function results. Typing arguments for a function procedure also helps you (or the function's user) enter arguments of the correct type, in the correct order, when the function is called.

To declare specific data types for a function procedure's arguments, simply use the As keyword, followed by the desired data type name, after the argument name in the argument list. Listing 6.3 shows the SLen function modified to accept only String type data in the **tStr** argument.

 Listing 6.3. Specifying the data type of the SLen function argument.

```
1:  Function SLen(tStr As String) As Long
2:  'returns length of tStr, excluding leading/trailing spaces
3:      SLen = Len(Trim(tStr))
4:  End Function
```

Analysis

Except for the function procedure declaration in line 1, Listing 6.3 is identical to Listing 6.2. Now that the argument type is declared, VBA only allows values of the String data type to appear as the argument when the **SLen** function is called. Calling **SLen** with any other data type value—even a Variant—as an argument produces a type mismatch error (specifically, an *argument type mismatch*).

Creating Optional Arguments

Usually, all of the arguments you list in a function procedure's argument list must be supplied each time you call the function; these arguments are *required* arguments. You've already learned about optional function arguments from working with VBA's InputBox and MsgBox functions. You can create optional arguments for your own function procedures, as well.

Use optional arguments to control how a function performs its task. For example, one of the optional arguments for the MsgBox function controls how many command buttons appear in the dialog box that MsgBox displays. The **FlipCase** function shown in Listing 6.4 uses an optional argument to control how many characters the function operates on.

When you include optional arguments in an argument list, you must list all of the required arguments first; after the first optional argument, all succeeding arguments in the argument list must also be optional. You cannot specify a data type for optional arguments; optional function arguments must always be a Variant type. VBA displays an error message if you attempt to specify the data type for an optional argument.

To create an optional argument, insert the VBA Optional keyword in front of the argument's name in the argument list of the function procedure declaration, as shown in line 1 of Listing 6.4.

Listing 6.4. The FlipCase function: optional arguments.

```
1:  Function FlipCase(tStr As String, Optional nChar) As String
2:  ' reverses the case — upper to lower, lower to upper — of
3:  ' the first nChar characters in tStr. If nChar omitted,
4:  ' flips the case of all chars in tStr
5:      Dim k As Long                    'loop counter
6:      Dim TestC As String * 1
7:
8:      If IsMissing(nChar) Then
9:          nChar = Len(tStr)
10:     End If
11:
12:     For k = 1 To nChar
13:         TestC = Mid(tStr, k, 1)
14:         If (StrComp(TestC, "A", 0) >= 0) And _
15:             (StrComp(TestC, "Z", 0) <= 0) Then
16:           Mid(tStr, k, 1) = LCase(TestC)
```

continues

Listing 6.4. continued

```
17:         ElseIf (StrComp(TestC, "a", 0) >= 0) And _
18:             (StrComp(TestC, "z", 0) <= 0) Then
19:            Mid(tStr, k, 1) = UCase(TestC)
20:         End If
21:      Next k
22:      FlipCase = tStr
23: End Function
```

Line 1 contains the function declaration for **FlipCase**, which has two arguments in its argument list. The first argument, **tStr** has the specific String type declared for it. When **FlipCase** is called, the first argument is required and must be a string. A comma separates the two arguments in the list; the second argument is prefaced with the Optional keyword, telling VBA that this argument may be omitted when the **FlipCase** function is called. (If the **FlipCase** function had more than the two arguments shown, any additional arguments in the list after the **nChar** argument would have to be optional, as well.) No data type is declared for the optional **nChar** argument; optional arguments must always be a Variant type. (Remember, any untyped variable, function, or argument automatically becomes a Variant type.)

Finally, the **FlipCase** function declaration ends by specifying that the data type returned by **FlipCase** must always be a String type.

The **FlipCase** function is more complex than any of the previous examples for either procedures or functions, and includes a couple of program structures that you have not seen before—one for decision-making, and one for repeating a group of actions. Although each of these structures is described in detail in later lessons, the next few paragraphs describe the essentials behind the operation of the **FlipCase** function procedure.

Lines 2 through 4 simply contain the function procedure's documenting comments. Lines 5 and 6 contain the declarations for the variables used by **FlipCase**.

Lines 8 through 10 illustrate a typical use of an important built-in VBA function: IsMissing. The IsMissing function exists for the sole purpose of determining whether or not an optional argument was included in a function procedure's call; it returns True only if the optional argument was *not* included.

Lines 8 through 10 use an If...Then decision structure (described in detail in Day 8) to alter the value of **nChar**, depending on whether or not the argument was included in the function call. If **nChar** is missing, then it is set to equal the length of the string in the **tStr** argument. In this way, **FlipCase** controls how many characters are affected by its manipulations—only a few, or the entire string.

Lines 12 through 21 carry out the actual work of the **FlipCase** function, and consist of two different control structures, one nested inside the other. The outermost control structure is a

For...Next loop, which begins in line 12. (For...Next loops are described in detail in Day 9.) A For...Next loop causes the statements it encloses to be repeated a set number of times. In this case, the statements enclosed by the For...Next loop are repeated the number of times specified by **nChar**.

The first statement inside the For...Next loop (line 13) uses the VBA Mid function to copy one character from **tStr** and store it in the **TestC** variable. (The variable **k** contains the current count of times through the For...Next loop, so the first time through the loop the first character of **tStr** is copied, the second time through the loop the second character of **tStr** is copied, and so on.) The character is copied to the **TestC** variable so that the Mid function only has to be called once, therefore saving some execution time—using the **TestC** variable to hold the character being tested also helps make the program code easier to read.

After copying the character to be tested, line 14 uses another If...Then structure to determine whether or not the character in **TestC** is an uppercase letter. Notice the line continuation character at the end of line 14. The logical expression in lines 14 and 15 is True if the character is greater than or equal to "A", and is less than or equal to "Z"—that is, whether the character is in the range of uppercase letters. The expression uses the VBA StrComp function to ensure that the comparisons are always binary comparisons, rather than text comparisons. Using the StrComp function ensures that this function will always work as expected, regardless of the Option Compare setting.

If the character in **TestC** is an uppercase letter, then line 16 executes. Line 16 uses the VBA Mid procedure, which replaces one or more characters in a string (don't be confused; VBA has both a Mid function and a Mid procedure). The Mid procedure statement in line 16 replaces the character in **tStr** that was originally copied into **TestC** with its lowercase equivalent, which is obtained by using the LCase function.

If the character in **TestC** is not an uppercase letter, execution passes to line 17, where **TestC** is again tested—this time to see if it is a lowercase letter. The logical expression establishes whether or not the character in **TestC** is in the range of lowercase letters. Again, the StrComp function is used in the expression to ensure that the string comparisons are binary comparisons, regardless of the Option Compare setting. (If a text comparison were made instead of a binary comparison, the **FlipCase** function wouldn't work, since it would be unable to distinguish between upper- and lowercase letters!)

If the character in **TestC** is a lowercase letter, then line 19 executes. Line 19 also uses the Mid procedure to replace the character in **tStr** that was originally copied into **TestC** with its uppercase equivalent, obtained by using VBA's UCase function.

Notice that, if the character in **TestC** is neither an uppercase nor a lowercase letter, the function makes no alteration in **tStr**—if the character isn't an uppercase or lowercase letter, then it must be a digit or punctuation character, and no case conversion is needed (or even possible).

Line 21 is the end of the `For...Next` loop; when the `For...Next` loop has executed the specified number of times (equivalent to the length of the string in **tStr**), execution passes to line 22, which contains the function assignment statement. The function has completed its work, and returns the altered value in **tStr** as the function result.

Understanding and Controlling How VBA Passes Arguments

Now that you know how to create function procedures with typed arguments and optional arguments, you're ready to take a closer look at the mechanisms VBA uses to actually pass argument data to a function procedure. Next, you learn how to control which mechanism VBA uses, and when to choose one mechanism over another.

Understanding Arguments Passed by Reference and by Value

There are two ways that VBA passes information into a function procedure: *by reference*, and *by value*. By default, VBA passes all arguments by reference. When VBA passes data through a function argument by reference, VBA really just passes a memory address which refers to the original data specified in the function's argument list at the time the function was called. This means that, if your function alters the values in any of its argument variables, the original data passed to the function through that argument variable is also changed.

When VBA passes an argument by value, however, VBA makes a *copy* of the original data and passes that copy to the function. If your function changes the value in an argument passed by value, only the copy of the data changes; the original data does not change. Passing by reference allows the original data passed through a function argument to be changed by the function; passing by value does not allow the original data value to be changed.

To better understand the difference between passing argument values by reference and by value, consider this analogy: A colleague tells you that there is a sales proposal in a basket on her desk, and asks you to read the proposal and write your comments in the margins. When you carry out the requested task, you get her proposal from the basket on the desk, and write your comments directly on it; when you are done, you leave the altered proposal in the same basket you found it in. Your colleague passed the data (the sales proposal) to you *by reference*. You received a reference to the location of the data, and changed that data.

If, on the other hand, your colleague gave you a photocopy of the sales proposal, and asked you to write your comments on the photocopy, she would have passed the data to you *by value*. You received a copy of the actual data (its value), changed that data, and returned the changed copy. Your colleague's original sales proposal remains unchanged and unaffected by the transaction.

Because passing by reference allows a function to change the original data value of its arguments, arguments passed by reference may have undesirable side effects. Listing 6.5 shows a procedure designed to test the **FlipCase** function in Listing 6.4.

Listing 6.5. Test procedure to demonstrate FlipCase function's side effects.

```
1:  Sub Test_FlipCase()
2:      Dim UserIn As String, Num As Integer
3:      UserIn = InputBox(prompt:="enter some text: ", _
4:                       Title:="FlipCase Test")
5:      Num = 5
6:      MsgBox FlipCase(UserIn, Num)
7:      MsgBox UserIn
8:      MsgBox FlipCase(UserIn)
9:      MsgBox UserIn
10: End Sub
```

Line 2 of this procedure declares some variables. Next, line 3 uses the InputBox function to ask the user to enter some text. Line 5 sets the variable **Num** to 5. Line 6 tests the **FlipCase** function with its optional argument (a numeric variable arbitrarily assigned a value of 5) and uses MsgBox to display the **FlipCase** function result. Line 7 displays the original value—the string stored in **UserIn**—passed to **FlipCase**. Line 8 tests the **FlipCase** function without its optional argument; line 9 again displays the contents of the **UserIn** variable.

If you enter both Listing 6.4 and 6.5, run the **Test_FlipCase** procedure, and then enter the string *FlipCase* as the test string, you may notice some peculiar results. In line 6 of Listing 6.5, VBA executes the first call to the **FlipCase** function. As expected, the function returns the string *fLIPcase*—a copy of the string stored in **UserIn** with the case of the first five characters reversed (shown in Figure 6.1). Line 7, however, displays the original string input by the user, and it too has changed to *fLIPcase* (line 7 displays a dialog box identical to the one in Figure 6.1). If you look again at Listing 6.4 (lines 16 and 19), you can see that the **FlipCase** function directly alters the string argument **tStr**. Because **tStr** is passed by reference (VBA, by default, passes all arguments by reference), any changes to **tStr** are really changes to the original data in the **UserIn** variable in the **Test_FlipCase** procedure.

Figure 6.1.
Both lines 6 and 7 in Listing 6.5 produce this dialog box, showing that the **FlipCase** *function has modified the contents of the argument variable passed to it.*

You can see the same thing happen again when lines 8 and 9 in Listing 6.5 execute: the function correctly returns the string *FlipCASE* as its result, but now the original string the user entered is also changed to *FlipCASE*.

Specifying Whether to Pass an Argument by Reference or by Value

Clearly, side-effects caused by a function altering values in arguments passed by reference are not necessary, and—in most cases—highly undesirable. Side-effects can cause serious problems elsewhere in your programs. Tracking down problems caused by side-effects is often very difficult, because there is seldom an immediately obvious cause for a variable's change in value. (*Side-effect* is a general term used to refer to any alteration in a variable's value, or in the environment of an executing program, that is not explicitly programmed.)

To prevent side-effects like this, the function needs to work with a copy of the argument value, instead of the original data. You could, of course, declare a local variable in the function procedure and copy the arguments into that local variable. Copying argument values into local function variables, however, is usually not desirable: the additional variables increase the memory required by the function, and increase the amount of work that you, the programmer must perform. The extra variables may also clutter up your program code, making it more difficult to understand and troubleshoot.

An easier and more desirable way to ensure that a function works only with copies of an argument value, rather than the original argument value, is to tell VBA that the argument should be passed by value, rather than by reference. (Remember, passing by value gives the function a *copy* of the argument value; passing by reference gives the function access to the *original* data in the argument.)

To specify whether VBA passes an argument by value or by reference, use the ByVal and ByRef keywords in front of the argument for which you want to specify the passing method. As you might expect from their names, ByVal causes VBA to pass the argument by value, and ByRef causes VBA to pass the argument by reference.

The following line shows the function declaration for the **FlipCase** function, modified so that the **tStr** argument is passed by value and the **nChar** argument is passed by reference:

```
Function FlipCase(ByVal tStr As String, Optional ByRef nChar) As String
```

The **nChar** argument can be safely passed by reference, because it is modified by the **FlipCase** function only when it is not present as an argument. If the ByRef keyword for the **nChar** argument is omitted from the declaration above, **nChar** is still passed by reference because VBA, by default, passes all arguments by reference.

If you change the **FlipCase** function declaration in Listing 6.4 to match the declaration shown above, and then run the **Test_FlipCase** procedure again, you can see that the original string entered by the user is no longer affected by the **FlipCase** function.

DO	DON'T

DO check carefully each time you write a function procedure to make sure that it does not alter its arguments.

DO add the ByVal keyword to each argument that your function procedure modifies.

DON'T declare arguments by value (ByVal) unless your function procedure modifies that argument, because passing arguments by value can use more memory and require slightly longer to execute than passing arguments by reference—passing an argument by value causes VBA to make a copy of the data for the argument.

DO go ahead and declare an argument with the ByVal keyword to pass it by value if you have doubts as to whether that particular argument should be passed by reference or by value—the memory and speed penalties of passing by value are not that great. Also, passing an argument by value is still more efficient, and makes for cleaner code, than making your own copy of the argument value in a local variable.

Using Function Procedures in Visual Basic for Applications

You use your own function procedures in VBA statements just as you do any of VBA's built-in functions; all of the same rules and conventions explained in Day 5 for using built-in functions apply to using your own function procedures. Lines 6 and 8 of Listing 6.5 show typical calls to a function procedure.

Remember, you must include the parentheses around the argument list when you call a function, unless you intend to ignore the function's result. (Like VBA's built-in functions, you can also ignore the result of your own function procedures—although you'll seldom need or want to.)

If you want to use named arguments when you use your own function procedures, just use the names from the argument list in your function procedure's declaration. For example, to use a named argument in a call to the **SLen** function (Listing 6.3), use a statement similar to the following (**AnyStr** and **MyString** are string variables):

```
AnyStr = SLen(tStr:=MyString)
```

To use named arguments in a call to the `FlipCase` function in Listing 6.4, use a statement similar to this next one (**AnyStr** and **UserIn** are string variables; **AnyNum** is an integer variable):

```
AnyStr = FlipCase(tStr:=UserIn, nChar:=AnyNum)
```

Using the Object Browser to Find and Insert Your Function Procedures

If you have trouble remembering all the named arguments for one of your own functions, you can use the Object Browser to see which of your function procedures are currently available, and to paste the function name and all its named arguments into your program—just like you would for one of VBA's built-in functions.

 To use the Object Browser with your own functions, start the Object Browser as you have already learned to do: choose the **View | O**bject Browser command or click the Object Browser button on the Visual Basic toolbar to display the Object Browser dialog box.

You already know how to use the Object Browser to display the available VBA or Excel functions. The **Libraries/Workbooks** drop-down list box lists all of the currently open application files, as well as the always-present **VBA** and **Excel** choices. To display the custom functions (and other procedures) in a particular workbook, follow these steps:

1. Select the workbook's filename in the **Libraries/Workbooks** drop-down list. Figure 6.2 shows the Object Browser dialog box with the DAY06.XLS workbook file selected in the **Libraries/Workbooks** box.

   Once you have selected a file in the **Libraries/Workbooks** list box, the **O**bjects/Modules list contains a list of all of the modules in the selected file.

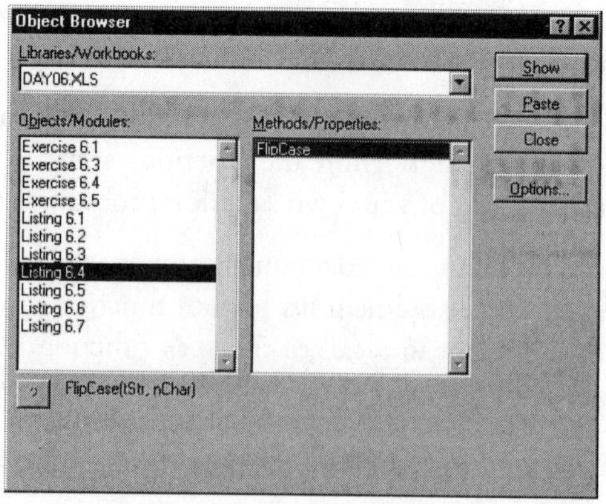

Figure 6.2.

Use the Object Browser to paste function or procedure names and arguments into your program, or to show the source code for a function or procedure.

2. Select a module in the **O**bjects/Modules list. Figure 6.2 shows the module titled **Listing 6.4** selected.

   After you select a module in the **O**bjects/Modules list, the **M**ethods/Properties list box contains a list of all procedures and function procedures declared in the selected module.

3. Select the function procedure that you want to use in the **M**ethods/Properties list box.

Refer again to Figure 6.2; the `FlipCase` function from Listing 6.4 is selected in the **M**ethods/ Properties list box. Notice that—just like the built-in VBA and host application functions—the function name and all of its arguments are displayed near the bottom of the Object Browser dialog box (underneath the **O**bjects/Modules and **M**ethods/Properties lists). Unlike the built-in functions, however, no description of the function's purpose appears, and the **?** help button is disabled. (Adding descriptions for your function procedures is described a little later in this section.)

To paste the function name and all its named arguments into your program code at the current position of the insertion point, choose the **P**aste button in the Object Browser dialog box—just as you would for a built-in VBA function.

Note: You can use the Object Browser to paste in your function calls in any VBA host application, not just Excel. The procedure for doing so is the same as that just described for Excel.

Using the Object Browser to Display a Function's Code

Notice, in Figure 6.2, that the **S**how button is enabled. The **S**how button has not yet been discussed, because it has always been disabled in previous examples and figures. The **S**how button is only enabled if the source code for a selected function or other procedure is available. When you display VBA's or Excel's built-in functions—or functions and procedures from an add-in program—the program source code is not available to you, and the **S**how button is disabled. With your own functions and procedures, however, the source code is available, and the **S**how button is enabled.

Click the **S**how button to view the source code for a function or procedure you have selected in the **M**ethods/Properties list box of the Object Browser dialog box. VBA makes the module containing the selected function or procedure the current module, and moves the insertion point to the first line of the source code after the function or procedure declaration. If you choose the

Show button to view the source code for a function or procedure that is in a hidden module or in a hidden file, VBA unhides the module or file before displaying the function or procedure source code.

> **Note:** You cannot use the Macro dialog box (opened by choosing the **Tools** | **Macro** command) to execute a function procedure. VBA expects function procedures, by their nature, to return a value, and assumes that there is no point in executing the function by itself; VBA therefore does not list function procedures in the **Macro** Name/Reference list in the Macro dialog box. You can only execute a function procedure by using it in a VBA statement, by calling it from Excel, or by using the function in an expression in the Immediate pane of the Debug window. (Using the Debug window is described in Day 14.)

Entering a Function Procedure Description with the Object Browser

In earlier lessons, you learned how to use the **O**ptions button in the Object Browser dialog box to enter or edit a description for a macro procedure, and to specify a **T**ools menu choice and a shortcut key for your macro procedures. Although it does not make sense to assign a function procedure to a menu choice or a shortcut key, adding a description to your function procedure is often useful. For example, the description you enter for a function by using the Object Browser appears not only in the Object Browser, but also in Excel's Function Wizard. Providing a description for your function procedure can therefore assist someone trying to use your function in a worksheet cell formula.

To enter a description for your function procedure, follow these steps:

1. Select your function procedure in the Object Browser, as already described.

2. Choose the **O**ptions button. VBA displays the Macro Options dialog box shown in Figure 6.3.

3. Enter a description for the function procedure in the **D**escription text box. Figure 6.3 shows a description of the `FlipCase` function already entered in the **D**escription text box.

4. Choose OK. Excel closes the Macro Options dialog box and returns you to the Object Browser. (You already know about the menu and shortcut key options in the Macro Options dialog box; the remaining options are described in later lessons, as they become relevant.)

Figure 6.3.

Enter a helpful description for your function procedures in the Macro Options dialog box.

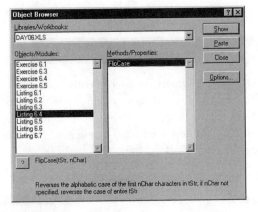

Figure 6.4 shows how the Object Browser dialog box appears after adding the description shown in Figure 6.3. Notice that the display of the function name and its arguments at the bottom of the Object Browser dialog box now includes the new description for the `FlipCase` function.

Figure 6.4.

The description you add in the Macro Options dialog box displays in the Object Browser dialog box.

Note: If the function procedure that you want to add or edit a description for is in a hidden module or hidden file (such as a workbook file), the **O**ptions button in the Object Browser dialog box is disabled. You must first unhide the module sheet or file before you can add or edit a function procedure's (or other procedure's) description.

Using User-Defined Functions in Excel

To use a user-defined function in Excel, enter the function name and its arguments as a formula in a worksheet cell the same way you would enter any of Excel's built-in functions. VBA even makes your user-defined functions available through Excel's Function Wizard. (Remember, a user-defined function is just a function procedure that meets certain requirements for use by Excel.)

If you can't remember the user-defined function's name or its arguments, you can usually find user-defined functions listed under the User-Defined category in Excel's Function Wizard. Figure 6.5 shows the Function Wizard - Step 1 of 2 dialog box, with **User Defined** selected in the Function Category list, and the `FlipCase` function selected in the Function Name list. (Refer to your Excel documentation or online help for complete information on using the Function Wizard.) Notice that the `FlipCase` function name and its arguments display at the bottom of the Function Wizard - Step 1 of 2 dialog box—along with any description that you entered for that user-defined function in the Object Browser (as described in the preceding section of this chapter).

Complete step 2 of the Function Wizard as you would for any of Excel's built-in functions, filling in values for the function arguments as necessary.

DO	DON'T
DO use the Object Browser to enter a description for your user-defined functions, especially if you intend to develop special-purpose functions in VBA and distribute them for use by other Excel users. You might also want to change the category of the function (as described next) from User Defined to some other category—depending on the purpose of the function.	

Figure 6.5.

Using Excel's Function Wizard to enter a user-defined function in a worksheet cell.

 Tip: If you use a UDF in a worksheet cell, and the displayed result of the function is the Excel #VALUE! error value, carefully double-check the code in your function procedure to make sure that it does not violate any of the rules for user-defined procedures. Neither Excel nor VBA prohibit you from using a function procedure that violates the rules for user-defined procedures in a worksheet cell. Because the function procedure violates the UDF rules, however, VBA does not execute the function; instead, it returns the Excel #VALUE! error value to the cell.

Changing a User-Defined Function's Category

By default, all of the user-defined functions that you write appear in the User Defined category of the Function Wizard. You may, however, prefer that a function appear in a different category. For example, it might be easier for you (or another Excel user) to find functions such as the **SLen** and **FlipCase** examples in this chapter under the Text category in the Function Wizard—since both of these functions perform operations on text and return text (string) results.

You can use the Object Browser to change the category of any user-defined function. To change a function's category, follow these steps:

1. Open the Object Browser dialog box, and select the function whose category you want to change in the **M**ethods/Properties list, as you have already learned to do.

2. Choose the **O**ptions button to display the Macro Options dialog box (pictured in Figure 6.3).

3. Select the function procedure's new category in the **F**unction Category drop-down list box near the bottom of the Macro Options dialog box.

4. Choose OK when you are satisfied with the function procedure's new option settings.

Figure 6.6 shows the Excel Function Wizard - Step 1 of 2 dialog box, this time showing the **FlipCase** function selected in the **Text** category.

Figure 6.6.

The `FlipCase` *user-defined function appears in the Text category in the Excel Function Wizard after using the Object Browser to change the function's category.*

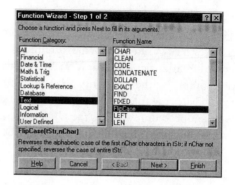

Designing Function Procedures and User-Defined Functions

Whenever you write a function procedure, always keep in mind that the special purpose of a function is to return a value of some kind. Keep your function procedures simple and to the point. Usually, a function should only contain the program code necessary to perform the desired computation or data manipulation; a function should never carry out actions not directly related to producing its return value.

Consider writing a function any time you find yourself using the same mathematical formula in a program or worksheet more than two or three times. As the examples in this chapter show, function procedures are also useful for manipulating data other than numbers. Consider writing a function any time you find yourself using the same expression or group of expressions more than two or three times.

Although the expression for a calculation might be quite simple, you should still write a function procedure if you use the expression frequently. By writing a function procedure, you eliminate any chance that you'll make a typing mistake when you enter the expression, and you also give the expression a meaningful name. For instance, you might find that you frequently enter a date expression—such as `Now + 30`—which computes a due date for an invoice based on the date the invoice is issued. By writing a function named **InvoiceDue** that returns the invoice's due date, you not only ensure that the calculation is performed the same way every time it is needed, you also make your program code self-documenting.

Although you can ignore the result of a function procedure, you should write your function procedures so that ignoring their result is meaningless. This is another way of saying that your functions should not perform actions beyond those absolutely necessary to produce the desired return result.

DO	**DON'T**

DON'T consider the VBA `MsgBox` function as a guiding example for writing functions. The `MsgBox` function fulfills truly unique needs in VBA; as a result, it performs much more work, with many more options, than functions typically should.

DO consider VBA functions such as `StrComp`, `Mid`, the data conversion functions `CStr`, `CDbl`, and so on as guiding examples of how a function procedure should perform. Each function performs a single task, and returns a single result without altering the original data contained in any arguments passed to it.

Although you may be tempted to use arguments passed by reference to create a function that returns more than one result—by using the function return and one or more modified arguments to get results—*don't* do this. A function should *never* change the original data in the arguments passed to it. As discussed later in Day 11, there are legitimate circumstances under which you will want to—and should—modify values in arguments passed by reference; in those circumstances, you should use a procedure, not a function. Make sure that your functions do not alter arguments passed by reference; use the `ByVal` keyword to pass arguments by value whenever necessary.

Many of the functions that you write will turn out to have uses in programs or worksheets other than the one for which you originally write the function procedure. The **SLen** and **FlipCase** functions used in this chapter, for example, are very general-purpose functions—they are likely to be useful in a number of different expressions in several different procedures, and possibly a few worksheets, as well.

Because any function procedure in any currently open workbook is available to any other currently open workbook, you can gather general-purpose functions together into a single workbook. By gathering general-purpose function procedures together into a single workbook, you create a *library* of functions. For example, you might put all of your general-purpose function procedures in a workbook file named MYFUNCS.XLS. Creating libraries of functions and procedures is described in Day 11.

DO	**DON'T**

DO double-check every function you write to make sure that the function contains a function assignment. That is, be certain that your function will return a result other than the default empty Variant, zero-length String, or zero numeric value.

DO avoid side-effects by being certain that you include the `ByVal` keyword for every argument that the function procedure modifies.

> **DO** make sure that your function procedure's program code adheres to all of the restrictions for user-defined functions explained at the beginning of this chapter if you expect to use your function as a UDF.

Designing Functions for Excel

When you write function procedures for use as UDFs in Excel worksheets, there are a few facts you should be aware of, above and beyond the general requirements for user-defined functions:

☐ User-defined functions that you intend to use in Excel cannot have names that resemble either A1 or R1C1 style cell reference notations.

☐ Any string (text) data returned from VBA to Excel cannot be greater than 255 characters in length. If your UDF returns a string greater than 255 characters in length to an Excel worksheet cell, Excel truncates the string to the maximum length of 255 characters before inserting it into the worksheet cell.

If you write a UDF for Excel that returns a date value, make certain that you specify the data type of the function's result as a Date type. Excel only applies a date format to a function result in a worksheet cell if it has the VBA Date data type. (Excel converts the VBA Date type to an Excel date automatically.)

One final concern exists regarding user-defined functions for Excel and centers around what point in time Excel actually calls the user-defined function in order to calculate or recalculate the worksheet cell formula of which the UDF is a part.

By default, Excel calls a UDF to recalculate the worksheet cell formula whenever the values used for the function's arguments change—much the same way Excel determines when to recalculate any worksheet formula. You can, however, set up a UDF so that Excel recalculates it whenever Excel recalculates *any* cell in the worksheet.

You should mark a UDF as volatile whenever its argument values don't come from other worksheet cell values. For example, assume you have a UDF named **PcntProfit** that computes a percentage profit. This UDF might have two arguments, one to specify the worksheet cell that contains the total income figure, and another to specify the worksheet cell that contains the total cost. Because the **PcntProfit** function's arguments specify cell coordinates, changing the *contents* of the cell doesn't change the **PcntProfit** function's argument value. If you edit the contents of either the total cost or total income cells, Excel will not recalculate **PcntProfit**; the **PcntProfit** function may then display erroneous results. If you mark this UDF as volatile, however, it will always display the correct value, because Excel will recalculate it whenever you change any cell on the worksheet.

A user-defined function that recalculates whenever Excel recalculates any cell in the worksheet is called a *volatile* function. To mark a UDF as a volatile function, add the following statement to the function, immediately after the function declaration:

```
Application.Volatile
```

This VBA statement that marks a UDF as a volatile function is really a type of procedure (called a *method*) that belongs to Excel. Because the method belongs to Excel, you must specify the `Application` object when you use the `Volatile` method—just like you must specify the `Application` object when you use an Excel function in a VBA statement. Listing 6.6 shows a volatile function, named **PcntProfit**, which returns a number representing the percent of profit earned, given gross sales and net costs.

Listing 6.6. A volatile user-defined function.

```
1:  Function PcntProfit(grSales As Currency, _
2:              netCosts As Currency) As Currency
3:      Application.Volatile
4:      PcntProfit = ((grSales - netCosts) / netCosts) * 100
5:  End Function
```

Lines 1 and 2 contain the function declaration for **PcntProfit**. (Notice the line continuation symbol at the end of line 1; this declaration was put on two lines to make it more readable.) **PcntProfit** has two arguments, **grSales** and **netCosts**; both arguments are required. Each argument has its data type declared as the Currency type. Because no argument passing method is specified, both arguments are passed by reference—the default passing method. The **PcntProfit** function declaration ends by specifying that the function's result is always a Currency data type. The Currency type was selected for both the function arguments and the function's result because this function is intended primarily for use with values representing money.

Line 3 contains the `Application.Volatile` statement; as required, it is the first statement in the function after the function declaration. The `Application.Volatile` statement "registers" the user-defined function with Excel, so that Excel calls the function to recalculate the worksheet cell formula in which the function appears whenever Excel recalculates *any* cell in the worksheet.

Understanding Recursion

Before ending this lesson on writing your own function procedures, there is one final concept that is important for you to understand, although it is not directly a part of creating VBA function procedures.

A *recursive* function or procedure is one which calls itself. Almost always, recursion is a mistake on the part of the programmer and results in outright program *crashes*, or failures—the most common symptom of a recursion problem is an out-of-memory or out-of-stack-space error. (A *stack* is a temporary working area of your computer's memory. VBA uses the stack memory area to hold interim expression results, copies of function arguments passed by value, function procedure results, and any other time it needs temporary working space. If your procedures use lots of memory while they are working, they can use up their temporary work space.)

Analyzing a Recursive Function's Operation

Listing 6.7 shows a function, named **Power**, that returns the power of a number, given the number and the power to raise it to.

Listing 6.7. The power function: a recursive example.

```
1:  Function Power(num As Double, pwr As Integer) As Double
2:  'recursively raises num to the power specified by pwr
3:      If pwr = 0 Then
4:          Power = 1                           'ends recursion
5:      Else
6:          Power = num * Power(num, pwr - 1)   'recursion
7:      End If
8:  End Function
```

Line 1 contains the **Power** function declaration. **Power** has two required arguments, **num** and **pwr**, and returns a Double type result.

Look closely at line 6 and notice that this line of the function calls itself. The **Power** function works by taking advantage of the fact that a number raised to a power *n* is the same as that number multiplied by itself to the *n-1* power. For example, 2^3 is the same as $2 \times 2^{3-1}$ or 2×2^2.

To understand how the **Power** function works, assume that you initially call the function with the following statement to display the result of raising 2 to the third power:

```
MsgBox Power(2, 3)
```

At this point, in the first call, the **num** argument contains 2 and the **pwr** argument contains 3. Line 3 starts an If...Then statement which determines whether or not it is time to stop the recursion. This line tests to see whether or not **pwr** is equal to 0. In this call, **pwr** is equal to 3, so execution skips to line 6.

Line 6 makes the function assignment; the expression assigned to the **Power** function result says that the function result is equal to **num** multiplied by the result of calling the **Power** function again, this time passing **pwr** minus 1 as the second argument.

If you substitute the literal interim values for this example into the expression, the call to the **Power** function in line 6 at this point is:

```
Power(2, 3-1)
```

In this, the second call to the **Power** function, **num** is still 2, but the **pwr** argument is now 2 (3-1=2), instead of 3. Again, line 3 tests the value of the **pwr** argument to see if it is equal to 0; it is not, so VBA again executes the function assignment in line 6. The expression in the function assignment calls the **Power** function again, once again passing **pwr** minus 1 as the second argument.

If you again substitute the literal interim values for this example into the expression in line 6, the call to the **Power** function at this point is:

```
Power(2, 2-1)
```

Once again, in this third call to the **Power** function, **num** is still 2, but **pwr** is now 1 (2-1=1). Yet again, line 3 tests the value of the **pwr** argument to see if it is equal to 0; again, it is not, so the function assignment in line 6 is executed a third time, resulting in a fourth call to the **Power** function.

In the fourth call to the **Power** function, **pwr** is 0 (1-1=0); when line 3 tests the value of the **pwr** argument to see if it is equal to 0, the comparison is finally true, and VBA executes line 4 of the **Power** function, ending the recursion. Line 4 is another function assignment statement, this time simply assigning the number 1 as the function result. (Any number raised to the 0 power is 1.)

In the first through third calls to the **Power** function, **Power** has not yet returned any results— VBA cannot completely evaluate the expression in the function assignment statement (line 6) until the series of recursive calls halts in the fourth call to **Power**. Now that the **Power** function actually returns a result, the recursive process ends, and each separate call to the **Power** function returns its result.

The fourth call to **Power** returns the number 1 into the expression in line 6 of the third call to the **Power** function. Substituting literal interim values from the example, this expression is now equal to 2×1. The result returned by the third call to the **Power** function is therefore 2.

VBA, in turn, returns this value—2—to the function assignment expression in the second call to the **Power** function, so that (substituting literal interim values) this expression is now equal to 2×2. The second call to the **Power** function therefore returns 4 to the function assignment expression of the first call to the **Power** function.

Substituting literal values again, the expression from the first call to **Power** is now equal to 2×4. Finally, the original, first call to the **Power** function returns the value 8—the correct result of raising 2 to the third power. The following list summarizes the function returns from each successive call to **Power**:

1	4th call
2×1=2	3rd call
2×2=4	2nd call
2×4=8	1st call

Incidentally, you don't really need to write a **Power** function, the VBA exponentiation operator (^) has the same effect. The **Power** function was chosen to illustrate recursion because it provides one of the simplest and easiest to understand examples of how recursion works.

Note: The **Power** function has one flaw—it won't work if you try to use it to raise a number to some negative power. If you pass a negative power value to the **Power** function, it will recurse infinitely—that is, it will never stop calling itself. (The value of the **pwr** argument is already less than 0; subtracting one just keeps making the negative number larger, and it will never be equal to 0.) If you feel adventurous, you can demonstrate for yourself the results of infinite recursion by calling **Power** with a negative value as the **pwr** argument.

Avoiding Accidental Recursion and Other Recursion Problems

Now that you understand a bit about how a recursive function procedure works, you are ready to understand the drawbacks of recursive routines, and how recursion is usually the result of a programmer mistake.

One of the most obvious drawbacks of recursive functions and procedures is that they are often difficult to understand. Another drawback of recursive functions and procedures is that they can use up a lot of memory: each time a recursive function calls itself, VBA passes all of its arguments again, and memory space is reserved for the function result. The amount of memory used by a series of recursive function calls may be significant, depending on the size of the arguments (in bytes) and the size of the function return (in bytes).

Almost any task you can perform with a recursive function you can also perform with a looping structure, without the extra memory penalty; it is also often easier to understand a looping structure rather than a function that accomplishes its job through recursion. (Looping structures are described in Day 9.)

Inadvertent recursion is a fairly common programmer error, especially for beginning programmers. As you begin writing functions, it is easy to get confused when you write the function assignment statement, and inadvertently create a statement which calls the function recursively, instead of assigning the function result. Because you tell VBA what value to return as the function result with a function assignment, it is also easy to forget that the function name is *not* a variable, and to attempt to treat the function name like a variable name—such attempts usually result in accidental recursive calls.

If you accidentally create a recursive function procedure, it is unlikely that the recursion will ever end, since recursive functions must be carefully constructed so that there is some condition that terminates the recursive calls. If a function does not test for some condition to explicitly end the recursion—like the **Power** function does—the recursive function calls continue until VBA runs out of memory, at which time a runtime error occurs.

Typically, when you execute a function that contains an inadvertent recursive call, your computer will seem to stop working for several seconds before VBA displays the out-of-memory runtime error.

Summary

In today's lesson, you learned how to create your own function procedures, and about the special restrictions on function procedures you intend to use with Excel or another host application. You learned how to declare a specific data type for a function's result, and how to declare data types for a function's arguments; you also learned how to create functions with optional arguments. This lesson taught you the difference between arguments passed by reference and arguments passed by value, and how to control which method VBA uses for specific arguments in your functions.

You learned how to use your function procedures in VBA statements and in Excel worksheets. You learned how to use the Object Browser to add a description to a function, and how to change a function's category in the Excel Function Wizard. Next, you received some tips and guidelines on designing function procedures for use in VBA, and for use in Excel.

Finally, you learned what a recursive function is, and saw an example of a recursive function procedure. You learned that recursion is a difficult programming technique, and you received some pointers on avoiding accidental recursion.

Q&A

Q **I can't find my function procedure in the Object Browser.**

A You may be looking at the wrong module. Try selecting a different module in the Objects/Modules list of the Object Browser. If you still can't find the function, then it might be in a different workbook. Try selecting another workbook in the Libraries/Workbooks drop-down list box. If you still can't find the function you are looking for, then it may be in a workbook that isn't currently open. The Object Browser only lists modules and functions in open workbooks.

The Object Browser lists functions and procedures whether or not the module or workbook containing the function is hidden—as long as a file is open, the Object Browser lists it.

Q **There is no description for my function procedure in Excel's Function Wizard.**

A If there is no description for your function procedure in the Excel Function Wizard, it just means that you did not enter a description for that function procedure by using the Object Browser. To have a description of your function procedure appear in the Function Wizard, follow the instructions at the end of the section "Using Function Procedures in Visual Basic for Applications," in this chapter.

Q **Do I really have to understand how recursion works? It seems sort of mysterious to me.**

A It is important that you understand what recursion is, and what a recursive function call looks like, so that you can avoid or recognize an accidental recursive function call. It is not essential, however, that you be able to write recursive functions right now, or ever. Recursion is a subtle programming technique; there are very few tasks that cannot be accomplished more obviously or easily some other way.

Q **I've written a function, but I'm not certain that it is returning the correct result. How can I verify its operation?**

A Always test your functions before relying on them. To test a function, write a procedure to call the function and display its result. Your test procedure should call the function with test values in the arguments for which you have manually calculated the correct answer. Next, call the function with argument values at the extreme limits of the range the function will accept. For example, if your function has an argument with a Single data type, test the function with the smallest and largest possible numbers the Single data type can hold.

If both of these tests produce the correct answer without any runtime error messages, then your function is probably working just fine.

Refer to the procedure in Listing 6.5 for an example of a procedure that tests a function. Notice that this testing procedure not only displays the value of the function

result, but also displays the original arguments after each function call to check whether or not the function arguments have been inadvertently modified. Notice also that the procedure tests the function both with and without its optional argument. If your function has optional arguments, be sure to test its behavior for every possible combination of present or missing arguments.

Q I understand what the `FlipCase` function does, but I'm not sure I understand exactly how the `For...Next` and `If...Then` structures work.

A As you may have gathered by now, it is difficult to get much work done without making some kind of a decision in your program code. If you understand the general flow of the function's operation, and, in particular, the function assignment statements, you're doing just fine. Any questions you have about the `For...Next` and `If...Then` structures should be answered in Days 8 and 9.

Workshop

Answers are in Appendix A.

Quiz

1. What distinguishes a function procedure from any other procedure you write?
2. Explain the difference between a function procedure and a user-defined function.
3. What are the rules that a user-defined function must observe?
4. What is a function assignment? Can a function procedure contain more than one function assignment?
5. What is recursion?
6. When would you use recursion?
7. When would you use the `IsMissing` function?
8. Why is the `StrComp` function used in the `FlipCase` function?
9. When (and why) should you pass function arguments by value?
10. If you wanted to find a particular function procedure, would you use the Tools | Macro command, or the View | Object Browser command? Why?

Exercises

1. As mentioned in the previous lesson, Excel does not have built-in functions for the `Xor`, `Eqv`, or `Imp` operators in VBA (although it does have built-in function equivalents for the `And`, `Or`, and `Not` operators). The following listing shows an example of a

function procedure that provides an equivalent to the VBA Xor operator, and can be used in an Excel worksheet:

```
1: Function uXOR(L1 As Boolean, L2 As Boolean) As Boolean
2:      uXOR = L1 Xor L2
3: End Function
```

The function is named **uXOR** for "user Xor"—remember, you cannot give your functions names that duplicate VBA restricted keywords such as Xor.

Write two functions, one named **uEQV** and the other named **uIMP** to provide equivalents that Excel can use for the VBA Eqv and Imp operators, respectively.

2. Use the Object Browser to add a description to the function procedures you just created in Exercise 1. Next, use the Object Browser to put at least one of these functions in the Logical category of functions.

3. Write a function, named **Yds2Inch**, to convert yards to inches, and also write a procedure to test the function. **Yds2Inch** should accept a single argument, which is assumed to be a measurement in yards, and return a value in inches. (Hint: Since there are 36 inches in a yard, multiply the number of yards by 36 to determine the number of inches.)

4. Write another function, this time named **Inch2Cm**, to convert inches to centimeters, and also write a procedure to test this function. **Inch2Cm** should accept a single argument, which is assumed to be a measurement in inches, and return a value in centimeters. (Hint: Divide inches by 0.3937 to get a measurement in centimeters.)

5. Write a procedure that uses the InputBox function to get a number representing a measurement in yards from the user and then prints the equivalent value in centimeters—use the two functions **Yds2Inch** and **Inch2Cm** from Exercises 3 and 4 to convert the yards to centimeters.

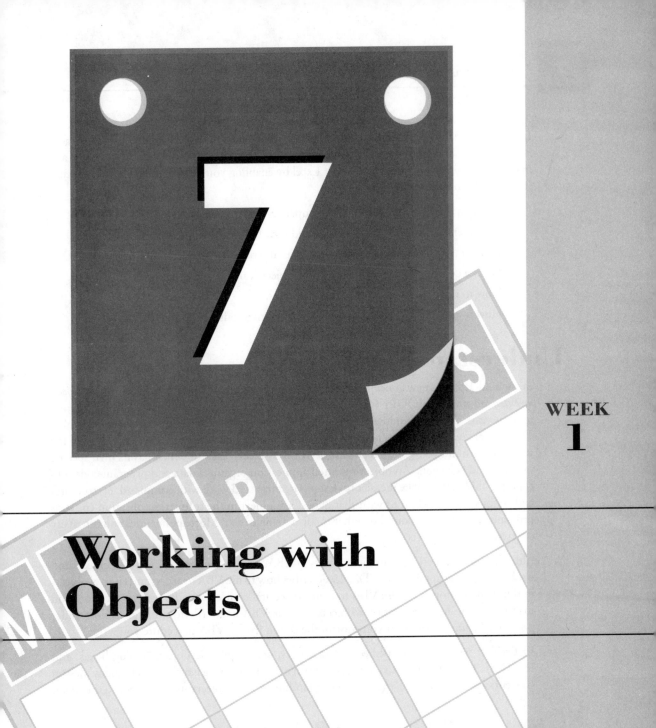

7

Working with Objects

Day 1 described how Visual Basic for Applications evolved, in part, from the original macro languages found in Excel and other applications. Visual Basic for Applications performs as a macro language, giving you control over Excel by enabling you to manipulate Excel's objects. In today's lesson, you learn:

☐ What an object is and what object properties and methods are.

☐ To understand the Object data type and how to use object variables in expressions.

☐ How to use object methods and properties in your VBA code.

☐ What a collection of objects is and how objects can contain other objects.

☐ How to use object collections and containers.

☐ How to use the Object Browser with objects, methods, and properties.

Understanding Objects

In the mid-1980s, a new concept in computer programming was developed, known as *object-oriented programming* (OOP). Object-oriented programming has become increasingly popular over the years; the new Windows 95 desktop, in fact, embodies many object-oriented principles. The central idea behind object-oriented programming is that a software application—like the real world around you—should consist of distinct objects, each of which has its own specific qualities and behaviors. An object-oriented application organizes data and program code into cohesive objects that make it easier to design, organize, and work with complex data structures and actions performed on or with that data. Each object in the software application contains program code and data bound together to form a single item. Most applications contain many different types of objects.

Although you can't create your own objects in VBA, you do have access to Excel's objects and to objects in other applications. (Day 19 describes how to use VBA to access and control objects in other applications.) To use VBA to gain procedural control over the host application, you manipulate the host application's objects in your VBA code. (Performing an action under *procedural control* means that you control the action from a VBA procedure you write.)

In Excel 7, workbooks, worksheets, data ranges, charts, graphic objects, dialog boxes, and Excel 7 itself, are all objects. In Day 18, you learn more about using Excel's objects; today's lesson concentrates on giving you a general understanding of what objects are and how you use them.

Note: What you learn in this lesson will help you work with VBA in applications other than Excel. All VBA host applications—such as Access 7 and Microsoft Project—have objects accessible to VBA in the same way that Excel's objects are. Objects in other VBA host applications exist for the same reasons and purposes as

objects in Excel. The specific objects in a VBA host application vary, depending on the application. The objects in Access 7, for example, all pertain to databases and database manipulation, while the objects in Excel 7 pertain to worksheets, workbooks, and so on.

Object Properties

Just like objects in the real world, VBA objects have various inherent qualities, or *properties*. A portable heater, for example, has properties such as how many watts of heat it puts out, how many cubic feet of air per minute the fan circulates, and what its current thermostat setting is. The heater also has properties such as its weight, color, length, height, and so on. Similarly, VBA objects also have properties that dictate their appearance and behavior: an Excel worksheet has the property of being visible or not, text has the properties of being bold or italic or neither, rows have a height property, columns have a width property, and so on.

Properties govern the appearance and behavior of an object. To change an object's appearance or behavior, you change its properties. To change the behavior of a portable heater, for example, you change its thermostat setting; to change its appearance, you might paint it a different color, thereby changing its color property. In Excel, you might change the behavior of a worksheet by changing the calculation property from automatic to manual, or change the worksheet's appearance by specifying a new color for the text or graphics in the sheet.

To find out about the current appearance and behavior of an object, you examine its properties. To find out the heat output of a heater, you read the heater's wattage from the name plate on the heater; to find out the name of an Excel workbook and what disk and directory it is stored in, you examine the workbook's `FullName` property.

Some of an object's properties you can change, others you cannot. With a portable heater, you can change the current thermostat setting—the heater's "thermostat" property—to determine when the heater will start or stop, but you cannot change the heater's wattage—its "heat output" property. Similarly, you can change some of a VBA object's properties, but not others. For example, in an Excel workbook, you can change the name of the workbook's author by changing the `Author` property, but you cannot change the workbook's `Name` property (the `Name` property of a workbook contains the workbook's disk filename and can't be changed without creating a new disk file, or renaming the workbook file outside of Excel).

Some objects have properties with the same or similar names—the `Application`, `Workbook`, and `Worksheet` objects in Excel all have a `Name` property, for example. Don't get confused: each object keeps the data for its own properties separate from other objects. Figure 7.1 shows a schematic representation of two worksheet objects, their properties, and their methods. Notice that each worksheet object stores the data for its properties within the worksheet itself, along with the user data. (*User data* just means any data that an object stores that comes directly from the user—like the data contained in a worksheet's cells.)

Figure 7.1.

Each object stores its own property information, but objects of the same type (like the worksheets shown here) share their method code.

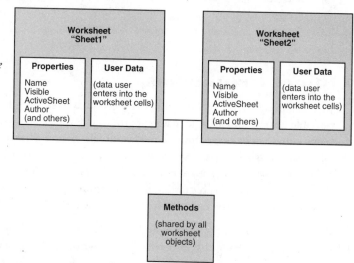

Object Methods

Objects in the real world almost always have some type of inherent behavior or action that they can perform. A video cassette recorder (VCR), for example, has a built-in capability to record television programs onto magnetic tape. You could say that the VCR has a method of recording video onto tape. VBA's objects also have inherent behaviors or abilities, called *methods*. A workbook object, for example, has the built-in ability to add a new worksheet to itself—it has a *method* for adding worksheets (called, in fact, Add).

Methods change the values of an object's properties; methods also perform actions upon or with data stored by the object. Methods are much like the VBA procedures you are already familiar with but are attached to an object; you must access an object's methods through the object.

One of the reasons object-oriented programming has become a popular design technique is because it enables software designers to create more efficient programs by sharing executable code more easily. Instead of keeping a separate copy of the code for each method for each object, VBA objects of the same type (like the worksheet objects shown in Figure 7.1) share their method code.

Although objects of the same type do share the code for their methods, a method is considered part of the object—when you access a particular method for a specific object, the method acts only on the object through which you access the method.

When you change the temperature setting of an oven, you don't need to know exactly how the oven regulates its temperature—you only need to know how to change the oven's thermostat property to set the desired temperature. When you use a VCR to record a television show, you don't worry about exactly how the VCR goes about recording the video images onto the tape— in fact, the details of a VCR's recording method may be a complete mystery to you. All you need to know to make the VCR record a show on tape is what settings you make to the VCR's controls to start the recording process—once you start the VCR's recording method, the VCR's internal mechanisms take over, and the VCR records the show onto tape without requiring any further knowledge or attention from you.

In the same way, you don't have to worry about how an Excel or VBA object's methods operate, nor do you have to worry about how an object stores or manipulates the user's data—all you need to know is how to specify a particular object, and how to specify the particular method you want to use (or the particular property you want to retrieve or change). The built-in code for the VBA object handles all the details for you, without further knowledge or attention from you.

Using Objects

VBA program statements that use objects typically perform one or more of the following actions:

- ☐ Examine the current condition or status of an object by retrieving the value stored in a particular property.
- ☐ Change the condition or status of an object by setting the value stored in a particular property.
- ☐ Use one of the object's methods to cause the object to carry out one of the object's built-in tasks.

As an example, you might determine the name of the currently active worksheet in Excel by retrieving the string stored in the worksheet's Name property. (A worksheet's Name property contains the name of the worksheet as shown on the sheet's tab.) To change the name of a worksheet, you assign a new string to that worksheet's Name property. To add a worksheet to a workbook, you use the workbook's Add method.

To use an object's properties or methods, you must specify the object whose properties or methods you want to use at the same time you specify the specific property or method to use.

In your VBA statements, use the general syntax shown below to specify an object property or method:

```
Object.identifier
```

Object is any valid reference to an object. You create object references by setting a variable to refer to an object, or by using object methods or properties that return an object reference. *Identifier* is any valid property or method name—VBA displays a runtime error message if you attempt to use properties or methods that are not actually part of the specified object. The first example below is a reference to a worksheet's Name property, and the second example is a reference to a workbook's Activate method (both use an object variable to supply the object reference):

```
aSheet.Name
```

```
aBook.Activate
```

In the syntax, and in both examples, notice that a period (.) separates the object reference from the property or method name. In a sense, this *dot separator* also connects the object reference to the property or method identifier. Because you access a property or a method through the object, you have to specify the object reference and the property or method identifier together. The dot separator tells VBA where the object reference ends and where the property or method identifier begins. At the same time, the dot separator connects the object reference and the property or method name to form a single identifier in the VBA statement.

You must remember to include the dot separator, or VBA won't be able to interpret your program instructions correctly. In the next two examples, the dot separator has been omitted:

```
aSheetName
aSheet Name
```

In the first line above, the object reference (a variable named **aSheet**) is not separated from the property identifier (Name) at all. VBA interprets this as a single variable or procedure identifier. Unless you actually have a variable or procedure named **aSheetName**, VBA either displays a runtime error or creates a new variable, depending on whether or not you have specified Option Explicit in the module.

In the second of the preceding examples, the object reference is not connected to the property identifier at all. In this case, VBA interprets the statement as a call to a procedure name **aSheet**, with a single argument in a variable named **Name**, and may produce one of several possible syntax or runtime errors.

Table 7.1 lists some of the more important objects (from a VBA programmer's point of view) in the Excel 7 version of VBA for Applications. The table shows the object's name and a brief description of the object. (Keep in mind that Excel 7 contains many more objects than the few listed in Table 7.1.)

Table 7.1. Common Excel 7 objects.

Object	Description
Application	The host application, itself.
Chart	A chart in a workbook.
DialogSheet	A dialog sheet in a workbook.

Object	Description
Font	This object contains the font and style attributes for text displayed in a worksheet.
Module	A module sheet in a workbook.
Range	A range of cells (1 or more) or a named range in a worksheet.
Window	Any window in Excel; windows are used to display worksheets, charts, modules, and so on.
Workbook	Any open workbook.
Worksheet	Any worksheet in a workbook.

Using Object Properties

You can use object properties in only two ways: you can *get* the value of the property, or you can *set* the value of a property. As mentioned earlier in today's lesson, not all of an object's properties are changeable. Object properties you cannot change are referred to as *read-only* properties; properties you can set are called *read-write* properties.

Typically, properties contain numeric, string, or Boolean data type values, although some properties may return Object or other data types.

You specify a property with this general syntax:

```
Object.property
```

Object represents any valid VBA object reference, while *property* represents any valid property name for the referenced object.

You retrieve or refer to the values in object properties by using the properties in expressions the same way you use any other variable or constant value. You can assign a property's value to a variable, use object properties in expressions, as arguments to functions and procedures, or as arguments for an object's methods.

To assign the value in an object property to a variable, use the following general syntax:

```
Variable = Object.Property
```

Variable is any variable of a type compatible with the object property; *Object* is any valid object reference, and *Property* is any valid property name for the referenced object. In the following example, the string stored in the Name property of the Excel worksheet referenced by the object variable **aSheet** is assigned to the **AnyStr** variable:

```
AnyStr = aSheet.Name
```

7

You can also use an object property directly in an expression, or as an argument to a function or procedure. The next few lines are all legitimate uses of an object's property (in each line, **aSheet** is an object variable set to refer to a worksheet):

```
MsgBox aSheet.Name
```

```
AnyStr = "This sheet is named: " & aSheet.Name
```

```
MsgBox LCase(aSheet.Name)
```

Almost every object in VBA has a property that contains its name. The following statement uses `MsgBox` to display the `FullName` property of a workbook object; the `FullName` property contains the disk, directory path, and filename of a workbook:

```
MsgBox aBook.FullName
```

In the above example, **aBook** is a variable set to refer to an open workbook object. If **aBook** refers to a workbook named SALES.XLS in the My Documents disk folder, for instance, then the message dialog box from the above statement displays `C:\My Documents\SALES.XLS`.

Syntax

To set an object property, simply assign the new value to the property, using the following basic syntax:

```
Object.Property = Expression
```

Object is any valid object reference, *Property* is any property of the referenced object, and *Expression* is any VBA expression that evaluates to a data type compatible with the property. The following line, for example, changes the name of the worksheet referenced by the object variable **aSheet** by assigning a value to the `Name` property of the sheet:

```
aSheet.Name = "First Quarter"
```

This next example changes the text displayed in the status bar at the bottom-left corner of the application window by assigning a string to the `StatusBar` property of the `Application` object (the `Application` object is VBA's host application, Excel in this case):

```
Application.StatusBar = "Generating 3rd Quarter Summary Report"
```

DO   DON'T

DO use the `Application.StatusBar` property in your procedures to display messages about actions your procedure performs, especially if some of those actions take a long time (like sorting a long list, querying a remote database, or updating OLE links). By adding a status bar message or prompt, you let the user know that your procedure is still working. Use a statement like the following:

```
Application.StatusBar = "Message about current actions"
```

> **DON'T** forget to set the `Application.StatusBar` property to `False` when your procedure is done, otherwise VBA continues to display the status bar message you set. Use a statement like the following to clear your status bar message and return control of the status bar to Excel:
>
> ```
> Application.StatusBar = False
> ```

Table 7.2 lists some of the most common or useful object properties in the Excel 7 version of Visual Basic for Applications. The table shows the property's name, a brief description of the property's data type and meaning, and the objects that have this property.

Table 7.2. Common and useful Excel 7 object properties.

Property	Type/Meaning	Found in These Objects
ActiveCell	Object: the active cell.	Application, Window
ActiveChart	Object: the active chart.	Application, Window, Workbook
ActiveSheet	Object: the active sheet.	Application, Window, Workbook
Count	Integer: the number of objects in a collection.	All collection objects
Formula	String: the formula for a worksheet cell.	Range
Index	Integer: the number of the object in a collection.	Worksheet, DialogSheet, Module
Name	String: name of the object.	Application, Workbook, others
Path	String: the disk drive and directory the object is stored in.	AddIn, Application, Workbook
Saved	Boolean: whether or not the workbook was saved since it last changed.	Workbook
Selection	Object: the current selection.	Application, Window
StatusBar	String: status bar message.	Application

continues

7

Table 7.2. continued

Property	Type/Meaning	Found in These Objects
ThisWorkBook	Object: workbook from which current procedure is executing.	Application
Type	Integer: a number indicating the type of the object.	Window, Worksheet, Chart
Visible	Boolean: whether or not Excel displays the object.	Application, Worksheet, Range, others
Value	(Varies): the actual value displayed in a cell.	Range

Using Object Methods

You use an object's methods in your VBA statements just as you would any of VBA's built-in procedures.

Syntax

The basic syntax to use an object method is:

```
Object.Method
```

For object methods that have required or optional arguments, use this syntax:

```
Object.Method Argument1, Argument2, Argument3...
```

In both syntax lines, *Object* represents any valid VBA object reference, and *Method* represents the name of any method belonging to the referenced object. In the second syntax line, *Argument1*, *Argument2*, etc. represent the arguments in the method's argument list. Just like the arguments for any VBA procedure call, you must list the method's arguments in order, separating each argument in the list with a comma, and including place holding commas for omitted optional arguments. A method may have none, one, or several arguments in its argument list; a method's arguments may be required or optional.

As an example, Excel workbooks have an Activate method that makes the workbook the current workbook and activates the first sheet in the workbook. If you set a variable, **aBook**, to refer to a workbook object, then the following statement activates that workbook (later sections in today's lesson describe how to set a variable to refer to an object):

```
aBook.Activate
```

Although the `Activate` method has no arguments, many object methods do have one or more arguments. The next example uses the `SaveAs` method of an Excel workbook object; the example uses the one required argument for the `SaveAs` method, and one of several optional arguments for the method.

```
ActiveWorkbook.SaveAs Filename:="C:\VBA21\NEWFILE.xls", FileFormat:=xlNormal
```

Many objects have methods that return values in the same way that a function returns a value. To use the value returned by a method, you must place parentheses around the method's argument list, and include the method call in an assignment statement or other expression—just like using a function. You can also ignore the result returned by a method the same way you can ignore the result of a function. To ignore a method's result (if it has one), call the method without parentheses around the argument list, as you would for a method that does not return a result.

As an example, the Excel `Address` method (which belongs to the `Range` object) returns the address of a range of cells in a worksheet as a string. The next example shows a VBA statement that uses the `Address` method (**myRange** is an object variable that references a range of cells on a worksheet):

```
MsgBox myRange.Address
```

If the variable **myRange** in the above line refers to the first cell in the worksheet, then the `MsgBox` statement in the above example line displays the string $A$1.

Although the example just given shows the `Address` method without any arguments, the `Address` method does have several optional arguments. These optional arguments specify the style of the worksheet cell address that the method returns, and whether the returned cell coordinates are absolute or relative. The next sample shows the `Address` method used with its third optional argument (which specifies the style of the cell coordinates returned):

```
MsgBox myRange.Address(, , xlR1C1)
```

In the preceding line, notice that you must include place holding commas for omitted optional arguments in the argument list of the method, just like any other procedure or function. Because the reference style argument is the third argument, two place holding commas precede it in the argument list. `xlR1C1` is a predefined Excel constant which indicates that the worksheet cell coordinates use the R1C1 notation style; if the **myRange** object variable refers to the cell in the second row and the third column, the example above displays the string R2C3.

Methods also have named arguments, just like other VBA procedures and functions. You can rewrite the last example using named arguments to appear as follows:

```
MsgBox myRange.Address(ReferenceStyle:=xlR1C1)
```

Use named arguments with methods to simplify both writing and reading your VBA code. The next two examples each show a statement that uses the `SaveAs` method of an Excel workbook

object (this method does not return a result) to save the workbook under a new name (the object variable **aBook** refers to a workbook):

```
aBook.SaveAs "NEWNAME.XLS", xlNormal, , , , True

aBook.SaveAs FileName:="NEWNAME.XLS", _
         FileFormat:=xlNormal, _
         CreateBackup:=True
```

Both these statements use only three of six optional arguments for the SaveAs method. The first statement uses a standard argument list, the second statement uses named arguments. You can tell how much easier it is to understand the purpose and action of the second statement than the first. (Notice the line continuation symbols and indentation used in the second statement to also help make the line more readable.)

> **Note:** If you don't see much difference between a method and a procedure, you're not confused or missing anything. There is really only one difference between an object method and any other VBA procedure (built-in or user-written)—a method belongs to a specific object, and you can only use the method by accessing it through that object. You can frequently recognize calls to methods in VBA code by the fact that the method is attached to an object reference with a dot separator, as shown in the examples in this section.

As you can see from the example statements in this section, using object methods in your VBA code is just like using any VBA procedure or method, except that you must specify the object to which the method belongs. Today's lesson only shows you the general rules and guidelines for using objects, methods, and properties. Day 18 describes many of the methods and properties used as examples in this lesson in more detail. Later sections of this lesson teach you how to use the Object Browser to get more information on the objects, methods, and properties available in VBA.

Table 7.3 lists some of the most common or useful methods in the Excel 7 version of VBA for Applications. The table shows the method's name, a brief description of the method's purpose, and the objects that have this method.

Table 7.3. Common and useful Excel 7 object methods.

Method	Purpose	Found in These Objects
Activate	Activates the object.	Window, Workbook, Worksheet, Range, others

Method	Purpose	Found in These Objects
Address	Returns the cell coordinates of the specified object.	Range
Calculate	Calculates open workbooks, a worksheet, or a range.	Application, Range, Worksheet
Cells	Returns a Range object.	Application, Range, Worksheet
Charts	Returns a collection of chart sheets.	Application, Workbook
Clear	Clears the data stored in the specified object.	Range
Close	Closes the specified object.	Window, Workbook, Workbooks
DialogSheets	Returns a collection of dialog sheets.	Application, Workbook
Justify	Justifies the text stored in the specified object.	Range
Run	Executes a specified procedure or function.	Application, Range
Save	Saves the workbook file.	Application, Workbook
SaveAs	Saves the specified object in another file.	Workbook, Worksheet
Select	Selects the specified object.	Range, Sheets, Worksheets
SendKeys	Sends keystrokes to dialog boxes in host application.	Application
Sheets	Returns a collection of all sheets in a workbook.	Application, Workbook
Volatile	Registers a function as volatile (see Day 6).	Application
Workbooks	Returns a collection of workbooks.	Application
Worksheets	Returns a collection of worksheets.	Application, Workbook

Declaring Object Variables

You may recall from the lesson in Day 3 on data types that, in addition to the Integer, Long, Single, Double, and String data types, VBA also has an Object data type. Variables or expressions of the Object data type refer to a VBA or Excel object, such as Excel's `Workbook`, `Worksheet`, and `Range` objects.

As with VBA's other data types, you can declare variables in your modules, procedures, and functions with the specific Object type, as shown in the following statement:

```
Dim myObject As Object
```

You can set the variable **myObject** created by the preceding `Dim` statement to contain a reference to any Excel or VBA object. If you intend to use an Object type variable for certain specific kinds of objects, you can also declare an object variable for that specific kind of object:

```
Dim aBook As Workbook
```

You can only use the **aBook** object variable created by this second `Dim` statement to store references to `Workbook` objects; if you attempt to set the **aBook** variable to refer to a `Range` or `Worksheet` object, VBA displays a type mismatch error.

Syntax

You can use the VBA `IsObject` function to determine whether a variable or expression forms a valid object reference. The syntax for the `IsObject` function is:

```
IsObject(Object)
```

Object represents the variable or expression that you want to test; `IsObject` returns `True` if *Object* is a valid object reference, `False` otherwise. You can also use the VBA `TypeName` function to determine the object type of a variable; Day 8 describes how to use the `TypeName` function.

Using Objects in Expressions and Assignments

An *object expression* is any VBA expression that specifies a particular object. All object expressions must evaluate to a single object reference; you use object expressions for the sole purpose of creating references to specific objects in your VBA programs.

An object expression may consist of object variables, specific object references, or an object method or property that returns an object. All the following examples are valid object expressions (using Excel objects):

`Application`	The object's name: refers to the application object.
`Application.ActiveSheet`	An object property that returns an object reference: the active sheet.
`Application.Workbooks`	An object method that returns a collection of objects: all open workbooks.
`aBook`	An object variable: initialized in a Set statement, refers to an object.

You cannot use Object type variables or object expressions in arithmetic, logical, or comparison operations. An object reference—whether created with an object expression or stored in an object variable—is really just a memory address that indicates the location in your computer's memory where the referenced object is stored. Because the object reference is really a memory address, arithmetic, logical, and comparison operations are not meaningful. For example, adding together the street address of the building you are sitting in right now with the address of the building next door will not necessarily produce another valid address on your street—so it is with object references.

Before you can use an object variable to refer to an object, you must set that variable to contain a reference to the desired object. Assigning an object reference to an object variable is not the same as making other variable assignments; to assign an object reference to an object variable, use the Set keyword.

Syntax

The Set keyword has this general syntax:

```
Set Var = Object
```

Var is any object variable or Variant type variable. *Object* is any valid object reference; it may be another object variable, or an object expression. If *Var* is a variable declared with a specific object type (like Range or Workbook), it must be of a type compatible with the object referenced by *Object*.

The following program fragment matches the variable and object types correctly:

```
Dim aSheet As Worksheet
Set aSheet = Application.ActiveSheet
```

The following VBA program fragment, however, results in a type mismatch error because the ActiveSheet property returns a Worksheet object, not a Workbook object:

```
Dim aBook As Workbook
Set aBook = Application.ActiveSheet
```

7

To specify a particular object in an expression, or to set an object variable to refer to that object, use methods and properties that return objects, such as the ActiveWorkbook and ActiveSheet properties of the Application object, or the Cells method of the Worksheet object.

Although the standard comparison operators (<, <=, >, >=, <>, =) are not meaningful when used with objects, VBA does provide one comparison operator designed exclusively for use with object expressions and variables—the Is operator.

The Is operator has the following syntax:

Object1 Is *Object2*

Object1 and *Object2* are any valid object references. Use the Is operator to determine whether or not two object references indicate the same object. The result of the Is comparison operation is True if the object references are the same, False otherwise.

Listing 7.1 shows a VBA procedure for Excel that makes a backup copy of the active workbook. You might use a procedure like this if you wanted to provide an easy way for a user to save a copy of the active workbook under a different name, without changing the filename of the active workbook in memory the way the **File | Save As** command (and the Workbook object's SaveAs method) does.

Type

Listing 7.1. The `Backup_ActiveBook` procedure.

```
1:  Sub Backup_ActiveBook()
2:  'Creates backup copy of active workbook under new filename
3:  'using the SaveCopyAs method. New name has extension ".BAK"
4:
5:     Dim FName As String
6:     Dim OldComment As String
7:                         'preserve original file comments
8:     OldComment = ActiveWorkbook.Comments
9:
10:    'Add new comments for the backup copy
11:    ActiveWorkbook.Comments = "Backup copy of " & _
12:                         ActiveWorkbook.Name & _
13:                         ", made by backup procedure."
14:
15:    'Make backup file name from original file name
16:    FName = Left(ActiveWorkbook.Name, _
17:               InStr(ActiveWorkbook.Name, ".")) & "BAK"
18:
19:    ActiveWorkbook.SaveCopyAs Filename:=FName
20:    ActiveWorkbook.Comments = OldComment    'restore comments
21: End Sub
```

Analysis This procedure uses a couple of different Excel objects, properties, and methods. The ActiveWorkbook object reference used throughout the **Backup_ActiveBook** procedure (lines 8, 11, 12, 16, 17, 19, and 20) is a property of the Application object that returns an object reference to the currently active workbook. (As you learn in the next section, you can usually omit the object reference for properties and methods of the Application object.)

Line 1 contains the procedure declaration for **Backup_ActiveBook**. Lines 2 and 3 are comments describing the purpose and action of the **Backup_ActiveBook** procedure.

Lines 5 and 6 of the procedure declare the **FName** and **OldComment** variables, respectively; both variables are strings. Line 8 copies the string in the Comments property of the ActiveWorkbook object to the **OldComment** variable. Next, lines 11 through 13 (notice the line continuation symbol at the end of lines 11 and 12) set a new value for the Comments property of the ActiveWorkbook object. The Comments property of a workbook object contains the comment text you enter in the Properties dialog box that Excel 7 displays whenever you save a workbook for the first time, or through the **File | Properties** command.

Lines 16 and 17 form a single VBA statement; notice the line continuation symbol at the end of line 16, indicating that these two lines are a single VBA statement. This statement uses the Left and InStr functions to help create a new filename for the backup copy of the active workbook. The InStr function returns the position of the filename separator (.) in the Name property of the ActiveWorkbook object. (The Name property of a workbook contains the workbook's filename.)

The result of the InStr function (line 17) determines how many characters the Left function copies from the Name property of the ActiveWorkbook. Because the InStr function returns the position of the filename separator (.), Left returns the workbook's filename up to and including the separator but does not copy the *XLS* extension. Instead, the extension *BAK* is concatenated to the filename string. If the ActiveWorkbook.Name property contains *DAY07.XLS*, for example, then this expression evaluates to *DAY07.BAK*. The assignment operator in line 16 stores this new filename in the **FName** variable.

Now, line 19 uses the ActiveWorkbook.SaveCopyAs method to save the active workbook under a new filename in the current drive and directory—the name of the active workbook file in memory remains the same.

Finally, line 20 restores the original contents of the ActiveWorkbook.Comments property; the active workbook file is now in exactly the same condition it was before this procedure started. The new copy of the workbook on disk is exactly the same as the workbook in memory, except that the comments in the Properties sheet for the workbook indicate that the new file is a backup copy, and gives the original workbook's filename.

7

> **Note:** The `Backup_ActiveBook` procedure in Listing 7.1 saves the copy of the workbook on the current disk drive in the current folder—which may be a different drive or folder than the one from which the workbook was loaded. The `Name` property returns only the name of the workbook, excluding disk drive and folder information. Later, you'll learn how to get the full disk and folder information from a workbook.

Referring to Objects by Using With...End With

As you can see from Listing 7.1, your procedures may refer to the same object frequently, with several statements in a row all referring to objects or methods that belong to the same object. Every statement in Listing 7.1, from line 8 to line 20, uses a property or method of the object referenced by `ActiveWorkbook`. VBA provides a special structure—the `With...End With` structure—that enables you to refer to properties or methods that belong to the same object without specifying the entire object reference each time.

The general syntax of the `With...End With` structure is:

```
With Object
' statements that use properties and methods of Object
End With
```

`Object` is any valid object reference. Listing 7.2 shows the `Backup_ActiveBook` procedure again, this time using the `With...End With` structure.

Syntax

Listing 7.2. Adding With...End With to the Backup_ActiveBook procedure.

```
1:  Sub Backup_ActiveBook()
2:  'Creates backup copy of active workbook under new filename
3:  'using the SaveCopyAs method. New name has extension ".BAK"
4:
5:      Dim FName As String
6:      Dim OldComment As String
7:
8:      With ActiveWorkbook
9:         OldComment = .Comments
10:
11:        'Add new comments for the backup copy
12:        .Comments = "Backup copy of " & .Name & _
13:                    ", made by backup procedure."
14:     .  'Make backup file name from original file name
15:        FName = Left(.Name, InStr(.Name, ".")) & "BAK"
16:
```

```
17:     .SaveCopyAs Filename:=FName     'save the file copy
18:     .Comments = OldComment          'restore original comments
19:   End With
20: End Sub
```

 This version of the **Backup_ActiveBook** procedure operates in exactly the same way as the version shown in Listing 7.1. The version shown in Listing 7.2, however, incorporates the With...End With structure. Line 8 starts with the keyword With, followed by the ActiveWorkbook object reference, therefore beginning the entire With statement.

Line 9 assigns the contents of the ActiveWorkbook.Comments property to the **OldComment** string variable. Notice that this time, only the dot separator (.) is included in front of the Comments property. Because this statement occurs inside the With ActiveWorkbook statement, VBA knows that the object reference for the .Comments property is the ActiveWorkbook—as long as the dot separator appears in front of the Comments property name.

Lines 12 and 13 are a single VBA statement which assigns a new value to the .Comments property. Line 15 assembles a new filename, as in Listing 7.1, and stores it in **FName**. In line 15, notice that the statement uses the .Name property the same way as the .Comments property. Because these statements are inside the With...End With statement, and they include the dot separator in front of the property name, VBA knows that the reference for the .Name property is the ActiveWorkbook object.

Line 17 uses the .SaveCopyAs method to save the backup copy, and line 18 restores the original comment to the .Comments property. In each of these lines, because the line is inside a With statement that specifies the ActiveWorkbook object, VBA knows that the correct object reference for each property or method preceded by a dot separator (.) is the ActiveWorkbook object.

Finally, line 19 completes the With statement with the End With keywords.

DO   DON'T

DO remember to preserve any data you wish to change only temporarily. The **Backup_ActiveBook** procedure, for example, alters the Comments property of the active workbook. The procedure therefore uses a variable to preserve the original comments *before* making the change, and then restores the original comment.

DON'T get input from the user unless you really need to or really want to. The **Backup_ActiveBook** procedure might have been written with an InputBox statement to get the filename, instead of assembling the filename automatically. In this case, generating the filename automatically ensures that the backup files created by this procedure are easily identifiable, and the user is saved the extra work of entering the filename. By generating the new filename within the procedure, you also eliminate any potential problems caused by a user entering an invalid filename, or mistakenly entering the file extension as *.BAT*, say, instead of *.BAK*.

You can see that Listing 7.2 obviously required less typing than Listing 7.1; it is also easier to read and understand. Simplify your code by using the `With...End With` structure whenever you have several program statements together that use properties or methods from the same object reference.

Working with Object Collections and Object Containers

An object *collection* is a group of related objects, such as all of the worksheets in a workbook, or all of the graphic objects in a worksheet. An object in a collection is called an *element* of that collection.

A collection is, itself, an object; collections have their own properties and methods. Every collection, for example, has a `Count` property that returns the number of elements in the collection. If the active workbook has 16 worksheets in it, the following expression evaluates to the number 16:

```
Application.ActiveWorkbook.Worksheets.Count
```

In the preceding expression, `Worksheets` is the collection of all worksheets in a workbook, `ActiveWorkbook` is a property of the `Application` object that returns the active workbook, and `Count` is the property of the `Worksheets` collection that returns the total number of worksheets in the collection.

This sample expression also helps illustrate how objects contain other objects. A *container* object is any object that contains one or more other objects. In the example, `Application` contains the object referenced by `ActiveWorkbook`, which in turn contains the collection object `Worksheets`. All the container object references are joined together with a dot separator (.) to form a single object expression.

Many objects contain other objects of differing types: a workbook contains `Module`, `Chart`, and `Worksheet` objects; a worksheet, in turn, may contain `DrawingObjects`, `ChartObjects`, or `OLEObjects`. Figure 7.2 shows a partial tree diagram of Excel 7 objects, showing how objects contain other objects.

You can see from Figure 7.2 that the `Application` object is the outermost container; the `Application` object contains all other objects. The `Application` object contains collections, such

as the Workbooks collection which, in turn, contains other collections: Worksheets and Sheets. Figure 7.2 shows only a partial diagram of the relationships between various objects and their containers. Visual Basic for Applications in Excel provides many more objects and collections than those shown in the diagram.

Figure 7.2.

The Application object contains object collections, such as Workbooks, which contain yet other objects, such as individual worksheets.

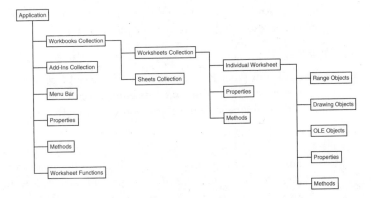

Figure 7.2 gives you an idea of how to specify complex object references. To make it clear to VBA which object you want to refer to, you may need to specify the object's container. To refer to a particular sheet in a workbook, for example, you may need to include a reference to the workbook that contains the worksheet:

```
Workbooks("SALES.XLS").Worksheets("Sales Report")
```

The preceding object expression uses the Workbooks collection to refer to the SALES.XLS workbook, and then uses the Worksheets collection contained in the SALES.XLS workbook to refer to a specific sheet. (How to indicate single items in a collection is described a little later in this lesson.) The following sample expression shows an even more complex object reference:

```
Application.Workbooks("SALES.XLS").Worksheets("Sales Report").Range("A1")
```

The object expression in the preceding line refers to the cell A1 on the *Sales Report* sheet of the SALES.XLS workbook. As you can see from these two examples, specifying a complete object reference through all of an object's containers can be quite tedious. Fortunately, VBA allows you to omit the Application object reference for almost all objects that the Application object contains. If you omit the Application object reference, VBA assumes that you mean the host application, and supplies the reference for you. The following object expression, therefore, refers to the same object as the preceding expression (cell A1 on the *Sales Report* sheet of SALES.XLS):

```
Workbooks("SALES.XLS").Worksheets("Sales Report").Range("A1")
```

You only have to specify the Application object when a reference might otherwise be ambiguous, or when using built-in Excel worksheet functions, as described in Day 5.

If you omit the Workbooks object reference, VBA usually—but not always—assumes that you mean the current active workbook. The next object expression is equivalent to the one just shown, provided the SALES.XLS workbook is the active workbook:

```
Worksheets("Sales Report").Range("A1")
```

If SALES.XLS is the active workbook, and *Sales Report* is the active sheet, this next object expression is also equivalent to the one just shown:

```
Range("A1")
```

In many of your procedures, however, you cannot be certain that any particular workbook or worksheet is active at the time your procedure executes, so you'll probably need to specify at least some of the containers for the object you want to refer to.

Tip: Remember to use methods and properties that return objects (such as ActiveWorkbook) to make object container references shorter. Using the With...End With statement is an ideal way to avoid writing lengthy object references more than once or twice in a procedure.

It is possible for the same object to be an element in more than one collection. For example, a Worksheet object is an element of both the Worksheets collection and the Sheets collection. Worksheets is a collection of all the worksheets in a workbook; Sheets is a collection of all sheets in a workbook, including worksheets, chart sheets, module sheets, and dialog sheets. Because the Sheets collection contains all sheets in a workbook, and Worksheets contains all worksheets, any worksheet belongs to both collections. Similarly, a particular Range object—which refers to a range of cells in a worksheet—may be contained by a Worksheet object, and also contained in a Column or Row object.

All these objects in containers and collections may be a little confusing to you; especially those objects that are contained in more than one object or collection at the same time. Although it may seem that objects in VBA can be in two places at once, this really isn't true. To better understand container objects and collections, you must keep in mind that VBA objects are not really a physical thing contained in another physical thing. Instead, remember that an object that contains another object really just has a memory address that refers to the contained object. VBA containers refer to the objects they "contain" through their memory addresses. Just as many different people may have your mailing address without your being physically present in their homes, any particular VBA object may be referred to by several other objects through its address.

Note: If you ever need to refer to an object's container, just use the object's `Parent` property. All objects have a `Parent` property, which returns an object reference to the object's container. The following object expression, for example, refers to the `Application` object, which contains the `Workbooks` collection:

```
Workbooks.Parent
```

Table 7.4 lists some of the most frequently used object collections in the Excel 7 version of Visual Basic for Applications. The table shows the collection's name, and a brief description of the collection's purpose.

Table 7.4. Common Excel 7 collections.

Collection	Purpose
Charts	The collection of all chart sheets in a workbook, or chart objects in a worksheet, depending on the container
DialogSheets	The collection of all dialog sheets in a workbook
Modules	The collection of all module sheets in a workbook
Windows	The collection of all windows in the application, whether or not the window is on-screen
Workbooks	The collection of all workbooks currently open in the application
Worksheets	The collection of all worksheets in a workbook

Adding to Collections

Most of the time, you work with elements that already exist in a collection. Occasionally, you may want or need to add an element to a collection, such as creating a new workbook, or adding a new worksheet to a workbook.

Every collection has an `Add` method, which adds a new element to the collection. Many of the `Add` methods have one or more arguments that allow you to specify various initial values or conditions for the new object's properties. The following statement shows the `Add` method of the `Workbooks` collection used to create a new Excel workbook:

```
Workbooks.Add
```

This statement creates a new workbook and makes it the active workbook. Day 18 gives you more information about adding elements to Excel's collections.

Referring to Specific Objects in a Collection or Container

To specify a single element of a collection, use the following general syntax:

```
Collection(Index)
```

Technically, this syntax specifying a single object in a collection is known as an *object accessor*. `Collection` is any valid object expression that refers to a collection. `Index` may be either a string or an integer designating the specific element you want. When the `Index` argument is a string, the string must contain the text name of the object, which may be the name of a worksheet as shown on the sheet's tab, the name of a named range in a worksheet, the filename of a workbook, the name of a toolbar button or menu command, and so on. For example, to refer to a worksheet named *July Data* in the active workbook, you would use the following statement:

```
Worksheets("July Data")
```

When the `Index` argument is an integer, it is the number of the element in the collection. VBA assigns this number to each element in the collection as it adds the object to the collection. For this reason, there is no easy way to determine the index number for any given collection element.

Usually, you should use a text name to refer to an element in a collection; this not only makes certain which element you want to refer to, but also makes your code easier to read. `Worksheets("July Data")` is much easier to understand than `Worksheets(5)`. (Many objects do have an `Index` property which returns the index number of the object in their collection, but you still have to be able to refer to the element in the collection before you can retrieve the `Index` property.)

If you want to refer to all of the elements in a collection, don't include any index. The following statement, for example, closes *all* of the visible, open workbooks:

```
Workbooks.Close
```

DO	DON'T

DO keep in mind that the methods and properties in the `Application` object belong to the host application (Excel), not to VBA. If you go on to work in other VBA applications, some of the methods and properties in the `Application` object may vary, depending on the specific host application: Excel 7, Access 7, or Microsoft Project.

DON'T forget that the `Application` object provides many useful methods and properties, as well as providing a container for the host application's objects. For example, remember that you access Excel's worksheet functions—such as SUM, MIN, MAX, and so on—through the `Application` object, as explained in Day 5.

Note: The `Application` object may contain methods with names that duplicate the names of VBA procedures or functions. When using a host application method that duplicates a VBA procedure or function name, you must specify the `Application` object, otherwise VBA assumes that you want to use the VBA procedure or function.

The Excel `Application` object, for example, contains an `InputBox` method. Excel's `InputBox` method isn't the same as VBA's `InputBox` function—the Excel `Application.InputBox` method has one more argument than the VBA `InputBox` method; this extra argument allows you to restrict the type of data (numeric, date, text) that the user enters in the dialog box. To use Excel's `InputBox` method, you must specify the `Application` object:

`Application.InputBox`

Otherwise, VBA assumes you want to use the VBA `InputBox` function.

Using the Object Browser with Objects, Methods, and Properties

You have already learned how to use the Object Browser to locate, get help on, and insert VBA and Excel functions, procedures, and constants into your code (Day 5). Using the Object Browser with objects, methods, and properties is very similar; in fact, the Object Browser's primary purpose—as its name suggests—is to enable you to browse through all of the objects available in VBA and Excel (or another host application), along with their various methods and properties.

You already know how to start the Object Browser: click the Object Browser button on the Visual Basic toolbar, or choose the **V**iew | **O**bject Browser command to display the Object Browser dialog box (shown in Figure 7.3).

7

Tip: You can also start the Object Browser by pressing F2 whenever a module sheet is active.

Figure 7.3.

Use the Object Browser to determine what objects are available, and to determine what properties and methods belong to a particular object.

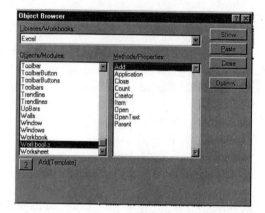

To view a list of the available Excel objects, and to view a list of properties and methods for a particular object, follow these steps:

1. Open the Object Browser dialog box.
2. Select **Excel** in the **Libraries/Workbooks** drop-down list at the top of the Object Browser dialog box. (Figure 7.3 shows Excel's Object Browser dialog box with **Excel** already selected in the **Libraries/Workbooks** list box.)

   After you select **Excel** in the **Libraries/Workbooks** list box, the **Objects/Modules** list contains all of the Excel objects available to VBA.
3. In the **Objects/Modules** list, select the object whose methods and properties you are interested in. Figure 7.3 shows the `Workbooks` collection object selected in the **Objects/Modules** list.
4. To get more information about the object you have selected in the **Objects/Modules** list, click the question mark (**?**) button (in the lower left of the Object Browser dialog box) to access the VBA online help system.

Note: You can only get help for an object selected in the **Objects/Modules** list if the object is selected *without* a selection in the **Methods/Properties** list. (Selecting an object in the **Objects/Modules** list clears any selection from the **Methods/Properties** list.)

After you select an object in the **Ob**jects/Modules list, the **Methods**/Properties list in the Object Browser dialog box then displays all of the methods and properties for the selected object.

5. In the **Methods**/Properties list, select the particular method or property you are interested in. The Object Browser now displays the method or property name at the bottom of the dialog box; if you select a method that has arguments, the Object Browser also lists all of the method's arguments. Figure 7.3 shows the Add method of the Workbooks collection selected.

Note: The Object Browser does not distinguish methods and properties from each other in the **Methods**/Properties list, it just lists them all together, alphabetically.

6. Click the question mark (**?**) button in the Object Browser dialog box to access the VBA online help system for detailed information on the method or property selected in the **Methods**/Properties list.

Note: You can use the Object Browser in any VBA host application to see what objects are available through the host application. In Access 7, for example, you could view available objects with the Object Browser by selecting **Access** (instead of **Excel**) in Step 2 of these instructions.

When you use the Object Browser to view the various objects and their methods and properties, only the **P**aste, Close, and question mark (**?**) buttons are enabled in the Object Browser dialog box. The following list summarizes the actions of these buttons:

☐ **P**aste. Enabled whenever you select a method or property in the **Methods**/Properties list. Choose this button to insert the selected method or property into the active module, at the current insertion point. If you paste a method that has arguments, the Object Browser pastes all of the method's named arguments into your source code, as well.

☐ **?**. Enabled whenever you select an object in the **Ob**jects/Modules list, or whenever you select a method or property in the **Methods**/Properties list. Choose this button to open the VBA online reference to the appropriate topic for the selected item(s). You can only get help for an object if there is *no* selection in the **Methods**/Properties list; selecting an object in the **Ob**jects/Modules list removes any selection from the **Methods**/Properties list.

☐ Close. Closes the Object Browser dialog box.

> ✓ **Tip:** You can get help on the Object Browser dialog box itself by clicking the question mark (**?**) button in the top-right corner of the dialog box and then clicking over any control or region of the Object Browser dialog box.

DO	**DON'T**

DO supply the object reference and dot separator (.) for each method or property that you paste into your code with the Object Browser. The Object Browser just pastes the method or property name; it cannot supply the object reference for you.

DON'T feel compelled to use all the arguments that the Object Browser pastes into your code if you don't need them. Simply delete any optional arguments you don't use from the argument list that the Object Browser inserts into your code.

DO remove the parentheses from the argument list that the Object Browser inserts in your code if the method does not return a result, or if you choose to ignore the result that the method returns.

DO use the Object Browser to become familiar with the various objects, methods, and properties available to you, and to speed up writing your program code.

Summary

In today's lesson, you learned that an object is a set of data and code bound together into a single unit. You learned that object properties store data about the condition and status of an object, and that object methods are special procedures and functions that provide the inherent behaviors and actions that an object has.

You learned how to use objects in your VBA code, and you learned the basic syntax for specifying an object's method or property. You learned how to declare variables of the Object data type, and you learned that you must use the VBA Set command to assign an object reference to an object variable. You also learned how to use the With...End With statement structure when several program statements refer to the same object in order to make it easier to write and read your program code.

Next, you learned what a collection of objects is, and how objects can contain other objects; you also learned how to specify a particular object by forming complex object references through an object's containers, and how to specify a particular object in a collection.

Finally, you saw how to use the Object Browser with VBA objects to view available objects, methods, and properties. You also saw how to access the VBA online help through the Object Browser for detailed information objects, methods, and properties, and how to paste methods and properties into your VBA code.

Q&A

Q **I'm trying to write a VBA procedure that changes the way the active worksheet gets displayed, but I don't know which object is the correct one to reference, and if I did know which object to reference, I still don't know which property to change, or whether there is a method to do what I want!**

A If you're not sure what objects or methods you should use to get a particular task done, then use the macro recorder to record the task (or a similar one), and then examine the recorded code to see which objects, properties, and methods it uses. You can then edit or copy the recorded statements to use in your procedure. You can also use the objects, properties, and methods you see in the recorded statements as the basis for doing research in the online help system or with the Object Browser.

Recording code with the macro recorder and then editing it to streamline or generalize its operation is a good programming technique for an environment like Visual Basic for Applications in Excel.

Q **Why should I declare a specific object type, such as `Range` or `Workbook`, instead of the more general `Object` type?**

A Declaring a specific object type helps you track programmer errors. If you make a mistake and set the object variable reference incorrectly, having a more specific object type might pinpoint the error for you, because VBA is likely to produce a type mismatch error. Otherwise, you may have trouble tracking down such errors.

Q **Does VBA create a new object when I declare an object variable and then use the `Set` command to assign an object to that variable?**

A When you declare an object variable and subsequently set it to refer to an object, you are *not* creating a new object—you create a new *reference* to the object. You can have several object variables that all reference the same object, if you want.

You use object variables to give meaningful short-hand names to the objects that your program manipulates. For instance, your code is easier to understand if it contains references like **DataSheet** rather than

```
Workbooks("CH07.XLS").Worksheets("DataSheet").
```

Q **If VBA understands the `Application` object reference tacitly, why should I ever specify the `Application` object in an object reference?**

A Although the `Application` object is optional for many object references, it is required for others. Usually, you must specify the `Application` object when there is a possibility of some ambiguity about which object you wish to reference. For example, to use Excel's worksheet functions, you must specify the `Application` object, as you learned in Day 5, and as shown in the following sample lines:

```
AnyVar = Application.Sum(Range("A1:A12"))
AnyVar = Application.Max(Range("A1:A12"))
AnyVar = Application.Min(Range("A1:A12"))
```

Each of the lines above uses a built-in Excel worksheet function (SUM, MAX, MIN), and assigns the result of the Excel function to a variable, **AnyVar**. To avoid any possible ambiguity between Excel's built-in functions, VBA's built-in functions, and functions you may have written yourself with the same names, VBA requires you to specify the `Application` object.

Q Does the index string to specify a particular element in a collection always have to be a quoted literal string?

A No. The index string may be a string variable, or any string expression that evaluates to a valid name for an element in the collection.

Q How do I figure out how to create the object reference for an object that I want to use?

A Create object references from the outermost container object to the innermost container, ending with the specific method or property you want:

```
Application.Container1.Container2.ThingYouWant
```

The `Application` object is always the outermost container. Remember that the `Application` object, and other objects, have properties and methods that return references to objects; use the `Application` object's `ActiveWorkbook`, `ActiveSheet`, and `ActiveWindow` properties to refer to the currently active workbook, sheet, or window, for example.

Also, you can use an object's `Parent` property to determine that object's container. As an example, you might want to determine whether or not the container for the current Window object—a worksheet with several charts, perhaps—has data displayed in more than one window. To determine which workbook contains the current active window, use the `ActiveWindow` property of the `Application` object to reference the active window, and then use the `Parent` property of the active window to reference the workbook containing that window. The following line, for example, uses the `MsgBox` statement to display the name of the workbook that contains the active window:

```
MsgBox ActiveWindow.Parent.Name
```

This next line again uses `MsgBox`, this time to display the count of windows that the parent workbook of the active window contains:

```
MsgBox ActiveWindow.Parent.Windows.Count
```

In general, you should create object references by working from the known towards the unknown. Both of the above sample lines begin by referencing a property of the Application object, (the Application object is always available, and therefore always "known"). Next, each statement uses a property of the Window object (Parent) to reference the object's container.

Workshop

Answers are in Appendix A.

Quiz

1. What is the main idea behind object-oriented programming?
2. In an object-oriented application, what is an object?
3. What is a property? What do you use object properties for?
4. Are all of an object's properties changeable?
5. If you change, say, the Name property of an object, does your change affect the Name property of other objects?
6. What is a method? What do you use object methods for?
7. Name three actions typically performed by VBA code that uses objects, properties, and methods.
8. What is the basic syntax required to use a property or method of an object?
9. What is the purpose of the dot separator (.) in an object reference?
10. What is an object expression, and what do you use object expressions for?
11. How do you create object references?
12. What is a collection of objects? What is an element in a collection?

Exercises

 1. **BUG BUSTER:** The following procedure uses the Workbooks collection's Add method to create a new workbook, and then fills in the new workbook's summary information with a combination of information obtained from the user in a series of InputBox statements and with information obtained from the Application object's OrganizationName property. (The summary information is the same information you can fill in manually by choosing the **File | Properties** command. The OrganizationName property of the Application object contains the organization name entered when you installed Excel.)

This procedure has a flaw in it, however, and does not correctly carry out its job. If Option Explicit is set in the module containing this procedure, VBA displays a runtime error message stating that there are undefined variables. If Option Explicit is not set, the procedure executes without errors but does not change the summary information of the new workbook.

Rewrite this procedure so that it works correctly.

```
1:  Sub NewBook()
2:  'Creates new workbook, and fills in the summary information
3:  'for the new workbook with some information from the user,
4:  'and some information from the Application object.
5:
6:     Const nbTitle = "New Book"
7:
8:     Workbooks.Add        'adds workbook to Workbooks collection
9:     With ActiveWorkbook
10:      Title = InputBox(prompt:= _
11:                       "Enter a title for this workbook:", _
12:                       Title:=nbTitle)
13:      Subject = InputBox(prompt:= _
14:                       "Enter the subject of this workbook:", _
15:                       Title:=nbTitle)
16:      Author = Application.OrganizationName
17:      Keywords = ""
18:      Comments = InputBox(prompt:= _
19:                       "Enter a comment regarding this workbook:", _
20:                       Title:=nbTitle)
21:     End With
22: End Sub
```

2. Rewrite the following procedure (which displays information about the Application object's operating environment and user) to use a With...End With statement.

```
1:  Sub Show_SystemInfo()
2:  'uses various properties of the host application to display
3:  'information about your computer system
4:
5:     Dim CR As String * 1
6:
7:     CR = Chr(13)      'a carriage-return
8:     MsgBox "Host Application: " & CR & _
9:            Application.Name & " v" & Application.Version & _
10:           ", Build " & Application.Build & CR & CR & _
11:           "Library Path: " & Application.LibraryPath & _
12:           CR & CR & "User: " & Application.UserName & CR & _
13:           "              " & Application.OrganizationName
14:
15:     MsgBox "Operating System:" & _
16:           Application.OperatingSystem & CR & CR & _
17:           "Mouse is Available: " & _
18:           Application.MouseAvailable & CR & CR & _
19:           "Total Memory: " & Application.MemoryTotal & _
20:           CR & "Used Memory: " & Application.MemoryUsed & _
21:           CR & "Free Memory: " & Application.MemoryFree _
22: End Sub
```

3. **BUG BUSTER:** Excel has an InputBox function that is slightly different from the VBA InputBox function. The Excel InputBox function has one more argument than the VBA InputBox function—a Type argument, that allows you to specify the type of data that the user may enter into the InputBox. A value of 1 in the Type argument causes Excel to restrict the user's input to some valid number; Excel displays an error message if the user enters any text that contains characters other than the digits 0 through 9, or a single decimal point (.).

The GetNumber function in the following listing is intended to return a number obtained from the user. It uses the Excel InputBox function with the Type argument to restrict the user's input to a number. The Test_GetNumber procedure simply uses VBA's MsgBox to display the result of the GetNumber function so that you can test the GetNumber function's operation.

The GetNumber function has a flaw in it, however. When you try to use this function, VBA displays a runtime error message stating that a named argument is not found. Alter the GetNumber function so that it performs correctly.

```
1:  Function GetNumber()
2:  'uses the application's InputBox function to return
3:  'a number obtained from the user.
4:
5:     GetNumber = InputBox(Prompt:="Enter a number:", _
6:                          Type:=1)
7:  End Function
8:
9:
10: Sub Test_GetNumber()
11:     MsgBox GetNumber
12: End Sub
```

4. When you use the **Insert | Worksheet** command in Excel to insert a worksheet, Excel gives the worksheet a name like *Sheet3* or *Sheet8*, depending on how many sheets you have inserted in the current working session. If you want the worksheet to have a different name, you must manually rename it by double-clicking the worksheet's tab, or by choosing the **Format | Sheet | Rename** command.

It might be more convenient for you to insert a worksheet and give it the desired name in a single operation. In this exercise, you write a general-purpose procedure that inserts a worksheet into the active workbook and gives the new worksheet a new name at the same time. You should write this procedure from scratch in a module sheet in the PERSONAL.XLS workbook. Name your procedure **SheetInsert**, and make sure that it performs the following actions:

(a) Use a variable to preserve an object reference to whatever sheet is active at the start of the procedure.

(b) Use VBA's InputBox function to obtain a new name from the user, and store this name in a string variable.

(c) Use the `Add` method of the `Worksheets` collection to add a worksheet to the active workbook.

(d) Assign the sheet name obtained from the user to the `Name` property of the new worksheet.

(e) Use the `Select` method and the object reference you preserved at the start of the procedure to restore the worksheet that was originally active at the time the procedure started.

Hints: Remember that the `ActiveSheet` property of the `Application` object returns an object reference to the active worksheet; also remember that when you use the `Add` method to insert a sheet, Excel inserts the new sheet and then makes it the active sheet.

After finishing your first week of learning how to program with VBA, you should feel comfortable using the Excel Macro Recorder to record and run a macro, and using the Object Browser to locate your recorded macros. You should also feel comfortable using the Visual Basic editor to edit recorded macros and procedures, and to write your own macro procedures and functions from scratch.

The following listing contains an entire Visual Basic module and pulls together many of the topics from the previous week.

Type

Listing R1.1. Week 1 review listing.

```
1:   Option Explicit
2:
3:
4:   Sub NewFile()
5:   'Creates a new file, then saves it with a name obtained
6:   'from the user. This procedure was created by editing a
7:   'recorded macro.
8:     Const nfTitle = "Creating New Workbook File"
9:     Const nfPrompt1 = "Enter the "          '1st part of prompt
10:
11:    Dim FName As String                     'file name from user
12:    Dim nfPrompt2 As String                 '2nd part of prompt
13:
14:    'display message in Excel's status bar
15:    Application.StatusBar = "Creating New Workbook " & _
16:                            "File: NewFile Procedure"
17:    'set up 2nd part of the prompt string for Input boxes
18:    nfPrompt2 = " for this new workbook." & Chr(13) & _
19:                "(Press Esc or choose Cancel to skip.)"
20:
21:    Workbooks.Add     'Add method creates new workbook
22:
23:    With ActiveWorkbook          'now get summary information
24:
25:       'get the title information from user
26:       .Title = InputBox(prompt:=nfPrompt1 & "title" & _
27:                         nfPrompt2, Title:=nfTitle)
28:
29:       'get the subject information from user
30:       .Subject = InputBox(prompt:=nfPrompt1 & "subject" & _
31:                           nfPrompt2, Title:=nfTitle)
32:
33:       'get author information from user, suggest logon
34:       'user name (in UserName property of Application object)
35:       'as the default value for the author information
36:       .Author = InputBox(prompt:=nfPrompt1 & "author" & _
37:                          nfPrompt2, Title:=nfTitle, _
38:                          default:=Application.UserName)
39:
40:       'get the list of keywords from user
41:       .Keywords = InputBox(prompt:=nfPrompt1 & "keywords" & _
42:                            nfPrompt2, Title:=nfTitle)
43:
44:       'get comments from user
45:       .Comments = InputBox(prompt:=nfPrompt1 & "comments" & _
46:                            nfPrompt2, Title:=nfTitle)
47:    End With
48:
49:       'Now get new file name from user by calling GetBookName
50:       'function. Call to GetBookName doesn't use nfPrompt2
51:       'string, because it's not appropriate to skip entering a
52:       'file name. Instead, call to GetBookName uses a prompt
53:       'suggesting the user store new file in Excel's examples
54:       'directory, with a name of NEWFILE.
```

```
55:    FName = GetBookName(lPrompt:=nfPrompt1 & "File Name " & _
56:          "for this workbook." & Chr(13) & _
57:          "You MUST enter a file name." & Chr(13) & _
58:          "Include the disk drive and directory name, " & _
59:          "if you want to store this workbook someplace " & _
60:          "other than the current drive and directory.", _
61:                   lTitle:=nfTitle, _
62:                   lDflt:="C:\EXCEL\EXAMPLES\NEWFILE.XLS")
63:
64:   'Now, save the new workbook file:
65:   ActiveWorkbook.SaveAs Filename:=FName, _
66:                   FileFormat:=xlNormal, _
67:                   ReadOnlyRecommended:=False, _
68:                   CreateBackup:=False
69:   'return control of status bar to Excel
70:   Application.StatusBar = False
71: End Sub      'NewFile
72:
73:
74: Function GetBookName(lDflt As String, _
75:                   Optional lPrompt, _
76:                   Optional lTitle) As String
77: 'Gets workbook name, and returns it as a string. The
78: 'function has a required argument for the default file
79: 'name used in the input dialog box, and has two optional
80: 'arguments used for the prompt string and title used in the
81: 'input dialog box. If the title is not supplied when this
82: 'function is called, no title appears in input dialog box.
83:
84:     'check to see if a prompt string was included
85:   If IsMissing(lPrompt) Then
86:     'if no prompt string, then set one.
87:     lPrompt = "Enter a workbook name:"
88:   End If
89:
90:     'use InputBox to get the file name.
91:   GetBookName = InputBox(prompt:=lPrompt, _
92:                   Title:=lTitle, _
93:                   default:=lDflt)
94: End Function    'GetBookName
95:
96:
97: Sub Test_GetBookName()
98: 'This procedure tests the GetBookName function
99:    MsgBox GetBookName("default only")
100:   MsgBox GetBookName(lPrompt:="Some prompt", _
101:                   lDflt:="default")
102:   MsgBox GetBookName(lDflt:="default", _
103:                   lTitle:="title")
104:End Sub
```

 After completing the quiz and exercises in Days 1 and 2, you should be able to record the macro on which the **NewFile** procedure is based, and then edit the **NewFile** macro to add the interactive features not found in the recorded macro. You should also feel comfortable entering the **GetBookName** function and the **Test_GetBookName** procedure.

The procedure and function listings here contain more comments than many of the other procedure and function examples you have seen so far. These comments are typical of real-world VBA programs, and provide enough information that any VBA programmer can easily read and understand the purpose and actions performed by the **NewFile** procedure and the **GetBookName** function. In particular, notice the comments at the beginning of each procedure and function declaration. The comments at the beginning of each procedure or function describe the purpose of the procedure or function; the comments for the **GetBookName** function also describe the function's arguments and return result.

Line 1 of this listing contains the module-level Option Explicit command, which tells Visual Basic that all of the variables used in this module must be explicitly declared with a Dim statement.

Line 4 contains the procedure declaration for the **NewFile** procedure. This procedure is based on the macro you recorded in Exercise 1 of Day 1 but has had several features added to it that cannot be incorporated into a procedure by recording alone. Lines 5, 6, and 7 contain comments about what the **NewFile** procedure does, and its origins. (The original recorded macro, you may recall, created a new workbook and saved it with the name NEWFILE.XLS.) The **NewFile** procedure creates a new workbook, gets the workbook's summary information from the user, gets a filename from the user, and then saves the workbook file, leaving the new file open as the active workbook.

Lines 8 and 9 declare constants for use within the **NewFile** procedure. The **nfTitle** constant contains a string used as a title for all the dialog boxes the **NewFile** procedure displays. The **nfPrompt1** constant contains a string used to form the first part of the prompt text displayed by every InputBox dialog box that **NewFile** displays.

Next, lines 11 and 12 declare the variables that **NewFile** uses. The **FName** variable stores the filename obtained from the procedure's user. The **nfPrompt2** variable provides the second part of the standard prompt used by almost all of the InputBox dialog boxes displayed by the **NewFile** procedure. **nfPrompt2** is a variable rather than a constant because—for cosmetic reasons—it must contain a carriage-return character to start a new line in the dialog box's text. The only way to include a carriage-return character in a string is to use the Chr function to provide the character equivalent of the carriage-return numeric code. Using a Visual Basic function such as Chr is not allowed in constant declarations, so the procedure declares a string variable instead, later assigning it the desired string value.

Line 15 begins the actual work that the **NewFile** procedure performs. This line, as explained in the comment in line 14, sets the Excel status bar to display the message Creating New Workbook File: NewFile Procedure. The Excel status bar message is changed so that the procedure's user has some additional information about what activity is occurring.

Lines 18 and 19 contain a single assignment expression, divided over two different lines with a line continuation symbol. This assignment expression sets the value for the **nfPrompt2** string variable.

Line 21 uses the `Workbooks` collection's `Add` method to create a new workbook. This line comes from the original recorded macro, with only a comment describing its action added. Remember, one of the best ways to find out which objects and methods to use to carry out a particular task in Visual Basic is to record that task, or one that is similar, and then edit or copy the resulting macro code. When line 21 executes, Excel creates a new workbook and makes it the active workbook.

Line 23 starts a `With...End With` statement in which the summary information for the new workbook is entered by the procedure's user. This `With...End With` statement was added to the original recorded macro. (You might want to take another look at the recorded macro listing in Appendix A for Exercise 1.1.) Remember that `ActiveWorkbook` is a property of the `Application` object that returns the current active workbook—in this case, the new workbook created in line 21.

Also added to the original recorded macro are the workbook's summary information properties (`Title`, `Subject`, `Author`, `Keywords`, and `Comments`). Each of these workbook properties is set by obtaining the information from the procedure's user with an `InputBox` statement. (This is the information that displays in the workbook's Summary tab in the Properties dialog box that you can display with the **File | Properties** command.)

Line 26 uses the `InputBox` function to get a string from the user, and then assigns that string to the `Title` property of the active workbook. Notice that the `InputBox` function call uses named arguments. The prompt argument is a string assembled by concatenating the **nfPrompt1** constant, a literal string, and the **nfPrompt2** string variable. The title of the dialog box displayed by `InputBox` is supplied by the **nfTitle** string constant.

Line 30 similarly obtains a string from the user for the workbook's `Subject` property. Notice that this call to `InputBox` also uses named arguments, and that the prompt string is assembled the same way as for the `Title` property, except that a different literal string is used in the string expression for the dialog box's prompt. By using a combination of constants, literal strings, and string variables, the programmer was able to provide specific, customized messages for each `InputBox` prompt, without typing the entire string each time; this technique also uses less memory, requires less code, and is clearer and easier to read than typing out the entire prompt string each time it is used in a statement.

Lines 33 through 35 are comments about the action performed in line 36. Line 36 also uses `InputBox` to get a string from the user; in this case, however, the `InputBox` function call includes an argument to specify the default value in the `InputBox` dialog box. The default value argument passed to InputBox comes from the UserName property of the Application object, which contains the user name you entered when you logged on to Windows 95. If your Windows 95 installation doesn't require you to logon, then the UserName property contains the user name you entered when you installed Excel.

Lines 41 and 45 get the keywords and subject summary information using the same techniques as lines 20 and 36. Line 47 signals the end of the With...End With statement.

Lines 49 through 54 are comments explaining what the next action in the procedure is, and explaining why the nfPrompt2 variable is not used in the prompt for obtaining the new workbook name from the user.

Line 55 calls the GetBookName function and assigns its result to the FName variable. The GetBookName function is a special function written for the general-purpose task of obtaining a workbook filename from the user. You can use the GetBookName function from any of your procedures or macros in which you need to get a workbook filename from the user—whether you intend to open, create, or close that workbook. The operation of the GetBookName function is described in a little more detail later in this section. Line 55 calls GetBookName and passes arguments for the InputBox prompt and title message, and for a suggested default workbook name.

Line 65 uses the SaveAs method of a workbook object (specified by ActiveWorkbook) to save the workbook. This command also appeared in the original recorded macro. In the original macro, the filename specified for the file copy was a literal string. For this version of the NewFile procedure, the SaveAs statement was edited so that the Filename:= named argument uses whatever string is stored in the FName variable as the name of the saved workbook. The statement was reformatted to be more easily readable. Also, a couple of the named arguments from the original, recorded statement were removed—they were optional arguments, and had zero-length strings assigned to them. The macro recorder often records object method arguments that are not really required; often, if you see named arguments in recorded macros that pass empty strings, you can safely delete those named arguments.

Finally, line 70 restores control of the status bar to Excel. This line is fairly important—without this line, Excel continues to display the status bar message specified in line 15 until you actually exit from Excel, or until another procedure changes the status bar message.

The NewFile procedure ends in line 71 of the listing, with the End Sub keywords. The remaining code in this listing defines other functions or procedures in the module. You may recall that the original recorded macro closed the workbook file after creating and saving it. Because a user is most likely to want to begin working immediately with a workbook that they create, the recorded instruction that closed the workbook file was removed from this version of the NewFile procedure.

Line 74 begins the function declaration for the **GetBookName** function. This function has three arguments and returns a string value. The first argument, **1Dflt**, is required; the remaining two arguments, **1Prompt** and **1Title**, are optional. Notice that the function declaration has been divided over several different lines in the module by using the line continuation symbol. The function declaration was split up like this so that it is easier to see what the various function arguments and their options are. Lines 77 through 82 are comments that explain the behavior and purpose of the **GetBookName** function.

Line 85 of the listing begins the actual code for the **GetBookName** function. This line uses the If...Then structure very briefly introduced in this week, and the IsMissing function to determine whether or not a prompt argument was included when **GetBookName** was called. If a prompt was not included, then line 87 assigns a sort of generic prompt suitable for the task that this function carries out.

Line 91 is the heart of the **GetBookName** function—it contains the function assignment statement to specify the function's return value, and uses the InputBox function to get that value at the same time. Notice that the **GetBookName** function arguments are simply passed on as arguments to the InputBox function.

The **GetBookName** function was written for use with the **NewFile** procedure for a couple of different reasons. First, getting a workbook name is likely to be a frequent activity in many different procedures. Second, using a function to obtain the workbook name makes it possible to concentrate all the relevant code in a single location, without repeating that code over and over again in every procedure that needs to get a workbook name. If you now ever decide to alter how various procedures obtain filenames from the user—say, by validating the filename in some way—you only have to modify the **GetBookName** function to have the changes applied in all procedures that use **GetBookName** to get workbook names from the user.

Line 94 contains the keywords End Function to end the **GetBookName** function definition.

Finally, lines 97 through 104 define a procedure named **Test_GetBookName** that tests the **GetBookName** function. Before relying on the **GetBookName** function to behave correctly in the **NewFile** procedure, **Test_Get BookName** was used to test **GetBookName**. Notice that **Test_GetBookName** tests all of the possible combinations of required and optional arguments for **GetBookName**, and simply displays the result of the **GetBookName** function. If the **GetBookName** function were slightly more complex, this procedure should also have used variables and displayed the original argument values to ensure that **GetBookName** did not alter its arguments. In this case, the function is short enough that you can easily see it does not alter its arguments—except for **1Prompt**, which only gets modified if it is missing in the first place.

2

AT A GLANCE

8

9

10

11

12

13

14

You've finished your first week of learning how to program in Visual Basic for Applications. By now, you should feel comfortable entering, editing, and using procedures and functions in your modules—whether you record a macro and then edit it, or whether you write a procedure or function from scratch.

What's Ahead?

The second week, like the first, covers a lot of material. You'll learn about many of the key features of Visual Basic for Applications.

In Day 8, "Making Decisions in Visual Basic for Applications," you'll learn how to use VBA's decision-making structures—If...Then and Select Case. In Day 9, "Repeating Actions in Visual Basic: Loops," you'll learn how to add efficient repetition to your procedures by using VBA's looping structures.

In Day 10, "Data Types and Variables: Advanced Topics," you'll learn more about VBA's scope rules, how to increase or limit the scope of variables, procedures, and functions. You'll also learn how to create your own custom data types. In Day 11, "Modular Programming Techniques," you learn how to create libraries of VBA procedures and functions. Day 11 also gets you started writing programs that consist of several procedures and functions working together. This lesson also shows you how to add argument lists to your procedures.

Day 12, "Managing Files with Visual Basic for Applications," you learn how to use VBA's file management functions and statements to get information about files, create or remove disk directories, and copy or delete files.

Day 13, "Arrays," shows you how to create and sort arrays. Finally, in Day 14, "Debugging and Testing Macros," you'll learn how to use VBA's built-in debugger to examine your program's operation, and to find and correct errors in your programs. The VBA debugger is an important tool that enables you to closely examine how your procedures and programs execute, and makes it possible for you to locate or trace various problems that would otherwise be almost impossible to find.

The material in this second week builds on what you learned in the first week. Be sure to answer all of the quiz questions at the end of each day, and that you also try to complete each of the exercises. The best way to make the new material that you learn a real part of your everyday knowledge is to put that knowledge to work. You must write programs in order to learn how to program.

By the end of the first week, you learned to write simple VBA functions and procedures to carry out a single task. By the time you finish the second week, you should be able to write complex programs that can perform just about any job. Like the first week, the second week covers a lot of material, but if you take the information one chapter a day, you shouldn't have any problems.

Making Decisions in Visual Basic for Applications

Today, you learn how to write procedures or functions that alter their behavior based on various conditions. You learn:

- ☐ To understand what decision-making and branching commands are and how they work.

- ☐ How to construct logical statements to determine which branch of code your procedure should execute.

- ☐ How to make simple decisions in a function or procedure with the If...Then decision-making structure.

- ☐ How to make more complex decisions by nesting If...Then structures.

- ☐ How to make decisions involving many choices at once with the Select...Case structure.

- ☐ How to unconditionally change the execution of your code with a GoTo statement.

- ☐ Why and how to end a procedure, function, or an entire program early.

- ☐ How to use the Buttons argument in MsgBox to let your procedure's user make simple choices.

Understanding Visual Basic for Applications' Decision-Making Commands

Up to this point, you've written procedures and functions that VBA executes in a completely linear fashion, much the same way that VBA executes a recorded macro: VBA begins executing statements, starting with the first statement after the procedure's or function's declaration line. VBA continues to execute each statement, line by line, until it reaches the End Sub or End Function statement that marks the end of that procedure's or function's definition, or until a runtime error occurs—the *flow* of VBA's execution goes straight through, from beginning to end, without alteration.

Procedures and functions like this, although able to carry out fairly sophisticated tasks, lack the capability to make decisions that result in performing different actions under different circumstances. You'll encounter many situations where you need or want your procedures or functions to perform different actions under different circumstances. For example, if you write a procedure that gets the name of a workbook from the user, and then opens that workbook, you might consider it desirable to have your procedure offer to create the workbook if it doesn't already exist. In a situation like this, your procedure would use VBA's decision-making statements to offer the user the chance to create the workbook. Your procedure would then use

VBA's decision-making commands again, to evaluate the user's choice and either create the workbook, or end the procedure's execution.

You will frequently use decision-making commands to evaluate specific items of data, and to then choose different actions based on that single data item. For example, you might write a procedure that checks a column in a worksheet to make sure that all of the numbers entered in that column are between 1 and 10. Your procedure might then examine each column entry separately, and execute some special action whenever it encounters a column entry outside the specified range.

Decisions do not always involve reacting to problems. If you want your procedure's user to make some kind of a choice about what your procedure should do next, you might use the InputBox function to get text input from the user, or use the MsgBox function to let the user make a choice by clicking a command button in the message dialog box. (Using MsgBox to let your procedure's user make choices is described at the end of this chapter.) Once you've gotten the user's choice, your procedure must be able to choose a course of action corresponding to the user's choice.

Your procedures, of course, can't really "make a decision" the same way that a human being can. Your procedures can, however, choose predefined courses of action based on simple conditions and make relatively complex decisions by combining smaller decisions.

When you use VBA's decision-making statements, you define a condition or set of conditions under which VBA executes one or another *branch* of your procedure's code. Because decision-making statements affect the top-to-bottom flow of execution in your program, they are often referred to as *flow control* or *program control* statements but are known more technically as *conditional* and *unconditional branching* statements.

A *conditional* branching statement is a decision-making structure that chooses one or another branch of the procedure's code based on some predefined condition or group of conditions. An *unconditional* branching statement is a statement that simply alters the flow of the procedure's execution, without depending on any specific condition. You'll use conditional branching with much greater frequency than you'll use unconditional branching.

When VBA encounters a conditional branching statement—such as If...Then—it first evaluates the specified condition. If the condition is true, VBA executes a specified group of statements. You use a logical expression to specify the condition for a conditional branching statement. When VBA encounters an unconditional branching statement—the GoTo—it immediately begins executing the statements indicated by the branching command.

You specify the criteria on which VBA makes decisions in conditional branching statements by constructing a logical expression, which describes the condition under which you want VBA to execute or not execute a particular series of statements. You use VBA's various comparison and logical operators (described in Day 4) to construct the logical expressions in your branching statements.

Making Simple Choices

VBA's simplest decision-making statements are the `If...Then` and `If...Then...Else` statements. The `If...Then` statement gives VBA the ability to choose a single alternative branch of a procedure's execution. The closely related `If...Then...Else` statement gives VBA the ability to choose between two alternative branches of a procedure's execution, based on whether or not the specified condition is true.

Choosing a Single Branch Using *If...Then*

You've already seen examples of the `If...Then` statement used to test whether or not a function's optional arguments were included when the function was called. The `If...Then` statement chooses a single alternative branch of execution in your procedure or function code.

Syntax

The `If...Then` statement has two different syntax forms. The simplest form is the single-line `If...Then` statement:

```
If condition Then statements
```

`condition` is any logical expression, and `statements` may be none, one, or many VBA statements—all of the statements must be on the same line, however. When VBA executes a statement like this, it first evaluates the logical expression represented by `condition`; if this logical expression evaluates to `True`, VBA executes the statement or statements after the `Then` keyword, up to the end of the line. VBA then resumes execution with the first statement after the line that contains the `If...Then` statement.

If the logical expression represented by `condition` is `False`, VBA immediately executes the first statement in the line after the line that contains the `If...Then` statement, without executing the alternate branch at all. The following procedure fragment shows a typical single-line `If...Then` statement:

```
If temperature > 100 then MsgBox "Too hot!"
```

Placing Several Statements on the Same Line

You can include multiple VBA statements on a single line by separating each statement with a colon (:), as shown following:

```
statement1 : statement2 : statementN
```

In this line, `statement1`, `statement2`, and `statementN` are any single, valid VBA statements. You may include as many statements on a single line as you want, up to the maximum line length limit for a module sheet.

Lines with many statements in them may be difficult to read and understand, however. In general, you should only place a single statement on each line.

8

Listing 8.1 shows a slightly modified version of the **GetBookName** function shown previously in the "Week 1 in Review" listings.

Listing 8.1. The GetBookName function.

```
 1:  Function GetBookName(lDflt As String, _
 2:                       Optional Prmpt, _
 3:                       Optional lTitle) As String
 4:
 5:     'check for prompt string included in the argument list
 6:     If IsMissing(Prmpt) Then Prmpt = "Enter a workbook name:"
 7:
 8:     'use InputBox to get the filename.
 9:     GetBookName = InputBox(prompt:=Prmpt, _
10:                       Title:=lTitle, _
11:                       default:=lDflt)
12:  End Function    'GetBookName
```

This function works exactly as described in the "Week 1 in Review" section. Line 1 contains the function declaration, which specifies one required argument and two optional arguments for the function, and also specifies the function's result as a String.

Pay close attention to line 6, which contains a single-line If...Then statement. When VBA executes line 6, it first evaluates the condition expression IsMissing(Prmpt). The IsMissing function returns True if the **Prmpt** argument was missing from the argument list at the time the **GetBookName** function was called. If IsMissing returns True, then VBA executes the statement Prmpt = "Enter a workbook name:", which assigns a default string to the **Prmpt** argument variable. If IsMissing returns False, then VBA does *not* execute the statement after the Then keyword, and the contents of the **Prmpt** argument variable remain unaltered.

In this way, the **GetBookName** function provides a default value for its own **Prmpt** argument, whenever the **Prmpt** optional argument is omitted. The assignment to the **Prmpt** argument variable occurs only when the IsMissing function returns True.

Finally, line 9 of **GetBookName** uses the InputBox function to obtain the return value of the function.

The second form of the If...Then statement is called a *block* If statement. In the block If...Then statement, the condition and statements are written on separate lines, as shown in the following general syntax:

```
If condition Then
   statements
End If
```

259

condition, like the single-line If...Then statement, represents the logical expression defining the condition under which VBA should execute the alternate statements. *statements* represents none, one, or several VBA statements; the statements may be on a single line, or on several lines. Finally, the keywords End If signal VBA that the end of the alternate branch of statements has been reached. The End If keywords must appear on a line by themselves, although you may include a trailing comment on that line.

Just like the single-line If...Then statement, VBA first evaluates the logical expression represented by *condition*. If this expression is True, VBA executes the statements in the alternate branch, starting with the first statement on the line after the line containing the If...Then keywords. VBA continues executing statements in the alternate branch until it reaches the End If keywords. VBA then continues executing statements starting with the first statement after the End If.

If the logical expression represented by *condition* evaluates to False, VBA does not execute any of the statements in the alternate branch; instead VBA immediately continues executing statements, beginning with the first statement after the End If.

You've already seen a couple of examples of the block If...Then statement, in previous lessons. The following lines show a typical block If...Then statement:

```
If temperature > 100 Then
    MsgBox "Too hot!"
End If
```

In the preceding statement, if the value stored in the **temperature** variable is greater than 100, then VBA executes the MsgBox statement to display the message *Too hot!* If the value stored in the **temperature** variable is 100 or less, VBA executes the first statement that appears after the End If keywords. Remember, the End If keywords must appear on a line by themselves.

DO	DON'T

DO use a single-line If...Then statement when the logical expression for the condition is not very long, and there are only one or two statements in the alternate program branch.

DO use the block If...Then statement if the logical expression is long, or if there are many statements in the alternate program branch. The block If form is usually much easier to read and understand.

Choosing between Branches Using *If...Then...Else*

The `If...Then` statement allows you to specify a single alternate branch of statements in your procedure. Frequently, however, you will need or want to choose between one of two different alternate statement branches, depending on a specific condition. VBA provides the `If...Then...Else` and `If...Then...ElseIf` statements for just that purpose.

Syntax

Like `If...Then`, VBA's `If...Then...Else` statement has two forms—a single-line form and a block form. The general syntax for the single-line `If...Then...Else` statement is:

```
If Condition Then Statements Else ElseStatements
```

`Condition` represents any valid logical expression. `Statements` and `ElseStatements` each represent any one or more VBA statements. Like the single-line `If...Then` statement, all the statements and keywords of the single-line `If...Then...Else` must appear on the same line.

When VBA executes the single-line `If...Then...Else` statement, it first evaluates the logical expression represented by `Condition`; if this expression evaluates as `True`, VBA executes the statements between the keywords `Then` and `Else` (represented by `Statements`), and resumes execution with the first statement after the line that contains the `If...Then...Else`.

If the logical expression represented by `Condition` evaluates to `False`, VBA executes the statements after the `Else` keyword, up to the end of the line (represented by `ElseStatements`), and continues execution with the first statement after the line that contains the `If...Then...Else`.

The following line shows a typical example of a single-line `If...Then...Else` statement:

```
If temperature > 100 Then MsgBox "Hot!" Else MsgBox "Less Hot!"
```

In this example, if the value in the **temperature** variable is greater than 100, the condition expression is `True`, and VBA executes the `MsgBox` statement to display the message *Hot!* on-screen. If **temperature** contains a number that is 100 or less, the condition is `False`, and VBA executes the `MsgBox` statement after the `Else` keyword to display the message *Less Hot!* on-screen.

As you can tell from this simple single-line `If...Then...Else` example, the single-line form may not be easy for a human being to read. Also, because all elements of a single-line `If...Then...Else` statement must appear on the same line, the size and number of statements you can include in the alternate execution branches are limited by the amount of space available in the line.

Syntax

The block If...Then...Else statement is easier to read and understand, and—because you can place statements on different lines within the block If...Then...Else statement—has no limit on the size or number of statements you can include in the alternate branches. The general syntax of the block If...Then...Else statement is:

```
If Condition Then
     Statements
Else
     ElseStatements
End If
```

Condition represents any valid logical expression; Statements and ElseStatements each represent none, one, or several VBA statements. When VBA executes a block If...Then...Else statement, it first evaluates the logical expression represented by Condition. If the expression evaluates to True, then VBA executes all of the statements (represented by Statements) between the Then keyword and the Else keyword. VBA then resumes execution with the first statement that appears after the End If keywords, which signal the end of the block If...Then...Else statement.

If the logical expression represented by Condition evaluates to False, VBA executes all the statements (represented by ElseStatements) between the Else keyword and the End If keywords. VBA then continues execution with the first statement that appears after the End If keywords. Like the block If...Then statement, the End If keywords must appear on a line by themselves, although you can add a trailing comment to that line.

The If...Then...Else statement chooses one or the other branch, but never both at the same time. The following example shows a typical block If...Then...Else statement:

```
If temperature > 100 Then
     MsgBox "Hot!"
Else
     MsgBox "Less Hot!"
End If
```

This example contains the same statement shown for the single-line If...Then...Else, but using the block form instead. When VBA executes this statement, it first evaluates the logical expression temperature > 100. If **temperature** contains a value greater than 100—the logical expression is True—VBA executes the MsgBox "Hot!" statement and then executes the first statement after the End If keywords. If the number stored in the **temperature** variable is 100 or less, then the logical condition expression is False, and VBA executes the MsgBox "Less Hot!" statement; VBA then continues execution with the first statement after the End If keywords.

Listing 8.2 shows another version of the **GetBookName** function, with a block If...Then...Else statement added to it.

Type

Listing 8.2. The block `If...Then...Else` statement.

```
1:  Function GetBookName(ByVal lDflt As String, _
2:                       Optional Prmpt, _
3:                       Optional lTitle) As String
4:
5:    'was a prompt string included in the argument list?
6:    If IsMissing(Prmpt) Then Prmpt = "Enter a workbook name:"
7:
8:    'if default name is not an empty string, convert it to
9:    'all upper-case letters, otherwise assign a name to it.
10:   If lDflt <> "" Then
11:      lDflt = UCase(lDflt)
12:   Else
13:      lDflt = "NEWFILE.XLS"
14:   End If
15:
16:   'use InputBox to get the filename.
17:   GetBookName = InputBox(prompt:=Prmpt, _
18:                          Title:=lTitle, _
19:                          default:=lDflt)
20: End Function
21:
22:
23: Sub Test_GetBookName()
24: 'This procedure tests the GetBookName function
25:    MsgBox GetBookName("")
26:    MsgBox GetBookName("default only")
27:    MsgBox GetBookName(Prmpt:="A prompt", lDflt:="default")
28:    MsgBox GetBookName(lDflt:="default", lTitle:="title")
29: End Sub
```

This version of **GetBookName** operates exactly like the version shown previously in Listing 8.1, with the exception of the added `If...Then...Else` statement in lines 10 through 14.

The first line in this function that VBA executes is line 6, which uses a single-line `If...Then` statement to test whether the optional **Prmpt** argument was supplied when the function was called. If the **Prmpt** argument is missing, VBA executes the assignment statement at the end of line 6 to assign a default value to the **Prmpt** argument variable.

The next line VBA executes is line 10, which begins a block `If...Then...Else` statement. When VBA executes this line, it first evaluates the logical expression `lDflt <> ""`. This expression evaluates to `True` if the value contained in the **lDflt** argument variable is *not* an empty (zero-length) string—although the **lDflt** argument is required, it is possible for you to call the **GetBookName** function with an empty string passed as the **lDflt** argument.

If the **lDflt** argument does not contain an empty string, VBA executes the `lDflt = UCase(lDflt)` statement, which uses the `UCase` function to convert the string in the **lDflt** argument to all

uppercase letters. VBA continues executing statements starting with line 17, the first statement after the `End If` keywords of the `If...Then...Else` statement.

If the `lDflt` argument *does* contain an empty string, VBA executes the `Else` branch of the `If...Then...Else` statement, and executes the `lDflt = "NEWFILE.XLS"` statement, which simply assigns a string to the `lDflt` argument variable. VBA continues executing statements starting with line 17, the first statement after the `End If` keywords of the `If...Then...Else` statement.

Line 17 assigns the result of the `InputBox` function as the `GetBookName` function result.

> **Note:** Notice that the function declaration (line 1) for this version of the `GetBookName` now passes the `lDflt` argument by value because the added `If...Then...Else` statement in lines 10 through 14 alters the `lDflt` argument variable. The `ByVal` keyword was added so that the source of the `lDflt` argument is not permanently changed outside of the `GetBookName` function. (Remember, passing by value provides your function with a copy of the argument data, as explained in Day 6.)

Finally, lines 23 through 29 of Listing 8.2 contain a procedure used to test the behavior of the `GetBookName` function. Now, whenever you call the `GetBookName` function, it always displays the suggested default workbook name in capital letters, and—if an empty string for the default book name is passed to the function, the function supplies its own default name: `NEWFILE.XLS`.

You will see many more examples of `If...Then` and `If...Then...Else` statements throughout the remaining lessons in this book.

Making Complex Choices

So far, you have seen how to construct branching statements that choose a single alternate branch of procedure execution, or choose between one of two alternate branches of procedure execution. Frequently, however, you will need or want to make more complex choices in your procedures, choosing between three, four, or more different alternate branches.

Nested *If...Then* Statements

For more complex decision-making requirements, you can place an `If...Then` or `If...Then...Else` statement inside another `If...Then` or `If...Then...Else` statement, called *nesting* statements. (*Nesting* means placing one type of flow control structure inside another.)

Although you can nest the single-line forms of If...Then and If...Then...Else statements, such statements are quite difficult for a human reader to understand. When you nest If...Then and If...Then...Else statements, use the block forms of these statements for clarity.

Listing 8.3 shows a simple procedure to illustrate how nested If...Then...Else statements work. The **EvalTemperature** procedure gets a number from the user, and then evaluates that number.

> **Note:** The example in Listing 8.3, for simplicity, nests only one If...Then...Else statement inside another. You can nest as many If...Then...Else statements inside each other as you want.

Listing 8.3. Nested If...Then...Else statements.

```
1:  Sub EvalTemperature()
2:
3:      Dim temperature
4:
5:      temperature = Application.InputBox( _
6:                          prompt:="Enter the temperature:", _
7:                          Title:="EvalTemp Procedure", _
8:                          Type:=1)
9:
10:     If temperature > 100 Then
11:       MsgBox "Too hot!"
12:     Else
13:       If temperature > 50 Then
14:         MsgBox "Stay cool!"
15:       Else
16:         MsgBox "Too cold!"
17:       End If
18:     End If
19: End Sub
```

Line 3 of the procedure declares the **temperature** variable to store input obtained from the user. Line 5 uses the Application object's version of the InputBox function and includes the Type:=1 optional argument to specify that only a numeric value may be entered in the input dialog box. VBA displays an error message if the user enters a non-numeric value, and waits until the user does enter a numeric value, or chooses Cancel in the input dialog box. (The Type:= argument is not available in VBA's InputBox function.)

Pay close attention to lines 10 through 18 in this listing. When VBA executes line 10, it first evaluates the logical expression temperature > 100. If the value stored in the **temperature** variable is greater than 100, VBA executes line 11, displaying the message *Too hot!* on-screen, and continues execution with the first statement after the End If keywords in line 18—in this case, the end of the procedure.

If the value in the **temperature** variable is 100 or less, however, the condition for the If statement beginning in line 10 is False, and VBA executes the Else branch beginning in line 13.

Line 13 starts another If...Then...Else statement, which is nested inside the If...Then...Else statement that begins in line 10. This second If...Then...Else statement in line 13 is the *inner* statement of the nested If...Then...Else statements, because it is contained completely inside the *outer* statement that begins in line 10.

If the logical expression temperature > 50 evaluates to True (the value in the **temperature** variable is greater than 50), VBA executes the MsgBox statement in line 14, which displays the message *Stay cool!* on-screen. VBA then continues execution with the first line after the End If statement in line 17—in this case, the end of the outer If...Then...Else statement.

If the value in the **temperature** variable is 50 or less, however, the logical expression in the inner If...Then...Else statement in line 13 evaluates to False, and VBA executes the Else branch of the inner If...Then...Else statement in line 16, which displays the message *Too cold!* on-screen. VBA then continues execution with the first line after the End If statement in line 17.

The If...Then keywords in line 10, the Else keyword in line 12, and the End If keywords in line 18 are all part of the outer If...Then...Else statement. The If...Then keywords in line 13, the Else keyword in line 15, and the End If keywords in line 17 are all part of the inner, nested If...Then...Else statement.

Notice how the statements and keywords that are part of the nested If...Then...Else statement are indented from the keywords and statements that form the outer If...Then...Else statement. This indentation helps you more easily identify which keywords and statements belong to the inner and outer nested If...Then...Else statements—the inner If...Then...Else statement is indented further from the left edge than the outer statement.

Like other indentation, there is nothing in VBA that forces you to indent your code, but you should always indent nested If...Then...Else statements to make your code easier to read, understand, and maintain.

DO	**DON'T**

DO use varying levels of indentation in your source code to make your code more readable and easier to understand—especially when nesting If...Then...Else statements.

DON'T write code that looks like this:

```
If temperature > 100 Then
MsgBox "Too hot!"
Else
If temperature > 50 Then
MsgBox "Stay cool!"
```

```
Else
MsgBox "Too cold!"
End If
End If
```

Although VBA will execute these statements in exactly the same way as lines 10 through 18 in Listing 8.3, you can see that it is almost impossible to tell which statements and keywords form the inner and outer nested If...Then...Else statements.

Using *If...Then...ElseIf*

VBA provides a short-hand version of the If...Then...Else statement to provide a more concise equivalent for the kind of nested If...Then...Else statements shown in Listing 8.3. This shorthand variation is the If...Then...ElseIf statement.

The general syntax for the If...Then...ElseIf statement is:

```
If Condition1 Then
        Statements
ElseIf Condition2
        ElseIfStatements
[Else
        ElseStatements]
End If
```

Condition1 and *Condition2* each represent any valid logical expression; *Statements*, *ElseIfStatements*, and *ElseStatements* each represent none, one, or several VBA statements.

When VBA executes an If...Then...ElseIf statement, it first evaluates the logical expression represented by *Condition1*. If the expression evaluates to True, then VBA executes all of the statements (represented by Statements) between the Then keyword and the ElseIf keyword. VBA then resumes execution with the first statement that appears after the End If keywords, which signal the end of the If...Then...ElseIf statement.

If the *Condition1* logical expression evaluates to False, then VBA evaluates the logical expression represented by *Condition2*. If the *Condition2* expression evaluates to True, then VBA executes all of the statements (represented by *ElseIfStatements*) between the ElseIf keyword and the End If (or optional Else) keywords. VBA then continues execution with the first statement that appears after the End If keywords. The End If keywords must appear on a line by themselves.

If the *Condition2* logical expression evaluates to False, then VBA skips the *ElseIfStatements*, and continues execution with the first statement after the End If keywords. You can optionally include an Else clause in the If...Then...ElseIf statement. If the *Condition1* logical expression *and* the *Condition2* logical expressions are False, and there is an Else clause, then VBA executes the statements represented by *ElseStatements*. After executing the *ElseStatements*, VBA continues execution with the first statement after the End If keywords.

The following example shows lines 10 through 18 of Listing 8.3 rewritten to use the `If...Then...ElseIf` statement:

```
If temperature > 100 Then
     MsgBox "Too hot!"
ElseIf temperature > 50 Then
     MsgBox "Stay cool!"
Else
     MsgBox "Too cold!"
End If
```

The preceding `If...Then...ElseIf` statement behaves exactly the same as the nested `If...Then...Else` statements in lines 10 through 18 of Listing 8.3, with the same results—this form is just more compact.

If you want, you can include more than one `ElseIf` clause in an `If...Then...ElseIf` statement, as long as all the `ElseIf` clauses come before the `Else` clause. VBA only executes the statements in an `ElseIf` clause if the logical expression in that clause is `TRUE`.

Using the `If...Then...ElseIf` statement is a matter of personal preference. Many programmers feel that their code is more understandable and maintainable by using nested `If...Then...Else` statements, and avoiding the `If...Then...ElseIf` statement. Originally, `If...Then...ElseIf` was added to BASIC to provide a functionality similar to the `Select...Case` statement described in the next section; it remains in VBA in order to make it easier to translate existing BASIC programs into VBA. For making very many choices, the `Select...Case` statement is superior to either nested `If...Then...Else` statements, or the more compact `If...Then...ElseIf` statement.

Using the *Select...Case* Statement

The example of nested `If...Then...Else` statements in Listing 8.3—and the `If...Then...ElseIf` statements explained previously—easily make a three-way decision, but what if you need to choose between five, eight, or ten different courses of action? What if several possible conditions all lead to the same branching choice?

To choose among several possible branches of procedure execution, you can nest `If...Then...Else` statements many levels deep, but following the course of the decision branches becomes progressively more difficult for the human reader. Alternatively, you could add additional `ElseIf` clauses to an `If...Then...ElseIf` statement, with one `ElseIf` clause for each conditional branch. The `If...Then...ElseIf` statement has a similar problem, however: when there are many `ElseIf` clauses, the `If...Then...ElseIf` statement becomes difficult to read and follow.

<table>
<tr><td>

DO

</td><td>

DON'T

</td></tr>
</table>

DON'T nest If...Then...Else statements too deeply, or they can be almost impossible for a human reader to follow.

DO use a Select Case statement if you need to choose among more than three or four possible branches of execution.

Fortunately, VBA offers a conditional branching statement for use when you must choose among a large number of different branches: the Select Case statement. Select Case operates much the same as multiple independent If statements but is a bit easier to follow. You use the Select Case keywords with multiple Case statements where each Case statement tests for the occurrence of a different condition. Only one of the Case branches will be executed. A Case branch may contain none, one, or several VBA statements.

Syntax

The Select Case statement has the following general syntax:

```
Select Case TestExpression
      Case ExpressionList1
            statements1
      Case ExpressionList2
            statements2
      .
      .
      .
      Case ExpressionListN
            statementsN
      [Case Else
            ElseStatements]
End Select
```

TestExpression is any numeric or string expression. *ExpressionList1*, *ExpressionList2*, and *ExpressionListN* each represent a list of logical expressions, separated by commas. *statements1*, *statements2*, *statementsN*, and *ElseStatements* each represent none, one, or several VBA statements. You can include as few or as many Case *ExpressionList* clauses in a Select Case statement as you wish.

When VBA executes a Select Case statement, it first evaluates the *TestExpression*, and then compares the result of that expression to each of the expressions listed in each *ExpressionList*. If the value represented by *TestExpression* matches an expression in the *ExpressionList* for one of the Case clauses, then VBA executes the statements for that clause. If the *TestExpression* value matches more than one Case clause, VBA only executes the statements in the first matching Case

clause. `TestExpression` is frequently just a single variable name, or a mathematical or numeric expression, rather than a logical expression. The expressions in the `ExpressionList` are typically logical expressions.

When VBA finishes executing the statements in the first matching `Case` clause, it continues execution with the first statement after the `End Select` keywords, which mark the end of the `Select Case` statement.

If the `TestExpression` value does *not* match any of the `Case` clauses, and the optional `Case Else` clause is present, then VBA executes the statements represented by `ElseStatements` before continuing on to the statement after the `Select Case` statement.

In the separate `Case` clauses, the `ExpressionList` may consist of one or more expressions, separated by a comma. `ExpressionList` has the following general syntax:

```
expression1, expression2, expressionN
```

Expressions in `ExpressionList` may be any numeric string or logical expression. The expressions in `ExpressionList` may also specify a range of values by using the `To` operator:

```
expression1 To expression2
```

For example, to specify a range of numbers from 1 to 10 in a `Case` `ExpressionList` clause, you use the following expression:

```
Case 1 To 10
```

To select branches based on whether `TestExpression` is greater than, less than, equal to, or some other relational comparison, use the following general syntax:

```
Is ComparisonOperator expression
```

In the preceding line, `ComparisonOperator` is any of VBA's relational operators, except for the `Is` and `Like` operators; `expression` is any VBA expression. To execute the statements in a `Case` branch when the `TestExpression` is greater than 10, for example, you would use the following expression:

```
Case Is > 10
```

> **Note:** The `Is` keyword used in `Select Case` statements is *not* the same as the `Is` comparison operator; you cannot use the `Is` comparison operator, nor the `Like` operator, in a `Select Case` statement.

Listing 8.4 shows an example of a `Select Case` statement.

 Listing 8.4. The Select Case statement.

```
 1:   Sub EvalTemperature()
 2:
 3:      Dim temperature
 4:
 5:      temperature = Application.InputBox( _
 6:                          prompt:="Enter the temperature:", _
 7:                          Title:="EvalTemp Procedure", _
 8:                          Type:=1)
 9:
10:      Select Case temperature
11:        Case Is > 100
12:          MsgBox "Too hot!"
13:        Case 75 To 100
14:          MsgBox "Stay cool!"
15:        Case 50 To 74
16:          MsgBox "Okay."
17:        Case Is > 32
18:          MsgBox "Pretty cold."
19:        Case Else
20:          MsgBox "Freezing and below!"
21:      End Select
22:   End Sub
```

Analysis

The `EvalTemperature` procedure in this listing works essentially the same as the procedure in Listing 8.3. Like the procedure in Listing 8.3, line 5 gets a number from the user.

Lines 10 through 21 contain a `Select Case` statement. Line 10 contains the start of the `Select Case` statement. The test expression in line 10 consists of a single variable: the **temperature** variable. As you know, the result of an expression containing a single variable is the value stored in the variable. VBA therefore compares whatever value is stored in the **temperature** variable to the conditions specified in each `Case` branch of the `Select Case` statement.

First, VBA checks to see if the value in the **temperature** variable matches the condition specified in the first `Case` clause, in line 11. This `Case` condition contains the expression `Is > 100`. If the value in **temperature** is greater than 100, then the `MsgBox` statement in line 12 executes, displaying the message *Too hot!* on-screen. The condition in this case branch is equivalent to the following `If` statement:

```
If temperature > 100 then MsgBox "Too hot!"
```

When VBA finishes executing the statement in line 12, it continues execution with the first statement in the procedure after line 21, which contains the `End Select` keywords that mark the end of the `Select Case` statement.

If the value in the **temperature** variable is 100 or less, VBA skips to the next `Case` condition in line 13. This `Case` condition uses the `To` operator to specify a range of numbers. If the value in

temperature is any number from 75 to 100, then VBA executes the MsgBox statement in line 14, and then continues execution with the first statement after the End Select keywords in line 21.

If the value in the **temperature** variable is not in the range of 75 to 100, VBA skips to the next Case condition in line 15, which also tests to see if the value in **temperature** falls within a particular range: this time the range of numbers is from 50 to 74. If the test expression (**temperature**) matches the condition, then VBA executes line 16 and then continues with the statements after the End Select statement; otherwise, VBA again skips to the next Case condition. VBA behaves the same way for the remaining Case condition in line 17.

Finally, if the value in the **temperature** variable does not match any of the Case conditions, VBA executes the Case Else branch of the Select Case statement.

If the user enters the number 8 in response to the Application.InputBox statement in line 5, VBA executes the Select Case statement in lines 10 through 21 by first evaluating the test expression, which—because it contains only the variable **temperature**—evaluates to the number 8.

When VBA evaluates the Case condition in line 11, the condition is not true; 8 is not greater than 100. VBA goes on to the Case condition in line 13; again the condition is not true (8 is not in the range 75 to 100). VBA skips to the Case condition in line 15. The number 8 is not in the range 50 to 74, either, so VBA again skips to the next Case condition, this time in line 17. This condition is not true either (8 is not greater than 32).

VBA has now tested the result of the test expression against all of the specified conditions in the Select Case statement and has not found a match for any of them. VBA therefore executes the Case Else branch of the Select Case statement in line 19, resulting in the message dialog box shown in Figure 8.1. When VBA has finished executing the Case Else branch, execution continues with the first statement after the End Select statement in line 21—the end of the procedure, in this case.

Figure 8.1.

If you enter the number 8 in the input dialog box in Listing 8.4, VBA displays this dialog box.

Note: If the user enters a number greater than 74, but less than 75, then VBA ends up executing the Case Else branch. A number such as 74.5, for example, does not match any of the specified conditions in any of the Case branches in the Select Case statement in Listing 8.4. Entering the value of 74.5 for the temperature causes the *Freezing and below* message to display, which is obviously incorrect. The range in line 15 of Listing 8.4 should really have been: 50 To 75. This way there is no gap in the ranges—because VBA executes only the first matching Case condition, numbers with a value of 75 are still handled by the first Case branch starting in line 13. A number such as 74.5, however, would now be handled correctly by the Case branch starting in line 15.

DO	DON'T

DO use a Select Case statement if you need to choose among more than three or four different courses of action.

DO use a Select Case statement if you need to choose the same course of action when several different conditions are true. The following Case clause, for example, will have its associated statements executed whenever the test expression evaluates to one of the numbers 2, 4, 6, or 8.

```
Case 2, 4, 6, 8
```

DON'T forget to carefully construct your ranges and various other Case conditions to avoid gaps in value ranges like the one noted for Listing 8.4.

Unconditional Branching

An unconditional branching statement *always* changes the flow of statement execution in a VBA procedure or function. VBA does not test any conditions (hence the term *unconditional*), it simply switches execution to a specified location.

VBA has only one unconditional branching statement: GoTo. There are very few reasons to use the GoTo statement; in fact, procedures that use many GoTo statements tend to be very difficult to understand. In almost every circumstance where you might use a GoTo statement, you can use one of the If statements, a Select Case statement, or one of the looping structures you learn about in the next lesson, to accomplish the same purpose with greater ease and clarity.

The GoTo statement is a hold-over from early versions of the BASIC programming language, which didn't have the sophisticated Select Case decision-making statement described in this chapter, or the powerful looping structures described in the next chapter. Programmers in early versions of BASIC used GoTo to simulate the effects of the more sophisticated VBA statements. In VBA, you should use the GoTo statement as little as possible.

You should take the time to understand how the GoTo statement works as an unconditional branching statement, mostly to help you understand how the error-handling GoTo operates, but also because you will occasionally see this command used by other programmers.

DO	DON'T

DON'T use a GoTo statement except as part of an On Error GoTo statement (described in Day 17).

DO try to use some other structure, such as a Select Case statement or one of the looping structures described in the next lesson, instead of a GoTo statement.

Syntax

The GoTo statement has the following general syntax:

```
GoTo line
```

line represents any valid line label or line number in the same procedure or function that contains the GoTo statement. When VBA executes a GoTo statement, it immediately shifts procedure execution to the line specified by *line*.

Syntax

A *line label* is a special type of identifier that identifies a particular line by name. Line labels have the following general syntax:

```
name:
```

name represents any valid VBA identifier. A line label can begin in any column on a line, as long as it is the first non-blank character on the line. A *line number* is essentially the same as a line label but is just a number, not an identifier. Using line numbers in VBA procedures is extremely unusual—you should always use a line label, instead.

Listing 8.5 shows a procedure that employs one of the most common legitimate uses for a GoTo statement in a VBA procedure: the procedure uses the GoTo statement to skip to the end of the procedure when the user chooses the Cancel command button in an input dialog box.

Listing 8.5. The GoTo statement.

```
1:  Sub MakeSalesRpt_Chart()
2:  'This procedure asks for a sheet name containing source
3:  'data, then asks for a range of cells containing the data
4:  'to chart. Next, the procedure asks for a sheet name to put
5:  'the pie chart on. The procedure then creates the chart,
6:  'and uses the ChartWizard method to make a pie chart.
7:
8:    Const sTitle = "Make Sales Report Chart"
9:
10:   Dim SrcShtName As String
```

```
11:    Dim SourceRng As String
12:    Dim DestShtName As String
13:
14:        'get source sheet name
15:    SrcShtName = InputBox(prompt:= _
16:                "Enter the name of the sheet " & _
17:                "containing the data to graph:", _
18:                        Title:=sTitle)
19:    'check to see if user entered name or chose Cancel
20:    If Len(Trim(SrcShtName)) = 0 Then
21:      MsgBox "Data sheet name not entered -ending procedure"
22:      GoTo GiveUp
23:    End If
24:     'select source sheet so user can refer to it
25:    Sheets(SrcShtName).Select
26:
27:       'get source range
28:    SourceRng = InputBox(prompt:= _
29:                "Enter the range of the data to graph " & _
30:                "using R1C1 notation:", _
31:                        Title:=sTitle)
32:     'check to see if user entered range or chose Cancel
33:    If Len(Trim(SourceRng)) = 0 Then
34:      MsgBox "Source range not entered - ending procedure"
35:      GoTo GiveUp
36:    End If
37:
38:       'get destination sheet name
39:    DestShtName = InputBox(prompt:="Enter the name of " & _
40:                   "the sheet to contain the graph:", _
41:                        Title:=sTitle)
42:     'check to see if user chose Cancel
43:    If Len(Trim(DestShtName)) = 0 Then
44:      MsgBox "Chart destination sheet name not entered" & _
45:        " - ending procedure"
46:      GoTo GiveUp
47:    End If
48:
49:     'select the destination sheet and create chart
50:    Sheets(DestShtName).Select
51:    ActiveSheet.ChartObjects.Add(96, 37.5, 234, 111).Select
52:
53:     'use ChartWizard Method to create chart.
54:    With Sheets(SrcShtName)
55:      ActiveChart.ChartWizard Source:=.Range(SourceRng), _
56:                                   Gallery:=xlPie, _
57:                                   Format:=7, _
58:                                   PlotBy:=xlColumns, _
59:                                   CategoryLabels:=1, _
60:                                   SeriesLabels:=1, _
61:                                   HasLegend:=1, _
62:                                   Title:="Sales Report"
63:    End With
64: GiveUp:
65:     'end of the procedure - canceling user input jumps here
66: End Sub
```

> **Note:** If you want to type this listing in and experiment with it, make sure that you use R1C1 notation, such as C5:D8. Make sure that the data you select is suitable for graphing with a pie chart.

Analysis

The MakeSalesRpt_Chart procedure is an edited version of a recorded macro. First, a macro to create a pie chart was recorded. The recorded macro was then copied to another module and edited. The macro's name was changed to MakeSalesRpt_Chart, and various constant and variable declarations were added. Next, VBA statements to get input from the user and to evaluate the user's input were added to the procedure.

Lines 10 through 12 each declare a string variable. SrcShtName holds the name of the worksheet that contains the data to graph, SourceRng holds the name or description of the range of data to graph, and DestShtName holds the name of the worksheet on which the procedure will put the resulting graph.

Line 15 starts the actual work of the MakeSalesRpt_Chart procedure. This line uses the InputBox function to get the name of the worksheet that contains the source data. The result of the InputBox function is assigned to the SrcShtName variable.

Line 20 starts a block If...Then statement. In the logical expression, the Trim function first trims any leading or trailing spaces from the string in SrcShtName, and the Len function returns the length of the trimmed string. If the length of the trimmed string is 0, the user either did not enter a name in the input dialog box or chose the Cancel command button—the InputBox function returns an empty string if the user presses Esc or chooses Cancel.

In either case, there is no point in continuing the procedure. The MsgBox statement in line 21 displays a message explaining that the procedure will now end. Line 22 contains a GoTo statement. When VBA executes this line, it immediately shifts execution to the line containing the line label GiveUp:, skipping over any statements between the line that contains the GoTo and the line that contains the specified line label. VBA then continues execution with the statement on the line following the line label. In this case, the GiveUp: label is in line 64, just before the End Sub statement.

Line 25 uses the Select method of the Sheets collection to select the worksheet named by SrcShtName, so that the user can see the data source sheet while entering the coordinates of the range of data to graph.

Next, line 28 uses InputBox to get the coordinates of the range of data to graph from the user, and assigns the user's entry to the SourceRng variable. As with the name of the source worksheet, line 33 tests to see whether or not the string obtained for the range of data to graph contains anything other than blank space, or the empty string returned when the user chooses the Cancel command button in the input dialog box.

Again, if the **SourceRng** variable does not contain any data, there is no point in continuing the procedure. When the string length comparison expression in line 33 is True, VBA executes lines 34 and 35. Line 34 displays a message to the user that the procedure will now end, and line 35 causes VBA to skip to the **GiveUp:** line label.

Line 39 gets the name of the sheet that will contain the finished pie chart, and assigns it to the **DestShtName** variable. Once again, in line 43, an If...Then statement tests to see whether or not the user entered a string or chose Cancel. Again, if the string entered by the user is empty or all blank space, there is no point in continuing the procedure; VBA executes the alternate statements in the If...Then statement. Again, VBA is directed to skip to the **GiveUp:** label at the end of the procedure.

VBA only gets to execute line 50 if the procedure's user actually enters all three requested values. In line 50, the Select method of the Sheets collection is used to select the worksheet that will contain the finished pie chart. Line 51 uses the Add method of the ChartObjects collection of the active sheet to create and select the new chart object. Lines 50 and 51 were obtained from a recorded macro.

Line 55 uses the ChartWizard method of the active sheet object to set the specifications for the chart object created in line 51. Although the line from the recorded macro was reformatted, and a With...End With statement was added (line 54) to make this method call more readable, it is essentially unchanged from the line in the original recorded macro. The programmer added only the **SrcShtName** and **SourceRng** variables, and removed only a couple of named arguments that were assigned empty strings.

> **Tip:** You can usually safely remove named arguments that are assigned empty strings from any recorded statement because empty strings are also the standard default value for most omitted optional arguments.

Finally, line 64 contains the **GiveUp:** line label. This line is the line to which all the GoTo statements in this procedure pass execution. Because line 64 is the last statement in the procedure before the end of the procedure in line 66, all of the GoTo statements have the effect of ending the procedure early. As you will learn in the next section, there is an even easier way to accomplish the same task.

Ending Procedures, Functions, and Entire Programs Early

As you can see from the procedure in Listing 8.5, there are circumstances—such as a user canceling an input dialog box, or the absence of some expected data—in which there is no point in continuing the execution of your procedure or function. If you have written an entire program that contains procedures that call other functions and procedures (as described in Day 11), you may even decide there are circumstances in which your entire program should stop running—such as a missing worksheet, allowing a user to cancel the program, and so on.

VBA provides the Exit and End statements to allow you to either terminate a procedure or function, or halt your entire program.

Using the *Exit* Statement

To make a single procedure or function stop executing, you use one of two available forms for the VBA Exit statement, depending on whether you want to terminate a function or a procedure.

The Exit statement has the following two syntax forms:

```
Exit Sub
Exit Function
```

Exit Sub and Exit Function both work exactly the same way, and have the same effects; you use Exit Sub to end a procedure, and Exit Function to end a function.

Listing 8.6 shows the same **MakeSalesRpt_Chart** procedure from Listing 8.5, but uses the Exit Sub statements to end the procedure early.

Type

Listing 8.6. Ending a procedure early with Exit Sub.

```
1:  Sub MakeSalesRpt_Chart()
2:  'This procedure asks for a sheet name containing source
3:  'data, then asks for a range of cells containing the data
4:  'to chart. Next, procedure asks for a sheet name to put
5:  'the pie chart on. The procedure then creates the chart,
6:  'and uses the ChartWizard method to make a pie chart.
7:
8:      Const sTitle = "Make Sales Report Chart"
9:
10:     Dim SrcShtName As String
11:     Dim SourceRng As String
12:     Dim DestShtName As String
13:
14:      'get source sheet name
15:     SrcShtName = InputBox(prompt:= _
16:                 "Enter the name of the sheet " & _
17:                 "containing the data to graph:", _
18:                        Title:=sTitle)
19:      'check to see if user entered name or chose Cancel
20:     If Len(Trim(SrcShtName)) = 0 Then
21:       MsgBox "Data sheet name not entered -ending procedure"
22:       Exit Sub
23:     End If
24:      'select source sheet so user can refer to it
```

```
25:     Sheets(SrcShtName).Select
26:
27:       'get source range
28:     SourceRng = InputBox(prompt:= _
29:                  "Enter the range of the data to graph " & _
30:                  "using R1C1 notation:", _
31:                      Title:=sTitle)
32:      'check to see if user entered range or chose Cancel
33:     If Len(Trim(SourceRng)) = 0 Then
34:       MsgBox "Source range not entered - ending procedure"
35:       Exit Sub
36:     End If
37:
38:       'get destination sheet name
39:     DestShtName = InputBox(prompt:="Enter the name of " & _
40:                       "the sheet to contain the graph:", _
41:                        Title:=sTitle)
42:      'check to see if user chose Cancel
43:     If Len(Trim(DestShtName)) = 0 Then
44:       MsgBox "Chart destination sheet name not entered" & _
45:             " - ending procedure"
46:       Exit Sub
47:     End If
48:
49:       'select the destination sheet and create chart
50:     Sheets(DestShtName).Select
51:     ActiveSheet.ChartObjects.Add(96, 37.5, 234, 111).Select
52:
53:       'use ChartWizard Method to create chart.
54:     With Sheets(SrcShtName)
55:       ActiveChart.ChartWizard Source:=.Range(SourceRng), _
56:                               Gallery:=xlPie, _
57:                               Format:=7, _
58:                               PlotBy:=xlColumns, _
59:                               CategoryLabels:=1, _
60:                               SeriesLabels:=1, _
61:                               HasLegend:=1, _
62:                               Title:="Sales Report"
63:     End With
64: End Sub
```

Analysis

This version of the **MakeSalesRpt_Chart** procedure works the same as the procedure shown in Listing 8.5, except that this version uses the Exit Sub statement to end the procedure early, rather than the GoTo and line label arrangement.

Notice lines 22, 35, and 46. Each of these lines contains an Exit Sub statement. Like the procedure shown in Listing 8.5, the If...Then statements cause VBA to execute the statements in lines 22, 35, and 46 whenever the user enters a blank string, chooses the Cancel command button, or presses Esc in any of the three input dialog boxes.

Each Exit Sub statement causes VBA to immediately stop executing statements in the procedure. After executing the Exit Sub statements, VBA stops executing the current procedure and returns to execution in the procedure or function that called the procedure containing the Exit Sub statement.

> **Note:** If you use an `Exit Sub` or `Exit Function` statement in a procedure or function called by another VBA procedure or function, that function continues to execute. The `Exit Sub` and `Exit Function` statements only stop execution of the current procedure or function.

DO	**DON'T**

DO use an `Exit Sub` or `Exit Function` statement to end a procedure or function early, instead of a `GoTo`. The `Exit Sub` statement makes it more obvious that your procedure will stop executing—and therefore easier to write, read, and understand your procedure.

Using the *End* Statement

You're now familiar with the `End Sub` and `End Function` keywords used to signal VBA that it has reached the end of a procedure or function. These keyword phrases tell VBA to stop executing statements in the current procedure or function, and to resume execution in the procedure or function that called the current procedure or function—if the current procedure was not called by another procedure, VBA ceases all statement execution.

For example, consider the listing in the "Week 1 in Review" section of this book. The **NewFile** procedure gets a workbook name from the user by calling a function named **GetBookName**. When VBA executes the **NewFile** procedure and encounters the statement in **NewFile** that calls the **GetBookName** function, VBA passes the function's arguments, and then begins executing statements in the **GetBookName** function. VBA executes statements in **GetBookName** until it reaches either the `End Function` statement at the end of the function definition, or until it executes an `Exit Function` statement. In either case, VBA stops executing the code in the **GetBookName** function and returns the function result to the **NewFile** procedure.

After VBA returns from the **GetBookName** function call, it finishes evaluating whatever expression uses the function result and continues executing the statements in the **NewFile** procedure, beginning with the statement after the one that called the **GetBookName** function. .

As it is, the **NewFile** procedure continues to execute, even if the user canceled the input dialog box displayed by the **GetBookName** function. Obviously, if the user canceled entering a workbook name, there is no point in continuing the **NewFile** procedure—without a workbook name there isn't any work for the **NewFile** procedure to perform.

In this situation, it would be nice if you could write the **GetBookName** function so that if the user cancels the input dialog box displayed by **GetBookName**, then the entire process of creating a new workbook is also canceled. As shown in the examples in Listing 8.6, you can use a combination of If...Then statements and the Exit Function statement to detect when the user cancels an input operation, and to end the function immediately, if that happens.

If you just end the **GetBookName** function early, however, VBA simply returns to the **NewFile** procedure and continues to execute it—which is not what you desire. Instead, you must completely end VBA's execution of your program. (A program can be a single procedure, or hundreds of procedures and functions working together.)

Syntax

To completely end VBA's execution of your program, use the End keyword on a line all by itself:

End

When VBA executes the preceding statement, it stops all execution of procedure and function statements. Any variables in existence cease to exist, and their values are lost.

Listing 8.7 shows the **GetBookName** function rewritten so that it completely ends whatever program VBA is executing if the user cancels the input dialog box.

Type

Listing 8.7. Ending program execution with End.

```
 1:  Function GetBookName(ByVal lDflt As String, _
 2:                    Optional Prmpt, _
 3:                    Optional lTitle) As String
 4:
 5:       'was prompt string included in argument list?
 6:     If IsMissing(Prmpt) Then Prmpt = "Enter a workbook name:"
 7:
 8:     'if default name is not an empty string, convert it to
 9:     'all upper-case letters, otherwise assign a name to it.
10:     If lDflt <> "" Then
11:        lDflt = UCase(lDflt)
12:     Else
13:        lDflt = "NEWFILE.XLS"
14:     End If
15:
16:       'use InputBox to get the filename.
17:     GetBookName = InputBox(prompt:=lPrompt, _
18:                        Title:=lTitle, _
19:                        default:=lDflt)
20:
21:       'check: did user cancel operation?
22:     If Len(Trim(GetBookName)) = 0 Then
23:        MsgBox prompt:="Program Canceled", Title:=lTitle
24:        End   'cancel entire program
25:     End If
26: End Function
27:
```

continues

Listing 8.7. continued

```
28:
29: Sub Test_GetBookName()
30: 'This procedure tests the GetBookName function
31:
32:     MsgBox GetBookName(lDflt:="", lTitle:="Cancel Test")
33: End Sub
```

 This version of the **GetBookName** function is the same—and works exactly the same way—as the function described in Listing 8.2. Only lines 21 through 25 were added to this function to give it the capability to end the entire program if the user cancels the input dialog box in line 17.

Line 17 uses the InputBox function to obtain a string from the user; the string returned by InputBox is assigned to the **GetBookName** function result. If the user presses the Esc key, or chooses the Cancel button, InputBox returns an empty string.

Line 22 is the start of a block If...Then statement. The test condition for the If...Then statement uses the Trim and Len functions to get the length of the string stored in the function's result, excluding any blank spaces in the string. If the length of the string returned by InputBox is zero, the user either entered a blank string as the workbook name, chose the Cancel command button in the input dialog box, or pressed the Esc key.

If InputBox returns an empty string, VBA executes line 23, which uses MsgBox to display a message on-screen, stating that the program has been canceled. Next, VBA executes the End statement in line 24. When VBA executes this line, it ceases all execution—it does *not* return to the procedure that called the **GetBookName** function. No additional statements are executed in any procedure or function.

Lines 29 through 33 are a simple procedure to test the **GetBookName** function. When VBA executes the test procedure, it begins executing **GetBookName** when it is called in line 32 of the test procedure. If the user cancels the input dialog box in the **GetBookName** function, VBA executes the End statement in **GetBookName**, and stops *all* execution—VBA does not even finish executing the MsgBox statement in line 32 of the test procedure!

DO	DON'T

DO write any of your procedures or functions that use the End statement to display some message or notification to the user explaining what is about to happen, and why, before the statement that actually contains the End statement. If you don't, your procedure's users may be completely mystified as to why the procedure or program they were using suddenly stopped working. If you end the program because of some user action—such as canceling an input dialog box—without an explanation, your

procedure's user may never figure out why the procedure ends—in fact, users are prone to consider such things to be a bug in your procedure!

DON'T forget to close workbooks, or do other "housekeeping" before your procedure executes an End statement, so that your program's user doesn't have to clean up things like half-finished charts, or deal with workbooks that have unsaved data when your program ends.

Using *MsgBox* to Let Users Make Choices

By now, you should be quite comfortable using the MsgBox statement to display messages to the user in titled dialog boxes. You can also use the VBA MsgBox procedure as a function to get choices from the user in response to messages or questions that your procedure displays by including the optional Buttons argument. For many simple choices, using the MsgBox function to get a response from the user is much easier than getting text input from the user with an InputBox function and then analyzing that text to determine what choice the user made.

When you include the Buttons argument—and the necessary parentheses for a function call—the MsgBox statement operates like a function and displays a message dialog box that contains a variety of command buttons. MsgBox returns a numeric result indicating which command button the user chose. You specify the number and type of command buttons displayed in the MsgBox dialog box through the Buttons argument.

Listing 8.8 shows a simple procedure that demonstrates the use of the Buttons argument.

Type

Listing 8.8. Using MsgBox and the Buttons argument to get user input.

```
1:  Sub Demo_MsgBoxFunction()
2:  'This procedure demonstrates the MsgBox used as a function
3:
4:      Const mTitle = "MsgBox Button Demonstration"
5:      Dim Resp As Integer
6:
7:      Resp = MsgBox(prompt:="Choose a button.", _
8:                  Title:=mTitle, _
9:                  Buttons:=vbYesNoCancel + vbQuestion)
10:     Select Case Resp
11:       Case Is = vbYes
12:         MsgBox prompt:="You chose the 'Yes' button.", _
13:               Title:=mTitle, _
14:               Buttons:=vbInformation
```

continues

Listing 8.8. continued

```
15:      Case Is = vbNo
16:        MsgBox prompt:="You chose the 'No' button.", _
17:               Title:=mTitle, _
18:               Buttons:=vbInformation
19:      Case Is = vbCancel
20:        MsgBox prompt:="You chose the 'Cancel' button.", _
21:               Title:=mTitle, _
22:               Buttons:=vbCritical
23:    End Select
24: End Sub
```

 The **Demo_MsgBoxFunction** procedure just demonstrates how to use the MsgBox statement as a function, the effects of various Buttons arguments, and how to evaluate the value that the MsgBox function returns.

Line 1 contains the procedure declaration, and line 2 contains a comment briefly describing the purpose of this procedure. Line 4 declares a constant for use as the title of the MsgBox dialog box, and line 5 declares an Integer type variable, **Resp**, to hold the result returned by the MsgBox function.

Line 7 contains the call to the MsgBox function, and assigns the MsgBox result to the **Resp** variable. Notice that the MsgBox function call spans three lines: 7, 8, and 9, using the line continuation symbol.

Notice that the MsgBox function call in lines 7 through 9 observes all of the requirements for using a function: the argument list is enclosed in parentheses, and the result of the function is used—assigned to a variable, in this case.

The argument list for the MsgBox function call starting in line 7 contains the familiar named arguments: prompt:=, to specify the text displayed in the message dialog box; and Title:=, to specify the title of the message dialog box. The function call also contains the new Buttons:= argument.

The Buttons argument passes the sum of two of VBA's predefined constants—you combine values for the Buttons argument by adding together the predefined constants. VBA defines several constants explicitly for use with the Buttons argument in MsgBox. (A complete list of the Buttons arguments for MsgBox is on the inside back cover of this book.)

The Buttons argument for MsgBox allows you to specify the number and type of buttons, and whether or not the message dialog box contains one of Windows' icons to indicate a Warning message, Query message, Information message, or Critical Warning message. You can also use the Buttons argument to specify which of the displayed buttons (button 1, 2, or 3) is the default button in the message dialog box. You can only specify one button style, one icon, and one default button option at a time.

In line 9 (part of the MsgBox function call beginning in line 7), the vbYesNoCancel constant specifies that the MsgBox dialog box should contain three command buttons: a **Y**es button, a **N**o button, and a Cancel button. The vbQuestion constant specifies that the message dialog box should contain the Windows' Query message icon.

When VBA executes the MsgBox function call in lines 7 through 9, it displays the dialog box shown in Figure 8.2. This dialog box remains on-screen until the user chooses one of the command buttons, or presses the Esc key. (Pressing the Esc key in a MsgBox dialog box, like pressing Esc in any Windows dialog box, is the same as choosing Cancel.)

Figure 8.2.

The MsgBox function call in line 7 of Listing 8.8 displays this dialog box. Notice the **Yes, No,** *and Cancel command buttons and the Windows Query message icon—all specified by the* Buttons *argument.*

As soon as the user chooses a command button in the message dialog box, VBA returns a numeric value corresponding to the user's choice. In line 7, the result of the MsgBox function is assigned to the **Resp** variable. VBA uses different values, depending on which command button the user chose. VBA uses one value to indicate the **Y**es button, another value to indicate the **N**o button, and yet another value for the Cancel button. The MsgBox function can also display dialog boxes with **A**bort, **R**etry, and **I**gnore buttons, in various combinations. Because each button has its own specific return value, VBA provides several predefined constants to represent the possible return values of the MsgBox function. The inside back cover of this book contains a complete list of the VBA constant values that MsgBox can return.

Line 10 begins a Select Case statement that evaluates the value returned by the MsgBox function in line 7, which is stored in the **Resp** variable. The test expression for the Select Case statement is the **Resp** variable itself, so VBA compares the value in the **Resp** variable to see if it matches any of the Case conditions in the Select Case statement.

Line 11 contains the first Case condition. It tests to see if the **Resp** variable is equal to the predefined constant vbYes. This constant represents the value returned by MsgBox when the user chooses the **Y**es command button (refer to Figure 8.3).

If the Case condition in line 11 is True, that is, the user did choose the **Y**es command button, then VBA executes the corresponding statements for this Case branch, starting in line 12. Lines 12 through 14 contain a single MsgBox statement. This time, the MsgBox statement is in its more familiar form as a procedure call but still uses the optional Buttons argument (line 14). When VBA executes this statement, it displays the dialog box shown in Figure 8.3.

The Buttons argument in line 14 uses the vbInformation constant to specify that the Windows' Information icon should be included in the message dialog box. Because no value specifying the number of buttons was included, the message dialog box contains the usual single OK command button. Notice that this call to MsgBox does not include parentheses; VBA therefore ignores the function's result. (You learned about ignoring a function's result in Day 5.)

Figure 8.3.

*VBA displays this dialog box if the user chose the **Yes** command button. Notice the Windows Information message icon.*

If the user chose the **No** button, the Case condition in line 15—which tests to see if the result in **Resp** is equal to the predefined vbNo constant—is True, and VBA executes the corresponding MsgBox statement in lines 16 through 18. This statement displays a message dialog box similar to the one shown in Figure 8.3, except that it announces that the user chose the **No** button. Once again, the Buttons argument was included in order to include the Windows' Information message icon in the message dialog box.

If the user chose the Cancel button, the Case condition in line 19 is True—which tests to see if the result in **Resp** is equal to the predefined vbCancel constant—and VBA executes the corresponding MsgBox statement in lines 20 through 22. When VBA executes this statement, it displays the dialog box shown in Figure 8.4.

Figure 8.4.

VBA displays this dialog box if the user chose the Cancel command button. Notice the Windows Critical Warning message icon.

The Buttons argument in line 22 uses the vbCritical constant to specify that the Windows' Critical Warning icon should be included in the message dialog box. Because no value specifying the number of buttons was included, the message dialog box contains the usual single OK command button.

Finally, the Select Case statement ends in line 23, and line 24 is the end of the **Demo_MsgBoxFunction** procedure.

You'll see many more examples of the MsgBox function used to obtain a choice from the user throughout the rest of this book.

DO	**DON'T**

DO use the VBA predefined constants for the `Buttons` argument in `MsgBox`, and for the `MsgBox` return values. Using the predefined constant names makes your code easy to write, read, and understand.

DON'T use literal numeric values for either the `Buttons` argument in `MsgBox` or the `MsgBox` return value. Using the literal numeric values makes your code difficult to read and understand.

DO remember that, to combine values in the `Buttons` argument of `MsgBox`, you add the values together with the addition operator (+).

DON'T try to specify more than one set of buttons, more than one icon, or more than one default button at one time. For example, using the expression `vbYesNoCancel + vbAbortRetryIgnore` as the `Buttons` argument value will *not* produce a dialog box with six buttons in it. The results of trying to specify more than one set of buttons, more than one icon, or more than one default button at one time may be unpredictable, and certainly will not have the desired effect.

There is one remaining item that you can specify with the `Buttons` argument for `MsgBox` that was not included in Listing 8.8: You can specify whether the first, second, or third command button in `MsgBox` dialog boxes are the initial default command buttons.

As you have seen so far, `MsgBox` usually makes the first command button in its dialog box the default button. Refer to Figure 8.2, and notice that the **Y**es button is marked as the initial default command button. If, after VBA displays the dialog box in Figure 8.2, the user just presses the Enter key, VBA behaves as if the user chose the **Y**es button.

You might prefer that the default button be some button other than the first one listed in the message dialog box. For example, if you use `MsgBox` to ask the user to confirm deleting a worksheet in a workbook, you might prefer that the default command button be the **N**o button, instead of the **Y**es button—because a deleted worksheet cannot be recovered, it makes sense to help the user avoid inadvertently confirming a deletion if they just keep hitting the enter key. (Almost everyone has had the experience of accidentally making a choice they didn't really want just because they hit the Enter key one time too many.)

To change the default command button, add one of the VBA predefined constants—`DefaultButton1`, `DefaultButton2`, or `DefaultButton3`—to the `Buttons` argument. The following procedure fragment shows the `MsgBox` statement from lines 7 through 9 of Listing 8.8, modified so that the default command button in the message dialog box is the **N**o button:

```
Resp = MsgBox(prompt:="Choose a button.", _
              Title:=mTitle, _
              Buttons:=vbYesNoCancel + vbQuestion + _
                  vbDefaultButton2)
```

When VBA executes the preceding statement, it displays the dialog box shown in Figure 8.5. This dialog box is identical to the one shown previously in Figure 8.2, except that the addition of the `vbDefaultButton2` value in the `Buttons` argument causes the second button—in this case the **No** button—to become the initial default command button.

Figure 8.5.

*Compare this dialog box to the one shown in Figure 8.2. Notice that the **No** button is now the default command button, as a result of adding `vbDefaultButton2` to the `Buttons` argument.*

Summary

In today's lesson, you learned how VBA's decision-making commands work, and about a few of the many circumstances under which you will want your procedures to make decisions and choose an alternate series of actions. You also learned the difference between conditional branching statements, and unconditional branching statements.

You learned how to use the `If...Then` statement to make simple, single branch choices, and how to use the `If...Then...Else` statement to make choices between two different branches of procedure statements. You then learned how to nest `If...Then...Else` statements inside each other to make more complex decisions, involving more than two alternate branches, and how to use the `If...Then...ElseIf` statement to simplify some nested `If...Then...Else` statements.

Next, you learned how to use the `Select Case` statement to choose one of several possible branches of execution; you learned that the `Select Case` statement is a powerful alternative to using nested `If...Then...Else` statements. You also learned about unconditional branching with VBA's `GoTo` statement, and you learned that the `GoTo` statement has very limited uses.

You learned when and how to use `Exit Function` and `Exit Sub` statements to end a procedure or function's execution early, as well as when and how to use the `End` statement to end an entire program's execution. This chapter also explained the specific differences between using one of the `Exit` statements, and using the `End` statement.

Finally, this chapter taught you how to use the optional `Buttons` argument with `MsgBox` to specify the type and number of command buttons in the message dialog box, and to specify which (if

any) Windows message icon to include in the message dialog box. You also learned how to use `MsgBox` as a function to return the user's choices.

Day 9 teaches you how to use VBA's looping commands to repeat actions.

Q&A

Q I'm not sure I understand exactly when I should use the `If...Then...ElseIf` statement.

A The `If...Then...ElseIf` statement is most useful when you need to choose among three or four different branches, depending on various conditions. The `If...Then...ElseIf` statement is really an alternative to the `Select Case` statement—both statements have much the same effect: they allow you to choose one of several different branches. If you don't feel comfortable using the `If...Then...ElseIf` statement, simply use the `Select Case` statement instead.

Q I'm not sure I understand how to write the logical test expressions for the various `If...Then` statements.

A Usually, you specify a condition for a branching statement by constructing a logical expression that evaluates to `True` when the desired condition for executing a particular procedure branch is also true, and evaluates to `False` when the desired condition is not true.

Most of the time, you can figure out how to write the correct logical expression by just carefully stating the condition in English, and then substituting VBA comparison or logical operators for parts of the English sentence. For example, if you want a particular branch of your procedure to execute whenever the value in a variable named `NetIncome` drops below 10,000, you can state the situation in English, first: *when* `NetIncome` *is less than 10,000.* From this English statement, you can see that you are comparing `NetIncome` to the constant value 10,000, and that the comparison operator is the less than comparison (<). With this information, you can construct the expression:

```
NetIncome < 10000
```

This logical expression is `True` whenever `NetIncome` drops below (is less than) 10,000. You can construct more complex logical statements the same way. Suppose you want a particular branch of your procedure executed whenever the value in `NetIncome` drops below 10,000, or whenever the percent profit (`PcntProfit`) drops below 15%. Carefully state the situation in English, first: *when* `NetIncome` *is less than 10,000; or when* `PcntProfit` *is less than 15.* In this English statement, you can see that two smaller expressions are connected together by the word *or*. Write the smaller expressions first.

The first expression (NetIncome < 10000) has already been determined. The second expression compares **PcntProfit** to 15 and uses the less than operator (<), again. With this information, you can construct the second part of the logical expression:

```
PcntProfit < 15
```

Now connect the two smaller expressions with the logical operator corresponding to the English word that connected the expressions—Or—as in the following expression (you must include parentheses around the smaller parts of the expression, or the expression may not produce the results you expect):

```
(NetIncome < 10000) Or (PcntProfit < 15)
```

Q One of the examples in this chapter used the Application.InputBox function instead of VBA's InputBox statement to restrict the user's input to a number. How do I find out more about using the Application.InputBox function?

A You can find out more about the Application.InputBox function, or any other object, property, or method that you see in recorded macros or examples in this book by using the Object Browser, as described in Day 5. To get more information about the Application.InputBox function specifically, open the Object Browser dialog box and select Excel in the **L**ibraries/Workbooks drop-down list, select Application in the **O**bjects/Modules list, and then select InputBox in the **M**ethods/Properties list. Finally, select the **?** button at the bottom of the Object Browser dialog box.

Q I understand how the GoTo statement works, but I'm not sure when or why to use the GoTo statement.

A Except in relation to the special error handling GoTo statements described in Day 17, you really should never have to use the GoTo statement. This chapter makes sure you know about the GoTo statement so you will be more ready to understand the error handling GoTo statements described in Day 17, and so that you will be able to understand source code written by other programmers that uses the GoTo statement. You should always try to use conditional branching commands and looping commands to structure your code, instead of using a GoTo statement. If you need to end a procedure or program early, use the Exit or End statements in preference to a GoTo statement.

Workshop

Answers are in Appendix A.

Quiz

1. What is a conditional branching statement? An unconditional branching statement?
2. How do you specify the condition that VBA uses to determine whether or not to execute a particular program branch?

3. What are VBA's conditional branching statements?

4. What are VBA's unconditional branching statements?

5. What is the term used to describe the situation when you enclose one `If...Then` or `If...Then...Else` statement inside another?

6. How many `ElseIf` clauses can an `If...Then...ElseIf` statement contain? Can an `If...Then...ElseIf` statement also include an `Else` clause? If you can include an `Else` clause in an `If...Then...ElseIf` statement, where would you place it, and how many can you include?

7. How many `Case` clauses can you include in a `Select Case` statement? How do you specify a branch of statements for VBA to execute if none of the `Case` clauses in a `Select Case` statement are met? Where does that specification go inside the `Select Case` statement?

8. When, and why, would you use a `Select Case` statement, instead of several nested `If...Then...Else` statements?

9. What do you use the `Exit Sub` statement for? What about `Exit Function`?

10. What effect does the `End` keyword, on a line by itself, have?

11. What purpose does the `Buttons` argument for `MsgBox` serve? What tools does VBA provide to help you specify values for the `Buttons` argument?

12. When you use `MsgBox` as a function, what does its result value represent? What tools does VBA provide to help you interpret this result?

Exercises

This chapter has only two exercises. Although Exercise 8.1 is fairly simple, Exercise 8.2 is fairly complex and contains the same amount of work usually spread over two or three exercises. Don't be discouraged by this exercise's apparent complexity—it is really fairly simple. Rather than trying to write the entire procedure for Exercise 8.2 all at once, first write a procedure that just accomplishes the first task in the list. When that procedure works okay, add the code to accomplish the second task in the list, and so on. If you get stumped, take a look at the answer in Appendix A.

1. **BUG BUSTER:** The `Select Case` statement in the following procedure is supposed to display a message dialog box stating whether the number stored in the **Num** variable is less than 0, between 0 and 10, between 10 and 20, or none of these. As it is, however, this `Select Case` statement erroneously reports that numbers such as 10.01 and 0.7 are greater than 20. Correct this `Select Case` statement.

```
1:  Sub Case_Demo()
2:
3:      Dim sNum As String
```

```
 4:        Dim Num As Double
 5:
 6:        sNum = InputBox("enter a number:")
 7:        Num = CDbl(sNum)
 8:
 9:        Select Case Num
10:            Case Is < 0
11:                MsgBox "Num is less than 0"
12:            Case 1 To 10
13:                MsgBox "Num is between 0 and 10"
14:            Case 11 To 20
15:                MsgBox "Num is between 10 and 20"
16:            Case Else
17:                MsgBox "Num is greater than 20"
18:        End Select
19: End Sub
```

2. The digits on a telephone dial (or number pad) are each associated with a specific group of alphabetic letters. Write a procedure that asks the user for a letter of the alphabet, and then prints out the corresponding telephone digit for that letter.

   The digits and their corresponding letters are:

   ```
   2 = ABC
   3 = DEF
   4 = GHI
   5 = JKL
   6 = MNO
   7 = PRS
   8 = TUV
   9 = WXY
   ```

   There is no digit corresponding to either *Q* or *Z*.

   Your procedure should perform each of the following actions:

   ☐ Use the `InputBox` function to ask the user to enter a single letter of the alphabet.

   ☐ Use the `Len` function in a logical expression to determine whether or not the user canceled the input dialog box. If so, your procedure should display a message stating that its operation was canceled and then terminate the procedure's execution. Your message dialog box should include the Windows exclamation mark (!) warning icon. (HINT: Use an `If...Then` statement to make this test and choose the alternate branch. Add the `vbExclamation` constant in the `MsgBox` statement to display the exclamation point icon.)

   ☐ Use the `Len` function in a logical expression to determine whether or not the user did, in fact, enter a single character. If the length of the string the user entered is greater than 1, display a message stating that the user entered a string that was too long, and then terminate the procedure's execution. This message dialog box also should contain the Windows Exclamation warning message icon.

   ☐ Evaluate the user's input, and display the digit corresponding to the letter the user entered. If the user entered a letter or other character that does not have a

digit equivalent, your procedure should display a message stating that fact. (HINT: To simplify the comparisons you have to make, convert the user's input to uppercase with the UCase function, and use the Select Case statement to evaluate the user's input.)

☐ When your message dialog box displays the telephone digit equivalent to the letter entered by the user, the message dialog box should repeat the user's letter as part of its message, and also include the Windows Information icon. (HINT: Add the vbInformation constant to the MsgBox statement.)

Most of the work that this procedure does is to check up on the user's input. As you will learn in the next chapter, validating the information that the user enters can avoid many different errors and problems in your VBA procedures.

Repeating Actions in Visual Basic: Loops

Now that you know how to choose different courses of action based on predetermined conditions, you are ready to learn how to make your VBA procedures repeat actions either a predetermined number of times, or while a particular condition does or does not exist. In today's lesson, you learn:

☐ To understand what looping commands do, and to understand the difference between loops that repeat a definite number of times, and loops that repeat an indefinite number of times.

☐ When and how to use VBA's For loop structures to repeat actions a fixed number of times.

☐ When and how to use VBA's Do loop statement to repeat actions a flexible number of times.

☐ To understand and use the four different configurations of the Do loop statement.

☐ How, and under what circumstances, to end a loop before it has finished executing.

☐ How to use nested loops.

Understanding Looping Commands

One of the drawbacks of recorded macros is their inability to repeat actions—unless you record the desired action repeatedly. VBA provides several powerful and versatile structures that allow you to repeat actions easily, and to control closely the manner in which VBA repeats those actions.

Program structures that cause one or more statements to execute repeatedly are called *looping* structures because the flow of the procedure's statement execution *loops* through the same statements repeatedly. Each time VBA finishes one complete cycle of executing all the statements enclosed by the looping structure is called an *iteration* of the loop.

Some looping structures are constructed so that they will always execute a set number of times. Loop structures that always execute a set number of times are called *fixed iteration* loops. Other types of looping structures repeat a flexible number of times, depending on some set of conditions. Because the number of times these flexible looping structures repeat is indefinite, they are called *indefinite loops*.

In both fixed and indefinite looping structures, there is some expression that determines how many times the loop repeats. This expression is called the *loop determinant*, or the *loop invariant*. In a fixed loop structure, the loop determinant is almost always a numeric expression. In an indefinite loop structure, the loop determinant is a logical expression that describes the conditions under which the loop may continue repeating or stop repeating. You construct and use logical expressions for indefinite loop determinants the same way you construct and use logical expressions in VBA's conditional branching (decision-making) statements.

There are two basic ways that you can construct an indefinite loop. You can construct the loop so that VBA tests the loop's determinant condition *before* it executes the loop. If the condition for repeating the loop is not true, VBA skips over the statements in the loop altogether. You can also construct the loop so that VBA tests the loop's determinant condition *after* it executes the statements in the loop.

Figure 9.1 shows how VBA executes a loop that tests the determinant condition before executing the statements inside the loop. At the top of the loop, VBA tests the determinant condition (represented by the diamond-shaped box). If the conditions for executing the loop are met, VBA executes the statements inside the loop. After executing the last statement inside the loop, VBA returns to the top of the loop, and evaluates the loop's determinant condition again. If the conditions for executing the loop are still met, VBA repeats the statements inside the loop, and again returns to the top of the loop to test the determinant. As soon as the conditions for executing the loop are no longer met, VBA stops executing the loop and begins executing any statements after the loop.

Notice that, if the conditions for executing the loop are *not* met the first time VBA tests the loop determinant condition, VBA does not execute the statements inside the loop at all; instead, VBA skips over the body of the loop. (The *body* of a loop is the block of VBA statements enclosed by the beginning and ending of the loop.)

Figure 9.1.
The flow of VBA's statement execution for a loop that tests its determinant condition before executing statements inside the loop.

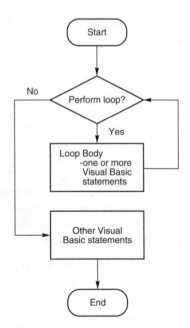

Figure 9.2 shows how VBA executes a loop that tests its determinant condition *after* executing the statements in the loop body. VBA first executes all statements in the loop body. When it reaches the end of the loop body, VBA evaluates the loop's determinant condition (represented by the diamond-shaped box). If conditions for executing the loop are met, VBA returns to the top of the loop and repeats the instructions in the body of the loop. At the end of the loop, VBA again tests the loop's determinant condition. As soon as the conditions for executing the loop are no longer met, VBA stops executing the loop and begins executing any statements after the loop.

Notice that VBA always executes the statements in this loop at least once.

Figure 9.2.

The flow of VBA's statement execution for a loop that tests its determinant condition after executing statements inside the loop.

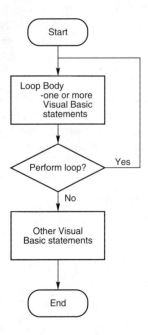

You can also construct an indefinite loop so that it does not have a determinant condition at all—loops that do not have a determinant condition repeat forever, and are called *infinite loops*. An infinite loop never ends; most infinite loops are the result of a programmer's error, although there are a few uses for an infinite loop.

The following sections in today's lesson explain the specific details of constructing fixed and indefinite loops, and how to construct loops that test determinant conditions before or after executing the loop body. The following sections also explain the circumstances under which you might use each type of loop.

Fixed Repetition: The *For* Loops

The simplest looping structure is the fixed loop. VBA provides two different fixed loop structures: `For...Next` and `For Each...Next`. Both fixed loop structures are called `For` loops because they always execute *for* a specified number of times.

Using the *For...Next* Loop

The first of VBA's For loops is the `For...Next` loop. Use the `For...Next` loop when you want to repeat an action or series of actions a set number of times.

The `For...Next` loop has the following general syntax:

```
For counter = start To end [Step StepSize]
       statements
Next [counter]
```

counter represents any VBA numeric variable, usually an Integer or Long type variable. *start* represents any numeric expression, and specifies the starting value for the *counter* variable. *end* is also a numeric expression and specifies the ending value for the counter variable.

By default, VBA *increments* (adds to) the *counter* variable by 1 each time it executes the statements in the loop. You can specify a different increment value by including the optional `Step` keyword. If you include the `Step` keyword, you must then specify the amount to increment the *counter* variable. In the preceding syntax sample, *StepSize* represents any numeric expression and specifies the amount to increment the *counter* variable.

statements represents none, one, or many VBA statements. These statements make up the body of the For loop; VBA executes each of these statements each time it executes the loop.

The `Next` keyword signals VBA that it has reached the end of the loop; the optional *counter* after the `Next` keyword must be the same *counter* variable you specified after the `For` keyword at the beginning of the loop structure. Include the optional *counter* variable after the `Next` keyword to improve the readability of your program code (especially with nested `For..Next` loops), and to improve the execution speed of your code (otherwise, VBA has to spend time figuring out which counter variable is the correct one to increment after encountering the `Next` keyword).

When VBA executes a `For...Next` loop, it first assigns the value represented by *start* to the *counter* variable. VBA then executes all the statements represented by *statements*, until it reaches the `Next` keyword. The `Next` keyword signals VBA that it has reached the end of the loop's body. VBA then increments the *counter* variable by *StepSize*—if the `Step` optional keyword is included. If `Step` is not specified, then VBA increments the *counter* variable by 1. VBA now returns to the top of the loop and compares the current value of the *counter* variable to the value represented by *end*. If *counter* is less than or equal to *end*, VBA executes the loop again. If *counter* is greater than *end*, VBA continues execution with the first statement after the `Next` keyword.

299

Using *For...Next* with a Count That Goes Up

Listing 9.1 shows a simple demonstration of the `For...Next` loop. This procedure obtains two numbers from the user, adds together every whole number in the range specified by the two numbers, and then displays the resulting sum on-screen. If you run this procedure and enter the numbers 4 and 8, for example, the procedure adds together the numbers 4, 5, 6, 7, and 8, and displays the number *30*.

Listing 9.1. A demonstration of the `For...Next` loop, counting up.

```
 1: Sub Demo_ForNext()
 2:
 3:     Dim k As Integer
 4:     Dim uStart As String
 5:     Dim uEnd As String
 6:     Dim uSum As Long
 7:
 8:     uStart = InputBox("Enter an integer number:")
 9:     uEnd = InputBox("Enter another integer number:")
10:
11:     uSum = 0
12:     For k = CInt(uStart) To CInt(uEnd)
13:         uSum = uSum + k
14:     Next k
15:
16:     MsgBox "The sum of the numbers from " & uStart & _
17:             " to " & uEnd & " is: " & uSum
18: End Sub
```

Lines 3 through 6 declare several variables for this procedure to use. The **k** variable is used as the `For...Next` loop's counter variable; the other variables are used to hold the starting and stopping values obtained from the user, and to hold the sum of numbers.

Line 8 uses `InputBox` to get a number from the user, and stores that number in **uStart**. Line 9 also uses `InputBox` to get a number from the user, this time storing it in **uEnd**. (This procedure assumes the first number entered is smaller than the second number entered.)

Line 11 sets the **uSum** variable to 0—no processing of the user's input has taken place yet, so the sum must be zero.

Finally, line 12 starts the `For...Next` loop. When VBA executes this line, it first executes the `CInt` function calls, which convert the user's string input into Integer numbers, and then inserts the resulting integer values into the statement.

VBA assigns the integer equivalent of the value stored in **uStart** to the counting variable, **k**. If you entered the number *4* in the first input dialog box, then the **k** counting variable receives the value 4 at the start of the loop.

Next, still in line 12, VBA compares the value in **k** to the integer equivalent of the number stored in **uEnd**. If **k** is less than or equal to the value in **uEnd**, VBA executes the body of the loop. If you entered the number *8* in response to the second input dialog box, VBA compares 4 to 8; 4 is indeed less than 8, so VBA executes the statement in line 13.

This loop has only one statement in its body: the addition and assignment expression in line 13. This line adds the current value of **k** to the current contents of the **uSum** variable, and then assigns the result of that addition to **uSum**. The first time through the loop, **k** is equal to 4 and **uSum** contains 0; after VBA finishes executing this statement, the value stored in **uSum** is the result of adding 0 + 4, so **uSum** ends up containing the number 4.

Now VBA encounters the Next statement in line 14. This statement signals the end of the For loop's body; VBA increments the counter variable, and returns to the top of the loop. At this point, the counter variable, **k**, still contains the number 4. The Step option was not specified in this For...Next loop, so VBA uses the default increment step, and adds 1 to the contents of **k**. The counting variable now contains the number 5.

VBA returns to the top of the loop in line 12, and compares the value in the counter variable, **k**, to the number represented by the contents of the **uEnd** variable. **k** currently contains 5, which is still less than 8, so VBA again executes the statement in line 13. After executing the statement in line 13, the **uSum** variable contains the value 9—the result of adding 4 (the previous contents of **uSum**) to 5 (the current counter value).

Again, VBA encounters the Next statement in line 14, increments the counter variable **k**, and returns to the top of the loop to compare the value in the counter variable to the ending value. The following table lists the values of the counter variable, **k**, and the **uSum** variable for each repetition of the loop:

Loop	Value of k	Value of uSum
0	0	0 (loop has not started)
1	4	4
2	5	9
3	6	15
4	7	22
5	8	30

The fifth time VBA executes the loop, **k** contains the value 8. After VBA increments the loop counter in line 14, **k** has the value *9*. When VBA returns to the top of the loop, the value in the counter variable is no longer less than or equal to the specified ending value of 8. At last, the value in the loop counter exceeds the value specified for the ending count, and VBA stops executing the loop.

Now that the loop has ended, VBA continues execution with the MsgBox statement in line 16, which displays the two numbers that you entered, and the sum of all integers in that range.

You'll see many other examples of For...Next loops throughout this book. You will frequently use For...Next loops with arrays (covered in Day 13).

> **Note:** If the first value the user enters (in **uStart**) is larger than the second value the user enters (in **uEnd**), the For...Next loop does not execute at all—the starting value for the loop counter exceeds the ending value before the loop has ever executed. When this happens, VBA does not execute the loop at all. For example, if you enter 8 first, and then enter 4, the loop does not execute—VBA skips over the statements in the loop and execution moves from line 12 to line 16.

DO	DON'T

DO use an Integer or Long data type variable for the counter in For...Next loops. Using an Integer or Long data type saves memory and speeds up the execution of your loop.

DO specify the counter variable after the Next statement; although placing the counter variable after the Next statement is optional, it greatly improves the readability of your program code. Also, VBA does not have to spend time determining which counter variable belongs with that Next statement, and your loops execute faster.

DO take advantage of the fact that you can count from any number up to any other number, if you wish.

Using *For...Next* with a Count That Goes Down

You don't always have to write For...Next loops that count up. Sometimes, it's easier or more useful to write a For loop that counts down. To make a For...Next loop count down, use the Step keyword, and a negative number for the step value.

Listing 9.2 shows the same procedure from Listing 9.1, but modified to include a For...Next loop that counts down from a higher starting value to a lower ending value. Like the procedure in Listing 9.1, this procedure gets two numbers from the user, adds together every whole number in the range specified by the two numbers, and then displays the resulting sum on-screen. If you run this procedure and enter the numbers 8 and 4, for example, then the procedure adds together the numbers 8, 7, 6, 5, and 4, and displays the number *30*.

 Listing 9.2. Making a `For...Next` loop that counts down.

```
 1:  Sub Demo_ForNextDown()
 2:
 3:      Dim k As Integer
 4:      Dim uStart As Integer
 5:      Dim uEnd As Integer
 6:      Dim uSum As Long
 7:
 8:      uStart = CInt(InputBox("Enter an integer number:"))
 9:      uEnd = CInt(InputBox("Enter another integer number:"))
10:
11:      uSum = 0
12:      For k = uStart To uEnd Step -1      'loop counts down
13:          uSum = uSum + k
14:      Next k
15:
16:      MsgBox "The sum of the numbers from " & uStart & _
17:              " to " & uEnd & " is: " & uSum
18:  End Sub
```

 Line 8 is different from the corresponding line in Listing 9.1. When VBA executes this statement, it first calls `InputBox` to get a number from the user. After the user enters a number, VBA calls the `CInt` function, and converts the String result of the `InputBox` function to an Integer type value. VBA stores the result of the `CInt` function (an integer number with the value corresponding to the string entered by the user) in the **uStart** variable.

Similarly, line 9 also uses `InputBox` to get a value from the user, calls the `CInt` function to convert the string entered by the user to an integer, and assigns the resulting integer to the **uEnd** variable. This procedure does not perform any checking of the user's input—it assumes that the first number entered is *larger* than the second number entered.

The `CInt` function was used directly in the statements that obtain input from the user in order to speed up the `For...Next` loop—in the procedure in Listing 9.1, VBA has to execute the `CInt` function each time it evaluates the loop's determinant condition (line 12 of Listing 9.1), slowing the loop down. In Listing 9.2, the strings entered by the user in the two `InputBox` statements have already been converted to numbers; the loop that starts in Line 12 of Listing 9.2 therefore executes that much faster.

Line 12 of Listing 9.2 starts the `For...Next` loop. When VBA executes this line, it assigns the value stored in **uStart** to the counting variable, **k**. If you entered the number *8* in the first input dialog box, the **k** counting variable receives the value 8 at the start of the loop.

Line 12 includes the `Step` keyword, so VBA also checks the *step value*—the amount by which VBA will increment the loop counter. In this loop, the step value is a negative number: -1. Because the step value is a negative number, VBA makes this loop count down rather than up. VBA *decrements* (subtracts from) the loop counter, instead of incrementing it.

Because VBA is counting down, it checks to see if the value of the loop counter is greater than or equal to the specified ending value—instead of checking whether the loop counter is less than or equal to the ending value.

Still in line 12, VBA now compares the value in **k** to the number stored in **uEnd**. If **k** is greater than or equal to the value in **uEnd**, VBA executes the body of the loop. If you entered the number *4* in response to the second input dialog box, VBA compares 8 to 4; 8 is greater than 4, so VBA executes the statement in line 13.

The statement in line 13 adds the current value of **k** to the current contents of the **uSum** variable, and then assigns the result of that addition to **uSum**. The first time through the loop, **k** is equal to 8 and **uSum** contains 0, so after VBA finishes executing this statement, the value stored in **uSum** is 8—that is, 0 + 8.

VBA encounters the Next statement in line 14. The Step option was specified in this For...Next loop, so VBA uses the specified step value, and subtracts 1 from the contents of **k**. The counting variable now contains the number *7*.

VBA returns to the top of the loop in line 12, and compares the value in the counter variable, **k**, to the number in the **uEnd** variable. **k** currently contains 7, which is still greater than 4, so VBA again executes the statement in line 13. After executing the statement in line 13, the **uSum** variable contains the value 15—that is, 8 + 7.

Again, VBA encounters the Next statement in line 14, decrements the counter variable **k**, and returns to the top of the loop. The following table lists the values of the counter variable, **k**, and the **uSum** variable for each repetition of the loop:

Loop	Value of k	Value of uSum
0	0	0 (loop has not started)
1	8	8
2	7	15
3	6	21
4	5	26
5	4	30

The fifth time VBA executes the loop, **k** contains the value *4*. After VBA decrements the loop counter in line 14, **k** has the value *3*. VBA then returns to the top of the loop and compares the value in **k** to the value in **uEnd**. The value in the counter variable is no longer greater than or equal to the ending value, and VBA stops executing the loop.

Now that the loop has ended, VBA continues execution with the MsgBox statement in line 16, which displays the two numbers that you entered, and the sum of all integers in that range.

Note: If the first value the user enters is smaller than the second value, the `For...Next` loop does not execute at all—for essentially the same reason that the loop in Listing 9.1 does not execute if the starting value is larger than the ending value. In Listing 9.2, for example, if you enter 4 first, and then enter 8, the loop will not execute—VBA skips over the statements in the loop and execution moves from line 12 to line 16.

DO	DON'T

DO use the `Step` keyword and a negative number to make VBA count down in a `For...Next` loop.

DO remember that when a `For...Next` loop counts *down*, it executes for as long as the counter variable is *greater than* or equal to the ending value and that when it counts *up*, it executes for as long as the counter variable is *less than* or equal to the ending value.

DO remember that you can specify any numeric value as the `Step` value in a `For...Next` loop. You can write `For...Next` loops that increment or decrement the counter variable by 0.1, 2, 5.1 or any decimal number.

Putting the *For...Next* Loop to Work

The example procedures in Listings 9.1 and 9.2 show how the `For...Next` loop operates with various options, but they don't actually accomplish a particularly useful task. Typically, you use `For...Next` loops when you want to perform an action a fixed number of times, or to perform operations on (or with) a fixed number of items.

You might use a `For...Next` loop to examine all the characters in a string, or to apply the same font and character formatting to the first three columns in a worksheet, or some similar task.

Listing 9.3 shows a `For...Next` loop used to repeat actions on every character in a string. The **PCase** function in Listing 9.3 returns a copy of its string argument with the first letter of each word capitalized, and all other letters in lowercase characters. For example, if you passed either of the strings *LEAPING LIZARDS* or *leaping lizards*, to the **PCase** function, it returns the string *Leaping Lizards*. Listing 9.3 also includes a procedure to test the **PCase** function.

Type

Listing 9.3. Using For...Next to perform an action with every character in a string.

```
 1: Function PCase(iStr As String) As String
 2: 'returns a copy of the string in the iStr argument with
 3: 'the first letter of each word capitalized — Proper Case
 4:
 5:    Dim oStr As String
 6:    Dim k As Long
 7:              'start output string with first letter
 8:    oStr = UCase(Left(iStr, 1))
 9:     'was prev char a space? if so, current char starts word
10:    For k = 2 To Len(iStr)
11:      If Mid(iStr, k - 1, 1) = " " Then
12:        oStr = oStr & UCase(Mid(iStr, k, 1))
13:      Else              'if not, force to lower case
14:        oStr = oStr & LCase(Mid(iStr, k, 1))
15:      End If
16:    Next k
17:
18:    PCase = oStr       'assign function result
19: End Function
20:
21:
22: Sub test_PCase()
23: 'this procedure tests the PCase function
24:
25:    Dim uStr As String
26:
27:    uStr = InputBox("Enter a string containing several " & _
28:                    "words separated by spaces:")
29:    MsgBox "You Entered: " & uStr & Chr(13) & _
30:            "PCase result: " & PCase(uStr)
31: End Sub
```

Analysis

Line 1 contains the **PCase** function declaration; this function has a single required argument (passed by reference), and the function's result is declared as a String type. Line 5 declares a string variable, **oStr**, to hold the modified copy of the **iStr** argument as it is assembled. Line 6 declares a Long type variable, **k**, for use as the loop counter variable. (VBA strings may be as large as 2 billion characters—the limit of a Long integer—so this procedure uses a Long type loop counter to accommodate the maximum possible string size.)

In line 8, the Left function copies the first character from the **iStr** argument, the UCase function then converts that character to its uppercase equivalent (if any); the result is then assigned to the **oStr** variable. Because the first letter in the **iStr** argument is also the start of a word, line 8 just converts the copy of that letter and stores it in **oStr**.

Line 10 begins the For...Next loop. The first time through this loop, VBA assigns the starting value 2 to the loop counter, **k**. The loop starts with the second character in **iStr** because the first character was already handled in line 8. The ending value for the counter variable in the For loop

is obtained by using the Len function to return the length of the string stored in **iStr**. This For...Next loop will execute starting from a count of 2, and going up to the number of characters in **iStr**, executing the loop body once for each remaining character in **iStr**.

Line 11 begins the body of the For...Next loop—this loop contains a single If...Then...Else statement in its body. Line 11 is also the beginning of the If...Then...Else statement that forms the body of the loop.

The **PCase** function is intended to capitalize the first letter of each word; it therefore has to be able to tell when a new word starts. The usual definition of a word—as far as most computer programs are concerned—is any group of characters separated from other characters in a string by a space. For the **PCase** function to identify the first letter of a word, it checks to see if the character immediately preceding it is a space.

Line 11 uses the Mid function to return one character from **iStr**. The starting position from which Mid copies the character is specified as k-1, and the number of characters to copy is specified as 1. The first time through the loop, **k** has the value 2, indicating the second character in **iStr**, so the Mid function in line 11 returns the first character of the string in **iStr** (2-1). The logical expression in the If...Then...Else statement tests whether the character returned by the Mid function is a space character.

If the character preceding the current character in **iStr** (specified by **k**) is a space, the character indicated by the value in **k** must be the beginning of a word in the string. When the logical expression in line 11 is True then VBA executes line 12, which again uses Mid to copy a single character from **iStr**. This time, Mid copies one character starting at position **k** in **iStr**; the result of the Mid function is passed to the UCase function, which converts it to uppercase. The result of the UCase function is concatenated to the end of the string already in **oStr**, and the result is stored in **oStr**. As the loop executes, **oStr** gradually gets longer and longer as each individual character from **iStr** is evaluated and copied to **oStr**. At the end of the loop, **oStr** will have the same length as **iStr**.

If the character preceding the current character in **iStr** (specified by **k**) is *not* a space, then the character indicated by the value in **k** must be somewhere in the middle of a word in **iStr**. When the logical expression in line 11 is False, then VBA executes line 14, which again uses Mid to copy a single character from **iStr**. Mid copies one character starting at position **k** in **iStr**; the result of the Mid function is passed to the LCase function, which converts it to lowercase (characters in the middle of a word should be lowercase). The result of the LCase function is concatenated to the end of the string already in **oStr**, and the result is stored in **oStr**.

Whether or not VBA executes line 12 or line 14, the next line it executes is line 16, which contains the Next statement. At this point, VBA increments the loop counter, **k**, by one (no Step value was specified) and returns to the top of the loop in line 10. If **k** is still less than or equal to the length of the string in **iStr**, then VBA executes the loop body again.

When the loop has finished executing, all the characters in **iStr** have been evaluated, and VBA then executes line 18, which assigns the function's return value. The value in **oStr** is assigned to the function result, and the function ends in line 19, returning its result.

Lines 22 through 31 contain a simple procedure to test the **PCase** function. Line 27 uses the InputBox function to get a string from the user. Line 29 uses the MsgBox function to display the string the user entered, and includes a call to the **PCase** function, displaying its result when passed the user's string. If you enter the string leaping lizards, then the MsgBox statement in lines 29 and 30 displays the dialog box shown in Figure 9.3.

Figure 9.3.

The test_PCase *function displays this dialog box if you enter the string* leaping lizards.

This type of manipulation—evaluating every character in a string, every column in a row, every row in a worksheet, and so on—is an ideal use for the For...Next loop.

DO	DON'T

DON'T change the value of a For...Next loop counter variable inside the body of the loop. Although you can assign a new value to the loop counter variable inside the loop, altering the loop counter's value may cause your For...Next loop to execute too many or too few times, leading to subtle bugs in your procedures.

DO allow VBA to handle incrementing or decrementing the loop counter "naturally," making your For...Next loops easier to understand and write.

Using the *For Each...Next* Loop

The second For loop is the For Each...Next loop. Unlike the For...Next loop, the For Each...Next loop does not use a loop counter. Instead, For Each...Next loops execute for as many times as there are elements in a specified group—such as a collection of objects, or an array. (You learned about collections of objects in Day 7; Day 13 describes arrays.) In other words, the For Each...Next loop executes once *for each* item in a group.

The For Each...Next loop has the following general syntax:

```
For Each element In group
        statements
Next [element]
```

element is a variable used to iterate through all the items in the specified group. *group* is either a collection object, or an array. If *group* is a collection object, then *element* must be a Variant type variable, an Object type variable, or a specific object type, such as Range, Worksheet, and so on. If *group* is an array, then *element* must be a Variant type variable. *statements* represents none, one, or several VBA statements making up the body of the loop.

The For Each...Next loop has fewer options than the For...Next loop. Counting up or counting down is not relevant to a For Each...Next loop; the For Each...Next loop always executes as many times as there are elements in the specified group.

Listing 9.4 shows a function named **SheetExists**, which uses the For Each...Next loop to determine whether or not a particular sheet exists in a workbook.

Type

Listing 9.4. Using For Each...Next.

```
 1: Function SheetExists(sName As String) As Boolean
 2: 'Returns True if sName sheet exists in the active workbook
 3:
 4:    Dim aSheet As Object
 5:
 6:    SheetExists = False   'assume sheet won't be found
 7:
 8:      'cycle through all sheets, compare each sheet's name to sName, as a text
 9:      'comparison.
10:    For Each aSheet In ActiveWorkbook.Sheets
11:      If (StrComp(aSheet.Name, sName, 1) = 0) Then
12:        SheetExists = True    'sheet names match, return true
13:      End If
14:    Next aSheet
15: End Function
16:
17:
18: Sub Test_SheetExists()
19: 'tests the SheetExists function
20:
21:    Dim uStr As String
22:
23:    uStr = InputBox("Enter the name of a sheet in the " & _
24:                    "current workbook:")
25:    If SheetExists(uStr) Then
26:      MsgBox "Sheet '" & uStr & _
27:             "' DOES exist in the current workbook."
28:    Else
29:      MsgBox "Sheet '" & uStr & _
30:             "' does NOT exist in the current workbook."
31:    End If
32: End Sub
```

9

Analysis This function has one required argument, **sName**, which contains a string representing the name of the sheet being searched for. **SheetExists** returns a Boolean type value—True if the sheet named by **sName** exists in the current workbook, False otherwise. You might use a function like this in one of your procedures to ensure that a worksheet, chart sheet, or module sheet exists before your procedure attempts to select that sheet—if your procedure tries to select a sheet that does not exist, VBA displays a runtime error message and stops executing your program. A function like **SheetExists** allows you to write your procedures so that they can detect and avoid possible errors that might occur, such as when a user enters a non-existent worksheet name.

Line 4 declares the **aSheet** object variable for use in the For Each...Next loop. Line 6 assigns the value False to the **SheetExists** function result. This statement assumes that the sheet named in **sName** will *not* be found. Assuming failure simplifies the decision-making task in the remaining portion of this function—now, the function only has to detect if the sheet is found and assign True to the function result.

Line 10 starts the For Each...Next loop, using the **aSheet** object variable as the element variable for the loop. The specified group is the ActiveWorkbook.Sheets collection. The ActiveWorkbook is a property of the Application object and returns an object reference to the current active workbook. Sheets is a workbook method that returns the collection of all sheets in the workbook, including worksheets, chart sheets, and module sheets.

Line 10 tells VBA to execute the statements in the loop body for as many times as there are sheets in the active workbook—that is, to repeat the actions once for each object in the Sheets collection. As VBA begins the For Each...Next loop, it assigns **aSheet** to refer to the first object in the Sheets collection, whatever that sheet happens to be.

Line 11 starts the body of the loop, which consists of a single If...Then statement. When VBA executes line 11, it first calls StrComp to compare the string in **sName** to the string stored in the Name property of the sheet currently referenced by **aSheet**. This call to StrComp specifies that the comparison should be a text comparison, and therefore unaffected by any differences in capitalization between the string in **sName** and the string in the sheet's Name property. Line 11 uses StrComp to compare the strings, rather than a simple relational operator, to ensure that the string comparison is always a text comparison, regardless of the Option Compare settings.

If the string in **sName** matches the string in the sheet's Name property, then VBA executes line 12, which assigns the value True to the function's result.

Whether or not the string in **sName** matches the string in the sheet's Name property, VBA next executes line 14, which contains the Next keyword ending the For Each...Next loop. VBA now returns to the top of the loop in line 10, and checks to see if all the elements in the group have been used. If not, VBA assigns the next element in the Sheets collection to the **aSheet** object variable and executes the loop again. If the active workbook contains 10 sheets, for example, the For Each...Next loop executes 10 times; if the active workbook contains 4 sheets, then the loop executes 4 times.

When VBA finishes executing the loop for all the elements in the ActiveWorkbook.Sheets collection, it continues execution with line 15, which ends the **SheetExists** function and returns the function result. If, at any time during the execution of the For Each...Next loop, the string in **sName** matched the string in one of the sheets' Name properties, then **SheetExists** returns True, indicating that the sheet specified by **sName** does exist in the active workbook; otherwise, the function returns False, indicating that the sheet does not exist.

Lines 18 through 29 declare a procedure, **Test_SheetExists** to test the **SheetExists** function. Line 23 of the test procedure uses InputBox to get a sheet name from the user, and lines 25 through 31 contain an If...Then...Else statement that calls the **SheetExists** function, evaluates its result, and then displays a message dialog box stating whether or not the sheet name entered by the user does in fact exist in the current workbook.

When VBA executes line 25, it calls the **SheetExists** function, passing the string entered by the user (**uStr**) as the argument to **SheetExists**. If the user entered a valid sheet name, then **SheetExists** returns True, and VBA executes line 26 to display a message to that effect. If the user entered an invalid sheet name, **SheetExists** returns False, and VBA executes line 29, displaying a message that the sheet does not exist.

You will see many more examples of the For Each...Next loop throughout the rest of this book, particularly in Day 13, where you learn how to use For Each...Next with arrays.

DO	**DON'T**

DO make sure that the For Each element variable is of a type compatible with the specified group. For example, if you specify a collection of worksheets, the element variable should be a Variant, a generic Object type, or a Worksheet object type.

DO use the trick of assuming a particular outcome of a test to simplify the decision-making process for that test, as shown in the **SheetExists** function in line 6.

DO use the StrComp function to compare strings when you want to ensure that a string comparison is either a binary or text comparison, and that the comparison is unaffected by the Option Compare settings.

Flexible Repetition: The *Do* Loops

VBA provides you with an extremely powerful looping statement to create indefinite looping structures in your procedures and functions. Essentially, you construct all of VBA's indefinite loops with a single indefinite looping statement—the Do statement. The Do statement has so many options and is so flexible, that, in effect, it provides you with four different loop constructions in two basic categories.

The two basic categories of Do loop constructions are: loops that test the determinant condition *before* executing the body of the loop, and loops that test the determinant condition *after* executing the body of the loop. Later sections in this chapter describe when and how to use these two categories of looping structure, and their specific syntax.

There are two basic ways to control how many times an indefinite loop executes, regardless of whether VBA tests the loop's determinant condition before or after it executes the body of the loop. The following paragraphs summarize these two techniques for controlling the number of times an indefinite loop executes:

☐ *Count-controlled* loops. In a count-controlled loop, the body of the loop executes while a particular count is above or below some specified limit—similar to a For...Next loop, except that you, the programmer, are responsible for initializing the counting variable and incrementing or decrementing the count. You might write a count-controlled loop using the Do statement if the counting step is irregular, or if there is no way to determine the ending limit until after the loop has started executing. For example, you might want to pace through the first 16 rows of a worksheet, sometimes advancing a single row at a time, and other times advancing two rows at time. Because the number of rows to advance (that is, the step for the count) changes, you cannot use a For...Next loop and must use a Do loop instead.

☐ *Event-controlled* loops. In an event-controlled loop, the determinant condition becomes true or false based on some event or action that occurs within the loop. For example, you might write a loop that executes indefinitely, until the user enters a particular value in an input dialog box. The user's input of that particular value is the event that ends the loop. As another example, you might perform operations on the cells in a worksheet until you reach an empty cell; reaching the empty cell is the event that ends the loop.

Understanding How Visual Basic for Applications Tests the Loop Determinant

You specify the determinant condition for an indefinite loop with a logical expression, in the same way you construct logical expressions for use with If...Then statements.

VBA provides two different ways of testing the determinant condition for a loop. You can construct a loop so that it executes for as long as the loop's determinant condition is True, and stops executing when the determinant condition becomes False. You can also construct a loop so that it executes for as long as the loop's determinant condition is False, and stops executing when the determinant condition becomes True.

To make a loop execute as long as its determinant condition is True, use the optional While keyword in the Do loop statement. VBA then executes the loop *while* the condition is True, and stops executing the loop as soon as the determinant condition becomes False.

Suppose you want to write a procedure that helps a user enter data into a worksheet. For a data entry procedure, you usually want the procedure to repeat whatever statements get information from the user while there is still more data to enter, and to stop repeating those statements when there is no more data. You might, therefore, write a Do loop that repeatedly gets data from the user, continuing to execute for as long as the user enters non-blank strings, and stopping as soon as the user enters a blank string. You would write the determinant condition for this loop so that the logical expression is True—and the loop continues to execute—as long as the user's input is *not* an empty string. If the user's input is stored in a variable named **uStr**, the logical expression for the loop determinant could be either of the following:

```
uStr <> ""
Len(Trim(uStr)) <> 0
```

Both of the preceding logical expressions are True when the string in **uStr** is not empty.

To make a loop execute as long as its determinant condition is False, use the optional Until keyword in the Do loop statement. VBA then executes the loop *until* the condition is True—that is, the loop continues to execute as long as the condition is False, and stops executing as soon as the determinant condition becomes True.

For example, you might want to write a procedure that advances column by column across a worksheet, applying a particular text and character formatting to column headings, and stopping at the first blank column. You might, therefore, write a Do loop that repeats the statements to format a column heading until a blank cell is encountered. You would write the determinant condition for this loop so that the logical expression is False as long as the current cell is not blank, and is True whenever the current cell is blank. Using the ActiveCell property of the Application object to return the current active cell, and using the Value property to obtain the cell's contents, your logical expression for the determinant could be either of the following:

```
ActiveCell.Value = ""
Len(Trim(ActiveCell.Value)) = 0
```

Both expressions evaluate True when the current cell is empty.

Whether you use the While or Until keywords depends mostly on how you think about the conditions that determine whether or not the loop should execute, and on how easily you can construct a logical expression for the loop's determinant condition:

- ☐ Use While if you want the loop to continue executing as long as the specified condition is True.
- ☐ Use Until when you want the loop to continue executing as long as the specified condition is False.

You can always write the same loop structure either way, depending on how you formulate your logical expression—the loop structure you choose is largely a matter of personal preference.

The following sections describe in detail how to use the specific options of the Do statement.

Caution: Be careful, as you construct your Do loops, to choose a determinant condition that will, at some point, really cause the loop to stop executing. The most common error that programmers make when constructing indefinite loops is making a mistake in formulating the loop's determinant condition, resulting in a loop that never stops executing because the determinant condition never becomes True (or False, in an Until loop). Loops that never stop executing are called *infinite* loops, because they execute infinitely.

If you end up with an infinite loop in one of your procedures, that procedure will never end, and your computer system may appear to have crashed or locked up. If the apparent computer system crash is the result of an infinite loop, you can interrupt your procedure as described in the sidebar in this section.

If you suspect that your computer has locked up due to an infinite loop in one of your procedures, try to interrupt the procedure by pressing the Esc key (see sidebar). *Only reboot your computer as a last resort*—rebooting your computer may cause loss of data in Excel or other programs that are active at the time you reboot the computer.

How to Interrupt an Executing Macro or Procedure

Because one of the most common problems you'll encounter while working with indefinite loop structures is inadvertently creating an infinite loop, it is important that you know how to interrupt VBA while it is executing your macros and procedures. Use the same technique to interrupt either recorded macros, or to interrupt the execution of procedures and functions you have written from scratch.

To interrupt VBA's execution, press the Esc key, or press the Ctrl+Break key combination. VBA finishes executing the current statement, suspends any further statement execution, and displays the runtime error dialog box shown in Figure 9.4. The command buttons in this runtime error dialog box are the same as those in any other runtime error dialog box (originally described in Day 2), and have the same effects, summarized following:

- **End.** Ends the program. All variables and their contents are lost. This is the command button you should usually choose after interrupting an infinite loop.

- **Continue.** Resumes VBA's execution of program statements. Usually, you should *not* make this choice after interrupting an infinite loop, because it will just start the infinite loop again.

- ☐ **Debug.** Activates VBA's debugger so you can examine the contents of variables, and pace through the execution of your loop to determine why it isn't stopping. Using the VBA debugger is the topic of Day 14.

- ☐ **Goto.** Jumps to the line that VBA was executing at the time you interrupted it.

You cannot interrupt VBA while it is displaying a dialog box; you must close any input, message, or other dialog boxes before you can interrupt a procedure—fortunately, the Esc key also closes open dialog boxes.

Depending on your exact loop, and the statements it contains, VBA may not respond to a single Esc or Ctrl+Break keystroke. In fact, you usually must press and hold down the Esc key to interrupt an executing procedure. If you do hold down the Esc key, you may inadvertently close the runtime error dialog box (see Figure 9.4). As a result, the error dialog box may flash on the screen too quickly for you to read it. If this does happen to you, don't worry—you'll probably have a good idea of which loop was stuck, based on how far your procedure got before it broke down, and the typical choice for this runtime error dialog box is to choose the **End** command button, which is the equivalent of the Esc key, anyway.

Figure 9.4.
*VBA displays this dialog box
when you press Esc to
interrupt an executing
procedure or macro.*

Using Loops That Test Conditions before Execution

To have VBA test the loop determinant condition before executing the body of the loop, you simply place the logical expression for the loop determinant at the beginning of the block of statements that make up the body of the loop. The following sections describe how to use the While and Until keywords to build loops that test their conditions before executing the loop body.

Building Loops with *Do While*

The first loop construction that tests its determinant condition before executing the loop is the Do While.

Syntax

The general syntax of the Do While statement is:

```
Do While condition
    statements
Loop
```

condition represents the logical expression for the loop's determinant. *statements* represents none, one, or several statements that make up the body of the loop. VBA executes all statements in the body of the loop each time it executes the loop. The Loop keyword after *statements* indicates the end of the loop's body and also indicates the point at which VBA returns to the top of the loop to check the determinant condition.

The Do While statement has the *condition* expression at the top of the loop, so VBA checks the determinant condition before executing the loop. Because this form uses the While keyword, VBA executes the loop as long as the logical expression represented by *condition* is True.

When VBA executes a Do While loop, it first tests the logical expression represented by *condition*; if it is True, then VBA executes the statements represented by *statements*. When VBA reaches the Loop keyword, it returns to the top of the loop and again checks to see if the *condition* logical expression is True. If *condition* is True, VBA executes the loop again; if it is False, VBA continues execution with whatever statements appear after the Loop keyword.

Notice that if the logical expression represented by *condition* is False the first time VBA executes the Do While statement, VBA simply skips the loop, without executing it at all.

Listing 9.5 shows a simple example of a Do While loop that repeatedly gets a number from the user, stopping only after the user has entered 10 odd numbers.

Type

Listing 9.5. Demonstrating the Do While loop.

```
1:  Sub Count_OddNums()
2:  'counts the odd numbers entered by the user, and stops
3:  'executing when a total of 10 odd numbers has been entered
4:
5:      Const ocTitle = "Odd Number Count"
6:
7:      Dim OddCount As Integer    'holds count of odd numbers
8:      Dim OddStr As String       'string to display odd nums
9:      Dim Num                    'Variant to hold user input
10:
11:     OddStr = ""
12:     OddCount = 0    'initialize the loop counter
13:     Do While OddCount < 10
14:         Num = InputBox("Enter a number:", ocTitle)
15:         If (Num Mod 2) <> 0 Then
16:             OddCount = OddCount + 1
17:             OddStr = OddStr & Num & " "
18:         End If
19:     Loop
20:
21:     MsgBox prompt:="You entered the following odd " & _
```

```
22:                        "numbers:" & Chr(13) & OddStr, _
23:                    Title:=ocTitle
24: End Sub
```

 Count_OddNums simply demonstrates how you go about constructing a Do While loop. The loop in this procedure executes while the user has entered less than 10 odd numbers (an *odd* number is any number that you cannot divide evenly by 2). At first, it might seem that you could accomplish this task with a For...Next loop, but that is not really possible. Although the loop in this procedure is a count-controlled loop, the counter that controls the loop's execution is not necessarily incremented every time the loop executes. If the user enters an even number, the loop does not increment the count of odd numbers. The only way to create a count-controlled loop that increments the counter variable at irregular intervals is with some variety of the Do statement.

Line 7 declares an Integer type variable, **OddCount**, to hold the count of odd numbers. Line 8 declares a String type variable, **OddStr**, to hold a string assembled from all the odd numbers the user enters while the loop is executing. Line 9 declares a Variant type variable, **Num**, to hold the user's input. This procedure uses a Variant type variable for the user's input to avoid having to explicitly convert the string from the InputBox function into a number.

Line 11 initializes the **OddStr** variable by assigning an empty string to it. Line 12 contains a very important assignment statement related to the loop's execution. Line 12 initializes the **OddCount** variable to 0, ensuring that the loop beginning in line 13 does start execution. (*Never* assume that a variable contains any particular value, unless you have assigned that value to the variable in one of your program statements.)

Line 13 starts the Do loop. This statement has the While keyword and loop determinant condition at the top of the loop, so VBA will execute this loop while the logical expression for the loop's determinant condition is True, and VBA will also test the determinant condition before executing the loop. The first time VBA evaluates this statement, the value stored in the **OddCount** variable is 0, so the expression OddCount < 10 is True, and VBA begins executing the loop, starting with line 14.

Line 14 is the first statement in the body of the loop; it uses InputBox to get a number from the user, and stores the user's input in the **Num** variable.

Line 15 is an If...Then statement that evaluates the number entered by the user. When VBA evaluates the expression (Num Mod 2) <> 0 it first performs the modulo division inside the parentheses. (Remember, VBA evaluates the portions of an expression enclosed in parentheses first.) The Mod division operator, as you may recall from Day 4, returns the remainder of a division operation. After performing the Mod division, VBA performs the indicated relational operation. If the result of the Mod division is not equal to 0, the expression is True; if the result of the Mod division operation is equal to 0, the expression is False. An odd number is a number that cannot be divided evenly by 2; therefore, if there is a remainder after dividing Num by 2, Num must contain an odd number.

If Num is an odd number, VBA executes the statements in lines 16 and 17. Line 16 increments the counter variable for the loop by adding one to the current value of OddCount, and then assigning the result of that addition to OddCount. The statement in line 17 concatenates the string equivalent of the odd number to the end of the string in the OddStr variable. (The loop assembles this string so that the user's input can be displayed when the loop has finished executing.)

When VBA executes line 19, the Loop keyword tells VBA that it has reached the end of the loop's body, and that it should go back to the top of the loop. VBA returns to line 13 and again evaluates the logical expression for the loop's determinant condition. If OddCount is still less than 10, VBA executes the body of the loop again, gets another number from the user, evaluates it to see if it is an odd number, and increments the OddCount variable, as necessary.

As soon as the user has entered 10 odd numbers, however, the value in the OddCount variable is also 10, and the logical expression of the loop's determinant condition is no longer True. VBA then skips over the body of the loop and continues execution with the first statement after the line that contains the Loop keyword: line 21, in this case.

The statement in line 21 displays a message to the user that includes the OddStr string variable to show the odd numbers entered by the user.

As you study this Do While loop, notice that the loop may actually execute many more than 10 times. For example, if you run this procedure and enter all the whole numbers from 1 to 20, then the loop executes 20 times, although only 10 odd numbers are entered.

Building Loops with *Do Until*

The Do While variation of the Do statement is only one way to construct a Do statement that tests its determinant condition before executing the body of the loop. You can also use the Do Until form of the Do statement to build a Do loop that tests its determinant condition before executing the body of the loop.

The general syntax of the Do Until statement is:

```
Do Until condition
     statements
Loop
```

condition represents the logical expression for the loop's determinant, and statements represents the VBA statements that make up the body of the loop. The Loop keyword after statements indicates the end of the loop's body, and also indicates the point at which VBA returns to the top of the loop to check the determinant condition.

The Do Until statement also has the condition expression at the top of the loop, so VBA tests the loop's determinant condition before executing the loop. Because this form includes the

Until keyword, VBA executes the loop as long as the logical expression represented by *condition* is False.

When VBA executes a Do Until loop, it first tests the logical expression represented by *condition*; if it is False, then VBA executes the statements represented by *statements*. When VBA reaches the Loop keyword, it returns to the top of the loop and again checks to see if the *condition* logical expression is False. If *condition* is False, VBA executes the loop again; if it is True, VBA continues execution with whatever statements appear after the Loop keyword.

If *condition* is True the first time VBA executes the Do Until statement, VBA skips the loop, without executing it at all.

Listing 9.6 shows a simple example of a Do Until loop that repeatedly gets a number from the user, stopping whenever the user enters an even number greater than 10.

Listing 9.6. Demonstrating the Do Until loop.

```
 1:  Sub Stop_AtEvenNums()
 2:  'receives numbers from the user until the user enters an
 3:  'even number greater than 10, and then stops executing.
 4:
 5:     Const evTitle = "Stop At Even Numbers"
 6:
 7:     Dim EvenFlag As Boolean
 8:     Dim Num                      'Variant to hold user's input
 9:
10:     EvenFlag = False   'initialize loop's control "flag"
11:     Do Until EvenFlag = True
12:       Num = InputBox("Enter a number:", evTitle)
13:       If ((Num Mod 2) = 0) Then
14:         If Num > 10 Then
15:           MsgBox prompt:="You entered an even number " & _
16:                      "greater than 10 - the loop ends.", _
17:                  Title:=evTitle
18:           EvenFlag = True
19:         Else
20:           MsgBox prompt:="You entered an even number " & _
21:                      "less than (or equal) 10 - the loop " & _
22:                      "continues.", _
23:                  Title:=evTitle
24:         End If
25:       Else
26:         MsgBox prompt:="You entered an odd number.", _
27:                 Title:=evTitle
28:       End If
29:     Loop
30:
31:     MsgBox prompt:="The loop has ended.", Title:=evTitle
32:  End Sub
```

Stop_AtEvenNums demonstrates how to construct a Do Until loop. The loop in this procedure executes until the user enters an even number. The loop in this procedure also demonstrates an event-controlled loop. The event that ends the loop's execution is the user's entry of an even number.

Line 7 declares a Boolean type variable, **EvenFlag**. This Boolean variable is used as a "flag" to signal whether or not the loop in the procedure should continue executing. Flag-controlled loops are a special variety of event-controlled loop. In this flag-controlled loop—because the loop uses the Until keyword—a *raised* flag (one with the value True) indicates that the loop should stop executing. In a loop that uses the While keyword, you would usually construct the loop so that it continues to execute when the flag value is True.

Line 8 declares a Variant type variable, **Num**, to store the user's input. Because the value is stored in a Variant type variable, VBA handles the string-to-number conversion automatically.

Line 10 initializes the **EvenFlag** variable to False. This initialization statement is very important to the loop that begins in line 11. By assigning the value False to the **EvenFlag** variable, this statement ensures that the loop in line 11 will actually start.

The first time VBA evaluates the statement in line 11, the value stored in the **EvenFlag** variable is False, so the expression for the loop determinant—which contains only the **EvenFlag** variable—is also False, and VBA begins executing the body of the loop, starting with line 12.

Line 12 uses InputBox to obtain a number from the user, and stores it in the **Num** variable. Next, the If...Then...Else statement in line 13 tests the number the user entered. First, VBA evaluates the expression (Num Mod 2) = 0—notice, this expression is *not* the same as the expression used in Listing 9.5 to test for an odd number. This time, the result of the Mod division is tested to see if it is equal to 0. If there is no remainder after dividing **Num** by 2, **Num** must be an even number.

If **Num** is an even number, VBA continues execution with line 14, which begins a nested If...Then...Else statement. The If...Then...Else statement in line 14 tests the value stored in **Num** to see if that value is greater than 10. If **Num** is greater than 10, VBA executes line 15, which uses the MsgBox statement to display a message stating that the user's number is even, and that it is greater than 10.

Line 18 is also very important in this loop. This line sets the **EvenFlag** variable True. After VBA executes this statement, the loop determinant condition is True, and the loop stops executing the next time VBA evaluates the loop determinant expression. Notice that VBA only executes this statement in line 18 when the value in **Num** is both even *and* greater than 10.

If the value in **Num** is not greater than 10, then VBA executes the Else clause starting in line 19, which consists of the single MsgBox statement in line 20. Line 20 displays a message stating that the user's number was even, but less than 10. No change is made to the **EvenFlag** variable, so the loop continues executing.

If the value in **Num** is not an even number, VBA executes the Else clause in line 25, which contains a single MsgBox statement in line 26 that displays a message stating the user's number was odd.

No matter which branch of the nested If...Then...Else statements ends up being executed, VBA continues execution with the Loop statement in line 29. The Loop keyword signals the end of the loop, and VBA returns to the top of the loop in line 11.

VBA again checks the expression for the loop determinant. If the **EvenFlag** variable is still False, VBA executes the loop again. If the user entered an even number greater than 10, causing the statement in line 18 to execute, then **EvenFlag** is True, and VBA does not execute the loop but continues execution with line 31. Line 30 contains a MsgBox statement that displays a message stating the loop has ended.

Using Loops That Test Conditions after Execution

To have VBA test the loop determinant condition after executing the body of the loop, you simply place the logical expression for the loop determinant at the end of the block of statements that make up the body of the loop, after the Loop keyword that signals the end of the loop. The following sections describe how to use the While and Until keywords to build loops that test their conditions after executing the loop body.

Building Loops with *Do...Loop While*

The first loop construction that tests its determinant condition after executing the loop body is the Do...Loop While.

The general syntax of the Do...Loop While statement is:

```
Do
      statements
Loop While condition
```

statements represents none, one, or several VBA statements making up the body of the loop. The Loop keyword after *statements* indicates the end of the loop's body, and also indicates the point at which VBA returns to the top of the loop. *condition* represents the logical expression for the loop's determinant.

In this syntax form, the Do...Loop While statement has the *condition* expression at the bottom of the loop, so VBA checks the determinant condition after executing the loop. Because this form of the Do statement uses the While keyword, VBA executes the loop as long as the logical expression represented by *condition* is True.

When VBA executes a Do...Loop While statement, it first executes the statements represented by *statements*. When VBA reaches the Loop While keywords, it tests the logical expression represented by *condition*; if the logical expression is True, then VBA returns to the top of the loop and again executes the body of the loop. When VBA again reaches the Loop While keywords at the bottom of the loop, it checks to see if the *condition* logical expression is still True. If *condition* is True, then VBA executes the loop again; if it is False, VBA continues execution with whatever statements appear after the line containing the Loop keyword.

Notice that regardless of the value of the logical expression represented by *condition*, this loop always executes at least once.

The **GetInput** procedure in Listing 9.7 is a prototypical form of a data-entry procedure, and uses a Do...Loop While loop construction to get input from the user until the user enters the word *exit*, indicating that data entry is complete.

Listing 9.7. A prototype data-entry loop that uses Do...Loop While.

```
 1: Sub GetInput()
 2: 'demonstrates Do...Loop While structure. Loops repeatedly
 3: 'while user's input does not equal the word "exit"
 4:
 5:    Const iTitle = "Data Entry"
 6:
 7:    Dim uStr As String
 8:
 9:    Do
10:      uStr = InputBox(prompt:="Enter a string " & _
11:                             "('exit' to end):", _
12:                    Title:=iTitle, _
13:                    default:="exit")
14:      'statements to process or validate user's input, or to
15:      'store user's input in worksheet cell, etc. go here.
16:      MsgBox prompt:="You entered: " & uStr, Title:=iTitle
17:    Loop While uStr <> "exit"
18:
19:    MsgBox prompt:="Data entry completed.", _
20:            Title:=iTitle, Buttons:=vbExclamation
21: End Sub
```

The **GetInput** procedure loops indefinitely, for as long as the user does *not* enter the word *exit*. You might use a procedure like this to help a user perform data entry for one of your worksheets. The Do loop in the **GetInput** procedure is a variety of event-controlled loop often referred to as a *sentinel-controlled* loop. Sentinel-controlled loops get their name from the fact that they watch for a particular value—called the *sentinel* value—to appear. In this procedure, the loop's sentinel value is a string containing the single word *exit*.

Line 9 begins the Do loop statement in this procedure. Because the Do keyword appears on the line by itself, it merely indicates to VBA the beginning of the loop's body. There is no additional

keyword (While or Until) and no logical expression for the loop's determinant condition in this line, so VBA simply continues execution with the first statement in the loop's body in line 10.

Line 10 uses InputBox to obtain a string from the user. In this procedure, the user is simply prompted to enter a string. Notice that the prompt string for InputBox includes instructions on how to end the data entry loop. This InputBox statement also suggests the word *exit* as the default value for the user's input.

The comments in lines 14 and 15 represent any additional processing of the user's input that you might want to include: storing the data in a worksheet cell, adding it to an array, ensuring that the data is numeric, non-numeric, or any other data validation or processing. Line 16 contains a MsgBox statement that simply echoes the user's input.

Line 17 contains the Loop keyword and indicates the end of the loop's body. This line also contains the While keyword, and the logical expression for the loop's determinant condition. When VBA executes this statement, it evaluates the logical expression for the loop determinant. Because this loop uses the While keyword, VBA continues to execute the loop as long as the logical expression for the loop's determinant condition is True. If the string entered by the user in line 10 does not contain the single word *exit*, then the expression uStr <> "exit" is True, and VBA returns to the top of the loop and repeats the body of the loop.

If the user did enter the word *exit* (either by accepting the suggested default for the InputBox function call in line 10, or by actually typing the word) then the expression uStr <> "exit" is False, and VBA continues execution with line 19, ending the loop.

Lines 19 and 20 contain a MsgBox statement that displays a message stating that the data entry is complete. Notice that this MsgBox statement uses the Buttons argument to display the Windows' Exclamation icon in the message dialog box. Line 21 contains the End Sub statement that ends the procedure.

DO	DON'T

DO make sure that your InputBox prompts give your procedure's user enough information about what kind of information you expect them to enter, and how to end or cancel (if possible) the task that your procedure carries out.

Building Loops with *Do...Loop Until*

You can also use the Do...Loop Until form of the Do statement to build a Do loop that tests its determinant condition after executing the body of the loop.

Syntax

The general syntax of the `Do...Loop Until` statement is:

```
Do
     statements
Loop Until condition
```

`statements` represents the VBA statements that make up the body of the loop. `condition` represents the logical expression for the loop's determinant.

The `Do...Loop Until` statement has the `condition` expression at the bottom of the loop, so VBA checks the determinant condition after executing the loop. Because this form of the `Do` statement uses the `Until` keyword, VBA executes the loop as long as the logical expression represented by `condition` is `False`.

When VBA executes a `Do...Loop Until` statement, it first executes the statements represented by `statements`. When VBA reaches the `Loop` keyword, it tests the logical expression represented by `condition`; if the logical expression is `False`, VBA returns to the top of the loop and again executes the body of the loop. When VBA reaches the `Loop` keyword at the bottom of the loop, it again checks to see if the `condition` logical expression is `False`. If `condition` is `False`, VBA executes the loop again; if it is `True`, VBA continues execution with whatever statements appear after the line containing the `Loop` keyword.

Notice that regardless of the value of the logical expression represented by `condition`, this loop always executes at least once.

Listing 9.8 shows another version of the prototypical data-entry loop shown in Listing 9.7. The **GetInput** procedure in Listing 9.8 uses a `Do...Loop Until` loop construction to get input from the user until the user cancels the input dialog box, or enters a blank string. Apart from using a different loop construction, **GetInput** in Listing 9.8 is also slightly more sophisticated than the version shown in Listing 9.7. **GetInput** in Listing 9.8 asks the user to confirm that he or she wants to end the data-entry process, before it actually ends the loop.

Type

Listing 9.8. A smarter version of `GetInput`, using a `Do...Loop Until` loop.

```
1:   Sub GetInput()
2:   'demonstrates Do...Loop Until structure. Loops repeatedly
3:   'until user cancels input dialog box or enters blank string
4:
5:      Const iTitle = "Data Entry"
6:
7:      Dim uStr As String
8:      Dim Check As Integer
9:
10:     Do
11:        uStr = InputBox(prompt:="Enter a string " & _
12:                               "(Cancel to end):", _
13:                       Title:=iTitle)
14:        If uStr = "" Then    'confirm ending data entry
```

```
15:        Check = MsgBox(prompt:="End data entry?", _
16:                       Title:=iTitle, _
17:                       Buttons:=vbYesNo + vbQuestion + _
18:                                vbDefaultButton2)
19:        If Check = vbNo Then uStr = "x"
20:      Else
21:        'statements to process or validate user input, or to
22:        'store user input in worksheet cell, etc. go here
23:        MsgBox prompt:="You entered: " & uStr, Title:=iTitle
24:      End If
25:   Loop Until uStr = ""
26:
27:      MsgBox prompt:="Data entry completed.", _
28:             Title:=iTitle, Buttons:=vbExclamation
29: End Sub
```

Analysis Line 10 begins the Do loop statement in this procedure. Because the Do keyword appears on the line by itself, it merely indicates to VBA the beginning of the loop's body. There is no additional keyword (While or Until) and no logical expression for the loop's determinant condition in this line, so VBA simply continues execution with the first statement in the loop's body in line 11, which uses InputBox to obtain a string from the procedure's user.

Line 14 begins an If...Then...Else statement to evaluate the user's input. If the string the user entered (stored in **uStr**) is empty (""), the user either canceled the input dialog box, or entered a blank string. This If...Then...Else statement ensures that the user really wants to end the data-entry process.

If **uStr** is empty, VBA executes the statements in lines 15 through 19. Line 15 starts a MsgBox function call that displays a Yes/No message box, asking the user whether data entry should end. Notice that this MsgBox function call uses the Buttons argument to specify that the message dialog box contains two buttons—**Y**es and **N**o—and specifies that the second button (the **N**o button) is the default. Notice also that the vbQuestion constant is also added to the Buttons argument so that the message dialog box displays the Windows' Query icon.

Line 19 contains an If...Then statement that evaluates the user's choice from the MsgBox function call in line 15. If the user chooses the **N**o button in the message dialog box, signifying that the data-entry process should continue, this statement assigns the single letter *x* to the **uStr** variable. This statement is necessary to keep the loop running because the loop stops executing whenever the **uStr** variable contains an empty string—this statement ensures that the **uStr** variable does *not* contain an empty string, so that VBA continues to execute the loop.

If the **uStr** variable is not empty when VBA performs the comparison for the If...Then...Else statement in line 14, VBA executes the Else clause in lines 20 through 23. This procedure, like Listing 9.7, just shows you how to set up a loop for a data entry process without actually doing anything with the data the user enters.

Line 25 contains the Loop keyword, indicating the end of the loop's body. This line also contains the Until keyword, and the logical expression for the loop's determinant condition. When VBA executes this statement, it evaluates the logical expression for the loop determinant. Because this loop uses the Until keyword, VBA continues to execute the loop as long as the logical expression for the loop's determinant condition is False. If the string entered by the user in line 14 is *not* empty (""), the expression uStr = "" is False—VBA returns to the top of the loop and executes the body of the loop again.

If the user did enter an empty string, or canceled the input dialog box, and also confirmed that the data entry should end, then the expression uStr = "" is True and VBA ends the loop, continuing execution with line 27. Notice that if the user did *not* confirm ending the data entry, **uStr** contains the single character *x*, and VBA does continue executing the loop because **uStr** is not empty.

DO	DON'T

DO use a Do...Loop While or Do...Loop Until loop construction if you want VBA to always execute the statements in the body of the loop at least once, no matter what.

DO consider including statements to confirm the cancellation of interactive looping processes, as shown in Listing 9.8.

Ending Loops Early

Many of the reasons why you might end a loop early are similar to the reasons you might end a procedure or entire program early: a user cancels an input dialog box, an expected value does not appear, and so on. There are additional reasons for ending a loop early, besides detecting some particular error. In some cases, you might want to terminate a loop early—particularly For...Next and For Each...Next loops—because their task is completed, and additional looping is simply a waste of time.

VBA provides two statements that allow you to terminate a loop early. The particular statement that you use depends on the type of loop that you want to end:

☐ Use the Exit For statement to end either a For...Next or a For Each...Next loop early. Usually, you end For loops early because the specific goal of the loop is accomplished, and you don't want VBA to waste time executing the loop unnecessarily.

☐ Use the Exit Do statement to end any of VBA's Do loops early. Usually, you end Do loops early because of some situation that not only makes continuing the loop unnecessary, but may affect the way VBA evaluates the logical expression for the loop's determinant condition.

With the exception that you use Exit For to end a For loop early, and you use Exit Do to end a Do loop early, both statements are essentially the same.

Listing 9.9 shows the same **SheetExists** function from Listing 9.4, but it is modified to include the Exit For statement.

 Listing 9.9. Using Exit For to end a loop early.

```
1:  Function SheetExists(sName As String) As Boolean
2:  'Returns True if sName sheet exists in active workbook
3:
4:    Dim aSheet As Object
5:
6:    SheetExists = False  'assume sheet won't be found
7:
8:      'cycle through all sheets, compare each sheet's
9:      'name to sName, as a text comparison.
10:   For Each aSheet In ActiveWorkbook.Sheets
11:     If (StrComp(aSheet.Name, sName, 1) = 0) Then
12:       SheetExists = True   'sheet names match, return true
13:       Exit For              'no point in continuing loop
14:     End If
15:   Next aSheet
16: End Function
17:
18:
19: Sub Test_SheetExists()
20: 'tests the SheetExists function
21:
22:   Dim uStr As String
23:
24:   uStr = InputBox("Enter the name of a sheet in the " & _
25:                   "current workbook:")
26:   If SheetExists(uStr) Then
27:     MsgBox "Sheet '" & uStr & _
28:             "' DOES exist in the current workbook."
29:   Else
30:     MsgBox "Sheet '" & uStr & _
31:             "' does NOT exist in the current workbook."
32:   End If
33: End Sub
```

 This version of **SheetExists** works exactly the same as the function shown in Listing 9.4, except that this version uses the Exit For statement to end the For Each...Next loop in the function early.

Notice line 13 in Listing 9.9. This line, containing the Exit For statement, is the only line that is different in this version of the **SheetExists** function.

Line 10 starts the For Each...Next loop, using the **aSheet** object variable as the element variable for the loop. The specified group is the ActiveWorkbook.Sheets collection object. Line 10 tells

VBA to execute the statements in the loop body for as many times as there are sheets in the active workbook—that is, to repeat the actions once for each object in the Sheets collection.

If the string in **sName** matches the string in the sheet's Name property, VBA executes line 12, which assigns the value True to the function's result.

The next statement that VBA executes is in line 13, the added Exit For statement. When VBA executes this statement, it immediately ends the For Each...Next loop, and continues execution with the first statement after the Next keyword—line 16, in this case, which ends the **SheetExists** function.

Because the purpose of **SheetExists** is to simply return True whenever it finds a sheet with the specified name in the active workbook, there is no point in continuing the For Each...Next loop once the first matching name is found—especially because Excel ensures that every sheet in a workbook has a unique name. As soon as a match between **sName** and a sheet's Name property is found, any additional executions of the statements inside the loop is just wasted processing time. By exiting a loop early in circumstances like this, you can speed up VBA's execution of your programs. Although the saved time in a function like **SheetExists** might be measured in milliseconds, the cumulative total of time saved in a complex program can be significant.

VBA executes line 15, which contains the Next keyword ending the For Each...Next loop, only if the string in **sName** does not match the string in the sheet's Name property. VBA now returns to the top of the loop in line 10 and checks to see if all the elements in the specified group have been used. If not, VBA assigns the next element in the Sheets collection to the **aSheet** object variable and executes the loop again.

In the **SheetExists** function in Listing 9.4, the For Each...Next loop always executed a number of times corresponding to the number of sheets in the active workbook. If the active workbook contained 10 sheets, for example, the For Each...Next loop executed 10 times; if the active workbook contained 4 sheets, the loop executed 4 times.

In this version, however, the number of times the For Each...Next loop executes may be fewer than the number of sheets in the active workbook, although it will never execute more times than there are sheets in the active workbook. If the active workbook contains 10 sheets, for example, and **sName** matches the Name property of the second sheet in the workbook, VBA only executes the For Each...Next loop twice. If **sName** matches the Name property of the eighth sheet in the workbook, VBA executes the For Each...Next loop eight times. VBA only ends up executing this loop all 10 times if it does not find a match, or if the matching sheet is also the tenth sheet in the workbook. Potentially, then, using the Exit For statement to end the loop early saves the time required to execute the loop as many as nine times, and as few as one time.

Many of the loops you write may execute hundreds of times; you can see that strategically ending a loop's execution early may save a lot of unnecessary processing.

In Listing 9.9, lines 19 through 33 declare a procedure, **Test_SheetExists**, to test the **SheetExists** function. This test procedure is identical to the test procedure in Listing 9.4.

DO	DON'T

DO use an Exit For statement to end a For Each...Next or For...Next loop early, if additional looping becomes unnecessary.

DON'T use a GoTo statement to jump out of an executing loop. Using GoTo statements makes your code difficult to read and understand.

DON'T use the Exit Do statement to end a Do loop unless absolutely necessary—that is, you can't figure out any other way to end the loop.

Nesting Loops

You can enclose loops inside of other loops, similar to the way you can enclose If...Then statements inside each other. Enclosing one looping structure inside another is referred to as *nesting* loops. You can nest looping structures of any type (mixed For and Do loops) to any level.

There are a few things you need to keep in mind when you nest loops, however. The following list summarizes points to watch for when you enclose one looping structure inside another:

☐ When you nest For...Next loops, each loop must have its own unique counter variable.

☐ When you nest For Each...Next loops, each loop must have its own unique element variable.

☐ If you use an Exit For or Exit Do statement in a nested loop, only the currently executing loop ends; VBA continues executing the next higher-level loop.

Nesting *For* Loops

Listing 9.10 shows a simple procedure that uses nested For...Next loops. The **FormatHeading** procedure applies a 12-point bold Arial font to the first three rows of the first six columns of the current active worksheet. The outer loop in the procedure counts down the rows, and the inner loop counts across the columns.

Listing 9.10. Nested For...Next loops.

```
 1:  Sub FormatHeading()
 2:  'This procedure applies 12-point bold Arial font to
 3:  'first 3 rows and first 6 columns of active worksheet
 4:
 5:    Dim Rnum As Integer, Cnum As Integer
 6:
 7:    For Rnum = 1 To 3
 8:      For Cnum = 1 To 6
 9:        Cells(Rnum, Cnum).Select
10:        With Selection.Font
11:          .Name = "Arial"
12:          .FontStyle = "Bold"
13:          .Size = 12
14:          .Strikethrough = False
15:          .Superscript = False
16:          .Subscript = False
17:          .OutlineFont = False
18:          .Shadow = False
19:          .Underline = xlNone
20:          .ColorIndex = xlAutomatic
21:        End With
22:      Next Cnum
23:    Next Rnum
24: End Sub
```

Analysis

You might use a procedure like **FormatHeading** to apply a uniform font, font style, and point size to the cells of a worksheet that you use for both the worksheet's heading, and for the column headings. **FormatHeading** uses two For...Next loops, one nested inside the other, to apply the 12-point bold Arial font.

The outer For...Next loop counts from 1 to 3, and the procedure uses the outer loop's counter variable to supply a row coordinate each time VBA executes the loop. Therefore, the outer loop counts 3 rows, from the top of the worksheet down.

The inner For...Next loop counts from 1 to 6, and the procedure uses the inner loop's counter variable to supply a column coordinate each time VBA executes the loop. Therefore, the inner loop counts 6 columns, from left to right across the worksheet.

As **FormatHeading** executes, it starts in the first row and the first column. As the inner loop's count increases, the procedure formats each column in the first row, moving across the worksheet from left to right. When the inner loop finishes executing, the first 6 columns in the first row are formatted. The outer For...Next loop then increments its counter variable, advancing to the next row, and again executes. Because VBA also executes the inner For...Next loop again (it is part of the outer loop's body), the first six columns of the second row are formatted. The same thing happens again for the third row. The outer For loop only executes three times, so the **FormatHeading** procedure ends after the third execution of the outer loop.

The outer For...Next loop begins in line 7. **Rnum** is the counter variable for this loop. The outer For loop stops executing as soon as **Rnum** is greater than 3—that is, after the loop executes three times.

The inner For...Next loop begins in line 8. **Cnum** is the counter variable for this loop. The inner For loop stops after it has executed six times.

Line 9 uses the Cells method of the Application object to return a Range object specified by using **Rnum** and **Cnum** as row and column coordinates. The statement also uses the Select method of the Range object to select the specified cell on the active worksheet. The Cells statement was copied from a recorded macro that contained only two actions: selecting a cell, and applying the desired formatting. The cell selection statement was copied into this procedure, and the literal values from the recorded statement were replaced with the **Rnum** and **Cnum** variables.

Line 10 begins a With statement. Selection is a property of the Application object that returns the current selection. In this case, the current selection is the single cell selected by the statement in line 9. The Selection.Font object contains all the font settings for the current selection. The statements inside the With statement in lines 11 through 20 all change properties of the Font object so that the selection has the desired bold Arial font at 12 points. These statements, like the statement in line 9, were copied from a recorded macro.

Line 22 contains the Next statement that marks the end of the body of the inner loop. Notice how including the counter variable name after the Next keyword, along with proper indentation, helps you tell the difference between the inner and outer loops. When VBA executes the statement in line 22, it increments the **Cnum** loop counter, and goes back to the top of the inner loop in line 8. In line 8, VBA checks the new value of the loop counter variable against the ending value, and executes the loop again, if necessary.

When the inner For...Next loop (lines 8 through 22) finishes executing, VBA executes line 23. This line contains the Next statement that marks the end of the outer loop's body. When VBA executes the statement in line 23, it increments the **Rnum** loop counter, and goes back to the top of the outer loop in line 7. In line 7, VBA checks the new value of the **Rnum** loop counter against the ending value, and executes the loop again, if necessary.

When the outer For...Next loop (lines 7 through 23) finishes executing, VBA executes line 24, which ends the procedure.

Note: You must run the **FormatHeading** procedure when the current sheet is a worksheet only. If you run **FormatHeading** when the current sheet is *not* a worksheet, you will receive a runtime error message stating that the Cells method failed—a completely reasonable error because module sheets do not have cells to select!

> **Tip:** You can also nest For Each...Next loops the same way you nest For...Next loops; use a technique similar to that shown in Listing 9.10.

Nesting *Do* Loops

Listing 9.11 shows a procedure that uses nested Do loops to help a user perform the data entry needed to generate an invoice. The outer loop in the **MakeInvoices** procedure gets invoice numbers from the user until there are no more invoices to enter—or the user cancels the input dialog box. The inner loop in the **MakeInvoices** procedure gets line-item numbers for the invoice until there are no more line-items to enter, or the user cancels the input dialog box. As you study this procedure, keep in mind that it is just a skeleton. In reality, you would probably need to collect much more information than this procedure does. This demonstration procedure was kept as simple as possible to make it easier for you to understand how the nested loops are constructed, and how they interact.

 Listing 9.11. Nested Do loops.

```
 1:  Sub MakeInvoices()
 2:  'provides data entry for invoices and line items on each
 3:  'invoice. Outer loop gets info about a single invoice,
 4:  'inner loop gets info about line-items in the invoice.
 5:
 6:      Const miTitle = "Invoice Data Entry "
 7:
 8:      Dim InvcNum As String * 5     'the invoice number
 9:      Dim ItemNum As String * 16    'line item stock ID number
10:      Dim ItemDone As Boolean       'done getting line items
11:      Dim InvcDone As Boolean       'done getting invoices
12:
13:      InvcDone = False    'make sure loop starts
14:      Do Until InvcDone       'loop for getting invoices
15:
16:          'ask for an invoice number
17:          InvcNum = InputBox(prompt:="Enter Invoice Number:", _
18:                      Title:=miTitle)
19:          If Trim(InvcNum) = "" Then    'invoice entry canceled
20:            MsgBox prompt:="Invoice Entry Canceled.", _
21:                    Title:=miTitle, Buttons:=vbExclamation
22:            InvcDone = True     'done getting invoices
23:            ItemDone = True     'no point in getting line items
24:          Else
25:            ItemDone = False    'prepare line item loop
26:          End If
27:
28:
29:          Do Until ItemDone         'loop to get line items
30:              'ask for a line item number
```

```
31:        ItemNum = InputBox(prompt:="Enter line #:", _
32:              Title:=miTitle & "- Line Items for " & InvcNum)
33:        If Trim(ItemNum) = "" Then       'line item canceled
34:          MsgBox prompt:="Line Item entry for Invoice #" & _
35:                         InvcNum & " ended.", _
36:                 Title:=miTitle
37:          ItemDone = True       'done getting line items
38:        Else
39:          'statements to store entered data, get more info
40:          'about the line item, and so on would go here.
41:          MsgBox prompt:="You entered line item #" & _
42:                         ItemNum & " on Invoice #" & InvcNum, _
43:              Title:=miTitle & "- Line Items for " & InvcNum
44:        End If
45:     Loop  'ending line item entry loop
46:   Loop  'ending invoice entry loop
47:
48:   MsgBox prompt:="Invoice Entry complete", Title:=miTitle
49: End Sub
```

Analysis

The **MakeInvoices** procedure uses the outer Do loop to get invoice numbers. Once the user enters an invoice number, the inner Do loop starts, and repeatedly gets line-item numbers from the user. The user signals that there are no more line-item numbers to enter by entering a blank string, or by canceling the input dialog box. (To keep this procedure fairly simple, no confirmation screening was added to any of the input dialog box cancellations.)

When the user signals that there are no more line-items to enter, the inner Do loop stops executing, and the outer Do loop resumes. The outer Do loop repeats, asking the user for another invoice number (the procedure assumes that the user has more than one invoice to enter).

Lines 8 through 11 declare several variables. **InvcNum** is for the invoice number, and **ItemNum** is for the line-item number. Notice that both of these strings are fixed-length strings. **ItemDone** and **InvcDone** are Boolean variables used to control the execution of the line-item and invoice Do loops, respectively.

Line 13 initializes the **InvcDone** variable as False, to ensure that the loop will actually start executing. Line 14 starts the outer Do loop. The logical expression for the loop determinant is the single Boolean variable **InvcDone**. This Do statement uses the Until keyword, so VBA checks this loop determinant's condition before executing the body of the loop, and continues executing the loop for as long as **InvcDone** is False.

The statement in line 17 uses the InputBox function to get an invoice number from the user, and assigns the InputBox result to the **InvcNum** variable. Lines 19 through 26 contain an If...Then...Else statement that evaluates the user's input in **InvcNum**.

In line 19, if **InvcNum** contains a blank string, then VBA executes the statements in lines 20 through 23, which display a message to the user that invoice entry will end, and then set *both* of the loop controlling flags to True, signifying that both line-item *and* invoice entry is complete.

If **InvcNum** is not blank, VBA executes line 25, which sets the **ItemDone** flag to False, signifying that line-item entry should be performed.

Whichever branch of the If...Then...Else statement was chosen in line 19, VBA next executes line 29, which is the start of the inner Do loop. This loop is constructed much the same as the outer loop; it just uses a different flag variable. The inner, nested, Do loop that starts in line 29 has its determinant condition tested before VBA executes the body of the loop, and the loop will execute for as long as **ItemDone** is False.

If the invoice entry is over (lines 20 through 23 were executed), **ItemDone** is True, and the inner loop starting in line 29 does *not* execute; instead, VBA skips over the body of the inner loop and executes line 46, which marks the end of the outer Do loop. VBA returns to the top of the outer loop in line 14, and checks the determinant condition—**InvcDone** is also True, so the outer loop ends as well.

If line 25 executed as a result of the If...Then...Else statement in line 19, **ItemDone** is False, and the inner Do loop in line 29 *does* begin to execute.

Line 31 uses the InputBox function to get a line-item number from the user, and assigns it to the **ItemNum** variable. Lines 33 through 44 contain an If...Then...Else statement that evaluates the user's input in **ItemNum**.

In line 33, if **ItemNum** contains a blank string, then VBA executes the statements in lines 34 through 37, which display a message to the user that line-item entry will end, and then sets the **ItemDone** flag to True, signifying that line-item entry is complete. If **ItemNum** is not blank, VBA executes the statements in lines 39 through 43. These statements merely display a message dialog box that echoes the user's input. If this procedure were really used to get data entry, this is where the statements that stored the data, or performed additional evaluation on the data would appear.

Whichever branch of the If...Then...Else statement was chosen in line 33, VBA next executes line 45, which is the end of the inner Do loop. VBA returns to the top of the inner loop in line 29, and checks the determinant condition of the loop again. If **ItemDone** is still False, VBA executes the loop again.

If **ItemDone** is True, VBA continues execution with the statement in line 46, which ends the outer Do loop. VBA returns to the top of the outer loop in line 14, and checks the loop's determinant condition again. If **InvcDone** is still False, VBA executes the outer loop again.

If **InvcDone** is True, VBA continues execution with line 48, which displays a message stating that the entry process is complete. Line 49 is the end of the **MakeInvoices** procedure.

Summary

In this lesson, you learned some of the different terminology used to describe different kinds of loops, and the various parts of a loop. You learned what a loop determinant is, and you learned the difference between a fixed and indefinite loop. You also learned how loops that test their determinant condition before executing the body of the loop are different from loops that test their determinant condition after executing the body of the loop.

First, you learned how to construct fixed loops with the `For...Next` and `For Each...Next` statements. You learned about the options for the `For...Next` loop, and you learned how to construct `For...Next` loops both with counts that go up, and counts that go down. You also learned how to use the `For Each...Next` loop to perform operations involving all of the elements in a particular group.

Next, you learned how to construct indefinite loops using the `Do` loop statement. This chapter showed you how VBA tests `Do` loop determinant conditions, how to use the `Do` statement to construct loops that test their determinant before execution, and to construct loops that test their determinant after execution. You learned about the four different ways to construct `Do` loops: `Do While`, `Do Until`, `Do...Loop While`, and `Do...Loop Until`.

This chapter also described some of the reasons why you might want or need to end a loop early, and showed you how to use the `Exit For` and `Exit Do` statements to end `For` and `Do` loops. Finally, this chapter showed you how to nest loops and gave you some examples of typical uses for nested `For...Next` loops and nested `Do` loops.

Q&A

Q I'm not sure if I should use a `For` loop or a `Do` loop.

A Deciding whether to use a `For` loop or a `Do` loop is pretty straightforward. If you want the loop to repeat a set number of times whenever it executes, and you can easily use constants or a mathematical expression to define the upper and lower limits for the loop's counting, use a `For` loop. If you're not sure how many times the loop might need to execute, or you cannot easily use constants or numeric expressions to set a lower and upper limit for the loop's count, then you should use a `Do` loop.

Q I think I understand how the fixed loop statements work, but I'm not sure whether I should use a `For...Next` loop, or a `For Each...Next` loop.

A Use a `For...Next` loop when you can control the loop's execution by counting the number of times it executes. Use a `For Each...Next` loop to operate on all of the elements in a collection, such as all the sheets in a workbook.

Q I'm pretty sure I should use a Do loop for a particular task, but how can I tell whether I've picked the right one of the four Do loop variations?

A Choosing the "right" loop structure is really mostly a matter of choosing the loop structure that is the easiest for you to set up, and involves the simplest logical expressions for the loop determinant conditions. Usually, carefully stating the looping conditions in English will give you a good idea of which Do loop variation you should use.

In English, try to express the looping operation you want to perform in one of the following sentence forms, and your loop will practically write itself:

☐ From the first (or 2nd or 3rd, etc.) up to the *n*th thing, do... (A For...Next loop.)

☐ From the *n*th thing down to the first (or 2nd or 3rd, etc.), do... (A For...Next loop with a negative Step value.)

☐ For the number of times specified by... (Another For...Next loop.)

☐ For every (or for each) item in the... (A For Each...Next loop.)

☐ While some condition exists, do... (A Do While loop.)

☐ Do this task at least once and, while these conditions exist, repeat it... (A Do...Loop While loop.)

☐ Until these conditions come into existence, do... (A Do Until loop.)

☐ Do this task at least once, repeating it until these conditions come into existence... (A Do...Loop Until loop.)

When you compose your English sentence to help you determine the correct looping structure, avoid sentences like "For as long as there is input, prompt the user for more input." By using a phrase like *For as long as* you may end up confusing yourself. In this example, you're really looking for an English sentence "While there is input, prompt the user for more input." This last sentence is very clear, and you can easily see that you would need to write a Do While loop statement to put this thought into action.

You could also express the same thought as "Prompt the user for input until there is no more input." Phrased this way, you might write a Do...Loop Until statement— either approach can work equally well, and both accomplish the same purpose. The only difference between the two is which is easier for *you* to phrase and understand.

Workshop

Answers are in Appendix A.

Quiz

1. What is the difference between a fixed loop and an indefinite loop?

2. Can you change the number of times a For...Next loop executes?

3. In a Do loop, how does VBA tell whether to test the determinant condition before or after executing the body of the loop?

4. In a Do loop, how does VBA tell whether to continue executing the loop while the determinant condition is True, or to continue executing the loop until the determinant condition is True?

5. What is a count-controlled Do loop? When would you use a count-controlled Do loop?

6. What is an event-controlled Do loop?

7. What is a flag-controlled Do loop?

Exercises

1. **BUG BUSTER:** The following procedure is supposed to repeatedly get a number from the user, and stop executing when the user enters the word *exit*. This procedure uses the Application.InputBox function to get input from the user. The procedure uses the Application.InputBox function instead of the VBA InputBox function because of the optional Type argument in the Application.InputBox function that allows you to specify that the user's input must be numeric.

   As written, the loop in this procedure has a fatal flaw: it will never stop executing. Find the problem with this loop, and correct it. (HINT: The problem lies with the manner in which the loop's determinant condition is defined.)

   NOTE: If you enter this procedure and execute it before you correct its problem, be prepared to use the Esc key to interrupt the procedure's execution—as described in the sidebar earlier in this chapter.

```
1:  Sub GetNumber()
2:  'loops indefinitely, getting numeric input from user
3:
4:    Dim iNum
5:
6:    Do
7:      iNum = Application.InputBox(prompt:="Enter number:", _
8:                                  Type:=1)
9:    Loop Until iNum = "exit"
10:
11:   MsgBox "Number entry ended."
12: End Sub
```

2. Write a procedure that gets three words from the user, assembles them into a single string, and then displays that string. Your procedure should include the following features:

   ☐ Use a For...Next loop to repeat the input statement that requests the user to input a word.

   ☐ Include statements to screen the user's input, and stop the loop if the user enters a blank string or cancels the input dialog box.

   ☐ Use no more than two string variables to get and assemble the three words.

3. Modify the procedure you wrote for the previous exercise so that it will loop indefinitely, collecting words from the user until the user enters a period (.) by itself. (HINT: Replace the For loop with a Do loop.)

4. Write a function named **IsBookOpen** that returns True if a particular workbook is open, False if it is not. Model your function on the **SheetExists** function shown earlier in this chapter. For your function, use the Workbooks collection—this collection contains all the currently open Excel workbooks. The name of the workbook is stored in the workbook's Name property, just like a worksheet's name. For a workbook, however, the string stored in the Name property is the workbook's filename on disk. For example, the personal macro workbook's Name property contains the string *PERSONAL.XLS*.

   As part of this exercise, write a procedure to test the **IsBookOpen** function.

5. Write a function named **SVal** that receives a String type argument, and returns a Double type result that contains the numeric equivalent of the value in its argument. Your function should remove all the non-digit characters (except the decimal point) from the argument string, and then use the VBA Val function to convert the string to a number.

   For example, if the argument contains the string *$1,000.00* your function should first convert the string to *1000.00* so that it can be converted to a number, and then pass the new string to the Val function to convert it into a number.

   As part of this exercise, write a procedure to test the **SVal** function.

Data Types and
Variables:
Advanced Topics

This chapter expands your knowledge of variable scope and persistence, tells you how to use VBA's functions to get information about the data type stored in a variable, and explains how you can create and use customized data types. Today, you learn:

☐ How to get information about the data type stored in a Variant or other type of variable, and how to get information about the data type of an expression's result.

☐ How to determine whether a Variant or Object type variable has ever been assigned a value.

☐ How to use data type information functions, combined with looping structures and If statements to validate the input that your procedure obtains from the user (or other sources).

☐ How to alter the persistence of variables to retain the value that the variable stores between function or procedure calls.

☐ How to create your own data types to fulfill special needs or to make it easier to manipulate groups of data values as a single unit.

Getting Information about Variables and Expressions

There are many different circumstances in which you'll find it useful to get more information about a variable or expression in your VBA code. This section starts out by describing a few of these circumstances, and then discusses the VBA information functions you can use to get more information about a variable or an expression.

One situation in which you may need to get more information about a variable occurs in your functions and procedures that have optional arguments. Optional arguments, as you may remember, must be Variants. As you also know, a Variant may contain any data type. So, your function may expect a numeric type in a particular optional argument, but—because the optional argument is a Variant—VBA allows you to pass a String, Date, or other data type when you actually call the function. To avoid runtime errors in your function, you might need to use VBA's data type information functions to determine what data type was actually passed to your function, and attempt to convert it—or display an error message—before your function uses the value.

You might also want to use VBA's information functions to get more information about a variable's data type to find out exactly what an object variable or object expression refers to. For example, if you are unsure whether an object reference refers to a Workbook or to a Worksheet object, you can use the TypeName function to find out—the TypeName function returns a string containing the object's specific name: *Workbook* for a Workbook object, *Range* for a Range object, and so on.

Yet another situation in which VBA's data type information functions become useful is when you use the InputBox function to get input from your procedure's user. The data type information functions can help you ensure your procedure's user does actually enter the information that your procedure asked for. The section "Validating User Input" in this chapter describes how to validate user input in more detail.

Table 10.1 summarizes VBA's data information functions. Some of these functions just give you general information about the type of data an expression represents, others give you more detailed information. The following sections of this chapter describe these data type information functions and their uses in more detail.

In Table 10.1, V represents any single variable name, and E represents any valid VBA expression. All function arguments shown in Table 10.1 are required, unless otherwise noted.

Table 10.1. Data type information functions.

Function	Purpose/Meaning
IsArray(V)	Returns True if V is an array variable; False otherwise. (Day 13 describes VBA's array data type.)
IsDate(E)	Returns True if E is a valid Date expression; False otherwise. E can be either a Date value or a string expression representing a date.
IsEmpty(E)	Returns True if expression E is empty; False otherwise. E can be a numeric or string expression, but is usually a Variant type variable (a Variant with no value). Always returns False if E contains more than one variable.
IsError(E)	Returns True if E is a numeric expression representing one of VBA's error codes, or a user-defined error code; returns False otherwise.
IsMissing(V)	Returns True if the optional argument variable V was *not* included in the argument list of a function or procedure; False otherwise. (Day 6 describes how to use the IsMissing function.)
IsNull(E)	Returns True if the expression E does *not* contain valid data, False otherwise. E may be any numeric or string expression; if any variable in the expression is Null, the entire expression evaluates to Null.
IsNumeric(E)	E may be any numeric or string expression. Returns True if E is a numeric data type (Integer, Long, Single, Double or Currency), or a string that VBA can convert to a number; returns False otherwise. IsNumeric always returns False if E is a Date expression. If E is Empty, IsNumeric returns True.

continues

Table 10.1. continued

Function	Purpose/Meaning
IsObject(E)	Returns True if the expression E refers to a valid OLE Automation object; False otherwise. (Some, but not all, OLE Automation objects are also VBA or host application objects; Day 20 describes OLE objects.)
TypeName(E)	Returns a string containing the name of the data type of expression E. E can be any expression or variable, except a user-defined type.
VarType(V)	Returns a number indicating the data type of variable V. V can be any variable, except a user-defined type.

Using Visual Basic for Application's Data Information Functions

VBA provides several functions that enable you to test if a variable or expression contains a particular type of data, and that give you a general idea of the variable's status. Each of these functions has a single argument and returns a Boolean value (True or False).

You can use these functions to get information about variables or expressions, including argument variables. These general information functions are: IsArray, IsDate, IsError, IsMissing, IsNumeric, IsObject, IsEmpty, and IsNull. Notice that each of these function names begins with the word *Is*, letting you know that the function tests the type and status of a variable or expression. Refer to Table 10.1 for a summary of each function's action, and what arguments it takes.

Using these testing functions is really quite straightforward. Because these functions return a Boolean result, you'll find yourself using them frequently in If...Then statements, and in logical expressions that define a Do loop's determinant condition.

Each of the following sample lines shows the general syntax for these functions:

```
IsArray(varname)
IsDate(expression)
IsError(expression)
IsMissing(argname)
IsNumeric(expression)
IsObject(expression)
```

varname represents any variable name, *expression* represents any VBA numeric, date, or string expression, and *argname* represents any argument variable name in the argument of one of your function procedures.

You have already learned how to use the IsMissing function (in Day 6), so this chapter does not describe the IsMissing function. This chapter does not describe the IsArray function in detail, either, because you have not yet learned about the Array data type. You use the IsArray function to determine whether or not a particular variable is an array. (An array is similar to a collection of objects; Day 13 explains in more detail what an Array data type is and how to use arrays.)

Because the IsEmpty and IsNull functions are so closely related to VBA's special Empty and Null values, these two functions are described in the later section of this chapter that describes the use and purpose of the Empty and Null values.

You use the remaining three functions—IsDate, IsNumeric, and IsObject—in similar ways, and for similar purposes. Listing 10.1 shows the **FlipCase** function from Day 6. This version of **FlipCase** not only uses the IsMissing function to determine whether the optional argument is present, but also uses the IsNumeric function to determine whether the argument contains the correct type of data.

Type

Listing 10.1. Verifying an optional argument's data type.

```
1:  Function FlipCase(ByVal tStr As String,
2:                    Optional ByVal nChar) As String
3:  'Reverses case of the first nChar characters in tStr.
4:  'If nChar omitted, flips the case of all chars in tStr
5:    Dim k As Long                    'loop counter
6:    Dim TestC As String * 1          'string for testing
7:
8:      'if nChar is missing, or is not numeric...
9:    If IsMissing(nChar) Or (Not IsNumeric(nChar)) Then
10:     nChar = Len(tStr)      'nChar gets entire tStr length,
11:    End If                  'thus avoiding a runtime error
12:
13:    For k = 1 To nChar
14:      TestC = Mid(tStr, k, 1)
15:      If (StrComp(TestC, "A", 0) >= 0) And _
16:         (StrComp(TestC, "Z", 0) <= 0) Then
17:        Mid(tStr, k, 1) = LCase(TestC)
18:      ElseIf (StrComp(TestC, "a", 0) >= 0) And _
19:             (StrComp(TestC, "z", 0) <= 0) Then
20:        Mid(tStr, k, 1) = UCase(TestC)
21:      End If
22:    Next k
23:    FlipCase = tStr
24: End Function
```

Analysis

The **FlipCase** function in Listing 10.1 operates essentially the same as the version shown in Day 6. The major difference in this version is the addition of the IsNumeric function to the If...Then statement in line 9. This If...Then statement now checks not only whether the **nChar** argument was included when the function was called, but also checks to see whether the value contained in **nChar** is numeric. The following paragraphs give a line-by-line

343

explanation of **FlipCase**. Some of the details of **FlipCase**'s operation that were explained in Day 6 are not repeated here.

As before, **FlipCase** takes two arguments. The first argument, **tStr**, is required and is passed by value. The second argument, **nChar** is optional and is also passed by value. The `ByVal` keyword was added to the **nChar** argument for this version of **FlipCase** because this version may modify **nChar**. Passing by value protects the source of the argument's data from being altered when the argument variable is altered within the function.

Lines 9 through 11 contain an `If...Then` statement that adjusts the value in **nChar**, if necessary. The first part of the logical expression in the `If...Then` statement, `IsMissing(nChar)`, is `True` if the **nChar** argument is missing. The second part of the logical expression (`Not IsNumeric(nChar)`) is `True` whenever the value in **nChar** is non-numeric—or can't be converted to a number. (Remember, the `Not` logical operator inverts the value of a logical expression; if `IsNumeric` returns `False`, meaning that **nChar** contains non-numeric data, `Not IsNumeric` returns `True`.)

Because the logical expressions in line 9 are connected with the `Or` logical operator, the entire logical expression is `True` whenever *either* of the two sub-expressions is `True`. As a result, VBA executes the statement in line 10 whenever **nChar** is missing, or whenever **nChar** contains non-numeric data. The statement in line 10 simply sets **nChar** to be equal to the length of the string in **tStr**.

Setting **nChar** to the length of the string in **tStr** whenever **nChar** starts out containing non-numeric data avoids a runtime error in line 13, which uses **nChar** to establish the ending count for the `For...Next` loop. For example, without the additional testing in line 9, if the statement that calls **FlipCase** passes the string *five*—which VBA cannot convert to a number—as the value for **nChar**, a type mismatch error occurs in line 13 when VBA tries to convert the string *five* to a number for use as the ending count of the loop. By including the `IsNumeric` test, and re-assigning a numeric value to **nChar**, there is no longer a possibility that a runtime error will occur in line 13—the test for missing or non-numeric data in lines 9 through 11 ensures that **nChar** will always have a numeric value by the time it gets used in line 13.

The `For` loop in lines 13 through 22 works as described in Day 6: Each character of the string in **tStr** is examined individually, and converted to either upper- or lowercase, as appropriate. Finally, line 23 assigns the function's result.

DO	DON'T

DO use the data information functions to ensure that optional arguments contain the correct data types, and convert or alter the data in the argument to the expected type if you want to avoid potential runtime errors in your functions and procedures.

DON'T assume that the statement that calls your function will always pass the right type of data to your function's optional arguments, especially if you write user-defined functions for use by other users.

The short procedure in Listing 10.2 shows another typical use of VBA's data information functions. The **InvoiceDate** procedure in Listing 10.2 uses the IsDate function to control a Do...Loop Until structure, forcing the loop to repeat until the user enters a valid date expression in the input dialog box.

 Listing 10.2. Verifying the data type of a user's input.

```
1:  Sub InvoiceDate()
2:  'repeats indefinitely, until the user enters a valid date.
3:
4:     Dim uDate As Variant
5:
6:     Do
7:       uDate = InputBox(prompt:="Enter the invoice date: ", _
8:                        Title:="Invoice Date")
9:     Loop Until IsDate(uDate)
10:    MsgBox "You entered the date: " & _
11:           Format(uDate, "long date")
12: End Sub
```

 In a practical application, the **InvoiceDate** procedure might be part of a larger procedure, or might actually be written as a function that gets a date from the user, and returns that date as the function's result.

Line 4 declares a variable, **uDate**, to hold the user's input. Notice that this variable is declared as a Variant, primarily to make any subsequent data type conversions a little easier.

Line 6 begins a Do...Loop Until statement. Because the determinant condition is at the end of the loop, VBA tests the loop determinant condition after executing the body of the loop. After reading the Do statement that starts the loop, VBA immediately moves on to execute the statement in line 7, which is the first—and only—statement in the loop's body.

The InputBox statement in lines 7 and 8 prompts the user to enter a date (the date of a hypothetical invoice), and stores the string entered by the user in the **uDate** variable. For simplicity, this procedure does not contain any statements to handle the possibility that the user canceled the input dialog box.

Line 9 marks the end of the loop and contains the loop's determinant condition. After VBA executes the body of the loop, it evaluates the logical expression in line 9. Because this loop uses the Until keyword, VBA will execute the loop until this logical expression becomes True. The logical expression contains the single call to the IsDate function. If the string the user entered represents a valid date—that is, the string contains information that VBA can convert to a Date type value—then IsDate returns True, and VBA stops executing the loop. Otherwise, IsDate returns False, and VBA executes the Do loop again.

For example, if you enter the string *Dec. 12, 1939*, the IsDate function returns True because VBA can convert this string to a Date type value. Similarly, if you enter strings like *4/1/94* or *5-12-97*, the IsDate function also returns True, ending the loop. If you enter a string like

December twelfth, 1939, however, `IsDate` returns `False`, because VBA cannot convert this string to a date, and the loop executes again. The `IsDate` function will also return `False` for date an invalid date, such as *February 30, 1996,* or *December 0, 1995.*

Finally, line 10 uses a `MsgBox` statement to display the date that the user entered.

DO	DON'T

DO use the VBA information functions to help you verify that a user enters the kind of data you expect.

DO use any of the VBA data information functions in ways similar to those just shown in Listing 10.1 and 10.2 for `IsNumeric` and `IsDate`.

DON'T use the *Is* information functions if you need specific information about the data type in a variable, use the `TypeName` or `VarType` functions (described in the next section) instead.

Determining the Specific Data Type of a Variable or Expression

VBA provides two functions—`TypeName` and `VarType`—especially for the purpose of determining what type of data a variable contains; or for determining the data type of an expression. `TypeName` and `VarType` give you more specific detail than the other data type information functions.

In general, you use the `TypeName` and `VarType` functions for the same reasons and purposes you use the more general information functions (`IsNumeric`, `IsDate`, and so on) described in the preceding section. You might use one of these two functions if you need to know specifically whether an expression or variable contains an Integer or a Double data type instead of just knowing that it is a numeric variable, or if you need to know the specific type of object that an object variable refers to, such as a `Range` or `Workbook` object.

You might also use the `TypeName` function if you're not sure how an expression will evaluate. For example, you can set up an expression just like the one you want to use in your procedure, and then use a `MsgBox` statement and the `TypeName` function to display the name of the data type for the expression's result. For instance, if you're uncertain whether an expression such as `tNum + tStr` results in a numeric or string data type when one variable contains a string and the other contains a number, you might use a test procedure like the one shown in Listing 10.3 to display the data type of the expression's result.

Listing 10.3. Using a test procedure to display the data type of an expression result.

```
1:   Sub Find_Type()
2:     Dim tNum As Variant
3:     Dim tStr As Variant
4:
5:     tNum = 5
6:     tStr = "2"
7:     MsgBox TypeName(tNum + tStr)
8:   End Sub
```

Listing 10.3 is very simple. Lines 2 and 3 declare a couple of variables, and lines 5 and 6 assign a numeric value to **tNum** and a string value that represents a number to **tStr**. (If you try to add the numeric and string constants together directly, VBA displays a type mismatch error.) Line 7 contains a MsgBox statement that displays the result of the TypeName function. In this statement, TypeName's result is a string containing the name of the data type to which the expression tNum + tStr evaluates.

If you enter and run this procedure, the resulting message dialog box displays the word *Double*, indicating that the result of this expression is a Double-precision floating-point number. This is a much more specific bit of information than you could obtain by using the IsNumeric function—with TypeName, you can determine not only that the value is numeric but what its specific numeric type is.

The next two sections describe the TypeName and VarType functions, and their return values, in detail.

Understanding the *TypeName* Function's Results

The TypeName function, as its name suggests, returns a string that contains the name of the data type for the variable or expression passed as its argument.

The general syntax of the TypeName function is:

```
TypeName(varname)
```

varname represents any VBA variable name or expression. Table 10.2 summarizes the possible strings that TypeName returns, depending on the specific data type of *varname*.

Table 10.2. Return values for the `TypeName` function.

Return String	Meaning
objecttype	An OLE Automation object whose type is *objecttype*. For example, `TypeName` returns *Worksheet* for a `Worksheet` object. (Some, but not all, VBA and Excel objects—such as `Worksheet`, `Workbook`, and `Range`—are OLE Automation objects.)
`Boolean`	A Boolean type.
`Currency`	A Currency type.
`Date`	A Date type.
`Double`	A Double-precision floating-point type.
`Empty`	An uninitialized Variant type.
`Error`	A Variant that contains one of VBA's or a user-defined error code. (Day 17 describes how to use error codes and handle various VBA errors.)
`Integer`	An Integer type.
`Long`	A Long integer type.
`Nothing`	An uninitialized `Object` type variable—that is, an `Object` type variable that does not refer to an object.
`Null`	A Variant variable that does not contain valid information.
`Object`	An object that does not support OLE Automation.
`Single`	A Single-precision floating-point type.
`String`	A string.
`Unknown`	An OLE Automation object with an unknown type—usually an object that belongs to an application other than VBA's host application. (Day 19 describes how to create OLE objects in VBA to manipulate objects in other applications.)

When you use the `TypeName` function, it returns one of the strings shown in Table 10.2. A few of the strings that `TypeName` returns require some additional explanation.

First, when you use the `TypeName` function to return the type of an object variable or object expression, `TypeName` returns a string with the specific object's name, if the object is an OLE Automation object. `TypeName` returns the generic string *Object* only if the object variable or expression references an object that does not support OLE Automation. Sometimes, `TypeName` cannot determine the specific type of an OLE Automation object; when this happens, `TypeName` returns the string *Unknown*. This last case usually occurs for OLE Automation objects that are not part of VBA for Applications but that you created by following the techniques described in Day 19.

Second, if the variable you test with TypeName is an array, TypeName adds a pair of empty parentheses to its return string. For example, an array of Long integers causes TypeName to return the string *Long()*. The *()* at the end of the data type name tells you that the variable you tested with TypeName is an array.

Usually, as in the demonstration procedure in Listing 10.4, you will use TypeName with a single variable as the argument, rather than a complex expression.

Listing 10.4. A demonstration of the results that TypeName returns under different circumstances.

```
 1:   Sub Demo_TypeName()
 2:     Dim V As Variant
 3:     Dim O As Object
 4:     Dim A() As Integer
 5:
 6:     MsgBox TypeName(V)      'uninitialized variant variable
 7:     MsgBox TypeName(O)      'uninitialized object variable
 8:     MsgBox TypeName(A)      'an array of integers
 9:
10:     Set O = ActiveWorkbook
11:     MsgBox TypeName(O)      'OLE Automation object: Workbook
12:     Set O = ActiveSheet
13:     MsgBox TypeName(O)      'OLE Automation object: depends on
14:                      'active sheet: "Module", "Worksheet", etc.
15:   End Sub
```

Analysis

The **Demo_TypeName** procedure just puts the TypeName function through some of its paces. Line 1 contains the procedure declaration, and lines 2 through 4 declare some variables. Notice that **V** is a Variant type variable, and that **O** is a generic Object type variable. The **A()** variable declared in line 4 is an Array type variable—the parentheses after the variable name indicate that it is an array. This array's elements are of type Integer. (Arrays contain several elements, sort of like a collection object—although you don't learn about arrays in detail until Day 13, showing the TypeName results for an array here is a useful part of this demonstration.)

Line 6 uses MsgBox to display the string returned by TypeName. The argument for TypeName in this statement is the Variant type variable, **V**. This variable has not yet had any value assigned to it, so TypeName reports that it is empty, and the message dialog box displays the word *Empty*.

Line 7 also uses MsgBox to display the string returned by TypeName. In this statement, the argument for TypeName is the Object type variable, **O**. This Object variable has not yet been used in a Set statement to make it refer to a particular object; as a result, **O** does not refer to any object. TypeName indicates this fact by returning the string *Nothing*. The message dialog box displayed by line 7 therefore contains the word *Nothing*.

Line 8, like the preceding two lines, displays the result of the TypeName function. In this statement, the argument for the TypeName function is the array variable, **A**. The message dialog box displayed by this line contains the string *Integer()*. TypeName is reporting that the basic data type of this variable is the Integer type, but that the variable is also an array of integers—TypeName adds the parentheses after the data type name to tell you that the variable is an array.

Line 10 contains a Set statement that sets the O object variable to refer to the current active workbook. Line 11 contains another statement that uses MsgBox to display the result of the TypeName function. In this case, the argument to TypeName is an Object type variable set to refer to a specific object. As a result, TypeName returns a string that contains the name of the specific object type that the variable references. Here, O was set to refer to a Workbook object, so TypeName returns the string *Workbook*. (Most of the objects in Visual Basic for Applications, Excel Edition are OLE Automation objects.)

Next, line 12 again contains a Set statement, this time setting the object variable, O, to refer to the current sheet in the active workbook. Again, line 13 displays the result of the TypeName function. The actual string that TypeName returns in this statement depends on the type of sheet active at the time you run this procedure. If you run this procedure while a module sheet is the current sheet, TypeName returns the string *Module*; if the current sheet is a worksheet, TypeName returns the string *Worksheet*.

The TypeName function has many practical uses. Listing 10.5 shows the **FormatArialBold12** procedure that you recorded in Day 1, modified to prevent a runtime error that occurs when you execute this procedure while the active sheet is not a worksheet.

FormatArialBold12 formats the current selection of the active worksheet to use the 12-point bold Arial font. If you execute the recorded macro when the active sheet is, for instance, a module sheet instead of a worksheet, VBA displays a runtime error, stating that an Object variable is not set. This error occurs because, on a module sheet, the text does not have a Font property that you can set. (This error message is not particularly clear; in this case Font is the object that is not set.)

Using the TypeName function, the **FormatArialBold12** procedure has been modified so that it simply refuses to carry out the character formatting unless the active sheet is really a worksheet, thus preventing a runtime error if you accidentally execute this macro when the current sheet is not a worksheet.

Listing 10.5. Using the TypeName function to prevent a runtime error.

```
1:  Sub FormatArialBold12()
2:
3:    If TypeName(ActiveSheet) <> "Worksheet" Then
4:      MsgBox prompt:="Current sheet is not a worksheet!" & _
5:                     " Format canceled.",
6:            Title:="Format Arial Bold, 12 Points"
7:      Exit Sub
8:    End If
9:    With Selection.Font
```

```
10:        .Name = "Arial"
11:        .FontStyle = "Bold"
12:        .Size = 12
13:        .Strikethrough = False
14:        .Superscript = False
15:        .Subscript = False
16:        .OutlineFont = False
17:        .Shadow = False
18:        .Underline = xlNone
19:        .ColorIndex = xlAutomatic
20:    End With
21: End Sub
```

 Lines 3 through 8 are the important lines in this version of **FormatArialBold12**. Line 3 begins an If...Then statement that tests whether or not the active sheet is a worksheet. When VBA executes the logical expression in line 3, it first uses the ActiveSheet property of the Application object to return an object reference to the current sheet. Next, VBA calls the TypeName function, passing the object reference returned by ActiveSheet. VBA then inserts the string returned by TypeName into the logical expression, and uses the inequality comparison operator (<>) to compare it to the constant string "Worksheet".

If the result of the comparison in line 3 is True, it indicates that the type of the current sheet—as returned by TypeName—is not a worksheet, and VBA executes lines 4 through 7. These lines display a message box to the user indicating the reason why the formatting will not take place, and then exit from the procedure.

In this way, the **FormatArialBold12** procedure ensures that it only tries to carry out the font formatting statements in lines 8 through 19 when the active sheet is really a worksheet, thereby avoiding a potential runtime error.

DO	DON'T

DO use the TypeName function—and VBA's other data type information functions—to help you write code that anticipates and avoids possible runtime errors, especially if you intend to distribute your procedures for use by other users.

Understanding the *VarType* Function's Results

The VarType function is similar to the TypeName function; you use both functions for the same purposes and in essentially the same way. The VarType function, however, returns a numeric code to indicate the data type of its argument, instead of the string returned by TypeName. Also, the use of VarType is slightly more restricted than TypeName.

10

The general syntax of the VarType function is:

VarType(*varname*)

varname represents any VBA variable name. Notice that, unlike TypeName, the *varname* argument must always be a single variable name. Table 10.3 summarizes the numeric codes that VarType returns, depending on the specific data type of *varname*.

Table 10.3. Return values for the VarType function.

VBA Constant	Value	Meaning
vbEmpty	0	Uninitialized Variant type.
vbNull	1	Variant that does not contain valid data.
vbInteger	2	Integer type.
vbLong	3	Long integer type.
vbSingle	4	Single-precision floating-point type.
vbDouble	5	Double-precision floating-point type.
vbCurrency	6	Currency type.
vbDate	7	Date type.
vbString	8	String type.
vbObject	9	OLE Automation object. (Use the TypeName function to find the specific object type.)
vbError	10	A VBA or user-defined error code. (Day 17 describes VBA's error codes.)
vbBoolean	11	Boolean type.
vbVariant	12	Variant type. VarType only returns this value combined with vbArray to indicate an array of Variants.
vbDataObject	13	An object that does not support OLE Automation.
vbArray	8192	Array type. VarType always combines this value (by arithmetic addition) with one of the other type codes listed in this table to indicate the specific type of the array's elements.) VarType never returns the vbArray type code alone.

When you use the VarType function, it returns one of the number values shown in Table 10.3. A few of the codes that VarType returns require some additional explanation.

First, when you use VarType to return the type of an object variable, notice that VarType can only tell you whether or not the variable is an Object type that supports OLE Automation, or an Object type that does not support OLE Automation. Also, if you use VarType on an uninitialized Object type variable, VBA displays a runtime error, complaining that the object variable is not set. If you need to find out the specific type of an object, or find out whether an object variable has ever been set to refer to an object, use the TypeName function instead.

Second, if the variable you test with VarType is an array, VarType arithmetically adds the code for an Array type to the code for the data type of the elements in the array. For example, an array of Long integers causes VarType to return the value *8195*, which is equal to 8192 (the code for an Array type) plus 3 (the code for a Long integer type). Therefore, any code value greater than 8192 tells you that the variable you tested with VarType is an array.

DO	DON'T

DO use the VBA constant names shown in Table 10.3 to refer to the various codes that VarType returns. Using VBA's predefined constant names makes your code more readable and easier to debug.

Understanding the Special *Empty* and *Null* Values

VBA provides two special values, indicated by the keywords Empty and Null, to represent uninitialized, absent, or invalid data. The two values have similar meanings, but different purposes.

The *Empty* Value

VBA uses the Empty value to indicate a Variant variable that has never had a value assigned to it. When VBA creates a new Variant type variable, it automatically assigns it the Empty value. The Variant variable keeps the Empty value until you assign some other value to the Variant variable.

The Empty value does not cause runtime or type mismatch errors if it ends up being included in an expression. When VBA encounters a Variant variable containing the Empty value in a numeric expression, or otherwise used as a number, VBA treats the Empty value as if it is zero (0). Whenever VBA encounters a Variant variable containing the Empty value in a string expression, VBA treats Empty as if it is an empty string (" ").

You can also directly assign the `Empty` value to a Variant variable, if you want to indicate that the variable does not contain any data. To assign the `Empty` value to a variable, use a statement like the following (where **v** is any Variant type variable):

```
V = Empty
```

Because VBA treats `Empty` as if it were 0 or an empty string (`""`), depending on the context of the expression, you can't use relational operators to find out if a Variant variable contains the special `Empty` value, or really contains 0 or an empty string. For this reason, VBA includes the `IsEmpty` function.

The general syntax of the `IsEmpty` function is:

```
IsEmpty(expression)
```

In the preceding syntax sample, *expression* represents any VBA Variant type variable or expression. `IsEmpty` returns `True` if *expression* is a single Variant type variable containing the special `Empty` value; `False` otherwise. Usually, you'll use the `IsEmpty` function with only a single variable name as the argument. Although you can pass a complex expression as the *expression* argument, `IsEmpty` always returns `False` if *expression* contains more than one variable.

You can also use the `TypeName` or `VarType` functions to find out whether or not a particular Variant variable contains the `Empty` value.

The *Null* Value

VBA provides the `Null` value to indicate a Variant type variable that does not contain any valid data. Unlike the `Empty` value, VBA does not assign the `Null` value to variables. The only way a variable can have the `Null` value is if you directly assign `Null` to that variable, or if you assign the result of an expression that contains a `Null` value to that variable.

The `Null` value does not cause runtime or type mismatch errors if it ends up being included in an expression, either. When VBA encounters a Variant variable containing the `Null` value in an expression, the entire expression results in `Null`. (This behavior is described by saying that the `Null` value *propagates*—that is, spreads—through expressions.)

VBA includes the `Null` value to help make it easier for you to deal with database information, and to program database type applications. Many database applications use the `Null` value to indicate missing or invalid data in the database. For example, you might have a procedure that helps perform data entry for a worksheet database in Excel. You might assign the `Null` value to a variable in your database program to indicate, for instance, that an invoice number has not yet been entered, or that an invalid invoice number was entered.

You can also use the `Null` value to indicate whether or not the value returned by a function is valid. For example, if you write a function that uses `InputBox` to get a value from a user, and the user cancels the input dialog box, you might want to have your function return `Null` to indicate that its operation was canceled, and that it is not returning any valid data.

To assign the Null value to a variable, use a statement like the following (where **v** is any Variant type variable):

```
V = Null
```

VBA includes the IsNull function to let you determine whether or not a Variant type variable contains the special Null value. You cannot use VBA's relational operators to determine whether a variable contains Null.

The general syntax of the IsNull function is:

```
IsNull(expression)
```

In the preceding syntax sample, *expression* represents any VBA Variant type variable or expression. The IsNull function returns True if *expression* is a single Variant type variable which contains Null; False otherwise. If *expression* contains more than one variable, and any one of the variables contains Null, then the entire expression evaluates to Null, and IsNull returns True.

DO	DON'T

DON'T confuse Empty and Null. VBA assigns Empty to indicate that the Variant variable has not yet been assigned a value (initialized). Null, on the other hand, requires you to deliberately assign the value to some variable to indicate invalid data.

DO use the IsEmpty and IsNull functions to test for the Empty and Null values in a variable. Standard comparison operators will not work for detecting either of these values.

Defensive Programming: Preventing Errors before They Happen

Defensive programming is just one of many names given to various programming techniques intended to reduce bugs and problems with your programs. The goal of defensive programming is to avoid runtime errors and other failures in your procedures by anticipating and preventing errors before they happen.

You have already seen several examples of "defensive programming" techniques in each of the chapters in this second week of teaching yourself Visual Basic for Applications. Decision-making structures, loops, and VBA's data type information functions are all essential tools to start making your procedures and programs "bulletproof"—that is, immune to unwanted runtime errors caused by invalid, missing, or erroneous data values.

Following these defensive programming practices is especially important if you expect to distribute your functions or procedures to other users. For example, you might be responsible for setting up computers with Excel for less experienced users. If so, you may end up writing or recording several macros to help less-experienced users perform routine tasks, such as adding data to certain spreadsheets, generating reports, and so on.

If this is your situation, your procedures and programs will get the best reception from their users if your procedures run without runtime errors. A procedure that fails in the middle of a complex task may leave a less-experienced user at a loss as to what to do next.

At the least, a procedure for use by inexperienced users should anticipate a runtime error and terminate its own execution more gracefully than VBA's runtime error dialog box. For example, it is much better for the **FormatArialBold12** procedure in Listing 10.5 to display a clear-cut message about why it is not going to carry out the requested formatting and then end, than for the user to receive VBA's somewhat obscure error message.

Even if you expect no one else to use your procedures except you, you should still practice defensive programming. If a procedure that performs some relatively complex task—such as data-entry in a worksheet, or creating and printing a report—fails due to a runtime error, you may find it difficult or annoying to recover from the partially completed task.

Checking Arguments and Other Internal Values

One defensive programming technique is to validate values that come from outside the function or procedure, such as a function's arguments. A related defensive programming technique is to ensure that the environment in which a procedure executes is actually the environment in which you intended it to execute.

Listings 10.1 and 10.5 (earlier in this chapter) both show examples of this kind of defensive programming in action. Both the **FlipCase** function and the **FormatArialBold12** procedure contain code that checks the status of various internal conditions, and prevents certain predictable errors from occurring.

The **FlipCase** function, for instance, has code that ensures that the optional **nChar** argument has the expected numeric type value. The same section of code also ensures that, if the **nChar** optional argument is missing, **FlipCase** provides a substitute value. Adding this extra code prevents a runtime error from occurring in the rest of the function's code, where the expected value from **nChar** actually gets used.

As another example, the **FormatArialBold12** procedure has code that ensures that the environment in which it executes is correct for the task that the procedure performs. This code checks to make sure that the active sheet is actually a worksheet, and avoids a runtime error from occurring later, when the procedure actually attempts to change the Font object's properties.

You can ensure that your procedures and functions run smoothly, without interruptions from runtime errors, by adding similar internal value and environment checking code to your procedures and functions.

Validating User Input

When you get one of your procedures working correctly, you can count on your computer and VBA to carry out the instructions in your procedure exactly the same, each time you run the procedure. You cannot count on a human being to behave the same way, however.

If your procedure or function gets input from a user—whether that user is yourself or someone else—you can't count on a human being to always perform the same way or to enter data without occasionally making mistakes. Even if you write absolutely error-free VBA code, an incorrect value entered by your procedure's user can end up producing a runtime error due to type mismatches or other problems.

For example, suppose you write a procedure that asks its user to enter a date value as a string. Suppose, also, that you wanted to save the user some typing, and you wrote your procedure so that it expects the user to enter only the month and day, and then concatenates a string containing the current year to the end of whatever string the user entered. If the user doesn't know—or ignores—the fact that the procedure adds the current year, and enters the complete date *10/29/95*, then your procedure still adds the current year (*/95*, for instance) to the date string the user entered, resulting in the string *10/29/95/95*, which is not a valid date expression. If your procedure tries to convert this value to a date, VBA displays a runtime error and stops executing your procedure.

As another example, if you write a procedure that needs to get a numeric value from a user, and the user enters a non-numeric string, you'll probably end up with a type mismatch runtime error at the point in your procedure where one of your VBA statements tries to use the non-numeric value from the user as a number.

For procedures that you use yourself, you can often prevent problems like this just by making sure that your input dialog box prompt text clearly states what kind of value to enter. For procedures that another person will use, you should add code to your procedure that analyzes the user's input to ensure it matches what your procedure expects, in addition to including clear and explicit prompt text. In the example of getting a date string, you might add code to your procedure that evaluates the string entered by the user, and only adds the year to the string if the user omits it.

You should also be sure to handle obvious issues, such as what happens if a user cancels an input dialog box. Many of the listings in Days 8 and 9 show If . . . Then and loop structures that evaluate the user's input, handling dialog box cancellations and blank strings appropriately. Listing 10.2 shows a rudimentary data entry loop that ensures that the value entered in the input dialog box is, in fact, the expected Date data type—or a string that VBA can convert to a Date.

DO	DON'T

DO evaluate a user's input to ensure that the user's value is really what the procedure needs. You should construct a loop to repeatedly get data from the user until the user enters a value of the expected type or range.

DON'T frustrate your procedure's users: if you refuse their input, display a message that tells the users why the data they entered is not acceptable.

Listing 10.6 shows a function, **GetInteger**, that gets an Integer type value from the user. This function clearly prompts the user for the type of information desired, and then carefully evaluates the string that the user types in to determine whether or not the user actually entered an integer value. If the user enters non-numeric data, a floating-point number, or a number outside the range for an Integer data type, the function displays a message stating the problem, and then repeats the request for an integer.

Type

Listing 10.6. Checking user input to ensure valid data values.

```
1:  Function GetInteger() As Variant
2:  'asks user for an integer value, and makes sure that the
3:  'entered value is really an integer
4:
5:    Const iTitle = "Get Integer"
6:    Const IntMax = 32767    'largest positive num for integer
7:    Const IntMin = -32768   'largest negative num for integer
8:
9:    Dim uNum As Variant
10:   Dim Okint As Boolean
11:
12:   OKint = False     'make sure loop starts
13:   Do Until OKint
14:     uNum = InputBox(prompt:="Enter an integer value: ", _
15:                     Title:=iTitle)
16:     If IsNumeric(uNum) Then      'value is at least numeric
17:       uNum = CDbl(uNum)          'convert to Double
18:       If ((uNum >= IntMin) And (uNum <= IntMax)) Then
19:         If (uNum - Int(uNum)) = 0 Then      'no fractions
20:           uNum = CInt(uNum)                 'final conversion
21:           OKint = True                 'it is an okay integer
22:         Else                       'user entered floating point
23:           MsgBox prompt:="Enter a number without " & _
24:                     "a decimal, only!", _
25:                 Title:=iTitle, Buttons:=vbExclamation
26:         End If
27:       Else          'user entered out-of-range number
28:         MsgBox prompt:="You must enter a number " & _
29:             "between " & IntMin & " and " & IntMax & ".", _
30:               Title:=iTitle, Buttons:=vbExclamation
31:       End If
```

```
32:     Else                'user entered non-numeric string
33:         If uNum = "" Then   'check to see if user canceled
34:             uNum = MsgBox(prompt:="Cancel Integer entry?", _
35:                             Title:=iTitle, _
36:                             Buttons:=vbYesNo + vbQuestion)
37:             If uNum = vbYes Then  'user canceled
38:                 GetInteger = Null       'assign Null to result
39:                 Exit Function              'end function
40:             End If
41:         Else
42:             MsgBox prompt:="You must enter a number!", _
43:                     Title:=iTitle, _
44:                     Buttons:=vbExclamation
45:         End If
46:     End If
47:     Loop
48:     GetInteger = uNum
49: End Function
50:
51:
52: Sub Test_GetInteger()
53:     Dim iNum As Variant
54:
55:     iNum = GetInteger
56:     If IsNull(iNum) Then
57:         MsgBox "Integer Entry was canceled"
58:     Else
59:         MsgBox "You entered: " & iNum
60:     End If
61: End Sub
```

 This function is fairly straightforward, although it may seem complex when you first look at it. This function gets input from the user, and then applies the following tests to the user input:

☐ Is the data numeric?

☐ If numeric, does the value fall within the range of permitted values for an Integer type number?

☐ If numeric, and within the range of an Integer, is the data a whole number, without a fractional part?

Only if the value entered by the user passes all three of these tests, does the function return the user's value. If the value entered by the user fails any of these tests, the function displays a message telling the user what's wrong with the data entered, and loops to get another value from the user. **GetInteger** also checks to see whether or not the user canceled the dialog box, confirms the cancellation, and returns Null if the user does cancel the input operation.

Line 1 contains the **GetInteger** function declaration. Notice that the function's return data type is a Variant, rather than an integer. **GetInteger** returns a Variant data type so that it is able to return a Null type value in case the user cancels the input dialog box.

Lines 5 through 7 declare several constants. **iTitle** supplies a title for all of the dialog boxes that this function displays. **IntMax** is the maximum value that an Integer data type can contain, and **IntMin** is the minimum value that an Integer data type can contain.

Line 9 declares the **uNum** variable, used to hold the user's input. Notice that this variable is a Variant type, which makes the evaluation and processing of this variable somewhat easier. Line 10 declares a Boolean type variable, **OKint**. **OKint** is used as a flag to control the execution of the loop that displays the input dialog box and evaluates the user's input.

Line 12 assigns False to the **OKint** variable, so that the loop in line 13 will start to execute.

Line 13 is the start of a Do Until loop. The body of this loop contains all of the statements from line 14 through line 46. This loop executes until **OKint** becomes True.

The first statement in the loop body is in line 14; this statement uses the InputBox function to prompt the user to enter an integer value, and then assigns the user's input to **uNum**.

Line 16 contains an If...Then...Else statement that checks whether the user's input is at least numeric. If the string in **uNum** is *not* numeric, VBA executes the Else clause for this statement in lines 32 through 46. In this Else clause, line 33 contains a nested If...Then...Else statement that checks whether or not the string in **uNum** is empty. If **uNum** is empty, line 34 uses MsgBox to ask the user whether or not the data entry should be canceled. If the user answers "Yes," line 38 assigns the Null value to the **GetInteger** function result, and line 39 ends the function. This way, you can test the function's result to determine whether the data-entry was canceled—if the **GetInteger** result is Null, the user canceled the data entry.

If **uNum** is not empty, VBA executes the Else clause for the nested If statement in lines 41 through 45. These lines use MsgBox to display a message to the user that they must enter a numeric value, and execution then passes to line 47, which marks the end of the loop body. (Remember, this branch of the code only executes if the user entered a non-numeric value.)

If, in line 16, the value in **uNum** is numeric then VBA continues execution with line 17. This statement converts the user's string to a Double type number, and stores the result back into **uNum**. (**uNum** is a Variant type, so it can contain any data type.) Converting the user's input to a Double type number makes the remaining tests somewhat easier—it is now possible to make simple arithmetic comparisons, instead of complex string analysis.

Line 18 begins a nested If...Then...Else statement that checks to see whether or not the value in **uNum** falls within the range of permissible values for an Integer data type. The expression ((uNum >= IntMin) And (uNum <= IntMax)) is True whenever **uNum** falls between −32768 and 32767, inclusive.

If the value in **uNum** is not within the range of acceptable values for an Integer, VBA executes the Else clause in lines 28 through 31. These lines simply display a message dialog box stating that the user must enter a number in the specified range. VBA then continues execution with line 47, which indicates the end of the loop body.

If, in line 18, the value in **uNum** is within the permissible range for an Integer, VBA continues execution with line 19, which contains yet another nested If...Then...Else statement.

In line 19, the If...Then...Else statement uses the expression (uNum - Int(uNum)) = 0 to determine which branch of code to execute. This expression subtracts the integer equivalent (returned by VBA's Int function) of the Double type number in **uNum** from **uNum** itself. If the difference between the two is 0, then the number in **uNum** has no fractional part. (This expression uses the Int function instead of CInt because CInt *rounds* numbers before converting them to integers, whereas Int *truncates*, or discards, the fractional part.)

If the expression in line 19 is False, the user entered a floating-point number, and VBA executes the nested Else clause in lines 22 through 26. These lines simply display a message dialog box to the user stating that they must enter a number with no decimal point. Execution then continues with line 47, marking the end of the loop's body.

If the expression in line 19 is True, the value the user entered is indeed an integer. VBA continues execution with line 20, which uses CInt to convert **uNum** to an integer. This conversion is required so that the Variant data type returned by **GetInteger** has the Integer type—otherwise, it will have a Double type.

Line 21 assigns True to **OKint**, indicating that the user successfully entered an integer value, thus ending the loop. VBA only executes this line when the user's value passes all three tests. If the user's value fails any of the tests, **GetInteger** displays the appropriate message, and repeats the entry loop.

When the user does enter an integer, the loop stops executing, and VBA executes line 48, which assigns the **GetInteger** function result, and the function ends.

Lines 52 through 61 contain a procedure to test the **GetInteger** function. Line 55 calls **GetInteger** and assigns its return value to the **iNum** variable declared in line 53. Notice the If...Then...Else statement in lines 56 through 60. This statement uses the IsNull function to determine whether the value returned by **GetInteger** and stored in **iNum** is Null. If it is Null, the user canceled the input dialog box in the **GetInteger** function, and the function result does not contain any valid data.

DO	DON'T

DO make your programming task easier by writing a list of all of the conditions that you want to test for, like the list at the beginning of the Analysis section for Listing 10.6. Writing a list like this before you start programming can help you avoid false starts, wasted effort, and possibly a great deal of frustration.

DO consider writing your own data type information functions to expand on the data type information functions that VBA provides, especially if you find yourself writing code to check whether a number is an Integer, Double, and so on. For example, if you find yourself writing many procedures or functions that check to make sure a value is, say, an Integer, then you might find it useful to write an **IsInteger** Boolean function to save yourself from writing the same value-testing code over and over again.

Validating Other Input

Your procedures may obtain data from other sources besides input entered into a dialog box by a user. Your procedures are also likely to use data values obtained from worksheet cells, or from external VBA data files.

Usually, you should apply some or all of the same kinds of data validation to any data your procedure obtains from any source. For instance, if your procedure obtains data from a worksheet cell, you should apply the same data checking routines as you would apply to data obtained directly from the user through an input dialog box. Use the same defensive programming techniques to validate data from other sources as those just described for validating a user's direct input.

Preserving Variables between Function and Procedure Calls

In Day 3, you learned about variable persistence, or how long a variable retains the value you assign to it. You learned that procedure-level variables retain their values only for as long as the procedure in which you declare the variable continues to execute.

There are, however, some circumstances under which you want a variable to retain its value. For example, you might want a procedure that creates charts to number each chart that it creates sequentially, even if the procedure only creates one chart at a time, by retaining a sequential count within the chart creating procedure. As another example, you might want to write a procedure that gets a worksheet name from the user, and retains the last worksheet name the user entered to suggest it as a default for the next time you call the procedure to get a worksheet name.

You can override VBA's normal variable persistence rules by adding the Static keyword to the variable's declaration, or by adding the Static keyword to the function or procedure declaration. By adding the Static keyword, you tell VBA not to dispose of the variable's contents, but to retain the variable and its stored data indefinitely. Static variables persist from the time they are created until you either close the workbook in which the variables are declared, or you end the current Excel work session.

The general syntax for using the Static keyword to create a single static variable is:

```
Static varname [As vartype]
```

varname represents any valid VBA variable name, and *vartype* represents any of VBA's data types: Integer, Long, Single, Double, Currency, String, or Date. Essentially, the syntax for creating a single static variable, including the optional As keyword, is the same as using Dim to declare a variable. By using the Static keyword instead of Dim, you tell VBA to create a variable that retains its value indefinitely. You can declare individual static variables only at the procedure level.

You can make all of the variables in a function or procedure static by placing the Static keyword at the beginning of the procedure or function declaration, as shown in the following general syntax samples:

```
Static Function name([arglist]) [As vartype]
Static Sub name()
```

name represents any valid VBA identifier for a function or procedure name. *arglist* represents any valid argument list definition for the function, and *vartype* represents the function result's data type.

If you declare an entire function or procedure with the Static keyword, all the variables declared within the function or procedure retain their values in between calls to that particular function or procedure.

Listing 10.7 shows the **MakeSalesRpt_Chart** procedure from Day 8, modified to use static variables. This version of **MakeSalesRpt_Chart** retains the values that the user enters for the source worksheet and the data range to graph the first time the procedure is executed during a particular work session, and suggests these values the next time the procedure is executed. **MakeSalesRpt_Chart** also keeps a running count of the charts generated and adds this number to the chart name for each chart the procedure creates.

Listing 10.7. Using static variables.

```
1:  Sub MakeSalesRpt_Chart()
2:  'asks for a sheet name that contains source data, and then
3:  'asks for a range of cells containing data to chart. Next,
4:  'asks for a sheet name to put the pie chart on. Procedure
5:  'then creates chart in a fixed location, and uses the
6:  'ChartWizard method to make a pie chart.
```

10

Listing 10.7. continued

```
 7:   'This procedure uses Static variables, so subsequent runs
 8:   'suggest the last used source sheet name and range.
 9:
10:     Const sTitle = "Make Sales Report Chart"
11:
12:     Static SrcShtName As String
13:     Static SourceRng As String
14:     Static ChartCount As Variant
15:     Dim DestShtName As String
16:
17:        'get source sheet name
18:     SrcShtName = InputBox(prompt:="Enter the name of " & _
19:             "the sheet containing the data to graph:", _
20:                      Title:=sTitle, _
21:                      default:=SrcShtName)
22:
23:        'check to see if user entered name or chose Cancel
24:     If Len(Trim(SrcShtName)) = 0 Then
25:        MsgBox "Data source not entered - ending procedure"
26:        Exit Sub
27:     End If
28:        'select source sheet so user can refer to it
29:     Sheets(SrcShtName).Select
30:
31:        'get source range
32:     SourceRng = InputBox(prompt:="Enter the range of " & _
33:                 "data to graph using R1C1 notation:", _
34:                      Title:=sTitle, _
35:                      default:=SourceRng)
36:
37:       'check to see if user entered range or chose Cancel
38:     If Len(Trim(SourceRng)) = 0 Then
39:        MsgBox "Source range not entered - ending procedure"
40:        Exit Sub
41:     End If
42:
43:       'get destination sheet name
44:     DestShtName = InputBox(prompt:="Enter the name of " & _
45:             "the sheet that will contain the graph:", _
46:                      Title:=sTitle)
47:
48:       'did user enter destination name or choose Cancel?
49:     If Len(Trim(DestShtName)) = 0 Then
50:        MsgBox "Chart sheet not entered - ending procedure"
51:        Exit Sub
52:     End If
53:
54:
55:       'select the destination sheet and create chart
56:     Sheets(DestShtName).Select
57:     ActiveSheet.ChartObjects.Add(96, 37.5, 234, 111).Select
58:
59:       'set up the chart count
60:     If IsEmpty(ChartCount) Then
```

```
61:      ChartCount = 1
62:    Else
63:      ChartCount = ChartCount + 1
64:    End If
65:
66:      'use ChartWizard Method to create chart.
67:    With Sheets(SrcShtName)
68:      ActiveChart.ChartWizard Source:=.Range(SourceRng), _
69:                              Gallery:=xlPie, _
70:                              Format:=7, _
71:                              PlotBy:=xlColumns, _
72:                              CategoryLabels:=1, _
73:                              SeriesLabels:=1, _
74:                              HasLegend:=1, _
75:                              Title:="Sales Report" & ChartCount
76:    End With
77: End Sub
```

10

Lines 12 through 15 declare the variables that this procedure uses. **SrcShtName**, **SourceRng**, and **ChartCount** are all declared as Static variables, so they will keep their value in between calls to **MakeSalesRpt_Chart**. The **DestShtName** variable is not declared as a static variable, so its value is lost as soon as **MakeSalesRpt_Chart** stops executing. The **ChartCount** variable is a new addition to this procedure and is used to supply a running count of the number of charts that this procedure has created in the current Excel work session. Declaring **ChartCount** as a Static Variant type variable makes it possible to use the IsEmpty function to determine whether this procedure has been executed previously during the current Excel work session.

Lines 18 through 21 get the name of the worksheet that contains the data to be charted. Notice that the InputBox function in these lines now uses the Default argument, and passes the **SrcShtName** variable as the suggested default. The first time **MakeSalesRpt_Chart** executes in the current Excel work session, these statements display the dialog box shown in Figure 10.1. Notice that the text box in this input dialog box is blank.

Figure 10.1.

MakeSalesRpt_Chart
displays this dialog box to get
the data source worksheet
name from the user the first
time you execute this
procedure in a particular
work session.

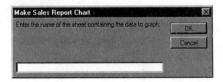

Lines 24 through 27 evaluate the user's input, checking to see whether or not the user canceled the input dialog box. If the user canceled the input dialog box, VBA executes the statements in lines 25 and 26, displaying a message that input was canceled, and ending the procedure.

Line 29 selects the worksheet that the user named, so the user can see the data sheet when asked to enter the range for the data to chart.

Lines 32 through 35 get the data range to be charted. Notice that this InputBox function also includes the Default argument, and passes the **SourceRng** variable as the suggested default value. The first time **MakeSalesRpt_Chart** executes during the current Excel work session, these statements display the dialog box shown in Figure 10.2. Notice that the text box in this input dialog box is also blank.

Figure 10.2.

MakeSalesRpt_Chart
displays this dialog box to get
the range of data to chart
from the user the first time
you execute this procedure in
a particular work session.

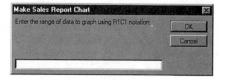

Lines 37 through 41 check to see whether the user canceled the range input dialog box, displaying a message and ending the procedure if the user did cancel.

Lines 44 through 46 get the name of the worksheet on which the completed chart should be placed. Notice that this InputBox function call does not suggest a default sheet name for the chart's destination, and that the **DestShtName** variable is the only variable in this procedure that is not static. **DestShtName** was not declared static because it is unlikely that you will want to place the new chart on top of the last chart you created. These statements display the dialog box shown in Figure 10.3. Notice that this text box, too, is blank.

Figure 10.3.

MakeSalesRpt_Chart
displays this dialog box to get
the name of the worksheet in
which to place the completed
chart.

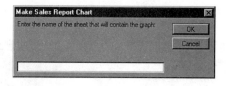

Once again, lines 49 through 52 check to see if the user canceled the operation. Now, lines 56 and 57 select the destination sheet and create the new chart object.

Lines 60 through 64 are also new to this version of **MakeSalesRpt_Chart**. This If...Then...Else statement checks to see if the **ChartCount** variable is Empty—remember, a Variant type variable that has never had a value assigned to it contains the special Empty value. If **ChartCount** is empty, then this is the first time in the current work session that you have executed this procedure, and the statement in line 61 assigns the value 1 to **ChartCount**. If **ChartCount** is not Empty, this

procedure has been executed at least once before in this work session, and the statement in line 63 increments **ChartCount** by 1. This **If...Then...Else** statement works only because **ChartCount** is a static variable, and retains its value in between calls to **MakeSalesRpt_Chart**. If **ChartCount** is not declared with the **Static** keyword, then it would be **Empty** every time this procedure executes because VBA would create it anew each time the procedure started execution, and would destroy it each time the procedure completed execution. Because it is static, however, **ChartCount** effectively keeps a running total of the number of charts created by this procedure in this work session.

Finally, lines 67 through 75 use the **ChartWizard** method to create the chart using the specified data range from the specified worksheet. Figure 10.4 shows a sample chart created with the **MakeSalesRpt_Chart** procedure. Notice that the chart title in Figure 10.4—Sales Report1— ends with the number 1. This is the result of concatenating the **ChartCount** value with the chart name in line 75.

Figure 10.4.

An example of a pie chart created by the **MakeSalesRpt_Chart** *procedure. Notice the number 1 at the end of the chart title.*

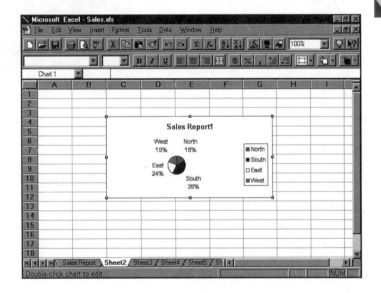

Now, if you execute **MakeSalesRpt_Chart** a second time in the same work session, the procedure behaves exactly the same as just described, but the contents of some of the dialog boxes it displays are different.

In lines 18 through 21, when **MakeSalesRpt_Chart** asks for the source data sheet name, it displays the dialog box shown in Figure 10.5 (assuming that *Sales Report* was the worksheet name you entered last time you executed **MakeSalesRpt_Chart**). Because the **SrcShtName** variable is static, it retained its value in between the first and second time the **MakeSalesRpt_Chart** was executed. Because the **InputBox** statement in lines 18 through 21 uses **SrcShtName** as the suggested input default, the **MakeSalesRpt_Chart** procedure is able to suggest the name of the last source worksheet as the source worksheet for this time.

367

Figure 10.5.

MakeSalesRpt_Chart

*displays this dialog box,
suggesting the last source
worksheet you used, each
additional time you execute
this procedure in a particular work session.*

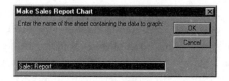

Similarly, when **MakeSalesRpt_Chart** asks for the source data range in lines 32 through 35, it displays the dialog box shown in Figure 10.6 (assuming that *b4:d8* was the range you entered last time you executed **MakeSalesRpt_Chart**).

Figure 10.6.

MakeSalesRpt_Chart

*displays this dialog box,
suggesting the last range you
used, each additional time
you execute this procedure in
a particular work session.*

When **MakeSalesRpt_Chart** asks for the destination worksheet in lines 44 through 46, it displays the same dialog box shown previously in Figure 10.3.

Finally, when **MakeSalesRpt_Chart** finishes creating its second chart, assuming you again charted the same data, the chart appears like the one shown in Figure 10.7. Notice that the chart title in Figure 10.7—Sales Report2—ends with the number 2. This is the result of concatenating the **ChartCount** (which increases by 1 each time you execute **MakeSalesRpt_Chart**) with the chart name in line 75.

Figure 10.7.

MakeSalesRpt_Chart

*created this pie chart the
second time it was used to
chart data. Notice the
number 2 at the end
of the chart title.*

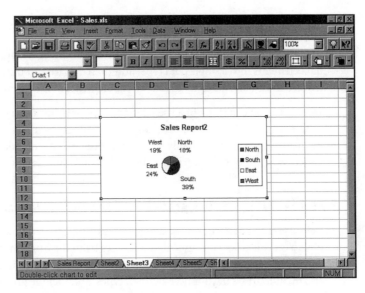

Creating Your Own Data Types

VBA allows you to create additional data types, called *user-defined types* that you can use in your
procedures and functions. A user-defined type lets you bind together several related pieces of
information into a single unit. You can then pass that single unit as an argument to a function,
or return that unit as a function result.

You create and use user-defined data types to simplify some programming tasks, and to reduce
the overall number of variables in your program. User-defined data types make it easier for you
to store and manipulate complex groups of data.

For example, if you want to write a procedure (or several procedures and functions) that help
you create invoices and enter each invoice's line-item information, you might end up declaring
several different variables to store all of the information your procedure needs to collect. You
might need a variable for the invoice number, a variable for the customer name, a variable for
the billing address, another variable for the shipping address, another variable for the invoice
total, yet another variable for the invoice date, and so on—and this partial list doesn't even begin
to include variables that store the invoice's line items.

As you can see, you might quickly end up with a large number of variables. Keeping track of so many variables is inconvenient at best, and sometimes gets downright confusing. By creating a user-defined data type for your invoice information, you can consolidate all of these different data elements into a single data type, and then declare and use a single variable to hold all of the invoice information, referring only to the elements in the variable that you need at any one time.

In a sense, you can think of a user-defined type as being a sort of suitcase in which you can pack different types of data. You can handle the suitcase as if it is a single unit, passing it back and forth as a single item. You only worry about the specific contents of the suitcase when you need to access or store some particular item inside the suitcase.

Defining a User-Defined Data Type

Before you can declare and use any variables with a user-defined type, you must first define the type. You construct your user-defined types from the fundamental VBA data types you learned about in Day 3: Integer, Long, Single, Double, Currency, Date, Boolean, and Variant. You can also include arrays in your user-defined types, and include previously-defined user-defined data types.

Syntax

To define a user-defined data type, use the `Type` statement in the definition area of a module. The `Type` statement has the following general syntax:

```
Type VarName
    ElementName As type
    [ElementName As type]
    [ElementName As type]
...
End Type
```

Both `VarName` and `ElementName` represent any valid VBA identifier. `type` represents any VBA data type name, or any previously defined user-defined type name. More specifically, `VarName` is the name for the new data type you are defining. `ElementName` is the name of a data element in the user-defined type. A user-defined type may contain one or more elements. You must specify the data type of each element in your user-defined type by following `ElementName` with the `As` keyword, and the name of the specific data type for that element. An element's type may be any of VBA's inherent data types, an array, or a previously defined user-defined data type.

VBA allows the `Type` statement to appear only at the module-level. You must place all of your user-defined type definitions in the definition area at the beginning of the module, before any procedure or function declarations, and before any variable declarations that use that user-defined type.

For example, you might define a user-defined type for a mailing address:

```
Type MailingData
    Street As String
    City As String
    State As String *2
    Zip As String * 5
End Type
```

This type definition creates a user-defined type named **MailingData**, which contains 4 elements: **Street** (the street name and number), **City** (the city's name), **State** (a two-letter state abbreviation), and **Zip** (a five-digit ZIP code).

As another example, to declare a user-defined type to hold invoice information, you might use the following definition:

```
Type InvoiceHeading
    Number As Integer
    DateIssued As Date
    Customer As String
    ShipAddress As MailingData
    BillAddress As MailingData
    Total As Currency
End Type
```

The preceding type definition creates a user-defined type named **InvoiceHeading**, which contains six elements: **Number** (the invoice number), **DateIssued** (the invoice date), **Customer** (the customer name), **ShipAddress** (the shipping address), **BillAddress** (the billing address), and **Total** (the total of the invoice).

Notice that the **BillAddress** and **ShipAddress** elements have the previously defined user-defined **MailingData** type. These two elements therefore also contain all of the same elements as the **MailingData** type. In a sense, the **InvoiceHeading** data type is a suitcase that contains other suitcases—the **BillAddress** and **ShipAddress** elements.

Each user-defined data type requires as much computer memory to store as the combined memory storage used by its elements. For example, a user-defined type that has four elements, each of which is an Integer, requires a total of 8 bytes of computer memory to store. Each Integer type element requires 2 bytes (the size of an Integer), and there are four elements, so the combined total storage is 8 bytes.

Note: You cannot use the TypeName, VarType, or any other VBA data type information functions with variables of user-defined types, although you can use the information functions with any individual elements of a user-defined type.

Declaring Variables That Have a User-Defined Type

You declare a variable with a user-defined type the same way you declare any other variable in your procedures and functions, as long as you declare the variable explicitly. Obviously, you cannot implicitly declare a variable with a user-defined type because VBA has no way of knowing which user-defined type you want the variable to have.

Use the Dim or Static keywords to declare a variable with a user-defined type. You can declare variables that have a user-defined type at either a procedure level, or at a module level. The following two statements each declare a variable with a user-defined type. The first statement declares a variable with the **InvoiceHeading** type, and the second statement declares a variable with the **MailingData** type.

```
Dim Invoice As InvoiceHeading
Dim Address As MailingData
```

Using Variables with User-Defined Types

You use variables that have user-defined types much the same way that you use other types of VBA variables. One of the few areas in which variables with user-defined types differ from other types of variables is when you need to refer to a particular element in a user-defined variable.

You are already familiar with the dot separator (.) used in object references. You know that the dot separator both joins and separates two different identifiers, so that VBA can tell when you want to refer to an object, property, or method that belongs to another object.

VBA also uses the dot separator to create references to the elements in a variable with a user-defined type. For example, if you have declared a variable named **Address** that has the user-defined type **MailingData**—as defined in the examples in the preceding sections—then you would refer to the **City** element of the variable with the following expression:

```
Address.City
```

Similarly, if you had variables named **MyAddress** and **YourAddress**, both declared with the user-defined type **MailingData**, you would refer to the **Zip** elements with the following expressions:

```
MyAddress.Zip
YourAddress.Zip
```

In all three of the preceding expressions, the dot (.) between the two names tells VBA that the two names together form a single identifier. VBA then first refers to the memory location referred to by the variable name, and then uses the element name to refer to the specific information stored in that element of the variable.

Look again at the user-defined type definition for the example of an invoice header information:

```
Type InvoiceHeading
    Number As Integer
    DateIssued As Date
    Customer As String
    ShipAddress As MailingData
    BillAddress As MailingData
    Total As Currency
End Type
```

Notice again that the **ShipAddress** and **BillAddress** elements in the **InvoiceHeading** user-defined type are declared as having the previously defined user-defined type **MailingData**. If you have a variable, **Invoice**, that has the user-defined type **InvoiceHeading**, and you want to refer to the **City** element of the shipping address, use an expression like this:

```
Invoice.ShipAddress.City
```

When VBA evaluates this expression, it first references the data stored in the **Invoice** variable. The first dot separator lets VBA know that you want to refer to the **ShipAddress** element in the **Invoice** variable, and the second dot separator lets VBA know that, in turn, you want to refer to the **City** element of the **ShipAddress** element. Just like with object references, the dot separator (.) connects the separate names into a single identifier, while also letting VBA—and you—know what the individual references are.

If you have two variables with the same user-defined type, you can directly assign one variable to the other, as shown in the following statement:

```
MyAddress = YourAddress
```

Assuming both variables in the preceding assignment statement have the user-defined type **MailingData**, VBA copies all of the information in each of the individual elements in **YourAddress** and stores them in the corresponding elements in **MyAddress**.

You cannot, however, assign a user-defined variable to another user-defined variable if they do not have the same type. For example, you could not assign the contents of a variable with the **MailingData** type to a variable with the **InvoiceHeading** type.

To assign values from or to individual elements in a user-defined type, you must specify an element in the user-defined type explicitly. For example, to assign a value to the **City** element of the variable **MyAddress** (assuming **MyAddress** has the user-defined type **MailingData**), you use the following statement:

```
MyAddress.City = "Oaktown"
```

In the preceding statement, VBA stores the string *Oaktown* in the **City** element of the **MyAddress** variable. Data that you assign to an element in a variable with a user-defined type must be compatible with the data type of that element.

To retrieve the information stored in a particular element of a user-defined type variable and assign it to another variable, use a statement like this:

```
AnyStr = MyAddress.City
```

In this statement, VBA retrieves whatever string is stored in the **City** element of the **MyAddress** variable and stores it in the string **AnyStr**.

You can use elements from a variable with a user-defined type in any expression, or as arguments for procedures and functions, where the data type of the specific element is compatible with that expression or argument type. You can even declare functions that return a result that has a user-defined type. (Listing 10.8 shows an example of such a function.)

DO	DON'T

DON'T try to assign a variable with a user-defined type to a Variant type variable; VBA will display a runtime error message if you do.

In Day 7, you learned how to use the With statement in object references to save yourself some typing, and to make your VBA code easier to read. You learned to use the With statement whenever you want to refer to several properties or methods of the same object at once. You can also use the With statement to simplify references to elements of a user-defined type variable. The following code fragment shows how you can use the With statement:

```
With MyAddress
    .Street = "123 American Lane, Suite 24"
    .City = "Oaktown"
    .State = "CA"
    .Zip = "94609"
End With
```

When VBA executes the preceding statements, it first encounters the With keyword, followed by the variable name. VBA then knows that it should reference data stored in the **MyAddress** variable. Notice that each element of the **MyAddress** variable that appears in the assignment statements has a dot separator (.) in front of it. When VBA executes these statements, it internally supplies the **MyAddress** variable reference for the missing reference (indicated by the dot separator) in each statement. As with object references and the With statement, you must include the dot separator. The End With keywords signal the end of the With statement.

Now you are ready to see a user-defined type put into action. Listing 10.8 shows the listing for an entire VBA module. This module contains a definition for a user-defined type, and also contains a single procedure and function declaration. The **UtilityBill** user-defined type is set up to store all of the relevant information for a single month's utility bill. It has elements (sometimes called *fields*) to store the billing date, the total cost of the bill, the number of therms

used in that month (a *therm* is a unit used to measure natural gas consumption), and another element to store the number of kilowatt-hours used (abbreviated KWH and used to measure consumption of electricity).

The **Enter_UtilityCosts** procedure controls data entry and storage for the monthly utility bill figures, and the **Get_UtilityItem** function handles the task of getting the individual values for a single utility bill from the user. Altogether, this module contains a single, simple program to handle the data entry of utility bills. You might use a program like this if you need to enter and analyze your company's (or your own) energy costs and consumption.

Listing 10.8. Defining, creating, and using user-defined types.

```
1:  Option Explicit
2:
3:  Const BillTitle = "Utility Bill Data Entry"
4:
5:  Type UtilityBill
6:      BillDate As Variant
7:      Cost As Currency
8:      Therms As Integer
9:      Kwh As Integer
10: End Type
11:
12:
13: Sub Enter_UtilityCosts()
14: 'this proc enters utility bill information. It calls the
15: 'Get_UtilityItem function to get data for a single utility
16: 'bill, and then transfers the data to a worksheet, looping
17: 'until there is no more data.
18:     Dim Bill As UtilityBill
19:     Dim Done As Boolean
20:     Dim RNum As Integer
21:
22:     Worksheets("sheet1").Select
23:
24:     RNum = 0
25:     Done = False
26:     Do Until Done
27:         Bill = Get_UtilityItem
28:         If IsNull(Bill.BillDate) Then
29:             Done = True
30:         Else
31:             RNum = RNum + 1
32:             With Bill
33:                 Cells(RNum, 1).Value = .BillDate
34:                 Cells(RNum, 2).Value = .Cost
35:                 Cells(RNum, 3).Value = .Therms
36:                 Cells(RNum, 4).Value = .Kwh
37:             End With
38:         End If
39:     Loop
40:     MsgBox prompt:="Data entry complete. " & RNum & _
41:             " records entered.", Title:=BillTitle
```

continues

Listing 10.8. continued

```
42: End Sub
43:
44:
45: Function Get_UtilityItem() As UtilityBill
46: 'gets all the data for a single utility bill, and
47: 'returns it in a utility bill user type.
48:
49:     Dim Item As UtilityBill
50:     Dim Tmp As Variant
51:
52:     With Item
53:       Do               'get the date of the bill
54:           Tmp = InputBox(prompt:="Enter the date of " & _
55:                          "the bill:", Title:=BillTitle)
56:           If Tmp = "" Then        'did user cancel?
57:               Tmp = MsgBox(prompt:="End data entry?", _
58:                            Title:=BillTitle, _
59:                            Buttons:=vbQuestion + vbYesNo)
60:               If Tmp = vbYes Then         'return null date
61:                   .BillDate = Null
62:                   Get_UtilityItem = Item
63:                   Exit Function
64:               End If
65:           End If
66:       Loop Until IsDate(Tmp)
67:       .BillDate = CDate(Tmp)       'fill billing date field
68:
69:       Do               'get the cost
70:           Tmp = InputBox(prompt:="Enter the total " & _
71:                          "cost of the bill:", Title:=BillTitle)
72:           If Tmp = "" Then        'not allowed to cancel
73:               MsgBox prompt:="You must enter the cost!", _
74:                      Title:=BillTitle, Buttons:=vbExclamation
75:           End If
76:       Loop Until IsNumeric(Tmp)
77:       .Cost = CCur(Tmp)           'store cost in cost field
78:
79:       Do               'get therms
80:           Tmp = InputBox(prompt:="Enter the total " & _
81:                   "Therms on this bill:", Title:=BillTitle)
82:           If Tmp = "" Then
83:               MsgBox prompt:="You must enter Therms!", _
84:                      Title:=BillTitle, Buttons:=vbExclamation
85:           End If
86:       Loop Until IsNumeric(Tmp)
87:       .Therms = CInt(Tmp)              'fill therms field
88:
89:       Do               'get KWH
90:           Tmp = InputBox(prompt:="Enter the total KWH " & _
91:                   "on this bill:", Title:=BillTitle)
92:           If Tmp = "" Then
93:               MsgBox prompt:="You must enter the KWH!", _
94:                      Title:=BillTitle, Buttons:=vbExclamation
95:           End If
```

```
96:        Loop Until IsNumeric(Tmp)
97:        .Kwh = CInt(Tmp)                'store KWH in Kwh field
98:      End With
99:      Get_UtilityItem = Item      'return filled UtilityBill
100:End Function
```

Analysis

Lines 1 through 12 of this module represent the module's definition area. Line 1 contains the Option Explicit command, which tells VBA that all variables in this module must be declared explicitly. Line 3 declares a module-level string constant to supply the text for the titles of all of the dialog boxes that all of the procedures or functions in this module display.

Lines 5 through 10 contain a user-defined type definition. The name of this user-defined type is **UtilityBill**, and it contains the following elements: **BillDate** (a Variant type element), **Cost** (a Currency type element), **Therms** (an Integer type element), and **Kwh** (another Integer type element). The programmer here chose the **BillDate** element's type to be a Variant type, rather than a Date type, so that it is possible to set the **BillDate** value to Null, indicating that there is no valid data stored in a variable that has the **UtilityBill** type. The End Type keywords in line 10 signal the end of the user-defined type definition for **UtilityBill**.

Lines 13 through 42 contain the **Enter_UtilityCosts** procedure. Line 13 contains the procedure declaration, and lines 14 through 17 contain comments about what the procedure does.

Lines 18 through 20 declare the variables that the **Enter_UtilityCosts** procedure uses. The **Bill** variable has the **UtilityBill** user-defined type. **Done** is a Boolean variable used to control a loop's execution, and **RNum** is an Integer variable used to keep track of which row in a worksheet the utility bill information should be stored in.

Line 22 uses the Select method of the Worksheets collection to select a worksheet named *sheet1*. This is the worksheet that will store the utility bill data that this procedure collects.

Lines 24 through 39 perform the real work of the **Enter_UtilityCosts** procedure. Line 24 sets the **RNum** variable to 0, because no data has yet been entered. Line 25 sets the **Done** variable to False so that the loop in lines 26 through 39 will start to execute.

Line 26 starts a Do Until loop that executes until the **Done** variable is True.

Pay special attention to line 27. This line contains a single assignment expression that assigns the result of the **Get_UtilityItem** function directly to the **Bill** variable. The **Get_UtilityItem** function's result (line 45) is declared as having the **UtilityBill** user-defined type, as does the **Bill** variable. (The details of the **Get_UtilityItem** function's operation is described a little later in this analysis.)

Lines 28 through 30 contain an If...Then...Else statement that chooses which branch of code to execute based on whether or not the **BillDate** element of the **UtilityBill** item returned by the **Get_UtilityItem** function contains the Null value. If the **BillDate** element of **Bill** contains Null, VBA executes line 29, which simply assigns True to the **Done** variable, signaling that it is time for the loop to end.

10

377

If the **BillDate** element of **Bill** is not Null, VBA executes the statements in lines 31 through 37. The statement in line 31 increments the value of **RNum** by one, advancing to the next row in the worksheet. Line 32 starts a With statement for the **Bill** variable, to make the next few statements easier to write and read.

Lines 33 through 36 each store one element from the **Bill** variable into a single cell in the worksheet. Each statement uses the Cells method of the Application object to return a reference to a cell on the active worksheet. The arguments for the Cells method are, first, the row coordinate, and, second, the column coordinate. Line 33 stores the contents of the **BillDate** element in the first column of the row indicated by **RNum**. Line 34 stores the contents of the **Cost** element in the second column of the row indicated by **RNum**—similarly, line 35 stores the contents of the **Therms** element in the third column, and line 36 stores the contents of the **Kwh** element in the fourth column of the worksheet. Line 37 contains the End With keywords, indicating the end of the With statement.

Line 39 contains the Loop keyword that marks the end of the loop. When VBA executes this line, it returns to the top of the loop, and checks the determinant condition before executing the loop body again. When the loop is complete, VBA executes line 40, which uses MsgBox to display a message to the user that the data entry operation is finished, and reports on how many items were entered, based on the row count stored in **RNum**.

Line 42 contains the End Sub keywords, marking the end of the **Enter_UtilityCosts** procedure.

Now, take a look at how the **Get_UtilityItem** function works. Lines 45 through 100 contain the **Get_UtilityItem** function's definition.

Line 45 contains the function's declaration. The **Get_UtilityItem** function has no arguments, but notice its return value type: this function returns the user-defined type **UtilityBill**.

Although this function might seem fairly long, it's operation is fairly simple. Lines 49 and 50 declare the variables that this function uses. **Item** has the user-defined **UtilityBill** type and is used to hold the data that this function gets from the user, until the function is ready to return its result. The **Tmp** variable has a Variant type and is used to temporarily hold the data obtained from the user with the InputBox function.

Line 52 starts a With statement that encloses almost the entire body of the function because so many of the statements in this function refer to elements of the **Item** variable.

Lines 53 through 66 contain a Do...Loop Until statement that loops repeatedly until the user enters a valid date value. Line 54 assigns the result of a call to the InputBox function to the **Tmp** variable. Lines 56 through 65 contain a couple of nested If...Then statements that evaluate the user's input from line 54.

If the user entered a blank string for the date, or canceled the input dialog box, VBA executes lines 57 through 64. Line 57 is just a little bit tricky. To avoid declaring more variables than absolutely necessary, this statement makes the **Tmp** variable do a little double-duty work. At the

point when VBA executes this statement, the value from the user, stored in **Tmp** has already been evaluated (line 56), and is no longer needed. It is therefore safe to use the **Tmp** variable again to hold the value returned by the **MsgBox** function in line 57. This **MsgBox** function asks the user whether or not the data entry should end and uses the **Buttons** argument to include **Yes** and **No** command buttons in the message dialog box, along with the Windows' Query icon.

Line 60 contains another **If...Then** statement to evaluate the user's response to the message dialog box displayed by line 57. If the user answered *yes* to ending the data entry, VBA executes lines 61 through 63. Line 61 assigns the **Null** value to the **BillDate** element of the **Item** variable (remember, this portion of the function's code is inside a **With** statement). By assigning the **Null** value to the **BillDate** element, this function makes it possible to determine whether or not its result contains any valid data. Line 62 then assigns the function's result, and line 63 exits the function.

If the user did not enter a blank string or cancel the input dialog box, or if the user answers *No* to ending the data entry, VBA continues execution with line 66, which contains the end of the **Do** loop, along with the loop's determinant condition. If the user input in **Tmp** is not a valid date value, or a value that VBA can convert to a date, VBA executes this loop again.

To keep this example function shorter and less complex, it does not include any code to let the user know why the loop is repeating. If you really wanted to write a program like this, and give it to other people to use, you should include code—as shown in previous examples—that would tell the user why the loop is repeating (they didn't enter a valid date).

As soon as the user enters a valid date, VBA executes line 67, which converts the string stored in **Tmp** (obtained from the user) to a Date, and stores it in the **BillDate** element of the **Item** variable. (Again, remember that the statements in this portion of the function are enclosed by a **With** statement.)

Next, lines 69 through 76 contain a **Do...Loop Until** loop that repeats until the user enters a numeric value for the utility bill's cost. Notice that, in lines 72 through 75, if the user cancels this input dialog box, or enters a blank string, the function refuses to allow a cancellation of data entry at this point, and simply displays a message insisting that the user must enter the cost.

As soon as the user enters a numeric value, VBA executes line 77, which converts the string entered by the user and stored in **Tmp** into a Currency type value, and stores it in the **Cost** element of the **Item** variable.

Now, lines 79 through 86 get the value for the therms. Again, this loop refuses to allow the user to cancel the data entry operation at this point, and insists that the user enter a value for the therms. As soon as the user enters a numeric value, the loop stops executing, and VBA executes line 87, which converts the string entered by the user to an Integer type value, and stores it in the **Therms** element of the **Item** variable.

Finally, lines 89 through 96 get the value for the kilowatt-hours used, and line 97 converts the string entered by the user to an Integer type value, and stores it in the **Kwh** element of the **Item** variable.

Now that the function has obtained data for all of the elements in the **Item** variable from the user, the **With** statement ends in line 98 with the **End With** keywords.

Line 99 assigns the **Item** variable to the function's result, and the **Get_UtilityItem** function ends, returning its result.

If you tried to collect all of this data without using a user-defined type, you would have to declare and keep track of four separate variables. You would have either had to include all of the code for getting the various data values from the user in the **Enter_UtilityCosts** procedure—which would make that procedure very long and probably rather difficult to understand because it would then contain five nested loop structures—or write four separate functions for obtaining each different value. By putting all four of the data values together in a single user-defined type, you can use a single function to get and return all of the data at once, greatly simplifying the **Enter_UtilityCosts** procedure.

The **Get_UtilityItem** function is also slightly less complex than it might be otherwise because the code in that function concentrates on getting the data values only, and does not have to deal with storing the data or recognizing when it is necessary to end data entry altogether—it just has to make sure that it gets the correct values in the correct elements of the user-defined type.

DO	DON'T

DO use user-defined types to simplify obtaining, storing, and manipulating groups of related data.

DON'T forget to include the dot separator (.) in front of the element names of a variable that has a user-defined type.

DO remember that all of your user-defined type definitions must appear at the module level, in the definition area of the module.

DO remember that variables and constants declared at the module level have module-level scope and are available to all of the procedures or functions in that module.

DON'T forget that Excel may not store date values from your VBA variables correctly, unless your variable has the explicit Date type.

Summary

Today, you learned how to use VBA's data type information functions to get more information about the type of data stored in Variant variables. In particular, you learned how to interpret the results of the TypeName and VarType functions, and the differences between these functions. You also learned about VBA's special Empty and Null values, their differences, and their uses. In particular, you learned that VBA automatically assigns the Empty value to a Variant type variable to indicate that the variable has not yet been assigned a value.

Next, you learned how to combine VBA's type information functions, decision-making statements, and looping structures to help avoid runtime errors by ensuring that the data values your functions and procedures use internally have the correct or expected values, and by ensuring that data values your functions and procedures obtain from a user or some other source also have the correct or expected values.

This chapter also showed you why and how to declare variables that retain their values between calls to a function or procedure by declaring them with the Static keyword.

Finally, this chapter taught you why and how to define your own customized data types. You learned how to create a user-defined type definition, how to declare variables that have a user-defined type, and how to access individual elements in a variable that has a user-defined type. You also saw an example of how to put user-defined data types to work for you.

Q&A

Q **Why is it so important to check internal data values? I'm writing the code, so I know what values will be passed when I call a function.**

A The main reason you should check internal data values is to guard against human error. No one can really remember everything about the functions or procedures that they write—especially if you want to use a function that you wrote several days, weeks, or months ago. Adding the internal value checking code can save you a great deal of frustration later on, especially if you make sure that your procedure or function makes an explicit complaint about what is wrong with its data values.

Frequently, your own error messages will be more clear than the runtime errors that VBA displays. Also, if VBA displays a runtime error that results from an incompatible value passed as an optional function argument, the point at which VBA detects the error may be far away in your code from the actual source of the error.

Finally, it is much better to have your procedures shut down in an orderly fashion when your own code detects some potential error, than to have to clean up a mess that might remain when a procedure fails unexpectedly with a runtime error.

Q **Why is it necessary to spend so much programming effort screening the values that a user enters in an input dialog box?**

A The amount of effort you spend adding program instructions to validate a user's data input depends greatly on who you expect to be the primary user of the procedures and functions that you write. If you want to distribute your procedures or functions to other users, you should really spend the extra effort making sure that your procedures and functions validate the data that the user enters. You'll only frustrate or confuse users if your procedures simply repeat input dialog boxes without any statement as to why, or if your procedures crash with runtime errors.

Even if you are the only person who uses your procedures, you should at least include some rudimentary data validation to guard yourself against having to clean up after a procedure that fails part way through its task with a runtime error.

Q **Why can't I store a user-defined type variable directly into a worksheet cell or into another variable?**

A You can only assign the contents of a variable with a user-defined type to another variable if they both have the same user-defined type. You can't assign a user-defined type variable directly to a worksheet cell or other variable because your user-defined type is an aggregate of several different data values. Your user-defined type makes it more convenient for you to store and pass several data items, but you must refer to specific elements of the variable in order to store those elements in a worksheet cell or a another variable.

Workshop

Answers are in Appendix A.

Quiz

1. What is the purpose of the VBA information functions that begin with the word Is?

2. What are the three VBA data type information functions that you are most likely to use on a regular basis?

3. Which of the VBA data type information functions give you the most specific information about the variable you are checking?

4. If you wanted to find out the specific type of an object reference, which data type information function should you use?

5. What does the IsMissing function tell you?

6. When the TypeName function returns the strings "Nothing" or "Unknown", what does that mean?

7. What does the `Empty` value signify? Does VBA ever assign this value to a variable?

8. What does the `Null` value signify? Does VBA ever assign this value to a variable?

9. What is *defensive programming*?

10. What is the purpose and effect of the `Static` keyword?

11. How do you use the `Static` keyword?

12. What is a user-defined type?

13. What VBA keyword starts a user-defined type definition?

14. Where do you place a user-defined type definition?

Exercises

1. Declare a user-defined data type that will hold all of the information necessary for a mailing list. Your user-defined type should include elements for the following information: first name, last name, company name, street address, city, state, and ZIP code.

2. Write both a function that gets data for the mailing list user-defined type you created in Exercise 1, preceding, and a procedure that calls that function and stores the data in a worksheet. Your function's result should be a user-defined type. (HINT: Copy the portions of the **Enter_UtilityCosts** procedure in Listing 10.8 that select a worksheet and store the data in the worksheet.)

3. Write a function named **IsMasterCard**, that returns `True` if the string in the argument represents a valid MasterCard credit card number, or `False` if the number is not a valid MasterCard number. Your function should have a single required string argument.

   A valid MasterCard credit card number always begins with the digit 5 and consists of four groups of four digits, with each digit group separated by a hyphen: 5234-5678-9012-3456. For this exercise, assume that the separating dashes are a required part of the credit card number. (HINT: Use the following logical expression with the `Like` operator (described on Day 4) to determine whether the function's argument is or is not a valid MasterCard credit card number: `StrVal Like 5###-####-####-####` where `StrVal` is the string that contains the MasterCard number. This expression is `True` if `StrVal` matches the pattern specified after the `Like` operator.)

4. Write a procedure that gets a MasterCard number from the user. Your procedure should loop indefinitely until the user enters a valid MasterCard number. Use the **IsMasterCard** function you wrote in Exercise 3, preceding, to validate the user's input. Make sure that your procedure allows the user to cancel the entry operation, and confirms the cancellation. Also, make sure that your procedure displays a message to the user stating *why* the loop is repeating.

11

Modular
Programming
Techniques

Today's lesson teaches you how to organize your procedures and functions when they are stored in several different modules. This chapter also teaches you how to get started writing programs that consist of several different procedures working together to complete a complex job. In today's lesson, you learn:

☐ How to use modules to organize commonly-used procedures and functions into libraries of procedures so those procedures or functions are available all the time.

☐ How to use the Public and Private keywords to increase or limit the availability of variables, constants, functions, and procedures in your modules.

☐ How to get started designing and creating large-scale programs using several different procedures, functions, and modules working together to complete a single task.

☐ How to use argument lists so that your procedures can receive information from, and return information to, the procedures that call them.

Using Modules More Effectively

You already know that you store your procedure and function source code in a module. In the first and second lessons in this book, you learned how the Macro Recorder chooses which module to store a recorded macro in, and you learned how to add new module sheets to your workbooks. This section teaches you how to use modules to organize your commonly used procedures and functions, and how to make them available for use in every Excel work session.

You can use modules to organize your recorded macros and procedures, and to make it easier to keep track of many different macros. Many users organize macros that carry out similar tasks, or have similar purposes, into various categories, and then store each category of macro in its own module, and sometimes in its own workbook.

For instance, you might decide that you want some or all of your worksheets to have a standardized look, and therefore choose certain fonts, font styles, and point sizes as standards for worksheet titles, column headings, row headings, subtotals, and so on. You might then end up recording or writing several different macros or procedures—like the **FormatArialBold12** macro you recorded in Day 1—that apply the specific font styles or other formatting for the various standards you decide upon.

For procedures that you use frequently, and want to have available in all (or most) of your workbooks, you probably don't want to copy all the module sheets into each and every workbook that uses those procedures. Apart from simply being a lot of work, duplicating frequently used procedures and macros in every workbook that uses them can cause a lot of confusion, and unnecessarily increases the size of your workbooks—both in terms of the amount of disk storage that they require, and in terms of the amount of memory that they require.

Also, if you decide to change a frequently used macro procedure that you have duplicated in several different workbooks, you must edit and test each and every copy of the procedure, or at least copy the altered macro procedure into all of the workbooks that use it. Going through such complex copying and editing tasks only increases the probability that something will go wrong, and that your results will be less than satisfactory.

You may think, at first, that creating an Excel template workbook, and storing your macro procedures in the template will resolve this problem, but it doesn't. When you create a new workbook based on an Excel template, Excel *copies* any module sheets in the template to the new workbook file, leading to the same problems with duplicate macro procedures just described.

Instead, the best way to make commonly-used macro procedures and functions available is to create a *library* of procedures and functions. A library of VBA procedures and functions works much like a public library filled with books and magazines—any time you (or one of your procedures) needs to use a particular function or procedure stored in the library, VBA looks up the necessary code in the library, and then executes it.

When describing the Personal macro workbook (stored in the PERSONAL.XLS workbook), Day 1 mentioned that you can run any macro or procedure as long as the workbook in which you stored it is open. The same situation is true for any sub functions or user-defined functions that you write. You can see this for yourself, by looking at the lists of procedures and functions in the Macro dialog box and the Object Browser—notice that the lists in these two dialog boxes always show all the functions and procedures in the currently open workbooks. (The Macro dialog box lists procedures only, the Object Browser lists both functions and procedures.)

Figure 11.1 is a diagram showing how all of the procedures or functions in the module sheets of all open workbooks are available to all other open workbooks.

Figure 11.1.
All macros, functions, and procedures in any open workbook are available to all other open workbooks.

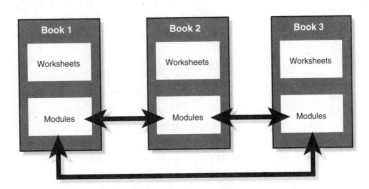

When VBA executes a procedure or function, it first searches the current module for the requested macro procedure or function. If VBA does not find the procedure or function in the current module, it then searches the other modules in the current workbook (if any). If VBA still cannot find the requested procedure or function, it then searches the modules in all open workbooks. Finally, if VBA cannot locate the requested procedure or function in any of the open workbooks, it then searches through any referenced workbooks to find the procedure or function. (Creating and using references to workbooks is described later in this section.)

This behind-the-scenes look-up process that VBA performs is the key to how libraries of procedures and functions work. In order to make a commonly used function or procedure universally available to any workbook, all you have to do is make sure that the procedure or function is stored in a workbook that will be among the workbooks that VBA searches—either an open workbook, or a workbook for which you have established a reference.

DO	**DON'T**

DON'T duplicate procedures and functions in multiple workbooks. Instead, create a library workbook that holds one copy that can be used by all other workbooks.

DO use the Object Browser to see a list of functions in a particular workbook. Remember that the Macro dialog box lists only procedures.

Creating Procedure and Function Libraries

To create a general- or special-purpose library of functions and procedures, simply create a workbook that contains only VBA modules. Although it doesn't really matter if the workbook contains worksheets as well as module sheets, there is no point in including worksheets or charts in a VBA library workbook—because they aren't used, they just use up disk space and computer memory unnecessarily. The PERSONAL.XLS workbook described in the first lesson is one example of a library workbook.

As an example of creating a library of procedures and functions, assume that you have recorded or written several different macros to help you create and format Excel charts. To create a library of chart-making and formatting functions and macro procedures, you might create an Excel workbook named CHARTMAC.XLS and then move all your chart-related macro procedures and functions into that workbook's modules. That simply, you have created a library of chart-making and formatting procedures and functions. The only remaining thing for you to do is to make your library of procedures available during your Excel work sessions.

To make the procedures and functions in any library workbook available, all you have to do is open the library workbook, or create a reference to that workbook. If you want, you can even have Excel open your library workbooks for you. The next section of this chapter describes both techniques of making libraries of procedures available.

Although it isn't required by VBA, most users further group related procedures together within a library workbook. For example, in the CHARTMAC.XLS library workbook, if you have several macros that help you create and format pie charts, you might group all of them together in a single module sheet named *Pie Charts*. Similarly, if you also have several macros that help you create and format bar charts, you might group all those macros together in another module sheet named *Bar Charts*, also in the CHARTMAC.XLS workbook.

By grouping all your chart-related macros and functions together in a single workbook, and further dividing them into specific categories within the library workbook, you not only make it possible to have your library of procedures and functions available at all times, but you also make it easier to find a particular procedure or function if you ever need to modify it, and you also make it easier to share your library workbook—or selected portions of it—with other users.

DO	DON'T

DO gather general-purpose functions (such as the `FlipCase`, `PCase`, and `SLen` functions given as examples in earlier chapters) together into a single library workbook so that you can use them in all your procedures.

DO consider using the PERSONAL.XLS workbook to store all your general-purpose procedures and functions.

Making Library Procedures and Functions Available

You can make any of the functions and procedures in one of your library workbooks available by opening that workbook with the **File | O**pen command. In the case of the chart-making macro library example in the previous section, opening the workbook manually in order to use the procedures or functions in the library may not be a problem, if you don't use the functions or procedures in that library on a daily basis.

With more general-purpose libraries, or any library whose functions and procedures you might want to have universally available to any workbook in any Excel work session, explicitly opening the library workbook with the **File | O**pen command will probably be inconvenient.

In fact, one of the main reasons to create a library of your commonly-used VBA procedures and functions is to make those functions available all the time, without having to perform any specific action to make them available. VBA and Excel provide you with two different ways to ensure that the procedures and functions in your library files are always, and automatically, available: you can put the library workbook in Excel's startup folder, or you can create a reference

to the library workbook. The next few paragraphs describe each technique for making your library procedures available in detail.

> **Tip:** You can use either of the techniques described in this section to make procedures and functions in any workbook available, even if you haven't formally organized those procedures into a library workbook.

Placing the Library Workbook in the Startup Folder

The easiest way to make your library workbooks available in every Excel work session is to put your library workbooks in Excel's startup folder, or in Excel's alternate startup folder. Whenever you start Excel, it opens any workbooks that are in the startup or alternate startup directories. As mentioned before, once your library workbook is open, all the functions and procedures stored in it become available to other open workbooks.

Figure 11.2 is a diagram showing how the macros, functions, and procedures in an open library workbook are available to other open workbooks.

Figure 11.2.
All the macros, functions, and procedures in an open library workbook are available to any other open workbooks.

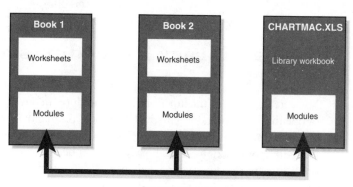

Either use Windows 95 to move or copy your library workbook to the startup or alternate startup folder, or use Excel's File | Save As command to save a copy of the library workbook file in the startup or alternate startup folder.

 Tip: You can also make Excel automatically load a workbook on startup by placing a Windows 95 shortcut in the Excel startup folder.

Excel's startup folder is named XLStart and is usually a subfolder in your Excel main disk folder. The names and location of Excel's main and startup folders are established at the time you install Excel, and cannot be changed. If you installed Excel on your computer using the default folder names and locations, then Excel is installed in a folder named \MSOffice\Excel, and the complete folder path for the startup folder is \MSOffice\Excel\XLStart. If you, or the person who installed Excel, performed a custom installation, then the startup folder name and location may be different.

If you're not sure what folder is Excel's startup folder, you can use the StartupPath property of the Application object to display the full path of Excel's startup folder. Enter the following procedure listing and then execute it; the resulting message dialog box displays the full folder path, including the drive letter, for Excel's startup folder:

 Listing 11.1. Using Visual Basic for Applications to display the Excel startup directory path.

```
1:    Sub ShowStartupPath()
2:        MsgBox Application.StartupPath
3:    End Sub
```

 Line 2 of the listing uses the MsgBox procedure to display the StartupPath property of the Application object. If you used the suggested defaults when you installed Excel with Microsoft Office 95, then this procedure displays the dialog box shown in Figure 11.3.

Figure 11.3.

The StartupPath property contains the full folder path to the Excel startup directory.

Excel's use of an alternate startup folder is optional. For Excel to use an alternate startup folder, you must use the **T**ools | **O**ptions command to enter the name and full folder path for the alternate startup folder. Unlike the startup folder, you can change the alternate startup folder at any time—although Excel looks only in the alternate startup folder when it first starts a new work session.

To set the alternate startup folder from the Excel menus, follow these steps:

1. Choose the **T**ools | **O**ptions command. Excel displays the Options dialog box.

2. Click the General tab, if necessary, to bring the General options to the front of the dialog box. Figure 11.4 shows the opened Options dialog box, with the General tab showing.

3. Enter the full folder path name, including the disk drive letter, in the Alternate Startup File **L**ocation text box. If you wish, you can use UNC (Universal Naming Convention) folder names to set the alternate startup file location to a folder accessible over the network.

4. Choose the OK command button. Excel closes the Options dialog box and changes the alternate startup directory.

   The next time you start Excel, it uses the directory path you just entered as the alternate startup directory.

Use the `AltStartupPath` property of the `Application` object to find out what the current alternate startup folder is, or to set a new alternate startup folder. Enter the following procedure listing and then execute it; the resulting message dialog box displays the full path, including the drive letter, for Excel's alternate startup directory.

Figure 11.4.

Use the General sheet in the Options dialog box to enter the name and directory path for Excel's alternate startup directory.

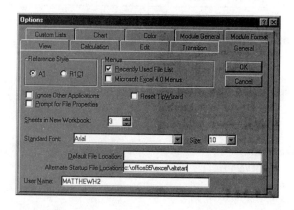

Listing 11.2. Using Visual Basic for Applications to display the Excel alternate startup directory.

```
1:    Sub ShowAlternateStartPath()
2:        MsgBox Application.AltStartupPath
3:    End Sub
```

Line 2 of the listing uses the MsgBox procedure to display the AltStartupPath property of the Application object. If you entered the alternate startup file location shown in Figure 11.4, then this procedure displays the dialog box shown in Figure 11.5.

Figure 11.5.

The AltStartupPath
*property contains the Excel
alternate startup directory.*

If the AltStartupPath property returns an empty string, then Excel is not currently using the alternate startup folder option. Although the StartupPath property is a read-only property (you can retrieve its value, but you can't change it), the AltStartupPath property is a read-write property (you can both retrieve or change its value).

To change Excel's alternate startup folder from within a VBA procedure, simply assign a string containing the new alternate startup folder name to the AltStartupPath property. Be sure to include the drive letter and full path, just as if you were entering the alternate startup folder in the Options dialog box. Listing 11.3 shows how to change the alternate startup folder with a VBA statement. (As when you change the alternate startup folder with the Options dialog box, Excel won't actually use the new alternate startup folder name until you restart Excel.)

Listing 11.3. Changing the Excel alternate startup folder with Visual Basic for Applications.

```
1:    Sub ChangeAlternateStartPath()
2:        Application.AltStartupPath = "C:\EXCEL\ALTSTART"
3:    End Sub
```

In Listing 11.3, substitute any string variable or constant containing the name and path of the alternate startup folder that you want for the quoted string in line 2.

DO   DON'T

DO use the **W**indow | **H**ide command to hide your library workbooks to reduce clutter in your work environment, and to help avoid making inadvertent changes in your library workbook. Excel will still open the hidden workbook in the startup or alternate startup folder. (Refer to your Excel documentation for more information on hiding and unhiding workbook files.)

> **DO** use the **Tools** | **Protection** | Protect **Workbook** command to protect your library workbook against inadvertent changes. If you plan to distribute your library workbook to other users, you may also want to use the password option of this command to prevent others from making changes in your library workbook. (Refer to your Excel documentation for more information on protecting workbooks.)
>
> **DO** remember that Excel opens all workbooks in *both* the startup folder and the alternate startup folder.

The only drawback involved in using a library workbook stored in the startup or alternate setup folder is that, because the library workbook is always open, it therefore always consumes a certain amount of computer memory. Also, the amount of time that Excel requires to start up and load itself into memory increases proportionally for each workbook file in the startup and alternate startup folders that Excel must open. You can avoid these two difficulties by creating a workbook reference (described in the next section) to make your library workbooks available instead of placing the library workbook in one of Excel's startup folders.

Using Excel References to Access Library Procedures and Functions

Usually, you can't use procedures or functions in a workbook that is closed—that is, you can only use procedures and functions in workbooks that are currently open. The one exception to this rule occurs when you establish a *reference* from one workbook to another.

When you execute a macro procedure or call a sub function stored in a referenced workbook, and the referenced workbook is not currently open, then Excel reads the closed workbook's disk file until it finds the VBA code for the requested macro procedure or function and then executes that code. The referenced workbook remains closed.

Figure 11.6 is a diagram showing how Excel makes macro procedures and functions in a referenced workbook available. Each individual workbook must have its own separate reference to the library workbook in order to access it.

Figure 11.6.

By creating a reference, Excel can access Visual Basic for Applications functions and procedures in a closed workbook.

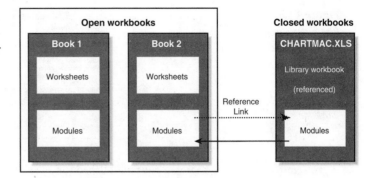

To create a reference to a library workbook (or any workbook), follow these steps:

1. Open the workbook in which you want to create the new reference to your library workbook, and display any module sheet.

2. Choose the **T**ools | **R**eferences command. Excel displays the References dialog box shown in Figure 11.7. (The **T**ools | **R**eferences command only appears on the **T**ools menu if the current sheet is a module sheet.)

   The **A**vailable References list in the References dialog box includes all open workbooks and any closed workbooks that are referenced by an open workbook.

3. Select the check box to the left of the workbook in the **A**vailable References list to create a reference to that workbook.

4. If the workbook that you want to reference is not listed in the **A**vailable References list, choose the **B**rowse command button. Excel displays the Browse dialog box, which looks and works just like a standard File Open dialog box.

   Select the workbook file that you want to reference in the Browse dialog box, and choose OK; Excel closes the Browse dialog box, and displays the selected workbook in the **A**vailable References list, with its check box selected.

5. After you have selected all the references you want for the current workbook, choose OK to close the References dialog box. Excel stores the new reference information in the current workbook.

   Now, whenever the workbook you set references for calls a macro procedure or function in the referenced workbook, Excel reads the necessary VBA code from the referenced workbook—whether it is open or closed—and executes that code.

Modular Programming Techniques

Figure 11.7.

Use Excel's References dialog box to establish references from one workbook to another, and to make VBA code in the referenced workbook available.

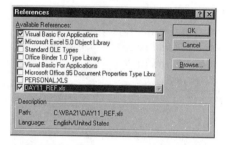

To remove a reference that you have established for a particular workbook, perform the same steps just given for creating a reference, but clear the check box for the reference that you want to remove, instead of selecting it.

Caution: Don't clear the check boxes for the Visual Basic For Applications reference or the Excel 7 Object Library reference, or your workbook will be unable to access those resources—such as Excel's `Workbook`, `Worksheet`, and `Application` objects, and VBA's built-in functions like `CInt`, `Len`, `MsgBox`, and so on.

Once you've established a reference, then whenever you call a procedure from the referenced workbook, Excel reads the referenced function or procedure from the referenced workbook. Excel only reads the VBA code from the referenced workbook; if the referenced workbook is closed, it remains closed.

Note: For any open workbook that contains references, the Object Browser—but *not* the Macro dialog box—lists the procedures and functions available in the referenced workbook. You can use the Object Browser to look up the functions or procedures in the referenced workbook, to paste the function or procedure name and its arguments into the current module, or to show the source code for the procedures and functions in the referenced workbook, just as you would for any other workbook's procedures or functions.

Using a reference to provide access to your library workbooks does have a couple of drawbacks. First, you must create each reference individually for each workbook. If you have five workbooks, and you want all of them to reference the same library workbook, then you must go through the process of creating a reference five times—once for each workbook that references the library. Also, because Excel must read the requested procedure or function code

from the closed workbook file, the execution of your procedures may be delayed by the amount of time required to access the disk drive.

> **Tip:** You can create a reference to a library workbook in an Excel template. Every workbook you create based on that template will then include the reference to the library workbook. (Refer to your Excel documentation for more information on creating Excel templates.)

Advanced Scope Rules for Cross-Module Programming

Now that you're learning how to share the code in your modules with other workbooks by creating libraries of VBA code, you are ready to learn how VBA applies its scope rules across modules. (Writing programs that have their source code distributed through more than one module is often referred to as *cross-module* programming, because the program crosses through several modules.) This knowledge of VBA's scope rules for multiple modules will also help you use and understand the large-scale programming techniques described in the next section of this chapter.

With programs that use procedures in more than one module, the scope rules are only slightly more complex than the scope rules you learned in Day 3. Also, VBA provides you with a couple of different ways to increase or limit the scope of your constants, variables, procedures, functions, and user-defined types among various different modules.

Understanding Private and Public Scope

All the scope rules you learned in Day 3 for single modules still apply in situations involving multiple modules. Local variables and constants—that is, variables and constants declared at the procedure level—are available only within the procedure or function in which you declare them. Variables and constants that you declare at the module level are available to all procedures or functions within that same module.

Although variables and constants that you declare at the module level are available to any procedure and function in that module, they are *not* available to procedures and functions in a *different* module. The scope of module-level variables and constants is limited to the module in which you declare those variables or constants.

In VBA, items such as variables and constants whose scope is limited to a single module have *private* scope, because their use is private within the particular module that contains their

declaration statements. All variables or constants that you declare at the module level (by using a `Dim` statement) have private scope, limited to the module in which they are declared.

As you learned in the preceding section about creating libraries of commonly-used procedures and functions, any procedure or function in any module in an open workbook (or a workbook for which you have created a reference) is available to any other workbook. Similarly, user-defined types in any module of any open or referenced workbook are also available to any other workbook.

In VBA, items that are available to all modules of all workbooks have *public* scope—because they are publicly available to all modules in all workbooks. All procedures, functions, or user-defined type definitions in a module have public scope and are available to all modules in all workbooks.

Incidentally, items with public scope are sometimes referred to as *global* variables, because they are available globally, that is, throughout the entire "world" of your program. You may also hear programmers with experience in programming languages other than Visual Basic for Applications refer to variables and constants with module-level scope as global variables because they are globally available within their particular module. To avoid any confusion, VBA (and this book), uses the term *private* to refer to items with a module-level scope, and *public* to refer to items that have a scope extending across several modules.

The following list summarizes VBA's three different scope levels:

- ☐ *Local Scope:* Variables and constants declared within a procedure or function. Items with local scope are available only within the particular procedure or function in which you declare them.

- ☐ *Private Scope:* Variables and constants declared at the module-level. Items with private scope are available to any procedure or function in the *same* module in which you declare the variables or constants, but are not available outside that module.

- ☐ *Public Scope:* Procedures, functions, and user-defined types. Items with public scope are available throughout the module in which you declare them, and to any other module in the same workbook, or to other workbooks—provided the workbook containing the module in which you declare the procedures, functions, or user-defined types is open or has a reference created for it.

DO	**DON'T**

DO remember that when variables, constants, functions, or procedures have the same name but different scope, VBA uses the variable, constant, function, or procedure with the more local scope.

> **DO** remember that variables, constants, functions, or procedures at the same scope level cannot have the same name. For example, you cannot have a module-level variable that has the same name as a function, procedure, or user-defined type in the same module.
>
> **DO** try to use unique names for all your variables, constants, functions, procedures, and user-defined types to avoid confusion and ambiguities that lead to subtle defects in your programs.

Overriding Visual Basic for Application's Scope Rules

Sometimes, you may want to limit or increase the availability of a particular variable, constant, procedure, function, or user-defined type, or even the contents of an entire module. VBA provides you with two different keywords—`Public` and `Private`—and a module-level compiler directive that enable you to change the scope of various items.

Making Entire Modules Private to a Single Workbook

Occasionally, you may want to make sure that the procedures, functions, and user-defined types in a particular module are *not* available to any workbooks other than the workbook in which you declare those items.

As an example, assume you have two different workbooks. One workbook contains data about gross sales, and another workbook contains budget data for your department. In both workbooks, you might have a group of procedures that you use to create quarterly reports from the data in that workbook. Your procedures might have names such as **FirstQuarterReport**, **SecondQuarterReport**, and so on. If you have both the sales and budget workbooks open, and you want to generate a sales report for the first quarter of the year, you might execute the **FirstQuarterReport** procedure to generate the report for you. If, however, you inadvertently execute the **FirstQuarterReport** procedure for the budget workbook, instead of the sales workbook, then your procedure may fail, or you won't get the report you were expecting.

To avoid accidentally executing a procedure with the same name in the wrong workbook, you can make the entire contents of a module *private*, so that the procedures and functions in that module cannot be used from any workbook except the workbook that contains that particular module.

As another example, you might have written some procedures or functions that you intend to call only from other procedures or functions, and should not be executed by themselves. By making the module private, you can reduce the possibility that you might accidentally execute one of these procedures or functions. Making a module private is, essentially, the reverse of creating a library—instead of ensuring that the procedures and functions are universally available, you ensure that the procedure and functions in that module can be used only from that particular workbook.

To make a module private, use the Option Private Module statement in the module, with this syntax:

Syntax

Option Private Module

The Option Private Module statement restricts the availability of all procedures, functions, user-defined types, and any module-level variables or constants declared in that module. You must place the Option Private Module statement on a line by itself in the definition area of the module, before any variable, constant, procedure, function, or user-defined type definitions.

To help you understand the effects of the Option Private Module statement, Figure 11.8 shows Excel's Macro dialog box. Notice that several procedures, named **Proc1**, **Proc2**, **Proc3**, and **Proc4** appear in the **M**acro Name/Reference list, all contained in the DAY11A.XLS workbook. Because the **M**acro Name/Reference list includes the workbook name in front of the procedure name, you can tell that the DAY11A.XLS workbook containing these procedures is not the current workbook. The DAY11A.XLS workbook module sheet that contains these procedure declarations does *not* include the Option Private Module statement, so the procedures are available to any other workbooks.

Figure 11.8.

Normally, all the procedures and functions in a module in an open workbook are available to any other workbook.

Now, look at Figure 11.9, which also shows Excel's Macro dialog box. The Option Private Module statement was added to the DAY11A.XLS workbook module sheet that contains the declarations for **Proc1**, **Proc2**, **Proc3**, and **Proc4**. Because the module containing these procedures is now private to the DAY11A.XLS workbook, they no longer appear in the **M**acro Name/Reference list of the Macro dialog box.

Figure 11.9.

Adding the `Option Private`
`Module` *statement to a
module restricts the availability of procedures and
functions in that module to
the workbook that contains
that particular module.*

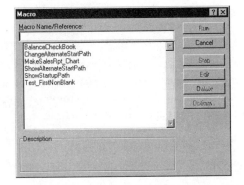

Note: Using the `Option Private Module` statement in a module only restricts the availability of procedures and functions to the single workbook that contains the module in which you declare those functions and procedures. Because procedures and functions, by default, have public scope, they are still available to other modules in the same workbook.

Using the *Private* Keyword to Limit Scope to a Single Module

The `Private` keyword restricts the scope level of a particular variable, constant, function, procedure, or user-defined type. Use the `Private` keyword if you have individual procedures, functions, or user-defined types in a module that you don't want available to other modules.

The `Private` keyword makes a VBA program item have private scope, overriding whatever scope level VBA would normally assign to that item. Use the `Private` keyword to reduce the scope level of items—such as procedures and functions—that otherwise would have a public scope level.

For instance, you might have a function that gets some data value from a user—like the data-entry functions in the previous lesson. If the data-entry function is specific to a particular workbook or task—like the **Get_UtilityItem** function in Listing 10.8—then you may not want this function to be publicly available. By adding the `Private` keyword to the function's declaration, you can change its scope so that it is only available within the module in which you declare it. The next few paragraphs show you the general syntax for using the `Private` keyword in variable, constant, procedure, function, and user-defined type declarations.

Syntax

To declare a private variable, use the following general syntax:

```
Private VarName [As TypeName]
```

VarName represents any valid VBA variable name. *TypeName* represents any valid VBA data type name or any user-defined data type name. Notice that this is exactly the same syntax you would use in a Dim statement, it just substitutes the Private keyword for Dim. You can only make Private variable declarations at the module level.

To declare a private constant, use this general syntax:

```
Private Const ConstName [As TypeName] = expression
```

ConstName represents any valid VBA constant name, *TypeName* represents any valid VBA data type name or any user-defined data type name, and *expression* represents any VBA expression. This is exactly the same syntax you use in a plain Const declaration statement. You can only make Private constant declarations at the module level.

To make a function or procedure private to the module in which you declare it, just add the Private keyword to the function or procedure declaration line, as shown in the following:

```
Private Function name([arglist]) [As TypeName]
Private Sub name([arglist])
```

name represents any valid VBA function name, *TypeName* represents any valid VBA data type name or any user-defined data type name, and *arglist* represents the function's or procedure's argument list. Notice that, except for the addition of the Private keyword, this is exactly the same syntax you would use for any function or procedure declaration. (A later section in this chapter describes procedures that use arguments.)

You can also restrict the availability of a user-defined type to a single module by adding the Private keyword to the first line of the type definition:

```
Private Type VarName
```

VarName represents any valid VBA identifier that you choose as the name for your user-defined type.

DO	DON'T

DO remember that you can only use the Private keyword at the module level, you cannot use it to change the scope of local variables or constants.

Using the *Public* Keyword to Increase Scope to All Modules

The `Public` keyword increases the scope level of a particular variable, constant, function, procedure, or user-defined type, making it available to all modules in all workbooks. Use the `Public` keyword if you have individual variables or constants that you want to make available to other modules in the same or other workbook.

The `Public` keyword makes a VBA program item have public scope, overriding whatever scope level VBA would normally assign to that item. Use the `Public` keyword to raise the scope level of items—such as variables and constants—that otherwise would have a private scope level.

For instance, you may recall that the section "Using String Characters You Cannot Type at the Keyboard" in Day 5 suggested using constants to supply commonly-used character codes for use with the `Chr` function. That section gave examples such as the **CR** constant for a carriage-return character (code 13), or the **CRightSym** constant for the copyright symbol (code 169), and suggested that you declare such constants at the module level, so that they would be available to all the procedures and functions in that module.

Constants like this, however, are useful in *all* your modules. In fact, constant declarations like **CR** and **CRightSym** are the kind of constant declarations that you would like to put in a library workbook, and make universally available to all of your VBA procedures and functions. Constants declared at the module-level, however, have a private scope—they are available throughout the module in which you declare them but are not available in other modules. By adding the `Public` keyword to the constant's declaration, you can change its scope so that it *is* available outside the module in which you declare it. The next few paragraphs show you the general syntax for using the `Public` keyword in variable, constant, procedure, function, and user-defined type declarations.

11

Syntax

To declare a public variable, use the following general syntax:

```
Public VarName [As TypeName]
```

VarName represents any valid identifier, and *TypeName* represents any valid data type name. This is the same syntax you use in a `Dim` statement, but uses the `Public` keyword instead of `Dim`. You can only make `Public` variable declarations at the module level.

To declare a public constant, use this general syntax:

```
Public Const ConstName [As TypeName] = expression
```

ConstName represents any valid identifier, *TypeName* represents any valid data type name, and *expression* represents any expression. This is the same syntax you use in a plain `Const` declaration statement, with only the `Public` keyword added. You can only make `Public` constant declarations at the module level.

To declare a public function or procedure, just add the `Public` keyword to the function or procedure declaration line:

```
Public Function name([arglist]) [As TypeName]
Public Sub name([arglist])
```

name represents any valid identifier, *TypeName* represents any valid data type, and *arglist* represents the function's or procedure's argument list. Except for the addition of the `Public` keyword, this is exactly the same syntax you would use for any function or procedure declaration.

Similarly, you can also add the `Public` keyword to a user-defined type definition (*VarName* represents any valid identifier):

```
Public Type VarName
```

DO	DON'T

DO use the `Public` keyword at the module level only; you cannot use it to change the scope of local variables or constants.

DON'T forget that, even if you add the `Option Private Module` statement to a module, the public scope items in that module remain available to other modules in the same workbook, but not outside that workbook.

If you add the `Option Private Module` statement to a module, so that the entire module is private to its workbook, you can still make module-level variables and constants in the private module available to other modules in the same workbook. To make variables and constants in a private module available to other modules in the same workbook, declare them with the `Public` keyword, as shown previously.

The `Option Private Module` statement restricts the availability of public scope items in that module to the workbook that contains the module. The `Public` keyword makes a variable or constant available outside of its module, so the combined effect is to make the variable or constant available to all the modules of that one workbook only.

Understanding and Avoiding Circular References

A *circular reference* occurs when an item—such as a constant—is defined by another item—such as another constant—which is defined by the first item. To better understand the concept of a circular reference, consider the following two English sentences:

> *Fast* means *quick.*
> *Quick* means *fast.*

In the first sentence, the word *fast* is defined as meaning *quick*; in the second sentence, *quick* is defined as meaning *fast*. No real definition of either word is given—the two definitions simply refer to each other, without supplying any additional information. This is a circular reference, also referred to as a *circular dependency.*

In VBA, you end up with circular references if your module contains constant declarations like the following:

```
Const A = B
Const B = A
```

In a single module, you probably won't make a mistake like this—the two statements are obviously wrong. If you do create a circular reference like this in a single module, VBA can tell that no real value is specified for the constant, and displays an error message stating that an expression is required for the first constant declaration.

When you declare `Public` constants, however, the likelihood increases that you will accidentally create a circular reference between two public constants in two different modules. If one module contains this declaration:

```
Public Const A = B
```

And another module contains this constant declaration:

```
Public Const B = A
```

VBA then displays a runtime error message stating that there are circular dependencies between modules.

DO	DON'T

DON'T create circular references. To avoid circular references, you just have to be careful with your constant declarations.

DO put all your public constant declarations in a single module; by gathering your public constants into a single module, you make it easier to check all of the constant definitions at once.

Understanding and Using Module Qualifiers

Occasionally, you may want to access a private variable, constant, procedure, or function in some other module, but you don't want to make the item public, or there is some reason you cannot make the item public. You can still access private variables, constants, procedures and functions in a module by specifying the particular module that contains the item you want access to. You specify the module by adding the module's name—called a *module qualifier*—to the name of the variable, constant, procedure, or function you want to use in that module.

Another reason to use a module qualifier is to avoid any ambiguity whenever you must refer to public variables, constants, procedures, or functions whose name duplicates the name of some other item that has public scope in a different module. As you know, identifiers must be unique within their scope level, so VBA prevents you from creating variables, constants, functions, procedures, or user-defined types whose names duplicate each other in the *same* module. When you work with several modules at once, however, it is possible that public identifiers in one module may duplicate a public identifier in another module. Specifying the precise module that contains the item you want with a module qualifier resolves any ambiguity in this situation.

> **Note:** To use module qualifiers, you must have established a reference (as described earlier in this chapter) to the workbook whose procedures you are using, if they are not in the same workbook as the calling procedure.

Syntax

The general syntax for adding a module qualifier is:

```
ModuleName.Identifier
```

`ModuleName` represents the name of the module as it appears in the tab at the bottom of the module sheet. Notice the dot separator (.) after the module name. Like object references, and references to elements in a user-defined type, the dot separator joins the two identifiers together into a single reference. `Identifier` is any VBA variable, constant, procedure, or function declared in the module indicated by `ModuleName`.

If the module name contains spaces, or otherwise violates VBA's identifier naming rules, then enclose the module name in square brackets, as shown following (in this case, the square brackets are actually part of the syntax—you *must* include them):

```
[Module Name].Identifier
```

In the preceding syntax sample, notice that the dot separator (.) still appears between the module qualifier and the identifier.

You may also need to include the workbook (sometimes referred to as the *project*) name as part of the module qualifier, particularly if you have two different workbooks that have modules whose names duplicate each other. To include the workbook name in the module qualifier, you add the workbook name to the module name, and use the syntax form that includes the square brackets:

```
[BOOK.XLS].[ModuleName].Identifier
```

In this syntax form, `BOOK.XLS` represents any Excel workbook name. Notice that the workbook name is also joined to the module name with a dot separator.

Going back to the CHARTMAC.XLS library workbook example described earlier in this chapter, if CHARTMAC.XLS contains module sheets named *PieCharts* (with no spaces) and *Bar Charts* (with a space between words), and each of these module sheets contains a procedure named **MkSalesChart**, then you could use the following module qualifiers to refer to the specific procedure in each module:

```
PieCharts.MkSalesChart
[Bar Charts].MkSalesChart
[CHARTMAC.XLS].[PieCharts].MkSalesChart
[CHARTMAC.XLS].[Bar Charts].MkSalesChart
```

The first line refers to the **MkSalesChart** procedure in the *PieCharts* module; the second line refers to the **MkSalesChart** procedure in the *Bar Charts* module. Because the name of the *Bar Charts* module contains a space, it must be enclosed in square brackets, otherwise VBA displays a runtime error message. The third and fourth lines refer to the same procedures in the same modules as the first and second lines, but also include the workbook's name.

DO	DON'T
DO consider choosing module names that follow VBA's identifier naming rules in order to make it easier to use module qualifiers. Use the underscore character (_) to represent a space, just as you would with a variable or constant name.	

Understanding Structured Programming Techniques

As you increasingly automate your work with VBA macros and procedures, you may realize at some point that, for some tasks, you're just executing several macro procedures, one right after the other. Usually, this is the point at which most people decide to organize the procedures related to a particular series of tasks into a single, cohesive program. This section is intended to help you design and create large-scale programs that consist of several procedures all working together—whether you sit down to write that program all at once, or you decide to reorganize and join together existing procedures.

Understanding Procedures That Call Other Procedures

In the examples in the last lesson, you may have noticed that some of the functions and procedures seemed rather long; you may even have found the longer function or procedure examples a little difficult to follow all at once. From these examples—which actually carry out pretty simple jobs—you can easily imagine how a single procedure to perform a complex task might quickly become overwhelmingly long and convoluted; so long, in fact, that creating, understanding, and maintaining such a procedure becomes almost impossible.

The solution to this problem is to divide the VBA code that performs a task into several different procedures that are called by another procedure. By dividing the task into smaller steps, and writing a separate procedure for each step, you make your procedures easier to write, debug, and update. To carry out all the steps to complete the task, you write another procedure that executes each of the smaller procedures in the correct order.

As an example, say you want to write a procedure that uses data in one of your workbooks to compute quarterly profit and loss statements, including a printed report, and creating some charts showing sales and costs for each quarter. You could write a single procedure that goes through all the steps needed to compute the various totals, create the charts, and print the reports. A single procedure to perform all the steps necessary for this job might be several hundred lines in length, contain many nested If...Then statements and looping structures, and will surely be so complex that its creation and maintenance may seem an absolute nightmare.

Writing several procedures that work together, however, makes this programming task manageable. By dividing the overall job into its component parts, and creating a procedure to carry out that single part of the overall job, you keep individual procedures at a level of complexity that remains comprehensible. This technique of dividing a large job into smaller jobs to make the overall task easier to program is often referred to as the *divide-and-conquer* approach to programming.

Applying the divide-and-conquer technique to the example of computing quarterly profit and loss statements, you might write several separate procedures: a single procedure that computes gross income, a procedure that computes gross expenses, a procedure that computes net income, another procedure that creates the printed report, and yet another procedure that creates the necessary charts.

Figure 11.10 shows how your separate procedures relate to various parts of the overall job. Notice that each part of the overall task has a corresponding procedure.

Figure 11.10.

You make large-scale programming tasks easier to manage by writing several smaller procedures to carry out individual parts of a task, instead of one large procedure for the whole task.

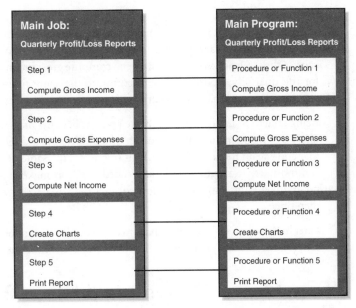

You may wonder what the benefit of writing several different procedures is, because you probably don't want to have to execute each procedure separately. To join all your separate procedures together into a single program (the Main Program box in Figure 11.10), you simply write a procedure that calls all of the other procedures or functions in the correct order.

You already know how to call a sub function from a procedure; calling procedures from another procedure is very much the same. If the procedures you write for steps 1 through 5 in Figure 11.10 are named **CompGrossIncome**, **CompGrossExpenses**, **CompNetIncome**, **CreateCharts**, and **PrintReport**, then the main procedure that executes all these procedures might look like this:

```
Sub QuarterlyReport()
    CompGrossIncome
    CompGrossExpenses
    CompNetIncome
    CreateCharts
    PrintReport
End Sub
```

As you can see, this procedure doesn't perform any work except to call, in the correct sequence, the procedures that carry out the necessary steps to complete the quarterly report. The **QuarterlyReport** procedure is short and simple—you can easily read this procedure and determine, in general, what tasks it performs. The specific details of each task are contained in the individual procedures called by the **QuarterlyReport** procedure.

Another benefit of dividing a large task into smaller pieces, and writing a separate procedure for each piece of the task is that you make it possible to re-use some of the VBA code that you write. For example, if you also generate annual profit and loss reports, you'll probably find that you can use the same procedures you wrote to compute gross income, gross expenses, and net income for the quarterly report when you compute the same figures for an annual report, just by changing the data that the procedures work with from quarterly to annual figures.

Being able to re-use code is one of the greatest benefits of a structured programming language like VBA. If you include all the code for a single task in a single procedure, then you must write that code again for any other task that might use the same or similar VBA code. By separating common activities into individual procedures, you make it possible to have several different programs use the same procedures, eliminating any necessity to program the same task more than once.

Later in this chapter, you'll learn how to use procedure arguments to exchange data values among different procedures, making your procedures even more flexible and powerful.

Top-Down Design and Step-Wise Refinement

One of the most accepted computer program design strategies is referred to as *top-down* design. When you design a program using a top-down approach, you start out by designing the most general part of the process you want to program—the "top"—and then proceed to more and more specific details of the process, working your way "down."

To apply top-down design techniques to your programs, follow this general process:

- ☐ Begin by outlining, in the most general terms, the tasks that your program will perform.

- ☐ Choose a procedure name for each step in your top-level general outline. If your top-level general outline has five steps in it, then you should choose five different procedure names.

- ☐ For each individual step from your top-level outline, create a more specific outline for all the tasks necessary to carry out that one step. After completing this second-level outline, choose procedure names to correspond to each step in this outline.

- ☐ For each individual step in your second-level outline, create a more specific outline of the tasks necessary to carry out that one step. Continue making successively more specific outlines for each sub-task, until you reach a level of simplicity where you can easily write the VBA code to carry out that task in a single, short procedure or function.

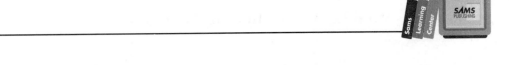

This process of successive outlining is also known as *step-wise refinement*, because you gradually refine each step into its component parts, successively reducing complex actions into their more easily understood component parts.

One of the benefits of top-down design and step-wise refinement is that it helps you focus your efforts for greatest effect. If you're stumped about exactly how to write the code for a particular sub-task, don't worry about it. Assign a procedure name to the task, pretend you have a friend who'll show up later and tell you how to write the code for that part, and continue with your outlining process.

Frequently, by the time you've completed outlining the other tasks in your program, it will become clear to you how to perform the task you were unsure of. Even it hasn't, you have still isolated your area of uncertainty down to a very few procedures, and you know where to concentrate your research or experimentation efforts. This is another way to apply the divide-and-conquer approach to computer programming.

Following this top-down design approach will also help you determine whether or not you really have all the data necessary to carry out a particular task, as well as helping you decide what kind of variables and constants you may need to declare, and what kinds of user-defined types you might need.

To use a top-down design approach for the quarterly profit and loss reporting example used in the preceding section, you might start out with the following English-language outline:

(A) Compute gross income
(B) Compute gross expenses
(C) Compute net income
(D) Create charts
(E) Print report, including charts

This outline describes the entire task you want your program to perform in very general terms. The main procedure of your program will correspond to this top-level outline and will consist of several statements that simply call the appropriate procedures in the correct order.

Now outline, in more detail, each separate task from the top-level outline. The second-level outline for step (A), computing the gross income, might look like the following:

(A.1) Total the sales figures for the Western region.
(A.2) Total the sales figures for the Eastern region.
(A.3) Total the sales figures for the Southern region.
(A.4) Add together the subtotals for the Western, Eastern, and Southern regions.

Looking at this second-level outline for the process of computing the gross sales, you can see that you'll need at least three different variables here, one for each regional sales subtotal. You can also see that the first three steps might require additional refinement, but that you can accomplish the fourth step with a simple arithmetic expression, once you have computed the various subtotals. Therefore, you will need to write procedures for the first three steps, but not for the fourth step, because it is simple enough that you can directly write the VBA statements for that step.

Now, working with step (A.1) from the second-level outline, you might produce this third-level outline:

(A.1.a) Select the worksheet that contains the sales figures for the Western region.

(A.1.b) Add together all of the numbers in column B of the worksheet (this column contains the figures for the weekly sales totals as submitted by the regional manager).

(A.1.c) Store the subtotal just computed in the variable for the Western regional sales total.

In this third-level outline, you can see that each of the three steps are simple enough that you can easily write the VBA code statements to carry out each step. In fact, each step in this outline corresponds to only one or two VBA statements. This particular level does not need any additional refinement—you have just outlined the steps for a single procedure.

When you make the third-level outline for step (A.2), you might end up with the following third-level outline:

(A.2.a) Select the worksheet that contains the sales figures for the Eastern region.

(A.2.b) Add together all of the numbers in column B of the worksheet (this column contains the figures for the weekly sales totals as submitted by the regional manager).

(A.2.c) Store the subtotal just computed in the variable for the Eastern regional sales total.

Notice that, except for the worksheet that contains the source data, and the variable that stores the regional subtotal, this outline is identical to the third-level outline for step (A.1). This situation tells you that you should use the same procedure to carry out both steps, and just tell the procedure which worksheet to select, and which variable to store the subtotal in. Because a function can return a result, you might even decide that it is more appropriate to write a function to carry out the task of computing a regional sales subtotal, and then create a function that takes the worksheet name for the source data as an argument, and returns the subtotal as its result.

This example only carries the outline process down three levels, and only fully outlines a couple of steps. There is no fixed rule about how many outline levels to create—just keep refining each outline to a lower and lower level until you reach the point where each step in your outline roughly corresponds to between one and four VBA statements.

DO	DON'T

DON'T forget the KISS principle—"Keep It Sweet and Simple"—when you write your procedures and functions.

DO write short procedures that perform a single, simple task. As a rule of thumb, you shouldn't let your procedures get much longer than 20 or 30 lines—about 1 or two screens full. If your procedure gets much longer than that, you're probably trying to make it do too much work.

DO avoid long procedures that perform many different tasks. The longer and more complex a single procedure gets, the more likely you are to make a programming mistake, or to have difficulty updating the procedure. Also, if you have very long procedures, it is likely that you are duplicating much more of your VBA code than necessary.

Using Modules to Organize Your Programming Projects

Usually, you should put all the code for a single program in a single workbook—with the exception of any general-purpose procedures or functions that you keep in a library workbook. Use different modules in your project workbook to help organize your program's code. (In Visual Basic for Applications, a *project* is a collection of modules, usually all in the same workbook.) Another reason for keeping all the VBA source code for a single program in a single project workbook is that, by starting out with all the code in a single workbook, you make it easier to convert your program to an add-in program, as described in Day 21.

With large projects, distribute the source code into several different modules, where each module contains the program source code to carry out specific tasks within the larger program. For example, it will be easier for you to develop and understand a VBA program that imports data into a worksheet, formats and charts the data, and then prints the chart and a report if you divide the program into several modules. One module, for example, might contain the procedures and functions that import the data, another module might contain the procedures and functions that format and chart the data, and so on.

Within a single module, you should organize your source code by following a few conventions. First, place all your Option statements at the very beginning of the module, before any other VBA statements. VBA's Option statements include Option Explicit, Option Compare, Option Private Module, and so on. Second, place all your user-defined type definitions after the Option statements, but before any variable, constant, procedure, or function declarations. Next, declare all your module-level or public variables and constants, and then declare all your functions and procedures.

The following code template, which does not contain any actual VBA code, shows how you should organize the code within individual modules:

```
'Beginning of module (also referred to as the "top" of the module)

'Option statements: Option Explicit, Option Compare, and so on

'User-defined type definitions

'Module-level variable and constant declarations

'Procedure and function declarations
```

Using Procedure Arguments to Communicate Data between Procedures

Just as you can create functions that receive data values passed in an argument list, you can also create procedures that receive data values passed as arguments. Essentially, creating argument lists for both procedures and functions is the same. The next few sections describe when and why you should create procedures with argument lists, and how to specify and use an argument list for a procedure.

Understanding When and Why You Should Use Argument Lists with Your Procedures

There are two main reasons to use an argument list in your procedures:

☐ An argument list is a convenient, efficient, and trouble-free way to pass information to a procedure that needs the information to complete its task. By using arguments to supply values to a procedure, you can make your procedures more flexible and more powerful.

☐ An argument list is also a convenient, efficient, and trouble-free way to *return* data from a procedure. To return data from a procedure, use an argument passed by reference—just like in a function, when a procedure changes the value of an argument passed by reference, the original data value changes.

In the section on top-down program design, you saw a case history of using top-down design and step-wise refinement to outline your program. You saw that the outlining process revealed how the steps for computing the sales subtotal for a single region were identical, except for the name of a worksheet containing figures to be totaled, and the name of a variable to hold the total. Because the code for computing each regional subtotal is so similar, you should use the same procedure to compute all the regional subtotals.

To use the same procedure to compute the subtotal for each region, you must be able to tell the procedure, somehow, what worksheet to select, and what variable to store the subtotal in. You can do both by passing arguments to the procedure: one argument for the worksheet name, and another argument—passed by reference—for the variable to store the regional subtotal in. You then write the procedure so that it computes a subtotal for whatever worksheet name you pass to it, and stores the subtotal in whatever variable you pass to it. By adding arguments to the procedure, you make it possible to use the same procedure to compute the regional sales subtotal for any of the sales regions, depending on the worksheet name you pass to it. In fact, you could use this same procedure to compute a subtotal for *any* worksheet you name.

Passing information to a procedure through its argument list also reduces the number of module-level or public variables that you need to declare. This is really quite helpful: it can reduce the amount of memory that your program needs, and definitely eliminates a potential source of errors and confusion. The greater the number of module-level or public variables in your program, the greater the chance is that you will inadvertently use the wrong variable—leading to various side-effects and subtle bugs. Use argument lists to make information available to a procedure, instead of a module-level variable.

Specifying a Procedure's Argument List

You specify argument lists for procedures exactly the same way you specify argument lists for functions. You already know that you must include parentheses after the procedure name in every procedure declaration—by now, you've probably realized that the empty parentheses indicate to VBA that the procedure has no arguments.

Syntax

The full syntax for a procedure declaration is:

```
Sub name([arglist])
    statements
End Sub
```

name represents the procedure name, *arglist* represents the procedure's optional argument list, and *statements* represents the VBA statements that make up the body of the procedure. The argument list may consist of one or more arguments, with each argument in the list separated by a comma. A single argument in the list has this general syntax:

```
[Optional] [ByVal | ByRef] varname [As typename]
```

Just like a function, the `Optional` keyword indicates that the argument is optional. You may include either the `ByVal` keyword, or the `ByRef` keyword, but not both. The `ByVal` keyword tells VBA to pass the argument by value, and the `ByRef` keyword tells VBA to pass the argument by reference. (You learned the difference between arguments passed by value and by reference in Day 6.) *varname* represents the argument name; it may be any valid VBA identifier. The final part of the argument syntax is the `As` keyword, followed by *typename*, which represents any valid

VBA or user-defined data type. Unless you specify the argument's data type, VBA passes the argument as a Variant data type.

DO	DON'T

DO list all of a procedure's required arguments first, with all optional arguments at the end of the argument list (VBA requires you to do this).

DO remember that you cannot specify the data type of an optional argument—optional arguments must be Variants.

DO use the `IsMissing` function to test for the presence or absence of optional arguments within the procedure, just as you do in a function with optional arguments.

DO remember that VBA, by default, passes arguments by reference. If you omit either the `ByRef` or `ByVal` keywords, then VBA passes the argument by reference.

DO remember that argument names have the same scope as variables declared locally within the procedure—that is, argument variables are not accessible outside the procedure in whose argument list you declare them.

DO check carefully each time you write a procedure to make sure it alters only the arguments you intend it to.

Using Procedures That Have Arguments

Although creating an argument list for a procedure is exactly like creating an argument list for a function, calling a procedure with arguments is slightly different. When you pass arguments to a procedure, you do not include any parentheses around the argument list—even though you must enclose the argument list in parentheses when you declare the procedure.

To call a procedure and pass arguments to it, just type the procedure's name, a space, and then list each argument value in the argument list, separating each value with a comma. You can also use named arguments when you specify the values in the procedure's argument list—just use the name of the argument as it appears in the argument list of the procedure's declaration.

Assume that you have a procedure named **CompGrossIncome** that has the following declaration:

```
Sub CompGrossIncome( SheetName As String, sTotal As Currency)
```

This declaration tells VBA that **CompGrossIncome** has two required arguments. The first argument, **SheetName**, is a string, while the second argument, **sTotal**, is a Currency type value. VBA passes both arguments by reference, because the `ByVal` keyword is not present.

To call the **CompGrossIncome** procedure and specify values for its argument list, you could use either of the following statements:

```
CompGrossIncome "Eastern", GrSales
CompGrossIncome SheetName:="Eastern", sTotal:=GrSales
```

The first line just lists the values for the arguments, in the correct order, separating each value in the argument list with a comma. The second line uses named arguments to specify the values in the procedure's argument list, also separating each argument with a comma.

If you try to pass arguments to a procedure that you did not declare with an argument list, VBA displays a syntax error at runtime, stating that the procedure has the wrong number of arguments. If your procedure has required arguments (any argument declared without the Optional keyword is required), and you leave one or more of them out, then VBA displays the same "wrong number of arguments" syntax error message.

Note: The Macro dialog box does *not* list procedures that have required arguments, because there is no way for you to supply the argument values. You can only execute procedures that have required arguments by calling the procedure in a VBA program statement. The Macro dialog box only lists procedures without arguments, although it will list a procedure if *all* of its arguments are optional.

Listing 11.4 shows two different procedures. The **MakeSalesRpt_Chart** procedure in Listing 11.4 is similar to the **MakeSalesRpt_Chart** procedure used as an example in previous lessons. The new feature in this listing is the fact that **MakeSalesRpt_Chart** now calls the **Make_LabeledPieChart** procedure to create the actual chart, instead of creating the chart itself.

Listing 11.4. Using a procedure's arguments to send information to the procedure.

```
1:   Sub Make_LabeledPieChart(srcSheet As String, _
2:                            sRng As String, _
3:                            destSheet As String, _
4:                            chTitle As String)
5:   'creates labeled pie chart in a fixed location, on the
6:   'worksheet named by destSheet, then uses ChartWizard method to
7:   'plot data from the range named by sRng on the sheet named by
8:   'srcSheet. New pie chart gets title specified by chTitle.
9:
10:      'select the destination sheet and create chart
11:   Sheets(destSheet).Select
12:   ActiveSheet.ChartObjects.Add(96, 37.5, 234, 111).Select
13:      'use ChartWizard Method to create chart.
14:   With Sheets(srcSheet)
15:     ActiveChart.ChartWizard Source:=.Range(sRng), _
```

417

Listing 11.4. continued

```
16:                                 Gallery:=xlPie, _
17:                                 Format:=7, _
18:                                 PlotBy:=xlColumns, _
19:                                 CategoryLabels:=1, _
20:                                 SeriesLabels:=1, _
21:                                 HasLegend:=1, _
22:                                 Title:=chTitle
23:     End With
24: End Sub
25:
26: Sub MakeSalesRpt_Chart()
27: 'Asks for a sheet name containing source data, and then
28: 'asks for a range of cells containing the data to chart.
29: 'Next, this procedure asks for a sheet name to put the pie
30: 'chart on. This procedure then calls Make_LabeledPieChart
31: 'procedure to make a pie chart.
32:     Const sTitle = "Make Sales Report Chart"
33:
34:     Static SrcShtName As String
35:     Static SourceRng As String
36:     Dim DestShtName As String
37:
38:     'get source sheet name
39:     SrcShtName = InputBox(prompt:="Enter the name of " & _
40:                 "the sheet containing the data to graph:", _
41:                         Title:=sTitle, _
42:                         default:=SrcShtName)
43:
44:     'check to see if user entered name or chose Cancel
45:     If Len(Trim(SrcShtName)) = 0 Then
46:       MsgBox "Data source not entered - ending procedure"
47:       Exit Sub
48:     End If
49:         'select source sheet so user can refer to it
50:     Sheets(SrcShtName).Select
51:
52:     'get source range
53:     SourceRng = InputBox(prompt:="Enter the range of " & _
54:                 "the data to graph using R1C1 notation:", _
55:                         Title:=sTitle, _
56:                         default:=SourceRng)
57:
58:     'check to see if user entered range or chose Cancel
59:     If Len(Trim(SourceRng)) = 0 Then
60:       MsgBox "Source range not entered - ending procedure"
61:       Exit Sub
62:     End If
63:
64:     'get destination sheet name
65:     DestShtName = InputBox(prompt:="Enter the name of " & _
66:                 "the sheet that will contain the graph:", _
67:                         Title:=sTitle)
68:
69:     'did user enter destination name or choose Cancel
```

```
70:    If Len(Trim(DestShtName)) = 0 Then
71:      MsgBox "Destination not entered - ending procedure"
72:      Exit Sub
73:    End If
74:
75:     'use Make_LabeledPieChart procedure to create chart.
76:     Make_LabeledPieChart srcSheet:=SrcShtName, _
77:                          sRng:=SourceRng, _
78:                          destSheet:=DestShtName, _
79:                          chTitle:="Sales Report"
80: End Sub
```

Analysis Lines 1 through 24 contain the definition for the **Make_LabeledPieChart** procedure. This procedure makes a labeled pie chart using the source data sheet, source data range, destination worksheet, and chart title passed to the procedure as arguments. Because the procedure receives all the information it needs to make the chart through its argument list, you can use this procedure to create a pie chart from data in any range of any worksheet, and place the chart on any worksheet.

The **Make_LabeledPieChart** procedure's declaration and argument list are in lines 1 through 4. Notice the line continuation symbol at the end of lines 1, 2, and 3. Lines 1 through 4 are a single sub procedure declaration. The argument list was divided over several physical lines in order to make it easier to read.

Make_LabeledPieChart has four different arguments, all of which are required, and all of which are strings. The **srcSheet** argument contains the name of the worksheet that has the source data to be charted, the **sRng** argument contains a string specifying the range of data from the source worksheet to chart, the **destSheet** argument contains the name of the worksheet on which the procedure places the resulting chart, and **chTitle** is a string containing the title for the new chart.

Line 11 selects the destination sheet for the chart, using the Sheets collection, and the **destSheet** argument variable to specify the destination sheet. Line 12 then creates the chart object on the destination sheet in a fixed location and selects the new chart objects.

Lines 15 through 22 are a single VBA statement that uses the ChartWizard method to create the desired pie chart. In line 15, notice that the source worksheet and range arguments, **srcSheet** and **sRng**, are used to specify the data source for the chart. In line 22, notice that the **chTitle** argument is used to supply the title for the pie chart.

The **Make_LabeledPieChart** procedure gets all the information it needs to carry out its task through its argument list. As long as you want a labeled pie chart with this format, you can use this procedure to chart data from any source, and insert the pie chart in any worksheet (provided the source and destination are in the same workbook). This is a classic example of a short, simple procedure that does one task well.

Lines 26 through 80 contain the definition for the `MakeSalesRpt_Chart` procedure. This procedure has no arguments. The `MakeSalesRpt_Chart` procedure carries out the task of getting a source worksheet name, data range, and destination worksheet name from the user.

Lines 39 through 42 get the worksheet name for the data source from the user, and lines 45 through 48 check to see whether or not the user canceled the input dialog box. If the user canceled the input dialog box, then the procedure ends, otherwise it continues on to line 50, which selects the named source data sheet.

Lines 53 through 56 get the source range from the user, and lines 58 through 62 again check to see if the user canceled the input dialog box. Lines 64 through 73 get the destination sheet name, and test again to see whether the user canceled the operation by entering a blank string or canceling the input dialog box.

Finally, lines 76 through 79 call the `Make_LabeledPieChart` procedure to actually create the new pie chart.

The advantage of creating the `Make_LabeledPieChart` procedure is that you gain a general-purpose procedure that can create a pie chart in a particular format for any source and destination. The procedure is short, simple, and easy to understand. You can use it to create similar charts for sales, expenses, net profit, and so on.

The example in Listing 11.4 only used the procedure's arguments to send information to a procedure. Listing 11.5 shows a procedure that uses its arguments, passed by reference, to return values to the procedure that called it. Listing 11.5 also shows two different procedures. The first procedure, `FirstNonBlankCell`, searches the first 10 columns of the first 16 rows of a worksheet. It returns the row and column coordinates of the first non-blank cell that it finds in its arguments. The second procedure simply helps you test the `FirstNonBlankCell` procedure.

Type

Listing 11.5. Using a procedure's arguments to return values from the procedure.

```
1:  Sub FirstNonBlankCell(nRow As Long, nCol As Long)
2:  'Loops through first 16 rows and 10 columns of the active
3:  'worksheet, looking for a non-blank cell. Returns the row
4:  'and column coordinates in nRow and nCol. If no non-blank
5:  'cell found in the first 16 rows and 10 columns,
6:  'returns 0 in both coordinates.
7:    Dim Rcount As Integer
8:    Dim Ccount As Integer
9:
10:   nRow = 0       'assume a non-blank cell is not found
11:   nCol = 0
12:
13:     'if active sheet is not a worksheet, then stop now
14:   If TypeName(ActiveSheet) <> "Worksheet" Then Exit Sub
15:
16:   For Rcount = 1 To 16
```

```
17:     For Ccount = 1 To 10
18:       If Not IsEmpty(Cells(Rcount, Ccount).Value) Then
19:         nRow = Rcount
20:         nCol = Ccount
21:         Exit Sub
22:       End If
23:     Next Ccount
24:   Next Rcount
25: End Sub
26:
27:
28: Sub Test_FirstNonBlank()
29:
30:   Dim Rows As Long
31:   Dim Cols As Long
32:   Dim OldSheet As Object
33:   Static sName As String
34:
35:   Set OldSheet = ActiveSheet
36:
37:   sName = InputBox("Enter a worksheet name:")
38:   Worksheets(sName).Select
39:   FirstNonBlankCell nRow:=Rows, nCol:=Cols
40:
41:   If Rows = 0 Then
42:     MsgBox "No non-blank cells were found."
43:   Else
44:     MsgBox "The first non-blank cell is in row " & _
45:             Rows & ", column " & Cols
46:   End If
47:   OldSheet.Select
48: End Sub
```

Analysis Lines 1 through 25 contain the definition for the **FirstNonBlankCell** procedure. The procedure has two required arguments, both of which are Long type numbers, and both of which are passed by reference. The first argument, **nRow** represents a row coordinate, and the second argument, **nCol**, represents a column coordinate. Because VBA passes these two arguments by reference (the default passing method in VBA), any time the **FirstNonBlankCell** procedure changes these argument values, the original data value is changed. The **FirstNonBlankCell** procedure uses the argument variables to pass values back to the procedure that called it.

Because 0 is not a legitimate value for a row or column coordinate in Excel, **FirstNonBlankCell** signals that it was unable to find a non-blank cell by setting the **nRow** and **nCol** values to 0.

This procedure must loop through rows and columns of a worksheet, so it needs to have a couple of loop counting variables, one for rows, and one for columns. Lines 7 and 8 declare the loop counting variables—**Rcount** for rows and **Ccount** for columns—for the **FirstNonBlankCell** procedure.

Lines 10 and 11 each assign 0 to the **nRow** and **nCol** argument variables. Assuming that the procedure will fail to find a non-blank cell simplifies the remaining tests that this procedure must make. The procedure now only has to determine whether or not it finds a non-blank cell, without testing for blank cells.

Line 14 use the TypeName function in a single-line If...Then statement to ensure that the current sheet is actually a worksheet, and to prevent a runtime error from occurring later in the procedure. If the active sheet is not a worksheet, there are no cells to examine, and the **FirstNonBlankCell** procedure should end immediately (Exit Sub). Because values indicating failure to locate a non-blank cell were already assigned to the argument variables in lines 10 and 11, no additional assignment or processing is necessary—the procedure simply exits.

Lines 16 through 24 contain a For...Next loop that paces through the first 16 rows of the worksheet. The upper limit of 16 was arbitrarily chosen because 16 rows roughly corresponds to the maximum number of rows that you can see in a full-window display of a worksheet (for most computer systems).

The first line in the body of the For...Next loop that counts through the rows (line 17) starts a nested For...Next loop (the nested loop occupies lines 17 through 23). The inner loop paces through the first 10 columns of a worksheet. The upper limit of 10 columns was arbitrarily chosen because 10 columns roughly corresponds to the maximum number of columns that you can see in a full-window display of a worksheet.

The body of the inner For...Next loop is a single If...Then statement that uses the IsEmpty function to test whether or not the worksheet cell specified by the current row and column count is empty. If the cell is not empty, then lines 19 and 20 assign the current row and column counts to the **nRow** and **nCol** argument variables respectively. Line 21 then exits the **FirstNonBlankCell** procedure. At this point, the values of **nRow** and **nCol** reflect the location of the first non-blank cell, and whatever procedure called **FirstNonBlankCell** now has those values available to it.

Lines 28 through 48 contain a simple procedure, **Test_FirstNonBlank**, that you can use to test the **FirstNonBlankCell** procedure. Line 28 contains the procedure definition, and lines 30 through 33 declare some variables for **Test_FirstNonBlank**. The first two variables, **Rows** and **Cols**, are used as the argument for **FirstNonBlankCell**. The **OldSheet** object variable is used, for convenience, to save and restore whatever sheet was active at the time you executed **Test_FirstNonBlank**. Finally, the static **sName** variable is used to hold the name of the worksheet you want **FirstNonBlankCell** to check. **sName** is declared as a static variable for convenience in successive testing runs.

Line 35 saves a reference to whatever sheet is active at the time you execute **Test_FirstNonBlank**. Line 37 uses the InputBox function to get the name of the worksheet you want to test **FirstNonBlankCell** on, and line 38 selects that sheet.

Line 39 calls the **FirstNonBlankCell** cell procedure, passing the **Rows** and **Cols** variables as the procedure's arguments. Notice that the **Test_FirstNonBlank** procedure has *not* assigned any value to either of these variables. When VBA executes this statement, it calls the **FirstNonBlankCell** procedure, which executes as described in the first few paragraphs of this analysis. When the **FirstNonBlankCell** procedure has finished executing, VBA continues execution with line 41 of the **Test_FirstNonBlank** procedure.

Line 41 begins an **If...Then...Else** statement that evaluates the value in the **Rows** variable. If the **Rows** variable contains 0, then the **FirstNonBlankCell** procedure did not find any non-blank cells, and VBA executes line 42, which displays a message dialog box stating that no non-blank cells were found.

If, however, the **Rows** variable contains a number other than 0, then the **FirstNonBlankCell** procedure *did* locate a non-blank cell, and the non-blank cell's row and column coordinates are now stored in the **Rows** and **Cols** variables. VBA then executes the statement in line 44, which displays a message dialog box reporting the row and column number of the non-blank cell.

Once again, notice that the **Test_FirstNonBlank** procedure does not contain any assignment statements to either the **Rows** or **Cols** variables. The values for these variables are assigned in the **FirstNonBlankCell** procedure; because the **FirstNonBlankCell** procedure's arguments are passed by reference, any changes to those arguments are reflected in the original source of the argument value specified when you call the procedure. The **FirstNonBlankCell** procedure uses its arguments to return values to the procedure that called it.

The advantage of using arguments passed by reference in a procedure to return values, rather than a function, is that you can use the **ByRef** arguments in a procedure to return more than one value at a time.

DO	DON'T

DO use **ByRef** arguments in a procedure's argument list to return values from a procedure *only* when you need to return more than one value at a time. (Remember, if you omit the **ByRef** or **ByVal** keyword, VBA's default method of passing arguments is by reference.)

DO use a function to return a single value.

DON'T use **ByRef** arguments in a function to return values other than the function result. Functions should always return a *single* value and should *never* modify their arguments.

DO remember that you can use the Object Browser to find, paste, or show your procedures in exactly the same way you do for your function procedures. You can also use the Object Browser's options to specify comments for your procedures as you do for your functions. Using the Object Browser was described in Day 6.

Summary

In this chapter you learned how to organize your commonly-used procedures into a library, and how to make that library available to other workbooks. You learned how to make library workbooks available by placing them in either Excel's startup directory, or the alternate startup directory, so that Excel opens the library workbook automatically every time you start Excel. You also learned how to create references from one workbook to another.

You learned how VBA determines the scope of variables, constants, procedures, functions, and user-defined types when your program uses code in different modules, and you learned the difference between local scope, private scope, and public scope. You also learned how to increase or limit the scope of variables, constants, procedures, functions, and user-defined types by adding the Public or Private keywords to their declarations. You then learned how to use module qualifiers to refer to specific items in specific modules and workbooks. You learned that you can only use module qualifiers to refer to items in workbooks to which there is a reference.

Next, this chapter showed you how to use the most prevalent techniques—top-down design combined with a process of step-wise refinement—to design large-scale programs. You learned how your procedures can call other procedures, and you learned how to use several different modules to organize the various procedures and functions that make up your programs.

This chapter showed you how to create and use argument lists with your procedures. You learned when and why to use arguments with your procedures, and you learned how to specify an argument list for your procedures. Finally, you saw examples of how to use procedure arguments to both send information to a procedure, and to return values from a procedure.

Q&A

Q Do I have to create a library workbook?

A No, you don't have to create a library workbook. Using a library workbook, however, can reduce the number of times you end up writing the same code over and over again. Also, if you attach macro procedures to toolbar buttons and menu choices, as described in Day 16, you need to make sure that the macro procedures for those menus and toolbar buttons are always available—the best way to do this is to put those macro procedures in a library workbook. In general, the benefits of creating a library workbook more than make up for the amount of work and care needed to create the library workbook.

Q When you talk about the scope level of user-defined types, I'm a little confused. Do you mean the scope of variables with user-defined types, or do you mean the definition of a user-defined type?

A The scope of a user-defined type refers to the scope level at which the user-defined type *definition* is available. You can only declare variables with a particular user-defined type if the user-defined type definition is available at the scope level in which you declare the variable. If you declare a user-defined type definition with the `Private` keyword, the user-defined type is only available within the module in which you declare it. This means that you can only declare variables with that user-defined type in the same module in which the type definition appears. If you want to declare variables with the user-defined type in another module, then you must allow the user-defined type definition to remain public, so that it is available outside its own module.

Q **I'm a little confused. If the scope of a module-level variable is already limited to the module in which I declared it, then what effect does using the `Private` keyword (instead of `Dim`) have?**

A You're right; this is a little confusing. There is absolutely no difference between using the `Private` keyword and the `Dim` keyword to declare a module-level variable. In both cases, the scope of the variable is limited to the module in which it is declared. The only reason you might use the `Private` keyword to declare a module-level variable is to reinforce the distinction between variables private to that module, and any variables in the same module that you declare with the `Public` keyword.

Q **I also don't understand the effect of adding the `Public` keyword to a procedure, function, or user-defined type definition, because they naturally have public scope. Why should I use the `Public` keyword to declare a procedure, function, or user-defined type?**

A There is absolutely no difference in the scope of a procedure, function, or user-defined type declared with or without the `Public` keyword. You use the `Public` keyword to reinforce the distinction between any public procedures and functions, and any procedures or functions declared with the `Private` keyword in the same module.

Q **When I use procedure arguments, do I have to send information, or only return information?**

A Although the two examples of procedures with argument lists in this chapter show one procedure whose arguments are only used to supply information, and another procedure whose arguments are only used to return values, you don't have to restrict yourself to doing only one or the other. For example, you could easily modify the **FirstNonBlankCell** procedure in Listing 11.7 so that it receives the name of the worksheet to test as one of its arguments. The procedure then might have the following declaration:

```
FirstNonBlankCell(ByVal SheetName As String, _
                ByRef nRow As Long, _
                ByRef nCol As Long)
```

The **SheetName** argument supplies information to the procedure (the name of the worksheet to test) and the other two arguments return values, as before. One thing you should *not* do, however, is use the same argument to *both* send information and then to return information—making an argument perform double-duty like that is kind of sneaky, which is why it might seem tempting, but it is also quite confusing and may lead to obscure problems with your programs.

Workshop

Answers are in Appendix A.

Quiz

1. How does VBA search for a particular procedure?

2. Do you use the Object Browser or Macro dialog box to see a list of available functions?

3. How do you create a library workbook?

4. What are two ways to make the procedures and functions in a library workbook available?

5. What `Application` object property returns the name of Excel's startup folder? Can you change the name of Excel's startup folder with this property?

6. What `Application` object property returns the name of Excel's alternate startup folder? Can you change the name of the alternate startup folder with this property?

7. What happens when you call a procedure or function stored in a referenced workbook?

8. How do you create a reference to another workbook? Can you create a reference to another workbook when the current sheet is a worksheet?

9. What is *private scope*? *Public scope*?

10. What is the effect of the `Option Private Module` statement?

11. What is the effect of using the `Private` keyword? The `Public` keyword?

12. Can you use the `Public` and `Private` keywords to change the scope of a local variable?

13. What are the two main reasons you should create an argument list for a procedure?

14. Does the Macro dialog box list procedures that have arguments? What about the Object Browser?

15. If you want to use a procedure's argument to return a value, would you pass that argument by reference, or by value?

Exercises

1. The following listing represents an entire module. Add the `Public` or `Private` keywords to each of the declarations in the module so that every item that normally has private scope has public scope, and every item that normally has public scope has private scope. Then, add the necessary statements so that none of the items in this module can be used in any workbook except the one that contains this module. (For simplicity, the actual code in the function procedures and bodies in this listing has been omitted.)

```
1:      Option Explicit
2:
3:      Type NodeRecord
4:          StatementText As String * agMaxStrLen
5:          NodeType As Integer
6:          NextIfYes As Integer
7:          NextIfNo As Integer
8:      End Type
9:
10:     Dim Spinning As Boolean
11:     Dim New_Animal As Boolean
12:     Dim Animals() As NodeRecord
13:
14:
15:     Sub AboutAnimal()
16:         ' procedure body
17:     End Sub
18:
19:
20:     Sub ShutDown()
21:         ' procedure body
22:     End Sub
23:
24:
25:     Sub Play_Game_Cycle()
26:         ' procedure body
27:     End Sub
28:
29:
30:     Sub ShowRules()
31:         ' procedure body
32:     End Sub
33:
34:     Function Do_Remember() As Boolean
35:         ' procedure body
36:     End Function
37:
38:
39:     Sub Still_Playing()
40:         ' procedure body
41:     End Sub
```

```
42:
43:
44:    Sub Animal()
45:        ' procedure body
46:    End Sub
```

2. Write a top-down design for a program to balance your checkbook. Your design should incorporate these features:

   ☐ The program should start by allowing you to enter the starting balance for your checking account.

   ☐ The program should allow you to enter transactions until there is no more data to enter. Enter credits (deposits) as positive numbers, and debits (checks or withdrawals) as negative numbers.

   ☐ When receiving the amount of a transaction, your program should check to make sure that the entry is numeric, and display appropriate error messages.

   ☐ After entering each transaction, the program should display the amount of the transaction, whether the transaction is a credit or debit, and the new balance. If the balance of the account drops below $100, the program should display a warning message.

3. Write the VBA program from the design you created in Exercise 2.

Managing Files
with Visual Basic
for Applications

At some point, you'll probably want your procedures to be able to copy or delete a workbook or other file, rename a file, or find a particular file on the disk. Visual Basic for Applications provides you with a variety of statements, functions, and methods to carry out common file management tasks. Today, you learn:

- ☐ How to make your procedures display the same File Open and File Save As dialog boxes that Excel uses to select or enter filenames interactively.

- ☐ How to search a disk directory for all files that match a particular file specification (like *.XLS).

- ☐ How to find out what the current directory and disk drive is, and how to change the current drive and directory.

- ☐ How to create or remove disk directories.

- ☐ How to copy, move, rename, or delete disk files.

- ☐ How to get information about a file, such as the file's length, or the date and time that the file was last changed.

- ☐ How to understand file attributes and to retrieve information about a file's attributes or to change a file's attributes.

Understanding File Management

This section first describes what file management is and discusses some of the typical activities you might perform as part of your file management activities. This section then gives you an overview of Visual Basic for Applications' file management functions, statements, and methods.

What Is File Management?

File management is the term used to describe the actions you perform with files stored on your disk drives. File management includes actions such as copying files to make a backup, deleting unused files to make more disk space available, moving files from one disk or directory to another, and creating or deleting disk directories. File management also includes activities such as viewing a list of files in a directory to find out the size of a file, or the date and time that the file was last modified.

Note: The new Windows 95 Desktop and help system uses the term *folder* to refer to what experienced Windows or DOS users know as *directories*. This book uses the term *folder* for consistency with Windows 95 terminology; in some cases, this book will also use the term *directory*.

You probably perform file management tasks every day, although you may not use that term to describe what you do. Any time you use the Windows 95 Desktop, Explorer, or use DOS commands to copy, delete, or rename files, to get a listing of files currently stored in a directory, or to create or remove a disk subdirectory, you are performing file management tasks. Visual Basic for Applications enables you to perform the most common file management tasks under the control of a procedure or function that you write.

Reviewing Visual Basic for Applications' File Management Capabilities

Table 12.1 summarizes all of VBA's file management functions, statements, and methods. The first column in the table shows the VBA keyword, and the second column in the table indicates whether the keyword is for a function, statement, or object method. Finally, the third column of Table 12.1 contains a brief description of the purpose of each function, statement, or method.

Table 12.1. File management functions, methods, and statements.

Name	Category	Purpose
ChDir	statement	Changes the current directory.
ChDrive	statement	Changes the current disk drive.
CurDir	function	Returns the current directory path as a string.
Dir	function	Returns the name of a directory or file that matches a particular filename (including wildcards) passed as a string argument. Use to find one or more files on a disk.
FileCopy	statement	Copies a file.
FileDateTime	function	Returns a Date type value containing the date and time the file was last changed.
FileLen	function	Returns the length of a file, in bytes.
FindFile	method	Displays the dialog box for Excel's Find File command.
GetAttr	function	Returns a number representing the combined attributes of a file or disk directory—such as System, Hidden, and so on.

continues

12

Table 12.1. continued

Name	Category	Purpose
GetOpenFileName	method	Displays Excel's Open File dialog box, and returns the filename selected by the user.
GetSaveAsFileName	method	Displays Excel's Save As dialog box, and returns the filename selected by the user.
Kill	statement	Deletes files from the disk drive.
MkDir	statement	Creates a disk directory.
Name	statement	Renames or moves a file.
RmDir	statement	Deletes a disk directory.
SetAttr	statement	Sets a file's attributes.

You may notice that Table 12.1 does not list any of the arguments for any of the items in the table. Several of these functions, statements, and methods have fairly complex argument lists and options. Beginning with the next section of this chapter, each VBA file management function, statement, or method in Table 12.1 is described in full, with all its arguments and options.

The file management statements, functions, and object methods that VBA provides divide roughly into six different areas of functionality:

☐ Getting or changing a file's attributes.

☐ Retrieving or locating filenames.

☐ Getting or changing the current disk drive and directory, or creating or removing disk directories.

☐ Copying and deleting files.

☐ Renaming or moving files.

☐ Getting information about files, such as the file length and the date and time the file was last modified.

Subsequent sections in this chapter each describe one of these areas of functionality, and describe all the VBA file management statements that relate to that type of file management activity.

Working with File Attributes

Before proceeding with a detailed discussion of VBA's file management functions, statements, and object methods, you should understand what file attributes are and what they mean. This

section starts out by explaining file attributes, and then describes the VBA function to retrieve a file's attribute information, and the VBA statement for changing a file's attributes.

Understanding File Attributes

Every file stored on any Windows 95 (or earlier DOS version) disk has *attributes*—regardless of the specific type of disk drive (hard disk, floppy disk, RAM drive, Bernoulli drive, and so on). Windows 95 and DOS use a file's attributes to determine what file management activities are permitted for that file. For example, Windows 95 (or DOS) prohibits you—and any application programs—from deleting, modifying, or renaming files that have a read-only attribute.

Windows 95 creates a file's attribute information when you, or an application program running on your computer, create the file. In a sense, a file's attributes are like object properties—a file's attributes give the file certain characteristics, depending on the specific attributes that it has. File attributes are part of the file information that Windows 95 stores on your disk drive. Windows 95 stores the file attribute information for a particular file along with the file's name, size, and date and time information.

Windows 95 automatically updates and maintains a file's attribute information for you. Most of the time, you'll never be aware of a file's attributes, and usually there is no reason for you to need to know what a file's attributes are. In some cases, though, being able to understand and use a file's attributes is very important. In particular, you need to understand file attributes and their meanings to get the full benefit from VBA's Dir function.

Windows 95 (and DOS) uses a total of seven different file attributes to specify different characteristics for a file. Each of the separate file attributes may be combined with other attributes—except the Volume Label attribute. For example, a file could have the Hidden, System, Directory, Archive, and Read-Only file attributes all at once. The following list gives the name of each file attribute and describes its meaning.

☐ **Archive.** The Archive attribute indicates whether or not a file has changed since the last time you backed it up with a backup program such as Windows 95's BACKUP or a third-party backup program such as Fastback!, BackIt, Norton Backup, or others.

   If a file has the Archive attribute, it means that the file needs to be backed up. If a file does *not* have the Archive attribute, then the file has *not* changed since the last time it was backed up.

☐ **Directory.** If a file has the Directory attribute, it means that the file is actually a disk directory or subdirectory (a *folder* in Windows 95 terminology). A disk directory is really a file that contains information about other files—when you create a directory, Windows 95 creates the special directory file and gives it the Directory attribute. The Directory attribute lets Windows 95 know that this file contains information about other files, and prevents the directory from being renamed, copied, or deleted like a regular data file.

☐ **Hidden.** If a file has the Hidden attribute, Windows 95 "hides" the file by omitting it from most directory displays—although Windows 95 does have a viewing option that displays the names of hidden files.

☐ **Normal.** The Normal file attribute is really the absence of any special file attributes. A so-called Normal (also sometimes called *general*) file attribute just means that the file does not have any of the other file attributes, except possibly the Archive attribute to indicate whether or not the file needs to be backed up.

☐ **Read-Only.** The Read-Only attribute means that you can read from the file, but you cannot change the file. Windows 95 prohibits you from changing, deleting, or renaming a file that has the Read-Only attribute.

☐ **System.** The System attribute tells Windows 95 that the file is part of your computer's operating system. Like Read-Only files, Windows 95 prohibits you from changing a file that has the System attribute. Also, if you create a startup disk with the DOS SYS command (or with the Windows 95 Control Panel), any files that have the System attribute are transferred to the new startup disk.

☐ **Volume Label.** The Volume Label informs Windows 95 that this file is a disk's volume label. (A *volume label* is the name you give to a hard disk or floppy disk when you format the disk, use the DOS LABEL command, or change the Label property on disk's properties sheet.) Volume Labels aren't really a complete file; they are just filename entries in the disk's root directory, with the Volume Label file attribute. A disk can have only one volume label at a time.

DO   DON'T

DON'T confuse opening an Excel workbook in read-only mode with the Read-Only file attribute. Excel's read-only mode for workbooks affects only workbooks in Excel. The Read-Only file attribute is maintained at the operating-system level of your computer's operation. A file with the Read-Only attribute cannot be changed or modified by any application.

Windows 95 represents each different file attribute with a unique code number, and stores the number with the file's name and size information. If a file has more than one attribute, Windows 95 adds the code numbers for each attribute together and stores their sum. The next section describes how you can retrieve and interpret the code number for a file's attributes.

Table 12.2 lists all the file attribute codes that Windows 95 uses, and the predefined VBA constants for those attribute codes. As with all other numeric codes for which VBA defines a constant, you should use the VBA constant for the code number instead of the code number itself.

Table 12.2. Visual Basic for Applications' file attribute constants.

VBA Constant	Value	Meaning
vbNormal	0	Normal
vbReadOnly	1	Read-Only
vbHidden	2	Hidden
vbSystem	4	System
vbVolume	8	Volume Label
vbDirectory	16	Disk directory or subdirectory
vbArchive	32	Archive. If set, indicates that file has changed since the last backup.

Getting a File's Attributes

To find out what attributes a particular file has, use VBA's GetAttr function.

Syntax

The GetAttr function has the following general syntax:

GetAttr(*pathname*)

pathname is any VBA string expression that represents a valid filename. *pathname* may include the drive letter and full directory path; if you don't include the drive letter, GetAttr searches for the specified file in the current disk drive; if you don't include the directory path, GetAttr searches in the current directory.

GetAttr returns a number that contains the sum of all the numeric codes for a file's attributes.

Listing 12.1 shows an example that uses the GetAttr function, and also demonstrates how to interpret the function's result.

12

Type

Listing 12.1. Using the GetAttr function and interpreting its result.

```
1:    Sub ShowFileAttr(fName As String)
2:    'displays a message box showing the file
3:    'attributes of the filename in the fName argument.
4:
5:      Dim fAttr As Integer
6:      Dim mStr As String
7:
8:      fAttr = GetAttr(fName)
9:      mStr = UCase(fName)
10:     mStr = mStr & " has these attributes: " & Chr(13)
11:     If (fAttr And vbReadOnly) Then _
```

continues

Listing 12.1. continued

```
12:                    mStr = mStr & "Read-Only" & Chr(13)
13:     If (fAttr And vbHidden) Then _
14:                    mStr = mStr & "Hidden" & Chr(13)
15:     If (fAttr And vbSystem) Then _
16:                    mStr = mStr & "System" & Chr(13)
17:     If (fAttr And vbVolume) Then _
18:                    mStr = mStr & "Volume" & Chr(13)
19:     If (fAttr And vbDirectory) Then _
20:                    mStr = mStr & "Directory" & Chr(13)
21:     If (fAttr And vbArchive) Then _
22:                    mStr = mStr & "Archive" & Chr(13)
23:     MsgBox mStr
24:  End Sub
25:
26:  Sub ListFileAttr()
27:     ShowFileAttr fName:="c:\io.sys"
28:     ShowFileAttr fName:="c:\msdos.sys"
29:     ShowFileAttr fName:="c:\MSOffice\Excel\XLStart"
30:     ShowFileAttr fName:="c:\MSOffice\Excel\Examples\Samples.xls"
31:  End Sub
```

Analysis

Listing 12.1 contains two different procedures. The first procedure, **ShowFileAttr**, occupies lines 1 through 24, and the second procedure, **ListFileAttr**, occupies lines 26 through 31. **ListFileAttr** simply calls **ShowFileAttr** several times, passing a different filename each time.

Line 1 contains the procedure declaration for **ShowFileAttr**; this procedure has a single, required argument named **fName** with a String data type. Line 5 declares an Integer type variable, **fAttr**, to store the value returned by the GetAttr function. Line 6 declares a String type variable, **mStr**, to store the message that this procedure assembles.

When VBA executes the statement in line 8, it calls GetAttr, passing whatever string is in the **fName** argument variable as the argument for GetAttr, and storing the function result in the **fAttr** variable. If the string in **fName** does not contain a valid filename, VBA displays a runtime error with the message "path not found."

Lines 9 and 10 put together the first part of the message that this procedure displays. Line 9 uses the UCase function to convert the filename in **fName** to uppercase, just for cosmetic reasons.

Lines 11 through 22 contain a series of If...Then statements that evaluate the number stored in **fAttr**, which contains the sum of all the code numbers for the file's attributes. Notice that these If...Then statements are *not* nested. Instead, the value in **fAttr** gets tested six different times, once for each possible attribute value. Remember, the attribute value that Windows 95 stores with the file is the sum of all the code numbers for each of the file attributes that the file has. If the file attribute that a particular If...Then statement tests for is present, then a string containing the appropriate attribute name gets added to the message string stored in **mStr**.

Bit-Wise Comparisons

It may not seem clear to you how the logical expressions in lines 11 through 22 in Listing 12.1 work. These expressions work because, when you use a logical operator (And, Or, Xor, Not, and so on) with numeric values, VBA operates on the individual *bits* that make up the numbers.

Look again at Table 12.1 and notice that the actual values of the attribute code numbers are not sequential. Each file attribute number is an even power of two, such that when you write the number using binary digits, the file attribute code number is either just 1, or a 1 with only zeroes after it: the Read-Only attribute is 1, Hidden is 10, System is 100, Volume is 1000, Directory is 10000, and Archive is 100000.

When VBA makes a bit-wise comparison, it compares the binary digits in each number. Depending on the specific logical operator, VBA performs an And, Or, Xor, Not, or Imp comparison on each pair of bits from the two numbers it is comparing. If the result of the comparison is True, VBA places a 1 in the corresponding digit for its answer, or a 0 if the comparison is False. Because an And logical operation is True whenever both of its arguments are True, the result of the expression 1 And 1 is True.

The expressions in Listing 12.1 work by performing a logical And on the **fAttr** variable's contents and one of the VBA file attribute constants, thus making a bit-wise comparison between the two numbers. If the file has the Hidden and Read-Only attributes, for example, then the value in **fAttr** is 3 (the sum of 1 + 2; refer to table 12.2). Written in binary notation, the number 3 is 11. The binary value for the Read-Only attribute is 01, and the binary value for the Hidden attribute is 10. The result of the expression 11 And 01 is True, indicating that the Read-Only attribute is present.

12

The MsgBox statement in line 23 displays the message string that the previous statements assembled, and line 24 is the end of the **ShowFileAttr** procedure.

Line 26 contains the declaration for the **ListFileAttr** procedure, which simply calls the **ShowFileAttr** procedure several times, passing it different filenames. Line 27 causes **ShowFileAttr** to display the file attributes for the IO.SYS file. This file is part of the Windows 95 operating system and is always located in the root directory of your startup disk. Because the IO.SYS file is part of the Windows 95 operating system, it has the System file attribute; it has a Read-Only attribute to prevent you from accidentally deleting this important file, and it also has the Hidden attribute, so it does not usually appear in Windows 95 desktop file windows' or in the Explorer's directory listings. When VBA executes line 27, it displays the dialog box shown in Figure 12.1.

Figure 12.1.

The **ShowFileAttr** *procedure displays this dialog box for the IO.SYS system file on your Windows 95 startup disk.*

The **ShowFileAttr** procedure displays a similar dialog box for the C:\MSDOS.SYS file. Notice that line 29 specifies a directory name (the Excel startup directory), rather than an actual filename. When this line executes, a dialog box stating that it has the Directory attribute appears. The final dialog box, depending on whether or not you have recently backed up the SAMPLES.XLS example file, either displays the Archive attribute, or no attributes.

Note: There is no test in the **ShowFileAttr** procedure for the Normal file attribute because the Normal file attribute is merely the absence of any other file attributes.

DO	**DON'T**

DO declare all variables that you use to store file attribute codes as Integer type variables. A file attribute code number will never exceed the permissible range of an Integer.

DON'T forget that file attribute codes are always handled as a single number containing the sum of all the individual code numbers for the file's attributes.

Changing a File's Attributes

Occasionally, you may want to change a file's attributes. For example, you might want to change a template workbook's file attributes to include the Read-Only attribute, to make sure that you can't accidentally delete that template workbook.

You can use the **SetAttr** statement to change a file's attributes. **SetAttr** fulfills the same purpose as the **File | Properties** command (available on any Windows 95 directory windows, or by right-clicking on a file's icon), or the DOS ATTRIB command.

The SetAttr statement has the following general syntax:

```
SetAttr pathname, attributes
```

pathname represents any string expression containing a valid Windows 95 file specification (a filename and, optionally, the full directory path and a drive letter). *attributes* represents a numeric expression. The numeric expression for attributes must be a number between 1 and 255, and must consist of one of the file attribute code numbers, or a sum of file attribute code numbers.

Listing 12.2 shows an example of how you might use the SetAttr statement.

Listing 12.2. Using the SetAttr statement to change a file's attributes.

```
1:  Sub DelProtectFile(fName As String)
2:  'sets Read-only attribute for file named in fName
3:
4:    Dim fAttr As Integer
5:
6:    fAttr = GetAttr(fName)
7:
8:        'don't set the attribute if it's already set
9:    If Not CBool((fAttr And vbReadOnly)) Then
10:     SetAttr fName, fAttr + vbReadOnly
11:    End If
12:
13:    MsgBox prompt:="Read-only file attribute for " & _
14:            fName & " set.", _
15:         Title:="Delete Protection"
16:  End Sub
17:
18:
19:  Sub Test_DelProtectFile()
20:    Dim iName As String
21:
22:    iName = Application.GetOpenFilename
23:    DelProtectFile iName
24:    ShowFileAttr iName
25:  End Sub
```

The **DelProtectFile** procedure protects files from accidental deletion by giving the file the Read-Only file attribute, without affecting the file's other attributes. **DelProtectFile** has a single required String type argument named **fName**, used to pass a filename into the procedure. Line 4 declares the **fAttr** variable; the procedure uses this variable to store a number for the file's attributes.

Line 6 uses GetAttr to retrieve the file attributes from the file specified by **fName**. Lines 9 through 11 contain an If statement that executes the SetAttr statement only if the file does not already have the Read-Only attribute. Line 10 contains the actual call to SetAttr. Notice that the old file attributes are arithmetically added to the vbReadOnly constant to specify the file's new attributes. This way, the file's original attributes are preserved.

Finally, lines 13 through 15 contain a MsgBox statement that displays a message notifying the user that the file has the Read-Only attribute set.

The **Test_DelProtectFile** procedure simply exercises the **DelProtectFile** procedure. Line 22 uses the GetOpenFileName method (described in the next section) to get a filename from you. Line 23 then calls the **DelProtectFile** procedure to set the file's attributes to include the Read-Only attribute. Finally, line 24 calls the **ShowFileAttr** procedure (shown in Listing 12.1) to display a message dialog box verifying the file's new attributes.

DO	DON'T

DON'T try to give a file the Directory (vbDirectory) or Volume Label (vbVolume) attributes with SetAttr, or VBA displays a runtime error.

DO keep in mind that, when you set a file's attributes, the file then has *only* the attributes you set. To add to a file's attributes without changing its existing attributes, you must retrieve its current attributes first, add the new attribute, and then set the file attributes.

DON'T add file attribute codes to an existing file attribute code number without ensuring that the attribute code does *not* already contain the attribute code you want to add. Otherwise, you may end up giving the file an attribute other than the ones you expected.

Tip: Use the Or operator to add a new file attribute to an existing set of file attributes. Using the Or operator to combine file attributes in a bitwise operation avoids any possible problems that might occur when using arithmetic addition to combine new attributes with existing attributes. The result of the expression 0 Or 1 is 1; the result of the expression 1 Or 1 is also 1. Because of this, you can combine a new file attribute into an existing file attribute number by using an expression similar to: OldAttr Or vbArchive. If the Archive attribute is not set in OldAttr, it will be set as a result of the Or operation. If the Archive attribute is already set, it will remain unchanged.

Getting or Finding Filenames

This section shows you how to use VBA to include Excel's own File Open and File Save As dialog boxes in your procedures, so that your procedure's user can easily and accurately supply filenames to your procedures. Next, this section shows you how to use the Dir function to search a disk directory for one or more files that match a particular filename.

Using the *GetOpenFilename* Method

Many of the examples earlier in this book use the InputBox function to get filenames from a procedure's user. Although getting a filename with InputBox works okay, it doesn't have the advantages of using a file-oriented dialog box such as Excel's File Open dialog box, which actually lets you see what files are on the disk, and lets you look at file lists from different disk drives and directories.

You can use Excel's GetOpenFilename method to display a dialog box that both looks and behaves the same as the dialog box that Excel displays when you choose the **File | Open** command. The GetOpenFilename method returns a string that contains the filename the user selects, including the drive letter and complete directory path. If the user cancels the dialog box, GetOpenFilename returns the Boolean value False as its result.

The GetOpenFilename method has this general syntax:

object.GetOpenFilename(*fileFilter*, *filterIndex*, *title*, *multiSelect*)

object must be a reference to the Application object. Although the *object* reference to the Application object is required, all the GetOpenFilename arguments are optional. *fileFilter* represents any valid String expression, specially formatted to specify the file filters listed in the Files of **T**ype drop-down list box in the File Open dialog box. If you omit the *fileFilter* argument, the file filter for the Files of **T**ype drop-down list box is All Files (*.*).

filterIndex represents any numeric expression and indicates which file filter VBA should use as the default for the Files of **T**ype drop-down list box. If you omit this argument, or specify a number greater than the actual number of file filters, the first file filter becomes the default. *title* represents any String expression and is the title VBA displays in the File Open dialog box. If you omit *title*, VBA displays the dialog box with the usual *Open* title.

Finally, *multiSelect* represents any Boolean expression or value. If *multiSelect* is True, then the File Open dialog box allows the user to select multiple file names. When *multiSelect* is True, GetOpenFilename returns an array containing the names of all of the selected files; you'll learn about arrays in tomorrow's lesson (Day 13).

Syntax

12

To specify the file filter string, format a string as follows:

"*FilterName1, filespec1, FilterName2, filespec2, FilterNameN, filespecN*"

FilterName represents the text that you want VBA to display in the Files of Type drop-down list box. *filespec* represents the file specification that Windows 95 uses to restrict the files listed in the File Open dialog box. You can list as many file filters as you want.

The following line shows a sample file filter string:

```
"XL 7 Templates (*.xlt),*.xlt,Workbooks (*.xls),*.xls"
```

The preceding filter string causes the two choices Xl 7 Templates (*.xlt) and Workbooks (*.xls) to appear in the Files of Type drop-down list box. When you select Xl 7 Templates (*.xlt) in the Files of Type list box, the file specification *.xlt appears in the Name text box, and the file list contains only files that match the *.xlt file specification.

Listing 12.3 shows an example that uses the GetOpenFilename method.

Type

Listing 12.3. Using GetOpenFilename to get a filename from your procedure's user.

```
 1:  Sub Open2DataEntry()
 2:  'opens a specified workbook to the Sales Report
 3:  'worksheet.
 4:
 5:    Const iTitle = "Data Entry Setup"
 6:    Const ShtName = "Sales Report"
 7:
 8:    Const FilterList = _
 9:    "Templates (*.xlt),*.xlt,Workbooks (*.xls),*.xls"
10:
11:    Dim fName As String
12:
13:    With Application
14:    fName = .GetOpenFilename(Title:=iTitle, _
15:                            filefilter:=FilterList, _
16:                            filterindex:=2)
17:    End With
18:    If fName = "False" Then
19:      MsgBox prompt:="Operation Canceled", _
20:            Title:=iTitle
21:      Exit Sub
22:    End If
23:
24:    Workbooks.Open Filename:=fName
25:    ActiveWorkbook.Sheets(ShtName).Select
26:    MsgBox prompt:="Workbook " & fName & _
27:                    " opened, " & ShtName & _
28:                    " selected.", _
29:            Title:=iTitle & " Complete"
30:  End Sub
```

The **Open2DataEntry** procedure opens a workbook selected by its user, and then selects a worksheet named *Sales Report* in the opened workbook. (This procedure assumes that any workbooks it opens will have a worksheet named *Sales Report*.) This procedure declares a couple of constants in lines 5 and 6. The **iTitle** constant is used to supply titles for dialog boxes that this procedure displays, and **ShtName** supplies the name for the worksheet.

Lines 8 and 9 require a close look. Notice the line continuation symbol at the end of line 8. These two lines together are a single constant declaration. The **FilterList** constant supplies the string for the file filters in the later call to the GetOpenFilename method.

Line 11 declares the **fName** variable to hold the filename obtained from the user. Lines 14 through 16 contain a single statement that calls the GetOpenFilename method and assigns its result to **fName**. Notice the dot separator in front of the GetOpenFilename method name, and notice that this statement is inside a With Application statement. Whenever you use the GetOpenFilename method, you must specify the Application object reference for the method.

When VBA executes this statement, it displays the dialog box shown in Figure 12.2. Figure 12.2 has the Files of Type list box opened so you can see the effect of the fileFilter argument. Notice that the dialog box in the figure is identical to the Excel File Open dialog box, except for the dialog's title and the contents of the Files of Type list box. Because the filterIndex argument (line 15) is set to 2, the Workbooks (*.xls) filter is the default filter rather than Templates (*.xlt).

Figure 12.2.

The OpenDataEntry
procedure uses the
GetOpenFilename *method to*
display this dialog box.
Notice the file filters in the
Files of **Type** *drop-down list.*

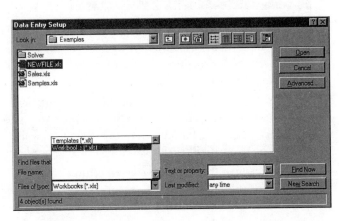

You select a name in the dialog box just as you would in Excel's File Open dialog box. When you choose Open, the GetOpenFilename method returns a string containing the filename, drive letter, and full directory path (the multiSelect argument wasn't used, so you can select only one filename). If you choose Cancel, GetOpenFilename returns the Boolean value False. Because, in this case, **fName** is a String variable, VBA automatically converts False to the string *False*.

> **Note:** The GetOpenFilename method restricts the files listed in the Files of type list box to ones that match the file types you specify with the fileFilter argument. For example, if you specify a file filter of "Workbooks,*.xls" then the GetOpenFilename dialog box will display *only* workbook files. In the **Open2DataEntry** procedure in Listing 12.3, the user's choices are restricted to Excel template and workbook files only—the user is unable to select any other type of file in the dialog box displayed by this procedure.

Lines 18 through 19 contain an If statement that checks to see whether you canceled the GetOpenFilename dialog box. If so, the MsgBox statement in lines 19 and 20 displays a message that the operation is canceled, and exits the procedure.

Line 24 opens the workbook you selected, and line 25 selects the *Sales Report* sheet. If you want to test this procedure, make sure the workbook you select has a worksheet named *Sales Report* in it or change the constant declaration in line 6 to match the name of a worksheet in one of your workbooks. Finally, lines 26 through 29 contain a MsgBox statement reporting a successful completion of the procedure's task.

DO	DON'T

DO remember that GetOpenFilename returns a string when you select a filename, and the Boolean value False when you cancel the dialog box. If you assign the GetOpenFilename result to a Variant type variable, you'll need to test for False instead of the string *False*.

DON'T be confused if you see an additional argument, buttonText, listed for the GetOpenFilename method in the Object Browser or the online Help. In Windows, GetOpenFilename ignores the buttonText argument; this argument is provided to maintain compatibility with Excel for the Macintosh.

DO remember that GetOpenFilename returns an array of strings if you use a value of True for the optional multiSelect argument—even if the user only selects one file. Arrays are the topic of the lesson in Day 13.

DON'T forget that the file types the user can select from are restricted by the fileFilter argument. To allow a user to select any type of file, you must include the *.* file type in the fileFilter argument.

DO remember that omitting the fileFilter argument causes the dialog box displayed by GetOpenFilename to list files of all types.

Using the *GetSaveAsFilename* Method

You can also use Excel's GetSaveAsFilename method to display a dialog box that looks and behaves the same as the dialog box that Excel displays when you choose the **File** | Save **As** command. The GetSaveAsFilename method also returns a string that contains the filename the user selects, including the drive letter and complete directory path. If the user cancels the dialog box, GetSaveAsFilename returns the Boolean value False.

Syntax

The GetSaveAsFilename method has this general syntax:

```
object.GetSaveAsFilename(initialFilename, fileFilter, filterIndex, title)
```

The GetSaveAsFilename method has almost exactly the same arguments and syntax as the GetOpenFilename method. *object* is a reference to the Application object, *fileFilter* is a String expression formatted to specify the file filters listed in the Save as **t**ype drop-down list box, *filterIndex* is a numeric expression indicating which file filter VBA should use as the default, and *title* is a String expression for the dialog box's title bar. If you omit *title*, VBA displays the dialog box with the usual *Save As* title.

The GetSaveAsFilename method has one more argument—*initialFilename*, which represents any valid filename. If you specify this optional argument, the filename you specify for *initialFilename* appears in the File **n**ame text box when the Save As dialog box first displays.

You specify file filter strings for GetSaveAsFilename the same way you format them for GetOpenFilename.

Listing 12.4 shows an example that uses the GetSaveAsFilename method.

Listing 12.4. Using GetSaveAsFilename to get a filename from your procedure's user.

```
1:  Sub Convert2Template()
2:  'saves the current workbook as a template file.
3:
4:     Const FilterList = "Templates (*.xlt),*.xlt"
5:     Const iTitle = "Convert WorkBook to Template"
6:     Static sName As String
7:     Static TCount As Variant
8:     Dim iName As String
9:
10:    If IsEmpty(TCount) Then
11:       TCount = 1
12:    Else
13:       TCount = TCount + 1
14:    End If
15:
16:    sName = "Template" & CStr(TCount) & ".xlt"
17:    With Application
```

continues

Listing 12.4. continued

```
18:        iName = .GetSaveAsFilename(InitialFilename:=sName, _
19:                                FileFilter:=FilterList, _
20:                                Title:=iTitle)
21:    End With
22:
23:    If iName = "False" Then
24:      MsgBox prompt:="Conversion to Template Canceled.", _
25:             Title:=iTitle
26:    Else
27:      ActiveWorkbook.SaveAs filename:=iName, _
28:                            FileFormat:=xlTemplate
29:    End If
30: End Sub
```

 The **Convert2Template** procedure saves the current workbook as an Excel template file, and uses the GetSaveAsFilename method to obtain the name for the new template file. Line 4 declares a constant for the file filter, and line 5 declares a constant to supply the titles for the dialog boxes that this procedure displays.

Lines 6 and 7 declare some Static variables. **sName** is used to supply a suggested name for the new template file, and **TCount** is used to number the default template names. Line 8 declares **iName** as a String type variable to hold the filename you select.

Lines 10 through 16 set up the template file counter and assemble the suggested template filename. Lines 18 through 20 contain a single statement that calls the GetSaveAsFilename method and assigns its result to **iName**. Notice the dot separator (.) in front of the GetSaveAsFilename method name, and notice also that this statement is inside a With Application statement. You must always specify the Application object when you call the GetSaveAsFilename method.

When VBA executes the statement in line 18, it displays the dialog box shown in Figure 12.3. Notice that the dialog box in the figure is exactly the same as Excel's Save As dialog box, except for the dialog box title and the contents of the Save as **t**ype list box.

Figure 12.3.

The **Convert2Template** *procedure uses the* GetSaveAsFilename *method to display this dialog box.*

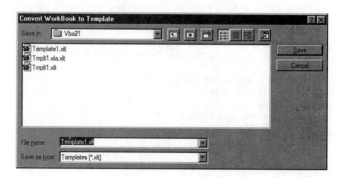

Note: The `fileFilter` argument for the `GetSaveAsFilename` method restricts not only the files listed in the dialog box, but also ensures that the file name entered by the user ends up with the three-letter file type extension specified by the current choice in the Save as **t**ype drop-down list.

Unless the user types the correct three-letter file type extension as part of the file name she enters, the `GetSaveAsFilename` method *always* adds the three-letter extension for the file type specified in the Save as **t**ype list.

Look again at Figure 12.3, and notice the file named `Tmplt1.xla.xlt`. This file was saved previously with the **Convert2Template** procedure. At that time, the user entered the file name `Tmplt1.xla` in the File **n**ame text box. Because long filenames in Windows 95 permit more than one period in a file name, and because the `.xla` file type extension did not match any of the file types specified in the `fileFilter` argument, the `GetSaveAsFilename` method added the `.xlt` file type extension (the current selection in the Save as **t**ype list) to the file name before creating the file.

You must include the `*.*` file type in the `fileFilter` argument to allow users to enter any file type extension.

Line 23 starts an `If...Then...Else` statement that evaluates whether the user canceled the `GetSaveAsFilename` dialog box. If the user chose the Cancel button (or pressed Esc), then the statement in line 24 executes, displaying a message dialog box informing the user that the conversion to a template has been canceled. If the user didn't cancel the `GetSaveAsFilename` dialog box, then the statement in line 27 calls the `SaveAs` method, saving the active workbook as an Excel template file. (You'll learn more about the `SaveAs` method in Day 18.)

DO	**DON'T**

DO keep in mind that both `GetOpenFilename` and `GetSaveAsFilename` may change the current disk drive and directory. You may want to use the `CurDir` function to get the current drive and directory, and store it in a variable so that you can switch back to the current disk drive and directory with `ChDrive` and `ChDir`. (These other functions and statements are described later in this chapter.)

DO use the `fileFilter` argument to ensure that your procedure's user can only enter filenames of particular types—that way you can ensure that your procedure only creates files with the specified types. For example, you might want to write all your Excel VBA procedures so that they are only capable of creating files with one of the file types known to Excel.

Using the *Dir* Function to Find Files

Occasionally, you may need to search a disk directory to see if it contains one or more files that match a particular filename specification, such as \EXCEL\EXAMPLES*.XLS. To search a disk directory, use the Dir function. The Dir function fulfills, for VBA, the same purposes as the file list in a Windows 95 directory window, or the DOS DIR command—it gives you an opportunity to see what files are stored in a particular directory, and to see what other directories are present.

The Dir function has the following general syntax:

```
Dir(pathname[, attributes])
```

pathname represents any String expression that results in a valid filename. The filename may contain a drive letter and the full directory path. The filename may also include wildcard file characters. The optional *attributes* argument is a number representing the attributes of the files you want to search for. If you include the *attributes* argument, Dir searches for files that have those attributes. If you omit the *attributes* argument, Dir searches for normal files—that is, any file except those with Hidden, Volume Label, Directory, or System file attributes.

When you call the Dir function with the *pathname* argument, it returns a string containing the name of the first file it finds that matches the filename in the *pathname* argument. If your filename contains wildcards (* or ?), then, to find *all* of the files in a directory that match your filename, you must use the Dir function in two stages. First, you call Dir with the *pathname* argument to get the *first* matching file, then you call Dir repeatedly *without* arguments, until Dir returns an empty string. As soon as Dir returns an empty string, there are no more files that match your filename. If you call Dir again, without specifying a filename, VBA generates a runtime error.

Listing 12.5 shows an example of Dir used to locate only one file.

Type

Listing 12.5. Finding a single file using Dir.

```
1:  Function IsDiskFile(fName As String) As Boolean
2:  'return True if fName is found on disk, False otherwise
3:
4:    If (Dir(fName) <> "") Then
5:      IsDiskFile = True
6:    Else
7:      IsDiskFile = False
8:    End If
9:  End Function
10:
11:
12:  Sub Test_IsDiskFile()
13:    Dim iName As String
14:
15:    iName = InputBox(prompt:="Enter a filename:", _
16:                     Title:="Testing IsDiskFile")
17:    MsgBox iName & " exists: " & IsDiskFile(iName)
18:  End Sub
```

 Lines 1 through 9 contain the **IsDiskFile** function, which has a single required String type argument, **fName**. **IsDiskFile** returns a Boolean result: True if the filename in **fName** exists on the disk drive, False if it does not.

The operation of the **IsDiskFile** function is quite simple. Line 4 contains an If...Then...Else statement that—as part of its logical expression—calls the Dir function, passing the contents of **fName** as the filename to search for. No argument for attributes is specified in this call to Dir, so it will find any file *except* ones that have Hidden, System, Directory, or Volume Label attributes.

Because the purpose of the **IsDiskFile** function is merely to determine whether a particular file does or does not exist, the return result of the Dir function is not used, except to compare it to an empty string. If the Dir function result is *not* an empty string, then Dir found the specified file, and VBA executes line 5, which assigns the function result True. If the Dir function result is an empty string, then no matching file was found, and VBA executes line 7, which assigns False to the function result.

Lines 12 through 18 declare a procedure to test the **IsDiskFile** function. This test procedure uses the InputBox function to get a filename from the user, and then calls the **IsDiskFile** function as part of a MsgBox statement, which displays a message stating whether or not the filename entered by the user exists.

Notice, if you call the **IsDiskFile** function with a filename that includes single (?) or multiple (*) wildcard characters, the function returns True if there is at least one file that matches the wildcard specification. (Refer to your Windows 95 online help for more information on wildcard characters in filenames.)

You can also use the Dir function to find all the files in a directory that match a particular filename. This feature of the Dir function is most useful when your filename contains wildcard characters. You might use the Dir function this way if you want to, say, find *all* the template files in a particular directory.

Listing 12.6 shows an example of how you use the Dir function to locate more than one file.

12

 Listing 12.6. Finding several files using Dir.

```
1:    Sub ShowFiles()
2:    'displays the names and attributes of all files in
3:    'the specified directory
4:
5:      Dim sAttr As Integer
6:      Dim fName As String
7:      Dim pName As String
8:      Dim fCount As Integer
9:
10:     pName = InputBox("enter a directory to search in:")
11:     If Trim(pName) = "" Then Exit Sub
12:     If Right(pName, 1) <> "\" Then pName = pName & "\"
13:
```

Listing 12.6. continued

```
14:     sAttr = vbDirectory + vbArchive + vbReadOnly + _
15:         vbHidden + vbSystem
16:
17:     'get the first file name and attributes
18:     fName = Dir(pName & "*.*", sAttr)
19:     If (fName <> "") And _
20:         ((fName <> ".") And (fName <> "..")) Then
21:       ShowFileAttr pName & fName
22:       fCount = 1
23:     End If
24:
25:     Do While (fName <> "")
26:       fName = Dir()
27:       If (fName <> "") And _
28:           ((fName <> ".") And (fName <> "..")) Then
29:         ShowFileAttr pName & fName
30:         fCount = fCount + 1
31:       End If
32:     Loop
33:
34:     MsgBox fCount & " files found."
35:   End Sub
```

The **ShowFiles** procedure asks the user to enter a directory name, and then uses the Dir function to find all the files in that directory. Lines 5 through 8 declare several variables. The **sAttr** variable is used to hold a file attribute number. **fName** is used to temporarily store the names of the files returned by Dir, and **pName** is used to store the name of the directory path that this procedure searches. The **fCount** variable is used to hold a count of all the files found.

Line 10 calls the InputBox function to get a directory name from the user. Line 11 checks to make sure that the user did not cancel the dialog box; if the dialog box is canceled, the procedure simply ends. Line 12 checks to make sure that the directory path the user entered ends with the path separator character (\), and adds it to the end of the directory path stored in **pName**, if it is missing.

Line 14 sets up the **sAttr** variable to contain the attributes for the files that Dir will search for. Notice that **sAttr** is set up to contain all the possible file attributes, except the Volume Label attribute.

Line 18 makes the first call to the Dir function, using the directory path in **pName**, and adds to it the file specification *.* (which will find all files), and also passes **sAttr** to specify which file attributes to search for. By specifying all the file attributes (except Volume Label), Dir will find any file in the specified directory, including any subdirectories in that directory. The Dir function result is assigned to **fName**.

Lines 19 through 23 contain an If...Then statement that evaluates the string returned by Dir, and stored in **fName**. Notice that the logical expression for this If statement is actually split over two lines: 19 and 20. The first part of the expression tests to see whether or not **fName** is empty. The second part of the expression (line 20), checks to make sure that **fName** does not contain either a string consisting of a single period (.), or a string consisting of two periods (..). These special strings are used by the Windows 95 file system to indicate the current directory (.) and the parent directory of the current directory (..). Although these special filenames are technically directories, and the Dir function will report their existence with the kind of attribute and wildcard specification used in this example, they don't actually exist on the disk, and any attempt to get their file attributes with GetAttr results in a runtime error.

If **fName** is not empty, and does not contain the special directory entries (. or ..), VBA executes line 21, which calls the **ShowFileAttr** procedure from Listing 12.1 to display a message box showing the filename and its actual attributes. VBA then executes line 22, which starts the count of found files by assigning 1 to **fCount**.

Now that the first matching file has been found, you must use the second-stage format of the Dir function to find the remaining files in the directory. Lines 25 through 32 contain a Do loop that executes for as long as **fName** does not contain an empty string. If at least one matching file was found in the Dir function call in line 18, then this loop will execute at least once.

Pay special attention to line 26. This statement calls the Dir function again, without any arguments. When you call Dir like this, VBA assumes that you want to find more files matching the specification for the pathname and attributes arguments you used last time you called Dir. The Dir function returns the next file in the directory that matches the previous filename and attribute specifications. If there are no more files, Dir returns an empty string.

Lines 27 through 31 contain an If...Then statement identical to the one in lines 19 through 23. If the string in **fName** is not empty, and does not contain the special directory entries (. and ..), VBA executes line 29 to call the **ShowFileAttr** procedure, and line 30 to increment the count of found files.

When all the matching files in the directory have been found, Dir returns an empty string, and the loop stops executing. Line 34 displays a message dialog box indicating how many matching files were found.

DO	**DON'T**
DO remember that VBA in Excel 7, Access 7, and any VBA host application designed for Windows 95 recognizes, and can use, Windows 95 long filenames.	

Working with Disk Drives and Directories

This section shows you how to use VBA's functions and statements to retrieve the current disk drive and directory, how to change the current drive or directory, and how to create or remove subdirectories. Remember, the *current drive* is the drive that Windows 95, and—by extension— Excel uses when you don't otherwise indicate a specific drive letter. Similarly, the *current directory* is the disk directory that Windows 95 uses if you don't specify a particular directory.

Getting the Current Directory Path and Drive Letter

Retrieving the current disk drive and directory path is quite simple. You get both pieces of information by using the `CurDir` function. `CurDir` returns a string that contains the full pathname for the current directory, including the drive letter.

`CurDir` has this general syntax:

`CurDir[(drive)]`

drive represents any String expression, and tells `CurDir` which disk drive's current directory you want. If you omit the *drive* argument, `CurDir` returns the current directory of the current disk drive. Usually, *drive* contains only a single letter; if you pass a string with more than one character in it, `CurDir` uses the first character in the string as the drive letter.

Listing 12.7 shows an example of the `CurDir` function.

Type

Listing 12.7. Using the `CurDir` function to obtain the current directory and drive.

```
1:  Sub ShowCurDriveDir()
2:  'displays current drive and directory
3:
4:      Dim DirName As String
5:      Dim DirLetter As String
6:
7:      DirName = CurDir()
8:      DirLetter = Left(DirName, 1)
9:      MsgBox "The current drive is: " & DirLetter
10:     MsgBox "The current directory is: " & DirName
11:
12:     DirName = CurDir("A")
13:     MsgBox "The current directory of drive A is: " & _
14:             DirName
15: End Sub
```

SAMS
PUBLISHING

Analysis This procedure just demonstrates how the CurDir function works. Lines 4 and 5 declare some variables for the procedure. **DirName** holds the result from the CurDir function, and **DirLetter** holds the drive letter extracted from the CurDir function's result.

Line 7 calls the CurDir function with no arguments, so that it returns the current directory of the current disk drive, and assigns its result to **DirName**. Line 8 uses the Left function to copy the first letter from **DirName**, and assigns it to **DirLetter**. Because CurDir returns the entire directory path, including the drive letter, the first character of the CurDir function result is always the drive letter. Lines 9 and 10 each display a message dialog box; the message displayed by line 9 states the current drive letter, and the message displayed by line 10 states the current directory of that drive.

Next, line 12 calls the CurDir function again, this time passing the single letter A as an argument. The argument tells CurDir to report the current directory of the disk in drive A:. (Be sure you have a disk in your drive A: when you execute this procedure, or you'll get a runtime error.) Finally, line 13 displays a message dialog box showing the current directory of drive A:.

Changing the Current Directory

If you want your VBA procedure to change the current directory to a different directory, use the ChDir statement. If you have experience using DOS, you'll recognize that VBA's ChDir fulfills the same purpose as the DOS CHDIR and CD commands.

Syntax The ChDir statement has the following general syntax:

ChDir *path*

path represents any String expression that results in a valid directory pathname. *path* may optionally contain a drive letter. If you do include a drive letter in the *path* argument, ChDir changes the current directory of the drive specified in *path* without changing the current drive. (To change the current drive, use the ChDrive statement described next.)

Listing 12.8 shows an example using the ChDir statement.

Listing 12.8. Using ChDir.

```
1:    Sub Demo_ChDir()
2:    'demonstrates the ChDir statement
3:
4:      Dim oldDir As String
5:
6:      MsgBox "Current directory: " & CurDir()
7:      oldDir = CurDir()
8:      ChDir "\excel"
9:      MsgBox "New directory: " & CurDir()
10:     ChDir oldDir
11:     MsgBox "Current directory: " & CurDir()
12:   End Sub
```

12

Analysis This procedure demonstrates the operation of the ChDir statement. Line 4 declares a String variable, **oldDir**, to store the current directory before it is changed. Line 6 uses MsgBox to display the current directory, and then line 7 stores the current directory (returned by CurDir) in the **oldDir** variable.

Line 8 uses the ChDir statement to change the current directory to the \EXCEL directory. (This procedure assumes that the \EXCEL directory is not the current directory, and that it is on the same disk drive as the current directory; if you enter this procedure, you'll probably want to choose your own directory name for this line.) Next, line 9 displays a message dialog box displaying the new current directory. Line 10 again uses the ChDir statement, this time to restore the original directory. Finally, line 11 displays another message dialog box to confirm that the current directory is back to the original directory.

DO	DON'T

DO save the current directory name in a variable so that you can restore that directory as the current directory.

Changing the Current Disk Drive

To change the current disk drive, you must use the ChDrive statement.

Syntax

The ChDrive statement has the following general syntax:

```
ChDrive drive
```

drive is any String expression that represents a disk drive letter. If *drive* contains more than one character, ChDrive uses only the first character in the string for the drive letter. If you specify an empty string for the *drive* argument, then the current drive doesn't change. If you specify a character other than one of the letters A through Z, VBA displays a runtime error. VBA also displays a runtime error if you specify a drive letter for a drive that does not actually exist on your computer system—although you can use drive letters of disks connected to your computer through a network.

Listing 12.9 demonstrates the use of the ChDrive statement.

Type

Listing 12.9. Using ChDrive to change the current disk drive.

```
1:   Sub Demo_ChDrive()
2:      Dim oldDir As String
3:
4:      oldDir = CurDir()
5:      MsgBox "The current directory is: " & oldDir
```

```
6:      ChDrive "A"
7:      MsgBox "The new drive and directory: " & CurDir()
8:      ChDrive oldDir
9:      ChDir oldDir
10:     MsgBox "The current directory is: " & CurDir()
11: End Sub
```

Line 2 declares a String variable, **oldDir**, to store the current directory. Line 4 calls the CurDir function and assigns its result to **oldDir**. Line 5 displays a message dialog box showing the current disk drive and directory, as returned by CurDir (and now stored in **oldDir**).

Line 6 uses the ChDrive statement to change the current disk drive to A:. (Make certain that there is a disk in drive A: before you run this procedure.) Line 7 displays another message dialog box, to confirm that the new current disk drive is drive A:.

Next, line 8 uses the ChDrive statement to restore the original disk drive as the current disk drive. Because CurDir always includes the drive letter in its return string, **oldDir** is used as the argument for ChDrive. ChDrive uses only the first letter of the string, which is the old current drive letter, and therefore restores the original disk drive as the current disk drive. To make certain that the original directory is also restored, line 9 uses the ChDir statement to restore the original directory as the current directory. Finally, line 10 displays another message dialog box to confirm that the current drive and directory are now restored.

Creating Disk Directories

Occasionally, you may want one of your procedures to create a new disk subdirectory to store new workbook files in, or for some other reason. To create a disk directory, use the MkDir statement. The MkDir statement fulfills the same purpose as the DOS MKDIR or MD commands, or the Windows 95's **F**ile | Ne**w** | **F**older command.

The MkDir statement has the following general syntax:

```
MkDir path
```

path represents any String expression that results in a valid directory pathname. *path* may optionally contain a drive letter. If you don't include a drive letter in the *path* argument, MkDir creates a new directory on the current disk drive. If *path* specifies a directory that already exists, or includes invalid filename characters, then VBA displays a runtime error. If you try to create a subdirectory in a directory that does not exist, VBA also displays a runtime error.

Listing 12.10 shows an example using the MkDir statement. Using MkDir does not change the current drive or directory.

Listing 12.10. Using MkDir to create a new disk directory.

```
1:    Sub Demo_MkDir()
2:    'demonstrates the MkDir statement
3:
4:      Dim newDir As String
6:
7:      newDir = "A:\test1"
8:      MkDir newDir
9:    ChDir newDir
10:     MsgBox "The current directory of A: is: " & _
11:            CurDir("A")
12:   End Sub
```

Analysis

Line 4 declares the **newDir** String type variable to hold the new directory name. Line 7 assigns the string A:\test1 to **newDir**, and then line 8 uses the MkDir statement to create the new directory (make sure you have a disk in drive A: when you run this procedure, or VBA displays a runtime error). After creating the new directory, line 9 changes the current directory on drive A: to the newly created directory, and the statement in lines 10 and 11 uses MsgBox to display the current directory of drive A:, verifying the creation of the new directory.

Removing Disk Directories

As well as creating new directories, you may occasionally want one of your procedures to remove a disk subdirectory. To remove a disk directory, use the RmDir statement. The RmDir statement fulfills the same purpose as the DOS RMDIR or RD commands (in Windows 95, you use the File | Delete command to delete both files and directories).

Syntax

The RmDir statement has the following general syntax:

RmDir *path*

path represents any String expression that results in a valid directory pathname. *path* may optionally contain a drive letter. If you don't include a drive letter in the *path* argument, RmDir removes the directory on the current disk drive. If *path* specifies a directory that does not already exist, or includes invalid filename characters, then VBA displays a runtime error.

Listing 12.11 shows an example using the RmDir statement.

Type

Listing 12.11. Using RmDir to remove a directory.

```
1:    Sub Demo_RmDir()
2:    'demonstrates the RmDir statement
3:
4:      Dim delDir As String
5:
6:      delDir = "A:\TEST1"
```

```
7:      If CurDir("A") = delDir Then ChDir "A:\"
8:      RmDir delDir
9:   End Sub
```

Analysis Line 4 declares a String type variable, **delDir**, to hold the name of the directory to remove. Line 6 assigns the directory name A:\TEST1 to **delDir** (this procedure assumes that you ran the procedure in Listing 12.10 to create the TEST1 directory on drive A:). Line 7 calls the CurDir function to determine the current directory for drive A:. If the current directory of drive A: is the same as the directory to be removed, then line 7 calls the ChDir function to change the current directory of drive A: to the root directory. You cannot remove a disk directory if it is the current directory or is not empty.

Next, line 8 uses the RmDir statement to remove the TEST1 subdirectory from the disk in drive A:.

DO	DON'T

DON'T try to remove a directory that contains files or other directories, or VBA will display a runtime error.

DO use the Dir function to determine whether or not a directory is empty before using RmDir, and use the Kill statement (described later in this chapter) to remove files from the directory. Use RmDir to remove any subdirectories from the directory you want to remove.

DON'T try to remove a directory if it is the current directory, or VBA will display a runtime error.

DO use the CurDir function to check whether or not the directory you want to remove is the current directory.

Copying and Deleting Files

Copying and deleting files are, perhaps, the two most common file management activities that most people perform. This section describes how you can copy or delete files under the control of your VBA procedures.

Copying a File

To copy a file, use the FileCopy statement. This VBA statement is equivalent to the DOS COPY command, or the Windows 95 **File | Copy** command.

The FileCopy statement has the following general syntax:

```
FileCopy source, destination
```

Both *source* and *destination* are String expressions that result in valid filenames. They may optionally include the full directory path and drive letter. If you try to copy a file onto itself, VBA displays a runtime error. VBA also displays a runtime error if you try to copy a file and there is not enough disk space to hold the copied file.

Listing 12.12. A procedure that uses the FileCopy statement.

```
 1:  Sub CopyFiles()
 2:  'copies a file selected by the user to a new name, drive
 3:  'or directory selected by the user.
 4:
 5:    Dim sName As String
 6:    Dim dName As String
 7:
 8:    Do
 9:      With Application
10:        sName = .GetOpenFilename(Title:= _
11:                            "File Copy - Source")
12:        If sName = "False" Then Exit Sub
13:        dName = .GetSaveAsFilename(Title:= _
14:                            "File Copy - Destination")
15:        If dName = "False" Then Exit Sub
16:      End With
17:      FileCopy source:=sName, destination:=dName
18:    Loop
19:  End Sub
```

Analysis

This procedure enables the user to select a file to copy, and then select the drive, directory, and filename to copy the file to. Lines 5 and 6 declare two String type variables to hold the source filename and the destination filename. Line 8 begins an infinite Do loop (a loop with no determinant condition). The loop in lines 8 through 18 executes until the user cancels one of the two file dialog boxes. Line 9 starts a With Application statement. Lines 10 and 11 contain a single statement that calls the GetOpenFilename method to display the file open dialog box, and assigns the filename (the method's result) to the **sName** variable.

Line 12 checks to see whether the user canceled the file opening dialog box. If so, the procedure exits. Otherwise, VBA continues on to execute the statement in lines 13 and 14, which uses the GetSaveAsFilename method to let the user select a filename, disk drive, and directory for the copied file. Line 15 checks to see whether the user canceled the file dialog box. If so, the procedure exits. Otherwise, VBA continues on to execute the FileCopy statement in line 17.

When VBA executes the FileCopy statement in line 17, it copies the file (whose name is stored in **sName**) to the new name, drive, and directory stored in **dName**. After copying the file, the Do loop repeats.

<table>
<tr><td>**DO**</td><td>**DON'T**</td></tr>
</table>

DON'T try to copy open workbook files, unless the workbook file was opened in Excel with a read-only status. Otherwise, VBA displays a runtime error.

DO determine whether an open workbook has read-only status by checking the value in the workbook's ReadOnly property. If the workbook's ReadOnly property is True, then it has read-only status.

Deleting a File

To delete a file, you use the dramatically named Kill statement. The Kill statement fulfills the same purpose as the DOS DEL command, or the Windows 95 **File** | **D**elete command.

Syntax

The general syntax of the Kill statement is:

```
Kill pathname
```

pathname is any String expression that results in a valid filename specification. *pathname* may include the drive letter, full directory path, and wildcard characters (* and ?). If *pathname* includes wildcard characters, Kill deletes *all* files that match the specification in *pathname*.

Listing 12.13 shows an example of the Kill statement in action.

Type

Listing 12.13. Using Kill to delete files.

```
1:   Sub DelFiles()
2:   'deletes files until user cancels file dialog box.
3:
4:     Dim fName As String
5:     Dim Ans As Integer
6:
7:     Do
8:       With Application
9:         fName = .GetOpenFilename(Title:="Delete File")
10:      End With
11:      If fName = "False" Then Exit Sub
12:      Ans = MsgBox(prompt:="Delete " & fName & "?", _
13:                   Title:="Delete File", _
14:                   Buttons:=vbQuestion + vbYesNo)
15:      If Ans = vbYes Then
16:        Kill fName
17:      End If
18:    Loop
19:  End Sub
```

12

Analysis This procedure uses the `GetOpenFilename` method to let the user select a filename, confirms the deletion, deletes the file, and then repeats. Line 4 declares a String type variable to store the filename, and line 5 declares an Integer type variable to store the user's response to the confirmation message dialog box.

Line 7 starts an infinite `Do` loop, which executes until the user cancels the file dialog box. Line 8 begins a `With` statement. Line 9 calls the `GetOpenFilename` method and assigns its result to `fName`. Line 11 checks to see if the user canceled the file dialog box and, if so, exits the procedure. Next, lines 12 through 14 contain a single `MsgBox` statement that asks the user to confirm deleting the selected file. If the user confirms the deletion, VBA executes the `Kill` statement in line 16, which deletes the file.

DO	DON'T

DON'T try to delete an open workbook file, or VBA displays a runtime error.

DO check a file's attributes before attempting to delete it. If you try to delete a file that has any of the Hidden, System, or Read-Only file attributes, VBA displays a runtime error. Use the `GetAttr` function to retrieve a file's attributes, and the `SetAttr` statement to change them, if you want to be able to delete files with the Hidden, System, or Read-Only file attributes.

Renaming or Moving Files

Occasionally, you may need to change the name of an existing file, or you may want to move the file to another directory on the same disk drive. To rename a file, or to move it to another directory, use the `Name` statement.

Syntax

The `Name` statement has the following general syntax:

```
Name oldpathname As newpathname
```

oldpathname and *newpathname* are String expressions that result in valid filenames. Both may optionally include the full directory path, including the drive letter. If you do include the drive letter, however, both *oldpathname* and *newpathname* must include the same drive letter, or VBA displays a runtime error. The filename in *newpathname* may not refer to a file that already exists, or VBA displays a runtime error. If *oldpathname* and *newpathname* refer to different directories, VBA moves the file to the new directory, and changes its name, if necessary.

Listing 12.14 shows a procedure that uses the `Name` statement to rename files.

Listing 12.14. Using `Name` to rename or move files.

```
1:  Sub RenameOrMoveFile()
2:  'renames or moves a disk file
3:
4:      Const iTitle = "Rename Or Move - "
5:      Dim oldName As String
6:      Dim newName As String
7:      Dim oldDir As String
8:
9:      oldDir = CurDir()
10:     With Application
11:       oldName = .GetOpenFilename(Title:=iTitle & "Source")
12:       If oldName = "False" Then Exit Sub
13:
14:       newName = .GetSaveAsFilename(InitialFilename:=oldName, _
15:                                    Title:=iTitle & "New Name")
16:       If newName = "False" Then Exit Sub
17:     End With
18:
19:     If Left(oldName, 1) = Left(newName, 1) Then
20:       Name oldName As newName
21:     Else
22:       FileCopy oldName, newName
23:       Kill oldName
24:     End If
25:
26:     ChDrive oldDir
27:     ChDir oldDir
28: End Sub
```

Analysis

This procedure renames or moves a file. The procedure's user selects the filename, directory, and disk drive for both the original file and for the file's new name and/or location. Line 4 declares a string constant to supply the titles for dialog boxes displayed by this procedure. Lines 5 through 7 declare the variables that this procedure uses. **oldName** is used to hold the file's old name, **newName** is for the file's new name, and **oldDir** is used to hold the name of the current drive and directory at the time this procedure starts, and to restore it when the procedure is complete.

Line 9 calls the CurDir function and stores its result in **oldDir**. Line 10 begins a With statement for the Application object. Line 11 uses the GetOpenFilename method to let the user select a file to rename or move. Line 12 uses an If statement to check whether the user canceled the GetOpenFilename dialog box; if so, the procedure exits.

Next, line 14 calls the GetSaveAsFilename method to let the user select the new filename, drive, and directory. Notice that this call to GetSaveAsFilename uses the InitialFilename argument to fill in the suggested new filename. Line 16 checks to see if the user canceled this dialog box and exits the procedure if he or she did.

Line 19 starts an If...Then...Else statement that evaluates whether or not the user selected a different drive to move the file to. The logical expression for the If statement in line 19 uses the Left function to return the first letter of both the **oldName** and the **newName** strings. If the two letters are the same, the user is renaming or moving the file on the same disk drive, and VBA executes the Name statement in line 20 to rename the file. If the directory paths in **oldName** and **newName** are different, Name moves the file to the new directory.

If the first letter of **oldName** and **newName** is different, then the user elected to move the file to a different disk drive. You cannot use Name to move files to another disk drive, so this procedure uses FileCopy to copy the file to the other disk drive, and then uses Kill to delete the original file.

Finally, the ChDrive and ChDir statements restore the original disk drive and directory that were current when this procedure started. (Remember, the GetOpenFilename and GetSaveAsFilename methods may change the current drive and directory.)

DO	DON'T

DON'T confuse the Name *statement* with the Name *property* that many objects have. The Name statement renames files, the Name property of an object stores that object's name.

DON'T try to move a file from one disk to another by using the Name statement.

DO move a file from one disk to another by copying the file with FileCopy, and then delete the source file with Kill, as shown in Listing 12.14.

DON'T try to rename an open file. If you do, VBA displays a runtime error. You must close open workbook files before renaming them.

Getting Information about Files

Sometimes, knowing the size of a file, or the date and time that a file was last modified, is important. If you have a procedure that backs up your workbook files, for example, you may want to program that procedure so that it checks to make sure that it is not replacing a more recent file with an older version.

Getting a File's Time and Date Stamp

Any time you, or one of your application programs like Excel, changes a disk file, the Windows 95 file system records the date and time—according to your computer's clock—with the file, so that you can tell when a file was last modified. To make this information available in your

VBA procedures, use the `FileDateTime` function. This function returns the date and time information from the file as a VBA Date type value.

The general syntax for the `FileDateTime` function is:

```
FileDateTime(pathname)
```

pathname is any String expression that results in a valid filename specification. *pathname* may optionally include the drive letter and full directory path but may not contain wildcard characters (* or ?).

Listing 12.15, in the next section, shows an example using the `FileDateTime` function.

Getting the Length of a File

To find out how big a file is, use the `FileLen` function. `FileLen` returns the length of a file in bytes.

The `FileLen` function has the following syntax:

```
FileLen(pathname)
```

pathname is any String expression that results in a valid filename specification. *pathname* may optionally include the drive letter and full directory path but may not contain wildcard characters. If *pathname* specifies an open workbook file, `FileLen` returns the size of the workbook the last time it was saved to disk.

Listing 12.15 shows an example using the `FileLen` function.

Type

Listing 12.15. Using the `FileDateTime` and `FileLen` functions.

```
 1:  Sub ShowFileDateSize(fName As String)
 2:  'displays the size and date a file was last changed.
 3:
 4:    Dim msg1 As String
 5:    Dim msg2 As String
 6:    Dim fDate As Date
 7:    Dim fLen As Long
 8:
 9:    fDate = FileDateTime(fName)
10:    fLen = FileLen(fName)
11:    msg1 = "Size: " & Format(fLen, "###,###,###") & _
12:           " bytes."
13:    msg2 = "Last modified: " & _
14:           Format(fDate, "long date") & _
15:           " at " & Format(fDate, "long time")
16:    MsgBox Title:="File Date and Size", _
17:           prompt:=fName & Chr(13) & _
18:           msg1 & Chr(13) & msg2
19:  End Sub
20:
```

continues

Listing 12.15. continued

```
21:  Sub Test_ShowFileDateSize()
22:    Dim sName As String
23:
24:    Do
25:      With Application
26:        sName = .GetOpenFilename(Title:="File Date/Size")
27:      End With
28:      If sName <> "False" Then ShowFileDateSize sName
29:    Loop Until sName = "False"
30:  End Sub
```

The **ShowFileDateSize** procedure uses the `FileLen` and the `FileDateTime` functions to display a message dialog box showing the current size of a file, and the date and time that the file was last modified. **ShowFileDateSize** has a single String type argument, **fName**, used to tell **ShowFileDateSize** which file's information to display.

Lines 4 through 7 declare several variables for this procedure. The first two variables, **msg1** and **msg2** are used to assemble the message text that this procedure displays. **fDate** and **fLen** are used to store the date and time information and the file size information, respectively. Notice that **fLen** is a Long data type, because a file's length may run into millions of bytes.

Line 9 calls the `FileDateTime` function, using **fName** to specify the filename argument, and stores the function's result in **fDate**. Next, line 10 calls the `FileLen` function, also using **fName** to specify the filename argument and stores this function's result in **fLen**.

Next, lines 11 through 12 contain a single statement that assembles the first part of the message that this procedure displays and stores it in **msg1**. Lines 13 through 15 contain a single statement that assembles the second part of the message that this procedure displays and stores it in **msg2**. Finally, the `MsgBox` statement in lines 16 through 18 displays the file's name, the size of the file, and the data and time the file was last modified.

Lines 21 through 30 contain a procedure that tests the **ShowFileDateSize** procedure. This procedure uses the `GetOpenFilename` method to let you select a file, and then calls the **ShowFileDateSize** procedure. The **ShowFileDateSize** procedure produces a dialog box similar to the one shown in Figure 12.4.

Figure 12.4.

The **ShowFileDateSize** *procedure uses the* `FileLen` *and* `FileDateTime` *functions to gather information about a file's size and the date and time it was last modified.*

Summary

In today's lesson, you learned how to use VBA's built-in functions and statements to perform all the file management tasks available in VBA. You also learned how to use the `GetOpenFilename` and `GetSaveAsFilename` methods to display Excel's File Open and File Save As dialog boxes from your own procedures.

You learned how to search a directory for a single filename, or several filenames. You learned how to find out what the current disk drive and directory are, and how to change the current directory or drive. This chapter taught you how to use VBA to create or remove disk directories, and how to copy, rename, move, or delete a file. Finally, this chapter showed you how to get the date and time that a file was last modified, and how to retrieve the file's length.

Q&A

Q How can I find out how much free space there is on a disk before I copy a file to it, so I don't get a runtime error if the disk is full?

A Unfortunately, VBA does not provide any way to find out how much free space is on a disk drive. If you want to avoid runtime errors when copying files (or using any of VBA's disk or other statements), use the error-handling features described in Day 17.

Q In the Object Browser and online Help, I notice there's another file-related method, `FindFile`. What does this method do, and how do I use it?

A The `FindFile` method opens the same dialog box as the Excel **F**ile | **O**pen command. When the user selects a file name, Excel opens that file. The `FindFile` method has no arguments; it returns `True` if a file was successfully opened, or `False` if the user canceled the dialog box. You can't control the `FindFile` dialog box from your procedure—it works the same as if you opened it by choosing the Excel **F**ile | **O**pen command. Because you can't control the `FindFile` dialog box from your procedure, the `FindFile` method's usefulness is fairly limited.

You can use the `FindFile` dialog box to allow your procedure's user to search for, preview, and open workbooks, but you can't get any information about what files the user searches for or previews. As soon as the user either cancels the `FileFind` dialog box or opens a workbook, your procedure continues execution. To use the `FindFile` method in a procedure, call it with a statement like the following (you must specify the `Application` object reference):

```
Application.FindFile
```

Workshop

Answers are in Appendix A.

Quiz

1. What are the seven different attributes that a disk file may have?
2. When a file has more than one attribute, how are the attributes combined into a single number?
3. Which function do you use to get a file's attributes? What is the function's result?
4. Can you use `SetAttr` to give a file the Directory or Volume Label attributes?
5. What do the `GetOpenFilename` and `GetSaveAsFilename` methods do?
6. How do you use the `Dir` function to find more than one file in a directory?
7. How do you find out the current disk drive and directory?
8. Which VBA statement would you use to copy a file?
9. Which VBA statement would you use to move a file from one directory to another on the same disk drive? Can you use the same statement to move a file to a different disk drive?

Exercises

1. **BUG BUSTER:** The following two code fragments each produce a runtime error. Can you spot what's wrong? (Assume that **fName** is a string variable.)

   (A)

   ```
   fName = GetOpenFilename
   ```

   (B)
   ```
   With Application
       fName = GetSaveAsFilename
   End With
   ```

2. **BUG BUSTER:** The following statement will produce a runtime error. Why?

   ```
   Name "C:\EXAMPLES\SALES.XLS" As "A:\SALES.XLS"
   ```

3. Using the **IsDiskFile** function in Listing 12.5 as a model, write a Boolean function named **IsDiskDirectory** that returns `True` if a specified disk directory exists, `False` if it does not.

4. Write a procedure that uses the InputBox function to get a directory name from the user and then changes the current directory to the directory entered by the user. Use the **IsDiskDirectory** function you wrote in Exercise 3 to test whether the directory exists before you try making it the current directory. If the directory does not exist, your procedure should ask whether or not to create it. Be sure to handle the situation correctly if the user cancels the input dialog box.

12

Arrays

This chapter teaches you about arrays. Arrays are a common and useful way of storing many different pieces of related data. Arrays are useful in creating sorted or unsorted lists of data, storing tables of information, and for many other tasks. You can access information stored in an array in any order. In today's lesson, you'll learn what an array is and how to:

- [ ] Declare arrays using the `Dim` statement.
- [ ] Use arrays in your VBA procedures.
- [ ] Get information about an array with the `IsArray`, `LBound`, and `UBound` functions.
- [ ] Perform operations on every element in an array using the `For...Each` loop structure.
- [ ] Redimension arrays using the `ReDim` statement.
- [ ] Clear and remove arrays using the `Erase` statement.
- [ ] Pass arrays as arguments to procedures or functions.
- [ ] Sort an array into a particular order.
- [ ] Search the elements in an array to find a particular item in the array.

Understanding Arrays

An *array* is a collection of variables that share the same name and basic data type. Like the user-defined data types that you learned about in Day 10, an array is a convenient way of storing several related data items together in a single container for greater programming convenience and efficiency. Unlike user-defined data types, however, every data item stored in an array must have the same data type—for example, if you create an array to store Integer data types, then all data items stored in that array must be integer numbers.

Arrays are typically used to represent lists or tables of information, where all of the entries in the list or table are the same type of data—that is, the list contains only Double numbers, Strings, Currency values, and so on. An array allows you to store and manipulate many data items through a single variable. In addition to reducing the total number of different variable names you must keep track of, another primary advantage of using arrays is that you can use loops to easily process the various elements of arrays. By combining arrays and looping structures (typically `For...Next` or `For...Each`), you can write a few statements that process a large amount of data. Performing the same tasks using separate variables might require hundreds of statements.

Understanding Single-Dimensional Arrays

The least complex array is simply a list of data items; this kind of array is called a *simple* or *single-dimensional* array. Single-dimensional arrays get their name from the fact that a list of data is like a line drawn on a sheet of paper; the list has only one dimension—length—and is therefore single-dimensional.

Figure 13.1 shows a diagram of a single-dimensional array. Each data item stored in an array is called an *element* of the array. The array in Figure 13.1 has ten elements in it; each element stores a Double type number. Notice that the elements in the array are numbered from 0 to 9, for a total of 10 elements. (This kind of numbering system is common in computer programming, and is called *zero-based* numbering.)

Figure 13.1.

A single-dimensional numeric array; single-dimensional arrays are essentially just lists of data of the same type.

Single-Dimensional Array

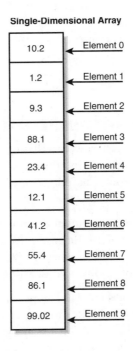

To access data stored in a particular array element, you specify the name of the array, followed by the number—called the *subscript* or *index*—of the element whose contents you want to retrieve or alter. The subscript must always be enclosed in parentheses. For example, if the array in Figure 13.1 is named **NumArray**, then the following statement assigns the number 55.4 to the variable **AnyNum**:

```
AnyNum = NumArray(7)
```

In this statement, the number 7 is the array subscript; notice that it is enclosed by parentheses, and is *not* separated with any spaces from the array's name. Because element numbering starts with 0, the element that this statement references is actually the 8th element of **NumArray**.

Look at Figure 13.1 again, and notice that the array element numbered 7 contains the value 55.4. When VBA executes the preceding statement, it retrieves the value 55.4 from the specified array element and stores that value in the **AnyNum** variable, just like any other variable assignment.

13

You also use a subscript whenever you want to store data in a particular array element. The next statement, for example, stores the number 12 in the 8th element of the array shown in Figure 13.1:

```
NumArray(7) = 12
```

When VBA executes this statement, it puts the value 12 into the specified array element, replacing the previous contents of that element—again, just like any other variable assignment. You can use an array element in any VBA expression the same way you would use any constant or variable value in an expression.

Mostly, you'll use single-dimensional arrays to represent various and different lists of data values.

Understanding Multi-Dimensional Arrays

Single-dimensional arrays work well to represent simple lists of data. Frequently, however, you'll need to represent tables of information in your programs, with the data organized in a row and column format—sort of like the cells in an Excel worksheet. To do so, you'll need to use a *multi-dimensional* array.

Figure 13.2 shows a diagram of the most common form of multi-dimensional array—a two-dimensional array. Multi-dimensional arrays get their name because they have more than one dimension—length (the number of rows in the array), width (the number of columns in the array), and even other dimensions, as you'll see later in this section.

The two-dimensional array in Figure 13.2 has two columns (numbered 0 and 1) and 10 rows (numbered 0 through 9) for a total of 20 elements. Like single-dimensional arrays, you access elements in a multi-dimensional array by *subscripting* the array—that is, you use the numbers of the column and row to specify a particular element in the array. Subscripting a two-dimensional array is a lot like specifying a cell in an Excel worksheet; the first dimension of the array corresponds to the worksheet's columns, and the second dimension of the array corresponds to the worksheet's rows.

If the array in Figure 13.2 is named **NumTable**, then the following statement assigns the value 10.2 (from the first row in the 2nd column of the array) to the variable **AnyNum**:

```
AnyNum = NumTable(1, 0)
```

Similarly, the following statement stores the value 2.5 in the second row of the 1st column of the array:

```
NumTable(0, 1) = 2.5
```

In both of the preceding statements, notice that the subscripts to the array are enclosed in parentheses, and that the column and row coordinates are separated by commas.

Figure 13.2.

A two-dimensional numeric array; two-dimensional arrays are typically used to represent tables of data in a row and column format.

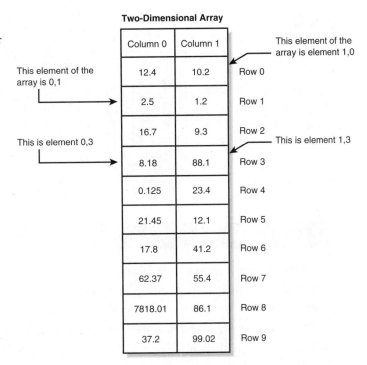

Arrays can have more than two dimensions. Figure 13.3 shows a three-dimensional array; this array has length, width, and height (so to speak). You can think of the elements in a three-dimensional array as being like a bunch of boxes stacked so many boxes wide, so many boxes deep, and so many boxes high. Another way to think of a three-dimensional array is as a series of pages in a book, with each page containing a table with the same number of rows and columns. Figure 13.3 shows an array with three "pages" (numbered 0 through 2); each page contains a table with two columns and ten rows. The subscripts for each array element are written into the element boxes in the figure.

You can also create arrays with more than three dimensions—in fact, VBA allows you to create arrays with up to 60 dimensions. Working with arrays with four or more dimensions quickly becomes rather mind-boggling—fortunately, you'll probably never have to. Mostly, you'll use single- and two-dimensional arrays in your programming. You'll seldom need to use arrays more complex than a list or table of data, so don't worry too much about arrays with more than two-dimensions—although you may occasionally use a three-dimensional array, the need for such complex arrays is small.

Figure 13.3.

A three-dimensional array,
used to represent pages of
tables; you don't usually
have to use arrays with more
than two dimensions.

Three-Dimensional Array

0	
Column 0	Column 1
Element 0,0,0	Element 0,1,0
Element 0,0,1	Element 0,1,1
Element 0,0,2	Element 0,1,2
Element 0,0,3	Element 0,1,3
Element 0,0,4	Element 0,1,4

1	
Column 0	Column 1
Element 1,0,0	Element 1,1,0
Element 1,0,1	Element 1,1,1
Element 1,0,2	Element 1,1,2
Element 1,0,3	Element 1,1,3
Element 1,0,4	Element 1,1,4

2	
Column 0	Column 1
Element 2,0,0	Element 2,1,0
Element 2,0,1	Element 2,1,1
Element 2,0,2	Element 2,1,2
Element 2,0,3	Element 2,1,3
Element 2,0,4	Element 2,1,4

DO	DON'T

DO remember to include the parentheses around an array's subscript.

DON'T separate the array's subscript value from the array's name—type both the array name, the parentheses, and the subscript value as one word in your VBA code.

DO remember to separate the subscripts for a multi-dimensional array with commas.

DO use integer numbers (whole numbers without a decimal fraction) for an array's subscripts.

Static and Dynamic Arrays

Usually, when you declare an array, you specify how many elements are in the array. As you'll learn in the next section of this lesson, you specify the number of elements in an array when you declare the array. The array declaration tells VBA how large the array's various dimensions are. Once you've declared the array, VBA allocates enough memory for all of the array's elements. For the array in Figure 13.1, VBA would allocate enough memory for 10 integers; for the array in Figure 13.2, VBA would allocate enough memory for 20 integers, and so on.

Note: Array variables are subject to the same scope and persistence rules as any other variable. Variable scope and persistence was explained in Day 3 and Day 10.

VBA keeps memory for all of the elements in the array reserved for as long as the array variable exists. Arrays like this are called *static* arrays, because the number of elements in the array doesn't change.

Sometimes, choosing the size of an array is difficult if you're not sure how much data is going to go into an array, or if the amount of data collected for an array varies greatly. If you sometimes have 100 values to store, and other times only have 10 values, you're potentially wasting the space required to store 90 values (the difference between the largest number of values and the smallest number).

For situations like this, VBA supports a special type of array, called a *dynamic* array. Dynamic arrays get their name because you can change the number of elements in the array as your VBA program executes. A dynamic array (combined with the right programming) can grow or shrink to accommodate exactly the required number of elements, without any wasted space. To change the size of a dynamic array, use the ReDim statement, described later in this lesson.

Now that you're acquainted with how arrays store data, you're ready to learn how to declare and use arrays, as described in the rest of this lesson.

The *Option Base* Statement

So far, you've seen arrays with zero-based numbering. In zero-based numbering, the subscript for the first element in any dimension of an array is 0; an array with 10 elements therefore has subscripts 0 through 9. Obviously, zero-based numbering can be confusing because the subscript 0 really indicates the 1st element in an array, the subscript 5 really indicates the 6th element of the array, and so on.

It would be much more convenient if an array's elements were numbered starting with 1, instead of 0. If an array's subscript numbering started at 1, then the subscript 1 would indicate the 1st element of the array, the subscript 5 would indicate the 5th element, and so on.

Fortunately, VBA does allow you to specify the starting number for an array's elements. You can either specify the low number for an array's subscripts when you declare the array (described later in this lesson), or use the Option Base compiler directive to specify whether you want array subscript numbering to start at 0 or 1.

13

Syntax

The general syntax for the Option Base compiler directive is:

```
Option Base 0 ¦ 1
```

The Option Base statement allows you to specify 0 or 1 as the default starting number for array subscripts. If you don't use the Option Base statement, then VBA starts array subscript numbering at 0 (the default). You must place the Option Base statement in the declaration area of a module, before any variable, constant, or procedure declarations. You can't place the Option Base statement inside a procedure.

The next two statements show examples of the Option Base compiler directive:

```
Option Base 0    ' the default setting
Option Base 1    ' array subscripts start with 1
```

> **Note:** You can only have a single Option Base statement in a module; the Option Base statement affects all of the arrays declared in a module, whether they are local to a procedure or declared at the module level.

Declaring Arrays

By now, you're familiar with the Dim statement used to declare variables. As you might expect, you also use the Dim statement to declare arrays. In fact, you may recall that the Dim keyword is an abbreviation for *dimension*. In the original BASIC programming language, the Dim keyword was used exclusively for *dimensioning* arrays, hence the abbreviation. Modern VBA has extended the Dim keyword for use with all variables, however. You can declare both single- and multi-dimensional arrays with Dim.

The general syntax for declaring an array with the Dim statement is:

```
Dim VarName([Subscripts])[As Type]
```

VarName represents any name for the array that meets VBA's rules for identifier names. The Subscripts clause represents the dimension(s) of the array. You may declare arrays with up to 60 dimensions. For a single-dimensional array, include one Subscripts clause; for a two-dimensional array, include two Subscripts clauses (separated by a comma), and so on, for as many dimensions as you want your array to have. Each Subscripts clause adds a new dimension to the array.

> **Note:** You can also declare static and dynamic arrays using the Public, Private, and Static keywords, just as you would any other variable—and with the same effects on the array's scope and persistence. Use the array declaration syntax shown here, and simply substitute the Public, Private, or Static keywords for the Dim keyword, as desired.

The Subscripts clause has this syntax:

```
[lower To] upper [,[lower To] upper] . . .
```

lower specifies the lower range of valid subscripts for the array. upper specifies the upper limit for the array's subscripts. Notice that only the upper limit is required; the lower To portion of the Subscripts clause is optional. If you specify only the upper limit, then VBA numbers the array's elements depending on the Option Base setting. If Option Base 1 is in effect, VBA

numbers the elements in the array from 1 to *upper*; otherwise VBA numbers the array elements from 0 to *upper*.

Including the *lower* To portion of the *Subscripts* clause can help make your code easier to understand and can help reveal programmer mistakes so that you can write more reliable programs. Including the *lower* To portion of the *Subscripts* clause also enables you to specify a starting subscript for an array other than 0 or 1. For example, you may want to create an array with elements numbered 5 through 10, or -5 through 0, depending on the specific job you're trying to accomplish.

Like standard variable declarations, you can declare a specific data type for an array by including the As *type* clause in the declaration. Every element in the array will have the data type you specify. *type* represents any valid VBA data type—Currency, Double, String, and so on. You can also declare arrays of a user-defined data type. If you omit *type*, all of the elements in the array have the Variant type. VBA initializes the elements of numeric arrays with zeros and the elements of string arrays with empty strings.

Notice that the *Subscripts* clause is optional. To create a dynamic array, omit the *Subscripts* clause altogether (you must include the parentheses in the array declaration, whether or not you specify *Subscripts*).

The following examples are all valid array declarations:

```
Dim January(1 To 31) As String
Dim January(31) As String    'assumes Option Base 1
Dim MailingList() As MailData    'dynamic array of user-defined type
Dim Grab_Bag()    'dynamic array of Variants
Dim LookupTable(2, 10)    'assumes Option Base 1
Dim HexMultiplication(0 To 15, 0 To 15) As String
Dim LookupBook(1 To 3, 1 To 2, 1 To 10)
```

In these examples, notice that (if Option Base 1 is selected) the first two statements declare identical arrays—both are single-dimensional, and both have 31 elements subscripted 1 through 31. The third array declaration (for MailingList) has a user-defined type as the data type of the array's elements. (User-defined data types were described in Day 10.) Both the third and fourth array declarations above omit the subscripts from the declaration—they are dynamic arrays. The fifth and sixth examples declare two-dimensional arrays, and the final example declaration declares a three-dimensional array.

13

DO / DON'T

DO remember that including the *Subscripts* clause in an array declaration creates a static array with a fixed number of elements.

DO remember that omitting the *Subscripts* clause in an array declaration creates a dynamic array.

> **DO** keep in mind that the `Option Base` setting can affect the total number of elements in an array. Consider the following declaration:
>
> ```
> Dim NumArray(10)
> ```
>
> If `Option Base` is 1, then this array's elements are subscripted with the numbers 1 through 10, for a total of ten elements. If, however, there is no `Option Base` statement, or `Option Base` is set to 0, this array's elements are subscripted with the numbers 0 through 10, for a total of *eleven* elements.

Using Arrays

Once you've declared an array, using it in your VBA code is straightforward. As explained at the beginning of this lesson, to access an element of an array you state the name of the array followed by a subscript value enclosed in parentheses.

Syntax

The general syntax for accessing an array element is:

```
arrayName(validIndex1, [validIndex2]...)
```

arrayName represents the name of an array. *validIndex1* represents a valid subscript value for the first dimension of the array. *validIndex2* represents a valid subscript value for the second dimension of the array, if there is one. You must supply a subscript value for every dimension in the array, every time you access an element in the array. For a two-dimensional array, for example, you must always specify two subscripts. A valid subscript is any VBA variable or expression that results in an integer number that falls within the range of the array's declared dimensions. For example, a valid subscript value for a single-dimensional array declared with subscripts from 1 to 10 could be any VBA expression that results in an integer number from 1 to 10. Using a subscript lower or higher than the range for a particular dimension in an array causes VBA to display a runtime error.

The following code fragment shows a typical array declaration and usage:

```
Dim Factorial(0 To 30) As Double
Factorial(0) = 1
For I = 1 To 30
    Factorial(I) = I * Factorial(I - 1)
Next I
```

Listing 13.1 shows the **DemoStaticArray** procedure, which declares and uses a numeric array to gather and subsequently process a group of numbers. As you study Listing 13.1, notice that it contains an entire module, including the compiler directives, module-level constant declarations, and two complete procedures.

When you execute the **DemoStaticArray** procedure, it first prompts you to enter a number specifying how many numbers the procedure should collect for processing. (**DemoStaticArray** requires you to enter a number between 3 and 15). Next, **DemoStaticArray** prompts you to enter the specified number of numeric values, storing each value you enter in an element of the array. After you've entered all the values, **DemoStaticArray** displays the values you entered on a worksheet—the worksheet display is for reference only, all data entry and data processing is based on the contents of the array. Finally, **DemoStaticArray** asks you to specify a range of array elements (such as the 1st through 15th numbers in the list, or the 2nd through 8th numbers in the list) for which **DemoStaticArray** will calculate the sum and average. **DemoStaticArray** first asks you for the low limit of the range, and then asks for the high limit of the range. After getting the range, **DemoStaticArray** adds together all of the numbers in the range, and displays both their sum and average.

Listing 13.1. The **DemoStaticArray** procedure declares and uses a static numeric array.

```
1:   Option Explicit
2:   Option Base 1
3:
4:   'Listing 13.1. The DemoStaticArray procedure, which declares
5:   '  and uses a static numeric array.
6:
7:   'maximum array elements
8:   Const ARRAY_MAX As Integer = 15
9:
10:  'minimum numbers to be entered
11:  Const ARRAY_MIN As Integer = 3
12:
13:  Sub DemoStaticArray()
14:     'declare single-dimensional array
15:     Dim NumArray(ARRAY_MAX) As Double
16:     Dim aSum As Double      'for sum of numbers
17:     Dim Count As Integer    'loop counter
18:     Dim NumCnt As Integer   'for count of numbers
19:     Dim cLow As Integer     'low limit for sum
20:     Dim cHigh As Integer    'high limit for sum
21:     Dim mStr As String      'message string
22:     Dim pStr As String      'prompt string
23:     Dim tRsp As String      'for input box responses
24:     Dim CR As String * 1    'for carriage-return
25:     Dim oldSheet As String  'original sheet name
26:
27:     'set up a carriage-return character
28:     CR = Chr$(13)
29:
30:     'preserve original sheet name
31:     oldSheet = ActiveWorkbook.ActiveSheet.Name
32:
33:     'select a new sheet
34:     ActiveWorkbook.Sheets("Sheet1").Select
```

continues

Listing 13.1. continued

```
35:
36:     'clear the worksheet cells for later display
37:     'of the array's contents
38:     For Count = 1 To (ARRAY_MAX + 2)
39:       Cells(Count, 1).Value = ""
40:       Cells(Count, 2).Value = ""
41:     Next Count
42:
43:     'prompt for number of values to be entered;
44:     'requires a minimum of ARRAY_MIN numbers
45:     Do
46:       pStr = "Type the number of values to enter (" & _
47:               ARRAY_MIN & " To" & _
48:               Str(ARRAY_MAX) & ") "
49:       tRsp = InputBox(prompt:=pStr, _
50:                        Title:="Integer Input", _
51:                        default:=ARRAY_MAX)
52:       If Len(Trim(tRsp)) = 0 Then
53:         CancelDemo cMsg:="Array sizing canceled.", _
54:                     rSheet:=oldSheet
55:       Else
56:         NumCnt = CInt(tRsp)
57:       End If
58:
59:       If (NumCnt < ARRAY_MIN) Or (NumCnt > ARRAY_MAX) Then
60:         MsgBox "Please enter a number between " & _
61:               ARRAY_MIN & " and " & ARRAY_MAX
62:       End If
63:     Loop Until (NumCnt >= ARRAY_MIN) And (NumCnt <= ARRAY_MAX)
64:
65:     'enter values into the array
66:     For Count = 1 To NumCnt
67:       pStr = "Enter value number " & Count
68:
69:       'get a value
70:       tRsp = InputBox(prompt:=pStr, _
71:                        Title:="Numeric Input", _
72:                        default:=Count)
73:       'check for cancellation
74:       If Len(Trim(tRsp)) = 0 Then
75:         CancelDemo cMsg:="Data entry canceled", _
76:                     rSheet:=oldSheet
77:       Else
78:         'store each value in a member of array NumArray
79:         NumArray(Count) = CDbl(tRsp)
80:       End If
81:     Next Count
82:
83:     'display the elements of NumArray on the worksheet
84:     For Count = 1 To NumCnt
85:       Cells(Count, 1).Value = "Value(" & Count & ")"
86:       Cells(Count, 2).Value = NumArray(Count)
87:     Next Count
88:
```

```
89:     'query repetitively for the range of elements in the
90:     'array for which to calculate the sum and average
91:     Do
92:       'get the low subscript of the elements to add
93:       Do
94:         tRsp = InputBox(prompt:="Enter subscript for " & _
95:                         "the low end of range to add:", _
96:                         Title:="Integer Input", _
97:                         default:="1")
98:         If Len(Trim(tRsp)) = 0 Then
99:           cLow = 0
100:        Else
101:          cLow = CInt(tRsp)
102:        End If
103:
104:        If (cLow < 1) Or (cLow >= NumCnt) Then
105:          MsgBox prompt:="You must enter a number " & _
106:                          "between 1 and " & (NumCnt - 1)
107:        End If
108:      Loop Until (cLow >= 1) And (cLow < NumCnt)
109:
110:      'get the high subscript of the elements to add
111:      Do
112:        tRsp = InputBox(prompt:="Enter subscript for " & _
113:                        "the high end of range to add:", _
114:                        Title:="Integer Input", _
115:                        default:=NumCnt)
116:        If Len(Trim(tRsp)) = 0 Then
117:          cHigh = 0
118:        Else
119:          cHigh = CInt(tRsp)
120:        End If
121:
122:        If (cHigh <= cLow) Or (cHigh > NumCnt) Then
123:          MsgBox prompt:="You must enter a number " & _
124:                          "between " & (cLow + 1) & _
125:                          " and " & NumCnt
126:        End If
127:      Loop Until (cHigh > cLow) And (cHigh <= NumCnt)
128:
129:      'add the elements of NumArray together, starting from
130:      'NumArray(cLow) to NumArray(cHigh)
131:
132:      'initialize the sum to 0, then loop through array
133:      'to compute the sum for the specified range
134:      aSum = 0
135:      For Count = cLow To cHigh
136:        aSum = aSum + NumArray(Count)
137:      Next Count
138:
139:      'display the results of the sum and average
140:      mStr = "Sum of NumArray(" & cLow & ") to NumArray(" & _
141:              cHigh & ") = " & aSum & CR
142:      mStr = mStr & "Mean of NumArray(" & cLow & _
143:              ") to NumArray(" & cHigh & ") = " & _
```

continues

Listing 13.1. continued

```
144:                 (aSum / (cHigh  cLow + 1)) & _
145:              CR & CR & "Add another set of values?"
146:    Count = MsgBox(prompt:=mStr, _
147:                      Buttons:=vbInformation + vbYesNo, _
148:                      Title:="Output")
149:    Loop Until Count = vbNo
150:
151:    'restore original sheet
152:    ActiveWorkbook.Sheets(oldSheet).Select
153: End Sub
154:
155: Sub CancelDemo(cMsg As String, rSheet As String)
156: 'displays the prompt specified by cMsg, makes the sheet
157: 'specified by rSheet the current sheet, and ends program
158:    MsgBox prompt:=cMsg, Title:="Static Array Demo"
159:    ActiveWorkbook.Sheets(rSheet).Select
160:    End   'ends entire program
161: End Sub
```

 The **DemoStaticArray** procedure demonstrates typical techniques for declaring a static array, filling the array with data, and then processing the data in the array. The **DemoStaticArray** procedure also demonstrates several of the programming practices mentioned in preceding lessons.

Listing 13.1 contains a couple of compiler directives, and a couple of module-level constant declarations. Line 2 is the Option Base 1 compiler directive, which tells VBA to use 1 as the starting number for elements of all arrays declared in this module. Line 8 declares a constant specifying the maximum size for an array, and line 11 specifies another constant, specifying the minimum number of elements for an array. (By using constants to specify things like the minimum and maximum dimensions for an array, you make it easier to change the code that handles an array if you later want to change the size of the array.)

Line 13 contains the **DemoStaticArray** function declaration. Line 15 declares a single-dimensional static array which will have **ARRAY_MAX** elements, all of which will have the Double data type. Because of the Option Base 1 directive, the array's elements will be numbered 1 through **ARRAY_MAX** (whatever the value of the **ARRAY_MAX** constant is). Lines 16 through 25 declare several other variables that the **DemoStaticArray** procedure uses—loop counters, high and low subscript values, prompt strings, message strings, and so on.

Line 28 sets up the **CR** variable to hold the special carriage-return character, used to format the text in various message dialog boxes later in the procedure. Because this procedure will change the active sheet, Line 31 stores the name of the current sheet in the **oldSheet** variable, so that this procedure can later restore the sheet that was current at the time the procedure started executing.

Line 34 uses the `Select` method of the `Sheets` property to change the active sheet to a worksheet named `"Sheet1"`. The `For...Next` loop in lines 38 through 41 clear the cells in the worksheet in which the procedure will later display the contents of the array's elements. Notice that the loop's ending value is calculated by using the **ARRAY_MAX** constant plus 2 (to clear an extra two rows on the worksheet). By using the constant value to set the ending limit of the loop, all you have to do to increase the maximum size of the array is change the **ARRAY_MAX** constant declaration—you don't have to fix all of the `For...Next` loops in the procedure or program.

Now the procedure's real work gets started. Lines 45 through 63 contain a `Do...Until` loop that gets a number from the user for how many array elements to fill. Lines 46 through 48 assemble a prompt string for the input dialog box displayed by lines 49 through 51. Notice that the `InputBox` statement suggests the maximum size of the array as the number of elements to be filled up. Lines 52 through 57 evaluate the user's input (stored in **tRsp**) to make sure that the user hasn't canceled the input dialog box. If the dialog box was canceled, then the **CancelDemo** procedure is called with appropriate arguments. (The **CancelDemo** procedure is in lines 155 through 161 of the listing.) If the input dialog box wasn't canceled, then the string in **tRsp** is converted to a Double type number (`CInt`), and stored in the **NumCnt** variable.

Next, lines 59 through 62 evaluate the value in **NumCnt** to make sure that it meets or exceeds the minimum size of the array, and is not greater than the maximum size of the array. Finally, the loop ends in line 63; the loop only ends if the user has entered a number that is between the minimum and maximum number of elements.

Line 66 starts a `For...Next` loop that prompts you for a numeric value, and then stores that value in an element of the array. The loop executes for the number of times entered in **NumCnt**. Line 67 assembles a prompt string for the input dialog box displayed by lines 70 through 72. Notice that the default value for this input dialog box is the current value of the loop counter—if you want, you can simply press Enter or OK to enter a number in each of the input dialog boxes displayed by this loop. The `If` statement that begins in line 74 checks to see whether the user has canceled the data entry—if so, the **CancelDemo** procedure is again called, ending the entire program. Otherwise, the statement in line 79 converts the user's input into a Double number (`CDbl`), and stores it in the array element referenced by the current value of the loop counter. The first time this loop executes, it stores the value entered by the user in element 1, the second time the loop executes, it stores the value in element 2, and so on. The `For...Next` loop ends in line 81.

> **Note:** Notice that the `For...Next` loops in the **DemoStaticArray** procedure all use the same loop-counting variable—**Count**. You can do this because none of the loops are nested inside of each other, and only one loop at a time executes, so they can all share the same loop counter variable, reducing the total number of variables that your program needs to use.

Lines 83 through 87 contain another `For...Next` loop counter that simply displays the contents of the array's elements on the worksheet selected earlier in the procedure. This display is just to help you see what's going on as the procedure executes—you could omit these statements without affecting the operation of the `DemoStaticArray` procedure.

Lines 91 through 153 are a `Do...Until` loop that first prompts for the lower and upper limits of a range of array elements to process, then adds together all of the array elements, and computes their average.

Line 93 begins a nested `Do...Until` loop that asks the user for the lower limit of array elements to process. Notice that this loop doesn't allow the user to cancel it—instead, it simply requires the user to enter a number somewhere between the first element in the array, and one element less than the number of data items in the array. (It's necessary to prohibit the user from selecting the last element in the array as the lower limit, otherwise the upper limit has to be beyond the end of the array.)

Line 111 begins another nested `Do...Until` loop, this time to get the upper limit of array elements to process. Notice that this loop also doesn't allow the user to cancel it, and simply requires the user to enter a number somewhere between the lower limit already chosen, and the maximum number of filled elements in the array (represented by **NumCnt**). The loop ends in line 127.

Line 134 makes sure that the **aSum** variable starts out initialized at 0, and then the `For...Next` loop in lines 135 through 137 computes the sum by looping through all of the array elements (from the low number to the high number) and successively adding their contents to the **aSum** variable.

Lines 140 through 145 assemble message text showing the low and high limits the user entered, the sum of all of the elements in the range and the average (mean) of the elements in the range. Notice that the average is calculated on-the-fly in line 144, as the message text is being assembled. The `MsgBox` function call in line 146 displays the just assembled message, and asks the user whether to process another range of elements in the array. The `Buttons` argument in line 147 causes the `MsgBox` statement to display the Information icon, and to display **Y**es and **N**o buttons in the dialog box. The return value from the `MsgBox` statement is stored in the **Count** variable— a somewhat sneaky use of the **Count** variable, but it eliminates a variable from the procedure.

Figure 13.4 shows a sample session with the **DemoStaticArray** procedure while displaying the `MsgBox` statement from line 146.

Finally, line 149 evaluates the contents of **Count** as the determinant condition for the loop—if the user chose **Y**es in the message dialog box displayed by line 146, then VBA executes the loop again (going back to line 91); otherwise, the loop ends. Finally, line 152 restores the sheet that was active when the **DemoStaticArray** procedure was called, and the procedure ends in line 153.

Figure 13.4.

A sample output display from the **DemoStaticArray** *procedure.*

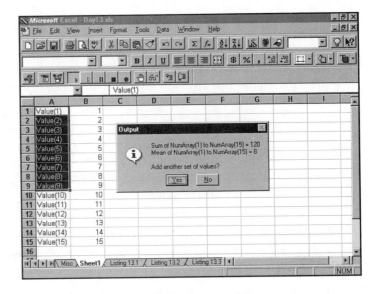

The **CancelDemo** procedure (lines 155 through 161) deserves just a few words of explanation. The **CancelDemo** procedure was written to help keep the **DemoStaticArray** procedure from getting too long, and to provide a generic method of canceling the entire procedure. There are two different places where the **DemoStaticArray** procedure allows the user to cancel data input, and thereby cancel the entire program. Both cancellation points require a message letting the user know that the operations were canceled, and to perform the "housekeeping" chore of restoring the sheet that was originally active at the time **DemoStaticArray** began executing. To avoid duplicating code, the **CancelDemo** procedure was written—it receives an argument for the message to display (so that the cancellation message can be specific) and an argument for the sheet to restore.

DO	DON'T

DO use constants to specify the maximum and minimum sizes of arrays—doing so makes it much easier to make changes in your code that processes arrays. In Listing 13.1, for example, if you wanted to change the maximum size of the array to 20 elements, you'd only have to change the **ARRAY_MAX** constant declaration. Because all of the array handling code uses that constant, you won't have to worry about the change affecting how For...Next loops operate on the array.

13

Using *ReDim* with Dynamic Arrays

As mentioned earlier in this lesson, there may be circumstances in which you don't know exactly how many elements you'll need in an array. The demonstration program in Listing 13.1 rather arbitrarily assumes that there will never be more than 15 numbers to process, although it does let you process less than 15 numbers.

If, in the procedure in Listing 13.1, you choose to process fewer than 15 numbers, then any unused array elements are still taking up memory (because the array is declared as a static array with 15 elements, it will always have 15 elements). Having unused array elements wastes memory, and uses up computer resources that may be needed by other procedures or programs. Another problem with the procedure in Listing 13.1 is that it won't allow you to process more than 15 numbers.

Using a dynamic array instead of a static array solves both problems. By using a dynamic array, you can create an array that is as small or as large as needed. You create dynamic arrays with the Dim statement, and then establish their size with the ReDim statement as your procedure executes.

Syntax

The general syntax for the ReDim statement is:

```
ReDim [Preserve] varname(subscripts) [As type][,varname(subscripts)[As type]] . . .
```

The optional keyword Preserve, as its name suggests, causes VBA to preserve the data in an existing array when you change the array's size with ReDim. *varname* represents the name of the array. *subscripts* represents the dimensions of the array. (The syntax for the *subscripts* clause in the ReDim statement is the same as for the Dim statement.) *type* represents any VBA or user-defined data type. You need to use a separate As *type* clause for each array you define. In the case of a Variant-type array, the *type* describes the type of each element of the array, but does not change the Variant to some other type.

The following are all valid examples of dynamic array declarations, and possible ReDim statements used with those dynamic arrays:

```
Dim aMonth() As String      'declares dynamic array aMonth
ReDim aMonth(1 To 30)       'resizes array to 30 elements
ReDim aMonth(1 To 31)       'resizes array to 31 elements
ReDim Preserve aMonth(1 To 31) 'resizes array to 31 elements, keeping contents
Dim LookupTable() As Integer 'declares dynamic array
ReDim LookupTable(3, 15)       'resizes array in two dimensions
ReDim LookupTable(4, 20)       'resizes two-dimensional array
ReDim Preserve LookupTable(4, 25)  'can only resize last dimension)
Dim Grab_Bag As Variant       'declares Variant type variable
ReDim Grab_Bag(20) As Integer  'creates array of 20 integers in Variant
```

The preceding examples illustrate some important points about dynamic arrays. First, you can only resize the last dimension of a multi-dimensional array when you use the Preserve keyword. Second, you can use ReDim to create a typed array inside a Variant type variable. Because Variant type variables can hold data of *any* type, you can use a Variant type variable to store a dynamic

array! (Using a Variant type variable to store a dynamic array makes it possible to ReDim the array *and* change the data type of the array.)

Typically, you'll use the ReDim statement to size or resize a dynamic array that you've previously declared using the Dim, Private, Public, or Static statements. You may use the ReDim statement to modify the number of elements and dimensions in a dynamic array as many times as you wish. You cannot, however, use the ReDim statement to change the data type of an array—unless the array is contained in a Variant type variable, or the array's elements themselves are Variants. If the dynamic array is stored in a Variant type variable, you can change the data type by using the As *type* clause in the ReDim statement.

> **Note:** Attempting to use ReDim on a static array (an array's whose dimensions you explicitly defined in a Dim, Public, Private, or Static declaration) causes VBA to display a runtime error.

Listing 13.2 demonstrates the use of a dynamic array. The **DemoDynamicArray** procedure in Listing 13.2 performs exactly the same job as the procedure in Listing 13.1, but uses a dynamic array to allow as many or as few numbers to be entered and processed as the user wants—without wasted memory.

Type

Listing 13.2. The DemoDynamicArray procedure declares and uses a dynamic array.

```
1:    Option Explicit
2:    Option Base 1
3:
4:    'minimum numbers to be entered
5:    Const ARRAY_MIN As Integer = 3
6:
7:    Sub DemoDynamicArray()
8:      Dim NumArray() As Double    'declare dynamic array
9:      Dim Array_Size As Integer   'for array size
10:     Dim aSum As Double       'for sum of numbers
11:     Dim Count As Integer     'loop counter
12:     Dim cLow As Integer      'low limit for sum
13:     Dim cHigh As Integer     'high limit for sum
14:     Dim mStr As String       'message string
15:     Dim pStr As String       'prompt string
16:     Dim tRsp As String       'for input box responses
17:     Dim CR As String * 1     'for carriage-return
18:     Dim oldSheet As String   'original sheet name
19:
20:     'set up a carriage-return character
21:     CR = Chr$(13)
22:
```

continues

Listing 13.2. continued

```
23:    'preserve original sheet name
24:    oldSheet = ActiveWorkbook.ActiveSheet.Name
25:
26:    'select a new sheet
27:    ActiveWorkbook.Sheets("Sheet1").Select
28:
29:    'prompt for number of values to be entered;
30:    'requires a minimum of ARRAY_MIN numbers
31:    pStr = "Type the number of values to enter (" & _
32:            ARRAY_MIN & " is the minimum):"
33:    Do
34:      tRsp = InputBox(prompt:=pStr, _
35:                      Title:="Specify Array Size", _
36:                      default:=ARRAY_MIN)
37:      If Len(Trim(tRsp)) = 0 Then
38:        CancelDemo cMsg:="Array sizing canceled.", _
39:                   rSheet:=oldSheet
40:      Else
41:        Array_Size = CInt(tRsp)
42:      End If
43:
44:      If (Array_Size < ARRAY_MIN) Then
45:        MsgBox "Please enter a number greater than " & _
46:               (ARRAY_MIN - 1) & "."
47:      End If
48:    Loop Until (Array_Size >= ARRAY_MIN)
49:
50:    'size the dynamic array
51:    ReDim NumArray(Array_Size)
52:
53:    'clear the worksheet cells for later display
54:    'of the array's contents
55:    For Count = 1 To (Array_Size + 2)
56:      Cells(Count, 1).Value = ""
57:      Cells(Count, 2).Value = ""
58:    Next Count
59:
60:    'enter values into the array
61:    For Count = 1 To Array_Size
62:      pStr = "Enter value number " & Count
63:      'get a value
64:      tRsp = InputBox(prompt:=pStr, _
65:                      Title:="Numeric Input", _
66:                      default:=Count)
67:      'check for cancellation
68:      If Len(Trim(tRsp)) = 0 Then
69:        CancelDemo cMsg:="Data entry canceled", _
70:                   rSheet:=oldSheet
71:      Else
72:        'store each value in a member of array NumArray
73:        NumArray(Count) = CDbl(tRsp)
74:      End If
75:    Next Count
76:
```

```
77:    'display the elements of NumArray on the worksheet
78:    For Count = 1 To Array_Size
79:      Cells(Count, 1).Value = "Value(" & Count & ")"
80:      Cells(Count, 2).Value = NumArray(Count)
81:    Next Count
82:
83:    'query repetitively for the range of elements in the
84:    'array for which to calculate the sum and average
85:    Do
86:      'get the low subscript of the elements to add
87:      Do
88:        tRsp = InputBox(prompt:="Enter subscript for " & _
89:                          "the low end of range to add:", _
90:                          Title:="Integer Input", _
91:                          default:="1")
92:        If Len(Trim(tRsp)) = 0 Then
93:          cLow = 0
94:        Else
95:          cLow = CInt(tRsp)
96:        End If
97:
98:        If (cLow < 1) Or (cLow >= Array_Size) Then
99:          RangeErrorMsg mLow:=1, mHigh:=Array_Size - 1
100:       End If
101:      Loop Until (cLow >= 1) And (cLow < Array_Size)
102:
103:     'get the high subscript of the elements to add
104:     Do
105:       tRsp = InputBox(prompt:="Enter subscript for " & _
106:                         "the high end of range to add:", _
107:                         Title:="Integer Input", _
108:                         default:=Array_Size)
109:       If Len(Trim(tRsp)) = 0 Then
110:         cHigh = 0
111:       Else
112:         cHigh = CInt(tRsp)
113:       End If
114:
115:       If (cHigh <= cLow) Or (cHigh > Array_Size) Then
116:         RangeErrorMsg mLow:=cLow + 1, mHigh:=Array_Size
117:       End If
118:     Loop Until (cHigh >= cLow) And (cHigh <= Array_Size)
119:
120:     'add the elements of NumArray together, starting from
121:     'NumArray(cLow) to NumArray(cHigh)
122:
123:     'initialize the sum to 0, then loop through array
124:     'to compute the sum for the specified range
125:     aSum = 0
126:     For Count = cLow To cHigh
127:       aSum = aSum + NumArray(Count)
128:     Next Count
129:
130:     'display the results of the sum and average
131:     mStr = "Sum of NumArray(" & cLow & ") to NumArray(" & _
132:            cHigh & ") = " & aSum & CR
```

continues

13

Listing 13.2. continued

```
133:       mStr = mStr & "Mean of NumArray(" & cLow & _
134:              ") to NumArray(" & cHigh & ") = " & _
135:              (aSum / (cHigh - cLow + 1)) & _
136:              CR & CR & "Add another set of values?"
137:       Count = MsgBox(prompt:=mStr, _
138:                      Buttons:=vbInformation + vbYesNo, _
139:                      Title:="Output")
140:     Loop Until Count = vbNo
141:
142:     'restore original sheet
143:     ActiveWorkbook.Sheets(oldSheet).Select
144: End Sub
145:
146: Sub RangeErrorMsg(mLow As Integer, mHigh As Integer)
147:    MsgBox prompt:="You must enter a number " & _
148:                   "between " & mLow & " and " & _
149:                   mHigh, _
150:           Title:="Dynamic Array Demo"
151: End Sub
152:
153: Sub CancelDemo(cMsg As String, rSheet As String)
154: 'displays the prompt specified by cMsg, makes the sheet
155: 'specified by rSheet the current sheet, and ends program
156:    MsgBox prompt:=cMsg, Title:="Dynamic Array Demo"
157:    ActiveWorkbook.Sheets(rSheet).Select
158:    End   'ends entire program
159: End Sub
```

 Analysis

The **DemoDynamicArray** procedure is very similar to the **DemoStaticArray** procedure from Listing 13.1, but has some important differences. This analysis will focus on the important similarities and differences between the two procedures.

First of all, line 2 of Listing 13.2 contains the Option Base 1 directive, so that all arrays in this module will start numbering their elements at 1. Notice that there is only a constant declaration for the minimum size of the array (line 5), but no constant specifying the maximum size of the array. In this procedure, the user specifies the maximum size of the array.

Line 8 declares the dynamic array **NumArray**. VBA knows this is a dynamic array because the parentheses in the array declaration are empty. The As clause specifies that all of the elements in the dynamic array are Double numbers. Lines 9 through 18 declare the variables that the **DemoDynamicArray** procedure uses while it is working. Notice that line 9 declares the **Array_Size** variable—this variable will hold the size of the array as entered by the user; it replaces the **ARRAY_MAX** constant from Listing 13.1. Notice also that the **NumCnt** variable is no longer used—because the **DemoDynamicArray** procedure simply creates an array of the desired size, there is no longer any need to separately keep track of how many elements in the array have valid data as compared to the maximum size of the array. In **DemoDynamicArray** the array never has unused elements in it.

Lines 21 through 28 perform the same housekeeping chores—setting up a carriage-return character, preserving the currently active sheet, and selecting the working sheet—as were performed in Listing 13.1.

In the **DemoDynamicArray** procedure, there's no point in doing anything until the desired size of the array has been obtained from the user, so lines 31 through 48 contain a Do...Until loop that asks the user to enter the total number of values to be entered into the array. This loop repeats until the user has entered a number greater than or equal to the minimum array size of 3 elements. Notice that the user's input is used to initialize the **Array_Size** variable.

Line 51 is the crucial statement in this procedure. This line uses the ReDim statement to establish the size of **NumArray**. This statement creates a single-dimensional array with **Array_Size** elements in it. If the user entered 3 in the input box, then **NumArray** ends up with 3 elements; if the user entered 20 in the input box, then **NumArray** ends up with 20 elements, and so on.

Lines 55 through 58 clear some space on the worksheet, as in Listing 13.1. Notice that this loop clears just enough space to display the data in the array—whatever the size of the array is—plus two blank rows to separate the current data from anything left over on the worksheet.

Lines 61 through 75 prompt the user for values to enter into the array's elements, just like the corresponding data-entry loop in Listing 13.1. Next, lines 78 through 81 display the contents of the array on the worksheet.

Finally, lines 85 through 140 ask the user for the upper and lower limits of the array elements for which the procedure will compute the sum and average. This loop, and the statements it contains, work the same way as in Listing 13.1. Notice, however, that the **Array_Size** variable is used in place of the **ARRAY_MAX** constant that was used in Listing 13.1. Also, the nested Do loops call another procedure, **RangeErrorMsg** to display error messages, instead of displaying their error messages themselves.

The **RangeErrorMsg** procedure (lines 146 through 151) was added to slightly shorten the **DemoDynamicArray** procedure, and to make your programming efforts more efficient—notice that Listing 13.2, which contains three complete procedures, is a couple of lines shorter than Listing 13.1. Although the savings in this short program isn't significant, a longer program might realize a substantial reduction in length and complexity by using a shorter, general-purpose procedure to carry out the task of displaying certain related kinds of error messages.

The **CancelDemo** procedure in lines 153 through 159 works the same as the corresponding procedure in Listing 13.1.

Figure 13.5 shows a sample session with the **DemoDynamicArray** procedure. In the figure, notice that the list of data items extends beyond the bottom edge of the visible portion of the worksheet—the user in this session selected an array with 20 elements in it.

13

Figure 13.5.

A sample session with the **DemoDynamicArray** *procedure.*

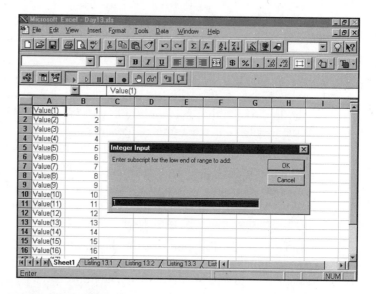

DO	**DON'T**

DO remember that you create dynamic arrays in a Dim, Public, Private, or Static declaration by using only empty parentheses.

DO remember that you can only use ReDim Preserve to change the size of the *last* dimension of a multi-dimensional array. You can change all the dimensions of a multi-dimensional array with the ReDim keyword alone, however.

DON'T forget that you can't change the data type of an array with ReDim, unless the array is contained in a Variant type variable or is a Variant array.

The *LBound* and *UBound* Functions

To keep track of the sizes of both static and dynamic arrays, you might find yourself using one or a pair of variables to store the minimum and maximum subscripts for an array. Unfortunately, if you rely on keeping track of the upper and lower limits of an array's subscripts with your own variables, you're taking on all the responsibility of keeping those variables up to date and accurate. If you don't, your procedure won't work correctly—you'll end up processing fewer elements than the array actually contains, or you'll get runtime errors from trying to access an array with subscripts beyond the actual size of the array. Such program bugs may be difficult to track down.

Fortunately, VBA includes a couple of functions that relieve you of the burden of manually keeping track of the upper and lower limits of an array yourself—the LBound and UBound functions. These functions return the lower and upper boundary subscript values of a static or dynamic array.

The general syntax for the LBound and UBound functions is:

```
LBound(arrayName [, dimension])
UBound(arrayName [, dimension])
```

The LBound function returns the first subscript of the array represented by *arrayName*. The UBound function returns the highest subscript of the array represented by *arrayName*. You can use these two functions with either static or dynamic arrays. *dimension* represents an integer number specifying the dimension of the array for which you want to obtain the lower or upper boundary. If you omit *dimension*, VBA returns the boundary for the first dimension of the array.

The following code fragments are examples of using the LBound and UBound functions:

```
Dim S(3 To 9) As String
For I = LBound(S) To UBound(S)
  S(I) = String$(10, 65 + I)
Next I
Dim Matrix(1 To 365, 1980 To 1989)
For DayNum = LBound(Matrix, 1) To UBound(Matrix, 1)
  For YearNum = LBound(Matrix, 2) To UBound(Matrix, 2)
    Matrix(DayNum, YearNum) = Rnd
  Next YearNum
Next DayNum
```

In the second example, notice that the LBound and UBound functions use the optional *dimension* argument. The outer For...Next loop executes for as many elements as there are in the first dimension of the **Matrix** array, while the inner For...Next loop executes for as many times as there are elements in the second dimension of the **Matrix** array.

There are some cases when the information returned by the UBound function won't necessarily be very useful to you. Frequently, you may not have completely filled an array with valid data (like the array in Listing 13.1), or you may need to perform some processing on the array before it is completely filled. Usually, you'll start storing data in the first element of an array, and gradually use elements with higher and higher subscripts. Often, the subscript of the last element in the array that contains meaningful data is less than the highest subscript in the array (as reported by the UBound function). In such a situation, you must use a separate variable to keep track of the *highest working index* of an array. You can also think of the highest working index as the *current working index* of the array. (An array's subscript and index are the same thing.)

To illustrate this point, Figure 13.6 shows a sample array named **WordList**, partway through a data-entry process. The first 6 elements of the array contain meaningful data (the list of words that has been entered so far), whereas the last 4 elements contain empty strings. Notice that the current, or highest, working index of the array is the 6th element. If you needed to manipulate

Syntax

the list in some way before data entry is complete, you'd need a variable (as suggested in the figure) to keep track of the current working index.

Figure 13.6.

A partially filled array. Notice that the variable **CurIndex** *stores the current working index of the* **WordList** *array. Only elements between the lower boundary of the array and the current working index contain meaningful data.*

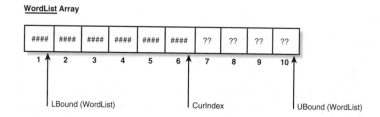

Using *Erase* to Clear or Remove Arrays

VBA provides a special statement—Erase—that allows you to perform one of two tasks, depending on whether you're manipulating a static or dynamic array. For static arrays, Erase allows you to clear all of the array's elements, essentially re-initializing the array to the same condition it had when VBA created it in memory. For dynamic arrays, Erase allows you to completely remove the array, and its contents, from your computer's memory.

Once you've filled an array's elements, the data in the array remains (whether the array is static or dynamic) until you either assign new values to the array's elements, or until VBA disposes of the array. (Arrays follow the same scope and persistence rules as any other variable in VBA, as explained in Day 3 and Day 10.)

In some circumstances, you may want to clear all of the values in the array—setting numeric values to 0, string values to empty strings, and so on. Generally, you'd write a For...Next or For...Each loop to set all of the elements in an array to a particular value. The following code fragments show both a For...Next and a For...Each loop used to initialize all of the values in a numeric array to 0:

```
For k = LBound(NumArray) To UBound(NumArray)
  NumArray(k) = 0
Next k
For Each Num In NumArray
  Num = 0
Next Num
```

The first code fragment uses a For...Next loop and the LBound and UBound functions to loop through all of the elements in the array; the second code fragment uses For...Each to loop through every element in the array, also setting each element to 0. Although these loops are quite short, you can accomplish the same task for a static array even more efficiently with a single `Erase` statement:

```
Erase NumArray
```

Arrays tend to consume relatively large quantities of memory—an array of 20 elements, for example, consumes as much memory as 20 separate variables of the same data type. Because arrays require so much memory, you should clear dynamic arrays from memory whenever they're not actually in use. (Static arrays cannot be removed from memory until VBA automatically disposes of the array.)

Just like any other locally declared variable, VBA removes arrays declared locally in a procedure from memory whenever the procedure stops executing. Arrays declared at the module-level, however, remain in existence as long as any procedure in that module is executing. If you have a large program, you may want (or need) to reclaim the memory used by module-level dynamic arrays. The `Erase` statement allows you to do just that.

Syntax

The general syntax for the `Erase` statement is:

```
Erase array1 [, array2, ...]
```

array1 and *array2* represent any valid VBA array name. You can list as many arrays in the `Erase` statement as you wish, separating each array name with a comma.

The `Erase` statement removes dynamic arrays from memory, freeing up the memory formerly in use by that array. If you `Erase` a dynamic array, you must re-create the array with a `ReDim` statement before you can use that particular dynamic array again. If you try to access elements in a dynamic array that you've used the `Erase` statement on without redimensioning it, VBA displays a runtime error.

The `Erase` statement's behavior for static arrays is slightly more complex, and depends on the specific data type of the array's elements. The following table summarizes the effect of the `Erase` statement on static arrays of various types (the `Empty` and `Nothing` values were discussed in Day 10):

Static Array Type	*Effect of* `Erase` *Statement*
any numeric type	Sets array elements to 0.
any string type	Sets array elements to zero-length string (`""`); sets fixed-length strings as all space characters.
Variant	Sets array elements to `Empty`.
Object	Sets array elements to `Nothing`.
any user-defined type	Sets each variable in the user-defined type individually: numeric types set to 0, String to zero-length, Variant to `Empty`, Object to `Nothing`.

13

You can place the Erase statement anywhere in your code that it's needed. The following code fragment shows an example of the Erase statement in use:

```
Dim NumArray(1 To 10) As Single   'declares static array
Dim k as Variant                  'multi-purpose loop counter

'fill an array with the squares of its subscripts
For k = LBound(NumArray) To UBound(NumArray)
  NumArray(k) = k * k
Next k

'display the squares
For k = LBound(NumArray) To UBound(NumArray)
  MsgBox "The square of " & k & " is " & NumArray(k)
Next k

're-initialize the array
Erase NumArray

For k = LBound(NumArray) To UBound(NumArray)
  MsgBox NumArray(k)    'displays zero
Next k
```

DO	**DON'T**

DO remember that Erase does *not* remove static arrays from memory, it only re-initializes the array's elements.

DO remember that Erase *does* remove a dynamic array from memory, destroying the contents of the array.

DON'T forget that you can use the For...Each looping structure to process all of the elements in an array.

Using Arrays as Arguments to Procedures and Functions

VBA allows you to pass arrays as arguments to your procedures and functions. This capability can be very useful—because you don't have to specify the size of the array that is passed as an argument, you can write general-purpose array processing procedures or functions. For example, you could write a function that receives a numeric array as an argument and returns the average of all of the numbers in the array as the function's result. As another example, you could write a procedure that receives an array as an argument passed by reference, and sorts that array (you'll learn about sorting arrays later in today's lesson.) In both of these examples, you can write the procedure or function to operate on an array of any size—5 elements, 10 elements, 100 elements, and so on.

Syntax

The general syntax for array arguments to a procedure or function is the same as that you've already learned for any procedure or function arguments (described in Day 6 and Day 11):

```
[ByVal ¦ ByRef] arrayname() As type
```

Like the procedure and function arguments you've already learned about, the ByVal keyword tells VBA to pass the array argument by value, and the ByRef keyword tells VBA to pass the array argument by reference. As usual, if you omit ByVal and ByRef, VBA passes the array argument by reference.

arrayname() represents the array argument; you may use any valid VBA identifier as the name of the array argument. You must always include the empty parentheses after the arrayname; the parentheses tell VBA that this argument is an array. type represents any valid VBA or user-defined data type.

The following code fragments show how to include arrays as arguments to procedures and functions:

```
Sub ShowText(Lines(), NumLines As Integer)
  'receives a Variant type array passed by reference
...
End Sub

Sub SortList(ByRef List() As String, NumLines As Integer)
  'receives a String type array passed by reference
...
End Sub

Function ComputeAve(Numbers() As Double) As Double
...'receives a Double type array passed by reference
End Function
```

DO	DON'T

DO remember that passing arguments by value (with the ByVal keyword) causes VBA to pass a *copy* of the data to the function or procedure.

DON'T pass arrays by value unless you absolutely must—passing large arrays by value can quickly exhaust your computer's memory resources, resulting in out-of-memory runtime errors.

Sorting Arrays

Note: Sorting and searching arrays are difficult topics. Don't be disheartened if the information in this section and the following section isn't clear the first time you read it. If you get the rudiments of how these processes work, and you can answer all of the Quiz questions at the end of this lesson, you're doing fine. You can refer back to these sections when you actually need to write a sorting or searching routine.

Apart from numerical or other computations involving data stored in an array, the two array manipulations you'll perform most frequently are sorting and searching an array. *Sorting* an array simply refers to the process of arranging the values in the array elements in either ascending or descending order. In an array sorted in ascending order, for example, the first element of the array contains the data with the lowest value, the second element of the array contains the data with the next highest value, and so on—the last element in the array holds the data with the greatest value. An array sorted in descending order has the highest value in the first element, and the lowest value in the last element of the array.

Usually, you sort an array if you need to process or display the data in the array in a particular order, or if you need to search for a particular data value in the array. Searching for specific data values stored in an array is usually much faster and efficient if the array has been sorted.

Over the years, computer scientists have spent a lot of effort developing various techniques for sorting arrays of data in an effort to increase the speed and efficiency of the sorting process. There is now a large number of sorting techniques available; each technique has various advantages and disadvantages. Unfortunately, there are far too many sorting techniques for this book to cover— many authors have written entire books on the subject of sorting arrays. Fortunately, there are a couple of sorting techniques that are both easy to understand and relatively easy to program.

Listing 13.3 shows a procedure that uses the *bubble-sort* technique to sort an array. The bubble-sort technique is one of the simplest sorting techniques. The bubble-sort works by comparing adjacent elements in the array, and exchanging their positions, as necessary. The bubble-sort gets its name because it causes the elements in the array to slowly move (or "bubble") upwards to their final location in the sorted array.

The following code outline—or pseudo-code—shows how the bubble-sort technique works for an ascending sort:

```
Given an array named Nums:
1:  Loop from 1st Nums element up to next-to-last Nums element, with counter I
1A:    Loop from Nums element after element indexed by the outer loop counter
          up to last Nums element, with counter J
1B:      If Nums(I) > Nums(J), then exchange contents of Nums(I) and Nums(J)
```

The preceding pseudo-code can be further refined into the following VBA statements:

```
'Given an array Nums with subscripts from 1 to N.
For I = LBound(Nums) To (UBound(Nums) - 1)
  For J = (I + 1) To UBound(Nums)
    If Nums(I) > Nums(J) Then
      tmp = Nums(I)
      Nums(I) = Nums(J)
      Nums(J) = tmp
    End If
  Next J
Next I
```

To create a descending sort order, simply change the greater-than comparison operator (>) to a less-than comparison operator (<)—the bubble-sort will then arrange the array in descending order.

Note: Code outlines like the one in this section, and those described in Day 11, are often called *pseudo-code*, because the English statements in the code outline only approximate the computer language statements that you'll have to write. Writing the pseudo-code for a complex process is a good design tool—it can help you more easily determine exactly how the actual program statements should be written to accomplish the task you desire.

Listing 13.3 contains the **DemoBubbleSort** procedure, which uses an Excel worksheet to graphically demonstrate how the bubble-sort operation works. The **DemoBubbleSort** procedure doesn't require any user input; it uses the Rnd function to fill an array with random numbers, and then sorts the array. As the **DemoBubbleSort** procedure executes, you'll see it display pointers indicating the array elements being compared and exchanged. As you watch this procedure execute, keep in mind that the display on the worksheet is only for effect—the sorting is taking place in the array.

13

Listing 13.3. The DemoBubbleSort procedure visually demonstrates the bubble-sort technique for sorting arrays.

```
1:   Option Explicit
2:   Option Base 1
3:
4:   Const DELAY_TIME As Single = 1
5:
6:   Sub DemoBubbleSort()
7:     'declare constants
8:     Const ARRAY_MAX As Integer = 10
9:     Const FORMATSTR As String = "####"
10:    Const COMPSTR1 As String = "<---- compare this element"
```

continues

Listing 13.3. continued

```
11:      Const COMPSTR2 As String = "<---- with this element"
12:      Const COMPSTR3 As String = "<---- swap this element"
13:
14:      'declare variables
15:      Dim IntArr(ARRAY_MAX) As Integer
16:      Dim I As Integer
17:      Dim J As Integer
18:      Dim oldSheet
19:
20:      'reseed random number generator
21:      Randomize Timer
22:
23:      'assign random numbers to the elements of array IntArr
24:      For I = 1 To ARRAY_MAX
25:        IntArr(I) = Int(Rnd * 1000)
26:      Next I
27:
28:      'preserve current sheet, switch to new sheet
29:      oldSheet = ActiveSheet.Name
30:      Sheets("Sheet1").Select
31:
32:      'display the array elements
33:      For I = 1 To ARRAY_MAX
34:        Cells(I, 1).Value = Format(IntArr(I), FORMATSTR)
35:      Next I
36:
37:      'start sorting the array
38:      For I = 1 To ARRAY_MAX - 1
39:        For J = I + 1 To ARRAY_MAX
40:          'display arrows that indicate the
41:          'elements being compared
42:          ShowCompare COMPSTR1, I, COMPSTR2, J
43:
44:          If IntArr(I) > IntArr(J) Then
45:            Beep 'sound the speaker
46:            'indicate that compared elements
47:            'will be swapped
48:            ShowCompare COMPSTR3, I, COMPSTR2, J
49:            'swap elements at index I and J
50:            Swap IntArr(I), IntArr(J)
51:            'display the new positions of the
52:            'swapped elements
53:            Cells(I, 1).Value = IntArr(I)
54:            Cells(J, 1).Value = IntArr(J)
55:          End If
56:        Next J
57:      Next I
58:      MsgBox prompt:="Array is now sorted!", _
59:             Buttons:=vbInformation, _
60:             Title:="Bubble-Sort Information"
61:      'restore original sheet
62:      Sheets(oldSheet).Select
63:  End Sub
64:
```

```
65:  Sub ShowCompare(S1 As String, I1 As Integer, _
66:                  S2 As String, I2 As Integer)
67:    Cells(I1, 2).Value = S1
68:    Cells(I2, 2).Value = S2
69:    WaitAWhile DELAY_TIME
70:    Cells(I1, 2).Value = ""
71:    Cells(I2, 2).Value = ""
72:  End Sub
73:
74:  Sub WaitAWhile(ByVal Interval As Single)
75:    Dim TheTime As Date
76:    TheTime = Timer
77:    Do
78:    Loop Until (Timer - TheTime) >= Interval
79:  End Sub
80:
81:  Sub Swap(I1 As Integer, I2 As Integer)
82:    Dim Temp As Integer
83:    Temp = I1
84:    I1 = I2
85:    I2 = Temp
86:  End Sub
```

 Figure 13.7 shows a sample run with the **DemoBubbleSort** procedure while comparing the data in the 4th and 6th elements of the array (displayed in cells A4 and A6 of the worksheet).

Figure 13.7.

A sample run of the
DemoBubbleSort *procedure*
in Listing 13.3.

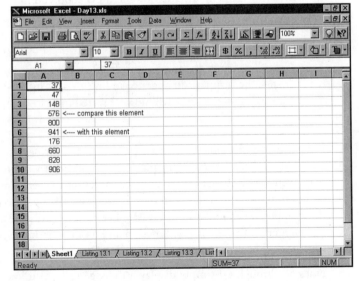

Notice that Listing 13.3 contains a complete module, and a total of 4 different procedures. Notice also that Line 2 contains the Option Base 1 statement, so that VBA will start array subscript numbering at 1.

Lines 6 through 63 contain the **DemoBubbleSort** procedure. The procedure's code begins with several constant declarations (lines 8 through 12). Notice the declaration of a constant for the array's maximum size, and the string constants used to form messages displayed by the procedure.

Lines 15 through 18 declare the variable that **DemoBubbleSort** uses. Line 15 declares the static array that will later be sorted, **I** and **J** are loop counter variables, and **oldSheet** is a string variable to hold the name of the current worksheet.

Line 21 uses the Randomize statement to initialize VBA's random number generator, while the For loop in lines 24 through 26 use the Rnd function to fill the array with random numbers.

Lines 29 and 30 preserve the current sheet's name (for later restoration) and select a worksheet on which to display the progress of the sorting process. Lines 33 through 35 display the unsorted arrays contents on the worksheet.

The real work of the **DemoBubbleSort** procedure begins on line 38. The nested For loops (the outer loop begins in line 38, the inner loop on line 39) result in every element of the array being compared with every other element of the array.

Line 42 calls the **ShowCompare** procedure to display markers on the worksheet showing which elements of the array are currently being compared. Line 44 makes the actual comparison test between the array elements; if the array element specified by the outer loop counter is greater than the array element specified by the inner loop counter, then the two values need to be swapped.

Note: To change the bubble-sort from an ascending sort to a descending sort, change the comparison operator in line 44 of Listing 13.3 to a less-than (<) comparison—the array will now be sorted in descending order.

If the values in the array elements are out of order, the Beep statement in line 45 gives you an audible alert that a swap is taking place, and the **ShowCompare** procedure is called again, this time to indicate which elements are being swapped. Beep makes Windows 95 play the default system beep sound (for computers with sound cards) or makes your computer's speaker sound a tone (for computers without sound cards). The Line 50 calls the **Swap** procedure, which actually exchanges the array elements. Lines 53 and 54 update the display of the array's values on the worksheet. The inner For loop ends in line 56, and the outer For loop ends in line 57.

Lines 58 through 60 simply display a message to let you know that the sorting operation is complete, and line 62 restores the sheet that was current when the **DemoBubbleSort** procedure began executing.

Lines 65 through 72 contain the **ShowCompare** procedure. This procedure simply displays its string arguments on the current worksheet at the specified row coordinates, calls the **WaitAWhile** procedure, and then clears the message strings from the worksheet.

Lines 74 through 79 contain the **WaitAWhile** procedure. This procedure waits for a set period of time by recording the system timer value when the procedure starts, and then looping until the difference between the old timer value and the current timer value exceeds the specified interval. (Your computer system's timer records the number of seconds that have elapsed since midnight—the VBA **Timer** function returns the computer system's timer value.)

Lines 81 through 86 contain the **Swap** procedure. Notice that this procedure's arguments are passed by reference (the VBA default), so that any changes that **Swap** makes to its argument's values are reflected in the original argument variables. **Swap** just exchanges the contents of its two argument variables—the **Temp** variable is just used to temporarily hold one of the values being exchanged.

You should enter the **DemoBubbleSort** procedure and then run it a few times to get a feel for how the bubble-sort works. Notice that each element in the array is successively compared to the remaining higher elements, gradually moving the high values to the end of the array. If the screen messages are too brief for you, increase the amount of time that the messages remain on-screen by increasing the value of the **DELAY_TIME** constant.

Now that you have a good feel for how the bubble-sort works, take a look at Listing 13.4. Listing 13.4 does essentially the same things as Listing 13.3, but all of the cosmetic code has been removed from the procedures, and the bubble-sort code itself has been moved into a couple of general-purpose sorting procedures with array parameters. One procedure provides a general-purpose ascending bubble-sort, and the other procedure provides a general-purpose descending bubble-sort. The **Sorter** procedure in Listing 13.4 is a practical implementation of the bubble-sort technique, executing the sorting process at its maximum speed.

Listing 13.4. The Sorter procedure sorts an array using the bubble-sort method and a couple of general-purpose sorting procedures.

```
 1:    Option Explicit
 2:    Option Base 1
 3:
 4:    Private Const FORMATSTR As String = "####"
 5:
 6:    Sub Sorter()
 7:       'declare constants
 8:       Const ARRAY_MAX As Integer = 10
 9:       Const iTitle As String = "Sorter Information"
10:
11:       'declare variables
12:       Dim IntArr(ARRAY_MAX) As Integer
```

continues

Listing 13.4. continued

```
13:     Dim Count As Integer
14:     Dim oldSheet As String
15:
16:     'reseed random number generator
17:     Randomize Timer
18:
19:     'assign random numbers to the elements of array IntArr
20:     For Count = 1 To ARRAY_MAX
21:       IntArr(Count) = Int(Rnd * 1000)
22:     Next Count
23:
24:     'preserve current sheet, switch to new sheet
25:     oldSheet = ActiveSheet.Name
26:     Sheets("Sheet1").Select
27:
28:     'display the array elements
29:     DisplayArray IntArr
30:
31:     MsgBox prompt:="Ready to start sorting.", _
32:            Buttons:=vbInformation, _
33:            Title:=iTitle
34:
35:     'sort the array in ascending order
36:     BubbleSortAscending IntArr
37:
38:     'display the sorted array elements
39:     DisplayArray IntArr()
40:
41:     MsgBox prompt:="Array now sorted in ascending order", _
42:            Buttons:=vbInformation, _
43:            Title:=iTitle
44:
45:     'sort the array in descending order
46:     BubbleSortDescending IntArr
47:
48:     'display the sorted array elements
49:     DisplayArray IntArr
50:
51:     MsgBox prompt:="Array now sorted in descending order", _
52:            Buttons:=vbInformation, _
53:            Title:=iTitle
54:
55:     'restore worksheet
56:     Sheets(oldSheet).Select
57: End Sub
58:
59: Sub BubbleSortAscending(AnyArray() As Integer)
60:     Dim I As Integer, J As Integer
61:
62:     'sorts any integer array in ascending order
63:     For I = LBound(AnyArray) To UBound(AnyArray) - 1
64:       For J = I + 1 To UBound(AnyArray)
65:         If AnyArray(I) > AnyArray(J) Then
66:           Swap AnyArray(I), AnyArray(J)
```

```
67:         End If
68:       Next J
69:     Next I
70: End Sub
71:
72: Sub BubbleSortDescending(AnyArray() As Integer)
73:    Dim I As Integer, J As Integer
74:
75:    'sorts any integer array in descending order
76:    For I = LBound(AnyArray) To UBound(AnyArray) - 1
77:      For J = I + 1 To UBound(AnyArray)
78:        If AnyArray(I) < AnyArray(J) Then
79:          Swap AnyArray(I), AnyArray(J)
80:        End If
81:      Next J
82:    Next I
83: End Sub
84:
85: Sub Swap(I1 As Integer, I2 As Integer)
86:    Dim temp As Integer
87:    temp = I1
88:    I1 = I2
89:    I2 = temp
90: End Sub
91:
92: Sub DisplayArray(AnyArray() As Integer)
93:    Dim k As Integer
94:
95:    For k = LBound(AnyArray) To UBound(AnyArray)
96:      Cells(k, 1).Value = Format(AnyArray(k), FORMATSTR)
97:    Next k
98: End Sub
```

The **Sorter** procedure in Listing 13.4 is an improved, no-frills version of the sorting procedure in Listing 13.3. This new version uses the procedures **BubbleSortAscending** and **BubbleSortDescending** to sort the array in either ascending or descending order, respectively. Each of these procedures has a single array argument, **AnyArray**, which is passed by reference. Consequently, when either **BubbleSortAscending** or **BubbleSortDescending** sorts the elements of the array argument passed to them, they are sorting the original array.

Note: Both the **BubbleSortAscending** and **BubbleSortDescending** procedures assume that the entire array is filled with valid data to be sorted. If you want to sort only a portion of the array, you must modify the sorting procedures to use a second argument specifying the maximum number of elements to sort, and then modify the loops to use that argument as the maximum count.

Notice that the **Sorter** procedure calls the **DisplayArray** procedure (which also has an array argument) to display the sorted array on the worksheet.

Searching Arrays

Frequently, you'll need to search an array to see if it contains a particular value. There are two basic techniques for searching arrays—a linear search and a binary search.

In a *linear* search, you simply start at the beginning of the array and examine each element in turn until you find an element that contains the value you're searching for. There are several variations on the basic linear search method. Use a linear search on an unsorted array, or if you need to find all occurrences of a particular value in the array.

For sorted arrays, the binary search method is much faster and more efficient. In a *binary* search, you successively divide the array in half (hence the name "binary"), and search only the half of the array that is likely to contain the value you're looking for. Binary searching only works on sorted arrays.

The next two sections of this lesson look at each searching technique in more detail.

Using Linear Searches

The basic linear search method is completely straightforward. Suppose you have an array which contains 10 unsorted integers and has subscripts from 1 to 10. To perform a linear search on this array, you simply start with element 1, testing to see if it contains the value you're looking for. If it does, the search is over; if it doesn't, you continue with the 2nd element, and test it for a match with the value you're searching for. The search continues until you either locate the desired value, or you run out of array elements to test. The pseudo-code for a linear search might look like this:

```
1:   Set a Not-Found Boolean flag to True.
2:   Set a variable, I, to the starting array subscript.
3:   Do the next step while these two conditions are true:
         I is less than or equal to the upper boundary of the array
         the Not-Found flag remains True
3A:    If the element referenced by I is not equal to the value being sought then:
         increment the subscript variable, I
       otherwise, set the Not-Found flag to false
```

The Not-Found Boolean flag indicates whether or not the linear search is successful. If the search is successful, the matching value in the array will be found in the array element subscripted by the value in the variable **I**.

Listing 13.5 shows the **LinearSearch** procedure, which visually demonstrates how a linear search on an array works. The **LinearSearch** procedure creates an array, fills the array with random numbers, and then searches the array for a number specified by the user.

Listing 13.5. The macro MacroSearch1 performs a visual demonstration of the linear search in an array.

```
1:    Option Explicit
2:    Option Base 1
3:
4:    Sub LinearSearch()
5:      'declare constants
6:      Const ARRAY_MAX As Integer = 10
7:      Const MSG_ROW As Integer = ARRAY_MAX + 2
8:      Const SHORT_DELAY = 1
9:      Const iTitle = "Linear Search"
10:
11:     'declare variables
12:     Dim IntArr(ARRAY_MAX) As Integer
13:     Dim I As Integer
14:     Dim NotFound As Boolean
15:     Dim oldSheet As String
16:     Dim SrchFor As Variant
17:     Dim Rsp As Integer
18:     Dim pStr As String
19:
20:     'preserve the current sheet, select worksheet
21:     oldSheet = ActiveSheet.Name
22:     Sheets("Sheet1").Select
23:
24:     Randomize Timer   'seed the random number generator
25:
26:     For I = 1 To ARRAY_MAX    'assign random values to array
27:       IntArr(I) = Int(Rnd * 1000)
28:     Next I
29:
30:     For I = 1 To ARRAY_MAX    'display the array elements
31:       Cells(I, 1).Value = IntArr(I)
32:     Next I
33:
34:     'get a value to search for from user, until the user
35:     'doesn't want to search anymore
36:     Do
37:       SrchFor = Application.InputBox( _
38:               prompt:="Enter a number to search for:", _
39:               Title:=iTitle & " Input", _
40:               Type:=1)
41:       SrchFor = CInt(SrchFor) 'convert value to integer
42:
43:       'display search status at bottom of number list
44:       Cells(MSG_ROW, 1).Value = "Searching for " & SrchFor
45:
46:       'start searching
47:       I = 1
48:       NotFound = True
49:       Do
50:         'display "?=?" near searched entry
51:         Cells(I, 2).Value = "?=? " & SrchFor
52:         WaitAWhile SHORT_DELAY
```

continues

Listing 13.5. continued

```
53:        Cells(I, 2).Value = ""
54:        'no match found?
55:        If IntArr(I) <> SrchFor Then  'increment search index
56:          I = I + 1
57:        Else    'set not-found flag to FALSE
58:          NotFound = False
59:        End If
60:      Loop Until I > ARRAY_MAX Or NotFound = False
61:
62:      If NotFound Then    'display no-match found message
63:        pStr = "No match for " & SrchFor
64:      Else  'display found-match message
65:        pStr = "Found " & SrchFor & " at IntArr(" & I & ")"
66:      End If
67:      Cells(MSG_ROW, 1).Value = ""   'clear message area
68:
69:      pStr = pStr & Chr(13) & Chr(13) & _
70:             "Search for another number?"
71:      Rsp = MsgBox(prompt:=pStr, _
72:                   Title:=iTitle, Buttons:=vbYesNo)
73:    Loop Until Rsp = vbNo
74:
75:    Sheets(oldSheet).Select   'restore original sheet
76:  End Sub
77:
78:  Sub WaitAWhile(Interval As Single)
79:    Dim TheTime As Date
80:    TheTime = Timer
81:    Do
82:    Loop Until (Timer - TheTime) >= Interval
83:  End Sub
```

Analysis

Figure 13.8 shows a sample session with the **LinearSearch** procedure while searching for the value 575.

Lines 6 through 9 declare various constants used by the **LinearSearch** procedure. Notice the **ARRAY_MAX** constant in line 6. Lines 12 through 18 declare the variables that this procedure uses. Notice the **IntArr** declaration in line 12.

Lines 21 through 32 set up the procedure's task: the current sheet name is preserved, a worksheet is selected, the array is filled with random numbers, and the contents of the array are displayed on the worksheet.

Line 36 starts a **Do...Until** loop; this loop executes until the user indicates that she no longer wishes to search the array for a number. Line 37 uses the Excel **InputBox** function to get a number from the user (the Excel **InputBox** function was used in order to ensure that the user does enter a number—line 41 converts the user's number to an integer). Line 44 displays a status message at the bottom of the list of numbers on the worksheet.

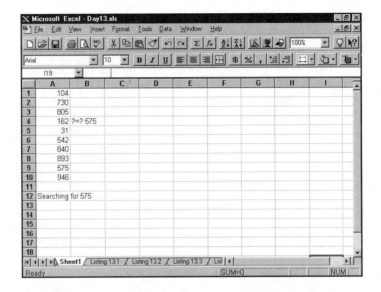

Figure 13.8.

A sample session with the
LinearSearch *procedure*
while searching for the
number 926 in the array.

The actual work of the search begins in lines 47 and 48, which set up the starting conditions for the Do...Until loop that starts in line 49. This Do loop executes until either a match is found, or the subscript counter has exceeded the maximum size of the array.

Lines 51 through 53 display a symbol on the worksheet, so you can see which array element is currently being tested.

Lines 55 through 59 perform the actual search test—the If...Then...Else statement tests to see whether the current array element matches the value being searched for. If it does not match, then the subscript variable is incremented by 1, and the loop continues; otherwise, the **NotFound** flag is set False.

Line 60 ends the loop, testing to see if the **NotFound** flag is False, or if the subscript variable (**I**) has exceeded the maximum size of the array. If either condition is true, the loop ends.

The If...Then...Else statement in lines 62 through 67 checks to see whether a match was found, and assembles an appropriate message. Finally, lines 69 through 72 complete the message string and display it in a MsgBox dialog box that also asks the user if they want to search for another number. If the user chooses **Y**es, then the loop starting in line 36 executes again. Otherwise, line 75 restores the original sheet, and **LinearSearch** ends.

Lines 78 through 83 contain the **WaitAWhile** procedure you're already familiar with from Listing 13.3.

13

Using Binary Searches

For sorted arrays, the binary search method is regarded by most programmers as the best general-purpose method for searching. Rather than searching the ordered array sequentially, the binary search takes advantage of the array's sorted order. Because the array is sorted, it is safe to assume that if an element in the middle of the array is greater than the value being searched for, then the sought after value can be found in the first half of the array. On the other hand, if the element in the middle of the array is less than the value you're searching for, then the sought after value can be found in the second half of the array. After determining which half of the array the sought after value is in, the binary search then takes that half of the array, and divides *it* in half. The binary search repeats this halving of the array until it either finds a match for the sought after value, or runs out of pieces of the array to search in.

To better understand the binary search, suppose you're looking for the name Harris in a 1,000 page phone book. Using the binary search method, you start by opening the phone book up at page 500 (half of 1,000). You see the name Maynard at the top of the page. Because Harris comes before Maynard, you know that the name you're looking for must be in the first half of the phone book. Now you have 500 pages to search in. Next, you open the phone book to page 250 (half of 500), and find the name Fogarty at the top of the page. Harris comes after Fogarty, so you now know that the name you're looking for is in the second half of the first 500 pages of the phone book. You now only have to search in pages 250 through 500. Next, you select the halfway point between 250 and 500, which is page 375. You can proceed with narrowing down the range of pages you're looking at until you either find the name Harris or you determine that there is no page in the phone book with that name on it.

The pseudo-code for a binary search looks like this:

```
1:  Set the low interval limit (called Low), to 1.
2:  Set the high interval limit (called High) to upper boundary of the array.
3:  Do the next steps until one of these two conditions is true:
        the element indexed by median of Low and High equals the sought value
        Low has become greater than High
3A: Set a half-way point (called Median) as the median value of Lo and High.
3B: If the sought value is less than the value subscripted by Median then
        set High to be the Median - 1
        otherwise, set Low to be the Median + 1
```

When the binary search is complete, you can determine whether it was successful by comparing the value of the array element subscripted by the contents of the median variable with the value being searched for—if they are equal, the search was successful; if they aren't, the search was unsuccessful. Figure 13.9 illustrates the steps of a binary search.

The **BinarySearch** procedure in Listing 13.6 visually demonstrates how a binary search works. The procedure creates an integer array, fills the array with random numbers, sorts the array, and then displays the array's contents on a worksheet. The procedure then asks the user for a number to search for.

Figure 13.9.

This sample binary search locates the element that contains the value 389.

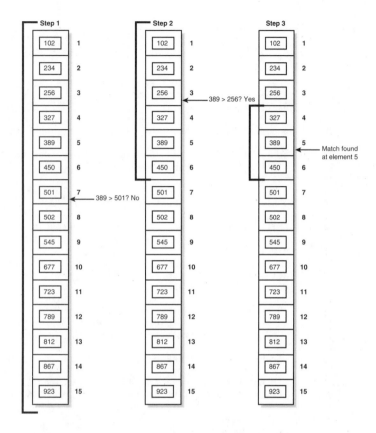

Listing 13.6. The `BinarySearch` procedure creates a visual demonstration of a binary search on an array.

```
1:    Option Explicit
2:    Option Base 1
3:
4:    Sub BinarySearch()
5:        'declare constants
6:        Const ARRAY_MAX As Integer = 10
7:        Const MSG_ROW As Integer = ARRAY_MAX + 2
8:        Const SHORT_DELAY = 1
9:        Const iTitle = "Binary Search"
10:
11:       'declare variables
12:       Dim IntArr(ARRAY_MAX) As Integer
13:       Dim I As Integer
14:       Dim Hi As Integer
15:       Dim Lo As Integer
16:       Dim Median As Integer
17:       Dim oldSheet As String
18:       Dim SrchFor As Variant
```

continues

Listing 13.6. continued

```
19:    Dim Rsp As Integer
20:    Dim pStr As String
21:
22:    'preserve the current sheet, select worksheet
23:    oldSheet = ActiveSheet.Name
24:    Sheets("Sheet1").Select
25:
26:    Randomize Timer  'seed the random number generator
27:
28:    For I = 1 To ARRAY_MAX  'assign random values to array
29:      IntArr(I) = Int(Rnd * 1000)
30:    Next I
31:
32:    BubbleSort IntArr  'sort array IntArr1
33:
34:    For I = 1 To ARRAY_MAX  'display the elements of array
35:      Cells(I, 1).Value = IntArr(I)
36:    Next I
37:
38:    'get a value to search for from user, until the user
39:    'doesn't want to search anymore
40:    Do
41:      SrchFor = Application.InputBox( _
42:              prompt:="Enter a number to search for:", _
43:              Title:=iTitle & " Input", _
44:              Type:=1)
45:      SrchFor = CInt(SrchFor) 'convert value to integer
46:
47:      'display search status at bottom of number list
48:      Cells(MSG_ROW, 1).Value = "Searching for " & SrchFor
49:
50:      'start searching
51:      Lo = LBound(IntArr)
52:      Hi = UBound(IntArr)
53:      Do
54:        Median = (Lo + Hi) \ 2  'integer division
55:        'display "?=?" near searched entry
56:        Cells(Median, 2).Value = "?=? " & SrchFor
57:        WaitAWhile SHORT_DELAY
58:        Cells(Median, 2).Value = ""
59:        If SrchFor < IntArr(Median) Then
60:          Hi = Median - 1
61:        Else
62:          Lo = Median + 1
63:        End If
64:      Loop Until (SrchFor = IntArr(Median)) Or (Lo > Hi)
65:
66:      'found match
67:      If SrchFor = IntArr(Median) Then  'found-match message
68:        pStr = "Found " & SrchFor & " at IntArr(" & _
69:               Median & ")"
70:      Else  'display no-match found message
71:        pStr = "No match for " & SrchFor
72:      End If
73:      Cells(MSG_ROW, 1).Value = ""   'clear message area
```

```
74:
75:        pStr = pStr & Chr(13) & Chr(13) & _
76:             "Search for another number?"
77:        Rsp = MsgBox(prompt:=pStr, _
78:                  Title:=iTitle, Buttons:=vbYesNo)
79:     Loop Until Rsp = vbNo
80:
81:     Sheets(oldSheet).Select   'restore original sheet
82:  End Sub
83:
84:  Sub WaitAWhile(Interval As Single)
85:     Dim TheTime As Double
86:     TheTime = Timer
87:     Do
88:     Loop Until (Timer - TheTime) >= Interval
89:    End Sub
90:
91:  Sub BubbleSort(AnyArray() As Integer)
92:  'sorts any integer array in ascending order
93:     Dim I As Integer, J As Integer
94:     For I = LBound(AnyArray) To UBound(AnyArray) - 1
95:       For J = I + 1 To UBound(AnyArray)
96:         If AnyArray(I) > AnyArray(J) Then
97:            Swap AnyArray(I), AnyArray(J)
98:          End If
99:        Next J
100:    Next I
101: End Sub
102:
103: Sub Swap(I1 As Integer, I2 As Integer)
104:    Dim temp As Integer
105:    temp = I1
106:    I1 = I2
107:    I2 = temp
108: End Sub
```

Analysis Figure 13.10 shows a sample session with the **BinarySearch** procedure while searching for the value 789.

Like the **LinearSearch** procedure in Listing 13.5, lines 6 through 20 declare the various constants and variables used in this procedure. Lines 23 through 30 perform the same housekeeping tasks as before.

Once the array has been filled with random numbers, however, line 32 calls the **BubbleSort** procedure (lines 91 through 101 in Listing 13.6) to sort the array in ascending order. (This is the same bubble-sorting routine that you're already familiar with from Listings 13.3 and 13.4.) After sorting the array, lines 34 through 36 display the contents of the sorted array on the worksheet.

Line 40 begins a Do...Until loop which, as before, executes until the user no longer wants to search for numbers in the array. Lines 41 through 48 get a number from the user, convert it to an integer, and display a status message on the worksheet.

513

Figure 13.10.

The BinarySearch procedure searching for the value 789.

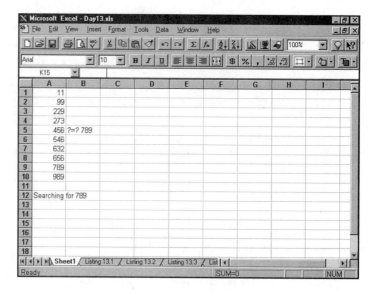

Line 51 begins the actual binary search process. Lines 51 and 52 set up the starting conditions for the Do...Until loop that starts in line 53. The Lo variable is the lower boundary of the array segment currently being searched, and Hi is the upper boundary of the array segment. When the loop first starts, the upper and lower boundaries are set equal to the array's actual physical boundaries. The Do loop starting in line 53 executes until either a match is found, or the low boundary of the array segment currently being searched ends up higher than the upper boundary of the array segment.

Line 54 sets the Median variable to point at an element halfway between the current upper and lower boundaries of the array segment currently being searched. Notice the use of the integer division operator (\) in this statement.

Lines 56 through 58 display a marker on the worksheet, so you can see which array element is currently being tested. Lines 59 through 63 actually perform a matching test. If the value being searched for is less than the value of the array element specified by Median, then the upper boundary of the array segment currently being searched (Hi) is set as being one less than the current Median; otherwise, the lower boundary is raised to be one more than the current Median.

Lines 67 through 72 check to see whether or not a match was found, and assembles an appropriate message string. Notice that determining whether a match was found simply involves checking to see if the array element referenced by Median matches the sought after value (SrchFor).

Lines 75 through 78 complete the message string, and use a MsgBox dialog box to ask the user whether to search for another number in the array.

The remainder of this module contains several procedures that you're already familiar with from listings earlier in this lesson: Lines 84 through 89 contain the **WaitAWhile** procedure, lines 91 through 101 contain the **BubbleSort** procedure (this one performs an ascending sort only), and lines 103 through 108 contain the **Swap** procedure used by **BubbleSort**.

DO	DON'T

DO use a linear search anytime you aren't certain whether the array you're searching is sorted.

DON'T use a binary search on an unsorted array—it won't work, and you'll get erroneous results from the search.

DON'T use a linear search when you know the array is sorted. Although the linear search will produce the correct result, binary searches are much faster and more efficient.

Summary

This chapter introduced you to arrays—the simplest and perhaps most useful data structure in many programming languages. You learned that an array is a collection of variables that share the same name. You learned that you access individual elements in an array through an integer subscript or index value.

This chapter showed you how to use the Option Base directive to control whether VBA starts numbering array elements with 0 or 1. Next, you learned how to declare static and dynamic arrays with the Dim statement, and you learned how to use ReDim to change the size and dimensions of a dynamic array. Then you learned how to use the Erase statement to re-initialize a static array, or to remove a dynamic array from memory. You also learned how to use the LBound and UBound functions to determine the upper and lower boundaries of an array.

Finally, you learned how to sort an array by using the classic bubble-sort technique, and you then learned reliable methods for searching both sorted and unsorted arrays.

Q&A

Q Why does VBA use zero-based numbering for arrays? It seems an awkward and difficult numbering system.

A VBA, and most other programming languages, use zero-based numbering for array subscripts because of the way arrays are stored in memory. When VBA creates an array, it simply reserves a single, contiguous block of memory large enough to

accommodate all of an array's elements. When you subscript the array, you're really telling VBA how far into the contiguous block of memory the data you want is stored—the array's subscript is translated into an offset value for the memory address. The first element of an array, therefore, is at offset 0, the second element is at offset 1, the third element at offset 2, and so on.

Q **Which `Option Base` statement should I use?**

A Use whichever `Option Base` statement makes you most comfortable. For many people, it's easiest to deal with arrays whose subscripts start with 1, so you'll probably want to include `Option Base 1` in your modules. If you feel comfortable with zero-based array numbering, use `Option Base 0` (or just omit the `Option Base` directive). Even if you do use the default zero-based numbering, you may want to add the `Option Base 0` directive to your modules to explicitly indicate which numbering scheme you're using in that module.

Q **Are there any side effects for not using `Option Base 1`?**

A Only if you consistently think of array subscripts beginning at 1. If you don't use `Option Base 1`, but write all your code using 1 as the beginning subscript, then you're wasting the array element at subscript 0. Also, if you sometimes use 1 as the beginning array subscript, and other times use the `LBound` function to obtain the lowest array index, you may end up with bugs in your programs that are difficult to track down.

Q **Can I alter the data types of the array elements in a `ReDim` statement?**

A You can only alter an array's data type if you created the array in a Variant variable with the `ReDim` statement in the first place; otherwise, VBA does *not* allow you to change the data type of an array's elements. The following code fragment shows how to use `ReDim` to create an array in a Variant variable.

```
Dim aList As Variant
ReDim aList(10) As Integer  'integer array inside Variant
ReDim aList(5)  'still an integer array
ReDim aList(10) As String  'now it's a String array in Variant
```

Q **Can I alter the data type of a dynamic array in a `ReDim` statement after I erase it with an `Erase` statement?**

A No. When you declare a dynamic array, VBA assigns a specific data type to the array's elements—Variant, by default, if you don't use the `As` clause to specify a data type. Although the `Erase` statement reclaims any memory used by the dynamic array, VBA does *not* destroy the array. VBA retains information about the array's name and data type in its internal table of variables and their corresponding memory addresses, although there is no memory allocated to the array. Consequently, whenever you `ReDim` the array, VBA still knows what data type the elements of the array should be, and prohibits you from changing it. This behavior actually supports good programming practice, discouraging you from using the same array to store different types of data.

Workshop

Answers in Appendix A.

Quiz

1. How many array elements are in the following declarations?

```
Option Base 1
Dim Lookup(10, 3, 5) As Integer
Dim Cube(3, 3, 3) As Double
```

2. Study the following multi-dimensional array declaration:

```
Option Base 1
Dim A(1980 To 1990, 10, 5 To 9)
```

   For the array declaration just shown, what are the values returned by the following function calls:

   (A) LBound(A, 1)
   (B) LBound(A, 2)
   (C) LBound(A, 3)
   (D) UBound(A, 1)
   (E) UBound(A, 2)
   (F) UBound(A, 3)

3. **BUG BUSTER:** What is wrong with the following set of statements?

```
1:   Option Base 1
2:   Dim X(10, 20) As Double
3:
4:   For I = 1 To 10
5:     For J = 1 To 20
6:       X(I, J) = Int(Rnd * 1000)
7:     Next J
8:   Next I
9:
10:  ReDim X(5, 10) As Single
11:
12:  For I = 1 To 5
13:    For J = 1 To 10
14:      X(I, J) = Int(Rnd * 1000)
15:    Next J
16:  Next I
```

4. Will inserting an Erase X statement before the ReDim statement (line 10) in the preceding program fix the problem?

5. Can you use an array element anywhere in a VBA statement where you could use a simple variable?

6. Will a linear search work correctly on a sorted array? An unsorted array?

7. Why should you use a binary search on a sorted array? Can you use a binary search on an unsorted array?

Exercises

1. Modify the **Sorter** procedure from Listing 13.4 to create another procedure, named **Sorter2**. The new procedure should declare a two-dimensional array, fill it with random numbers, and then sort the two-dimensional array. The **Sorter2** procedure's array should have 5 columns and 15 rows. When sorting the array, **Sorter2** should then sort the array based on the values in the second column. Keep in mind that your sorting process will need to swap entire rows, not just the elements in the 2nd column of the array.

2. Given the following code fragment, what values are stored in the array **A**?

```
Dim A(1 To 9) As Long
Dim I As Integer
A(LBound(A)) = 2
For I = LBound(A) + 1 To UBound(A)
    A(I) = 2 * A(I - 1) - 1
Next I
```

3. **BUG BUSTER:** What is wrong with the following statements?

```
1:  Dim ProjIncome(1995 To 1999) As Double
2:  Dim I As Integer
3:  ProjIncome(1995) = 1000
4:  For I = 1995 To 2000
5:    ProjIncome(I) = 1.1 * ProjectIncome(I - 1)
6:  Next I
```

4. **BUG BUSTER:** What is wrong with the following statements?

```
1:  Option Base 1
2:  Dim X(100) As Double
3:  Dim I As Integer
4:  For I = 1 To 100
5:    X(I) = I * I
6:  Next I
7:  For I = 1 To 100
8:    Cells(I, 1).Value = X(I)
9:  Next I
10: ReDim X(10) As Integer
11: For I = 1 To 10
12:   X(I) = I * I
13: Next I
14: For I = 1 To 10
15:   Cells(I, 1).Value = X(I)
16: Next I
```

5. **BUG BUSTER:** What is wrong with these statements?

```
1:  Option Base 2
2:  Dim A(9) As Long
3:  Dim I As Integer
4:  A(LBound(A)) = 2
5:  For I = LBound(A) + 1 To UBound(A)
6:    A(I) = 2 * A(I - 1) - 1
7:  Next I
```

6. **BUG BUSTER:** What is the error in the following statements?

```
1:  Option Base 1
2:  Dim A(9) As Long
3:  Option Base 0
4:  Dim B(9) As Long
5:  Dim I As Integer
6:  A(LBound(A)) = 2
7:  For I = LBound(A) + 1 To UBound(A)
8:     A(I) = 2 * A(I - 1) - 1
9:     B(I) = 2 * A(I - 1)
10: Next I
```

7. **BUG BUSTER:** What is the error in the following statements?

```
1:  Dim A(9) As Long
2:  Option Base 0
3:  Dim B(9) As Long
4:  Dim I As Integer
5:  A(LBound(A)) = 2
6:  For I = LBound(A) + 1 To UBound(A)
7:     A(I) = 2 * A(I - 1) - 1
9:     B(I) = 2 * A(I - 1)
10: Next I
```

13

14

Debugging and
Testing Macros

Bugs are errors in your code that cause your programs to produce erroneous results, or prevent them from executing altogether. Today's lesson teaches you about VBA's debugging tools. The VBA Debugger provides several powerful features to help you track down and correct the sources of bugs in your procedures and functions. In this lesson, you'll learn about:

☐ The basic types of bugs you're likely to encounter as you develop your procedures and functions.

☐ Using breakpoints and the Debugger's break mode to suspend the execution of your program code, and to control and monitor the execution of your code.

☐ Working with Watch variables and expressions to monitor the values that your code produces as it executes.

☐ Using the Step Into and Step Over commands to see your code execute line by line and procedure by procedure.

☐ Tracing the order of procedure calls.

☐ Using the Immediate pane of the Debug window to view special debugging output from your program, or to test the results of various expressions as your program executes.

Today's lesson starts by discussing the basic techniques for *debugging* (that is, locating and eliminating bugs), and then presents examples of using those techniques.

Basic Types of Program Bugs

In computer programming, Murphy's Law ("If anything can go wrong, it will") is especially applicable. Just about any aspect of a program can go wrong. Every computer programmer, regardless of experience or computer language, must spend a certain amount of time tracking down errors and defects in their code. Such defects and errors typically result in programs which stop executing suddenly (they *crash*) or which produce erroneous results. Any defect or error in a computer program is called a *bug*.

You'll encounter four basic types of bugs as you program in VBA:

☐ *Syntax errors* are the result of typing errors, such as misspelling a VBA keyword, a variable, or procedure name; syntax errors usually occur as you write your code. As you learned in Day 2, VBA's editor can detect most syntax errors as you edit or type each line in your program. (VBA checks syntax when you move the insertion point away from a newly edited or typed line.) Other syntax errors may occasionally show up as compile errors.

☐ *Compile errors* are the result of statements that VBA cannot correctly compile, and may occur as you attempt to run a VBA procedure. If VBA detects any problems with your code during compilation, it displays an error message, and does not execute any code. For example, if you have `Option Explicit` in a module, and you use a variable without first declaring it in a `Dim` statement, VBA moves the insertion point to the point where it detected the undeclared variable, and displays a compile error.

☐ *Runtime errors* are the result of expressions or statements that VBA cannot evaluate or execute, such as invalid operations, invalid procedure and function arguments, or illegal mathematical operations. Runtime errors occur as your program code executes. Typical examples of causes of runtime errors are expressions that result in mathematical underflow or overflow, type mismatches in assignment expressions or procedure arguments, attempting to open non-existent files, or attempting to divide by zero.

☐ *Logical errors* are the result of a programmer's error in reasoning. Erroneous results are the typical symptoms of logical errors in a program—your procedures or functions may produce numerical results that are incorrect, a task may be performed incorrectly or incompletely, or your procedure may even perform the wrong task. Some, but not all, logical errors will also result in a runtime error, depending on the specific results of the reasoning flaw.

The VBA Compiler

Whenever VBA executes any code in a newly created or edited module, VBA *compiles* the code in that module. As VBA compiles a module, it reads through all of the source code in the module. During compilation, VBA builds its internal tables of variables and constants, and ensures that all of the decision-making and looping structures, as well as procedure and function declarations, are correctly formed. VBA also checks all procedure and function calls to make sure that the correct number and type of required arguments are provided. This compilation process is an essential step in VBA's preparation to execute your code. It is also during the compilation step that VBA processes the compiler directives (such as `Option Explicit`, `Option Compare`, and `Option Base`) and ensures that all the code in the module meets any restrictions established by the compiler directives.

Using the Break Mode

In order to debug your VBA code, you'll frequently need to see exactly how VBA is executing your program statements, and what values are stored in various variables at particular moments in your program's execution. For example, you might have a bug in a procedure that sorts an array, resulting in the array remaining unsorted. It will be a lot easier to find the bug in your sorting procedure if you can tell which branches of `If...Then` statements are being executed, check to make sure that Do loops execute correctly, or inspect the values stored in variables *as your sorting procedure executes.*

The Debugger's *break mode* gives you the ability to interact more intimately with your VBA code than when you simply execute one of your programs. When you execute a procedure, your code executes from start to finish, at the greatest speed that VBA is capable of—you can't see exactly which parts of your code are executing at any given moment, nor can you tell what value a variable holds at any particular moment. In break mode, however, you gain the ability to execute your code (or parts of it) one line or procedure at a time—sort of like executing your programs in slow motion. Executing your programs one statement at a time is called *single-stepping* through your program.

VBA provides a total of five different ways to activate the Debugger's break mode:

- ☐ Click the Debug button in a runtime error dialog box.
- ☐ Set one or more breakpoints.
- ☐ Use the Stop statement in your code.
- ☐ Use the **R**un | Step **I**nto command (or press F8).
- ☐ Press Esc or Ctrl+Break to interrupt VBA code execution.

Each of these different techniques for activating the Debugger's break mode is described in the following sections of this lesson.

VBA provides toolbar buttons for the most frequently used Debugger commands. Figure 14.1 shows the VBA toolbar (in its floating window), with only the Debugger command buttons identified. Use this figure to help identify the toolbar buttons for the commands discussed in the remainder of this lesson.

Figure 14.1.
The Debugger command buttons on the VBA toolbar.

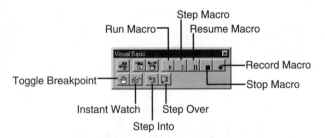

Entering Break Mode from an Error Dialog Box

Whenever a runtime error occurs while one of your VBA procedures or functions is executing, VBA displays an error dialog box like the one shown in Figure 14.2 (the specific error message will vary, depending on the actual runtime error that occurred). This Macro Error dialog box

displays the runtime error number, a brief explanation of the nature of the error, and several command buttons. In Figure 14.2, for example, the runtime error was number 11, and is described briefly as `Division by zero`.

Figure 14.2.

A typical runtime error dialog box.

Runtime error dialog boxes contain the following command buttons:

☐ **E**nd—Ends all VBA code execution.

☐ **C**ontinue—Continues execution of interrupted VBA code. The **C**ontinue command button is usually disabled when a runtime error occurs, as shown in Figure 14.2.

☐ **D**ebug—Starts Debugger's break mode and displays the Debug window.

☐ **G**oto—Opens the module that contains the code that produced the runtime error, and positions the insertion point in the VBA statement that was executing at the time the error occurred. Use the **G**oto command button to quickly jump to the statement that contains the problem.

Tip: To get help about the specific runtime error, click the help button (**?**) at the top right corner of the Macro Error dialog box, and then click over the text for the error message. VBA displays the online help for that particular runtime error.

To enter the Debugger break mode from a runtime error message dialog box, simply click the Debug button. VBA will open a Debug window, similar to the one shown in Figure 14.3.

Notice that the Debug window is divided into two main areas. The *Code pane* is at the bottom of the Debug window; the Code pane displays your VBA code, and marks the current VBA statement. The upper portion of the Debug window is a tabbed display area; the *Watch pane* is showing in Figure 14.3. The Watch pane permits you to observe the current values in your program's variables. The Immediate pane (not shown in Figure 14.3) allows you to view special Debugger output from your program, and to perform on-the-fly tests of expressions using current variable values in your program. You'll learn more about the Debug window's various panes as this lesson progresses.

Figure 14.3.

A typical Debug window, showing the Code pane and the Watch pane.

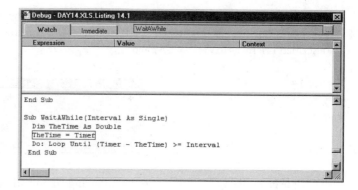

Setting and Using Breakpoints

To locate the cause of both runtime and logical bugs, you'll almost always need to single-step through the statements in your program. Single-stepping through your program's statements allows you to either see exactly which code executes before and as a runtime error occurs, or lets you observe the operation of a group of statements that don't seem to be working correctly.

Single-stepping through all of the statements in a procedure or a program can be fairly time-consuming and tedious. You'll seldom want or need to single-step through *all* of the statements in your program. Fortunately, VBA's Debugger allows you to execute most of your code at full speed, entering break mode only when certain, specific statements in your code execute. (Remember, you must be in the Debugger's break mode before you can single-step through your code.)

A *breakpoint* is a line in your code that you have specially marked; when VBA encounters a breakpoint, it switches from normal code execution to the Debugger's break mode. By using breakpoints, you can execute most of your program at full speed, entering break mode only when VBA reaches the particular statements that you're interested in examining closely. Once set, a breakpoint remains in effect until you either remove it, or until you close the file that contains the module in which you set the breakpoint.

You can set a breakpoint on any line in your source code that contains an executable statement. Usually, you'll set breakpoints slightly ahead of the statements that you know or suspect are causing problems. To set a breakpoint, follow these steps:

1. Display the VBA module containing the statements you want to single-step through.

2. Place the insertion point on the line in the module where you want VBA to switch from normal execution into break mode. This line will become the new breakpoint, and must contain an executable VBA statement.

3. Choose the **R**un | Toggle **B**reakpoint command to insert the breakpoint. VBA color-codes the line (in both the module and the Code pane of the Debug window) to indicate that it is selected as a breakpoint, as shown in Figure 14.4. (You can also press F9 or use the Toggle Breakpoint button on the VBA toolbar to set a breakpoint.)

Figure 14.4.

A breakpoint in a VBA module.

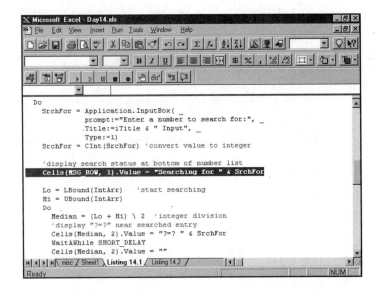

Note: To remove a breakpoint, perform the same steps as for adding a breakpoint—if you use the Toggle Breakpoint command on a line that already has a breakpoint set, VBA removes the breakpoint. To clear all of the breakpoints in a module, choose the **R**un | **C**lear All Breakpoints command.

Using the *Stop* Statement

Breakpoints set with the Toggle Breakpoint command only remain in effect for the current work session. Sometimes, and particularly for complex programs, your debugging efforts may extend over several work sessions. As a result, you may want to set a more-or-less permanent breakpoint. VBA provides the Stop keyword for exactly that purpose.

Whenever VBA encounters the Stop statement, it stops executing your code, opens the Debug window, and enters break mode. When you use the Stop statement, you create a *hard-coded*

breakpoint; that is, the breakpoint becomes an actual part of your VBA code. The only way to remove the breakpoint created by the Stop statement is to remove the Stop statement from your source code.

Typically, you'll insert the Stop statement in your code whenever you need a persistent breakpoint; when you have finished debugging your program, you'll edit your source code to remove the Stop statement.

DO	**DON'T**
DO keep in mind that breakpoints set with the Toggle Breakpoint command only remain in effect for the current work session. **DO** use the Stop statement to create a breakpoint that remains permanently in your code. **DON'T** forget to remove Stop statements when you are finished developing your macros.	

Entering Break Mode Using the Step Into Command

You already know that you can execute a procedure directly from its source code by using the **R**un | **S**tart command or clicking the Run Macro button on the VBA toolbar.

Similarly, you can start executing any procedure in break mode. Simply place the insertion point inside the procedure you want to execute in break mode, and choose the **R**un | Step **I**nto command. (You can also press F8 or click the Step Into command button on the VBA toolbar.) VBA opens the Debug window, and makes the procedure declaration the current executing statement.

Entering Break Mode by Interrupting Code Execution

As you've already learned, VBA allows you to interrupt code execution by pressing the Esc key (or by pressing the Ctrl+Break key combination). When you interrupt code execution, VBA displays an error dialog box; this dialog box indicates that code execution was interrupted, and offers you the same choices as VBA's runtime error dialog box: **E**nd, **C**ontinue, **D**ebug, and **G**oto. To work with your code in break mode, choose the **D**ebug command button; VBA opens the Debug window, and displays the statement that was executing at the time you interrupted the procedure.

Ending Break Mode

Often, you may single-step through part of your code, and then want the rest of your program to execute at full speed. The rest of the time, you'll probably want to end both the break mode and execution of your code, so you can make changes in your source code to correct the problems you've identified while using break mode.

To end break mode and continue executing your program at full speed, choose the **R**un | Con**t**inue command. VBA closes the Debug window and continues executing your code at full speed until VBA encounters the normal end of your program. If VBA encounters a breakpoint or a Stop statement before it reaches the end of your program, VBA will again enter break mode. (You can also end break mode and continue program execution by pressing F5, or by clicking the Resume Macro toolbar button.)

To end break mode and also end all program execution, choose the **R**un | **E**nd command. VBA closes the Debug window and halts all code execution. (You can also end break mode and halt program execution by clicking the Stop Macro button on the VBA toolbar.)

DO	DON'T

DO remember that the Continue command only appears on the **R**un menu when you are in break mode.

DO remember that you may not always be able to continue code execution—either single-stepping or normally—if you entered break mode from a runtime error dialog box. Usually, an error serious enough to produce a runtime error prevents VBA from being able to execute any more statements in your program.

Using the Step Into Command

Now that you understand how to enter and end break mode, you're ready to learn how to use the Step Into command to single-step through your code while in break mode. Stepping into statements allows you to thoroughly examine the execution of a procedure, function, or of an entire program in order to debug it.

When you use the Step Into command to single-step through your source code, VBA steps *into* every procedure or function call that it encounters, so that you end up single-stepping each and every statement that VBA executes. The single-stepping process with the Step Into command allows you to follow the execution of every statement in the main procedure, and every statement in every function or procedure called directly or indirectly by the main routine.

Before using the Step Into command, you need some code to single-step through. Listing 14.1 contains a slightly shortened version of the module from Listing 13.6 in the preceding lesson. The procedures in Listing 14.1 are for you to have some code to work with in the Debug window.

Type

Listing 14.1. Some code to demonstrate the VBA Debugger.

```
 1:   Option Explicit
 2:   Option Base 1
 3:
 4:   Sub DebugDemo1()
 5:     Const ARRAY_MAX As Integer = 10
 6:     Const MSG_ROW As Integer = ARRAY_MAX + 2
 7:     Const SHORT_DELAY = 1
 8:     Const iTitle = "Binary Search"
 9:
10:     Dim IntArr(ARRAY_MAX) As Integer
11:     Dim I As Integer
12:     Dim Hi As Integer
13:     Dim Lo As Integer
14:     Dim Median As Integer
15:     Dim oldSheet As String
16:     Dim SrchFor As Variant
17:     Dim Rsp As Integer
18:     Dim pStr As String
19:
20:     oldSheet = ActiveSheet.Name   'preserve current sheet
21:     Sheets("Sheet1").Select        'select new worksheet
22:
23:     Randomize Timer   'seed the random number generator
24:     For I = 1 To ARRAY_MAX   'assign random values to array
25:       IntArr(I) = Int(Rnd * 1000)
26:     Next I
27:
28:     BubbleSort IntArr   'sort array IntArr1
29:     For I = 1 To ARRAY_MAX   'display the elements of array
30:       Cells(I, 1).Value = IntArr(I)
31:     Next I
32:
33:     'get a value to search for from user, until the user
34:     'doesn't want to search anymore
35:     Do
36:       SrchFor = Application.InputBox( _
37:                 prompt:="Enter a number to search for:", _
38:                 Title:=iTitle & " Input", _
39:                 Type:=1)
40:       SrchFor = CInt(SrchFor) 'convert value to integer
41:
42:       'display search status at bottom of number list
43:       Cells(MSG_ROW, 1).Value = "Searching for " & SrchFor
44:
45:       Lo = LBound(IntArr)    'start searching
46:       Hi = UBound(IntArr)
47:       Do
48:         Median = (Lo + Hi) \ 2  'integer division
49:         'display "?=?" near searched entry
```

```
50:          Cells(Median, 2).Value = "?=? " & SrchFor
51:          WaitAWhile SHORT_DELAY
52:          Cells(Median, 2).Value = ""
53:          If SrchFor < IntArr(Median) Then
54:            Hi = Median - 1
55:          Else
56:            Lo = Median + 1
57:          End If
58:        Loop Until (SrchFor = IntArr(Median)) Or (Lo > Hi)
59:
60:        If SrchFor = IntArr(Median) Then    'found a match
61:          pStr = "Found " & SrchFor & " at IntArr(" & _
62:                  Median & ")"
63:        Else  'display no-match found message
64:          pStr = "No match for " & SrchFor
65:        End If
66:        Cells(MSG_ROW, 1).Value = ""     'clear message area
67:
68:        pStr = pStr & Chr(13) & Chr(13) & _
69:                "Search for another number?"
70:        Rsp = MsgBox(prompt:=pStr, _
71:                     Title:=iTitle, Buttons:=vbYesNo)
72:      Loop Until Rsp = vbNo
73:      Sheets(oldSheet).Select  'restore original sheet
74:    End Sub
75:
76:    Sub WaitAWhile(Interval As Single)
77:      Dim TheTime As Double
78:      TheTime = Timer
79:      Do: Loop Until (Timer - TheTime) >= Interval
80:     End Sub
81:
82:    Sub BubbleSort(xArray() As Integer)
83:    'sorts integer array in ascending order
84:      Dim I As Integer, J As Integer
85:      For I = LBound(xArray) To UBound(xArray) - 1
86:        For J = I + 1 To UBound(xArray)
87:          If xArray(I) > xArray(J) Then _
88:            Swap xArray(I), xArray(J)
89:        Next J
90:      Next I
91:    End Sub
92:
93:    Sub Swap(I1 As Integer, I2 As Integer)
94:      Dim temp As Integer
95:      temp = I1: I1 = I2: I2 = temp
96:    End Sub
```

14

Analysis The module in Listing 14.1 is essentially the same as the module presented from Listing 13.6—some of the code statements and comments have been reformatted to take up less vertical space, but the functionality of the procedures in the module is unchanged. The **DebugDemo1** procedure works exactly the same as the **BinarySearch** procedure from Listing 13.6—it creates an array, fills it with random numbers, sorts the array, and then searches the array for values entered by the user. The **WaitAWhile**, **BubbleSort**, and **Swap** procedures all work the same as described for Listing 13.6.

The only differences between Listing 14.1 and Listing 13.6 are in how some of the VBA statements are formatted. Notice the colon (:) characters in lines 79 and 95. The colon separates VBA statements on the same line—sort of the opposite of the line continuation character, the colon (:) character tells VBA that there is more than one logical statement on the same physical line. Also notice the line-continuation character in line 87; using this line continuation character makes this If...Then statement a single-line If...Then, eliminating the need for an End If statement.

After you enter Listing 14.1, you're ready to use the Step Into command. To practice using the Step Into command (and setting a breakpoint), follow these steps:

1. Move the insertion point to line 28 (the statement that calls the **BubbleSort** proce-dure), and choose the **R**un | Toggle Breakpoint command to set a breakpoint. VBA highlights the line in your source code to indicate that you have set a breakpoint there. (Setting breakpoints was described in the preceding section of this lesson.)

2. Now run the **DebugDemo1** procedure. VBA will execute the code in the **DebugDemo1** procedure until it reaches the statement where you've set the breakpoint, and then switches to break mode, displaying the Debug window. You'll see a Debug window similar to the one shown in Figure 14.5. At this point, VBA is ready to execute the procedure call to the **BubbleSort** procedure.

Figure 14.5.

VBA displays this Debug window when it halts at the breakpoint set in line 28 of Listing 14.1.

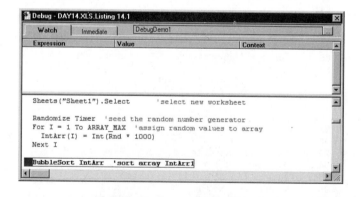

3. Choose the **R**un | Step **I**nto command. VBA executes the statement that calls the **BubbleSort** procedure, stepping into the **BubbleSort** procedure's code. (You can also press F8, or click the Step Into command button on the VBA toolbar.)

After choosing the Step Into command, the Code pane of the Debug window displays the procedure declaration for the **BubbleSort** procedure—VBA is now ready to start executing the statements in that procedure. (In the Code pane of the Debug window,

VBA displays a box around the statement it will execute next, as shown in Figure 14.6—this box indicates the current statement.)

Figure 14.6.

When single-stepping in break mode, VBA indicates the current statement in the Code pane of the Debug window by drawing a box around it.

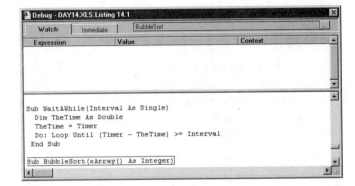

4. Continue using the **R**un | Step **I**nto command to execute statements. VBA executes a single statement each time you issue the Step Into command. As you continue to single-step through Listing 14.1 with the Step Into command, notice that—when you reach the call to the **Swap** procedure in line 97—the Step Into command also single-steps through the statements of the **Swap** procedure.

> **Tip:** The easiest and most practical way to single-step through your code with the Step Into command is to use one of the command shortcuts—either press F8 to issue the Step Into command, or click the Step Into command button on the VBA toolbar.

If you continue using the Step Into command to step through all of the statements in both **BubbleSort** and **Swap**, you'll follow VBA's code execution until you eventually return to the main procedure. After stepping through all of the statements in **BubbleSort**, VBA execution returns to line 29. If you spend a little more time using the Step Into command, you can watch the **For...Next** loop in lines 29 through 31 execute. If you continue to use the Step Into command, you'll eventually reach the **WaitAWhile** procedure call in line 51. If you use the Step Into command at this point, the Debugger will take you stepping into the statements of the **WaitAWhile** procedure.

 When you're tired of single-stepping through the code in Listing 14.1, you can end all code execution by choosing the **R**un | **E**nd command, or by clicking the Stop Macro command button on the VBA toolbar.

If you want to finish executing the code in Listing 14.1 at normal speed, choose the **Run | Continue** command, or click the Resume Macro command button on the VBA toolbar.

Using the Step Over Command

As you can see from the preceding exercise, stepping into every procedure call in your code can be quite tedious—it may not always be useful to you, either. For example, if you're stepping through the **BubbleSort** procedure because you suspect it has a bug in it, but you're confident that the **Swap** procedure is working fine, you won't want (and don't need) to step through all of the instructions in the **Swap** procedure every time you step through the **BubbleSort** procedure.

Fortunately, the VBA Debugger provides the Step Over command, which complements the action of the Step Into command. When you use the Step Over debugging command on a statement that calls a procedure or user-defined function, VBA doesn't step into that procedure's code; instead, it executes the called procedure's code at normal speed, and resumes single-stepping with the first statement *after* the procedure call. Stepping over procedure calls helps you focus on debugging the statements in the current procedure, without wasting time stepping through the statements in subsidiary procedures which you already know work correctly.

To get some practice using the Step Over command, follow these steps:

1. If you have not already set a breakpoint in line 28 of Listing 14.1, do so now.

2. Execute the **DebugDemo1** procedure. As in the previous exercise, VBA executes **DebugDemo1** until it reaches the statement containing the breakpoint and then displays a Debug window similar to the one already shown in Figure 14.5.

 3. Choose the **Run | Step Over** command (you can also press Shift+F8, or use the Step Over command button on the VBA toolbar).

   As soon as you choose the Step Over command, VBA executes the statement that calls the **BubbleSort** procedure—executing the entire **BubbleSort** procedure (including any procedures called by **BubbleSort**) at normal execution speed, *without* single-stepping through any of the statements in the **BubbleSort** procedure's code at all. VBA resumes single-stepping with the first statement in **DebugDemo1** after the one that called the **BubbleSort** procedure—line 29 of Listing 14.1.

4. Continue using the **Run | Step Over** command to execute statements. VBA executes a single statement each time you issue the Step Over command, except when the statement calls one of your procedures or functions. As you continue to single-step through Listing 14.1 with the Step Over command, notice that—when you reach the call to the **WaitAWhile** procedure in line 51—the Step Over command causes VBA to execute the **WaitAWhile** procedure *without* single-stepping through any of its statements—the Step Over command "steps over" the statements in the called procedure.

Tip: The easiest and most practical way to use the Step Over command is with one of its shortcuts—either press Shift+F8 to issue the Step Over command, or click the Step Over command button on the VBA toolbar.

When you're tired of single-stepping through the code in Listing 14.1, you can resume full speed code execution by choosing the **R**un | Continue command, or by clicking the Resume Macro command button on the VBA toolbar. To stop all code execution, choose the **R**un | **E**nd command, or click the Stop Macro command button on the VBA toolbar.

Understanding and Using Watched Variables

Single-stepping through your code alone won't provide all the clues you need to find and eliminate bugs in your programs. By single-stepping through your code, you may be able to tell, for example, that VBA is executing the wrong branch of an If...Then...Else statement. In this situation, there's clearly something wrong with the value produced by the logical expression in the If statement. How can you tell whether there is something wrong with the expression you've written, or whether the problem is due to an incorrect value in one of the variables used in the expression?

A *watched* variable allows you to inspect the contents of a variable while your code is executing. By using a watched variable, the Watch pane of the Debug window, and the Debugger's break mode, you can monitor the values generated by your program as it executes. For example, when trying to find out what's wrong with the logical expression of an If...Then...Else statement, you would watch the values of any variables in the logical expression, and might also watch the value of the logical expression itself. By watching those variables and the expression result, you'll be able to tell why the If...Then...Else statement doesn't have the expected results.

Typically, you watch variables or expressions whose values are associated with logical or runtime errors. You'll probably want to watch all of the variables in any expression that produces a runtime error—division by zero, for example—in order to determine which variable is responsible for the runtime error, and at which point in your program they acquire the offending value. Such information is invaluable in detecting and correcting bugs in your programs. VBA uses the Debugger window's Watch pane to enable you to monitor the contents of a variable, or the values produced by an expression.

Figure 14.7 shows the Debugger's Watch pane with several watched variables and one watched expression listed. Notice that the Watch pane lists the name of expression, the value currently

resulting from the expression, and the context of the expression. The expression itself may be either a single variable name, or any expression from your code.

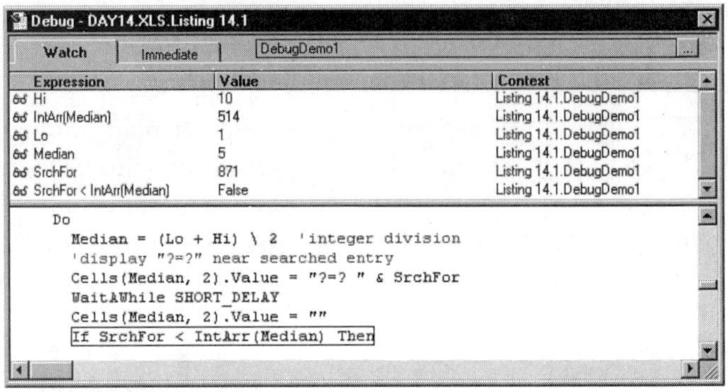

Figure 14.7.

The Debug window's Watch pane, with several watched variables and expressions.

Expression	Value	Context
66 Hi	10	Listing 14.1.DebugDemo1
66 IntArr(Median)	514	Listing 14.1.DebugDemo1
66 Lo	1	Listing 14.1.DebugDemo1
66 Median	5	Listing 14.1.DebugDemo1
66 SrchFor	871	Listing 14.1.DebugDemo1
66 SrchFor < IntArr(Median)	False	Listing 14.1.DebugDemo1

```
    Do
        Median = (Lo + Hi) \ 2    'integer division
        'display "?=?" near searched entry
        Cells(Median, 2).Value = "?=? " & SrchFor
        WaitAWhile SHORT_DELAY
        Cells(Median, 2).Value = ""
        If SrchFor < IntArr(Median) Then
```

In Figure 14.7, the first five items listed in the Watch pane are single variables, the last item is an expression. In the case of a single variable, the Value column displays the value currently stored in the variable; for expressions, the Value column displays what the expression's result is when evaluated using current variable values. If a listed watched variable is outside of its current scope, the Value column displays <out of context>. For array elements with invalid subscript values, the Value column of the Watch pane displays <subscript out of range>.

The Context column of the Watch pane tells you which module and procedure the watched variable or expression is in. All of the watched variables in the Watch pane in Figure 14.7 are in the same module and from the same procedure.

Note: Watch expressions only remain in effect for the current work session.

Adding a Watch Expression

Before you can watch a variable or expression, you must add it to the Watch pane of the Debug window. You can add any variable or expression from your source code to the list in the Watch pane.

To add a variable or expression to the Watch pane, follow these steps:

1. Either directly in a module sheet, or while already in the Debug window, select the text containing the variable or expression you want to add to the Watch pane.

2. Choose the **T**ools | **A**dd Watch command. VBA displays the Add Watch dialog box shown in Figure 14.8.

3. Fill in the dialog box options (described next), and choose OK. VBA closes the Add Watch dialog box and adds the selected variable or expression to the Watch pane.

Figure 14.8.

An Add Watch dialog box, showing the variable Median *being entered as a watched variable.*

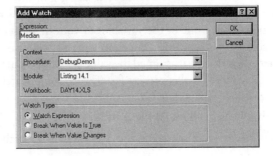

Note: You can open the Debug window at any time by choosing the **V**iew | **D**ebug Window command (or pressing Ctrl+G). VBA updates the Watch pane—and the Immediate pane, which you'll learn about later in this lesson—whether or not the Debug window is open. To view the updated Watch or Immediate panes, you must display the Debug window.

The Add Watch dialog box allows you to specify the following options for the new watch expression:

☐ The **E**xpression edit box allows you to enter the variable or expression that you want to watch. If you've selected text in your source code before opening the Add Watch dialog box, the selected text is filled in as the default. You must enter a valid variable name or VBA expression.

☐ The Context group box contains the **P**rocedure and **M**odule drop-down list boxes. By default, VBA uses the current module and procedure. You may specify a watch variable or expression in a different module or procedure by selecting the desired module in the **M**odule drop-down list, and the desired procedure in the **P**rocedure drop-down list.

☐ The Watch Type group box contains three radio buttons—**W**atch Expression, Break When Value Is **T**rue, and Break When Value **C**hanges. You use these options to give the Debugger special instructions about how you want to handle this watched variable or expression. If you select **W**atch Expression, VBA simply adds the variable or expression to the Watch pane. If you select Break When Value Is **T**rue, VBA enters break mode whenever the variable or expression you're watching evaluates to True. The Break When Value Changes option tells VBA to enter break mode whenever the value of the watched variable or expression changes.

Use the last two options in the Watch Type group box (Break When Value Is True and Break When Value Changes) to reduce the amount of time that you spend single-stepping through your code. For example, you might be trying to track down the source of a divide-by-zero runtime error—one of the variables in your division expression ends up with the value zero, causing the runtime error. To eliminate this bug, you need to find the point in your program where that variable is assigned the value 0—or find out whether any value is ever assigned to the variable. To make this process faster, you would watch the suspected variable with the Break When Value Changes option. You could then execute your code at full speed, entering break mode and viewing the Watch pane only when the value in the suspected variable changes.

To get some practice setting and using watched variables, follow these steps:

1. Clear all the breakpoints from Listing 14.1 by choosing the **R**un | **C**lear All Breakpoints command.

2. Set a breakpoint in line 43 of Listing 14.1. (Setting breakpoints was described earlier in this lesson.)

3. Execute the **DebugDemo1** procedure. VBA executes the procedure until it reaches the breakpoint. VBA then enters break mode, and displays the Debug window.

4. Click the Watch tab to display the Watch pane, if the Watch pane is not already visible.

5. Choose the **T**ools | **A**dd Watch command. VBA displays the Add Watch dialog box, already shown in Figure 14.8.

6. Enter the variable name **Lo** in the **E**xpression edit box, and choose OK. VBA closes the Add Watch dialog box and adds the **Lo** variable to the Watch pane.

7. Repeat steps 5 and 6 to add the variables **Hi**, and **Median** to the Watch pane, and again to add the expression **IntArr(Median)**.

8. Use the Step Over command (described in the preceding section of this lesson) to single-step through the Do loop in lines 47–58. Notice the changes in the Watch pane's display of the watched variables.

Figure 14.7 shows a Watch pane similar to the one you set up when you followed the preceding instructions. If you want, keep single-stepping through subsequent repetitions of the Do loop, noticing how the variable values in the Watch pane change as the code in the loop executes.

Editing a Watch Expression

Occasionally, you may want to edit a watched expression. You may just want to change the name of a variable to another similarly named variable to avoid adding a completely new watch variable, or for some other reason. VBA allows you to edit the expressions in the Watch pane.

To edit a watched expression, follow these steps:

1. Choose the **View** | **D**ebug Window command to display the Debug window (if the Debug window isn't already open).
2. Click the Watch tab to display the Watch pane (if the Watch pane isn't already displayed).
3. Select the watch expression you want to edit.
4. Choose the **Tools** | **E**dit Watch command. This command invokes the Edit Watch dialog box, which is essentially identical to the Add Watch dialog box already shown in Figure 14.8.
5. Make whatever changes you want in the watched expression's name, context, or watch type.
6. Choose OK to close the Edit Watch dialog box. VBA updates the edited watch expression in the Watch pane.

Deleting a Watch Expression

As you work with watched variables and expressions, you'll find that your list in the Watch pane tends to grow. At some point, you'll probably realize that you don't really need all of the watch expressions that you have set, and you'll want to delete some of them from the Watch pane. You can delete a watch expression in one of two ways:

☐ Select the watch expression you want to delete in the Watch pane, and then press the Del key. VBA deletes the selected watch expression from the Watch pane, without confirmation.

☐ Select the watch expression you want to delete, and then choose the **Tools** | **E**dit Watch command. VBA displays the Edit Watch dialog box. Choose the **D**elete command button in the Edit Watch dialog box. VBA deletes the selected watch expression from the Watch pane.

Using the Instant Watch

Sometimes, you may just want to take a peek at the value of a variable or expression, without adding it to the Watch pane. For example, you may want to get a glance at the current value of a loop counter as you're single-stepping through your code, without actually creating a watch for the loop counter.

VBA allows you to take a quick peek at variable and expression values by using the Instant Watch dialog box. To use the Instant Watch dialog box, follow these steps:

1. In the Debug window's Code pane, place the insertion point inside the expression or variable you wish to view.

2. Choose the **T**ools | Instant **W**atch command (you can also press Shift+F9 or click the Instant Watch command button on the VBA toolbar). VBA displays the Instant Watch dialog box. Figure 14.9 shows a sample Instant Watch dialog box.

3. If you want to add this variable or expression to the Watch pane, click the **A**dd button in the Instant Watch dialog box. VBA adds the variable or expression to the Watch pane as a standard watch expression, with the context shown in the Instant Watch dialog box.

4. To close the Instant Watch dialog box *without* adding the selected variable or expression to the Watch pane, choose the Cancel button.

Figure 14.9.

An Instant Watch dialog box showing the current context and value for the array element `IntArr(Median)`.

Tracing Procedure Calls

Frequently, you'll need to determine the exact *chain*, or sequence, of procedure calls leading up to a particular statement that generates errors. The chain of procedure calls may be important because often the exact sequence of procedure calls plays an important role in determining the source of an error. For example, you may find a statement that results in a divide-by-zero error, but you don't know why one of the variables in the statement contains a zero. Knowing the exact chain of procedure calls may help you determine, for example, that a procedure was called with an optional argument missing, or simply with a bad value in a required argument.

VBA allows you to view the chain of procedure calls through the Debug window. To view the chain of procedure calls, click on the command button labeled with an ellipsis (…) in the Debug window. (This button is located near the top right corner of the Debug window; refer to Figure 14.7.)

When you click on the ellipsis button in the Debug window, VBA displays the Calls dialog box shown in Figure 14.10 (the exact chain of procedure calls will vary). As Figure 14.10 shows, the

Calls dialog box lists the sequence of procedure and function calls leading up to the currently executing procedure or function.

Figure 14.10.

A Calls dialog box, showing the chain of procedure calls for the **Swap** *procedure in Listing 14.1.*

To reproduce the Calls dialog box shown in Figure 14.10, follow these steps:

1. Choose the **R**un | **C**lear All Breakpoints command to remove all breakpoints from Listing 14.1.
2. Set a breakpoint in line 95 of Listing 14.1 (inside the **Swap** procedure).
3. Execute the **DebugDemo1** procedure. VBA executes the procedure until it reaches the breakpoint in line 95, and then enters break mode, displaying the Debug window.
4. Choose the ellipsis (...) command button in the Debug window. VBA displays the Calls dialog box already shown in Figure 14.10. The list in the Calls dialog box shows all of the procedure calls leading up to the **Swap** procedure: **Swap** was called by **BubbleSort**, which in turn was called by **DebugDemo1**.

Notice that the Calls dialog box contains two command buttons—**S**how and Cancel. The Cancel button simply closes the Calls dialog box and returns you to the Debug window. The **S**how button, however, performs a very useful function.

Use the **S**how button in the Calls dialog box to see the statement that contains the call to a particular procedure. You can use the **S**how button to help backtrack the argument values passed to a particular procedure. Assume, for example, that you're trying to resolve a divide-by-zero runtime error, and you determine that the offending value has been passed into the current procedure as one of the procedure's arguments. Open the Calls dialog box, select the name of the procedure that called the current procedure, and then choose the **S**how command button. VBA closes the Calls dialog box and displays the statement that called the current procedure in the Debug window's Code pane. You can use the **S**how button and the Calls dialog box to work backwards through the entire chain of procedure calls.

Using the Immediate Pane

Sometimes, even the combination of single-stepping, watched expressions, and tracing procedure calls won't be enough to help you track down a bug in your code. VBA's Debugger offers one final tool to help you locate defects in your code.

The Debug window's Immediate pane is a free-form editor that allows you to inspect the values in variables, inspect the values of expressions, perform on-the-fly computations, alter the values of variables, and test the results of a function—all while your VBA code's execution is suspended in break mode. To view or use the Immediate pane, open the Debug window and click the Immediate tab; VBA displays the Immediate pane.

You use Print commands (or the shorthand ? for Print) to display information in the Immediate pane. You use the Print command in the Immediate pane along with a list of variables or expressions. As soon as you type a Print command and press Enter, VBA evaluates the expressions you listed with the Print command and displays their results on the line below the Print command. Figure 14.11 shows a sample session using the Immediate pane.

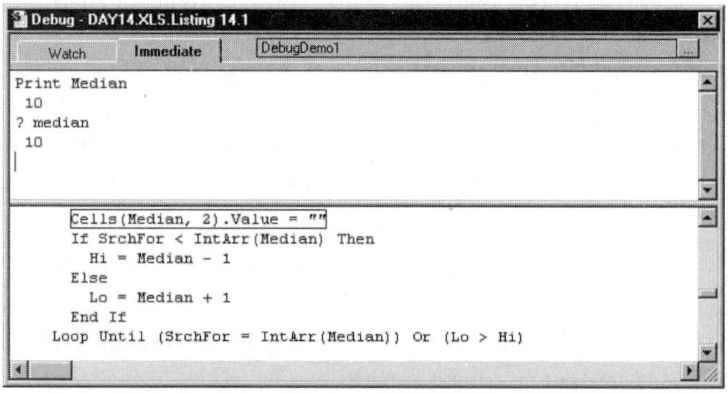

Figure 14.11.

A session with the Immediate pane showing the output of some Print commands.

```
Debug - DAY14.XLS.Listing 14.1                                    ×
  Watch     Immediate      DebugDemo1                          ...
Print Median
  10
? median
  10

  Cells(Median, 2).Value = ""
  If SrchFor < IntArr(Median) Then
     Hi = Median - 1
  Else
     Lo = Median + 1
  End If
  Loop Until (SrchFor = IntArr(Median)) Or (Lo > Hi)
```

Using the *Debug.Print* Statement

The VBA Debugger, like many other features in VBA, is an object. The VBA Debugger object has only one method, the Print method. You use the Debug.Print method to display information in the Immediate pane of the Debug window as your code executes. To use the Debug.Print method, you write VBA statements that call the Debug.Print method.

Usually, you'll use the Debug.Print method in combination with the Stop statement you learned about earlier in this lesson. Combining these two elements allows you to run your programs at full speed, but still generate debugging information similar to the information you can get by watching variables or expressions. Typically, you'll add one or more statements calling the Debug.Print method, and displaying the value of certain variables or expressions on the Immediate pane. Although the Immediate pane is not visible when VBA executes your code normally, VBA will enter break mode whenever it encounters a Stop statement, displaying the Debug window and making the Immediate pane available. The Immediate pane then allows you to view any output generated by the Debug.Print statements in your code. By using this technique, you can save a lot of debugging time by avoiding single-stepping through code. After

you've viewed the information in the Immediate pane, you can then resume execution of your program at normal speed.

Listing 14.2 contains the **DebugDemo2** procedure and module.

Listing 14.2. The DebugDemo2 procedure, used to illustrate the use of Debug.Print.

```
1:    Option Explicit
2:    Option Base 1
3:
4:    Sub DebugDemo2()
5:      Const ARRAY_MAX As Integer = 10
6:      Const MSG_ROW As Integer = ARRAY_MAX + 2
7:      Const SHORT_DELAY = 1
8:      Const iTitle = "Binary Search"
9:
10:     Dim IntArr(ARRAY_MAX) As Integer
11:     Dim I As Integer
12:     Dim Hi As Integer
13:     Dim Lo As Integer
14:     Dim Median As Integer
15:     Dim oldSheet As String
16:     Dim SrchFor As Variant
17:     Dim Rsp As Integer
18:     Dim pStr As String
19:
20:     oldSheet = ActiveSheet.Name   'preserve current sheet
21:     Sheets("Sheet1").Select       'select new worksheet
22:
23:     Randomize Timer   'seed the random number generator
24:     For I = 1 To ARRAY_MAX  'assign random values to array
25:       IntArr(I) = Int(Rnd * 1000)
26:     Next I
27:
28:     BubbleSort IntArr   'sort array IntArr1
29:     For I = 1 To ARRAY_MAX   'display the elements of array
30:       Cells(I, 1).Value = IntArr(I)
31:     Next I
32:
33:     'get a value to search for from user, until the user
34:     'doesn't want to search anymore
35:     Do
36:       SrchFor = Application.InputBox( _
37:               prompt:="Enter a number to search for:", _
38:               Title:=iTitle & " Input", _
39:               Type:=1)
40:       SrchFor = CInt(SrchFor) 'convert value to integer
41:
42:       'display search status at bottom of number list
43:       Cells(MSG_ROW, 1).Value = "Searching for " & SrchFor
44:
45:       Lo = LBound(IntArr)    'start searching
```

continues

543

Listing 14.2. continued

```
46:        Hi = UBound(IntArr)
47:
48:        Debug.Print "IntArr(Median) SrchFor", "Lo", "Hi", _
49:                      "Median"
50:        Do
51:          Median = (Lo + Hi) \ 2   'integer division
52:          Cells(Median, 2).Value = "?=? " & SrchFor
53:          WaitAWhile SHORT_DELAY
54:
55:          Debug.Print IntArr(Median), SrchFor, Lo, Hi, Median
56:
57:          Cells(Median, 2).Value = ""
58:          If SrchFor < IntArr(Median) Then
59:            Hi = Median - 1
60:          Else
61:            Lo = Median + 1
62:          End If
63:        Loop Until (SrchFor = IntArr(Median)) Or (Lo > Hi)
64:
65:        Stop   'enter break mode
66:
67:        If SrchFor = IntArr(Median) Then   'found a match
68:          pStr = "Found " & SrchFor & " at IntArr(" & _
69:                  Median & ")"
70:        Else   'display no-match found message
71:          pStr = "No match for " & SrchFor
72:        End If
73:        Cells(MSG_ROW, 1).Value = ""    'clear message area
74:
75:        pStr = pStr & Chr(13) & Chr(13) & _
76:                "Search for another number?"
77:        Rsp = MsgBox(prompt:=pStr, _
78:                      Title:=iTitle, Buttons:=vbYesNo)
79:      Loop Until Rsp = vbNo
80:      Sheets(oldSheet).Select   'restore original sheet
81:    End Sub
82:
83:    Sub WaitAWhile(Interval As Single)
84:      Dim TheTime As Double
85:      TheTime = Timer
86:      Do: Loop Until (Timer - TheTime) >= Interval
87:    End Sub
88:
89:    Sub BubbleSort(xArray() As Integer)
90:    'sorts integer array in ascending order
91:      Dim I As Integer, J As Integer
92:      For I = LBound(xArray) To UBound(xArray) - 1
93:        For J = I + 1 To UBound(xArray)
94:          If xArray(I) > xArray(J) Then _
95:            Swap xArray(I), xArray(J)
96:        Next J
97:      Next I
98:    End Sub
99:
```

544

```
100: Sub Swap(I1 As Integer, I2 As Integer)
101:    Dim temp As Integer
102:    temp = I1: I1 = I2: I2 = temp
103: End Sub
```

Analysis

This listing is identical to Listing 14.1, but has had some Debug.Print statements and a Stop statement added to it. The Debug.Print statement in line 48 was added to create a heading for subsequent values displayed in the Immediate pane. The Debug.Print statement in line 55 was added to display the values of the **Median**, **Hi**, **Lo**, **SrchFor** variables, and the **IntArr** array element subscripted by **Median**. Finally, the Stop statement in line 65 was added to cause VBA to enter break mode and allow you to see the values displayed by the Debug.Print statements. Figure 14.12 shows the Immediate pane after a sample session with **DebugDemo2** completed a single search.

Figure 14.12.

The Immediate pane, showing the output of the Debug.Print statements in Listing 14.2.

IntArr(Median)	SrchFor	Lo	Hi	Median
431	750	1	10	5
589	750	6	10	8
594	750	9	10	9
750	750	10	10	10

```
            Hi = Median - 1
        Else
            Lo = Median + 1
        End If
    Loop Until (SrchFor = IntArr(Median)) Or (Lo > Hi)

    Stop    'enter break mode
```

When you execute **DebugDemo2**, VBA executes the procedure at normal speed, until it encounters the Stop statement in line 65. VBA then enters break mode, and opens the Debug window. You may need to click the Immediate tab to display the Immediate pane. The exact list of values you see printed will depend on the actual list of random numbers that **DebugDemo2** generates, and the number you entered to search for.

After reviewing the contents of the Immediate pane, continue executing the **DebugDemo2** procedure by pressing F5 or clicking the Resume Macro command button on the VBA toolbar. Each time you search for a number in the list, the **DebugDemo2** procedure will pause at the Stop statement, and you'll see a new set of output values in the Immediate pane (these values are generated by the Do loop in lines 50 through 63).

Summary

This lesson discussed the various debugging features offered by VBA. You learned that there are four basic types of errors you'll encounter: syntax, compile, runtime, and logical. You also learned the typical causes for these types of errors.

In this lesson, you learned what VBA's break mode is, and how to use the break mode in combination with the Step Into and Step Over commands to suspend your code's execution and then step through your VBA code one statement or procedure at a time. You learned about VBA's Debug window, the Code pane, the Watch pane, and the Immediate pane.

This lesson taught you how to set and clear breakpoints, and showed you how to use them. You were shown how to watch particular variables or expressions in the Watch pane, and how to add, edit, or delete watched variables. You also learned how to use the Stop statement as a hard-coded breakpoint.

Next, you learned how and why to trace the chain of calling procedures, and, finally, you learned how to use the Immediate pane of the Debug window. As part of learning how to use the Immediate pane, you also learned how to use the Debug.Print method in your VBA code to display information on the Immediate pane while your code is executing.

Q&A

Q Isn't there some way I can turn Debug.Print statements on or off, so I don't have to edit my entire program or procedure again once it's working correctly?

A No, not directly. There is, however, an indirect way to turn Debug.Print statements on and off. Write each Debug.Print statement as part of an If...Then statement, and use a public, module-level Boolean constant (named, for example **DEBUGGING**) to indicate whether or not you're debugging your code. The following code fragment demonstrates how to use this technique:

```
If DEBUGGING Then
   Debug.Print "Debugging is on."
End If
```

If the **DEBUGGING** constant is False, then the Debug.Print statement won't execute.

Q Is there a statement that counteracts the Stop statement?

A No. To resume program execution, you must use the **R**un | Con**t**inue command.

Workshop

Answers are in Appendix A.

Quiz

1. Where do you place a breakpoint in a procedure or function?

2. How can multiple breakpoints help you debug a program?

3. Does VBA allow you to watch the values of an entire array?

4. How can you experiment with calling a function without writing VBA code to call that function?

5. What command do you use to reset single-stepping a macro in order to rerun it?

Exercises

1. Change line 63 of Listing 14.2 from the following:

   ```
   63:        Loop Until (SrchFor = IntArr(Median)) Or (Lo > Hi)
   ```

   to the following:

   ```
   63:        Loop Until (SrchFor = IntArr(Median)) Or (Lo >= Hi)
   ```

   Run the modified procedure and examine the values generated by the Debug.Print statement. What kind of effect does replacing the > operator with >= have on the procedure's operation?

2. Change the following If statement in Listing 14.2:

   ```
   58:        If SrchFor < IntArr(Median) Then
   59:          Hi = Median - 1
   60:        Else
   61:          Lo = Median + 1
   62:        End If
   ```

   into the following:

   ```
   58:        If SrchFor < IntArr(Median) Then
   59:          Hi = Median
   60:        Else
   61:          Lo = Median
   62:        End If
   ```

   Run the modified procedure and examine the values generated by the Debug.Print statement. What effect does this modification have? Does the procedure still work correctly?

3. **BUG BUSTER:** What is the error in this following loop?

   ```
   1:  Dim I As Integer
   2:  Dim S As String
   3:  Dim FindChar As String * 1
   4:  Dim ReplChar As String * 1
   5:
   6:  S = "Hello World!! How are you?"
   7:  FindChar = "!"
   8:  ReplChar = " "
   ```

14

```
9:  I = 1
10:
11: Do While I < Len(S)
12:   If Mid(S, I, 1) = FindChar Then
13:     Mid(S, I, 1) = FindChar
14:   End If
15: Loop
```

4. **BUG BUSTER:** Where is the error in the following statements? What category of errors does it belong to?

```
1:  I = 55
2:
3:  If I < 10 And I > 100 Then
4:    Debug.Print "I = ", I
5:  End If
6:  Debug.Print "Hello!"
```

5. **BUG BUSTER:** Where is the error in the following statements? How can you fix it?

```
1:  Dim S As String
2:  Dim SubStr As String
3:  Dim I As Integer
4:
5:  S = "The rain in Spain stays mainly in the plain"
6:  SubStr = "ain"
7:  I = InStr(S, SubStr)
8:  Do While I > 0
9:    Debug.Print "Match at "; I
10:   I = InStr(I, S, SubStr)
11: Loop
```

2

You've finished your second week of learning how to program in Visual Basic for Applications. By now you should feel relatively comfortable with VBA. You have covered all of the core concepts in Visual Basic for Applications.

The following listings contain two complete VBA modules that pull together many of the VBA programming elements and concepts from the previous week. The two modules together make up a single VBA program that allows a user to create a new workbook file and give it a name in a single operation, without duplicating the names of any workbooks that might already be open or on the disk in the same directory. The program also allows the user to optionally specify the number and names of the worksheets in the workbook, and to optionally add named VBA modules to the workbook.

This program was designed using the top-down and step-wise refinement techniques described in Day 11. The pseudo-code below shows the major design outline for this program:

1. Get a workbook filename from the user.
2. Make sure the workbook doesn't already exist.
   a. If the workbook is already open, offer to make it the active workbook.
   b. If the workbook isn't open, but exists in the current folder, offer to open the workbook.
3. Create the new workbook, using the standard Excel workbook defaults.
4. Get summary information for the new workbook.
   a. Require the user to enter the author information.
   b. Require the user to enter the title of the workbook.
   c. All other summary information is optional.
5. Ask user if she/he wants to adjust the number of worksheets in the workbook.
   a. Get the number of worksheets from user, requiring at least 1 worksheet, and don't allow user to cancel.
   b. Create or eliminate sheets from the workbook until it contains the user's specified number of worksheets.
6. Ask user if she/he wants to change the default names of the worksheets in the workbook.
   a. Get worksheet names from user for as many worksheets as are in the workbook; ensure that names are unique.
   b. Ask user whether to sort the worksheet names alphabetically.
      b.1 If so, sort the array of worksheet names.
   c. Rename all worksheets in the workbook, using array of worksheet names previously obtained from user.
7. Ask user if she/he wants to add module sheets to the workbook.
   a. Get number of module sheets from user; allow user to enter 0 sheets as a way of cancelling the operation.
   b. Ask user if she/he wants to change the default module names.
      b.1 For the user's number of modules, ask user for new module name. Ensure that module names are unique.
   c. Add modules, renaming each module as it is added to the workbook, for the specified number of modules.
8. Save the new workbook, but leave it open as the current workbook, with the first sheet selected.

As you study the following listings, pay attention to how each task is handled by its own procedure or function, and how various procedures call several different functions or procedures to accomplish their own tasks. Notice also that the source code has been divided into three different modules—one module for the main program, another module to hold the supporting procedures and functions highly specific to the main task, and a third module to hold the more generic functions used by the program.

Type

Listing R2.1. The `OpenNewBook` program's main module and procedure.

```
1:   Option Explicit
2:
3:   Type SmryInfo    'same data as summary info properties page
4:       Title As String
5:       Subject As String
6:       Author As String
7:       Keywords As String
8:       Comments As String
9:   End Type
10:
11:  Sub OpenNewBook()
```

```
12:     'Creates a new workbook, ensuring that the chosen workbook
13:     'is not already open, and does not already exist in the
14:     'current disk folder. Optionally allows user to select the
15:     'number of worksheets and modules, and allows user to give
16:     'them specific names when creating the workbook.
17:
18:     Const nfTitle = "Open New Workbook"
19:
20:     Dim fName As String         'filename, including path
21:     Dim BName As String          'filename, without path
22:     Dim OKName As Boolean
23:     Dim Smry As SmryInfo              'book's summary info
24:     Dim Ans As Integer               'answers from MsgBox
25:     Dim mPrompt As String             'prompt for MsgBox
26:     Dim nBook As Workbook        'object for new workbook
27:
28:     'display status bar message
29:     Application.StatusBar = "Creating New Workbook..."
30:
31:     BName = "New Workbook"          'get new filename from user
32:     OKName = False
33:     Do
34:         fName = GetBookName(Dflt:=BName, Title:=nfTitle & _
35:                     " - Select Save As Name for New Workbook")
36:         If fName = "False" Then EndNewBook     'user canceled
37:
38:         BName = FullName2BookName(fName)
39:         If IsBookOpen(BName) Then
40:           mPrompt = BName & " is already open. " & _
41:                     "Would you like to switch to it?"
42:           Ans = MsgBox(Prompt:=mPrompt, Title:=nfTitle, _
43:                     Buttons:=vbQuestion + vbYesNo)
44:           If Ans = vbYes Then
45:             Workbooks(BName).Activate
46:             EndNewBook
47:           End If
48:         ElseIf IsDiskFile(fName) Then
49:           mPrompt = fName & Chr(13) & _
50:                 " already exists. Would you like to open it?"
51:           Ans = MsgBox(Prompt:=mPrompt, Title:=nfTitle, _
52:                     Buttons:=vbQuestion + vbYesNo)
53:           If Ans = vbYes Then
54:             Workbooks.Open fName
55:             EndNewBook
56:           End If
57:         Else
58:           OKName = True   'book is neither open nor exists
59:         End If
60:     Loop Until OKName
61:
62:     'create new workbook with one worksheet
63:     Set nBook = Workbooks.Add(xlWorksheet)
64:
65:     'get summary information
66:     GetSmryInfo Info:=Smry, Title:=nfTitle
```

continues

Listing R2.1. continued

```
67:     With nBook     'fill in summary information
68:       .Title = Smry.Title
69:       .Subject = Smry.Subject
70:       .Author = Smry.Author
71:       .Keywords = Smry.Keywords
72:       .Comments = Smry.Comments
73:     End With
74:
75:     mPrompt = "Adjust number of worksheets in workbook?" & _
76:                 Chr(13) & "Workbook currently has " & _
77:                 nBook.Worksheets.Count & " worksheets."
78:     Ans = MsgBox(Prompt:=mPrompt, Title:=nfTitle, _
79:                 Buttons:=vbQuestion + vbYesNo)
80:     If Ans = vbYes Then 'set up new worksheets
81:       NewBook_Worksheets nBook, nfTitle
82:     End If
83:
84:     mPrompt = "Add module sheets to this workbook?"
85:     Ans = MsgBox(Prompt:=mPrompt, Title:=nfTitle, _
86:                 Buttons:=vbQuestion + vbYesNo)
87:     If Ans = vbYes Then
88:       NewBook_Modules nBook, nfTitle     'set up new modules
89:     End If
90:
91:     'Finally, save the new workbook file
92:     nBook.SaveAs fileName:=fName, _
93:                 FileFormat:=xlNormal, _
94:                 ReadOnlyRecommended:=False, _
95:                 CreateBackup:=False
96:     nBook.Activate
97:     nBook.Sheets(1).Activate
98:     EndNewBook 'do housekeeping
99:   End Sub
```

 Listing R2.1 is the first module of the program, and contains only one procedure, **OpenNewBook**. This procedure is a more fully developed version of the **NewFile** procedure from last week's review, and incorporates almost all of the VBA features that you've learned in the past week.

Notice the user-defined data type (Day 10) declared in lines 3 through 9. **OpenNewBook** uses this user-defined type to pass the summary information back and forth between this procedure and the procedure that actually gets the information from the user. A Do loop (Day 9) starts in line 33, and repeats until the filename chosen by the user does not duplicate the name of a workbook that is already open or already exists on the disk in the current folder.

The **OpenNewBook** procedure calls many other procedures and functions that help it do its work. These other procedures avoid duplication of code, and make it possible for the **OpenNewBook** procedure to operate in a flexible and efficient manner. All of the procedures and functions that **OpenNewBook** calls are in the second and third modules (Listing R2.2 and Listing R2.3).

Line 34 of **OpenNewBook** calls the **GetBookName** procedure to get the workbook filename from the user. Line 38 calls the **FullName2BookName** function to get just the workbook name out of the filename selected by the user. (The filename returned by **GetBookName** contains the full directory path, including the drive letter.)

Lines 39 through 59 contain several nested If...Then...Else statements that test to ensure that the workbook filename selected by the user doesn't duplicate the name of a workbook that is already open or the name of a workbook that is already stored on the disk. In the process of testing whether the workbook already exists, **OpenNewBook** calls the functions **IsBookOpen**, and **IsDiskFile** (both of these are in the third module).

Line 63 uses the Add method of the Workbooks collection to create a new workbook containing only one worksheet; the statement in line 63 also sets an object variable (Day 7) to refer to the newly created workbook. The original statement for the Add method was taken from a recorded macro. The Add method was then researched in the online help system, which revealed that the Add method returns an object reference to the newly created workbook object, and has an optional argument to specify that the new workbook should contain only a single worksheet. If an object method returns a result, you can use that method in your VBA code like a function—just remember to include the parentheses, and to use the result in an expression somehow.

> **Note:** Several of the statements in all three modules shown here were created by copying statements from recorded macros. The methods and procedures from the recorded macro statements were then researched in the online help system to find out about additional options for those methods. You can use this technique to help develop your own VBA code.

Line 66 calls the **GetSmryInfo** procedure, which uses a procedure argument passed by reference (Day 11) to return the summary information for the new workbook to **OpenNewBook**.

Lines 75 through 82 carry out the task of asking the user whether or not to adjust the number of worksheets in the workbook. If the user does choose to adjust the number of workbooks, the statement in line 81 calls the **NewBook_Worksheets** procedure. **NewBook_Worksheets** carries out the task of getting the desired number of worksheets from the user, optionally allowing the user to rename the worksheets and alphabetically sort their names.

Lines 84 through 89 carry out the task of asking the user whether or not to add module sheets to the workbook. If the user does decide to add module sheets, line 88 calls the **NewBook_Modules** procedure to set the number of module sheets, and optionally get and sort their names.

Finally, lines 92 through 95 save the new workbook, and lines 96 and 97 ensure that the new workbook is the active workbook, with its first worksheet selected.

The next listing shows another complete module that contains all of the procedures called directly by **OpenNewBook**. (All three modules must be in the same workbook for **OpenNewBook** to operate correctly.)

Type

Listing R2.2. The **OpenNewBook** program's supporting procedures module.

```
 1:    Option Private Module
 2:    Option Explicit
 3:
 4:    Public Const BINCOMP As Integer = 0   'binary comparison
 5:    Public Const TXTCOMP As Integer = 1   'text comparison
 6:    Public Const STREQUAL As Integer = 0  'StrComp: equality
 7:    Public Const STRLESS As Integer = -1  'StrComp: less than
 8:    Public Const STRGREAT As Integer = 1  'StrComp: greater than
 9:
10:    Sub EndNewBook()
11:    'ends OpenNewBook program, after cleaning up
12:       Application.StatusBar = False
13:       End
14:    End Sub
15:
16:
17:    Sub GetSmryInfo(ByRef Info As SmryInfo, _
18:                    ByVal Title As String)
19:    'returns workbook summary information
20:       Title = Title & " Summary Information"
21:       With Info     'get summary information
22:         .Author = GetSmryItem(Item:="author", Title:=Title, _
23:                               Dflt:=Application.UserName, _
24:                               Required:=True)
25:         .Title = GetSmryItem(Item:="title", Title:=Title, _
26:                              Required:=True)
27:         .Subject = GetSmryItem(Item:="subject", Title:=Title)
28:         .Keywords = GetSmryItem(Item:="keywords", Title:=Title)
29:         .Comments = GetSmryItem(Item:="comments", Title:=Title)
30:       End With
31:    End Sub
32:
33:
34:    Function GetSmryItem(Item As String, _
35:                         Optional ByVal Title, _
36:                         Optional Dflt, _
37:                         Optional Required) As String
38:    'gets file summary info for specified Item
39:
40:       Const Prmpt1 = "Enter the "
41:       Dim Prmpt2 As String        '2nd part of prompt
42:       Dim tStr As String
43:
44:       If IsMissing(Title) Then Title = UCase(Item)
45:       If IsMissing(Required) Or _
46:          VarType(Required) <> vbBoolean Then
47:          Required = False
```

```
48:      Title = Title & " - Optional Entry"
49:    Else
50:      Title = Title & " - Required Entry"
51:    End If
52:
53:    Prmpt2 = " for this workbook."
54:    If Not Required Then
55:      Prmpt2 = Prmpt2 & Chr(13) & _
56:                "(Press Esc or choose Cancel to skip.)"
57:    End If
58:
59:    Do
60:      tStr = InputBox(Prompt:=Prmpt1 & Item & Prmpt2, _
61:                    Title:=Title, Default:=Dflt)
62:      If Required And (Trim(tStr) = "") Then
63:        MsgBox Prompt:="You must enter the " & Item & "!", _
64:               Title:=Title & " - ERROR", _
65:               Buttons:=vbExclamation
66:      End If
67:    Loop Until (Not Required) Or (Trim(tStr) <> "")
68:    GetSmryItem = tStr
69:  End Function
70:
71:
72:  Sub NewBook_Worksheets(ByRef Book As Workbook, _
73:                        ByVal Title As String)
74:  'Get and set number of worksheets for the new workbook
75:
76:    Dim shtNames() As String       'array for workbook names
77:    Dim numSheets As Integer   'number of worksheets from user
78:    Dim Ans As Integer         'MsgBox answers
79:    Dim k As Integer           'loop counter
80:    Dim Sht As Worksheet
81:    Dim Sht2 As Worksheet
82:
83:    Title = Title & " - Select Worksheets"
84:
85:    Do     'get desired number of worksheets
86:      numSheets = GetInteger(Prompt:="Enter number of " & _
87:                       "worksheets for this workbook:", _
88:                       Title:=Title, Default:=1)
89:      If numSheets < 1 Then
90:        MsgBox Prompt:="You must have at least one " & _
91:               "worksheet in a workbook!", _
92:               Title:=Title, _
93:               Buttons:=vbExclamation
94:      End If
95:    Loop Until numSheets >= 1
96:
97:    Ans = MsgBox(Title:=Title, _
98:               Buttons:=vbQuestion + vbYesNo, _
99:               Prompt:="Change default worksheet names?")
100:   If Ans = vbNo Then   'just add sheets
101:     For k = (Book.Worksheets.Count + 1) To numSheets
```

continues

Listing R2.2. continued

```
102:        Set Sht = Book.Worksheets(Book.Worksheets.Count)
103:        Set Sht2 = Book.Worksheets.Add
104:        Sht2.Move after:=Sht
105:     Next k
106:     Exit Sub 'no more work to do
107:    End If
108:
109:    ReDim shtNames(1 To numSheets)   'size the array of names
110:    For k = 1 To numSheets
111:      shtNames(k) = "Sheet" & k    'make default names
112:    Next k
113:
114:    'get names of worksheets from user
115:    Get_NameList Book:=Book, List:=shtNames, _
116:                 Prompt:="Enter a worksheet name:", _
117:                 Title:=Title
118:    Ans = MsgBox(Title:=Title, _
119:                 Buttons:=vbQuestion + vbYesNo, _
120:             Prompt:="Sort worksheet names alphabetically?")
121:    If Ans = vbYes Then BubbleSortStrings shtNames
122:
123:    'create the worksheets with names
124:    With Book
125:      'start by just renaming the first sheet
126:      .Worksheets(1).Name = shtNames(1)
127:      For k = 2 To numSheets
128:        Set Sht = .Worksheets(.Worksheets.Count)
129:        Set Sht2 = .Worksheets.Add
130:        Sht2.Move after:=Sht
131:        Sht2.Name = shtNames(k)
132:      Next k
133:    End With
134: End Sub
135:
136:
137: Sub Get_NameList(Book As Workbook, _
138:                  List() As String, _
139:                  Prompt As String, _
140:                  Title As String)
141: 'gets a list of worksheet names as strings
142:    Dim k As Long, tStr As String, GoodName As Boolean
143:
144:    For k = LBound(List) To UBound(List)
145:      Do 'ask for a unique name
146:        tStr = InputBox(Prompt:=Prompt, _
147:                        Title:=Title, _
148:                        Default:=List(k))
149:        If Trim(tStr) = "" Then
150:          Exit Sub   'user canceled, no more work
151:        Else
152:          If StrComp(tStr, List(k), TXTCOMP) = STREQUAL Then
153:            GoodName = True
154:          Else
155:            If InListSoFar(List, tStr, k - 1) Or _
```

```
156:                SheetExists(Book, tStr) Then
157:                MsgBox Prompt:="Use a different name. " & _
158:                        "This name already exists; " & _
159:                        "sheet names must be unique.", _
160:                        Title:="Sheet Name Error", _
161:                        Buttons:=vbExclamation
162:               GoodName = False
163:           Else
164:               GoodName = True
165:               List(k) = tStr
166:           End If
167:         End If
168:       End If
169:     Loop Until GoodName
170:   Next k
171: End Sub
172:
173:
174: Sub NewBook_Modules(ByRef Book As Workbook, _
175:                      ByVal Title As String)
176: 'Get number of worksheets for the new workbook
177:   Dim shtNames() As String
178:   Dim numSheets As Integer
179:   Dim Ans As Integer
180:   Dim k As Integer
181:   Dim Sht As Object
182:   Dim Sht2 As Object
183:
184:   Title = Title & " - Select Modules"
185:
186:   Do      'get desired number of modules
187:     numSheets = GetInteger(Prompt:="Enter the number " & _
188:                     "of modules for this workbook:" & _
189:                     Chr(13) & "(Enter 0 to cancel)", _
190:                 Title:=Title, Default:=0)
191:     If numSheets < 0 Then Beep
192:   Loop Until numSheets >= 0
193:
194:   If numSheets = 0 Then Exit Sub
195:
196:   Ans = MsgBox(Title:=Title, _
197:             Prompt:="Change default module names now?", _
198:             Buttons:=vbYesNo + vbQuestion)
199:   If Ans = vbNo Then
200:     For k = 1 To numSheets
201:       Set Sht = Book.Sheets(Book.Sheets.Count)
202:       Set Sht2 = Book.Modules.Add
203:       Sht2.Move after:=Sht
204:     Next k
205:     Exit Sub  'end this procedure
206:   End If
207:
208:   'get a list of names from the user
209:   ReDim shtNames(1 To numSheets)
```

continues

Listing R2.2. continued

```
210:     For k = 1 To numSheets
211:        shtNames(k) = "Module" & k
212:     Next k
213:     Get_NameList Book:=Book, _
214:                  List:=shtNames, _
215:                  Prompt:="Enter module name: ", _
216:                  Title:=Title
217:     Ans = MsgBox(Title:=Title, _
218:              Prompt:="Sort module names alphabetically?", _
219:              Buttons:=vbQuestion + vbYesNo)
220:     If Ans = vbYes Then BubbleSortStrings shtNames
221:
222:     'create module sheets
223:     For k = 1 To numSheets
224:        Set Sht = Book.Sheets(Book.Sheets.Count)
225:        Set Sht2 = Book.Modules.Add
226:        Sht2.Move after:=Sht
227:        Sht2.Name = shtNames(k)
228:     Next k
229: End Sub
230:
231:
232: Sub BubbleSortStrings(Arr() As String)
233: 'sorts any string array in ascending order
234:    Dim I As Integer, J As Integer
235:    For I = LBound(Arr) To UBound(Arr) - 1
236:       For J = I + 1 To UBound(Arr)
237:          If StrComp(Arr(I), Arr(J), BINCOMP) = STRGREAT Then
238:             Swap Arr(I), Arr(J)
239:          End If
240:       Next J
241:    Next I
242: End Sub
243:
244:
245: Sub Swap(T1 As Variant, T2 As Variant)
246:    Dim tmp As Variant
247:    tmp = T1: T1 = T2: T2 = tmp
248: End Sub
```

  All of the functions and procedures in this second module must be called by another procedure or function—almost all of them are intended to be called only by the **OpenNewBook** procedure. Notice the Option Private Module compiler directive (Day 11) in line 1. This directive means that none of the procedures or functions in this module are available outside of the workbook that contains this module.

The module begins with several constant declarations at the module level (lines 4 through 8). These constants need to be available to all of the modules in the program, so they have been declared with the Public keyword (Day 11). The Public keyword makes the constants available outside of this module, while the Option Private Module directive limits their scope

to the workbook that contains this module, only. These constants are used to provide argument values for StrComp and to represent the StrComp function's results—thus making the VBA code that uses StrComp easier to understand.

Lines 10 through 14 contain the **EndNewBook** procedure. The **EndNewBook** procedure simply makes sure that Excel gets back control of its status bar, and then uses the End statement to stop program execution. A procedure like this is useful because there are several places in **OpenNewBook** where the procedure should stop. Because the **OpenNewBook** procedure does use the StatusBar property to display a status message while it is running, the two statements to restore the status bar control to Excel and to exit the sub procedure were repeated several times. By using the **EndNewBook** procedure, the **OpenNewBook** procedure is made shorter and easier to understand. If, in the future, you modify **OpenNewBook** so that it changes other parts of Excel's environment (like whether or not Excel updates the screen), you can add any other "housekeeping" chores to the **EndNewBook** procedure.

Lines 17 through 31 contain the **GetSmryInfo** procedure. Notice that this procedure not only has arguments, but uses the **Info** argument to return data to the procedure that called it (Day 11). The **Info** argument has the user-defined **SmryInfo** data type; this procedure fills all of the elements in the **Info** argument variable. Notice also that **GetSmryInfo** calls a function, **GetSmryItem**, to obtain the values for the specific elements.

Lines 34 through 69 contain the **GetSmryItem** function, which returns a single string value. **GetSmryItem** has several arguments; most of them are optional. The **Item** argument is the name of the summary information item that **GetSmryItem** is asking the user for. The optional **Dflt** argument is a string suggesting the contents of the particular summary information item being obtained. The optional **Required** argument is used to determine whether or not **GetSmryItem** should require the user to enter the requested information, or if it's acceptable to skip entering it. Notice how the **GetSmryItem** function checks for missing optional arguments, optional arguments with the correct data type, and sets appropriate default values for missing or bad optional arguments.

Lines 72 through 134 contain the **NewBook_Worksheets** procedure. This procedure has two arguments—one for an object reference to the workbook being created, and another argument for a title to be displayed by this procedure's message dialog boxes. The procedure declares several variables; notice the dynamic array (Day 13) declared in line 76, and the object variables (Day 7) declared in lines 80 and 81.

The **NewBook_Worksheets** procedure starts out with a Do loop that asks the user for the number of worksheets to put in the workbook until the entered number is at least 1. Notice that this procedure calls a general-purpose function, **GetInteger**, to get an integer number. (**GetInteger** is in the third module.) The statements in lines 97 through 100 check to see whether the user wants to change the default worksheet names. If not, the For loop in lines 101 through 105 create the needed number of new worksheets, moving each new worksheet to the end of the workbook. Line 106 exits from the **NewBook_Worksheets** procedure, because there is no further work to be done.

If the user does want to change the default worksheet names, then lines 109 through 112 dimension the **shtNames** dynamic array so it is large enough to hold all of the needed worksheet names, and then fills the array with faked default worksheet names. Next, lines 115 through 117 call the **Get_NameList** procedure to fill the **shtNames** array with worksheet names from the user. The **Get_NameList** procedure uses an argument passed by reference to return values in the **shtNames** array. Lines 118 through 121 ask the user whether or not to sort the list of worksheet names alphabetically, and calls the **BubbleSortStrings** procedure to sort the **shtNames** array.

Finally, lines 124 through 133 create and rename the new worksheets in the workbook. Because the workbook was created with a single worksheet in it, line 126 simply renames that worksheet, and the For loop (line 127) creates and names only the additionally required worksheets.

Lines 137 through 171 contain the **Get_NameList** procedure. This procedure generically fills a list (passed by reference as a string array argument) with sheet names, ensuring that no sheet name entered into the list duplicates an existing sheet name in the workbook or any sheet name entered into the list so far. In order to know which workbook to check for duplicate names, **Get_NameList** takes an object reference to a workbook as a required argument, along with arguments for the string array, a prompt to display, and a title for its message dialog boxes.

The **Get_NameList** procedure uses the LBound and UBound functions so that it can work with any string array. This procedure uses the StrComp procedure in order to ensure that strings are always compared as text (that is, without regard to capitalization). **Get_NameList** calls the **InListSoFar** and **SheetExists** functions to help determine whether the user has entered a unique sheet name. This procedure loops until either all the elements in the array have been processed, or the user cancels one of the input dialog boxes.

Lines 174 through 229 contain the **NewBook_Modules** procedure, which performs essentially the same task as the **NewBook_Worksheets** procedure. At first glance, it may seem as if the **NewBook_Worksheets** and **NewBook_Modules** procedures could have been combined into a single procedure that creates both worksheets and modules, but this isn't actually possible without a lot of extra effort. The **NewBook_Modules** procedure works a little differently than **NewBook_Worksheets** because the newly created workbook must contain at least one worksheet, but does not contain any module sheets. As a result, not only the text prompts, but For loops and some other structures must be written differently. Combining the two procedures would require more programming effort than creating a single procedure tailored for each specific task.

Lines 232 through 242 contain the **BubbleSortStrings** procedure. This procedure is exactly the same as the bubble-sort procedures you saw in Day 13, but has been modified to alphabetically sort strings, instead of numbers. Notice that line 237 uses the StrComp function to compare the strings. This way, the string comparison is controlled, and not affected by the Option Compare settings—this procedure will always make a case-sensitive alphabetic comparison of strings, which is what it is supposed to do.

Finally, lines 245 through 248 contain the **Swap** procedure used by **BubbleSortStrings**. Notice that this version of **Swap** has been modified to use Variant type variables—it can swap the values of any data type. The advantage of changing the **Swap** procedure this way is that it can now be used by *any* bubble-sort procedure, whether the bubble-sort is sorting strings or numbers.

The third and final module that makes up this complete program is a group of supporting functions.

 Listing R2.3. The OpenNewBook program's supporting functions module.

```
1:   Option Private Module
2:   Option Explicit
3:
4:   Function GetBookName(Dflt As String, _
5:                     Optional Title) As String
6:   'gets a workbook file name, returns "False" if canceled
7:     Dim Fltr As String, tName As String
8:
9:     If IsMissing(Title) Then     'was Title in argument list?
10:      Title = "Enter Workbook Name"
11:     End If
12:
13:     Fltr = "Excel Workbooks,*.xls"  'allow only workbooks
14:     With Application
15:       tName = .GetSaveAsFilename(InitialFilename:=Dflt, _
16:                         FileFilter:=Fltr, _
17:                         Title:=Title)
18:     End With
19:     GetBookName = tName     'return filename
20:   End Function
21:
22:
23:   Function FullName2BookName(fileName As String) As String
24:   'returns workbook filename from a filename with full path
25:     Dim tName As String, k As Long
26:
27:     tName = ReverseStr(fileName)     'reverse the filename
28:     k = InStr(tName, "\")       'find the first backslash
29:
30:     If k = 0 Then  'copy everything in front of backslash
```

continues

Listing R2.3. continued

```
31:        FullName2BookName = fileName
32:     Else
33:        tName = Left(tName, k - 1)
34:     End If
35:
36:     'reverse it again, and return result
37:     FullName2BookName = ReverseStr(tName)
38: End Function
39:
40:
41: Function IsBookOpen(ByVal BName As String) As Boolean
42: 'returns True if book is open
43:     Dim aBook As Object
44:
45:     IsBookOpen = False    'assume failure
46:     BName = Trim(BName)
47:     For Each aBook In Workbooks
48:        If StrComp(aBook.Name, BName, TXTCOMP) = STREQUAL Then
49:           IsBookOpen = True
50:           Exit For
51:        End If
52:     Next aBook
53: End Function
54:
55:
56: Function IsDiskFile(fName As String) As Boolean
57: 'return True if fName is found on disk, False otherwise
58:     If (Dir(fName) <> "") Then
59:        IsDiskFile = True
60:     Else
61:        IsDiskFile = False
62:     End If
63: End Function
64:
65:
66: Function InListSoFar(List() As String, _
67:                      SrchFor As String, _
68:                      Limit As Long) As Boolean
69: 'performs linear search of List for SrchFor
70:     Dim k As Long
71:
72:     InListSoFar = False 'assume failure
73:     For k = LBound(List) To Limit
74:        If StrComp(List(k), SrchFor, TXTCOMP) = STREQUAL Then
75:           InListSoFar = True
76:           Exit Function
77:        End If
78:     Next k
79: End Function
80:
81:
82: Function SheetExists(Book As Workbook, _
83:                      ShtName As String) As Boolean
```

```
84:    'returns true if sheet exists in specified book.
85:       Dim Sht As Object
86:
87:       SheetExists = False 'assume failure
88:       For Each Sht In Book.Sheets
89:         If StrComp(Sht.Name, ShtName, TXTCOMP) = STREQUAL Then
90:           SheetExists = True
91:           Exit Function
92:         End If
93:       Next Sht
94:    End Function
95:
96:
97:    Function GetInteger(Prompt As String, _
98:                        Optional Title, _
99:                        Optional Default) As Long
100:   'returns an integer number
101:      Dim tRsp As Variant
102:
103:      If IsMissing(Title) Or VarType(Title) <> vbString Then
104:        Title = "Integer Input"
105:      End If
106:      If IsMissing(Default) Or _
107:         (Not IsNumeric(Default)) Then
108:        Default = ""
109:      Else
110:        Default = CLng(Default)
111:      End If
112:
113:      Do   'get input until numeric, no cancel
114:        tRsp = InputBox(Prompt:=Prompt, _
115:                        Title:=Title, _
116:                        Default:=Default)
117:        If (Not IsNumeric(tRsp)) Or _
118:           (Len(Trim(tRsp)) = 0) Then _
119:          MsgBox Prompt:="You must enter an integer!", _
120:                 Title:=Title, Buttons:=vbExclamation
121:      Loop Until IsNumeric(tRsp) And (Len(Trim(tRsp)) > 0)
122:      GetInteger = CLng(tRsp)   'assign function result
123:   End Function
124:
125:
126:   Function ReverseStr(Str As String) As String
127:   'reverses the order of characters in the Str argument
128:      Dim k As Long, tStr As String
129:
130:      tStr = ""
131:      For k = 1 To Len(Str)
132:        tStr = Mid(Str, k, 1) & tStr
133:      Next k
134:      ReverseStr = tStr
135:   End Function
```

 This module contains the supporting functions used by procedures in both Listing R2.1 and Listing R2.2. The functions in this module are more general-purpose than the procedures and functions in Listing R2.2, and were segregated into a third module to make it easier to later copy them into another workbook that might need similar support functions, or to put these functions into a library workbook.

Notice that this module, like Listing R2.2, contains the `Option Private Module` compiler directive, making all of the procedures and functions in this module private to the workbook that contains them.

Lines 4 through 20 contain the **GetBookName** function. This version of the **GetBookName** function is similar to the one from the Week 1 review, but has been greatly enhanced. This version of **GetBookName** has different arguments than the previous version. Instead of using `InputBox`, this version uses the `GetSaveAsFilename` method (Day 12) to get the filename from the user in line 15. Because the specified filter string includes only the `.XLS` extension, `GetSaveAsFilename` does not permit the user to select a filename for a file type other than an Excel workbook. Notice that **GetBookName** returns the string `"False"` if the user cancels the file selection.

Lines 23 through 38 contain the **FullName2BookName** function. This function returns just the filename part of a string that contains a full file path specification (a full path specification includes the drive letter and complete directory path—like the strings returned by the `GetSaveAsFilename` method described in Day 12).

Notice that **FullName2BookName** calls yet another function, **ReverseStr**, to help it accomplish its task. In a full directory path, the filename is the part after the last backslash (\) in the path. Since all of VBA's string searching functions only search from right to left, it's difficult to find the *last* occurrence of a particular character, so **FullName2BookName** works by reversing the full path name, and then copying all of the characters up to the *first* backslash. For example, if the directory path is `C:\BUDGET\JUNE.XLS` then **FullName2BookName** reverses it to `SLX.ENUJ\TEGDUB\:C`, copies `SLX.ENUJ` from it, and then reverses it again to get `JUNE.XLS`.

> **Note:** For an interesting practice session with the Debugger (Day 14), set a breakpoint at line 23 of Listing R2.3, and set a Watch expression for the **tName** variable in the **FullName2BookName** procedure. When you run the **OpenNewBook** procedure, it will stop at the **FullName2BookName** procedure, and you can see how the value in **tName** changes.

Lines 41 through 53 contain the **IsBookOpen** function, which returns a Boolean result indicating whether or not the workbook specified in its argument is open. This function uses

a For Each...Next loop (Day 9) to check all of the currently open workbooks in the Workbooks collection.

Lines 56 through 63 contain the **IsDiskFile** function, which returns a Boolean value indicating whether or not there is a file on the disk matching the drive, directory, and filename in the **fName** argument. Notice the call to the Dir function in line 58. **IsDiskFile** is identical to the function of the same name described in Day 12.

Lines 66 through 79 contain the **InListSoFar** function, which returns a Boolean result, depending on whether or not the value in the **SrchFor** argument is found in the **List** array up to the element specified by **Limit**. **InListSoFar** performs a simple linear search on the array (Day 13). (**InListSoFar** uses a linear search, instead of the more efficient binary search, because the array isn't sorted at this point, and binary searches only work on sorted arrays.)

Lines 82 through 94 contain the **SheetExists** function, which also returns a Boolean value, this time depending on whether or not the worksheet specified by **ShtName** exists in the workbook specified by **Book**.

Lines 97 through 123 contain the **GetInteger** function, which returns a Long integer number. This function has a required argument for a prompt string to be displayed by the InputBox dialog box, and two optional arguments for the dialog box title and default input value. Notice the code in lines 103 through 111 that checks for the presence of the optional arguments, and assigns reasonable default values if the optional arguments are missing or of the wrong type. Line 113 starts a Do loop that repeats until the user enters a numeric value—the user isn't allowed to cancel the input dialog box. As soon as the user enters a numeric value, the user's number is converted to a Long integer (discarding any decimal fraction) and returned as the **GetInteger** function result.

Finally, lines 126 through 135 contain the **ReverseStr** function. This function simply returns a copy of the string passed as its argument, with the order of its characters reversed. Line 131 starts a For...Next loop (Day 9) that loops for as many times as there are characters in the **Str** argument string, assembling them in reverse order.

This program uses almost all of what you've learned in your first two weeks of VBA programming. As you can see, much of what you learned in the second week makes it easier (and possible) to create powerful and flexible programs, using several procedures and functions working together. In the coming week, you'll continue to build on what you have learned so far.

You have finished your second week of learning how to program in Visual Basic for Applications. By now, you should feel comfortable using Visual Basic for Applications—you've covered all the core features of the language. Now you're ready to learn about some of VBA's advanced features.

What's Ahead?

Now that you have a firm grasp of the core features of the Visual Basic for Applications programming language, you have all the resources necessary to take advantage of VBA's advanced features. In this third week, you'll learn how to make your Visual Basic for Applications programs perform as if they are part of Excel, and how to give your programs a polished, professional appearance and behavior.

In Day 15, "Dialog Boxes and Custom Controls," you'll learn how to create and use custom dialog boxes for your programs. Day 16, "Menus and Toolbars," teaches you how to use VBA's menu and toolbar statements to create and manage Excel's menus and toolbars under the control of your procedures.

Day 17, "Error Handling," teaches you how to use VBA's error-handling capabilities so that your programs and procedures can handle runtime errors gracefully and professionally without crashing. Day 18, "Working with Excel," gives you additional information about controlling Excel's objects through your VBA procedures and programs. In Day 19, "Working with Other Applications: OLE and OLE Automation," you learn how to use program objects from other Windows applications, such as MS Word for Windows. Day 20, "Working with Other Applications: DDE, DLLs, and Sending Keystrokes," shows you how to use Dynamic Data Exchange messages to control other Windows applications, how to use functions and procedures in DLL files, and how to control other applications by sending keystrokes.

Finally, Day 21, "Using Automatic Procedures, Event Procedures, and Add-Ins," describes how to use procedures that execute automatically whenever you open or close a workbook, and how to tell VBA and Excel to execute a particular procedure whenever a particular event occurs. Day 21 concludes with an explanation of how you can convert your own programs into an Excel add-in program.

Although not formally part of the third week of instruction, Appendix B contains a complete sample application—a simple game—that illustrates almost all of the VBA language features that you have learned throughout this book. Appendix A contains all of the Quiz answers and solutions to most of the Exercises in each chapter.

Dialog Boxes and Custom Controls

So far, you've learned to use the dialog boxes that VBA predefines for you—the MsgBox procedure and function, and the InputBox function. Although MsgBox and InputBox give your programs the flexibility that only interactive programs can have, they are fairly limited. As you develop more complex programs, you'll want to display dialog boxes that allow your program's user to select more than one option at a time, to select items from a list, or to input several values at the same time—just like the dialog boxes that Excel and other Windows applications display.

Fortunately, VBA allows you to create and use custom dialog boxes in your programs and procedures. By using VBA custom dialog boxes, you can display data, or get values from your program's user in a specific manner that meets your program's needs. For example, you can display a dialog box to display a list of various date formats, allowing the user to select only one date format from the list.

As another example, you might have a program that searches for a specific string in a workbook. For such a program, you might use a dialog box that contains controls allowing the user to select the workbook file to search in, a text box in which to enter the text to be searched for, and option buttons or check boxes to select how the search is conducted. Custom dialog boxes enable your program to interact with its user in a sophisticated way, providing a versatile form of data input and output.

This lesson gets you started with creating and managing VBA custom dialog boxes in Excel. Today, you'll learn how to:

☐ Insert a new dialog sheet.

☐ Add controls to the dialog sheet.

☐ Set the tab order of controls in the dialog box.

☐ Attach code to dialog box's controls.

☐ Set the dialog box control properties.

☐ Invoke the custom control.

Understanding Custom Dialog Box Controls

The custom dialog boxes you can create in VBA have controls just like those you find in other dialog boxes displayed by Excel or other Windows applications. Dialog box *controls* are the elements of a dialog box that enable a user to interact with your program. These elements include option buttons, scrollbars, command buttons, and so on. This section acquaints you with the dialog box controls that you can include in your own dialog boxes.

In VBA, each dialog box control is an object with specific properties and methods. (Objects were discussed in Day 7.) Table 15.1 lists the controls that you can place in a VBA custom dialog box,

and summarizes the purpose of each control. As you'll see from the table, VBA's custom dialog box controls include all of the controls that you see in other Windows applications, with one exception—you can't create tabbed dialog boxes in Excel VBA.

Table 15.1. VBA custom dialog box controls.

Control	Purpose
Label	Provides caption labels for controls that don't have their own inherent captions. Use this control to put static text on a dialog box, such as instructions or tips on filling in the other dialog box controls.
Button	A command button. Use command buttons for actions such as Cancel, Save, OK, and so on. When a user clicks the command button, a VBA procedure attached to the control is executed.
Edit Box	A free-form text editing box for data entry; can be either single-line or multi-line.
Group Box	Visually and logically groups other controls (especially check boxes and option boxes). Use a group box to show the user which controls in a dialog box are related to each other, or to set a particular group of controls off from other dialog box controls.
Check Box	A standard check box (a square box; when selected, it contains a checkmark). Use check boxes for user selections that are on/off, true/false, and so on. Use check boxes for option selections which are *not* mutually exclusive—for example, you can search text for a case-sensitive match, whether or not you search for whole words only, so you'd use check boxes for selecting these search options.
Option Button	A standard option button (a round box; when selected, it is filled in with a black dot). Use option buttons for user selections that are not only on/off or true/false, but are also mutually exclusive—for example, you can't search both forward and backward at the same time, so you'd use an option button for selecting the search direction. Option buttons are typically gathered together in a group box.
Spinner	Spinner controls are a special variety of text box. You typically use spinner boxes to enter numeric, date, or other sequential values that fall within a specified range. Clicking the up-arrow

continues

Table 15.1. continued

Control	Purpose
	on the spinner control increases the value in the box, and clicking the down-arrow decreases the value in the box.
ScrollBar	Scrollbar controls allow you to select a linear value, similar to a spinner control.
List Box	Displays a list of values that the user selects from. You can set list boxes to allow the user to select only a single value, or to select multiple values. Use list boxes for things like workbook names, sheet names, range names, months in the year, and so on.
Combo List-Edit Box	This control combines an edit box with a list box. Use a combo list-edit box whenever you want to suggest values for the user to choose from, but want to allow the user to enter a value that isn't already in the list.
Dropdown List Box	A variation on the list box, in which the list of items to choose from drops down when the user clicks the down-arrow at the right of the control. You can use drop-down list boxes only to select a single item.
Combo Dropdown-Edit List Box	Essentially the same as a combo list-edit box, but operates the same as a drop-down list box.

Table 15.2 lists the most common dialog box control properties that you'll need to work with in your VBA code—the properties that let you change the control's label, retrieve the state of the control (that is, find out what selections the user made), and so on.

> **Note:** Listing all of the properties and methods for all of the custom dialog box controls is, unfortunately, beyond the scope of this book—amongst all of the dialog box controls there are literally hundreds of properties and methods. This chapter shows you the most common methods and properties that you'll need to use. Refer to the VBA online help for additional information about specific dialog box controls. After finishing this book, you may also want to read Sams' *Database Developer's Guide with Visual Basic*.

Table 15.2. Selected properties for some dialog box controls.

Control	Property Name	Purpose
Label	Caption	The text displayed by the control.
Button	Caption	The text displayed on the command button.
Button	OnAction	Specifies the VBA procedure to be executed when this command button is clicked.
EditBox	Caption	The text displayed in the edit box.
CheckBox	Value	The value stored in the check box control, representing whether the check box is selected; may be one of the Excel VBA constants xlOn, xlOff, or xlMixed.
OptionButton	Value	The value stored in the option button control, representing whether the option control is selected; may be one of the Excel VBA constants xlOn or xlOff.
ScrollBar	Value	The scroll bar's value.
Spinner	Value	The spinner's value.
ListBox	List	Returns a collection object containing the text for the list displayed by the list control—essentially an array of strings. The List property is common to all list-oriented dialog controls.
ListBox	Value	The index (a number between 1 and the total number of items in the list) of the currently selected item—use the index number in Value as a subscript in the List collection to retrieve the text for the selected list item.
ListBox	Selected	Used with lists that permit multiple selections. Returns an array of Boolean values; each element in the array contains one element corresponding to each item in the list. If an element in the Selected array is True, then the corresponding list item has been selected.
All dialog box controls	Enabled	Stores a Boolean value to determine whether or not the dialog box control is enabled. If Enabled is False, then it is still displayed in the dialog box but is grayed out.

continues

Table 15.2. continued

Control	Property Name	Purpose
DropDown	Value	The index (a number between 1 and the total number of items in the drop-down list) of the currently selected item—use the index number in Value as a subscript in the List collection to retrieve the text for the selected list item.

Note: Don't confuse an edit box control on a custom dialog box with the text box graphic object that you find elsewhere in Excel. A TextBox object is a graphic object used to display text labels on a chart sheet, dialog sheet, or worksheet. In contrast, an EditBox object is the special data-entry box in which you can type or edit text.

After you learn the general steps for creating custom dialog boxes, later sections in this lesson present and explain examples of most of the controls listed in Table 15.1, and several of the properties listed in Table 15.2. The example listings in this lesson also demonstrate how you can make some of the dialog box controls change their behavior or otherwise respond to specific events.

Creating Custom Dialog Boxes

Creating a custom dialog box is a fairly straightforward process. You don't have to write any VBA code to create the dialog box, itself. Instead, you interactively use Excel to graphically create the dialog box on a special workbook sheet, called a *dialog sheet*. Essentially, you just draw the custom dialog box on the dialog sheet. You can create only one dialog box on each dialog sheet.

To create a custom VBA dialog box in Excel, follow these basic steps:

1. Insert a dialog sheet for the new dialog box.
2. Use the Forms toolbar to place the controls you want onto the custom dialog box and to set the properties of the controls.
3. Adjust the tab order of the dialog box controls.
4. Add or attach VBA code to dialog box controls—such as command buttons—to carry out the actions you want.
5. Write the VBA code to display the dialog box and retrieve values from the dialog box's controls.

The next few parts of this section show you how to interactively create a custom dialog box, place controls on it, and adjust the controls' tab order and properties. The last section of this lesson shows you how to attach code to dialog box controls, and how to use the custom dialog box in your code.

Inserting a New Dialog Sheet

The first step in creating a custom dialog box is to insert a new dialog sheet. The dialog sheet contains the dialog box that you draw, as well as providing the workspace in which you draw the dialog box. Because dialog sheets are part of the workbook, and are contained in the workbook's Sheets collection, the dialog sheet also provides a way to access the dialog box from your VBA code.

To insert a new dialog sheet, use the Insert | Macro | Dialog command. Excel inserts a new dialog sheet before the active sheet, and gives it a default name—DialogN—using the same numbering system as Excel does for worksheets and module sheets.

Figure 15.1 shows a newly inserted dialog sheet. Notice that the new dialog sheet already contains a minimal dialog box—one that contains the OK and Cancel buttons found in almost all dialog boxes. Notice also that Excel displays the Forms toolbar whenever the active sheet is a dialog sheet.

Figure 15.1.

A new dialog sheet. Notice that Excel automatically includes the OK and Cancel buttons on the new dialog box.

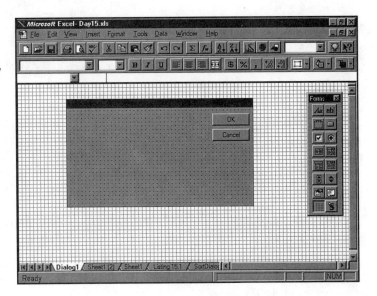

DO	**DON'T**

DO give your dialog sheets descriptive names, so that you can easily tell what the dialog box on that sheet is for. To rename a dialog sheet, double-click its name tab, and enter the new name.

DON'T leave a new dialog sheet with its default name, such as Dialog1 or Dialog2. Instead, rename the new dialog sheet as soon as you create it.

Using the Forms Toolbar

Whenever Excel displays a dialog sheet, it also displays the Forms toolbar. Figure 15.2 shows the Forms toolbar in its floating toolbar window. The command buttons on the Forms toolbar activate various tools to insert controls on the dialog sheet, or allow you to test the dialog box or alter the properties of the dialog box or of the dialog box's controls.

Figure 15.2.

Use Excel's Forms toolbar to place controls on the dialog sheet.

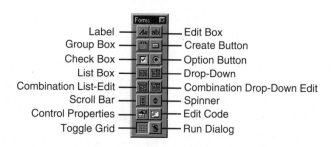

Tip: If the Forms toolbar display has been turned off by using the **V**iew | **T**oolbars command, then Excel may not display the Forms toolbar when you open or insert a dialog sheet. If the Forms toolbar doesn't appear when a dialog sheet is the active sheet, use the **V**iew | **T**oolbars command to display it.

To use the commands on the Forms toolbar to insert controls on your dialog box, follow these steps:

1. Click the command button on the Forms toolbar that corresponds to the dialog box control you want to add to the dialog box. The mouse pointer will change to a crosshair pointer.

2. Position the crosshair pointer over the dialog box where you want the top-left corner of the control to be.

3. Click and hold down the left mouse button.

4. Drag down and to the right until the control is the size you want, then release the mouse button. Excel inserts the control onto the dialog box, and the mouse pointer returns to the arrow shape.

Tip: You can resize the dialog box itself by clicking on its title bar to select it, and then dragging one of the sizing handles to increase or decrease the size of the dialog box. (Sizing handles are the small black squares that appear when an object on the dialog sheet is selected.)

The following list summarizes the action of each command button on the Forms toolbar (refer to Figure 15.2):

☐ *Label.* Activates the label tool. Use the label tool to insert text—such as instructions or tips for using the dialog—into the dialog box.

☐ *Edit Box.* Activates the edit box tool. Use the edit box tool to insert edit boxes.

☐ *Group Box.* Activates the group box tool to add a group box. You usually use group boxes to visually group together option button and check box controls.

☐ *Create Button.* Activates the button tool. Use the button tool to add command buttons to the dialog box.

☐ *Check Box.* Activates the check box tool to add a check box and accompanying label to the dialog box.

☐ *Option Button.* Activates the option button tool to add an option button and accompanying label to the dialog box.

☐ *List Box.* Activates the list box tool to insert a list box.

☐ *Drop-Down.* Activates the drop-down list box tool to place a drop-down list in the dialog box.

☐ *Combination List-Edit.* Activates the list-edit tool to insert a combination list-edit box. Combination list-edit boxes are really two separate controls linked together—an edit box and a list box.

☐ *Combination Drop-Down Edit.* Activates the drop-down edit tool to insert a combination drop-down edit list box.

☐ *Scroll Bar.* Activates the scroll bar tool to insert scroll bar controls.

☐ *Spinner.* Activates the spinner tool to insert a spinner control.

☐ *Control Properties.* Displays the properties sheet for the currently selected dialog box control. You use the properties sheet to set the properties for a dialog box control, such as the font style for text in the control, binding list boxes to worksheet cell ranges, colors for the control, whether the control is enabled, attaching VBA code to the control, and so on.

☐ *Edit Code.* If a dialog box control has a VBA procedure attached to it, the Edit Code command button causes Excel to display the source code for the attached procedure. (Attaching code to a dialog box control is described in the next section of this lesson.)

☐ *Toggle Grid.* Turns the display of drawing gridlines on and off. In Figure 15.1, the gridlines are turned on.

☐ *Run Dialog.* Allows you to test the appearance and behavior of the dialog box. When you select this command button on the Forms toolbar, Excel displays the dialog box in an active mode—all of the command buttons, edit boxes, and so on become active, and you can check how they work.

> **Note:** If you use the Run Dialog command to test a dialog box, remember that any variables or arrays used by code attached to your dialog box controls won't be initialized because the Run Dialog command only exercises the dialog box—it doesn't cause any code not directly attached to the dialog box to execute. As a result, some of the code attached to a dialog box control may fail with various runtime errors when you use the Run Dialog command.

Adding Controls to the Custom Dialog Box

When you create a new dialog sheet, Excel automatically presents you with a dialog box that already contains OK and Cancel command buttons. The OK and Cancel command buttons are the standard buttons that should appear in almost every dialog box—Excel saves you a little bit of work by adding these command buttons for you. You'll need to add any other controls that you want in the dialog box yourself, however. You add controls to a custom dialog box by displaying a dialog sheet and then graphically drawing the controls onto the dialog box using the various tools from the Forms toolbar.

To add a control to a dialog box, use the Forms toolbar as described in the preceding section of this lesson. As an example of adding a specific control to a custom dialog box, add an edit box control to a new dialog sheet by following these steps:

1. Choose the **I**nsert | **M**acro | **D**ialog command; Excel inserts a new dialog sheet, similar to the one already shown in Figure 15.1.

2. Click the Edit Box command button on the Forms toolbar. The mouse cursor changes to a crosshair.

3. Move the mouse pointer over the dialog box on the dialog sheet, and position the crosshair where you want the top-left corner of the edit box to be.

4. Drag the mouse cursor down and to the right to draw the edit box control. VBA displays a box outline showing the size of the edit box while you drag the mouse cursor.

5. Release the mouse button when the edit box is the size you want. VBA creates the edit box control and inserts it into the dialog box. Figure 15.3 shows a new dialog sheet as it appears immediately after drawing the edit box.

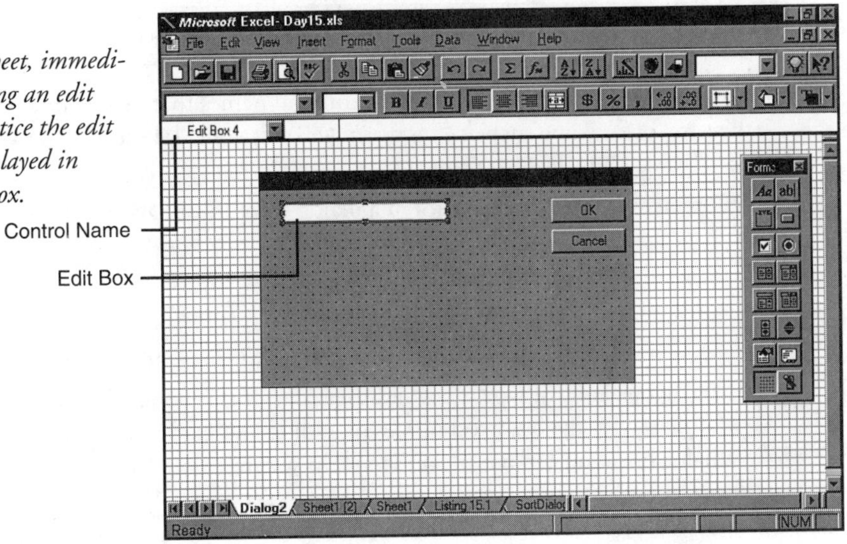

Figure 15.3.

A new dialog sheet, immediately after adding an edit box control. Notice the edit box's name displayed in Excel's Name box.

Control Name

Edit Box

Note: As you draw the edit box in this example, you may notice that the top-left corner of the edit box—as well as the outline of the edit box itself—jumps to align itself with the grid pattern on-screen. This action—called *snap to grid*—helps you align controls and text on the dialog box. The grid is always active, although you can turn its display on and off by clicking the Toggle Grid command button on the Forms toolbar.

All dialog box controls must have a unique name—you use this name to refer to the dialog control in your VBA code, as explained later in this lesson. Whenever you add a control to a dialog box, VBA gives the new control a default name consisting of the control's type name followed by a number. VBA ensures that the control has a unique name by including the number in the control's name—the number in the name is higher than any other control number.

For example, the edit box you just created has the name `Edit Box 4`—Excel displays the name of the selected control in the Name text box; refer to Figure 15.3. In this case, the control's name indicates that it is an edit box, and that it is also the fourth object to be created on the dialog sheet. (The first three objects on the dialog sheet are the dialog box itself, the OK command button, and the Cancel command button—all of which were automatically inserted into the new dialog sheet when you created it.)

If you want, you can change a control's name by making an assignment to its `Name` property, or by interactively editing the control's properties.

DO	DON'T

DO give your dialog box controls meaningful names that help you remember what they are for. A name such as `FirstName Box` tells you a lot more about what a control does than a name like `Edit Box 10`.

DO remember that each control in a dialog sheet must have a unique name.

Note: Unfortunately, covering all details of adding and editing each and every dialog box control type is beyond the scope of this book. Once you've gotten familiar with the basic techniques of adding and editing controls on a custom dialog box, you can use the online Help system to get more information on specific controls and their properties.

Editing Custom Dialog Box Controls

After you draw a control on a dialog sheet you can resize the control, move it, copy it, delete it, change its formatting (font size, style, typeface), or alter its properties (such as the control's caption, attached VBA procedure, and so on). You'll need to edit or move dialog box controls as you fine-tune the design and appearance of your dialog box—for example, you may decide that an edit box is too small or too large for the values that will be entered into it, and want to change its size. As another example, you may want to edit the caption of the default OK and Cancel default buttons that VBA places on the dialog box. You'll certainly want to edit the caption of any command button that you place, because VBA gives new command buttons a caption that is the same as the control's default name—you probably don't need a command button labeled "Button 7."

Selecting Controls

To edit a control, you must first select it by clicking on it. Selected controls have a gray border with sizing handles—as shown for the edit box that appears in Figure 15.3. To select several controls at once, hold down the Shift key while you click on the controls you want to select. Selecting multiple controls at once is useful if you want to make a formatting change that affects all of the controls on the dialog box—such as changing the font size, style, or typeface. Selecting multiple controls is also useful if you want to move several controls all at the same time.

> **Tip:** You can semi-permanently group several controls together by using the Format | Placement | Group command. When the controls are grouped, they behave as a single object when you select, move, copy, or otherwise edit them. The controls will remain grouped until you use the Format | Placement | Ungroup command on the selected group.

Moving a Control

To move a control to a new location in the dialog box, first select the control. Next, position the mouse pointer over any part of the gray outline around the selected control *except* one of the sizing handles. Now, click and drag the control to its new position.

Changing a Control's Size

To change the size of a control, first select it. Next, move the mouse pointer over one of the sizing handles (the square boxes that appear at the corners and at the center of the sides of the gray border around the selected object). When the pointer is over a sizing handle, the pointer changes to a double-headed arrow indicating the direction in which you can now resize the selected control. Now, click and drag the sizing handle; VBA displays an outline showing you the new size of the control. When the control is the desired size, release the mouse button; VBA redraws the control to the new size.

Copying, Pasting, and Deleting Controls

One of the easiest ways to create several similar controls—such as several check box or command button controls—is to first create one control, copy it, and then paste the copied control into the dialog sheet as many times as needed. To copy a dialog box control, simply select it, and then use the Edit | Copy command (or press Ctrl+C).

Once you've copied a control, you can paste it into the same or a different dialog box by using the Edit | Paste command. After you paste the control, move it to its desired location.

You may occasionally want to delete a dialog box control. You may have placed a control you later decide you don't really need, or you may accidentally make too many copies of a control, or for some other reason. To delete a dialog box control, select the control and then press the Delete key. VBA deletes the selected control(s).

Editing or Formatting a Control's Caption Text

To edit the caption text on a control, just click over the text. VBA will place the insertion point into the caption text. You can now edit the text using any of the standard Windows text editing commands you're already familiar with. To change the typeface, style, or font size, use the Format toolbar the same way you would with any other text in Excel. You may need to resize label, check box, option box, command button, or other objects to display the entire caption that you type.

Tip: You can edit or format the dialog box's title bar the same way you do a control's caption—just click over the custom dialog box's title bar to place the insertion point into the title bar, allowing you to edit or format it.

Note: Some controls, like edit boxes, list boxes, and drop-down lists don't have an inherent caption (more properly called a *label*). Use the label tool to place labels in the dialog box near controls that don't have their own inherent labels.

Renaming a Control

A control's name is how you refer to a specific control in your VBA code. When a control is selected, its name appears in Excel's Name text box (refer to Figure 15.3). You'll frequently want to rename your dialog box controls, in order to give them meaningful names.

To rename a dialog box control, first select it, and then type the new name in the Name text box, the same as you would to rename any Excel range or cell.

Controlling the Tab Order

When your custom dialog box is active, it will behave like other Windows dialog boxes. Your dialog box's user can move forward from control to control with the Tab key, and backwards through the dialog box's controls by using the Shift+Tab key. The order in which the controls

become active in response to the user pressing the Tab or Shift+Tab key is called the *tab order* of the controls. Usually, you want the controls' tab order to be (approximately) left-to-right and top-to-bottom—in general, you should make sure that the tab order provides a logical movement sequence through the controls in the dialog box.

VBA assigns a default tab order to each control, as you add it to the custom dialog box. The default tab order therefore corresponds to the order in which you place the controls on the dialog sheet. Frequently, by the time you've placed all the controls on the dialog sheet and moved them around until you're satisfied with their appearance, the default tab order no longer provides a logical sequence of movement through the dialog box's controls.

To change the tab order of the controls in a dialog box, follow these steps:

1. Choose the **Tools | Ta b** Order command; VBA displays the Tab Order dialog box shown in Figure 15.4. The Tab Order list displays all of the controls in the dialog box in their current tab order.

Figure 15.4.

Use the Tab Order dialog box to change the tab order of controls in your custom dialog box.

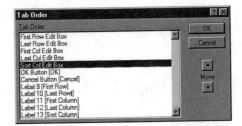

2. In the Tab Order list, select the control whose position in the tab order you want to change. Figure 15.4 shows a control named `Sort Col Edit Box` selected.

Note: Although label controls do appear in the Tab Order dialog box, and you can change their position in the tab order, VBA doesn't actually make a label control active—label controls are intended only to display text.

3. Use the Move arrow buttons to change the selected control's position in the tab order. Click the up-arrow to move the control up in the list, or the down-arrow to move the control lower in the list.

4. Repeat steps 2 through 3 for each control, until you are satisfied with the tab order for the dialog box.

5. Choose the OK button to confirm your changes; VBA closes the Tab Order dialog box, and returns you to the dialog sheet.

DO	DON'T

DO remember to check the tab order of your dialog boxes to ensure that it provides a logical movement sequence through the controls in your dialog box.

Setting Control Properties Interactively

Each custom dialog box control has its own set of properties, just like any other VBA or Excel object. There are several dialog box control properties that are both easier and more practical to set interactively—that is, while the dialog sheet is displayed, rather than through your VBA code.

For example, an OK or Close button in a dialog box should also dismiss the dialog box. Command buttons have a property that you can set so that whenever that command button is chosen, the dialog box is closed. Because you want this behavior to be permanent for a particular command button, it's most practical to set this property interactively in the dialog sheet. Properties that you interactively set for a dialog box control become the new default properties for that control.

Understanding the Interactively Set Control Properties

Table 15.3 shows a partial list of the control properties that you can set interactively. The table indicates which controls have the listed properties, and summarizes each property's use and purpose.

Table 15.3. Control properties set interactively.

Property	Belongs To:	Purpose
Value	OptionButton, CheckBox	Indicates whether the box is checked, unchecked, or (for check boxes only) mixed—that is, neither checked nor unchecked. Mixed check boxes are filled in with gray instead of a checkmark.
Edit Validation	EditBox	Restricts that entry in the edit box to one of: Text, Integer, Number, Reference, or Formula.
Accelerator Key	GroupBox, Button, Label, CheckBox, OptionButton	Indicates which letter in the control's caption to use as the accelerator key. Pressing Alt+ the accelerator key causes that control to become the active control.

Property	Belongs To:	Purpose
Cell Link	ListBox, DropDown, ScrollBar, Spinner, CheckBox, OptionButton	Links a worksheet cell to the control's Value property—as the control's value property changes, the value stored in the linked worksheet cell is continuously updated.

As you can see from Table 15.3, you can preset the value for option buttons and check boxes on your dialog sheet by setting the value property for those controls interactively.

Tip: You can also preset the value for a text box by typing the preset value directly into the text on the dialog sheet. Then, whenever you display the dialog box, it will display the default text that you typed.

The Button object has several other properties, in addition to having an accelerator key property. (Command buttons in a dialog box are Button objects.) These additional Button object properties require some special attention. Table 15.4 lists the Button object properties, and describes each property's purpose; the table lists both the property names as they appear in the properties sheet, and their formal VBA names.

Table 15.4. The Button object's properties.

On Property Sheet	Formal Name	Purpose/Usage
Default	DefaultButton	Makes this the default command button—this is the selected button when the dialog box is displayed. If more than one command button has this property, the command button lowest in the tab order is the default button.
Cancel	CancelButton	Makes this command button cancel the dialog box. Whenever a button with this property is clicked, the custom dialog box returns False, indicating it was canceled. (Using values returned by custom dialog boxes is described later in this lesson.)

continues

Table 15.4. continued

On Property Sheet	Formal Name	Purpose/Usage
Dismiss	`DismissButton`	Whenever a command button with this property is clicked, the action for the button is carried out, and then the dialog box is closed. Typically, the OK button has this property.
Help	`HelpButton`	Indicates that pressing F1 for online help has the same effect as clicking the button with this property. The command button's action code would then use the `Application` object's `Help` method to display a particular help topic.

Changing the Control Properties

To interactively change a dialog box control's properties, follow these steps:

1. Select the control whose properties you want to modify.

2. Choose the Format | Object command to display the Format Object dialog box.
3. Click the Control tab in the Format Object dialog box to bring the Control property sheet to the front of the dialog box if it isn't already displayed.
4. Fill in the options you want for the selected dialog box control.
5. Choose OK to close the Format Object dialog box.

> **Tip:** You can also display the Format Object dialog box by right-clicking on the dialog box control you want to format, and selecting Format Object from the resulting shortcut pop-up menu.

DO	DON'T

DO make sure that your dialog box contains at least one command button that cancels the dialog box (provided you want to allow the user to cancel the dialog).

DO make sure that you have at least one command button with the Dismiss property set, or you won't be able to close the dialog box except by canceling it (either through a Cancel button or by pressing Esc).

Displaying a Custom Dialog Box with VBA

To define a dialog box in Excel VBA, you first visually create the custom dialog box on a dialog sheet. VBA then uses the graphical design on the dialog sheet to get all the information it needs to display the dialog box: the size of the dialog box, the controls on it, and so on. As a result, Excel VBA enables you to display the custom dialog box with a single statement.

Syntax

There are two syntax forms for displaying a custom dialog box; both use the Show method of the DialogSheets collection:

```
DialogSheets(n).Show
DialogSheets(dialogName).Show
```

The Show method displays the specified dialog box, leaving it on-screen until the user clicks a command button in the dialog box that has either the DismissButton or the CancelButton property set. Although code attached to the dialog box's controls will execute, the overall execution of your program is suspended until the dialog box is closed.

In the first syntax form, *n* represents any numeric expression that results in a valid index number for a dialog sheet (that is, the number of the specific dialog sheet in the DialogSheets collection). In the second syntax form, *dialogName* represents any string expression that results in a valid name for a dialog sheet. You'll use the second syntax form more often, since it is usually easier to refer to a dialog sheet by its name.

You can use the Show method as either a procedure or a function. When used as a function, the Show method returns a Boolean result, depending on how the dialog box was closed. Show returns True if the dialog box was closed as the result of the user clicking any command button that has the DismissButton property set. Show returns False if the dialog box was closed as the result of the user clicking any command button with the CancelButton property set, or if the user pressed the Esc key. The code examples later in this lesson show more specific examples of how to use the Show method and its return result. The following two code fragments demonstrate the use of the Show method:

```
If DialogSheets(2).Show Then
   ' statements to process the data in the controls of the
   ' dialog box
Else
   ' statements to respond to the canceled dialog box
End If

If DialogSheets("SortingDialog").Show Then
   ' statements to process the data in the controls of the
   ' dialog box
Else
   ' statements to respond to the canceled dialog box
End If
```

> **Note:** When VBA executes the Show method to display a dialog box, execution in the procedure containing the call to the Show method is suspended until the displayed dialog box is closed by the user. VBA will, however, execute the code for any event procedures attached to the dialog box's controls (event procedures are described in the next section).

Using VBA with Custom Dialog Box Controls

Displaying a dialog box alone usually isn't enough to accomplish your purpose. In almost every case, you'll need to sample the state of the dialog box controls to find out what data or choices the user made in your dialog box. For example, if you use a dialog box to get information from a user about which columns and rows in a worksheet should be sorted (as the next program example does), you need to be able to find out what values the user entered after the dialog box has been closed, and before you actually start the sorting operation.

In other cases, you may want to dynamically change the captions of the command buttons (or other controls) in the dialog box, or dynamically validate data entered into the dialog box. For example, you may have a dialog box used for data entry in an accounting program you're developing. You may want to validate an account code or department name entered into a text box as soon as the user enters the data.

For the first task, you need to be able to access and manipulate the dialog box's controls after the dialog box has been closed. For the second task, you need to be able to attach code to the dialog box's controls so that your VBA procedure can be automatically executed by the dialog box control, itself. Attaching code to a VBA control is also how you make a command button carry out an action.

The next few sections show you how to attach a procedure to a dialog box control, and how to test the different kinds of controls in a custom dialog box.

Attaching VBA Procedures to Dialog Box Controls

As you work with your custom dialog boxes and their controls, you'll find there are many instances when clicking a control or modifying its data requires the control (or some other part of your program) to respond promptly. VBA allows you to define procedures that cause specific controls to respond to specific events. An *event* is something that happens to a dialog box control,

such as clicking a command button, option button, or check box; another type of event occurs when the contents of an edit box or a list selection changes.

You can attach any VBA procedure to a dialog box control, or create a procedure directly from the dialog sheet. Whichever method you use to attach code to a control, a reference to the attached procedure is stored in the control's OnAction property. Whenever the control is clicked or changed, VBA executes the procedure referenced by the OnAction property. Procedures attached to a control through the control's OnAction property are called *event handlers*, or just *event procedures*.

Assigning a Procedure to a Control

To assign a VBA procedure to a control, first display the dialog sheet with the dialog box whose control(s) you want to assign an action procedure to, and then follow these steps:

1. Select the dialog box control that you want to attach a procedure to. Usually, this will be a command button.
2. Choose the **Tools | Assign** Macro command. Excel displays the Assign Macro dialog box shown in Figure 15.5.

Figure 15.5.

Use the Assign Macro dialog box to assign a VBA procedure to a custom dialog box control, such as a command button.

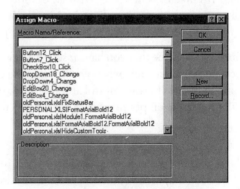

3. Select the name of the procedure that you want to attach to the control in the **M**acro Name/Reference list, and then choose OK. VBA assigns the procedure to the control, and closes the Assign Macro dialog box.

The Assign Macro dialog box also offers you the opportunity to write a new macro from scratch by clicking the **N**ew button. Clicking the **N**ew command button in the Assign Macro dialog box has the same effect as using the Edit Code command button on the Forms toolbar, described in the next part of this section. If you wish, you can also choose the **R**ecord command button to record the macro procedure that you're assigning to the dialog box control. Recording a procedure from the Assign Macro dialog box is essentially the same as using the **T**ools | **R**ecord Macro | **R**ecord New Macro command.

Editing or Creating Code from the Dialog Sheet

You can also assign a procedure to a dialog box control from the dialog sheet. Also, if you need to edit a procedure assigned to a particular dialog box control, you can access the code directly from the dialog sheet without having to search through a module to find the correct procedure.

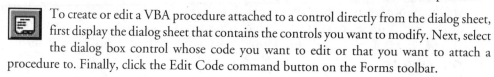

To create or edit a VBA procedure attached to a control directly from the dialog sheet, first display the dialog sheet that contains the controls you want to modify. Next, select the dialog box control whose code you want to edit or that you want to attach a procedure to. Finally, click the Edit Code command button on the Forms toolbar.

As soon as you click the Edit Code button on the Forms toolbar, VBA does one of two things: If the selected control already has a procedure attached to it, VBA displays the appropriate module and procedure declaration for that control. If the control does *not* already have a procedure attached to it, VBA creates a new procedure declaration, and positions the insertion point in the procedure body, ready for you to begin writing new code.

When VBA creates a new procedure declaration for a procedure to be attached to a control, it may insert a new module sheet. VBA will give the new module sheet a default name—both the sheet insertion and the default name for the module sheet follow the same rules as when you record a VBA macro. When VBA writes the empty procedure declaration for a new dialog box control's OnAction event procedure, it gives the procedure a name consisting of the control's name, followed by the name of the event that the procedure handles.

As an example, assume that you have inserted a new dialog sheet. The OK button in the dialog sheet (created automatically when you inserted the dialog sheet) has the name *Button 2*. If you select this command button control and then click the Edit Code command button, VBA will create the following empty procedure declaration for you:

```
Sub Button2_Click()
End Sub
```

The above procedure's name tells you some useful information—it indicates which control the procedure is for, and what action the procedure is supposed to handle. You should follow similar naming conventions if you write procedures from scratch that you later intend to attach to a dialog box control.

DO	DON'T

DO remember that only command button controls that have either the `DismissButton` or `CancelButton` properties set to `True` will close a dialog box when they are clicked. Command buttons without these properties will execute the attached procedure, but the dialog box remains open.

DON'T forget that, if a command button has the `DismissButton` or `CancelButton` properties, it will still execute any attached code before closing the dialog box.

DO rename your dialog box controls *before* using the Edit Code button to create an event procedure for the control. That way, the default event procedure name that VBA creates will already have the control's meaningful name as part of the procedure name.

DON'T forget that you can assign only one procedure to a control at a time.

DO keep in mind that you can assign the same procedure to more than one control.

Removing an Attached Procedure from a Control

Occasionally, you may want to replace or remove a dialog box control's event procedure. Deleting the event procedure's source code, or deleting the module that contains the event procedure's source code won't disassociate the control from that procedure.

To replace an event procedure for a dialog box control with another procedure, use the **Tools** | **Assign** Macro command, and select a different procedure in the **Macro** Name/Reference list, then choose OK. VBA will link the new procedure to the control.

To remove an event procedure's association with a particular dialog box control, use the **Tools** | **Assign** Macro command, and clear the **Macro** Name/Reference list (so that it is blank), and then choose OK. VBA will disassociate the control from any event procedures.

Using the Edit Box Control

This first example program, **RowSorter1**, uses a simple dialog box to get information about which rows and columns to sort, and which column to use as the basis for sorting the rows. Listing 15.1 demonstrates the basics of using the edit box control.

Before you can execute the **RowSorter1** procedure, you need to create both a custom dialog box and a worksheet with some data in it. To get started with this demonstration procedure, follow these steps:

1. Create a new workbook.
2. On Sheet1 of the workbook, enter the following data in the first three columns and the first five rows of the worksheet:

1	222	1
3	123	3
4	34	5
5	11	4
22	2	2

3. Insert a dialog sheet, and rename it `SortDialog1`.

4. Add five edit box controls to the dialog sheet, using the techniques for adding controls you learned earlier in this lesson. As you add each edit box control, also add a label control to correspond to that edit box.

5. Edit the label controls' captions, so that your edit boxes are labeled **First Row**, **Last Row**, **First Column**, **Last Column**, and **Sort Column**. Your dialog box should now appear similar to the one shown in Figure 15.6.

6. Now, rename each edit box control (as described earlier in this lesson), so that your edit boxes are named `First Row Edit`, `Last Row Edit`, `First Col Edit`, `Last Col Edit`, and `Sort Col Edit`. Be careful when you complete this step—make sure that the edit box's new name and its corresponding label are the same, otherwise your dialog box won't produce the results you expect.

7. Edit the dialog box's title bar caption, and change the dialog box's title to **Row Sorter**.

8. Insert a module sheet, and enter the code from Listing 15.1.

Figure 15.6.

A sample session with the **RowSorter1** *program. Before you can use this program, you must create the Row Sorter custom dialog box, and enter some data for the program to work with.*

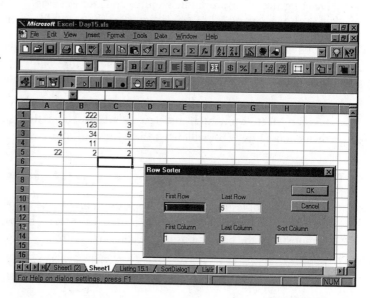

The **RowSorter1** program shown in Listing 15.1 uses a custom dialog box to get five numbers from the user all at once. These numbers define a range of columns, a range of rows, and specify a column on which to base a sorting operation. After the user clicks the OK button, **RowSorter1** sorts the block of rows in ascending order, using the specified sort column to determine the sorted order of the rows. The **RowSorter1** program is similar to the sorting programs from the preceding lesson, but uses a custom dialog box to conveniently get several values from the user at once, instead of using constant values, or values obtained through a series of InputBox statements.

Listing 15.1. Using edit box controls in a custom dialog box.

```
 1:    Sub RowSorter1()
 2:
 3:      Const lTitle = "Row Sorter"
 4:
 5:      Dim FirstRow As Integer
 6:      Dim LastRow As Integer
 7:      Dim FirstCol As Integer
 8:      Dim LastCol As Integer
 9:      Dim SortCol As Integer
10:      Dim oldSheet As String
11:
12:      ' preserve current sheet, change to new sheet
13:      oldSheet = ActiveSheet.Name
14:      Worksheets("Sheet1").Select
15:
16:      If DialogSheets("SortDialog1").Show Then
17:        With DialogSheets("SortDialog1")
18:          FirstRow = Int(.EditBoxes("First Row Edit").Caption)
19:          LastRow = Int(.EditBoxes("Last Row Edit").Caption)
20:          FirstCol = Int(.EditBoxes("First Col Edit").Caption)
21:          LastCol = Int(.EditBoxes("Last Col Edit").Caption)
22:          SortCol = Int(.EditBoxes("Sort Col Edit").Caption)
23:        End With
24:      Else
25:        MsgBox Title:=lTitle, prompt:="Sort Canceled", _
26:               Buttons:=vbExclamation
27:        Sheets(oldSheet).Select
28:        Exit Sub
29:      End If
30:
31:      ' ensure that 1st row is less than last row
32:      If FirstRow > LastRow Then
33:        Swap FirstRow, LastRow
34:      End If
35:
36:      ' ensure that 1st column is less than last column
37:      If FirstCol > LastCol Then
38:        Swap FirstCol, LastCol
39:      End If
40:
41:      ' ensure that sorting column is within specified range
42:      If (SortCol < FirstCol) Or (SortCol > LastCol) Then
43:        MsgBox Title:=lTitle, _
44:               prompt:="Sort column is out of range!", _
45:               Buttons:=vbCritical
46:        Sheets(oldSheet).Select
47:        Exit Sub
48:      End If
49:
50:      'sort the rows and return to original sheet
51:      SortRows FirstRow, LastRow, FirstCol, LastCol, SortCol
52:      MsgBox Title:=lTitle, prompt:="Rows are sorted.", _
53:             Buttons:=vbInformation
54:      Sheets(oldSheet).Select
55:    End Sub
```

Listing 15.1. continued

```
56:
57:  Private Sub Swap(I1 As Variant, I2 As Variant)
58:     Dim Temp As Integer
59:     Temp = I1
60:     I1 = I2
61:     I2 = Temp
62:  End Sub
63:
64:  Private Sub SortRows(ByVal FirstRow As Integer, _
65:                       ByVal LastRow As Integer, _
66:                       ByVal FirstCol As Integer, _
67:                       ByVal LastCol As Integer, _
68:                       ByVal SCol As Integer)
69:     Dim I As Integer
70:     Dim J As Integer
71:     Dim k As Integer
72:     Dim Temp As Variant
73:
74:     For I = FirstRow To LastRow - 1
75:       For J = I To LastRow
76:         If Cells(I, SCol).Value > Cells(J, SCol).Value Then
77:           ' swap columns
78:           For k = FirstCol To LastCol
79:             Temp = Cells(I, k).Value
80:             Cells(I, k).Value = Cells(J, k).Value
81:             Cells(J, k).Value = Temp
82:           Next k
83:         End If
84:       Next J
85:     Next I
86:  End Sub
```

Listing 15.1 contains an entire module. The **RowSorter1** procedure occupies lines 1 through 55 of the listing. Lines 3 through 10 declare the variables and constants used by **RowSorter1**, while lines 13 and 14 preserve the current sheet's name, and make the sheet containing the sample data (Sheet1) the active sheet.

Line 16 is the crucial statement in the **RowSorter1** procedure—the If statement invokes the Show method of the dialog sheet to display the custom dialog box, using the method's Boolean return value to determine the course of action carried out in the remainder of the procedure. (Remember, the dialog sheet Show method returns True if the dialog box is dismissed normally, or False if the dialog box is canceled.)

Note: By default, the OK and Cancel buttons that VBA automatically includes on any new dialog sheet have the DismissButton and CancelButton properties set, respectively.

In line 16, notice that the desired dialog sheet is accessed through the DialogSheets collection, in the same way you'd specify a worksheet in the Worksheets collection.

If the user clicks the OK button in the Row Sorter dialog box, then the Show method returns True, and the statements in lines 17 through 23 are executed. If the user cancels the dialog box, the Show method returns False, and the statements in lines 25 through 28 are executed, ending the procedure.

In lines 17 through 23, the values stored in the edit box controls are retrieved, converted to integer values, and assigned to the corresponding variables declared in the **RowSorter1** procedure. Notice that the value stored in the edit box is retrieved from the edit box's Caption property, and that the edit boxes are accessed through the EditBoxes collection object by using the control's name. In turn, the EditBoxes collection is accessed through the DialogSheets collection (specified by the With statement in line 17). The full object reference, written as a single statement, for the First Row edit box's Caption property would be:

```
DialogSheets("SortDialog1").EditBoxes("First Row Edit").Caption
```

Lines 32 through 48 make sure that the various values that the user entered are reasonable. If the last row or column value is smaller than the first row or column value, the values are simply swapped by calling the **Swap** procedure. If the sort column isn't within the range of columns specified by the first and last column values, then an error message is displayed, and the procedure stops executing.

After all of the data values entered by the user are validated, the actual sorting operation takes place through a call to the **SortRows** procedure in line 51. Lines 52 through 54 display a message announcing the completion of the sorting process, and restoring the original active sheet.

Lines 57 through 62 contain the **Swap** procedure, and lines 64 through 86 contain the **SortRows** procedure. The **SortRows** procedure is similar to the sorting procedures you learned about in yesterday's lesson, and uses a bubble-sort to sort the specified rows and columns.

Figure 15.6 shows an example of using the **RowSorter1** procedure.

Using Option Button Controls and Group Boxes

Listing 15.2 presents **RowSorter2**, which performs the same task as **RowSorter1**, but allows the user to select either an ascending or descending sort order. The dialog box in this example uses a pair of option buttons to allow the user to select the sort order. For convenience and clarity in using the dialog box, the option buttons are grouped together with a group box control.

To prepare for using the **RowSorter2** procedure, you'll need to create the SortDialog2 dialog sheet and dialog box. Create this dialog sheet in the same workbook you used for the last example program, and make the SortDialog2 dialog box identical to the SortDialog1 dialog box, but add the following controls, giving them the specified name and label:

Control	Name	Label
Option Button	Sort Up Option	Ascending
Option Button	Sort Down Option	Descending
Group Box	Sort Group	Sort Order

You can use the same sample data with this example as you did for Listing 15.1. Figure 15.7 shows a sample session with **RowSorter2**, showing how the completed dialog box appears.

 Tip: To simplify creating the SortDialog2 dialog box, copy the SortDialog1 dialog sheet from the preceding example, and then just add the new controls to it.

Figure 15.7.

A sample session with the RowSorter2 program. Before you can use this program, you must create the Row Sorter 2 custom dialog box on a dialog sheet named SortDialog2.

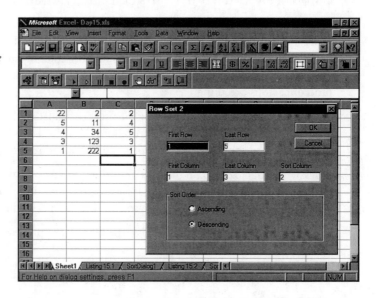

After you've prepared the SortDialog2 dialog sheet and dialog box, you're ready to enter and run the code in Listing 15.2.

Type

Listing 15.2. Using option button controls.

```
1:    Option Explicit
2:
3:    Sub RowSorter2()
4:
5:      Const lTitle = "Row Sorter 2"
```

```
6:
7:     Dim FirstRow As Integer
8:     Dim LastRow As Integer
9:     Dim FirstCol As Integer
10:    Dim LastCol As Integer
11:    Dim SortCol As Integer
12:    Dim IsAscending As Boolean
13:    Dim oldSheet As String
14:
15:    ' preserve current sheet, change to new sheet
16:    oldSheet = ActiveSheet.Name
17:    Worksheets("Sheet1").Select
18:
19:    If DialogSheets("SortDialog2").Show Then
20:      With DialogSheets("SortDialog2")
21:        FirstRow = Int(.EditBoxes("First Row Edit").Caption)
22:        LastRow = Int(.EditBoxes("Last Row Edit").Caption)
23:        FirstCol = Int(.EditBoxes("First Col Edit").Caption)
24:        LastCol = Int(.EditBoxes("Last Col Edit").Caption)
25:        SortCol = Int(.EditBoxes("Sort Col Edit").Caption)
26:        If .OptionButtons("Sort Up Option").Value = xlOn Then
27:          IsAscending = True
28:        Else
29:          IsAscending = False
30:        End If
31:      End With
32:    Else
33:      MsgBox Title:=lTitle, prompt:="Sort Canceled", _
34:             Buttons:=vbExclamation
35:      Sheets(oldSheet).Select
36:      Exit Sub
37:    End If
38:
39:    ' ensure that 1st row is less than last row
40:    If FirstRow > LastRow Then
41:      Swap FirstRow, LastRow
42:    End If
43:
44:    ' ensure that 1st column is less than last column
45:    If FirstCol > LastCol Then
46:      Swap FirstCol, LastCol
47:    End If
48:
49:    ' ensure that sorting column is within specified range
50:    If (SortCol < FirstCol) Or (SortCol > LastCol) Then
51:      MsgBox Title:=lTitle, _
52:             prompt:="Sort column is out of range!", _
53:             Buttons:=vbCritical
54:      Sheets(oldSheet).Select
55:      Exit Sub
56:    End If
57:
58:    'sort the rows and return to original sheet
59:    If IsAscending Then
60:      SortRowsUp FirstRow, LastRow, _
61:                 FirstCol, LastCol, SortCol
```

continues

Listing 15.2. continued

```
 62:    Else
 63:      SortRowsDown FirstRow, LastRow, _
 64:                   FirstCol, LastCol, SortCol
 65:    End If
 66:    MsgBox Title:=lTitle, prompt:="Rows are sorted.", _
 67:           Buttons:=vbInformation
 68:    Sheets(oldSheet).Select
 69: End Sub
 70:
 71: Private Sub Swap(I1 As Variant, I2 As Variant)
 72:    Dim Temp As Variant
 73:    Temp = I1
 74:    I1 = I2
 75:    I2 = Temp
 76: End Sub
 77:
 78: Private Sub SortRowsUp(ByVal FirstRow As Integer, _
 79:                        ByVal LastRow As Integer, _
 80:                        ByVal FirstCol As Integer, _
 81:                        ByVal LastCol As Integer, _
 82:                        ByVal SCol As Integer)
 83:    Dim I As Integer
 84:    Dim J As Integer
 85:    Dim k As Integer
 86:    Dim Temp As Variant
 87:
 88:    For I = FirstRow To LastRow - 1
 89:      For J = I To LastRow
 90:        If Cells(I, SCol).Value > Cells(J, SCol).Value Then
 91:          ' swap columns
 92:          For k = FirstCol To LastCol
 93:            Temp = Cells(I, k).Value
 94:            Cells(I, k).Value = Cells(J, k).Value
 95:            Cells(J, k).Value = Temp
 96:          Next k
 97:        End If
 98:      Next J
 99:    Next I
100: End Sub
101:
102: Private Sub SortRowsDown(ByVal FirstRow As Integer, _
103:                          ByVal LastRow As Integer, _
104:                          ByVal FirstCol As Integer, _
105:                          ByVal LastCol As Integer, _
106:                          ByVal SCol As Integer)
107:    Dim I As Integer
108:    Dim J As Integer
109:    Dim k As Integer
110:    Dim Temp As Variant
111:
112:    ' start sorting the rows
113:    For I = FirstRow To LastRow - 1
114:      For J = I To LastRow
115:        If Cells(I, SCol).Value < Cells(J, SCol).Value Then
116:          ' swap columns
```

```
117:          For k = FirstCol To LastCol
118:              Temp = Cells(I, k).Value
119:              Cells(I, k).Value = Cells(J, k).Value
120:              Cells(J, k).Value = Temp
121:          Next k
122:        End If
123:      Next J
124:   Next I
125: End Sub
```

Analysis

Listing 15.2 contains a complete module. Lines 3 through 76 contain the **RowSorter2** procedure. This procedure operates almost exactly the same as the **RowSorter1** procedure from Listing 15.1, with a few notable differences.

Notice the If...Then...Else statement in lines 26 through 30. This statement tests the Sort Up Option option button's state. If that button's Value property is equal to the predefined constant xlOn, then the user chose the ascending sort order; otherwise, the user chose a descending sort order. In this case, because there are only two option buttons, and because option buttons are mutually exclusive, it is correct to assume that if the ascending option button is checked, then the descending button is *not* checked—and the other way around.

Notice that the option button is accessed through the OptionButtons collection, using the control's name to indicate the specific control. The OptionButtons collection is accessed in turn through the DialogSheets collection (specified in the With statement starting in line 20). The full object reference for the Value property of the option button, written out altogether in a single expression, is:

```
DialogSheets("SortDialog2").OptionButtons("Sort Up Option").Value
```

Lines 58 through 65 contain another If...Then...Else statement, which evaluates the **IsAscending** variable, and calls the appropriate sorting procedure. **SortRowsUp** (declared in lines 78 through 100) sorts the rows in ascending order, and **SortRowsDown** (declared in lines 102 through 125) sorts the rows in descending order. Both sorting procedures use the bubble-sort technique you're now familiar with.

Except for the differences just noted, and the dialog box's use of option buttons to select the sort order, the **RowSorter2** procedure's operation is the same as **RowSorter1** in Listing 15.1. Refer to Figure 15.7 for a sample view of using the **RowSorter2** procedure.

DO	DON'T

DO use Excel's predefined constants—xlOn, xlOff, and xlMixed—when assigning or evaluating the Value property of an option button or check box.

DON'T forget that option buttons can only contain either the value x1On or x1Off, although check boxes may contain all three values, including x1Mixed.

DO use the x1Mixed value for a check box's value to indicate special cases, such as a check box that has never had user input in it before.

Using Check Box Controls

In the preceding sample, the custom dialog box (on the SortDialog2 dialog sheet) used option buttons to specify the sort order. You could easily represent the same choice with a check box. Instead of asking the user to choose between ascending and descending sort order with option buttons, you can ask the user whether or not to sort the list in descending order with a check box—that is, if the check box is checked, then the list should be sorted in descending order.

The next example, **RowSorter3**, uses a check box control to obtain the sort order choice. Of course, you'll need to create the dialog box containing the check box control before using the **RowSorter3** procedure.

To prepare for this example, insert another dialog sheet, and rename it SortDialog3, create the five edit boxes as you did before—or just copy the SortDialog1 dialog sheet, rename it, and add the check box control to the dialog. Since you're only adding one control, you don't need a group box—just add a single check box control to the dialog, and give it the name Sort Down Check. Figure 15.8 shows the SortDialog3 dialog box. Use the same sample data you've used for the preceding two examples.

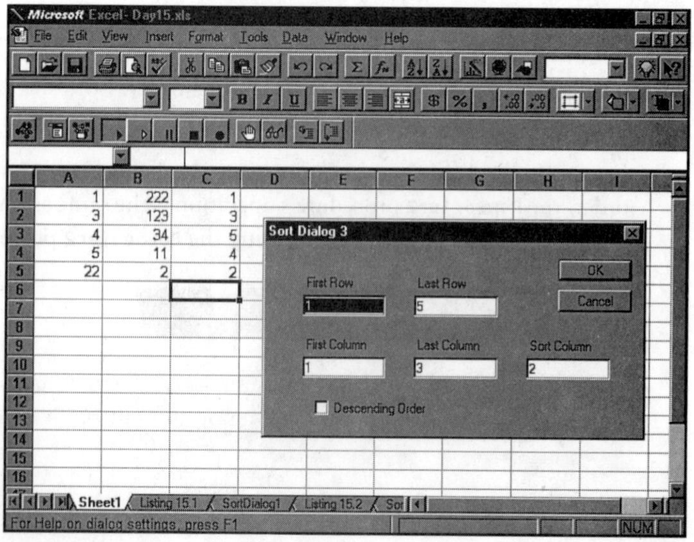

Figure 15.8.

This dialog box, used by the **RowSorter3** *procedure in Listing 15.3, uses a single check box control to determine whether the list should be sorted in descending order (checked) or ascending order (unchecked).*

Listing 15.3 shows the **RowSorter3** procedure. Because **RowSorter3** differs from **RowSorter2** so little, you may want to just copy the module sheet that you entered from Listing 15.2, and just edit it to match Listing 15.3.

 Listing 15.3. Using check box controls.

```
1:    Option Explicit
2:
3:    Sub RowSorter3()
4:
5:      Const lTitle = "Row Sorter 3"
6:
7:      Dim FirstRow As Integer
8:      Dim LastRow As Integer
9:      Dim FirstCol As Integer
10:     Dim LastCol As Integer
11:     Dim SortCol As Integer
12:     Dim IsAscending As Boolean
13:     Dim oldSheet As String
14:
15:     ' preserve current sheet, change to new sheet
16:     oldSheet = ActiveSheet.Name
17:     Worksheets("Sheet1").Select
18:
19:     If DialogSheets("SortDialog3").Show Then
20:       With DialogSheets("SortDialog3")
21:         FirstRow = Int(.EditBoxes("First Row Edit").Caption)
22:         LastRow = Int(.EditBoxes("Last Row Edit").Caption)
23:         FirstCol = Int(.EditBoxes("First Col Edit").Caption)
24:         LastCol = Int(.EditBoxes("Last Col Edit").Caption)
25:         SortCol = Int(.EditBoxes("Sort Col Edit").Caption)
26:         If .CheckBoxes("Sort Down Check").Value = xlOff Then
27:           IsAscending = True
28:         Else
29:           IsAscending = False
30:         End If
31:       End With
32:     Else
33:       MsgBox Title:=lTitle, prompt:="Sort Canceled", _
34:             Buttons:=vbExclamation
35:       Sheets(oldSheet).Select
36:       Exit Sub
37:     End If
38:
39:     ' ensure that 1st row is less than last row
40:     If FirstRow > LastRow Then
41:       Swap FirstRow, LastRow
42:     End If
43:
44:     ' ensure that 1st column is less than last column
45:     If FirstCol > LastCol Then
46:       Swap FirstCol, LastCol
47:     End If
48:
```

continues

601

Listing 15.3. continued

```
 49:     ' ensure that sorting column is within specified range
 50:     If (SortCol < FirstCol) Or (SortCol > LastCol) Then
 51:       MsgBox Title:=lTitle, _
 52:              prompt:="Sort column is out of range!", _
 53:              Buttons:=vbCritical
 54:       Sheets(oldSheet).Select
 55:       Exit Sub
 56:     End If
 57:
 58:     'sort the rows and return to original sheet
 59:     If IsAscending Then
 60:       SortRowsUp FirstRow, LastRow, _
 61:                  FirstCol, LastCol, SortCol
 62:     Else
 63:       SortRowsDown FirstRow, LastRow, _
 64:                    FirstCol, LastCol, SortCol
 65:     End If
 66:     MsgBox Title:=lTitle, prompt:="Rows are sorted.", _
 67:            Buttons:=vbInformation
 68:     Sheets(oldSheet).Select
 69:   End Sub
 70:
 71:   Private Sub Swap(I1 As Variant, I2 As Variant)
 72:     Dim Temp As Variant
 73:     Temp = I1
 74:     I1 = I2
 75:     I2 = Temp
 76:   End Sub
 77:
 78:   Private Sub SortRowsUp(ByVal FirstRow As Integer, _
 79:                          ByVal LastRow As Integer, _
 80:                          ByVal FirstCol As Integer, _
 81:                          ByVal LastCol As Integer, _
 82:                          ByVal SCol As Integer)
 83:     Dim I As Integer
 84:     Dim J As Integer
 85:     Dim k As Integer
 86:     Dim Temp As Variant
 87:
 88:     For I = FirstRow To LastRow - 1
 89:       For J = I To LastRow
 90:         If Cells(I, SCol).Value > Cells(J, SCol).Value Then
 91:           ' swap columns
 92:           For k = FirstCol To LastCol
 93:             Temp = Cells(I, k).Value
 94:             Cells(I, k).Value = Cells(J, k).Value
 95:             Cells(J, k).Value = Temp
 96:           Next k
 97:         End If
 98:       Next J
 99:     Next I
100:   End Sub
101:
102:   Private Sub SortRowsDown(ByVal FirstRow As Integer, _
103:                            ByVal LastRow As Integer, _
104:                            ByVal FirstCol As Integer, _
```

```
105:                        ByVal LastCol As Integer, _
106:                        ByVal SCol As Integer)
107:    Dim I As Integer
108:    Dim J As Integer
109:    Dim k As Integer
110:    Dim Temp As Variant
111:
112:    ' start sorting the rows
113:    For I = FirstRow To LastRow - 1
114:       For J = I To LastRow
115:          If Cells(I, SCol).Value < Cells(J, SCol).Value Then
116:             ' swap columns
117:             For k = FirstCol To LastCol
118:                Temp = Cells(I, k).Value
119:                Cells(I, k).Value = Cells(J, k).Value
120:                Cells(J, k).Value = Temp
121:             Next k
122:          End If
123:       Next J
124:    Next I
125: End Sub
```

Analysis Listing 15.3 is a complete module, and is almost identical to Listing 15.4, with the exception of line 26. In this statement, the Value property of the check box control is compared to the Excel constant xlOff. If the check box is off—that is, not checked—then the list should be sorted in ascending order, and the **IsAscending** variable is set accordingly. If the check box is on—that is, checked—then the list should be sorted in ascending order.

Notice that the check box is accessed through the CheckBoxes collection, using the control's name to indicate the specific control. The CheckBoxes collection, like the other control collections, is accessed through the DialogSheets collection (specified in the With statement starting in line 20). The full object reference for the Value property of the check box, written out altogether in a single expression, is:

```
DialogSheets("SortDialog2").CheckBoxes("Sort Down Check").Value
```

DO	DON'T

DO remember that you access a specific control through the appropriate collection object, using the control's name—set through the Name property or while editing the dialog sheet. You reference a check box through the CheckBoxes collection, an edit box through the EditBoxes collection, an option button through the OptionButtons collection, and so on. Refer to the Excel VBA online help to find out about other dialog box control collections.

> **DO** remember that you access a particular dialog box's controls through the dialog sheet object; you reference specific dialog sheets by name through the `DialogSheets` collection object of a workbook.

Using Scrollbar and Spinner Controls with Dynamically Updated Labels in a Floating Dialog Box

Scrollbar and spinner controls present a special difficulty—when you click a scrollbar or spinner control, its value changes, but VBA does not automatically update the control's label, because scrollbar and spinner controls don't have inherent captions. It is up to you, the programmer, to update the labels in the dialog box to reflect the changing values of scrollbar and spinner controls. The next program example shows you how to use an event procedure attached to a scrollbar or spinner control to update that control's label.

This next custom dialog box example also demonstrates how you can create floating dialog boxes, and carry out actions without having your custom dialog box close. (A *floating* dialog box remains open, even after clicking a button to perform an action.) As you work in Excel and other Windows programs, you've probably noticed that they sometimes use floating dialog boxes. A common example of a floating dialog box is the Find dialog box in Excel—you specify the text you want to find, and then click the Find Next button. Even after Excel finds the text you specified, it leaves the Find dialog box open so that you can easily conduct additional searches. To close the Find dialog box, you must specifically choose the Close command button.

As an incidental part of creating the floating dialog box in the next example, you'll also gain some experience in attaching an event procedure to a command button.

For this example, you can use the same sample data that you've used for the preceding examples in this listing. Creating the dialog box is somewhat more complex, however. Follow these steps to set up the next demonstration dialog box:

1. Insert a new module sheet in the same workbook in which you've entered the other examples from this lesson, and enter all of the code from Listing 15.4.

2. Insert a new dialog sheet into the workbook, and rename it `SortDialog4`.

3. Change the dialog box's title bar to **Row Sort 4**.

4. Add four scrollbar controls to the dialog sheet, using the techniques for adding controls you learned earlier in this lesson. As you add each scrollbar control, also add a label control to correspond to that scrollbar control. (Refer to Figure 15.9.) Label the scrollbars as **First Row**, **Last Row**, **First Column**, and **Last Column**.

As you add each scrollbar control, rename it so that your scrollbars are named `First Row SBar`, `Last Row SBar`, `First Col SBar`, and `Last Col SBar`.

5. Add a spinner control to the dialog sheet, and add a label control for the spinner. For the spinner control, it doesn't matter what the label control says, you just need to make sure you have a label control that corresponds to the spinner control. After adding the spinner control, rename it as `Sort Col Spin`.

6. Add a check box control to the dialog sheet; edit the check box's caption to read: **Descending Sort Order**. After adding the check box control, rename it as `Sort Down Check`.

7. Change the caption on the OK command button (which was automatically included in the dialog box), so that it now reads: **Sort**, and rename it as `Sort Button`. Edit the newly renamed Sort command button's properties (use the Control Properties command button on the Forms toolbar) and clear the Dismiss check box; this button will then no longer dismiss the dialog box.

8. Change the caption on the Cancel command button (which was automatically included in the dialog box), so that it now reads: **Close**, and rename it as `Close Button`.

Figure 15.9.

The dialog box in the SortDialog4 dialog sheet should look like this one when you've finished adding all the controls and changing the command button captions.

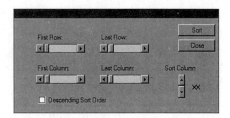

At this point, your custom dialog box should look similar to the one shown in Figure 15.9. Now you're ready to assign procedures to the controls on your dialog box. Follow the steps for attaching procedures to a dialog box control that you learned earlier in this lesson, and use the following table as a guide for assigning procedures from Listing 15.4 to the various dialog box controls:

Control	Attached Procedure
First Row SBar	**FirstRowScroll_Change**
Last Row SBar	**LastRowScroll_Change**
First Col SBar	**FirstColScroll_Change**
Last Col SBar	**LastColScroll_Change**
Sort Col Spin	**SortColSpinner_Change**
Sort Button	**SortButton_Click**

When you execute the **RowSortMain** procedure in Listing 15.4, it displays the custom dialog box you just created (from the SortDialog4 dialog sheet). The scrollbar controls are used to select the boundaries for the block of rows and columns to be sorted, and the spinner control selects the column used for sorting. When the user clicks the scrollbar or spinner controls, the attached event procedure updates the control's label so that the user can see what the value selected by the control is. As before, the check box control selects whether or not the rows should be sorted in descending order.

When the user clicks the Sort command button, the rows are sorted, but the dialog box is *not* closed—instead, it remains open so that the user can choose additional sort criteria and resort the rows. To close the dialog box, the user chooses the Close command button, or presses the Esc key.

Type

Listing 15.4. Using scrollbar and spinner controls in a floating dialog box.

```
1:   Option Explicit
2:
3:   Private Const lTitle = "Row Sort 4"
4:
5:   Sub RowSortMain()
6:   'sets up and displays the SortDialog 4 dialog box
7:
8:      Dim oldSheet As String
9:
10:     'preserve old sheet, select data sheet
11:     oldSheet = ActiveSheet.Name
12:     Worksheets("Sheet1").Select
13:
14:     'make sure of accurate labels when dialog first displayed
15:     With DialogSheets("SortDialog4")
16:       .Labels("First Row Label").Caption = _
17:         "First Row: " & .ScrollBars("First Row SBar").Value
18:       .Labels("Last Row Label").Caption = _
19:         "Last Row: " & .ScrollBars("Last Row SBar").Value
20:       .Labels("First Col Label").Caption = _
21:         "First Column: " & .ScrollBars("First Col SBar").Value
22:       .Labels("Last Col Label").Caption = _
23:         "Last Column: " & .ScrollBars("Last Col SBar").Value
24:       .Labels("Sort Col Label").Caption = _
25:                   CStr(.Spinners("Sort Col Spin").Value)
26:     End With
27:
28:     DialogSheets("SortDialog4").Show   'show the dialog box
29:
30:     Sheets(oldSheet).Select    'restore original sheet
31:   End Sub
32:
33:   Sub SortButton_Click()
34:   'carries out the sorting task when Sort button is clicked
35:
```

```
36:     Dim FirstRow As Integer
37:     Dim LastRow As Integer
38:     Dim FirstCol As Integer
39:     Dim LastCol As Integer
40:     Dim SortCol As Integer
41:     Dim IsAscending As Boolean
42:
43:     With DialogSheets("SortDialog4")
44:       FirstRow = .ScrollBars("First Row SBar").Value
45:       LastRow = .ScrollBars("Last Row SBar").Value
46:       FirstCol = .ScrollBars("First Col SBar").Value
47:       LastCol = .ScrollBars("Last Col SBar").Value
48:       SortCol = .Spinners("Sort Col Spin").Value
49:       If .CheckBoxes("Sort Down Check").Value = xlOff Then
50:         IsAscending = True
51:       Else
52:         IsAscending = False
53:       End If
54:     End With
55:
56:     ' ensure that 1st row is less than last row
57:     If FirstRow > LastRow Then Swap FirstRow, LastRow
58:
59:     ' ensure that 1st column is less than last column
60:     If FirstCol > LastCol Then Swap FirstCol, LastCol
61:
62:     ' ensure that sorting column is within specified range
63:     If (SortCol < FirstCol) Or (SortCol > LastCol) Then
64:       MsgBox Title:=lTitle, _
65:               prompt:="Sort column is out of range!", _
66:               Buttons:=vbCritical
67:       Exit Sub
68:     End If
69:
70:     'sort the rows
71:     If IsAscending Then
72:       SortRowsUp FirstRow, LastRow, _
73:                   FirstCol, LastCol, SortCol
74:     Else
75:       SortRowsDown FirstRow, LastRow, _
76:                   FirstCol, LastCol, SortCol
77:     End If
78:     MsgBox Title:=lTitle, prompt:="Rows are sorted.", _
79:           Buttons:=vbInformation
80: End Sub
81:
82: Private Sub Swap(I1 As Variant, I2 As Variant)
83:     Dim Temp As Variant
84:     Temp = I1: I1 = I2: I2 = Temp
85: End Sub
86:
87: Private Sub SortRowsUp(ByVal FirstRow As Integer, _
88:                        ByVal LastRow As Integer, _
89:                        ByVal FirstCol As Integer, _
90:                        ByVal LastCol As Integer, _
91:                        ByVal SCol As Integer)
```

continues

Listing 15.4. continued

```
 92:    Dim I As Integer
 93:    Dim J As Integer
 94:    Dim k As Integer
 95:    Dim Temp As Variant
 96:
 97:    For I = FirstRow To LastRow - 1
 98:      For J = I To LastRow
 99:        If Cells(I, SCol).Value > Cells(J, SCol).Value Then
100:          For k = FirstCol To LastCol  'swap columns
101:            Temp = Cells(I, k).Value
102:            Cells(I, k).Value = Cells(J, k).Value
103:            Cells(J, k).Value = Temp
104:          Next k
105:        End If
106:      Next J
107:    Next I
108: End Sub
109:
110: Private Sub SortRowsDown(ByVal FirstRow As Integer, _
111:                          ByVal LastRow As Integer, _
112:                          ByVal FirstCol As Integer, _
113:                          ByVal LastCol As Integer, _
114:                          ByVal SCol As Integer)
115:    Dim I As Integer
116:    Dim J As Integer
117:    Dim k As Integer
118:    Dim Temp As Variant
119:
120:    For I = FirstRow To LastRow - 1
121:      For J = I To LastRow
122:        If Cells(I, SCol).Value < Cells(J, SCol).Value Then
123:          For k = FirstCol To LastCol  'swap columns
124:            Temp = Cells(I, k).Value
125:            Cells(I, k).Value = Cells(J, k).Value
126:            Cells(J, k).Value = Temp
127:          Next k
128:        End If
129:      Next J
130:    Next I
131: End Sub
132:
133: Sub FirstRowScroll_Change()
134: 'updates label of First Row Scrollbar control
135:    With DialogSheets("SortDialog4")
136:      .Labels("First Row Label").Caption = _
137:        "First Row: " & .ScrollBars("First Row SBar").Value
138:    End With
139: End Sub
140:
141:
142: Sub LastRowScroll_Change()
143: 'updates label of Last Row Scrollbar
144:    With DialogSheets("SortDialog4")
```

```
145:      .Labels("Last Row Label").Caption = _
146:         "Last Row: " & .ScrollBars("Last Row SBar").Value
147:    End With
148: End Sub
149:
150: Sub FirstColScroll_Change()
151: 'updates label of First Col Scrollbar
152:    With DialogSheets("SortDialog4")
153:      .Labels("First Col Label").Caption = _
154:         "First Column: " & .ScrollBars("First Col SBar").Value
155:    End With
156: End Sub
157:
158: Sub LastColScroll_Change()
159: 'updates label of Last Col Scrollbar
160:    With DialogSheets("SortDialog4")
161:      .Labels("Last Col Label").Caption = _
162:         "Last Column: " & .ScrollBars("Last Col SBar").Value
163:    End With
164: End Sub
165:
166: Sub SortColSpinner_Change()
167: 'updates label of Sort Col Spinner
168:    With DialogSheets("SortDialog4")
169:      .Labels("Sort Col Label").Caption = _
170:            CStr(.Spinners("Sort Col Spin").Value)
171:    End With
172: End Sub
```

Analysis

Listing 15.4 contains a complete module. Line 1 of the module contains the Option Explicit compiler directive to require that all variables be declared explicitly. Line 3 declares a constant for use in the title bar of message boxes displayed by procedures in this module. The Private keyword restricts the scope of this constant to this module.

To display the SortDialog4 custom dialog box, execute the **RowSortMain** procedure (lines 5 through 31). The **RowSortMain** procedure begins by preserving the current sheet name (line 11), and then selecting the worksheet with sample data (line 12). Next, the statements in lines 15 through 26 adjust the Caption property of all of the label controls on the dialog sheet to ensure that the dialog box displays the correct control values when it is first displayed. Because of this action, you can see why it was important to create and name a label control corresponding to each scrollbar and spinner control, but that it didn't really matter what caption you gave the label controls when you placed them on the dialog box—the VBA code is controlling the label controls' captions.

Notice that each label control is accessed through the Labels collection, using the label control's name to indicate the specific control. The Labels collection is accessed through the DialogSheets collection (specified in the With statement starting in line 15). The full object reference for the

Caption property of the label control for the first row scrollbar control, written out in a single expression, is:

```
DialogSheets("SortDialog4").Labels("First Row Label").Caption
```

Line 28 uses the Show method to display the dialog box. Since this dialog box carries out all its work without having to be closed, it's not important to check the Show method's return value—there is no reason to be concerned whether the user canceled the dialog box or not. The actual sorting operation is carried out when the user clicks the Sort button in the dialog box.

When VBA executes the statement in line 28, it displays the specified dialog box, and execution of the **RowSortMain** procedure is suspended until the dialog box is closed. When the user closes the dialog box by clicking the Close button, or pressing the Esc key, execution in **RowSortMain** resumes with line 30, which restores the original worksheet; **RowSortMain** ends in line 31.

Lines 33 through 80 contain the **SortButton_Click** procedure. This procedure is attached to the Sort button in the dialog box. Whenever the dialog box is displayed, and the user clicks the Sort command button, this procedure is executed. Most of the code in the **SortButton_Click** procedure is familiar to you, by now—it's essentially the same statements from the preceding two examples.

Lines 43 through 54 of **SortButton_Click** retrieve the values from the dialog box controls—the row and column limits are retrieved from the scrollbar controls, the sort column is retrieved from the spinner control, and the sort direction is obtained by testing the value of the Sort Down Check check box. Notice that the scrollbar controls are accessed through the ScrollBars collection, the spinner control is accessed through the Spinners collection, and the check box is accessed through the CheckBoxes collection.

After retrieving the row and column limits and obtaining the sort direction, lines 56 through 68 make sure that the lower limits are actually smaller than the upper limits, and that the selected sort column falls between the upper and lower column limits. If the sort column number is outside the limits, a warning message is displayed, and the **SortButton_Click** procedure's execution is stopped (lines 64 through 67).

Notice that if the sort column number is out of range, only the **SortButton_Click** procedure ends—the dialog box will remain open, and the user can easily select another sort column value with the spinner control.

Lines 71 through 77 call the appropriate sorting procedure, depending on the value of the **IsAscending** variable. Finally, lines 78 through 79 display a message box signaling that the sort is complete.

Again, notice that when the **SortButton_Click** procedure stops executing, the dialog box remains open and active—the **RowSortMain** procedure's execution is still suspended at the statement calling the Show method in line 28 of the listing.

Lines 82 through 131 contain the **Swap**, **SortRowsUp**, and **SortRowsDown** procedures. These procedures are all called by the **SortButton_Click** procedure, and are the same as the procedures you've already seen in Listing 15.3 of the same name.

The procedures in lines 133 through 172 all require some special attention, however. Each of these procedures is an event procedure that updates the label control corresponding to one of the scrollbar or spinner controls in the dialog box. Each procedure is attached to its corresponding control.

For example, the **FirstRowScroll_Change** procedure in lines 133 through 139 is attached to the First Row Sbar scrollbar control. Whenever that scrollbar control is changed, VBA executes this attached event procedure. **FirstRowScroll_Change** simply retrieves the value from the First Row Sbar scrollbar control, assembles it into a string, and assigns the new string to the First Row Label control's Caption property. As soon as the new value is assigned to the label control's Caption property, VBA updates the on-screen display of the dialog box. This way, the user immediately sees the change made by clicking the scrollbar control. It may seem like a lot of work to create the dialog box, enter the code, and run the example, but it's really worth it to see these event procedures working.

All of the remaining event procedures—**LastRowScroll_Change**, **FirstColScroll_Change**, **LastColScroll_Change**, and **SortColSpinner_Change**—work essentially the same way by retrieving the scrollbar or spinner control's value, assembling it into a string, and then assigning that string to the corresponding label control.

Figure 15.10 shows a session using the **RowSortMain** procedure from Listing 15.4.

Figure 15.10.

*The **RowSortMain** procedure in Listing 15.4 uses this dialog box to get information from the user. This dialog box sorts the selected rows and columns without closing; you must click the Close button to close this dialog box.*

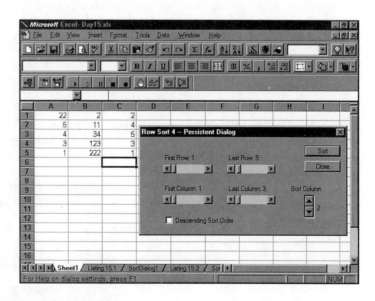

611

DO	DON'T

DO keep in mind that you can use the technique illustrated in Listing 15.4 for updating label controls associated with other controls to dynamically update any control in a dialog box, including edit boxes, list boxes, and so on.

DON'T forget that an event procedure is executed whenever the dialog box control's state changes—when a command button is clicked, text is typed in an edit box, a scrollbar or spinner is clicked, a list selection is made, and so on.

DO remember that any procedure can be an event procedure—what makes a procedure an event procedure is the fact that you've attached the procedure to a dialog box control.

DO use event procedures attached to command buttons to carry out actions, whether or not the command button dismisses the dialog box.

Using List Box Controls

The final example in this lesson is a dialog box that uses a list box control. In this example, the dialog box shows a list box containing the names of various cities. The dialog box also contains the default OK and Cancel command buttons, and a label control at the bottom of the dialog box to echo the current list selection. When you select an item in the list, the label control is updated to display the new selection; when you close the dialog box by clicking the OK command button, the procedure displays the chosen list item in a MsgBox dialog box.

This example shows you how to add items to a list in a list box, as well as retrieve the list selection value. To use this example, you'll need to create a dialog box like the one in Figure 15.11, which shows a sample session using the example dialog box and code from Listing 15.5.

After you've entered Listing 15.5 into a module sheet, insert a new dialog sheet, rename it to ListBoxDialog1, and create the dialog box. Rename the list box as City List, and rename the label control as City List Label. To complete the dialog box preparation, attach the **CityList_Change** procedure to the list box control.

Figure 15.11.

This dialog box displays the choice from the list in the label control under the list.

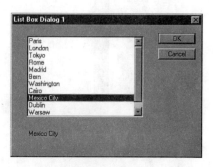

Type

Listing 15.5. Using a list box control.

```
 1:  Option Explicit
 2:
 3:  Sub DemoListBox()
 4:      Dim Choice As String
 5:      Dim Index As Integer
 6:
 7:      With DialogSheets("ListBoxDialog1")
 8:        ' clear the list box
 9:        .ListBoxes("City List").RemoveAllItems
10:        ' insert data
11:        .ListBoxes("City List").AddItem ("Paris")
12:        .ListBoxes("City List").AddItem ("London")
13:        .ListBoxes("City List").AddItem ("Tokyo")
14:        .ListBoxes("City List").AddItem ("Rome")
15:        .ListBoxes("City List").AddItem ("Madrid")
16:        .ListBoxes("City List").AddItem ("Bern")
17:        .ListBoxes("City List").AddItem ("Washington")
18:        .ListBoxes("City List").AddItem ("Cairo")
19:        .ListBoxes("City List").AddItem ("Mexico City")
20:        .ListBoxes("City List").AddItem ("Dublin")
21:        .ListBoxes("City List").AddItem ("Warsaw")
22:        .ListBoxes("City List").AddItem ("Vienna")
23:
24:        'update label control
25:        Index = .ListBoxes("City List").Value
26:        If Index > 0 Then
27:          Choice = .ListBoxes("City List").List(Index)
28:          .Labels("City List Label").Caption = Choice
29:        End If
30:      End With
31:
32:      If DialogSheets("ListBoxDialog1").Show Then
33:        With DialogSheets("ListBoxDialog1")
34:          Index = .ListBoxes("City List").Value
35:          Choice = .ListBoxes("City List").List(Index)
36:        End With
37:        MsgBox prompt:=Choice, Buttons:=vbInformation, _
38:               Title:="List Box Selection"
39:      End If
40:  End Sub
41:
42:  Sub CityList_Change()
43:  'updates label control, reflecting list choice
44:      Dim I As Integer
45:
46:      With DialogSheets("ListBoxDialog1")
47:        I = .ListBoxes("City List").Value
48:        .Labels("City List Label").Caption = _
49:                    .ListBoxes("City List").List(I)
50:      End With
51:  End Sub
```

Like the other listings in this lesson, Listing 15.5 is a complete module. The **DemoListBox** procedure occupies lines 3 through 40 of the listing. Lines 4 and 5 declare the variables used by this procedure.

Look closely at line 9. This statement uses the RemoveAllItems method of the list box control to empty the list—if the dialog box were displayed at this point, nothing would be shown in the list. By completely removing all items from the list, this statement helps ensure that the list's contents will be precisely known—that is, the list won't contain any items that this procedure didn't put there.

Next, lines 11 through 22 each use the AddItem method of the list box control to add a single item to the list. There is one statement for each item in the list.

Tip: You could also fill a list box's list by adding items from a VBA array, or by linking the list box control to a range of cells in a worksheet—each cell's value becomes an item in the list.

Notice that the list box control object is accessed through the ListBoxes collection, using the list box's name to indicate the specific control. The ListBoxes collection is accessed through the DialogSheets collection (specified in the With statement starting in line 7).

Lines 25 through 29 assign the Value property of the list box control to the **Index** variable, and then tests to see if the **Index** variable contains a number greater than 0. If it does, the City List Label label control's Caption property is updated to reflect the current list choice, ensuring that the text in the dialog box is accurate when the dialog box is first displayed.

Note: The list box control's Value property contains a number indicating the current list selection. For example, if the second item in the list is selected, then the Value property contains the number 2. You then get the text for the list selection by using the List collection property of the list box control—just use the number from the Value property as a subscript in the List collection, as you would in an array.

Lines 32 through 39 contain an If statement that uses the Show method to display the dialog box. If the user chooses the OK button, the Show method returns True, and lines 33 through 38 are executed. If the user cancels the dialog box, the **DemoListBox** procedure simply ends.

Lines 33 through 36 retrieve the list selection by first assigning the Value property of the list box to the **Index** variable, and then using the **Index** variable as a subscript in the list box's List

collection. The value returned by the List collection is assigned to the **Choice** variable. The complete object reference for retrieving the list box's selection text, written as a single expression, is:

```
DialogSheets("ListDialogBox1").ListBoxes("City List").List(Index)
```

The MsgBox statement in lines 37 through 38 simply displays the contents of the **Choice** variable in a message box on-screen.

The **CityList_Change** procedure in lines 42 through 51 is an event procedure attached to the list box control. Whenever the selection in the list box changes, VBA executes this procedure, which simply retrieves the text for the selected list item and assigns it to the Caption property of the label control of the dialog box.

 Tip: Managing drop-down lists is essentially the same as managing a list box.

Summary

In today's lesson, you learned the basic skills required to work with VBA's custom dialog boxes in Excel. You learned how to create, use, and manage custom dialog boxes and their controls. You learned that you create custom dialog boxes by drawing them visually on a dialog sheet. You learned about the basic features of a variety of dialog box controls, and how to control them with your VBA code. In particular, you learned how to attach event procedures to command buttons and other controls, how to create a floating dialog box, and how to use event procedures to update a dialog box's controls while the dialog box is still displayed.

Q&A

Q My dialog box never closes; what's wrong with it?

A Any command button on your dialog box that should close the dialog box must have either the DismissButton property or the CancelButton property set. You can set these properties interactively on the dialog sheet by selecting the command button control and then clicking the Control Properties button on the Forms toolbar. Check either the Dismiss check box or the Cancel check box on the properties sheet to set these properties. Remember, although they both close the dialog box, the DismissButton property causes the Show method to return True, and the CancelButton property causes the Show method to return False.

Q How can I specify where my custom dialog box appears on-screen?

A You can't control where your custom dialog box appears on-screen. VBA displays custom dialog boxes on-screen with the top-left corner of your custom dialog box at the same position as the top-left corner of the last dialog box displayed on-screen, whether it was a custom dialog box or an Excel dialog box.

Q How can I disable a custom dialog box control?

A You can disable a custom dialog box control by assigning False to the Enabled property of that control. To enable the control again, assign True to the Enabled property.

Q How can I hide a control?

A You can hide a control by assigning False to the Visible property of that control. To show the control, assign True to the Visible property.

Q How can I make an edit box display multiple lines?

A You can make an edit box show multiple lines by assigning True to its MultiLine property. You can also set this property interactively on the dialog sheet by selecting the edit box and then using the Control Properties command button on the Forms toolbar.

Q How can I add and delete items from a list box and a drop-down control?

A You can add and delete items using the AddItem and RemoveItem methods. The AddItem method takes a string expression as its argument. The RemoveItem method takes two numeric expressions as its arguments—the first number specifies the index of the first list item to be deleted. The second number specifies the number of items to delete.

Q How do I obtain the number of items in a list box?

A Use the ListCount property of the list box control.

Workshop

Answers are in Appendix A.

Quiz

1. **BUG BUSTER:** Where is the error in the following set of statements?

```
' clear the list box
.ListBoxes("AnyList").RemoveAllItems
' insert data
.ListBoxes("AnyList").AddItem ("Paris")
.ListBoxes("AnyList").AddItem ("London")
.ListBoxes("AnyList").AddItem ("Tokyo")
.ListBoxes("AnyList").AddItem ("Rome")
.ListBoxes("AnyList").AddItem ("Madrid")
```

```
        .ListBoxes("AnyList").AddItem ("Bern")
        .ListBoxes("AnyList").AddItem ("Washington")
```

2. **BUG BUSTER:** Where is the error in the following set of statements?

```
With DialogSheets("ListBoxDialog1")
  ' clear the list box
  ListBoxes("AnyList").RemoveAllItems
  ' insert data
  .ListBoxes("AnyList").AddItem ("Paris")
  .ListBoxes("AnyList").AddItem ("London")
  .ListBoxes("AnyList").AddItem ("Tokyo")
  .ListBoxes("AnyList").AddItem ("Rome")
  .ListBoxes("AnyList").AddItem ("Dublin")
  .ListBoxes("AnyList").AddItem ("Warsaw")
  .ListBoxes("AnyList").AddItem ("Vienna")
End With
```

3. **BUG BUSTER:** Is the syntax of the following statements correct?

```
With DialogSheets("ListBoxDialog1")
  ' clear the list box
  .ListBoxes("AnyList").RemoveAllItems
  ' insert data
  With .ListBoxes("AnyList")
    .AddItem ("Paris")
    .AddItem ("London")
    .AddItem ("Tokyo")
    .AddItem ("Rome")
    .AddItem ("Dublin")
    .AddItem ("Warsaw")
    .AddItem ("Vienna")
  End With
End With
```

Exercises

1. Modify the **DemoListBox** procedure, along with the ListBoxDialog1 dialog sheet to create a **DemoDropDown** procedure and DropDownDialog1 dialog box, respectively. The new procedure and dialog box should handle the drop-down list the same way the procedures in Listing 15.5 handle the list box. Figure 15.12 shows how the DropDownDialog1 dialog box might appear, when completed. HINT: Drop-down list controls are accessed through the DropDowns collection of the dialog sheet.

Figure 15.12.
Create this dialog box for
*your **DemoDropDown***
procedure.

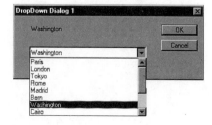

2. Create a procedure named **COCA** (which stands for Common Command-Oriented Calculator) that uses a dialog box to get two operands and a mathematical operator, and then displays the result of combining the operands with the specified mathematical operation when the user clicks the Calculate command button. Make the COCA dialog box a floating dialog box, as demonstrated in Listing 15.4. HINT: Create two procedures—one to display the COCA dialog box, and one to work as the event procedure for the Calculate button. HINT: Make sure that the Dismiss property for the Calculate button is cleared. Figure 15.13 shows what the COCA dialog box might look like.

Figure 15.13.

The COCA should use a floating dialog box like this one.

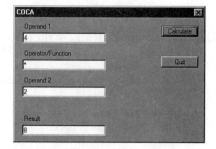

You should make the COCA able to handle all of the following operations: + (add), - (subtract), * (multiply), / (divide), ^ (exponentiation), and Sqr (square root). Make sure you prevent division by zero, and attempting to find the square root of a negative number. HINT: Use a Select Case statement to evaluate the operator that the user enters; include a Case clause for each operator, containing statements that perform the requested operation on the operands.

16

Menus and Toolbars

Now that you know how to use Excel VBA's custom dialog boxes, you're ready to learn about another VBA feature that allows you to create complete, professional programs—menus and toolbars. Visual Basic for Applications makes it possible for you to customize existing menus and toolbars by adding new commands and submenus, or to create your own complete menus and toolbars. By creating your own menus and toolbars, or customizing an existing menu or toolbar, you can add sophisticated extensions to the standard Excel user interface, or create complete menu and toolbar systems for your own applications. In today's lesson, you'll learn:

☐ About Excel's menu bars and menu structure, and their corresponding VBA objects.

☐ How to add commands or submenus to Excel's predefined menu bars and menus.

☐ How to use VBA to create and manage your own custom menu bars, menus, submenus, and menu commands.

☐ How to manipulate Excel's built-in toolbars.

☐ How to create and manage custom toolbars and the buttons on the toolbars.

Understanding Menu Structures

VBA makes it possible for you to customize Excel's built-in menu bars and to create your own menu bars. Before getting into the details of manipulating menu bars and menu objects with your VBA code, you need to understand the menu and menu bar structure; you'll also need to know a bit about the VBA objects that enable you to create and modify menus.

The Parts of a Menu

Figure 16.1 shows the expanded Insert menu from the Visual Basic menu bar. (Excel displays the Visual Basic menu bar whenever the active window contains a module sheet.) Although you're probably already familiar with the end-user terminology used for the various parts of a menu, you need to understand VBA's menu terminology, as well.

Figure 16.1.

The expanded Insert menu of the Visual Basic menu bar, showing all the essential menu elements: menu bar, menu, submenu, and menu item.

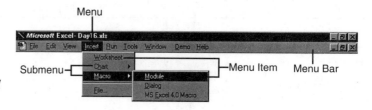

A *menu bar* is the bar that extends across the top of the application's window (underneath the window's title bar) and lists the first-level menu choices currently available. Each word on the menu bar represents a menu. When you click the menu name on the menu bar, Excel displays that menu.

Menus list a series of commands or additional menus that you may choose from. In VBA, the commands listed on a menu are called *menu items*. Clicking the menu item causes the listed command to be carried out. In Figure 16.1, the **W**orksheet and **F**ile choices are both menu items on the **I**nsert menu. The **M**odule, **D**ialog, and MS E**x**cel 4.0 Macro choices are all menu items on the **M**acro menu.

From an end-user's point of view, additional menus contained in another menu—just as the **I**nsert menu contains the **M**acro and C**h**art menus in Figure 16.1—are called *submenus*. VBA, however, doesn't make a distinction in terminology between menus and submenus; both are referred to as menus. VBA considers submenus to simply be a menu attached to another menu.

> **Note:** As you already know, menu choices that lead to other menus are designated by a right-facing arrowhead at the right of the menu choice. Menu choices that lead to dialog boxes are designated by an ellipsis (...) at the right of the menu choice. Choices without either symbol at the right immediately carry out the indicated command. In Figure 16.1, the C**h**art and **M**acro choices lead to additional menus, while the **F**ile choice leads to a dialog box. The **W**orksheet choice is a command that will be carried out immediately when clicked.
>
> When you create and display your custom menus, Excel and VBA will automatically add the arrow that indicates a submenu; *you*, however, must remember to provide the ellipsis to indicate that your custom command leads to a dialog box.

VBA Menu Objects and Properties

VBA uses objects to represent menu bars, menus, and menu items. VBA also uses a couple of object collections to represent the hierarchical structure of the menu system. Table 16.1 lists the VBA menu objects and collections that you'll use in your code to customize and manipulate various parts of either Excel's or your own custom menus.

Table 16.1. VBA menu objects.

Menu Object	Purpose
MenuBar	A menu bar object. Represents a single menu bar, such as the Visual Basic menu bar, or the Worksheet menu bar. A MenuBar object typically contains a collection of menus.
Menu	A menu object. Represents a single menu on a menu bar, or a submenu on another menu. A Menu object typically contains a mixed collection of menu items and additional menus.
MenuItem	A menu command. Represents a single command on a menu or submenu. A MenuItem typically invokes a VBA procedure which may, in turn, invoke a custom dialog box.
MenuBars	A collection of MenuBar objects. Used as a method of the Application object, MenuBars returns the collection of all currently existing menu bars—both built-in and custom menu bars.
Menus	A collection of Menu objects. Used as a method of the MenuBar object, Menus returns a collection of all the menus attached to a particular menu bar.
MenuItems	A collection of MenuItem objects. Used as a method of the Menu object, MenuItems returns a mixed collection of MenuItem and Menu objects attached to a particular menu. Menu objects in the MenuItems collection represent submenus. For example, the **Macro** submenu in Figure 16.1 is a Menu object contained in the MenuItems collection of the **Insert** Menu object, just as the **W**orksheet command is a MenuItem object in the same MenuItems collection.

The objects listed in Table 16.1 have a variety of properties and methods that you will need to use in order to create and manipulate menus with your VBA code. Table 16.2 lists the most frequently used properties and methods of the VBA menu objects listed in Table 16.1.

Table 16.2. VBA menu object properties and methods.

Property/Method	Belongs To	Purpose
Activate	MenuBar	Method. Causes VBA and Excel to display the menu bar on-screen, replacing the current menu bar.
Add	MenuBars, Menus, MenuItems	Method. Adds a new object to the specified collection—a menu bar, a menu, or a menu item.

Property/Method	Belongs To	Purpose
AddMenu	MenuItems	Method. Use this method to add a submenu to a menu. The Add method for the Menus collection adds only MenuItem objects. By using AddMenu, you can add a Menu object to the MenuItems collection to create a submenu.
BuiltIn	MenuBar	Property. True if the menu bar is one of Excel's built-in menu bars.
Caption	MenuBar, Menu, MenuItem	Property. The menu and menu item captions are the text that appears on-screen for that choice. A menu bar's caption just identifies the menu bar.
Count	Menus, MenuItems, MenuBars	Property. The total number of elements in the specified collection.
Delete	MenuBar, Menu, MenuItem	Method. Deletes the specified object from the collection.
Enabled	Menu, MenuItem	Property. Whether or not the menu or menu item is available. When set to False, the menu or menu item is displayed as a disabled choice.
Checked	MenuItem	Property. When True, causes a checkmark to displayed to the left of the menu item.
OnAction	MenuItem	Property. Contains a string specifying the VBA procedure to execute when this menu item is clicked. Use OnAction to specify the event procedure for a menu command.
StatusBar	MenuItem	Property. Contains a string specifying the text to display in Excel's status bar when the mouse pointer is over that menu item. Use StatusBar to provide hints for users about what a command does.

You'll learn about specific details of using the menu-related objects, properties, and methods in the code examples later in this lesson.

Excel's Built-In Menus

Excel has several different built-in menu bars. Excel displays different menu bars, depending on the type of the active sheet. For example, you already know that when a worksheet is active, Excel displays a different menu than the one that Excel displays when a module sheet is active. Each of these different menu configurations is actually a separate MenuBar object, with its attached collections of menus and menu items.

You can refer to Excel's built-in menus either by their full name, or by using one of Excel's predefined constants. Table 16.3 lists the four built-in Excel menu bars that you see most often, showing their full name and the corresponding predefined constant value. Accessing specific menu bars in the MenuBars collection is explained later in this lesson.

Table 16.3. The four most common Excel menu bars and their constants.

Menu Bar Name	Constant	Displayed When
Worksheet	xlWorksheet	Active window is a worksheet.
Chart	xlChart	Active window is a chart sheet.
No Documents Open	xlNoDocuments	No documents are open.
Visual Basic Module	xlModule	Active window is a module sheet.

You can write VBA code to customize any of Excel's built-in menus, using any of the techniques described in the remaining parts of this lesson.

Custom Menu Bars

With a custom menu bar, you can give your VBA programs the same kind of professional menu interface that Excel itself uses. VBA's menu objects allow you to create your own, completely customized menu system. Creating a custom menu system involves three basic steps:

1. Create a menu bar object.
2. Add menus to the menu bar.
3. Add menu items to the menus.

The next few sections of this lesson show you how to write the VBA code needed to create new menu bars, their menus, and their menu commands.

Using the Interactive Menu Editor

Excel's Menu Editor is a powerful interactive menu editing tool. If all you want to do is permanently add a customized menu choice to a built-in menu bar (or a menu on a built-in menu bar), then you might be better off using the Menu Editor.

Note: You can't use the Menu Editor to create new menu bars. You can only edit, add to, or delete the menu choices on Excel's built-in menu bars.

To use the Menu Editor, click the Menu Editor command button on the Visual Basic toolbar, or use the **T**ools | Menu E**d**itor command. Excel will display the Menu Editor dialog box shown in Figure 16.2. When you use the Menu Editor, the custom menus that you create are permanently attached to the workbook that is active at the time you invoke the Menu Editor. For example, the menu being edited in Figure 16.2 will be attached to the DAY16.XLS workbook.

Figure 16.2.

Use the Menu Editor dialog box to interactively create your custom menus.

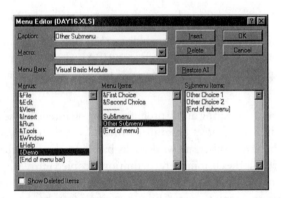

Using the menu editor is fairly straightforward. The following list summarizes the Menu Editor's dialog box options:

☐ *Menus.* Select the menu that you want to customize in this list box, or the menu you want to insert a new menu in front of. Clicking a selection in this list deselects any items in the Menu Items and Submenu Items lists.

☐ *Menu Items.* Select the menu item or submenu that you want to customize in this list box, or the menu item you want to insert a new item in front of. Clicking a selection in this list deselects any item in the Submenu Items list.

☐ *Submenu Items.* Select the submenu item you want to customize in this list box, or the submenu item you want to insert a new item in front of.

☐ *Caption.* Enter or edit the text for the selected menu choice in this text box.

☐ *Macro.* Use this drop-down list to select the VBA procedure that you want executed as a result of clicking this menu choice.

☐ *Menu Bars.* Use this drop-down list to select the menu bar whose menus you want to edit or customize.

☐ *Insert.* Click this command button to insert a new menu choice. The new menu or menu item is inserted in front of the currently selected item.

☐ *Delete.* Click this command button to delete the selected menu or menu item. It is possible, but not recommended, to delete menu choices from Excel's built-in menus.

☐ *Restore All.* Restores the selected Excel built-in menu bar to its original, default state. Use this command button to revert to a built-in menu's original state.

☐ *OK.* Confirms your changes to the menus, and closes the Menu Editor dialog box. As soon as the Menu Editor dialog closes, Excel updates its menu bar display to reflect any changes you've made.

☐ *Cancel.* Cancels your changes and closes the Menu Editor dialog box.

Unfortunately, it's not possible to go into all of the details on how to use the Menu Editor dialog box. Instead, this book focuses on VBA code for manipulating menus. The Menu Editor is such a useful tool, however, it deserves to be mentioned in any discussion about customizing Excel's menus.

If you're creating utility programs that you intend to use yourself, you may want to use the Menu Editor to create a customized menu, and then convert the workbook to a template. Then, whenever you create workbooks based on that template, your custom menu will be present. Because the custom menu definition is copied into each workbook, however, you're likely to run into the same problems as if you stored all your program code in the template—changing the custom menu means editing every single workbook that contains that menu. Instead, if you use code in a library workbook, or some other workbook, that creates menus under program control, all you have to do is update the procedure(s) that create the custom menu to update the custom menu for all workbooks that use your program. If you intend to distribute your programs for other people to use, you should probably create custom menus under control of your VBA code.

Managing Custom and Built-In Menu Bars

If you're creating an entire add-in application, you'll need to know how to create your own custom menu bar(s), and how to display or remove them. This section shows you how to use VBA's objects and methods to create, display, or remove a custom menu bar, and how to restore

a built-in menu bar to its default condition. A code example tying all of these elements together appears at the end of this section.

Adding a New Menu Bar

The first step in creating a customized menu system is to add a new menu bar object to the collection of menu bars. To do this, use the Add method of the MenuBars collection.

16

The general syntax for creating a new menu bar is:

```
MenuBars.Add menuName
```

menuName represents any valid string expression, and specifies the name you want to assign to the new menu bar. You'll use this name to access the new menu bar. If the menu bar specified by *menuName* already exists, a runtime error occurs. The Add method creates an empty menu bar and adds it to the MenuBars collection, but does not display the new menu bar. The following statement shows an example of the Add method:

```
MenuBars.Add "AccountingAppMenu"
```

Displaying a Menu Bar

After you've created a menu bar, you can display it on-screen. A newly-created menu bar, of course, is completely blank, and has no menus on it, so it will appear completely blank when displayed. Usually, you'll add menu items and submenus (as described later) to a menu bar before displaying it.

> **Note:** When you display one of your custom menu bars, it becomes the only menu system available to an interactive user—only the menus on your menu bar will be available. Displaying a blank menu bar, therefore, will leave you unable to carry out any actions!

To display a menu bar on-screen, you make it the active menu bar by using the Activate method of the MenuBars collection.

The general syntax for activating and displaying a menu bar is:

```
MenuBars(menuName).Activate
```

menuName represents any string expression that evaluates to a valid menu bar name—either for an Excel built-in menu, or your own custom menu bar. (For a custom menu bar, use the same name you specified when you created the menu bar with the Add method.) You can also use one of Excel's predefined constants to specify a built-in menu bar, as shown in the second example below.

When VBA executes the `Activate` method, it makes the specified menu bar the active menu bar—the menu bar is displayed across the top of the screen, and only the choices on that menu bar are available to the user. The following two code fragments show examples of the `Activate` method:

```
' Example 1
MenuBars.Add "MyCustomMenu"
MenuBars("MyCustomMenu").Activate

' Example 2
' display the built-in worksheet menu
MenuBars(xlWorksheet).Activate
```

Tip: You can use the `Activate` method to display any built-in Excel menu bar, as well as your own custom menus.

Deleting a Menu Bar

A menu bar, and its accompanying menus and menu items, does take up a certain amount of memory. In order to recover the memory resources used by your custom menu bar, you should delete any menu bars that your program no longer needs.

Note: A custom menu bar isn't like a VBA variable—it doesn't go away when your VBA procedure stops running. When you create a new menu bar, it remains in the `MenuBars` collection (which is part of the Excel `Application` object) for the remainder of the current work session, unless you delete it.

To delete a menu bar, use the menu bar's `Delete` method.

The general syntax for deleting a menu bar is:

```
MenuBars(menuName).Delete
```

menuName represents any string expression that evaluates to a valid custom menu bar name. When VBA executes the `Delete` method, the menu bar is removed from the `MenuBars` collection, and any memory used by that menu bar is returned to the general pool of available memory. The following sample procedure shows an example of using the `Delete` method:

```
Sub DeleteCustMenu()
  ' switch to the built-in worksheet menu
  MenuBars(xlWorksheet).Activate
```

```
    ' now delete the custom menu
    MenuBars("CustomMenu").Delete
End Sub
```

> **Note:** You cannot delete any of Excel's built-in menu bars.

16

Resetting a Built-In Menu Bar

If you have edited or modified a built-in menu bar, you may want to remove your custom commands or menus from the menu bar at some point. Instead of writing all the VBA statements to undo any changes you may have made, you can use the `Reset` method of the `MenuBar` object to return the built-in menu bar to its original, default state.

Syntax

The general syntax for restoring a built-in menu bar is:

```
MenuBars(menuName).Reset
```

menuName represents any string expression that evaluates to a valid Excel built-in menu bar name—you can also use the Excel predefined constants listed in Table 16.3 for the *menuName* argument. When VBA executes the `Reset` method, it restores the specified built-in menu to its default state—*all* custom menus and menu items are removed, no matter when or how they were created. The following sample procedure shows an example of the `Reset` method:

```
Sub ResetWorkSheetMenuBar()
    ' reset the built-in worksheet menu
    MenuBars(xlWorksheet).Reset
    ' reactivate the worksheet menu
    MenuBars(xlWorksheet).Activate
End Sub
```

> **Note:** If you use the `Reset` method on a menu bar that has been customized with the Menu Editor, or by some other VBA program, you may remove commands that you don't intend to. Exercise caution when using the `Reset` method.

A Blank Menu Bar Example

Listing 16.1 shows an example of creating, displaying, and removing a custom menu bar. You haven't yet learned to add menus or menu items to a menu bar, so this example uses a blank menu bar. The **DemoMenuBar** procedure in Listing 16.1 creates a menu bar, activates it, and then removes it after a brief interval. **DemoMenuBar** starts by displaying a message box telling you that it is going to create a blank new menu bar, and then displays the empty custom menu bar for about two seconds before removing it.

Type

Listing 16.1. The **DemoMenuBar** procedure displays and then removes a blank new custom menu bar.

```
 1:   Option Explicit
 2:
 3:   Private Const DELAY1 As Integer = 2
 4:
 5:   Sub DemoMenuBar()
 6:     Dim oldMenu As MenuBar
 7:
 8:     MsgBox prompt:="Ready to create a blank new menu bar", _
 9:           Buttons:=vbInformation, Title:="Demo Menu Bar"
10:
11:     'preserve a reference to currently active menu
12:     Set oldMenu = Application.ActiveMenuBar
13:
14:     MenuBars.Add "CustMenu1"              'add new menu bar
15:     MenuBars("CustMenu1").Activate        'activate it
16:     Wait DELAY1                           'wait a while
17:     oldMenu.Activate                'reactivate the old menu
18:     MenuBars("CustMenu1").Delete    'delete the custom menu
19:     MsgBox prompt:="Restored '" & oldMenu.Caption & _
20:                   "' menu bar", _
21:           Buttons:=vbInformation, Title:="Demo Menu Bar"
22:   End Sub
23:
24:   Private Sub Wait(Delay As Single)
25:     Dim TheTime As Single
26:
27:     TheTime = Timer
28:     Do
29:     Loop Until (Timer - TheTime) >= Delay
30:   End Sub
```

The **DemoMenuBar** procedure's operation is relatively simple. The **DemoMenuBar** procedure occupies lines 5 through 22 of Listing 16.1. Line 6 declares a MenuBar object variable, **oldMenu**, in order to store a reference to the menu bar that is active at the time you execute this procedure.

Line 12 uses the ActiveMenuBar property of the Application object to set the **oldMenu** variable to refer to whatever menu bar is currently active. (The ActiveMenuBar property returns an object reference to the active menu bar.)

Line 14 uses the Add method of the MenuBars collection to add a new menu bar name CustMenu1 to the collection of menu bars. Next, line 15 uses the Activate method to display the new menu

bar on-screen. Line 16 calls the **Wait** procedure delay for the number of seconds specified by the constant **DELAY1**.

After the delay, line 17 uses the Activate method, this time to restore the original menu bar. Because the object variable **oldMenu** contains a reference to the original menu bar object, the statement in line 17 can access the Activate method as shown.

Finally, line 18 uses the Delete method to remove the custom menu bar. Notice that the Delete method belongs to the menu bar object, *not* the menu bar collection.

Lines 19 through 21 simply display a message dialog box announcing the completion of the **DemoMenuBar** procedure. Notice that the old menu bar's Caption property is used to include the name of the restored menu bar in the message dialog box's text.

Lines 24 through 30 contain the **Wait** procedure, which simply loops until the number of seconds elapsed is equal to or greater than the specified value.

DO	DON'T

DO delete menu bars as soon as you're done with them.

DO add menus and menu items to a custom menu bar before making it active. (Adding menus and menu items is described in the next section.)

DON'T forget to use the ActiveMenuBar property to find out which menu bar is currently active.

Managing Menus with VBA

In order to make a custom menu bar useful, you'll have to create and manage the menus that it contains. This section shows you how to use VBA's methods and objects to create, display, or remove menus on a menu bar—whether a custom menu bar, or one of Excel's built-in menu bars.

Adding Menus

When you create a new menu bar, it has no menus—as you saw in the sample procedure in Listing 16.1. You'll need to add menus to the menu bar as the second step in creating your custom menu system.

> **Note:** In order to conform to the user-interface design standards for Windows programs, you need to incorporate certain standard menus in every custom menu you create. You should always include a **File** menu, for example, and usually an **Edit** menu, as well.

Keep in mind that adding menus does not automatically add any commands—you'll still need to add menu items to your menus, as described in the next section of this lesson.

Syntax

To add a new menu to a menu bar, use the Add method with this general syntax:

```
MenuBars(menuName).Menus.Add(caption[, before, restore])
```

menuName represents any string expression that evaluates to a valid menu bar name. *caption* is a required argument, and may be any string expression; it specifies the name of the new menu, and is also the text displayed for that menu on the menu bar.

> **Note:** To create a hot key for your custom menus, include the ampersand (&) character in front of the letter you want to define as the hot key. For example, to make the letter F the hot key in the menu name `File`, you would use the following string as the *caption* argument in the Add method:
>
> `&File`
>
> Now, the user can press Alt+F to open the file menu, and the letter F is underlined in the menu name on-screen.

The *before* and *restore* arguments are both optional. The *before* argument can be any string expression that evaluates to a valid menu caption; VBA inserts your new menu to the left of the menu specified by the *before* argument. If you omit the *before* argument, and you're adding a menu to a built-in menu bar, VBA adds the new menu choice to the left of the **Help** menu. If you omit the *before* argument when you add a menu to a custom menu bar, VBA adds the new menu choice at the end of the menus on the menu bar.

The optional *restore* argument can be any Boolean expression. When `True`, the *restore* argument allows you to restore a previously deleted built-in menu. (Although you cannot delete built-in menu bars, you can delete built-in menus from a built-in menu bar.) When *restore* is omitted, VBA assumes a value of `False`. The following two code fragments show examples of the Add method used to add a menu to a menu bar. In the second example, notice that you don't have to include the ampersand (&) character when deleting the Windows menu; you must include the ampersand to set the shortcut key letter when restoring the Windows menu, however.

```
' example 1
MenuBars.Add "MyCustomMenu"
With MenuBars("MyCustomMenu")
    .Menus.Add caption := "&Calculate", before := "Windows"
End With
' example 2
' delete the Windows menu
MenuBars(xlWorksheet).Menus("Windows").Delete
' other statements here
' now restore the Windows menu
With MenuBars(xlWorksheet)
    Menus.Add caption := "&Windows", restore := True
End With
```

16

Deleting Menus

You may want to remove menus from a menu bar for a variety of reasons. For example, you might want to remove the **Fo**rmat menu to prevent users from reformatting data on the worksheet, or you may want to remove a menu from one of your custom menu bars. Whatever the reason, you can delete menus from both custom and built-in menu bars.

Syntax

To delete a menu, use the `Menu` object's `Delete` method, with the following syntax:

```
MenuBars(menuName).Menus(caption).Delete
```

menuName is any string expression that evaluates to a valid menu bar name, and *caption* is any string expression that evaluates to a valid menu caption. When VBA executes the `Delete` method, the specified menu is deleted from the menu bar. The following code fragment shows an example of the `Delete` method:

```
MenuBars.Add "MyCustomMenu"
MenuBars("MyCustomMenu").Menus.Add _
                        caption := "&Calculate", _
                        before := "Windows"
MenuBars("MyCustomMenu").Menus("Calculate").Delete
```

A Menu Bar with Non-Working Menus

You already know how to create a menu bar. The sample program in Listing 16.2 shows you how to add menus to a menu bar. The next section covers adding menu items to a menu, so the menus produced in this example don't contain any commands—the **DemoMenu** procedure in Listing 16.2 merely demonstrates how to add menus to a menu bar.

DemoMenu is similar to the **DemoMenuBar** procedure from Listing 16.1, but displays a menu bar with **F**ile, **E**dit, **W**indow, and **H**elp menus on it, as shown in Figure 16.3. As before, **DemoMenu** merely displays the menu bar and then removes it—because there are no menu items on any of the menus, the menu bar and menus are not yet useful.

Figure 16.3.

The menu bar created by the **DemoMenu** *procedure in Listing 16.2.*

Listing 16.2. The DemoMenu procedure displays and then removes a custom menu bar with several menus.

```
 1:  Option Explicit
 2:
 3:  Private Const DELAY1! = 2
 4:
 5:  Sub DemoMenu()
 6:     Dim oldMenu As MenuBar
 7:     Dim aMenu As Menu
 8:
 9:     MsgBox prompt:="Ready to create a new menu bar", _
10:            Buttons:=vbInformation, Title:="Demo Menus"
11:
12:     'preserve a reference to currently active menu
13:     Set oldMenu = Application.ActiveMenuBar
14:
15:     MenuBars.Add "CustMenu"              'add new menu bar
16:
17:     With MenuBars("CustMenu").Menus     'add menus to menu bar
18:        .Add Caption:="&File"
19:        .Add Caption:="&Edit"
20:        .Add Caption:="&Window"
21:        .Add Caption:="&Help"
22:     End With
23:
24:     MenuBars("CustMenu").Activate  'activate the menu
25:
26:     Wait DELAY1            'wait a while
27:     oldMenu.Activate       'restore old menu
28:
29:     'delete all the menus
30:     For Each aMenu In MenuBars("CustMenu").Menus
31:        aMenu.Delete
32:     Next aMenu
33:
34:     MenuBars("CustMenu").Delete     'delete custom menu bar
35:
36:     MsgBox prompt:="Restored '" & oldMenu.Caption & _
37:                    "' menu bar", _
38:            Buttons:=vbInformation, Title:="Demo Menus"
39:  End Sub
40:
41:  Private Sub Wait(Delay As Single)
42:     Dim TheTime As Single
```

```
43:
44:     TheTime = Timer
45:     Do
46:     Loop Until (Timer - TheTime) >= Delay
47: End Sub
```

The **DemoMenu** procedure, which occupies lines 3 through 39 of Listing 16.2 works very much like the **DemoMenuBar** procedure from Listing 16.1; this analysis focuses on the differences between the two listings.

After preserving the current menu bar, **DemoMenu** creates a new menu bar, as before. This time, however, lines 17 through 22 add menus to the CustMenu menu bar before it is displayed. Line 17 starts a With statement that references the custom menu's Menus collection. Each of lines 18 through 21 uses the Menus collection's Add method to add a menu to the custom menu bar. Notice the use of the ampersand (&) character to specify a hot-key letter for each menu choice (compare the Caption arguments in lines 18 through 21 with the menu names shown in Figure 16.3).

Lines 24 through 27 activate the custom menu, wait a while, and then restore the menu bar that was active at the time this procedure started execution.

Lines 30 through 32 contain a For Each loop. This loop executes once for every menu in the custom menu's Menus collection. The statement in line 31 therefore calls the Delete method of each menu, in turn, until all of the menus have been deleted. Finally, line 34 uses the Delete method to delete the custom menu bar.

The **Wait** procedure in lines 41 through 47 is the same as shown previously.

Managing Menu Items

So far, you've learned how to create new menu bars and add menus to them. To create a completely functioning menu system, however, you still need to add commands and submenus to your menus. As explained at the beginning of this lesson, a menu command in VBA is a *menu item*, and submenus are just another Menu object added to a menu's collection of menu items.

To create, manipulate, and manage the menu item commands, you'll need to perform some or all of the following operations:

- ☐ Add a menu item.
- ☐ Specify or change an action to be carried out when the menu item is clicked.
- ☐ Set the status bar hint text for a menu item.
- ☐ Enable and disable a menu item.
- ☐ Delete a menu item.

☐ Check a menu item. (*Checking* a menu item means placing a check mark to the left of the menu item.)

☐ Rename a menu item.

☐ Add a submenu to a menu.

The next sections show you how to use the VBA menu objects, methods, and properties to carry out each of these menu item management tasks.

Adding Menu Items

To make your custom menu system functional, you must add menu items to them, and specify a VBA procedure to be executed when the menu item command is clicked. To add a menu item, you use the Add method of the MenuItems collection. (Every menu on a menu bar contains a MenuItems collection.) When you add a menu item to a menu, you must specify the name of the menu item (as it will appear on the menu on-screen). You can optionally specify the menu item's location on the menu, and the name of the event procedure to be executed by the new menu command.

Note: You make menu items carry out a specific action in much the same way you make a custom dialog box button carry out a specific action—by attaching a VBA procedure to the menu item as an event procedure. Whenever the menu item is clicked, VBA executes the attached procedure.

Syntax

The general syntax for adding a menu item is:

```
object.MenuItems.Add(caption[, OnAction, before, restore])
```

In this syntax sample, `object` represents any valid object reference to a Menu object. The required `caption` argument can be any string expression. The `caption` argument specifies both the name of the menu item and the name that will appear in the on-screen menu, as well. To specify a hot-key for the menu choice, use the ampersand (&) character as you would for a menu bar menu.

The optional `OnAction` argument may be any string expression that evaluates to a valid reference to a VBA procedure, including the workbook name, the module name, and the actual procedure name. Use this syntax when specifying the value for the `OnAction` argument:

```
bookName!moduleName.procName
```

where `bookName` is any valid workbook name (optionally including the drive letter and directory path), `moduleName` is the name of the module sheet in the workbook, and `procName` is the name of the specific procedure you want the menu item command to execute. (The code example at the end of this section contains an example of setting the OnAction property while creating a new menu item.)

The optional *before* argument may be any string expression that evaluates to a valid name of a menu item already in the MenuItems collection you are adding to. VBA inserts the new menu item above the existing menu item specified by the *before* argument. If you omit the *before* argument, VBA inserts the new menu item at the end of the menu.

The optional *restore* argument may be any Boolean expression. The *restore* argument causes VBA to restore a previously deleted built-in menu item on the menu specified by the *caption* argument. The following code fragment demonstrates how to add a menu item:

```
MenuBars.Add "MyCustomMenu"
MenuBars("MyCustomMenu").Menus.Add caption := "&Calculate", _
                                   before := "Windows"
With MenuBars("MyCustomMenu").Menus("Calculate")
  .MenuItems.Add caption:="&Initialize", _
                 onAction:="DAY16.XLS!Module1.InitCalc"
End With
```

The preceding example adds a menu item command (**Initialize**) to the **Calculate** custom menu. The example specifies the procedure Module1.InitCalc in the DAY16.XLS workbook as the event procedure for this menu item command—whenever the user clicks the **Initialize** command on the **Calculate** menu, the InitCalc procedure will be executed.

Specifying a Menu Item's Event Procedure

You can also specify the event procedure for a menu item by altering the menu item's OnAction property, as well as when you create the menu item. You might want to change the specific procedure that a given menu command carries out because of changing conditions in your program, or you just might prefer to set the event procedure after creating your menu items. Frequently, you'll need to change a menu item's event procedure in conjunction with changing the menu item's name (described later in this section).

Syntax

To assign an event procedure to a menu item, use this general syntax:

```
object.MenuItems(caption).OnAction = procName
```

object represents any valid object reference to a Menu object. The required *caption* argument can be any string expression that evaluates to a valid name of a menu item in the MenuItems collection. *procName* is any valid string expression, and specifies the event procedure to be executed when the specified menu item is clicked. The *procName* string argument must use this syntax:

```
bookName!moduleName.procName
```

bookName is any valid workbook name (optionally including the drive letter and directory path), *moduleName* is the name of a module sheet in the workbook, and *procName* is the name of the specific procedure you want the menu item command to execute.

Displaying Hints for Menu Item Commands in the Status Bar

You've probably noticed that Excel, and most Windows programs, display hints about menu actions in the application's status bar. When you place the mouse pointer over a particular menu item, a brief message about the actions that command performs appears in the status bar. For example, if you place the mouse pointer over Excel's **File** | **Save As** menu item, the text `Saves document with new name, file format, or password` appears in Excel's status bar.

You can make your custom menu items display similar hints in the application's status bar by setting the `StatusBar` property of the menu item. Adding these status bar hints to your custom menu items not only gives your VBA program a professional look and feel, but makes it easier for people to use.

To add a status bar message to your custom menu items, use this general syntax:

```
object.MenuItems(caption).StatusBar = message
```

`object` represents any valid object reference to a `Menu` object. The required `caption` argument can be any string expression that evaluates to a valid name of a menu item in the `MenuItems` collection. `message` is any string expression, and represents the text you want displayed in the status bar when the mouse pointer is over the referenced menu item. The following code fragment shows an example of setting the `StatusBar` property:

```
With MenuBars("MyCustomMenu").Menus("Calculate")
  .MenuItems.Add caption:="&Initialize", _
             onAction:="DAY16.XLS!Module1.InitCalc"
  .MenuItems("Initialize").StatusBar = "Initializes the calculator"
End With
```

The preceding example adds the **I**nitialize menu item to the Calculate menu, and then sets the `StatusBar` property so that the message `Initializes the calculator` appears in the application's status bar whenever the mouse pointer is over the **I**nitialize menu item.

Deleting Menu Items

You may want to delete a menu item from a menu. For example, you may want to make one of Excel's built-in menu item commands unavailable, or you may want to make one of your own custom commands unavailable. When a menu item is no longer needed or valid, you can use the `Delete` method to remove it from the menu.

The general syntax for deleting a menu item is:

```
object.MenuItems(caption).Delete
```

In this syntax example, `object` represents any valid object reference to a `Menu` object—either a custom menu or one of the built-in menus. The required `caption` argument is any string expression that evaluates to a valid menu item name on the referenced `Menu` object. When VBA executes the `Delete` method, it removes the specified menu item from the referenced menu. The following code fragment, for example, deletes the custom menu item **I**nitialize from the **C**alculate menu, on the `MyCustomMenu` menu bar:

```
With MenuBars("MyCustomMenu").Menus("Calculate")
   .MenuItems("&Initialize").Delete
End With
```

Enabling or Disabling Menu Items

There are many times when you may want to make a particular menu item unavailable. For example, you might have written a program that adds a to-do list manager to Excel, and has a custom Print command to print the to-do list. If the to-do list is empty, you might want to disable the Print command because there is nothing to print. In this case, you could delete the Print menu, but this might confuse users of your program—they may not understand why various menu choices appear and disappear.

A better technique than deleting a menu item is to disable it. If you disable the menu item for your custom Print command, then the menu item is still displayed as part of the menu, but is grayed to show that the choice is currently unavailable. Almost every Windows user is familiar with the appearance of a disabled menu choice, and will understand that the choice is temporarily unavailable.

To enable or disable menu items, simply change the menu item's `Enabled` property. The `Enabled` property stores a Boolean value; if `Enabled` is `True`, then the menu item is enabled. If `Enabled` is `False`, then the menu item is disabled. You can also use the `Enabled` property to determine whether a particular menu item is currently enabled or disabled.

The following code fragment shows an example of using the `Enabled` property:

```
With MenuBars("MyCustomMenu").Menus("Calculate")
   MenuItems("&Intialize").Enabled = False
End With
```

Note: The `Enabled` property is `True`, by default, for any new menu items you create.

Checking Menu Items

Some types of menu item command just turn a particular program feature on or off—that is, they are *toggle* commands. For example, the **F**ormula Bar command on Excel's **V**iew menu turns the display of the formula bar on and off. When the formula bar is displayed, a checkmark appears to the left of the **Formula Bar** command, indicating that the feature is on. When the formula bar is not displayed, there is no checkmark next to the **Formula Bar** command.

At some point, you'll probably end up creating your own menu item toggle commands. To display or remove a checkmark next to a menu item, you use the `Checked` property. Each `MenuItem` object has a `Checked` property. This property stores a Boolean value; if it is `True`, then VBA displays a checkmark to the left of that menu item. By default, the `Checked` property is `False` when you create a new menu item. You can also use the `Checked` property to determine whether a menu item is currently checked. The following code fragment shows an example of using the `Checked` property (these statements cause VBA to display a checkmark next to the **I**nitialize menu item on the Calculate menu of the `MyCustomMenu` menu bar):

```
With MenuBars("MyCustomMenu").Menus("Calculate")
  .MenuItems("&Initialize").Checked = True
End With
```

Renaming Menu Items

Occasionally, you'll find cases where you need to change a menu item's name at some point after creating the menu item, while your VBA program is still running. The most common example is a menu that allows a choice of recently opened workbooks or recently viewed worksheets—such as Excel's **File** menu, which provides menu choices to quickly open any of the last five workbooks that you opened. To make this part of the menu work, the menu item's name must be periodically changed as additional files are opened.

Changing a menu item's caption is simple—just assign a new value to the menu item's `Caption` property. The following code fragment demonstrates the use of the `Caption` property to rename a menu item (these statements change the menu item's name from **I**nitialize to **I**nit):

```
With MenuBars("MyCustomMenu").Menus("Calculate")
  .MenuItems("&Initialize").Caption = "&Init"
End With
```

Adding Submenus

So far, you've learned how to create and manipulate menu items. Most menu systems include one or more submenus, though. Instead of giving your users long lists of commands, it makes more sense to group related commands together and then put them on a submenu.

To add a submenu to a menu, you must use the special `AddMenu` method of the `MenuItems` collection. The `AddMenu` method adds a `Menu` object to the `MenuItems` collection, instead of a `MenuItem` object. The `Menu` object added by the `AddMenu` method has all of the same methods and properties as any other `Menu` object. (Managing `Menu` objects was described earlier in this lesson.)

Sams Learning Center · SAMS PUBLISHING

Syntax

The general syntax for adding a submenu to a command is:

```
object.MenuItems.AddMenu(caption[, before, restore])
```

In this syntax example, *object* represents any valid object reference to a Menu object—either a custom menu or one of the built-in menus. The required *caption* argument can be any string expression. The *caption* argument specifies the name of the new menu. To specify a hot-key for the menu choice, use the ampersand (&) character before the letter that you want to use as the hot-key.

The optional *before* argument may be any string expression that evaluates to a valid name of a menu item already in the MenuItems collection you are adding to. VBA inserts the new submenu above the existing menu item specified by the *before* argument. If you omit the *before* argument, VBA inserts the new submenu at the end of the menu.

The optional *restore* argument may be any Boolean expression. The *restore* argument causes VBA to restore a previously deleted built-in menu item on the menu specified by the *caption* argument. The following code fragment shows an example of adding a submenu:

```
MenuBars.Add "MyCustomMenu"
MenuBars("MyCustomMenu").Menus.Add caption := "&Calculate", _
                                   before := "Windows"
With MenuBars("MyCustomMenu").Menus("Calculate").MenuItems
   .Add caption:="&Initialize", _
        onAction:="DAY16.XLS!Module1.InitCalc"
   .AddMenu caption:="&Spreadsheet"
End With
```

The above example adds the submenu **S**preadsheet to the menu **C**alculate. Thus, the MenuItems collection for the **C**alculate menu contains the menu item named **I**nitialize, and a menu object named **S**preadsheet.

Putting It Together: A Functioning Menu Example

You've learned a lot about menu bars, menus, and menu items in the last few sections of this lesson. Now you're ready to put all this new knowledge to work, and create a working menu system. The menu system in Listing 16.3 doesn't do much in the way of real work, but it does demonstrate using all of the important VBA menu objects.

The menu system created by Listing 16.3 also illustrates an important requirement for any menu system: making sure there is some kind of exit command available. If you don't include a way to exit from the menu system you activate, you won't ever be able to get Excel's built-in menus back in the current work session—you'll have to exit from Excel and restart it to get the standard menus back.

The custom menu bar created by Listing 16.3 has only two choices on it: **F**ile and **D**emo. The **F**ile menu has only one menu item—the E**x**it command. Selecting **F**ile | E**x**it restores whatever menu bar is appropriate to the currently active sheet, and then deletes the menu bar.

The **D**emo menu has two menu item commands, and one submenu on it. The submenu has three menu items on it; the first menu item demonstrates how to toggle a menu checkmark on and off, and also demonstrates changing a menu item's caption. All of the menu items on the **D**emo menu and its submenu call the same dummy command procedure—in a real menu system you'd have separate event procedures for each menu command. Figure 16.4 shows the custom menu bar created by Listing 16.3, with the **D**emo menu dropped down and the submenu expanded. As shown in Figure 16.4, the first submenu selection has the checkmark turned on.

Figure 16.4.

The menu bar created by the **DemoMenuSystem,** *showing a menu with two levels of submenus.*

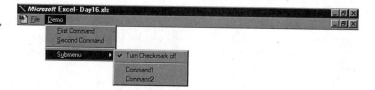

Listing 16.3. The `DemoMenuSystem` procedure produces a minimally working menu.

```
1:  Option Explicit
2:
3:  Sub DemoMenuSystem()
4:  'creates and installs a demonstration menu system.
5:
6:    Dim myMenuBar As MenuBar
7:
8:    Set myMenuBar = MenuBars.Add("Demo Menu")   'add menu bar
9:    With myMenuBar.Menus   'add menus to menu bar
10:     .Add Caption:="&File"
11:     .Add Caption:="&Demo"
12:   End With
13:
14:   With myMenuBar.Menus("File")  'populate the File menu
15:     .MenuItems.Add Caption:="E&xit", _
16:                 OnAction:="ExitCommand"
17:     .MenuItems("Exit").StatusBar = "Close this menu bar"
18:   End With
19:
20:   With myMenuBar.Menus("Demo").MenuItems  'fill Demo menu
21:     .Add Caption:="&First Command", _
22:         OnAction:="DummyCommand"
23:     .Add Caption:="&Second Command", _
24:         OnAction:="DummyCommand"
25:     .Add Caption:="-"    'adds a menu separator
26:     .AddMenu Caption:="S&ubmenu"
27:   End With
```

```
28:
29:     'populate the Demo ¦ Submenu menu.
30:     With myMenuBar.Menus("Demo").MenuItems("Submenu")
31:        .MenuItems.Add Caption:="Turn checkmark on", _
32:             OnAction:="CheckToggle"
33:        .MenuItems.Add Caption:="-"
34:        .MenuItems.Add Caption:="Command1", _
35:             OnAction:="DummyCommand"
36:        .MenuItems.Add Caption:="Command2", _
37:             OnAction:="DummyCommand"
38:     End With
39:
40:     myMenuBar.Activate   'activate the menu
41:   End Sub
42:
43:
44:   Sub CheckToggle()
45:   'toggles the checkmark, and changes caption
46:
47:     With MenuBars("Demo Menu").Menus("Demo")
48:       With .MenuItems("Submenu").MenuItems(1)
49:         .Checked = Not .Checked
50:         If .Checked Then
51:           .Caption = "Turn Checkmark off"
52:         Else
53:           .Caption = "Turn Checkmark on"
54:         End If
55:       End With
56:     End With
57:   End Sub
58:
59:
60:   Sub DummyCommand()
61:     MsgBox prompt:="Simulated menu command.", _
62:           Buttons:=vbInformation, _
63:           Title:="Menu System Demonstration"
64:   End Sub
65:
66:
67:   Sub ExitCommand()
68:   'closes and removes the custom menu bar
69:
70:     Dim mType As String
71:
72:     mType = UCase(TypeName(ActiveSheet))
73:     Select Case mType
74:       Case Is = "WORKSHEET"
75:         MenuBars(xlWorksheet).Activate
76:       Case Is = "MODULE"
77:         MenuBars(xlModule).Activate
78:       Case Is = "DIALOGSHEET"
79:         MenuBars(xlDialogSheet).Activate
80:     End Select
81:
82:     MenuBars("Demo Menu").Delete
83:   End Sub
```

The **DemoMenuSystem** procedure (lines 3 through 41 in Listing 16.3) starts out by adding a custom menu bar to the **MenuBars** collection with the statement in line 8. For convenience, the result of the **Add** method (an object reference to the newly created menu bar) is assigned to the **myMenuBar** object variable.

Lines 9 through 12 add the **File** and **Demo** menus to the custom menu bar. Line 15 adds the **Exit** menu item to the **File** menu and simultaneously sets the **OnAction** property of the new menu item. When the **File | Exit** menu command is chosen, VBA will execute the **ExitCommand** procedure (in lines 67 through 81 of Listing 16.3). Line 17 sets the **StatusBar** property of the **Exit** menu item so that the specified hint text will be shown in Excel's status bar when the mouse pointer is over that menu item. Notice that, although the **Exit** command was created with an ampersand (**&**) character in the caption, you don't have to include the ampersand in subsequent references to the **Exit** menu. (Contrast line 15 with line 17.)

Note: Enter all of the code in Listing 16.3 before running the **DemoMenuSystem** procedure. After running the **DemoMenuSystem** procedure, notice that you can still select worksheets, choose buttons from on-screen toolbars, enter data, or even edit your VBA modules while your custom menu bar is on-screen. You must choose the **File | Exit** command from the custom menu bar to restore access to Excel's built-in menu bars.

Lines 20 through 27 add menu items to the **Demo** menu, also setting the **OnAction** property for the menu item's event procedure at the same time. Lines 21 and 22 create the **First Command** menu item, while lines 23 and 24 create the **Second Command** menu item.

Line 25 deserves special attention—it creates a separator on the menu. Refer to Figure 16.4 and notice the line separating the first two menu items from the submenu item in the **Demo** menu. The statement in line 25 creates that separator.

Line 26 also deserves some special attention. This line uses the **AddMenu** method to add a **Menu** object to the menu items collection of the **Demo** menu. Line 26 creates the submenu that you can see at the bottom of the **Demo** menu in Figure 16.4.

Next, lines 30 through 38 create the menu items for the **Demo | Submenu** menu object. Like the other menu item creation lines, these lines add the new menu item and simultaneously specify the menu item's event procedure. Notice that the first menu item on the submenu has a special event procedure, different from the **DummyCommand** procedure specified for all of the other menu items. The **CheckToggle** procedure (lines 44 through 57 of Listing 16.3) adds or removes the checkmark next to the menu item, and changes the menu item's caption accordingly. When first created, the checkmark is not on, and the menu item's caption is Turn checkmark on.

Lines 44 through 57 contain the **CheckToggle** procedure. This procedure begins by simply inverting the state of the Checked property, and then evaluating whether Checked is True or not. If the Checked property is True (a checkmark is displayed to the left of the menu item), then line 51 changes the menu item's caption to Turn Checkmark off, as shown in Figure 16.4. Otherwise, the menu item's caption is set to read Turn Checkmark on. The **CheckToggle** procedure is executed whenever the **D**emo I **Su**bmenu I Turn Checkmark off (or **D**emo I **Su**bmenu I Turn Checkmark on) command is selected.

Lines 60 through 64 contain the **DummyCommand** procedure, which exists solely to simulate the event procedures that might be called by various menu commands. The **DummyCommand** procedure is executed whenever the **D**emo I **F**irst Command, **D**emo I **S**econd Command, **D**emo I **Su**bmenu I Command**1**, or **D**emo I **Su**bmenu I Command**2** menu items are selected.

Finally, lines 67 through 81 contain the **ExitCommand** procedure. This procedure is executed whenever the **F**ile I **E**xit command is selected. Line 72 uses the Application object's ActiveSheet method to return an object reference to the currently active sheet—the same statement calls the TypeName function to return a string containing the name of the sheet object's type, uses the UCase function to convert the type name string to all uppercase, and assigns the result to the **mType** variable.

Lines 73 through 80 contain a Select Case statement that activates the built-in menu bar that matches the currently active sheet type—you'll get a runtime error if you attempt to activate, for example, the Visual Basic Module menu bar while a worksheet is active. Finally, line 82 deletes the custom menu bar.

DO	DON'T
DO remember that you can create menu separators by adding a menu item with a caption consisting of only a hyphen (-) character.	
DO remember to always provide a File menu with an Exit or Close command on it that will shut down your program and remove your custom menu bar.	
DO use code similar to that in Listing 16.3 to determine which is the correct built-in menu bar to activate when you remove your custom menu bar.	

Understanding Toolbars

Toolbars are becoming an increasingly popular part of the Windows interface. Excel itself provides a variety of toolbars for you to use. VBA enables you to work with the built-in toolbars as well as to create and manage custom toolbars. You can give your own VBA programs a

professional touch by utilizing either Excel's built-in toolbars or by creating your own custom toolbars. The next few sections of this lesson discuss working with both built-in and custom toolbars. Use your VBA code to manipulate Excel's built-in toolbars or to create your own custom toolbars for the same reasons you create your custom menus with VBA code.

> **Note:** You can also create custom toolbars interactively in Excel. Unfortunately, creating custom toolbars interactively is too complex a topic for this book. Refer to your online help system for more information on interactively creating custom toolbars in Excel.

Toolbar Objects, Properties, and Methods

VBA allows you to manipulate both built-in and custom menu bars through four different objects, and a variety of object properties. Using Toolbar objects is similar to using the menu objects you've just learned about. Table 16.4 lists VBA's toolbar objects and their purpose.

Table 16.4. VBA toolbar objects.

Toolbar Object	Purpose
Toolbar	A single toolbar, such as the Forms toolbar. Toolbars may be built-in or custom.
ToolbarButton	A single toolbar button, such as the Edit Code button on the Forms toolbar.
Toolbars	The collection of all toolbars, both custom and built-in, currently available to the application.
ToolbarButtons	The collection of all toolbar buttons on a particular toolbar.

The toolbar objects listed in Table 16.4 have a variety of properties and methods that you'll need to use in order to create or manipulate toolbars with your VBA code. Table 16.5 lists the most frequently used properties and methods of the VBA toolbar objects listed in Table 16.4.

Table 16.5. VBA toolbar object properties and methods.

Property/Method	Belongs To	Purpose
Add	Toolbars, ToolbarButtons	Method. Adds an object to the specified collection.
BuiltIn	Toolbar, ToolbarButton	Property. True if the toolbar or toolbar button is one of Excel's built-in toolbars or toolbar buttons.
Delete	Toolbar, ToolbarButton	Method. Deletes the object from its collection.
Enabled	ToolbarButton	Property. If False, the toolbar button is shown grayed to indicate it is temporarily unavailable.
Name	Toolbar, ToolbarButton	Property. A string containing the name of the toolbar or button. Also provides the ToolTip text when the mouse pointer is over the toolbar button.
OnAction	ToolbarButton	Property. A string specifying the VBA procedure to be executed when the button is clicked.
Position	Toolbar	Property. The position of the toolbar: docked, or one of several floating toolbar formats.
Pushed	ToolbarButton	Property. If True, indicates that the button should be displayed as pushed-down. You can change this property only for custom toolbar buttons.
Reset	Toolbar, ToolbarButtons	Method. Restores a built-in toolbar to its default condition.
Reset	Toolbar, ToolbarButtons	Method. Restores a built-in toolbar to its default condition.
StatusBar	ToolbarButton	Property. A string that is displayed in Excel's status bar when the mouse pointer is over the toolbar button.
Visible	Toolbar	Property. Whether or not the toolbar is visible on-screen.

16

You'll learn about specific details of using the toolbar-related objects, properties, and methods in the code examples later in this lesson.

Accessing Excel's Built-In Toolbars

Excel has several built-in toolbars. You access these (and any) toolbar through the `ToolBars` collection. As with almost every other object accessor, you can reference toolbars in the `ToolBars` collection either by name or by numeric index. Table 16.6 shows the names and indexes of Excel's built-in toolbars. The names shown in Table 16.6 are the same toolbar names that appear in the Toolbars dialog box (displayed by choosing the **V**iew | **T**oolbars command).

Table 16.6. The names and indexes of Excel's built-in toolbars.

Toolbar Name	Index
Standard	1
Formatting	2
Query and Pivot	3
Chart	4
Drawing	5
TipWizard	6
Forms	7
Stop Recording	8
Visual Basic	9
Auditing	10
Workgroup	11
Microsoft	12
Full Screen	13

In general, you should refer to Excel's built-in toolbars by name, rather than by index number. There are no predefined constants for accessing toolbars, so you'll have to keep track of the appropriate index numbers yourself—it's better to just use the toolbar name. You'll learn more about accessing specific toolbars in the remaining sections of this lesson.

Creating and Managing Toolbars

You can use VBA's toolbar objects and methods to create your own custom toolbars. Your custom toolbars can contain built-in toolbar buttons from Excel, or buttons that you have

assigned an event procedure to. For example, you might want a custom toolbar for an accounting worksheet that contains Excel's built-in toolbar button to print the worksheet, and a customized toolbar button that creates a specific chart of your accounting data.

To create a custom toolbar, you need to perform two basic steps:

1. Create a new custom toolbar.
2. Add toolbar buttons to the toolbar.

VBA also allows you to manage both built-in and custom toolbars by displaying them, deleting specific toolbar buttons or entire toolbars, and restoring built-in toolbars to their default states. The next few sections of this lesson introduce the basic techniques for creating and managing toolbars.

Creating a Custom Toolbar

You use custom toolbars to support categories of tasks by providing toolbar button shortcuts to specific commands. In general, you should create your own custom toolbars, instead of modifying Excel's built-in toolbars. Although you can always restore a built-in toolbar to its default condition, it may have already been customized, and the toolbar defaults won't really restore the toolbar to the condition that a particular user is used to seeing.

You create a custom toolbar by using the `Add` method of the `Toolbars` collection with the following general syntax:

```
Toolbars.Add toolbarName
```

toolbarName represents any string expression. *toolbarName* specifies the name given to the new toolbar. When the `Add` method executes, it creates a new toolbar and adds it to the `Toolbars` collection; by default, the new toolbar's `Visible` property is false, so the new toolbar is not displayed on-screen. The following statement is a typical example of the `Add` method of the `ToolBars` collection:

```
ToolBars.Add "MyCustomToolbar"
```

> **Note:** You can also create custom toolbars by using Excel's interactive toolbar customization features. Although Excel usually stores toolbars created interactively in a special .XLB file in your Windows directory, you can use Excel's interactive commands to attach a toolbar to a particular workbook. The custom toolbar is then stored in that workbook and has access to the custom toolbar, whether or not it still has access to the .XLB file in your Windows directory.

Hiding, Displaying, and Positioning Toolbars

You can use your VBA code to display or hide either Excel's built-in toolbars or your custom toolbars. The Visible property of a toolbar controls whether or not Excel displays the toolbar on-screen. You can also test the Visible property's current value to determine whether the toolbar is already displayed on-screen.

You can also specify the position of a toolbar by using the Position property, and one of several predefined constant values to specify the toolbar's position—floating, or one of several docked positions. Table 16.7 lists the constants for the Position property, and explains their effect on the toolbar's position.

Table 16.7. Excel's predefined constants for a toolbar's Position property.

Constant	Effect
xlTop	Places toolbar in top docking area
xlBottom	Places toolbar in bottom docking area
xlLeft	Places toolbar in left docking area
xlRight	Places toolbar in right docking area
xlFloating	Floats toolbar

The next two code fragments show how to use the Visible and Position properties to display and position a built-in toolbar:

Here are examples of using the preceding property to display a built-in toolbar:

```
With Toolbars("Chart")
  .Position = xlBottom
  .Visible = True
End With

With Toolbars("Visual Basic")
  .Position = xlFloating
  .Visible = True
End With
```

Both examples set the Visible property to True, so the toolbar will be displayed on-screen. The first example specifies that the built-in Chart toolbar should appear in the bottom toolbar docking area (near the bottom of the Excel window). The second example specifies that the built-in Visual Basic toolbar is a floating toolbar; the exact position of the floating toolbar window is determined by Excel.

Listing 16.4 demonstrates using these properties by hiding and displaying the Visual Basic toolbar in all its docked positions, and in a floating toolbar window.

Listing 16.4. The `DemoToolbarPosition` procedure changes the visibility and position of the Drawing toolbar.

```
1:    Option Explicit
2:
3:    Private Const DELAY1 As Integer = 2
4:
5:    Sub DemoToolbarPosition()
6:
7:       Const dTitle = "Demo Toolbar Positioning"
8:
9:       Dim oldVisible As Boolean
10:      Dim oldPosition As Integer
11:      Dim tBar As Toolbar
12:
13:      MsgBox prompt:="About to change the Visual Basic " & _
14:                    "toolbar settings", _
15:           Buttons:=vbInformation, Title:=dTitle
16:
17:      Set tBar = Toolbars("Visual Basic")
18:      oldVisible = tBar.Visible     'preserve current settings
19:      oldPosition = tBar.Position
20:
21:      If tBar.Visible Then
22:        MsgBox prompt:="VB toolbar will be hidden.", _
23:              Buttons:=vbInformation, Title:=dTitle
24:      Else
25:        MsgBox prompt:="VB toolbar will be dislayed.", _
26:              Buttons:=vbInformation, Title:=dTitle
27:      End If
28:
29:      tBar.Visible = Not tBar.Visible   'invert Visible property
30:
31:      'let user know what's going to happen
32:      MsgBox prompt:="The Visual Basic toolbar will be " & _
33:                    "shown floating, and then top, bottom " & _
34:                    "left and right docked, with a brief " & _
35:                    "delay between position changes.", _
36:           Buttons:=vbInformation, Title:=dTitle
37:
38:      tBar.Position = xlFloating   'show the toolbar floating
39:      tBar.Visible = True          'force visibility
40:      Wait DELAY1
41:
42:      tBar.Position = xlTop   'show toolbar at top dock
43:      Wait DELAY1
44:
45:      tBar.Position = xlBottom   'show toolbar at bottom dock
46:      Wait DELAY1
47:
```

continues

16

Listing 16.4. continued

```
48:     tBar.Position = xlLeft       'show toolbar at left dock
49:     Wait DELAY1
50:
51:     tBar.Position = xlRight      'show toolbar at right dock
52:     Wait DELAY1
53:
54:     'restore old toolbar settings.
55:     MsgBox prompt:="Restoring original toolbar settings.", _
56:            Buttons:=vbInformation, Title:=dTitle
57:     tBar.Visible = oldVisible
58:     tBar.Position = oldPosition
59: End Sub
60:
61:
62: Private Sub Wait(Delay As Integer)
63:     Dim TheTime As Single
64:     TheTime = Timer
65:     Do
66:     Loop Until (Timer - TheTime) >= Delay
67: End Sub
```

The `DemoToolbarPosition` procedure (lines 5 through 59 of Listing 16.4) is really quite simple—it just exercises the use of the `Visible` and `Position` properties of the `Toolbar` object. Lines 13 through 15 display a message dialog box informing the user that changes will be made to the Visual Basic toolbar settings.

Line 17 uses the `Toolbars` method to set the **tBar** object variable to refer to the Visual Basic toolbar. An object variable is used to refer to the toolbar in order to save a lot of typing and to keep the VBA code shorter and more concise.

Lines 18 and 19 preserve the Visual Basic toolbar's current values for the `Visible` and `Position` properties, so that they can be restored later.

Lines 21 through 27 use an `If...Then...Else` statement to test the value of the toolbar's `Visible` property. If the toolbar is currently visible on-screen, lines 22 and 23 use a message dialog box to tell the user that the toolbar will now be hidden; otherwise, lines 25 and 26 display a message telling the user that the toolbar will now be displayed.

Line 29 simply uses the `Not` logical operator to invert the current value of the `Visible` property, and assigns the inverted value as the new value of the `Visible` property. If the toolbar is displayed on-screen, line 29 has the effect of hiding it; if the toolbar is not displayed, line 29 causes it to become visible on-screen.

Lines 32 through 36 contain a single `MsgBox` statement that informs the user about what the `DemoToolbarPosition` procedure will do next.

Line 38 assigns the xlFloating constant to the toolbar's Position property, causing the toolbar to be displayed in a floating toolbar window. Because it's not known for certain whether the toolbar is actually displayed at this point, line 39 forces the toolbar to appear on-screen by assigning True to the Visible property. Line 40 calls the **Wait** procedure to delay for an amount of time specified by the **DELAY1** constant—about 2 seconds, in this case.

Next, line 42 changes the toolbar's position so that it is docked at the top of the Excel window, and again delays for about 2 seconds. Now, line 45 changes the toolbar's docked position to the bottom of the Excel window, again delaying for about 2 seconds so that you can see the change on-screen. Similarly, lines 48 and 51 change the toolbar's docked position to the left and right of the Excel window, respectively.

Finally, lines 55 through 58 display a message dialog box letting the user know that the Visual Basic toolbar's original settings will now be restored, and then assigns the preserved values to the toolbar's Visible and Position properties.

Lines 62 through 67 contain the **Wait** procedure that you're already familiar with.

DO	DON'T

DO preserve a toolbar's original Position and Visible properties before changing them, so that you can restore those settings later.

DON'T assume that all toolbars (whether built-in or custom) can be docked in all of the docking positions. Some toolbars, like the Drawing toolbar, are too long to be docked in the left or right docking positions. If you attempt to dock the Drawing toolbar at the left edge of the Excel window by assigning xlLeft to the Drawing toolbar's Position property, for example, VBA will generate a runtime error because the toolbar won't fit in that space.

DO avoid runtime errors in your VBA code by manually checking to see whether a particular toolbar will fit into a particular docking position before you attempt to do so under the control of your VBA procedures.

Deleting a Toolbar

As soon as you no longer need a custom toolbar, you should delete it from the Toolbars collection in order to make the memory used by the custom toolbar available to Excel and other applications.

Syntax

To delete a custom toolbar, use the `Delete` method with this general syntax:

`ToolbarObject.Delete`

ToolbarObject is any valid object reference to a `Toolbar` object. You cannot delete built-in toolbars—VBA ignores an attempt to delete a built-in toolbar, without generating a runtime error. This code fragment shows a typical use of the `Delete` method:

```
Dim tBar As Toolbar
For Each tBar in Toolbars
   tBar.Delete
Next tBar
```

Because VBA ignores an attempt to delete a built-in toolbar, the above code fragment deletes all of the custom toolbars, but leaves the built-in toolbars unaffected, and no runtime errors occur.

Restoring a Built-In Toolbar

In case you do modify a built-in toolbar—by adding or removing toolbar buttons—and you want to restore it to its original configuration, VBA provides you with the `Reset` method, which restores the specified built-in toolbar to its default state.

Syntax

The general syntax for restoring a toolbar is:

`ToolbarObject.Reset`

ToolbarObject represents any valid object reference to a Toolbar object. When the `Reset` method executes, the referenced toolbar is restored to its default toolbar button configuration. An example of the `Reset` method used with a toolbar object:

```
Dim tBar as Toolbar
For Each tBar in Toolbars
   'reset toolbar if it is built-in
   If tBar.BuiltIn Then
     tBar.Reset
   Else
     'delete the toolbar
     tBar.Delete
   End If
Next tBar
```

The preceding code fragment uses a `For...Each` loop to process all of the currently existing toolbars. The `If...Then` statement checks the toolbar's `BuiltIn` property, which is `True` if the toolbar is an Excel built-in toolbar. If the toolbar is built-in, it is reset to its original default configuration; otherwise, it is a custom toolbar and is deleted.

Adding Toolbar Buttons

When you create a custom toolbar, it is empty—it does not contain any toolbar buttons. To make your custom toolbar useful, you need to add toolbar buttons to it—if you add custom toolbar buttons, you'll also need to specify the event procedure that you want executed when the toolbar button is clicked. In some cases, you may also want to add a custom toolbar button to one of Excel's built-in toolbars.

To add toolbar buttons to a custom or built-in toolbar, use the Add method of the ToolbarButtons collection with this general syntax:

```
ToolbarObject.ToolbarButtons.Add(button, before, OnAction, pushed, enabled)
```

ToolbarObject is any valid object reference to a Toolbar object. All of the Add method's arguments are optional.

The *button* argument is any numeric expression that specifies the ID number of the toolbar button to add to the toolbar. VBA has approximately 200 predefined toolbar buttons, and you must specify the toolbar ID number for one of these toolbar buttons when you include this argument. (Search the online help system for Toolbar Button ID Values to see a list of all of the available toolbar buttons and their ID numbers—there are too many to list in this book.) If you omit the *button* argument, then VBA inserts a gap—that is, a blank space—into the toolbar. You can't add a gap to a toolbar as either the first or last toolbar button.

The *before* argument is any numeric expression and specifies which button on the toolbar the new button should be inserted in front of. If you omit this argument, then VBA inserts the new toolbar button at the end of the toolbar.

The OnAction property is any string expression that evaluates to a valid specification for the event procedure to be executed when this toolbar button is clicked. Use the same syntax for specifying the OnAction argument for a toolbar button as you would for a menu item. If you omit this argument and you've specified a toolbar button ID for one of Excel's built-in toolbar buttons, the toolbar button will carry out its built-in task when clicked from your custom toolbar. If you specify the OnAction argument for a built-in toolbar button, the event procedure you specify will over-ride the toolbar button's built-in action.

The *pushed* argument is any Boolean expression. If *pushed* is True, then the toolbar button is initially displayed in a "down" condition; otherwise, the toolbar button is initially displayed in an "up" condition. You can't use the *pushed* argument for a built-in toolbar button.

The *enabled* argument is any Boolean expression. If *enabled* is True, then the toolbar button is initially displayed in an enabled state; otherwise the toolbar button is initially displayed in a disabled state. You can't use the *enabled* argument for a built-in toolbar button.

```
TB = "MyCustomToolbar"
ToolBars.Add TB
ToolBars(TB).ToolbarButtons.Add button:= 225, _
                             before:=1, _
                             onAction:="OpenFile"
```

The preceding code fragment creates the new toolbar "MyCustomToolbar" and adds a button whose ID number is 225 (a trashcan icon). The Add method also specifies that the new toolbar button is inserted to the left of any other toolbar button and that the procedure OpenFile is executed when you click this new toolbar button.

Note: Use the Button Image Editor to create your own toolbar faces. You can't add to the predefined toolbar buttons in Excel, but you can edit the faces of any of Excel's toolbar buttons to get the appearance you want. Refer to Excel's online help for more information on editing toolbar button faces.

Deleting Toolbar Buttons

You can delete toolbar buttons from both your own custom toolbars, and from Excel's built-in toolbars. You might delete a toolbar button from your custom toolbars because it is no longer needed, or you might want to delete a toolbar button from a built-in toolbar because you want to make it unavailable for some reason.

To delete a toolbar button, use the Delete method with the following general syntax:

ToolbarObject.ToolbarButtons(*button*).Delete

ToolbarObject is any object reference to a Toolbar object. The *button* argument is any numeric expression that evaluates to a valid toolbar button ID number of a toolbar button on the referenced toolbar. The following statement demonstrates the use of the Delete method:

Toolbars("MyCustomToolbar").ToolbarButtons(225).Delete

Manipulating Toolbar Buttons

As with menu item commands, you can disable toolbar buttons to indicate that their associated tasks are temporarily unavailable. This is usually a better technique than deleting the toolbar button. Also, you can indicate whether a toolbar button should remain "down" after it has been clicked—you would use this feature with toolbar buttons that represent a toggled command, similar to placing a checkmark to the left of a menu item.

You can manipulate these two toolbar button states by using the Boolean Pushed and Enabled properties of the toolbar button. If a toolbar button's Pushed property is True, then that button

is displayed in a "down" state. If the Pushed property is False, then the toolbar button is displayed in an "up" state. If a toolbar button's Enabled property is True, then the button is enabled; when Enabled is False, the toolbar button is displayed in a disabled state.

Although you can change the Enabled property for a built-in toolbar button, you can't change the Pushed property of a built-in toolbar button—unless you've overridden that toolbar button's built-in behavior by assigning your event procedure to it with the OnAction property.

Putting It Together: A Working Toolbar

The DemoToolbarSystem procedure in Listing 16.5 creates a custom toolbar, populates it with a few buttons, and displays it in a floating toolbar window. Although the custom toolbar created by DemoToolbarSystem doesn't do any real work, it demonstrates several of the toolbar and toolbar button objects and properties discussed in the preceding sections of this lesson, and shows you can construct your own working toolbars.

Figure 16.5 shows what the toolbar created by the DemoToolbarSystem looks like when displayed on-screen in a floating toolbar window. Clicking the happy-face button enables the three right-most buttons on the toolbar. When these last three buttons are enabled, the happy-face button remains "down," as shown in Figure 16.5. The sad-face button disables the last three buttons on the toolbar. When the buttons are disabled, the sad-face button remains "down." Clicking the sad-face button makes the happy-face button return to its "up" position, and the other way around.

Figure 16.5.

The DemoToolbarSystem procedure in Listing 16.5 creates this custom toolbar.

Clicking the toolbar button with the Info symbol on it displays a message dialog box with some information about VBA's current operating environment. Clicking the toolbar button with the bell symbol causes the system's default beep noise to sound, while clicking the button with the red diamond shape on it causes the custom toolbar to be removed from the on-screen display and deleted from the Toolbars collection.

After you've executed the DemoToolbarSystem procedure to create the custom toolbar and display it on-screen, experiment with dragging the toolbar to different docking locations. Notice that the custom toolbar also shows up in the list of toolbars displayed by the **View | Toolbars** command (until you delete it). Also notice how Excel's status bar changes and the ToolTips that appear when you position the mouse cursor over the toolbar's buttons. (ToolTips is a switchable

Excel feature; if your ToolTips don't appear, choose the **View** | **Toolbars** command and check the **S**how ToolTips option.)

Listing 16.5. Creating a working custom toolbar.

```
 1:  Option Explicit
 2:
 3:  Private Const Demo_tbName = "Demo Toolbar"
 4:  Private Const HappyButton = 211
 5:  Private Const SadButton = 212
 6:  Private Const InfoButton = 243
 7:  Private Const BellButton = 226
 8:  Private Const DmndButton = 222
 9:
10:
11:  Sub DemoToolbarSystem()
12:
13:    Dim myToolBar As Toolbar
14:
15:    'create a new toolbar
16:    Set myToolBar = Toolbars.Add(Name:=Demo_tbName)
17:
18:    With myToolBar.ToolbarButtons
19:      .Add Button:=HappyButton, OnAction:="HappyButton_Click"
20:      .Add Button:=SadButton, OnAction:="SadButton_Click"
21:      .Add Button:=InfoButton, OnAction:="InfoButton_Click"
22:      .Add Button:=BellButton, OnAction:="BellButton_Click"
23:      .Add Button:=DmndButton, OnAction:="RemoveDemoToolbar"
24:      .Add before:=.Count - 1
25:      .Add before:=.Count - 3
26:    End With
27:
28:    With myToolBar   'button properties
29:      With .ToolbarButtons(1)
30:        .Name = "Happy Button"
31:        .StatusBar = "Enables toolbar buttons"
32:        .Pushed = True
33:      End With
34:      With .ToolbarButtons(2)
35:        .Name = "Sad Button"
36:        .StatusBar = "Disables toolbar buttons"
37:      End With
38:      With .ToolbarButtons(4)
39:        .Name = "VBA Info"
40:        .StatusBar = "Display Information about VBA"
41:      End With
42:      With .ToolbarButtons(6)
43:        .Name = "Beep"
44:        .StatusBar = "Makes the system Beep noise"
45:      End With
46:      With .ToolbarButtons(7)
47:        .Name = "Remove"
48:        .StatusBar = "Deletes the demo toolbar"
49:      End With
50:    End With
```

```
51:
52:    myToolBar.Position = xlFloating    'floating by default
53:    myToolBar.Visible = True           'make it visible
54: End Sub
55:
56:
57: Sub HappyButton_Click()
58: 'enables all buttons on demo toolbar
59:    Dim k As Integer
60:
61:    With Toolbars(Demo_tbName)
62:      If Not .ToolbarButtons(1).Pushed Then
63:        For k = 4 To .ToolbarButtons.Count
64:          With .ToolbarButtons(k)
65:             If Not .IsGap Then .Enabled = True
66:          End With
67:        Next k
68:        .ToolbarButtons(1).Pushed = True
69:        .ToolbarButtons(2).Pushed = False
70:      End If
71:    End With
72: End Sub
73:
74:
75: Sub SadButton_Click()
76: 'disables all buttons on demo toolbar except Happy and Sad buttons
77:    Dim k As Integer
78:
79:    With Toolbars(Demo_tbName)
80:      If Not .ToolbarButtons(2).Pushed Then
81:        For k = 4 To .ToolbarButtons.Count
82:          With .ToolbarButtons(k)
83:             If Not .IsGap Then .Enabled = False
84:          End With
85:        Next k
86:        .ToolbarButtons(2).Pushed = True
87:        .ToolbarButtons(1).Pushed = False
88:      End If
89:    End With
90: End Sub
91:
92:
93: Sub InfoButton_Click()
94: 'displays info about VBA's environment
95:    MsgBox Buttons:=vbInformation, _
96:          Title:="VBA Info—Toolbar Demo", _
97:          prompt:="VBA is running in:" & Chr(13) & _
98:                  Application.Name & Chr(13) & _
99:                  "Build: " & Application.Build
100: End Sub
101:
102:
103: Sub BellButton_Click()
104: 'sound system Beep tone
```

continues

Listing 16.5. continued

```
105:    Beep
106: End Sub
107:
108:
109: Sub RemoveDemoToolbar()
110: 'removes the demo toolbar
111:    With Toolbars(Demo_tbName)
112:       If .Visible Then .Visible = False
113:       .Delete
114:    End With
115: End Sub
```

The **DemoToolbarSystem** procedure (lines 11 through 54 of Listing 16.5) starts out by creating a new toolbar object in line 16. This statement assigns the result of the Add method (which, when used as a function, returns an object reference to the newly created toolbar) and assigns it to the **myToolBar** object variable. An object variable is used to save some typing, and to make the ensuing code more concise.

Lines 18 through 26 add five buttons and two gaps to the toolbar. A *gap* is like a menu separator—it's a blank space between buttons on a toolbar. The button with the Info icon is separated from the other buttons on the toolbar with a gap on either side (see Figure 16.5). Because you can't create gaps at the end of a toolbar—VBA will display a runtime error if you try—lines 19 through 23 first create all of the toolbar buttons, simultaneously setting their event procedures with the OnAction argument of the Add method. After the toolbar buttons have been created, lines 24 and 25 add the two gaps.

Line 24 adds a gap in front of the next-to-last button on the toolbar (.Count - 1), which is the position occupied by the button with the bell icon on it. Adding the gap in line 24 increases the value in the Count property of the ToolbarButtons collection because the ToolbarButtons collection treats gaps as a special kind of button. After adding the gap in line 24, the ToolbarButtons collection now contains six buttons. The button with the Info icon on it is now the fourth button from the end of the toolbar. Line 25 adds a gap in front of the Info button, specified by .Count - 3. After adding this second gap, there are seven buttons in the ToolbarButtons collection, and the Info button now has a gap in front and behind.

Lines 28 through 50 contain a series of nested With statements that finalize the toolbar button properties for the custom toolbar. First, lines 30 through 32 set the Name, StatusBar, and Pushed properties of the first button on the toolbar—the button with the happy-face on it. The happy-face button must start out pushed down because all of the buttons on the toolbar are enabled by default, and this button's purpose is to enable all of the toolbar buttons.

Note: Excel displays the text in a toolbar button's Name property as the ToolTip for that toolbar button. Excel displays the text in a toolbar's StatusBar property in the status bar at the bottom of the Excel window.

Lines 34 through 37 set the Name and StatusBar properties for the second button on the toolbar—the toolbar button with the sad face on it. This button needs to be initially displayed in the "up" position, so only the Name and StatusBar properties are altered—the default values for all other properties are appropriate for this toolbar button.

Similarly, lines 38 through 41 set the properties for the fourth button on the toolbar, lines 42 through 45 set the properties for the sixth button on the toolbar, and lines 46 through 49 set the properties for the seventh button on the toolbar. Remember that this toolbar contains two gap buttons, so the Info button (which is separated from the first two buttons by a gap) is actually the fourth toolbar button, and the last two buttons are the sixth and seventh toolbar buttons because there is another gap button after the Info button.

Finally, line 52 sets the custom toolbar's position as a floating toolbar, and makes the new toolbar visible on-screen. At this point, you should see the toolbar shown in Figure 16.5—your toolbar may be displayed vertically rather than horizontally, however.

The remaining procedures in Listing 16.5 are the event procedures for the various toolbar buttons.

The **HappyButton_Click** procedure (lines 57 through 72) is executed whenever the happy-face button on the toolbar is clicked. Line 62 checks to see if the happy-face button is already "down"—if the button is down, then all of the toolbar buttons should be enabled. Only if the happy-face button is up (that is, not pushed) are lines 63 through 70 executed. Lines 63 through 67 begin a For loop which executes starting at the fourth button (the Info toolbar button) and ending with the last toolbar button. If the toolbar button isn't the special gap button—determined by testing the IsGap property, which is True for gap buttons—then its Enabled property is set to True. Line 68 sets the happy-face button's Pushed property to True, so the button will remain "down." (Remember, the happy-face button is the first button on the toolbar, so it is button number 1). Line 69 sets the sad-face button's Pushed property to False, so the button will be "up." (The sad-face button is the second button on the toolbar, so it is button number 2.)

The **SadButton_Click** procedure (lines 75 through 90) is executed whenever the sad-face button on the toolbar is clicked. This button's job is to disable the last four buttons on the toolbar, and works just like the **HappyFace_Click** procedure, except that it performs the reverse process. Line 80 checks to make sure that the sad-face button isn't already pushed "down"—if it isn't, then lines 81 through 85 proceed to disable the remaining toolbar buttons by setting their `Enabled` property to `False`. Line 86 sets the sad-face button's `Pushed` property so the button will remain "down," and sets the happy-face button's `Pushed` property so it will return to the "up" position.

Note: This example uses two toolbar buttons to show an on/off situation—when the happy-face button is down, the other buttons are enabled. When the sad-face button is down, the other buttons are disabled. More often, you'll probably want to just use a single toolbar button—with down being "on" and up being "off." Use whatever technique you think will be most intuitive for the command or feature controlled by the toolbar button.

Lines 93 through 100 contain the **InfoButton_Click** procedure. This procedure executes whenever the Info button on the custom toolbar is clicked. It simply uses a `MsgBox` statement to display some information about VBA's current operating environment. The `MsgBox` statement uses the `Application.Name` property and the `Application.Build` property to display a message on-screen showing the name and build number of the VBA host application.

Lines 103 through 106 contain the **BellButton_Click** procedure, which merely calls the VBA `Beep` procedure to sound the system's default beep noise. The specific sound you'll hear (and where it comes from) will depend on your computer hardware and software. With a default configuration on a multimedia computer, you'll hear a "ding" sound from your stereo speakers—if you don't have multimedia hardware, you'll hear a beep from your computer's built-in speaker.

Finally, lines 109 through 115 contain the **RemoveDemoToolbar** procedure. This procedure is executed whenever the button with the diamond icon is clicked. Line 112 hides the toolbar if it is currently visible on-screen, and then uses the `Delete` method to delete the custom toolbar from the `Toolbars` collection.

DO	**DON'T**

DO remember that adding a toolbar button without the button argument creates a gap on the toolbar. Gaps are similar to separators on a menu.

DON'T try to add gaps at the end of a toolbar, or VBA will display a runtime error.

DO remember that you have to access toolbar buttons in the `ToolbarButtons` collection by using the button's index number (that is, whether the button is the first, second, third, and so on). You can't use the toolbar button's name to access it in the `Toolbars` collection.

> **DO** use a toolbar button's `Name` and `StatusBar` properties to provide clues to a user about what the specific tasks or actions that the various custom toolbar buttons on your custom toolbar carry out.

Summary

This chapter taught you how to create and manipulate custom menus and toolbars in Excel by using VBA objects and their properties and methods. You learned about the various VBA objects that you can use to create custom menu bars and menus, as well as to alter Excel's built-in menu bars and menus.

This lesson gave you details on creating custom menu bars, menus, and menu item commands with VBA code. Specifically, you learned how to create, display, and delete menu bars, their menus, submenus, and command items. You also learned how to change menu captions, and assign event procedures to menu items. The material in this lesson on menus concluded with a working example of a complete menu system. You learned that you can use the `Reset` method to restore built-in menu bars to their original default configuration.

Next, this lesson showed you how to create custom toolbars and how to add custom toolbar buttons to a toolbar. You learned how to display and position both custom and built-in toolbars, and how to add gaps to a toolbar. The portion of this lesson on toolbars concluded with a working toolbar example, which demonstrated how to enable and disable toolbar buttons, and how to show a toolbar button in its "down" position.

Q&A

Q How can you tell if a toolbar is built-in?

A Use the Boolean property `BuiltIn`.

Q How can I pass information to a procedure's arguments if that procedure is an event procedure for a menu item or toolbar button?

A You can't assign procedures that have arguments to the `OnAction` property of a menu item or toolbar button. Instead, use a procedure without arguments, and make the needed information available to it through private module-level variables.

Q Do I have to always use Excel's built-in toolbar buttons to perform their built-in tasks?

A No. You can add Excel's built-in toolbar buttons to your own custom toolbars. If you don't specify an `OnAction` event procedure, the toolbar button uses its built-in behavior. You can, however, assign a new action to the built-in toolbar button by specifying an event procedure. Make sure that the tasks you assign to built-in toolbar buttons are similar to their usual tasks, or you'll confuse your toolbar's users.

Workshop

Answers are in Appendix A.

Quiz

1. How do you add a submenu to a menu?

2. Why should you always include a **File | Exit** or similar command on your custom menu bars?

3. **BUG BUSTER:** What is wrong with the following statement?

```
ToolbarButtons("Happy Button").Enabled = False
```

4. **BUG BUSTER:** What is wrong with the following set of statements?

```
Dim tbName as String
tbName = "Custom Toolbar"
Toolbars.Add(tbName)
With ToolBars(tbName).ToolbarButtons
  .Add Button:=211
  .Add Button:=212
  .Add
  .Add Button:=243
  .Add
  .Add Button:=226
  .Add Button:=222
End With
```

5. Do you have to specify an event procedure when you create a toolbar button?

6. Can you set the `Checked` property of a menu item when you create it?

7. Can you change the `Pushed` property of a built-in toolbar button?

Exercises

1. Write a procedure named **AddVBA_MenuExtras** that adds a custom menu to the built-in Visual Basic menu bar. This new menu choice should be named **P**rogrammer, and should contain these menu items: the first menu item should be named **V**BA Help (which displays the VBA online help contents), the second menu item should be named **I**nsert Named Module (which inserts a module sheet and asks you to rename it), the third menu item should be a separator line, and the fourth menu item should be named **R**emove Menu (which removes this custom menu from the Visual Basic menu bar).

HINT: The Visual Basic menu bar is named Visual Basic Module. So you can concentrate on creating the new menu choice and its menu items, use the following two procedures. Use **VBAHelp_Command** as the event procedure for the **P**rogrammer | **V**BA Help menu item, and use **InsNamedModule_Command** as the event procedure for the **P**rogrammer | **I**nsert Named Module menu item. Write the event procedure for the **P**rogrammer | **R**emove Menu command yourself.

```
Sub VBAHelp_Command()
  Application.Help "VBA_XL.HLP"
End Sub
Sub InsNamedModule_Command()
  Static sName As String
  sName = InputBox(prompt:="Enter the new sheet name:", _
                   Title:="Insert Named Module", _
                   default:=sName)
  If Trim(sName) = "" Then Exit Sub

  Modules.Add
  ActiveSheet.Name = sName
  With ActiveWorkbook    'move module to end of workbook
    .Sheets(sName).Activate
    .Sheets(sName).Move after:=.Sheets(.Sheets.Count)
  End With
End Sub
```

2. Write a procedure named **AddVBA_ToolbarExtras** that creates and displays a custom toolbar (named VBA Programmer) that contains three custom toolbar buttons. Separate the last button from the first two with a gap. The first toolbar button should perform the same task as the **P**rogrammer | **V**BA Help menu item from the preceding exercise, while the second toolbar button should perform the same task as the **P**rogrammer | **I**nsert Named Module menu item. The last toolbar button should remove the custom toolbar. HINT: Use toolbar button ID numbers 179, 219, and 225 for the first, second, and last toolbar buttons.

17

Error Handling

Your VBA procedures and programs, especially during the development stages, will often contain logical errors, or fail to properly handle certain data values acquired from a user or read from a disk file. These logic errors and other failures produce runtime errors that bring your VBA programs to an abrupt end. By now, you've probably gotten a lot of experience with VBA's runtime error dialog box—it's something that happens to all programmers, because no one can write perfect code all the time.

In today's lesson, you'll learn about VBA's special error-handling mechanisms. These mechanisms allow you to write code that will gracefully handle various runtime errors, allowing your VBA program to either circumvent the error, or to at least shut down in an orderly fashion. Error-handling is an important feature of professional programs. Today's lesson covers the following topics:

- ☐ An overview of error-handling strategies.
- ☐ How to trap errors by using the On Error GoTo statement.
- ☐ How to handle errors by using the Resume statement.
- ☐ How to use the Err and Erl functions to find out the type of error and where it occurred.
- ☐ How to force a user-defined error condition by using the Error statement.

Strategies for Error Handling

Basically, there are two general error-handling strategies that you can adopt: defensive programming, and error-trapping. In most programs, you'll use a combination of both strategies.

Defensive programming is a lot like defensive driving. When you drive defensively, you attempt to anticipate dangerous road situations, and avoid them. In a defensive programming strategy, you attempt to anticipate conditions that will result in runtime errors, and to write your code to detect and avoid those conditions.

Defensive programming can take many guises. You've already seen one example of defensive programming—screening a user's input to make sure that the values the user enters are the kind of values that your program expects. For example, if you display an InputBox dialog box to get an integer value, and the user instead types in a string that can't be converted to a numeric value, you'll probably end up with a type-mismatch runtime error at some point in your program after the InputBox statement. To use defensive programming for this situation, you add code to your input procedure so that it checks the value that the user enters (by using the IsNumeric function, say), and repeats the input request until an appropriate value has been entered. By making sure that the input meets expectations, you defensively avoid possible runtime errors.

Another example of defensive programming is shown in the following code fragment. Because dividing a number by zero is mathematically impossible, VBA will always generate a runtime error if you attempt to divide a number by zero. You might, therefore, use an If statement to guard against division by zero:

```
X = Val(InputBox("Enter first number ", "Input", ""))
Y = Val(InputBox("Enter second number ", "Input", ""))
If Y <> 0 Then
  MsgBox Str(X) & "/" & Str(Y) & "=" & Str(X / Y)
Else
  MsgBox "Cannot divide by zero!"
End If
```

The preceding statements prevent a runtime error by checking the values in the division operation first, and only performing the division if the divisor isn't 0. Another way of handling this issue is to use a looping structure to get input from the user until a non-zero divisor is entered.

You've seen many examples of defensive programming throughout this book. By now, you should have a pretty good sense of how to use defensive programming techniques. It isn't always possible, however, to imagine all of the possible situations that might produce a runtime error in your VBA programs. Frequently, runtime errors occur as the result of unexpected and unanticipated events. For example, your program might use a particular workbook to store data. If a user deletes or moves your program's workbook to another disk folder, your program is likely to produce a runtime error when it tries to open the missing workbook. There really isn't a way to anticipate this kind of problem, or to write defensive code for it.

In an *error-trapping* strategy, you use special VBA commands to "trap" the error, which prevents VBA from generating the usual runtime error dialog box. The VBA error-trapping statements tell VBA that you want to handle the runtime error yourself, and specify which part of your code to execute when a runtime error occurs. You then write the code to gracefully handle runtime errors under your program's control.

To handle something like a missing workbook disk file, as an example, you could use error-trapping statements in the procedure that opens the workbook file. Instead of getting a runtime error and having your program halt its execution over the missing file, you could use the error-trapping feature to invoke a special error-handling procedure that informs the user about exactly what file is missing, gives advice on solving the problem, removes menu bars, and otherwise shuts your program down in an orderly fashion—instead of leaving a mess for the user to clean up as a result of your program's unexpected termination.

In some cases, you can even resolve runtime errors without halting your program. Using error-trapping can also sometimes reduce the amount of defensive programming code that you have to write.

VBA uses an interdependent system of statements and functions for error-trapping and error-handling. The next few sections of this lesson first explain VBA's error-trapping statements and their syntax, and then present several examples of putting these error-trapping and error-handling statements and functions to work.

The *On Error GoTo* Statement

Before you can handle an error, you must be able to trap it. The VBA runtime system will always detect runtime errors whenever they occur. By trapping the error, you prevent the VBA runtime system from displaying the usual runtime error dialog box as a result of detecting a runtime error. When you trap errors, you also must specify which statements VBA should execute to handle the error. You use the On Error GoTo statement to both trap runtime errors, and to specify which part of your own code VBA should execute in order to handle the error. You can also use On Error GoTo to turn off error-trapping.

The On Error GoTo statement is has these two syntax forms:

```
On Error GoTo Label
On Error GoTo 0
```

In the first syntax form, *Label* represents either a line label or a line number. (You learned about line labels and numbers on Day 8.) When VBA executes the On Error GoTo *Label* statement, it installs an error trap. If a runtime error occurs after VBA has executed the On Error GoTo *Label* statement, execution is passed to the source code line specified by *Label*, instead of producing a runtime error dialog box. The *Label* must be in the same procedure as the On Error GoTo statement that refers to it, or VBA will display an error message when it compiles your source code before executing it. When the procedure that contains the On Error GoTo *Label* statement ends, VBA removes the error trap—error traps installed with On Error GoTo *Label* have the same persistence as local variables. If more than one procedure in the calling chain installs an error trap, VBA uses the error trap with the most local scope. If a procedure installs more than one error trap, VBA uses the most recently executed On Error GoTo *Label* statement to determine which error trap to use.

Using On Error GoTo 0, as shown in the second syntax form, causes VBA to remove any error trap you might have previously installed with the On Error GoTo *Label* form. Any runtime error that occurs after VBA executes an On Error GoTo 0 statement will again produce the usual runtime error dialog box. Use the On Error GoTo 0 statement to clear any error handlers that you may have installed with On Error GoTo *Label*. For example, you may want to install an error-handler for a particular segment of code within a procedure, and then want VBA to generate the standard runtime error dialog box for any statements that occur after that particular code segment. In this case, you would set up the error-handler with an On Error GoTo *Label* statement, followed by the VBA statements for which you want to handle the error yourself, and then followed by the On Error GoTo 0 statement to clear the error-handling trap.

The following code fragment uses an `Error GoTo` statement to trap a division-by-zero error, and then clears the error-handler after the critical statements have been executed:

```
X = Val(InputBox("Enter first number ", "Input", ""))
Y = Val(InputBox("Enter second number ", "Input", ""))

'set up the error trap
On Error GoTo DivideByZero

MsgBox Str(X) & "/" & Str(Y) & "=" & Str(X / Y)
Goto Skip1      'skip over the error-handling code
DivideByZero:
MsgBox "Cannot divide by zero"Skip1:
On Error GoTo 0    'resume normal error-handling
```

The *Resume* Statement

The `On Error GoTo Label` statement directs VBA's execution of statements to a specific point in your procedure, specified by a line number or label, where your code to handle the error is located. If the error is not a fatal error, you can handle the error and then resume your procedure's execution at the point where the runtime error originally occurred, or at some other specified point in your procedure's code. (A *fatal* error is any error from which you can't recover, such as a missing data file or insufficient memory; a *non-fatal* error is any error you can correct or recover from, such as bad user input.)

You use the `Resume` statement in your error-handling code to tell VBA whether to resume program execution, and where. Also, whenever VBA encounters a `Resume` statement, it considers the runtime error resolved, and resets its internal runtime error-handling mechanisms for the next error.

Syntax

The `Resume` statement has four different syntax forms:

```
Resume
Resume 0
Resume Next
Resume Label
```

The `Resume` and `Resume 0` syntax forms both have the same effect—they cause VBA to resume execution with the same statement that originally caused the runtime error—essentially, `Resume` and `Resume 0` direct VBA to retry the statement that caused the error. Typically, you'll use `Resume` or `Resume 0` to retry a statement after attempting to correct the conditions that caused that statement to produce an error. Use one of these forms to resolve errors such as a failed attempt to open a disk file—your error-handling code, for example, might get an alternate file location or perhaps even create the missing file, and then try the same file opening statement again by using the `Resume` or `Resume 0` statements.

The `Resume Next` syntax form causes VBA to resume execution with the first statement *after* the statement that originally caused the runtime error. Use this form of the `Resume` statement if the statement that caused the runtime error is one that can be successfully skipped. It's unusual to have a procedure whose correct operation won't be adversely affected by simply skipping over statements that cause runtime errors, so you probably won't use the `Resume Next` statement very often—unless, of course, you make certain that your error-handling code contains statements that accomplish the same (or a parallel) task as the statement that caused the runtime error.

The final syntax form, `Resume Label`, causes VBA to resume execution with the first statement after the specified `Label`, which may be any line label or line number. Use the `Resume Label` statement if you need to resume execution at a point in your code before the statement that caused the runtime error, or if you want to resume execution at a point several statements after the one that caused the runtime error.

> **Note:** VBA considers a runtime error to be resolved whenever it executes a `Resume` statement (in any of its syntax forms). Until then, any additional runtime errors that occur *will not* be trapped and will result in a runtime error dialog box, halting your procedure's execution. VBA must execute a `Resume` statement in order to reset its internal runtime error-handling mechanisms.

The following series of code fragments each shows an example of using one of the forms of the `Resume` statement:

```
' example 1
X = Val(InputBox("Enter first number ", "Input", ""))
Y = Val(InputBox("Enter second number ", "Input", ""))
On Error GoTo DivideByZero
Z = X / Y
MsgBox Str(X) & "/" & Str(Y) & "=" & Str(Z)
Goto Skip1     'skip over the error-handling code
DivideByZero:
Do
  Y = Val(InputBox("Enter a non-zero second number "))
Loop Until Y <> 0
Resume 0          'try the offending statement again
Skip1:
On Error GoTo 0  'restore normal error handling
```

The error-handling code in the preceding example executes a loop to get a non-zero number from the user, and then resumes at the same statement that originally caused the runtime error—the division operation. An `On Error GoTo 0` statement is included after the error-handling code to remove the error-handling trap. Assuming that this is not the end of the procedure, it may no longer be appropriate for future runtime errors in this procedure to be handled by the error-handling code at the `DivideByZero` label.

```
' example 2
X = Val(InputBox("Enter first number ", "Input", ""))
Y = Val(InputBox("Enter second number ", "Input", ""))
On Error Goto DivideByZero
```

```
Z = X / Y
MsgBox Str(X) & "/" & Str(Y) & "=" & Str(Z)
Goto Skip2
DivideByZero:
Resume Next
Skip2:
On Error GoTo 0     'restore normal error-handling
```

The preceding example essentially ignores the runtime error, and resumes execution with the next statement after the one that caused the error—the `MsgBox` statement that displays the division result. An `On Error GoTo 0` statement is also included after the error-handling code in this example, for the same reasons as in the preceding example.

```
' example 3
X = Val(InputBox("Enter first number ", "Input", ""))
Retry:
Y = Val(InputBox("Enter second number ", "Input", ""))
On Error Goto DivideByZero
Z = X / Y
MsgBox Str(X) & "/" & Str(Y) & "=" & Str(Z)
Goto Skip3
DivideByZero:
MsgBox "Division by 0 not allowed. Try again."
Resume Retry
Skip3:
On Error GoTo 0     'restore normal error-handling
```

This final example uses a line label (`Retry:`) in front of the statement that gets the divisor from the user. If a division-by-zero runtime error occurs, the user sees a message explaining the problem, and the `Resume` statement directs VBA to resume execution at the `Retry` label—the user is then prompted for another divisor, and the division operation is repeated. This behavior will repeat itself until the user enters a non-zero divisor.

DO	**DON'T**

DO make sure that you have somehow resolved the error before resuming code execution. In particular, if you use `Resume` or `Resume Next` to retry the offending statement without resolving the conditions responsible for the error, your procedure may end up looping infinitely: the runtime error will occur again, your procedure will execute the error-handling code, then return to the error-causing statement which starts the cycle over again.

DON'T end your procedure unless the runtime error is truly a fatal error, and there is no way to recover from it. Professional programs should always handle runtime errors as gracefully as possible, and only terminate their execution if there is no other way to resolve the problem.

DO remember to remove any custom menu bars, close workbooks, and save data (if possible) before shutting down a program as a result of a fatal error.

Finding the Runtime Error's Type, Message, and Location

Frequently, you'll need to know the exact type of runtime error that occurred in order to successfully resolve a problem. It may also be useful for you to retrieve the error message text that corresponds to the runtime error that occurred. Less frequently, you'll need to know the exact location where a runtime error occurred. VBA provides the Err function to let you determine the exact runtime error that occurred, the Error function to determine what message text corresponds to a particular runtime error, and the Erl function to determine where in your code the runtime error occurred.

To understand why you might need to know the exact type of a runtime error, and the exact location of the offending statement, consider the following code fragment:

```
X = CDbl(InputBox("Enter first number ", "Input", ""))
Y = CDbl(InputBox("Enter second number ", "Input", ""))
MsgBox Str(X) & "/" & Str(Y) & "=" & Str(X / Y)
```

In the preceding code, the results of the InputBox functions in the first two lines are converted to double-precision numbers by the CDbl function. Not only is it possible for the user to enter 0 in the second input dialog box (resulting in a divide-by-zero runtime error), but it is also possible for the user to enter a string that can't be converted to a number. With the CDbl function, this produces a runtime error. (The Val function was used in earlier examples because it returns 0 when it can't convert a string to a number.)

To know how to handle a runtime error in the preceding code fragment, you need to know whether the error stems from division-by-zero or a string value that can't be converted to a number. To know the most suitable point to resume program execution, you need to be able to determine which statement produced the error—one of the two input dialog boxes, or the division operation.

The next few sections of this lesson show you how to retrieve the specific error type, the corresponding error message text, and the location of the error.

Determining the Runtime Error Type: Using the *Err* Function

To find out the specific runtime error that occurred, use the Err function, which returns an integer number code for the specific runtime error.

SAMS
PUBLISHING

Sams
Learning
Center

Syntax

The `Err` function has this syntax:

```
Err
```

The `Err` function has no arguments, and simply returns an integer number which indicates the specific runtime error (this number is called an *error code*). Table 17.1 lists VBA's runtime error codes, and briefly describes their meaning. The `Err` function will always return one of these codes, or a user-defined error code (creating user-defined error codes is described later in this lesson). The following code fragment shows an example of using the `Err` function to return the error code:

```
On Error Goto HaveError
X = 1 / 0
Goto Skip1
HaveError:
MsgBox "Error number " & Str(Err)
Skip1:
```

17

Table 17.1. VBA's trappable runtime error codes.

Error Code	Description
3	Return without `GoSub`
5	Invalid procedure call
6	Overflow
7	Out of memory
9	Subscript out of range
10	Duplicate definition
11	Division by zero
13	Type mismatch
14	Out of string space
16	String formula too complex
17	Can't perform requested operation
18	User interrupt occurred
20	Resume without error
28	Out of stack space
35	Sub or Function not defined

continues

Table 17.1. continued

Error Code	Description
48	Error in loading DLL
49	Bad DLL calling convention
51	Internal error
52	Bad filename or number
53	File not found
54	Bad file mode
55	File already open
57	Device I/O error
58	File already exists
59	Bad record length
61	Disk full
62	Input past end of file
63	Bad record number
67	Too many files
68	Device unavailable
70	Permission denied
71	Disk not ready
74	Can't rename with different drive
75	Path/File access error
76	Path not found
91	Object variable not set
92	For loop not initialized
93	Invalid pattern string
94	Invalid use of Null
95	User-defined error
323	Can't load module; invalid format
423	Property or method not found
424	Object required
430	Class does not support OLE Automation
438	Object doesn't support this property or method
440	OLE Automation error
445	Object doesn't support this action

Error Code	Description
446	Object doesn't support named arguments
447	Object doesn't support current locale setting
448	Named argument not found
449	Argument not optional
450	Wrong number of arguments
451	Object not a collection
452	Invalid ordinal
453	Specified DLL function not found
454	Code resource not found
455	Code resource lock error
1000	Classname does not have `propertyname` property
1001	Classname does not have `methodname` method
1002	Missing required argument `argumentname`
1003	Invalid number of arguments
1004	`Methodname` method of `classname` class failed
1005	Unable to set the `propertyname` property of the `classname` class
1006	Unable to get the `propertyname` property of the `classname` class

Getting the Runtime Error Message Text: Using the *Error* Function

To find out what the text for a specific error code is, use the `Error` function, which returns a string containing the text that corresponds to a particular error code.

The `Error` function has this syntax:

```
Error([errorcode])
```

The optional *errorcode* argument can be any numeric expression that evaluates to one of the error codes listed in Table 17.1. If you omit the *errorcode* argument, `Error` returns the error message text corresponding to the last unresolved runtime error that occurred. If there is no unresolved runtime error, then the `Error` function returns an empty string (`""`). As an example, the next code fragment displays a message dialog box containing the error number and the string corresponding to that error:

```
On Error GoTo ShutDown
X = 1 / 0   'illegal operation
GoTo Skip1
ShutDown:
```

```
MsgBox Str(Err) & " means " & Error
End  'halts all program execution
Skip1:
```

This code fragment installs an error trap with the On Error statement, then executes the illegal division-by-zero operation. The MsgBox statement displays the text 11 means Division by zero, by concatenating the error code number with its corresponding text message.

Determining the Runtime Error Location: Using the *Erl* Function

To find out where an error occurred, VBA provides the Erl function. This function reports the line number closest to, but still preceding, the line that produced the runtime error.

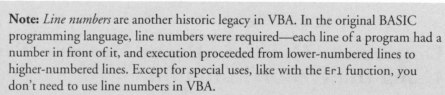

The general syntax for the Erl function is:

```
Erl
```

The Erl function returns the last line number that appears before the line containing the offending statement. Erl does *not* return line labels—only line *numbers*. In order to use the Erl function, you'll need to add line numbers to some of the lines in your procedure, as shown in the following code example. If the procedure does not contain any line numbers, or no error has occurred, then Erl returns 0.

> **Note:** *Line numbers* are another historic legacy in VBA. In the original BASIC programming language, line numbers were required—each line of a program had a number in front of it, and execution proceeded from lower-numbered lines to higher-numbered lines. Except for special uses, like with the Erl function, you don't need to use line numbers in VBA.
>
> To create a line number in your VBA code, simply make sure that the first character in a line is a number, and that the VBA statements on the line are separated from the number by at least one space character—VBA assumes that the number at the beginning of the line is a line number.

In the following code fragment, the first 3 lines of code have line numbers (1 through 3). The MsgBox statement displays the message Runtime Error on line 2 by calling the Erl function to get the last line number before the line containing the error—in this case, the same line as the line containing the error.

```
1 On Error GoTo ShutDown
2 X = 1 / 0  'illegal operation
3 GoTo Skip1
```

```
ShutDown:
MsgBox "Runtime Error on line " & Str(Erl)
End   'halts all program execution
Skip1:
```

DO	DON'T

DO use a Select Case statement when evaluating the Err function's result to identify the specific runtime error and the appropriate action to take.

DO use the Error function to get text corresponding to a specific error code.

DON'T frustrate your procedure's end-user with cryptic error messages. Make your error messages as clear as possible, and offer suggestions on correcting the problem as often as possible.

17

Forcing Runtime Errors and Creating User-Defined Error Codes: The *Error* Statement

VBA permits you to either artificially force a runtime error to occur, or to create your own runtime error codes by using the Error statement. Use the Error statement to force runtime errors with a user-defined error code any time you want to handle a situation as if it were a runtime error.

Note: Don't confuse the Error *function* with the Error *statement*. The Error function returns a text message corresponding to a particular runtime error code. The Error statement allows you to create your own error codes.

Use the Error statement to force a runtime error with one of the error codes from Table 17.1 in situations where you want to handle an improper condition or value in your procedure as if it were a runtime error. For example, you might have a procedure that has an optional argument but expects the optional argument to always contain an integer value, or a value that can be converted to an integer. Because optional arguments must be Variant data types, you can't rely on VBA to generate a type-mismatch runtime error to let you know you've made a programming mistake and are passing the wrong data type in that procedure's optional argument. Instead, you might check the data type passed in the optional argument, and then use the Error statement to force the production of a type-mismatch runtime error.

Whether you use the Error statement to force a runtime error with a predefined error code, or with a user-defined error code, VBA behaves exactly the same as for any other runtime error. VBA will use any error trap that you've installed with an On Error GoTo statement; if there is no error trap, VBA displays a runtime error dialog box, as usual.

Syntax

The general syntax for the Error statement is:

```
Error errorNumber
```

errorNumber represents any numeric expression that results in a number from 0 to 65,535. If the *errorNumber* argument is one of the error code numbers listed in Table 17.1, then VBA behaves as if that runtime error had occurred—the Err function, Erl function, and Error functions will all return results corresponding to the runtime error code you specified in *errorNumber*.

If you use a number higher than the error codes listed in Table 17.1, VBA sets the Err function to return that number, and sets the Erl function to report on the last line number before the Error statement. The Error function will return the string User-defined error.

The following code fragment, for example, sets up an error trap, and then uses the Error statement to generate a user-defined error whenever the value in **A** is zero.

```
' example 1
  Dim A As Double
  On Error Goto BadValue
Retry:
  A = Val(InputBox("Enter a non-zero number "))
  'create user defined error for zero-number input
  If A = 0 Then Error 65535
  MsgBox "1 /" & A & "=" & (1/A)
  Goto EndIt
BadValue:
  MsgBox "Non-zero numbers only! Try again."
  GoTo Retry
EndIt:
```

The next code fragment sets up an error trap, and then uses the Error statement to generate runtime error 11, division by zero whenever the contents of **A** are zero.

```
' example 2
  Dim A As Double
  On Error Goto BadValue
Retry:
  A = Val(InputBox("Enter a non-zero number "))
  'force divide-by-zero error BEFORE it actually occurs
  If A = 0 Then Error 11
  MsgBox "1 /" & A & "=" & (1/A)
  Goto EndIt
BadValue:
  MsgBox "Cannot divide by zero"
  GoTo Retry
EndIt:
```

> **Tip:** To avoid any potential conflict with VBA's predefined runtime error codes, it's usually a good idea to start your custom error code numbering at 65,535 and work downwards.

Putting It Together: Examples of Error Handling

The remaining sections of this lesson show examples of the different ways you can use the error-handling statements and functions described in the first few sections of this lesson. The first four listings are all variations on each other and show different ways of handling the same runtime error. The final example shows how to use forced runtime errors to help make your own procedures behave more like VBA's built-in procedures.

Handling Fatal Errors

The first error-handling example is Listing 17.1, which contains the **DemoFatalError** procedure. The basic task performed in this (and the next three listings) is to display a table of square roots from 5 to –2, computed by using VBA's Sqr function. The Sqr function, however, requires its argument to be a non-negative number, and produces a runtime error anytime you pass a negative number to it—runtime error code 5, Invalid procedure call, to be precise. Listings 17.1 through 17.4 each demonstrate a different error-handling technique to resolve this problem.

> **Note:** VBA's Sqr function produces a runtime error for negative numbers because negative numbers don't really have a square root. (Whenever you multiply two negative numbers together, the result is a positive number.) However, it doesn't seem to make sense that the number 4 has a square root, while the number -4 doesn't. To resolve this apparent contradiction, mathematicians invented an imaginary number, represented by the symbol i, to represent the square root of -1. By using i, it becomes possible to represent the square roots of negative numbers. For example, while the square root of 4 is 2, the square root of -4 is $2i$—that is, 2 multiplied by the square root of -1.

The **DemoFatalError** procedure in Listing 17.1 treats the runtime error as being unresolvable—that is, as a fatal error. When the call to the Sqr function generates a runtime error, the error-handling code displays a message about the error, and the procedure ends. **DemoFatalError** uses the Err and Erl functions to identify the error type and line number that contains the offending statement.

> **Note:** As you enter the code in Listing 17.1, pay special attention to lines 26 through 30 of the listing. The additional line numbers in the VBA statements really are part of the VBA code you should enter. These line numbers are included so that the Erl function will be able to report where the runtime error occurred.

Type

Listing 17.1. The DemoFatalError procedure uses the Err and Erl functions.

```
1:    Option Explicit
2:
3:    Sub DemoFatalError()
4:
5:       Const tblHead = "Table of Square Roots"
6:       Const FIRST As Integer = 5
7:       Const LAST As Integer = -2
8:       Const INCR As Integer = -1
9:
10:      Dim Count As Integer
11:      Dim cRow As Integer
12:      Dim oldSheet As String
13:
14:      oldSheet = ActiveSheet.Name   'preserve original sheet
15:      Worksheets("Sheet1").Select   'change to worksheet
16:
17:      On Error GoTo BadValue        'set error trap
18:
19:      Cells(1, 2).Value = tblHead      'set up table headings
20:      Cells(2, 1).Value = "   X"
21:      Cells(2, 2).Value = "  Sqr(X)"
22:      Cells(3, 1).Value = String$(35, "-")
23:      Cells(3, 2).Value = String$(35, "-")
24:
25:      cRow = 4
26: 1:   For Count = FIRST To LAST Step INCR
27: 2:      Cells(cRow, 1).Value = Count
28: 3:      Cells(cRow, 2).Value = CStr(Sqr(Count))
29: 4:      cRow = cRow + 1
30: 5:   Next Count
31:
32:      MsgBox Buttons:=vbInformation, TITLE:=tblHead, _
33:             prompt:="Square root table completed."
34:
35:      GoTo Ending  'skip over error handling code
36:
```

```
37:   BadValue:
38:     MsgBox Buttons:=vbCritical, TITLE:=tblHead, _
39:            prompt:="Error! " & Err & ": " & Error() & _
40:                    " in line " & Erl & Chr(13) & _
41:                    "Bad value was: " & Count & Chr(13) & _
42:                    "Procedure Terminating."
43:
44:   Ending:    'stuff that should be done regardless of error
45:     Sheets(oldSheet).Select
46:   End Sub
```

If you enter Listing 17.1 exactly as shown, the **DemoFatalError** procedure will display the dialog box shown in Figure 17.1.

Figure 17.1.

*The **DemoFatalError** procedure in Listing 17.1 displays this dialog box describing the runtime error.*

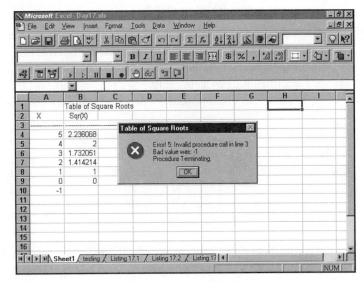

DemoFatalError is the only procedure in Listing 17.1. Lines 5 through 8 declare several constants used by this procedure: a title for the square root table and the dialog boxes displayed by this procedure, a starting value for the square root table, an ending value for the square root table, and an increment value for a For loop. Lines 10 through 12 declare the variables used by **DemoFatalError**: a counting variable, a variable for the current worksheet row, and a variable to store the name of the sheet that was active when this procedure started. Line 14 preserves the current worksheet's name, and then line 15 switches to the worksheet named Sheet1.

Line 17 installs the error trap with an On Error GoTo statement, and lines 19 through 23 set up table and column headings on the worksheet for the square root table.

Pay special attention to lines 26 through 30. These statements contain a `For...Next` loop that builds the square root table. Each line in the loop has a line number in front of it—the statements are numbered 1 through 5. These line numbers make it possible for `Erl` to identify the line that generates the runtime error. Otherwise, `Erl` would return 0.

Lines 32 and 33 display a message dialog box announcing that the square root table is complete. Actually, these lines never get executed in this procedure because it is written so that a runtime error always occurs. Because this procedure's error-handling code treats the error as a fatal error, execution never gets to this point. (As an experiment, change the **LAST** constant to 1, instead of -2, and then run the **DemoFatalError** procedure.)

Line 35 contains a `GoTo` statement that directs statement execution to the line indicated by the **Ending** line label in order to skip over the error handling code in lines 37 through 42. (`GoTo` statements were covered in Day 8.)

The actual error-handling code is in lines 37 through 42. Because the `On Error GoTo` statement specifies the **BadValue** line label when it installs the error trap, VBA begins executing statements in line 37 whenever a runtime error occurs in the **DemoFatalError** procedure. For this procedure, the error-handling code simply displays a message dialog box stating what the error number and error text are, in what line the error occurred, and what the offending value was (see Figure 17.1).

Tip: You can sometimes use your own error-handling code to deliver more information about a runtime error than VBA can. Notice that the dialog box produced by Listing 17.1 (in Figure 17.1) also reports what the offending value is—something that VBA isn't able to do.

Because the error-handling code is at the end of the procedure, and because there is no `Resume` statement, VBA continues code execution with the first statement after line 42.

Notice the **Ending** line label in line 44, and the statement in line 45, which restores the sheet that was active at the time this procedure started. The statement in line 45 should be executed whether or not a runtime error occurs.

Note: When you install an error-handling trap in a procedure, it is only in effect for the particular procedure. As soon as that procedure stops executing, the error trap is no longer in effect. Each procedure must install its own error-handling trap, and have its own error-handling code. Your error-handling code can, however, call other procedures or functions.

DO	DON'T

DO always make sure that your procedure does whatever housekeeping is necessary—such as closing workbooks, removing menu bars, or saving data—before you end it due to a fatal error you have detected.

DON'T number all of the lines in all of your VBA code. Just number lines that you think might cause problems.

Resolving Runtime Errors without Halting

The **DemoFatalError** procedure in Listing 17.1 simply halts after displaying the error number, message, and location. It makes no effort to resolve the error and resume execution of the procedure. The **DemoResolveError** procedure in Listing 17.2, however, resolves the error condition by entering a value for an imaginary number into the square root table (the square root of a negative number is an imaginary number). **DemoResolveError** deals with the runtime error internally, and gives the user the impression that everything is working without problems by resolving the condition that produced the runtime error, and using the Resume Next statement to continue program execution.

Listing 17.2. The DemoResolveError procedure uses the Resume Next statement.

```
1:    Option Explicit
2:
3:    Sub DemoResolveError()
4:
5:       Const tblHead = "Table of Square Roots"
6:       Const FIRST As Integer = 5
7:       Const LAST As Integer = -2
8:       Const INCR As Integer = -1
9:
10:      Dim Count As Integer
11:      Dim cRow As Integer
12:      Dim oldSheet As String
13:
14:      oldSheet = ActiveSheet.Name    'preserve original sheet
15:      Worksheets("Sheet1").Select    'change to worksheet
16:
17:      On Error GoTo BadValue         'set error trap
18:
19:      Cells(1, 2).Value = tblHead    'set up table headings
20:      Cells(2, 1).Value = "   X"
21:      Cells(2, 2).Value = "  Sqr(X)"
22:      Cells(3, 1).Value = String$(35, "-")
23:      Cells(3, 2).Value = String$(35, "-")
```

continues

Listing 17.2. continued

```
24:
25:     cRow = 4
26:     For Count = FIRST To LAST Step INCR
27:       Cells(cRow, 1).Value = Count
28:       Cells(cRow, 2).Value = Sqr(Count)
29:       cRow = cRow + 1
30:     Next Count
31:
32:     MsgBox Buttons:=vbInformation, TITLE:=tblHead, _
33:            prompt:="Square root table completed."
34:
35:     Sheets(oldSheet).Select
36:     Exit Sub   'no more work to do
37:
38:   BadValue:
39:     Cells(cRow, 2).Value = Sqr(Abs(Count)) & "i"
40:     Resume Next
41:
42:   End Sub
```

The **DemoResolveError** procedure from Listing 17.2 displays the worksheet and dialog box shown in Figure 17.2. Notice that this time, the procedure is able to complete the square root table—even for the negative numbers.

Figure 17.2.

*The **DemoResolveError** procedure can complete the square root table, even for negative numbers.*

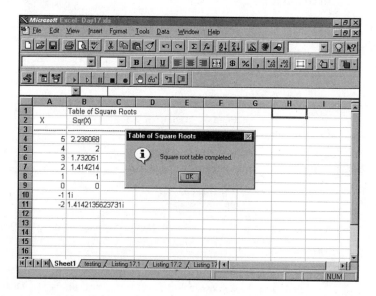

DemoResolveError works exactly the same as the procedure from Listing 17.1, with the exception of how the runtime error is handled, and the placement of the housekeeping code.

As before, the On Error GoTo statement in line 17 installs the error trap for this procedure. Lines 19 through 23 create the table's column headings, and lines 25 through 30 fill the table. Notice that this time, there are no line numbers in the VBA statements—this procedure doesn't use the Erl function, so there is no reason to include line numbers.

When the inevitable runtime error occurs (passing a negative number to the Sqr function), the error trap causes execution to pass to the first statement after the **BadValue** line label—in this case, line 39. Line 39 sidesteps the reason for the runtime error—it uses the Abs function to get the absolute value of the Count variable, and then finds the Sqr of that. (The *absolute value* of a number is the number's value, regardless of its sign—the absolute value of both 2 and -2 is 2, for example.) After computing the square root of the absolute value, the statement in line 39 then concatenates the letter *i* to the end of the number to show that it is an imaginary number.

Line 40 is important. After computing the imaginary square root of a negative number in line 39, the Resume Next statement in line 40 causes VBA to resume execution at the statement immediately after the statement that caused the runtime error—in this case, line 29 (inside the For loop). This has the effect of letting the procedure continue running as if the runtime error had never occurred—in a sense, it never did.

Because this procedure resolves the runtime error caused by passing a negative number to the Sqr function, the procedure will actually finish executing the For loop in lines 26 through 30, and will then execute the statements in lines 32 through 36. Line 32 starts a MsgBox statement that lets the user know the square root table is finished. Line 35 restores the sheet that was active when this procedure started, and line 36 exits the procedure. The only remaining statements in the procedure are the error-handling code, and the procedure has accomplished its work, so it is safe and appropriate to exit the procedure.

Retrying the Error-Causing Statement

Listing 17.3 shows yet another way to resolve the runtime error that occurs while building the square root table. This solution uses the Resume 0 statement to retry the statement that caused the runtime error, after manipulating the offending values so that the runtime error no longer occurs.

 Listing 17.3. The DemoRetryError procedure uses the Resume 0 statement to retry the error-causing statement.

```
1:   Option Explicit
2:
3:   Sub DemoRetryError()
4:
5:     Const tblHead = "Table of Square Roots"
6:     Const FIRST As Integer = 5
7:     Const LAST As Integer = -2
8:     Const INCR As Integer = -1
9:
```

DAY 17

Listing 17.3. continued

```
10:     Dim Count As Integer
11:     Dim cRow As Integer
12:     Dim oldSheet As String
13:     Dim Temp As Integer
14:     Dim tStr As String
15:
16:     oldSheet = ActiveSheet.Name   'preserve original sheet
17:     Worksheets("Sheet1").Select   'change to worksheet
18:
19:     On Error GoTo BadValue        'set error trap
20:
21:     Cells(1, 2).Value = tblHead      'set up table headings
22:     Cells(2, 1).Value = "   X"
23:     Cells(2, 2).Value = "  Sqr(X)"
24:     Cells(3, 1).Value = String$(35, "-")
25:     Cells(3, 2).Value = String$(35, "-")
26:
27:     cRow = 4
28:     For Count = FIRST To LAST Step INCR
29:       tStr = ""
30:       Temp = Count
31:       Cells(cRow, 1).Value = Temp
32:       Cells(cRow, 2).Value = CStr(Sqr(Temp)) & tStr
33:       cRow = cRow + 1
34:     Next Count
35:
36:     MsgBox Buttons:=vbInformation, TITLE:=tblHead, _
37:           prompt:="Square root table completed."
38:
39:     Sheets(oldSheet).Select
40:     Exit Sub     'no more work to do
41:
42:  BadValue:
43:     Temp = -Temp
44:     tStr = "i"
45:     Resume 0
46:  End Sub
```

The **DemoRetryError** procedure in Listing 17.3 produces the same worksheet and dialog box as already shown in Figure 17.2—the technique for achieving those results is different, however.

Listing 17.3 is the same as Listing 17.2, with a few exceptions. First, notice the addition of two new variables declared in lines 13 and 14. The **Temp** variable is used to temporarily store and work with the loop counter's value. The **tStr** variable is used to add the designation for imaginary numbers, when necessary.

As before, the current sheet's name is preserved, Sheet1 is selected, the error trap is installed, and the column headings are written onto the worksheet.

The For loop in lines 28–34 has changed, however. Notice that line 29 sets the **tStr** variable to be an empty string, and line 30 assigns the current **Count** value to the **Temp** variable. Lines 31 and 32, which fill in the current row of the square root table, now use the **Temp** variable instead of the loop counter variable. This is because the error-handling code (lines 42 through 45) changes the contents of the variable causing the runtime error. If this procedure actually changed the value of the **Count** variable, the For loop would not execute the correct number of times.

As soon as the loop counter becomes a negative number, the usual runtime error will occur. As before, VBA directs statement execution to the statements after the **BadValue** label because of the error trap installed in line 19. Line 43 simply inverts the sign of the number stored in **Temp** and assigns the result back into the **Temp** variable. Line 44 assigns the letter "i" to the **tStr** variable. Finally, line 45 uses the Resume 0 statement to cause VBA to resume execution with the *same* statement that originally caused the runtime error. The value in **Temp** is now a positive number (because its sign was inverted in line 43), so the Sqr function in line 32 won't cause a runtime error. Because the **tStr** variable contains the letter "i", the square root is entered into the worksheet with the appropriate suffix to indicate it is an imaginary number. (The next time through the loop, **tStr** will again be set to contain an empty string.)

17

DO	DON'T

DON'T modify a For loop counter's variable unless you really want to change the number of times the loop executes.

Resuming Execution at a Specified Point

Another way to handle a runtime error is to ignore it, or to skip over the operation that produces the runtime error. This technique can be particularly useful in looping situations—you can simply ignore the runtime error and assume that it will not occur in the next iteration of the loop. The example in Listing 17.4 uses exactly that technique to resolve its runtime error. When the runtime error occurs due to attempting to find the square root of a negative number, the **DemoResumeError** procedure ignores the runtime error, and allows the loop to continue executing.

Listing 17.4. The DemoResumeError procedure uses the Resume *label* statement.

```
1:  Option Explicit
2:
3:  Sub DemoResumeError()
4:
5:      Const tblHead = "Table of Square Roots"
```

continues

Listing 17.4. continued

```
 6:    Const FIRST As Integer = 5
 7:    Const LAST As Integer = -2
 8:    Const INCR As Integer = -1
 9:
10:    Dim Count As Integer
11:    Dim cRow As Integer
12:    Dim oldSheet As String
13:    Dim Temp As Double
14:
15:    oldSheet = ActiveSheet.Name    'preserve original sheet
16:    Worksheets("Sheet1").Select    'change to worksheet
17:
18:    On Error GoTo BadValue         'set error trap
19:
20:    Cells(1, 2).Value = tblHead      'set up table headings
21:    Cells(2, 1).Value = "   X"
22:    Cells(2, 2).Value = "  Sqr(X)"
23:    Cells(3, 1).Value = String$(35, "-")
24:    Cells(3, 2).Value = String$(35, "-")
25:
26:    cRow = 4
27:    For Count = FIRST To LAST Step INCR
28:      Temp = Sqr(Count)
29:      Cells(cRow, 1).Value = Count
30:      Cells(cRow, 2).Value = CStr(Temp)
31:      cRow = cRow + 1
32: ResumeLoop:
33:    Next Count
34:
35:    MsgBox Buttons:=vbInformation, TITLE:=tblHead, _
36:           prompt:="Square root table completed."
37:
38:    Sheets(oldSheet).Select
39:    Exit Sub     'no more work to do
40:
41: BadValue:
42:    Resume ResumeLoop
43: End Sub
```

Analysis

Figure 17.3 shows the worksheet and dialog box displayed by the **DemoResumeError** procedure in Listing 17.4. Notice that the table of square roots stops with 0 and does *not* contain any negative numbers.

The **DemoResumeError** procedure works essentially the same as the procedures you've already seen in this lesson. Again, only the error-handling technique is different.

Notice that line 13 declares a **Temp** variable of type Double. This variable is used to temporarily store the computed square root value. In the For loop in lines 27 through 33, notice that the result of the Sqr function is assigned to the **Temp** variable—if the argument for the Sqr function is negative, line 28 is the statement that will cause a runtime error. Notice also the addition of the **ResumeLoop** line label in line 32. This is the point where the loop's execution will resume after the runtime error.

Figure 17.3.

The DemoResumeError procedure completes the square root table but ignores negative numbers that cause runtime errors.

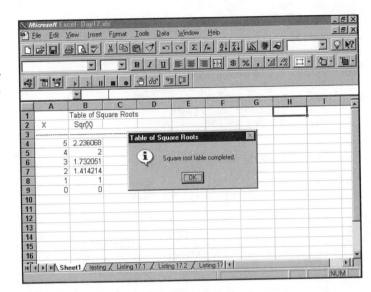

When a runtime error occurs, VBA shifts execution to the first statement after the **BadValue** line label, because of the error trap installed in line 18. The error-handling code in this procedure consists of the single Resume ResumeLoop statement in line 42. When VBA executes this statement, it shifts program execution to the first statement after the **ResumeLoop** line label—the Next statement in line 33. The For...Next loop then continues executing normally, as if no error had occurred. Handling the error this way has the effect of simply ignoring any negative numbers in the square root table, allowing the procedure to complete its operation without interruption.

Forcing a Runtime Error

This final example uses the Error statement to generate the runtime error *before* it actually occurs in a call to the Sqr function. You can use a similar technique with user-defined error codes.

Listing 17.5. The DemoForcedError procedure uses the Error statement to force a runtime error.

```
 1:   Option Explicit
 2:   Option Base 1
 3:
 4:   Const rtBadProcedureCall As Integer = 5
 5:   Const BINCOMP As Integer = 0
 6:   Const StrCmpLess As Integer = -1
 7:   Const StrCmpGreat As Integer = 1
 8:
 9:
10:   Sub DemoForcedError()
11:
```

continues

Listing 17.5. continued

```
12:    Const dTitle = "Forced Error"
13:
14:    Dim oldSheet As String
15:    Dim strArray(6) As String
16:    Dim tmpArray As Variant
17:    Dim intArray(6) As Integer
18:    Dim Count As Integer
19:    Dim Ans As Integer
20:    Dim ErrLine As Long
21:
22:    On Error GoTo rtError         'set error trap
23:
24:    oldSheet = ActiveSheet.Name   'preserve original sheet
25:    Worksheets("Sheet1").Select   'change to worksheet
26:
27:    Cells(1, 2).Value = dTitle
28:
29:    strArray(1) = "a": strArray(2) = "b": strArray(3) = "c"
30:    strArray(4) = "A": strArray(5) = "B": strArray(6) = "C"
31:
32:    intArray(1) = 2: intArray(2) = 6: intArray(3) = 4
33:    intArray(4) = 5: intArray(5) = 1: intArray(6) = 3
34:
35: Test1:
36:    tmpArray = strArray
37: 1  SortStringList List:=tmpArray, Descending:=True
38:    For Count = 1 To UBound(tmpArray)
39:      Cells(Count + 1, 1).Value = tmpArray(Count)
40:    Next Count
41:
42: Test2:
43:    tmpArray = strArray
44: 2  SortStringList List:=tmpArray
45:    For Count = 1 To UBound(tmpArray)
46:      Cells(Count + 1, 2).Value = tmpArray(Count)
47:    Next Count
48:
49: Test3:
50:    Ans = MsgBox(Buttons:=vbQuestion + vbYesNo, _
51:                 TITLE:=dTitle, _
52:                 prompt:="Test invalid direction argument?")
53:    If Ans = vbYes Then
54:      tmpArray = strArray
55: 3    SortStringList List:=tmpArray, Descending:="True"
56:      For Count = 1 To UBound(tmpArray)
57:        Cells(Count + 1, 3).Value = tmpArray(Count)
58:      Next Count
59:    End If
60:
61: Test4:
62:    Ans = MsgBox(Buttons:=vbQuestion + vbYesNo, _
63:                 TITLE:=dTitle, _
64:                 prompt:="Test invalid array argument?")
65:    If Ans = vbYes Then
66:      tmpArray = intArray
```

```
67:  4    SortStringList List:=tmpArray
68:       For Count = 1 To UBound(tmpArray)
69:         Cells(Count + 1, 4).Value = tmpArray(Count)
70:       Next Count
71:     End If
72:
73:  AfterTests:
74:     MsgBox Buttons:=vbInformation, TITLE:=dTitle, _
75:            prompt:="Sorting test completed."
76:     Sheets(oldSheet).Select
77:     Exit Sub      'no more work to do
78:
79:  rtError:   'handles runtime error
80:     ErrLine = Erl
81:     MsgBox Buttons:=vbCritical, TITLE:=dTitle, _
82:            prompt:="Error! " & Err & ": " & Error() & _
83:                    " in line " & ErrLine & Chr(13)
84:     Select Case ErrLine
85:       Case Is = 3
86:         Resume Test4
87:       Case Is = 4
88:         Resume AfterTests
89:       Case Else
90:         MsgBox Buttons:=vbCritical, TITLE:=dTitle, _
91:                prompt:="Unable to Continue!"
92:     End Select
93:  End Sub
94:
95:
96:  Sub SortStringList(ByRef List As Variant, _
97:                     Optional Descending)
98:  'sorts on ascending or descending order,
99:  'depending on value of Descending argument
100:
101:    Dim uCount As Integer, dCount As Integer
102:    Dim CmpResult As Integer
103:
104:    If IsMissing(Descending) Then Descending = False
105:    If TypeName(Descending) <> "Boolean" Then
106:      Error rtBadProcedureCall
107:    End If
108:
109:    If TypeName(List) <> "String()" Then
110:      Error rtBadProcedureCall
111:    End If
112:
113:    For uCount = LBound(List) To UBound(List) - 1
114:      For dCount = uCount + 1 To UBound(List)
115:      CmpResult = StrComp(List(uCount), List(dCount), BINCOMP)
116:        If Descending Then
117:          If CmpResult = StrCmpLess Then _
118:            Swap List(uCount), List(dCount)
119:        Else
120:          If CmpResult = StrCmpGreat Then _
121:            Swap List(uCount), List(dCount)
122:        End If
```

continues

693

Listing 17.5. continued

```
123:    Next dCount
124:   Next uCount
125: End Sub
126:
127: Sub Swap(I1 As Variant, I2 As Variant)
128:    Dim Temp As Variant
129:    Temp = I1: I1 = I2: I2 = Temp
130: End Sub
```

Analysis

Listing 17.5 shows a practical way of using the `Error` statement to make your own procedures and functions behave more like VBA's built-in procedures and functions by forcing a runtime error. By now, you know that VBA's built-in procedures and functions generate a runtime error if you pass an argument of the wrong type or with an invalid value. These runtime errors can help you spot your programming mistakes. By adding similar behavior to your own procedures—especially if you intend to distribute them to other users, you can make them easier to use.

Listing 17.5 contains several procedures. The **DemoForcedError** procedure (lines 10 through 93) simply sets up the variables needed to test the **SortStringList** procedure and then calls that procedure several times with both valid and invalid arguments. Figure 17.4 shows the worksheet and dialog box displayed by **DemoForcedError** after performing the third test of the **SortStringList** procedure.

Figure 17.4.

The **DemoForcedError** *procedure displays this message dialog box when it tries to test the* **SortStringList** *procedure with an invalid argument.*

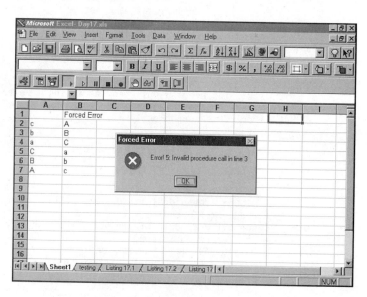

The **SortStringList** procedure (lines 96 through 125) is a version of the bubble-sort designed to sort arrays of strings in either ascending or descending order. **SortStringList** has two arguments. The first, required argument, is a Variant type; **SortStringList** expects it to contain an array of strings. The second, optional argument, is (as required by VBA for optional arguments) also a Variant type; **SortStringList** expects this argument to be a Boolean value indicating whether the list should be sorted in descending order. If either argument is *not* of the expected type, then the **SortStringList** procedure uses the Error statement to force VBA to generate an Invalid Procedure Call error message. The next few paragraphs take a closer look at how the code in Listing 17.5 works.

Listing 17.5 contains an entire module. Notice the Option Base 1 directive in line 2, which forces all arrays in this module to have a starting subscript of 1. Lines 4 through 7 declare some module-level constants. Line 4 declares a constant for the runtime error value, line 5 declares a constant to specify the type of string comparison desired, and lines 6 and 7 declare constants representing some of the return values of the StrComp function.

The **DemoForcedError** procedure starts in line 10. Lines 12 through 20 declare constants and variables. Notice that line 15 declares a string array, line 17 declares an integer array, and line 16 declares a Variant type variable.

Line 22 installs an error-handling trap for the **DemoForcedError** procedure, and lines 24 and 25 preserve the current sheet name and switch the active sheet to Sheet1, while line 27 enters a title on the worksheet. Lines 29 and 30 fill the string array with some test values, while lines 32 and 33 fill the integer array with test values. Notice that these lines contain multiple statements, separated with a colon (:).

Lines 35 through 40 form the first test of the **SortStringList** procedure. First, the string array is assigned to the **tmpArray** Variant variable. Because Variant type variables can store any data type, the result of the assignment operation in line 36 is to store a copy of the string array in the **tmpArray** variable.

Line 37 calls the **SortStringList** procedure, passing **tmpArray** as the array to be sorted, and specifying a descending sort order. Notice that this line also has a line number—it is line number 1 (because this is the first line that tests the **SortStringList** procedure). After the array is sorted, lines 38 through 40 contain a For loop that displays the sorted array in the first column of the worksheet. Because both arguments are of the correct type, this test of the **SortStringList** procedure does not produce any runtime errors.

Lines 42 through 47 contain the second test of the **SortStringList** procedure. This test works the same as the first test, except it calls the **SortStringList** procedure without the optional argument. The **SortStringList** procedure assumes that if the sort direction is not specified, then the list should be sorted in ascending order. Because the second argument is optional (and can be omitted), and because the first argument is of the correct data type (an array of strings), this call to **SortStringList** does not produce any runtime errors. Notice that line 44, which calls the **SortStringList** procedure has a line number—it is line 2, because this is the second call to **SortStringList**.

Lines 49 through 59 contain the third test of the **SortStringList** procedure. The user is first asked if they want to perform this test; if the user clicks the **Yes** command button, then the **SortStringList** procedure test is performed. Line 55 calls the **SortStringList** procedure, deliberately passing a string value for the optional **Descending** argument. Because this argument should be a Boolean value, not a string value, the **SortStringList** procedure generates a runtime error, and the **DemoForcedError** procedure's error-handling code is invoked. (The exact operation of the **SortStringList** procedure is described later). Notice that line 55, which calls **SortStringList**, has line number 3, because this is the third line that calls **SortStringList**.

Lines 61 through 71 contain the fourth, and final, test of the **SortStringList** procedure. Again, the user is asked whether to perform the test. If so, the **SortStringList** procedure is called by the statement in line 67. Notice that the statement in line 66 assigns the integer array to the **tmpArray** variable. When **SortStringList** is called in line 67, the **List** argument is an integer array, not a string array. Because this argument has the wrong data type, **SortStringList** generates a runtime error.

Lines 73 through 77 of **DemoForcedError** display a message informing the user that testing is completed, restores the original sheet. Line 77 exits the procedure because there is no more work to be done, and because the error-handling code at the end of the procedure needs to be skipped over—it's simplest to just end the procedure at this point.

Lines 79 through 92 contain the **DemoForcedError** procedure's error-handling statements. When a runtime error occurs, VBA shifts execution to the first statement after the **rtError** line label because of the error trap installed by the On Error GoTo statement in line 22. First, line 80 preserves the result of the Erl function in the **ErrCode** variable. Next, lines 81 through 83 contain a MsgBox statement that informs the user of the runtime error, reporting the precise error code number, its corresponding text, and the error line number. Now, lines 84 through 92 contain a Select Case statement that selects the appropriate point to resume the **DemoForcedError** procedure, based on which line produced the runtime error. If the runtime error occurred in the third test, then the procedure resumes with the fourth test; if the runtime error occurred in the fourth test, then the procedure resumes at a point after all the tests.

Note: As an experiment, replace the Select Case statement in lines 84 through 92 of Listing 17.5 with a single Resume Next statement, and observe how the **DemoForcedError** procedure's behavior changes.

Line 96 through 125 contain the **SortStringList** procedure. Lines 101 and 102 declare the variables used by **SortStringList**. Line 104 checks to see whether the optional **Descending** argument was included—if that argument is missing, then it's set to a default value of False so the list will be sorted in ascending order.

Line 105 tests to see what the data type of the **Descending** argument is by using the TypeName function. If the **Descending** argument doesn't have a Boolean type, then line 106 uses the Error statement to force a runtime error—in this case, the runtime error specified by the **rtBadProcedureCall** constant (which stores the error code number for an Invalid Procedure Call error). Because of the forced runtime error, VBA immediately stops executing the **SortStringList** procedure and returns to the **DemoForcedError** procedure. After returning to the **DemoForcedError** procedure, VBA sets its internal error mechanisms to indicate that an invalid procedure call has been made, and also interrupts the execution of the **DemoForcedError** procedure. Because the **DemoForcedError** procedure has an error trap installed, it handles the runtime error itself.

> **Note:** As an experiment, remove the On Error GoTo statement from line 22 of Listing 17.5, and see what happens when the **SortStringList** procedure is called with invalid arguments.

If the **Descending** argument has the correct type, then execution continues with line 109, which also uses the TypeName function to test the type of the **List** argument. If the **List** argument is an array of strings, then the TypeName function returns String() as its result. If the **List** argument is *not* an array of strings, then the Error statement in line 110 is executed, forcing a runtime error. This statement has the same effect as line 106—**SortStringList** terminates, and the runtime error is reported in the context of the procedure that called **SortStringList** (**DemoForcedError** in this case). The remainder of the **SortStringList** procedure carries out the bubble-sort that you're already familiar with.

Lines 127 through 130 contain the **Swap** procedure used by **SortStringList**. You already know how this procedure works.

Summary

This lesson presented the mechanisms for trapping and handling errors in your VBA procedures. You learned that there are two basic error-handling strategies: defensive programming and error trapping. The first strategy detects conditions that will cause a runtime error and takes the necessary steps to avoid the error. Error trapping involves installing an error trap (by using the On Error GoTo statement) that causes VBA to automatically branch to a particular spot in your procedure, which usually contains code to handle the error without halting the procedure's execution.

This lesson showed you how to use the On Error GoTo statement to install an error trap. You learned that the On Error GoTo statement uses a line label to specify a location in your procedure to which VBA switches program execution if a runtime error occurs. You also learned how to use the Resume statement to determine where your procedure's code should resume execution. Typically, your error-handling code will end with a Resume statement of some kind, after dealing with the runtime error.

This lesson also taught you how to use the Err, Erl, and Error functions to find out the specific runtime error code, the line number of the statement that caused the runtime error, and the corresponding text for the error message. Finally, you learned how to use the Error statement to force a runtime error to occur with either a predefined VBA error code, or an error code which you define.

This lesson concluded with several examples of putting the various error-handling statements and functions to work.

Q&A

Q At what point in my procedure should I install an error trap with the On Error GoTo statement?

A Usually, you should install the error trap at the beginning of your procedure, especially if it's intended to handle any runtime error that might occur while the procedure is executing. Alternatively, you can install the error trap immediately in front of any error-prone statement—your procedure can even contain more than one On Error GoTo statement, with each statement pointing to a different section of error-handling statements. In general, though, you should use only one On Error GoTo statement.

Q What happens if another runtime error occurs as a result of one of the statements in my procedure's error-handling code?

A VBA will stop executing your procedure's code and display a runtime error dialog box for the additional runtime error, because it can't deal with the new runtime error until you've reset VBA's internal runtime error mechanisms with a Resume statement.

Q Well, can I use an On Error GoTo statement in my error-handling code to take care of any additional runtime errors that occur while my code resolves the first runtime error?

A Yes, but you must first use a Resume statement to clear VBA's internal runtime error-handling mechanisms. Here is the general form for a nested error handler:

```
FirstError:
    'statements to record the error number, etc.
    Resume NextLine1
NextLine1:
    'install second error handler
    On Error GoTo SecondError
    'statements that handle first error
    GoTo ReturnLabel
SecondError:
    'statements to handle second error
    Resume ReturnLabel
```

Notice that the first Resume statement simply directs execution to resume at the label on the following line. This programming trick satisfies VBA's need to handle the first error. The On Error GoTo statement then sets the internal error handler.

Q What happens if I just use a Resume 0 statement to handle an error?

A Your procedure will enter an infinite loop, because the error isn't actually being resolved, and the statement causing the error isn't being skipped over. A runtime error will occur, VBA will execute the Resume 0 statement in your error-handling code, return to the offending statement, and the same runtime error will occur again. Only use the Resume 0 statement after your error-handling code has resolved the conditions that produced the runtime error (by modifying variable values, changing to another worksheet or workbook, and so on).

17

Workshop

Answers are in Appendix A.

Quiz

1. What statement can you use to cause your procedure to resume execution at the statement immediately following the one that caused a runtime error?

2. What happens if a new runtime error occurs while your procedure is still handling a previous runtime error?

3. Can a procedure have multiple sets of error-handling statements?

4. Which statement can you use to cause your procedure to resume execution with the same statement that caused a runtime error?

5. How do you disable your error trap?

6. What statement clears VBA's internal runtime error-handling mechanisms?

7. What function returns the error message text corresponding to a particular runtime error code?

8. What statement forces a runtime error to occur?

Exercises

1. Write a procedure named **MyErrorHandler** that traps and handles the runtime error produced when you call the Mid function with invalid indices. (Mid returns a specified portion of a string.) Here is the pseudo-code for the **MyErrorHandler** procedure:

```
1. Install the error trap.
2. Prompt the user to enter a string.
```

3. Prompt user to enter the starting index.
4. Prompt user to enter the number of characters to extract.
5. Call the Mid function, and assign its result to a variable.
6. Display the original string and the extracted string.
7. End the procedure.

The Mid function produces a runtime error any time its arguments are negative or zero. Your procedure should handle the error along the lines of the following pseudo-code:

1. Assign an empty string to the variable for the extracted string.
2. Display an error message.
3. Resume execution at the statement following the one that caused the runtime error.

2. What is displayed in the message dialog box after the following statements are executed?

```
Dim S As String
Dim L As Integer
On Error GoTo RunTimeError
S = "Hello"
L = 0
Mid(S, L, 1) = "J"
MsgBox S
GoTo EndIt
RunTimeError:
  Resume Next
EndIt:
```

3. What is displayed in the message dialog box after these statements execute?

```
Dim S As String
Dim L As Integer
On Error GoTo RunTimeError
S = "Hello"
L = 0
Mid(S, L, 1) = "J"
MsgBox S
GoTo EndIt
RunTimeError:
  L = 1
  Resume 0
EndIt:
```

4. What is displayed in the message dialog box after the following statements are executed? What does it tell you about the number of times the macro calls the error-handling statements?

```
Dim S As String
Dim L As Integer
Dim Count As Integer
Count = 0
On Error GoTo RunTimeError
S = "Hello"
L = -10
Mid(S, L, 1) = "J"
MsgBox S & Chr(13) & Chr(10) & Count
```

```
            GoTo EndIt
        RunTimeError:
          Count = Count + 1
          L = L + 1
          Resume 0
        EndIt:
```

5. What is displayed in the message dialog box after the following statements are
executed?

```
        Dim S As String
        Dim L As Integer
        On Error GoTo RunTimeError
        S = "Hello"
        L = 0
        Mid(S, L, 1) = "J"
        MsgBox S
        GoTo EndIt
        RunTimeError:
          MsgBox "Runtime error number" & Err
        EndIt:
```

Working with Excel

As you have already learned, Visual Basic for Applications is a programming language designed primarily to work with and enhance existing software programs. The Excel version of VBA has many objects, properties, and methods that enable you to control almost every aspect of Excel. In today's lesson, you'll learn:

- ☐ How to work with Workbook objects.
- ☐ How to work with Worksheet objects.
- ☐ Various methods that return Range objects.
- ☐ How to work with and define range names.
- ☐ How to select ranges.
- ☐ How to enter values and formulas.
- ☐ Techniques for cutting, copying, and clearing ranges.

Working with Workbook Objects

Excel 5 introduced a new workbook format, still used in Excel 7. This workbook format is a great way to make common spreadsheet tasks faster and easier. The Excel 5 and Excel 7 workbooks are a significant improvement over the file formats used in previous versions of Excel. VBA includes a number of methods and properties that enable you to perform basic chores on your workbooks. The next few sections look at some of the most common methods and properties.

Returning a Workbook Object

In Excel, each workbook is a Workbook object, and Workbooks is the collection of all the open workbooks in the current Excel session. To refer to a specific workbook, use the Application object's Workbooks method:

Syntax

```
Workbooks(Index)
```

Index can be either of the following:

A numeric expression representing the workbook that you want to use. 1 signifies the first workbook opened in this session, 2 signifies the second workbook opened, and so on.

A string expression representing the name of the open workbook that you want to use.

The most common—and usually the most readable—way of using *Index* is as a text string. Listing 18.1 shows an example.

Listing 18.1. Using the `Workbooks` method to return a workbook.

```
1:  Sub SetWorkbookProtection()
2:  'Activates workbook protection
3:
4:     Workbooks("DAY18.XLS").Protect _
5:          Structure:=True, _
6:          Windows:=True
7:     MsgBox "Workbook protection for DAY18.XLS activated."
8:  End Sub
```

The statement in line 4, `Workbooks("DAY18.XLS")`, returns the DAY18.XLS workbook object, and the `Protect` method sets up protection for the workbook's structure and windows. The `MsgBox` statement in line 7 displays a message telling you that protection has been activated for this workbook. (This procedure assumes that a workbook named DAY18.XLS is currently open—if it isn't, you'll get a runtime error.)

DO	DON'T

DO use `ActiveWorkbook` to refer to the active workbook.

DO use `ThisWorkbook` to refer to the workbook that contains the currently running procedure, especially if you intend to convert your program to an Excel add-in program.

DON'T use numbers for the `Index` argument of the `Workbooks` method if you don't have to. The meaning of a statement such as `Workbooks("DAY18.XLS")` is much clearer than, say, `Workbooks(2)`. Using the text name of the workbook is also more accurate. Unless all the workbooks in the current Excel session are opened by your program, you cannot be sure that the DAY18.XLS workbook is, in fact, the second workbook.

18

Opening a Workbook

If the workbook that you need is not open, use the `Open` method to load the workbook into memory:

```
Workbooks.Open(Filename)
```

The **Filename** argument is a text string representing the full path name—drive, directory, and filename—of the workbook. If you don't specify the drive or directory name, Excel looks for the workbook file in the current drive or directory. Listing 18.2 shows the `Open` method in action.

Listing 18.2. Using the `Open` method to open a workbook.

```
 1:  Sub OpenWorkbook()
 2:  'Prompts for, and then opens a workbook
 3:
 4:     Dim WorkbookName As String
 5:
 6:     WorkbookName = _
 7:        InputBox("Enter the full path name of the workbook to open:")
 8:     If WorkbookName <> "" Then
 9:        Workbooks.Open Filename:=WorkbookName
10:     End If
11:  End Sub
```

Analysis In this procedure, a variable called **WorkbookName** is declared as a String (line 4), and an `InputBox` function prompts the user for the name of a workbook file (line 7). The `If...Then` statement in line 8 checks whether the user canceled the input dialog box. If not—in other words, if **WorkbookName** isn't blank—the `Open` method uses **WorkbookName** to open the file (line 9).

DO	DON'T

DO take advantage of Excel's built-in Open dialog box, if you need or want the user to select a file to open. You can use Excel's built-in Open dialog box either by using the `GetFileOpenName` method (discussed in Day 12), or by using the `Dialogs` methods shown here:

`Application.Dialogs(xlDialogOpen).Show`

DON'T use the `Open` method and expect the workbook's `Auto_Open` macros to execute. They won't. Instead, use the `Open` method to open the workbook, and then use the following method to run the workbook's `Auto_Open` macro procedure:

`Object.RunAutoMacros(xlAutoOpen)`

Here, **Object** is a reference to any Workbook object. `xlAutoOpen` is an Excel constant that specifies which auto procedure to run.

DON'T despair if you want to open a file as read-only or with a password. The `Open` method has no less than a dozen arguments that cover situations like these. Use the Object Browser to see, paste, or get help on the various arguments for the `Open` method.

Creating a New Workbook

If your procedure needs to create a new workbook, use the Workbooks collection's Add method to get the job done:

```
Workbooks.Add([Template])
```

The optional **Template** argument determines the kind of workbook that Excel creates. If you omit **Template**, Excel creates a default workbook.

To create a new workbook based on an existing template, enter **Template** as a string specifying the name of the template that you want to use. If the template that you want to use is not in the startup or alternate startup directory, include the full path—drive, directory, and template filename—in the string for the **Template** argument.

To create a workbook that contains only a single sheet, use one of the following predefined constants for **Template**: xlWorksheet, xlChart, xl4MacroSheet, or xl4IntlMacroSheet.

Listing 18.3 shows an example procedure that creates a new workbook.

Type

Listing 18.3. Using the Add method to create a new workbook.

18

```
 1:   Sub CreateMonthlyReport()
 2:   'Creates new workbook based on Excel's Invoice template
 3:
 4:      Dim dPath As String
 5:
 6:      dPath = "C:\MsOffice\Templates\Spreadsheet Solutions\"
 7:      Workbooks.Add Template:=dPath & "Invoice"
 8:      With ActiveWorkbook
 9:         .Title = "Invoice to the Absolutely Huge Co."
10:         .Subject = "Invoice for January 1996"
11:         .Author = "Lisa Simpson"
12:      End With
13:
14:   End Sub
```

Analysis

Listing 18.3 creates a new workbook from the Invoice template supplied with Excel and Microsoft Office (line 7). (The path used in this example is for Microsoft Office installed into its default directories—your template file may be in a different location.) Any new workbook automatically becomes the active workbook. Lines 8 through 12 use the ActiveWorkbook object to add some summary information for the new workbook file—Title, Subject, and Author.

Activating a Workbook

If your VBA program keeps several workbooks open at once, you might need to switch from one workbook to another to display, for example, a report or a data entry screen.

Use the `Activate` method to make any open workbook the active workbook:

```
Object.Activate
```

Here, **Object** represents any valid object reference to the worksheet you want to activate. Listing 18.4 displays an example procedure that uses the `Activate` method.

Listing 18.4. Using the `Activate` method to switch to a workbook.

```
 1:  Sub ActivateTest()
 2:  'Activates two workbooks without changing the screen.
 3:
 4:    Dim SaveBook As String
 5:
 6:    SaveBook = ActiveWorkbook.Name
 7:
 8:    Application.ScreenUpdating = False
 9:    Workbooks("DATA.XLS").Activate
10:
11:    'Code that does stuff to DATA.XLS goes here
12:
13:    Workbooks(SaveBook).Activate
14:    Application.ScreenUpdating = True
15:  End Sub
```

Analysis

This simple procedure demonstrates two tenets of good programming.

☐ Whenever possible, hide your program's intermediate operations from the user. For example, if the procedure has a number of statements that format ranges and enter data, perform these tasks "behind the scenes." Present the user only with the finished screen. You do this by setting the `Application` object's `ScreenUpdating` property to `False`.

☐ If you're activating a workbook because your code needs to—and not because you want the user to see a different file—your procedure should always return the user to where she started. Especially for novice users, it is highly disconcerting to start a procedure and to end up suddenly in a different workbook for no obvious reason.

The purpose of the procedure in Listing 18.4 is to switch from the current workbook to another workbook (DATA.XLS), to make some modifications to it by means of code, and to return to the original workbook. First, in line 4, the name of the current active workbook is saved in the **SaveBook** string variable. Next, to keep the user from seeing the details of the procedure's action,

line 8 sets the `ScreenUpdating` property to `False`. Line 9 activates the DATA.XLS workbook. The following lines would perform actions in the DATA.XLS workbook—the actual code that modifies DATA.XLS has been omitted from this example. To get the user back to the original workbook, line 13 reactivates the original workbook. Line 14 sets `ScreenUpdating` back to `True`.

DO	**DON'T**

DO let the user know what's happening if you've switched from one workbook to another. A simple `MsgBox` statement can tell the user where she is now and what she should expect.

DON'T activate a workbook if you don't have to. You can almost always modify or get information about a workbook simply by referring to the appropriate `Workbook` object. For example, to find out the format of DATA.XLS by using the `FileFormat` property, you can use the following statement without activating the workbook:

```
FileFmt = Workbooks("DATA.XLS").FileFormat
```

18

Saving a Workbook

If your VBA program makes changes to a workbook, you should give the user an opportunity to save those changes or have your program save them outright. This is easily accomplished either by including Excel's built-in Save command in your program's menu, or by adding the Save button to your program's toolbar if your program has menus or toolbars.

There might be times, though, when you need to save a workbook under the control of a procedure. For example, you might want to create your own version of the File | Save command. Likewise, you might be trying to protect a novice user from performing actions with unfortunate consequences, such as closing a workbook or exiting your program or Excel without saving his work. To save a workbook, you use—appropriately enough—the `Save` method:

```
Object.Save
```

With this method, **Object** is an object reference to the open `Workbook` object that you want to save.

A slightly different, but handy, method is called `SaveCopyAs`. This method saves a copy of the specified workbook to disk without affecting the workbook in memory. This method is useful, for example, if you want to create a Revert command that returns a workbook to its original state. You use `SaveCopyAs` at the beginning of your program to make another copy of the workbook file to disk before any changes are made in the workbook. Then, you can revert to this saved copy by opening it and saving it again with its original filename. Here is the general form of the `SaveCopyAs` method:

```
Object.SaveCopyAs(Filename)
```

Object is an object reference to the Workbook to be saved, and **Filename** is a string expression for the name you want to use for the saved workbook copy.

Listing 18.5 shows an example procedure that uses both Save and SaveCopyAs.

Listing 18.5. Using the Save and SaveCopyAs methods.

```
 1:  Sub BackUpToFloppy()
 2:  'Saves and backs up the active workbook to floppy A:
 3:
 4:     Const FloppyDrv = "A:"
 5:
 6:     With ActiveWorkbook
 7:        If Not .Saved Then .Save
 8:        .SaveCopyAs Filename:=FloppyDrv & .Name
 9:     End With
10:  End Sub
```

This procedure saves the active workbook and makes a backup copy on a floppy disk in drive A. The procedure begins by declaring a single constant for the floppy drive letter. The With statement processes several commands for the ActiveWorkbook object.

An If...Then test (line 7) checks the workbook's Saved property. If this property is False, the workbook has changes that haven't been saved yet, so the procedure calls the Save method.

The name of the backup file is created by concatenating the **FloppyDrv** constant value with the workbook's Name property. The result is used as the Name argument to the SaveCopyAs method (line 8), which saves a copy of the workbook to the floppy drive.

DO	**DON'T**

DON'T use the Save method for a new workbook that has never been saved before. If you do, Excel saves the new workbook with its current name—for example, BOOK1.XLS. Instead, use the SaveAs method to assign a name to the workbook the first time you save it:

Object.SaveAs(**Filename**)

The SaveAs method includes several other arguments that enable you, among other things, to specify a file format or assign a password to the file. Use the Object Browser to see, paste, or get help on all the SaveAs method arguments. You can also refer to the Visual Basic Reference in the Help system.

> **DO** use the Workbook object's `Path` property to check whether a new file has been saved. If `Path` returns an empty string (`""`), then the workbook has never been saved before.

Closing a Workbook

When you're finished with a workbook, you should close it to save memory and to avoid cluttering the screen. You close a workbook by using one of the following forms of the `Close` method:

```
Workbooks.Close
Object.Close(SaveChanges)
```

The first syntax form simply closes every open workbook. Excel prompts you to save changes in the workbooks before closing them, if necessary. The second syntax form closes a specific workbook, denoted by **Object**. Use the **SaveChanges** argument as follows:

☐ If **SaveChanges** is `True`, Excel saves the workbook automatically before closing it.

☐ If **SaveChanges** is `False`, Excel closes the workbook without saving any changes.

☐ If you omit **SaveChanges**, Excel prompts you to save changes, if necessary.

Listing 18.6 demonstrates the `Close` method.

Listing 18.6. Using the `Close` method.

```
1:  Sub CloseAll()
2:  'Closes all open workbooks and prompts to save changes
3:
4:     Const qButtons = vbYesNo + vbQuestion
5:
6:     Dim Book As Workbook
7:     Dim Ans As Integer
8:     Dim MsgPrompt As String
9:
10:    For Each Book In Workbooks
11:      If Not Book.Saved Then
12:        MsgPrompt = "Save changes to " & Book.Name & "?"
13:        Ans = MsgBox(prompt:=MsgPrompt, Buttons:=qButtons)
14:        If Ans = vbYes Then
15:          Book.Close SaveChanges:=True
16:        Else
17:          Book.Close SaveChanges:=False
18:        End If
19:      Else
20:        Book.Close
21:      End If
22:    Next Book
23:  End Sub
```

This procedure closes all the open workbooks and prompts the user to save changes for each workbook with unsaved changes. Use a procedure like this one instead of the Workbooks.Close method when you need to prevent a user from canceling the operation; Excel's built-in Save prompts have a Cancel button. After declaring a constant and several variables (lines 4 through 8), the procedure starts a For Each loop to process all of the workbooks in the Workbooks collection.

If the workbook has changes that haven't been saved (line 11), a MsgBox function (line 12) asks whether to save the changes. If the user chooses the Yes button (so that vbYes is returned in the Ans variable), the procedure runs the Close method with SaveChanges set to True (line 14 and 15). Otherwise, the procedure closes the workbook with SaveChanges set to False (line 17). If the workbook doesn't have unsaved changes, the procedure runs the Close method without arguments (line 20).

DO	DON'T

DON'T assume that Excel runs a workbook's Auto_Close macros when you use the Close method; it doesn't. To run these macros, use the following method:

```
Object.RunAutoMacros(xlAutoClose)
```

Here, **Object** is a reference to the Workbook object you're closing.

DO investigate the full syntax of the Close method in the Object Browser or the Visual Basic Reference in the Help system. This method includes two other arguments that enable you to specify a filename for a workbook that has never been saved, and to route a workbook over a network.

Working with Worksheet Objects

Worksheet objects contain a number of properties and methods that you can exploit in your VBA code. With these properties and methods, you can activate and hide worksheets; add new worksheets to a workbook; and move, copy, rename, and delete worksheets. The next sections discuss each of these worksheet operations.

Returning a Worksheet Object

Each worksheet is a Worksheet object, and Worksheets is the collection of all the worksheets in a given workbook. To refer to a specific worksheet, use the Workbook object's Worksheets method:

Syntax

```
Object.Worksheets(Index)
```

Here, **Object** is an object reference to the Workbook object that contains the worksheet. **Index** can be either of the following:

☐ A number representing the worksheet that you want to use. 1 signifies the first worksheet in the workbook, 2 signifies the second worksheet, and so on.

☐ The name, as a string, of the worksheet you want to use. This is the name as it appears on the worksheet's tab.

Listing 18.7 shows an example of the most common way of using the Worksheets method—using a text string to identify a worksheet.

Type

Listing 18.7. Using the Worksheets method to return a worksheet.

```
1:    Sub SetWorksheetProtection()
2:    'Activates worksheet protection
3:
4:        Workbooks("DAY18.XLS").Worksheets("Sheet1").Protect _
5:                            Contents:=True, Scenarios:=True
6:        MsgBox "Protection for ""Sheet1"" sheet now active."
7:    End Sub
```

Analysis

Workbooks("DAY18.XLS").Worksheets("Sheet1") returns an object reference to the sheet named Sheet1 in the DAY18.XLS workbook. The Protect method sets up protection for the worksheet's contents and scenarios. The MsgBox statement tells the user that worksheet protection has been activated.

DO	DON'T

DO use the ActiveSheet object if you need to refer to the active worksheet.

DO use the Sheets collection, instead of the WorkSheets collection, when you need to refer to *every* sheet in a workbook (or you're not sure what kind of sheet you're selecting). The Sheets collection contains not only Worksheet objects but also Chart, Module, and DialogSheet objects.

DON'T specify the Workbook object if the procedure and worksheet are in the same workbook.

DON'T use numbers for the Index argument if you don't have to. Something such as Worksheets("June Sales") is clearer and easier to read than, say, Worksheets(6).

Activating a Worksheet

Most workbooks contain more than one worksheet, so your VBA program might need to switch from one worksheet to another. For example, you might need to display one worksheet for data entry and then switch to another worksheet to view a report or chart. You can switch among worksheets by using the `Activate` method:

`Object.Activate`

In this statement, **`Object`** is an object reference to the `Worksheet` object that you want to activate. Listing 18.8 shows an example of the `Activate` method.

Type

Listing 18.8. Using the `Activate` method to switch to a worksheet.

```
 1:  Sub DisplayReport()
 2:  'Activates the "Sheet1" sheet if the user wants to see it
 3:
 4:     Dim Ans As Integer, qBtns As Integer
 5:     Dim mPrompt As String
 6:
 7:     mPrompt = "Do you want to view ""Sheet1""?"
 8:     qBtns = vbYesNo + vbQuestion + vbDefaultButton2
 9:     Ans = MsgBox(prompt:=mPrompt, Buttons:=qBtns)
10:     If Ans = vbYes Then
11:       Workbooks("DAY18.XLS").Worksheets("Sheet1").Activate
12:     End If
13:  End Sub
```

Analysis

This procedure asks whether the user wants to see a particular worksheet—the default Sheet1, in this case (lines 7-9). If the user chooses the Yes button, the worksheet named *Sheet1* is activated (line 11).

DO	DON'T

DO use the `Select` method if you need to select a worksheet:

`Object``.Select`

This method is useful for creating three-dimensional references and for defining the sheets that you want printed. (A three-dimensional reference is a reference to a range of cells on more than one worksheet.)

DON'T activate a worksheet if you don't have to. For most `Worksheet` object properties and methods, you can simply use the `Worksheets` method to refer to the worksheet that you want to use. The following statement, for example, returns the standard width of the `June Sales` worksheet without activating the sheet:

`StdWidth = Worksheets("June Sales").StandardWidth`

Creating a New Worksheet

The Worksheets collection has an Add method that you can use to insert new worksheets into a workbook. The syntax for this method is

```
Object.Worksheets.Add([Before] [,After] [,Count] [,Type])
```

Here, **Object** is the Workbook object to which you want to add the new worksheet. The **Before** argument specifies the sheet before which the new sheet is added, and the **After** argument specifies the sheet after which the new sheet is added. (You can't use the **Before** and **After** arguments together in the same statement.) If you omit both **Before** and **After**, VBA adds the new worksheet before the active sheet.

Count is the number of new worksheets to add. (VBA adds one worksheet if you omit **Count**.) **Type** is the type of worksheet that you want. You have three choices for the **Type** argument: xlWorksheet (which is the default), xlExcel4MacroSheet, or xlExcel4IntlMacroSheet. Listing 18.9 shows the Add method in action.

Listing 18.9. Using the Add method to create a new worksheet.

```
 1:  Sub CreateTempWorksheet()
 2:  'Creates a new, temporary, worksheet and then hides it
 3:
 4:     Application.ScreenUpdating = False
 5:     Worksheets.Add
 6:     With ActiveSheet
 7:        .Name = "Temporary"
 8:        .Visible = False
 9:     End With
10:     Application.ScreenUpdating = True
11:  End Sub
```

This procedure is useful for creating a new worksheet that will hold intermediate results or other data that you don't want the user to see. After it turns off screen updates (line 4), the procedure adds a new worksheet (line 5). In the With statement (lines 6 through 9) two operations are performed on this new, active sheet. First, line 7 uses the Name property (described in the next section) to change the name of the new worksheet to Temporary. Second, line 8 hides the new worksheet by setting its Visible property to False.

Renaming a Worksheet

The name of a worksheet is the text that appears inside the sheet's tab. If you need to rename a worksheet, change the sheet's Name property:

```
Object.Name
```

Object is the worksheet you want to rename. Listing 18.9, which you've just seen, has an example procedure that changes a worksheet's Name property.

Copying and Moving a Worksheet

If you need to rearrange the sheets in a workbook, use the Copy and Move methods. For both methods, the syntax is identical:

```
Object.Copy([Before] [,After])
Object.Move([Before] [,After])
```

Object is an object reference to the worksheet you want to copy or move. *Before* specifies the worksheet before which the sheet is copied or moved, and *After* specifies the worksheet after which the sheet is copied or moved. (You can't use the *Before* and *After* arguments together in the same statement.) If you omit both *Before* and *After*, VBA creates a new workbook for the copied or moved sheet.

Listing 18.10 takes you through a procedure that uses the Move method.

Type

Listing 18.10. Using the Move method to move a worksheet.

```
 1:  Sub CreateWorksheetAtEnd()
 2:  'Creates a new worksheet at the end of the workbook
 3:
 4:     Dim NewSheet As String
 5:
 6:     Application.ScreenUpdating = False
 7:
 8:     Worksheets.Add before:=Worksheets(Worksheets.Count)
 9:     NewSheet = ActiveSheet.Name
10:     With Worksheets(NewSheet)
11:       .Move after:=Worksheets(Worksheets.Count)
12:       .Activate
13:     End With
14:
15:     Application.ScreenUpdating = True
16:  End Sub
```

After **CreateWorksheetAtEnd** declares a variable and turns off screen updating, it uses the Add method to add a worksheet (line 8). This call to the Add method uses the optional before argument to insert the new worksheet directly in front of the last worksheet already in the workbook. Line 8 determines the number of the last sheet in the workbook by using the Count property, which simply returns a count of the worksheets in the workbook. Then, the new worksheet's name is saved in the **NewSheet** variable.

Line 11 uses the Move method to move the new worksheet behind the last worksheet of the workbook. Again, the Count property is used to get the number of worksheets in the workbook. The new sheet is activated (line 12), and screen updates are turned on again (line 15).

DO	**DON'T**

DON'T forget to turn screen updating back on, if your procedure turns it off.

DO remember that you can also insert sheets after a specified sheet. The procedure in Listing 18.10 inserts a sheet before the last sheet and then moves it because Excel doesn't allow you to insert sheets at the end of a workbook. Use the `After` argument with the `Add` method to insert a worksheet anywhere except as the last sheet.

Deleting a Worksheet

To keep your workbooks manageable and to save disk space, you should delete worksheets that you don't need. This is especially true if your application creates temporary sheets to hold intermediate results (as shown in an example earlier in this lesson). Use the `Delete` method to delete a worksheet:

```
Object.Delete
```

Object is an object reference to the `Worksheet` you want to delete. Listing 18.11 shows an example of the `Delete` method.

18

Listing 18.11. Using the `Delete` method to delete a worksheet.

```
1:  Sub DeleteTemporarySheets()
2:  'Deletes all temporary worksheets
3:
4:     Dim Sheet As Worksheet
5:
6:     Application.DisplayAlerts = False
7:
8:     For Each Sheet In Workbooks("DAY18.XLS").Worksheets
9:        If InStr(1, Sheet.Name, "Temporary") Then
10:          Sheet.Delete
11:       End If
12:    Next Sheet
13:
14:    Application.DisplayAlerts = True
15: End Sub
```

This procedure cycles through every worksheet in a workbook and deletes all the temporary sheets that have been created. The procedure assumes that the temporary sheets have names such as *Temporary 1* and *Temporary 2*.

The procedure declares a `Worksheet` object variable—**Sheet**—and sets the `Application` object's `DisplayAlerts` property to `False` (line 6). This suppresses Excel's normal confirmation dialog box, which you see whenever you delete a worksheet. Line 8 starts a `For Each` loop to go through all the worksheets in the DAY18.XLS workbook. For each sheet, an `InStr` function tests whether the string `Temporary` is in the sheet name. If it is, line 10 deletes the sheet. When this process is complete, the `DisplayAlerts` property is set back to `True` (line 14).

DO	DON'T

DO use the *compare* argument in the `InStr` function to make a text comparison for sheet names, so that the comparison is not case-sensitive. The procedure in Listing 18.11 assumes that `Option Compare Text` is the current global comparison setting.

DON'T forget to turn Excel's alerts back on, if your procedure turns them off.

Methods That Return Range Objects

Most worksheet chores—whether entering information, cutting or copying data, or applying formatting options—involve cells, ranges, and range names. It should come as no surprise that many Excel object methods in VBA end up doing *something* to a range.

Just as you must select a worksheet range before you do anything to it, you must reference a worksheet range in a VBA procedure before you can do anything to it. To do that, you need to work with the most common of all Excel objects—the `Range` object. A `Range` object can be a single cell, a row or a column, a selection of cells, or even a three-dimensional range (that is, a range that includes selected cells on more than one worksheet). The following sections look at various methods and properties that return `Range` objects.

Using the *Range* Method

The easiest and most straightforward way of identifying a cell or range is with the `Range` method:

Object.Range(*Name*)

Object is a reference to the `Worksheet` object that contains the range. If you omit ***Object***, VBA assumes that the method applies to the `ActiveSheet` object. The ***Name*** argument is a range reference or range name entered as text.

Listing 18.12 shows an example of the `Range` method.

 Listing 18.12. Using the `Range` method to work with a range.

```
1:    Sub FormatRangeFont()
2:    'Sets the font of a range using the Range method
3:
```

```
4:      With Worksheets("Sheet1")
5:          .Range("A1:L1").Font.Size = 24
6:          .Range("A1:L1").Font.Bold = True
7:          .Range("A1:L1").Font.Name = "Times New Roman"
8:      End With
9:  End Sub
```

In this example, all three statements (lines 5 through 7) return the range A1:L1 on the worksheet named Sheet1. (Notice that you must enclose the range coordinates in quotation marks.)

The procedure in Listing 18.12 sets several font attributes for the specified range. In VBA, a Font is a property of the Range object, but Fonts are also objects in themselves. Their properties are simply the normal font attributes that you assign with the Font dialog box. Here's a sample of Font properties. In each case, **Object** is a Range object. Use the Object Browser or refer to the help system's Visual Basic Reference to see a full list of Font properties.

- ☐ **Object**.Font.Bold: Turns the bold font style on (True) or off (False).

- ☐ **Object**.Font.Italic: Turns the italic font style on (True) or off (False).

- ☐ **Object**.Font.Underline: Turns the underline font effect on (xlSingle or xlDouble) or off (xlNone).

- ☐ **Object**.Font.Name: Sets the name of the font's typeface. You enter the name as text.

- ☐ **Object**.Font.Size: Sets the size of the font in points.

The Range method also works with named ranges, as you can see in Listing 18.13.

Listing 18.13. Using a range name in the Range method.

```
1:  Sub PlayWelcomeMessage()
2:  'Plays a message using a range name in the Range method
3:
4:      If Application.CanPlaySounds Then
5:        With Worksheets("Sheet1")
6:            .Range("WelcomeMessage").SoundNote.Play
7:        End With
8:      Else
9:        MsgBox "This computer can't play sounds."
10:     End If
11: End Sub
```

This example assumes that a worksheet named *Sheet1* contains a cell named *WelcomeMessage*, and that this cell contains a sound note. The procedure uses the Application object's CanPlaySounds property to check whether the computer can play sounds. If the computer can play sounds, the cell that contains the note is specified by using both the *Sheet1* worksheet and the *WelcomeMessage* range name. Playing the sound involves running the Play method on the range's SoundNote property.

18

DO	**DON'T**

DO take advantage of the alternative syntax for the Range method that requires two arguments:

Object.Range(*Cell1*, *Cell2*)

As before, *Object* is the Worksheet object that contains the range. The *Cell1* argument defines the upper left corner of the range and *Cell2* defines the lower right corner. Each can be a cell address as text, a Range object consisting of a single cell, or an entire column or row.

The advantage of this syntax is that it separates the range corners into separate arguments, which enables you to modify each corner under procedural control. For example, you could set up variables named, for example, UpperLeft and LowerRight, and return Range objects of different sizes, as in

Range(UpperLeft, LowerRight)

DON'T use range coordinates in the Range method if you have range names available. Range names make your code much easier to decipher and debug.

Using the *Cells* Method

Although you can use the Range method to return a single cell, the Cells method also does the job and it gives you much greater flexibility. Its syntax is as follows:

Object.Cells(*RowIndex*, *ColumnIndex*)

Object is a reference to either the Worksheet or the Range object that contains the cell with which you want to work. If you omit *Object*, the method applies to the ActiveSheet object.

RowIndex is the row number of the cell. If *Object* is a worksheet, a *RowIndex* of 1 refers to row 1 on the sheet. If *Object* is a range, a *RowIndex* of 1 refers to the first row of the range.

ColumnIndex is the column of the cell. You can enter either a letter (as a literal constant or as a string variable) or a number to specify the column. If *Object* is a worksheet, a *ColumnIndex* of "A" or 1 refers to column A on the worksheet. If *Object* is a range, a *ColumnIndex* of "A" or 1 refers to the first column of the range.

Listing 18.14 shows an example of the Cells method.

Syntax

 Listing 18.14. Using the `Cells` method to return a cell.

```
 1:  Sub WriteNewData()
 2:  'Enters data from a dialog box into a worksheet
 3:
 4:      Dim I As Integer, DBRows As Integer, DBColumns As Integer
 5:      Dim DBTopRow As Integer, DBNewRow As Integer
 6:
 7:      'Get Database range data
 8:      With Range("Database")
 9:          DBRows = .Rows.Count
10:          DBColumns = .Columns.Count
11:          DBTopRow = .Row
12:          DBNewRow = DBTopRow + DBRows
13:      End With
14:
15:      'Enter dialog box data into cells in new row
16:      For I = 1 To DBColumns
17:          Cells(DBNewRow, I).Value = _
18:              DialogSheets("Dialog").EditBoxes(I).Caption
19:      Next I
20:  End Sub
```

 This procedure is part of a database maintenance application. The user enters the database information into a custom dialog box, and this procedure writes the new data into the worksheet at the bottom of the database range. The `With` statement in line 8 uses the range named `Database` to calculate the following variables:

DBRows: This is the number of rows in the `Database` range. It is calculated using the Range property `Rows.Count`.

DBColumns: This is the number of columns in the `Database` range. It is calculated using the `Columns.Count` property.

DBTopRow: This is the top row of the `Database` range. It is calculated using the `Row` property.

DBNewRow: This is the row immediately below the `Database` range—in other words, the row where the new data should be stored. It is calculated by adding **DBTopRow** and **DBRows.**

The `For...Next` loop performs the actual data entry. The loop counter (**i**) runs from 1 (because, in this case, the `Database` range starts in column A) to `DBColumns`. Inside the loop, the `Cells` method returns each cell in the new row and the cell's `Value` property is set to the appropriate edit box caption. This code assumes there is a one-to-one correspondence between the edit boxes in the dialog box and the fields in the database. This means that the first edit box corresponds to the first database field, the second edit box to the second field, and so on. (The "Entering Values and Formulas" section later in this chapter has more information on the `Value` property.)

18

Using the *Offset* Method

When you define your Range objects, you often don't know the specific range address to use. For example, you might need to refer to the cell that is two rows down from and one column to the right of the active cell. Although you could find the address of the active cell and calculate the address of the other cell, VBA gives you an easier and more flexible way—the Offset method. Offset returns a Range object that is offset from a specified range by a certain number of rows and columns.

```
Object.Offset([RowOffset] [,ColumnOffset])
```

Object is a reference to the original Range object. *RowOffset* is the number of rows to offset *Object*. You can use a positive number (to move down), a negative number (to move up), or 0 (to use the same rows). If you omit *RowOffset*, VBA uses 0.

ColumnOffset is the number of columns to offset *Object*. Again, you can use a positive number (to move right), a negative number (to move left), or 0 (to use the same columns). If you omit *ColumnOffset*, VBA uses 0.

Listing 18.15 shows a procedure that uses the Offset method.

Type

Listing 18.15. Using the Offset method to return a range.

```
 1:  Sub SelectData()
 2:  'Selects the data area of a database range
 3:
 4:      Dim DBRows As Integer
 5:
 6:      Worksheets("Sheet1").Select
 7:      With Range("Database")
 8:          DBRows = .Rows.Count
 9:          .Offset(1, 0).Resize(DBRows - 1).Select
10:      End With
11:  End Sub
```

This procedure selects the data area of a range named Database—that is, the range that includes only the data and not the column headings. This is handy if you need to perform a global operation on the data, such as sorting or applying a format.

Line 6 selects the Sheet1 worksheet, and the With statement in line 7 specifies the Range object on the worksheet named Database. Line 8 obtains the number of rows in the range by using the Rows.Count property of the Range object, storing it in the **DBRows** variable.

Line 9 is where all the interesting things happen. The Offset(1, 0) method returns a range that is offset from the Database range by one row down. Because this new range includes a

(presumably) blank row below the Database range, you must eliminate this extra row. To do that, you can use the Resize method to change the size of the range:

```
Object.Resize([RowSize] [,ColumnSize])
```

Object is an object reference to the range you want to resize. **RowSize** is the number of rows in the returned range. **ColumnSize** is the number of columns in the returned range. If you omit **RowSize** or **ColumnSize**, the returned range uses the same number of rows or columns, respectively. In line 9, the Resize(DBRows - 1) expression removes the unneeded bottom row from the offset range.

The Select method in line 9 selects the new range. (The "Selecting a Range" section later in this chapter has more information on the Select method.)

Other Methods and Properties That Return Ranges

Range, Cells, and Offset are the most common methods for returning Range objects, but they are by no means the only ones. In Listing 18.15 you saw how the Resize method can return a range of a specific size. A few more methods and properties that return Range objects are

- [ ] **[cellRef]**: You can return a single cell by enclosing the cell reference in square brackets. For example, [A1].Font.Size = 16 sets the font in cell A1 to size 16. Notice that, in this case, no quotation marks are used around the cell reference (**cellRef**).

- [ ] **Object**.Rows(**Index**): This method returns a row in the worksheet or range specified by **Object**. If you omit **Object**, VBA uses ActiveSheet. **Index** is the row number. If **Object** is a worksheet, an **Index** of 1 refers to row 1 on the sheet. If **Object** is a range, an **Index** of 1 refers to the first row of the range.

- [ ] **Object**.EntireRow: This property returns the entire row or rows that contain the range specified by **Object**.

- [ ] **Object**.Columns(**Index**): This method returns a column in the worksheet or range specified by **Object**. If you omit **Object**, VBA uses ActiveSheet. **Index** is the column letter or number. If **Object** is a worksheet, an **Index** of "A" or 1 refers to column A on the sheet. If **Object** is a range, an **Index** of "A" or 1 refers to the first column of the range.

- [ ] **Object**.EntireColumn: This property returns the entire column or columns that contain the range specified by **Object**.

- [ ] **Object**.CurrentRegion: This property returns the *current region* of the range **Object**. The current region is defined as the area surrounding the current cell or range that is bounded by blank rows on the top and bottom and blank columns on the left and right.

Working with Cells and Ranges

Now that you know how to return a Range object, you can take advantage of the long list of Range properties and methods. The next section examines a few of these properties and methods. Use the Object Browser to see all of the Range object's methods and properties and to access the online help text for the Range object.

Selecting a Cell or Range

To select a cell, or range of cells, use the Select method:

```
Object.Select
```

Object is a reference to the Range object you want to select. Listing 18.16 shows an example.

 Listing 18.16. Using the Select method to select a range.

```
 1:  Sub CreateChart()
 2:  'Creates a chart with data from the Sales range
 3:
 4:     With Workbooks("DAY18.XLS").Worksheets("Sheet1")
 5:        .Activate
 6:        .Range("Sales").Select
 7:     End With
 8:
 9:     Charts.Add
10:  End Sub
```

 This procedure creates a new chart sheet from a selected range. Line 5 activates the Workbooks("DAY18.XLS").Worksheets("Sheet1") worksheet. Line 6 selects the range on the worksheet named Sales. Line 9 executes the Charts object's Add method to create the chart sheet.

DO	**DON'T**
DO use the Selection property to return the Range object that is currently selected. **DON'T** select a range if you don't have to. Select is one of the slowest of all VBA methods, so avoiding it wherever possible speeds up your code.	

Working with Values and Formulas

Most of your VBA programs for Excel will utilize worksheet data in one form or another. For example, a procedure might need to read the contents of a cell to perform a data validation

routine. Alternatively, your program might gather data by using a custom dialog box, and you might need to transfer the data entered in the dialog box's edit boxes into the appropriate worksheet cells. (See Listing 18.14 for an example of doing this.)

If you need to get the contents of a cell, or if you need to enter data into a range, VBA offers two Range object properties—Value and Formula. The syntax for each one is

```
Object.Value
```

```
Object.Formula
```

In both cases, **Object** represents an object reference to the Range object with which you want to work. To get the contents of a cell, follow these guidelines:

- ☐ If all you want is the cell's result, use the Value property. For example, if cell A1 contains the formula =2*2, Range("A1").Value returns 4.

- ☐ If you want the cell's formula, use the Formula property. For example, if Cell A1 contains the formula =2*2, Range("A1").Formula returns the text string =2*2.

To enter data in a cell or range, you can use Value or Formula interchangeably. Listing 18.17 shows several examples.

Type

Listing 18.17. Using the `Value` and `Formula` methods to enter data.

```
 1:  Sub CreateLoanPmtCalculator()
 2:  'Creates a loan payment calculator on Sheet2
 3:
 4:     Worksheets("Sheet2").Select
 5:
 6:     With Range("A1")       'Enter labels
 7:       .Value = "Loan Payment Calculator"
 8:       .Font.Bold = True
 9:       .Font.Italic = True
10:       .Font.Size = 18
11:       .Offset(1).Value = "Rate"
12:       .Offset(2).Value = "Period"
13:       .Offset(3).Value = "Amount"
14:       .Offset(5).Value = "Payment"
15:     End With
16:
17:     'Enter number formats and formula
18:     With Range("A1")
19:       .Offset(1, 1).NumberFormat = "0.00%"
20:       .Offset(3, 1).NumberFormat = "$#,##0_);[Red]($#,##0)"
21:       .Offset(5, 1).NumberFormat = "$#,##0.00_);[Red]($#,##0.00)"
22:       .Offset(5, 1).Formula = "=PMT($B$2/12, $B$3*12, $B$4)"
23:     End With
24:  End Sub
```

This procedure creates a simple loan payment calculator on Sheet2 in the active workbook. The first With statement (line 6) uses cell A1 as a starting point. This cell's Value property is set to contain the text "Loan Payment Calculator" (line 7), and some font options are set (lines 8-10). The next four lines (11-14) use the Value property of cells A2, A3, A4, and A6 to enter the labels. Notice the use of the Offset method to work with these cells.

The second With statement (line 18) also uses cell A1. The actions in this procedure have been divided into two different With statements for extra clarity; there is no technical requirement that they be divided this way. The next three lines (19-21) set the numeric format of cells B2, B4, and B6. This is accomplished by using the NumberFormat property of the referenced range:

```
Object.NumberFormat = FormatString
```

Object is an object reference to the cell or range to format, and **FormatString** is a text string that specifies the formatting.

Finally, line 22 uses the Formula property to enter the payment formula in cell B6.

Defining a Range Name

Range names in VBA are Name objects. To define them, you use the Add method for the Names collection, which usually is the collection of defined names in a workbook. Here is an abbreviated syntax for the Names collection's Add method. (This method has a total of nine arguments, so use the Object Browser to see all the available arguments and to access the online help for full details on the Add method.)

Syntax

```
Names.Add(Name, RefersTo, RefersToR1C1)
```

The **Name** argument is any string expression specifying the name that you want to use for the new named range. The **RefersTo** and **RefersToR1C1** arguments describe the range to which the name refers. Use these arguments as follows:

☐ **RefersTo**: Use this argument to enter the range description in A1-style—for example: "=Sales!$A$1:$C$6".

☐ **RefersToR1C1**: Use this argument when the range description either is in R1C1-style— for example, "=Sales!R1C1:R6C3"—or when the range description is a method or property that returns a range—for example, Range("A1:C6") or Selection.

Listing 18.18 shows an example of the Names collection's Add method.

Listing 18.18. Naming a range using the `Names` object's `Add` method.

```
1:   Sub WriteNewData()
2:   'Enters data from a dialog box, then renames
3:   'the Database1 range
4:
5:       Dim I As Integer, DBRows As Integer, DBColumns As Integer
6:       Dim DBTopRow As Integer, DBNewRow As Integer
7:
8:       Worksheets("Sheet3").Select
9:
10:      With Range("Database1")    'Get Database range data
11:          DBRows = .Rows.Count
12:          DBColumns = .Columns.Count
13:          DBTopRow = .Row
14:          DBNewRow = DBTopRow + DBRows
15:      End With
16:
17:      'Enter dialog box data into cells in new row
18:      For I = 1 To DBColumns
19:          Cells(DBNewRow, I).Value = _
20:              DialogSheets("Dialog1").EditBoxes(I).Caption
21:      Next I
22:
23:      'Define new Database range name
24:      Range("Database1").Resize(DBRows + 1).Select
25:      Names.Add Name:="Database1", RefersToR1C1:=Selection
26:
27:      Cells(DBNewRow, 1).Activate 'Activate 1st cell in new row
28:  End Sub
```

Analysis

The first 21 lines of this procedure are identical to Listing 18.14, except that the named range is called Database1, and the selected worksheet is Sheet3. As in Listing 18.4, these first lines take data from a custom dialog box and enter it in the next line below a range named Database1. This revised version of the procedure adds two lines that redefine the Database1 range name. Line 24 resizes the Database1 range to include the new row and uses the Select method to select this new range. Line 25 uses Names.Add method to rename the range—in this case, the range is given the same name as before, but the new named range now includes more rows than it did before. Notice this statement uses the RefersToR1C1 argument with the Selection property. To unselect the range, line 27 uses the Cells and Activate methods to activate the first cell in the new row.

Cutting, Copying, and Clearing Data

If your procedures must do some basic worksheet editing chores, the Cut, Copy, and Clear methods can handle the job.

The Cut and Copy methods use identical syntax:

Syntax

```
Object.Cut([Destination])
Object.Copy([Destination])
```

Object is an object reference to the Range object you want to cut or copy. **Destination** is the cell or range where you want the cut or copied range to be pasted. If you omit the **Destination** argument, the data is cut or copied to the Windows Clipboard.

To remove data from a range, you can use the Cut method with or without the destination argument, or you can use any of the following methods:

```
Object.Clear
Object.ClearContents
Object.ClearFormats
Object.ClearNotes
```

In each case, **Object** is an object reference to the range you want to clear. The Clear method removes everything from the range—content, formatting, and notes. ClearContents clears the contents of **Object**. ClearFormats clears the formatting of **Object**. ClearNotes clears the notes, including sound notes, from **Object**.

Listing 18.19 shows examples of the Cut, Copy, and Clear methods.

Type

Listing 18.19. Using the Cut, Copy, and Clear methods.

```
1:    Sub CopyToTempSheet()
2:    'Copies data to a temporary worksheet
3:
4:        Dim LastCell As Range
5:        Dim oldSheet As String
6:
7:        Application.ScreenUpdating = False
8:
9:        oldSheet = ActiveSheet.Name        'current sheet name
10:       Worksheets.Add                     'create temp worksheet
11:       ActiveSheet.Name = "Temporary"
12:       Worksheets("Sheet1").Select        'select Sheet1
13:
14:       Set LastCell = Range("A1").SpecialCells(xlLastCell)
15:       With Worksheets("Temporary")
16:          .Cells.Clear
17:          Range("A1", LastCell).Copy Destination:=.Range("A1")
18:       End With
19:
20:       Sheets(oldSheet).Select  'restore original sheet
21:       Application.ScreenUpdating = True
22:    End Sub
23:
24:
25:    Sub RestoreFromTempSheet()
26:    'Restores data from temporary worksheet
27:
```

```
28:     Dim LastCell As Range
29:     Dim oldSheet As String
30:
31:     Application.ScreenUpdating = False
32:     oldSheet = ActiveSheet.Name
33:
34:     Worksheets("Sheet1").Select
35:     With Worksheets("Temporary")
36:        Set LastCell = .Range("A1").SpecialCells(xlLastCell)
37:        .Range("A1", LastCell).Cut Destination:=Range("A1")
38:     End With
39:
40:     Sheets(oldSheet).Select
41:     Application.ScreenUpdating = True
42:  End Sub
```

Analysis

The first procedure, **CopyToTempSheet**, adds a worksheet named Temporary, and selects the worksheet named Sheet1. Next, the procedure copies all the data from the active worksheet and stores it in the temporary worksheet. This procedure uses the SpecialCells(xlLastCell) method (line 14) to return the last cell in the active sheet, and stores the resulting Range object reference in the **LastCell** variable. Then, inside a With statement, two actions are performed on the Temporary worksheet. Line 16 uses Clear to clear the entire sheet. (The Cells method without any arguments returns every cell in a sheet.) Line 17 uses Copy to copy the range defined by A1 in the upper-left corner and **LastCell** in the lower-right corner. The destination is cell A1 in the Temporary worksheet.

The second procedure, **RestoreFromTempSheet**, essentially reverses the process. This time, **LastCell** is set to the last cell in the Temporary worksheet (line 36). The range from A1 to **LastCell** is cut and pasted to cell A1 in the active worksheet (line 37). (The active worksheet is Sheet1, selected in line 34.)

DO	DON'T

DO use the Paste or PasteSpecial methods with a Worksheet or Range object to paste data from the Clipboard to a worksheet. The syntax for the Paste method is

Object.Paste ([*Destination*], [*Link*])

Object is any valid object reference to a worksheet. The optional argument *Destination* is any range object. The data is pasted beginning at the top-left corner of the range. If you omit the *Destination* argument, the data is pasted to the current selection. You can specify the *Destination* argument only if the contents of the Clipboard can be pasted to a range; using the *Destination* argument is the same as using the Paste editing command. The optional *Link* argument, if True, indicates that a link should be established to the data source; using the *Link* argument is the same as using the Paste Link editing command. You cannot use the *Destination* and *Link* arguments together in the same statement.

DO remember that the various Clear methods delete the data outright; it is *not* preserved on the Clipboard. Use the Cut method with no arguments to remove data from the worksheet and place the data in the Clipboard for later use.

Summary

Today's lesson showed you how to use Visual Basic for Applications to control Excel. You learned basic techniques for working with workbooks, worksheets, and ranges.

You saw that you use the Workbooks(*Index*) method to return a Workbook object, where *Index* is usually the name of the workbook as a string. You also learned how to use the Open method to open a workbook, the Workbooks.Add method to create a new workbook, the Save method to save a workbook, and the Close method to close a workbook.

To return a Worksheet object, you learned how to use the Worksheets(*Index*) method, where *Index* is the name of the worksheet. Other important Worksheet methods and properties include Activate (for activating a worksheet), Worksheets.Add (for creating a new worksheet), Name (for returning or setting a worksheet's name), and Delete (for deleting a worksheet).

You also learned that VBA provides a number of methods for returning a Range object. The most common is Range, but you can also use Cells (for returning a single cell) and Offset (for returning a range offset from a specified range). Range objects have dozens of properties and methods, and you learned about a few of them. These included Select (for selecting a range), Value and Formula (for returning cell contents and entering values and formulas), Names.Add (for defining range names), as well as Cut, Copy, and Clear.

Q&A

Q I want to create a new workbook based on a template, so I'm using the Template argument in the Workbooks.Add method. Unfortunately, Excel keeps giving me an error. What am I doing wrong?

A The likely problem is that your template isn't stored in Excel's XLStart subdirectory. When you use the Template argument, Excel looks in the XLStart directory for the template file. If it doesn't find the file there, Excel then looks in the alternate startup directory (if there is one); if Excel still can't find the specified template file, Excel displays an error message. You can solve the problem in one of two ways: you can change your VBA code to specify the full path for the template you want to use, or

you can designate the directory that contains the template file as your alternate startup directory.

There are two techniques that you can use to create an alternate startup directory:

☐ Use the **Tools | O**ptions command, select the General tab in the Options dialog box, and then enter the directory in the Alternate Startup File **L**ocation edit box.

☐ Set the `Application` object's `AltStartupPath` property equal to a text string that defines the directory.

Whichever technique you use to designate the alternate startup directory, you'll need to restart Excel to put the change into effect.

Q **The Workbook object's `Name` property returns the name of the workbook as it appears in the title bar. Is there any way to get the full path name of the workbook, including the drive and directory where the file is stored?**

A Yes. You just need to use the `FullName` property:

`Object.FullName`

Here, `Object` is a reference to the workbook for which you want the path name. If all you want is the workbook's drive and directory, use the `Path` property instead.

Q **What if I want to print a workbook or worksheet from a VBA procedure?**

A No problem. Just use the `PrintOut` method with the following syntax:

`Object.PrintOut([From] [,To] [,Copies] [,Preview])`

`Object` is a reference to any printable object, such as a `Workbook`, `Worksheet`, or `Range`. `From` is an optional argument that specifies the first page to print. `To` is also optional; it specifies the last page to print. `Copies` determines the number of copies you want. If you omit `Copies`, Excel prints one copy. `Preview` determines whether the print preview screen is displayed before printing. The screen is displayed if `Preview` is `True`; the screen is not displayed if `Preview` is `False` or is omitted. The `PrintOut` method also has arguments to specify the active printer and whether to print to a file. Refer to VBA's online help for more information on the `PrintOut` method.

Q **In the "Opening a Workbook" section, you showed me how to display Excel's built-in Open dialog box. Can I access any other built-in dialog boxes in my VBA procedures?**

A Absolutely. Just use the `Application.Dialog(xlConstant).Show` method, where `xlConstant` is one of Excel's predefined constants. `xlConstant` specifies the dialog box that you want to display, such as `xlDialogOpen`. To see a complete list of Excel's predefined constants, select the **View | O**bject Browser command from any module. In the Object Browser dialog box, select Excel in the **L**ibraries/Workbooks drop-down list, select Constants in the **O**bjects/Modules list, and look in the **M**ethods/Properties list for constants that begin with `xlDialog`. You'll see there are dozens of these constants that enable you to display just about any Excel dialog box.

18

Workshop

Answers are in Appendix A.

Quiz

1. If you use the Open method to load a workbook, does Excel automatically run the workbook's Auto_Open procedures?

2. What's the difference between the Save method, the SaveAs method, and the SaveCopyAs method?

3. What happens if you run the Save method on a new, unsaved workbook?

4. When you use the Copy or Move methods on a worksheet, what happens if you omit both the Before and After arguments?

5. What's the difference between the Worksheets collection and the Sheets collection?

6. What are the three main methods for returning a range, and how do they differ?

7. The following two procedures perform similar tasks. Can you figure out what they're doing?

```
Sub FillAcross()
  Dim SheetArray As Variant
  SheetArray = Array("Sheet1", "Sheet2", "Sheet3")
  Worksheets("Sheet1").Range("A1").Value = "Sheet Title"
  Worksheets(SheetArray).FillAcrossSheets _
    Range:=Worksheets("Sheet1").Range("A1")
End Sub

Sub SpearTest()
Dim SheetArray As Variant
  SheetArray = Array("Sheet1", "Sheet2", "Sheet3")
  Worksheets(SheetArray).Select
  Worksheets("Sheet1").Range("A1").Activate
  Selection.Value = "Sheet Title"
End Sub
```

8. For returning the contents of a cell, what's the difference between the Value and Formula properties?

9. Under which circumstances should you use the RefersToR1C1 argument in the Names.Add method instead of RefersTo?

10. Name the five methods that you can use to remove data from a range.

Exercises

1. Write a procedure that saves every open workbook. The code should check for new, unnamed workbooks. If the workbook is unnamed, the procedure should ask whether the workbook should be saved. If so, the procedure should display the Save As dialog box to enable the user to supply a filename and storage location.

2. Excel doesn't allow you to cut or copy a *multiple selection*—that is, a selection that includes multiple, noncontiguous ranges. Write a procedure that enables you to cut or copy multiple selections to the same position in a different worksheet. (HINT: The Areas method returns a collection that consists of all the ranges in a multiple selection.)

3. **BUG BUSTER:** The following procedure executes three Names.Add methods. None of these statements causes an error, but each one creates unexpected results. Can you see why?

```
Sub NameTests()
    Names.Add Name:="Test1", RefersTo:="Sheet4!$A$1"
    Names.Add Name:="Test2",
RefersTo:=Worksheets("Sheet4").Range("A1:E10")
    Names.Add Name:="Test3", RefersTo:="='June Sales'!A1:A10"
End Sub
```

4. **BUG BUSTER:** The following code produces an error. Can you find the culprit?

```
Sub ApplyTitleFont()
    Dim TitleRange As Range
    TitleRange = ActiveWindow.Selection
    With TitleRange
        .Font.Size = 24
        .Font.Bold = True
        .Font.Underline = True
    End With
End Sub
```

5. Listing 18.14 showed you how to enter the results of a custom dialog box into a new row of a worksheet database. Write a procedure that performs the opposite function. It should load the contents of a database record—a row—into the edit boxes of a custom dialog box. As in Listing 18.14, assume that there is a one-to-one correspondence between the database fields and the dialog box edit boxes; you don't have to create the dialog box.

Working with Other Applications: OLE and OLE Automation

The next two chapters show you how to use Visual Basic for Applications to work with and control other applications, such as Microsoft Word, Microsoft Access, or any other application that supports OLE and OLE automation. In today's lesson, you'll learn:

☐ What OLE is and what you can do with it.

☐ How to link and embed objects in a worksheet.

☐ How to work with linked and embedded objects.

☐ How to use OLE automation to control other applications.

What Is OLE?

Before you learn how to use Visual Basic for Applications to work with OLE and OLE automation, you need to understand what OLE is and what you can do with it.

A Brief History of OLE

Object linking and embedding—abbreviated OLE and pronounced *oh-lay*—Version 2.0 is Microsoft's latest attempt at enabling users to create a true *compound document*. A compound document is any file that contains data from more than one application. For example, an Excel worksheet that contains annotations from a word processor, pictures from a paint program, and recordings from a sound program in addition to its native numbers and formulas is a compound document. As you'll see, OLE 2.0 makes it much easier and simpler for applications to interact with one another.

With early versions of Microsoft Windows, you could exchange data between applications only by using the Clipboard. You copied the data from one program to the Clipboard and then pasted it from the Clipboard into another application. If you needed to make changes to the data, you had to open the original application, open the appropriate file, make the changes, and then repeat the entire copying and pasting process.

Although using the Clipboard to transfer information between applications is better than not being able to transfer information at all, it still isn't the most efficient way to work. Microsoft introduced Dynamic Data Exchange (DDE) as a way of reducing the number of steps involved in transferring and updating information between two different applications. To use DDE, you still begin the process by creating data in one application—the *server*—and then copying that data to the Clipboard. However, an application that supports DDE—the *client*—enables you to use the Paste Link command instead of the regular Paste command to paste the data from the Clipboard into another application. The Paste Link command establishes a communications link between the two applications. This communications link gives you two advantages:

☐ If both applications are running at the same time and the data created by the server application changes, the client document is updated automatically.

☐ If you edit the linked data in the server application while the client application is closed, the linked data is updated in the client application automatically. The linked data is updated either when you reopen the file containing the linked data in the client application, or when you use an explicit Update command in the client application.

DO	DON'T

DON'T confuse the terms *client* and *server*. These terms are used throughout this chapter and the remaining chapters of this book, so it's important that you understand what they mean. The client is always the application that receives the data; the server is always the application that supplies the data. An analogy to keep in mind is the relationship between a customer and a business. The customer (that is, the client) requests goods and services (data) from the business that provides those goods and services (the server).

DDE is a significant improvement over the original copy-and-paste technique, but it still has some deficiencies. First, data pasted from the Clipboard, regardless of whether it is pasted with a DDE link, is simply inserted into the client application with little or no formatting. Second, making changes to the data can be difficult. To make changes in DDE linked data, you must switch to, or start, the server application for the linked data. At best, this situation remains somewhat inconvenient. However, it poses special difficulties if you're not sure which application is the server for the DDE linked data, or if you can't remember which server document contains the source data.

To address these issues, Microsoft took a new approach to sharing data: Object Linking and Embedding. With OLE, data pasted from the server application appears in the client document as an *object*. Each object can be pasted in one of two ways: *linked* or *embedded*. Both types of OLE object store the OLE server's name, and any information that the server needs. The features of the two types of OLE object are:

☐ **Linked**: The object contains an image of the server data and maintains a link between the client and the server, much as DDE does. The original data remains in a separate file under the control of the server application. If the data changes, the link ensures that the client object is updated automatically. In general, you should paste an object as linked when other applications might require access to the same data file.

☐ **Embedded**: The object contains a stand-alone version of the server data—essentially a copy of the server data. No link is established between the server and the client because none is needed. The client object contains not only the data but also all the underlying information associated with the server application, such as the name of the application, the file structure, and formatting codes. In general, you should paste an object as embedded when you'll be working with the data only from inside the client application.

19

Another advantage of OLE is that, in many cases, you don't need a server document. You can create the data by starting the server application within the client application and then inserting the data into the client document as an embedded object. This means, for example, you could insert an empty Word document into an Excel worksheet as an embedded OLE object, and *then* type the letter, memo, note, or whatever.

Whether you link or embed data, an OLE object retains the original formatting of the data. This means that OLE objects appear in the client document exactly as they do in the server application. An OLE object stores the name of its server application, and, if the OLE object is linked, the name of the server file the object came from is stored in the OLE object as well. This means that you never need to know which application and which file are the source of the embedded data. You simply double-click the object: OLE loads the server application and, if necessary, opens the correct source data file.

OLE 2.0 also gives you the following advantages:

☐ **Drag-and-drop data sharing**: You can move information between two open OLE 2.0 applications simply by dragging selected data from one application and dropping it in the other. If you want to copy the data, hold down the Ctrl key while dragging.

☐ **In-place inserting**: If you insert an OLE 2.0 object from within the client application, the client activates in-place inserting. With in-place inserting, certain features of the client window—for example, toolbars and menu commands—are temporarily replaced by the OLE server's features; the server application is not displayed in a separate window. In other words, the *document* stays the same and the surrounding application changes.

☐ **In-place editing**: With in-place editing, when you double-click an OLE 2.0 object to edit it, the object remains in the document, and the client window changes as it does with in-place inserting.

☐ **OLE automation**: For a VBA programmer, the most exciting development in OLE 2.0 is OLE automation. This feature exposes an OLE 2.0 application's objects, such as a Worksheet or Range object in Excel, to other OLE 2.0 applications. This makes it possible for you to write VBA procedures in one application that control objects in another application as easily as VBA controls objects in its own host application. For example, a VBA procedure in Excel can use OLE to control application objects in another OLE 2.0 application, such as Microsoft Access or Microsoft Project. Any application that supports OLE automation exposes some or all of its objects, whether or not it also supports VBA. This means that you can use your VBA programs to control objects in applications such as Microsoft Word, which does not have VBA, but *does* function as an OLE server.

How Does Visual Basic for Applications Fit In?

Microsoft designed Visual Basic for Applications with OLE in mind—in fact, many of the Excel objects that you work with in VBA are also OLE automation objects. In particular, VBA provides you with a special object and object collection—OLEObject and OLEObjects—specifically for the purpose of accessing OLE features in other applications. OLEObject and its related collection, OLEObjects, have many properties and methods that enable you to create and work with either linked or embedded data.

In addition, VBA supports OLE automation. This means that a VBA procedure in Excel, for example, can access and manipulate the objects in another OLE 2.0 automation application just as though the VBA procedure is working in the other application itself. VBA's OLE automation techniques are examined later in this lesson.

Adding Linked and Embedded Objects

OLE adds powerful features to your application. The price that end-users pay for this advanced technology is added complexity. This is especially true for novice users, who might be uncomfortable with the various choices available in a typical OLE operation. For example, if you've copied data from an OLE server application, the client's Paste Special command gives you a number of choices: you can paste the information as an object, or as a picture or text (depending on the data); you can paste the data linked or unlinked; and you can paste the data as an icon or in full view.

You can use VBA procedures that manipulate OLE objects to simplify tasks for your program's users, because VBA gives you control over each of these decisions at the procedural level. For example, you can give your users a single command or toolbar button that creates a specified OLE object but hides all the details and choices involved in creating that OLE object. The next sections show you how to create OLE objects with VBA.

Using the *Add* Method for the *OLEObjects* Collection

In Excel VBA, each linked or embedded OLE object is an OLEObject, and the collection of all OLE objects in a worksheet is OLEObjects. To insert a new OLE object in a sheet, use the Add method with the following syntax:

Syntax

```
Sheet.OLEObjects.Add([ClassType] [,FileName] [,Link] [,DisplayAsIcon]
➥                      [,IconFileName] [,IconIndex] [,IconLabel])
```

For this method, *Sheet* represents any valid object reference to a `Worksheet` object. The `OLEObjects.Add` method has these arguments:

☐ *ClassType*: This optional argument is a string expression specifying the class name of the object you want to insert. Use this argument when you want to insert a new (blank or empty) OLE object. For example, to insert a new Word for Windows document, you would use the string `Word.Document.6` for the *ClassType* argument. (The next section, "Looking Up an Object's Class Type," explains how to determine the class type of various OLE objects.) You must include either the *ClassType* argument or the *FileName* argument when you use the `OLEObjects.Add` method.

☐ *FileName*: This optional argument is a string expression specifying the filename of the object you want to insert; the filename must have an extension corresponding to a registered OLE server application. Use *FileName* argument to insert an existing file into a worksheet as an OLE object. For example, if you wanted to insert an existing Word for Windows document file named MYWORDS.DOC from a folder named ACCOUNTS on drive C, you would use the string `C:\ACCOUNTS\MYWORDS.DOC` as the *FileName* argument. If you include the *ClassType* argument, the `Add` method ignores the *FileName* argument.

☐ *Link*: This optional argument is a Boolean value that determines whether the object created from *FileName* is linked or embedded. If `True`, the OLE object inserted by the `Add` method is linked to the original file. If `False` or omitted, the object is embedded. The *Link* argument is ignored if you use the *ClassType* argument.

☐ *DisplayAsIcon*: This optional argument is a Boolean value that determines how the object is displayed. If `True`, the object is displayed as an icon. If `False` or omitted, the object is displayed in its normal form.

☐ *IconFileName*: Use this optional argument only if *DisplayAsIcon* is `True`. *IconFileName* is a string specifying the name of the file that contains the icon you want to display for the inserted OLE object. If you omit *IconFileName*, or the specified file doesn't contain any icons, the default icon for the OLE class is used.

☐ *IconIndex*: Some files contain more than one icon; use the *IconIndex* argument to select which icon in the file you want to display. Icon numbering starts at 0; the first icon in a file is 0, the second is 1, and so on. Use *IconIndex* only if *DisplayAsIcon* is `True` and you've included the *IconFileName* argument. If you specify an icon number that doesn't exist, the first icon in the icon file is used.

☐ *IconLabel*: Use this optional argument (only if *DisplayAsIcon* is `True`) to customize the label for the OLE object's icon. The *IconLabel* argument can be any string expression.

The next few sections show you how to use the `Add` method.

Looking Up an Object's Class Type

Before you learn how to put the Add method of OLEObjects to work, you need to know how to
determine an object's class type, so you can supply legitimate values for the ClassType argument.

> **Note:** OLE objects are divided into various object groups, known formally as *object
> classes*. An OLE object's *class* indicates exactly what kind of object it is—an Excel
> worksheet, an Access database, a Word for Windows document, and so on. Each
> class has a unique name and identifier code that designates its specific OLE object
> class. Windows 95 and OLE 2.0 use the class type to determine which application
> is the server for a particular linked or embedded OLE object.

Windows 95 maintains a Registry database which contains, among other things, information
about the applications installed on your system—including specific information about OLE
objects. To find out the class type—also called the *programmatic ID*—of any OLE object
available on your system, you can look up the object's type in the Windows 95 Registry database.

Starting the Windows 95 Registry Editor

To view the contents of the Registry database, you'll need to use the Registry Editor utility
program provided with Windows 95. (The Registry Editor is typically installed in the Windows
95 directory but is not placed on the Windows 95 Start menu.) To start the Registry Editor
program, follow these steps:

1. From the Windows 95 Start menu, choose the **R**un command.
2. In the **O**pen edit box, type **C:\Windows\Regedit.exe** (assuming Windows 95 is
   installed in the Windows folder on drive C) and then choose OK. Windows 95 starts
   the Registry Editor, which displays the window shown in Figure 19.1. The exact
   appearance of the tree diagram on your system may be different, depending on your
   specific system's configuration.

> **Note:** The Windows 95 Registry database replaces the WIN.INI, SYSTEM.INI,
> and REG.DAT files used by previous versions of Windows by combining the
> information into a single database structure. The Windows 95 Registry actually
> consists of several files: SYSTEM.DAT, USER.DAT, and POLICY.POL. The
> POLICY.POL file is an optional component used in Windows 95 network
> configurations. Every Windows 95 system will have the SYSTEM.DAT and
> USER.DAT files. The Windows 95 Registry Editor reads both data files simulta-
> neously and displays them as if they are a single database file.

Figure 19.1.

The Registry Editor window contains a tree diagram of the data about your computer's software and hardware.

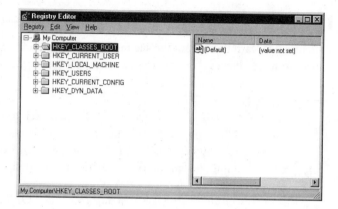

The Registry Editor displays a tree diagram of the Registry database's contents in the left pane of the window, and the specific data contained by the selected database entry in the right pane of the window. It is normal for many of the tree branches in the Registry database to show (value not set) in the Data column of the right-hand window pane, as does the HKEY_CLASSES_ROOT branch in Figure 19.1. This doesn't mean that there is no data entered into that branch of the database; instead, it usually means that the selected branch of the Registry database tree leads to additional branches or entries in the Registry.

Finding OLE Object Classes in the Registry Database

The Registry stores information about OLE objects in the HKEY_CLASSES_ROOT branch of the database tree, shown selected in Figure 19.1. To view the registered OLE object classes on your system, follow these steps:

1. Click the square box to the left of the HKEY_CLASSES_ROOT branch of the tree diagram to expand that branch. The Registry editor now displays a list of all of the registered file types and OLE objects. (This list is usually *very* long.)

2. Scroll through the tree diagram in the left pane of the Registry Editor window until you find the names of the registered OLE object classes. (Because there are many different file extensions, and because they alphabetize before most of the OLE object class names, you may need to scroll quite a bit before reaching the OLE object class names.)

You can recognize OLE object class types in the Registry because they usually begin with the name of the server application. Figure 19.2 shows the expanded HKEY_CLASSES_ROOT branch of the Registry database, scrolled to the point where Excel OLE objects appear in the list. The Excel.Application.5 OLE object class is shown selected in Figure 19.2; this OLE object class represents the Excel application itself.

Figure 19.2.

HKEY_CLASSES_ROOT branch of the Registry database contains the registered OLE object classes for your system.

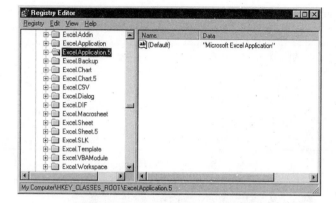

Notice that the data shown in the right pane of the Registry Editor window in Figure 19.2 gives the name of the selected OLE object—"`Microsoft Excel Application`". Notice also the other Excel OLE objects visible in the left pane of the Registry Editor window—`Excel.Addin`, `Excel.Chart`, `Excel.Dialog`, `Excel.Sheet.5`, `Excel.Template`, and so on. Each of these entries is an OLE object, and could be used as the value for the *ClassType* argument of the `OLEObjects.Add` method. (To create Excel objects from Excel VBA, however, it would be much easier to manipulate the object directly through Excel.)

Once you've found the OLE object class you want to use in the Registry database, make a note of the object's class name for future use. Table 19.1 lists the class types for a few common objects.

Table 19.1. Class types for common objects.

Object	Class type
1-2-3 Release 4 Worksheet	`123Worksheet`
Microsoft Equation 2.0	`Equation.2`
Microsoft Excel Application	`Excel.Application.5`
Excel 5.0 or 7 Chart	`Excel.Chart.5`
Excel Worksheet (5.0 or 7)	`Excel.Sheet.5`
Microsoft Graph 5.0	`MSGraph.Chart.5`
MS PowerPoint 7 Presentation	`PowerPoint.Show.7`
MS PowerPoint 7 Slide	`PowerPoint.Slide.7`
MS Project 4.0 Project	`MSProject.Project.4`
MS Word Document (6 or 7)	`Word.Document.6`
MS Word Picture (6 or 7)	`Word.Picture.6`

continues

Table 19.1. continued

Object	Class type
MS WordArt 2.0	MSWordArt.2
Package (Object Packager)	Package
Paintbrush Picture	PBrush
Wave Sound	SoundRec
Visio 2.0 Drawing	ShapewareVISIO20

DO	**DON'T**

DON'T edit, rename, or otherwise alter the contents of the Registry database, unless you are a Windows 95 expert. Incorrect or missing entries in the Registry database can prevent your computer from starting or operating correctly.

DON'T assume that every entry you see in the Registry database has full OLE capabilities. Some are only OLE servers, such as Microsoft Draw. Some are only OLE clients. Others don't do OLE at all.

DO check an application's documentation or its developer's technical support department to find out whether that specific application supports OLE 2.0.

Inserting a New Embedded Object

To insert a new embedded object into a worksheet, you must execute the `Add` method of `OLEObjects` with the `ClassType` argument. Listing 19.1 provides an example by inserting a new WordArt object into an Excel worksheet.

 Listing 19.1. Using the `Add` method to embed a new object in a worksheet.

```
 1:    Sub InsertNewWordArt()
 2:    'Inserts a new embedded WordArt object in the active cell
 3:
 4:       Dim Ans As Integer
 5:
 6:       Ans = MsgBox(Prompt:="Insert a new WordArt object now?", _
 7:                 Buttons:=vbOKCancel + vbQuestion, _
 8:                 Title:="Insert New Word Art")
 9:       If Ans = vbOK Then
10:         Application.StatusBar = "Inserting WordArt object..."
11:         Worksheets("Sheet1").OLEObjects.Add _
```

```
12:                                    ClassType:="MSWordArt.2"
13:         Application.StatusBar = False
14:     End If
15: End Sub
```

Analysis The **InsertNewWordArt** procedure is designed to insert a new Microsoft WordArt object into a worksheet. The procedure begins by displaying a message dialog box to get the user's confirmation for inserting the object (lines 6 through 8). The If...Then statement in line 9 tests the user's response. If the user chose the OK button, then MsgBox returned the value vbOK, and lines 10 through 13 are executed. Line 10 displays a message in the status bar to let the user know that the WordArt object is being inserted. Lines 11 and 12 contain the statement invoking the OLEObjects.Add method, inserting a new WordArt OLE object into the worksheet named Sheet1. Finally, line 13 gives control of the status bar back to Excel. Figure 19.3 shows the results of executing the **InsertNewWordArt** procedure.

Figure 19.3.

*The **InsertNewWordArt** procedure from Listing 19.1 inserts this WordArt object into the worksheet—the text in the WordArt object is part of the WordArt default object.*

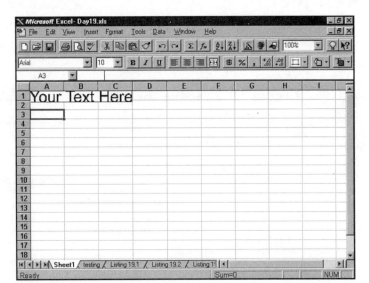

19

Unless you add the object as an icon, the appearance of the OLE object you insert depends largely on the server application. In some cases, the server application loads into memory and presents you a blank document. Other server applications, such as WordArt, display a default object (it contains the words "Your Text Here"). In most cases, though, you just get a container—that is, a blank picture box—for the object. If you want to make sure the server application loads so that the user can work with the new object, add the Activate method to the end of your Add statement. For example,

```
Worksheets("Sheet1").OLEObjects.Add(ClassType:="MSDraw").Activate
```

<table>
<tr><td>**DO**</td><td>**DON'T**</td></tr>
</table>

DON'T forget to position the active cell where you want the OLE object to appear before you insert the new object, because Excel uses the active cell to position the top-left corner of the object.

DO remember that the length of time it takes to insert an object depends on whether the server application is already running. If it is, the insertion may take only a second or two. Otherwise, you must wait for the server application to load itself into memory.

Inserting an Existing File as an Embedded Object

To embed an OLE object from an existing file, you need to use the Add method with the FileName argument and you need to either set the Link argument to False or omit it altogether. Listing 19.2 shows you how this is done.

Listing 19.2. Using the Add method to embed an existing file in a worksheet.

```
 1:   Sub EmbedPaintPicture()
 2:   'Embeds an existing MSPaint file
 3:
 4:      With Worksheets("Sheet1")
 5:         .OLEObjects.Add FileName:="C:\WINDOWS\BUBBLES.BMP", _
 6:                  DisplayAsIcon:=True, _
 7:                  IconFileName:="C:\WINDOWS\PBRUSH.EXE", _
 8:                  IconIndex:=0, _
 9:                  IconLabel:="Bubbles.bmp - Double-click to open"
10:      End With
11:   End Sub
```

Analysis This procedure embeds a Microsoft Paint bitmap picture into a worksheet by specifying the filename in the Add method (line 5) and by omitting the Link argument. (The BUBBLES.BMP file is a wallpaper file provided with Windows 95; it is located in the directory in which you installed Windows 95—you may need to change the directory path in lines 5 and 7 for this procedure to work on your system.) The procedure also displays the object as an icon by setting the DisplayAsIcon argument to True (line 6), and specifying an icon file (the MS Paint executable in line 7), an icon index (line 8), and an icon label, which appears beneath the icon (line 9). Figure 19.4 shows the icon and label inserted by this procedure.

Figure 19.4.

The `EmbedPaintPicture`
procedure in Listing 19.2
embeds the BUBBLES.BMP
bitmap into the worksheet as
an icon with a customized
caption.

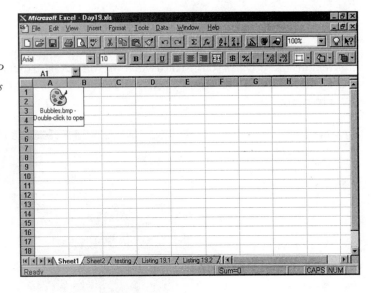

Inserting an Existing File as a Linked Object

If you would rather insert an existing file as linked instead of embedded, you need to set the Add method's Link argument to True, as shown in Listing 19.3.

19

 Listing 19.3. Using the Add method to insert an existing file as a linked object.

```
1:  Sub LinkPaintPicture()
2:  'Inserts a bitmap (BMP) file as a linked object
3:
4:    Application.ScreenUpdating = False
5:    With Worksheets("Sheet1")
6:      .Activate
7:      .Cells(1, 1).Select
8:      .OLEObjects.Add FileName:="C:\WINDOWS\FOREST.BMP", _
9:                      Link:=True
10:   End With
11:   Application.ScreenUpdating = True
12: End Sub
```

Analysis This procedure inserts a bitmap file into a worksheet as a linked object. The first few statements set up the worksheet, and screen updating is turned off (line 4). Then, the worksheet is activated (line 6), and the cell where the upper-left corner of the object will appear is selected (line 7).

Next, the Add method is executed to insert the file (lines 8 and 9). The `FileName` argument specifies the bitmap file, and the `Link` argument is set to `True` to establish the link. (The FOREST.BMP file, like the BUBBLES.BMP file, is supplied with Windows 95, and resides in the directory in which you installed windows; you may need to change the drive or directory path for this procedure to work.) Figure 19.5 shows the linked bitmap object inserted by this procedure.

Figure 19.5.

The `LinkPaintPicture` procedure inserts this linked bitmap file onto the worksheet.

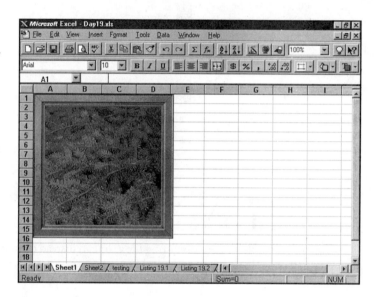

Working with Linked and Embedded Objects

After you've linked or embedded an OLE object into a worksheet, you can manipulate it by using `OLEObject` properties and methods. Among other things, you can change the object's size and formatting, update the OLE object's data, edit the object, and delete the object from the worksheet.

Before you examine these techniques, though, you need to know how to refer to OLE objects once you've added them to a worksheet. One way of doing this is to use the `OLEObjects` collection as the object accessor:

Syntax

Sheet.OLEObjects(*Index*)

Sheet represents any valid object reference to a worksheet containing the OLE object you want to work with. The *Index* argument can be either of the following:

☐ A number representing the OLE object that you want to use. 1 signifies the first object inserted into the worksheet, 2 signifies the second object inserted, and so on.

□ The name, as text, of the OLE object that you want to use. Excel assigns each object a name in the form *Picture n*, where *n* is a number corresponding to the order in which the object was inserted into the worksheet. The first OLE object is *Picture 1*, the second is *Picture 2*, and so on. You can find out the name of any OLE object by clicking it and looking in the formula bar's Name box.

DO	DON'T

DO rename OLE objects after you insert them into a worksheet, giving them meaningful names. The problem with leaving an OLE object with its default name is that neither technique of using the OLEObjects collection to access an OLE object is particularly enlightening—OLEObjects(3) is just as obscure as OLEObjects("Picture 4"). To remedy this, either store a reference to the object in a module-level variable, or change the object's Name property (see the next section, "Using OLE Object Properties," for details).

DON'T confuse regular picture objects—such as those inserted into the worksheet by using the Insert Picture command—with OLE objects. Both have names of the form *Picture n*, so it's easy to get them mixed up. When in doubt, select the object and look in the formula bar. An OLE object displays information about its class type and, if applicable, its filename.

19

Using OLE Object Properties

Like every other object in Excel and VBA, an OLEObject has a number of properties that you can use in your VBA code to change OLE object's appearance or behavior. Table 19.2 summarizes some of the more commonly used OLEObject properties.

Table 19.2. Common OLEObject properties.

Property	Meaning/Purpose
Name	The name of the object. Use this property to retrieve or rename the OLE object.
AutoUpdate	True if the OLE object is automatically updated when the server data changes. Applies only to linked OLE objects.
Border	Returns an object reference to the OLE object's border. Use this property to set or alter the appearance and style of the OLE object's border.

continues

Table 19.2. continued

Property	Meaning/Purpose
Shadow	Set this property to True if you want to add a shadow to the object's container. Use False to remove a shadow.
Top	Sets or returns the position of the top edge of the object. The distance is measured in points from the top edge of row 1—there are 72 points to an inch.
Left	Sets or returns the position of the left edge of the object. The distance is measured in points from the left edge of column A.
Height	Sets or returns the height of the OLE object in points.
Width	Sets or returns the width of the OLE object in points.
BottomRightCell	Returns a Range object specifying the worksheet cell underneath the bottom-right corner of the OLE object.
TopLeftCell	Returns a Range object specifying the worksheet cell underneath the top-left corner of the OLE object. Use the TopLeftCell and BottomRightCell properties to determine which worksheet cells are covered by the OLE object.
Object	Returns the OLE automation object associated with the object. Refer to the "Using OLE Automation" section later in this chapter.
OLEType	Indicates whether the OLE object is a linked or embedded file. If the file is linked, the property returns the constant xlOLELink. If the file is embedded, the property returns the constant xlOLEEmbed.
OnAction	Use this property to set or retrieve the name of the event procedure for this OLE object.
Visible	Set this property to False if you want to hide an object. Use True to unhide an object.

Listing 19.4 shows a procedure that demonstrates the use of some of these properties.

Type

Listing 19.4. A procedure that uses several OLEObject properties.

```
 1:  Sub OLEObjectProperties()
 2:  'This procedure embeds a new object
 3:  'and then sets a few of its properties
 4:
 5:      Dim BMPObj As OLEObject
 6:
 7:      With Worksheets("Sheet1")
 8:        .Activate
 9:        .Cells(2, 2).Value = "Double-click to edit picture"
10:        .Cells(3, 2).Select
11:        Set BMPObj = .OLEObjects.Add( _
12:                           FileName:="C:\WINDOWS\GOLD WEAVE.BMP")
13:      End With
14:
15:      With BMPObj
16:        .Border.Weight = xlMedium
17:        .Name = "Gold Weave Bitmap"
18:        .Shadow = True
19:      End With
20:  End Sub
```

Analysis

The **OLEObjectProperties** procedure inserts an embedded bitmap picture, and then sets some properties for the new object. The procedure begins by declaring an OLE object type variable named **BMPObject** to store a reference to the new object (line 5). Lines 8 through 10 set up the worksheet.

Like the Add methods of most object collections, you can use the OLEObjects.Add method as a function, creating the new object and returning a reference to that object at the same time. The statement in lines 11 and 12 does just that—it invokes the Add method to insert the CARS.BMP file as an embedded OLE object on the worksheet and assigns the resulting object reference to the **BMPObject** variable.

Lines 15 through 19 contain a With statement that uses the **BMPObject** variable to refer to the newly inserted OLE object. Line 16 sets the thickness of the OLE object's border to a medium weight by assigning the xlMedium constant to the Weight property of the OLE object's border—accessed through the OLEObject.Border property. Line 17 changes the name of the inserted object by assigning the string "Gold Weave Bitmap" to the Name property. Finally, line 18 sets the OLE object's Shadow property to True, so that the OLE object is displayed with a drop-shadow. Figure 19.6 shows the resulting worksheet appearance after executing the **OLEObjectProperties** procedure.

19

Figure 19.6.

The `OLEObjectProperties` *procedure inserts the GOLD WEAVE.BMP embedded object shown here, sets the border style, and adds a shadow to the image.*

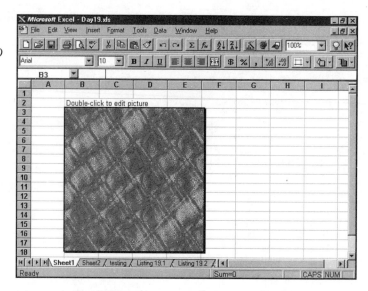

Using OLE Object Methods

OLE objects also come equipped with several methods that you can use to manipulate objects once you've inserted them. Many of these methods, such as `Copy`, `Cut`, `Delete`, `Activate`, and `Select`, are straightforward. They operate in much the same way as the methods of the same name do for the Excel `Worksheets` object described in Day 18. However, there are two methods—`Update` and `Verb`—that have special significance for OLE objects. The next two sections take a closer look at these methods.

The Update Method

If you insert a linked OLE object, the link between the object and the server file is usually automatic. This means that whenever the server file changes, the client object is updated automatically. There are two circumstances where updating is *not* automatic:

☐ If you have changed the link to manual. (You can do this by choosing the **Edit | Links** command, selecting the source file in the Links dialog box, and then selecting the **M**anual update option.)

☐ If you closed and then reopened the client document and chose **No** when Excel asked whether you wanted to re-establish the links.

In these situations, you need to use the `Update` method to update the object:

```
Object.Update
```

Here, `Object` is a reference to the OLE object that you want to update.

Listing 19.5 provides an example of how to use the `Update` method.

Listing 19.5. Using the `Update` method to update an OLE object.

```
1:  Sub UpdateAllObjects()
2:  'This procedure updates OLE objects
3:
4:    Dim aSheet As Worksheet
5:    Dim Obj As Object
6:
7:    For Each aSheet In ActiveWorkbook.Worksheets
8:      Application.StatusBar = "Now updating objects in " _
9:                          & aSheet.Name
10:       For Each Obj In aSheet.OLEObjects
11:         If Obj.OLEType = xlOLELink Then Obj.Update
12:       Next Obj
13:    Next aSheet
14:    Application.StatusBar = False
15:    MsgBox prompt:="Link update complete.", _
16:           Title:="Update All Objects"
17:  End Sub
```

This procedure updates all of the linked OLE objects on each worksheet in the active workbook. The first `For Each` loop (line 7) uses the **aSheet** variable to loop through each worksheet in the active workbook. The `StatusBar` property displays the name of each worksheet in the status bar so the user can watch the progress of the operation (lines 8 and 9). A nested `For Each` loop, starting in line 10, uses the **Obj** variable to loop through every OLE object in the current worksheet. If the object is linked—that is, its `OLEType` property equals `xlOLELink`— then it gets updated with the `Update` method (line 11). When both loops are complete, the procedure resets the status bar (line 14) and displays a completion message (lines 15 and 16).

The Verb Method

Each OLE object has one or more verbs, which specify the actions that can be performed on it. Unlike methods, which tell you what actions you can perform on the object from Excel's point of view, verbs tell you what actions you can perform on the object *from the server's point of view*— in other words, actions performed on the OLE object by the application you used to create the object. For example, a typical verb is `Edit`; sending the `Edit` verb to the OLE object opens the server application so that you can edit the object.

To send a verb to an OLE object, use the `Verb` method:

Syntax

`Object.Verb(Verb)`

Here, `Object` represents any object reference to an `OLEObject`. The `Verb` argument is a constant or integer that specifies the verb you want to send. If you omit the `Verb` argument, then the default verb is sent. If you include parentheses around the `Verb` argument, as shown in the syntax sample, the `Verb` method returns a Boolean result: `True` if the `Verb` method completed successfully, `False` otherwise.

Here are some notes to keep in mind as you deal with the `Verb` argument:

☐ All OLE objects have a *primary* verb, which is the same as the action taken when you double-click the object. To specify the primary verb, use the constant `xlPrimary`.

☐ For most objects, the primary verb lets you edit the object. If you want to edit an object, but you're not sure what its primary verb does, use the constant `xlOpen`.

☐ If the object supports a secondary verb, you can specify this verb by using 2 for the `Verb` argument.

☐ For embedded objects that support OLE 2.0, the primary verb (`xlPrimary`) lets you edit the object in place, and the secondary verb (`xlOpen`) lets you open the object in a separate server window.

Table 19.3 lists the available verbs for some common OLE objects.

Table 19.3. Verbs for common OLE objects.

Object	Primary verb	Other verb
1-2-3 Release 4 Worksheet	`Edit`	None
Microsoft Drawing	`Edit`	None
Microsoft Equation 2.0	`Edit`	None
Excel 5.0 Chart	`Edit` (in-place)	`Open`
Excel 5.0 Worksheet	`Edit` (in-place)	`Open`
Microsoft Graph 5.0	`Edit`	None
PowerPoint Presentation	`Slide Show`	`Edit`
PowerPoint Slide	`Edit`	None
Microsoft Project 4.0 Project	`Edit` (in-place)	`Open`
Word for Windows 6.0 Document	`Edit` (in-place)	`Open`
Word for Windows 6.0 Picture	`Edit` (in-place)	`Open`
WordArt 2.0	`Edit` (in-place)	`Open`
Object Packager	`Activate Contents`	`Edit Package`

Object	Primary verb	Other verb
Paintbrush Picture	Edit	None
Sound	Play	Edit
Visio 2.0 Drawing	Edit (in-place)	Open

Listing 19.6 contains an example of the Verb method.

Listing 19.6. Using the Verb method to edit an OLE object.

```
1:   Sub InsertAndEditWordDoc()
2:   'This procedure adds and edits an OLE object
3:
4:      Const lTitle = "Insert and Edit Word Document"
5:
6:      Dim mPrompt As String
7:      Dim mBtns As Integer
8:      Dim WordDoc As Object
9:      Dim Ans As Integer
10:
11:     Set WordDoc = Worksheets("Sheet1").OLEObjects.Add( _
12:                          ClassType:="Word.Document.6")
13:
14:     mPrompt = "Do you want to edit the document in-place?"
15:     mBtns = vbYesNoCancel + vbQuestion
16:     Ans = MsgBox(prompt:=mPrompt, Buttons:=mBtns, _
17:               Title:=lTitle)
18:     If Ans = vbYes Then
19:        WordDoc.Verb xlPrimary
20:     Else
21:        WordDoc.Verb xlOpen
22:     End If
23:  End Sub
```

This procedure embeds a new Word for Windows 6.0 document (which is the document format used by both Word 6 and Word 7) and then gives the user the choice of editing the document in-place or in a separate window.

Line 11 inserts the embedded document; the statement in line 11 uses the Add method as a function, and the resulting object reference is stored in the **WordDoc** variable. The **mPrompt** and **mBtns** variables are used to construct a MsgBox message (lines 14 and 15) that asks the user how she wants to edit the document. The message is displayed (line 16), and the result is stored in the **Ans** variable. If **Ans** is vbYes—that is, the user wants to edit in-place—the Verb method is used with the xlPrimary constant (line 19). Otherwise, the Verb method uses xlOpen (line 21). There are no parentheses used around the argument to the Verb method, because the method's result is not used (remember, you can ignore the result of a function or method by omitting the parentheses around the argument list).

Using OLE Automation

One of the advantages of OLE (especially OLE 2.0) is the fact that you gain access to the OLE object's original tools. With a simple double-click or a Verb method, you can edit the OLE object with the full power of the server's menus and commands.

Until recently, the one thing that has been missing is the ability to control an OLE server by means of programming. To edit or create an OLE object, whether it is in-place or in a separate window, you had to be at least familiar with the server application. Although *you* might be willing to spend time and effort learning a new program, the users of your VBA programs might not.

This situation has changed with the advent of OLE automation and Visual Basic for Applications. Windows applications that support OLE automation expose their objects to VBA, as well as to any other applications and development tools that support the OLE automation standard.

Just as VBA can recognize and manipulate, for example, an Excel worksheet range (a Range object), it can also recognize and manipulate objects from other OLE automation applications. Microsoft Access 7, Visio 2.0, Microsoft Graph 5.0, Microsoft Word 7, and PowerPoint 7 are a few of the applications that expose a number of objects to VBA. Visio 2.0, for example, exposes objects such as documents, pages, shapes, and windows; Microsoft Access 7 exposes objects such as forms, reports, and modules. Each of these objects has its own collection of methods and properties that can be read or altered by a VBA program, just like Excel's methods and properties.

Although the number of Windows applications that currently support OLE automation is still fairly small, it is growing rapidly. Many experts believe that OLE automation may become *the* standard for application interoperability in the near future. Certainly, any other applications that use Visual Basic for Applications will be OLE-automated. Indeed, Microsoft has announced that Visual Basic for Applications will become a part of all its major Windows applications—the current roster of Microsoft applications that host VBA and OLE automation includes Excel 5 and 7, Access 7, Project 4.0, PowerPoint 7, and Visual Basic 4.

Accessing OLE Automation Objects

How you access an OLE automation object from VBA depends on whether the object provides an object library file. An example of an .OLB file is XL5EN32.OLB, which comes with Excel 7.

If the application provides an object library, you can refer to the objects directly, just as you do with Excel's objects. (To make sure of this, select the Tools | References command from any module, and make sure that the object library's check box is activated in the References dialog box.) Some applications, including Word for Windows, don't have an object library, but they do enable you to access some of their objects directly.

If the application doesn't provide an object library and you want to access a new object, use the CreateObject function. If the application doesn't have a library and you want to access an existing object, use the GetObject function.

The next few sections discuss these techniques in more detail.

Accessing Objects Directly

Accessing objects directly is the easiest way to work with OLE automation. The syntax is

```
Application.ObjectName
```

Here, *Application* is the name of the application, and *ObjectName* is the name of the object. If you're not sure what to use for the application name, each OLEObject has an Object property that can supply you with the application name:

```
MyOLEObject.Object.Application
```

Here, *MyOLEObject* is an existing OLEObject. For example, suppose that you have an embedded Word for Windows document named WordObject. To refer to Word's WordBasic object—the only OLE automation object exposed by Word—you would use a statement such as:

```
Set WBObject = WordObject.Object.Application.WordBasic
```

This statement sets an Object variable named **WBObject** equal to a WordBasic object that can work directly with the Word document. To insert text in the document, for example, you would use:

```
WBObject.Insert = "This is the text that will be inserted."
```

Listing 19.7 shows an example of accessing an object directly.

Type

Listing 19.7. Referring to OLE automation objects directly.

```
1:   Sub AutomateWordObject()
2:   'This procedure embeds a new Word document and then
3:   'works with the document using the WordBasic object
4:
5:      Dim DocObject As Object
6:      Dim WBObject As Object
7:
8:      'Select the upper left cell
9:      With Worksheets("Sheet1")
10:        .Activate
11:        .Cells(2, 1).Select
12:        Set DocObject = .OLEObjects.Add( _
13:                            ClassType:="Word.Document.6")
14:     End With
15:
```

continues

757

Listing 19.7. continues

```
16:     DocObject.Activate
17:     Set WBObject = DocObject.Object.Application.WordBasic
18:
19:     'Access the WordBasic object directly
20:     With WBObject
21:        .Insert "I'm an OLE automated object!"
22:        .EditSelectAll
23:        .Bold
24:     End With
25:
26:     Cells(1, 1).Select
27: End Sub
```

This procedure embeds a new Word for Windows document and invokes Word's WordBasic object in order to edit the document. The procedure begins by declaring two Object type variables. **DocObject** will store a reference to the embedded document object, and **WBObject** will store a reference to the WordBasic object.

In the With statement in lines 9 through 14, the procedure activates a worksheet (line 10), selects the first cell in the second row (line 11), and then adds an embedded Word 6 document, simultaneously setting the **DocObject** variable to refer to the new document object (lines 12 and 13).

Next, line 16 activates the embedded OLE object, so that it can be edited. Line 17 sets the **WBObject** variable to refer to the WordBasic OLE automation object that is exposed by Word for Windows 6 or 7.

The With statement in lines 20 through 24 edits the word document object by using Word Basic programming instructions accessed through the WordBasic OLE automation object referenced by **WBObject**. Line 21 inserts some text, line 22 selects all of the text in the document, and line 23 makes the selected text in the document bold.

Finally, line 26 selects a different worksheet cell, ending the editing of the embedded Word document. (If the procedure stopped without this statement, the embedded document would still be opened in Word, ready for more editing.)

Creating a New OLE Automation Object

If an OLE automation application provides an object library, you can use the library functions to create new objects. If the application does not have an object library, you can use VBA's CreateObject function to create new OLE automation objects:

SAMS
PUBLISHING

Sams
Learning
Center

```
CreateObject(Class)
```

The *Class* argument is the *programmatic identifier*—in other words, the class type—which specifies the OLE server application and the type of object you want to create. For example, the programmatic identifier for WordBasic is `Word.Basic`. For a Visio application, you would use `Visio.Application`; for an Access 7 application, you would use `Access.Application.7`. The `CreateObject` method returns an object reference to the newly created object. Listing 19.8 provides an example of the `CreateObject` function.

Type

Listing 19.8. Using `CreateObject` to create an OLE automation object.

```
1:    Sub CreateAccessDBObject()
2:    'This procedure starts Access, creates a new database,
3:    'and then inserts the database in the worksheet
4:
5:      Dim Access7 As Object
6:      Dim CurrDB As Object
7:      Dim NewTable As Object
8:      Dim fName As String        'database name
9:      Dim iconfName As String    'icon file name
10:
11:     'Create an instance of the Access application
12:     Set Access7 = CreateObject("Access.Application.7")
13:
14:     'set up a filename using the activeworkbook's folder
15:     fName = ActiveWorkbook.Path
16:     fName = fName & "\A DB Created by Excel VBA.MDB"
17:
18:     'create a new database
19:     Access7.NewCurrentDatabase FilePath:=fName
20:
21:     'set an object reference to the new database
22:     Set CurrDB = Access7.CurrentDb
23:
24:     'create a new table definition in the database
25:     Set NewTable = CurrDB.CreateTableDef("Name Table")
26:
27:     'create fields and append them to the table definition
28:     With NewTable
29:       .Fields.Append .CreateField("Last Name", dbText, 20)
30:       .Fields.Append .CreateField("First Name", dbText, 10)
31:       .Fields.Append .CreateField("Middle Initial", dbText, 1)
32:     End With
33:
34:     'Append the table definition to the database
35:     CurrDB.TableDefs.Append NewTable
36:
```

19

continues

Listing 19.8. continued

```
37:     Access7.Quit      'Quit Access
38:
39:     'Insert the linked database into Excel
40:     iconfName = "C:\MSOFFICE\ACCESS\MSACCESS.EXE"
41:     With ActiveWorkbook.Worksheets("Sheet1")
42:        .Select
43:        .Cells(2, 2).Activate
44:        .OLEObjects.Add Filename:=fName, _
45:                        Link:=True, _
46:                        DisplayAsIcon:=True, _
47:                        IconFileName:=iconfName, _
48:                        IconIndex:=1, _
49:                        IconLabel:="Database of Names"
50:     End With
51: End Sub
```

 This procedure starts Access 7, creates a new database, adds a table to the database, and then inserts the new database as a linked object on a worksheet.

To start Access, the procedure uses the `CreateObject` function to create an `"Access.Application.7"` object (line 12). This object is stored in the **Access7** variable. Through the Access application object, you now have complete access to all of Access' objects, methods, and properties.

For example, you can create a new Access database by using the `NewCurrentDatabase` method, as shown in line 19. Next, line 22 uses Access' `CurrentDb` method to set another Object type variable—**CurrDB**—to refer to the current database. Line 25 uses yet another method, `CreateTableDef`, to create a new table in the database. Lines 28 through 32 add three fields to the new table definition by calling the `CreateField` method (which returns a new table field object) and passing its result as the argument to the `Append` method of the `Fields` collection (which adds the field object to the table). After creating fields in the table, line 35 uses another `Append` method to add the new table object to the database. Finally, line 37 uses the `Quit` method to terminate the Access working session that was started by the `CreateObject` function call (back in line 12).

 **Note:** The `CreateTableDef`, `CreateField`, and a few other methods and properties used in Listing 19.8 actually belong to the Data Access Objects library (DAO) rather than directly to the Access 7 application. If you get errors when you try to execute the **CreateAccessObject** procedure, use the **Tools | References** command, and make sure that both the `Microsoft Access 7.0` and the `Microsoft DAO 3.0 Object Library` are selected in the list of available references.

Line 40 sets up the `iconfName` variable to hold the full path and name of the Access 7 program file; this file will be used as the source of an icon for the inserted OLE object. (If your copy of Access 7 is installed on a different drive or directory, you'll need to change this line to match your system.) Line 42 selects the worksheet named `Sheet1` in the active workbook, and line 43 selects the second cell in the second row (remember, the `OLEObjects.Add` method inserts the OLE object in the current active worksheet cell). Lines 44 through 49 contain a single `OLEObjects.Add` method statement, using several of its arguments. The object is inserted as a linked object from a filename (using the `fName` variable initialized at the beginning of the procedure). The inserted object is displayed as an icon, using the second icon from the Access 7 program file, and with a customized icon label. Figure 19.7 shows the resulting worksheet display.

Figure 19.7.

The `CreateAccessDBObject` procedure creates a new Access 7 database and links it to the worksheet.

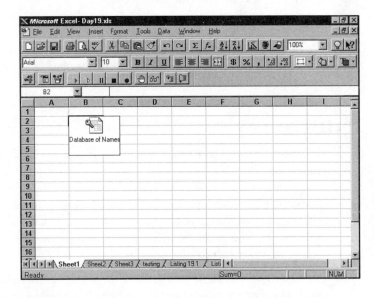

 Note: The Access 7 database isn't directly inserted into the worksheet—it is actually inserted through the Object Packager.

Accessing an Existing OLE Automation Object

Instead of creating a new object, you might need to work with an existing object. If the server application is already running, use VBA's `GetObject` function to access an existing OLE automation object:

```
GetObject(Class)
```

The *Class* argument is the programmatic identifier of the object you want to work with. For example, the following code fragment declares an Object type variable named **AppVisio** and uses this variable to refer to a running instance of Visio. The code then opens a Visio file named DRAWING.VSD.

```
Dim AppVisio As Object
Set AppVisio = GetObject(Class:="Visio.Application")
AppVisio.Documents.Open "C:\VISIO\DRAWING.VSD"
```

If an OLE automation application exposes its files as objects, you can use the slightly different GetObject syntax to access the file directly:

```
GetObject(PathName [,Class])
```

The *PathName* argument is the full path name for the file that you want to open. The *Class* argument is optional; you can use it to specify the object type. Whichever syntax form you use, the GetObject method returns an object reference.

Summary

This chapter showed you how to work with object linking and embedding (OLE) and OLE automation. The lesson began with a look at OLE's history. You saw that OLE is Microsoft's latest attempt at making true compound documents; the earlier attempts were the Clipboard and dynamic data exchange (DDE). OLE works by inserting data from a server application into a client document. You can either link the object (in which case the data remains with the server application) or you can embed the object (in which case the data is stored entirely in the client document). OLE 2.0 provides new features such as in-place editing and OLE automation.

You learned how to use the Add method of the OLEObjects collection to insert OLE objects in a worksheet. For new objects, you specify a class type; for existing objects, you specify a filename. If you want to embed the object, set the Link argument to False. To link the object, set Link to True.

You also learned that you can use VBA to work with an OLE object once you've inserted it. The OLEObjects method returns individual OLE objects. Several properties (such as AutoUpdate, Border, Name, and OLEType) and methods (such as Update and Verb) are available for OLE objects.

The lesson finished with a look at OLE automation. This is a software standard that enables applications to expose their objects to languages such as Visual Basic for Applications. Your procedure can work with these objects by executing their methods and reading or setting their properties. For applications with object libraries, you can refer to their objects directly. Otherwise, you use the CreateObject and GetObject functions.

Q&A

Q **How do the items in the Registry database get entered?**

A Typically, these items are added automatically when you install your software, so you never need to worry about it. Although the Registry Editor does enable you to add, delete, or edit information in the Registry database, it is *highly recommended* that you *avoid altering the registration database*, unless you are instructed by a technical support engineer or by someone else who is extremely knowledgeable about the workings of the Registry database.

Q **When I use the `Add` method to insert a new embedded object I get an error message telling me that Excel `cannot insert object`. What am I doing wrong?**

A You're not doing anything wrong. It's just that some applications don't support embedding. Instead, you should try inserting these objects from existing files, and linking them rather than embedding them. Refer to Listings 19.3 and 19.8 for examples of inserting linked OLE objects from existing files.

Q **Is there a way to find out what verbs exist for each OLE object?**

A Yes, there is. The easiest way is to select the object, pull down the **E**dit menu, and select the `ObjectType` **O**bject command. (`ObjectType` is the type of object you've selected, such as Microsoft Drawing.) This displays a cascade menu, the top half of which lists the object's verbs.

Alternatively, you can use the Registry database. This file contains much more information than discussed in this book so far. To see this additional information, simply locate the OLE class type as already explained in this lesson, and then keep expanding branches of the database tree. Figure 19.8 shows the database tree for the `Excel.Chart.5` class type expanded to show the two available verbs. To find out what each verb is, select it, and read the verb's name from the Data pane of the Registry Editor window, as shown for the Edit verb in Figure 19.8. Use the verb number in the left pane as the `Verb` argument—for example, you'd use `0` as the argument value to send the `Edit` verb for the `Excel.Chart.5` class type. You just need to look through the Registry database tree to find both the object with which you want to work and its corresponding `Verb` branch.

Q **How do I know whether an OLE automation application provides an object library?**

A In any VBA module, select the **T**ools | **R**eferences command. The References dialog box shows you a list of all the object libraries on your system. If an object library appears in the list, you can see its exposed objects in the Object Browser dialog box (select the **V**iew | **O**bject Browser command).

19

Figure 19.8.

The Excel.Chart.5 *OLE object class in the Registry; its branch in the database has been expanded to reveal the object's available verbs.*

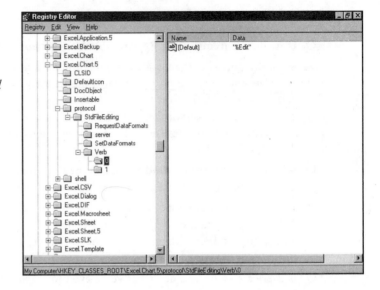

Workshop

Answers are in Appendix A.

Quiz

1. In OLE terminology, what is a server and what is a client?

2. What is the difference between a linked object and an embedded object?

3. Name three advantages that OLE provides over DDE.

4. Name and give a brief explanation of the four main features found in OLE 2.0.

5. What is the purpose of the Windows 95 Registry database?

6. What arguments would you use with the OLEObjects.Add method to perform the following tasks. Ignore the icon-related arguments.

   A. Insert a linked, existing word processing document.

   B. Insert a new presentation slide.

   C. Insert an embedded, existing bitmap image.

7. What is an OLE verb? What does the primary verb usually do?

8. What is OLE automation?

9. What are the three techniques that you can use to access OLE automation objects?

Exercises

1. **BUG BUSTER:** The following procedure produces an error. Can you see why?

```
Sub InsertWordObject()
  Dim WordObject As Object
  'Select the upper left cell
  Worksheets("Sheet1").Activate
  Range("A2").Select
  'Insert the object
  Set WordObject = ActiveSheet.OLEObjects.Add _
                (ClassType:="Word.Document.6")
  'Edit it
  WordObject.Verb xlPrimary
  'Set its properties
  With WordObject
    .Border.Weight = xlMedium
    .Name = "Annotation"
    .Shadow = True
  End With
End Sub
```

2. **BUG BUSTER:** The following procedure is supposed to enter some text in a Word document object. Unfortunately, when the procedure finishes, the text doesn't appear inside the object. Do you know why?

```
Sub InsertText()
  Dim DocObject As Object, WBObject As Object
  Set DocObject = ActiveSheet.OLEObjects(1)
  With DocObject
    Set WBObject = .Object.Application.WordBasic
    WBObject.Insert "Some text."
  End With
  Range("A1").Select
End Sub
```

19

Working with Other Applications: DDE, DLLs, and Sending Keystrokes

Yesterday's lesson showed you how to use object linking and embedding to work with ot‍
Windows applications. Unfortunately, not all Windows applications support the OLE standard; you must use other techniques to work with those applications. Today's lesson investigates
some of these other techniques. In particular, you'll learn:

- [ ] How to start other applications within a VBA procedure.
- [ ] What dynamic data exchange (DDE) is and what you can do with it.
- [ ] How to use VBA's DDE methods.
- [ ] How to send keystrokes to other running applications.
- [ ] How to declare and use dynamic-link library (DLL) functions.

Starting Another Application

One of the most obvious ways of working with another application is simply to start it and work
with it directly. You can use VBA's `Shell` function to start another application from a VBA
procedure:

Syntax

```
Shell(PathName [,WindowStyle])
```

The *PathName* argument is a string expression for the name of the file that starts the application.
To start Microsoft Access, for example, you would use the filename for the Access program:
MSACCESS.EXE. Unless the file's directory is in the DOS path, you must include the drive
and directory to ensure that VBA can find the file. You can also include any command-line
switches or arguments for the application you're starting in the *PathName* argument's string. For
example, to start Microsoft Access and open the MYDATA database, you would use a string like
the following for the *PathName* argument (assuming Access is installed on drive C, in the
\MSOFFICE\ACCESS folder):

```
C:\MSOFFICE\ACCESS\MSACCESS.EXE MYDATA.MDB
```

The *WindowStyle* argument is a number that specifies how the application window will appear.
Values for the *WindowStyle* argument are listed in Table 20.1. For those entries in Table 20.1
that show more than one value, it doesn't matter which value you use; for example, the values
1, 5, and 9 all have the same effect. There are no predefined constants for the *WindowStyle*
argument. If you omit the *WindowStyle* argument, then the application is started minimized,
with focus.

If the `Shell` function is successful, it returns a numeric value—the *task identification number* for
the application just started. (Windows internally identifies every currently running application
with a unique task identification number; the task identification number for an application
changes from work session to work session.) If `Shell` is unsuccessful, it generates an error. Listing
20.1 shows an example of the `Shell` function.

Table 20.1. The `WindowStyle` argument and the appearance of the application window.

WindowStyle	Window Appearance
1, 5, or 9	Normal size with focus
2 or omitted	Minimized with focus
3	Maximized with focus
4 or 8	Normal size without focus
6 or 7	Minimized without focus

 Listing 20.1. Using the `Shell` function to start an application.

```
1:   Option Explicit
2:
3:   Const shellNormFocus = 1
4:   Const shellMinFocus = 2
5:   Const shellMaxFocus = 3
6:   Const shellNormNoFocus = 4
7:   Const shellMinNoFocus = 6
8:
9:
10:  Sub StartControlPanel(sIcon As String)
11:  'Starts the Control Panel icon specified by sIcon argument.
12:
13:    On Error GoTo BadStart
14:
15:    Shell PathName:="CONTROL.EXE MAIN.CPL " & sIcon, _
16:          WindowStyle:=shellNormFocus
17:    Exit Sub
18:
19:  BadStart:
20:    MsgBox prompt:="Could not start Control Panel!", _
21:          Buttons:=vbOKOnly + vbExclamation, _
22:          Title:="Start Control Panel: " & sIcon
23:  End Sub
24:
25:
26:  Sub ChangePrinter()
27:  'Calls StartControlPanel to open Printers folder
28:    StartControlPanel ("PRINTERS")
29:  End Sub
```

Analysis The Windows Control Panel, a frequently used applet, allows you to control many aspects of the Windows environment, including printer settings, fonts, and colors. The **StartControlPanel** procedure takes advantage of the fact that you can start many Control Panel icons directly by using the following command line syntax:

`CONTROL.EXE MAIN.CPL IconName`

Here, MAIN.CPL is a .CPL—short for Control Panel Library—file of icons. *IconName* is the name of the Control Panel icon that you want to run—for example, PRINTERS, or FONTS.

Listing 20.1 starts out by declaring several module-level constants for the possible window styles that can be used with the Shell function. These constants are declared to help make any code that uses the Shell function more readable.

The **StartControlPanel** procedure (lines 10 through 23) takes an **sIcon** argument that specifies the Control Panel icon with which you want to work. The procedure sets up an On Error handler (line 13) in case Control Panel doesn't start properly. Line 15 executes the Shell function (ignoring its result) to load Control Panel and run the module specified by **sIcon**. If all goes well, the procedure exits normally with Exit Sub (line 17). If an error occurs, the procedure jumps to the **BadStart** label (line 19), and a MsgBox function displays the bad news (lines 20 through 22).

The **ChangePrinter** procedure (lines 26 through 29) is an example of how you would call **StartControlPanel**.

DO	DON'T

DO save the result of the Shell function—the task identification number of the application you started—in a module-level or public scope variable if you intend to have your VBA program refer to this application again later in the procedure or program.

DO use the VBA ChDir statement if you need to change to an application's directory before starting the program (refer to Day 12).

DON'T enter statements after a Shell function if you want the statements to execute only when you've finished with the other application. The Shell statement runs an application *asynchronously*, which means that VBA starts the program and then immediately continues executing the rest of the procedure.

Activating a Running Application

After you have some other programs running, your application might need to switch among them. For example, you might want the user to switch between Excel and Control Panel to change various settings. To switch to any running application, use the AppActivate statement:

SAMS
PUBLISHING

Syntax

```
AppActivate(Title [,Wait])
```

The *Title* argument can be either a numeric expression that evaluates to a valid task identification number (as returned by the Shell function), or a string expression containing the name of the application to which you want to switch. In this case, the name of the application is the text that appears in the application's title bar. For some applications, the title bar includes both the name of the application and the name of the active document. If *Title* doesn't match any application's title bar exactly, VBA tries to find a title bar that begins with the string passed in the *Title* argument. If *Title* matches the beginning of more than one running application's title bar, one of the applications is arbitrarily activated.

The optional *Wait* argument is a Boolean value that determines when Excel switches to the application. If *Wait* is True, AppActivate waits until the calling application is active before it switches to the other application—in Excel VBA, this means AppActivate waits until Excel is activated before switching. If *Wait* is False or is omitted, AppActivate switches to the other application immediately. Set *Wait* to True whenever you want to ensure that your VBA program activates the other application *only* when Excel is active, and *not* when Excel is executing in the background. Listing 20.2 shows AppActivate in action.

Type

Listing 20.2. Using the `AppActivate` statement to switch to a running application.

```
 1:  Option Explicit
 2:
 3:  Const shellNormFocus = 1
 4:  Const shellMinFocus = 2
 5:  Const shellMaxFocus = 3
 6:  Const shellNormNoFocus = 4
 7:  Const shellMinNoFocus = 6
 8:
 9:  Dim NPad_ID As Long
10:
11:  Sub LoadExcelReadMe()
12:  'Loads Excel's Read Me text file into Notepad
13:
14:     Const lTitle = "Load Excel Read Me Text File"
15:     Const xlReadMe = "C:\MSOFFICE\EXCEL\XLREADME.TXT"
16:
17:     If Dir(xlReadMe) <> "" Then
18:        NPad_ID = Shell(PathName:="NOTEPAD.EXE " & xlReadMe, _
19:                        WindowStyle:=shellNormNoFocus)
20:        Application.OnKey Key:="^+E", _
21:                          Procedure:="ActivateNotepad"
22:        MsgBox prompt:="Excel Read Me loaded!" & Chr(13) & _
23:                  "Press Ctrl+Shift+E to activate.", _
24:              Buttons:=vbInformation, Title:=lTitle
25:     Else
```

continues

20

Listing 20.2. continued

```
26:            MsgBox prompt:="Can't find " & xlReadMe, _
27:                    Buttons:=vbExclamation, Title:=lTitle
28:        End If
29:    End Sub
30:
31:
32:    Sub ActivateNotepad()
33:    'Activates Notepad when user presses Ctrl+Shift+E
34:
35:        On Error GoTo NotRunning
36:
37:        AppActivate Title:=NPad_ID
38:        Exit Sub
39:
40:    NotRunning:
41:        MsgBox prompt:="Notepad is not loaded!", _
42:                Buttons:=vbExclamation, _
43:                Title:="Hot Key Switch To NotePad"
44:    End Sub
```

In this example, the **LoadExcelReadMe** procedure loads the file XLREADME.TXT into Notepad and sets up a shortcut key for activating Notepad.

Listing 20.2 is a complete module. Lines 3 through 7 declare constants for use with the Shell function, as in Listing 20.1. Notice line 9, which declares a module-level variable, **NPad_ID**, which is used to store the task identification number returned by the Shell function. Declaring this as a module-level variable ensures that the task identification number for the running copy of NotePad will be available to all of the procedures in this module.

The **LoadExcelReadMe** procedure starts in line 11. Lines 14 and 15 declare constants local to the procedure—a title for the message boxes displayed by this procedure, and a constant for the name and directory path of the Excel Read Me text file. (This file is installed with Excel, in Excel's installed directory; you may need to change this constant declaration if Excel is installed in a different drive or directory on your computer.)

Lines 17 through 28 perform the real work of this procedure. First, line 17 starts an If...Then statement that calls the Dir function (explained in Day 12) to ensure that the Excel Read Me file is in the specified directory. If it is, then lines 18 through 24 are executed; otherwise, lines 26 and 27 display a message box announcing that the file can't be found.

Line 18 calls the Shell function to start the NotePad program. Notice that the PathName argument concatenates the name of the NotePad program with the **xlReadMe** constant—when NotePad starts, it will automatically load the specified filename. The result of the Shell function—the task identification number for this running copy of NotePad—is assigned to the **NPad_ID** variable for later use.

Next, line 20 creates an OnKey event that causes the **ActivateNotePad** procedure to be invoked whenever the user presses the Ctrl+Shift+E key combination. (OnKey events are described in more detail in Day 21.) Finally, lines 22 through 24 display a message dialog box announcing the successful loading of the Excel Read Me text file into NotePad.

The **ActivateNotepad** procedure (lines 32 through 44) activates the NotePad application. Line 35 sets up an On Error GoTo handler in case the copy of NotePad started by the **LoadExcelReadMe** procedure is no longer running. If all is well, the AppActivate statement in line 37 activates NotePad. If an error occurs, the code jumps to the **NotRunning** label (line 40), and an error message is displayed (lines 41 through 43).

Using Dynamic Data Exchange

In the preceding lesson, you learned how the advanced technologies of OLE and OLE automation make it possible for you to work and exchange data with other Windows applications. Of the thousands of Windows applications that exist, however, only a few support the OLE standard, and a mere handful—for now—support OLE automation. OLE may one day be the *de facto* standard for application interoperability, but until then you must use other techniques to work with applications that do not support OLE.

One of those techniques is the predecessor of OLE—*dynamic data exchange* (DDE). DDE is an internal communications protocol that enables some Windows applications to exchange data and even execute each other's commands. Because it is implemented unevenly in different applications, DDE is nowhere near as clean or straightforward as OLE, but is often the only choice you have. VBA provides a variety of tools that enable you to utilize the DDE protocol in your procedures. The next few sections examine each of those tools.

DDE: The Basics

20

Human conversations can take two forms: static and dynamic. A static conversation, such as the exchange of letters or e-mail, is one in which information is passed back and forth intermittently. A dynamic conversation, on the other hand, is one in which information is exchanged continuously. Face-to-face meetings or telephone calls are examples of dynamic conversations.

A *dynamic* data exchange, then, is one in which two applications continuously send data and commands to each other. As in OLE, the two applications involved in this process are called *client* and *server*. The client is the application that initializes the conversation and sends requests for data. The client is also called the *destination*. The server is the application that responds to the client's requests by executing its own commands and sending its data. The server is also called the *source*.

DDE conversations have three stages:

1. **Initiating a link between the client and the server:** This link—called a *channel*—is the path along which the two applications communicate. Initiating a DDE link is sort of like dialing the telephone to establish a connection with someone you want to talk to. Because your VBA procedures initiate the conversation, VBA is the client, or destination, for the DDE link.

2. **Working with the server:** Once the link is established, the client can exchange data with the server, and it can control the server by invoking the server's internal macro commands or by sending keystrokes to the server.

3. **Terminating the link:** When the client is done working with the server, your procedure needs to close the DDE channel.

Initiating and Terminating a Link between VBA and a DDE Server

Just as you need to dial someone's telephone number and establish a connection before you can have a telephone conversation, so too must your VBA procedure establish a connection with a server application in order to initiate a DDE conversation. To establish a channel between VBA and another DDE application, use the DDEInitiate method:

Syntax

`object.DDEInitiate(App, Topic)`

In this syntax, `object` is optional, and represents the Application object (DDEInitiate is a method belonging to the VBA host application). The `App` argument is a string containing the DDE name of the server application with which you want to establish a link. The DDE name depends on the application you're linking to, and is almost always the name, without the extension, of the executable file that starts the application. For example, the DDE name for Excel is Excel and the DDE name for Word for Windows is WinWord.

The `Topic` argument is a string specifying the part of the server with which you want to work. You can think of this as the "topic of conversation" between the client and server. For most applications, you use either the System topic—which accesses the server application as a whole—or the name of a specific server file with which you want to work.

If DDEInitiate is successful, it returns an integer that identifies the channel. You must refer to this number in all subsequent DDE exchanges between the client and server.

DO	**DON'T**

DO include the full path name of a document in the DDEInitiate method's *Topic* argument if you're trying to access a document that isn't already open. Here's an example:

```
DDEInitiate("WinWord", "C:\WINWORD\MEMO.DOC")
```

DON'T forget that your other DDE commands need to refer to the channel number returned by DDEInitiate. If these commands exist in other procedures, be sure to use a global variable to store the channel number, or pass the channel number as a procedure argument.

DO remember that the task identification number returned by the Shell function and the DDE channel number returned by the DDEInitiate methods are *not* the same, and they *cannot* be used interchangeably.

DON'T assume that a server's executable filename is always the same as its DDE name. For example, the executable file for FoxPro for Windows is FOXPROW.EXE, but its DDE name is FoxPro. If you're not sure, you may need to contact the application's tech support department to find out the DDE name of the application.

If the server application is already open when you execute the DDEInitiate method, a DDE channel is opened. If the DDE server isn't running, then the DDEInitiate method will cause the server application to be started. There are a couple of reasons, however, why allowing DDEInitiate to start the server application for you may be inconvenient:

☐ Whenever the server application is started by executing DDEInitiate, the VBA host application (Excel, in this case) will display a dialog box like the one shown in Figure 20.1. To continue, the user must choose the **Y**es command button—if the user chooses the **N**o button, then the DDEInitiate method generates a VBA run-time error. Even if you attempt to work around this problem by setting the Application.DisplayAlerts property to False, VBA will still generate a runtime error.

Figure 20.1.
Excel displays this dialog box if it has to start the DDE server application in order to complete a DDEInitiate *method call.*

☐ If there is more than one instance of the DDE server application currently executing, the user is presented with a dialog box asking which instance of the server to use. Figure 20.2 shows the Dynamic Data Exchange dialog box produced if you execute the **OpenHailingFrequencies** procedure in Listing 20.3 when there are already two copies of Word for Windows running. (The procedure starts its own copy, for a total of three instances.)

Figure 20.2.

Excel displays this dialog box if it needs the user to choose among more than one instance of the DDE server application in order to complete the DDEInitiate *call.*

☐ If the DDE server application is not in the current drive or directory, nor in a drive or directory in the DOS search path, DDEInitiate cannot find it. To solve this problem, first use the VBA ChDir statement to change to the directory of the DDE server before running DDEInitiate:

```
ChDir "C:\WINWORD"
```

Most of the time, you should use the Shell function to start the server application, before using DDEInitiate to open the DDE channel. Listing 20.3 shows an example procedure that uses the DDEInitiate method.

Listing 20.3. Using the DDEInitiate method to open a DDE channel.

```
1:   Option Explicit
2:
3:   Const shellNormFocus = 1
4:   Const shellMinFocus = 2
5:   Const shellMaxFocus = 3
6:   Const shellNormNoFocus = 4
7:   Const shellMinNoFocus = 6
8:
9:   Dim ddeChannel As Integer      'global to this module
10:
11:  Sub OpenHailingFrequencies()
12:  'This procedure opens a channel between Excel and Word
13:
14:     Const lTitle = "Open DDE Channel"
15:
16:     On Error GoTo BadConnection
17:
```

```
18:     Shell PathName:="C:\MSOFFICE\WINWORD\WINWORD.EXE", _
19:          WindowStyle:=shellMinNoFocus
20:     ddeChannel = DDEInitiate(App:="WinWord", Topic:="System")
21:
22:     MsgBox prompt:="A channel to WinWord is now open.", _
23:            Buttons:=vbInformation, Title:=lTitle
24:     Exit Sub
25:
26:  BadConnection:
27:    MsgBox prompt:="Could not open channel!", _
28:           Buttons:=vbExclamation, Title:=lTitle
29:  End Sub
```

The **OpenHailingFrequencies** procedure opens a DDE channel between Excel and Word for Windows. Lines 3 through 7 contain module-level constants for the arguments to the Shell function.

Line 9 declares a variable named **ddeChannel**, also at the module level—this gives other procedures in this module (if there were any) access to the channel number returned by the DDEInitiate method.

The procedure actually starts in line 11. The statement in line 16 sets up an error-handling trap, in case something goes wrong. Including an error handler in your DDE procedures is always a good idea, because DDE connections are notoriously unreliable.

A call to the Shell function (lines 18 and 19) starts Word for Windows minimized, without focus; this call to the Shell function ignores the function's result. Line 20 invokes the DDEInitiate method—Word for Windows is already running as a result of the Shell function call, so DDEInitiate just opens a DDE channel. If all goes well, the channel number is stored in the **ddeChannel** variable, and a MsgBox statement tells the user that the connection has been established (lines 22 and 23). If an error occurs, the code jumps to the **BadConnection** label (line 26) and displays an error message (lines 27 and 28).

Note: If you already have at least one copy of Word for Windows running when you execute the procedure in Listing 20.3, you'll see a dialog box similar to the one shown in Figure 20.2.

When your procedure has finished its DDE conversation, you must terminate the link between the client and server. To do this, you use the DDETerminate method:

DDETerminate *Channel*

Here, *Channel* is the channel number returned by the DDEInitiate method.

20

Controlling the Server Application

Once you have an open channel, you can use the DDEExecute method to control the DDE server application. You can send commands that the server application understands—such as commands from its macro language, if it has one—or you can send keystrokes. The syntax for DDEExecute is

Syntax

DDEExecute(*Channel*, *String*)

Channel is the channel number returned by the DDEInitiate method. *String* is a string expression that represents the commands or keystrokes to send to the server. The format you use for commands depends on the DDE server application. Some applications, such as Word for Windows, permit you to use their macro language commands. Other applications use special DDE commands. (For information about the DDE commands used by a particular application, refer to the server application's documentation, or contact the application developer's technical support department.) To send keystrokes, use a string containing the keystroke symbols explained later in this chapter for the SendKeys method. The DDEExecute method returns a Boolean value indicating whether or not the method was successful.

DO	DON'T

DON'T use DDEExecute to send keystrokes to a server application's dialog box. For that you need to use the SendKeys method. (See "Sending Keystrokes to an Application" later in this chapter.)

Listing 20.4 demonstrates several examples of the DDEExecute method.

Type

Listing 20.4. Using DDEExecute to control a server application.

```
 1:  Option Explicit
 2:
 3:  Const shellMinNoFocus = 6
 4:
 5:  Sub CreateWordLink()
 6:  'Copies data from Word; pastes it with a DDE link in Excel
 7:
 8:      Dim Channel As Integer
 9:
10:      On Error GoTo BailOut
11:
12:      Application.StatusBar = "Starting WinWord..."
13:      Shell PathName:="C:\MSOFFICE\WINWORD\WINWORD.EXE", _
14:          WindowStyle:=shellMinNoFocus
15:
16:      'Initiate channel with System topic
17:      Application.StatusBar = "Opening test document..."
```

```
18:     Channel = DDEInitiate(App:="WinWord", Topic:="System")
19:     DDEExecute Channel:=Channel, _
20:        String:="[FileOpen ""C:\My Documents\TEST DDE.DOC""]"
21:     DDETerminate Channel
22:
23:     'Initiate new channel with document
24:     Application.StatusBar = "Copying text..."
25:     Channel = DDEInitiate(App:="WinWord", _
26:                     Topic:="C:\My Documents\TEST DDE.DOC")
27:     DDEExecute Channel:=Channel, String:="[StartOfDocument]"
28:     DDEExecute Channel:=Channel, String:="[EndOfLine 1]"
29:     DDEExecute Channel:=Channel, String:="[EditCopy]"
30:     DDETerminate Channel
31:
32:     'Paste and link copied text
33:     Application.StatusBar = "Pasting text..."
34:     Worksheets("Sheet1").Activate
35:     Range("A1").Select
36:     ActiveSheet.Paste Link:=True
37:     Application.StatusBar = False
38:     Exit Sub
39:
40: BailOut:
41:     DDETerminate Channel
42:     Application.StatusBar = False
43: End Sub
```

Analysis

The **CreateWordLink** procedure loads Word for Windows, executes several Word commands—including copying some text—and pastes the copied text to Excel with a DDE link. Line 3 declares a constant for use with the Shell function; the actual procedure begins in line 5.

Line 10 sets up an error-handler, and line 12 sets the application's status bar so the user knows what's going on. The statement in lines 13 and 14 starts Word for Windows by calling the Shell function (and ignoring its result). If Word for Windows is installed in a different drive or directory on your system, you may need to alter the directory paths in line 13.

Line 17 again sets the application's status bar, while line 18 opens a DDE channel with the System topic to Word; the DDE channel number is stored in **Channel**. The first call to the DDEExecute method (lines 19 and 20) runs WordBasic's FileOpen command to open a file named TEST DDE.DOC. The DDE conversation with the System topic is now complete, so DDETerminate closes the channel (line 21).

Note: Before you execute the **CreateWordLink** procedure, you'll need to create the TEST DDE.DOC document file; it should contain at least one line of text. Make sure that the drive and directory paths in lines 20 and 26 match the drive and directory where you've stored your test document.

Next, the procedure starts a new DDE exchange. This time the TEST DDE.DOC file is the topic (line 26). Now, the procedure uses the DDEExecute method three times to execute three WordBasic commands. These commands move to the start of the document (line 27), select the entire first line (line 28), and copy the selection to the Clipboard (line 29). Another DDETerminate statement closes the second channel (line 30).

The rest of the procedure pastes and links the copied data. Lines 34 and 35 select the cell to which the data will be pasted—selecting the destination cell is mandatory when pasting linked data. Then, the Paste method uses its Link argument to paste the text with a DDE link to Word (line 36).

Exchanging Data with the DDE Server Application

As you've seen, each DDE conversation between the client and server is established on a specified topic. Everything else the two applications discuss in the current DDE session is limited to subjects related to the specified topic. In the last section, you saw how the server's commands are included in a DDE exchange. This section examines another subject you can use in your DDE exchanges: data items.

Each server application that supports DDE defines one or more items that the server application can share with the client. For example, a typical worksheet item is a cell, and a typical word processor item is a bookmark (a bookmark is a named block of text). These items are always composed of only text and numbers. Therefore, you cannot transfer graphics and other high-level objects in a DDE exchange.

The next two sections show you how to use the DDERequest and DDEPoke methods to exchange data items between the client and server.

Receiving Data from the DDE Server

If the server has data that you want to transfer to a worksheet cell, you can establish a DDE link between the two applications and use the DDERequest method to retrieve the data:

Syntax

DDERequest(*Channel*, *Item*)

The *Channel* argument is the channel number returned by the DDEInitiate method. *Item* is a string specifying the data item that you want to retrieve from the server. As with other DDE methods, DDERequest returns a Boolean value indicating the success of failure of the operation. Listing 20.5 shows an example of the DDERequest method.

Type

Listing 20.5. Using `DDERequest` to retrieve data from an application.

```
 1:    Option Explicit
 2:
 3:    Const shellMinNoFocus = 6
 4:
 5:    Sub RequestWordData()
 6:    'Sets up a bookmark in Word, then retrieves bookmark text
 7:
 8:        Dim Channel As Integer
 9:        Dim WordData As Variant
10:
11:        On Error GoTo Retreat
12:
13:        Application.StatusBar = "Starting Word for Windows..."
14:        Shell PathName:="C:\MSOFFICE\WINWORD\WINWORD.EXE", _
15:              WindowStyle:=shellMinNoFocus
16:
17:        Application.StatusBar = "DDE: Opening test document..."
18:        Channel = DDEInitiate(App:="WinWord", Topic:="System")
19:        DDEExecute Channel:=Channel, _
20:           String:="[FileOpen ""C:\My Documents\TEST DDE.DOC""]"
21:        DDETerminate Channel
22:
23:        'open new DDE channel with document topic
24:        Channel = DDEInitiate(App:="Winword", _
25:                      Topic:="C:\My Documents\TEST DDE.DOC")
26:
27:        'Find keyword and add a bookmark
28:        Application.StatusBar = "DDE: Searching for keyword..."
29:        DDEExecute Channel:=Channel, String:="[StartOfDocument]"
30:        DDEExecute Channel:=Channel, _
31:                   String:="[EditFind .Find = ""ACME""]"
32:        DDEExecute Channel:=Channel, _
33:                   String:="[SelectCurSentence]"
34:        DDEExecute Channel:=Channel, _
35:                   String:="[EditBookmark .Name = ""Gotcha""]"
36:
37:        Application.StatusBar = "DDE: Retrieving text..."
38:        WordData = DDERequest(Channel:=Channel, Item:="Gotcha")
39:
40:        Application.StatusBar = "Inserting retrieved text..."
41:        Worksheets("Sheet1").[A1].Value = WordData
42:        DDETerminate Channel
43:        Application.StatusBar = False
44:        Exit Sub
45:
46:    Retreat:
47:        DDETerminate Channel
48:        Application.StatusBar = False
49:    End Sub
```

20

The **RequestWordData** procedure in Listing 20.5 finds a particular section of text in a Word document and then reads it into Excel. Listing 20.5 contains an entire module; notice the usual module-level constant declaration (line 3) for the Shell function's WindowStyle arguments.

The **RequestWordData** procedure starts in line 5, and declares two variables: **Channel**, to store the DDE channel number, and **WordData** to store the data returned from Word for Windows. Line 11 sets up an error-handling trap, in case something goes wrong with the DDE exchange.

Line 14 uses the Shell function to start Word for Windows. Line 18 opens a DDE channel to WinWord with the System topic, and lines 19 and 20 contain a single statement that uses DDEExecute to open the document file in WinWord. After the document file is open, this DDE channel is no longer needed, so line 21 uses DDETerminate to close the System topic channel.

Next, line 24 opens a new DDE channel to WinWord, this time using the opened document as the topic of the exchange. Lines 29 through 35 contain four different DDEExecute statements which execute WordBasic commands. Line 29 moves to the start of the document, line 30 searches for a particular word in the document, line 32 selects the line containing the searched-for text, and line 34 inserts a bookmark for the selected text.

> **Note:** For the procedure in Listing 20.5 to work correctly, you must have prepared a Word for Windows document named TEST DDE.DOC that contains a line with the word ACME in it ahead of time. If your test document doesn't contain the word ACME, the procedure in Listing 20.5 will appear to hang up—what's really happening is that Word has generated an error that isn't detected in the DDE exchange.

Line 38 uses the DDERequest method to retrieve the text marked by the new bookmark and stores it in the **WordData** variable. Line 41 inserts the **WordData** contents into the first cell of the Sheet1 worksheet in the active workbook. Finally, line 42 terminates the DDE connection, line 43 returns control of the status bar to Excel, and line 44 ends the procedure. If any errors occur during the DDE exchange, control jumps to the error-handling code after the **Retreat** line label. The error-handling code in lines 47 and 48 simply terminates the DDE channel and returns control of the status bar to Excel.

Sending Data to the DDE Server

Like all good conversations, the exchange between the DDE client and DDE server is a two-way street. Just as your procedures can request data from the server, so too can the client send data to the server by using the DDEPoke method:

Syntax

DDEPoke(*Channel, Item, Data*)

As usual, *Channel* is the channel number generated by the DDEInitiate method. The *Item* argument is a string specifying the server item where you want the data sent. The *Data* argument is the data that you want to send; it must be plain text or numbers. The DDEPoke method returns a Boolean result indicating the success or failure of the operation. Listing 20.6 shows you how DDEPoke works.

Type

Listing 20.6. Using DDEPoke to send data to an application.

```
 1:  Option Explicit
 2:
 3:  Const shellMinNoFocus = 6
 4:
 5:  Sub SendDataToWord()
 6:  'Sends data to a bookmark in Word
 7:
 8:     Dim Channel As Integer
 9:     Dim PokeData As Object
10:
11:     On Error GoTo BadNews
12:
13:     Application.StatusBar = "Starting Word for Windows..."
14:     Shell PathName:="C:\MSOFFICE\WINWORD\WINWORD.EXE", _
15:           WindowStyle:=shellMinNoFocus
16:
17:     Application.StatusBar = "DDE: Opening test document..."
18:     Channel = DDEInitiate(App:="WinWord", Topic:="System")
19:     DDEExecute Channel:=Channel, _
20:        String:="[FileOpen ""C:\My Documents\TEST DDE.DOC""]"
21:     DDETerminate Channel
22:
23:     'open new DDE channel with document topic
24:     Application.StatusBar = "DDE: Making insert bookmark..."
25:     Channel = DDEInitiate(App:="Winword", _
26:                    Topic:="C:\My Documents\TEST DDE.DOC")
27:
28:     DDEExecute Channel:=Channel, String:="[EndOfDocument]"
29:     DDEExecute Channel:=Channel, String:="[InsertPara]"
30:     DDEExecute Channel:=Channel, _
31:             String:="[EditBookmark .Name = ""NewStuff""]"
32:
33:     Application.StatusBar = "DDE: Checking new data..."
34:     With Worksheets("Sheet1")
35:        If .Cells(1, 1).Value = "" Then
36:          .Cells(1, 1).Value = "This is the new stuff."
37:        End If
38:        'Get the data to be sent
39:        Set PokeData = .Cells(1, 1)
40:     End With
41:
42:     'Send new data to the "NewStuff" bookmark
43:     Application.StatusBar = "DDE: Inserting new data..."
```

continues

Listing 20.6. continued

```
44:      Application.DDEPoke Channel:=Channel, _
45:                          Item:="NewStuff", _
46:                          Data:=PokeData
47:      DDETerminate Channel
48:      Application.StatusBar = False
49:      Exit Sub
50:
51:  BadNews:
52:      DDETerminate Channel
53:      Application.StatusBar = False
54:  End Sub
```

In a sense, this procedure performs the inverse of the task performed by the procedure in Listing 20.5. Here, VBA takes text from a worksheet cell and sends it to a bookmark in Word for Windows.

The **SendDataToWord** procedure begins by setting up an error-handler in line 11, then starts Word for Windows (line 14), and establishes a DDE link (line 18). Line 19 uses DDEExecute to open the test document file, and then line 21 terminates the current DDE exchange.

As before, the procedure initiates a new DDE exchange (line 25), with the test document as the topic of the exchange. Lines 28 through 31 use DDEExecute to issue three different WordBasic commands: line 28 moves to the end of the test document, line 29 inserts a new paragraph in the document, and line 30 inserts a new bookmark into the document.

Now, lines 35 through 37 check to see if the first cell of the Sheet1 worksheet has any data in it; if not, line 36 inserts some text into the cell. Line 39 sets the **PokeData** variable to contain an object reference to the first cell of the Sheet1 worksheet.

Finally, a DDEPoke statement (lines 44 through 46) inserts the data from the worksheet cell into the Word for Windows document. The DDE channel is no longer needed, so line 47 terminates the DDE connection, the status bar's control is returned to Excel, and the procedure exits in line 49.

If an error occurs during the DDE exchanges, the error-handling code in lines 52 and 53 is executed.

Sending Keystrokes to an Application

In yesterday's lesson, "Working with Other Applications: OLE and OLE Automation," you saw how OLE automation makes it easy to program a server application's objects. In today's lesson, you've seen how to use DDE to run the server application's macro commands. The majority of Windows applications, however, don't support OLE automation and don't have a macro language that you can control with DDE. You're probably wondering, then, how you can control these less-sophisticated programs with a VBA for Applications program.

One solution is to load the application with the Shell function and have the user work with the program directly. Usually, this solution isn't satisfactory, because the typical goal of a VBA program is to automate a task so that the user doesn't have to perform any actions herself.

Another solution is to send keystrokes to the other application with the SendKeys statement. You can send any key or key-combination—including those that use the Alt, Ctrl, and Shift keys— to a DDE server application. The result is exactly the same as if you typed those keystrokes directly in the application. Here is the syntax of the SendKeys statement:

Syntax

```
SendKeys(String [,Wait])
```

The *String* argument is the key or key-combination that you want to send to the active application. For letters, numbers, or punctuation marks, you simply enclose the character in quotes, as in "a". For other keys, use the strings listed in Table 20.2.

The optional *Wait* argument is a Boolean value indicating whether or not VBA waits for the keystrokes to be processed by the receiving application before VBA continues. If *Wait* is True, VBA waits for the application to finish processing the keys you send before moving on to the next statement in the procedure; otherwise, VBA continues with procedure execution without waiting.

You don't need to initiate a DDE link to use SendKeys. All you have to do is activate a program with Shell or AppActivate. Then, you can send whatever keystrokes you want. For example, you can close any active Windows application by sending the Alt+F4 key combination, as follows:

```
SendKeys String:="%{F4}"
```

Table 20.2. Strings to use for the SendKeys method's String argument.

For...	Use...
Backspace	"{BACKSPACE}" or "{BS}"
Break	"{BREAK}"
Caps Lock	"{CAPSLOCK}"
Delete	"{DELETE}" or "{DEL}"
Down Arrow	"{DOWN}"
End	"{END}"
Enter (keypad)	"{ENTER}"
Enter	"~" (tilde)
Esc	"{ESCAPE}" or "{ESC}"
Home	"{HOME}"
Insert	"{INSERT}"

continues

Table 20.2. continued

For...	Use...
Left Arrow	"{LEFT}"
Num Lock	"{NUMLOCK}"
Page Down	"{PGDN}"
Page Up	"{PGUP}"
Right Arrow	"{RIGHT}"
Scroll Lock	"{SCROLLLOCK}"
Tab	"{TAB}"
Up Arrow	"{UP}"
F1 through F12	"{F1}" through "{F12}"

By combining the keys from Table 20.2 with the Alt, Ctrl, and Shift keys, you can create any key-combination. Just precede a string from Table 20.2 with one or more of the codes listed in Table 20.3.

Table 20.3. Codes for the Alt, Ctrl, and Shift keys.

For...	Use...
Alt	% (percent)
Ctrl	^ (caret)
Shift	+ (plus)

Listing 20.7 shows an example of sending keystrokes that uses the Windows 95 Phone Dialer applet to dial a phone number from the current cell in a worksheet.

Listing 20.7. Controlling an application using the SendKeys statement.

```
1:   Option Explicit
2:
3:   Const shellNormFocus = 1
4:
5:   Sub DialIt()
6:   'Use the Phone dialer applet to dial a phone number
7:   'from the active worksheet cell.
8:
9:      Dim PhoneNumber As String
10:     Dim Ans As Integer
11:
```

```
12:    With ActiveCell
13:      Ans = MsgBox(prompt:="About to dial " & .Value & _
14:                   Chr(13) & "Make sure modem is on.", _
15:                   Buttons:=vbOKCancel + vbExclamation, _
16:                   Title:="Invoking Phone Dialer")
17:      If Ans = vbCancel Then Exit Sub
18:      .Copy
19:    End With
20:
21:    Shell PathName:="C:\WIN95\DIALER.EXE", _
22:         WindowStyle:=shellNormFocus    'Start Phone Dialer
23:    SendKeys String:="^v", Wait:=True   'Paste phone number
24:    SendKeys String:="%d", Wait:=True   'Start Dialing
25:
26:    Application.Wait Now + TimeValue("00:00:15")
27:
28:    SendKeys String:="~", Wait:=True
29:    SendKeys String:="%h", Wait:=True
30:    SendKeys String:="%{F4}", Wait:=True
31:
32:    Application.CutCopyMode = False
33: End Sub
```

Analysis The **DialIt** procedure uses the Windows 95 Phone Dialer applet to dial a telephone number entered in the active worksheet cell. To execute this procedure, you need to first enter a phone number in any worksheet cell, make that cell active, and then execute the **DialIt** procedure through the **T**ools | **M**acro command.

Using ActiveCell in a With statement (lines 12 through 19), the procedure first displays a message dialog box showing the phone number that will be dialed and warning the user to make sure that their modem is turned on. If the user chooses Cancel (or presses Esc), the procedure exits (line 17). Otherwise, the contents of the active cell are copied to the Clipboard (line 18).

Next, the procedure starts the Phone Dialer applet by using the Shell function (line 21). Two SendKeys statements send the following keys to the Phone Dialer (lines 23 and 24):

Ctrl+V—to paste the phone number from the Clipboard

Alt+D—to dial the number

At this point, Phone Dialer displays a "Pick up the phone" dialog box. Go ahead and pick up the receiver, but don't press Enter to clear the dialog box. The **DialIt** procedure waits 15 seconds to give your telephone time to dial (line 26), and then another group of SendKeys statements sends the following keys:

Enter—to remove the dialog box

Alt+H—to cause phone dialer to hang up

Alt+F4—to close the Phone Dialer applet

20

Finally, the CutCopyMode property is set to False (line 32) to take Excel out of Copy mode.

DO	**DON'T**

DO keep in mind that the SendKeys statement is case-sensitive. For example, the strings "^P" and "^+p" both send the key combination Ctrl+Shift+P. If you want to send only Ctrl+P, use "^p".

DO include the following characters in braces—{}—if you want to send them in a SendKeys string:

~ % ^ ( ) + { } [ ]

For example, you send a percent sign as follows:

SendKeys "{%}"

DON'T forget that you can also send keystrokes with the DDEExecute method. Use the same strings listed in Tables 20.2 and 20.3. For example, the following DDEExecute method sends the key combination Ctrl+S to an application linked with **Channel**:

DDEExecute Channel, "^s"

The advantage of using DDEExecute is that you don't need to activate the server application in order to send the keys. The disadvantage is that you can't send keys to dialog boxes.

Accessing DLLs from Visual Basic for Applications

Dynamic-link libraries (DLLs) are collections of functions and procedures that are available to all Windows applications. Windows itself comes with a number of DLL files that provide developers with hundreds of specialized—and very fast—functions. Tapping in to these procedures is an easy way to include powerful Windows functionality in applications—such as reading strings from and writing strings to the Registry database. Together, the DLL libraries supplied with Windows form what is known as the Windows *Application Programming Interface* (API).

Although most of the API functions are highly technical, you can take advantage of a few of them in your VBA procedures. The next sections show you how to access DLLs in your VBA code. You also get to see a few examples.

Declaring DLL Procedures

Before you can use a function from a DLL, you must tell VBA where to find the DLL file and what arguments the function needs. You do this by entering a `Declare` statement at the module level—that is, before any procedure declarations in the module. Depending on whether the procedure is a `Function` or `Sub` procedure, you use one of the following forms:

```
[Public ¦ Private] Declare Function Name Lib "LibName" [Alias AliasName]
➥(Arguments) [As Type]
[Public ¦ Private] Declare Sub Name Lib "LibName" [Alias AliasName] (Arguments) [As
➥Type]
```

As with VBA variables and constants, you can declare DLL procedures to be either `Public` (to make the procedure available to all modules in all workbooks), or `Private` (to make the procedure available only in the module in which it is declared).

`Name` represents the name of the procedure, and `LibName` is the name of the DLL file—for example, `"USER32"`. If the procedure has the same name as a VBA keyword or a `Public` variable, you can't use the procedure's own original name in your code. Instead, use `AliasName` to specify a different name for the procedure.

`Arguments` is the list of arguments required by the procedure. This list uses the following syntax:

```
[Optional][ByVal¦ByRef][ParamArray] VarName [As Type]
```

`Optional` specifies that the argument isn't required. `ByVal` means that the argument is passed by value, as is the case with most DLL procedures. `ByRef` means that the argument is passed by reference. `ParamArray` is used with arrays of Variant type data. `ParamArray` must be the last argument in the argument list; you cannot use `ParamArray` in combination with `Optional`, `ByVal`, or `ByRef`. `VarName` is the name of the argument, and `Type` specifies the data type of the argument.

The following statement, for example, declares a function named `MessageBeep` from the USER32.EXE DLL:

```
Declare Sub MessageBeep Lib "USER32" (ByVal BeepType As Integer)
```

Once you've declared the DLL procedure, you can use it in your VBA code just like any other `Sub` or `Function` procedure.

Note: When a DLL filename ends with the digits 32, it signifies that the DLL contains 32-bit code. Whenever you have a choice, you should use the 32-bit versions of any DLL in your VBA code.

Some DLL Examples

This section provides you with several examples of how to use DLL procedures in VBA code. To learn more about DLLs and the Windows API, you might want to get yourself a copy of *Win32 API Desktop Reference* by James McCord. This book provides complete coverage of the subjects.

Beeping the Speaker

VBA provides you with a simple `Beep` statement you can use to get the user's attention. Unfortunately, `Beep` produces only a single sound. This isn't a problem most of the time, but there are plenty of situations for which you'll want to do more. For example, you usually want to beep the speaker at the end of a long operation to bring the user's attention back to the screen. But what if an error occurs during the operation? It would be nice to have a different sound to go with your error message.

If different sounds are what you want, the DLL procedure `MessageBeep` gives you access to five individual sounds. To take advantage of `MessageBeep`, you or the users of your VBA program need a sound card supported by Windows 95.

Note: The DLL that contains the `MessageBeep` procedure—USER32—is stored in a disk file named USER32.DLL in your \WINDOWS\SYSTEM directory. It is supplied with Windows 95. USER32.DLL contains other useful functions and procedures in addition to `MessageBeep`, all of which are part of the standard 32-bit Windows API. To get full information on the functions and procedures in USER32.DLL, refer to the Win32 Software Developer's Kit documentation, available from Microsoft.

Here's the `Declare` statement to use with `MessageBeep`:

```
Declare Sub MessageBeep Lib "USER32" (ByVal BeepType as Long)
```

The `BeepType` argument takes one of five values, which are listed in Table 20.4.

Table 20.4. Values for the `BeepType` argument.

BeepType	Sound Produced
0	Default beep
16	Critical stop

BeepType	Sound Produced
32	Question
48	Exclamation
64	Asterisk

These sounds are all defined in the Sounds icon of Control Panel. Listing 20.8 displays a procedure that plays all five sounds.

 Listing 20.8. Using the `MessageBeep` DLL procedure.

```
1:  Option Explicit
2:
3:  Declare Sub MessageBeep Lib "USER32" (ByVal BeepType As Long)
4:
5:  Sub BeepTest()
6:  'This procedure plays all five MessageBeep sounds.
7:
8:    Dim I As Integer
9:
10:   For I = 0 To 64 Step 16
11:     Select Case I
12:       Case 0
13:         Application.StatusBar = "Default Beep"
14:       Case 16
15:         Application.StatusBar = "Critical Stop"
16:       Case 32
17:         Application.StatusBar = "Question"
18:       Case 48
19:         Application.StatusBar = "Exclamation"
20:       Case 64
21:         Application.StatusBar = "Asterisk"
22:     End Select
23:     MessageBeep I
24:     Application.Wait Now + TimeValue("00:00:02")
25:   Next I
26:
27:   Application.StatusBar = False
28: End Sub
```

 This procedure simply runs through all the values accepted by `MessageBeep` and plays the associated sounds. Line 3 contains the `Declare` statement for the `MessageBeep` procedure; this is the statement that makes that routine in the USER32.DLL available to VBA in this module.

The `For...Next` structure (lines 10–25) loops through values of the variable `I` from 0 to 64 in steps of 16. A `Select Case` statement (line 11) looks for each value of `I` and displays the sound name in the status bar. `MessageBeep` plays the sound (line 23), and the procedure delays for 2 seconds (line 24) before it moves on to the next value.

<table>
<tr><td>

DO

</td><td>

DON'T

</td></tr>
</table>

DO declare the `MessageBeep` arguments as constants if you'll be using them throughout a procedure or module. For example, the following statement declares the `QuestionBeep` constant as 32:

```
Const QuestionBeep = 32
```

DON'T worry about running `MessageBeep` on a system without a sound card or sound driver. If the system can't play the sound, `MessageBeep` uses the computer's default beep.

Determining the Windows Directory

The `GetWindowsDirectory` DLL function determines the path name of the Windows directory. This is handy if you need to find out which directory Windows is installed in, or if you need to find out where one of Windows' accessory applets is located—such as the Phone Dialer applet used in Listing 20.7. You declare the `GetWindowsDirectory` function as follows (in this case, the `Alias` portion of the declaration is required):

```
Declare Function GetWindowsDirectory Lib "kernel32" _
                Alias "GetWindowsDirectoryA" _
                (ByVal Buffer As String, _
                 ByVal Size As Long) As Long
```

The `Buffer` argument is a string variable into which `GetWindowsDirectory` places the Windows path name. You must ensure that the string you pass is already long enough to hold the path name, because DLLs can't increase the length of strings passed to them. If the string is not long enough to accommodate the directory path name, the string returned in the `Buffer` argument may overwrite memory locations not reserved for use by VBA—with disastrous consequences. Anything from General Protection Fault errors to an outright system crash is possible. The `Buffer` argument is an ideal use for a fixed-length string. The following declaration, for example, is an appropriate string to use as the `Buffer` argument:

```
Dim WinDir As String * 255
```

The `Size` argument is the maximum size of the buffer. You can use the `Len` function to determine the length of the buffer variable, and use the result as the `Size` argument.

The `GetWindowsDirectory` function returns the length of the pathname string copied into `Buffer`. Listing 20.9 shows an example.

Listing 20.9. Using the `GetWindowsDirectory` DLL function.

```
1:  Option Explicit
2:
3:  Const shellMaxFocus = 3
4:
5:  Declare Function GetWindowsDirectory Lib "kernel32" _
6:                  Alias "GetWindowsDirectoryA" _
```

```
7:                          (ByVal Buffer As String, _
8:                           ByVal Size As Long) As Long
9:
10:   Sub LaunchWordPad()
11:   'Loads WordPad applet
12:
13:      Dim WinDir As String * 255
14:      Dim DirLength As Long
15:      Dim FullName As String
16:
17:      DirLength = GetWindowsDirectory(Buffer:=WinDir, _
18:                              Size:=Len(WinDir))
19:      If DirLength = 0 Then
20:        MsgBox "Unable to determine Windows directory!"
21:      Else
22:        FullName = Left(WinDir, DirLength) & "\WRITE.EXE"
23:        Shell PathName:=FullName, WindowStyle:=shellMaxFocus
24:      End If
25:   End Sub
```

Analysis
This procedure just loads the WordPad applet provided with Windows 95, and leaves it open, ready for editing. Listing 20.9 contains an entire module. Lines 5 through 8 contain the `Declare` statement for the `GetWindowsDirectory` function. In this case, the `Alias` portion of the statement is required—the actual name of the DLL procedure is `GetWindowsDirectoryA`; without the `Alias` information, VBA can't find the routine in the DLL.

The **LaunchWordPad** procedure begins by declaring the **WinDir** variable as a fixed-length string 255 characters long (line 13). **WinDir** is used as the buffer for the `GetWindowsDirectory` function (line 17). The size of the directory string copied to **WinDir** is stored in the **DirLength** variable. If **DirLength** is **0**, it means that the function failed (line 19). In this case, a message to that effect is displayed (line 20). Otherwise, the full directory path name for the WordPad applet (whose executable filename is WRITE.EXE) is created by concatenating the Windows directory—as given by the `Left(WinDir, DirLength)` function—with `"\WRITE.EXE"` (line 22). The `Shell` statement runs WordPad in a maximized window with focus (line 23).

Summary

This chapter walked you through a few more techniques for working with other applications. The most straightforward of these techniques was the simple `Shell` function, which starts another application. By specifying an executable file, you can use this function to start any other application. You can choose a window style, such as maximized or minimized, and specify whether the application gets the focus at startup.

You can activate any running application by using the `AppActivate` statement. You must specify the name of the application as it appears in the application's title bar.

20

You also learned about dynamic data exchange (DDE). This protocol lets DDE-enabled applications talk to each other and exchange data items. VBA has several DDE functions that enable you to initialize a DDE channel, execute the server application's commands, send data back and forth, and terminate the link.

You learned that you can control applications that don't support either OLE or DDE by sending keystrokes. The SendKeys statement can send any key or key-combination to an active Windows application. The results are the same as though you had typed the keys yourself.

You also learned how to work with dynamic-link libraries (DLLs) in your VBA code. DLLs offer hundreds of specialized functions and procedures that enable you to perform tasks that are otherwise extremely difficult, if not impossible, with VBA alone.

Q&A

Q When I try to run the StartControlPanel procedure in Listing 20.1 with the Password, Time and Date, International, Desktop or other options, I get a display other than the one I expect, or nothing at all happens. Is something wrong with Control Panel?

A No, Control Panel is fine. The problem is that many of the Control Panel setting icons are actually located in different .CPL files. For example, the Password settings are in the PASSWORD.CPL file, the International settings are in the INTL.CPL file, and so on. To find out what .CPL files are available for you to use, use Windows 95's Start | Find | Files or Folders command, and search for files named *.CPL.

Q Can I use the Shell function to run DOS commands?

A Sure. For external DOS commands—in other words, commands such as FORMAT or ATTRIB that have their own executable files—just execute Shell with the name of the appropriate .EXE or .COM file—for example, FORMAT.COM or ATTRIB.EXE. For internal DOS commands, such as DIR and COPY, you can use the following syntax:

```
Shell "COMMAND.COM /C DOSCommand"
```

Here, another copy of the DOS command interpreter, COMMAND.COM, is loaded into memory. The /C parameter tells DOS that this copy of COMMAND.COM in memory is temporary. DOSCommand is a string containing the internal command you want to execute and any additional switches or parameters. Use the exact syntax for the command that you would use at the DOS command line. For example, the following statement redirects the output of a DIR command to a file named DIR.TXT:

```
Shell "COMMAND.COM /C DIR /-P > DIR.TXT"
```

You should remember from Days 5 and 12, however, that VBA includes several functions and statements that can perform many of the duties for which you might use DOS commands.

Q Once I've pasted data with a DDE link, is there any way to update the link using Visual Basic for Applications?

A Sure. First, use the `LinkSources` method to return an array of the names of all the links in a workbook:

```
Object.LinkSources(xlOLELinks)
```

Here, `Object` is a reference to the Workbook object that contains the link (or links) you want to update. Next, use the `UpdateLink` method to update a specific link:

```
Object.UpdateLink(Name)
```

Again, `Object` is a reference to the Workbook object that contains the links and `Name` is the name of the link from the array returned by `LinkSources`.

The following code fragment updates every link in the active workbook:

```
With ActiveWorkbook
    .UpdateLink .LinkSources
End With
```

Q I've used DDE to link some Word for Windows text to an Excel worksheet. However, when I change the text in Word, Excel doesn't update its version of the text despite the fact that both programs are running. What's the problem?

A Your problem could be one of two things. First, the link might have been set to a manual link. This means that the text is updated only if you run the `UpdateLink` method or if you select the **U**pdate button in the Links dialog box (select the **E**dit | **L**inks command).

Second, Excel might be set up to ignore updates from server applications. To check this, select the **T**ools | **O**ptions command, select the Calculation tab in the Options dialog box, and take a look at the Update **R**emote References check box. This check box must be activated for Excel to automatically update DDE links.

You can check the status of the Update Remote References check box in the Options dialog box by testing whether the `UpdateRemoteReferences` property of a particular `Workbook` object is `True` or `False`. If `UpdateRemoteReferences` is `True`, the Update **R**emote References check box is selected; if it is `False`, the Update **R**emote References check box is not selected.

```
AnyBoolean = ActiveWorkBook.UpdateRemoteReferences
```

You can also change the status of the Update **R**emote References check box in the Options dialog box by making an assignment to the `UpdateRemoteReferences` property. The following statement sets the `UpdateRemoteReferences` property for the active workbook to `True` so that remote references are updated automatically:

```
ActiveWorkBook.UpdateRemoteReferences = True
```

Workshop

Answers are in Appendix A.

Quiz

1. What does it mean to say that the Shell function executes applications asynchronously?

2. What is dynamic data exchange?

3. What are the three basic steps in a DDE conversation? Be sure to include the appropriate DDE methods in your answer.

4. What are the three main disadvantages of letting the DDEInitiate method start the server application?

5. In a DDEInitiate method, what does the System topic do?

6. Under what circumstances is it better to use SendKeys instead of DDEExecute for sending keystrokes to another application?

7. In a SendKeys statement, what does the Wait argument do?

8. What is a dynamic-link library?

9. What is the Windows API?

Exercises

1. **BUG BUSTER:** The following procedure looks for a file named MEM.TXT and deletes it if it exists. The first Shell function runs the DOS MEM command and redirects the output to MEM.TXT. The second Shell statement is supposed to open MEM.TXT in NotePad, but an error occurs instead. Do you know why?

```
Sub GetMEMText()
    If Dir("C:\WINDOWS\MEM.TXT") <> "" Then _
        Kill "C:\WINDOWS\MEM.TXT"
    Shell "COMMAND.COM /C MEM.EXE > C:\WINDOWS\MEM.TXT"
    Shell "NOTEPAD.EXE C:\WINDOWS\MEM.TXT, 3
End Sub
```

2. Write a function procedure that uses DDE to determine whether a file is open in the server application. The function should return True if the file is open and False if not. (Hint: Running a DDERequest method with "Topics" as the Item argument returns an array of all the server's current topics, including the full path names of the open files.)

3. One of the problems with the Shell function is that it doesn't warn you whether an application is already running. In most cases, it simply starts up a second instance of

the program. Besides using up precious memory—especially if you're dealing with a large application—this can be disastrous if you're using DDE to exchange data with the application.

Unfortunately, VBA gives you no way of determining whether an application is already running. That isn't a problem, though; the GetModuleHandle DLL function can do the job. Here's how you declare this function:

```
Declare Function GetModuleHandle Lib "Kernel32" _
                Alias "GetModuleHandleA" _
                (ByVal ModuleName As String) As Long
```

The ModuleName argument is a string that specifies the name of an executable file. If this function returns 0, the application isn't running. Write a procedure that checks whether Word for Windows is running. If it is, your procedure should activate it; otherwise, your procedure should start it.

20

Using Automatic Procedures, Event Procedures, and Add-Ins

As you've seen throughout this book, Visual Basic for Applications doesn't skimp on the number of ways in which you can run your procedures. You can start them by using the Macro dialog box, by using a shortcut key, by assigning the procedure to the Tools menu, by using a customized menu command, or by using a customized toolbar button.

The common feature of these methods is that you have to do *something* to run the procedure—choosing a menu command, pressing a key combination, or clicking a toolbar button. VBA also has several techniques that enable you to create procedures that run automatically when a certain event occurs, such as opening a workbook. Your final lesson covers these automatic routines. You'll learn:

☐ How to run a procedure when you open, close, or save a workbook.

☐ How to run a procedure when you activate or deactivate a worksheet, or when you activate a window.

☐ How to create procedures that run in response to specified keystrokes, key combinations, or mouse actions.

☐ How to run a procedure at a specific time.

☐ How to set up procedures that respond when the user enters data or when the worksheet recalculates.

☐ How to create and work with add-in applications.

What Are Automatic Procedures and Event Procedures?

VBA makes it possible for you to create *event-driven* programs. An event-driven program is one that loops indefinitely, waiting for—and responding to—various events, instead of simply following a linear path from the beginning of a routine to the end. An *event* is something that happens in the program, such as a particular keystroke, a mouse click, the activating or deactivating of a worksheet, or the opening or closing of a workbook file. Because the specific events that occur while the program is executing guide the program's behavior, the program is said to be *driven* by those events, hence the term event-driven.

When an event occurs, the program executes one or more procedures related to that event. These procedures are generally referred to as *event handlers*. Visual Basic for Applications divides event handlers into two categories: automatic procedures and event procedures. Depending on the specific event, VBA executes either an automatic procedure or an event procedure.

Automatic procedures are associated with the following four events:

☐ Opening a workbook

☐ Closing a workbook

- [ ] Installing an add-in application
- [ ] Removing an add-in application

VBA associates automatic procedures with these events by requiring the event handler to have a special name. VBA in Excel requires, for example, that the automatic procedure it executes on opening a workbook be named `Auto_Open`. If a workbook contains a procedure named `Auto_Open`, VBA automatically executes that procedure whenever that workbook is opened manually from the Excel menus. (You will recall from Day 18 that using the `Open` and `Close` methods of the host application to open or close files doesn't result in the execution of automatic procedures; you must use the `RunAutoMacros` method to execute the automatic procedures.)

Event procedures are associated with the following events:

- [ ] Saving a workbook
- [ ] Activating a worksheet or window
- [ ] Deactivating a worksheet
- [ ] Pressing a key or key combination
- [ ] Double-clicking the mouse
- [ ] Entering data in a worksheet
- [ ] Recalculating a worksheet

Unlike automatic procedures, event procedures don't need a special name. Instead, you use one of VBA's `OnEvent` properties or methods to associate a procedure with a specific event. For example, you use the `OnKey` method to associate a procedure with a specific keystroke. When the user presses the key, the procedure associated with that keypress executes automatically.

Working with Automatic Procedures

The next two sections give you basic details about two of the automatic procedures, `Auto_Open` and `Auto_Close`. (See the "Working with Add-In Applications" section later in this chapter to learn more about the automatic procedures associated with add-in applications.)

Auto_Open Procedures

To function properly, most large-scale VBA programs require the host application's environment to be modified in some way. These modifications might involve adding custom menu commands, displaying a custom toolbar, or setting options for the host application. In most cases, these modifications must be made to the host application as soon as the user starts your VBA program, so that your program's menu commands and toolbars are available from the start.

If you want your VBA program to be well received, you shouldn't impose the chore of adding menus and toolbars or changing option settings on the user. Instead, you should make these adjustments automatically at startup with an `Auto_Open` procedure. Simply include a `Sub` procedure named `Auto_Open` in any of the modules of your program. The host application will run this procedure automatically whenever a user opens the file containing your program.

Some items you can include in an `Auto_Open` procedure are

- [ ] Custom menu bars, menus, and menu commands.
- [ ] Custom toolbars.
- [ ] Program-wide settings, such as the calculation mode, the default file path, the standard font, and the objects displayed on-screen (including the status and formula bars).
- [ ] Event procedure assignments.
- [ ] A custom dialog box of application options.
- [ ] DDE links.

Listing 21.1 shows an example of an `Auto_Open` procedure.

Listing 21.1. Using the `Auto_Open` procedure.

```
 1: Sub Auto_Open()
 2: 'This procedure runs automatically when workbook is opened
 3:
 4:    Application.StatusBar = "Loading VBA application..."
 5:
 6:    'Initialize environment
 7:    With Application
 8:      .AlertBeforeOverwriting = True
 9:      .Calculation = xlManual
10:      .Caption = "VBA Rules!"
11:      .DefaultFilePath = "C:\EXCEL\STUFF"
12:      .DisplayRecentFiles = False
13:      .MoveAfterReturn = False
14:      .PromptForSummaryInfo = False
15:      .SheetsInNewWorkbook = 8
16:      .UserName = InputBox("Enter your name:")
17:    End With
18:
19:    'Display toolbar
20:    With Toolbars("Visual Basic")
21:      .Visible = True
22:      .Position = xlFloating
23:      .Left = 400
24:      .Top = 40
25:    End With
26:
27:    Application.StatusBar = False
28: End Sub
```

 The procedure begins by setting the `Application` object's `StatusBar` property to a text string (line 4). This string appears in the status bar to tell the user what's going on. (You can use the `StatusBar` property in any procedure. It's an easy way of keeping the user informed, and it's less intrusive than the `MsgBox` function.)

Lines 7 through 17 contain a `With` statement which sets several properties of the `Application` object. Most of these properties are available in the Options dialog box; you would use the **Tools | O**ptions command to set these properties manually. The `Caption` property (line 10), however, is different. This property controls the text that appears in the title of the host application's main window. In Excel, for example, this is normally *Microsoft Excel*, but you can change it to the name of your application, the name of your company, or whatever you like.

The next `With` statement (lines 20 through 25) displays and positions the Visual Basic toolbar. The procedure ends by setting the `StatusBar` property to `False` (line 27), which clears the status bar and returns control back to Excel.

DO	DON'T

DO hold down the Shift key while opening a workbook to prevent Excel from executing the `Auto_Open` procedure.

DO remember that Excel doesn't run an `Auto_Open` procedure if you open a workbook with the `Open` method, which is explained in Day 18, "Working with Excel." Instead, you must run the following method:

`Object.RunAutoMacros(xlAutoOpen)`

`Object` is a reference to the Workbook object that contains the `Auto_Open` procedure.

DON'T create more than one `Auto_Open` procedure. If you do, you create an ambiguous situation, and Excel can't tell which `Auto_Open` procedure should be executed. As a result, Excel does not execute any of them.

Auto_Close **Procedures**

When you close a workbook, you often need to reset the host application's environment, especially if an `Auto_Open` procedure has added menu commands or toolbars. To make this chore easier, you can create an `Auto_Close` procedure in any module of the file. The host application executes this procedure automatically when you close the file. Listing 21.2 shows an example of an `Auto_Close` procedure.

Type

Listing 21.2. Using the `Auto_Close` procedure.

```
 1:  Sub Auto_Close()
 2:  'This procedure runs automatically when the workbook closes
 3:
 4:      Application.StatusBar = "Closing VBA application..."
 5:
 6:      'Reset environment
 7:      With Application
 8:        .Caption = Empty
 9:        .DefaultFilePath = "C:\EXCEL"
10:        .DisplayRecentFiles = True
11:        .Calculation = xlAutomatic
12:        .MoveAfterReturn = True
13:        .PromptForSummaryInfo = True
14:        .SheetsInNewWorkbook = 16
15:      End With
16:
17:      'Hide toolbar
18:      Toolbars("Visual Basic").Visible = False
19:
20:      'Quit Excel
21:      Application.Quit
22:  End Sub
```

Analysis

This procedure resets many of the environment options that were modified in the previous `Auto_Open` procedure (lines 7-15). Notice that the `Caption` property is assigned the value `Empty` in line 8. Assigning the special `Empty` value to the `Caption` property restores the original application's caption in the title bar of the main window. Line 17 hides the custom toolbar, and line 21 quits Excel with the `Quit` method.

DO	**DON'T**

DO use the `RunAutoMacros` method to execute an `Auto_Close` procedure before you close a workbook with the `Close` method:

`Object.RunAutoMacros(xlAutoClose)`

`Object` is a reference to the Workbook object that contains the `Auto_Close` procedure.

DON'T create more than one `Auto_Close` procedure because, as with `Auto_Open`, Excel can't tell which one to run, and consequently won't run any of them.

Working with Event Procedures

The way you work with event procedures is slightly different from the way you work with automatic procedures. Instead of creating a procedure with a special name, you associate an existing procedure with a specific event by using one of VBA's OnEvent properties or methods. These properties and methods correspond to various Excel or system events, such as pressing a key or recalculating a workbook. Once the association is set up, Excel executes the procedure automatically as soon as, and whenever, the event occurs. This is known as *event trapping*. The next few sections take you through each of the OnEvent properties and methods. (Day 16 described how to attach event procedures to custom menus and toolbar buttons.)

The *OnSheetActivate* Property

The Auto_Open procedure demonstrated earlier in this lesson is useful for setting up menus, toolbars, and global settings used by every workbook and worksheet in a VBA program. Many programs that use multiple workbooks and multiple sheets in each workbook, however, require different settings as the user moves from sheet to sheet and book to book. For example, you might need to display a custom data entry dialog box whenever the user selects a certain sheet, or you might need to customize a menu or display a different toolbar when the user moves to another workbook.

In these cases, the user is activating different objects—worksheets and workbooks. Activating a specific object is an event, and you can trap these events by using the OnSheetActivate property with this general syntax:

Syntax

Object.OnSheetActivate = "*ProcedureName*"

Object is a reference to any of the Excel objects listed in Table 21.1. *ProcedureName* represents a text string specifying the name of the procedure to be executed whenever Excel traps the event—that is, whenever the user activates the object indicated by *Object*.

To cancel the event procedure, set the object's OnSheetActivate property equal to a zero-length string:

Object.OnSheetActivate = ""

Listing 21.3 shows you how to use the OnSheetActivate property.

Table 21.1. Excel objects that use the OnSheetActivate property.

Object	Runs the Event Procedure When...
Application	Any sheet in any open workbook is activated.
Chart	A specified chart sheet is activated.
DialogSheet	A specified dialog sheet is activated.
Module	A specified VBA module is activated.
Workbook	Any sheet in the specified workbook is activated.
Worksheet	A specified worksheet is activated.

21

Listing 21.3. Using the `OnSheetActivate` property.

```
1:  Option Explicit
2:
3:  Sub Auto_Open()
4:  'This simple Auto_Open procedure initializes
5:  'the event trapping
6:
7:    Worksheets("Data Entry").OnSheetActivate = _
8:                         "DAY21.XLS!DataEntryHandler"
9:  End Sub
10:
11:
12: Sub DataEntryHandler()
13: 'This is the event handler that runs whenever the
14: 'Data Entry sheet is activated
15:
16:   Application.Calculation = xlManual
17:
18:   Do While True
19:     If DialogSheets("Data Entry Dialog").Show Then
20:       ProcessData
21:     Else
22:       Exit Do
23:     End If
24:   Loop
25: End Sub
26:
27:
28: Sub ProcessData()
29:   MsgBox prompt:="Stand-in for a data-processing routine.", _
30:         Title:="Demo OnSheetActivate event procedure"
31: End Sub
```

The `Auto_Open` procedure (lines 3 through 9) in Listing 21.3 sets the `OnSheetActivate` property of a worksheet named `Data Entry`. After completing the `Auto_Open` procedure, Excel will now execute the **DataEntryHandler** procedure whenever the Data Entry worksheet is activated.

The **DataEntryHandler** procedure (lines 12 through 25) begins by setting the `Calculation` property to `xlManual` (line 14). Then, a `Do While` loop displays a dialog box (line 19). If the user selects OK, line 18 executes a procedure named **ProcessData**. Otherwise, an `Exit Do` statement exits the loop (line 22). The **ProcessData** procedure in lines 28 through 31 is just a dummy procedure to represent whatever processing might be needed for the data entered into the dialog box.

DO	DON'T

DO use the `Auto_Open` procedure to initialize all your event procedures. This ensures that event trapping is turned on immediately. If you don't want event trapping

available from the start, you can always include the initialization statements in another procedure.

DON'T leave out the event procedure's workbook and module names if the procedure resides in a different workbook.

The *OnSheetDeactivate* **Property**

As you learned earlier in this chapter, the Auto_Close procedure is useful for resetting any changes made to the Excel environment by an Auto_Open routine. The OnSheetDeactivate property performs a similar function. A sheet's OnSheetDeactivate event procedure executes as soon as you exit the sheet. This means that you can use the procedure to restore menus, hide toolbars, or reset program options. The objects that have the OnSheetActivate property use OnSheetDeactivate in the same way (refer to Table 21.1). The general form for an OnSheetDeactivate statement is shown in the following syntax.

Object.OnSheetDeactivate = "*ProcedureName*"

Object represents an object reference to any of the Excel objects from Table 21.1. *ProcedureName* represents a string containing the name of the procedure that executes when Excel traps the event—that is, when the user deactivates the referenced *Object*.

To cancel the event handler, assign a zero-length string to the object's OnSheetDeactivate property:

Object.OnSheetDeactivate = ""

Listing 21.4 shows an example of the OnSheetDeactivate property.

Listing 21.4. Using the OnSheetDeactivate property.

```
 1:  Sub Auto_Open()
 2:  'This procedure sets up the event trapping
 3:
 4:    With Worksheets("Budget Analysis")
 5:      .OnSheetActivate = "SetUpBudgetSheet"
 6:      .OnSheetDeactivate = "ResetBudgetSheet"
 7:    End With
 8:  End Sub
 9:
10:
11:  Sub SetUpBudgetSheet()
12:  'Prepares budget sheet for use.
13:  'Executed whenever Budget Analysis sheet is activated
14:
15:    Toolbars.Add "Budget Buttons"
```

21

continues

Listing 21.4. continued

```
16:     With Toolbars("Budget Buttons")
17:        .ToolbarButtons.Add Button:=221, OnAction:="ButtonFill"
18:        .ToolbarButtons.Add Button:=223, OnAction:="ButtonFill"
19:        With .ToolbarButtons(1)
20:           .Name = "Budget Button 1"
21:           .StatusBar = "Doesn't do anything"
22:        End With
23:        With .ToolbarButtons(2)
24:           .Name = "Budget Button 2"
25:           .StatusBar = "Doesn't do anything"
26:        End With
27:        .Position = xlFloating
28:        .Width = 200 * 2
29:        .Visible = True
30:     End With
31:
32:     With Application
33:        .Calculation = xlManual
34:        .Caption = "Budget Analysis Demo"
35:     End With
36: End Sub
37:
38:
39: Sub ResetBudgetSheet()
40: 'This is the event handler that runs whenever
41: 'the Budget Analysis sheet is deactivated
42:
43:     Toolbars("Budget Buttons").Delete
44:
45:     With Application
46:        .Calculation = xlAutomatic
47:        .Caption = Empty
48:     End With
49: End Sub
50:
51:
52: Sub ButtonFill()
53:     MsgBox prompt:="Demo Button only", _
54:            Title:="OnSheetActivate/OnSheetDeactivate Demo"
55: End Sub
```

Analysis

The Auto_Open procedure in this listing sets up event trapping for both the OnSheetActivate and OnSheetDeactivate properties of a worksheet named Budget Analysis. Notice that the **SetUpBudgetSheet** procedure (lines 11 through 36) is the procedure executed whenever the Budget Analysis worksheet is activated; it creates a toolbar for use with that particular worksheet (creating custom toolbars was discussed in Day 16). The toolbar created in the **SetUpBudgetSheet** procedure has only two buttons, both of which call the same dummy procedure (**ButtonFill**, in lines 52 through 55). The **SetUpBudgetSheet** procedure also sets a couple of application properties: the calculation mode is set to manual (line 33), and the application's caption is changed (line 34).

The event for `OnSheetDeactivate` is the deactivation of the `Budget Analysis` worksheet, and the procedure that Excel executes is called **ResetBudgetSheet**.

The **ResetBudgetSheet** procedure occupies lines 39 through 49 of Listing 21.4. Line 43 deletes the custom toolbar that was created by the `OnSheetActivate` event procedure, and then lines 45 through 48 reset the application properties that were previously modified. The calculation mode is returned to automatic (line 46), and the application's original caption is restored (line 47).

DO	DON'T

DO keep in mind that Excel doesn't run an `OnSheetActivate` or `OnSheetDeactivate` event procedure if you use the `Activate` method to switch between workbooks or worksheets. If you want to run these procedures, you must include the appropriate procedure calls in your code.

DON'T use the `ActiveWorkbook` or `ActiveSheet` objects within the `OnSheetDeactivate` event procedure. Excel switches to the new workbook or sheet before it runs the procedure. Therefore, any code that references the active workbook or active sheet might not run properly.

The *OnWindow* Property

The `OnWindow` and `OnSheetActivate` properties are similar. However, `OnWindow` specifies an event procedure that runs whenever the user activates a particular window instead of a particular sheet. Use the `OnWindow` property if you want to execute a particular procedure whenever any window on a particular worksheet becomes the active window. Another use for the `OnWindow` property is if you need to evaluate the contents of the current window, and enable or disable menu commands or toolbars in your application, depending on the window's specific contents. (Remember, you can have multiple windows open for the same worksheet.) The syntax for setting the `OnWindow` property is:

Syntax

```
Object.OnWindow = "ProcedureName"
```

Here, *Object* is an object reference to either a `Window` object or the `Application` object. If *Object* references a `Window` object, the event procedure executes whenever the user switches to the specified window. If *Object* references the `Application` object, then the event procedure executes whenever the user switches to any window.

To cancel an event procedure associated with a window, assign a zero-length string to the `OnWindow` property:

```
Object.OnWindow = ""
```

Listing 21.5 shows an example of the `OnWindow` property.

Listing 21.5. Using the `OnWindow` property.

```
1:  Option Explicit
2:
3:  Sub SetWindowHandler()
4:  'Sets up the event trapping for the OnWindow property
5:
6:     Windows("DAY21.XLS:2").OnWindow = "WindowHandler"
7:  End Sub
8:
9:
10: Sub WindowHandler()
11: 'Runs whenever the DAY21.XLS:2 window is activated
12:
13:    With Windows("DAY21.XLS:2")
14:       .SplitVertical = 150
15:       .DisplayFormulas = True
16:       .DisplayGridlines = False
17:       .DisplayZeros = False
18:       .FreezePanes = True
19:       .WindowState = xlMaximized
20:    End With
21: End Sub
22:
23:
24: Sub ClearWindowHandler()
25: 'Removes event trapping for the OnWindow property
26:
27:    Windows("DAY21.XLS:2").OnWindow = ""
28: End Sub
```

Listing 21.5 contains a complete module listing. In this example, a procedure named **SetWindowHandler** (lines 3 through 7) sets the `OnWindow` property for a window named DAY21:2.XLS (line 6). The event procedure—**WindowHandler**—sets several of the window's properties inside a `With` statement (lines 13 through 20). The window is split vertically (line 14), formulas are displayed (line 15), gridlines are turned off (line 16), zeros are hidden (line 17), the panes are frozen (line 18), and the window is maximized (line 19). (The **WindowHandler** procedure only works if the sheet currently displayed in the window is a worksheet—otherwise it will produce runtime errors.)

The *OnKey* Method

As you know, you can assign shortcut key combinations to your VBA procedures interactively, by using the **Tools | Macro** command, selecting a macro, and then clicking the **Options** command button. You can also install custom shortcut key combinations in your VBA code by using the `OnKey` method. The keystroke shortcuts generally take the form Ctrl+*key*, where *key* is a letter of the alphabet. Excel differentiates between uppercase and lowercase letters. Although your choice of letters is limited—especially since Excel uses some letters for its built-in shortcut keys, such as Ctrl+C for the **Edit | C**opy command—this technique works fine in most applications.

What happens, though, if you need to trap different kinds of keys or key combinations? For example, what if you don't want a user to delete anything? You can remove the Cut button from the toolbar and the Cut and Clear commands from the menus, but what about the Delete key? Ideally, you would like to disable the Delete key, or to trap it and run a procedure that displays a message.

For these situations, you need to use the OnKey method to trap a specific key or key combination:

Syntax

```
Application.OnKey(Key [,Procedure])
```

The *Key* argument is a string specifying the key or key combination that you want to trap. For letters, numbers, or punctuation marks, simply enclose the character in quotes—for example, "a". For other keys, use the text strings outlined in Table 21.2. You can also create key combinations by combining a letter key or one of the keys from Table 21.2 with the Alt, Ctrl, and Shift keys by preceding the key letter or code with one or more of the codes listed in Table 21.3. (The key values shown in Tables 21.2 and 21.3 are the same as the key values you use with the SendKeys method described in Day 20.)

The *Procedure* argument is a string specifying the name of the procedure that is to be executed whenever the user presses the specified key. If you enter a zero-length string ("") for the *Procedure* argument, the shortcut key is disabled. If you omit the *Procedure* argument, Excel resets the key to its normal state.

Table 21.2. Text strings to use for the OnKey method's Key argument.

For...	Use...
Backspace	"{BACKSPACE}" or "{BS}"
Break	"{BREAK}"
Caps Lock	"{CAPSLOCK}"
Delete	"{DELETE}" or "{DEL}"
Down Arrow	"{DOWN}"
End	"{END}"
Enter (keypad)	"{ENTER}"
Enter	"{~}" (tilde)
Esc	"{ESCAPE}" or "{ESC}"
Home	"{HOME}"

continues

Table 21.2. continued

For...	Use...
Insert	"{INSERT}"
Left Arrow	"{LEFT}"
Num Lock	"{NUMLOCK}"
Page Down	"{PGDN}"
Page Up	"{PGUP}"
Right Arrow	"{RIGHT}"
Scroll Lock	"{SCROLLLOCK}"
Tab	"{TAB}"
Up Arrow	"{UP}"
F1 through F12	"{F1}" through "{F12}"

Table 21.3. Codes for the Alt, Ctrl, and Shift keys.

For...	Use...
Alt	% (percent)
Ctrl	^ (caret)
Shift	+ (plus)

Listing 21.6 shows you how to use the OnKey method.

Listing 21.6. Using the OnKey method.

```
1:   Option Explicit
2:
3:   Sub SetShortcutKeys()
4:   'Sets the Ctrl+Shift+O and Ctrl+Shift+G shortcut keys
5:     With Application
6:       .OnKey Key:="^+O", Procedure:="DisplayGeneralOptions"
7:       .OnKey Key:="^+G", Procedure:="ToggleGridlines"
8:     End With
9:   End Sub
10:
11:
12:  Sub DisplayGeneralOptions()
13:  'Displays the General tab of the Options dialog box
14:    Application.Dialogs(xlDialogOptionsGeneral).Show
15:  End Sub
16:
17:  Sub ToggleGridlines()
18:  'This procedure toggles gridlines on and off
```

```
19:    With ActiveWindow
20:        .DisplayGridlines = Not .DisplayGridlines
21:    End With
22: End Sub
23:
24: Sub ResetShortcutKeys()
25: 'Resets the Ctrl+Shift+O and Ctrl+Shift+G shortcut keys
26:    With Application
27:        .OnKey Key:="^+O"
28:        .OnKey Key:="^+G"
29:    End With
30: End Sub
```

Analysis

Listing 20.6 contains a complete module with four different procedures in it. The first procedure—**SetShortcutKeys**—uses two OnKey methods to define two shortcut keys. The first OnKey statement (line 6) assigns the procedure **DisplayGeneralOptions** to be executed whenever the Ctrl+Shift+O key combination is pressed. The second OnKey statement (line 7) assigns the procedure **ToggleGridlines** to be executed whenever the Ctrl+Shift+G key combination is pressed.

The **DisplayGeneralOptions** procedure (lines 12 through 15) invokes the Show method (line 14) to display the General tab in the Options dialog box (specified by the xlDialogOptionsGeneral constant). The **ToggleGridlines** procedure (lines 17 through 22) simply toggles the DisplayGridlines property for the ActiveWindow (line 20).

The **ResetShortcutKeys** procedure (lines 24 through 30) restores the two shortcut key combinations (Ctrl+Shift+O and Ctrl+Shift+G) to their original actions—nothing—by using the OnKey method without the Procedure argument (lines 27 and 28).

The *OnDoubleClick* Property

Double-clicking the mouse in Excel produces different results, depending on the object involved. For example, double-clicking a cell activates in-cell editing, and double-clicking a graphic object displays the Format Object dialog box for that object. Either of these behaviors could be dangerous, for they enable the user to edit cells or objects that you might not want edited. To trap double-clicks, you can set the OnDoubleClick property to execute one of your procedures whenever the user double-clicks the mouse. Use this syntax with the OnDoubleClick property:

Syntax

Object.OnDoubleClick = "*ProcedureName*"

Object is an object reference to the Application object (to trap double-clicks in any sheet), or it can be a reference to a Worksheet, Chart, DialogSheet, or Module object (to trap double-clicks in a specific sheet).

If you want only to disable double-clicks, assign a zero-length string ("") to the OnDoubleClick property. You also could assign a different behavior to a double-click. Listing 21.7 shows an example.

Listing 21.7. Using the `OnDoubleClick` property.

```
1:   Option Explicit
2:
3:   Sub SetDoubleClick()
4:   'Activates double-click trapping
5:     Application.OnDoubleClick = "DAY21.XLS!DisplayTime"
6:   End Sub
7:
8:   Sub DisplayTime()
9:   'Displays the system time whenever the user double-clicks
10:    MsgBox prompt:=Format(Time, "h:mm AM/PM"), _
11:           Title:="Time"
12:  End Sub
13:
14:  Sub ResetDoubleClick()
15:  'This procedure resets double-clicks
16:    Application.OnDoubleClick = ""
17:  End Sub
```

Analysis

The module in Listing 21.6 contains three different procedures. The **SetDoubleClick** procedure (lines 3 through 6) assigns the `Application` object's `OnDoubleClick` property to the **DAY21.XLS!DisplayTime** procedure. The **DisplayTime** procedure (lines 8 through 12) uses the `MsgBox` procedure to display the current system time. The VBA `Time` function (line 10) returns the current time, and the `Format` function converts the time to text using the specified format—`h:mm AM/PM`, in this case.

When you want to disable `OnDoubleClick`, execute the **ResetDoubleClick** procedure (lines 14 through 17), which sets `OnDoubleClick` to a zero-length string, restoring the default double-click behavior.

The *OnTime* Method

The `OnTime` method enables you to execute a VBA procedure at a specific time, even on a specific day. Why would you need to do such a thing? Well, here are a few possibilities:

☐ Day 18 showed you a procedure that backs up a workbook to a floppy disk. You could set up `OnTime` to run this program at, say, 5:00 p.m. every day.

☐ If you're going to be away from your desk for a while, you could schedule a few time-consuming chores, such as recalculating a large worksheet or printing a report.

☐ You could have Excel display reminders about meetings, appointments, coffee breaks, and so on.

☐ You could run another program at a certain time to check your e-mail or perform some other task.

The general syntax for the `OnTime` method is:

SAMS
PUBLISHING

Syntax

```
Application.OnTime(EarliestTime, Procedure [,LatestTime] [,Schedule])
```

The *EarliestTime* argument is a number representing the time—and date, if desired—when you want the designated procedure to run. Use a serial date number for the *EarliestTime* argument. (Serial date numbers were described in Day 3.) The *Procedure* argument is a string containing the name of the procedure that you want executed when the time specified by *EarliestTime* arrives.

If Excel isn't ready to execute the specified procedure at *EarliestTime*—that is, if Excel isn't in Ready, Cut, Copy, or Find mode—it will keep trying to execute the procedure until a time specified by the optional *LatestTime* argument. The *LatestTime* argument is also a serial date number. If you omit *LatestTime*, Excel executes the specified procedure as soon as possible after the *EarliestTime*.

The optional *Schedule* argument is a Boolean value that tells Excel whether to execute the designated procedure at the designated time. If the *Schedule* argument is True or omitted, then Excel will execute the event procedure at the scheduled time. If the *Schedule* argument is False, then Excel cancels the OnTime setting.

Listing 21.8 shows an example of the OnTime method.

Tip: The easiest way to enter a serial date number to specify a time or date in the OnTime method arguments is to use either VBA's TimeValue or DateValue functions. Use the TimeValue function to create a serial date number containing only a time value:

```
TimeValue(Time)
```

Here, *Time* is a string representing what time you want—for example, "5:00 PM" or "17:00". Similarly, if you want to obtain a date serial number with both date and time values, use the DateValue function:

```
DateValue(Date)
```

The *Date* argument is a string representing what date and time you want—for example, "3/15/94 5:00 PM".

Type

Listing 21.8. Using the OnTime method.

```
1:  Sub SetReminder()
2:  'Installs an OnTime event
3:    Application.OnTime EarliestTime:=TimeValue("3:22 PM"), _
4:                   Procedure:="DAY21.XLS!RemindMe"
5:  End Sub
6:
7:
```

Listing 21.8. continued

```
8:   Sub RemindMe()
9:   'This procedure displays a reminder message
10:    Beep
11:    MsgBox prompt:="The time is now " & _
12:                   Format(Time, "h:mm AM/PM") & "." & _
13:                   Chr(13) & _
14:                   "Don't forget your meeting with Simpson!"
15:  End Sub
```

Analysis

Listing 21.8 contains two procedures. The first procedure, **SetReminder** (lines 1 through 5) uses the OnTime method to install the **RemindMe** procedure to be executed at 3:22 p.m. (lines 3 and 4). The **RemindMe** procedure (lines 8 through 15) beeps the speaker (line 10) and displays a reminder message (lines 11-14). The Chr(13) function in line 13 inserts a carriage return character in the message. This is handy when you need to start a new line in a message box.

DO	DON'T

DO remember that Excel runs an OnTime event procedure only once. If you run a procedure at noon today, the same procedure will not run again at noon tomorrow, even if you leave your computer on and keep Excel loaded.

DON'T try to cancel an OnTime method that has already expired, or Excel will generate an error message.

The *OnEntry* Property

To ensure the accuracy of your worksheet data, it helps if you can verify each cell entry. For example, you might check to make sure that a date field entry is really a date, or that an entered number satisfies a particular condition, such as being a positive number. You can do this by setting up an OnEntry event procedure:

Syntax

`Object.OnEntry = "ProcedureName"`

`Object` is a reference to either the Application object or to a Worksheet object. If you use Application, Excel calls *ProcedureName* whenever you enter or edit data in any worksheet. If you use a Worksheet object, Excel calls *ProcedureName* whenever you enter or edit data in the specified worksheet. *ProcedureName*, as you might expect, is a string specifying the name of the procedure to be executed.

To cancel a data entry event handler, assign a zero-length string (`""`) to the OnEntry property:

`Object.OnEntry = ""`

Listing 21.9 shows you how to use OnEntry for data verification.

Type

Listing 21.9. Using the OnEntry property.

```
 1:   Option Explicit
 2:
 3:   Sub SetDataEntryHandler()
 4:   'Sets up an OnEntry event procedure to validate data
 5:     Application.MoveAfterReturn = False
 6:     Worksheets("Sales Entry").OnEntry = "VerifyData"
 7:   End Sub
 8:
 9:   Sub VerifyData()
10:   'Verifies data entered in the Data Entry worksheet
11:     With ActiveCell
12:       Select Case .Column
13:         Case 1          'Date field
14:           If Not IsDate(.Value) Then
15:             MsgBox "Invalid entry in Date field."
16:             .ClearContents
17:           Else
18:             .NumberFormat = "mmmm d, yyyy"
19:           End If
20:
21:         Case 2          'Discount field
22:           If IsNumeric(.Value) Then
23:             If .Value > 1 Or .Value < 0 Then
24:               MsgBox "Discount must be between 0 and 1."
25:               .ClearContents
26:             Else
27:               .NumberFormat = "0.0%"
28:             End If
29:           Else
30:             MsgBox "Invalid entry in discount field."
31:             .ClearContents
32:           End If
33:
34:         Case 3          'Amount field
35:           If IsNumeric(.Value) Then
36:             If .Value < 0 Then
37:               MsgBox "Amount cannot be negative."
38:               .ClearContents
39:             Else
40:               .NumberFormat = "$#,##0.00_);($#,##0.00)"
41:             End If
42:           Else
43:             MsgBox "You must enter a numeric value."
44:             .ClearContents
45:           End If
46:       End Select
47:     End With
48:   End Sub
49:
50:
```

21

continues

Listing 21.9. continued

```
51:   Sub ResetDataEntryHandler()
52:   'This procedure resets OnEntry
53:     Application.MoveAfterReturn = True
54:     Worksheets("Sales Entry").OnEntry = ""
55:   End Sub
```

The module in Listing 21.9 contains three procedures. The first procedure, **SetDataEntryHandler** (lines 3 through 7) begins by setting the MoveAfterReturn property to False. This leaves the current worksheet cell selected after the user presses Enter. This setting is changed for convenience only—it isn't required for the OnEntry property. Next, the OnEntry event procedure is established for the Sales Entry worksheet (line 6).

The second procedure, called **VerifyData** (lines 9 through 48), is the data verification procedure assigned to the OnEntry property. After the **SetDataEntryHandler** procedure has been executed, Excel will execute the **VerifyData** procedure whenever new data is entered into a cell on the Sales Entry worksheet. The With statement in line 11 uses ActiveCell because the cell where data entry has just occurred is still activated. (This is true even if the user presses an arrow key or clicks another cell to confirm the data. Excel doesn't move to the new cell until after the OnEntry event procedure is complete.)

The Select Case structure (line 12) uses the Column property of ActiveCell (which returns the column number of the active cell) to determine how the data should be validated. Column 1 in the worksheet is supposed to contain only Date type values, so Case 1 (which is executed whenever the Column property is 1) ensures that the value in the cell is a date (line 14). If the value isn't a date, then a message dialog box stating so is displayed (line 15), and the cell's contents are cleared (line 16). Otherwise, a date format is applied to the cell's contents (line 18).

Similarly, all values in column 2 of the worksheet are supposed to be percentages. If the value in the cell is numeric (line 22), the value is next checked to make sure it represents a percentage—that is, the number is a decimal fraction between 0 and 1, inclusive (line 23). If the number isn't a percentage, a message dialog box stating the problem is displayed (line 24) and the cell contents are cleared (line 25). Otherwise, the cell entry meets both conditions, and a number format is applied to the entry in line 27. If the entry in the cell isn't numeric, line 30 displays a message dialog box stating the problem, then line 31 clears the cell contents.

All values in column 3 are supposed to be dollar amounts, so the Case branch beginning in line 34 checks to make sure that the entry is a numeric value (line 35). If the entry isn't a numeric value, line 43 displays an error message, and line 44 clears the cell's contents. If the entry is a numeric value, then line 36 checks to make sure that the entry is a positive number; if so, a currency format is applied to the cell (line 40). If the entry in the cell isn't greater than 0, an error message is displayed (line 37), and the cell is cleared (line 38).

The last procedure in this module, **ResetDataEntryHandler** (lines 51 through 55) resets the `MoveAfterReturn` property (line 53) and cancels the `OnEntry` event handler (line 54).

DO	DON'T

DO use the `ActiveCell` object's `Address` property to return the address of the cell where the data entry occurred.

DON'T expect the `OnEntry` event procedure to run after the user uses the Cut or Paste command to change the contents of a cell. Excel traps the data entry event only if the user enters data through in-cell editing or with the formula bar.

The *OnCalculate* Property

In a worksheet with a large and complex model, changing one variable can affect dozens of formulas. If you can't keep an eye on all these formulas—to check, for example, that a boundary condition is still being met—you can have Excel do it for you. You can set the `OnCalculate` property to make Excel trap the calculate event and run a procedure:

Object.OnCalculate = "*ProcedureName*"

Object is an object reference to either the `Application` object or to a `Worksheet` object. If *Object* is the `Application` object, Excel executes the procedure specified by the *ProcedureName* argument whenever any worksheet recalculates. If *Object* is a `Worksheet` object, Excel executes *ProcedureName* whenever that particular worksheet recalculates. To cancel an `OnCalculate` event handler, assign a zero-length string (`""`) to it. Listing 21.10 shows an example.

Type

Listing 21.10. Using the `OnCalculate` property.

```
1:   Option Explicit
2:
3:   Sub SetCalculateHandler()
4:   'Installs an event handler for the calculation event
5:     Workbooks("DAY21.XLS").Worksheets("Budget Analysis") _
6:         .OnCalculate = "CheckMargin"
7:   End Sub
8:
9:   Sub CheckMargin()
10:  'Executes whenever Budget Analysis worksheet recalculates
11:    If Range("GrossMargin") < 0.2 Then
12:        MsgBox "Gross margin is less than 20%!"
13:    End If
14:  End Sub
15:
16:  Sub ClearCalculateHandler()
```

continues

Listing 21.10. continued

```
17:    'Removes event handler for the calculation event
18:    Workbooks("DAY21.XLS").Worksheets("Budget Analysis") _
19:       .OnCalculate = ""
20:    End Sub
```

The first procedure in this module—**SetCalculateHandler** in lines 3 through 7—sets the OnCalculate property of the Budget Analysis worksheet in the DAY21.XLS workbook so that Excel will execute the **CheckMargin** procedure when the worksheet is recalculated. The **CheckMargin** procedure (lines 9 through 14) tests the result of a formula in a cell named GrossMargin in the Budget Analysis worksheet (line 11). If GrossMargin falls below 20%, a message is displayed (line 12). The **ClearCalculateHandler** procedure (lines 16 through 20) removes the **CheckMargin** event handling procedure by assigning a zero-length string to the OnCalculate property.

Working with Add-In Applications

If you've used any of Excel's add-in applications, you know how handy they are. They add extra functions and commands that look as though they were built in to Excel. For your own VBA programs, you can convert your workbooks to add-ins and gain the following advantages:

☐ Your Sub procedures don't appear in the Macro dialog box. This means that users must access your add-in procedures with shortcut keys, menu commands, toolbar buttons, or other indirect means, such as event handlers.

☐ Add-ins execute faster than normal files.

☐ The code is compiled into a compressed format that no one else can read or modify.

It is important to keep in mind that add-in applications are *demand-loaded*. This means that when you install your application, it gets read into memory in two stages:

1. The add-in application's functions are added to the Function Wizard; its shortcut keys are enabled; its menus and menu commands are added to the appropriate menu bar; and its toolbars are displayed.

2. The rest of the application is loaded into memory when the user either chooses one of the add-in functions, presses an add-in shortcut key, selects an add-in menu item, or clicks an add-in toolbar button.

The exception to the preceding demand-loading rules occurs when the add-in application has an Auto_Open procedure. In this case, the entire add-in is loaded at the start.

Creating an Add-In Application

After you've fully debugged and tested your code, you're ready to distribute it to your users. Follow these steps to convert the workbook into the add-in format:

1. Activate a module in the workbook that you want to save as an add-in.

2. Select the **T**ools | Ma**k**e Add-In command to display the Make Add-In dialog box.

3. Enter a new name, drive, and directory, if required, for the file. Be sure to leave the file extension as .XLA.

4. Make sure that Microsoft Excel Add-In is selected in the Save as **t**ype drop-down list.

5. Select **S**ave or press Enter.

DO	DON'T

DO be sure to remove any debugging code from your procedures. Any Stop or Debug.Print statements still in your code will cause problems when the user tries to run the add-in.

DO fill in the Title and Comments boxes in the Summary tab of the workbooks properties sheet *before* you convert the workbook to an add-in. The Title text supplies the name of your add-in program in the Add-Ins dialog box, and the Comments appear as the add-in's description at the bottom of the Add-Ins dialog box. Select the File | Properties command to display a workbook's properties sheet; click the Summary tab to display the Title and Comments text boxes.

DO use ThisWorkbook instead of ActiveWorkbook to refer to objects inside the add-in workbook. The ActiveWorkbook method won't return a reference to an add-in workbook.

DON'T forget that you can't change an add-in workbook after you've created it. Although your VBA code can add worksheets and data to an add-in workbook while the add-in is loaded, you can't save them in the add-in workbook.

Controlling Add-Ins with Visual Basic

VBA provides several methods and properties that enable you to control add-in applications at the procedural level. From a VBA point of view, an AddIn object is an individual add-in application, and AddIns is the collection of all the add-in applications available to Excel. The AddIns collection is identical with the list of add-ins that you see when you display the Add-Ins dialog box by selecting the **T**ools | Add-**I**ns command.

Syntax

To refer to an `AddIn` object, use the `AddIns` method:

`AddIns(Index)`

The `Index` argument can be any of the following:

- [ ] A number representing the add-in that you want to use. 1 signifies the first add-in that appears in the Add-Ins dialog box, 2 signifies the second, and so on.

- [ ] The name, as text, of the add-in that you want to use. For the add-ins that come with Excel, the name of the add-in is the name that appears in the Add-Ins dialog box. For your own add-ins, the name is either the filename, minus the extension, or the text that you entered in the Title edit box of the Summary tab of the workbook's properties sheet (accessed through the File | Properties command).

For example, the following statement refers to the Solver add-in application:

`AddIns("Solver Add-In")`

Before you can work with your own add-ins, you must add them to the `AddIns` collection. To do that, use the `Add` method:

`AddIns.Add(FileName [,CopyFile])`

The `FileName` argument is a string containing the full path name of the add-in file. `CopyFile` is an optional logical argument to use when the add-in file is stored on a floppy disk, CD-ROM, or network drive. If `CopyFile` is `True`, Excel copies the add-in file to your hard disk. If `CopyFile` is `False`, Excel leaves the file where it is. If you omit `CopyFile`, Excel displays a dialog box that asks what you want to do. The `CopyFile` argument is ignored if `FileName` references a file on your hard disk.

Using the `Add` method merely makes the new `AddIn` object available to Excel. To actually *use* the add-in—that is, to make its commands and functions available to the user—you must install it by setting its `Installed` property to `True`. Setting an `AddIn` object's `Installed` property to `True` is the equivalent of activating the add-in's checkbox in the Add-Ins dialog box, and does two things:

- [ ] The first part of the demand-loading sequence is performed. The add-in's functions, shortcut keys, menus, and toolbars become available.

- [ ] The add-in's `Auto_Add` procedure—if it has one—is executed. The `Auto_Add` procedure is similar to the `Auto_Open` procedures you learned about earlier in this lesson, but can only be used in an add-in. The `Auto_Add` procedure is useful for things such as initializing the add-in and telling the user that the add-in is loaded.

Listing 21.11 shows you how to work with add-ins from a VBA procedure.

Listing 21.11. Working with add-in applications.

```
 1:    Sub InstallBudgetTools()
 2:    'Installs an add-in application
 3:      AddIns.Add FileName:="D:\VBA21\BUDGET TOOLS.XLA"
 4:      With AddIns("Budget Tools")
 5:          .Installed = True
 6:          MsgBox "The " & .Title & _
 7:            " add-in is now installed.", _
 8:             vbInformation
 9:      End With
10:    End Sub
11:
12:    Sub RemoveBudgetTools()
13:    'Removes an add-in application
14:      With AddIns("Budget Tools")
15:          .Installed = False
16:          MsgBox "The " & .Title & _
17:            " add-in is now UNinstalled.", _
18:             vbInformation
19:      End With
20:    End Sub
```

The **InstallBudgetTools** procedure adds and installs an add-in named Budget Tools. Line 3 uses the Add method to make the add-in available to Excel. The With statement (line 4) installs the Budget Tools add-in (line 5) and displays a message telling the user that the add-in has been installed (lines 6-8).

Notice the use of the Title property in line 6. AddIn objects share many of the same properties found in Workbook objects. These properties include Author, Comments, FullName, Name, Path, Subject, and Title.

When you no longer need to work with an add-in, you can remove it by setting its Installed property to False, as shown in the **RemoveBudgetTools** procedure. Setting the Installed property to False also executes Auto_Remove, the other automatic procedure for add-ins.

Summary

Excel offers a number of ways to execute your VBA procedures. They include the Macro dialog box, shortcut keys, menu commands, and toolbar buttons. In each case, you or the user of your application has to do something to execute the procedure. This chapter showed you two types of procedures that execute automatically: automatic procedures and event procedures.

Automatic procedures run either when you open a workbook or when you close a workbook. To execute one or more VBA statements every time you open a workbook, include them in a Sub procedure named Auto_Open. This is handy for creating menu systems, displaying toolbars, and setting Excel program options. Similarly, to run one or more VBA statements every time you close a file, place them inside a `Sub` procedure named `Auto_Close`. Excel permits you to have only one `Auto_Open` and one `Auto_Close` procedure in each workbook.

Event procedures are `Sub` procedures that have been assigned to an `OnEvent` property or method. When Excel traps the event associated with the property or method, it automatically executes the associated event procedure. Example properties are `OnKey`, which executes a specified procedure whenever you press a designated key or key combination; `OnTime`, which executes a procedure when a specified time arrives; and `OnCalculate`, which runs a procedure when a worksheet recalculates.

Q&A

Q I have a workbook that contains several procedures I want to run automatically when I open the file. I can't combine them into one procedure or add procedure calls because I use the individual routines from time to time while I'm working. If I can't create multiple `Auto_Open` procedures, how can I force Excel to run each procedure at startup?

A The simplest approach is to simply write an **`Auto_Open`** procedure that calls all the procedures you want to execute. As an alternative, Excel has a feature called *defined-name automatic procedures,* which enables you to specify as many startup or shutdown procedures as you like. Activate any worksheet in the workbook, and select the Insert | Name | Define command to display the Define Name dialog box. In the Names in Workbook box, enter a name that begins with either `Auto_Open` or `Auto_Close`—for example, `Auto_Open_DisplayDialog`. In the Refers to box, type an equals sign followed by the name of the procedure that you want to run—for example, **`=DisplayDialogProc`**. Select the Add button to define the name. Repeat this procedure for any other defined-name procedures that you want to create. Just make sure that each name begins with either `Auto_Open` or `Auto_Close`.

Q Does Excel execute either an `OnSheetActivate` or `OnWindow` event handler when you first open a workbook?

A No. Even though, technically, you're activating a sheet and a window when you first open a workbook, Excel doesn't run these event procedures at startup.

Q The `OnDoubleClick` method is handy, but I want to run a procedure when the user clicks a picture or chart. Is that possible?

A Not only is it possible, it's extremely easy to do. Click the object to select it, and select the Tools | Assign Macro command. In the Assign Macro dialog box, use the Macro Name/Reference list to highlight the procedure that you want to run, and choose OK.

Click an empty part of the worksheet to deselect the object. Now, position the mouse pointer over the object. You'll see the pointer change to a hand with a pointing finger. Click the object, and Excel will execute the procedure.

You can also assign an event procedure to a picture or chart by assigning a string specifying the desired event procedure to the object's `OnAction` property. Many Excel objects have an `OnAction` property—graphic objects, buttons, drawing objects, charts, and so on.

Q I have several event procedures that I use every day—shortcut keys, `OnTime` events, and so on. Is there any way to install all of these event procedures automatically every time I start Excel?

A Absolutely. First, unhide the Personal Macro Workbook (PERSONAL.XLS). In this workbook's module sheet, create an `Auto_Open` procedure; include in it all the statements that set up your event procedures. In each of these statements, be sure to enter the procedure string as follows:

```
"PERSONAL.XLS!procedureName"
```

Here, *procedureName* is the name of the event procedure. This tells Excel where to find each procedure. Copy the event procedures to the PERSONAL.XLS module as well, so that they are always available. After you save your changes, don't forget to hide PERSONAL.XLS again.

If you don't have a Personal Macro Workbook, you can create one easily. Simply start a new workbook, add a module, and save the workbook as PERSONAL.XLS in your XLSTART directory. Then, add your code to the module, save the workbook again, and hide it.

Q My `OnKey` event procedures don't seem to work while another procedure is running. Am I doing something wrong?

A Not at all. That's simply the default behavior of the `OnKey` property. Excel traps the key or key combination only when other procedures are not running.

Q How can I find out if an event procedure has been assigned to a particular `OnEvent` property?

A All the `OnEvent` properties—as opposed to the methods—have read/write status. This means that you can assign values to them (write), and you also can find out whether a procedure has been assigned (read). The following statement, for example, stores the value of the `Application` object's `OnCalculate` property in a variable named **calcProc**:

```
calcProc = Application.OnCalculate
```

You could then test this variable. If it equals a zero-length string (`""`), no event procedure has been assigned.

Workshop

Answers are in Appendix A.

Quiz

1. What is an automatic procedure?

2. Name the four types of automatic procedures, and describe what each one does.

3. What is an event procedure?

4. How do you cancel event procedures associated with OnEvent properties, such as OnSheetActivate and OnWindow?

5. What events are trapped if you set the Application object's OnSheetActivate property?

6. Why is it dangerous to use the ActiveWorkbook or ActiveSheet objects within an OnSheetDeactivate event procedure?

7. In an OnKey method, what happens if you assign a zero-length string ("") to the Procedure argument? What happens if you leave out the Procedure argument altogether?

8. In the OnTime method, what's the difference between the EarliestTime and LatestTime arguments?

9. Does the OnEntry event procedure execute when you paste data to the worksheet?

10. If you have an event procedure defined for the OnCalculate property, under what circumstances will Excel recalculate the worksheet but not run the event procedure?

11. What does it mean to say an add-in application is *demand-loaded*?

Exercises

1. A well-designed VBA program always resets the environment when it exits. Using the Application object's DefaultFilePath, PromptForSummaryInfo, and SheetsInNewWorkbook properties, create an Auto_Open procedure that saves the current state of each property. Then, write an Auto_Close procedure that resets each property to its original state.

2. **BUG BUSTER:** The **ResetSheet** procedure shown below does not work correctly. Can you tell why?

```
Sub SetSheetHandler()
  Worksheets("Scratch Pad").OnSheetDeactivate = "ResetSheet"
End Sub
```

```
Sub ResetSheet()
  With ActiveSheet
    .UsedRange.Clear
    .OnEntry = ""
    .OnCalculate = ""
    .OnDoubleClick = ""
  End With
End Sub
```

3. Create procedures that test which event procedure runs first—OnSheetActivate or OnWindow.

4. Pressing the Delete key normally wipes out only a cell's contents. Write the necessary procedures that set up the Ctrl+Delete key combination to delete everything in a cell—contents, formats, and notes.

5. It's possible to set up the OnTime method to run a procedure at regular intervals—say, every 60 minutes—instead of at a specific time. For example, if you have a procedure that backs up the active workbook to a network file server, you could have OnTime run this procedure every 5 or 10 minutes, so that you don't have to worry about backing up your work. Write a procedure that sets up an OnTime method to run a procedure at a regular interval specified by the user.

6. **BUG BUSTER:** Can you spot the flaw in the OnEntry event procedure shown below? Under what circumstances might this procedure work correctly?

```
Sub VerifyNumber()
'Check the active cell
  With ActiveCell
    'If it's not a number...
    If Not IsNumeric(.Value) Then
      'Display an error message
      MsgBox "Invalid entry in cell " & .Address
      'Clear the cell's contents
      .ClearContents
      'Activate in-cell editing so
      'the user can enter a new value
      SendKeys ("{F2}")
    End If
  End With
End Sub
```

21

Congratulations! You have completed your third and final week of learning to program in VBA. This final week covered advanced VBA topics, including custom dialog boxes, error handling, custom menus and toolbars, and controlling other Windows applications from your VBA programs. This final week ended by showing you how to create worksheets with automatic procedures, and how to create add-in applications. The listings in this review put together several of the concepts you have learned, in particular, creating custom menus.

The following listings represent two complete modules. For all the code in these two modules to work, the two modules from the Week 2 review must be in the same workbook (all four modules fit together).

The module in Listing R3.1 is a collection of useful utility procedures. As you study this listing, notice that some of the procedures use support routines from the support library module in Listing R2.2 (from the Week 2 review).

 Listing R3.1. The Utilities module—a library of utility procedures.

```
1:   Option Explicit
2:
3:   'MessageBeep routine from Windows DLL
4:   Declare Sub MessageBeep Lib "USER32" _
5:               (ByVal BeepType As Long)
6:
7:   'MessageBeep constants
8:   Const mBeepDefault = 0
9:   Const mBeepCritical = 16
10:  Const mBeepQuestion = 32
11:  Const mBeepExclamation = 48
12:  Const mBeepAsterisk = 64
13:
14:  Sub CopyFiles()
15:  'copies a file selected by the user to a new name, drive
16:  'or directory selected by the user.
17:
18:    Dim sName As String     'source file name
19:    Dim dName As String     'destination file name
20:    Dim orgDrive As String  'original drive/directory
21:
22:    On Error GoTo BadNews    'set up error handler
23:
24:    orgDrive = CurDir()  'preserve logged drive/directory
25:
26:    With Application
27:      .StatusBar = "Select file to be copied."
28:      sName = .GetOpenFilename(Title:="File Copy - Source")
29:      If sName = "False" Then GoTo CancelJob
30:      .StatusBar = "Select destination or new file name."
31:      dName = .GetSaveAsFilename( _
32:              Title:="File Copy - Destination", _
33:              initialFilename:=FullName2BookName(sName))
34:      If dName = "False" Then GoTo CancelJob
35:      .StatusBar = "Copying " & sName & " to " & dName
36:      FileCopy source:=sName, destination:=dName
37:    End With
38:
39:  CancelJob:  'jump here if job is canceled
40:    ChDrive orgDrive    'restore original drive
41:    ChDir orgDrive      'restore original directory
42:    Application.StatusBar = False
```

```
43:    Exit Sub
44:
45:  BadNews:   'only executed if there's a runtime error
46:    MessageBeep mBeepCritical
47:    MsgBox Prompt:="Unable to complete File Copy." & _
48:                    Chr(13) & Error(), _
49:          Title:="File Copy", _
50:          Buttons:=vbCritical
51:    ChDrive orgDrive
52:    ChDir orgDrive
53:    Application.StatusBar = False
54:  End Sub
55:
56:
57:  Sub Convert2Template()
58:  'saves the current workbook as a template file.
59:
60:    Const FilterList = "Templates (*.xlt),*.xlt"
61:    Const ititle = "Convert WorkBook to Template"
62:
63:    Dim dName As String        'destination filename
64:    Dim iName As String        'file name from user
65:    Dim orgDrive As String     'original drive/directory
66:
67:    On Error GoTo BadNews  'set error-handling
68:
69:    'ensure that it's safe to change workbook format
70:    With ActiveWorkbook
71:      If Not .Saved Then
72:        MessageBeep mBeepAsterisk
73:        MsgBox Prompt:=.Name & " has unsaved changes." & _
74:                        Chr(13) & "Save the workbook " & _
75:                        "before creating a template.", _
76:              Buttons:=vbInformation, _
77:              Title:=ititle
78:        Exit Sub
79:      End If
80:    End With
81:
82:    orgDrive = CurDir()       'preserve original drive/directory
83:
84:    'set up default destination filename
85:    dName = Left(ActiveWorkbook.Name, _
86:                  Len(ActiveWorkbook.Name) - 4)
87:
88:    With Application
89:      'change drive/directory to Excel's templates path
90:      ChDrive .TemplatesPath
91:      ChDir .TemplatesPath
92:      .StatusBar = "Select new template name."
93:
94:      'get the SaveAs filename from user
95:      iName = .GetSaveAsFilename(Title:=ititle, _
96:                                  initialFilename:=dName, _
97:                                  FileFilter:=FilterList)
```

continues

Listing R3.1. continued

```
98:     End With
99:
100:    If iName <> "False" Then
101:       Application.StatusBar = "Creating template..."
102:       ActiveWorkbook.SaveAs fileName:=iName, _
103:                            FileFormat:=xlTemplate
104:       MessageBeep mBeepAsterisk
105:       MsgBox Prompt:="Template created successfully.", _
106:              Buttons:=vbInformation, _
107:              Title:=ititle
108:    End If
109:
110:    'restore original logged drive/directory
111:    ChDrive orgDrive
112:    ChDir orgDrive
113:
114:    Application.StatusBar = False
115:    Exit Sub 'no more work to do
116:
117: BadNews:    'only get here if there's a runtime error
118:    MessageBeep mBeepCritical
119:    MsgBox Prompt:="Can't convert workbook to template" & _
120:                   Chr(13) & Error(), _
121:           Title:=ititle, _
122:           Buttons:=vbCritical
123:    Application.StatusBar = False
124:    ChDrive orgDrive
125:    ChDir orgDrive
126: End Sub
127:
128:
129: Sub Backup_ActiveBook()
130: ' Creates backup copy of active workbook by using the
131: 'SaveCopyAs method. New filename has extension ".BAK"
132:
133:    Dim fName As String
134:    Dim OldComment As String
135:    Dim Indx As Integer
136:
137:    With ActiveWorkbook
138:       OldComment = .Comments  'preserve original comments
139:
140:       'Add new comments for backup copy
141:       .Comments = .Comments & " Backup of " & .Name & _
142:                   ", made by backup procedure."
143:
144:       'Make backup filename from original full filename
145:       fName = ReverseStr(.FullName)
146:       Indx = (Len(fName) - InStr(fName, ".")) + 1
147:       fName = Right(fName, Indx)
148:       fName = ReverseStr(fName) & "BAK"
149:
150:       .SaveCopyAs fileName:=fName     'save file copy
151:       .Comments = OldComment         'restore original comments
152:    End With
```

```
153: End Sub
154:
155:
156: Sub RecoverBackup()
157: 'recovers a workbook from backup by copying from the
158: 'filename with the .BAK extension a filename with the
159: '.XLS extension to make the file usable as a workbook
160: 'again.
161:
162:    Const Fltr = "Backup Workbooks (*.bak),*.bak"
163:    Const rtitle = "Recover Backup Workbook"
164:
165:    Dim fName As String       'backup filename
166:    Dim dName As String       'recovered filename
167:    Dim Ans As Integer        'MsgBox answer
168:    Dim orgDrive As String    'original drive/directory
169:
170:    On Error GoTo BadNews     'install error-handler
171:
172:    orgDrive = CurDir()       'save original drive/directory
173:
174:    'get filename of backup file to recover
175:    Application.StatusBar = "Select backup file to recover."
176:    fName = Application.GetOpenFilename(FileFilter:=Fltr, _
177:                                 Title:=rtitle & " - Source")
178:    If fName = "False" Then GoTo CancelJob
179:
180:    Do     'get filename for recovered file
181:      dName = FullName2BookName(fName)
182:      dName = Left(dName, Len(dName) - 3) & "XLS"
183:
184:      With Application
185:        .StatusBar = "Select recovered workbook name."
186:        dName = .GetOpenFilename(Title:=rtitle, _
187:                       FileFilter:="Excel Workbooks,*.xls")
188:        If dName = "False" Then GoTo CancelJob
189:        .StatusBar = ""
190:      End With
191:
192:      'ensure that we're not restoring an open workbook
193:      If IsBookOpen(FullName2BookName(dName)) Then
194:        MessageBeep mBeepExclamation
195:        MsgBox Prompt:="You can't recover open workbooks!", _
196:               Title:=rtitle, _
197:               Buttons:=vbExclamation
198:        GoTo CancelJob
199:      End If
200:
201:      'make sure it's okay to overwrite an existing workbook
202:      If IsDiskFile(dName) Then
203:        MessageBeep mBeepQuestion
204:        Ans = MsgBox(Prompt:=dName & " already exists." & _
205:                            Chr(13) & Chr(13) & _
206:                            "Overwrite it anyway?", _
207:                     Title:=rtitle, _
208:                     Buttons:=vbQuestion + vbYesNoCancel)
```

continues

Listing R3.1. continued

```
209:          If Ans = vbCancel Then
210:            GoTo CancelJob
211:          ElseIf Ans = vbNo Then
212:            dName = ""
213:          End If
214:        End If
215:      Loop Until dName <> ""
216:
217:      Application.StatusBar = "Recovering workbook file..."
218:      FileCopy fName, dName     'copy from backup to workbook
219:      MessageBeep mBeepExclamation
220:      MsgBox Prompt:=fName & " recovered as:" & _
221:                    Chr(13) & dName, _
222:            Buttons:=vbInformation, _
223:            Title:=rtitle
224:
225: CancelJob:    'jumps here if canceled
226:      Application.StatusBar = False
227:      ChDrive orgDrive
228:      ChDir orgDrive
229:      Exit Sub
230:
231: BadNews:   'only get here if there's a runtime error
232:      MessageBeep mBeepCritical
233:      MsgBox Prompt:="Unable to recover backup workbook." & _
234:                    Chr(13) & Error(), _
235:            Buttons:=vbCritical, _
236:            Title:=rtitle
237:      Application.StatusBar = False
238:      ChDrive orgDrive
239:      ChDir orgDrive
240: End Sub
```

Listing R3.1 is a complete module. Lines 4 and 5 contain a declaration for the external DLL procedure, MessageBeep (Day 20), while lines 8 through 12 declare global constants for use in selecting the tone to be played by MessageBeep.

Lines 14 through 54 contain the **CopyFiles** procedure. This is a version of a procedure that appeared in Day 12. Notice the On Error GoTo statement (Day 17) in line 22. If any errors occur when this procedure executes—such as a full disk—the runtime error-handling code in lines 46 through 53 displays an error message, and performs some housekeeping.

Lines 57 through 126 contain the **Convert2Template** procedure, which converts the active workbook to an Excel template file. This procedure also uses an On Error GoTo statement (line 67) to set up an error-handling routine.

Lines 129 through 153 contain the **Backup_ActiveBook** procedure, which makes a backup copy of the current workbook, giving the new file a name that ends with .BAK. This procedure is similar to one that appeared in Day 7 but is a somewhat more sophisticated

version. Notice that, in lines 145 through 148, this version uses the ReverseStr function declared in the support module in the Week 2 review.

Lines 156 through 240 contain the **RecoverBackup** procedure, which lets the user rename one of the backup files created by the **Backup_ActiveBook** procedure so that Excel can open it as a workbook. **RecoverBackup** ensures that the user is not trying to recover a workbook file that is currently open, and asks the user to confirm overwriting an existing file on the disk. Notice that **RecoverBackup** makes use of the **IsBookOpen** (line 193) and the **IsDiskFile** (line 202) functions from the Week 2 review.

The next listing shows another complete module. This second module contains some automatic procedures that customize Excel's menus whenever the workbook containing this module is opened.

Listing R3.2. The Automatic Procedures module.

```
 1:    Option Explicit
 2:    Option Private Module
 3:
 4:
 5:    Sub Auto_Open()
 6:    'creates the Utilities menu, and modifies the File Menu
 7:
 8:       Dim aMenu As MenuBar
 9:       Dim tItem As MenuItem
10:
11:    For Each aMenu In MenuBars     'for all existing menus
12:      If aMenu.BuiltIn Then    'only modify built-in menus
13:        Create_UtilityMenu mBar:=aMenu  'add Utilities menu
14:        With aMenu.Menus("File").MenuItems  'add to File menu
15:          Set tItem = .Add( _
16:                      Caption:="C&reate Named Workbook...", _
17:                      OnAction:="OpenNewBook", _
18:                      Before:="Open...")
19:          tItem.StatusBar = _
20:                "Creates a new workbook with a specific name"
21:        End With
22:      End If
23:    Next aMenu
24:    End Sub
25:
26:
27:    Sub Auto_Close()
28:      Dim aMenu As MenuBar
29:
30:      For Each aMenu In MenuBars
31:        If aMenu.BuiltIn Then               'remove utility menu
32:          aMenu.Menus("Utilities").Delete
33:          With aMenu.Menus("File")          'clean up File menu
34:            .MenuItems("Create Named Workbook...").Delete
35:          End With
```

continues

Listing R3.2. continued

```
36:        End If
37:      Next aMenu
38:  End Sub
39:
40:
41:  Private Sub Create_UtilityMenu(mBar As MenuBar)
42:  'adds Utility menu to specified menu bar
43:    Dim tItem As MenuItem
44:
45:    With mBar
46:      .Menus.Add Caption:="&Utilities", Before:="Help"
47:      With .Menus("Utilities").MenuItems
48:        Set tItem = .Add(Caption:="&Copy File", _
49:                         OnAction:="CopyFiles")
50:        tItem.StatusBar = _
51:              "Copy any filename to any other filename"
52:        .Add Caption:="-"
53:        Set tItem = .Add(Caption:="&Backup Active Book", _
54:                         OnAction:="Backup_ActiveBook")
55:        tItem.StatusBar = _
56:              "Make backup copy of active workbook."
57:        Set tItem = .Add(Caption:="&Recover Back Up Book", _
58:                         OnAction:="RecoverBackup")
59:        tItem.StatusBar = _
60:            "Convert backup workbook to usable XLS file."
61:        .Add Caption:="-"
62:        Set tItem = .Add(Caption:="Convert To &Template", _
63:                         OnAction:="Convert2Template")
64:        tItem.StatusBar = _
65:          "Convert the active workbook to an Excel template"
66:      End With
67:    End With
68:  End Sub
```

First of all, notice that this module uses the Option Private Module statement (line 2). You should always make the module that contains the **Auto_Open** and **Auto_Close** procedures a private module so that your automatic procedures aren't listed in the Macro dialog box and are not available to other workbooks.

Lines 5 through 24 contain the **Auto_Open** procedure. This procedure essentially consists of a single For Each...Next loop (line 11) that loops through all of Excel's menu bars, and adds a Utilities menu to each built-in menu bar. Only built-in menu bars are altered, so as to avoid interfering with any other custom menu bars that might have been installed by another VBA program or an add-in program.

To add the custom Utilities menu, the **Auto_Open** procedure calls the **Create_UtilityMenu** procedure. Lines 15 through 18 add a single menu choice to the Excel File menu, creating the new custom File | Create Named Workbook command. Notice that this new menu command executes the **OpenNewBook** procedure from the Week 2 review (the OnAction

argument in line 17). Line 19 sets the `StatusBar` property of the new menu item, in order to provide a hint to the user about what this command does.

Lines 27 through 38 contain the **Auto_Close** procedure, which removes all the custom menus and commands when the workbook containing this module is closed. The **Auto_Close** procedure removes the custom **U**tilities menu and the custom **F**ile | C**r**eate Named Book command from each of Excel's built-in menu bars.

Finally, lines 41 through 68 contain the **Create_UtilityMenu** procedure, which adds the custom **U**tility menu to the menu bar specified by the **mBar** argument. Notice that this procedure is declared with the `Private` keyword, so that it is not available outside of this particular module.

Line 46 adds the **U**tilities menu choice, itself. Lines 48 through 51 add the **U**tilities | C**o**py File command (specifying that this menu item should execute the **CopyFiles** procedure), and sets the new menu item's `StatusBar` property. Line 52 places a separator bar into the menu, and then lines 53 through 56 add the **U**tilities | **B**ackup Active Book command (specifying that this menu item should execute the **Backup_ActiveBook** procedure), and also set this menu item's `StatusBar` property. Similarly, lines 57 through 60 add the **U**tilities | **R**ecover Backed Up Book command, specify the **RecoverBackup** procedure as the event procedure, and set the `StatusBar` property. Line 61 places another separator bar into the menu, and then lines 62 through 65 add the **U**tilities | Convert To **T**emplate command with the **Convert2Template** procedure as its event procedure.

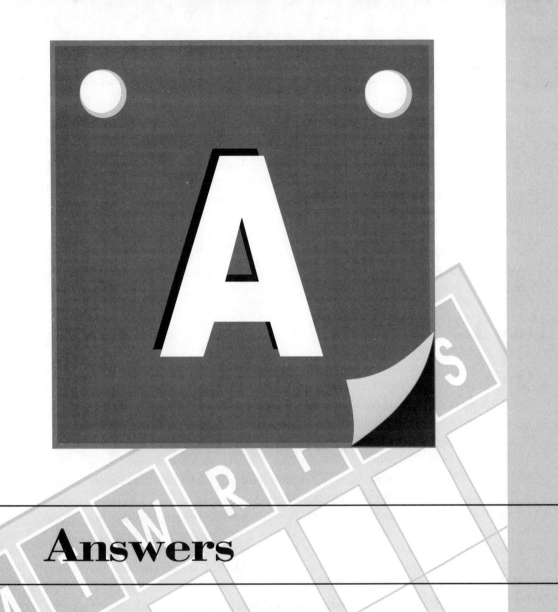

Answers

In a few of the code listings in this appendix, you will notice a special symbol in some of the longer code lines. This symbol is not part of VBA. This symbol is used for code lines that are too wide for the page margins in this book, and which must be continued on a second line. The symbol lets you know that, in the VBA module, the code is really one single physical line. An example of this special line-break symbol is shown in the following:

```
16:  ActiveWorkbook.SaveAs Filename:="NEWFILE.XLS",
↪FileFormat:=xlNormal
```

Notice the arrow-shaped symbol at the left edge of the second line in the preceding code, indicating that this line is a continuation of the line above it. Notice that the continued line does not have a line number.

Day 1

Quiz

1. A plain, recorded macro is inflexible. It cannot efficiently repeat actions or make decisions based on conditions that occur while the macro is executing.

2. The core portions of Visual Basic for Applications and Visual Basic are identical. Visual Basic for Applications has these differences from Visual Basic:

   ☐ VBA stores its macro source code in the application's files (for example, an Excel workbook) instead of separate text files.

   ☐ Programs written in VBA must be started from inside the application in which the program was written. For example, a VBA program written inside Excel must always be executed from Excel. (You could, however, have another application use OLE Automation or send a DDE message to cause Excel to run a particular VBA macro program.)

   ☐ VBA contains many extensions to the core portion of Visual Basic; the specific extensions depend on the application in which you use VBA. In Excel 7, for example, VBA contains added features that relate to manipulating workbooks, worksheets, and to making financial and statistical calculations.

3. Three major benefits obtained by adding VBA program elements to a recorded macro are:

   ☐ Ability to repeat actions efficiently.

   ☐ Ability to have a macro execute different instructions, depending on conditions that occur while the macro is operating or depending on choices that the macro's user makes.

   ☐ Ability to connect several smaller macros into a large program in order to perform highly complex tasks.

4. Yes, you can assign an Excel macro to the **T**ools menu when you first record it. To do so, choose the **O**ptions command button in the Record New Macro dialog box and select the Men**u** Item on Tools Menu option box after filling in the text box with the name that you want the macro to have on the **T**ools menu.

5. The Excel Macro dialog box lists *all* of the macros in *all* of the currently opened workbooks, whether or not the workbooks are hidden.

Exercises

1. Your recorded macro should be similar to the following macro. (The macro recorder does not include the line numbers; line numbers are added to the listings in this book to make it easier to identify specific lines in a listing.) In the following listing, lines 1 through 6 are comments inserted by the macro recorder, and include the text you typed in the **D**escription text box of the Record New Macro dialog box. Line 9 is a VBA command which changes the current disk and folder. The ChDir command will only occur in your recorded macro if you used the drive and folder list box in the Save As dialog box to change the current drive and/or folder.

```
 1:    '
 2:    ' NewFile Macro
 3:    ' Macro recorded 5/9/95 by MATTHEWH2
 4:    ' Creates a new workbook, and then saves it with the name NEWFILE
 5:    '
 6:    '
 7:    Sub NewFile()
 8:        Workbooks.Add
 9:        ChDir "C:\Test Data"
10:        ActiveWorkbook.SaveAs Filename:= _
11:            "C:\OFFICE95\EXCEL\Examples\NEWFILE.xls", FileFormat:=xlNormal, _
12:            Password:="", WriteResPassword:="", ReadOnlyRecommended:=False _
13:            , CreateBackup:=False
14:        ActiveWorkbook.Close
15:    End Sub
```

2. Running your recorded macro creates and saves another workbook in the same drive and folder, also named NEWFILE.

3. Because the **NewFile** macro attempts to save the new workbook file to disk with a name that duplicates a file already on the disk, Excel displays a dialog box asking whether you want to replace the existing file. This dialog box contains four buttons: **Y**es, **N**o, Cancel, and **H**elp. If you choose **Y**es, Excel replaces the existing workbook file (its contents, if any, are consequently lost) and the recorded macro completes executing normally.

   If you choose **N**o (or Cancel), the file save operation is canceled. Because the canceled operation causes an instruction in the recorded macro to fail, the macro is interrupted and does not continue running.

This exercise illustrates that, if an instruction in a recorded macro does not complete normally, the recorded macro does not continue executing. As you learn in later lessons, adding VBA program elements helps you control the behavior of a macro more closely. For example, it would be more desirable if the **NewFile** macro asked the user to enter a different filename, and then attempted the save operation again, instead of failing with an error message.

Day 2

Quiz

1. A module stores the source code for macros. A module may contain none, one, or several macros, up to the maximum of approximately 4,000 lines. In Excel, modules are stored in workbook files in special module sheets. In other VBA host applications, modules are also stored in the files that the application normally stores information in—Access 7 modules, for example, are stored in Access database files.

2. You add comments to a recorded macro to document the use and purpose of the macro, and to describe any special conditions that must exist before the macro will execute correctly. Adding comments to a recorded macro immediately after recording it can help you remember which parts of the recorded code are the result of specific actions that you performed, and make it easier to change the macro later, if necessary. You should also add comments whenever you make changes in a macro; these comments make it easier to determine which parts of a macro you edited, and what those changes accomplish.

   You should also add comments to macros that you write yourself, for similar reasons.

3. A VBA keyword is any word or symbol that is part of the VBA programming language, as opposed to words (like macro names) that you create.

4. To produce a syntactically correct macro, you must define the macro with the keyword Sub, followed by the macro name and a pair of parentheses on the same line. End the macro with the keywords End Sub, on a line by themselves. None, one, or many program statements may occur between the macro declaration line and the line ending the macro. The following sample shows the required elements of a macro:

```
Sub AnyMacro()
    'None, one, or any number of program statements
End Sub
```

5. A macro declaration is the first line of a macro (containing the Sub keyword) that indicates the name of the macro.

6. The body of a macro is the part of the macro that contains the actual commands and program statements that the macro executes. The body of the macro is the part of a

macro between the line containing the macro declaration, and the End Sub line that ends the macro.

7. The Object Browser allows you to view a list of all of the currently available macros. The Object Browser lists all of the macros in all of the currently opened workbooks.

8. Recorded VBA source code is indented in order to make the code more readable by a human being. You should indent your source code as you write macros for the same reason: to enhance the readability (and understandability) of your macro programs.

9. The MsgBox procedure provides a simple way for a macro to display messages to the macro's user.

10. An argument is information passed to a VBA procedure, for use by that procedure. Some procedures may use more than one argument; in this case, the arguments are written in a list and separated with commas, forming an argument list.

11. The line continuation symbol consists of a space character followed by an underscore character (_). The line continuation symbol is used to indicate to VBA that the following line should be joined with the current line to form a single VBA statement. By using the line continuation symbol, you can divide VBA statements onto several lines in order to enhance the readability of your macro source code. The following source code fragment shows five lines containing line continuation symbols. The result of these line continuation symbols is to join all six of the physical lines in the code fragment into one logical line containing a single VBA statement.

```
ActiveWorkbook.SaveAs Filename:="NEWFILE.XLS", _
                      FileFormat:=xlNormal, _
                      Password:="", _
                      WriteResPassword:="", _
                      ReadOnlyRecommended:= False, _
                      CreateBackup:=False
```

12. A syntax error is an error resulting from an improperly formed VBA program statement. Syntax errors usually result from such things as missing or improperly placed commas, parentheses, quotation marks, and so on. Syntax errors also frequently result from missing keywords, such as omitting the Sub or End Sub keywords in a macro definition.

   VBA usually notifies you of syntax errors as you write each line of code. If you do not correct syntax errors when they are first detected, then VBA will again display an error message when you run the macro.

13. A runtime error is an error that occurs while your macro is executing. Runtime errors have many different causes; they result most frequently from statements that are syntactically correct but contain data of the wrong type, attempts to operate on files or parts of a file (such as a specific worksheet) that are not present at the time the macro executes, and so on.

14. Three reasons for recording new macro instructions directly into a macro are:

☐ Recording new instructions directly into an existing macro is frequently less error-prone than adding the new code manually.

☐ Recording new instructions into an existing macro is easier than writing the code manually if you need to add or change a lengthy series of instructions in a macro.

☐ Recording instructions into an existing macro ensures that the recorded code goes into a particular module (otherwise, VBA determines which module to store the recorded macro in).

Exercises

1. The purpose of this exercise is to give you some practice entering code with the VBA editor and modules. This macro uses a command—line 6 of the listing—which invokes the application's (and hence Windows') help system, and specifies that the VBA reference is the help file to open. (The help file for VBA is separate from the application's main help file; in Excel 7, the VBA help file is named VBA_XL.HLP.)

If this macro does not execute, or does not display the VBA reference at the table of contents, check to make sure you copied the listing exactly. Specifically, check to make sure that you included both the Sub and End Sub keywords, as well as the quotation marks around the help filename in line 6. Also, make sure that you included the period (.) between the word Application and the word Help in line 6.

You may want to attach this macro to the **Tools** menu, and/or specify a hotkey for it, since the macro provides a shortcut into the VBA help system, which is not otherwise easily accessible from Excel.

2. This one is just a little tricky. If you get syntax errors while writing the line that uses the MsgBox procedure, remember that you must include the place-holding comma for the missing second argument.

Your macro should appear similar to the following listing, although you probably chose a different name for your macro:

```
'
'Exercise 2.2
'This macro displays a message.
'
Sub MyMessage()
    MsgBox "I am a Visual Basic message", , "VBA Message"
End Sub
```

3. Line 2 of the original macro did not contain the quotation marks around the message text. As a result, VBA detected a syntax error. If you typed this macro in as-is to see what VBA's error messages were, you might have noticed that the syntax error message did not directly relate to the actual problem. Instead, because VBA interpreted the unquoted text as variable names, you received error messages stating that a comma or parenthesis was expected.

This exercise illustrates the fact that VBA cannot always report the exactly correct syntax error. Sometimes, as with these missing quotation marks, the syntax error that VBA reports is actually caused by a different syntax error that occurred earlier in the program source code—perhaps earlier in the same line, perhaps one or more lines earlier. If you get syntax errors regarding missing commas or parentheses, and the syntax error does not seem appropriate, look for things such as missing quotation marks earlier in the line.

The corrected macro program is shown below:

```
'
'Exercise 2.3
'This macro was broken, but now it's fixed
'
Sub Broken()
    MsgBox "Yet Another Message"
End Sub
```

4. When you run the macro resulting from this exercise, the macro should carry out all of the actions that you recorded, and then display a dialog box containing the message that the recorded instructions are complete. The following listing shows how your completed macro might appear.

```
1:   'Exercise 2.4
2:   'Contains instructions recorded directly into the macro
3:   '
4:   Sub InsertByRecording()
5:
6:       ChDir "C:\OFFICE95\EXCEL\Examples"
7:       Workbooks.Open Filename:="C:\OFFICE95\EXCEL\Examples\SAMPLES.XLS"
8:
9:       'Instructions above recorded directly into the macro
10:      MsgBox "Recorded Instructions Completed"
11:  End Sub
```

All of the instructions above the comment in line 9 were inserted by using the macro recorder. The comments in lines 1 through 3, the macro declaration in line 4, the MsgBox statement in line 10, and the End Sub statement in line 11 were all written manually (as was the comment in line 9). The recording mark was inserted at the beginning of line 9.

Day 3

Quiz

1. There are five numeric data types in VBA: Integer, Long, Single, Double, and Currency.

2. The primary difference between the Integer and Single data types is that an Integer data type can store only whole numbers (numbers with no decimal point), while the Single data type can store numbers with a decimal point; secondarily, the range of the Single data type is much greater than that of the Integer.

   Both the Integer and the Long data type can store whole numbers only; the only difference between an Integer and a Long is that the range of values that you can store in a Long is much greater than the range you can store in an Integer.

3. A type definition character is a special symbol that, when added to the end of a variable or constant name, specifies the data type of that variable or constant.

4. You declare variables implicitly by simply using the variable. If the variable does not already exist, VBA understands that the variable needs to be created, and does so. To explicitly declare a variable, you use the VBA Dim statement to specifically instruct VBA to create the variable.

5. Identifier names must begin with a letter of the alphabet, and may optionally be followed by any combination of letters or digits; although the underscore character (_) is permitted in an identifier, you cannot use spaces, a period (.), or any other symbols (except type definition characters) in an identifier. When choosing identifier names, you should choose names which are descriptive, and reflect the use or purpose of the identifier—whether the identifier is a variable, constant, or procedure name. Finally, use capital letters and the underscore character to make long identifiers easier to read and understand.

6. The advantages of explicitly declaring variables include:

   ☐ Speeds up execution of VBA code.

   ☐ Helps avoid errors due to misspelling variable names.

   ☐ Makes your source code easier to read and understand.

   ☐ Regularizes capitalization of every occurrence of a variable name to match the capitalization in the variable declaration.

7. The advantages of declaring a variable's type include:

   ☐ Speeds up execution of VBA code.

   ☐ Makes your programs use memory more efficiently.

    ☐ Makes your source code easier to read and understand.

    ☐ Helps prevent bugs in your program.

8. You should use named constants in your programs to make them easier to read and understand and easier to maintain. Use named constants for values that are used repeatedly, or for values that are difficult to remember or whose meaning is not immediately clear.

9. The purpose of the InputBox function is to obtain input from the user for use by the macro program, such as filenames, numbers to use in calculations, and so on. The InputBox function displays a dialog box containing text (which you supply) that prompts the user to enter some value, and also contains a text box for the user to type the requested value in.

10. The first argument for the InputBox function—the string containing the text which prompts the user to enter a value—is required. All other arguments are optional.

11. The InputBox function always returns a String data type value.

Exercises

1. One of the keys in choosing whether to declare a data item as a variable or a constant is whether or not the value is computed by the program as it executes or the value is known ahead of time. The variable and constant names here were chosen to be as descriptive as possible. Notice that several of the variable names attempt to strike a balance between being easily understood and avoiding having to type very long words. Although you may have chosen different names for the various items, your declarations should look like this:

    (a) A computed count of columns in a worksheet must be a variable, since the value it contains is determined after the program starts running. Because it is unlikely that there will be more than 32,767 columns in a worksheet, an Integer data type was chosen as the smallest and fastest numeric type able to hold the anticipated data. The second line below shows the declaration using a type definition character:

```
Dim NumCols As Integer
Dim NumCols%            'using Integer type definition character
```

    (b) Since this is a value computed by the program, it must be stored in a variable. The Currency data type is specified because the numeric value to be stored represents a dollar value; the Currency data type is the fastest, most accurate data type for dollar values. The second line below shows the declaration using a type definition character:

```
Dim EastCoast_Sales As Currency
Dim EastCoast_Sales@ 'using Currency type definition character
```

Answers

(c) This item is a little tricky. If the projected number of respondents from a marketing survey is computed by the macro, this would be a variable. Usually, however, an item like this is a constant, representing a quantity known ahead of time. The constant declaration below assumes that the response from the marketing survey will be about two percent and will be declared as a Double in order to have the greatest accuracy in computations using this constant. The second line below shows the declaration using a type definition character:

```
Const ProjectedResp As Double = 2
Const ProjectedResp# = 2        'Double type definition character
```

(d) Again, because this value is calculated by the macro, a variable is chosen. Again, a Double data type is declared in order to have the greatest range and accuracy when calculating the cylinder's surface area.

```
Dim CylinderArea As Double
Dim CylinderArea#        'using Double type definition character
```

(e) The multiplier to convert inches to centimeters is a constant. This is the kind of data that is ideal for a named constant. (Notice how the numeral *2* is included in the constant name as a sort of phonic synonym for the word *to*. This is a common practice among programmers to make identifiers expressive, but to avoid extra typing.)

```
Const Inch2Cm As Double = 0.3937
Const Inch2Cm# = 0.3937        'using Double type definition character
```

(f) Once again, a variable is declared because the value for the percent profit is calculated by the program. Notice how an underscore, numeral, and capitalization were used to make this variable name both expressive and still relatively short. A Single data type was chosen because percentage values are typically only worked out to two decimal places. If your program needed more accuracy, you might want to use a Double; if, on the other hand, you are more concerned about rounding errors, or if you expect to use the value in other computations involving money values, you might want to use a Currency data type instead.

```
Dim PcntProfit_1stQ As Single
Dim PcntProfit_1stQ!        'Single type definition character
```

(g) A self-employment tax rate, of course, is a constant. This, also, is the ideal type of data for a named constant. Because this tax rate may change at some point in time, you make the program easy to update by using a named constant—you simply alter the constant declaration. A Currency data type was chosen for this value, since it will be used in computations with values representing money.

```
Const SelfEmp_Tax As Currency = 12
Const SelfEmp_Tax@        'Currency type definition character
```

2. Your macro procedure should look something like the following listing. Notice lines 7 and 8; these lines declare a constant for the dialog box title bars and declare all of the variables used in the procedure. Lines 9 and 10 do the work. Line 9 uses InputBox to

get a string from the user, and line 10 uses MsgBox to display the string typed by the user.

```
1:   '
2:   'Exercise 3.2
3:   'Procedure:  EchoThis
4:   'takes a string from the user, and echoes it with MsgBox
5:   '
6:   Sub EchoThis()
7:     Const BoxTitle = "Echo"
8:     Dim User$
9:     User$ = InputBox("Type any text:", BoxTitle)
10:    MsgBox User$, , BoxTitle
11: End Sub
```

3. The listing below shows how the recorded macro should appear before editing. (The file name you opened may be different, of course.) Since opening the workbook was the first action taken, and since the name of the opened workbook is known (SAMPLES.XLS, in this case), it is fairly easy to determine that line 6 is the VBA statement that actually opens the workbook. Therefore, the InputBox statement to ask the user for the workbook filename should be inserted immediately before line 6.

```
1:   '
2:   ' OpenSheet3 Macro -- Unedited version
3:   ' Opens a workbook and selects sheet named "Sheet3"
4:   '
5:   Sub OpenSheet3()
6:     Workbooks.Open Filename:="C:\OFFICE95\EXCEL\Examples\SAMPLES.XLS"
7:     Sheets("Sheet3").Select
8:   End Sub
```

The following listing shows the macro after adding InputBox. Line 7 declares a variable to store the string for the filename. Line 8 uses the InputBox function to ask the user for the filename and assigns the function result to the FName variable. Line 10 is the same VBA statement from line 6 in the unedited listing; here, the line has been changed so that the FName variable replaces the literal quoted string from before. Now, when the macro executes, whatever filename is stored in the FName variable is opened.

```
1:   '
2:   ' OpenSheet3 Macro
3:   ' Opens a workbook and selects sheet named "Sheet3"
4:   ' Modified to ask macro user for file to open.
5:   '
6:   Sub OpenSheet3()
7:     Dim FName As String
8:     FName = InputBox("Enter the name of the file to open:", _
9:                        "Open Sheet 3")
10:      Workbooks.Open Filename:=FName
11:     Sheets("Sheet3").Select
12: End Sub
```

4. The following listing shows how the macro from Exercise 1 in Day 1 might be modified to ask the user for the filename to open. The changes made to this macro are similar to the changes made in the preceding exercise.

```
 1:  ' NewFile Macro
 2:  ' Creates new file, and saves it with the name NEWFILE
 3:  ' Modified to ask user for the name of newly created file
 4:  '
 5:  Sub NewFile()
 6:    Dim FName As String
 7:    Workbooks.Add
 8:    'The next line gets the new file name from the user
 9:    FName = InputBox("Enter a name for the new file:", _
10:                    "New File")
11:    ActiveWorkbook.SaveAs Filename:=FName, _
12:        FileFormat:=xlNormal, Password:="", _
13:        WriteResPassword:="", ReadOnlyRecommended:=False, _
14:        CreateBackup:=False
15:    ActiveWorkbook.Close
16:  End Sub
```

Day 4

Quiz

1. An expression is a value or group of values representing a single quantity. An expression result is the value obtained when all operations specified in an expression have been carried out, and the expression has been reduced to a single quantity.

2. An expression may contain one or more different values. Values in an expression are connected by operators.

3. Yes.

4. Expression results are assigned to variables, or used as function or procedure arguments. The result of an expression must be used in some way.

5. The equals sign (=) is used to indicate both the assignment operation and the test for equality.

6. The / symbol indicates a floating-point division operation; the result of this division is always a floating-point number, usually a Double type. The \ symbol indicates integer division; the result of integer division is always an integer number, either an Integer or Long type.

7. The results of the expressions are:

    (a) the Boolean value False

    (b) the number 40

    (c) the string 1723

    (d) the number 0

    (e) the string 23Skidoo

Exercises

1. The expressions, with parentheses added, are:

   (a) `3 * (5 - 7)`

   (b) `(4.7 + 26) / 10`

   (c) `312 / ((47 + 16) - 2)`

   (d) `((17 - 5) - (44 / 2)) ^ 2`

2. Your procedure, when finished, should look something like the following listing:

```
 1:  'Exercise 4.2
 2:  'Get three words from the user, assemble them into a single
 3:  'string, and display that string on the screen
 4:  Sub ThreeWords()
 5:      Const Title1 = "Input: "
 6:      Const Title2 = " Word"
 7:      Const Prmpt = "Enter a word:"     'prompt for InputBox
 8:      Dim Echo As String          'assembled string for display
 9:      Dim Word As String          'temporarily store user word
10:
11:      Word = InputBox(Prmpt, Title1 & "First" & Title2)
12:      Echo = Word
13:      Word = InputBox(Prmpt, Title1 & "Second" & Title2)
14:      Echo = Echo & " " & Word
15:      Word = InputBox(Prmpt, Title1 & "Third" & Title2)
16:      Echo = Echo & " " & Word
17:
18:      MsgBox Echo, , "Three Words"
19: End Sub
```

Lines 5 through 7 declare the necessary constants for this procedure. Notice that this procedure uses two separate named constants for the unchanging part of the title used for the InputBox dialog boxes. Lines 8 through 9 declare all of the variables needed for this procedure. Lines 11 through 16 ask the user for a word and add each word to the **Echo** string as it is entered. Line 18 displays the three words assembled into a single string.

Day 5

Quiz

1. Any three of the following is correct:

   ☐ Converting text strings to other data types.

   ☐ Converting other data types to text strings, or returning information about text strings.

   ☐ Formatting numbers or other data types for display.

    ☐ Manipulating or generating date values.

    ☐ Performing trigonometric, logarithmic, statistical, financial, and other calculations.

    ☐ Getting information about files, disk drives, or the environment in which VBA or your application is currently running.

2. You can use a function to supply a value anywhere in any VBA statement where you can legitimately use a constant or variable value (except at the left side of an assignment operation).

3. Omit the parentheses from the argument list of the function to tell VBA that you want to ignore the function's result. You cannot ignore the result of every VBA function, only those which carry out a specific task as well as returning a result.

4. The VBA functions are inherent to VBA and are available in any version of VBA, regardless of the host application (whether it is Microsoft Excel, Access, Project, or some other application). The functions provided by Excel (or any host application) exist only in Excel. Although some or all of a host application's functions may be available to Visual Basic for Applications, they are not part of VBA and may not be available in every host application.

5. You must include the `Application` keyword and a period (.) in front of the name of the host application function that you intend to use.

6. No.

7. The Object Browser allows you to determine which VBA and Excel (or other host application) functions are available, and provides easy access to the on-line help for these functions. The Object Browser can also paste the function call and all its named arguments into your source code for you.

8. Manipulating string data is important because text string data is your program's primary means of exchanging information (displaying messages and receiving input) with your program's user. The more effectively you can manipulate string data, the more likely you are to successfully display attractive, coherent messages for your program's user, or to be able to analyze the data that your program's user enters.

Exercises

1. The corrected expressions are:

    (a) `Sum$ = CStr(12 + 15)`

    (b) `Num% = CInt("47") + CInt("52")`

    (c) `Num@ = 12.98 * CCur("16")`

    (d) `Root! = Sqr(CSng(User_Input$))`

2. Your completed procedure should look something like the following:

```
1:  'Exercise 5.2
2:  Sub Demo_Min()
3:      Const InPrompt = "Enter a number:"
4:      Const InTitle = "Number "
5:      Dim N1 As String, N2 As String, N3 As String
6:      Dim NMin As String
7:      N1 = InputBox(Prompt:=InPrompt, Title:=InTitle & "1")
8:      N2 = InputBox(Prompt:=InPrompt, Title:=InTitle & "2")
9:      N3 = InputBox(Prompt:=InPrompt, Title:=InTitle & "3")
10:      NMin = Application.Min(N1, N2, N3)
11:      MsgBox "The minimum of " & N1 & ", " & N2 & ", and " _
12:          & N3 & " is: " & Nmin
13: End Sub
```

Lines 7 through 9 use the InputBox function to get numbers from the user and assign them to variables. Line 10 calls the Excel MIN function, and line 11 displays the results of the function to the user. You may have displayed the function result directly with the MsgBox function; this is perfectly acceptable.

Notice that this procedure attempts to produce the most complete, coherent, and cosmetically appealing messages for the user. In general, all of your procedures should do the same.

3. Your completed procedure should look something like the following:

```
1:  'Exercise 5.3
2:  Sub Demo_Substrings()
3:      Const InTitle = "Substring Extraction"
4:      Dim UserIn As String
5:      UserIn = InputBox(Prompt:="Enter some text:", _
6:                      Title:=InTitle, Default:="Suggested")
7:      MsgBox Left(UserIn, 3)
8:      MsgBox Right(UserIn, 4)
9:      MsgBox Mid(UserIn, 3, 4)
10: End Sub
```

4. Your completed procedure should look something like the following:

```
1:  'Exercise 5.4
2:  Sub SearchDemo()
3:      Const BoxTitle = "Substring Search Demo"
4:      Dim UserIn As String, SrchFor As String
5:      UserIn = InputBox(Prompt:="Enter some text:", _
6:                  Title:=BoxTitle, Default:="Default string")
7:      SrchFor = "L"
8:      MsgBox Prompt:=InStr(1, UserIn, SrchFor, 1), _
9:              Title:=BoxTitle & ": Text Comparison"
10:      MsgBox Prompt:=InStr(1, UserIn, SrchFor, 0), _
11:              Title:=BoxTitle & ": Binary Comparison"
12:      MsgBox Prompt:=InStr(UserIn, SrchFor), _
13:              Title:=BoxTitle & ": Using Option Compare Setting"
14: End Sub
```

In this procedure, lines 7 through 9 display the results of the InStr search using each of the possible comparison options (if you have only one of these in your procedure,

that's fine). All three lines begin searching at the first character of the **UserIn** string. Line 7 performs a text comparison, line 8 performs a binary comparison, and line 9 uses whatever the current Option Compare setting is.

Try changing the case of **SrchFor** from "L" to "l", and see how the results returned by InStr change. Also try changing the Option Compare setting in the module and see how the result changes.

Day 6

Quiz

1. Function procedures are enclosed by the Function and End Function keywords, instead of the Sub and End Sub keywords. A function returns a result; a procedure does not.

2. A user-defined function is the same thing as a function procedure, except that *user-defined function* is the term used for any function procedure that observes the restrictions against altering Excel's environment, so that the function procedure can be used by Excel. Similar conditions hold true for UDFs in other VBA host applications.

3. A user-defined function must not alter Excel's environment in any way. This means that a user-defined function cannot add, delete, edit, or format data in Excel.

4. A function assignment is a statement in a function procedure that tells VBA what value the function returns. A function can have more than one function assignment statement. The function will return whatever value was specified by the last function assignment executed before the function stops executing.

5. Recursion is when a function (or other procedure) calls itself.

6. Sorry, this one is a bit of a trick question. Generally, you should never use recursive function procedures. Recursive procedures are often difficult to understand and may consume a great deal of memory—sometimes too much for them to complete the computation or manipulation. The main reason this lesson explained recursion is so that you can understand what happens when you accidentally create a recursive function or procedure.

7. Use the IsMissing function to test whether or not a particular optional argument was present when a function (or other) procedure was called.

8. The StrComp function was used in the **FlipCase** function because it compares two strings and allows you to specify the exact comparison method to use for that specific comparison. The entire operation of the **FlipCase** function centers around determining whether or not a particular letter is upper- or lowercase. If a plain relational operator is used, its action is affected by the Option Compare setting; if Option Compare

is set to Text, then a test with plain relational operators would not be able to tell the difference between the letter "A" and the letter "a". By using StrComp, the tests are guaranteed to use a binary comparison, regardless of the Option Compare setting.

9. You should specify that a function argument is passed by value whenever your function alters any of the values in its argument variables. Passing the argument by reference gives the function a copy of the original data in the argument, so that the function can safely change the value without affecting the original data.

10. You would use the **View | O**bject Browser command. Function procedures are not listed in the Macro dialog box opened by the **Tools | M**acro command.

Exercises

1. Your equivalent functions should be similar to the following two listings.

   A user-defined function equivalent for Visual Basic Eqv operator:

   ```
   1:  Function uEQV(L1 As Boolean, L2 As Boolean) As Boolean
   2:      uEQV = L1 Eqv L2
   3:  End Function
   ```

   A user-defined function equivalent for Visual Basic Imp operator:

   ```
   1:  Function uIMP(L1 As Boolean, L2 As Boolean) As Boolean
   2:      uIMP = L1 Imp L2
   3:  End Function
   ```

2. If you carry out the steps described in this lesson correctly, you should see the description you enter in the Object Browser appear in Excel's Function Wizard. Similarly, if you successfully changed the function's category, it will now appear listed in the category of Logical functions in Excel's Function Wizard, instead of the User Defined category.

3. Your function procedure should be similar to the one shown below:

   ```
   1:  Function Yds2Inch(yds As Double) As Double
   2:  'returns a measurement in inches equivalent to the number
   3:  'of yards in yds
   4:      Yds2Inch = yds * 36
   5:  End Function
   ```

   In this function, the Double data type was chosen for both the argument data type and the function result data type to offer the greatest possible range of values for both this function's input and its return value. An Integer or Long type is not suitable for either the function argument or the function result, because you may have a fractional number of yards, resulting in an equivalent in inches which also has a fractional part. If you used Variant or Single data types for this function, that's fine, too.

   Your testing procedure should be similar to the following listing:

   ```
   1:  Sub Test_Yds2Inch()
   2:      Dim UserIn
   3:      UserIn = InputBox("Enter a measurement in yards:", _
   ```

A

```
4:                         "Yds2Inch")
5:        MsgBox UserIn & " yards is " & Yds2Inch(CDbl(UserIn)) _
6:                & " inches"
7:        MsgBox "The value of the user input after " & _
8:                "Yds2Inch is called: " & UserIn
9:    End Sub
```

In this testing procedure, the test values are obtained by using the InputBox function. This is usually easier than using literal constants and editing the test program several times. Notice that the test procedure not only displays the result of calling the function, but checks the original input value to the function argument to ensure that the function does not change its argument in any way. (In a function this simple, this last step is not really necessary, but it's a good idea to get into the habit of checking whether your functions modify their arguments.)

4. Your function procedure should be similar to the one shown in the following listing:

```
1:  Function Inch2Cm(inches As Double) As Double
2:  'returns a measurement in centimeters equivalent to the _
3:  'number of inches
4:       Inch2Cm = inches / 0.3937
5:  End Function
```

The data types for the function arguments and function result are the same as in the function in Exercise 6.3, and for the same reasons.

Your testing procedure for this function should be similar to the following listing:

```
1:  Sub Test_Inch2Cm()
2:     Dim UserIn
3:     UserIn = InputBox("Enter a measurement in inches:", _
4:                        "Inch2Cm")
5:     MsgBox UserIn & " inches is " & Inch2Cm(CDbl(UserIn)) _
6:             & " centimeters"
7:     MsgBox "The value of the user input after Inch2Cm " & _
8:             "is called: " & UserIn
9:  End Sub
```

Notice that this test procedure also gets the test values from the user, and also tests to ensure that the function does not alter its arguments.

5. Your procedure to display a measurement in yards converted to centimeters should be similar to the following listing:

```
1:  Sub Yds2Cm()
2:      Dim UserIn As String
3:      UserIn = InputBox(prompt:="Enter a measurement in " & _
4:                             "yards:", _
5:                        Title:="Yards to Centimeters")
6:      MsgBox UserIn & " yards is " & _
7:             Inch2Cm(Yds2Inch(CDbl(UserIn))) & " centimeters."
8:  End Sub
```

Notice, in line 7 of the above listing, that the CDbl conversion function is used to explicitly convert the string entered by the user into a Double type number; because the function argument's data type is a Double, VBA requires that the data type passed to the function also be a Double.

Day 7

Quiz

1. The main idea behind object-oriented programming is that a software application, like the world around you, should consist of individual objects, each with its own properties and behaviors.

2. A program object consists of code and data bound together so that you can treat it as a single entity.

3. A property is an inherent quality of a program object, such as whether it is visible, its color, its filename, and so on. Properties control an object's appearance and behavior. You use object properties to alter an object's appearance or behavior, or to find out about an object's current appearance and behavior.

4. No. Some properties you can alter, others you cannot. Whether or not you can alter an object property, you can always retrieve its value.

5. No. Each object stores the data for its own properties separately. Although objects have properties with the same names, they do not share the values stored in the property.

6. A method is an inherent behavior of a program object, such as a workbook's ability to add a new worksheet to itself, a workbook's ability to save itself to a disk file, or the application's ability to open a workbook or to create a new workbook. You use an object's methods to perform actions on or with the properties and user data stored by an object.

7. (a) Examine current condition or status of an object by retrieving a property value.

   (b) Change the condition or status of an object by setting a property value.

   (c) Use a method to cause the object to carry out one of its built-in actions.

8. *Object.Identifier* where *Object* is any valid object reference, and *Identifier* is any property or method valid for the referenced object. The dot separator (.) between the object reference and the property or method identifier is required.

9. The dot separator (.) both separates and joins the identifiers that make up the object reference. You must write the object identifiers together, without spaces, to form a single identifier that VBA uses to determine which object you intend to reference. The dot separator lets you join the identifiers together, but also separates one identifier from another, so that VBA can recognize each separate piece of the object reference.

10. An object expression is any VBA expression that specifies an object. Object expressions must evaluate to a single object reference; you use object expressions to create references to specific objects in your VBA programs.

11. Use object methods and properties (starting with the Application property, if necessary) that return object references; for ease of typing or conciseness in your program, you can also assign object references to a variable by using the Set command.

12. An object collection is a group of related objects, such as all of the worksheets in a workbook, or all of the graphic objects in a worksheet. An element is a single object in the collection.

Exercises

1. The flaw in the NewBook procedure relates to the With...End With statement and the object references inside it.

   The problem is that the programmer left out the dot separator (.) in front of the property names for the active workbook. As a result, VBA interprets the Title, Subject, Author, Keywords, and Comments properties as variable names, rather than references to the ActiveWorkbook's properties—this is why VBA complains that there are undefined variables if the Option Explicit statement is on.

   To correct the problem, add the dot separator (.) in front of each property name, as shown in the following listing:

```
1:  Sub NewBook()
2:  'Creates new workbook, and fills in the summary information
3:  'for the new workbook with some information from the user,
4:  'and some information from the Application object.
5:
6:      Const nbTitle = "New Book"
7:
8:      Workbooks.Add       'adds workbook to Workbooks collection
9:      With ActiveWorkbook
10:       .Title = InputBox(prompt:= _
11:                         "Enter a title for this workbook:", _
12:                         Title:=nbTitle)
13:       .Subject = InputBox(prompt:= _
14:                           "Enter the subject of this workbook:", _
15:                           Title:=nbTitle)
16:       .Author = Application.OrganizationName
17:       .Keywords = ""
18:       .Comments = InputBox(prompt:= _
19:               "Enter a comment regarding this workbook:", _
20:               Title:=nbTitle)
21:     End With
22: End Sub
```

2. After rewriting the **Show_SystemInfo** procedure to use a With...End With statement, it should appear similar to the following:

```
1:  Sub Show_SystemInfo()
2:  'uses various host application properties to display
3:  'information about your computer system
4:
5:      Dim CR As String * 1
6:
```

```
 7:    CR = Chr(13)     'a carriage-return
 8:    With Application
 9:      MsgBox "Host Application: " & CR & .Name & " v" _
10:              & .Version & ", Build " & .Build & CR & CR & _
11:              "Library Path: " & .LibraryPath & CR & CR & _
12:              "User: " & .UserName & CR & "            " & _
13:              .OrganizationName
14:      MsgBox "Operating System: " & .OperatingSystem & _
15:              CR & CR & "Mouse is Available: " & _
16:              .MouseAvailable & CR & CR & _
17:              "Total Memory: " & .MemoryTotal & CR & _
18:              "Used Memory: " & .MemoryUsed & CR & _
19:              "Free Memory: " & .MemoryFree
20:    End With
21: End Sub
```

Notice that the dot separator is included in front of each Application object property within the With...End With statement. Incidentally, notice how line 5 and line 7 declare a variable and then assign the character equivalent of a carriage-return keystroke to that variable. The carriage-return character in a string causes VBA to start a new line—this is how the MsgBox text is broken into several lines for display.

3. The problem with the **GetNumber** function is that it is supposed to use the Excel InputBox function, *not* the VBA InputBox function. Because both the Excel host application *and* VBA have functions named InputBox, you must specify the Application object to use the Excel host application's version of this function. Because **GetNumber** omitted the object reference to the Application object, VBA assumed that the VBA InputBox function is intended—which does not have the Type argument.

The corrected **GetNumber** function appears below; notice the change to line 5:

```
 1:   Function GetNumber()
 2:   'Uses the application's InputBox function to return
 3:   'a number obtained from the user.
 4:
 5:     GetNumber = Application.InputBox(Prompt:="Enter a " & _
 6:                                      "number:", _Type:=1)
 7:   End Function
 8:
 9:
10:  Sub Test_GetNumber()
11:       MsgBox GetNumber
12:  End Sub
```

Lines 10 through 12 are the same test procedure to test the **GetNumber** function.

You might want to use a function like **GetNumber** in your procedures to ensure that the user enters numeric data only. By using a function like this, you also avoid having to supply a prompt each time you use InputBox, which can help you make your code shorter and more concise.

4. Your completed procedure should be similar to the following:

```
 1:   Sub SheetInsert()
 2:   'Adds new worksheet to current workbook, then renames that
 3:   'sheet, using a name supplied by the user.
```

```
 4:
 5:     Dim sName As String
 6:     Dim oldSheet As Object
 7:
 8:     Set oldSheet = ActiveSheet
 9:     sName = InputBox(Prompt:="Enter name for new " & _
10:                     "worksheet:", Title:="Add New Sheet")
11:     Worksheets.Add
12:     ActiveSheet.Name = sName
13:     oldSheet.Select
14: End Sub
```

Line 8 uses the Set statement to assign an object reference to the current active sheet
to the **oldSheet** variable. Next, line 9 uses the InputBox function to get a name for the
new worksheet from the user, storing it in the **sName** variable. Line 11 uses the Add
method of the Worksheets collection to add a new worksheet to the active workbook.
Excel adds a new worksheet and makes it the active sheet. Line 12 renames the new
worksheet by assigning the string stored in **sName** to the Name property of the active
sheet. Finally, line 13 switches back to the sheet that was active at the time this
procedure began executing. The Select method causes an object to select itself; the
oldSheet variable supplies the object reference to the original active sheet.

Day 8

Quiz

1. A conditional branching statement alters the flow of VBA's execution of statements in
   a procedure, based on whether a particular condition is true or false. An unconditional
   branching statement redirects VBA's execution of statements without testing for any
   particular condition.

2. You use logical expressions to specify the condition under which VBA should or
   should not execute a particular program branch.

3. VBA's conditional branching statements are:

   (a) If...Then

   (b) If...Then...Else

   (c) If...Then...ElseIf

   (d) Select Case

4. VBA has only one unconditional branching statement: the GoTo statement.

5. Nesting.

6. An If...Then...ElseIf statement may contain an unlimited number of ElseIf
   clauses. You may include *one* Else clause in an If...Then...ElseIf statement; the
   Else clause must come after all of the ElseIf clauses and before the End If keywords.

7. You can include as many `Case` clauses in a `Select Case` statement as you wish. You can specify a branch of statements for VBA to execute if none of the `Case` clauses is met by adding a `Case Else` clause to the `Select Case` statement. The `Case Else` clause must be the last clause in the `Select Case` statement, before the `End Select` keywords.

8. Use `Select Case` when you need to make more than three or four choices; using `Select Case` makes it easier to write, read, and understand your code when you need to make several choices.

9. You use `Exit Sub` to end a procedure early, and `Exit Function` function to end a function early.

10. The `End` keyword, on a line by itself, ends all VBA statement execution, terminating your entire program. All variable values are lost.

11. You use the `Buttons` argument for `MsgBox` to:

    (a) Specify how many and what type of buttons appear in the message dialog box.

    (b) Specify which Windows' icon (Information, Query, Warning, or Critical) appears in the message dialog box.

    (c) Specify which command button is the initial default command button in the message dialog box.

    VBA provides several predefined constants (listed on the back cover of this book, and in the VBA online reference) to help you specify values for the `Buttons` argument.

12. The return value from the `MsgBox` function represents which button the user chose in the dialog box. VBA provides you with several predefined constants (listed on the back cover of this book, and in the VBA online reference) to help you interpret the `MsgBox` function's return values.

Exercises

1. The corrected listing is shown below. The problem with the `Select Case` statement in this procedure involved the `Case` condition statements in lines 12 and 14.

   In the original version of this procedure, the `Case` condition in line 12 checked to see if **Num** was between 1 and 10, inclusive. This allowed any numbers with values between 0 and 1 to be missed—since they didn't match any of the `Case` conditions, they were handled by the `Case Else` statement. Line 12 in the corrected version correctly checks to see if **Num** is between 0 and 10, eliminating the gap.

   Similarly, the `Case` condition in line 14 checks to see if **Num** is between 11 and 20, missing numbers between 10 and 11. Again, the corrected line 14 now checks to see if the number is between 10 and 20.

   ```
   1:  Sub Case_Demo()
   2:
   3:     Dim sNum As String
   ```

```
 4:      Dim Num As Double
 5:
 6:      sNum = InputBox("enter a number:")
 7:      Num = CDbl(sNum)
 8:
 9:      Select Case Num
10:         Case Is < 0
11:             MsgBox "Num is less than 0"
12:         Case 0 To 10
13:             MsgBox "Num is between 0 and 10"
14:         Case 10 To 20
15:             MsgBox "Num is between 10 and 20"
16:         Case Else
17:             MsgBox "Num is greater than 20"
18:      End Select
19: End Sub
```

2. One possible way of completing this exercise appears in the following listing:

```
 1:  Sub TeleDigits()
 2:  'displays the telephone number pad digit corresponding to
 3:  'the alphabetic letter entered by the user.
 4:
 5:      Const tdTitle = "TeleDigits"
 6:
 7:      Dim Letter As String
 8:      Dim Msg As String
 9:
10:
11:      Letter = InputBox(prompt:="Enter a single letter " & _
12:                        "of the alphabet:", Title:=tdTitle)
13:      If Len(Trim(Letter)) = 0 Then
14:        MsgBox prompt:="Entry operation canceled.", _
15:               Title:=tdTitle, _
16:               Buttons:=vbExclamation
17:        Exit Sub
18:      End If
19:
20:      If Len(Trim(Letter)) > 1 Then
21:        MsgBox prompt:="You must enter a single " & _
22:               "character - Canceled.", Title:=tdTitle, _
23:               Buttons:=vbExclamation
24:        Exit Sub
25:      End If
26:
27:      Letter = UCase(Letter)
28:
29:      Msg = "The telephone digit for " & Letter & " is: "
30:
31:      Select Case Letter
32:        Case "A" To "C"
33:          MsgBox prompt:=Msg & "2", _
34:                 Title:=tdTitle, _
35:                 Buttons:=vbInformation
36:        Case "D" To "F"
37:          MsgBox prompt:=Msg & "3", _
38:                 Title:=tdTitle, _
```

```
39:                 Buttons:=vbInformation
40:       Case "G" To "I"
41:         MsgBox prompt:=Msg & "4", _
42:                 Title:=tdTitle, _
43:                 Buttons:=vbInformation
44:       Case "J" To "L"
45:         MsgBox prompt:=Msg & "5", _
46:                 Title:=tdTitle, _
47:                 Buttons:=vbInformation
48:       Case "M" To "O"
49:         MsgBox prompt:=Msg & "6", _
50:                 Title:=tdTitle, _
51:                 Buttons:=vbInformation
52:       Case "P", "R", "S"
53:         MsgBox prompt:=Msg & "7", _
54:                 Title:=tdTitle, _
55:                 Buttons:=vbInformation
56:       Case "T" To "V"
57:         MsgBox prompt:=Msg & "8", _
58:                 Title:=tdTitle, _
59:                 Buttons:=vbInformation
60:       Case "W" To "Y"
61:         MsgBox prompt:=Msg & "9", _
62:                 Title:=tdTitle, _
63:                 Buttons:=vbInformation
64:       Case Else
65:         MsgBox prompt:="There is no telephone digit " & _
66:                 "match for " & Letter, Title:=tdTitle, _
67:                 Buttons:=vbExclamation
68:     End Select
69: End Sub
```

Line 27 converts the character in **Letter** to uppercase, in order to simplify later tests. Line 29 assembles a standard string used by message boxes later in the procedure.

Finally, lines 31 through 68 contain a Select Case statement that evaluates the letter that the user entered. The first eight Case condition branches test the character in **Letter** to find out which range of characters it falls into, and then displays the appropriate message for that digit. Notice that all but one of the Case condition expressions use the To keyword to set a range of characters, and that all of the characters in the Case condition expressions are uppercase. Using all uppercase characters eliminates worrying about making lowercase comparisons, also.

Pay special attention to line 52, which is the only Case condition expression that lists the values to match. There is no digit match for the letter *Q*—the range "P" To "S" includes the letter *Q*, which is not desired, so this expression must list each of the letters individually.

If the character in **Letter** does not match any of the first eight Case expressions, then VBA executes the Case Else clause in lines 64 through 67. These statements simply display a message dialog box with the message that the character has no match.

Day 9

Quiz

1. A fixed loop always repeats a fixed number of times. An indefinite loop repeats an indefinite number of times, depending on conditions that occur while the loop executes.

2. No. The For...Next loop is a fixed loop and always executes a set number of times, although you can end a For loop early with the Exit For statement.

3. If the logical expression for the determinant condition appears at the top of the loop, then VBA tests the condition before executing the loop. If the logical expression for the determinant condition appears at the bottom of the loop, then VBA tests the condition after executing the loop.

4. If you use the While keyword, VBA executes the loop as long as the determinant condition is True, and stops executing the loop when the determinant condition becomes False. If you use the Until keyword, VBA executes the loop until the determinant condition becomes True—that is, VBA executes the loop as long as the determinant condition is False and stops executing the loop when the determinant becomes True.

5. A count-controlled loop is a Do loop that executes while a count is above or below a particular limit. A count-controlled Do loop is very similar in concept to a For...Next loop. You use a count-controlled Do loop, however, whenever the count is incremented at irregular intervals.

6. An event-controlled Do loop is a loop whose determinant condition becomes True or False depending on events that occur while the loop executes, such as the user entering a particular value.

7. A flag-controlled loop is a Do loop that uses a Boolean variable as the determinant condition. You use statements both before and within the loop to change the value of the flag variable, indicating whether or not the loop should continue to execute.

Exercises

1. The problem with this loop is that it is impossible for the user to enter the value that will end the loop! The Excel Application.InputBox function, when used with the optional Type argument to specify that the user should enter numeric-only data prohibits the user from entering a string such as *exit*. Therefore, the determinant condition for the loop can never become True, and the loop executes infinitely.

There are two ways you can correct the loop in this procedure. In the first listing below, the determinant condition (line 9) was changed to end the loop any time the value 0 is entered. By experimenting with the Application.InputBox function a little, you can determine that it returns 0 if the user cancels the input dialog box.

```
1:  Sub GetNumber()
2:  'loops indefinitely, getting numeric input from the user
3:
4:     Dim Num
5:
6:     Do
7:       Num = Application.InputBox(prompt:="Enter a number:", _
8:                                       Type:=1)
9:     Loop Until Num = 0
10:
11:    MsgBox "Number entry ended."
12: End Sub
```

The second way to correct the problem with this loop is to use the VBA InputBox function instead of the Excel Application.InputBox function (line 7). This solution may not be as desirable as the first, since it means giving up the number-only screening provided by the Application.InputBox function's Type argument. (The next lesson describes how you can write your own data-screening code.)

```
1:  Sub GetNumber()
2:  'loops indefinitely, getting numeric input from the user
3:
4:     Dim iNum
5:
6:     Do
7:       iNum = InputBox(prompt:="Enter a number:")
8:     Loop Until iNum = "exit"
9:
10:    MsgBox "Number entry ended."
11: End Sub
```

2. There are several different solutions that will produce the desired results for this exercise. The following listing shows one of them:

```
1:  Sub Three_Words()
2:  'gets three words from the user, and assembles them into
3:  'a single sentence.
4:
5:     Const lTitle = "Three Words"
6:
7:     Dim uStr As String          'string for user input
8:     Dim Sentence As String      'string for output sentence
9:     Dim k As Integer            'loop counter
10:
11:    Sentence = ""
12:    For k = 1 To 3
13:      uStr = InputBox(prompt:="Enter a word:", Title:=lTitle)
14:      If Trim(uStr) = "" Then
15:        MsgBox prompt:="Word entry canceled.", Title:=lTitle
16:        Exit For
```

```
17:      Else
18:         Sentence = Sentence & " " & Trim(uStr)
19:      End If
20:    Next k
21:
22:    'if uStr empty, then last input was canceled
23:    If Trim(uStr) <> "" Then
24:      MsgBox prompt:="You entered the following sentence:" _
25:                     & Chr(13) & Chr(13) & Sentence, _
26:             Title:=lTitle
27:    End If
28: End Sub
```

Line 12 starts a For...Next loop, set to execute 3 times. The statements to get a word from the user are in the body of this For...Next loop, so the loop will ask the user for a word three times.

Line 13 uses the InputBox function to assign the user's input to the **uStr** variable. Lines 14 through 19 contain an If...Then...Else statement to evaluate the user's input. If **uStr** is empty (or consists of only space characters), then the statements in lines 15 and 16 display a message stating that word entry is canceled, and then exits the For loop. If **uStr** is not empty, then line 18 concatenates the user's string with the string in the **Sentence** variable, including a space between words. By cumulatively assembling the sentence inside the loop, you can avoid using more than two string variables. The Trim function is used several times to avoid unnecessary leading and trailing spaces.

Lines 23 through 27 contain an If...Then statement that checks to make sure that **uStr** is not empty. If **uStr** is not empty, then the MsgBox statement in lines 24 through 26 displays the assembled sentence. If **uStr** is empty, it means that the user canceled the last input operation, and the assembled sentence should not be displayed.

3. One possible solution is:

```
1:  Sub Sentence()
2:  'repeatedly gets words from the user, assembles them into
3:  'a single sentence. Stops collecting words from the user
4:  'when the user enters a period (.)
5:
6:    Const lTitle = "Build a Sentence"
7:
8:    Dim uStr As String          'string for user input
9:    Dim Sentence As String      'string for output sentence
10:
11:   Sentence = ""
12:   Do
13:     uStr = InputBox(prompt:="Enter a word ('.' to end):", _
14:                     Title:=lTitle)
15:     If Trim(uStr) = "" Then
16:        MsgBox prompt:="Word entry canceled.", Title:=lTitle
17:        Exit Do
18:     Else
19:        If Trim(uStr) = "." Then
```

```
20:            Sentence = Sentence & Trim(uStr)
21:          Else
22:            Sentence = Sentence & " " & Trim(uStr)
23:          End If
24:       End If
25:    Loop Until Trim(uStr) = "."
26:
27:       'if uStr is empty, then the last input was canceled
28:    If Trim(uStr) <> "" Then
29:      MsgBox prompt:="You entered the following sentence:" _
30:                     & Chr(13) & Chr(13) & Sentence, _
31:             Title:=lTitle
32:    End If
33: End Sub
```

Line 12 starts the Do loop. Because the determinant condition is at the end of the loop, VBA immediately begins to execute the loop's body, starting in line 13.

Line 13 uses the InputBox function to assign the user's input to **uStr**. Lines 15 through 24 contain a pair of nested If...Then statements. The outer If...Then statement, like the one in the procedure from Exercise 9.2, evaluates the user's input. If **uStr** is empty (or consists only of space characters), VBA executes lines 16 and 17, which display a message stating that word entry was canceled, and exits the loop, this time using an Exit Do statement because this is a Do loop.

If **uStr** is not empty, then VBA executes the outer If...Then statement's Else clause in lines 19 through 23, which contain another If...Then statement. This inner If...Then statement was included mostly for cosmetic reasons. If the user's input is a period (.), then it is concatenated to the string in **Sentence** without a space. If it is not a period, then the **uStr** is concatenated to **Sentence** with a space between the two words.

As soon as the user enters a period (.) by itself, the loop determinant condition in line 25 becomes True, and VBA stops executing the loop.

4. The completed **IsBookOpen** function and a testing procedure for it are shown below:

```
1:  Function IsBookOpen(bName As String) As Boolean
2:  'Returns True if workbook named by sName is currently open
3:
4:     Dim aBook As Object
5:
6:     IsBookOpen = False   'assume book won't be found
7:
8:        'cycle through all books, compare each book's name to
9:        'bName, as a text comparison.
10:    For Each aBook In Workbooks
11:      If (StrComp(aBook.Name, bName, 1) = 0) Then
12:        IsBookOpen = True   'if book names match, return true
13:        Exit For
14:      End If
15:    Next aBook
16: End Function
17:
```

```
18:
19: Sub Test_IsBookOpen()
20: 'tests the IsBookOpen function
21:
22:    Dim uStr As String
23:
24:    uStr = InputBox("Enter a workbook name (include " & _
25:                    "the .XLS extension):")
26:    If IsBookOpen(uStr) Then
27:      MsgBox "Book '" & uStr & "' IS open."
28:    Else
29:      MsgBox "Book '" & uStr & "' IS NOT open."
30:    End If
31: End Sub
```

This function and testing procedure work in exactly the same way as the **SheetExists** function shown in Listing 9.10, except that it uses the Workbooks collection instead of the Sheets collection.

5. The **SVal** function and testing procedure shown below are one possible solution:

```
1:  Function SVal(ByVal iStr As String) As Double
2:  'removes non-digit characters from iStr argument, and then
3:  'returns the numeric equivalent of the string. Returns 0 if
4:  'input string does not contain any digits, or has more than
5:  'one decimal place
6:    Dim oStr As String        'working string for output
7:    Dim k As Long             'loop counter
8:    Dim PCount As Long        'count for number of periods (.)
9:
10:   iStr = Trim(iStr)     'remove spaces from the input string
11:   oStr = ""             'make sure working string is empty
12:   PCount = 0            'make sure period count starts at 0
13:
14:   For k = 1 To Len(iStr)
15:       'is the kth character a digit or decimal place?
16:     If (InStr(1, "0123456789.", Mid(iStr,k,1),1) <> 0) Then
17:       oStr = oStr & Mid(iStr, k, 1) 'copy the character
18:         'keep track of how many decimal places (.)
19:       If Mid(iStr, k, 1) = "." Then PCount = PCount + 1
20:     End If
21:   Next k
22:
23:   If (PCount > 1) Or (oStr = "") Then
24:     SVal = 0     'return zero as the result
25:   Else
26:     SVal = Val(oStr)
27:   End If
28: End Function
29:
30:
31: Sub Test_Sval()
32: 'this procedure tests the SVal function
33:
34:    Dim uStr As String
35:    Dim Num As Double
```

```
36:
37:    uStr = InputBox("Enter a string: ")
38:    Num = SVal(uStr)
39:    MsgBox "You entered: " & uStr & " which converted to: " _
40:       & Num
41: End Sub
```

Line 14 begins a For...Next loop that executes for as many characters as there are in **iStr**.

When the loop has finished executing, **oStr** contains a copy of **iStr**, excluding any non-digit characters. The If...Then statement in lines 23 through 28 evaluates both the **PCount** and the **oStr** variables. If **PCount** is greater than 1, then the input string had too many decimal places. If **oStr** is still empty, then the input string did not contain *any* digit characters. If either condition is True, then the string cannot be converted to a number, and the return result of **SVal** is assigned 0.

If neither of these conditions is True, then VBA executes the Else clause in line 26, which assigns the **SVal** function result as the result of converting **oStr** to a number with the VBA Val function.

Lines 31 through 40 contain a procedure to test the **SVal** function.

Day 10

Quiz

1. The VBA information functions that begin with the word Is are all used to determine whether or not a variable has a particular data type.

2. You are most likely to use IsNumeric, IsDate, and IsObject.

3. The TypeName and VarType functions provide the most specific information about the data contained in a particular variable.

4. Use the TypeName function to return a string containing the specific name of the object; VarType can only tell you whether or not the object supports OLE Automation.

5. IsMissing tells you whether or not a particular optional argument was included at the time a function was called.

6. The *Nothing* return means that the object variable you tested has not yet been set to refer to any object. The *Unknown* return means that TypeName was unable to determine the specific type of the referenced object.

7. The Empty value indicates that a Variant variable has not yet had a value assigned to it. VBA assigns this value to every Variant variable at the time it creates the variable.

8. The Null value indicates that a Variant variable does not contain valid data. VBA does not assign this value to any variables. The only way a Variant variable can end up containing the Null value is if you, the programmer, assign Null to a variable.

9. Defensive programming is just a name given to the techniques used to validate data values in a program in order to avoid runtime errors, or to handle runtime errors more gracefully than VBA alone.

10. The purpose of the Static keyword is to indicate to VBA which variables in a function or procedure that you want to keep in between function or procedure calls. Unlike other procedure-level variables, VBA does *not* dispose of the contents of a static variable when a procedure or function ends. Instead, VBA preserves the variable's value.

11. You use the Static keyword instead of the Dim keyword to declare a static variable. If you want all of the variables in a procedure or function to be static, then place the Static keyword at the beginning of the function or procedure's declaration.

12. A user-defined type is a data type that you construct by combining elements based on VBA's fundamental data types. A user-defined data type binds together several different, but related, types of data.

13. The Type keyword begins a user-defined type definition.

14. You must place user-defined type definitions in the definition area of a module, at the module level—usually before any procedure or function declarations.

Exercises

Starting with this chapter, the Exercise answers will no longer include an analysis of the programming solutions, except occasionally to point out a particularly useful or tricky part of the solution. Although this Appendix will continue to provide programming solutions to the Exercises, keep in mind that there are often many different solutions to a particular exercise, all of which might have equal merit. Don't be dismayed if your solutions differ from the ones shown here—these solutions are here to help you get going again if you're stumped by a particular exercise. Also, you might find it useful to see a solution besides the one you come up with.

1. Your user-defined type for the mailing list information should look something like this (the State and Zip elements are declared as fixed-length strings so that they will automatically get truncated to the correct length):

```
1:  Type MailAddress
2:      FName As String
3:      LName As String
4:      Company As String
5:      Street As String
6:      City As String
```

```
7:      State As String * 2
8:      Zip As String * 5
9:  End Type
```

2. Your function and procedure should look something like this (notice that the following listing contains a complete module):

```
1:  Option Explicit
2:
3:  Type MailAddress
4:      FName As String
5:      LName As String
6:      Company As String
7:      Street As String
8:      City As String
9:      State As String * 2
10:     Zip As String * 5
11: End Type
12:
13: Const MailTitle = "Mailing List Data Entry"
14:
15: Sub Enter_MailingData()
16: 'enters information for a mailing list. It calls
17: 'Get_MailAddress to get data for a single mailing address,
18: 'and then transfers the data to a worksheet, looping until
19: 'there is no more data.
20:
21:     Dim Person As MailAddress
22:     Dim Done As Boolean
23:     Dim RNum As Integer
24:
25:     Worksheets("Sheet2").Select       'put the data in Sheet2
26:
27:     RNum = 0
28:     Done = False
29:     Do Until Done
30:       Person = Get_MailAddress
31:       If Len(Trim(Person.LName)) = 0 Then    'no more data
32:         Done = True
33:       Else                            'store data in worksheet
34:         RNum = RNum + 1
35:         With Person
36:           Cells(RNum, 1).Value = .LName
37:           Cells(RNum, 2).Value = .FName
38:           Cells(RNum, 3).Value = .Company
39:           Cells(RNum, 4).Value = .Street
40:           Cells(RNum, 5).Value = .City
41:           Cells(RNum, 6).Value = .State
42:           Cells(RNum, 7).Value = .Zip
43:         End With
44:       End If
45:     Loop
46:     MsgBox prompt:="Data entry complete. " & RNum & " _
47:               "records entered.", Title:=MailTitle
48: End Sub
```

```
49:
50:
51: Function Get_MailAddress() As MailAddress
52: 'gets all the data for a single mailing list entry, and
53: 'returns it in a MailAddress user type.
54:
55:    Dim Item As MailAddress
56:    Dim Tmp As Variant
57:
58:    With Item
59:      Do               'get the person's last name
60:        .LName = InputBox(prompt:="Enter person's LAST " & _
61:                              name:", Title:=MailTitle)
62:        If Len(Trim(.LName)) = 0 Then        'cancel?
63:          Tmp = MsgBox(prompt:="End mail list data entry?", _
64:                          Title:=MailTitle, _
65:                          Buttons:=vbQuestion + vbYesNo)
66:         If Tmp = vbYes Then
67:           .LName = ""
68:           Get_MailAddress = Item
69:           Exit Function
70:         End If
71:        End If
72:      Loop While Len(Trim(.LName)) = 0
73:
74:      Do               'get the person's first name
75:        .FName = InputBox(prompt:="Enter person's FIRST " & _
76:                              "name:", Title:=MailTitle)
77:      Loop While Len(Trim(.FName)) = 0
78:
79:      Do               'get the company name
80:        .Company = InputBox(prompt:="Enter company " & _
81:                              "name:", Title:=MailTitle)
82:      Loop While Len(Trim(.Company)) = 0
83:
84:      Do               'get street address
85:        .Street = InputBox(prompt:="Enter street number " & _
86:                              "and name:", Title:=MailTitle)
87:      Loop While Len(Trim(.Street)) = 0
88:
89:      Do               'get city
90:        .City = InputBox(prompt:="Enter the city name:", _
91:                          Title:=MailTitle)
92:      Loop While Len(Trim(.City)) = 0
93:
94:      Do               'get the state
95:        .State = InputBox(prompt:="Enter 2 letter State " & _
96:                              "name:", Title:=MailTitle)
97:      Loop While Len(Trim(.State)) = 0
98:
99:      Do               'get zip code
100:       .Zip = InputBox(prompt:="Enter 5 digit zip code:", _
101:                         Title:=MailTitle)
102:     Loop While Len(Trim(.Zip)) = 0
```

```
103:   End With
104:   Get_MailAddress = Item      'return filled MailAddress
105: End Function
```

3. Your function should look something like this:

```
1:    Function IsMasterCard(CardNum As String) As Boolean
2:    'evaluates the string in CardNum, and returns True if the
3:    'string represents a valid MasterCard number. Valid
4:    'MasterCard numbers always begin with the digit 5, and
5:    'consist of four groups of four digits, with each group
6:    'separated by a hyphen.
7:
8:    IsMasterCard = (CardNum Like "5###[-]####[-]####[-]####")
9:    End Function
10:
11:
12: Sub Test_IsMasterCard()
13: 'This procedure tests the IsMasterCard function.
14:
15:    Dim uStr As String
16:
17:    Do
18:      uStr = InputBox("Enter a MasterCard number " & _
19:                       "(include the hyphens):")
20:      MsgBox IsMasterCard(uStr)
21:    Loop Until Len(Trim(uStr)) = 0
22: End Sub
```

4. Your procedure should look something like this one:

```
1:    Sub Get_MasterCardNum()
2:    'gets a MasterCard credit card number from user, looping
3:    'repeatedly until user enters a valid MasterCard number.
4:
5:      Dim uStr As String
6:      Dim Ans As Integer
7:
8:      Do
9:        uStr = InputBox("Enter a MasterCard number " & _
10:             "(include the hyphens):", "Credit Card Data Entry")
11:        If Len(Trim(uStr)) = 0 Then
12:          Ans = MsgBox(prompt:="Cancel Card Number Entry?", _
13:                       Title:="Card Entry - Confirm Cancel", _
14:                       Buttons:=vbQuestion + vbYesNo)
15:          If Ans = vbYes Then Exit Sub
16:        ElseIf Not IsMasterCard(uStr) Then
17:              MsgBox prompt:="You entered an invalid " & _
18:                      "MasterCard number." & Chr(13) & _
19:                      "Please try again.", _
20:                      Title:="Error: Invalid Card Number", _
21:                      Buttons:=vbExclamation
22:        End If
23:      Loop Until IsMasterCard(uStr)
24:
25:      'code to store or use valid MasterCard number goes here.
26: End Sub
```

Answers

Day 11

Quiz

1. VBA first searches for the procedure in the current module, then searches the other modules in the current workbook. VBA then searches other open workbooks, and finally searches any workbooks referenced by the workbook calling the procedure.

2. Use the Object Browser. The Macro dialog box lists procedures only.

3. Any workbook can be a library workbook. You create a library workbook by placing procedures and functions in the workbook, and then making sure that the workbook is available.

4. You can either make sure that the workbook is always open by placing it in Excel's startup or alternate startup directories, or you can create a reference to the library workbook.

5. The StartupPath property returns the name of Excel's startup directory. This property is a read-only property; you cannot change it.

6. The AltStartupPath property returns the name of Excel's alternate startup directory. This is a read-write property; you *can* use this property to change Excel's alternate startup directory.

7. When you execute a procedure or function stored in a referenced workbook, VBA reads the necessary code from the referenced workbook, and executes that code, without actually opening the referenced workbook.

8. Use the Tools | References command to create a reference. The Tools | References command only appears when the current sheet is a module sheet.

9. Private scope means that an item's availability is limited to the module in which it is declared. Public scope means that an item is available to any module, in any workbook.

10. Option Private Module limits the availability of items in the module that contains the statement to the workbook that contains that module.

11. The Private keyword causes an item—such as a procedure or function—that would normally have public scope to have private (module-level) scope, instead. The Public keyword causes an item—such as a module-level variable or constant—that would normally have private scope to have public scope, instead.

12. No. Local variables, declared inside a procedure or function, are never available outside the procedure or function in which you declare them. If you need to make the value in one procedure available to another procedure, pass it as an argument to the second procedure.

A

13. To pass information to a procedure, or to return a value from a procedure.

14. The Macro dialog box does not list procedures if they have required arguments. If *all* of a procedure's arguments are optional, then the Macro dialog box will list that procedure. The Object Browser lists all available procedures, whether or not their arguments are optional or required.

15. By reference.

Exercises

1. The changed listing is:

```
 1:       Option Explicit
 2:       Option Private Module
 3:
 4:       Private Type NodeRecord
 5:           StatementText As String * agMaxStrLen
 6:           NodeType As Integer
 7:           NextIfYes As Integer
 8:           NextIfNo As Integer
 9:       End Type
10:
11:       Public Spinning As Boolean
12:       Public New_Animal As Boolean
13:       Public Animals() As NodeRecord
14:
15:
16:       Private Sub AboutAnimal()
17:         ' procedure body
18:       End Sub
19:
20:
21:       Private Sub ShutDown()
22:         ' procedure body
23:       End Sub
24:
25:
26:       Private Sub Play_Game_Cycle()
27:         ' procedure body
28:       End Sub
29:
30:
31:       Private Sub ShowRules()
32:         ' procedure body
33:       End Sub
34:
35:       Private Function Do_Remember() As Boolean
36:         ' procedure body
37:       End Function
38:
39:
40:       Private Sub Still_Playing()
41:         ' procedure body
42:       End Sub
```

```
43:
44:
45:        Private Sub Animal()
46:          ' procedure body
47:        End Sub
```

All items that normally have private scope now have public scope, and all items that normally have public scope now have private scope.

2. No answer for this exercise is provided. Refer to the listing for exercise 3 of Day 11 (following) for an example of the VBA code resulting from this design exercise.

3. Your completed program might look like the following (this listing contains one entire module):

```
1:  Option Explicit
2:
3:  Sub BalanceCheckBook()
4:
5:      Dim Balance As Currency        'the check book balance
6:      Dim Transaction As Currency    'the transaction amount
7:      Dim Done As Boolean            'flag to end transaction loop
8:
9:
10:     Get_StartBalance Amt:=Balance       'get starting balance
11:     MsgBox "Your Starting Balance is: $" & Balance
12:
13:     Do                          'get transactions
14:       Get_Transaction Amt:=Transaction, LastItem:=Done
15:       If Not Done Then
16:         Balance = Balance + Transaction
17:         Display_NewBal Bal:=Balance, Amt:=Transaction
18:       End If
19:     Loop Until Done
20:                                     'Display ending balance
21:     Display_NewBal Bal:=Balance
22: End Sub
23:
24:
25: Sub Get_StartBalance(Amt As Currency)
26: 'gets starting balance from user, and returns it in Amt
27:
28:     Dim iStr As String
29:
30:     Amt = 0
31:     Do
32:       iStr = InputBox("Enter the starting balance:")
33:       If Len(Trim(iStr)) = 0 Then    'canceled input?
34:         If ConfirmCancel("Do you want to stop program?") Then
35:           End  'stop entire program
36:         End If
37:       ElseIf Not IsNumeric(iStr) Then
38:         MsgBox prompt:="Please enter a number, only.", _
39:                     Buttons:=vbExclamation
40:       End If
```

```
41:    Loop Until IsNumeric(iStr)
42:    Amt = CCur(iStr)
43: End Sub
44:
45:
46: Sub Get_Transaction(Amt As Currency, LastItem As Boolean)
47: 'gets a single transaction from user, and signals whether
48: 'or not it is last transaction by setting LastItem True.
49:
50:    Dim iStr As String
51:
52:    Amt = 0
53:    LastItem = False    'assume this is not the last item
54:    Do
55:      iStr = InputBox("Enter the transaction amount: ")
56:      If Len(Trim(iStr)) = 0 Then    'canceled?
57:        If ConfirmCancel("Stop entering transactions?") Then
58:          LastItem = True
59:          Exit Sub
60:        End If
61:      ElseIf Not IsNumeric(iStr) Then
62:        MsgBox prompt:="Please enter numbers only. & _
63:              "Enter negative numbers for debits, " & _
64:              "positive numbers for credits.", _
65:                Buttons:=vbExclamation
66:      End If
67:    Loop Until IsNumeric(iStr)
68:    Amt = CCur(iStr)
69: End Sub
70:
71: Sub Display_NewBal(Bal As Currency, Optional Amt)
72: 'displays the balance. If the optional Amt argument is
73: 'included, it is assumed to be a transaction amount.
74:
75:    Dim Msg1 As String      'message to display, in two parts
76:    Dim Msg2 As String
77:    Dim Btns As Integer     'buttons options for message box
78:
79:    Msg1 = ""
80:    Msg2 = "Your "
81:    If IsMissing(Amt) Then    'is Amt present?
82:        Msg2 = Msg2 & "Ending "
83:      Else              'is transaction a credit or debit?
84:        If Amt < 0 Then Msg1 = "Debit" Else Msg1 = "Credit"
85:        Msg1 = Msg1 & " amount is: $" & Abs(Amt) & " " & _
86:              Chr(13) & Chr(13)
87:    End If
88:    Msg2 = Msg2 & "Balance is: $" & Bal
89:
90:            'add warning, if necessary
91:    If Bal < 100 Then
92:      Btns = vbExclamation
93:      Msg2 = Msg2 & Chr(13) & Chr(13) & _
94:            "CAUTION, your balance is very low!"
```

```
95:    Else
96:        Btns = 0
97:    End If
98:    MsgBox prompt:=Msg1 & Msg2, Buttons:=Btns
99: End Sub
100:
101:
102: Function ConfirmCancel(pStr As String) As Boolean
103: 'returns true or false, depending on whether or not user
104: 'answers yes to the question posed in pStr.
105:
106:    Dim Ans As Integer
107:
108:    Ans = MsgBox(prompt:=pStr, _
109:                    Buttons:=vbQuestion + vbYesNo)
110:    If Ans = vbYes Then
111:        ConfirmCancel = True
112:    Else
113:        ConfirmCancel = False
114:    End If
115: End Function
```

Day 12

Quiz

1. Archive, Directory, Hidden, Normal, Read-Only, System, Volume Label.

2. By adding them together. The file attribute code number for a file is the sum of all of its attributes.

3. Use the GetAttr function to retrieve a file's attributes. The function returns a single number, containing the sum of the file's attribute code numbers.

4. No. You cannot assign the Directory or Volume Label attributes to a file with SetAttr. To create a directory, use the MkDir statement. VBA does not provide a way to create or remove disk Volume Labels.

5. GetOpenFilename displays a dialog box that looks and behaves exactly like the Excel File Open dialog box. GetSaveAsFilename displays a dialog box that looks and behaves exactly like Excel's File Save As dialog box.

6. You use the Dir function in two stages. First, you call it *with* arguments, in order to find the first matching file. Then, you call Dir repeatedly, *without* arguments, to find any additional matching files. Dir returns an empty string when there are no more matching files.

7. Use the CurDir function, which returns a string containing the complete path of the current directory, including the drive letter.

8. The FileCopy statement.

9. Use the `Name` statement to move a file from one directory to another on the same disk. You cannot use `Name` to move a file to a different disk drive, you must use `FileCopy` to copy the file.

Exercises

1. In (A) the `Application` object reference is missing. In (B), the dot separator (.) in front of the `GetSaveAsFilename` method is missing. The corrected fragments are:

   (A):

   ```
   fName = Application.GetOpenFilename
   ```

   (B):

   ```
   With Application
     fName = .GetSaveAsFilename
   End With
   ```

2. The statement attempts to use `Name` to move a file to a different disk drive, which is not possible. Use the following code to move the file, instead:

   ```
   FileCopy "C:\EXAMPLES\SALES.XLS", "A:\SALES.XLS"
   Kill "C:\EXAMPLES\SALES.XLS"
   ```

3. Your **IsDiskDirectory** function might look like this:

   ```
   1:   Function IsDiskDirectory(dirName As String) As Boolean
   2:   'return True if dirName is found on disk
   3:
   4:       If (Dir(dirName, vbDirectory) <> "") Then
   5:           IsDiskDirectory = True
   6:       Else
   7:           IsDiskDirectory = False
   8:       End If
   9:   End Function
   ```

4. Your procedure might look like this:

   ```
   1:   Sub SwitchDir()
   2:   'switches to a new subdirectory,
   3:   'creating it if it does not already exist.
   4:
   5:       Const iTitle = "Switch Directory"
   6:       Dim iName As String
   7:       Dim Ans As Integer
   8:
   9:       iName = InputBox(prompt:="Enter a directory name: ", _
   10:                   Title:=iTitle)
   11:      If Trim(iName) = "" Then Exit Sub
   12:
   13:      If IsDiskDirectory(iName) Then
   14:         ChDrive iName
   15:         ChDir iName
   16:      Else
   17:         Ans = MsgBox(prompt:=iName & " does not exist. " & _
   18:                     Chr(13) & Chr(13) & "Create it?", _
   ```

```
19:                     Title:=iTitle, _
20:                     Buttons:=vbQuestion + vbYesNo)
21:         If Ans = vbYes Then
22:            MkDir iName
23:            ChDrive iName
24:            ChDir iName
25:         End If
26:      End If
27:   End Sub
```

Day 13

Quiz

1. The **Lookup** array has 150 elements (5 times 3 times 10); the **Cube** array has 27 elements (3 times 3 times 3). You compute the number of elements in an array by multiplying the number of elements in each dimension together.

2. The values returned by the various function calls are:

   (A) 1980
   (B) 1
   (C) 5
   (D) 1990
   (E) 10
   (F) 9

3. The ReDim statement in line 10 is incorrect. You cannot use ReDim to alter the data type of the array's elements.

4. No. Not even using the Erase statement will let you alter the data type of the array's elements.

5. Yes. VBA treats a single array element just like any simple variable.

6. Yes, a linear search will work correctly on both a sorted and unsorted array.

7. You should use a binary search on a sorted array because binary searches take advantage of the fact that the elements in the array are in order, resulting in a much faster and more efficient search. Binary searches only work on sorted arrays. Using a binary search on an unsorted array will produce incorrect results.

Exercises

1. Your procedure might look something like this (notice that the **BubbleSort** procedure in this module uses an optional argument to specify whether the sort is ascending or descending):

```
1:    Option Explicit
2:    Option Base 1
3:
```

```
 4:    Private Const FORMATSTR As String = "####"
 5:
 6:    Sub Sorter2()
 7:      Const NUM_ROWS As Integer = 15
 8:      Const NUM_COLS As Integer = 4
 9:      Const iTitle As String = "Sorter2 Information"
10:      Const SortCol As Integer = 2
11:
12:      Dim NumTable(NUM_ROWS, NUM_COLS) As Integer
13:      Dim I As Integer
14:      Dim J As Integer
15:      Dim oldSheet As String
16:
17:      oldSheet = ActiveSheet.Name   'preserve current sheet
18:      Sheets("Sheet1").Select        'switch to new sheet
19:
20:      Randomize Timer   'reseed random number generator
21:      For I = 1 To NUM_ROWS   'fill array w/random numbers
22:        For J = 1 To NUM_COLS
23:          NumTable(I, J) = Int(Rnd * 1000)
24:        Next J
25:      Next I
26:      DisplayArray NumTable         'display the array elements
27:      MsgBox prompt:="Ready to start sorting.", _
28:             Buttons:=vbInformation, _
29:             Title:=iTitle
30:
31:      'sort array ascending
32:      BubbleSort xArray:=NumTable, sCol:=SortCol, Ascend:=True
33:      DisplayArray NumTable  'display sorted array elements
34:      MsgBox prompt:="Array now sorted in ascending order.", _
35:             Buttons:=vbInformation, _
36:             Title:=iTitle
37:
38:      'sort array descending
39:      BubbleSort xArray:=NumTable, sCol:=SortCol, Ascend:=False
40:      DisplayArray NumTable  'display sorted array elements
41:      MsgBox prompt:="Array now sorted in descending order.", _
42:             Buttons:=vbInformation, _
43:             Title:=iTitle
44:      Sheets(oldSheet).Select    'restore worksheet
45:    End Sub
46:
47:    Sub BubbleSort(xArray() As Integer, _
48:                   sCol As Integer, _
49:                   Optional Ascend)
50:    'sorts on ascending or descending order,
51:    'depending on value of Ascend argument
52:      Dim I As Integer, J As Integer
53:
54:      If IsMissing(Ascend) Or _
55:         TypeName(Ascend) <> "Boolean" Then Ascend = True
56:      For I = LBound(xArray, 1) To UBound(xArray, 1) - 1
57:        For J = I + 1 To UBound(xArray, 1)
58:          If Ascend Then
59:            If xArray(I, sCol) > xArray(J, sCol) Then _
```

```
60:              SwapRow xArray, I, J
61:           Else
62:             If xArray(I, sCol) < xArray(J, sCol) Then _
63:               SwapRow xArray, I, J
64:           End If
65:         Next J
66:       Next I
67:     End Sub
68:
69:     Sub SwapRow(xArray() As Integer, _
70:                   sRow1 As Integer, _
71:                   sRow2 As Integer)
72:     'swap elements at rows sRow1 and sRow2
73:       Dim k As Integer
74:       For k = LBound(xArray, 2) To UBound(xArray, 2)
75:         Swap xArray(sRow1, k), xArray(sRow2, k)
76:       Next k
77:     End Sub
78:
79:     Sub Swap(I1 As Integer, I2 As Integer)
80:       Dim temp As Integer
81:       temp = I1
82:       I1 = I2
83:       I2 = temp
84:     End Sub
85:
86:     Sub DisplayArray(xArr() As Integer)
87:       Dim k1 As Integer, k2 As Integer
88:       For k1 = LBound(xArr, 1) To UBound(xArr, 1)
89:         For k2 = LBound(xArr, 2) To UBound(xArr, 2)
90:           Cells(k1, k2).Value = Format(xArr(k1, k2), FORMATSTR)
91:         Next k2
92:       Next k1
93:     End Sub
```

2. The elements in array **A** have the following values:

```
A(1) contains 2
A(2) contains 3
A(3) contains 5
A(4) contains 9
A(5) contains 17
A(6) contains 33
A(7) contains 65
A(8) contains 129
A(9) contains 257
```

3. This listing actually has two problems. First, the For...Next loop in line 4 causes a runtime error because the element ProjIncome(I-1) is not valid when **I** equals 1995—1995 minus 1 is 1994, which is below the lower limit of array subscripts. Second, the upper limit of the For loop will also produce a runtime error because 2000 is not a valid subscript to the **ProjIncome** array—this time it is past the upper limit of array subscripts.

4. The array **X** is declared as a static array in line 2; the ReDim statement in line 10 causes an error, because you can't redimension a static array.

5. The `Option Base` statement in line 1 is at fault—you can only use 0 or 1 with the `Option Base` compiler directive.

6. The `Option Base` statement in line 3 is at fault—a module can contain only one `Option Base` directive.

7. The `Option Base` statement in line 2 is at fault—the `Option Base` directive must appear in a module before any arrays are declared.

Day 14

Quiz

1. You place a breakpoint before a statement which is causing a runtime error, or which you suspect as being the cause of a logical error.

2. Place multiple breakpoints before several statements that are involved (or at least suspected of being involved) with a runtime error. When the procedure execution stops at each breakpoint, inspect the watched variables and then resume executing the procedure at normal speed until the next breakpoint is reached. This scheme allows you to quickly move between trouble spots.

3. False. You can watch only watch the value in an individual array element.

4. Use the `Print` command in the Immediate pane of the Debug window. The `Print` command allows you to supply various arguments to the function to determine whether or not it works correctly.

5. The **Run | R**eset command resets a macro.

Exercises

1. No answer is provided for this exercise.

2. No answer is provided for this exercise.

3. The `Do` loop does not increment the variable **I**, which allows the loop to examine the characters of string **S**. Consequently, the loop repeats indefinitely. Here is the corrected version of the loop:

```
11: Do While I < Len(S)
12:    If Mid(S, I, 1) = FindChar Then
13:      Mid(S, I, 1) = FindChar
14:    Else
15:      I = I + 1
16:    End If
17: Loop
```

4. The condition of the `If` statement is never true (no number can be both less than 10 and greater than 100 at the same time). This error is a logical error.

5. The call to function `InStr` in line 10 has a logically incorrect first argument. The correct code is:

```
1:  Dim S As String
2:  Dim SubStr As String
3:  Dim I As Integer
4:
5:  S = "The rain is Spain stays mainly in the plain"
6:  SubStr = "ain"
7:  I = InStr(S, SubStr)
8:  Do While I > 0
9:     Debug.Print "Match at "; I
10:    I = InStr(I + 1, S, SubStr)
11: Loop
```

Day 15

Quiz

1. The statements lack a `With` block.

2. The first statement inside the `With` block is missing the dot separator (.).

3. Yes, the syntax for the statements is correct. Using nested `With` statements with the complex object references required for dialog box controls is not only acceptable, it's recommended.

Exercises

1. Here is one version of the **DemoDropDown** procedure. This procedure assumes that the drop-down list box is named `City Drop List`, and that it has the **CityDropList_Change** procedure attached to it. The label control is named `City Label`. Notice that nested `With` statements have been added to the procedure to reduce the amount of typing required. Refer to Figure 15.12 to see a sample of the dialog box used by this procedure, which must be stored in a dialog sheet named `DropDownDialog1`.

```
1:    Sub DemoDropDown()
2:       Dim Choice As String
3:       Dim Index As Integer
4:
5:       With DialogSheets("DropDownDialog1")
6:          With .DropDowns("City Drop List")
7:             .RemoveAllItems   'clear the list box
8:             .AddItem ("Paris")    'insert data
9:             .AddItem ("London")
```

```
10:          .AddItem ("Tokyo")
11:          .AddItem ("Rome")
12:          .AddItem ("Madrid")
13:          .AddItem ("Bern")
14:          .AddItem ("Washington")
15:          .AddItem ("Cairo")
16:          .AddItem ("Mexico City")
17:          .AddItem ("Dublin")
18:          .AddItem ("Warsaw")
19:          .AddItem ("Vienna")
20:
21:          Index = .Value
22:          If Index > 0 Then
23:            Choice = .List(Index)
24:            .Caption = Choice
25:          End If
26:       End With
27:     End With
28:
29:     If DialogSheets("DropDownDialog1").Show Then
30:       With DialogSheets("DropDownDialog1")
31:         With .DropDowns("City Drop List")
32:            Index = .Value
33:            Choice = .List(Index)
34:         End With
35:       End With
36:       MsgBox prompt:=Choice, Buttons:=vbInformation, _
37:              Title:="DropDown Box Selection"
38:     End If
39:   End Sub
40:
41:   Sub CityDropList_Change()
42:   'updates the label control with current list selection
43:     Dim I As Integer
44:
45:     With DialogSheets("DropDownDialog1")
46:       I = .DropDowns("City Drop List").Value
47:       .Labels("City Label").Caption = _
48:             .DropDowns("City Drop List").List(I)
49:     End With
50:   End Sub
```

2. Here is one possible version of the **COCA** procedure, which displays the COCA dialog box, and the **CalculateButton_Click** procedure that performs the actual computations. This procedure assumes that the dialog box is stored on a dialog sheet named COCADialog, and that the dialog box contains four edit boxes named Operand1, Operand2, Operator, and Result. This procedure also assumes that you have attached the **CalculateButton_Click** procedure as the event procedure for a Calculate command button on the dialog box. Refer to Figure 15.13 for an illustration of the COCA dialog box's controls.

```
1:   Option Explicit
2:
3:   Sub COCA()
```

```
 4:      DialogSheets("COCADialog").Show
 5:   End Sub
 6:
 7:   Sub CalculateButton_Click()
 8:   'performs the specified calculation
 9:      Dim Operand1 As Double
10:      Dim Operand2 As Double
11:      Dim Result As Double
12:      Dim OpStr As String
13:
14:      With DialogSheets("COCADialog")
15:         'get the operands and operator/function. Use Val to
16:         'convert strings to numbers so that blank strings
17:         'are converted as zero
18:         Operand1 = Val(.EditBoxes("Operand1").Caption)
19:         OpStr = UCase(Trim(.EditBoxes("Operator").Caption))
20:         Operand2 = Val(.EditBoxes("Operand2").Caption)
21:
22:         'check for missing operator
23:         If Len(OpStr) = 0 Then
24:            MsgBox prompt:="No operator/function specified", _
25:                   Buttons:=vbExclamation, Title:="Error!"
26:            Exit Sub
27:         End If
28:
29:         Select Case OpStr
30:           Case Is = "+"
31:              Result = Operand1 + Operand2
32:           Case Is = "-"
33:              Result = Operand1 - Operand2
34:           Case Is = "*"
35:              Result = Operand1 * Operand2
36:           Case Is = "^"
37:              Result = Operand1 ^ Operand2
38:           Case Is = "/"
39:              If Operand2 <> 0 Then
40:                 Result = Operand1 / Operand2
41:              Else
42:                 MsgBox prompt:="Division-by-zero error", _
43:                        Buttons:=vbExclamation, Title:="Error!"
44:              Exit Sub
45:              End If
46:           Case Is = "SQR"
47:              If Operand1 > 0 Then
48:                 Result = Sqr(Operand1)
49:              Else
50:                 MsgBox prompt:="Bad function argument", _
51:                        Buttons:=vbExclamation, Title:="Error!"
52:              Exit Sub
53:              End If
54:           Case Else
55:              MsgBox prompt:="Invalid operator", _
56:                     Buttons:=vbExclamation, Title:="Error!"
57:              Exit Sub
```

```
58:        End Select
59:
60:        'display the result
61:        .EditBoxes("Result").Caption = CStr(Result)
62:    End With
63: End Sub
```

Day 16

Quiz

1. By using the `AddMenu` method of the `MenuItems` collection for the menu to which you want to add the submenu.

2. It's important to make sure the user has a way to exit from your program, or from the menu system that you've installed—otherwise, the user can never get back to the original Excel menus.

3. The `ToolbarButtons` method is being used with a string argument. You must use a numeric expression to specify a member of the `ToolbarButtons` collection. For example, if the statement was intended to access the first button on the toolbar, then it should be:

   ```
   ToolbarButtons(1).Enabled = False
   ```

4. The block of statements produces a runtime error whenever VBA attempts to execute the first `Add` method with no arguments. This call to the `Add` method is intended to create a gap in the toolbar. Any time you omit the `Before` argument with the `Add` method, VBA tries to add the new toolbar button to the end of the toolbar—inserting a gap at the beginning or end of a toolbar is simply forbidden by VBA, so the statement results in a runtime error. Always use the `Before` argument when inserting gaps on a toolbar. To add gaps, you usually need to add most or all of the toolbar buttons first, and then insert the special gap buttons in between the other buttons.

5. You don't have to include the `OnAction` argument when you create a custom toolbar button. Of course, your toolbar button won't be able to carry out an action until you do assign an event procedure to the `OnAction` property—unless the toolbar button is one of Excel's built-in toolbar buttons, in which case it will carry out its predefined task.

6. No. If you want a menu item to be checked when a menu is initially displayed, you'll need to set the `Checked` property separately. Make sure that the condition you're indicating as true when you check the menu item really is true!

7. No. You can't change the `Pushed` property of a built-in toolbar button.

Answers

Exercises

1. Your solution to this exercise should look something like this:

```
1:    Option Explicit
2:
3:    Sub AddVBA_MenuExtras()
4:        Dim mBar As MenuBar
5:
6:        Set mBar = MenuBars("Visual Basic Module")
7:        mBar.Menus.Add Caption:="&Programmer"
8:        With mBar.Menus("Programmer").MenuItems
9:          .Add Caption:="&VBA Help", _
10:             OnAction:="VBAHelp_Command"
11:          .Add Caption:="&Insert Named Module", _
12:             OnAction:="InsNamedModule_Command"
13:          .Add Caption:="-"
14:          .Add Caption:="&Remove Menu", _
15:             OnAction:="RemoveMenu_Command"
16:        End With
17:
18:        With mBar.Menus("Programmer")
19:          .MenuItems("VBA Help").StatusBar = _
20:                             "Show VBA Help Contents"
21:          .MenuItems("Insert Named Module").StatusBar = _
22:                               "Inserts and renames module"
23:          .MenuItems("Remove Menu").StatusBar = _
24:                               "Removes this menu"
25:        End With
26:    End Sub
27:
28:
29:    Sub VBAHelp_Command()
30:        Application.Help "VBA_XL.HLP"
31:    End Sub
32:
33:    Sub InsNamedModule_Command()
34:        Static sName As String
35:        sName = InputBox(prompt:="Enter the new sheet name:", _
36:                         Title:="Insert Named Module", _
37:                         default:=sName)
38:        If Trim(sName) = "" Then Exit Sub
39:
40:        Modules.Add
41:        ActiveSheet.Name = sName
42:        With ActiveWorkbook       'move module to end of workbook
43:          .Sheets(sName).Activate
44:          .Sheets(sName).Move after:=.Sheets(.Sheets.Count)
45:        End With
46:    End Sub
47:
48:
49:    Sub RemoveMenu_Command()
50:        With MenuBars("Visual Basic Module")
51:          .Menus("Programmer").Delete
52:        End With
53:    End Sub
```

2. One solution to this exercise might look something like the following listing. Notice the Width property used in line 28. By specifying a width for your toolbar you can ensure that the toolbar is displayed horizontally instead of vertically.

```
1:    Option Explicit
2:
3:    Sub AddVBA_ToolbarExtras()
4:      Dim tBar As Toolbar
5:
6:      Set tBar = Toolbars.Add("VBA Programmer")
7:      With tBar.ToolbarButtons
8:        .Add Button:=179, OnAction:="VBAHelp_Command"
9:        .Add Button:=219, OnAction:="InsNamedModule_Command"
10:       .Add Button:=225, OnAction:="RemoveToolbar"
11:       .Add before:=.Count
12:     End With
13:
14:     With tBar
15:       With .ToolbarButtons(1)
16:         .Name = "VBA Help"
17:         .StatusBar = "Show VBA Help Contents"
18:       End With
19:       With .ToolbarButtons(2)
20:         .Name = "Insert Named Module"
21:         .StatusBar = "Inserts and renames module"
22:       End With
23:       With .ToolbarButtons(4)
24:         .Name = "Remove Toolbar"
25:         .StatusBar = "Removes this toolbar"
26:       End With
27:       .Position = xlFloating
28:       .Width = 200 * 4
29:       .Visible = True
30:     End With
31:   End Sub
32:
33:
34:   Sub RemoveToolbar()
35:     Toolbars("VBA Programmer").Visible = False
36:     Toolbars("VBA Programmer").Delete
37:   End Sub
```

Day 17

Quiz

1. The On Error Resume Next statement.

2. VBA stops code execution and displays a runtime error dialog box.

3. Certainly! Each set of statements handles a specific kind of error.

4. The Resume 0 statement, which is usually placed at the end of your error-handling statements.

5. Use the On Error Goto 0 statement.

6. The Resume statement clears VBA's internal runtime error handling mechanisms.

7. The Error function returns the error message text corresponding to a particular runtime error code.

8. The Error statement forces a runtime error to occur. (Don't confuse the Error statement, which forces a runtime error, with the Error function, which returns the text of an error message.)

Exercise

1. Your procedure might look something like this one:

```
1:   Sub MyErrorHandler()
2:
3:       'declare constants
4:       Const ERR_MSG = "Invalid indexes for Mid function"
5:       Const dTitle = "My Error Handler"
6:
7:       'declare variables
8:       Static iStr As String
9:       Dim eStr As String
10:      Dim pStr As String
11:      Dim Start As Integer
12:      Dim Count As Integer
13:
14:      On Error GoTo BadIndex  'install error trap
15:
16:      'get source string, start index, and number of chars
17:      iStr = InputBox(prompt:="Enter a string", _
18:                      TITLE:=dTitle, default:=iStr)
19:      pStr = "Enter the index for the first character " & _
20:              "to be extracted."
21:      Start = Val(InputBox(prompt:=pStr, TITLE:=dTitle))
22:      pStr = "Enter the number of characters to extract."
23:      Count = Val(InputBox(prompt:=pStr, TITLE:=dTitle))
24:
25:      eStr = Mid(iStr, Start, Count)
26:      MsgBox Buttons:=vbInformation, TITLE:=dTitle, _
27:             prompt:="'" & iStr & "'" & Chr(13) & _
28:                     "'" & eStr & "'"
29:      Exit Sub
30:
31:  BadIndex:
32:      eStr = ""
33:      MsgBox Buttons:=vbCritical, TITLE:=dTitle, _
34:             prompt:=ERR_MSG
35:      Resume Next
36:  End Sub
```

2. The statements display the string: Hello.

3. The statements display the string: Jello.

A

4. The statements display the following in a message box:

```
Jello
11
```

The number 11 indicates that the Mid statement caused a runtime error eleven times.

5. The statements display the following:

```
Runtime error number 5
```

Day 18

Quiz

1. No. To execute the Auto_Open macros you must use the
   `Object.RunAutoMacros(xlAutoOpen)` method. Note that this applies to Auto_Close procedures as well. To run these procedures, use the RunAutoMacros method with xlAutoClose. (See Day 21, "Using Automatic Procedures, Event Procedures, and Add-Ins," for more information.)

2. The Save method saves the specified workbook to disk, with the same filename it had before. The SaveAs method works like the File | Save As command, saving the workbook under a new name, and also changing the open workbook's name to the new name. The SaveCopyAs method, however, saves a *copy* of the specified workbook to a different file and leaves the original file unaltered, both on disk and in memory.

3. Excel saves the workbook using its current name. For example, if the workbook is called Book1, Excel names the file BOOK1.XLS. You should use the SaveAs method to assign a name to a new file. You can tell whether a file has been saved before by checking whether the FullName property returns a zero-length string (" ").

4. Excel creates a new workbook to store the copied or moved worksheet.

5. The Worksheets collection contains only the worksheets in the current workbook, whereas the Sheets collection contains worksheets, charts, modules, and dialog sheets.

6. The three main methods are Range, Cells, and Offset. Range uses either range coordinates or a range name to return a cell or range. Cells uses row and column numbers to return a single cell. Offset returns a range that is offset from another range by a specified number of rows and columns.

7. Both procedures create three-dimensional references across multiple sheets and enter data into the same cell in each sheet. Both sheets use an array (SheetArray) to hold the names of three sheets (Sheet1, Sheet2, and Sheet3).

   In the first procedure (FillAcross), a label is entered in cell A1 of Sheet1, and the FillAcrossSheets method is applied to the Worksheets object. This method, which is the VBA equivalent of the Edit | Fill | Across Worksheets command, uses the following syntax:

891

```
Object.FillAcrossSheets(Range [,Type])
```

Object is an object reference to a `Worksheets` collection. *Range* is the range to fill across the worksheets; it must be from one of the sheets in *Object*. *Type* specifies how to copy the range—`xlAll`, `xlContents`, or `xlFormulas`.

The second procedure uses `Select` to group the array of worksheets, activates cell A1 in `Sheet1`, and enters the label in the `Selection`. This is the equivalent of a technique known as *spearing*, where you select a group of sheets, type in a value, and press Ctrl+Enter.

Of these two procedures, the first is probably better because you can fill a range—not just a single cell—across the sheets. Likewise, it doesn't use the slow `Select` and `Activate` methods.

8. `Value` always returns the value of a cell—that is, the data stored in the cell, or the result of the cell's formula. `Formula`, on the other hand, either returns the cell's value (if the cell contains a constant) or the cell's formula as a string (if the cell contains a formula).

9. Use `RefersToR1C1` when your range description either is in R1C1-style or is a method or property that returns a range.

10. `Cut` without the `Destination` argument, `Clear`, `ClearContents`, `ClearFormats`, and `ClearNotes`.

Exercises

1. Your solution should look something like this:

```
1:   Option Explicit
2:
3:   Sub SaveAllWorkbooks()
4:   'saves all workbooks
5:
6:     Dim wBook As Workbook
7:     Dim Ans As Integer
8:     Dim mPrompt As String
9:     Dim qBtns As Integer
10:    Dim mTitle As String
11:    Dim NewName As Variant
12:
13:    For Each wBook In Workbooks
14:      'workbook has unsaved changes or a zero-length path?
15:      If (Not wBook.Saved) Or (wBook.Path = "") Then
16:        'If so, check for new, unnamed workbook
17:        If wBook.Path = "" Then
18:          'Ask user if they want to save it
19:          mPrompt = "Do you want to save " & wBook.Name & "?"
20:          qBtns = vbYesNoCancel + vbQuestion
21:          mTitle = "Save All Workbooks"
22:          Ans = MsgBox(Prompt:=mPrompt, Buttons:=qBtns, _
```

```
23:                         Title:=mTitle)
24:             Select Case Ans
25:               Case vbYes  'display GetSaveAsFileName dialog
26:                 NewName = Application.GetSaveAsFilename( _
27:                       InitialFilename:=wBook.Name, _
28:                       FileFilter:="Excel Workbooks,*.xls", _
29:                       Title:=mTitle & " -Select Name")
30:                 If NewName <> False Then
31:                    wBook.SaveAs filename:=NewName
32:                 End If
33:               Case vbCancel
34:                  Exit Sub    'canceled, bail out
35:             End Select
36:           Else  'Otherwise, just save it
37:             wBook.Save
38:           End If
39:         End If
40:     Next wBook
41:   End Sub
```

2. Here's the code for a multiple selection copy. To convert this procedure to a multiple selection cut, just change the `Copy` method to a `Cut` method.

```
1:   Option Explicit
2:
3:   Sub CopyMultipleSelection()
4:
5:     Dim R As Range
6:     Dim SheetStr As String
7:     Dim DestSheet As Worksheet
8:
9:     'Request the name of the sheet
10:    SheetStr = InputBox("Enter the destination sheet name:", _
11:                    "Multiple Selection Copy")
12:
13:    'Check to see if user pressed Cancel
14:    If SheetStr <> "" Then
15:      'If not, convert InputBox string to Worksheet object
16:      Set DestSheet = Worksheets(SheetStr)
17:      'Loop through each area in selection and copy
18:      'it to destination sheet
19:      For Each R In Selection.Areas
20:        R.Copy Destination:=DestSheet.Cells(R.Row, R.Column)
21:      Next R
22:    End If
23:  End Sub
```

3. The first `Names.Add` method defines the name `Test1` to refer to the string constant `Sheet1!$A$1`. The problem is an incorrect range description in the `RefersTo` argument:

`Names.Add Name:="Test1", RefersTo:="Sheet1!$A$1"`

The argument should read `RefersTo:="=Sheet1!$A$1"`.

The second `Names.Add` method defines `Test2` to refer to the *contents* of the cell `Sheet1!A1`, instead of the cell itself. The problem is the use of the `RefersTo` argument instead of `RefersToR1C1`.

The third `Names.Add` method defines a range name, but the definition of the range changes depending on which cell is the active cell. The problem is that the `RefersTo` argument uses a relative range (`'June Sales'!A1:A10`). Unless you specifically need a relative range name, always use absolute references when you define range names.

4. The following line produces the error:

```
TitleRange = ActiveSheet.Selection
```

The problem is that the `TitleRange` variable is declared as an object—namely, a `Range`—but the statement above doesn't use `Set` to assign a value to the variable. When you work with `Workbook`, `Worksheet`, and `Range` objects, always remember to use `Set` to assign the object reference to an object variable.

5. Your procedure should look something like this:

```
1:    Sub EditData()
2:
3:        Dim I As Integer
4:        Dim CurrRow As Integer
5:        Dim DBColumns As Integer
6:
7:        'Get current row
8:        CurrRow = ActiveCell.Row
9:        'Get number of columns in Database range
10:       DBColumns = Range("Database").Columns.Count
11:
12:       'Load record data in dialog box
13:       For I = 1 To DBColumns
14:           DialogSheets("Dialog1").EditBoxes(I).Caption = _
15:           Cells(CurrRow, I).Value
16:       Next I
17:   End Sub
```

Day 19

Quiz

1. The server is the application that supplies the OLE object, and provides services for that object. The client is the application that contains the OLE object. Client applications are also sometimes called *container* applications.

2. A linked object contains an image of the server data and maintains a link between the client and server. An embedded object contains not only the server data but also all the underlying information associated with the server application, such as the name of the application, the file structure, and all the formatting codes.

3. The first advantage is that you don't need a server document because you can create the data within the client application and then insert it into the client document as an embedded object.

   The second advantage is that OLE objects retain the original formatting of the data. This means that they appear in the client document exactly as they do in the server application.

   The third advantage is that OLE objects contain the name of the server application and the name of the server file from which the object came, if the object is linked. This means that you need only to double-click the object, and OLE will load the server application and open the correct file, if necessary.

4. The first advantage that you get with OLE 2.0 is that you can drag and drop data between two open OLE 2.0 applications. The second advantage is that you can insert objects in-place—that is, you can stay in the same document and the surrounding menus and toolbars change to that of the server application. The third advantage is that you can edit objects in-place—that is, when you double-click an object to edit it, the object remains in the document and the server's tools appear in place of the client's. The fourth advantage is that you can use OLE automation to control the exposed objects of another OLE 2.0 application.

5. The Registry database contains information about the Windows applications installed on your computer. The database records data related to the OLE support of each application, such as the class type for the application's objects.

6. a. Set `FileName` equal to the name of the document, and set `Link` to `True`.

   b. Set `ClassType` equal to the class type of the presentation graphics program.

   c. Set `FileName` equal to the name of the bitmap file, and either omit `Link` or set it to `False`.

7. A verb tells you what actions can be performed on an OLE object from the point of view of the object's native application.

   The primary verb is the default action that can be performed on an object—in other words, the action that occurs when you double-click the object. Typically, the primary verb will open or edit the OLE object.

8. OLE automation is a standard by which applications expose their objects to other applications running on the system. Languages such as Visual Basic for Applications can recognize and manipulate these objects by running methods and setting properties.

9. You can refer to the server application's objects directly. You can create new objects with the `CreateObject` function. And you can access existing objects by using the `GetObject` function.

Exercises

1. The problem here is that when you activate in-place editing, which is the primary verb for Word for Windows 6.0, the OLE object becomes unavailable. Remember: With in-place editing you don't leave the document. VBA, however, continues processing the rest of the procedure. Therefore, it chokes when it tries to set any of the object's properties. The solution is either to set the properties elsewhere—such as when you're finished editing—or to use the x10pen verb to open a separate editing window for the object.

2. Some applications, such as Word for Windows, require you to activate their objects before you can see any changes. To fix this procedure, simply include an Activate method at the beginning of the With statement to activate the document object.

Day 20

Quiz

1. Executing an application asynchronously means that once VBA has started the application, it immediately returns to the procedure that contains the Shell function and continues executing the other statements in the procedure.

2. Dynamic data exchange is an internal Windows communications protocol that enables you to exchange data between a client application and a server application and to execute the server's macro or DDE commands.

3. a. Use DDEInitiate to open a channel between the client and the server.

   b. Use the DDEExecute, DDERequest, and DDEPoke methods to send commands to the server and exchange data.

   c. Use the DDETerminate method to close the channel.

4. Excel displays a dialog box that asks whether you want to start the application, and DDEInitiate fails if it can't find the server's executable file either in the current directory or on the search path.

5. The System topic gives you access to the DDE server application as a whole.

6. If you need to control one of the application's dialog boxes, you must use the SendKeys method.

7. The Wait argument determines whether your procedure waits for the application to process the keystrokes before it continues. If you set Wait to True, the procedure waits for the application. If you set Wait to False, the procedure continues executing without waiting for the application.

8. Dynamic link libraries are collections of functions and procedures that are available to all Windows applications. You can use DLL procedures in your VBA code by declaring the procedures at the module level.

9. The API is the Applications Programming Interface. It is the sum-total of the functions and procedures in the DLLs that come with Windows.

Exercises

1. Because Shell is asynchronous, the second Shell—the one that runs Notepad— begins to execute *before* the first Shell (which creates MEM.TXT), is finished. Therefore, Notepad can't find MEM.TXT, and it displays an error message. The solution is to insert a delay between the two Shell statements. For example, the following statement creates a three-second delay, which should be long enough in most cases:

```
Application.Wait Now + TimeValue("00:00:03")
```

2. Your function, and its accompanying test procedure, might look something like the following:

```
 1:   Function IsOpenInWord(FileName As String) As Boolean
 2:   'Checks Word's "Topics" item to see if FileName is one of
 3:   'the open documents.
 4:
 5:      Dim Channel As Integer
 6:      Dim I As Integer
 7:      Dim TopicArray As Variant
 8:
 9:      On Error GoTo Retreat   'set up error handling
10:
11:      'Open a channel to Word's "System" topic
12:      Channel = DDEInitiate(App:="Winword", topic:="System")
13:
14:      'Get complete topic list; list is returned in an array
15:      TopicArray = DDERequest(Channel, "Topics")
16:
17:      'Loop through array
18:      For I = LBound(TopicArray) To UBound(TopicArray)
19:        'If FileName is in one of the topics
20:        If InStr(1, TopicArray(I), FileName, 1) Then
21:          IsOpenInWord = True   'Return True and end function
22:          DDETerminate Channel
23:          Exit Function
24:        End If
25:      Next I
26:
27:   Retreat:
28:      DDETerminate Channel
29:      IsOpenInWord = False      'return False if we get here
30:   End Function
31:
```

```
32:
33:   Sub test_IsOpenInWord()
34:     Dim wStr As String
35:
36:     wStr = InputBox(prompt:="Enter Word document name:", _
37:                     Title:="Testing IsOpenInWord function")
38:     If IsOpenInWord(wStr) Then
39:       MsgBox wStr & " is open."
40:     Else
41:       MsgBox wStr & " is NOT open."
42:     End If
43:   End Sub
```

3. Your procedure might look like this:

```
1:    Declare Function GetModuleHandle Lib "kernel32" _
2:                     Alias "GetModuleHandleA" _
3:                     (ByVal ModuleName As String) As Long
4:
5:    Sub SwitchToWinWord()
6:    'Switches to WinWord. If WinWord is already running,
7:    'activates that copy, otherwise starts WinWord
8:
9:      If GetModuleHandle("WINWORD.EXE") Then
10:       AppActivate "Microsoft Word"
11:     Else
12:       Shell PathName:="C:\MSOFFICE\WINWORD\WINWORD.EXE", _
13:             WindowStyle:=3
14:     End If
15:   End Sub
```

Day 21

Quiz

1. An automatic procedure is a Sub procedure that executes automatically when certain Excel events occur. The names of automatic procedures begin with Auto_.

2. Auto_Open procedures run automatically when you open a workbook, and Auto_Close procedures run automatically when you close a workbook. For add-in applications, Auto_Add procedures run automatically when you install the add-in, and Auto_Remove procedures run automatically when you uninstall the add-in.

3. An event procedure is a Sub procedure associated with an Excel or system event. When Excel traps the event, the event procedure runs automatically.

4. Set the appropriate property equal to a zero-length string ("").

5. The Application.OnSheetActivate property traps the activation of any sheet in any open workbook.

6. When you switch to a different workbook or worksheet, Excel makes the new book or sheet active before it runs the appropriate `OnSheetDeactivate` event procedure. Therefore, code in the procedure that references the `ActiveWorkbook` or `ActiveSheet` objects does not apply to the workbook or worksheet that has just been deactivated.

7. If you assign a zero-length string to the `Procedure` argument, Excel disables the key. If you omit the `Procedure` argument, the key reverts to its normal behavior, which may be nothing.

8. The `EarliestTime` argument is the time when you want the specified event procedure to run. `LatestTime` is the time until which Excel will wait in order to run the procedure if the program is not ready at `EarliestTime`.

9. No, it doesn't. The `OnEntry` event handler runs only when you enter or edit data using either the formula bar or in-cell editing.

10. An `OnCalculate` event procedure does not run if you recalculate the worksheet using the `Calculate` method.

11. *Demand-loaded* means that the add-in gets loaded into memory in two stages. First, the add-in's functions, menus, and toolbars are made available. Then, the entire add-in is loaded when the user selects one of the add-in functions, menu commands, or toolbar buttons.

Exercises

1. As the code below shows, you first declare three variables to hold each of the original settings. You declare these variables at the module level—in other words, outside of any procedures in the module—so that they are available to each procedure. In `Auto_Open`, store the current setting in the appropriate variable and change the property to the new value. In `Auto_Close`, use the variables to reinstate each property.

```
Dim OldDefaultFilePath As String
Dim OldPromptForSummaryInfo As Boolean
Dim OldSheetsInNewWorkbook As Integer

Sub Auto_Open()
  With Application
    OldDefaultFilePath = .DefaultFilePath
    .DefaultFilePath = "D:\EXCEL\STUFF"
    OldPromptForSummaryInfo = .PromptForSummaryInfo
    .PromptForSummaryInfo = False
    OldSheetsInNewWorkbook = .SheetsInNewWorkbook
    .SheetsInNewWorkbook = 8
  End With
End Sub
```

```
Sub Auto_Close()
  With Application
    .DefaultFilePath = OldDefaultFilePath
    .PromptForSummaryInfo = OldPromptForSummaryInfo
    .SheetsInNewWorkbook = OldSheetsInNewWorkbook
  End With
End Sub
```

2. At first glance, it appears that the **ResetSheet** procedure is trying to clean up the Scratch Pad worksheet before it moves on to the next sheet. However, **ResetSheet** uses the ActiveSheet object to perform its tasks. This is a no-no because Excel activates the sheet you're moving to before it runs the OnSheetDeactivate event procedure. This means that every statement inside the With affects the new sheet, not the Scratch Pad.

   If you want to perform tasks on the sheet you're leaving, you must spell out the appropriate Worksheet object—for example, Worksheets("Scratch Pad"). If you want to use the OnSheetDeactivate event procedure for multiple worksheets, you could declare a Public variable to hold the name of the current sheet. You could set this variable in the sheet's OnSheetActivate event procedure and use it again in the OnSheetDeactivate code. You could also pass the current sheet's name as an argument to the OnSheetDeactivate procedure.

3. Use the following procedures to ensure that Excel runs the OnWindow event procedure before it runs the OnSheetActivate event procedure:

```
Sub SetHandlers()
  Workbooks("FINANCES.XLS") _
    .Worksheets("Budget") _
    .OnSheetActivate = "SheetEventHandler"
  Windows("FINANCES.XLS") _
    .OnWindow = "WindowEventHandler"
End Sub

Sub SheetEventHandler()
  MsgBox "This is the OnSheetActivate procedure."
End Sub

Sub WindowEventHandler()
  MsgBox "This is the OnWindow procedure."
End Sub
```

4. Your solution might look something like this:

```
Sub SetKey()
  Application.OnKey _
        Key:="^{Del}", _
        Procedure:="DeleteAll"
End Sub

Sub DeleteAll()
  Selection.Clear
End Sub
```

5. The **GetInterval** procedure uses InputBox to get the number of minutes between events. This is stored in a global variable named **Interval**. Then, **GetInterval** calls the

SetRegularInterval procedure to initialize the OnTime property. **SetRegularInterval** converts the number of minutes in **Interval** to a day fraction—CInt(interval) / (60 * 24)—and adds this fraction to the Now function. This is stored in the **nextTime** variable. In the OnTime property, the EarliestTime argument is set to **nextTime**, and the Procedure argument is set to **SaveWorkbook**. The **SaveWorkbook** procedure saves the workbook and runs the **SetRegularInterval** procedure again to create the next event trap. The **SetRegularInterval** procedure will be called for as long as the **Continue** variable remains True. The **RemoveIntervalProc** stops the renewal of the OnTime event by setting **Continue** to False.

```
Dim Interval As String
Dim Continue As Boolean

Sub GetInterval()
  Interval = InputBox("Enter the interval, in minutes:")
  Continue = True
  SetRegularInterval
End Sub

Sub SetRegularInterval()
  Dim nextTime As Date

  If Interval <> "" Then
    nextTime = Now + CInt(Interval) / (60 * 24)
    Application.OnTime EarliestTime:=nextTime, _
                       Procedure:="IntervalProc"
  End If
End Sub

Sub IntervalProc()
  Beep
  With Application
    .StatusBar = "Interval Procedure now executing."
    .Wait Now + TimeValue("00:00:07")
    .StatusBar = False
  End With
  If Continue Then SetRegularInterval
End Sub

Sub RemoveIntervalProc()
  Continue = False
End Sub
```

6. The idea behind this procedure is to verify that the user is entering numeric values in the worksheet. If an entry isn't a number, the procedure is supposed to display an error message, clear the contents of the cell, and activate in-cell editing by sending an F2 keypress by means of the SendKeys statement. The user can then enter a correct value and move on.

The problem is related to the SendKeys statement. When Excel encounters a SendKeys, it takes the specified keystroke, sends it to the keyboard buffer, and returns control to the procedure. Unfortunately, there's a good chance that the keyboard buffer already

Answers

contains a keystroke—the key that the user pressed to confirm the cell entry, such as Enter or one of the arrow keys. This means that Excel waits until after the procedure is finished before it flushes the buffer. It first processes the confirmation keystroke— this moves the cursor—and then processes the F2. This means that the wrong cell gets activated.

There are two circumstances under which this procedure works as advertised:

☐ If the Application object's MoveAfterReturn property is set to False and the user presses Enter to confirm the cell entry.

☐ If the user confirms the entry by clicking the Enter button in the formula bar.

Sample Application

This appendix contains all the module listings for a complete VBA program, which has been written expressly for easy conversion to an Excel add-in (XLA) program, as discussed in Day 21. This sample program is a game called Guess The Animal. This game is a very simple form of an artificial-intelligence program, and models a process known as *heuristic learning*, which means learning through asking questions.

The Guess The Animal game demonstrates many of the important programming concepts and VBA features that you have learned about in this book. You've put in so much hard work learning VBA that now it's time for you to have a little fun.

Creating the Sample Application

Like any full-scale program you might create in VBA, the Guess The Animal game has all of its code in a single workbook, divided among several module sheets. The following sections of this appendix presents each of the module code listings separately, and gives a brief discussion of each module. To get this sample application up and running, follow these steps:

1. Create a new workbook named ANIMAL.XLS. (This is important, because the Guess The Animal program will not work unless it is stored in a workbook with this name.)

2. Choose the **File | Properties** command, and click the Summary tab to display the new workbook's summary information. Enter **Animal Game** in the **T**itle text box, and a brief description of the game in the **C**omments text box, as shown in Figure B.1. This is important, or the add-in version of the game won't work correctly—the Summary title and comments supply the add-in program's name and description for the Add-ins dialog box in Excel.

3. Enter each code listing in a separate module. Be sure you give each module the correct name, or the Guess The Animal program will not work.

4. Create the four dialog boxes that this program uses, according to the descriptions given later in this appendix. Follow the dialog box instructions carefully—make sure that you give the controls the specified names, and that you assign the correct macros to the various dialog box controls.

5. Run the game, and have fun!

Tip: To save space on your disk, you can delete all worksheets from the ANIMAL.XLS workbook. The Guess The Animal program stores its data in an external workbook—as must any Excel VBA program designed to become an add-in.

Figure B.1.

You must enter the workbook's title (Animal Game) into the Title field of the workbook Properties sheet, or the add-in version of the Guess The Animal game won't work properly.

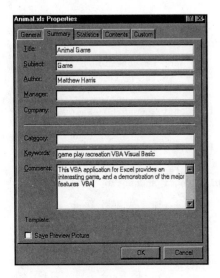

Entering the Code Listings

To enter the code listings, insert a new module sheet for each listing, and type in the code for each module exactly as it appears in the listing (without line numbers, of course). Make sure that you give each module the correct name, as stated in each listing section.

The Constants Module

Insert a new module sheet and rename it *Constants*. The Constants module contains all of the constant declarations that the Guess The Animal game uses.

Listing B.1. The Constants module.

```
 1:  Option Explicit
 2:
 3:                  'used to specify binary string comparison
 4:  Public Const agBinComp = 0
 5:
 6:                  'used to specify text string comparison
 7:  Public Const agTxtComp = 1
 8:
 9:                  'WorkBook that contains data
10:  Public Const agDataBook = "Animal Game Data.XLS"
11:
12:                  'Worksheet to store data for animals known
13:  Public Const agData = "AnimalData"
14:
15:                  'Maximum animals that can be learned
```

continues

Listing B.1. continued

```
16:   Public Const agMax_Animals As Integer = 3000
17:
18:            'end of question chain - must learn new animal
19:   Public Const agLEARN As Integer = -1
20:
21:            'end of question chain - guessed animal correctly
22:   Public Const agGUESSED As Integer = -2
23:
24:               'character code for carriage return
25:   Public Const agCR = 13
26:
27:     'indicates whether a data item is a question or an answer
28:   Public Const agQuestion = 1, agAnswer = 2
29:
30:        'the title for most MsgBox dialog boxes in this game
31:   Public Const agTitle = "Guess The Animal"
```

Notice that this module contains no procedures, only constant declarations. Some of these constants you might want to consider declaring and making available in your own VBA libraries, such as the **agBinComp** and **agTxtComp** constants for specifying the string comparison type for the VBA StrComp and InStr functions, or the **agCR** constant that specifies the character code for a carriage-return character.

Notice that all of the Guess The Animal program's constants begin with the two letters **ag**, so that you can tell these constants belong to the Animal game—just like VBA's constants all begin with the letters vb and Excel's constants begin with the letters xl.

The AnimalMain Module

Insert a new module sheet and rename it *AnimalMain*. The AnimalMain module contains all of the public procedures in the Guess The Animal program, including the main procedure that starts the game.

Listing B.2. The AnimalMain module.

```
1:   Option Explicit
2:   Option Base 1       'all arrays begin with 1
3:
4:   Dim Spinning As Boolean          'whether the game is going
5:
6:   'indicates that new animals were learned
7:   Public New_Animal As Boolean
8:
9:   Type NodeRecord
10:      StatementText As String
11:      NodeType As Integer
12:      NextIfYes As Integer
13:      NextIfNo As Integer
```

```
14:   End Type
15:
16:                   'array of known animals and Questions/Data
17:   Public Animals() As NodeRecord
18:
19:
20:     'Program Start
21:   Sub Animal()
22:     Spinning = True              'playing the game
23:     New_Animal = False           'haven't learned new animals
24:     AnimalRetrieval.Read_AnimalFile  'read animal data
25:
26:     Do While Spinning
27:       DoEvents 'process any pending system events
28:       ThisWorkbook.DialogSheets("DialogMain").Show
29:     Loop
30:
31:     If New_Animal Then           'we learned new animals
32:       If Do_Remember Then        'make new animals permanent
33:         AnimalRetrieval.Remember_Animals
34:       End If                'close down game, save new animals
35:     End If
36:
37:     Erase Animals  'remove array when not in use
38:   End Sub      ' Animal
39:
40:
41:   Sub Play_Game_Cycle()
42:   'Traverse the animal tree, asking questions of the user,
43:   'and selecting the new branches, depending on player
44:   'response.  When an animal (answer) node is reached, ask
45:   'the user if that is the correct animal.  If it is not,
46:   'then a new animal must be learned by the program.
47:
48:     Dim AnimalNDX As Integer
49:     Dim Prompt_String As String
50:     Dim Ans As Integer
51:
52:     AnimalNDX = 1               'start with the first question
53:
54:     Do While (Animals(AnimalNDX).NodeType <> agAnswer)
55:       'show question, get input, (yes or no only),
56:       'and move to next node until we reach an answer node
57:       With Animals(AnimalNDX)
58:         Prompt_String = Trim(.StatementText) & "?"
59:         Ans = MsgBox(prompt:=Prompt_String, _
60:             Title:=agTitle & ":  - Guessing Your Animal", _
61:             Buttons:=vbQuestion + vbYesNo)
62:         If Ans = vbYes Then
63:           AnimalNDX = .NextIfYes
64:         Else
65:           AnimalNDX = .NextIfNo
66:         End If
67:       End With
68:     Loop      'while node is question - 'answer' after this
69:
```

continues

907

Listing B.2. continued

```
70:    Prompt_String = "I think I know what your animal is..." _
71:                   & Chr(agCR) & Chr(agCR) & "Is it " & _
72:             Preposition(Animals(AnimalNDX).StatementText) & _
73:                Trim(Animals(AnimalNDX).StatementText) & "?"
74:
75:    Ans = MsgBox(prompt:=Prompt_String, _
76:            Title:=agTitle & ":  - Guessed Your Animal", _
77:            Buttons:=vbQuestion + vbYesNo)
78:    If Ans = vbNo Then          'need to learn a new animal
79:      Learn_New_Animal (AnimalNDX)
80:    Else                        'successful guess
81:      MsgBox prompt:="I knew I was right!", _
82:            Title:=agTitle
83:    End If
84: End Sub  'Play_Game_Cycle
85:
86:
87: Sub Still_Playing()
88: 'player clicked the Close button. Find out if they really
89: 'want to stop playing.
90:
91:    Dim Ans As Integer
92:
93:    Ans = MsgBox(prompt:="Do you still want to play?", _
94:               Title:=agTitle, _
95:               Buttons:=vbYesNo + vbQuestion)
96:    If Ans = vbNo Then Spinning = False
97: End Sub  ' Still_Playing
98:
99:
100: Sub ShowRules()
101: 'Display the dialog box with the rules of the game.
102:    ThisWorkbook.DialogSheets("DialogRules").Show
103: End Sub   'ShowRules
104:
105:
106: Sub AboutAnimal()
107: 'This procedure tells the user a little bit about ANIMAL
108:
109:    Dim pStr As String
110:
111:    If IsAddIn(ThisWorkbook) Then
112:      pStr = "Add-In Program"
113:    Else
114:      pStr = "standard workbook format"
115:    End If
116:
117:    MsgBox Title:="About " & agTitle, _
118:           prompt:="GUESS THE ANIMAL v 2.0" & Chr(agCR) & _
119:           "Running from code in: " & pStr & Chr(agCR) & _
120:           Chr(agCR) & "Executing under: " & _
121:           Application.Name & Chr(agCR) & "Build: " & _
122:           Application.Build
123: End Sub
124:
```

```
125:
126: Sub ShutDown()
127: 'shuts down the animal game, and closes the ANIMAL workbook.
128:
129:    Dim Ans As Integer
130:
131:    Ans = MsgBox(Title:="Shut Down " & agTitle, _
132:                 prompt:="Are you sure you want to " & _
133:                         "close the Guess the Animal " & _
134:                         "game and remove its menus?", _
135:                 Buttons:=vbQuestion + vbYesNo)
136:    If Ans = vbYes Then
137:      If IsAddIn(ThisWorkbook) Then
138:        MsgBox prompt:="Animal Game add-in will be " & _
139:                       "uninstalled. Use the Tools ¦ " & _
140:                       "Add-ins command to reactivate " & _
141:                       "the Animal Game add-in.", _
142:               Buttons:=vbInformation, _
143:               Title:=agTitle
144:        AddIns("Animal Game").Installed = False
145:      Else
146:        With ThisWorkbook
147:           .RunAutoMacros xlAutoClose   'run auto close proc
148:           .Close savechanges:=False    'close the workbook
149:        End With
150:      End If
151:    End If
152: End Sub
153:
154:
155: Private Function Do_Remember() As Boolean
156: ' Ask player if any new animals that were learned should
157: ' be made a permanent part of the program's "knowledge"
158:
159:    Dim Ans As Integer
160:
161:    Ans = MsgBox(prompt:="I have learned some new animals." _
162:                         & Chr(agCR) & Chr(agCR) & _
163:                     "Shall I remember them permanently? ", _
164:                 Title:=agTitle, _
165:                 Buttons:=vbQuestion + vbYesNo)
166:    If Ans = vbYes Then
167:      Do_Remember = True
168:    Else
169:      Do_Remember = False
170:    End If
171: End Function     'Do_Remember
```

Analysis

This is the main module for the Guess The Animal program. Notice that the module begins with several variable declarations, and a user-defined type definition.

Lines 21 through 38 contain the **Animal** procedure, which is the main procedure of this program. The **Animal** procedure shows the main dialog box repeatedly, until the game is no longer being played. The global Boolean flag, **Spinning**, is used to indicate whether or not the game is still being played. In particular, notice the DoEvents statement line 27. DoEvents allows Excel to process any events that might occur while the Guess The Animal game is running. You should include a DoEvents statement in any intensive loops or long-executing loops that you write, so that other Excel event-processing doesn't come to a standstill. The **Animal** procedure is executed whenever the user chooses the **G**ame | **G**uess the Animal custom menu command.

Lines 41 through 84 contain the **Play_Game_Cycle** procedure, which conducts one complete cycle of asking questions and guessing the animal. Notice that the procedure loops for as long as the statements it presents to the user are *not* answers. As soon as the procedure presents a statement that is an answer, the loop stops executing, and the procedure continues on to find out whether or not the answer coincides with the animal the user was thinking of. The **Play_Game_Cycle** procedure is only executed by being called from the **Animal** procedure.

Lines 87 through 97 contain the **Still_Playing** procedure, which simply confirms whether or not the user really wants to stop playing. If the user does confirm ending play, **Still_Playing** sets the module-level variable **Spinning** to False so that the loop in the **Animal** procedure will stop. The **Still_Playing** procedure is executed whenever the user chooses the **C**lose command button in the Are You Thinking of An Animal? dialog box (described later).

The **ShowRules** procedure occupies lines 100 through 103. This procedure simply displays a custom dialog box that contains an explanation of the rules of the game. (Creating the dialog boxes for this program is described in a later section of this appendix). This procedure is called by choosing either the **G**ame | **R**ules command on the custom menu of this program, or by clicking the **R**ules of the Game command button in the Are You Thinking of An Animal? dialog box.

Lines 106 through 123 contain the **AboutAnimal** procedure, which is executed whenever the user chooses the **G**ame | **A**bout command on the custom menu of this program. This procedure displays a message dialog box showing whether the Guess The Animal program is executing from code in an XLS workbook, or from an XLA add-in program, and displays the name and build number of the host application. Notice that **AboutAnimal** calls the **IsAddIn** function to determine which code version is executing.

The **ShutDown** procedure is in lines 126 through 152. This procedure is executed whenever the user chooses the **G**ame | **R**emove Animal Game command on the custom menu. **ShutDown** first confirms that the user wants to close the game and remove its custom menus. If removal is confirmed, then **ShutDown** checks to see if the code is running from an add-in workbook. If the program is an add-in, then **ShutDown** displays an additional message dialog box explaining how to reactivate the Animal game's menus, and then sets the Installed property of the add-in game to False. (The game's **Auto_Close** procedure runs automatically when the Installed property changes to False.) If the Animal game isn't running from an add-in, then **ShutDown** uses the RunAutoMacros method to execute the **Auto_Close** procedure (Day 21) and closes the workbook without saving any changes.

The **Do_Remember** function in lines 155 through 171 is private to this module; it returns True if the user wants to save any new animals that the game "learned," or False if the new animals are to be discarded.

The AnimalRetrieval Module

Insert a new module sheet and rename it *AnimalRetrieval*. The AnimalRetrieval module contains all of the procedures needed to store and retrieve the data about animals that the Guess The Animal program keeps.

 Listing B.3. The AnimalRetrieval module.

```
 1:    Option Explicit
 2:    Option Base 1        'all arrays begin with 1
 3:    Option Private Module
 4:
 5:
 6:    Dim agDataDir As String   'directory where data is stored
 7:
 8:
 9:    Sub Read_AnimalFile()
10:    'This procedure reads all of the data from the source
11:    'data sheet into an array. The data is read into the array
12:    'to make the program a little faster and to make handling
13:    'the list a little easier. For this program, it is easier
14:    'to handle the data in an array than to continually refer
15:    'to the data worksheet.
16:
17:    'The animal data is expected in a worksheet named
18:    '"AnimalData" in a workbook named "Animal Game Data".
19:    'Storing the data externally makes it possible to convert
20:    'this program into an add-in.
21:    'If this is the first time the Animal program has been used,
22:    'or the data workbook doesn't exist, the program must create
23:    'the data workbook and seed it with the minimum amount
24:    'of data to get started.
25:
26:       Dim Rec_Count As Integer
27:       Dim DataStart As Object
28:
29:       On Error GoTo NoLoad    'install error-handler
30:
31:       agDataDir = ThisWorkbook.Path    'set data directory
32:
33:       Application.StatusBar = "Remembering Animals, wait..."
34:
35:       'make sure data workbook exists
36:       If Dir(agDataDir & "\" & agDataBook) = "" Then
37:         Seed_Self noFile:=True
38:       End If
39:
40:       'open data workbook, and make sure it's hidden
```

continues

Listing B.3. continued

```
41:      Application.ScreenUpdating = False
42:      Workbooks.Open agDataDir & "\" & agDataBook
43:      Windows(agDataBook).Visible = False
44:      Application.ScreenUpdating = True
45:
46:      'if data sheet doesn't exist, then build it
47:      If Not SheetExists(agDataBook, agData) Then
48:        Seed_Self noFile:=False
49:      End If
50:
51:      ReDim Animals(1) 'ensure animal array exists and is empty
52:
53:      'set an object variable to point to the data
54:      With Workbooks(agDataBook)
55:        Set DataStart = .Worksheets(agData).Range("DataStart")
56:      End With
57:
58:      'load the array from the worksheet columns
59:      Rec_Count = 0
60:      Do While (DataStart.Offset(Rec_Count, 0).Value <> "") _
61:              And (Rec_Count <= agMax_Animals)
62:        ReDim Preserve Animals(Rec_Count + 1)
63:        With Animals(Rec_Count + 1)
64:          .StatementText = DataStart.Offset(Rec_Count, 0).Value
65:          .NodeType = DataStart.Offset(Rec_Count, 1).Value
66:          .NextIfYes = DataStart.Offset(Rec_Count, 2).Value
67:          .NextIfNo = DataStart.Offset(Rec_Count, 3).Value
68:        End With
69:        Rec_Count = Rec_Count + 1
70:      Loop
71:
72:      Workbooks(agDataBook).Close savechanges:=False
73:      Application.StatusBar = False
74:      Exit Sub    'no more work to do
75:
76:  NoLoad:
77:  'inability to load list of animals is a fatal error
78:      MsgBox prompt:="ERROR: Unable to load animal list!" & _
79:                  Chr(agCR) & Chr(agCR) & Error() & _
80:                  Chr(agCR) & Chr(agCR) & _
81:                  "Animal Game Program Will Terminate", _
82:            Title:=agTitle & ":  ERROR", _
83:            Buttons:=vbCritical
84:      Application.StatusBar = False
85:      Application.ScreenUpdating = True
86:      End  'end all program execution
87:  End Sub      'Read_AnimalFile
88:
89:
90:  Private Sub Seed_Self(noFile As Boolean)
91:  'To seed the question and answer tree, this procedure
92:  'establishes the root and first two branches of the tree.
93:  'To do this requires creating a minimum of 3 nodes.
94:  'The root of the tree is a question, each branch is an
```

```
 95:   'answer. This triad is the smallest viable configuration
 96:   'for this type of tree.
 97:
 98:   'Each animal is stored in a single row, with first column
 99:   'as the text for the animal or question, 2nd column is the
100:   'row to skip to if the user answers yes, 3rd column is the
101:   'row to skip to if the user answers no.
102:
103:   'If the noFile argument is True, Seed_Self creates a new
104:   'workbook with a single worksheet in the same directory
105:   'in which the Animal.XLS or Animal.XLA file resides.
106:   'If the noFile argument is False, Seed_Self just inserts
107:   'the needed worksheet into the workbook.
108:
109:   Dim k As Integer       'two loop counters
110:   Dim k1 As Integer
111:   Dim nThing As Object   'new workbook
112:
113:   On Error GoTo BadSeed      'set up error handling
114:
115:   If noFile Then    'need to create data workbook
116:     Application.StatusBar = "Creating data workbook..."
117:     Application.ScreenUpdating = False
118:     Set nThing = Workbooks.Add(xlWorksheet)
119:     Windows(nThing.Name).Visible = False
120:     nThing.Worksheets(1).Name = agData
121:     nThing.SaveAs agDataDir & "\" & agDataBook
122:     Application.ScreenUpdating = True
123:   End If
124:
125:   With Workbooks(agDataBook)
126:     If Not noFile Then  'workbook exists, but no datasheet
127:       Set nThing = .Worksheets.Add
128:       nThing.Name = agData
129:     End If
130:
131:     With .Worksheets(agData).Cells(1, 1)
132:       .Name = "DataStart"              'give data range a name
133:       .Value = "Is it a mammal"      '1st question in 1st col
134:       .Offset(0, 1).Value = agQuestion  'statement type
135:       .Offset(0, 2).Value = 2        'next if yes in 3rd col
136:       .Offset(0, 3).Value = 3        'next if no in 4th col
137:       .Offset(1, 0).Value = "dolphin"            '2nd row
138:       .Offset(1, 1).Value = agAnswer
139:       .Offset(1, 2).Value = agGUESSED
140:       .Offset(1, 3).Value = agLEARN
141:       .Offset(2, 0).Value = "rainbow trout"       '3rd row
142:       .Offset(2, 1).Value = agAnswer
143:       .Offset(2, 2).Value = agGUESSED
144:       .Offset(2, 3).Value = agLEARN
145:     End With
146:   End With
147:
148:   Workbooks(agDataBook).Save  'save the new data sheet
```

continues

Listing B.3. continued

```
149:   If noFile Then   'calling procedure expects closed book
150:     Workbooks(agDataBook).Close savechanges:=False
151:   End If
152:
153:   Exit Sub      'exit this sub procedure, work is done
154:
155: BadSeed:
156: 'inability to create workbook or insert data sheet is
157: 'a fatal error.
158:   MsgBox prompt:="ERROR: Unable to create Data Source!" & _
159:               Chr(agCR) & Chr(agCR) & Error() & _
160:               Chr(agCR) & Chr(agCR) & _
161:               "Animal Game Program Will Terminate", _
162:         Title:=agTitle & ":  ERROR", _
163:         Buttons:=vbCritical
164:   Application.StatusBar = False
165:   Application.ScreenUpdating = True
166:   End     'end the entire program
167: End Sub    'Seed_Self
168:
169:
170: Sub Remember_Animals()
171: 'Write the new animals in the tree structure onto the
172: 'data sheet. Since all of the current animals are stored
173: 'in the Animals array, the entire data sheet is rewritten.
174:
175:   Dim Rec_Count As Integer
176:   Dim DataStart As Object
177:
178:   On Error GoTo BadSave   'set up error-handler
179:
180:   Application.StatusBar = "Memorizing animals, wait..."
181:
182:   'open the data workbook
183:   If Dir(agDataDir & "\" & agDataBook) = "" Then
184:     'force "Unable to Open File" runtime error
185:     Error 53
186:   Else
187:     'open the workbook and make sure it's invisible
188:     Application.ScreenUpdating = False
189:     Workbooks.Open agDataDir & "\" & agDataBook
190:     Windows(agDataBook).Visible = False
191:     Application.ScreenUpdating = True
192:   End If
193:
194:   With Workbooks(agDataBook).Worksheets(agData)
195:     Set DataStart = .Range("DataStart")
196:     With DataStart
197:       Rec_Count = 1
198:       Do While Rec_Count <= UBound(Animals)
199:         .Offset(Rec_Count - 1, 0).Value = _
200:                           Animals(Rec_Count).StatementText
```

```
201:            .Offset(Rec_Count - 1, 1).Value = _
202:                        Animals(Rec_Count).NodeType
203:            .Offset(Rec_Count - 1, 2).Value = _
204:                        Animals(Rec_Count).NextIfYes
205:            .Offset(Rec_Count - 1, 3).Value = _
206:                        Animals(Rec_Count).NextIfNo
207:            Rec_Count = Rec_Count + 1
208:        Loop
209:    End With
210:  End With
211:
212:  Workbooks(agDataBook).Close savechanges:=True
213:  Application.StatusBar = False
214:  Exit Sub  'no more work to do
215:
216: BadSave:
217: 'not a fatal error - just tell user it wasn't possible to
218: 'save the animal list
219:  MsgBox prompt:="ERROR: Unable to save animal list!" & _
220:               Chr(agCR) & Chr(agCR) & Error(), _
221:         Title:=agTitle & ":  ERROR", _
222:         Buttons:=vbCritical
223:  Application.StatusBar = False
224:  Application.ScreenUpdating = True
225: End Sub      'Remember_Animals
```

This module contains functions and procedures private to the Animal game (line 3). Notice the module-level variable declaration in line 6; this variable is used to hold the data directory for the animal game's data.

The **Read_AnimalFile** procedure in lines 9 through 87 copies all of the data from the data worksheet (which is stored in a separate workbook) into the array of animals. If the data workbook or worksheet does not exist (that is, this is the first time the program has ever been run), then **Read_AnimalFile** calls the **Seed_Self** procedure to create the data workbook and data worksheet. Notice the error-handling code (line 29 and lines 76 through 86).

The **Seed_Self** procedure in lines 90 through 167 creates the data workbook and worksheet that the Animal game requires, and fills in just enough data—one question, and two answers—to get the game started. Notice the error-handling that gets set up in line 113, and the nested With statements in lines 125 and 131. Make sure you include all the dot separators (.) in the code.

Lines 170 through 225 contain the **Remember_Animals** procedure, which permanently saves any new animals and questions that the Animal game learns while you are playing. Because the game starts out knowing only two animals and one question, you are assured of teaching it more animals. **Remember_Animals** works by transcribing the array of animals and questions into the data worksheet (overwriting any previous data), then saving the workbook.

Tip: The code listings for the Guess the Animal game contain many comments about how the code in each procedure works. In general, you should document your programs in a similar fashion; in particular, you should include comments about any conditions required for a procedure or function to be used correctly.

The LearnNewAnimals Module

Insert a new module sheet and rename it *LearnNewAnimals*. The LearnNewAnimals module contains all the procedures needed for the Guess The Animal game to learn a new animal.

Type

Listing B.4. The LearnNewAnimals module.

```
1:  Option Explicit
2:  Option Base 1      'all arrays begin with 1
3:  Option Private Module
4:
5:
6:  Public Sub Learn_New_Animal(AnimalNDX As Integer)
7:  'Get the name of the player's animal, and a yes/no question
8:  'distinguishing that animal from the one the program picked
9:  'as a match. Record the correct yes/no response to the
10: 'distinguishing question.  Confirm all of the input
11: 'from the player, and link the new question and answer
12: 'nodes into the tree.
13:
14:    Dim NewAnimal As String
15:    Dim NewQuestion As String
16:    Dim NewAnswer As Integer
17:    Dim Confirmed As Boolean
18:    Dim Ans As Integer
19:
20:    If ((UBound(Animals) + 2) > agMax_Animals) Then
21:      MsgBox prompt:="I couldn't guess your animal, " & _
22:                 "but I don't have" & Chr(agCR) & _
23:                 "enough memory to learn any more!", _
24:          Title:=agTitle & ": Too Many Animals to Learn", _
25:          Buttons:=vbExclamation
26:      Exit Sub 'don't bother if max number of animals reached
27:    End If
28:
29:    MsgBox prompt:="I give up." & Chr(agCR) & Chr(agCR) & _
30:               "I'll just have to learn a new animal!", _
31:          Title:=agTitle, _
32:          Buttons:=vbExclamation + vbOKOnly
33:
34:    NewAnimal = ""
35:    NewQuestion = ""
36:    NewAnswer = vbYes
```

```
37:    Do                      'get the new question and answer
38:      Get_New_Animal nAnimal:=NewAnimal, _
39:                     nQuestion:=NewQuestion, _
40:                     nAnswer:=NewAnswer, _
41:                     aNDX:=AnimalNDX
42:
43:      Confirmed = Confirmed_Animal(NewAnimal, _
44:                                   NewQuestion, _
45:                                   NewAnswer, _
46:                                   AnimalNDX)
47:      If Not Confirmed Then
48:        Ans = MsgBox(prompt:="Do you want to cancel " & _
49:                            "learning a new animal?", _
50:                     Title:=agTitle, _
51:                     Buttons:=vbQuestion + vbYesNo)
52:       If Ans = vbYes Then Exit Sub
53:      End If
54:    Loop Until Confirmed
55:                             'add new animal to data chains
56:      Link_New_Animal nAnimal:=NewAnimal, _
57:                      nQuestion:=NewQuestion, _
58:                      nAnswer:=NewAnswer, _
59:                      aNDX:=AnimalNDX
60:
61:    New_Animal = True        'we just learned a new animal
62: End Sub        'Learn_New_Animal
63:
64:
65: Private Sub Get_New_Animal(ByRef nQuestion As String, _
66:                            ByRef nAnswer As Integer, _
67:                            ByRef nAnimal As String, _
68:                            ByRef aNDX)
69: 'Show dialog box to get new animal and differentiating
70: 'question from the player.
71:
72:    Dim Okay As Boolean
73:
74:    'prep the dialog box labels and controls
75:    With ThisWorkbook.DialogSheets("DialogNewAnimal")
76:      .Labels("Question Label").Caption = _
77:        "What yes-or-no question would distinguish " & _
78:        "your animal from " & _
79:        Preposition(Animals(aNDX).StatementText) & _
80:        Trim(Animals(aNDX).StatementText) & "?"
81:      .EditBoxes("AnimalName Box").Caption = nAnimal
82:      .EditBoxes("Question Box").Caption = nQuestion
83:      If nAnswer = vbYes Then
84:        .OptionButtons("QYes Option").Value = xlOn
85:        .OptionButtons("QNo Option").Value = xlOff
86:      Else
87:        .OptionButtons("QYes Option").Value = xlOff
88:        .OptionButtons("QNo Option").Value = xlOn
89:      End If
90:
91:      Do      'show the dialog box
92:        .Show
```

continues

Listing B.4. continued

```
93:          nAnimal = Trim(.EditBoxes("AnimalName Box").Caption)
94:          nQuestion = Trim(.EditBoxes("Question Box").Caption)
95:          If .OptionButtons("QYes Option").Value = xlOn Then
96:            nAnswer = vbYes
97:          Else
98:            nAnswer = vbNo
99:          End If
100:
101:          'make sure no entries are blank
102:          If (Trim(nAnimal) = "") Or _
103:             (Trim(nQuestion) = "") Then
104:            MsgBox prompt:="Please complete all of the " & _
105:                          "fields in the dialog box!", _
106:                   Buttons:=vbExclamation, _
107:                   Title:="Learning New Animal"
108:            Okay = False
109:          Else
110:            Mid(nQuestion, 1, 1) = UCase(Left(nQuestion, 1))
111:            Okay = True
112:          End If
113:        Loop Until Okay
114:      End With
115: End Sub        'Get_New_Animal
116:
117:
118: Private Function Confirmed_Animal(ByVal nAnimal As String, _
119:                                   ByVal nQuestion As String, _
120:                                   ByVal nAnswer As Integer, _
121:                                   ByVal aNDX As Integer) As Boolean
122:
123: 'get the player to confirm the new animal and
124: 'question information.
125:
126:    Dim pStr As String
127:    Dim Ans As Integer
128:
129:    pStr = _
130:      "I want to be sure I've got this straight now. . ." & _
131:      Chr(agCR) & Chr(agCR) & "You were thinking of " & _
132:      Preposition(nAnimal) & nAnimal & "."
133:    pStr = pStr & Chr(agCR) & Chr(agCR) & _
134:      "The distinguishing question between " & _
135:      Preposition(nAnimal) & nAnimal & " and " & _
136:      Preposition(Animals(aNDX).StatementText) & _
137:      Trim(Animals(aNDX).StatementText) & " is: " & _
138:      Chr(agCR) & Chr(agCR) & "      " & nQuestion & "?" & _
139:      Chr(agCR) & Chr(agCR)
140:    pStr = pStr & "The correct answer for " & _
141:          Preposition(nAnimal) & nAnimal & " is: "
142:
143:    If nAnswer = vbYes Then
144:      pStr = pStr & "'YES'"
```

B

```
145:    Else
146:      pStr = pStr & "'NO'"
147:    End If
148:    ·
149:    pStr = pStr & Chr(agCR)
150:
151:    Ans = MsgBox(prompt:=pStr, _
152:                 Title:=agTitle & ":    Confirm Question and Answer", _
153:                 Buttons:=vbQuestion + vbOKCancel)
154:    If Ans = vbOK Then
155:      Confirmed_Animal = True
156:    Else
157:      Confirmed_Animal = False
158:    End If
159: End Function        'Confirmed_Animal
160:
161:
162: Private Sub Link_New_Animal(ByVal nAnimal As String, _
163:                             ByVal nQuestion As String, _
164:                       '      ByVal nAnswer As Integer, _
165:                             ByVal aNDX As Integer)
166:
167: ' Attach a new animal to the chain - the new question is
168: 'inserted at the current node position, the old answer and
169: 'new answer are moved to the end of the chain.
170:
171:    Dim OldAns As Integer, NewAns As Integer
172:
173:    OldAns = UBound(Animals) + 1
174:    NewAns = UBound(Animals) + 2
175:
176:    ReDim Preserve Animals(1 To NewAns)   'allocate new nodes
177:
178:    Animals(OldAns) = Animals(aNDX)       'move existing animal
179:
180:    With Animals(aNDX)          'move new question to old node
181:      .StatementText = nQuestion
182:      .NodeType = agQuestion
183:      If nAnswer = vbYes Then          'make the chain links
184:        .NextIfYes = NewAns
185:        .NextIfNo = OldAns
186:      Else
187:        .NextIfYes = OldAns
188:        .NextIfNo = NewAns
189:      End If
190:    End With
191:
192:    With Animals(NewAns)              'put new animal in new node
193:      .StatementText = nAnimal
194:      .NodeType = agAnswer
195:      .NextIfYes = agGUESSED
196:      .NextIfNo = agLEARN
197:    End With
198: End Sub      'Link_New_Question
```

Lines 6 through 62 contain the `Learn_New_Animal` procedure. This procedure is executed whenever the Animal game failed to correctly guess the animal, and needs to "learn" a new animal. The `Learn_New_Animal` procedure calls several other procedures, all of which are private to this particular module. Notice that `Learn_New_Animal` repeats the process of displaying the dialog box for learning a new animal until the user confirms that the information is all correct.

One of the procedures `Learn_New_Animal` calls is the `Get_New_Animal` procedure in lines 65 through 115. `Get_New_Animal` displays a dialog box that has fields for the user to enter the animal they were thinking of, along with a question (and its answer) distinguishing their animal from the one that the game guessed. Before displaying the dialog box, though, `Get_New_Animal` customizes the label control that prompts the user to enter a question—this allows the dialog box to display a more specific prompt, so the user has a better idea of what's expected. `Get_New_Animal` also sets the dialog box's controls with default values from the procedure's arguments before showing the dialog. After showing the dialog box, `Get_New_Animal` makes sure that all text boxes were filled in, makes sure that the first letter of the question sentence is upper-case, and finally passes the user's data back through its argument variables—all of which are passed by reference.

The `Confirmed_Animal` function in lines 118 through 159 displays a message dialog box that repeats the information entered so far: the name of the animal, the question that distinguishes the user's animal from the animal the computer guessed, and the correct answer for that question. The user gets the choice of confirming the new animal information, answering **No** to try entering the information again, or canceling the new animal entry.

Lines 162 through 198 contain the `Link_New_Animal` procedure. This procedure links the new animal, question, and answer data into the database of animals. Notice the use of the `ReDim Preserve` statement to increase the size of the `Animals` array without destroying any of the data it contains.

The ListAnimals Module

Insert a new module sheet and rename it *ListAnimals*. The ListAnimals module contains the procedure that the Guess The Animal game uses to sort and display a list of all of the animals it knows.

     Listing B.5. The ListAnimals module.

```
1:  Option Explicit
2:  Option Base 1       'all arrays begin with 1
3:
4:
5:  Sub List_Animals()
6:  'Transcribe the list of animals from the array to a
```

```
7:     'temporary worksheet, then sort the list alphabetically,
8:     'and finally display it in a scrolling list box.
9:
10:    Dim k As Integer
11:    Dim Ofst As Integer
12:    Dim lSheet As Object
13:
14:    'create temporary worksheet for animal list
15:    Set lSheet = ThisWorkbook.Worksheets.Add
16:
17:    Ofst = 0
18:    With lSheet.Cells(1, 1)        'transcribe the animals list
19:      For k = LBound(Animals) To UBound(Animals)
20:        If Animals(k).NodeType = agAnswer Then
21:          .Offset(Ofst, 0).Value = _
22:                               Trim(Animals(k).StatementText)
23:          Ofst = Ofst + 1
24:        End If
25:      Next k
26:    End With
27:
28:    With lSheet        'name and sort range for list of animals
29:      .Range(.Cells(1, 1), .Cells(Ofst, 1)).Name = "ListStart"
30:      .Cells(1, 1).Sort Key1:=.Cells(1, 1), _
31:                              Order1:=xlAscending, _
32:                              MatchCase:=False
33:    End With
34:
35:    With ThisWorkbook.DialogSheets("DialogList")
36:      With .ListBoxes("ListOfAnimals")
37:        .ListFillRange = "ListStart"
38:        .LinkedCell = ""
39:        .MultiSelect = 1
40:      End With
41:      .Show
42:    End With
43:
44:    Application.DisplayAlerts = False
45:    lSheet.Delete    'remove the temporary sheet
46:    Application.DisplayAlerts = True
47:  End Sub      'List_Animals
```

Analysis

This module contains only one procedure, **List_Animals**, which displays the list of animals that are in the game's database (the array of animals and questions). This procedure works by creating a temporary worksheet (line 15), and then transcribing the list of animals to that worksheet (the loop in lines 19 through 25). Next, **List_Animals** gives the start of the list a name, and uses the Sort method to sort the list in the worksheet. Finally, **List_Animals** attaches the named range for the sorted list to the list box on the *DialogList* dialog sheet, and shows the dialog box (lines 35 through 42). When the procedure is done, it deletes the temporary list worksheet.

The Functions Module

Insert a new module sheet and rename it *Functions*. The Functions module contains all the utility functions used by the Guess The Animal program.

 Listing B.6. The Functions module.

```
1:   Option Explicit
2:
3:
4:   Function Preposition(Str As String) As String
5:   'Returns one of the prepositions, "a" or "an", depending
6:   'on whether or not the first letter of Str is a vowel.
7:
8:     If InStr(1, "AEIOU", Left(Str, 1), agTxtComp) Then
9:       Preposition = "an "
10:    Else
11:      Preposition = "a "
12:    End If
13:  End Function   'Preposition
14:
15:
16:  Function SheetExists(bName As String, _
17:                       sName As String) As Boolean
18:  'Returns True if the sheet named by sName exists in the
19:  'workbook specified by bName.
20:
21:    Dim aSheet As Object
22:
23:    'cycle through all sheets, comparing each sheet's name
24:    'to sName, as a text comparison
25:    For Each aSheet In Workbooks(bName).Sheets
26:      If (StrComp(aSheet.Name, sName, agTxtComp) = 0) Then
27:        SheetExists = True       'names match, return true
28:        Exit Function            'and exit function
29:      End If
30:    Next aSheet
31:
32:    'if loop completes, then match not found: return false
33:    SheetExists = False
34:  End Function
35:
36:
37:  Function IsAddIn(ByVal aBook As Object) As Boolean
38:  'reports whether aBook object is an add-in
39:
40:    On Error GoTo Default
41:
42:    If UCase(Right(aBook.Name, 3)) = "XLA" Then
43:      IsAddIn = True
44:      Exit Function
45:    End If
46:
```

```
47:    Default:
48:       IsAddIn = False
49:    End Function
```

This module contains a few general-purpose functions. The first function, **Preposition** (lines 4 through 13), fulfills a cosmetic purpose when assembling messages. This function returns the correct preposition "a" or "an," depending on whether or not the string passed as an argument begins with a vowel.

The second function, **SheetExists** (lines 16 through 34), checks to see whether or not a particular sheet exists in a particular workbook. **SheetExists** returns True if the sheet exists in the specified workbook, False otherwise.

The final function, **IsAddIn** (lines 37 through 49), returns True if the object passed as **aBook** argument is a workbook and has a name that ends with XLA; otherwise it returns false. Notice the error-handling code in lines 40 and 48—any runtime error that occurs in this function causes it to return a value of False.

The Automatic Module

Insert a new module sheet and rename it *Automatic*. The Automatic module contains the **Auto_Open** and **Auto_Close** procedures for the Guess The Animal program, including the menu-building procedure called by **Auto_Open**.

 Listing B.7. The Automatic module.

```
1:    Option Explicit
2:    Option Base 1      'all arrays begin with 1
3:    Option Private Module
4:
5:
6:    Sub Auto_Open()
7:       Dim aMenu As MenuBar
8:
9:       Application.StatusBar = "Installing Animal Game..."
10:
11:      'if we're a workbook, hide ourselves
12:      If Not IsAddIn(ThisWorkbook) Then
13:        Windows(ThisWorkbook.Name).Visible = False
14:      End If
15:
16:      'install Game menu on all Excel built-in menu bars
17:      For Each aMenu In MenuBars
18:        If aMenu.BuiltIn Then
19:          agSetMenu mBar:=aMenu
20:        End If
21:      Next aMenu
```

continues

Listing B.7. continued

```
22:
23:      Application.StatusBar = False
24:   End Sub
25:
26:
27:   Sub Auto_Close()
28:     Dim aMenu As MenuBar
29:
30:     'remove Game menus from built-in Excel menus
31:     For Each aMenu In MenuBars
32:       If aMenu.BuiltIn Then
33:         aMenu.Menus("Game").Delete
34:       End If
35:     Next aMenu
36:   End Sub
37:
38:
39:   Private Sub agSetMenu(mBar As MenuBar)
40:   'Adds the Animal game menu to the menu bar specified
41:   'by the aMenu argument.
42:
43:     Dim tItem As MenuItem
44:     Dim bStr As String
45:
46:     If IsAddIn(ThisWorkbook) Then
47:       bStr = "ANIMAL.XLA!AnimalMain."
48:     Else
49:       bStr = "ANIMAL.XLS!AnimalMain."
50:     End If
51:
52:     With mBar
53:       .Menus.Add Caption:="&Game"
54:       With .Menus("Game").MenuItems
55:         Set tItem = .Add(Caption:="&Guess the Animal", _
56:                          OnAction:=bStr & "Animal")
57:         tItem.StatusBar = "Play ""Guess the Animal"" game"
58:         Set tItem = .Add(Caption:="&Rules", _
59:                          OnAction:=bStr & "ShowRules")
60:         tItem.StatusBar = "Display game rules"
61:         .Add Caption:="-"   'adds separator bar
62:         Set tItem = .Add(Caption:="R&emove Animal Game", _
63:                          OnAction:=bStr & "ShutDown")
64:         tItem.StatusBar = "Remove ""Guess the Animal"" game"
65:         .Add Caption:="-"   'adds separator bar
66:         Set tItem = .Add(Caption:="&About", _
67:                          OnAction:=bStr & "AboutAnimal")
68:         tItem.StatusBar = "Info about ""Guess the Animal"""
69:       End With
70:     End With
71:   End Sub
```

Analysis This final module contains the automatic procedures for the ANIMAL.XLS workbook and one supporting procedure. Notice that this is a private module (line 3), so no other workbooks can use these procedures.

The **Auto_Open** procedure executes whenever Excel opens the ANIMAL.XLS workbook (or whenever the ANIMAL.XLA add-in is loaded). This procedure consists, essentially, of a For Each...Next loop that loops through all of the menu bars in the MenuBars collection, calling the **agSetMenu** procedure for each built-in menu bar. This procedure modifies only built-in menus to avoid altering another workbook's or add-in program's custom menus.

Lines 27 through 36 contain the **Auto_Close** procedure, which executes each time Excel closes the ANIMAL.XLS workbook (or whenever the ANIMAL.XLA program is uninstalled). This procedure, like the automatic opening procedure, consists of a For Each...Next loop that cycles through all of the menu bars in the MenuBars collection. In this case, though, the custom **G**ame menu is deleted from each built-in menu bar.

The **agSetMenu** procedure in lines 39 through 71 adds the **G**ame custom menu to whatever MenuBar object is passed as its argument. Lines 46 through 50 adjust the prefix for the event procedure's name, depending on whether this program is executing from a workbook or an add-in. Line 53 adds the **G**ame custom menu to the menu bar, and lines 54 through 69 add the individual commands (with their status bar text) to the **G**ame menu.

Creating the Guess The Animal Game's Dialog Boxes

In order to use the Guess The Animal game, you must create a total of four dialog boxes. You don't have to make the dialog boxes look exactly like the dialog boxes shown in the figures, but you should make sure that your dialog boxes contain the same number of buttons and list box controls, and that the buttons and list boxes have the same labels and names as shown.

Note: After you create the dialog boxes, you'll need to assign procedures to the dialog box command buttons, so you should enter all of the source code listings before you create the dialog boxes.

The DialogMain Dialog Box

Insert a new dialog sheet and rename it *DialogMain.* This is the dialog box through which you operate the Guess The Animal game.

Sample Application

Figure B.2 shows the *DialogMain* dialog box, as it appears on the dialog sheet. Creating custom dialog boxes was covered in Day 15. You don't have to make your dialog box look exactly like this one, but you must include four command buttons to correspond to the four buttons shown in Figure B.2: Yes, I'm thinking of an Animal, Rules of the Game, List the Animals I Know, and Close.

Figure B.2.

The Guess The Animal game's main dialog box. You must assign procedures to the command buttons when you create this dialog box.

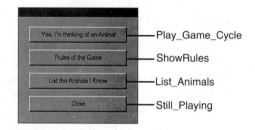

Once you have created the dialog box and its four command buttons, you must assign the correct procedures to each command button in order to make the game work. The following table lists the four command buttons, and the name and module of the procedure you should assign to that command button. The procedure names to assign to each button are also marked in Figure B.1.

Procedure Assignments for the DialogMain Dialog Box

Command Button	Procedure	Module
Yes	Play_Game_Cycle	AnimalMain
Rules	ShowRules	AnimalMain
List	List_Animals	ListAnimals
Close	Still_Playing	AnimalMain

To assign the procedures to the dialog box command buttons, follow these steps:

1. Display the *DialogMain* dialog sheet, if it is not already on-screen.

2. Click on the command button on the dialog sheet that you want to assign the procedure to. For example, to assign the procedure to the "Yes" button, click on that button.

3. Choose the **Tools** | **Assign** Macro command. VBA displays the Assign Macro dialog box.

4. Select the correct procedure in the **Macro** Name/Reference list box. Refer to Figure B.1 and the preceding table to see which procedure to assign to which button. For example, to assign the procedure for the "Yes" button, select **Play_Game_Cycle** in the **Macro** Name/Reference list box.

5. Choose OK. VBA assigns the selected procedure to the selected command button, and closes the Assign Macro dialog box.

6. Repeat the above steps for each of the four command buttons.

You have now finished creating the main dialog box for the Guess The Animal game.

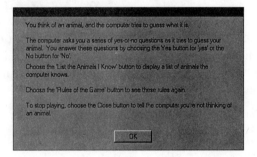

The DialogRules Dialog Box

Insert a new dialog sheet and rename it *DialogRules*. This is the dialog box that the Guess The Animal game displays in response to the Game | Rules command, or in response to the Rules of the Game command button in the DialogMain dialog box. Figure B.3 shows how this dialog box should look. It has only one command button, the OK button. There are no procedures attached to this command button.

> **Tip:** You can't see it in the figure, but the DialogRules dialog box's text is actually entered into two different label controls—although Excel will allow you to enter a lot of text into a label control, you can't really display all of it. The text for the rules of the game is about twice as long as a single label control can display.

Figure B.3.

The dialog box for display-ing the rules of the game merely contains two label controls, and a single command button control with no event procedures.

The text for the DialogRules dialog box is:

```
You think of an animal, and the computer will try to guess what it is.

The computer asks you a series of yes-or-no questions as it tries to guess your
animal. You answer these questions by choosing the Yes button for 'yes', or the
No button for 'No'.

Choose the 'List the Animals I Know' button to display a list of animals the
computer knows.

Choose the 'Rules of the Game' button to see these rules again.
```

```
To stop playing, choose the Close button to tell the computer you're not thinking
of an animal.
```

The DialogList Dialog Box

Insert a new dialog sheet and rename it *DialogList*. This is the dialog box that the Guess The Animal game uses to display the list of animals that it knows.

Figure B.4 shows the DialogList dialog box, as it appears on the dialog sheet. You don't have to make your dialog box look exactly like this one, but you must include the OK command button and the list box, or the Guess The Animal program won't work correctly.

Figure B.4.

The DialogList dialog box. You must rename the list box control when you create this dialog box.

ListOfAnimals

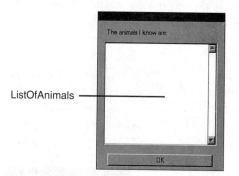

Once you have created the dialog box with the single OK button and its list box control, you must rename the list box, so that the Guess The Animal program will work correctly. (Look at Listing B.5, and notice that the **List_Animals** procedure refers to the list box control on this dialog box by name.)

To rename the list box control, follow these steps:

1. Display the DialogList dialog sheet, if it is not already on-screen.
2. Click on the list box control to select it.
3. Enter the name **ListOfAnimals** in the Name Box. (The Name Box is the text box on the left side of the formula bar.)

You have now finished creating the dialog box for the list of animals that the game knows.

The DialogNewAnimal Dialog Box

Insert a new dialog sheet and rename it *DialogNewAnimal*. This is the dialog box that the Guess The Animal game uses to get new animals, questions, and answers from the user. For this dialog

box, it's very important that you include the controls shown, and give them the specified names, or the program won't work correctly. (Notice that `Get_New_Animal` in Listing B.4 references the controls on this dialog box by name.)

Figure B.5 shows the `DialogNewAnimal` as it appears on the dialog sheet. There are no event procedures assigned to any of the controls on this dialog box—it's default values and labels are assigned before it is displayed, and the data is read from the controls after the dialog box is dismissed.

Figure B.5.

The Animal game uses this dialog box to get a new animal's name and a differentiating question (with its corresponding answer) from the player.

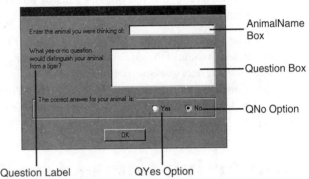

After you've placed the controls and labels on the dialog box, be sure to rename the controls as shown in the figure callouts. Rename these controls the same way you did the list box for the `DialogList` dialog box.

Using the Game

Once you have entered all of the source code and created the dialog boxes, you're ready to run the Guess The Animal Game. To get ready to run the Guess The Animal Game, follow these steps:

1. Save the ANIMAL.XLS workbook, and then close it. (You'll probably see a runtime error when the workbook closes, because the `Auto_Close` procedure is trying to remove menus that don't exist—just choose **End** in the runtime error dialog box to let the workbook finish closing.)

2. Open the ANIMAL.XLS workbook.

When you open the completed workbook, it will execute the **Auto_Open** procedure, which hides the workbook and adds a **G**ame choice to all of Excel's built-in menus. To play the game, choose the custom **G**ame | **G**uess The Animal command. All of the commands on the custom **G**ame menu are summarized in the following list:

☐ **G**uess The Animal. This command starts the game.

☐ **R**ules. This command displays a dialog box explaining the rules of the game.

☐ **R**emove Animal Game. This command removes the custom **G**ame menu, and closes the ANIMAL.XLS workbook. To make the game available again, just open the ANIMAL.XLS workbook again. (If you convert the game to an add-in, this command will uninstall the add-in program—you'll need to use the **T**ools | Add-**I**ns command to make the game available again.)

☐ **A**bout. This command displays a dialog box containing some information about the game.

The code in the game deliberately avoids turning off Excel's screen updating in most cases, so you can watch some of the game's behind-the-scenes manipulations, if you want. To watch what happens to the data worksheets when you list the animals that the game knows, or when you save new animals on exiting the game, just use the **W**indow | **U**nhide command to unhide the ANIMAL.XLS workbook (the automatic opening procedure will hide it again, the next time you open ANIMAL.XLS).

Converting Guess The Animal to an Add-In Program

The Guess The Animal program was designed specifically with the goal of converting it to an add-in procedure. After you're sure that your version is working correctly in workbook form, you can turn it into an XLA add-in program, as described in Day 21.

Notice that the Animal game has followed the two important rules for programming an add-in program:

☐ Uses `ThisWorkbook` to refer to the workbook from which the code is running instead of `ActiveWorkbook`.

☐ Stores all data in an external file.

To convert the Animal game to an add-in, follow these steps:

1. Open the ANIMAL.XLS workbook, and unhide it.

2. Make sure that the **T**itle field of the Summary information contains the words: `Animal Game`.

3. Choose the **T**ools | Ma**k**e Add-In command, and save the workbook with the name ANIMAL.XLA. (If you don't use this name, the add-in program won't work correctly.)

4. Choose the **G**ame | **Re**move Animal Game custom menu command to close the workbook version of the Animal game and remove its menus.

5. Install the ANIMAL.XLA add-in program.

After you've saved the workbook with the Animal game as an XLA add-in file, you need to add the new add-in to Excel's Add-Ins dialog box. To do so, follow this procedure:

1. Choose the **T**ools | Add-**I**ns command. Excel displays the Add-Ins dialog box.

2. Choose the **B**rowse command button. Excel opens a standard file open dialog box.

3. Select the ANIMAL.XLA add-in file, and click the OK button. Excel adds the Animal game add-in to the list in the Add-Ins dialog box, and installs the add-in program.

If you filled in the **T**itle field of the Summary information for the ANIMAL.XLS workbook as directed at the beginning of this appendix, the Animal game add-in will now be listed in the Add-Ins dialog box list as `Animal Game`.

The add-in version of the Animal game will perform exactly the same as the workbook version, with two exceptions. First, the dialog box displayed by the **G**ame | **A**bout custom menu command should now indicate that the program code is executing from within an add-in. Second, the **G**ame | **Re**move Animal Game menu command now has the effect of uninstalling the add-in (it will still be listed in the Add-Ins dialog box, but will be unchecked). The **Re**move Animal Game command will also display an additional dialog box with instructions on how to re-install the add-in game.

How Guess The Animal Works

Guess The Animal stores its data in a worksheet named `AnimalData`, which is stored in a workbook named `Animal Game Data.XLS`. The Animal game program creates this workbook and worksheet automatically the first time you run the program, and fills in enough data to get the game started. (Actually, the Animal game creates this workbook and worksheet any time you try to play the game and it can't find an existing data workbook in the directory from which the Animal game is running.)

The first column of each row in the data worksheet holds a yes or no question about an animal or the name of an animal. The second column holds a numeric code indicating whether the data in the first column is a question or an animal name. (These numeric codes are represented by the constants **agQuestion** and **agAnswer**, declared in the `Constants` module.)

The third column of each row in the data worksheet holds a numeric code representing the action to take if the user answers "yes" when asked a question, and the fourth column holds a numeric code representing the action to take if the user answers "no." If the number is positive, then it is the row number of the next item in the chain of questions. If the number is negative, then it is a code indicating whether the computer successfully guessed the animal you were thinking of, or if the computer needs to learn a new animal. (These two codes are represented by the constants **agGUESSED** and **agLEARN**, declared in the Constants module.)

When the program tries to "guess" the animal you are thinking of, it starts with the first row in the data sheet—which must be a question—and asks that question. Depending on whether you answer "yes" or "no" to the question, the program then skips to the row specified by the number in either the third (yes) or fourth (no) columns.

The program then checks the code number from the second column of the new row, to find out whether this new statement is an animal, or another question. If the statement is a question, the program asks you that question about the animal you're thinking of. If the statement is an animal, the program tells you that it has guessed your animal, and asks if it has guessed correctly.

Again, depending on whether you answer "yes" or "no," the program looks up the code number in the third or fourth columns of the data worksheet, and determines what to do next. If the numbers are positive, the program skips to the indicated row, and repeats the questioning process just described. If the code number is negative, and you answered that the animal the computer guessed was not the animal you were thinking of, then the program asks you to enter a new question to distinguish the animal it guessed from the animal you were thinking of.

After you enter the new question and animal, the program adds the question and animal to its database array of animals and questions.

As the program runs, it actually copies the data from the worksheet into an array that uses a user-defined type (declared in the AnimalMain module). The program copies the data on the worksheet to its array for reasons of convenience and speed. It requires less programming effort to manipulate the data in an array with a user-defined type than to continuously fetch data values from the worksheet. When you stop playing, the Guess The Animal program asks if you want to save any new animals permanently. If you answer "yes," then the program transcribes the contents of the array to the correct rows and columns in the data worksheet, and saves the data.

In technical terms, this kind of data representation is referred to as an *unbalanced binary tree*. It gets this name from the fact that each data item (one row in the worksheet, called a *node*) has two possible branches—one for "yes," and one for "no." Also, if you diagram the connections between the various nodes, you end up with a diagram that sort of looks like a tree. This tree structure is called "unbalanced" because it is possible for, say, the "yes" branches to continue much further than the "no" branches, depending on the kinds of questions the user teaches the program. Each time a chain of questions leads to an animal, that particular branch in the tree comes to an end.

When the Guess The Animal program learns a new animal, it adds a new node to the tree, extending that particular branch one more level. The first node of the tree must always be a question. Each branch away from a node is either a "yes" branch, or a "no" branch. A chain of

branches is terminated by a node that represents an animal, rather than a question. Going through the chain of questions and answers in the tree is called *traversing* the tree, and ends whenever an answer node is reached.

This entire process implements a simple example of how heuristic learning can be modeled by a computer program. As the program "learns" new animals, it grows a simple expert system on animals, using yes/no rules ("does it have feathers?" or "is it a mammal?") to determine which animal is being considered.

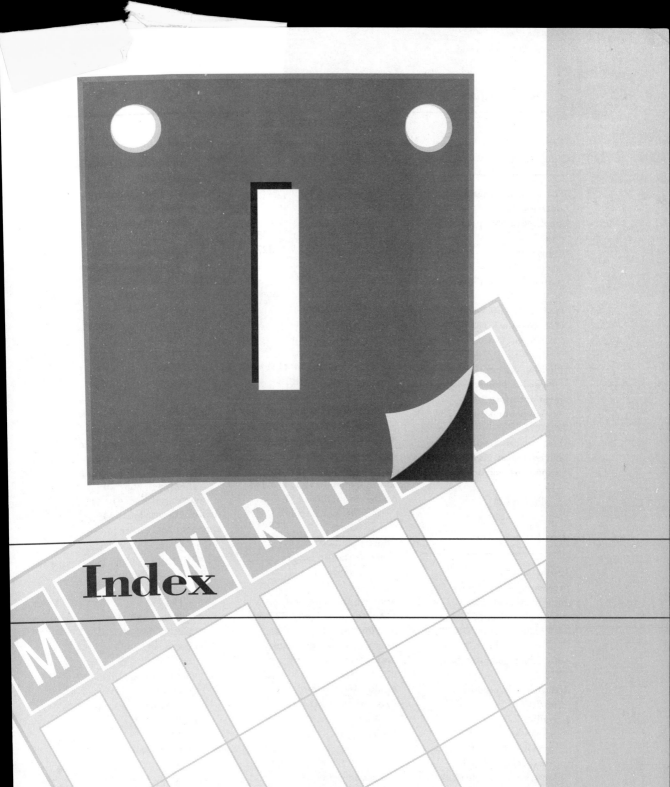

Index

Symbols

Symbols

& (string concatenation) operator, 106
* (multiplication operator), 114
+ (plus sign)
    addition operator, 112-113
    string concatenation operator, 130-131
- (subtraction operator), 113
. (dot separator), 158
    with user-defined data types, 372-373
/ (division operator), 115
:= (named-argument assignment operator), 146
= (assignment operator), 73, 109-112
[ ] (square brackets), returning cell references, 723
^ (exponentiation operators), 116
… (ellipsis), 621

A

Abs function, 147
Accelerator Key property, 584
Activate method, 222, 622
    MenuBar object, 627-628
    Workbook object, 708-709
    Worksheet object, 714
ActivateNotepad procedure, 772-773
ActivateTest procedure, 708-709
activating
    applications, 770-773
    windows, 809-810
    workbooks, 708-709
    worksheets, 714, 805-807
ActiveCell property, 219
ActiveChart property, 219
ActiveSheet property, 219

Add method, 622, 647
    AddIns collection, 822
    MenuBars collection, 6
    MenuItems collection, 636-637
    Menus collection, 632-6
    Names collection, 726-7
    OLEObjects collection, 739-740, 744-748
    ToolbarButtons collection, 655-656
    Toolbars collection, 649
    Workbooks collection, 707
    Worksheets collection, 715
Add Watch command (Tools menu), 29, 537-538
add-in applications, 820-823
    converting Guess The Animal application to, 930-931
AddIn.Installed property, 822
AddIns method, 822
AddIns.Add method, 822
addition (+) operator, 112-113
AddMenu method, 623
    MenuItems collection, 640-641
Address method, 223
alternate startup folders, library workbooks in, 391-394
AltStartupPath property (Application object), 392-393
And operator, 125-126
AnotherMessage procedure, 80
AppActivate statement, 770-773
Application keyword, 158
Application object, 216
    Workbooks method, 704
applications
    activating, 770-773
    add-in, 820-823
    canceling, 280-283
    Guess The Animal, 904
        AnimalMain module, 906-911

..., 930-931
        creating, 904
        Functions module, 922-923
        LearnNewAnimals module, 916-920
        ListAnimals module, 920-921
        playing, 931-933
        running, 929-930
    OpenNewBook, 549-565
    Registry Editor, 741-742
    sending keystrokes to other applications, 785-788
    starting from VBA procedures, 768-770
    top-down design, 410-413
Archive file attribute, 433
argument lists (procedures), 414-423
arguments
    function procedures
        declaring data types for, 186-187
        optional, 187-190
        passing, 190-193
    functions, 142-143
        named, 145-147
        passing arrays as, 496-497
        validating, 356-357
    procedures, passing arrays as, 496-497
    required, 187
arithmetic operators
    addition (+), 112-113
    comparison, 116-118
    division (/), 115
    exponentiation (^), 116

integer division (/), 115
modulo division, 116
multiplication (*), 114
subtraction (-), 113-114
Variant type exceptions,
112-113
Array data type, 62
arrays, 470
declaring, 476-478
dynamic, 474-475
deleting, 494-496
redimensioning, 486-492
multi-dimensional, 472-474
passing as arguments to
procedures/functions,
496-497
searching
binary searches, 506,
510-515
linear searches, 506-509
single-dimensional (simple),
470-472
sorting, 498-506
static, 474-475, 478-485
clearing elements,
494-496
subscripts
starting number,
changing, 475-476
upper/lower boundaries,
492-494
using, 478-485
arrows beside commands, 621
As keyword, 84-85
Asc function, 149
ascending order sorts, 498
Assign Macro command (Tools
menu), 589
assignment operators
assignment (=), 73, 109-112
named-argument (:=), 146
assignments
functions in, 139-142
objects, 224-228
Atn function, 147

Attach Toolbars command
(Tools menu), 29
attributes (files), 432-440
Auto_Close procedure,
803-804, 807-809
Auto_Open procedure,
801-803, 805-807
AutomateWordObject
procedure, 757-758
automatic indenting, 46
automatic procedures,
800-801, 835-837
AutoUpdate property
(OLEObject object), 749

B

Backup_ActiveBook procedure,
226-230
BackUpToFloppy procedure,
710
beeps, MessageBeep DLL
procedure, 790-792
BeepTest procedure, 791
BellButton_Click procedure,
662
binary
searches of arrays, 506,
510-515
string comparisons, 120
BinarySearch procedure,
510-515
bit-wise comparisons, 437
bits, 62
block If statements, 259-260
Boolean data type, 62, 68
constants, 92
Truth tables, 125
value conversion, 108
Border property (OLEObject
object), 749
BottomRightCell property
(OLEObject object), 750
brackets ([ ]), returning cell
references, 723

branches
conditional branching
statements, 257
If...Then, 258-260
If...Then...Else, 261-264
If...Then...ElseIf, 267-268
nested If...Then, 264-267
nested If...Then...Else,
264-267
Select Case, 268-273
On Error GoTo statement,
670-671
unconditional branching
statements, 257, 273-277
break mode (Debugger),
523-529
single-stepping, 529-534
breaking strings into compo-
nent parts, 169-170
breakpoints, 526-527
bubble-sort technique, 498-506
BubbleSortAscending
procedure, 505
BubbleSortDescending
procedure, 505
bugs, 522-523
built-in menu bars, restoring,
629
built-in menus (Excel), 624
built-in toolbars
Excel, 648
restoring, 654
BuiltIn property, 623, 647
Button object properties,
585-586
buttons
check boxes (custom dialog
boxes), 571, 600-604
command
custom dialog boxes, 571
default, 290
in message dialog boxes,
283-288
Forms toolbar, 577-578
option (custom dialog boxes),
571, 595-600

toolbars, 655-657
Visual Basic toolbar, 31
  Instant Watch, 540
  Menu Editor, 625
  Record Macro, 11
  Resume Macro, 529
  Step Into, 528, 532
  Step Over, 534
  Stop Macro, 529
  Toggle Breakpoint, 527
bytes, 62

C

Calc_CircleArea procedure, 90, 96-98
Calculate method, 223
calculations
expressions, 103
recalculating worksheets, 819-820
calling functions, 139
Calls dialog box, 540-541
CancelButton property, 585
CancelDemo procedure, 485
canceling
functions, 278-280
input dialog boxes, 274-277
procedures, 278-280
programs, 280-283
Caption property, 573, 623
MenuItem object, 640
CBool function, 150
CCur function, 150
CDate function, 150
CDbl function, 150
Cell Link property, 585
cells
cutting/copying/clearing data, 727-730
entering data, 724-726
selecting, 724
verifying contents, 816-819
Cells method, 223
Worksheet/Range objects, 720-721

channels, 774
disconnecting, 777
establishing, 774-777
Chart object, 216
Charts collection, 233
Charts method, 223
ChDir statement, 431, 453-454
ChDrive statement, 431, 454-455
Check Box button (Forms toolbar), 577
check boxes (custom dialog boxes), 571, 600-604
Checked property, 623
MenuItem object, 640
CheckMargin procedure, 819-820
CheckToggle procedure, 645
Chr function, 149, 171-172
CInt function, 150
circular references, 404-405
CityList_Change procedure, 615
classes (OLE objects), determining types, 741-744
Clear All Breakpoints command (Run menu), 29, 527
Clear method, 223
Range object, 728-730
clearing
static-array elements, 494-496
worksheet data, 727-730
clients
DDE
  establishing channels with servers, 774-777
  exchanging data with, 780-784
OLE, 737
Clipboard, moving/copying macros, 39-40
CLng function, 150
Close method, 223
Workbook object/Workbooks collection, 711-712

CloseAll procedure, 711-712
closing workbooks, 711-712
Auto_Close procedure, 803-804
code
multiple statements on single lines of code, 258-259
organizing within modules, 413-414
collections, 230-235
colors, macro text, 37
columns
formatting headings, 329-332, 350-351
sorting, 591-604
Columns method (Range object), 723
Combination Drop-Down Edit button (Forms toolbar), 577
Combination List-Edit button (Forms toolbar), 577
combo dropdown-edit list boxes (custom dialog boxes), 572
combo list-edit boxes (custom dialog boxes), 572
command buttons
custom dialog boxes, 571
default, 290
in message dialog boxes, 283-288
commands, 25-27, 621
adding submenus, 640-641
adding to menus, 636-637
deleting from menus, 638-639
Edit menu, 28
enabling/disabling, 639
event procedures, specifying, 637
Format menu, Object, 586
hints, displaying in status bar, 638
Insert menu
  Macro | Dialog, 575
  Macro | Module, 41-42

macro recorder, 5
macros, 4-5
  renaming, 640
Run menu, 28-29
  Clear All Breakpoints, 527
  Continue, 529
  End, 529
  Step Into, 528-534
  Step Over, 534-535
  Toggle Breakpoint, 527
toggle, 639-640
Tools menu, 29
  Add Watch, 537-538
  Assign Macro, 589
  Edit Watch, 539
  Instant Watch, 540
  Macro, 18-19
  Make Add-In, 821
  Menu Editor, 625
  Protection, 41
  Protection | Protect
    Workbook, 394
  Record Macro | Record
    New Macro, 11-14
  References, 395
  Tab Order, 583
View menu, 28
  Debug Window, 537
Window menu, Hide, 393
comparing strings, 166-169
comparison operators, 116-118
  function description list, 117
  Is, 123
  sample expressions, 117
  strings, 118-120
compile errors, 522-523
compilers, 523
**complex expressions,
  evaluating, 131-134**
concatenation operators, 128
  & (ampersand), 106, 130
  + (plus), 130-131
**conditional branching
  statements, 257**
  If...Then, 258-260
    nested, 264-267

  If...Then...Else, 261-264
    nested, 264-267
  If...Then...ElseIf, 267-268
  Select Case, 268-273
constants
  Boolean, 92
  literal, 87-88
    date, 91-92
    numeric, 91
  named, 88
  predefined, 93
    locating with object
      browser, 94-95
  private, 401-402
  public, 403-404
  scope declaration, 89-90
  specifying data types, 92-93
container objects, 230-231
**Continue command (Run
  menu), 529**
**Control Properties button
  (Forms toolbar), 577-578**
**controls (custom dialog boxes),
  570-574**
  attaching procedures to,
    588-591
  check boxes, 600-604
  edit boxes, 591-595
  editing, 580-582
  group boxes, 595-600
  list boxes, 612-615
  option buttons, 595-600
  placing/setting properties,
    576-580
  scrollbars, 604-612
  setting properties
    interactively, 584-586
  spinner boxes, 604-612
  tab order, 582-584
conversations (DDE)
  exchanging data, 780-784
  initiating, 774-777
  terminating, 777
**Convert2Template procedure,
  445-447**

Copy method
  Range object, 728-730
  Worksheet object, 716-717
CopyFiles procedure, 458
copying
  custom dialog-box controls,
    581-582
  files, 457-459
  worksheet data, 727-730
  worksheets, 716-717
**CopyToTempSheet procedure,
  728-729**
Cos function, 148
Count property, 219, 623
count-controlled loops, 312
**Count_OddNums procedure,
  316-318**
**Create Button button (Forms
  toolbar), 577**
**CreateAccessDBObject
  procedure, 759-761**
**CreateLoanPmtCalculator
  procedure, 725-726**
**CreateMonthlyReport
  procedure, 707**
**CreateObject function,
  758-761**
**CreateTempWorksheet
  procedure, 715**
**CreateWordLink procedure,
  778-780**
**CreateWorksheetAtEnd
  procedure, 716**
**cross-module programming,
  scope, 397-407**
CSng function, 150
CStr function, 139, 150
CurDir function, 431, 452-453
Currency data type, 63, 67-68
**CurrentRegion property
  (Range object), 723**
custom dialog boxes
  controls, 570-574
    attaching procedures to,
      588-591
    check boxes, 600-604

edit boxes, 591-595
editing, 580-582
group boxes, 595-600
list boxes, 612-615
option buttons, 595-600
placing/setting properties,
576-580
scrollbars, 604-612
setting properties
interactively, 584-586
spinner boxes, 604-612
tab order, 582-584
creating, 574-575
displaying, 587-588
inserting dialog sheets for,
575-576
custom menu bars, creating,
624
custom toolbars
creating, 649, 657-663
deleting, 653-654
Cut method (Range object),
728-730
cutting worksheet data,
727-730
CVar function, 150

D

data
bits, 62
input, 95
text strings, 68
values, storing in variables
(assignment operator), 73
data conversion functions,
148-151
data types, 62-65
automatic conversion,
105-107
Boolean, 68
compatibility, 104-105
Currency, 67-68
Date, 65-66
conversion, 108-109

declaring
for function-procedure
arguments, 186-187
for function-procedure
results, 184-186
floating point numbers, 67
information about, obtaining,
340-355
Integer, 66-67
validating user input,
358-361
numeric, 66-68
conversion, 107
scientific notation, 64-65
specifying
in constants, 92-93
in variables, 84
storage in variables, 69-71
string variables, declaring
fixed length variables, 87
user-defined
creating, 370-380
private, 401-402
public, 403-404
Variant, 69
see also expressions
DataEntryHandler procedure,
806-807
date
expressions, 103
functions, 151-153
literal constants, 91-92
stamps, 462-463
Date data type, 63, 65-66
conversion, 108-109
testing for corrrect type of
data, 345-346
Date function, 151
DateSerial function, 152
DateValue function, 153
Day function, 152
DDE (dynamic data exchange),
773-784
DDEExecute method, 778-780
DDEInitiate method, 774-777
DDEPoke method, 782-784

DDERequest method, 780-782
DDETerminate method, 777
Debug window, 525
Immediate pane, 542-545
Watch pane, 535-540
Debug Window command
(View menu), 28, 537
Debug.Print method, 542-545
DebugDemo1 procedure,
530-534
DebugDemo2 procedure,
543-545
debugging
break mode, 523-529
single-stepping through
statements, 529-534
stepping over procedures,
534-535
tracing procedure calls,
540-541
watched variables/expressions,
535-540
decision-making statements,
256-257
End Sub/Function, 280-283
Exit Sub/Function, 278-280
GoTo, 273-277
If...Then, 258-260
nested, 264-267
If...Then...Else, 261-264
nested, 264-267
If...Then...ElseIf, 267-268
MsgBox, 283-288
Select Case, 268-273
declaration line, 36
Declare statement, 789
declaring
arrays, 476-478
data types
for function-procedure
arguments, 186-187
for function-procedure
results, 184-186
DLL procedures, 789
explicit variables, 74-76,
81-83

object variables, 224
variables with user-defined
   types, 372
**default command buttons,
   287-288**
DefaultButton property, 585
**defensive programming,
   355-356, 668-669**
   function arguments,
      validating, 356-357
   non-user input, validating,
      362
   procedure environments,
      validating, 356-357
   user input, validating,
      357-362
   see also error handling
**defining user-defined data
   types, 370-371**
Delete method, 623, 647
   Menu object, 633
   MenuBar object, 628-629
   MenuItem object, 638-639
   Toolbar object, 654
   ToolbarButton object, 656
   Worksheet object, 717-718
**DeleteCustMenu procedure,
   628-629**
**DeleteTemporarySheets
   procedure, 717-718**
deleting
   attached procedures from
      custom dialog-box control,
      591
   commands from menus,
      638-639
   custom dialog-box controls,
      581-582
   custom toolbars, 655-656
   directories, 456-457
   dynamic arrays, 494-496
   files, 459-460
   leading or trailing space
      characters, 164-165
   menu bars, 628-631

menus from menu bars,
   633-635
toolbar buttons, 656
watched variables/expressions,
   539
worksheets from workbooks,
   717-718
DelFiles procedure, 459-460
**DelProtectFile procedure,
   439-440**
**Demo_ChDir procedure,
   453-454**
**Demo_ChDrive procedure,
   454-455**
**Demo_ForNext procedure,
   300-302**
**Demo_ForNextDown proce-
   dure, 302-305**
**Demo_InStr procedure,
   168-169**
Demo_MkDir procedure, 456
**Demo_MsgBoxFunction
   procedure, 283-288**
**Demo_RmDir procedure,
   456-457**
**Demo_StrComp procedure,
   167**
**Demo_TypeName procedure,
   349-350**
**DemoBubbleSort procedure,
   499-505**
**DemoDynamicArray proce-
   dure, 487-491**
**DemoFatalError procedure,
   681-684**
**DemoForcedError procedure,
   691-697**
**DemoListBox procedure,
   613-615**
**DemoMenu procedure,
   633-635**
**DemoMenuBar procedure,
   629-631**
**DemoMenuSystem procedure,
   641-645**

**DemoResolveError procedure,
   685-687**
**DemoResumeError procedure,
   689-691**
**DemoRetryError procedure,
   687-689**
**DemoStaticArray procedure,
   478-485**
**DemoToolbarPosition
   procedure, 651-653**
**DemoToolbarSystem
   procedure, 657-662**
descending order sorts, 498
**designing function procedures,
   200-203**
DialIt procedure, 786-788
dialog boxes
   Add Watch, 537-538
   Assign Macro, 589
   Calls, 540-541
   custom
      attaching procedures to
         controls, 588-591
      check boxes, 600-604
      controls, 570-574
      creating, 574-575
      displaying, 587-588
      edit boxes, 591-595
      editing controls, 580-582
      group boxes, 595-600
      inserting dialog sheets for,
         575-576
      list boxes, 612-615
      option buttons, 595-600
      placing/setting control
         properties, 576-580
      scrollbars, 604-612
      setting control properties
         interactively, 584-586
      spinner boxes, 604-612
      tab order, 582-584
   Edit Watch, 539
   floating, 604-612
   Format Object, 586
   Function Wizard (Excel),
      198-199

input, canceling, 274-277
Instant Watch, 540
Macro, 18-19
Make Add-In, 821
Menu Editor, 625-626
message, with command
   buttons, 283-288
Object Browser, 32-33,
   94-95, 160-163, 194-197,
   235-238
Open, 441-444
Record New Macro, 11-14
References, 395
runtime error, 51-52,
   314-315, 524-525
Save As, 445-447
Tab Order, 583
dialog sheets
   assigning procedures to dialog
      box controls, 590-591
   inserting, 575-576
DialogSheet object, 216
DialogSheets collection, 233
   Show method, 587-588
DialogSheets method, 223
Dim statement, 75-76, 476-478
   declaring fixed length string
      variables, 87
   declaring variables, 84-85
Dir function, 431, 448-451
directories
   creating, 455-456
   current, changing, 453-454
   deleting, 456-457
   paths, retrieving current,
      452-453
   searching for files, 448-451
   Windows, path name,
      792-793
Directory file attribute, 433
disabling commands, 639
DismissButton property, 586
DisplayArray procedure, 506
DisplayGeneralOptions
   procedure, 812-813
DisplayReport procedure, 714

DisplayTime procedure, 814
division
   integers, 115
   modulo, 116
division operator (/), 115
DLLs (dynamic-link libraries),
   788-793
Do statements
   nesting, 332-334
   testing loop determinants
      (loop invariants), 312-315
Do Until statement, 318-321
Do While statement, 315-318
Do...Loop Until statement,
   323-326
Do...Loop While statement,
   321-323
dot separator (.), 158
   with user-defined data types,
      372-373
Double data type, 63
double-clicking, 813-814
drives, current
   changing, 454-455
   retrieving, 452-453
Drop-Down button (Forms
   toolbar), 577
drop-down list boxes (custom
   dialog boxes), 572
DummyCommand procedure,
   645
dynamic arrays, 474-475
   deleting, 494-496
   redimensioning, 486-492
dynamic data exchange (DDE),
   773-784
dynamic-link libraries (DLLs),
   788-793

E

Edit Box button (Forms
   toolbar), 577
edit boxes
   combo dropdown-edit list
      boxes, 572

combo list-edit boxes, 572
custom dialog boxes, 571,
   591-595
versus TextBox objects, 574
Edit Code button (Forms
   toolbar), 578
Edit menu commands, 28
   source codes in macros, 37-39
Edit Validation property, 584
Edit Watch command (Tools
   menu), 29, 539
editing
   custom dialog-box controls,
      580-582
   text in custom dialog-box
      controls, 582
   watched variables/expressions,
      539
ellipsis (...), 621
embedded objects, 737
   inserting into worksheets
      existing files, 746
      new objects, 744-746
EmbedPaintPicture procedure,
   746
Empty keyword, 353
Empty value (Variant
   variables), 353-355
Enabled property, 573, 623,
   647
   MenuItem object, 639
   ToolbarButton object,
      656-657
enabling commands, 639
End command (Run menu),
   28, 529
End Function statement,
   280-283
End Sub statement, 36,
   280-283
Enter_UtilityCosts procedure,
   375-380
EntireColumn property (Range
   object), 723
EntireRow property (Range
   object), 723

Eqv operators, 127
Erase statement, 494-496
Erl function, 678-679
Err function, 674-677
Error function, 677-678
error handling
    fatal errors, 681-684
    On Error GoTo statement,
      670-671
    resuming program execution,
      671-673
    runtime errors, 674
      forcing, 679-681,
        691-697
      ignoring/skipping,
        689-691
      locations, 678-679
      message text, 677-678
      resolving errors without
        halting, 685-687
      retrying error-causing
        statements, 687-689
      types, 674-677
    strategies, 668-670
    see also defensive
      programming
Error statement, 679-681,
  691-697
error-trapping, 669-670
    On Error GoTo statement,
      670-671
errors
    compile, 522-523
    fatal, 671
    logical, 523
    non-fatal, 671
    runtime, 51-56, 523
    syntax, 48-50, 522
EvalTemperature procedure,
  265-267, 270-273
event handlers, 800
event procedures, 801, 804-805
    OnCalculate property,
      819-820
    OnDoubleClick property,
      813-814

OnEntry property, 816-819
OnKey method, 810-813
OnSheetActivate property,
  805-807
OnSheetDeactivate property,
  807-809
OnTime method, 814-816
OnWindow property,
  809-810
  specifying, 637
event-controlled loops, 312
Excel functions, 157-159
  viewing/inserting, 162-163
Exit Do statement, 326-329
Exit For statement, 326-329
Exit Function statement,
  278-280
Exit Sub statement, 278-280
ExitCommand procedure, 645
Exp function, 148
explicit variable declarations,
  74-76, 81-83
exponentiation (^) operator,
  116
expressions
    assigning to variable with
      specific data type, 111
    calculations, 103
    complex evaluations, 131-134
    data type compatibility,
      104-105
    data type conversions
      automatic, 105-107
      Boolean, 108
      numeric, 108
      string, 108
    date, 103
    evaluation precedence order,
      133-134
    functions in, 139-142
    in values, 102-104
    information about, obtaining,
      340-355
    logical, 104
    numeric, 104
    objects, 104, 224-228

    operators, 103-104
      assignment (=), 109-112
      string concatenation (&),
        106
    strings, 104
    types, 103-104
    watched, 535-540

F

fatal errors, 671
    handling, 681-684
file management, 430-432
FileCopy statement, 431,
  457-459
FileDateTime function, 431,
  463-464
FileLen function, 431, 463-464
files
    attributes, 432-440
    copying, 457-459
    date and time stamps,
      462-463
    deleting, 459-460
    extensions
      .OLB, 756
      .XLA, 821
    inserting into worksheets
      as embedded objects, 746
      as linked objects, 747-748
    lengths, determining,
      463-464
    moving, 460-462
    opening, 441-444
    renaming, 445-447, 460-462
    saving, 445-447
    searching directories for,
      448-451
Find_Type procedure, 346-347
FindFile method, 431
finding
    macros, 32-34
    OLE object classes in Registry
      database, 742-744
FirstColScroll_Change
  procedure, 611

FirstNonBlankCell procedure,
420-423
FirstRowScroll_Change
procedure, 611
Fix function, 148
fixed iteration loops, 296
   For Each...Next, 308-311
   For...Next, 299-308
      nested, 329-332
fixed length strings, variable
length comparison, 119
FlipCase function procedure,
187-190, 192-193, 343-344
floating dialog boxes, 604-612
floating point numbers (data
type), 67
folders (startup), library
workbooks in, 390-394
Font object, 217
For Each...Next statement,
308-311
For...Next statement, 299-308
   nested, 329-332
forcing runtime errors,
679-681, 691-697
Format function, 149
Format menu, Object
command, 586
FormatArialBold12 macro, 16,
35-37
FormatArialBold12 procedure,
350-351
FormatHeading procedure,
329-332
FormatRangeFont procedure,
718-719
formatting
   column headings, 329-332,
      350-351
   text in custom dialog-box
      controls, 582
Forms toolbar, 576-578
Formula property, 219
   Range object, 725-726
FuncDemo procedure, 140-142
Function keyword, 180

function libraries, 386-397
function procedures, 178-179
   arguments
      optional, 187-190
      passing, 190-193
   declaring data types
      for arguments, 186-187
      for results, 184-186
   designing, 200-203
   in VBA, 193-197
   Get_UtilityItem, 375-380
   IsDiskFile, 448-449
   recursion, 203-207
   user-defined functions
      (UDFs), 179
      creating, 183
      in Excel, 198-199
   writing, 180-183
Function Wizard (Excel),
198-199
functions, 138
   arguments, 142-143
      named, 145-147
      passing arrays as, 496-497
      validating, 356-357
   calling, 139
   canceling, 278-280
   Chr, 171-172
   CreateObject, 758-761
   CStr, 139
   CurDir, 431, 452-453
   data conversion, 148-151
   date and time, 151-153
   Dir, 431, 448-451
   Erl, 678-679
   Err, 674-677
   Error, 677-678
   Excel, 157-159
      viewing/inserting,
      162-163
   FileDateTime, 431, 463-464
   FileLen, 431, 463-464
   GetAttr, 431, 435-438
   GetBookName, 250-251,
      259-260, 262-264, 280-283
   GetInteger, 358-361

   GetObject, 761-762
   GetWindowsDirectory DLL,
      792-793
   in assignments and
      expressions, 139-142
   InputBox, 153-154
   inserting, 159-163
   InStr, 168-169
   IsArray, 341
   IsDate, 341, 345-346
   IsEmpty, 341, 354
   IsError, 341
   IsMissing, 341
   IsNull, 341, 355
   IsNumeric, 341, 343-344
   IsObject, 342
   LBound, 493-494
   Left, 169
   Len, 165-166
   LTrim, 164-165
   mathematical, 147-148
   Mid, 170
   MsgBox, 154-155
   Now, 139
   PCase, 305-308
   private, 401-402
   public, 403-404
   recursion, 203-207
   results, 142-143
      ignoring, 143-145
   retaining variable values
      between calls, 362-368
   Right, 169-170
   RTrim, 164-165
   SheetExists, 309-311,
      327-329
   Shell, 768-770
   Sqr, 681
   StrComp, 166-167, 311
   string, 156-157, 163-172
   Trim, 164-165
   TypeName, 139, 342,
      346-351
   UBound, 493-494
   user interaction, 153-155

VarType, 342, 346-347, 351-353
viewing, 159-163
volatile, 203

G

games, Guess The Animal, *see* Guess The Animal application
Get_UtilityItem function procedure, 375-380
GetAttr function, 431, 435-438
GetBookName function, 250-251, 259-260, 262-264, 280-283
GetInput procedure, 322-326
GetInteger function, 358-361
GetObject function, 761-762
GetOpenFilename method, 432, 441-444, 447
GetSaveAsFilename method, 432, 445-447
GetWindowsDirectory DLL function, 792-793
global variables, 398
GoTo statement, 273-277
Group Box button (Forms toolbar), 577
group boxes (custom dialog boxes), 571, 595-600
Guess The Animal application, 904
converting to add-in application, 930-931
creating, 904
modules
AnimalMain, 906-911
AnimalRetrieval, 911-916
Automatic, 923-925
Constants, 905-906
Functions, 922-923
LearnNewAnimals, 916-920
ListAnimals, 920-921

playing, 931-933
running, 929-930

H

HappyButton_Click procedure, 661
headings (columns), formatting, 329-332, 350-351
Height property (OLEObject object), 750
HelloDave procedure, 79-80, 82
HelloMacro procedure, 43-45, 47-48, 75-80, 82, 86-87
HelpButton property, 586
Hex function, 149
Hidden file attribute, 434
Hide command (Window menu), 393
hiding toolbars, 650-653
hints about commands, displaying in status bar, 638
Hour function, 152

I

identifiers, 71-73
If...Then statement, 258-260
nested, 264-267
If...Then...Else statement, 261-264
nested, 264-267
If...Then...ElseIf statement, 267-268
ignoring results of functions, 143-145
Immediate pane (Debug window), 542-545
Imp operator, truth table, 128
implicit variable declaration, 73-75
prohibition, 82

indefinite loops, 296
testing
conditions after execution, 321-326
conditions before execution, 315-321
loop determinants (loop invariants), 312-315
types, 311-312
indenting, automatic, 46
Index property, 219
InfoButton_Click procedure, 662
input (user)
in message dialog boxes with command buttons, 283-288
invoice numbers, entering, 332-334
obtaining through interactive procedures, 95-98
testing indefinite-loop conditions after execution, 322-326
validating, 357-362
input dialog boxes, canceling, 274-277
InputBox function, 95, 153-154
Insert menu, Macro command
Dialog, 575
Module, 41-42
Insert Module button (Visual Basic toolbar), 31
InsertAndEditWordDoc procedure, 755
InsertNewWordArt procedure, 744-745
InstallBudgetTools procedure, 823
Installed property (AddIn object), 822
Instant Watch button (Visual Basic toolbar), 31, 540
Instant Watch command (Tools menu), 29, 540
InStr function, 156, 168-169

Int function, 148
Integer data type, 63
　user input, validating,
　　358-361
integer division operator (/),
115
interactive procedures, 95-98
interrupting
　code execution, 528
　executing macros/procedures,
　　314-315
invoice numbers, entering,
332-334
InvoiceDate procedure,
345-346
Is keyword, 270
Is operator, 226
　object type expression
　　comparison, 123
IsArray function, 341
IsDate function, 341, 345-346
IsDiskFile function procedure,
448-449
IsEmpty function, 341, 354
IsError function, 341
IsMissing function, 341
IsNull function, 341, 355
IsNumeric function, 341,
343-344
IsObject function, 342
iterations of loops, 296

J–K

Justify method, 223

keyboard shortcuts
　assigning macros, 13
　custom, installing in VBA
　　code, 810-813
　Debug Window (Ctrl+G),
　　537
　Instant Watch (Shift+F9),
　　540
　Interrupt (Esc or Ctrl+Break),
　　314

Resume Macro (F5), 529
Step Into (F8), 528, 532
Step Over (Shift+F8), 534
Toggle Breakpoint (F9), 527
keystrokes
　sending to other applications,
　　785-788
　trapping, 810-813
keywords
　Application, 158
　As, 84-85
　Empty, 353
　Function, 180
　Is, 270
　Next, 299, 302
　Null, 353
　Preserve, 486
　Private, 401-402
　Public, 403-404
　Set, 225
　Static, 363-368
　Step, 305
Kill statement, 432, 459-460

L

Label button (Forms toolbar),
577
labels
　custom dialog boxes, 571
　scrollbars/spinner boxes,
　　dynamically updating,
　　604-612
LastColScroll_Change
procedure, 611
LastRowScroll_Change
procedure, 611
LaunchWordPad procedure,
793
LBound function, 493-494
LCase function, 156
leading space characters,
deleting, 164-165
Left function, 156, 169

Left property (OLEObject
object), 750
Len function, 156, 165-166
libraries
　DLLs (dynamic-link
　　libraries), 788-793
　procedures/functions,
　　386-397
Like operator, 121
line continuation symbol, 37
linear searches of arrays,
506-509
LinearSearch procedure,
506-509
linked objects, 737
　inserting existing files into
　　worksheets, 747-748
LinkPaintPicture procedure,
747-748
List Box button (Forms
toolbar), 577
list boxes
　combo dropdown-edit, 572
　combo list-edit boxes, 572
　custom dialog boxes, 572,
　　612-615
　drop-down, 572
List property, 573
ListFileAttr procedure,
436-438
listings
　2.1. The FormatArialBold12
　　macro, 35
　2.2. The NewFile macro, 35
　2.3. Adding a comment to
　　the NewFile macro, 38
　2.4. The HelloMacro
　　procedure, 43
　2.5. Displaying a customized
　　title bar with MsgBox, 47
　2.6. The NewBook macro
　　creates a new workbook file,
　　53
　2.7. The NewBook macro
　　with recorded code inserted
　　directly, 54-55

3.1. The HelloMacro procedure, with an explicit variable declaration, 75

3.2. Procedure-level scope, 77

3.3. Module-level variable scope, 79

3.4. Combined module-level and procedure-level scope, 80

3.5. The Option Explicit module command, 82

3.6. Explicit and Implicit type declaration, 86

3.7. Using constants: Computing the area of a circle, 90

3.8. Getting input with the InputBox statement, 96

4.1. String concatenation, 129-136

5.1. Using functions, 140

5.2. Demonstration of RTrim, LTrim, and Trim functions, 164

5.3. Demonstration of StrComp function, 167

5.4. Demonstration of InStr function, 168-175

6.1. A simple function procedure: SLen, 182

6.2. Specifying the data type of the Slen function result, 185

6.3. Specifying the data type of the Slen function argument, 186

6.4. The FlipCase function: optional arguments, 187-188

6.5. Test procedure to demonstrate FlipCase function's side effects, 191

6.6. A volatile user-defined function, 203

6.7. The power function: a recursive example, 204

7.1. The Backup_ActiveBook procedure, 226

7.2. Adding With...End With to the Backup_ActiveBook procedure, 228-229

8.1. GetBookName function, 259

8.2. Block If...Then...Else statement, 263

8.3. Nested If...Then...Else statements, 265-271

8.4. Select Case statement, 271

8.5. GoTo statement, 274-275

8.6. Ending a procedure early with Exit Sub, 278-279

8.7. Ending program execution with End, 281-282

8.8. Using MsgBox and the Buttons argument to get user input, 283-284

9.1. A demonstration of the For...Next loop, counting up, 300

9.2. Making a For...Next loop that counts down, 303

9.3. Using For...Next to perform an action with every character in a string, 306

9.4. Using For Each...Next, 309

9.5. Demonstrating the Do While loop, 316-317

9.6. Demonstrating the Do Until loop, 319

9.7. A prototype data-entry loop that uses Do...Loop While, 322

9.8. A smarter version of GetInput, using a Do...Loop Until loop, 324-325

9.9. Using Exit For to end a loop early, 327

9.10. Nested For...Next loops, 330

9.11. Nested Do loops, 332-333

10.1. Verifying an optional argument's data type, 343

10.2. Verifying the data type of a user's input, 345

10.3. Using a test procedure to display the data type of an expression result, 347

10.4. A demonstration of the results that TypeName returns under different circumstances, 349

10.5. Using the TypeName function to prevent a runtime error, 350-351

10.6. Checking user input to ensure valid data values, 358-359

10.7. Using Static variables, 363-365

10.8. Defining, creating, and using user-defined types, 375-377

11.1. Using Visual Basic for Applications to display the Excel startup directory path, 391

11.2. Using Visual Basic for Applications to display the Excel alternate startup directory, 392

11.3. Changing the Excel alternate startup folder with Visual Basic for Applications, 393

11.4. Using a procedure's arguments to send information to the procedure, 417-419

11.5. Using a procedure's arguments to return values from the procedure, 420-421

listings

12.1. Using the GetAttr function and interpreting its result, 435-436

12.2. Using the SetAttr statement to change a file's attributes, 439

12.3. Using GetOpenFilename to get a filename from your procedure's user, 442

12.4. Using GetSaveAsFilename to get a filename from your procedure's user, 445-446

12.5. Finding a single file using Dir, 448

12.6. Finding several files using Dir, 449-450

12.7. Using the CurDir function to obtain the current directory and drive, 452

12.8 shows an example using the ChDir statement, 453

12.9. Using ChDrive to change the current disk drive, 454-455

12.10. Using MkDir to create a new disk directory, 456

12.11. Using RmDir to remove a directory, 456-457

12.12. A procedure that uses the FileCopy statement, 458

12.13. Using Kill to delete files, 459

12.14. Using Name to rename or move files, 461

12.15. Using the FileDateTime and FileLen functions, 463-464

13.1. The DemoStaticArray procedure declares and uses a static numeric array, 479-482

13.2. The DemoDynamicArray procedure declares and uses a dynamic array, 487-490

13.3. The DemoBubbleSort procedure visually demonstrates the bubble-sort technique for sorting arrays, 499-501

13.4. The Sorter procedure sorts an array using the bubble-sort method and a couple of general-purpose sorting procedures, 503-505

13.5. The macro MacroSearch1 performs a visual demonstration of the linear search in an array, 507-508

13.6. The BinarySearch procedure creates a visual demonstration of a binary search on an array, 511-513

14.1. Some code to demonstrate the VBA Debugger, 530-531

14.2. The DebugDemo2 procedure, used to illustrate the use of Debug.Print, 543-545

15.1. Using Edit Box Controls in a Custom Dialog Box, 593-594

15.2. Using Option Button Controls, 596-599

15.3. Using Check Box Controls, 601-603

15.4. Using Scrollbar and Spinner Controls in a Floating Dialog Box, 606-609

15.5. Using a List Box Control, 613

16.1. The DemoMenuBar procedure displays and then removes a blank new custom menu bar, 630

16.2. The DemoMenu procedure displays and then removes a custom menu bar with several menus, 634-635

16.3. The DemoMenuSystem procedure produces a minimally working menu, 642-643

16.4. The DemoToolbarPosition procedure changes the visibility and position of the Drawing toolbar, 651-652

16.5. Creating a working custom toolbar, 658-660

17.1. The DemoFatalError procedure uses the Err and Erl functions, 682-683

17.2. The DemoResolveError procedure uses the Resume Next statement, 685-686

17.3. The DemoRetryError procedure uses the Resume 0 statement to retry the error-causing statement, 687-688

17.4. The DemoResumeError procedure uses the Resume label statement, 689-690

17.5. The DemoForcedError procedure uses the Error statement to force a runtime error, 691-694

18.1. Using the Workbooks method to return a workbook, 705

18.2. Using the Open method to open a workbook, 706

18.3. Using the Add method to create a new workbook, 707

18.4. Using the Activate method to switch to a workbook, 708

18.5. Using the Save and SaveCopyAs methods, 710

18.6. Using the Close method, 711

18.7. Using the Worksheets method to return a worksheet, 713

18.8. Using the Activate method to switch to a worksheet, 714

18.9. Using the Add method to create a new worksheet, 715

18.10. Using the Move method to move a worksheet, 716

18.11. Using the Delete method to delete a worksheet, 717

18.12. Using the Range method to work with a range, 718-719

18.13. Using a range name in the Range method, 719

18.14. Using the Cells method to return a cell, 721

18.15. Using the Offset method to return a range, 722

18.16. Using the Select method to select a range, 724

18.17. Using the Value and Formula methods to enter data, 725

18.18. Naming a range using the Names object's Add method, 727

18.19. Using the Cut, Copy, and Clear methods, 728-729

19.1. Using the Add method to embed a new object in a worksheet, 744-745

19.2. Using the Add method to embed an existing file in a worksheet, 746

19.3. Using the Add method to insert an existing file as a linked object, 747

19.4. A procedure that uses several OLEObject properties, 751

19.5. Using the Update method to update an OLE object, 753

19.6. Using the Verb method to edit an OLE object, 755

19.7. Referring to OLE automation objects directly, 757-758

19.8. Using CreateObject to create an OLE automation object, 759-760

20.1. Using the Shell function to start an application, 769

20.2. Using the AppActivate statement to switch to a running application, 771-772

20.3. Using the DDEInitiate method to open a DDE channel, 776-777

20.4. Using DDEExecute to control a server application, 778-779

20.5. Using DDERequest to retrieve data from an application, 781

20.6. Using DDEPoke to send data to an application, 783-784

20.7. Controlling an application using the SendKeys statement, 786-787

20.8. Using the MessageBeep DLL procedure, 791

20.9. Using the GetWindowsDirectory DLL function, 792-793

21.1. Using the Auto_Open procedure, 802

21.2. Using the Auto_Close procedure, 804

21.3. Using the OnSheetActivate property, 806

21.4. Using the OnSheetDeactivate property, 807-808

21.5. Using the OnWindow property, 810

21.6. Using the OnKey method, 812-813

21.7. Using the OnDoubleClick property, 814

21.8. Using the OnTime method, 815-816

21.9. Using the OnEntry property, 817-818

21.10. Using the OnCalculate property, 819-820

21.11. Working with add-in applications, 823

B.1. The Constants module, 905-906

B.2. The AnimalMain module, 906-909

B.3. The AnimalRetrieval Module, 911-915

B.4. The LearnNewAnimals module, 916-919

B.5. The ListAnimals module, 920-921

B.6. The Functions module, 922-923

B.7. The Automatic module, 923-924

R1.1. Week 1 review listing, 246-247

R2.1. The OpenNewBook program's main module and procedure, 550-552

R2.2. The OpenNewBook program's supporting procedures module, 554-558

listings

R2.3. The OpenNewBook program's supporting functions module, 561-563

R3.1. The Utilities module—a library of utility procedures, 830-834

R3.2. The Automatic Procedures module, 835-837

literal constants
date, 91-92
macros, 87-88
numeric, 91-92

LoadExcelReadMe procedure, 771-773

local scope, 398

Log function, 148

logical
errors, 523
expressions, 104
operators, 124
values (data types), 68

Long data type, 63

loop determinants (loop invariants), 296
testing, 312-315

looping structures, 296-298
fixed iteration loops
For Each...Next, 308-311
For...Next, 299-308
indefinite loops
testing conditions after execution, 321-326
testing conditions before execution, 315-321
testing loop determinants (loop invariants), 312-315
types, 311-312
nesting, 329-334
terminating early, 326-329

LTrim function, 156, 164-165

M

Macro command
Insert menu
Dialog, 575
Module, 41-42
Tools menu, 18-19

macro declaration line, 36

macro recorder, 5
compared to VBA, 7-9

macros, 4-5
assigning to Tools menu, 13
assigning to shortcut keys, 13
components, 34-37
copying, 39-40
displaying messages to user, 46-48
End Sub keywords, 36
finding, 32-34
FormatArialBold12, 16
inserting new module sheet into workbook, 41-42
interrupting execution, 314-315
literal constants, 87-88
in strings, 90-91
modules, 24-25
moving/copying, 40-41
moving, 39-40
naming, 12-14
NewBook, recording new actions to, 54
preparing starting conditions, 10
printing, 55-56
recorded macro limitations, 8
recording, 11
actions to existing macro, 52-56
ending recording session, 16
with VBA, 9
runtime errors, 51-56
selecting existing module sheets, 42

source code, 17-18
editing, 37-39
security, 41
writing source code text, 43-46
syntax errors, 48-50
text color, 37
using recorded macros, 18-19
while editing, 46
VBA statements, 36
see also procedures

Make Add-In command (Tools menu), 29, 821

Make_LabeledPieChart procedure, 417-420

MakeInvoices procedure, 332-334

MakeSalesRpt_Chart procedure, 274-280, 363-368, 417-420

mathematical functions, 147-148

menu bars, 621
adding menus, 631-635
built-in, restoring, 629
creating, 627, 629-631
custom, creating, 624
deleting, 628-631
deleting menus, 633-635
displaying, 627-631

Menu Editor, 625-626

Menu Editor button (Visual Basic toolbar), 31, 625

Menu Editor command (Tools menu), 29, 625

menu items, *see* commands

Menu object, 622

menu system, creating, 641-645

MenuBar object, 622
Reset method, 629

MenuBars collection, 622
Activate method, 627-628
Add method, 627
Delete method, 628-629

MenuItem object, 622

MenuItems collection, 622
Add method, 636-637
AddMenu method, 640-641
Caption property, 640
Checked property, 640
Delete method, 638-639
Enabled property, 639
OnAction property, 637
StatusBar property, 638
menus, 621
adding commands, 636-637
adding to menu bars, 631-635
built-in (Excel), 624
commands, 25-32
components, 620-621
deleting commands, 638-639
deleting from menu bars, 633-635
objects, 621-622
properties/methods, 622-623
Menus collection, 622
Add method, 632-633
Delete method, 633
message dialog boxes with command buttons, 283-288
MessageBeep DLL procedure, 790-792
messages (runtime errors), 677-678
methods
Activate, 622
MenuBar object, 627-628
Workbook object, 708-709
Worksheet object, 714
Add, 622, 647
AddIns collection, 822
MenuBars collection, 627
MenuItems collection, 636-637
Menus collection, 632-633
Names collection, 726-727

OLEObjects collection, 739-740, 744-748
ToolbarButtons collection, 655-656
Toolbars collection, 649
Workbooks collection, 707
Worksheets collection, 715
AddIns, 822
AddMenu, 623
MenuItems collection, 640-641
Cells (Worksheet/Range objects), 720-721
Clear (Range object), 728-730
Close (Workbook object/Workbooks collection), 711-712
Columns (Range object), 723
Copy
Range object, 728-730
Worksheet object, 716-717
Cut (Range object), 728-730
DDEExecute, 778-780
DDEInitiate, 774-777
DDEPoke, 782-784
DDERequest, 780-782
DDETerminate, 777
Delete, 623, 647
Menu object, 633
MenuBar object, 628-629
MenuItem object, 638-639
Toolbar object, 654
ToolbarButton object, 656
Worksheet object, 717-718
FindFile, 431
GetOpenFilename, 432, 441-444, 447
GetSaveAsFilename, 432, 445-447

Move (Worksheet object), 716-717
objects, 214-215, 220-223
browsing, 235-238
referring to, 228-230
Offset (Range object), 722-723
OLE objects, 752-755
OnKey, 810-813
OnTime, 814-816
Open (Workbooks collection), 705-706
Print (Debug), 542-545
Range (Worksheet object), 718-720
Reset, 647
MenuBar object, 629
Toolbar object, 654
Rows (Range object), 723
Save (Workbook object), 709-711
SaveCopyAs (Workbook object), 709-711
Select (Range object), 724
Show (DialogSheets collection), 587-588
Workbooks (Application object), 704
Worksheets (Workbook object), 712-713
Mid function, 156, 170
Minute function, 152
MkDir statement, 432, 455-456
modes, break (Debugger), 523-529
module level scopes, 78-79
Module object, 217
module qualifiers, 406-407
modules, 24-25
copying, 40-41
cross-module programming, scope, 397-407
inserting new sheet in workbook, 41-42
moving, 40-41

moving/copying macros,
39-40
organizing programming
code, 413-414
printing sheets, 55-56
procedure/function libraries,
386-397
selecting existing sheets, 42
sheets, 24
Modules collection, 233
modulo divisions, 116
Month function, 152
**Move method (Worksheet
object), 716-717**
moving
custom dialog-box controls,
581
files, 460-462
worksheets, 716-717
MsgBox function, 154-155
**MsgBox statement, 46-48,
283-288**
**multi-dimensional arrays,
472-474**
**multiple statements on single
lines of code, 258-259**
**multiplication operator (*),
114**

N

Name property, 219, 647
OLEObject object, 749
Worksheet object, 715-716
Name statement, 432, 460-462
named
arguments (functions),
145-147
constants, 88
**named-argument assignment
operator (:=), 146**
names
commands, renaming, 640
custom dialog-box controls,
renaming, 582

data types of variables/
expressions, determining,
347-351
files, renaming, 445-447,
460-462
ranges, 726-727
variables, 71-73
workbooks, 549-565
worksheets, renaming,
715-716
Names.Add method, 726-727
nested
If...Then statement, 264-267
If...Then...Else statement,
264-267
looping structures, 329-334
NewBook macro, 53-55
NewFile macro, 35-39
**NewFile procedure, 248-250,
280-283**
Next keyword, 299, 302
non-fatal errors, 671
Normal file attribute, 434
Not operator, 126-127
Now function, 139, 151
Null keyword, 353
**Null value (Variant variables),
354-355**
numeric
data types, 66-68
conversions, 107-108
floating point numbers,
67
integers, 66-67
testing for corrrect type of
data, 343-344
expressions, 104
literal constants, 91-92

O

Object Browser
browsing objects, methods,
and properties, 235-238

finding/displaying macros,
32-34
function procedures, 194-197
locating predefined constants,
94-95
viewing/inserting functions,
159-163
**Object Browser button (Visual
Basic toolbar), 31**
**Object Browser command
(View menu), 28**
**Object command (Format
menu), 586**
Object data type, 63
object expressions, 104
**Object property (OLEObject
object), 750**
objects, 212-213
browsing, 235-238
collections, 230-235
in expressions and assignments, 224-228
menus, 621-622
methods, 214-215, 220-223,
228-230
properties, 213-214,
217-220, 228-230
toolbars, 646
uses, 215-217
variables, declaring, 224
Oct function, 149
**Offset method (Range object),
722-723**
.OLB file extension, 756
**OLE (object linking and
embedding)**
embedded objects
inserting existing files into
worksheets, 746
inserting new objects into
worksheets, 744-746
history, 736-738
linked objects, inserting
existing files into
worksheets, 747-748

private

SAMS
PUBLISHING
Sams
Learning
Center

OLE objects
  determining class types, 741-744
  inserting in sheets, 739-740
  methods, 752-755
  properties, 749-751
  referring to, 748-749
  VBA support, 739
OLE automation, 756
  accessing OLE automation objects, 756-757
    directly, 757-758
    existing objects, 761-762
  creating OLE automation objects, 758-761
OLEObjectProperties procedure, 751
OLEObjects.Add method, 739-740, 744-748
OLEType property (OLEObject object), 750
On Error GoTo statement, 670-671
OnAction property, 573, 623, 647
  MenuItem object, 637
  OLEObject object, 750
OnCalculate property, 819-820
OnDoubleClick property, 813-814
OnEntry property, 816-819
OnKey method, 810-813
OnSheetActivate property, 805-807
OnSheetDeactivate property, 807-809
OnTime method, 814-816
OnWindow property, 809-810
OOP (object-oriented programming), 212
Open dialog box, 441-444
Open method (Workbooks collection), 705-706
Open2DataEntry procedure, 129, 442-444

OpenHailingFrequencies procedure, 776-777
opening
  files, 441-444
  workbooks, 705-706
    Auto_Open procedure, 801-803
OpenNewBook program, 549-565
OpenWorkbook procedure, 706
operands, *see* **operators**
operators
  And, 125-126
  arithmetic, 112-116
  assignment
    =, 109-112
    := (named-argument), 146
  automatic data conversion, 105-107
  comparison, 116-119
  division (/), 115
  Eqv, 127
  exponentiation (^), 116
  Imp, 128
  in expressions, 103-104
  integer division (/), 115
  Is, 123, 226
  Like, 121
  logical, 124
  modulo division, 116
  multiplication (*), 114
  Not, 126-127
  Or, 126, 440
  precedence, 131-134
  string concatenation, 128, 130-131
  subtraction (-), 113-114
  Xor, 127
Option Base statement, 475-476
Option Button button (Forms toolbar), 577
option buttons (custom dialog boxes), 571, 595-600

Option Compare statement, 120
Option Explicit statement, 82-83
Option Private Module statement, 400-401
optional arguments (function procedures), 187-190
Or operator, 126, 440
outlines, top-down design, 410-413

P–Q

passing
  arguments (function procedures), 190-193
  arrays as arguments to procedures/functions, 496-497
pasting custom dialog-box controls, 581-582
Path property, 219
paths (directories)
  retrieving current, 452-453
  Windows directory path name, 792-793
pattern-matching for Like operators, 121
PCase function, 305-308
PcntProfit function procedure, 203
persistence (variables), 81
PlayWelcomeMessage procedure, 719
plus (+) string concatenation operator, 130-131
Position property, 647
  Toolbar object, 650-653
Power function procedure, 204-206
Preserve keyword, 486
printing macros, 55-56
private
  modules, 399-401

scope, 397-399
variables/constants/functions/
    procedures/user-defined
    data types, 401-402
Private keyword, 401-402
**Procedure Definition com-
    mand (View menu), 28**
procedure level scope, 77-78
procedure libraries, 386-397
procedures
    ActivateNotepad, 772-773
    ActivateTest, 708-709
    AnotherMessage, 80
    argument lists, 414-423
    attaching to custom dialog-
        box controls, 588-591
    Auto_Close, 803-804,
        807-809
    Auto_Open, 801-803,
        805-807
    AutomateWordObject,
        757-758
    automatic, 800-801, 835-837
    Backup_ActiveBook,
        226-230
    BackUpToFloppy, 710
    BeepTest, 791
    BellButton_Click, 662
    BinarySearch, 510-515
    BubbleSortAscending, 505
    BubbleSortDescending, 505
    Calc_CircleArea, 90, 96-98
    calling other procedures,
        408-410
    CancelDemo, 485
    canceling, 278-280
    CheckMargin, 819-820
    CheckToggle, 645
    CityList_Change, 615
    CloseAll, 711-712
    Convert2Template, 445-447
    CopyFiles, 458
    CopyToTempSheet, 728-729
    Count_OddNums, 316-318
    CreateAccessDBObject,
        759-761

CreateLoanPmtCalculator,
    725-726
CreateMonthlyReport, 707
CreateTempWorksheet, 715
CreateWordLink, 778-780
CreateWorksheetAtEnd, 716
DataEntryHandler, 806-807
DebugDemo1, 530-534
DebugDemo2, 543-545
DeleteCustMenu, 628-629
DeleteTemporarySheets,
    717-718
DelFiles, 459-460
DelProtectFile, 439-440
Demo_ChDir, 453-454
Demo_ChDrive, 454-455
Demo_ForNext, 300-302
Demo_ForNextDown,
    302-305
Demo_InStr, 168-169
Demo_MkDir, 456
Demo_MsgBoxFunction,
    283-288
Demo_RmDir, 456-457
Demo_StrComp, 167
Demo_TypeName, 349-350
DemoBubbleSort, 499-503
DemoDynamicArray,
    487-491
DemoFatalError, 681-684
DemoForcedError, 691-697
DemoListBox, 613-615
DemoMenu, 633-635
DemoMenuBar, 629-631
DemoMenuSystem, 641-645
DemoResolveError, 685-687
DemoResumeError, 689-691
DemoRetryError, 687-689
DemoStaticArray, 478-485
DemoToolbarPosition,
    651-653
DemoToolbarSystem,
    657-662
DialIt, 786-788
DisplayArray, 506

DisplayGeneralOptions,
    812-813
displaying messages to user,
    46-48
DisplayReport, 714
DisplayTime, 814
DLL (dynamic-link library)
    declaring, 789
    MessageBeep, 790-792
DummyCommand, 645
EmbedPaintPicture, 746
Enter_UtilityCosts, 375-380
environments, validating,
    356-357
EvalTemperature, 265-267,
    270-273
event procedures, 801,
    804-805
    OnCalculate property,
        819-820
    OnDoubleClick property,
        813-814
    OnEntry property,
        816-819
    OnKey method, 810-813
    OnSheetActivate
        property, 805-807
    OnSheetDeactivate
        property, 807-809
    OnTime method,
        814-816
    OnWindow property,
        809-810
    specifying, 637
execution time, specifying,
    814-816
ExitCommand, 645
Find_Type, 346-347
FirstColScroll_Change, 611
FirstNonBlankCell, 420-423
FirstRowScroll_Change, 611
FormatArialBold12, 350-351
FormatHeading, 329-332
FormatRangeFont, 718-719
FuncDemo, 140-142

function procedures, 178-179
  declaring data types for
    arguments, 186-187
  declaring data types for
    results, 184-186
  designing, 200-203
  in VBA, 193-197
  optional arguments,
    187-190
  passing arguments,
    190-193
  user-defined (UDFs),
    179, 183
  user-defined functions in
    Excel, 198-199
  writing, 180-183
GetInput, 322-326
HappyButton_Click, 661
HelloDave, 79-80, 82
HelloMacro, 43-45, 47-48,
  75-80, 82, 86-87
InfoButton_Click, 662
InsertAndEditWordDoc, 755
InsertNewWordArt, 744-745
InstallBudgetTools, 823
interactive, 95-98
interrupting execution,
  314-315
InvoiceDate, 345-346
LastColScroll_Change, 611
LastRowScroll_Change, 611
LaunchWordPad, 793
LinearSearch, 506-509
LinkPaintPicture, 747-748
ListFileAttr, 436-438
LoadExcelReadMe, 771-773
Make_LabeledPieChart,
  417-420
MakeInvoices, 332-334
MakeSalesRpt_Chart,
  274-280, 363-368, 417-420
NewFile, 248-250, 280-283
OLEObjectProperties, 751
Open2DataEntry, 129,
  442-444

OpenHailingFrequencies,
  776-777
OpenWorkbook, 706
passing arrays as arguments,
  496-497
PlayWelcomeMessage, 719
private, 401-402
public, 403-404
RangeErrorMsg, 491
recording actions to existing
  procedure, 52-56
recursion, 203-207
RemindMe, 816
RemoveBudgetTools, 823
RemoveDemoToolbar, 662
RenameOrMoveFile,
  461-462
RequestWordData, 781-782
ResetBudgetSheet, 808-809
ResetDataEntryHandler,
  818-819
ResetDoubleClick, 814
ResetShortcutKeys, 813
retaining variable values
  between calls, 362-368
RowSorter1, 591-595
RowSorter2, 595-600
RowSorter3, 600-604
RowSortMain, 606-612
SadButton_Click, 661-662
SelectData, 722-723
SendDataToWord, 783-784
SetCalculateHandler,
  819-820
SetDataEntryHandler,
  817-819
SetDoubleClick, 814
SetReminder, 815-816
SetShortcutKeys, 812-813
SetUpBudgetSheet, 807-809
SetWindowHandler, 810
SetWorkbookProtection, 705
SetWorksheetProtection, 713
ShowCompare, 503
ShowCurDriveDir, 452-453

ShowFileAttr, 435-438
ShowFileDateSize, 463-464
ShowFiles, 449-451
SortButton_Click, 610
SortColSpinner_Change, 611
Sorter, 503-506
SortRows, 595
SortRowsDown, 599
SortRowsUp, 599
SortStringList, 695-697
StartControlPanel, 769-770
stepping over, 534-535
Stop_AtEvenNums, 319-321
Swap, 503
Test_DelProtectFile, 439-440
Test_FlipCase, 191-192
Test_GetBookName, 251
ToggleGridlines, 812-813
top-down design, 410-413
tracing calls, 540-541
TrimDemo, 164-165
UpdateAllObjects, 753-756
using while editing, 46
VerifyData, 817-819
Wait, 631
WaitAWhile, 503
WindowHandler, 810
WriteNewData, 721, 727
  see also macros

programs, *see* **applications**
properties
  AltStartupPath (Application
    object), 392-393
  BuiltIn, 623, 647
  Button object, 585-586
  Caption, 623
    MenuItem object, 640
  Checked, 623
    MenuItem object, 640
  Count, 623
  CurrentRegion (Range
    object), 723
  dialog box controls, 573-574
    setting, 576-580
    setting interactively,
      584-586

Enabled, 623, 647
    MenuItem object, 639
    ToolbarButton object,
        656-657
EntireColumn (Range
    object), 723
EntireRow (Range object),
    723
Formula (Range object),
    725-726
Installed (AddIn object), 822
Name, 647
    Worksheet object,
        715-716
objects, 213-214, 217-220
    browsing, 235-238
    referring to, 228-230
OLE objects, 749-751
OnAction, 623, 647
    MenuItem object, 637
OnCalculate, 819-820
OnDoubleClick, 813-814
OnEntry, 816-819
OnSheetActivate, 805-807
OnSheetDeactivate, 807-809
OnWindow, 809-810
Position, 647
    Toolbar object, 650-653
Pushed, 647
    ToolbarButton object,
        656-657
StatusBar, 623, 647
    MenuItem object, 638
Value (Range object),
    725-726
Visible, 647
    Toolbar object, 650-653
**Protection command (Tools
    menu), 41**
    Protect Workbook, 394
public
    scope, 397-399
    variables/constants/functions/
        procedures/user-defined
        data types, 403-404
Public keyword, 403-404

Pushed property, 647
    ToolbarButton object,
        656-657

R

**Range method (Worksheet
    object), 718-720**
Range object, 217
    Cells method, 720-721
    Clear method, 728-730
    Columns method, 723
    Copy method, 728-730
    CurrentRegion property, 723
    Cut method, 728-730
    EntireColumn property, 723
    EntireRow property, 723
    Formula property, 725-726
    Offset method, 722-723
    Rows method, 723
    Select method, 724
    Value property, 725-726
RangeErrorMsg procedure, 491
ranges
    cutting/copying/clearing data,
        727-730
    entering data, 724-726
    names, 726-727
    returning, 718-723
    selecting, 724
Read-Only file attribute, 434
real numbers, 67
**recalculating worksheets,
    819-820**
**Record Macro button (Visual
    Basic toolbar), 11, 31**
**Record Macro command
    (Tools menu), Record New
    Macro, 11-14**
recorded macros
    components, 34-37
    finding, 32-34
recorders (macro), 5
    compared to VBA, 7
    limitations, 8

recursion, 203-207
ReDim statement, 486-492
references
    circular, 404-405
    workbooks, 394-397
**References command (Tools
    menu), 29, 395**
Registry database, 741-744
RemindMe procedure, 816
**RemoveBudgetTools proce-
    dure, 823**
**RemoveDemoToolbar
    procedure, 662**
**RenameOrMoveFile procedure,
    461-462**
renaming
    commands, 640
    custom dialog-box controls,
        582
    files, 445-447, 460-462
    worksheets, 715-716
**repeating actions on every
    character in strings, 305-308**
**RequestWordData procedure,
    781-782**
required arguments, 187
**Reset command (Run menu),
    28**
Reset method, 647
    MenuBar object, 629
    Toolbar object, 654
**ResetBudgetSheet procedure,
    808-809**
**ResetDataEntryHandler
    procedure, 818-819**
**ResetDoubleClick procedure,
    814**
**ResetShortcutKeys procedure,
    813**
**resizing custom dialog-box
    controls, 581**
restoring
    built-in menu bars, 629
    built-in toolbars, 654

results
    of function procedures,
        declaring data types for,
        184-186
    of functions, 142-145
Resume 0 statement, 687-689
**Resume label statement,
    689-691**
**Resume Macro button (Visual
    Basic toolbar), 31, 529**
**Resume Next statement,
    685-687**
Resume statement, 671-673
RGB function, 149
Right function, 156, 169-170
**RmDir statement, 432,
    456-457**
Rnd function, 148
rows, sorting, 591-604
**Rows method (Range object),
    723**
**RowSorter1 procedure,
    591-595**
**RowSorter2 procedure,
    595-600**
**RowSorter3 procedure,
    600-604**
**RowSortMain procedure,
    606-612**
RTrim function, 156, 164-165
**Run Dialog button (Forms
    toolbar), 578**
**Run Macro button (Visual
    Basic toolbar), 31**
Run menu commands, 28-29
    Clear All Breakpoints, 527
    Continue, 529
    End, 529
    Step Into, 528-534
    Step Over, 534-535
    Toggle Breakpoint, 527
Run method, 223
runtime error codes
    trappable, 675-677
    user-defined, 679-681

**runtime error dialog boxes,
    51-52, 314-315**
    entering break mode from,
        524-525
runtime errors, 51-56, 523
    forcing, 679-681, 691-697
    handling, 674
        ignoring/skipping,
            689-691
        locations, 678-679
        message text, 677-678
        types, 674-677

S

**SadButton_Click procedure,
    661-662**
Save As dialog box, 445-447
Save method, 223
    Workbook object, 709-711
SaveAs method, 223
**SaveCopyAs method (Work-
    book object), 709-711**
Saved property, 219
saving
    files, 445-447
    workbooks, 709-711
scientific notation, 64-65
scope
    cross-module programming,
        397-407
    duplicate name variables, 79
    module level, 78-79
    named constant declaration,
        89-90
    procedure level, 77-78
**Scroll Bar button (Forms
    toolbar), 577**
**scrollbars (custom dialog
    boxes), 572, 604-612**
searching
    arrays
        binary searches, 506,
            510-515
        linear searches, 506-509
    directories for files, 448-451

Second function, 152
Select Case statement, 268-273
Select method, 223
    Range object, 724
SelectData procedure, 722-723
Selected property, 573
selecting
    cells/ranges, 724
    custom dialog-box controls,
        581
Selection property, 219
**SendDataToWord procedure,
    783-784**
**sending keystrokes to other
    applications, 785-788**
SendKeys method, 223
SendKeys statement, 785-788
servers
    DDE
        controlling, 778-780
        establishing channels with
            clients, 774-777
        exchanging data with,
            780-784
    OLE, 737
Set keyword, 225
**SetAttr statement, 432,
    438-440**
**SetCalculateHandler proce-
    dure, 819-820**
**SetDataEntryHandler proce-
    dure, 817-819**
**SetDoubleClick procedure,
    814**
**SetReminder procedure,
    815-816**
**SetShortcutKeys procedure,
    812-813**
**SetUpBudgetSheet procedure,
    807-809**
**SetWindowHandler procedure,
    810**
**SetWorkbookProtection
    procedure, 705**
**SetWorksheetProtection
    procedure, 713**

Sgn function, 148
Shadow property (OLEObject object), 750
SheetExists function, 309-311, 327-329
sheets
    determining existence, 309-311, 327-329
    dialog
        assigning procedures to dialog box controls, 590-591
        inserting, 575-576
    inserting OLE objects, 739-740
    module, printing, 55-56
Sheets method, 223
Shell function, 768-770
shortcut keys, *see* keyboard shortcuts
Show method (DialogSheets collection), 587-588
ShowCompare procedure, 503
ShowCurDriveDir procedure, 452-453
ShowFileAttr procedure, 435-438
ShowFileDateSize procedure, 463-464
ShowFiles procedure, 449-451
Sin function, 148
Single data type, 63
single-dimensional (simple) arrays, 470-472
single-stepping through statements, 526-527, 529-534
sizes of custom dialog-box controls, resizing, 581
skipping runtime errors, 689-691
SLen function procedure, 182-183, 185-187
SortButton_Click procedure, 610
SortColSpinner_Change procedure, 611

Sorter procedure, 503-506
sorting
    arrays, 498-506
    rows/columns, 591-604
SortRows procedure, 595
SortRowsDown procedure, 599
SortRowsUp procedure, 599
SortStringList procedure, 695-697
sound, MessageBeep DLL procedure, 790-792
source code, 17-18
    editing, 37-39
    modules, 24-25
    security, 41
    writing for macros, 43-46
space characters, deleting leading/trailing, 164-165
Space function, 156
spinner boxes (custom dialog boxes), 571-572, 604-612
Spinner button (Forms toolbar), 577
Sqr function, 148, 681
square brackets ([ ]), returning cell references, 723
Start command (Run menu), 28
StartControlPanel procedure, 769-770
starting
    applications from VBA procedures, 768-770
    Registry Editor utility program, 741-742
startup folder, library workbooks in, 390-394
statements
    AppActivate, 770-773
    ChDir, 431, 453-454
    ChDrive, 431, 454-455
    decision-making, 256-257
    Declare, 789
    Dim, 75-76, 476-478
        declaring fixed length string variables, 87

declaring typed variables, 84-85
Do
    nesting, 332-334
    testing loop determinants (loop invariants), 312-315
Do Until, 318-321
Do While, 315-318
Do...Loop Until, 323-326
Do...Loop While, 321-323
End Function, 280-283
End Sub, 36, 280-283
Erase, 494-496
Error, 679-681, 691-697
Exit Do, 326-329
Exit For, 326-329
Exit Function, 278-280
Exit Sub, 278-280
FileCopy, 431, 457-459
For Each...Next, 308-311
For...Next, 299-308
    nested, 329-332
GoTo, 273-277
If...Then, 258-260
    nested, 264-267
If...Then...Else, 261-264
    nested, 264-267
If...Then...ElseIf, 267-268
Kill, 432, 459-460
MkDir, 432, 455-456
MsgBox, 46-48, 283-288
multiple on single lines of code, 258-259
Name, 432, 460-462
On Error GoTo, 670-671
Option Base, 475-476
Option Compare, 120
Option Explicit, 82-83
Option Private Module, 400-401
ReDim, 486-492
Resume, 671-673
Resume 0, 687-689
Resume label, 689-691
Resume Next, 685-687

ThisWorkBook property

Sams
Learning
Center

SAMS
PUBLISHING

RmDir, 432, 456-457
Select Case, 268-273
SendKeys, 785-788
SetAttr, 432, 438-440
single-stepping through,
    529-534
Stop, 527-528
Type, 370-371
VBA, 36
With, 374
With...End With, 228-230
see also commands
static arrays, 474-475, 478-485
    clearing elements, 494-496
Static keyword, 363-368
status bar, displaying hints
    about commands, 638
StatusBar property, 219, 623,
    647
    MenuItem object, 638
Step Into button (Visual Basic
    toolbar), 31, 528, 532
Step Into command (Run
    menu), 29, 528-534
Step keyword, 305
Step Macro button (Visual
    Basic toolbar), 31
Step Over button (Visual Basic
    toolbar), 31, 534
Step Over command (Run
    menu), 29, 534-535
step-wise refinement, 410-413
Stop Macro button (Visual
    Basic toolbar), 31, 529
Stop statement, 527-528
Stop_AtEvenNums procedure,
    319-321
storage of data types in
    variables, 69-71
Str function, 149
StrComp function, 156,
    166-167, 311
string concatenation operators,
    128
    & (ampersand), 106, 130
    + (plus), 130-131

string conversions (expres-
    sions), 108
String data type, 63
string expressions, 104
String function, 157
string functions, 156-157,
    163-172
strings (text data), 68
    breaking into component
        parts, 169-170
    comparing, 118-120,
        166-169
    declaring fixed length
        variables, 87
    deleting leading or trailing
        space characters, 164-165
    lengths, 165-166
    literal constants in macros,
        90-91
    repeating actions on every
        character, 305-308
    special-meaning/non-typeable
        characters, 170-172
submenus, 621
    adding to commands,
        640-641
    see also menus
subscripts of arrays
    starting number, changing,
        475-476
    upper/lower boundaries,
        492-494
subtraction operator (-),
    113-114
Swap procedure, 503
syntax errors, 48-50, 522
syntax forms in assignment
    operators (=), 109
System file attribute, 434

T

tab order (custom dialog-box
    controls), 582-584
Tab Order command (Tools
    menu), 583

tables, Boolean truth, 125
Tan function, 148
temperatures, evaluating,
    265-267, 270-273
templates, saving workbooks
    as, 445-447
terminating looping structures
    early, 326-329
Test_DelProtectFile procedure,
    439-440
Test_FlipCase procedure,
    191-192
Test_GetBookName procedure,
    251
testing
    indefinite-loop conditions
        after execution, 321-326
        before execution, 315-321
    loop determinants (loop
        invariants), 312-315
text
    color (macros), 37
    custom dialog-box controls,
        582
    editing in macros, 37-39
    strings, 68
        breaking into component
            parts, 169-170
        comparing, 118-120,
            166-169
        declaring fixed length
            variables, 87
        deleting leading or trailing
            space characters,
            164-165
        lengths, 165-166
        literal constants in macros,
            90-91
        repeating actions on every
            character, 305-308
        special-meaning/non-
            typeable characters,
            170-172
TextBox objects versus edit
    boxes, 574
ThisWorkBook property, 220

three-dimensional arrays,
473-474
time
functions, 151-153
specifying for executing
procedures, 814-816
stamps, 462-463
Time function, 151
Timer function, 153
TimeSerial function, 152
TimeValue function, 153
Toggle Breakpoint button
(Visual Basic toolbar), 31,
527
Toggle Breakpoint command
(Run menu), 29, 527
toggle commands, 639-640
Toggle Grid button (Forms
toolbar), 578
ToggleGridlines procedure,
812-813
Toolbar object, 646
Delete method, 654
Position property, 650-653
Reset method, 654
Visible property, 650-653
ToolbarButton object, 646
Delete method, 656
Enabled property, 656-657
Pushed property, 656-657
ToolbarButtons collection, 646
Add method, 655-656
toolbars, 645-646
built-in
Excel, 648
restoring, 654
buttons, 655-657
custom
creating, 649, 657-663
deleting, 655-656
Forms, 576-578
hiding/displaying/position-
ing, 650-653
objects, 646
properties/methods, 646-648
Visual Basic, 30-31

Toolbars collection, 646
Add method, 649
Tools menu commands, 29
Add Watch, 537-538
Assign Macro, 589
assigning macros, 13
Edit Watch, 539
Instant Watch, 540
Macro, 18-19
Make Add-In, 821
Menu Editor, 625
Protection, 41
Protect Workbook, 394
Record Macro | Record New
Macro, 11-14
References, 395
Tab Order, 583
Top property (OLEObject
object), 750
top-down design, 410-413
TopLeftCell property
(OLEObject object), 750
tracing procedure calls,
540-541
trailing space characters,
deleting, 164-165
trappable runtime error codes,
675-677
trapping keystrokes, 810-813
Trim function, 157, 164-165
TrimDemo procedure,
164-165
truth tables, 125
two-dimensional arrays,
472-474
type definition characters, 85
Type property, 220
Type statement, 370-371
TypeName function, 139, 342,
346-351

U

UBound function, 493-494
UCase function, 157

unary minus (-) subtraction
operator, 113-114
unconditional branching
statements, 257, 273-277
Update method (OLEObject
object), 752-753
UpdateAllObjects procedure,
753-756
updating labels in scrollbars/
spinner boxes, 604-612
user data, obtaining through
interactive procedures, 95-98
user input
entering invoice numbers,
332-334
in message dialog boxes with
command buttons, 283-288
testing indefinite-loop
conditions after execution,
322-326
validating, 357-362
user interaction functions,
153-155
user-defined
data types
creating, 369-380
private, 401-402
public, 403-404
functions (UDFs), 179
creating, 183
designing for Excel,
202-203
in Excel, 198-199
runtime error codes, 679-681

V

Val function, 149
validating
function arguments, 356-357
non-user input, 362
procedure environments,
356-357
user input, 357-362

Value property, 220, 573-574, 584
  Range object, 725-726
values
  Boolean type conversion, 108
  expressions, 102-104
  operators (in expressions), 103-104
  persistence (variables), 81
variable length strings, fixed length comparison, 119
variables, 69-71
  assignment operator (=), 109-112
  creating, 73-76
  declaring
    explicit, 74-76, 81-83
    fixed length strings, 87
    implicit, 73-75
    objects, 224
    types, 84-85
  duplicate names, 79
  expression assignment to with specific data type, 111
  global, 398
  information about, obtaining, 340-355
  module level scope, 78-79
  naming, 71-73
  private, 401-402
  procedure level scope, 77-78
  public, 403-404
  retaining values between function/procedure calls, 362-368
  specifying data types, 84
  storing data values (assignment operator), 73
  user-defined data types, creating, 369-380
  value persistence, 81
  Variant type arithmetic exceptions, 112-113
  watched, 535-540
Variant data type, 64, 69
  Empty value, 353-355
  Null value, 354-355

VarType function, 342, 346-347, 351-353
VBA (Visual Basic for Applications)
  compared to macro recorders, 7-9
  compiler, 523
  history, 5-7
  statements, 36
Verb method (OLEObject object), 753-755
VerifyData procedure, 817-819
verifying cell contents, 816-819
View menu commands, 28
  Debug Window, 537
Visible property, 220, 647
  OLEObject object, 750
  Toolbar object, 650-653
Visual Basic toolbar, 30-31
  Instant Watch button, 540
  Menu Editor button, 625
  Record Macro button, 11
  Resume Macro button, 529
  Step Into button, 528, 532
  Step Over button, 534
  Stop Macro button, 529
  Toggle Breakpoint button, 527
volatile functions, 203
Volatile method, 223
Volume Label file attribute, 433-434

W

Wait procedure, 631
WaitAWhile procedure, 503
Watch pane (Debug window), 535-540
watched variables/expressions, 535-540
Weekday function, 152
Width property (OLEObject object), 750
Window menu, Hide command, 393

Window object, 217
WindowHandler procedure, 810
Windows
  Clipboard, moving/copying macros, 39-40
  directory path name, 792-793
windows
  activating, 809-810
  Debug, 525
    Immediate pane, 542-545
    Watch pane, 535-540
Windows collection, 233
With statement, 374
With...End With statement, 228-230
Workbook object, 217
  Activate method, 708-709
  Close method, 711-712
  Save method, 709-711
  SaveCopyAs method, 709-711
  Worksheets method, 712-713
workbooks
  activating, 708-709
  adding worksheets, 715
  backing up, 226-228
  closing, 711-712
    Auto_Close procedure, 803-804
  creating, 549-565, 707
  deleting worksheets, 717-718
  inserting new module sheet, 41-42
  naming, 549-565
  opening, 705-706
    Auto_Open procedure, 801-803
  private modules, 399-401
  referencing, 394-397
  referring to, 704-705
  saving, 709-711
    as templates, 445-447
  selecting existing module sheets, 42
  sheets, determining existence, 309-311, 327-329

Workbooks collection, 233
Add method, 707
Close method, 711-712
Open method, 705-706
Workbooks method, 223
Application object, 704
Worksheet object, 217
Activate method, 714
Cells method, 720-721
Copy method, 716-717
Delete method, 717-718
Move method, 716-717
Name property, 715-716
Range method, 718-720
worksheets
activating, 714, 805-807
cells
selecting, 724
verifying contents,
816-819
copying, 716-717
creating, 715
cutting/copying/clearing data,
727-730

deactivating, 807-809
deleting from workbooks,
717-718
entering data, 724-726
moving, 716-717
ranges
names, 726-727
returning, 718-723
selecting, 724
recalculating, 819-820
referring to, 712-713
renaming, 715-716
Worksheets collection, 233
Add method, 715
Worksheets method, 223
Workbook object, 712-713
**WriteNewData procedure, 721,
727**
**writing function procedures,
180-183**

X–Z

.XLA file extension, 821
Xor operator, 127

Year function, 152

**zero-based numbering of
arrays, 475**

Add to Your Sams Library Today with the Best Books for Programming, Operating Systems, and New Technologies

The easiest way to order is to pick up the phone and call

1-800-428-5331

between 9:00 a.m. and 5:00 p.m. EST.

For faster service please have your credit card available.

ISBN	Quantity	Description of Item	Unit Cost	Total Cost
0-672-30739-1		Excel for Windows 95 Unleashed (Book/CD-ROM)	$39.99	
0-672-30771-5		Essential Visual Basic 4	$25.00	
0-672-30620-4		Teach Yourself Visual Basic 4 in 21 Days, 3E	$29.99	
0-672-30792-8		Teach Yourself Access 95 in 14 Days, 3E	$29.99	
0-672-30640-9		Master Visual Basic 4, 2E (Book/CD-ROM)	$49.99	
0-672-30596-8		Develop a Professional Visual Basic Application in 21 Days (Book/CD-ROM)	$35.00	
0-672-30779-0		Real-World Programming with Visual Basic 4 (Book/CD-ROM), 2E	$45.00	
0-672-30837-1		Visual Basic 4 Unleashed (Book/CD-ROM)	$45.00	
0-672-30743-X		Gurewich OLE Controls for Visual Basic 4 (Book/CD-ROM)	$35.00	
0-672-30624-7		Peter Norton's Inside the PC, 6E	$35.00	
0-672-30614-X		Peter Norton's Complete Guide to DOS 6.22 Premier Edition	$29.99	
0-672-30708-1		Peter Norton's Complete Guide to Windows 95	$29.99	
0-672-30615-8		Peter Norton's Guide to Visual Basic 4 for Windows 95	$39.99	
❏ 3 ½" Disk		Shipping and Handling: See information below.		
❏ 5 ¼" Disk		TOTAL		

Shipping and Handling: $4.00 for the first book, and $1.75 for each additional book. Floppy disk: add $1.75 for shipping and handling. If you need to have it NOW, we can ship product to you in 24 hours for an additional charge of approximately $18.00, and you will receive your item overnight or in two days. Overseas shipping and handling adds $2.00 per book and $8.00 for up to three disks. Prices subject to change. Call for availability and pricing information on latest editions.

201 W. 103rd Street, Indianapolis, Indiana 46290

1-800-428-5331 — Orders   1-800-835-3202 — FAX   1-800-858-7674 — Customer Service

Book ISBN 0-672-30782-0

GET CONNECTED
to the ultimate source of computer information!

The MCP Forum on CompuServe

Go online with the world's leading computer book publisher!
Macmillan Computer Publishing offers everything
you need for computer success!

Find the books that are right for you!
A complete online catalog, plus sample
chapters and tables of contents give
you an in-depth look at all our books.
The best way to shop or browse!

➤ Get fast answers and technical support for
MCP books and software

➤ Join discussion groups on major computer
subjects

➤ Interact with our expert authors via e-mail
and conferences

➤ Download software from our immense
library:

  ▷ Source code from books
  ▷ Demos of hot software
  ▷ The best shareware and freeware
  ▷ Graphics files

Join now and get a free CompuServe Starter Kit!

To receive your free CompuServe Intro-
ductory Membership, call **1-800-848-
8199** and ask for representative #597.

The Starter Kit includes:
➤ Personal ID number and password
➤ $15 credit on the system
➤ Subscription to *CompuServe Magazine*

Once on the CompuServe System, type:

GO MACMILLAN

for the most computer information anywhere!

MACMILLAN
COMPUTER
PUBLISHING

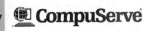

PLUG YOURSELF INTO...

THE MACMILLAN INFORMATION SUPERLIBRARY™

Free information and vast computer resources from the world's leading computer book publisher—online!

FIND THE BOOKS THAT ARE RIGHT FOR YOU!

A complete online catalog, plus sample chapters and tables of contents give you an in-depth look at *all* of our books, including hard-to-find titles. It's the best way to find the books you need!

- **STAY INFORMED** with the latest computer industry news through our online newsletter, press releases, and customized Information SuperLibrary Reports.

- **GET FAST ANSWERS** to your questions about MCP books and software.

- **VISIT** our online bookstore for the latest information and editions!

- **COMMUNICATE** with our expert authors through e-mail and conferences.

- **DOWNLOAD SOFTWARE** from the immense MCP library:
    - Source code and files from MCP books
    - The best shareware, freeware, and demos

- **DISCOVER HOT SPOTS** on other parts of the Internet.

- **WIN BOOKS** in ongoing contests and giveaways!

TO PLUG INTO MCP: ➔   **WORLD WIDE WEB: http://www.mcp.com**

GOPHER: gopher.mcp.com

FTP: ftp.mcp.com